# Straley's Programming with Clipper 5.2

*Second Edition*

# Straley's Programming with Clipper 5.2

*Second Edition*

Stephen J. Straley

Random House
Electronic Publishing

Straley's Programming with Clipper 5.2, Second Edition

Copyright © 1993 by Stephen J. Straley

Produced by MicroText Productions
Composed by Context Publishing Services

All rights reserved. No part of the contents of this book may be reproduced in any form or by any means without the written permission of the publisher.

Published in the United States by Random House, Inc., New York, and simultaneously in Canada by Random House of Canada, Limited.

Manufactured in the United States of America.

0   9   8   7   6   5   4   3   2

First edition

ISBN 0-679-79154-X

The author(s) and publisher have used their best efforts in preparing this book, and the programs contained herein. However, the author(s) and publisher make no warranties of any kind, express or implied, with regard to the documentation or programs contained in this book, and specifically disclaim without limitation, any implied warranties of merchantability and fitness for a particular purpose with respect to program listings in the book and/or the techniques described in the book. In no event shall the author or publisher be responsible or liable for any loss of profit or any other commercial damages, including but not limited to special, incidental, consequential or any other damages in connection with or arising out of furnishing, performance, or use of this book or the programs.

**Trademarks**
A number of entered words in which we have reason to believe trademark, service mark, or other proprietary rights may exist have been designated as such by use of initial capitalization. However, no attempt has been made to designate as trademarks or service marks all personal computer words or terms in which proprietary rights might exist. The inclusion, exclusion or definition of a word or term is not intended to affect, or express any judgment on, the validity or legal status of any proprietary right which may be claimed in that word or term.

New York   Toronto   London   Sydney   Auckland

# *Dedication*

As with the first edition, I would like to dedicate this book to a special teacher. Mr. Essor "Smoke" Maso is not only a wizard with computer theory, but he has also brought human compassion and understanding to a world that seems at times to lack it. His patience to teach me about life, people, and the art of having fun with computers has made possible not only this book, but every endeavor hereafter. Essor, you give me the determination to try new things, the strength to change those things I can, the peace for those I can't, and simplistic wisdom to see the difference. Much love and thanks!

In addition, I would also like to dedicate this to Ron Petrusha, who, over the past couple of years, has been a true friend in helping me finish all of these books. They would not be what they are without his hand helping mold the ideas into printed words.

# Contents

Preface  xv
Acknowledgments  xix
How to Use This Book  xxi
What Is New  xxxiii

## Part I  The Clipper Package  1

## 1  Clipper, the Compiler  3

What Is a Compiler?  3
Compiling Switches  4

/A Automatic Declaration of Public, Private, and Parameters 5  /B Include Debugging Information 5  /CREDIT Display Listing of Credits 5  /D Define a Manifest Constant 5  /ES Set Clipper Exit Severity Level 6  /I Include File Directory Search List 7  /L Line Number Suppression 7  /M Compile Only the Current Program Module 8  /N Suppress Automatic Main Procedure 8  /O Object Filename Specified 10  /P Generate a Preprocessed Output Listing 11  /Q Quiet Mode 11  /R Resolve and Search for Unresolved Externals 12  /S Syntax Check Only 12  /T Temporary File Location 12  /U User-Defined Standard Header File 12  /V Variable References 13  /W Warning Messages for Ambiguous Variable References 14  /Z Suppress "Shortcutting" Optimization 14

Standard Compiling Switches and Options  14

CLIP Files and Batch Compiling  15
The DOS Environment  18
    CLIPPERCMD 18   TMP 19   INCLUDE 19   CLIPPER 20

Clipper Error Messages  23
Tips and Pointers  23

## 2  RTLink, the Linker  25

What Is a Linker?  25
What Is RTLink?  27
RTLink Command Summary  28
Environmental Variables  32
Dynamic and Static Overlays  34
Incremental Linking and Prelinked Libraries  35
    Incremental Linking 36   Prelinked Libraries 36

Contents of Libraries  41
    CLIPPER.LIB 41   EXTEND.LIB 63   TERMINAL.LIB 68
    DBFNTX.LIB 68   DBFNDX.LIB 69   DBFMDX.LIB 69
    DBFCDX.LIB 70   ANSITERM.LIB 73   DBPX.LIB 74
    PCBIOS.LIB 86   NOVTERM.LIB 86   SAMPLES.LIB 86

Other Linkers  88
Linking Ideas  88
Virtual Memory Manager (VMM)  89
    What Is VMM? 89   Segmented Virtual Object Store (SVOS) 90   Working with Dynamic Overlays and VMM 91

Summary  91

## 3  The Preprocessor and UDCs  93

The Preprocessor: An Overview  93
Syntax  95
    #define 95   #undef 101   #ifdef/#else/#endif and #ifndef/#else/#endif 102
    #include 111   #translate, #xtranslate, #command, and #xcommand 116
    #error 125   #stdout 126

Making Your Own Language  127
    User-Defined Commands vs. User-Defined Functions 129
    Pseudofunctions 130  User-Defined Commands 138  The Basics 139
    Intermediate Uses 142  Advanced Uses 145  Other Possibilities 147

Summary  148

## 4 Operators and Conditions  149

Basic Symbols  149
    Strings and Dates 152  Mathematics 155

Rules of Precedence  159

Tips on Expressions and Operators  163
    Concise Boolean Expressions 163  Aliased Memory Variables or Aliased Fields? 164  Multiple Commands for the Preprocessor and Line Continuations 165  Fields and In-Line Assignments 166  Working with == and ! 167  Working with Zeros, %, and / 168  Using the Minus Operator on Strings in Indexes 168  Evaluating Expressions 169

## 5 Data Types, Parameters, Statements, and UDFs  171

Variable Initialization and Storage Class  172
    PUBLIC 173  PRIVATE 174  LOCAL 176  STATIC 179  FILEWIDE Static Variables 181

Declaration Statements  182
    MEMVAR and FIELD 182  EXTERNAL 185  REQUEST 186

The Order of Variable and Field Statements  186

Parameter Passing  187
    Parameters by Value 187  Parameters by Reference 191  Passing Arrays as Parameters 194  Obtaining Values from the DOS Command Line 199  Obtaining Values from Environmental Values 201

Statements  203
    Static Function and Static Procedure 203  INIT Procedure 203  EXIT Procedure 204  ANNOUNCE 204

User-Defined Functions  205

Summary  207

## 6 Clipper Command Reference 209

## 7 Clipper Function Reference 327

The Functions, Pseudofunctions, and Expressions 328

# Part II   Clipper Concepts 563

## 8 Clipper Utilities and Debugging 565

RMAKE.EXE 565

Commands 565   RMAKE Optional Switches 566   RMAKE Command Statements 566   Invoking RMAKE.EXE 568   Environmental Variables 569   RMAKE Operation and Rules 569

PE.EXE 579

DBU.EXE 579

RL.EXE 579

NG.EXE 579

The Clipper Debugger 579

Preparing Code and Restrictions 580   Calling the Debugger 581   Debugging Points 589

The Keyboard Interface 589

Debugging Commands 592   Debugger Command Reference 594

## 9 Macros and Expressions 601

What Is a Macro? 601

Illegal Substitutions 602   Macros and Array Declarations and Definitions 603   Macros and Code Blocks 604

Expressions and Parentheses 608

The Concept 608   Macro-Expanded Expressions 609   Extended Use of Expressions 610

## 10 Arrays 623

Arrays in Clipper 5.2 623

Initializing Arrays 626

Parameter Passing  631
Supporting Functions and AEVAL( )  632
    AADD( ) 633  ACHOICE( ) 633  ACLONE( ) 642  ACOPY( ) 643
    ADEL( ) 645  AEVAL( ) 646  AFILL( ) 652  AINS( ) 653
    ARRAY( ) 655  ASCAN( ) 656  ASIZE( ) 658  ASORT( ) 659

Arrays and User Entry Possibilities  662
Data Caching and Transaction Rollback  668
Environmental Control: SET KEYs, the SET Environment, SET RELATION  672
Passing an Array Element by Reference  676
The QU Program: A Look at Nested Arrays  678

# 11 Memos: Memo Fields and Large Strings  685

The Basics of Memo Handling  685
Individual Functions for Memo Handling  686
MEMOEDIT( )  691
    MEMOEDIT( ) Basics 691  Using the Keystroke Function for MEMOEDIT( ) 695  Restricting the Size of MEMOEDIT( ) 698

Form( ) Function for Output  700
A Major Text Editor  702
Summary  717

# 12 Database Management  719

The Files  719
    The Database File 719  The Memo File 721  The Index File 722

Rules and Tips for Database Management  723
Creating a Database File  725
    CREATE 725  DBCREATE( ) 728

Using a Database, Index, and Relations  729
Looking at Internal Information  732
Working with the Fields  735
Traversing the Database  738

Simple DBEVAL( ) 739
    Working with the FOR and WHILE Conditions 741

Building a Database of Another Data Format 744

Summary 745

## 13 Indexes and RDDs 747

The NTX File Format 747

Basics of the RDDs 749

The Clipper 5.2 Database and Index System 761

Using other RDDs 768
    DBFCDX 768   DBFMDX 773   DBFNDX 777   DBFNTX 779
    DBPX 780

Summary 782

## 14 Low-Level File and Binary Functions 783

The Basics 783

DOS and File Handles 783

Low-Level File Functions and RMAKE.EXE 784

Seeing If a Drive or Path Exists 787

Using the Preprocessor 790

Reading Files 791
    Text Files 791   .MEM Files 795   .NTX Files 799

Writing Arrays to Disk 801

Building New Types of System Files 805

Summary 810

## 15 Code Blocks 811

What Are Code Blocks? 811

Syntax for Code Blocks 812

Code Block Functions for Clipper 813

Code Block Usage 813
    Basic Programming 813   Intermediate Programming 823   Advanced Programming 828   GET/SET Block Functions 832

Contents **xiii**

More Advanced Features: Building Generic Subroutines 835
Summary 839

## 16 Clipper Objects 841

### TBROWSE and TBCOLUMN 844

Initial Steps 851 Basics 853 Intermediate Examples 862 Advanced Examples 888

### TBROWSENEW( ) 906

Basics 906 Intermediate and Advanced Examples 909 An Advanced Example Using DICT( ) 928

The GET Object 932
The Error Object 936
Conclusion 939

## 17 Windowing, Screens, and Menus 941

Basic Screen Control 941
Menus 946

Bounce-Bar Menus 946 Lotus-Like Menus 955 Pull-Down Menus 960

Virtual Screens 970
Windows 973
Conclusion 982

## 18 Data Entry Options 983

Parts of a GET 983

Rows and Columns 984 Memory Variables and Fields 984 Picture Clauses for Formatting 986 WHEN and VALID Clauses 986 The READ Command and READMODAL( ) Function 986 The SET KEY Command and SETKEY( ) Function 986 Object-Oriented Programming 987

The Basic Data Screen 987

Working with VALID Clauses 990 Working with WHEN Clauses 993 Working with the SET KEY TO Command 998

List Boxes 1000
Saving GETs 1007

SET KEY Applications 1013
Working with User-Defined Readers 1015
Modifying GETSYS.PRG 1022
Summary 1041

## 19 The Help and Error Systems 1043

The Help System 1043
The Error System 1066
Conclusion 1075

## 20 Epilogue 1077

# Part III   Appendixes 1079

### Appendix 1: Data Generation Program 1081

### Appendix 2: STUBSTD.CH 1101

### Appendix 3: RMAKE Script Files 1111

### Appendix 4: Include Files 1115

### Appendix 5: ASCII Codes and the IBM Extended Character Set 1137

### Appendix 6: Color Tables 1141

### Appendix 7: Table of Tones 1147

### Appendix 8: DOS Error Messages 1149

### Appendix 9: Warning and Error Messages 1151

**Index** 1161

# *Preface*

This book is designed to be used in conjunction with Computer Associates' CA-Clipper 5.2 compiler. It is a wonderful time for all of us in the Clipper community, for with Computer Associates' purchase of the product, the entire Clipper family has been embraced as well. A commitment to this language as "the" answer to application development under DOS is now secure. This book has been restructured to reflect this new commitment and is geared to get you into building applications as quickly as possible. It is also designed to work in conjunction with our other books: *The Steve Straley Seminars: Clipper 5.0*, *Clipper 5.2 Power Tools*, and the forthcoming *Object-Oriented Clipper*.

However, before moving into this work, the philosophy of Clipper must be touched on briefly. As with any philosophy, certain personal convictions and opinions are interwoven not only in the approach, but also in coding styles and code fragments. It seems that only time and the continued growth of a belief will turn programming theories into standards. Carrying this further, with time, hybrid languages will be transformed into cutting-edge technologies, and simple user groups will suddenly become the information processing centers of major corporations. This is what happened with Clipper.

In the beginning, Clipper aimed at satisfying a small subset of the dBASE world: those who wanted a compiler. These were application-oriented programmers who refused to adhere to the gospel of dBASE and purchase multiple copies of a slow interpreter just to sell their applications. In those days, the concept of building something bigger, better, and faster prevailed, and so Nantucket was formed. While I worked there, this philosophy was apparent not only in the personnel, but also in those who waited patiently for us to deliver the first version: Winter '84. Along with it came the enhanced features and capabilities that only a handful began to test and extend. Slowly, people started to convert dBASE code to Clipper code and to incorporate new additions into the language, like user-defined functions, open architecture, and multiple open files. These marketing buzzwords became reality, and the move away from dBASE began.

With each new version, Clipper introduced a new standard. While the .DBF file remained constant, what Clipper did with the language changed. And as people began to see the potential of this language, they flocked together to form user groups and corporate information centers. More and more, people preferred to program in Clipper, to the point where Clipper programmers and C programmers now form the backbone of many corporate development and information hubs.

The belief, in the early days, that Clipper was a superset of the dBASE dialect did not do the language or the company justice. Clipper is actually C-Base. The philosophy of the language has now evolved to its next logical step. This version of Clipper includes concepts—such as code blocks, static variables, preprocessor directives, database drivers, APIs, and many more—that are not new to the C programmer.

But what makes Clipper clearly superior to dBASE as a development platform is the ease with which you can develop sophisticated applications. Development time is drastically reduced, while the potential for pushing the language grows. With Clipper, reducing development time and support costs also means including additional features that a program written in C or any other dBASE-like language would not normally have. Clipper is a complete development library: Screen, data entry, database, variable, and simple memory management functions are all handled within the Clipper environment.

For this and for other reasons, there will be no further reference to the dBASE ancestry that was given up long ago for the more productive language that we now have. This book will look at Clipper in its present form; therefore, you should have some understanding of basic programming concepts and practice. While a certain "look-and-feel" that is similar to dBASE remains, your key to success is to use the language on its own merits. When you do this, you are half-way to pushing the Clipper language to its ultimate potential.

The remaining half is up to you—to your desire, dedication, and commitment to ask yourself "What if?" If you come from the past history of the language, you have the most difficult job: You must remove your dBlinders. Look at this as a complete environment that gives you the ability to create your wildest ideas. It is even possible to use this language to realize the next generation of database management concepts and environments. If this language can go beyond the feeble beginnings of the past, you must take it upon yourself to find that road to success. Ask yourself "What if?" Think about the problems, and "mix and match" the Clipper command and function set to achieve your goals.

Everything comes down to your dedication to read, think, and try. It is no longer acceptable to have functions and ideas simply handed to you: You must be a programmer. That means you have the ability to create your own file structure, your own menuing format, your own style. Satisfy your customers and yourself by finding out what this language can really do for you. Unless you try, you might as well return to a past of sluggish interpreters and limited possibilities. Remember, you are vital to the continued growth and success of this environment. Exercise it and use it. When you push it, not only will your individual abilities grow, but so will your expectations. And in those expectations lies the wonderful future of Clipper. You will begin to demand more and expect more; and Computer Associates will continue to provide a quality development tool. This relationship means that Clipper will not only expand but prosper, and we—those of us dedicated to flex our muscles and to think—will be constantly rewarded.

Clipper is now a language not only for former Clipper programmers, but also for C, Pascal, and COBOL people as well. And in the future, Visual Objects for Clipper, promises to add C++ programmers to the camp as well. If you understand the new philosophy of Clipper 5.2—building smaller functions (known as objects) which intuitively know what to do based on the coding parameters passed to them (known as code blocks)—you will build applications differently, just as you now build applications differently than in the early days of dBASE III Plus.

So sit back, enjoy, and remember: A language is only alive if there are people willing to speak in it. With that, you will begin to see the Clipper revolution: a ride that can make you feel as if you were young again and as if the world were new. Happy Clipping!

Stephen J. Straley

# *Acknowledgments*

In the past year, many people have contributed to this book in a variety of ways. First to mind is Ron Petrusha of Random House. This book is as much his creation as it is mine. Damian Pearson also played a significant though indirect role in this book. Without Damian taking care of the office at Sirius Software, I would not have been able to focus on writing this edition. Larry Eiss, Savanah Brentnall, Dr. Charles Beattie, Al Acker, and a host of user group presidents and coordinators, both domestic and international: They were able to be friends in difficult times as well as in prosperous times. Finally, a brief word for the friends who have passed away due to two illnesses: AIDS and fear. Our industry is based on creativity, and it suffers a direct loss when some of our brightest minds are lost to a disease, to fear, and to hatred. The Clipper community has been directly impacted since its early days, and it is to these people and their families that I acknowledge and extend my deepest thanks—for being who they were and for the tenacity to bring down the walls of ignorance, prejudice, fear, and hatred. Many thanks.

# How to Use This Book

Before talking about the specific parts of this book, it should be duly noted that this book is just one volume dedicated to the Clipper language. This book is written to quickly educate and assist you in developing an application at the time you need it most: while programming. It is therefore a complete "data dump" of the language and the concepts underlying the language. It is geared to a wide base of Clipper users, from novices to experts: There is something in here for everyone. To go with this tome, there are three additional books, each with a different focus and audience. For those just beginning in the Clipper language who want to learn just the concepts in an overall perspective, *The Steve Straley Seminars: Clipper 5.0* adds this dimension to the series. If a book filled with application-oriented techniques that comes with a library of over 500 functions is needed, then *Clipper 5.2 Power Tools* is an excellent companion to this book. Finally, for those topics that are considered "heavy"— the APIs, working with C and ASM in Clipper, graphics, networking, object-oriented programming, and event-driven application development—*Object-Oriented Clipper* is the work of choice. This series of four books, each of which approaches the language from a different perspective, should provide you with ample information to complete the task at hand.

This book is written in two parts—The Clipper Package and Clipper Concepts—with one common purpose: to provide you with as much technical and practical information about the Clipper language as possible. All coding examples are presented along with detailed textual explanations—that is, the remarks about the code and the points that need to be highlighted are not found in the remark statements within the code, but are nestled within the themes of each chapter.

Part I is a reference guide to Clipper. It contains samples of many programming tips and provides cross-references to more information where this is appropriate. Chapters 1 and 2 cover compiling techniques and linking concepts; both chapters contain detailed examples. Chapter 3 explains the preprocessor in detail, while Chapter 4 looks at the operators and conditions, again with many examples. Chapter 5 explores Clipper data types, conventions regarding passing parameters, functions, procedures, and some of the new features of Clipper

5.2. Chapters 6 and 7 explain Clipper commands and functions in outline form and can be used as a quick reference to see how a specific command or function may work for you. These chapters contain cross-references to similar functions and/or commands, along with programming examples. It is always our intent to provide a reference section that is complete and comprehensive. This means that you will not have to search in one place for database and RDD functions, while you need to turn to another volume for information on all of the other functions. Statements, commands, and functions are grouped together in alphabetical order to provide quick and easy access.

Part II explains and discusses the concepts that make Clipper such a powerful language. These chapters cover programming techniques, styles, and tips which, in conjunction with Part I, show you how to push the language to its limits. In reading these chapters, keep in mind that no one programmer's style is "the" way to do an operation. This is the beauty of the language. Different command and function sets can and will yield similar results. You should look at all of the code throughout this book and apply it to your coding style. Like a professional painter, pick and choose the code possibilities that are right for you. So for this part of the book, you should go through each chapter, read it once, try a few of the coding techniques, and reexamine the point that is being made.

Make sure that, if you use any of the book's complete programs, you code, compile, and link the program in Appendix A. This program will generate the data necessary for most of the sample programs to work. Also note that most programming examples and ancillary support files within the chapters contain line numbers. These are included to facilitate the book's general discussion and are *not* part of the actual programming examples. Clipper does *not* support line numbers; therefore, do *not* include them when coding the examples yourself.

Before going further, there are two points to be made on the overall direction of the book, which is part of a series and as such lays the foundation on which a vast array of technical information will be built; it is the technical reference book to the Clipper language. But in addition to providing this solid mass of technical information, the book has a second goal—what can be classically called "determining the motivational factor." In other words, behind each function, command, and concept in Clipper 5.2, there must be a motivational factor that will help you learn it, try it, think about it, and, if it can aid in your daily programming challenges, use it. The book attempts to keep you from looking at any piece of this language and thinking, "Oh, that's nice . . . so what?"

The most important thing to remember when programming with Clipper 5.2 is to think. To help this process out, take the file named STD.CH that comes with your Clipper distribution copy and print it out. Make several copies and keep them handy at all times. Read them over and over again as you read this book. Refer to the file and look at it for insightful tips on the new approach to the language. You will be able to see how typical commands that you are familiar with are treated in the native Clipper environment.

Also, keep in mind that to really push the technology within Clipper 5.2, not only should any dBASE remnants be shucked away, but so should any deeply rooted prejudices about previous releases of Clipper. This version is radically different: You have more control, more power, and more of a say in how you program. Accepting Clipper 5.2 as merely an "upgrade" means you will not push the language; you will not look deeper to explore other possibilities. Clipper 5.2 is about tapping the possible and the potential. There are obvious relationships within any version of Clipper, including this one. However, if you think about the concepts outlined in this book and practice those ideas in your own coding conventions and programs, you will see significant differences in your programming style and approach and, ultimately, in your productivity.

To successfully use the programming examples in this book, you must follow these few guidelines.

- Set the compiling environmental variable to the following:

  ```
  set clippercmd=/m /p /v /w /a /b /n /es2
  ```

  Unless it is specifically stated, this DOS environmental variable is used. Otherwise, the SAMPLE.RMK file can be used to make most of the programs found in this book. That file contains the various switches for each program module and therefore does not require any DOS environmental switch to be established.

- Set the environmental variable for the linker to the following:

  ```
  set lib=\clipper5\lib
  set pll=\clipper5\pll
  ```

- Compile and execute the program named MAKEDATA.PRG found in Appendix A. Keep in mind that both the DOS FILES= and Clipper "F" switch needs to be set to a number greater than 79.

## Converting from Summer '87 to Clipper 5.2

There are two basic things to think about before converting to Clipper 5.2. First, to best determine the desirability of converting, look at your coding style and your current application base. If most of the code in question is based on Clipper '87, the conversion process should be relatively safe—that is, of course, if your code is devoid of any of the Clipper "programming secrets" based on unique features or idiosyncracies that were discovered in Summer '87. These types of features include having list boxes in VALID clauses automatically pop up from null GETS or using the SET TYPEAHEAD command to disable LASTKEY( ). Since none of these features were ever considered to be "documented," future compatibility is left to chance. On the other hand, if the code is within the realm of Clipper-documented features, upward compatibility may not be an issue.

The second thing to look at are the added benefits of Clipper 5.2 over Summer '87. Most developers try to push the language with internal corporate libraries, third-party libraries, or the enhanced technology within the language. These developers, like yourself, will want to push the technology within Clipper 5.2, which is drastically different from Summer '87, to achieve maximum benefit for your customer and client base. For example, can one convert an application and realize the desire to push the language without tapping into the Clipper preprocessor, code-block technology, true pointer-based arrays and structures, extended expression handling, or object-oriented GET, ERROR, and BROWSING? Probably not. If speed is the motive in converting from Summer '87 to Clipper 5.2, stick with Summer '87. If memory fragmentation is the issue (as well as the enhanced memory management capabilities of RTLink and Clipper's repooling of available memory), look at your coding style and make the determination. If the code is too Summer '87-based, perhaps acquiring a third-party linker such as BLINKER (r), which is a dynamic overlay linker, would be a better decision. If you want to start your next application using all of the features available to you that are "appropriate," Clipper 5.2 is your ticket.

But conversion from Summer '87 to 5.0 and 5.2 is rarely completely seamless. What follows are just a few examples of the problems that can occur with converting. If, in order to save memory, we convert all of our PRIVATE variables to LOCAL, thus removing their symbol table references, we would reduce the basic load module. However, we could, with this one simple conversion, break our application, as shown below:

```
PROCEDURE Top_gun

    PRIVATE x

    * do some work within the routine and
    * now call an exclusively dependent
    * subroutine.

    DO Sub_routine

    ? x

*****************

PROCEDURE Sub_routine

    * At this point, the variable X in the
    * parent routine needs to be worked on

    x = x + 23

    * do some more stuff, and return

* End of example.
```

Although this is not good structured coding because the variable *X* is being manipulated at a lower level without being passed as a formal parameter, a majority of Clipper programmers do this every day. It gets the job done, and there is nothing wrong with that! Now if we take all PRIVATES and made them LOCAL command statements, we would have the following:

```
procedure TopGun()

    local nNumber   // This was a private variable
    //  do some work within the routine and now call an exclusively
    //  dependent subroutine

    SubRoutine()

    ? nNumber

*****************
```

```
static procedure SubRoutine()

   // At this point, the variable nNumber in the parent routine needs to
   // be worked on

   nNumber += 23

   // do some more stuff, and return

// End of Example
```

In this case, LOCAL variables are not visible to those subroutines called by the creator of the LOCAL variable; PRIVATE variables are. How many times do we look at, evaluate, or even modify a PRIVATE variable in subroutines?

Or how about the following example:

```
local cVariable := fieldname(1)
local cArea     := alias(1)

set relation to &cVariable. INTO &cArea
```

This is legal code; the preprocessor output (.PPO) file looks fine. It will, however, not work. Why? Because LOCAL variables have no reference in the symbol table and therefore cannot undergo macro-expansion in some cases. Once again, if this were a PRIVATE variable, the desired effect would be achieved.

In these two examples, the conversion of PRIVATE to LOCAL variables could ruin the application. And this is just one issue. The preprocessor, pointer logic, code blocks, and object-oriented programming have yet to be considered.

Additionally, if you are in the middle of a project and are thinking about finishing the application in Clipper 5.2 while keeping the rest in the previous version, avoid the temptation. First, object modules from the two versions are not compatible within the same executable module. This means that all Summer '87 code would have to be recompiled under Clipper 5.2, and that those nuances new to Clipper commands and functions would appear in those once-solid object files. In addition, the temptation to cross over and alter older, functional Summer '87 program files would be too great.

In these pseudocode examples, as well as in all of the examples in this book, we follow a modified Hungarian notational style of coding. This coding style is consistent with all of our other books and products. It is discussed extensively in *Clipper 5.2 Power Tools*, which outlines why this coding style was chosen over others. In addition, we have tried to use the various header files and ancillary files found in those books in this book whenever appropriate. This means a reduction in disk space should you have the source code for any of the other books.

Finally, one of the biggest features of Clipper is its ability to let us control how the language operates. This means that if we want to alter the behavior of a GET, we can do it; if we want to alter the behavior of typical commands like COUNT and RECALL, we can. And we can customize the language to fit how we code and solve problems in a way which is not necessarily based on an archaic manner of programming commonly known as dBASE III.

Organization of Your Machine

```
                                    /
    ┌───────────────────────────────┼───────────────────────────────┐
CLIPPER 87                     CLIPPER 52
CLIPPER.EXE                    README
CLIPPER.LIB
EXTEND.LIB
PLINK86.EXE
            ┌──────────────┬──────────────┬──────────────┬──────────────┐
           BIN           INCLUDE          LIB            NG           SOURCE

CLD.EXE              ACHOICE.CH      ANSITERM.LIB   C52G01B.NG
CLD.HLP              ASSERT.CH       CLD.LIB        C52G02B.NG
CLIPPER.EXE          BOX.CH          CLIPPER.LIB    C52G04B.NG
DBT52.EXE            COLOR.CH        DBFCDX.LIB     C52G05B.NG
RMAKE.EXE            COMMON.CH       DBFMDX.LIB     C52G06B.NG
RTLINK.DAT           DBEDIT.CH       DBFNDX.LIB     C52G07B.NG
RTLINK.EXE           DBSTRUCT.CH     DBFNTX.LIB     NG.EXE
RTLINK.HLP           DIRECTRY.CH     DBPX.LIB       NG.INI
RTLINKST.COM         ERROR.CH        EXTEND.LIB
                     EXTEND.CH       NOVTERM.LIB
                     FILEIO.CH       PCBIOS.LIB
                     GETEXIT.CH      RTLUTILS.LIB
                     INKEY.CH        SAMPLES.LIB
                     MEMOEDIT.CH     TERMINAL.LIB
                     RESERVED.CH
                     SET.CH
                     SETCURS.CH
                     SIMPLEIO.CH
                     STD.CH
```

## DBU

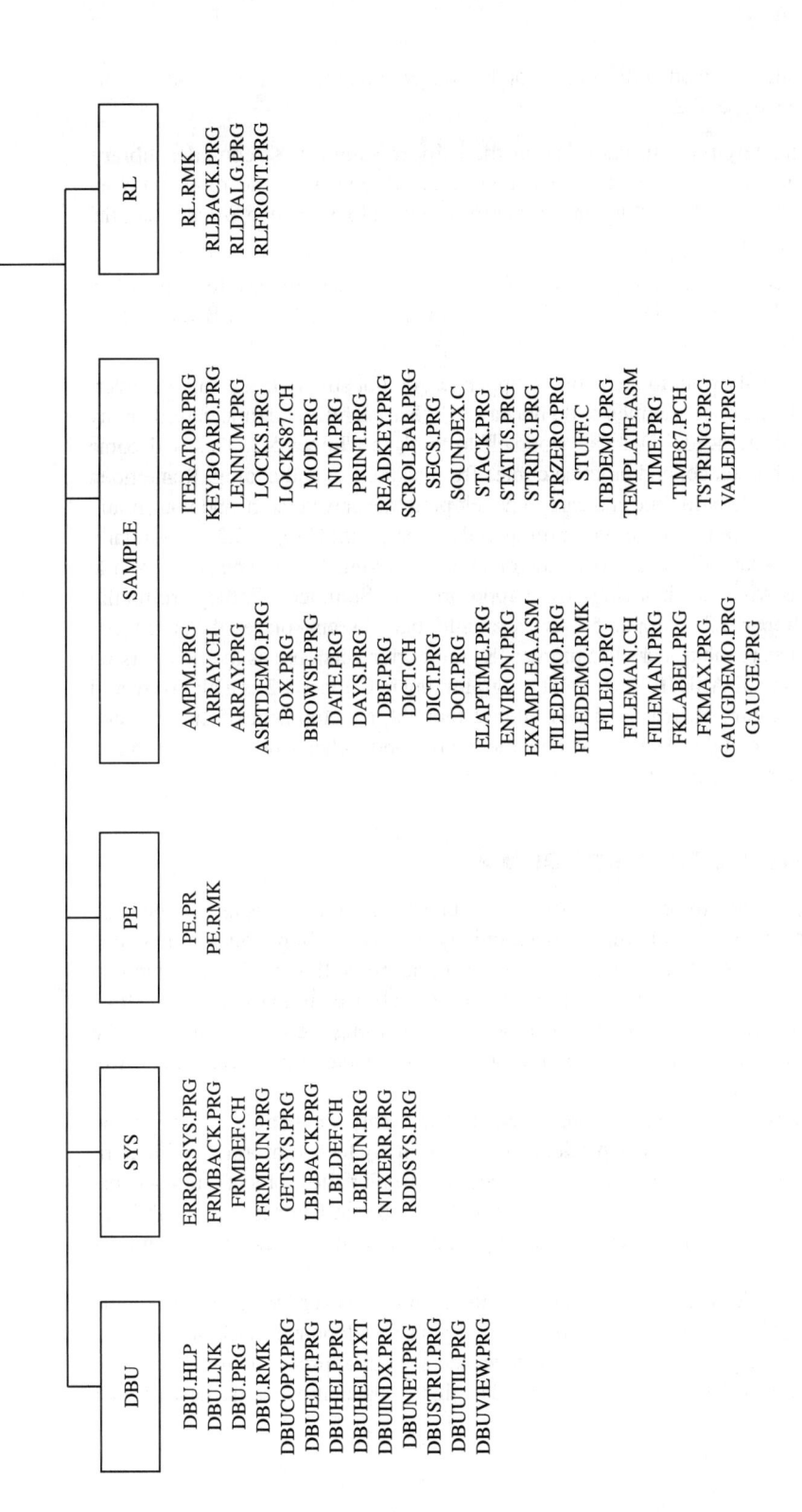

- DBU.HLP
- DBU.LNK
- DBU.PRG
- DBU.RMK
- DBUCOPY.PRG
- DBUEDIT.PRG
- DBUHELP.PRG
- DBUHELP.TXT
- DBUINDX.PRG
- DBUNET.PRG
- DBUSTRU.PRG
- DBUUTIL.PRG
- DBUVIEW.PRG

## SYS

- ERRORSYS.PRG
- FRMBACK.PRG
- FRMDEF.CH
- FRMRUN.PRG
- GETSYS.PRG
- LBLBACK.PRG
- LBLDEF.CH
- LBLRUN.PRG
- NTXERR.PRG
- RDDSYS.PRG

## PE

- PE.PR
- PE.RMK

## SAMPLE

- AMPM.PRG
- ARRAY.CH
- ARRAY.PRG
- ASRTDEMO.PRG
- BOX.PRG
- BROWSE.PRG
- DATE.PRG
- DAYS.PRG
- DBF.PRG
- DICT.CH
- DICT.PRG
- DOT.PRG
- ELAPTIME.PRG
- ENVIRON.PRG
- EXAMPLEA.ASM
- FILEDEMO.PRG
- FILEDEMO.RMK
- FILEIO.PRG
- FILEMAN.CH
- FILEMAN.PRG
- FKLABEL.PRG
- FKMAX.PRG
- GAUGDEMO.PRG
- GAUGE.PRG
- ITERATOR.PRG
- KEYBOARD.PRG
- LENNUM.PRG
- LOCKS.PRG
- LOCKS87.CH
- MOD.PRG
- NUM.PRG
- PRINT.PRG
- READKEY.PRG
- SCROLBAR.PRG
- SECS.PRG
- SOUNDEX.C
- STACK.PRG
- STATUS.PRG
- STRING.PRG
- STRZERO.PRG
- STUFF.C
- TBDEMO.PRG
- TEMPLATE.ASM
- TIME.PRG
- TIME87.PCH
- TSTRING.PRG
- VALEDIT.PRG

## RL

- RL.RMK
- RLBACK.PRG
- RLDIALG.PRG
- RLFRONT.PRG

Now, in view of these and other difficulties of the conversion process, a few points should be made regarding Clipper 5.2:

- Do not immediately rid your hard disk of the Clipper Summer '87 compiler, library, third-party routines, or your original source code. If you have the room on your development machine, try setting up a directory structure for Clipper 5.2 that is parallel to the one for Summer '87.

- If you want to convert some of your older Summer '87-based routines into Clipper 5.2, start with smaller .PRG files, preferably those based on CLIPPER.LIB rather than EXTEND.LIB.

- Finally, if you really want to delve into Clipper 5.2, do not simply make small conversions with existing code fragments; do not say, "I'll learn a little at a time, based on my experience and my need." Dedicate yourself to think in Clipper 5.2. This will come about only with practice, and practice comes from actual use and coding. Remember, the developers took extra time and care in developing this new version, and you should devote the same care to each programming undertaking with Clipper 5.2. Continually ask yourself, "What if?" and do not settle for someone saying, "It can't be done." While there are areas where such sayings were appropriate in Summer '87, they are totally passe' for Clipper 5.2. Clipper 5.2 is as evolutionary as any piece of "upgraded" software. It is as revolutionary to Summer '87 (and prior versions) as the first version of Clipper was to dBASE III Plus! Treat programming in Clipper 5.2 as a pianist would treat his craft: hours of dedicated and intense thought, development of thought, and employment of thought. As Clipper becomes richer and richer with subtle treasures, you *must* devote more time to uncovering them.

## Disk Configurations for Clipper 5.2

There are two approaches to setting up your development machine to install Clipper 5.2, depending on whether you want to maintain a previous version of Clipper on your machine while working with Clipper 5.2. Consider this question carefully. If a considerable amount of code is written in a previous version, it may be beneficial to keep it around for a while. You may also consider the time that you can devote to learning the new compiler while maintaining your workload and client commitments, or servicing current customers. Remember, Clipper 5.2 is different.

While it maintains the industry practice to remain "upwardly compatible" from version to version, in reality it is a brand new product. Until you finally feel comfortable with all of the aspects of Clipper 5.2 (code blocks, preprocessors, header files, objects, replaceable database drivers, dynamic overlays) or until you feel certain that Clipper 5.2 is stable for your environment, keeping a previous version on your machine may be a safe and comfortable avenue.

The first approach adds Clipper 5.2 without deleting a previous version. The chart on the previous pages graphically shows the organization of your development machine.

If you want only Clipper 5.2 on your machine, the second approach is to remove the subdirectory for Clipper '87 or for Clipper 5.0 and begin the installation from a new Clipper subdirectory.

Clipper 5.2 requires at least 3 MB of free space, but it is preferable to have 4 MB of free space. Clipper 5.2 requires at least 512K of RAM and DOS version 3.1 or higher.

As you scan through your directory listing, pay particular attention to the time stamp of each file. Make sure that the files you have are the most recent ones from Computer Associates. To verify this, if necessary, call customer service for a complete run-down. If you are experiencing problems that do not correspond to this book or to the Clipper manual and you believe that your coding fragment is correct, verify the time stamp on all of the library files that come with Clipper, and also of any other original distribution files that you may be using.

## Suggested Enhancements and Programs

Perhaps far more than any other database development tool, Clipper has spawned a huge market for add-on software that, in one way or another, supplements the functionality provided by Clipper itself. Listed below are just a few of the additional third-party utilities, programs, libraries, periodicals, and educational resources for Clipper 5.2.

### EXTENDING LIBRARIES

- *Straley's Power Pack*
- *Pleiades—The Code That Tutors*
- *Helios Subsystems*
- *Hermes Dialog and Event System*

  **Sirius Software Development, Inc.**
  564 Mission St. - Suite 343
  San Francisco, CA 94105-2921
  415-399-9810
  415-399-9857 (fax)

- *R&R Relational Report Writer*

  **Concentric Data Systems, Inc.**
  18 Lyman St.
  Westboro, MA 01581
  508-366-1122

### GRAPHICS LIBRARY

- *Straley's Power Pack*

  **Sirius Software Development, Inc.**
  564 Mission St. - Suite 343
  San Francisco, CA 94105-2921
  415-399-9810
  415-399-9857 (fax)

- *Flipper*

  **ProWorks**
  P.O. Box 1635
  Hermiston, OR 97838
  503-567-1459

- *DGE*

  **Pinnacle Publishing, Inc.**
  P.O. Box 8099
  Federal Way, WA 98003
  206-941-2300

## NETWORKING LIBRARY

- *RaSQL*
- NetLib

  **Pinnacle Publishing, Inc.**
  P.O. Box 8099
  Federal Way, WA 98003
  206-941-2300

## COMMUNICATION LIBRARIES

- *SilverComm*

  **Silver Ware, Inc.**
  3010 LBJ Freeway - Suite 740
  Dallas, TX 75234
  214-247-0131

- *AddComm*

  **Pinnacle Publishing, Inc.**
  P.O. Box 8099
  Federal Way, WA 98003
  206-941-2300

## LINKERS and EDITORS

- *Blinker*

  **Blink, Inc.**
  P.O. Box 7154
  Richmond, VA 23221-0154
  804-353-0137

- *WarpLink*

  **Hyperkinetix, Inc.**
  666 Baker St. - Suite 405
  Costa Mesa, CA 92626
  714-668-9234

- *Multi Edit (Evolve is optional)*

  **American Cybernetics**
  1830 W. University Drive - Suite 112
  Tempe, AZ 85281
  602-968-1945
  602-966-1654 (Fax)

## PERIODICALS

- *Reference Clipper*

  **Pinnacle Publishing, Inc.**
  P.O. Box 8099
  Federal Way, WA 98003
  206-941-2300

## TRAINING AND EDUCATION

- *Pleiades*
- *Sirius Software University*

  **Sirius Software Development, Inc.**
  —A Computer Associates Recognized Training Center—
  564 Mission St. - Suite 343
  San Francisco, CA 94105-2921
  415-399-9810
  415-399-9857

# Summary

Get as much information you can on this product, review the various resources available, and use this book to help you to develop applications in Clipper.

# What Is New

With each new version of CA-Clipper comes the chance to try out new ideas, to refine old ideas, and to attempt to write a better book. So while on the surface there is not much different in Clipper 5.2, much has changed within the two covers of this book.

One of the first things we tried to do is to make this book consistent with our other books in the series: *Clipper 5.2 Power Tools*, *The Steve Straley Seminars: Clipper 5.0*, and *Object-Oriented Clipper 5.2*. In addition, we have tried to make the book fit all of the products and personalities at Sirius Software Development, Inc. This means that the coding style used here will be uniform. For example, we will be using the same header files in the various books; however, we will not duplicate coding examples or concepts. This means, to the reader, a reduction in confusion as well as in code to be typed or in files on the disk. We have incorporated a modified version of Hungarian notation. This can be summarized as follows:

- *Manifest Constants* will be prefixed with the lower-cased letter "p" followed by all upper-cased letters.
- All variables will be un-aliased and will contain a root name preceded by a single letter *metasymbol*. This one-letter abbreviation depicts the data type of the variable. If a variable or a parameter may be of more than one data type, then the letter "x" will be used as the metasymbol.
- All fields will be aliased. In addition, extended expressions will be used as often as possible in preference to the SELECT command or the SELECT( ) function.
- Arrays will adhere to the Pascal notation for subscripts.
- Header files will be identical to those used in *Clipper 5.2 Power Tools*. This will avoid a major duplication of effort and files.
- Local and static variables will be used as often as possible.

- Headers in the sample programs are absent from the text.

   All files, unless otherwise stated, will be compiled with the following compiling switches:

   ```
   Clipper <file> /es2 /p /n /m /a /w /v /b
   ```

   In addition, all files will be linked in the following manner, unless stated otherwise:

   ```
   RTlink fi <file> pll Base52
   ```

   This means that the .PLL file needs to be created with BASE52.LNK.

- The := operator will be used for all assignments, while the == operator will be used for comparisons. The single equal sign (=) will be dropped. In addition, to negate a comparison, the != operator will be dropped in favor of the !( *value* == *value*) expression. This style removes ambiguity in the code between a comparison and an assignment.

Another thing new in this book is its all new collection of sample programs, which focus on relating the point or topic under discussion to application development. Much of this is handled by the uniform style. However, some samples are taken from working applications.

Chapters on C and ASM, making .LIB files, and networking have all been removed and will be expanded upon in *Object-Oriented Clipper 5.2*, the next book in Random House's ongoing series on CA-Clipper.

This book also includes the code for an enhanced and fully functional error system as well as an enhanced DBU utility. In addition, some of the chapters have been condensed and grouped together with other topics. For example, the chapter on user-defined commands has been incorporated into the chapter on the preprocessor.

The optional companion disk that may be purchased for this book contains all of the example programs, along with a mouse-aware screen painter, source code documentor, and application generator. Technical support for this book is made available free for only those who purchase the Companion Disk.

# Part I

*The Clipper Package*

# 1

# Clipper, the Compiler

When people think of Clipper, they often think of only the word *compiler*—in reality there is much more. Actually, as a language, Clipper's fundamental philosophy is based on building applications in Clipper, on linking with Clipper, and of course on compiling with Clipper. While working with the compiler is a vital step, it is not the only step. And even this step consists of several components, each of which is vital to the total picture that makes up the basic compiler. These components include compiling switches, clip files, environmental variables, preprocessing statements, and header files.

## What Is a Compiler?

Before we look at the specifics of the Clipper compiler, two questions need to be addressed. First, what is a compiler, and second, why should we compile rather than interpret.

Starting with the last question first, programs generated from compilers execute much faster than programs generated from interpreters. Ironically, most interpreters are programs that have been compiled. Therefore the *why* to compile is simple: (a) to have a faster-running application; and (b) to have an independent .EXE file, free of the need to have an interpreter present to execute a program. In addition, to properly code for a compiler, programmers must think and plan ahead, which forces them to use a more structured programming style.

Before discussing the job of the compiler, let's define a few terms.

A compiler is a programming routine that allows a computer to translate a program from a pseudocode language into machine language. A compiler may also preprocess or "translate" the pseudocode into another pseudocode language for later compilation.

Pseudocode is a program requiring a conversion of its code for use by the computer; it is also called *symbolic code*. This code is independent of the hardware.

Clipper is a two-pass compiler; it is a compiler as well as a translator/preprocessor. The preprocessor portion of the compiler basically uses a template file to help it match command patterns with those patterns required by the compiler. In other words, Clipper first matches the code patterns in your program files with those patterns expected by the compiler and/or by the libraries. Once these translations are made, they are compiled and converted into machine relocatable object code. The code within the object file will match the calls required in the library, either CLIPPER.LIB, EXTEND.LIB, TERMINAL.LIB, or one of the database driver libraries, typically DBNTX.LIB.

In essence, the compiler takes our code, which is written in an English-like language, and turns it into machine-level symbols known as *tokens*. A single token can, and often does, represent several lines of compiled code. For example, what we normally see as a loop statement—consisting of a beginning, an ending (and in the case of a FOR . . . NEXT loop, a variable and an incrementing/decrementing value as well), and perhaps a break point—is one token to the compiler. The compiler breaks the code down into logical chunks so that it and the library can better understand what it is that we want the computer to do. This does not mean that the information in our code has been understood—that is what an interpreter does. It simply means that the words and phrases that we use to symbolically represent a computer action have been reduced to a minimal number of computer instructions.

After all tokens have been generated, the compiler's second pass actually groups like symbols (producing only one token in the symbol table), builds the individual tables (code, constant, and symbol tables), and eventually produces an object file. Think of the basic compiling process in terms of a dictionary. The dictionary consists of an alphabetical listing of all of the words in a language. Along with these words are the pronunciations, etymologies, and definitions of each word. Your program files are nothing more than a low-level dictionary with all of the words mixed up and out of order. The compiler translates what you are trying to say in common, human-based lingo and arranges the commands to fit the machine. It then lists them in a file in an order that the machine can understand and tie to the proper definitions. The definitions themselves are not kept in the compiler: They reside in a library. The process by which an object file is filled with computer-based words (or tokens) is called linking (which is discussed in Chapter 2). Keep in mind that the words listed in the object file do not necessarily **do** anything; they merely point to those locations in the library that do.

## Compiling Switches

You can specify different compiling options through compiling switches, which may use either upper- or lowercase letters. Each compiling switch is delimited on the command line with either the slash character (/) or the hyphen character (-). Additionally, compiling switches may be used in any order and may be passed to the compiler either on the command line or in an environmental variable (explained later in this chapter). Normally, the switches appear after the name of the file that is to be compiled. The basic format will be the following:

```
Clipper <filename> [<compiler switches>]
```

What follows is a list of the compiling switches supported by Clipper, along with an explanation for each.

## /A   AUTOMATIC DECLARATION OF PUBLIC, PRIVATE, AND PARAMETERS

This means that any variable that is declared in a PUBLIC, PRIVATE, or PARAMETER command statement is automatically initialized as a MEMVAR. This is an internal declaration and cannot be seen in the preprocessor's intermediate file, if one is generated.

One of the peculiarities of the /A switch is worth noting: It effectively prevents a parameter from being macro-expanded into a PUBLIC variable, as the following code fragment attempts to do:

```
function Dull( cName )

  public &cName.
```

Since the variable that is to be declared PUBLIC is not yet known at compile-time, no memory variable can be properly defined. As a result, compiling with the /A switch will force this to be flagged as a syntax error. However, if the /A is omitted from the compiling process, then the compiler will accept this and the program will work as expected.

## /B   INCLUDE DEBUGGING INFORMATION

This compiler switch causes Clipper to generate an object file that includes source filenames, names of local and static variables, and other related information for the debugger. Line numbers are automatically included with the .OBJ file unless this feature is suppressed via another compiler switch.

## /CREDIT   DISPLAY LISTING OF CREDITS

This merely shows a screen of the various people who were directly or indirectly involved with the development of Clipper 5.x. It has no relevance to the compiler, the linker, or the executable.

## /D   DEFINE A MANIFEST CONSTANT

```
/D<constant>[=<definition>]
```

This switch creates a manifest constant—a keyword that is defined as a literal constant before the compilation process. Using the /D switch, a manifest constant can be defined directly from the command line or by the CLIPPERCMD environmental variable. It follows the same rules as the #define preprocessor directive. If there is no <definition> for <constant>, <constant> will have an empty value but will be considered defined. Such a constant with an empty value would be useful in an example like the following:

```
Clipper Myprog /DDEMO
```

In MYPROG.PRG, the following code may appear:

```
#ifdef DEMO
   record_limit := 50
#else
   record_limit := 99999999999999999
#endif
```

In this example, if the program is compiled with the /DDEMO switch and the preprocessor tests whether DEMO is defined, the value of the variable *record_limit* would be set to 50, thus allowing only 50 records to be added to a database. Otherwise, the variable would be set to such a high number that there would be, in practice, no limit. Such a technique could be used in a variety of programming situations.

## /ES  SET CLIPPER EXIT SEVERITY LEVEL

```
/ES[<nErrorLevel>]
```

The setting of the /ES switch controls how Clipper responds to warning messages—to a class of errors detected by the compiler that are not necessarily fatal. The value of <nErrorLevel> determines, on the one hand, whether Clipper will generate an .OBJ file if it encounters warnings, and whether it assigns a value to the DOS ERRORLEVEL after it completes compilation. The default value, /ES, does not set the value of ERRORLEVEL and will nevertheless allow the .OBJ file to be generated if warnings are encountered. The following, however, are also possible variations on the /ES switch:

- /ES0 This is the same as /ES and does not set the DOS ERRORLEVEL should a warning appear.
- /ES1 This is similar to /ES and /ES0 in that it does generate an .OBJ file, but it also sets the DOS ERRORLEVEL.
- /ES2 Should warnings appear during the compilation process, then the DOS ERRORLEVEL is set and Clipper does not generate an .OBJ file.

Consider the following batch file:

```
Clipper %1 /m /n /v /a /w /p /b /es2
if not errorlevel 1 rtlink %1 lib Ptool52
```

This means, for example, that should the name of a memory variable be misspelled in a routine, the DOS ERRORLEVEL will be set, no object module will be generated, and the call to RTLINK will not be executed.

If you prefer using .BAT files for your compile and link cycle for simple files, the /ES switch provides a way to stop the link cycle should a warning message be generated during a compile. In the past, if a variable was misspelled (for example) and the /W switch was used in the compiling process, a warning message might be generated. Typically, the variable is declared to be one thing and due to the misspelling, it is not seen:

```
local nTypeAhead

// executing code or other statements

set typeahead to nTyepAhead
```

Since the misspelling is obvious, the immediate need is to stop the batch file, fix the problem, and then return to the batch file to reexecute the process. However, this is not always that easy when the batch file looks like this:

```
clipper %1 /m /n /a /w /v /p
if not errorlevel 1 rtlink fi %1
```

Even if there was a warning, Clipper would still return an ERRORLEVEL of 0 and generate an object module, and our batch file would then in turn go through an unnecessary link cycle. We could try to halt the batch file by slamming a few control-C characters into the process, only to find them (more likely than not) ignored. In Clipper 5.2, the new /ES2 switch may be added to the batch file so that, in cases of a warning message being detected by the compiler, the DOS ERRORLEVEL is set so that the link does not take place and an .OBJ file is not generated.

## /I  INCLUDE FILE DIRECTORY SEARCH LIST

```
/I<search path>
```

This switch adds the directory designated in <search path> to the front of the list of directories to be searched for included files. Any directory specified will be searched before the directories defined by the DOS SET INCLUDE command. The following example, for instance, instructs Clipper to search the \RANDOM\INCLUDE directory for any Clipper header files:

```
Clipper MAKEDATA /I\RANDOM\INCLUDE
```

## /L  LINE NUMBER SUPPRESSION

This switch tells the compiler not to include line numbers from the source program files in the compiled object file. This reduces the object file size by three (3) bytes and the code table size by three bytes for each recognized command line in the source program file. Line continuations are not counted. By default, line numbers will be included.

Only specify the /L compiling option when disk or memory space is critical and/or the application has been completely debugged. Leaving in the line numbers, as well as specifying the /B option to include additional debugging information in the .OBJ file, gives you greater flexibility and power in debugging an application.

```
Clipper Makedata /A /L
Clipper Makedata /B /L
```

The first example generates the MAKEDATA object file without line numbers and automatically declares all variables declared in PUBLIC, PRIVATE, and PARAMETER statements to be internally aliased as M-> or MEMVAR->. In the second example, the line numbers are again suppressed, but debugging information is added. This means that additional information will be available for the debugger in the MAKEDATA.OBJ file, but it will not include the line numbers that point to the original source file.

## /M  COMPILE ONLY THE CURRENT PROGRAM MODULE

This compiler switch tells Clipper to compile only the specified program module. This will not work in conjunction with .CLP (script file or batch compilation) files. This directive will keep Clipper from including any other program module that may be specified via a DO, SET FORMAT TO, or SET PROCEDURE TO command statement. References to modules from these commands will still be generated within the object file. These external references must be resolved at link time to avoid warning messages from the linker.

```
Clipper Makedata /M
```

This example generates an object module named MAKEDATA.OBJ that may contain external references to subroutines; however, these will not be included in the object file.

## /N  SUPPRESS AUTOMATIC MAIN PROCEDURE

This switch prevents the compiler from automatically defining a procedure with the same name as the program module. Normally, the top of a .PRG file contains code that directs program flow to other procedures and/or functions. Clipper automatically assigns this code at the top of the file the name of the .PRG file, which explains how Clipper can treat the start-up procedure the same as any other procedure. The /N switch, however, tells the compiler that there is no start-up procedure, or to put it another way, that the symbol in the symbol table that is generally reserved for the .PRG file will not be created.

The start-up procedure or function for an application is the first routine encountered at link time. Ordinarily, when compiling without the /N option, no procedure or function is formally defined at the top of the program file; this is consistent with Clipper's assigning the top of a program file the same name as the program file itself, and with executing the code at the top of the file when the program filename is called. In contrast, when compiling with the /N switch, only the first explicitly defined procedure or function serves as the start-up procedure when the program's filename is called.

In a sense, the /N switch can be used to create an object module that corresponds to a procedure file under Summer '87. A procedure file was a program file that contained only individual procedures and generally served as a library of procedures or functions. However, in the past, Clipper still treated the procedure file itself as a procedure and generated a reference to it in the symbol table. This meant that procedures within an application could not have the same name as a program file. While this limitation still exists if the /N switch is not used, it can be avoided if program modules are compiled with the /N switch.

To make this somewhat clearer, let's take the following simple program, which we'll name SIMPLE.PRG:

```
* SIMPLE.PRG

function Main()

   local GetList := {}

   cls
   ? "We are in function Main()"

   return(NIL)
```

If the /N switch is not used in compiling this program file, the result will be two distinct modules: the .PRG file itself (since it can also be a self-running executable) and the function Main( ). In this case, if we attempt to run the program, nothing happens, since the module Simple contains no code, while the function Main( ) is never called.

Note that, had we named our program file MAIN.PRG instead of SIMPLE.PRG and compiled without the /N switch, Clipper would have generated a compile-time error, since there would have been two modules named Main: the .PRG file itself and the Main( ) function. This is the case because Clipper does not differentiate between a .PRG file acting like a procedure, a function, or a procedure; all are represented by a symbol in the symbol table.

On the other hand, if we compile with the /N switch, Clipper generates a single reference in the symbol table—for the function Main( ). When SIMPLE.EXE is executed, however, Main( ) is executed first, since it is the topmost procedure.

The /N switch corresponds closely to a function-based, Clipper 5.x style of programming. In contrast, compiling without the /N switch resembles the pre-Clipper 5.x approach to programming. The following code fragment, although very simple, is typical of Summer '87:

```
* SIMPLE.PRG

local GetList := {}

cls
? "We are executing the procedure Simple"

return
```

When compiled without the /N switch, it executes as expected. But it cannot be compiled with the /N switch, since it generates the error message "Statement not allowed outside procedure or function." Clipper has not been able to identify a single procedure or subroutine inside our program file, and as a result can make no sense of our source code.

A variation on this last example is the following:

```
* SIMPLE.PRG

Main()

function Main()

   local GetList := {}

   cls
   ? "We are executing the procedure Main"

   return(NIL)
```

Note that the /N switch is also useful in supporting filewide STATIC variables. Consider the following code:

```
* SIMPLE.PRG

static cFilename := "SIMPLE.PRG"
static GetList := {}

function Main()

   qout("This is program "+cFilename)

   return(NIL)
```

If compiled with the /N switch, the static variables are visible throughout the program file, and Main( ), as the topmost procedure or function, executes automatically when the program is called. In contrast, without the /N switch, the topmost procedure, SIMPLE, contains only the STATIC variable declarations and does not call Main( ); the program once again seems to do nothing.

This example can only be compiled without the /N switch. Since the function Main( ) is called within the topmost routine, that routine must have a symbol in the symbol table in order for Main( ) to be called. If this example were compiled with the /N switch, an error message would again be generated and no .OBJ file would be created.

## /O  OBJECT FILENAME SPECIFIED

```
/O<filename>
```

This switch generates an .OBJ file which will be named <filename>. Specify only the root name of the file; the file extension will always be .OBJ.

The /O switch can also be used to place the .OBJ file in an explicit drive and directory. If only a directory path is specified in <filename>, make certain that the path concludes with the backslash (\) character. If this is the case, the .OBJ file will take on the root name of the first module compiled, with an .OBJ file extension.

```
Clipper Makedata /M /L /O\RANDOM\OBJECT\
Clipper Makedata /OData
Clipper Makedata /B /O\RANDOM\OBJECT\DATA
```

In the first example, the source file MAKEDATA.PRG will be compiled without line numbers and in a single module only. The object file that Clipper will create will by default be named MAKEDATA.OBJ and will be stored in the \RANDOM\OBJECT directory. Note that the extra backslash character is used in this example. In the second example, the object module will be named DATA.OBJ, and it will be placed in the default directory. Finally, in the third example, the source file MAKEDATA.PRG will be compiled with additional debugging information, and it will be written to the \RANDOM\OBJECT directory under the name of DATA.OBJ.

## /P  GENERATE A PREPROCESSED OUTPUT LISTING

```
/P[<filename>]
```

This generates an output listing after the preprocessor has finished scanning the program module or file. The preprocessed output listing is a Clipper intermediate file that is made prior to the actual compilation step. It is normally held in memory and is not visible to you; it is part of the compiling process.

By default, the output file will have the same root name as the .PRG or .CLP file, but it will have a .PPO (preprocessor output) file extension. You may specify the name of the output file as well as its path. Make certain that the backslash character is part of the directory path. If you want to redirect the output file to a specific directory yet wish to keep the default filename, specify the directory path as the <filename> but end the expression with the backslash (\) character.

```
Clipper Makedata /P\RANDOM\C5\PPO\
Clipper Makedata /P
Clipper Makedata /P\RANDOM\C5\PPO\Output
```

In the first example above, the preprocessed file would be MAKEDATA.PPO, and it would be placed in the directory named \RANDOM\C5\PPO. Note that the extra backslash is needed here for this to happen; otherwise, the file would be named PPO.PPO and would be stored in the \RANDOM\C5 subdirectory. In the second example, the output file will be MAKEDATA.PPO and it will be written to the current drive and directory. In the final example, the output file will be named OUTPUT.PPO and will be found in the \RANDOM\C5\PPO directory.

## /Q  QUIET MODE

This switch prevents source code line numbers from being displayed on the screen while the compiler is active. This only affects the visual display and has no effect on line numbers being written to the .OBJ file. Use the /L option for that.

## /R RESOLVE AND SEARCH FOR UNRESOLVED EXTERNALS

```
/R<filename>
```

The Clipper programming environment provides two major ways of specifying library references to the linker. The most obvious is to explicitly specify them with the LIB argument to the RTLINK command. However, in addition, the Clipper compiler automatically embeds the names of four major libraries in the object file itself: CLIPPER, EXTEND, TERMINAL, and DBFNTX. The /R switch allows additional library references to be embedded in the .OBJ file generated by the Clipper compiler, and (provided that the library or libraries are either in the current directory or in a directory defined by the LIB environmental variable) frees the programmer from having to explicitly specify library names as parameters to the RTLINK command. For example, the following command line instructs Clipper to embed the PTOOLS.LIB filename in the object file, where the linker can find it when it searches for any unresolved external references:

```
Clipper MAKEDATA /RPTOOLS
```

Note that using the /R switch with no parameters, however, instructs Clipper to generate an object file that contains no embedded library references. In this case, all libraries' references needed by an application, including the four libraries that Clipper by default names in the .OBJ file, must be provided as parameters to the RTLINK command.

## /S SYNTAX CHECK ONLY

This tells the compiler to check the specified modules for syntactical correctness. No object file is generated. The .PPO file (using the /P switch) may still be generated even though no object file was generated.

## /T TEMPORARY FILE LOCATION

```
/T<pathname>
```

This specifies a different directory path for all temporary files that may be generated during the compiling process. If no path is specified, the current directory will be used.

## /U USER-DEFINED STANDARD HEADER FILE

```
/U<filename>
```

This switch tells the compiler to use an alternate header file for the preprocessor; <filename> should include both the name and extension of the header file, as well as the directory path if it is not located in the current directory or in a directory not defined by the INCLUDE environmental variable. Unless this compiler option is being used to supply the exact location of STD.CH to the compiler, the alternate header file will replace STD.CH. Therefore, it must contain only preprocessor directives. If no <filename> is specified, no standard header will be used for the preprocessor, and the source code will not be put through a preprocessing step.

```
Clipper Makedata /M /U\RANDOM\C5\HEADER\STD.CH
Clipper Makedata /UMYSTD.CH
Clipper Makedata /U
```

The first example tells the compiler that the preprocessor header file to be used will be STD.CH, and that it is located in the directory \RANDOM\C5\HEADER. The object file will also be compiled in a single module only. The second example tells the compiler that the header file for the preprocessor is not STD.CH; rather, it is MYSTD.CH. Since a path is not specified, the compiler will search for it in the logged drive's current directory, in the directories defined by the /I switch, and, finally, in the directory defined by the DOS INCLUDE environmental variable. In the final example, the switch tells Clipper that there will be no standard header file for the preprocessor.

To speed up the compiling process, a header file named STUBSTD.CH may be used that contains only those commonly used commands that need translating. The translations removed from STUBSTD.CH include the rarely used UPDATE, LOCATE, and JOIN commands. This file, provided in Appendix 2, can be further modified to speed up the compiling process even more.

## /V  VARIABLE REFERENCES

This option applies to cases in which fields and memory variables have the same name. It determines how Clipper will resolve ambiguous references that may be either fields or memory variables.

When programs are compiled without the /V switch, Clipper assumes that all unaliased references are fields; in this case, memory variables with the same names as fields must be indicated by the M-> or MEMVAR-> alias. However, this convention may make it impossible to pass a variable by reference to the function, since these aliases cannot be used with the @ symbol.

Therefore, it is preferable to compile with the /V switch. This means that Clipper will assume that unaliased references are variables, and that, in cases in which variable names and field names are identical, fields should be explicitly specified with either their alias name, the alias of their work area, or the dynamic field alias FIELD->.

```
Clipper Makedata /M /P /V
```

This example tells the compiler to generate the object file for the source program MAKEDATA.PRG, to compile only that module, to generate a preprocessed file with the name MAKEDATA.PPO in the directory that is logged at the time of the compilation, and to assume that ambiguous references are to variables instead of fields.

## /W  WARNING MESSAGES FOR AMBIGUOUS VARIABLE REFERENCES

The /W switch merely instructs Clipper that it should display a warning message on the screen that warns the programmer of a potential hazard without stopping the compilation process. For example, the Clipper compiler will produce a warning message if a function does not end with a RETURN statement or if a variable is not explicitly defined as PUBLIC, PRIVATE, MEMVAR, LOCAL, STATIC or FIELD.

## /Z  SUPPRESS "SHORTCUTTING" OPTIMIZATION

Normally, Clipper will optimize code using a technique whereby the evaluation of expressions that contain logical connectives like .AND. and .OR. will stop as soon as the result of the expression as a whole can be determined. As an example, let's look at the following code extract:

```
if ( One() .OR. Two() .OR. Three() )
   // Perform operation
endif
```

Clipper 5.2 would evaluate the One( ) function, and, if it returned a logical true (.T.) value, it would not call either the Two( ) or Three( ) function, since the expression must necessarily result in the value of true. This technique, called "shortcutting," suppresses the execution or evaluation of parts of any expression so long as the results of the expression can be determined without executing those coded fragments. This technique did not appear in versions of Clipper prior to Clipper 5.0, which means that in these versions, the above expression would cause sequential evaluation of each of the three functions, even if the results of the expression were already known. For compatibility with previous versions, this shortcutting technique can be suppressed with the /Z compiler option. However, this optimization technique cannot be turned off within those expressions that are macro-expanded.

# Standard Compiling Switches and Options

Typically, for most compiling processes, the following switches will be used. They may appear within a .RMK file, the SET CLIPPERCMD= environmental switch, or issued on the command line with the filename:

```
/m /n /v /w /a /p /es2
```

If the debugger is to be used in building the application, the /b switch should be added to the list.

If a test mode is used in building an application in which test functions may be dropped into the compilation but not designed for the final output, then the following might be issued in conjunction with the standard set:

```
/dpTEST
```

## CLIP Files and Batch Compiling

Files with a .CLP extension are known as CLIP files. They are script files that contain the names of individual source program files to be compiled together into one .OBJ file. Each source program file must be named on a separate line, without its file extension. Files listed in these text files may also contain specific paths. Regardless of the name of the first file in the script file list, the default name of the object file will be the root name of the CLIP file. In other words, if the following files are listed in a script file named ONE.CLP, the object file would be ONE.OBJ:

```
Ledger
Ledopen
Ledmakes
Ledger1
Ledger2
```

This name could be changed by the /O compiler directive switch.

To compile a script file, the @ sign is used in front of the root name of the script file. In the above example, one possible calling convention would be

```
Clipper @One
```

Each program file listed in ONE.CLP would be opened and compiled into a single object file named ONE.OBJ. The name of the object file could be altered as follows:

```
Clipper @One /OLedger
```

This would compile all of the files listed in the CLIP file named ONE.CLP into a file named LEDGER.OBJ. Specifying any compiler directive with a script file would tell Clipper to apply that compiler switch to all files listed in the file. For example, if the /L and /B switches were used when compiling with a CLIP file, line numbers for each program listed in the CLIP file would be removed from the output object file and the remaining debugging information would be added.

In the past, CLIP files were used to optimize your linking strategy. Now they are used to batch like files, allowing the compiler to symbolically build the best structured object file. For example, if there are two separate program files with references to a variable named $x$, there would be two object files with separate symbolic references to this variable. When linked, the two symbols would reside in the main load; each reference would be looked up at the appropriate time in the execution of the program. However, in essence, they are the same variable.

If the linker could reduce these two references to one reference, we would have a reduction in load memory, which would in turn give us more free pool memory to run our application. But linkers cannot make these assumptions; compilers, on the other hand, can. Instead of having two separate symbol tables, one for each object file, the compiler can generate one object file by combining the two program files. This way, the compiler would generate only one token for the variable $x$, which would be referenced by either of the two procedures or functions.

It is not feasible to go through an entire application's layout and reorganize the contents of each program file for that application. It is, however, possible to use a CLIP file to accomplish the same thing. For example, consider the following scenario. An accounting package contains seven modules: General Ledger, Accounts Receivable, Accounts Payable, Inventory, Payroll, Order Entry, and Purchasing. Each subsystem contains a unique set of program modules with similar variables that appear not only in individual program files, but also in program files across subsystems. One possible CLIP file arrangement would be to have one unique object module for each subsystem. Another possibility would be to combine those files with similar symbolic references (fields and variables) into a single object file.

One restriction on the number of program modules that can be combined into a single object file should be noted here. A single Clipper object file can contain only 512 entries in a symbol table. Two entries per object file will contain the root name of the CLIP file, and an additional 14 entries are used by the compiler for overhead. Each function or procedure generates two entries. This means that the maximum number of procedures and functions allowed in a single object file is about 240. If you exceed this number, you could get either of the following errors:

```
C3024 Too many procs
```

or

```
C3020 Too many segments
```

To illustrate the use of a CLIP file to generate an object file, here is a series of individual source files that could be compiled separately and linked, or compiled using a CLIP file:

```
* File:     Clip1.prg
* Note:     Clipper @Clipdemo /P /V

  local cScreen := savescreen()  // Save the current screen
  local nRow    := row()         // Save the current row and
  local nCol    := col()         // then the column status

  cls
  @ 1,0 say "This is the first screen..."
  SubRoutine1()
  setpos( nRow, nCol )      // Put the cursor back
  restscreen(,,,,cScreen)   // restore the screen

// End of File: Clip1.prg


* File:     Clip2.prg

procedure SubRoutine1()

  @ 3,5 SAY " And now I am in the next screen"
  @ 4,5 SAY " Press any key to move onto the"
  @ 5,5 SAY " next procedure..."
  inkey(0)
  SubRoute2( date() )

********************

static procedure SubRoute2( dInDate )
```

```
   @  7,10 SAY "Now that we are here, we have a date that was passed"
   @  8,10 SAY "to this procedure.  This parameter is a local memory"
   @  9,10 SAY "variable that will be explained later in this book..."

   setpos(20,00)    // Set the cursor position for the WAIT command
   wait
   SubRoute3()

// End of File: Clip2.prg


*  File:      Clip3.prg

procedure SubRoute3()

   local nLevel := 0

   while !empty( procname( nLevel ) )
      devpos( row()+1, 15 )
      devout( "Program Level is: " )
      devout( nLevel )
      devout( padl( "Procedure is ", 20 ) )
      devout( procname( nLevel++ ) )        // Post incrementing!
   enddo

   wait

// End of File: Clip3.prg
```

And the CLIP file that compiles all of this is the following:

```
*  File:      Clipdemo.clp
clip1
clip2
clip3
*  End of File: ClipDemo.clp
```

The command to compile each of the individual program files into the object file named **CLIPDEMO.OBJ** is

```
CLIPPER @Clipdemo /P /V
```

Once the object file has been generated, the command for the linker would be

```
RTLINK FI Clipdemo LIB Clipper
```

Treat the object file generated via the script file CLIPDEMO.CLP as a regular object file, as if it were generated from a .PRG file. So the important thing to remember with .CLP files and the object files they build is that duplicate symbols are eliminated in the process of compiling.

In addition, keep in mind that if the /P compiler switch is used, an intermediate file for each of the files listed in the .CLP file will be generated. Also, regular Clipper comments may be embedded in a .CLP file. They will not disrupt the contents and compiling order of those files listed in the CLIP file.

## The DOS Environment

There are also several DOS environmental variables that may be defined to aid in the compiling process. Setting these environmental variables consumes some of the fixed memory available within the DOS environment. If an "out of environment space" message appears, this indicates that all memory in the DOS environment has been used. Check your DOS version to see if you can set your environment size within CONFIG.SYS using the SHELL command with the /E switch. Remember, your default search path, DOS prompt, environmental variables for your editor (such as MultiEdit), and any other environmental variables all take up room in your DOS environment.

Clipper 5.2 can make use of several DOS environmental variables. These can be issued directly on the command line or included in your AUTOEXEC.BAT. They are

```
CLIPPERCMD
TMP
INCLUDE
CLIPPER
```

There are additional DOS environmental variables that pertain either to linking an application or to a particular Clipper utility. These DOS variables, listed below, will be discussed in their appropriate chapters:

```
LIB
OBJ
PLL
RTLINKCMD
RMAKE
```

## CLIPPERCMD

CLIPPERCMD is defined as follows:

```
SET CLIPPERCMD=<compiler directives>
```

The list of <compiler directives> defines the Clipper compiler switches that will be processed each time the compiler is called, as long as this environmental variable is still active. Any compiler switch specified in the <compiler directives> list will be processed before those specified on the command line. In some cases, if a switch is specified in both the DOS environment and on the command line, the switch is not invoked (that is, it is turned off).

The CLIPPERCMD variable might be defined as follows:

```
SET CLIPPERCMD=/m /p /v /u\random\b2\std.ch
```

To turn off the CLIPPERCMD variable, type in the following:

```
SET CLIPPERCMD=
```

The equal sign must immediately follow the string CLIPPERCMD in order to completely turn off the environmental variable; no spaces should separate the two. To verify that it has been removed from the environmental table, simply type the word *SET* on the command line.

Keep in mind that in a group environment, many applications and machines require different settings. Therefore, while it is possible to set up any one machine with a series of CLIPPERCMD settings, it is highly recommended that these switches either be used directly on the command line with the application being compiled or, preferably, be used in conjunction with an RMAKE .RMK file. This way, the compiler switches used in the process will not be machine dependent and will be documented through the use of a .RMK file.

## TMP

The TMP environmental variable is set by issuing the following statement on the DOS command line:

```
SET TMP=<path name>
```

In some cases, the compiler will generate temporary files to complete the preprocessing step, the compilation step, or both. This usually takes place when the application is larger than the amount of available memory, or the amount of available memory is not adequate to complete all of the steps necessary to turn a program file into an object file. In these cases, Clipper will create temporary files. These files can be directed to another directory on your hard disk, or even to a RAM disk. After Clipper is finished, the files will be automatically deleted.

The directory in which these special files will be written is set via the SET TMP command. The linker for Clipper will also use the path specified by the SET TMP command.

```
SET TMP=H:\
```

This command, for example, will create any temporary files in the H:\ directory. To turn off this DOS environmental command, issue the following:

```
SET TMP=
```

If the compiler switch /T is used to specify the location of temporary files, this switch will override any TMP environmental variable.

## INCLUDE

This DOS environmental variable allows you to tell the compiler the default location of all INCLUDE files. To set it, issue the following DOS command:

```
SET INCLUDE=<path name>
```

<path name> may include more than one directory path; in these cases, paths should be separated from one another by a semicolon. For example:

```
SET INCLUDE=C:\CLIPPER5.2\INCLUDE;C:\PTOOLS\INCLUDE
```

This path may also be issued directly with the include preprocessor directive, as follows:

```
#include "\PTOOLS\PTVerbs.ch"
```

To avoid making a specific reference to a directory path, the search path for the include files should be set either by the SET INCLUDE= statement or by the /I compiling switch.

If both the DOS environmental variable and the /I compiling switch are used, the path defined by SET INCLUDE will take precedence over the path prescribed by the /I switch. SET INCLUDE will not take precedence over the current directory. However, if the INCLUDE files are not first found in the current directory and are not then found in the directory or directories defined by the SET INCLUDE statement, the path specified in the /I switch will be used.

To undefine the INCLUDE environmental variable, issue the following command at the DOS prompt:

```
SET INCLUDE=
```

## CLIPPER

This environmental variable is used to handle several things, including Clipper's new Virtual Memory Manager, the setting for expanded memory, the setting for the number of files to open at any one time, the setting used to allocate memory for an external RUN command, and the settings used for the overlay manager. Multiple settings can be defined by the SET CLIPPER command, provided that a semicolon is used to separate each one.

Note that, although all of the environmental variables that we have discussed previously affect the operation of the Clipper compiler, the CLIPPER environmental variable affects the operation of the application at run time, after it has been compiled by Clipper and subsequently linked.

**SET CLIPPER=BADCACHE**   This switch forces the virtual memory manager (VMM) that is a part of the Clipper environment to maintain and preserve the "restore state" of an EMM page before and after each time the EMM is accessed. It is designed to resolve potential conflicts between the running Clipper application and other programs using the EMM. However, this may adversely affect the performance of VMM with some EMM systems. Computer Associates advises that this feature should be used only if there is some experience with disk and/or file corruption due to a conflict between the Clipper application and a disk caching or other RAM-resident software package.

**SET CLIPPER=CGACURS**   This parameter ensures that Clipper will not take advantage of the extended cursor capabilities of EGA and VGA systems. While this may preclude some cursor modes, it is useful in making sure that an application will run on a computer with TSRs loaded or in some multitasking environments.

**SET CLIPPER=DYNF:<expN1>**   The value of DYNF determines the number of file handles that the dynamic overlay system uses. Its value can range from 1 to 8. By default, the value of DYNF is 2.

**SET CLIPPER=E:<expN1>**   Programs compiled and linked with Clipper 5.2 can use expanded memory that conforms to the LIM 4.0 (or higher) Expanded Memory Specification. All available expanded memory is allocated at start-up. To set a maximum amount of expanded memory that will be allocated to a Clipper application, the E parameter can be used. For example, the following command restricts the amount of expanded memory available to the application to one megabyte:

```
SET CLIPPER=E:1024
```

There are four items to keep in mind with respect to the maximum amount of total memory allocated:

- The amount of EMS available
- The SET CLIPPER=E: setting
- A theoretical maximum of 32 MB of memory
- The amount of conventional memory available

It is important to remember that a certain amount of conventional memory will be used to hold tables for Clipper's VMM system. The more memory that is available (both conventional and EMS memory), the more that will be consumed by the VMM system.

**SET CLIPPER=F:<expN1>**   While the number of files that can be open at a single time is defined by the FILES= command in the CONFIG.SYS file, Clipper also has its own setting for controlling the number of files that can be open at a single time within the Clipper application. By default, 20 files can be open at once (unless FILES has been set to less than 20 in CONFIG.SYS). This setting can be changed with the F parameter. The following example would allow Clipper to open up to 50 files at a single time, provided that CONFIG.SYS contains a FILES= value that would also allow this:

```
SET CLIPPER=F:50
```

**SET CLIPPER=INFO**   This setting will provide information regarding Clipper's memory use for that application at the start-up of the application and then at the conclusion of the program as well. For example, if the following program were to be compiled:

```
function Main()

  inkey(0)
  cls
  ? "Now for a test"
  inkey(0)

  return( NIL )
```

and if the INFO switch is engaged, the following would be displayed to the screen prior to the execution of the first INKEY(0) function call:

```
Clipper (R) 5.2 Rev. 1.97 ASCII
DS=2FA7:0000   DS avail=40KB   OS avail=186KB   EMM avail=1427KB
```

and then, at the conclusion of the program, the following will be displayed:

```
(Fixed heap=12KB/2)
```

Those numbers have the following significance:

| | |
|---|---|
| DS=<offset>:0000 | Address for the data segment known as DGROUP. |
| DS avail=<mem>KB | Shows the amount of available memory in DGROUP. |
| OS avail=<mem>KB | Shows the amount of conventional memory for VMM to swap with. |

EMM avail=<mem>KB    Shows the amount of expanded memory allocated to the program.

Fixed Heap=<x>KB    Shows the size of the fixed heap in kilobyte increments as well as the number of fixed segments.

**SET CLIPPER=NOIDLE**   The Clipper NOIDLE switch turns off the internal setting that enables Clipper to detect and take advantage of idle time during the execution of a program. The syntax is

```
SET CLIPPER=NOIDLE
```

Typically, a Clipper-compiled application will use idle time, such as while it is awaiting user input (a WAIT state), to perform garbage collection, file updates, and other memory management and overlay maintenance operations. Setting the NOIDLE switch will suppress this and thus reduce the overall performance of an application. However, it is useful for those applications that use C modules with reserved memory locations that cannot be moved during a Clipper "wait" state.

**SET CLIPPER=SWAPK:<expN1>**   The SWAPK parameter determines the maximum size in kilobytes (KB) that the swap file can be, where <expN1> is in the range of 256 to 65,535, inclusive, with a default of 16 megabytes (MB). Be careful not to suppress the disk-swapping mechanism with SET CLIPPER=SWAPK:0. This will cause an application to fail. For example, the following would set the swap file size to 2 MB.

```
SET CLIPPER=SWAPK:2048
```

**SET CLIPPER=SWAPPATH:<expC>**   The SWAPPATH switch tells where the swap file is to be placed. A drive and a directory name may be used; RAM drives may also be used. If not specified, the current drive and directory will be used. For example, if a RAM disk is located on the H: drive, the following command may be used:

```
SET CLIPPER=SWAPK:2048;SWAPPATH:"H:"
```

**SET CLIPPER=TEMPPATH:<expN>**   The TEMPPATH switch defines where temporary files created during any sorting or indexing operation are located. The default location for those files will be the current directory. It should be noted that these files may be quite large, a factor that must be considered before redirecting them to a RAM disk.

**SET CLIPPER=X:<expN1>**   X defines how much memory should be allocated when running a program. This switch is particularly useful for testing and debugging programs when the development machine has much more memory than the hardware that will be running the application. For example, if the development machine has a full 640K of memory but the computer that will run the application has only 512K, the following will exclude 128K of the development machine's conventional memory:

```
SET CLIPPER=X:128
```

## Using the CLIPPER Switches

What is cumbersome about executing an application that requires one of these Clipper settings is that these environmental settings are not "burned" into the executable file. One solution is to use a batch file to set up the application before calling it. You can specify many of these switches by using the following example:

```
SET CLIPPER=NOIDLE; F:79? E:0; CGACURS
```

While all of these settings could be defined by the DOS CLIPPER environmental variable, it is also possible to pass these settings to any Clipper application directly on the command line along with any parameters that are to be passed to the application. The format for calling a Clipper application with any of these switches is as follows:

```
<application> [<switches] [<application parameters>]
```

So, for example, the following could be specified when calling the MakeData application which generates all of the data files for the other example programs in this book:

```
MakeData F:70 E:0 NOIDLE \PWC\SOURCE
```

# Clipper Error Messages

There are several types of error messages. Some of these messages pertain to your code, some pertain to the preprocessor, some are embedded within your application and are displayed at run-time, and others are just internal errors for Computer Associates. A list of Clipper errors, preprocessor, compiler, and run-time errors is given in Appendix 9.

If the compiler encounters an error or if compilation is prematurely terminated by pressing Ctrl-C, the DOS ERRORLEVEL code would be 1. If the compilation process is successful, regardless of any warning messages, the DOS ERRORLEVEL will be 0.

# Tips and Pointers

Environmental variables take precedence over command line specifications; however, in some cases, specifying a compiler switch in an environmental setting as well as on the command line could turn off the compiler directive:

```
set clippercmd=/m /p /v /u\random\b2\std.ch
CLIPPER Makedata /P
```

This actually turns off the output file that would have been generated by the preprocessor because the /P compiler switch would negate the environmental /P directive.

You may add to an environmental condition with additional command-line compiling directives:

```
set clippercmd=/m /p /v /u\random\b2\std.ch
CLIPPER MAKEDATA /OData
```

This simply tells Clipper to adhere to the rules outlined in the environmental SET command, but to add to it the output object switch. In this case, the program file MAKEDATA.PRG will be compiled in single-module mode only, all ambiguous references will be tagged as variables (not fields), and a file named MAKEDATA.PPO will be created, as will an object file named DATA.OBJ.

**WARNING** Do not mix object modules compiled with previous versions of the Clipper compiler with object modules generated with Clipper 5.2. And do not try to link object modules generated with prior versions of Clipper with the libraries that come with Clipper 5.2.

# 2

# RTLink, the Linker

## What Is a Linker?

Compiling is only half of the equation; linking an application together is the second piece of the Clipper puzzle. A compiler makes a list of symbolic references; the linker attempts to match them (tie them together) as best it can with their meanings. Again, thinking in terms of a dictionary, a compiler is the word-list portion of each entry. A linker takes the symbolic references of routines—namely, procedures and functions—and finds their definitions within other object files (.OBJ) or within a library file (.LIB). To continue with our dictionary analogy, the other half of the dictionary entry—the half containing what the words mean—must be added to the words to get both word and definition to make sense.

Here is a basic code example:

```
Hello()

* * * * * * * * * * * * * *

function Hello

  qout( "Hello world!" )
  return( NIL )
```

In this example, the call to the Hello( ) subroutine is found within the same program module as the Hello function. The definition of Hello( ) is the formal declaration of Hello( ) as a function. The compiler will resolve this (match the call to the definition) during the compilation stage. However, within Hello( ) there is a call to the QOUT( ) function, which is Clipper's ? command in a function format. This function is found in part within CLIPPER.LIB. The linker will match this call with the definition of QOUT( ) found within the library.

A library file (.LIB) is nothing more than a file that contains one or more object files. The linker will find the reference to a called subroutine and link in or add to the application the object module within the .LIB file that contains that specific procedure or function. The linker will not pull in those object modules that are not specifically referenced within the application or within other dependent object modules in the library file. However, if a routine is compiled with several other subroutines and that individual routine is called, the linker will not separate only the functional reference; instead, the entire object module will be linked into the application.

If a .PRG file contains several independent functions or procedures which could, for all practicality, stand on their own, it is said that the .PRG file, and subsequently the .OBJ and .LIB files, are ungranulated. The concept here is that when a function is called, the .OBJ file in which it is defined is initially linked into the executable program, causing excess bloating. Before VMM, a call to that single function would also bring that entire module into memory. Sometimes, ungranulated libraries and object files are necessary: dependent subroutines are required if any general function or procedure should be needed. However, in many cases, some overhead may be reduced by simply using proper library management techniques.

The definitions for all of the Clipper functions are grouped together in four individual library files. The basic Clipper functions and dBASE command dialect, including a macro-parsing/run-time object module (known as PLANKTON.OBJ) are in CLIPPER.LIB. Extended functions and operations, including added user-defined functions to add backward compatibility, are in EXTEND.LIB. TERMINAL.LIB contains the object modules that specifically pertain to video output and control, while DBFNTX.LIB is the library file that contains the object module to handle the .NTX file format. These four libraries are specifically hard-coded into the header of any object file created by Clipper 5.2; this can be seen in Figure 2.1, which is a screen dump of a sample object file, as shown by The Norton Utilities.

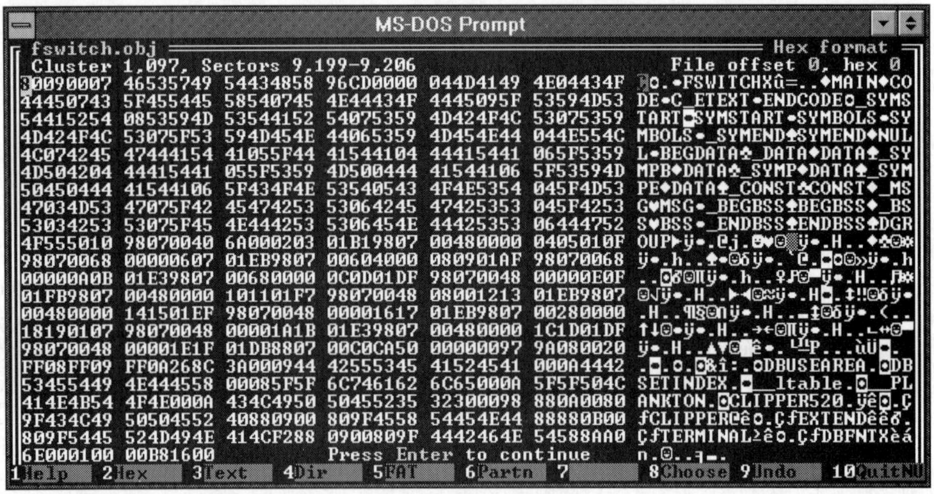

Figure 2.1  Library references in an object file

Near the end of this chapter there is a section which shows the individual components of each of these four Clipper libraries. This information is very handy when you need to know what modules are involved in a link cycle and in planning to build a .PLL.

## What Is RTLink?

Included with Clipper is a special linker named RTLink, which consists of the following five files:

**RTLINK.EXE**   This is the actual linker. It will create both executable (.EXE) files and prelinked (.PLL and .PLT) libraries.

**RTLINKST.COM**   This contains start-up information for RTLINK to use each time a prelinked library is created. It is only used to create the library and is not required when executing a program using a .PLL file. This file must be in the same directory as RTLINK.EXE.

**RTUTILS.LIB**   This library file contains the static overlay manager. It is needed when the linker puts together programs that use any of the static overlay linking options.

**RTLINK.DAT**   This file contains all of the error messages for the linker. In addition, it contains information needed to parse the commands used in *Freeformat* mode. This file must reside in the same directory as RTLINK.EXE.

**RTLINK.HLP**   This file contains the help information that is displayed when the *HELP* clause is specified. This file must reside in the same directory as RTLINK.EXE.

RTLink has been especially designed to take Clipper-compiled code and build a dynamic overlay area that can swap Clipper code in and out of memory. This allows large applications to run in a limited memory environment. However, it is not the ultimate answer to memory management problems. The way we code and our approach to application design has as much of an impact on memory management as does the methodology we choose to employ in linking. RTLink tries to assist us by compacting the symbol tables of Clipper object files. With other linkers in the past, the only way to pack a symbol table was to allow the compiler to make as few object files as possible, allowing it to match like symbols in one table. This was accomplished via .CLP (Clip) files.

Along with the linking question comes the issue of memory management, which is handled automatically by Clipper's Virtual Memory Management (VMM) system (discussed later in this chapter). One thing to keep in mind is that VMM is never turned off; and it is handled by the internals of CLIPPER.LIB and not by the linker. Memory management issues are therefore handled in two parts: the overlaying of Clipper code in a set area of memory, which is handled by the linker; and allocating available free pool memory to handle database information, indexing, memory variables, arrays, objects, and the like, which is handled by the language itself. Do not get the two confused.

There are three ways in which RTLink makes an executable file: from the DOS command line; from RTLink's own interactive prompt; and from a script file, commonly with the default extension of .LNK. The .LNK script file is similar in nature to the script file for making object files (.CLP files) and for putting together an application with RMAKE.EXE

(.RMK files). All three methods for linking have two potential interfaces with RTLink; one is known as *Positional*, and the other is known as *Freeformat*. The *Positional* interface is patterned after Microsoft's LINK style, while the *Freeformat* is patterned after PLINK86-Plus' style. The latter style is more flexible; however, either style is acceptable to RTLink.

The difference between Freeformat and Positional format is based on previous stylistic preferences. Most C programmers are familiar with the way in which executable files are created from Microsoft's LINK program, while others are accustomed to previous versions of Clipper and the PLINK86-Plus linking style. While the latter style is more *free-form*, both methods are acceptable.

In addition to the two different interface styles, there are different linking methodologies. These include standard linking, linking with dynamic overlays, linking with a prelinked library, and incremental linking. Each linking strategy is different and applies to different programming scenarios and situations.

## RTLink Command Summary

Keep in mind that, when issuing linker commands in *positional* mode, every command must be preceded by a forward slash (/). The *freeformat* mode does not make such a requirement; however, a forward slash (/) is acceptable. In addition, some of the commands in positional mode require a colon character (:). However, as with the (/) character, some commands do not require this in either mode. Below is a complete listing of the commands, the proper syntax for each linking mode, and their meaning. Following this is a brief template showing the items required by each linking mode to produce an executable file.

**/FREEFORMAT** This command specifies to the linker that commands and options will be issued in FREEFORMAT mode, which represents a PLINK86-Plus linking command style. The (/) character is required with this command. If neither the /FREEFORMAT nor the /POSITIONAL argument is specified, FREEFORMAT will be the default mode of the linker.

**/POSITIONAL** This command tells the linker that commands and options will be issued in POSITIONAL mode, which represents a Microsoft LINK command style. The / character is required with this command.

**DYNAMIC [INTO <expC1>] (freeformat) and /DYNAMIC[:<expC1>] (positional)** This command instructs RTLink to place Clipper-compiled modules into a dynamic overlay; this is the default option. DYNAMIC is the opposite of RESIDENT, which will locate these modules in the root section; this will cause the memory *footprint* of an application to be large. By contrast, a dynamic overlay will reduce the initial memory footprint of an application. However, the application's speed of execution will be affected by disk access time and the extra time needed to load dynamic overlays. If specified, <expC1> is the name of an external overlay (.OVL) file which will contain the code for the dynamic overlay. If not specified, the overlay will be internal to the application and will be written into the executable (.EXE) file. This is the default mode for the linker.

**/RESIDENT** This command tells the linker to place all of the Clipper-compiled modules into the main load or "root section" of the application. This will speed up the execution of an application but will require more memory. This command will override the default mode, which is *DYNAMIC*.

**/DEBUG and DEBUG**   This instructs the memory manager to display a message during the execution of an application that shows the name of each overlay as it is being loaded into memory.

**/HELP and HELP**   This command lists all of the linker options available to the standard output device (console). It may be directed to a file by issuing the following command at the DOS prompt:

```
RTLINK /HELP > <filename>
```

**MAP [= <expC2>] [<expC1>] (freeformat) and /MAP[:<expC1>] (positional)**
This command will generate a file named <expC2> which will contain one or more reports describing the transactions that occurred during the linking session. If no map filename is specified in either linking mode command, the name of the map file will be the same as the root name of the executable program with a .MAP default file extension. The option <expC1> represents the available reports that this command can generate:

| | |
|---|---|
| S | Report segments with assigned addresses |
| N | Report public symbols with addresses sorted by symbol |
| A | Report public symbols with addresses sorted by address |

If <expC1> is not specified, all three reports are written to the map file.

**/SILENT**   This command suppresses the display of the prompts generated by the linker when it is called with a script file.

**/VERBOSE[:<expN1>]**   This command tells the linker what level of information it is to display in status messages while linking. The value of <expN1> determines how much information is displayed; it can be 0, 1, or 2. A value of 0 instructs the linker to suppress the display of informational messages except for one containing the name of the temporary swap file generated by the linker. Values of 1 and 2 instruct the linker to indicate which object modules (and, when <expN1> equals 2, the names of the libraries in which they are found) are being linked into the application and in what order. If the /VERBOSE argument is omitted, it defaults to /VERBOSE:0. If the /VERBOSE argument is used but <expN1> is omitted, it defaults to 1.

**/INCREMENTAL[:<expN1>]**   The INCREMENTAL command tells the linker to perform an incremental link. If activated, only those object modules that have changed will be relinked into the application. If specified, <expN1> represents the percentage of *wasted space* allowed in the output executable file (.EXE). Wasted space is generated for incremental linking to allow a program module to grow or shrink. Each time a section of Clipper code is worked on, the amount of compiled information will vary, and as a result, the size of that particular module will either decrease or increase. To handle this fluctuation during the coding stages of an application, this parameter will instruct the linker to control wasted space. This numeric parameter controls the linker's tolerance level before it automatically performs a complete relink of the application. Once this level is reached, a complete relink will be performed. The default tolerance of wasted space is 25%; the amount of wasted space may be tracked using the VERBOSE command switch.

If the INCREMENTAL option is specified, a special file of incremental information will be generated with the root name of the executable file (.EXE), but with an .INF file extension. Deleting this file will cause the linker to perform a complete relink cycle during the next link session.

**/NOINCREMENTAL**   The NOINCREMENTAL command switch—the default—instructs the linker to perform a complete link cycle.

**/BATCH and /NOBATCH**   The BATCH command prevents the linker from issuing a prompt to the user to indicate or correct an error; usually it does this when it is unable to find a particular file. The default is NOBATCH.

**/DEFAULTLIBRARYSEARCH and /NODEFAULTLIBRARYSEARCH**   As we have seen, the names of the four default libraries—CLIPPER, EXTEND, TERMINAL, and DBFNTX—are placed in the header of every .OBJ file compiled by Clipper. (This assumes, of course, that the /R compiling option is not used.) The linker will automatically search the library path and the DOS path for these four libraries (if they are needed) in order to perform the link cycle if the DEFAULTLIBRARYSEARCH command is used. Specifying the NODEFAULTLIBRARYSEARCH command tells the linker to ignore these embedded library names when resolving any compiled symbol. This allows you to replace Clipper functions with your own procedures and/or functions. The default is the DEFAULTLIBRARYSEARCH command.

**/EXTDICTIONARY and /NOEXTDICTIONARY**   The NOEXTDICTIONARY command instructs the linker to not search through the extended dictionary. This dictionary is a list of symbol locations, references, and dependencies that the linker will use in order to speed up library searches. In essence, it is an index of internal references and cross-references. Specifying NOEXTDICTIONARY turns off this option. The default is the EXTDICTIONARY command.

**/IGNORECASE and /NOIGNORECASE**   The NOIGNORECASE command forces the linker to observe the case of symbolic references, names, and segment names. All Clipper-compiled symbols are automatically forced to uppercased reference; therefore, this command would have no effect on them. However, in C and ASM, case is an issue, and the linker can become case sensitive with this command option. The default is the IGNORECASE command.

**/STACK:<expN1>**   This command specifies the size of a program stack and overrides the stack size for a particular object module. The value of <expN1> may be any positive number up to 65,535 (64K).

**/EXCLUDE:<expC1> and EXCLUDE <expC1>**   In PRELINK mode, this command tells the linker to exclude the object module that includes a definition of the symbol <expC1>.

**/PLL:<expC1>**   This command specifies the name of a prelinked library to be used in the link cycle. The name of the prelinked library is specified in <expC1>. In addition, this command will tell the linker the name of a dependent prelinked library, <expC1>, if the link cycle is in PRELINK mode. Prelinked libraries may only be nested one level deep.

**/PRELINK** This command instructs the linker to operate in prelink mode. This mode generates two output files. One is the prelinked library itself, with a file extension of .PLL; the other is a .PLT file, which represents a prelinked transfer file. Note that prelink mode does not generate the customary executable file (.EXE).

Prelinking and the use of prelinked libraries are discussed further later in the chapter.

**/REFER:<expC1> and REFER <expC1>** In PRELINK mode, this command causes the linker to search through all of the specified and default libraries to load the code associated with the symbol <expC1>.

**BEGINAREA <freeformat option> and ENDAREA** These two commands partition a static overlay area. Any command between these two linker statements will be part of a static overlay section within the overlay area. Static overlays may be nested by nesting these two commands.

**MODULE <expC1>** This command moves the appropriate segments from the module <expC1> into the current static overlay section. It will override the FILE and LIBRARY command options.

**PRELOAD** This command forces the current static overlay section to be loaded prior to the normal execution of the application. Normally, only the resident section of an application is brought into memory before program execution.

**SECTION [= <expC1>] [INTO <expC2>]** This command creates a static overlay section. It also forces the segments within any non-Clipper object module in any FILE or LIBRARY command statement to become part of that static section. The name of the section is specified as <expC1>, and, if present, <expC2> represents the name of an external overlay file with a default file extension of .OVL. If <expC2> is not specified, the static overlay area will reside within the executable file (.EXE). A SECTION command will be treated as a DYNAMIC command.

The command structure for the *Positional* mode is as follows:

```
RTLINK [<expC1> [, <expC2> [, <expC3> [, <expC4> [, <expC5>]]]]] [;]
```

| | |
|---|---|
| <expC1>: | Object file list |
| <expC2>: | Name of output file |
| <expC3>: | Name of MAP file |
| <expC4>: | Library file list |
| <expC5>: | Linking option list |

The command structure for the *Freeformat* mode is as follows:

```
RTLINK [FILE <expC1> [OUTPUT <expC2> [LIBRARY <expC3>]]] [<expC4>]
```

| | |
|---|---|
| <expC1>: | Object file listing |
| <expC2>: | Name of output file |
| <expC3>: | Library file listing |
| <expC4>: | Linking option list |

Two points are worth noting about the command syntax needed for invoking RTLINK, and particularly for including particular libraries in the link cycle. First, it is important to recognize that libraries are nothing more than a collection of object files (.OBJ), which means that a library may appear in the list of .OBJ files instead of in the .LIB list. This requires, however, that the .LIB file extension accompany the root name of the file. Second, when using a number of private or third-party libraries, it is frequently the case that the same function name exists in more than one library. In this case, the order in which the libraries are listed when RTLink is invoked determines which library will be used to resolve the function call.

## Environmental Variables

To help with the linking process, several DOS environmental variables are available to help the linker find files, to provide the linker with a default set of instructions, or to direct the path of output files. As with the environmental variables used with the compiler, be sure there is enough environment space before issuing one of these commands. If there is not enough space, DOS will truncate the value, which will either cause an error or give unexpected results.

**SET RTLINKCMD=<expC1>**  This command sets the default command-line directives for the linker, where <expC1> is a list of command options. For example, one possible option would be

```
SET RTLINKCMD=/INCREMENTAL:30
```

Here, the default condition will be to link incrementally with a wasted-space allocation size set to 30%. Additional commands may be added to the environmental variable by separating each command with a space. For example,

```
SET RTLINKCMD=/INCREMENTAL:30 /NOIGNORECASE /VERBOSE
```

In this example, three default linking instructions are given. First, as stated earlier, the linker will default to incremental linking with a 30% allocation of wasted-space. Second, the linker is instructed to not ignore the case of a symbol (a procedure or function name). And finally, /VERBOSE tells the linker to display the names of those modules that are being linked into the application and to show in what order they are being included as the linker is building the application.

Perhaps one of the most common uses of the RTLINKCMD environmental variable is to define the interface that will be used by RTLink. The first SET command, for example, informs RTLink that it is to operate in freeformat mode, while the second configures it to operate in positional mode:

```
SET RTLINKCMD=/FREEFORMAT

SET RTLINKCMD=/POSITIONAL
```

**WARNING** Make sure that any RTLINKCMD switch does not make reference to a /PLL if making a .PLL file. This will result in the creation of an erroneous file. If making a .PLL file, the SET RTLINKCMD= command should be issued in order to remove any previous value that might cause a cyclical linking operation.

**SET TMP=<EXPC1>**   With some linking operations, the linker may generate temporary files. By default, these will usually be written to the currently logged drive and directory. It is possible to redirect this output to a specified drive or directory via the value of <expC1>. To increase the speed of some operations, it may be beneficial to redirect the temporary files to a RAM drive. For example,

```
SET TMP=H:\
```

**SET LIB=<expC1>**   When typical Clipper object files are being linked, the default library names "burned" into the header of the object files will tell the linker which libraries are needed. The linker will then automatically search the current directory for the libraries (or for any other library specified without a directory path). If the files are not in the current directory, the path specified in <expC1> in the LIB environmental variable will be searched. In addition, if a prelinked library is used, the path defined by this environmental variable will be used to search for it as well. However, if the SET PLL command is used to define a PLL environmental variable, its path will be used to search for .PLL and .PLT files before the set LIB path setting.

For example,

```
SET LIB=\CLIPPER\LIB
```

directs the linker to search for any library file not found in the current directory in the \CLIPPER\LIB directory. If a PLL is involved and if no set PLL environmental variable is present, the linker will search in this directory for both .PLL and .PLT files.

To specify multiple directories, separate the directory names with a semicolon:

```
SET LIB=\CLIPPER\LIB;\PTOOLS\LIB
```

**SET PLL=<expC1>**   This command creates an environmental variable that is similar to the LIB variable except that it pertains only to the prelinked library files with .PLL and .PLT file extensions. For example,

```
SET PLL=\CLIPPER\PLL;\PCAP\PLL
SET LIB=\CLIPPER\LIB
```

In this example, when the linker is called, it will search through \CLIPPER\LIB for any library files it may need to resolve any missing external references (such as functions or procedures). In addition, the needed prelinked library file (.PLL) and prelinked transfer file (.PLT) may be found in either the \CLIPPER\PLL directory or the \PCAP\PLL directory.

**SET OBJ=<expC1>**   In some cases, the symbols that need to be located in order to resolve missing external references may be found in other object files (.OBJ). If these files reside in locations other than the current directory, the OBJ variable may be needed. If it is not specified, the directory designated in the LIB variable will be used for object files as well as for library files (and for prelinked files as well, if PLL is not defined).

## Dynamic and Static Overlays

By default, RTLink supports dynamic overlays, which it handles automatically; this frees the programmer from the need to be concerned with the nitty-gritty details of memory management. RTLink also supports static overlays, which can be used to load C and assembly language modules into memory.

An overlay, whether it is static or dynamic, is a portion of code that is read from disk and stored in memory only when it is needed. In essence, a main load module must be memory-resident, and it makes calls to all overlays. These are then swapped into and out of a portion of memory called the overlay area. This use of overlays contrasts with the technique of making a program entirely memory-resident, which means that all of its code is loaded into memory at the time the program is first called and remains there until the program terminates.

A dynamic overlay is a single area of memory that the run-time memory manager uses to swap code in and out of as it is needed. The amount of memory used for the overlay area is set aside when the application first executes, and is determined in part by the amount of free memory available on the machine on which the application is running; the dynamic overlay area does not necessarily require a fixed amount of memory. Code is then swapped in and out of this dynamic overlay area as it is needed, with the least recently used code being replaced as new code is needed.

Note that the need to carefully determine which modules must be resident in memory at a particular time or to nest overlays is no longer necessary with a dynamic overlay linker; these details are handled automatically by the run-time memory manager. If a routine is not available in memory when it is needed, the overlay manager will simply swap out enough unused code, read the necessary code fragment from disk, and execute the function or procedure. When this is finished, control returns to the calling procedure or function.

It may help you understand what goes on in your application if you think of a dynamic overlay as nothing more than a run-time linker. In other words, the complete link cycle is not performed until the application is executed. Therefore, every Clipper application built with a dynamic overlay includes a run-time linking library that helps control every procedure and every function.

The only times that it is not advantageous to have a dynamic overlay are when the application is small enough to fit in a conventional 640K environment, and when speed is an issue. Since the default mode of the linker is to build a dynamic overlay, the RTLink command to prevent this from happening is RESIDENT. Again, the RESIDENT mode forces the Clipper code to be in the memory-resident footprint of an application, which increases its memory requirements. However, since all of the code is loaded into memory, there is no longer any need to swap code out to disk or to pull in the required Clipper code.

To get a better picture of this, compile the data generating program named MAKEDATA.PRG and link that program in the following two fashions:

```
RTLINK FI Makedata
```

or

```
RTLINK RESIDENT FI Makedata
```

The RESIDENT mode requires an additional 21K of memory just to load the program; all of the Clipper code is in memory. The application linked in RESIDENT mode will execute faster than the one linked in the default DYNAMIC mode.

By default, the dynamic overlays created by the linker are located WITHIN the executable file; there is no separate overlay file. If it is required, it is possible to place Clipper's dynamic overlays in an external overlay file, normally one with an .OVL file extension. It is also possible to mix a dynamic internal overlay with a dynamic external overlay.

RTLink allows only Clipper-compiled object files to be placed in a dynamic overlay area. Blinker®, by Blink Inc., allows most C and ASM code to be linked in a dynamic overlay area as well, including EXTEND.LIB—which contains DBEDIT( ) and MEMOEDIT( ). The only exception is those C or ASM routines that are interrupt drivers (making direct calls to hardware devices). Those modules need to reside in the main load module.

Static overlays are similar to dynamic overlays, in that both are sections of code that are not loaded into memory until they are needed. But there are two significant areas of difference. First, whereas the amount of memory required for the dynamic overlay area is variable and depends in part on the amount of memory available on the host computer, the amount of memory required for the static overlay area is fixed; it is determined by the size of the largest static overlay. Second, whereas the overlay manager in an application using dynamic overlays will load only those modules that are needed by the application, the overlay manager in an application using static overlays must load an entire overlay module at the same time.

Static overlays are not designed to work with Clipper-compiled modules. The only purpose for a static overlay is to store C- or ASM-generated object code in a special overlay area. These object files, and those for C in particular, must be compiled in large-module format.

As with a dynamic overlay, the static overlay may reside in a separate file, usually with an .OVL file extension. However, if this option is not explicitly specified, the overlay will be placed within the executable (.EXE) file.

A static overlay may require you to make a few more decisions about linking. First, you may tell the linker to force a particular SECTION of a static overlay to be loaded along with the main load module. The PRELOAD command does this; it appears in *Freeformat* mode after the SECTION command that designates a particular static overlay section. Also, you may explicitly tell the linker to place C- or ASM-based code segments into the current static overlay SECTION with the MODULE command. Again, only those applications using extensive C or ASM routines would require such a command.

## Incremental Linking and Prelinked Libraries

As applications become more and more complex, the time required to link them together grows proportionally. And when applications are being developed, it is not uncommon to recompile and relink for each minor change made to source code. There are two methods to help with this problem. The first is incremental linking, which relinks into an existing executable file only that section of code which has changed. This means that the entire application does not need to be put together from scratch every time one small change is made to a function or procedure. An alternative available to us is the prelinked library. Here, the code that is not changed is placed into a prelinked library, which is similar in concept to incremental linking. However, with a prelinked library, there are some disadvantages to be aware of (these are discussed below).

## INCREMENTAL LINKING

Basically, the idea behind incremental linking is that the space used by the various tables in an .OBJ file (symbol, code, and constant) will be bloated or exaggerated. This way, during the linking process, should any .OBJ module change in size, so long as the new size is within the boundaries of the originally bloated .OBJ file, there will be room for any new .OBJ module to replace an old one within the .EXE file. This means that the link cycle is drastically reduced. However, inconsistent results and a huge strain on memory and performance makes this an impractical option.

## PRELINKED LIBRARIES

A prelinked library is a library of those functions and procedures that have already been linked and are available by reference to one or many executable files. A prelinked library consists of two files; the first is the actual library with a .PLL extension, which is needed at run-time for the application to work properly. The other is a file with a .PLT file extension, which is called a transfer file and contains symbolic information concerning the .PLL file. This file is needed only at link time.

A prelinked library has three advantages over a full link cycle: (1) the drastic reduction in the time required to compile and link an application; (2) the reduced size of the executable file (.EXE); and (3) the amount of disk space saved when multiple executable files access one prelinked library. In other words, one prelinked library can support multiple executable files. So if, for example, CLIPPER.LIB is the main crux of the prelinked library, and if there are 20 Clipper applications on a machine, the savings in disk space would be in the order of 19 * 150K, or 2850K. In addition, if you are working from a remote site and wish to transmit modified executables, the size of the altered executable is drastically smaller than the entire application if it is not prelinked; the result is a dramatic reduction in connect time and online charges if a Clipper application is routinely transmitted across phone lines.

The disadvantages are just as important, and can be staggering. For example, deleting a prelinked library for 20 executables means that all 20 programs no longer work. While the use of prelinked libraries can significantly conserve disk space if a number of applications draw on a common .PLL, it does so at the expense of memory. First, a minor increase in an application's memory requirements occurs because an application requires an additional file handle; separate handles are needed for the .EXE and the .PLL, whereas applications that execute without a .PLL require only one handle for the .EXE. More significantly, however, using a prelinked library results in a substantially larger load module for most applications. This is the case because the bulk of the prelinked library is resident in memory once the application is loaded. A final consideration involves testing methodology. If the application is to be in the commercial mainstream and all beta tests of the application use a .PLL, yet the final version will not use a .PLL, there is no assurance that the beta cycle is valid. In other words, if the application will eventually work with a .PLL, all phases of development should be done with a .PLL. If, on the other hand, the finished application is to be a single executable file, then spare a few seconds during each link cycle to guarantee software integrity. The environment of release should be identical to the beta environment.

In the development cycle of an application, procedures and functions can be broken down into two categories: static and in-process. The static routines may be viewed as those routines that do not change (this is not the same as a *static function* or *static procedure*). When a routine is no longer changing as the development cycle progresses, the need to constantly relink it as if it were still being modified decreases. It becomes a perfect candidate for inclusion in a prelinked library.

Once you know what routines will never change, you need to know what routines you will use in your application. It is easy to know some of them: We can build functions and procedures ourselves. For example, in our earlier example of the Hello( ) function at the beginning of this chapter, we both defined and called the Hello( ) subroutine. However, within the Hello( ) function there is a call to Clipper's QOUT( ) function; therefore, we need to determine which object module within CLIPPER.LIB contains this reference so that we can include it in our prelinked library. (To help with this, at the end of this chapter is a complete listing of the object modules and internal function and procedure references within CLIPPER.LIB, EXTEND.LIB, DBFNTX.LIB, and TERMINAL.LIB.) Within CLIPPER.LIB, there is an object module named TERM, and within it is a reference to QOUT. Look at this in the same way as you would your own .PRG files: Each .PRG file contains a series of procedures and functions, each with a unique name, yet they are all compiled within a single object module with the same root name as the .PRG file. Looking at the internal library we can see the following:

```
Object Filename:   term

TERM              Offset:  0003b910H   Code and data size: 16bcH
   DEVOUT           DISPOUT         LASTKEY          NEXTKEY
   QOUT             QQOUT           SETKEY           SETPRC
   _Now             _COL            _ConOut          _cQOut
   _dbgtermx        _DEVPOS         _EJECT           _INKEY0
   _INKEY1          _KEYBOARD       _modal_key       _nbuff
   _PCOL            _PrintOut       _PROW            _ROW
   _SETPOS          _SETPOSBS       _termSLR         _XHELP
   _xSetCursor
```

This object module within CLIPPER.LIB contains 29 functions that we know of (there may be "static functions" that support these 29 functions and that cannot be called from outside this module). While not all 29 functions may be called by our application, we nevertheless must work with the TERM object module as a whole—we cannot segregate individual routines within it. Since the object module TERM will not change and since we are making a reference to it, this object module may be placed in a prelinked library. This step in building a prelinked library is referred to as identifying needed symbols; you need to do this to properly build a prelinked library.

Prelinked libraries always contain all of the object modules that were specifically placed there. And indeed, another one of the major advantages of a .PLL file is the removal of the redundant Clipper functions and base routines that every Clipper application would otherwise have but may not need. So it is important to take particular care to insure that unnecessary modules are not included in a .PLL. For example, if a .PLL contains the MEMOEDIT( ), ACHOICE( ), and low-level file functions but the application never calls them, they will all nevertheless be resident in memory for the whole time that the application executes. The increased size of the load module, and the increased memory requirements, may drag on performance, especially on a network.

To build a prelinked library, several linker commands need to be invoked: PRELINK, REFER, and EXCLUDE. Included on the distribution disks is a file called BASE52.LNK. It illustrates how these commands look in Freeformat mode:

```
#
#   Base52.lnk
#
#   Link script for base PLL creation
#
#   Copyright (c) 1990-1993, Computer Associates International, Inc.
#   All rights reserved.
#

prelink
output base52
lib clipper
lib extend


#
#   The following lines are provided to allow inclusion of one of the
#   various general terminal (GT) drivers.  By default, Terminal.lib
#   will be used.  If another driver is desired, simply comment out
#   the reference to Terminal.lib below and uncomment one of the other
#   terminal drivers.  The PCBIOS and ANSITerm GT drivers require that
#   the object file gt.obj be linked in.  This file is located in the
#   \OBJ directory of the default installation.  If the OBJ environment
#   variable is set to the \OBJ directory, RTLink will locate it
#   automatically.
#
lib terminal
#   lib pcbios     fi gt
#   lib ansiterm   fi gt
#   lib novterm


#
#   The following lines are provided to allow inclusion of one or more
#   of the various Replaceable Database Drivers (RDDs).  The system
#   program file Rddsys.prg defines which driver will operate as the
#   default.  The version of Rddsys.prg provided makes Dbfntx.lib the
#   default RDD.  To change the default RDD, this file must be
#   changed to refer to the RDD desired.  Rddsys.prg can be found
#   in the SOURCE\SYS subdirectory of the installation.  To include any
#   of the RDDs listed below uncomment its line.  For example, to include
#   the Dbfmdx RDD, uncomment the line "lib dbfmdx  refer dbfmdx" below.
#
lib dbfntx   refer dbfntx
#   lib dbfndx   refer dbfndx
```

```
#   lib dbfmdx    refer dbfmdx
#   lib dbfcdx    refer dbfcdx
#   lib dbpx      refer dbpx

refer _VOPS, _VMACRO, _VDB
refer _VTERM, _VPICT, _VGETSYS
refer _VDBG

#
# If you are providing an alternate Rddsys (Rddsys.obj) to establish
# another RDD as the default driver, uncomment the "file RDDSYS" line
# and comment out the "exclude RDDSYS" line below.
#
# file RDDSYS
#
exclude RDDSYS

exclude ERRORSYS
```

The following command invokes the linker and instructs it to use the BASE52.LNK script file:

```
RTLINK @BASE52
```

Before linking, remember to redefine the RTLINKCMD environmental variable so that it does not contain the value /PLL:<filename>. This will prevent erroneous error messages and cyclical links.

As RTLink processes the script file, it displays five error messages; these are normal and are to be ignored at this stage. When the linker has completed execution, you can see that it has generated two files: BASE52.PLL (which is 353,280 bytes in size) and BASE52.PLT (33,215 bytes). Whenever an application is to be linked with BASE52.PLL, the file BASE52.PLT is needed to complete the linking cycle. Once the link cycle is complete, the .PLT file does not need to be present with the .PLL when the application is executing.

The linker will search the four libraries listed (CLIPPER.LIB, EXTEND.LIB, TERMINAL.LIB, and DBFNTX.LIB) for the seven references listed after the three REFER commands. If they are found, their code will be placed in the prelinked library file. For example, the reference to _VTERM is found within the VTERM object module in CLIPPER.LIB. This module will therefore be included in the prelinked library.

In this example, the EXCLUDE command is not needed. However, if a reference to a function normally defaults to a Clipper function and you do not want that reference to be pulled into the .PLL and .PLT files, the EXCLUDE command must be used. This happens when a reference is meant to be a user-defined function but it has the same name as an internal Clipper function. To avoid being forced to globally change the name of your function, the EXCLUDE command allows you to prevent a Clipper reference from being included in the .PLL. This way, at link time, your function will resolve the symbolic reference and not the internal Clipper function. Just be careful to make certain that you reference the user-defined function in the link list to avoid a run-time warning message from the linker.

Once a prelinked library has been created, the next step is to link it with the remainder of an application's code. For instance, if the code example at the start of this chapter was in a

.PRG file named SAYING.PRG, we could first compile it and then use the following positional mode syntax to invoke the linker:

```
RTLINK FI Saying PLL BASE52
```

The result is a SAYING.EXE file that is 5120 bytes. The drawback is that the required load module is roughly 278K, while a standard link yields a basic load module of 137K. The .PLL pulls everything into the main load; it is not a dynamic overlay area.

You may add calls to one existing .PLL in a new .PLL. For example, consider a .PLL file that is made up of most of the Clipper functions from EXTEND.LIB. The script file to create that special .PLL file may look something like the following:

```
#copyright(c) 1991-1993 - Sirius Software Development, Inc.
# note: this is a PLL script building file for EXTEND.PLL. It may be
# used in conjunction with COMPLETE.LNK

prelink
output Extend

lib clipper
lib extend
lib terminal
lib dbfntx
refer fopen, curdir
refer dbedit, _vdb, _vdbg

#end of file
```

To invoke this, do the following:

```
RTLINK @Extend
```

Once EXTEND.PLL file has been created, another .PLL file may be built that depends on EXTEND.PLL. This nesting can go only one level deep. The secondary link file that we are building here is named COMPLETE.LNK, and it looks like this:

```
#copyright(c) 1991-1993 - Sirius Software Development, Inc.
#Author: Steve Straley
#note: this is a PLL script building file that depends on EXTEND.PLL
#       having been built previously

prelink
output complete

/PLL:extend

lib clipper, extend, terminal, dbfntx
refer _VOPS, _VMACRO, _VDBF, _VDBFNTX
refer _VTERM, _VPICT, _VGETSYS

# End of File
```

Again, the command to build this is

```
RTLINK @COMPLETE
```

Now, if a program file uses DBEDIT( ), the program can be compiled and linked with COMPLETE.PLL. This would include the .PLL for EXTEND.PLL. The DOS call would look like this:

```
RTLINK FI Clients PLL Complete
```

where CLIENTS.PRG consists of the following:

```
USE Clients NEW
DBEDIT()
```

The result is a 5K executable file and a 263K load module.

## Contents of Libraries

Below is a listing of the object files found in a number of the standard libraries that accompany Clipper 5.2. This listing may change as these libraries are updated. To generate a library listing, a library manager (e.g., Microsoft's LIB.EXE) is needed. Some of these are documented references that may be called directly; others are internal functions that are not documented. Making direct calls to these latter functions is not recommended—without knowing the parameters that each may require, you cannot call them properly. In some cases, it is possible, of course, to determine what the correct parameters are by examining STD.CH. Even here, however, making direct calls to internal functions within the library is not recommended, since there is no guarantee that these functions will remain in place "as is" from version to version. However, there is nothing wrong with building your own superset, a super STD.CH header file that will make direct translations of the pseudofunctions within your programs to the internal functions in CLIPPER.LIB or EXTEND.LIB. This listing is provided only as a guide to assist in creating prelinked libraries and deciding which objects are to be placed in it.

### CLIPPER.LIB

Object Module Name: crt0

```
__abrkp           __abrktb          __abrktbe         __acrtused
__aexit_rtn       __amsg_exit       __asizds          __astart
__atopsp          __cintDIV
```

Object Module Name: crt0dat

```
_environ          _errno            _exit             __acfinfo
__aintdiv         __child           __cinit           __ctermsub
__doserrno        __dosvermajor     __dosverminor     __exit
__fac             __fpinit          __intno           __nfile
__oserr           __osfile          __osmajor         __osminor
__osmode          __osversion       __ovlflag         __ovlvec
__pgmptr          __psp             __pspadr          __umaskval
___argc           ___argv
```

**Object Module Name: crt0fp**

    `__fptrap`

**Object Module Name: crt0msg**

    `__acrtmsg`        `__adbgmsg`        `__FF_MSGBANNER`

**Object Module Name: chksum**

    `__nullcheck`

**Object Module Name: nmsghdr**

    `__NMSG_TEXT`      `__NMSG_WRITE`

**Object Module Name: stdenvp**

    `__setenvp`

**Object Module Name: stdargv**

    `__setargv`

**Object Module Name: afhdiff**

    `__aFahdiff`

**Object Module Name: hdiff**

    `__ahdiff`

**Object Module Name: diffhlp**

    `__AHINCR`        `__AHSHIFT`

**Object Module Name: affaldiv**

    `__aFFaldiv`

**Object Module Name: affalmul**

    `__aFFalmul`      `__aFFaulmul`

**Object Module Name: afldiv**

    `__aFldiv`

**Object Module Name: aflmul**

    `__aFlmul`        `__aFulmul`

**Object Module Name: aflshl**

    `__aFlshl`

**Object Module Name: aflshr**

    `__aFlshr`

**Object Module Name:** aflrem

    \_\_aFlrem

**Object Module Name:** afulrem

    \_\_aFulrem

**Object Module Name:** afuldiv

    \_\_aFuldiv

**Object Module Name:** afnalmul

    \_\_aFNalmul     \_\_aFNaulmul

**Object Module Name:** afnaldiv

    \_\_aFNaldiv

**Object Module Name:** fltuseda

    \_\_fltused

**Object Module Name:** huge

    \_HUGE     \_\_matherr_flag

**Object Module Name:** ccall

| B$FCMP | B$FIL2 | B$FILD | B$FIS2 |
|---|---|---|---|
| B$FIST | B$FUST | OpTab | \_\_dcvt |
| \_\_eaddd | \_\_eadds | \_\_edivd | \_\_edivdr |
| \_\_edivs | \_\_edivsr | \_\_eldd | \_\_eldl |
| \_\_elds | \_\_eldw | \_\_emuld | \_\_emuls |
| \_\_estd | \_\_estdp | \_\_ests | \_\_estsp |
| \_\_esubd | \_\_esubdr | \_\_esubs | \_\_esubsr |
| \_\_fabs | \_\_fadd | \_\_faddd | \_\_fadds |
| \_\_fchs | \_\_fcmp | \_\_fcompp | \_\_fdiv |
| \_\_fdivd | \_\_fdivdr | \_\_fdivr | \_\_fdivs |
| \_\_fdivsr | \_\_fdup | \_\_fldd | \_\_fldl |
| \_\_flds | \_\_fldt | \_\_fldw | \_\_fldz |
| \_\_fmul | \_\_fmuld | \_\_fmuls | \_\_fstd |
| \_\_fstdp | \_\_fsts | \_\_fstsp | \_\_fstt |
| \_\_fsttp | \_\_fsub | \_\_fsubd | \_\_fsubdr |
| \_\_fsubr | \_\_fsubs | \_\_fsubsr | \_\_ftol |
| \_\_ftst | \_\_fxch | \_\_fxchq | \_\_saddd |
| \_\_sadds | \_\_sdivd | \_\_sdivdr | \_\_sdivs |
| \_\_sdivsr | \_\_sldd | \_\_sldl | \_\_slds |
| \_\_sldt | \_\_sldw | \_\_smuld | \_\_smuls |
| \_\_sstd | \_\_sstdp | \_\_ssts | \_\_sstsp |
| \_\_sstt | \_\_ssttp | \_\_ssubd | \_\_ssubdr |
| \_\_ssubs | \_\_ssubsr | | |

### Object Module Name: ccalle

```
$i4_errdiv0        $i4_errinf         $i4_errinvld       $i4_errminf
$i4_errpinf        $i8_errdiv0        $i8_errinf         $i8_errinvld
$i8_errminf        $i8_errpinf        $i8_errstack       __fcsp
__fpsignal
```

### Object Module Name: ifcall

```
$i4_result         $i8_result         __dcvtdisi         __dcvtst0
__dcvtst0a         __dmovtmpesbx      __dmovtmpessi      __fctmp
__fctopst          __fpmath           __fpsigadr         __smovtmpesbx
__smovtmpessi
```

### Object Module Name: cdisp

```
__ctrandisp1       __ctrandisp2
```

### Object Module Name: cfin

```
__fltin            __fltinf
```

### Object Module Name: cfout

```
__fltout
```

### Object Module Name: ixcomp

```
$i4_cmp            $i8_cmp
```

### Object Module Name: ixconv

```
$i4_8              $i4_fix            $i4_fixirnd        $i4_fixrnd
$i4_l              $i4_q              $i4_s              $i4_to_l
$i4_to_lirnd       $i4_to_lrnd        $i4_to_q           $i4_to_qirnd
$i4_to_qrnd        $i4_to_s           $i4_to_sirnd       $i4_to_srnd
$i4_to_w           $i4_to_wirnd       $i4_to_wrnd        $i4_w
$i8_4              $i8_fix            $i8_fixirnd        $i8_fixrnd
$i8_l              $i8_q              $i8_s              $i8_to_l
$i8_to_lirnd       $i8_to_lrnd        $i8_to_q           $i8_to_qirnd
$i8_to_qrnd        $i8_to_s           $i8_to_sirnd       $i8_to_srnd
$i8_to_w           $i8_to_wirnd       $i8_to_wrnd        $i8_w
```

### Object Module Name: i4math

```
$i4_ac_hi          $i4_ac_lo          $i4_add            $i4_div
$i4_divrev         $i4_mul            $i4_norm           $i4_round
$i4_round_exp      $i4_round_flag     $i4_sub            $i4_subrev
```

### Object Module Name: i8math

```
$i8_ac_hi          $i8_ac_lo          $i8_add            $i8_div
$i8_divrev         $i8_mul            $i8_norm           $i8_round
$i8_round_exp      $i8_round_flag     $i8_sub            $i8_subrev
```

**Object Module Name: i8tran**

| $i8_exp | $i8_expadjust | $i8_lgt | $i8_log |

**Object Module Name: i8powr**

$i8_c_pwr  $i8_pf_pwr  $i8_pf_pwr_1  $i8_pwr
$i8_pwr_1

**Object Module Name: i8sqr**

$i8_sqr

**Object Module Name: i8help**

$i8_addf     $i8_addfsi      $i8_arg       $i8_clearac
$i8_divf     $i8_divfsi      $i8_divr      $i8_divrdi
$i8_even     $i8_half        $i8_movac     $i8_movac_arg
$i8_movarg   $i8_movarg_ac   $i8_movtemp   $i8_mulf
$i8_mulfsi   $i8_one         $i8_poly      $i8_popac
$i8_poparg   $i8_popsi       $i8_pshac     $i8_psharg
$i8_pshsi    $i8_subf        $i8_subfsi    $i8_subr
$i8_subrdi   $i8_temp        $i8_two

**Object Module Name: i8trhlp**

$i8_exphrange    $i8_expm1           $i8_expm1reduced   $i8_exprange
$i8_lnreduce     $i8_lnreduceac_hi                      $i8_log_hi
$i8_log_lo       $i8_overflowrange                      $i8_range
$i8_retone       $i8_retzero

**Object Module Name: i8comm**

$i8_pzz     $i8_p_q    $i8_reduce   $i8_z
$i8_z2p_q   $i8_z3p_q  $i8_zz

**Object Module Name: i8tmul**

$i8_tmul   $i8_tpwr10

**Object Module Name: i8fin**

$i8_implicit_exp   $i8_input   $i8_input_ws

**Object Module Name: i8fout**

$i8_output

**Object Module Name: flrceil**

_ceil   _floor

**Object Module Name: fmod**

_fmod

**Object Module Name: ctran**

| _exp | _log | _log10 | _pow |

**Object Module Name: csqrt**

_sqrt

**Object Module Name: stdalloc**

__myalloc

**Object Module Name: wrt2err**

__wrt2err

**Object Module Name: NATION**

| __ch_type    | __day_name  | __errordesc | __locase  |
| __month_name | __nascii    | __ncopylc   | __ncopyuc |
| __ndbcs      | __nget      | __nLexId    | __nnexti  |
| __node_search| __nprevi    | __nput      | __nScanId |
| __ntrimlen   | __nversion  | __scann     | __scanw   |
| __s_order    | __tcmp      | __upcase    | __ynstr   |

**Object Module Name: SORTBLOC**

| __sfcount | __sfields | __slbase | __srbase |
| __srsize  |           |          |          |

**Object Module Name: ASUPPORT**

| _stccpy      | _stpblk  | _stpchr  | _strcat  |
| _strcpy      | _strlen  | _strncpy | __asmcall|
| __bcmp       | __bcopy  | __bcopyf | __bmove  |
| __bscan      | __bset   | __dosfunc| __lcopy  |
| __pToAbsAddr | __u2hex  |          |          |

**Object Module Name: TSUPPORT**

| __tclose  | __tcommit | __tcreat | __tlock   |
| __tlseek  | __topen   | __tread  | __trename |
| __tunlink | __twrite  |          |           |

**Object Module Name: FILESYS**

| __dspace   | __fsClose  | __fsCommit | __fsCreate |
| __fsDelete | __fsError  | __fsLock   | __fsOpen   |
| __fsRead   | __fsRename | __fsSeek   | __fsWrite  |
| __f_first  | __f_next   | __horror   | __tchdir   |
| __tchdrv   | __tctemp   | __tcurdir  | __tcurdrv  |
| __tdevraw  | __tend     | __terror   | __thcount  |
| __tinit    | __tisdevice| __tisdrv   | __tmkdir   |
| __tmname   | __trmdir   | __tversion | __txaction |
| __txclass  | __txerror  | __txlocus  |            |

**Object Module Name: DATE**

__dAlphaToDateDBF  __dAlphaToDateFmt
__dDateToAlphaDBF  __dDateToAlphaFmt
__dDateToDMYD   __dDMYToDate   __dSetEpoch   __dSetFmt
__dSysDate

**Object Module Name: OSDATE**

__osdate   __ostime

**Object Module Name: TXOPEN**

FILE   __scan_filename   __txopen

**Object Module Name: GETENV**

__getenv

**Object Module Name: DVA**

_matherr   __aton     __dvadd   __dvdiv
__dvfma    __dvfmi    __dvfml   __dvfmq
__dvinit   __dvmul    __dvsub   __dvtoi
__dvtol    __dvtoq    __lntoa   __ntoa

**Object Module Name: DVDUMMY**

__cfltcvt     __cfltcvt_tab   __cftoe     __cftof
__cftog       __cropzeros     __fassign   __forcdecpt
__MSCONFLICT1 __positive

**Object Module Name: DVC**

__dvabs   __dvdec   __dveq    __dveqz
__dvexp   __dvge    __dvgt    __dvinc
__dvint   __dvle    __dvlog   __dvlt
__dvltz   __dvmod   __dvne    __dvneg
__dvpow   __dvrnd   __dvsqr

**Object Module Name: SQUAWK**

__awk   __squ

**Object Module Name: INITEXIT**

ERRORLEVEL     __QUIT        __sysErrorLevel   __sysExit
__sysInit      __sysLevel    __sysPostArgs     __sysResume
__sysSuspend   __XARGC       __XARGV

**Object Module Name: APPINIT**

__appInitRegister   __appMain

**Object Module Name: APPEXIT**

__appExit   __appExitRegister

**Object Module Name: HARDINIT**

```
__sysHardInit
```

**Object Module Name: MAIN**

```
C50R100          CLIPPER520       _main            _term
```

**Object Module Name: UPREF**

```
__upref          __uprefp
```

**Object Module Name: _APPINI**

```
SYSINIT
```

**Object Module Name: RUN**

```
__RUN            __system
```

**Object Module Name: SYSCALL**

```
__syscall
```

**Object Module Name: EVE**

```
__eveEntry       __evLow
```

**Object Module Name: EVENT**

```
ALTD             SETCANCEL        __break_cycle    __evBreakEnable
__evDeregReceiver                 __event_init     __evKbdEntry
__evModalRead    __evPost         __evPostId       __evPostStruct
__evRegReceiverFunc               __evRegType      __evScrollPause
__evSend         __evSendId       __evSendStruct   __evStrobe
__evTranslate    __sysRegLow
```

**Object Module Name: DYNC**

```
__dynFreeModule  __dynGetNamedAddr __dynGetOrdAddr
__dynini         __dynInit         __dynLoadModule
```

**Object Module Name: DYNA**

```
_dinit_init      _dmod_count      _dmod_table
```

**Object Module Name: DYNINA**

```
__dynina
```

**Object Module Name: WEEDBED**

```
__start_proc     __weedbed        __weedend        __weed_eatr
___sympb         ___sympe
```

**Object Module Name: STARTSYM**

```
__START_SYM
```

## Object Module Name: SYMSYS

| _weed_digestr | __chk_sym    | __get_sym | __next_sym |
| __sym_init    | __sym_search |           |            |

## Object Module Name: OM

| ARRAY        | ASIZE        | _ARRAYNEW    | _BLOCKNEW    |
| _BYTESNEW    | _BYTESNEW2   | _CSCANCHECK  | _OSTRDUP     |
| _VARRAY      | _VARRAYLEN   | _VARRAYX     | _VSTR        |
| _VSTR2       | _VSTRCOLD    | _VSTRLOCK    | _VSTRUNLOCK  |
| _VSTRX       | __AADD       | __cAt        | __cAtAt      |
| __cAtPut     | __cAtPutStr  | __cBecome    | __cCopy      |
| __cResize    | __iarrayat   | __iarrayc2   | __iarrayput  |
| __imakea     | __imakela    | __oBounds    | __oCopy      |
| __oEstimate  | __oGen       | __oGen0      | __oGen1      |
| __om_init    | __opf        | __opx        | __oScavengeAll |
| __VDict      | __VSetDict   | __xcheck     | __xgrip1     |
| __xgrip2     | __xgrip3     | __xlock      | __xsafe      |
| __xsegmin    | __xunlock    | __xxlock     |              |

## Object Module Name: STACK

| __actcount   | __actinfo    | __callerpopm | __cEval0     |
| __cEval1     | __DropGrip   | __eextent    | __estat      |
| __estatlow   | __eval       | __evalhigh   | __fbase      |
| __fixlen     | __fzzcount   | __GetGrip    | __ibEvalTran |
| __ibPushTran | __igetm      | __imvclean   | __imvwipe    |
| __iparams    | __ipopm      | __iprivates  | __ipublics   |
| __ipushblock | __ipushflr   | __ipushlr    | __ipushm     |
| __ipushmr    | __ipushsr    | __isaveret   | __isframe    |
| __isinit     | __ixblock    | __izzact     | __izzblock   |
| __lbase      | __line_num   | __lparam     | __mbp        |
| __mcount     | __mlink      | __mstack     | __mtop       |
| __param      | __pcount     | __ptop       | __putc       |
| __putcl      | __putl       | __putln      | __putq       |
| __putsym     | __QQPUB      | __retc       | __retl       |
| __retq       | __sbase      | __sptol      | __sptoq      |
| __stack_exit | __stack_init | __SymEVAL    | __sysflags   |
| __tos        | __xline      | __xpopm      | __xpushm     |

## Object Module Name: FIELD

| __fcheck  | __ipopf  | __ipopqf | __ipushf |
| __ipushqf | __ipushv | __xpopf  | __xpushf |

## Object Module Name: EXTEND

| __exmback  | __exmgrab  | __parc    | __parclen  |
| __parcpeek | __parcsiz  | __pards   | __parinfa  |
| __parinfo  | __parl     | __parnd   | __parni    |
| __parnl    | __ret      | __reta    | __retclen  |
| __retds    | __retnd    | __retni   | __retnl    |
| __storc    | __storclen | __stords  | __storl    |
| __stornd   | __storni   | __stornl  |            |

**Object Module Name: CALL**

```
__icall
```

**Object Module Name: FGET**

```
FIELDGET        FIELDPOS        FIELDPUT
```

**Object Module Name: SEND**

```
__CLASSADD      __CLASSINS      __CLASSNAM      __CLASSNEW
__CLASSSEL      __isendp        __mdAdd         __mdAssociate
__mdCreate
```

**Object Module Name: TB**

```
PROCFILE        PROCLINE        PROCNAME        __tbname
```

**Object Module Name: SET**

```
SET             __Set           __SetHandler    __SetStruct
```

**Object Module Name: OPS**

```
LEFT            __ASC           __AT            __CDOW
__CHR           __CMONTH        __CTOD          __DATE
__DAY           __DOW           __DTOC          __DTOS
__EMPTY         __EXPON         __INSTR         __INT
__LEFT          __LEN           __LOGQ          __LOWER
__LTRIM         __MAX           __MIN           __MODULUS
__MONTH         __QEXP          __QSQRT         __REPLICATE
__ROUND         __SECONDS       __SPACE         __STR1
__STR2          __STR3          __strminus      __SUB2
__SUB3          __TIME          __TRIM          __UPPER
__VAL           __VALTYPE       __WORD          __YEAR
```

**Object Module Name: EXACTCMP**

```
__exactcmp
```

**Object Module Name: ACOPY**

```
ACOPY
```

**Object Module Name: ADEL**

```
ADEL
```

**Object Module Name: AINS**

```
AINS
```

**Object Module Name: ATAIL**

```
ATAIL
```

**Object Module Name: MSAVE**

```
__MRESTORE          __MSAVE
```

**Object Module Name: MRELEASE**

```
__MCLEAR            __MRELEASE          __MXRELEAS
```

**Object Module Name: ERRORSYS**

```
ERRORSYS
```

**Object Module Name: _CENTURY**

```
__SETCENTU
```

**Object Module Name: _ERRSYS**

```
_EINSTVAR
```

**Object Module Name: ERRSYS0**

```
__CreateErrorDict
```

**Object Module Name: ERRSYS1**

```
DOSERROR            ERRORBLOCK          ERRORINHAN          ERRORNEW
NETERR              _tb                 __afail             __eArg
__eCancel           __ECANDEFA          __ECANRETR          __ECANSUBS
__ECARGO            __ECLASSNA          __EDESCRIP          __eError
__eErrorp           __EFILENAM          __EGENCODE          __eNoAlias
__eNoFunc           __eNoMethod         __eNoTable          __eNoVar
__eOp               __EOPERATI          __EOSCODE           __EPARAMS
__ePStack           __eRegNFHandler     __ErrorDict         __ESETCAND
__ESETCANR          __ESETCANS          __ESETCARG          __ESETDESC
__eSetDosError      __ESETFILE          __ESETGENC          __eSetNetErr
__ESETOPER          __ESETOSCO          __ESETPARA          __ESETSEVE
__ESETSUBC          __ESETSUBS          __ESETTRIE          __ESEVERIT
__ESUBCODE          __ESUBSYST          __ETRIES            __ierror
__neterr            __salt              __salty_dyn         __sodium
```

**Object Module Name: SEQ**

```
__END_SEQ           __ibeginseq         __ibreakcont        __iendseq
__seqReg
```

**Object Module Name: AEVAL**

```
AEVAL
```

**Object Module Name: VERSION**

```
OS                  VERSION
```

**Object Module Name: ALLOC**

| __AllocF | __CycleF | __FreeF | __FSegs |
| __LoneSegs | __xalloc | __xfree | __xgrab |

**Object Module Name: VM**

| _DSNormal | _OverlayLevel | _OverlayLine | _OverlayTop |
| _Preserve1 | _Preserve2 | _ReceiverHandle | _SwapLowEventId |
| __DiskioDrop | __efault | __memcount | __mem_exit |
| __mem_init | __mem_init2 | __mem_resume | __mem_suspend |
| __OSegs | __stackbase | __stackslop | __v16 |
| __v32 | __vmAdd | __vmAlloc | __vmAllocD |
| __vmAllocF | __vmAllocO | __vmDirtyPtr | __vmDiscard |
| __vmFix | __vmFree | __vmLock | __vmLockOvl |
| __vmLockSeg | __vmPendingOvl | __vmPreAlloc | __vmPtr |
| __vmRealloc | __vmSize | __vmStat | __vmStatE |
| __vmStatN | __vmTwo | __vmUnlock | __vmUnlockOvl |
| __vmXchg | __vmXfr | | |

**Object Module Name: VMAPIY**

| __vAlloc | __vFree | __vLock | __vLockCount |
| __vRealloc | __vSize | __vUnlock | __vUnwire |
| __vWire | | | |

**Object Module Name: VMAPI**

| __xvalloc | __xvfree | __xvheapalloc | __xvheapdestroy |
| __xvheapfree | __xvheaplock | __xvheapnew | __xvheapresize |
| __xvheapunlock | __xvlock | __xvlockcount | __xvrealloc |
| __xvsize | __xvunlock | __xvunwire | __xvwire |

**Object Module Name: KMAP**

| __kmapClear | __kmapScan | __kmapSet |

**Object Module Name: SUBAL**

| __memSubAlloc | __memSubAllocFirst | | __memSubAvail |
| __memSubCheck | __memSubEmpty | __memSubExtent | __memSubFree |
| __memSubInfo | __memSubInit | __memSubMax | __memSubNext |
| __memSubReinit | | | |

**Object Module Name: OSMEM**

| __osAlloc | __osAllocDefSeg | __osAvail | __osSize |

**Object Module Name: OSME**

__osStackBase

**Object Module Name: CMEM**

| _free | _malloc | __ffree | __fmalloc |
| __nfree | __nmalloc | | |

**Object Module Name: MEMORY**

MEMORY

**Object Module Name: MACRO**

| _Accessor | _ambigBlock | _dostuff | _D_red |
| _H_symbol | _macro_error | _N_start | _N_tran |
| _P_length | _rez_alias | _R_prod | _R_start |
| _R_symb | _stuff | _T_start | _T_tran |
| __dbgmacro | __lex_ | __mac_immed | __TYPE_ |
| __WAVEA_ | __WAVEF_ | __WAVEL_ | __WAVEPOPF_ |
| __WAVEPOPQ_ | __WAVEPOP_ | __WAVEP_ | __WAVEQ_ |
| __WAVE_ | __WSYMBOL_ | | |

**Object Module Name: MPAR**

__parse_

**Object Module Name: XMACRO**

| __bmacro | __macrop | __vmacro |

**Object Module Name: VBLOCK**

| FIELDBLOCK | FIELDWBLOC | MEMVARBLOC |

**Object Module Name: MACROINA**

__macroina

**Object Module Name: PLANKTON**

| _CoerceDnums | _CoerceNums | _DbgEntry | _DbgExit |
| _ErrorBuild | _ErrorCycle | __0ABS | __0AND |
| __0ARRAYAT | __0ARRAYATI | __0ARRAYPUT | __0ARRAYPUTI |
| __0BEGIN_SEQ | __0BREAK | __0CALL | __0DEC |
| __0DIVIDE | __0DO | __0DOOP | __0EEQ |
| __0ENDPROC | __0END_SEQ | __0EQ | __0ERR |
| __0EVENTS | __0FALSE | __0FRAME | __0FUNC |
| __0GE | __0GT | __0INC | __0JDBG |
| __0JF | __0JFPT | __0JISW | __0JMP |
| __0JNEI | __0JT | __0JTPF | __0LE |
| __0LINE | __0LT | __0MAKEA | __0MAKELA |
| __0MINUS | __0MPOPF | __0MPOPM | __0MPOPQF |
| __0MPUSHA | __0MPUSHF | __0MPUSHM | __0MPUSHMR |
| __0MPUSHP | __0MPUSHQF | __0MPUSHV | __0MSYMBOL |
| __0MSYMF | __0MULT | __0NE | __0NEGATE |
| __0NOP | __0NOT | __0NULL | __0ONE1 |
| __0OR | __0PARAMS | __0PCOUNT | __0PLUS |
| __0POP | __0POPF | __0POPFL | __0POPL |
| __0POPM | __0POPQF | __0POPS | __0PRIVATES |
| __0PUBLICS | __0PUSHA | __0PUSHBL | __0PUSHC |
| __0PUSHF | __0PUSHFL | __0PUSHFLR | __0PUSHI |
| __0PUSHL | __0PUSHLR | __0PUSHM | __0PUSHMR |
| __0PUSHN | __0PUSHP | __0PUSHQF | __0PUSHRV |

| | | | |
|---|---|---|---|
| __0PUSHS | __0PUSHSR | __0PUSHV | __0PUSHW |
| __0QSELF | __0SAVE_RET | __0SEND | __0SFRAME |
| __0SINIT | __0SYMBOL | __0SYMF | __0TRUE |
| __0UNDEF | __0XBLOCK | __0ZERO | __0ZZBLOCK |
| __dbgcomm | __ddo | __DPLANKTON | __DynBadNews |
| __dyn_getpp | __NoCode | __pflock | __pfversion |
| __PLANKTON | __plank_init | __SPLANKTON | __TPLANK |
| __xdo | __xeq | __xeval | __xlt |

### Object Module Name: VNONE

__ltable

### Object Module Name: VALL

_VALL

### Object Module Name: VOPS

_VOPS

### Object Module Name: VDB

_VDB

### Object Module Name: VDBG

_VDBG

### Object Module Name: VMACRO

_VMACRO

### Object Module Name: VPICT

_VPICT

### Object Module Name: VTERM

_VTERM

### Object Module Name: DYNAMIC

| | | |
|---|---|---|
| __dyn_fname | __dyn_getnbrpages | __dyn_getpage |
| __dyn_init | __dyn_release | |

### Object Module Name: DYNX

| | | |
|---|---|---|
| __dynxSLR | __dynx_read | __dyn_used |

### Object Module Name: DYNXINA

__dynxhook

### Object Module Name: INSTD

__instd_

### Object Module Name: OUTSTD

| ALERT | OUTERR | OUTSTD | __alertP |
|---|---|---|---|
| __couterr | __coutstd | __errmsg | __errmsgn |
| __NONOALER | __outini | __postExtP | __preExtP |

### Object Module Name: GT

| DISPBEGIN | DISPCOUNT | DISPEND | __gtBeginWrite |
|---|---|---|---|
| __gtBox | __gtBoxD | __gtBoxS | __gtDispBegin |
| __gtDispCount | __gtDispEnd | __gtEndWrite | __gtFlushCursor |
| __gtGetColor | __gtGetCursor | __gtGetPos | __gtIsColor |
| __gtMaxCol | __gtMaxRow | __gtModalRead | __gtPostExt |
| __gtPreExt | __gtRectSize | __gtRepChar | __gtRest |
| __gtSave | __gtScrDim | __gtScroll | __gtSetBlink |
| __gtSetBorder | __gtSetColor | __gtSetCursor | __gtSetMode |
| __gtSetPos | __gtSetSnowFlag | __gtSLR | __gtWApp |
| __gtWCreate | __gtWCurrent | __gtWDestroy | __gtWFlash |
| __gtWPos | __gtWrite | __gtWriteAt | __gtWriteCon |
| __gtWVis | | | |

### Object Module Name: GTAPI

| __gtColorSelect | __gtGetColorStr | __gtSetColorStr |
|---|---|---|

### Object Module Name: GX

| ISCOLOR | NOSNOW | SETMODE | __no_snow |
|---|---|---|---|

### Object Module Name: TERM

| DEVOUT | DISPOUT | LASTKEY | NEXTKEY |
|---|---|---|---|
| QOUT | QQOUT | SETKEY | SETPRC |
| _Now | __COL | __ConOut | __cQOut |
| __dbgtermx | __DEVPOS | __EJECT | __INKEY0 |
| __INKEY1 | __KEYBOARD | __modal_key | __nbuff |
| __PCOL | __PrintOut | __PROW | __ROW |
| __SETPOS | __SETPOSBS | __termSLR | __XHELP |
| __xSetCursor | | | |

### Object Module Name: BOX

DISPBOX

### Object Module Name: OLDCLEAR

| __ATCLEAR | __CLEAR |
|---|---|

### Object Module Name: OLDBOX

| __BOX | __BOXD | __BOXS |
|---|---|---|

### Object Module Name: TCVT

| __tclen | __tcstr | __tcvt |
|---|---|---|

**Object Module Name: MAXROW**

```
MAXCOL              MAXROW
```

**Object Module Name: COLOR**

```
COLORSELEC          SETBLINK            SETCOLOR            _CParse
_sParse             __ColorCount        __Colors            __xSetColor
```

**Object Module Name: SETCURS**

```
SETCURSOR
```

**Object Module Name: SAVEREST**

```
RESTSCREEN          SAVESCREEN
```

**Object Module Name: _SAVESCR**

```
__XRESTSCR          __XSAVESCR
```

**Object Module Name: SCROLL**

```
SCROLL
```

**Object Module Name: _WAIT**

```
__WAIT
```

**Object Module Name: ACCEPT**

```
__ACCEPT            __ACCEPTST
```

**Object Module Name: _INPUT**

```
__INPUT
```

**Object Module Name: _SETFUNC**

```
__SETFUNCT
```

**Object Module Name: _SETTA**

```
SETTYPEAHE
```

**Object Module Name: _HELPKEY**

```
__SETHELPK
```

**Object Module Name: TERMINA**

```
__termhook
```

**Object Module Name: GTINA**

```
__gthook
```

## Object Module Name: PICT

```
DEVOUTPICT        TRANSFORM         __DateTemplate    __ParseAts
__PictLiteral     __tbuff           __tbuffPrep       __tbuffsize
__TRANS           __xtran           __ytran           __ztran
__zztran
```

## Object Module Name: GETS0

```
__GETCLASS        __GetDict         __GetSetup
```

## Object Module Name: GETS1

```
_DisplayTheGET    _GetGETContext    _SetGETContext    __GET
__GETA            __GETCDISP        __GETCOL          __GETCOLOR
__GETROW          __GETSETCO        __GETSETCS        __GETSETRO
__GETVARGE        __GETVARPU        __TOGET
```

## Object Module Name: GETS2

```
_VGETSYS          __GETASSIG        __GETBACKS        __GETCHANG
__GETCLEAR        __GETDECPO        __GETDELET        __GETDISPL
__GETEND          __GETHOME         __GETINSER        __GETKILLF
__GETLEFT         __GETMINUS        __GETOVERS        __GETPOS
__GETREFOR        __GETREJEC        __GETRESET        __GETRIGHT
__GETRITED        __GETSETCH        __GETSETCL        __GETSETFO
__GETSETMI        __GETSETPO        __GETTYPE         __GETTYPEO
__GETUNTRA        __GETUPDAT        __GETWORDD        __GETWORDL
__GETWORDR
```

## Object Module Name: _GETMSG

```
GETNEW            __GETBADDA        __GETBUFFE        __GETDWLEF
__GETHASFO        __GETORIGI        __GETSETBL        __GETSETBU
__GETSETCA        __GETSETEX        __GETSETNA        __GETSETPB
__GETSETPI        __GETSETPR        __GETSETRE        __GETSETSU
__GETTODEC        __GETUNDO
```

## Object Module Name: _GETSYS

```
GETACTIVE         GETAPPLYKE        GETDOSETKE        GETPOSTVAL
GETPREVALI        GETREADER         RANGECHECK        READEXIT
READFORMAT        READINSERT        READKILL          READMODAL
READUPDATE        UPDATED           __KILLREAD        __SETFORMA
```

## Object Module Name: _READVAR

```
READVAR
```

## Object Module Name: _ATPROMP

```
__ATPROMPT        __MENUTO
```

## Object Module Name: _TEXT

```
__TEXTREST        __TEXTSAVE
```

## Object Module Name: ITEMAPI

| | | | |
|---|---|---|---|
| __evalLaunch | __evalNew | __evalPutParam | __evalRelease |
| __itemArrayGet | __itemArrayNew | __itemArrayPut | __itemGetC |
| __itemGetDS | __itemGetL | __itemGetND | __itemGetNL |
| __itemNew | __itemParam | __itemPutC | __itemPutCL |
| __itemPutDS | __itemPutL | __itemPutND | __itemPutNL |
| __itemRelease | __itemReturn | __itemSize | __itemType |

## Object Module Name: _RDDORD

| | | | |
|---|---|---|---|
| DBCLEARIND | DBCREATEIN | DBREINDEX | DBSETINDEX |
| DBSETORDER | INDEXEXT | INDEXKEY | INDEXORD |
| _DTXCONDSE | | | |

## Object Module Name: RDDORD

| | | | |
|---|---|---|---|
| ORDBAGEXT | ORDBAGNAME | ORDCONDSET | ORDCREATE |
| ORDDESTROY | ORDFOR | ORDKEY | ORDLISTADD |
| ORDLISTCLE | ORDLISTREB | ORDNAME | ORDNUMBER |
| ORDSETFOCU | | | |

## Object Module Name: RDDSVR

| | | | |
|---|---|---|---|
| RDDLIST | RDDREGISTE | __dbUnloadAll | __isRdd |
| __isRddType | __rddDisinherit | __rddInherit | __rddServerShutdown |
| __xftableDiscardPtr | | __xftableGetPtr | |

## Object Module Name: DBCMD0

| | | | |
|---|---|---|---|
| DBCLOSEALL | DBCLOSEARE | DBSETDRIVE | DBTABLEEXT |
| DBUSEAREA | RDDNAME | RDDSETDEFA | __dbcmdSLR |
| __defDriver | | | |

## Object Module Name: DBCMD1

| | | | |
|---|---|---|---|
| ALIAS | DBAPPEND | DBCOMMIT | DBCOMMITAL |
| DBDELETE | DBEVAL | DBGOBOTTOM | DBGOTO |
| DBGOTOP | DBRECALL | DBRLOCK | DBRLOCKLIS |
| DBRUNLOCK | DBSEEK | DBSELECTAR | DBSKIP |
| DBUNLOCK | DBUNLOCKAL | USED | __AXPRIN |
| __AXPROUT | __BOF | __DBPACK | __DBZAP |
| __DELETED | __EOF | __FCOUNT | __FIELDNAME |
| __FLOCK | __FOUND | __FSELECT0 | __FSELECT1 |
| __LASTREC | __LOCK | __RECNO | __v2alias |
| __xappend | | | |

## Object Module Name: DBCMD2

| | | | |
|---|---|---|---|
| DBCLEARFIL | DBCLEARREL | DBFILTER | DBRELATION |
| DBRSELECT | DBSETFILTE | DBSETRELAT | |

## Object Module Name: DBCMD3

| | | | |
|---|---|---|---|
| __dbFieldIndex | __DBTRANS | __DBTRANSR | ___dbBuildTrans |

**Object Module Name: DBCMD4**

__DBARRANG

**Object Module Name: DBCMD5**

__DBSETFOU    __DBSETLOC

**Object Module Name: LUPDATE**

HEADER    LUPDATE    RECSIZE

**Object Module Name: DBNUBS**

| __DBAPPEND | __DBCLEARI | __DBCLEARR | __DBCLOSE |
| --- | --- | --- | --- |
| __DBCLOSEA | __DBCOMMIT | __DBCOMMITA | __DBCREATI |
| __DBDELETE | __DBGOBOTT | __DBGOTO | __DBGOTOP |
| __DBRECALL | __DBREINDE | __DBSEEK | __DBSELECT |
| __DBSETFIL | __DBSETIND | __DBSETORD | __DBSETREL |
| __DBSKIP | __DBUNLALL | __DBUNLOCK | __DBUSE |

**Object Module Name: DBJUNCT**

| __selection | __sTrimToUpper | __Workareas | __xNoTableError |
| --- | --- | --- | --- |
| __xParamError | __xselect | | |

**Object Module Name: DBCMDINA**

__dbcmdhook

**Object Module Name: WORKAREA**

__waFuncTable

**Object Module Name: DBSTRUCT**

DBSTRUCT

**Object Module Name: DBCREATE**

DBCREATE    __DBOPENSD

**Object Module Name: JOINLIST**

__DOJOINLI    __JOINLIST

**Object Module Name: _DBLOCAT**

__DBCONTIN    __DBLOCATE

**Object Module Name: _DBSTRUX**

__DBCOPYST    __DBCOPYXS    __DBCREATE

**Object Module Name: _DBCOPY**

__DBAPP    __DBCOPY

## Object Module Name: _DBJOIN

__DBJOIN

## Object Module Name: _DBSORT

__DBSORT

## Object Module Name: _DBTOTAL

__DBTOTAL

## Object Module Name: _DBUPDAT

__DBUPDATE

## Object Module Name: _FLEDIT

__FLEDIT

## Object Module Name: _AFIELDS

AFIELDS

## Object Module Name: _DBLIST

__DBLIST

## Object Module Name: DISKIO

| | | | |
|---|---|---|---|
| __diskioSLR | __page_append | __page_clear | __page_error |
| __page_flush | __page_got | __page_read | __page_readlock |
| __page_unlock | __page_update | __page_write | __xpage_read |
| __xpage_update | | | |

## Object Module Name: DIOINA

__diskiohook

## Object Module Name: DBF1

| | | | |
|---|---|---|---|
| __dbfAddField | __dbfAppend | __dbfBof | __dbfChildEnd |
| __dbfChildStart | __dbfChildSync | __dbfClose | __dbfCreate |
| __dbfDelete | __dbfDeleted | __dbfEof | __dbfFlush |
| __dbfForceRel | __dbfFound | __dbfGetValue | __dbfGetVarLen |
| __dbfGoBottom | __dbfGoCold | __dbfGoHot | __dbfGoto |
| __dbfGotoId | __dbfGoTop | __dbfInfo | __dbfLock |
| __dbfNew | __dbfOpen | __dbfPack | __dbfPlaceRec |
| __dbfPutRec | __dbfPutValue | __dbfRecall | __dbfReccount |
| __dbfRecno | __dbfSetFieldExtent | | __dbfSetFilter |
| __dbfSkip | __dbfSkipRaw | __dbfSort | __dbfStructSize |
| __dbfSuper | __dbfSysName | __dbfTrans | __dbfTransRec |
| __dbfUnlock | __dbfZap | __xDefAlias | |

## Object Module Name: DBF0

| | | | |
|---|---|---|---|
| _DBFINIT | __DBFGETFUNCTABLE | | __dbfPlaceRecP |

**Object Module Name: DBFDYN**

```
_VDBF
```

**Object Module Name: _DBF**

```
DBFONLY
```

**Object Module Name: SORTOF**

```
_Merge            __sortAdvance     __sortComplete    __sortEnd
__sortInit        __sortSetField    __sortSort

Object Module Name:  NET

NETNAME           __IndexExclLock   __IndexExclUnlock
__netalck         __netaunl         __netflck         __netfunl
__netmess         __netrlck         __netrunl         __netwho
```

**Object Module Name: _DBSDF**

```
__DBSDF
```

**Object Module Name: _DBDELIM**

```
__DBDELIM
```

**Object Module Name: DLM1**

```
_sdwrite          __dlmAddField     __dlmAppend       __dlmClose
__dlmCreate       __dlmDelete       __dlmDeleted      __dlmEof
__dlmGetValue     __dlmGoTop        __dlmInfo         __dlmNew
__dlmOpen         __dlmPutValue     __dlmSetFieldExtent
__dlmSkip         __dlmStructSize   __dlmSuper        __dlmSysName
```

**Object Module Name: DELIMDYN**

```
_VDELIM
```

**Object Module Name: SDF1**

```
__sdfAddField     __sdfAppend       __sdfClose        __sdfCreate
__sdfDelete       __sdfDeleted      __sdfEof          __sdfGetValue
__sdfGoTop        __sdfNew          __sdfOpen         __sdfPutValue
__sdfSetFieldExtent                 __sdfSkip         __sdfStructSize
__sdfSuper        __sdfSysName
```

**Object Module Name: SDFDYN**

```
_VSDF
```

**Object Module Name: SDF0**

```
_SDFINIT          __SDFGETFUNCTABLE
```

**Object Module Name: DLM0**

```
_DLMINIT          __DLMGETFUNCTABLE
```

Object Module Name: _SDF

  SDF

Object Module Name: _DELIM

  DELIM

Object Module Name: PHILES

| FCLOSE | FCREATE | FERASE | FERROR |
|---|---|---|---|
| FOPEN | FREAD | FREADSTR | FRENAME |
| FSEEK | FWRITE | | |

Object Module Name: DBGAPI

| __BNAMES | __dbgAbort | __dbgActCount | __dbgActInfo |
|---|---|---|---|
| __dbgAssign | __dbgDispA | __dbgGetCommArea | __dbgStrToVal |
| __dbgValToStr | __dbgValType | __dbgVarInfo | __LNAMES |
| __SNAMES | __SRCNAME | | |

Object Module Name: DBGINIT

  dbgInit           __dbgina

Object Module Name: DBGSHADO

  DBGSHADOW       DISPOUTAT

Object Module Name: _DBGMENU

| __DBGCLR | __DBGCMD | __DBGCMDS | __DBGCPICK |
|---|---|---|---|
| __DBGCTEXT | __DBGDOS | __DBGMBAR | __DBGMENU |
| __DBGMKEY | __DBGRESTS | __DBGSAVES | __DBGSBAR |
| __DBGSCLR | __DBGSET | __DBGSTATE | __DBGTEXT |

Object Module Name: _DBGINSP

| INSPECTCOL | __DBGDELP | __DBGERROR | __DBGFILE |
|---|---|---|---|
| __DBGHFILE | __DBGINSP | __DBGLN | __DBGLOOK |
| __DBGNP | __DBGPATH | __DBGPATHS | __DBGSETS |
| __DBGSS | __DBGSTEP | __DBGTABW | __DBGTERMA |
| __DBGTP | __DBGWFILE | __DBGWP | |

Object Module Name: _DBFLIST

  __DBFLIST

Object Module Name: _DBGHELP

  __DBGHELP

Object Module Name: _DBGBROW

  _ABAPPLYKE      _ABNEW         _ABSETCOLU

Object Module Name: EMMALLOC

   \_\_emmAllocPages

Object Module Name: EMMCONTX

   \_\_emmContextRest   \_\_emmContextSave

Object Module Name: EMMCOUNT

   \_\_emmGetAllocPageCount      \_\_emmGetTotalPageCount
   \_\_emmGetUnAllocPageCount

Object Module Name: EMMFREE

   \_\_emmDeAllocPages

Object Module Name: EMMINST

   \_\_emmInstalled

Object Module Name: EMMMAP

   \_\_emmMapUnMapPage

Object Module Name: EMMPAGE

   \_\_emmGetPageFrameSeg

Object Module Name: EMMREALL

   \_\_emmReAllocPages

Object Module Name: EMMSTAT

   \_\_emmGetStatus

Object Module Name: EMMVERS

   \_\_emmGetVersion

# EXTEND.LIB

Object Module Name: RDDSYS

   RDDSYS

Object Module Name: AMPM

   AMPM

Object Module Name: TSTRING

   TSTRING

**Object Module Name: SECS**
```
SECS
```

**Object Module Name: STRZERO**
```
STRZERO
```

**Object Module Name: READKEY**
```
READKEY
```

**Object Module Name: MOD**
```
MOD
```

**Object Module Name: DAYS**
```
DAYS
```

**Object Module Name: LENNUM**
```
LENNUM
```

**Object Module Name: ELAPTIME**
```
ELAPTIME
```

**Object Module Name: DBF**
```
DBF
```

**Object Module Name: FKLABEL**
```
FKLABEL
```

**Object Module Name: FKMAX**
```
FKMAX
```

**Object Module Name: GETE**
```
GETE            GETENV
```

**Object Module Name: DISKSPAC**
```
DISKSPACE
```

**Object Module Name: _DIR**
```
__DIR
```

**Object Module Name: COPYFILE**
```
__COPYFILE
```

**Object Module Name: TYPEFILE**
```
__TYPEFILE
```

**Object Module Name: EXAMPLEA**
```
BIN2I           BIN2L           BIN2W           CURDIR
I2BIN           ISPRINTER       L2BIN           TONE
```

**Object Module Name: _BROWSE**
```
BROWSE
```

**Object Module Name: ALLTRIM**
```
ALLTRIM
```

**Object Module Name: RIGHT**
```
RIGHT
```

**Object Module Name: DESCEND**
```
DESCEND
```

**Object Module Name: RAT**
```
RAT
```

**Object Module Name: PADL**
```
PADL
```

**Object Module Name: PADR**
```
PADR
```

**Object Module Name: PADC**
```
PADC
```

**Object Module Name: PAD**
```
PAD
```

**Object Module Name: IS**
```
ISALPHA         ISDIGIT         ISLOWER         ISUPPER
```

**Object Module Name: STRTRAN**
```
STRTRAN
```

**Object Module Name: SOUNDEX**
```
SOUNDEX
```

**Object Module Name: STUFF**
```
STUFF
```

**Object Module Name: HARDCR**
```
HARDCR
```

**Object Module Name: MEMOREAD**
```
MEMOREAD
```

**Object Module Name: MEMOWRIT**
```
MEMOWRIT
```

**Object Module Name: MEMOTRAN**
```
MEMOTRAN
```

**Object Module Name: MEMOLINE**
```
MEMOLINE
```

**Object Module Name: MLCOUNT**
```
MLCOUNT
```

**Object Module Name: MLPOS**
```
MLPOS
```

**Object Module Name: MLCTOPOS**
```
MLCTOPOS        MPOSTOLC
```

**Object Module Name: LINELEN**
```
_fetchar        _linelen
```

**Object Module Name: ASCAN**
```
ASCAN           _AScanSub
```

**Object Module Name: ASORT**
```
ASORT
```

**Object Module Name: _ARRAY**
```
ACLONE          AFILL
```

**Object Module Name: _DEFPATH**
```
DEFPATH         __DEFPATH
```

**Object Module Name: _ADIR**
```
ADIR
```

**Object Module Name: DIRECT**

```
DIRECTORY
```

**Object Module Name: MEMOEDIT**

```
MEMOEDIT
```

**Object Module Name: TBROWSE0**

```
__CCLASSNA        __TOTBCOLU        __TOTBROWS        __xTbrSetup
```

**Object Module Name: TBROWSE1**

```
_pan              __TAUTOLIT        __TBBANG          __TBEND
__TCLASSNA        __TCOLORRE        __TCOLWIDT        __TCURSCOL
__TCURSROW        __TDEHILIT        __TDOWN           __TEBANG
__TFORCEST        __TFREEZE         __TGOBOTTO        __TGOTOP
__THILITE         __THOME           __TINVALID        __TLEFT
__TLEFTVIS        __TLINEFRE        __TPANEND         __TPANHOME
__TPANLEFT        __TPANRIGH        __TPGDN           __TPGUP
__TREFRESH        __TRIGHT          __TRIGHTVI        __TROWCOUN
__TSETAUTO        __TSETBBAN        __TSETCONF        __TSETCURC
__TSETCURR        __TSETEBAN        __TSETFREE        __TSETSTAB
__TSTABILI        __TSTABLE         __TUP
```

**Object Module Name: _TBROWSE**

```
TBCOLUMNNE        TBROWSENEW        __CSETBLOC        __CSETCOLO
__CSETCOLS        __CSETDEFC        __CSETFOOT        __CSETFSEP
__CSETHEAD        __CSETHSEP        __CSETPICT        __CSETWIDT
__TADDCOLU        __TCARGO          __TCOLCOUN        __TCOLUMN
__TDELCOLU        __TINSCOLU        __TSETBOTT        __TSETCARG
__TSETCOLO        __TSETCOLS        __TSETCOLU        __TSETFOOT
__TSETHEAD        __TSETRBOT        __TSETRLEF        __TSETRRIG
__TSETRTOP        __TSETSKIP        __TSETTOP
```

**Object Module Name: _TBRDB**

```
TBROWSEDB
```

**Object Module Name: _DBEDIT**

```
DBEDIT
```

**Object Module Name: ACHOICE**

```
ACHOICE
```

**Object Module Name: _FRMBACK**

```
PARSEHEADE        __FRMLOAD
```

**Object Module Name: _FRMRUN**

```
__REPORTFO
```

Object Module Name: _LBLBACK

    __LBLLOAD

Object Module Name: _LBLRUN

    __LABELFOR

## TERMINAL.LIB

Object Module Name: BEEP

    __beep_

Object Module Name: DISPIBM

    _VDISPLAY

Object Module Name: KBDIBM

    _VKEYBOARD

Object Module Name: MOUSEIBM

    _VMOUSE

## DBFNTX.LIB

Object Module Name: DTX1

| | | | |
|---|---|---|---|
| __dtxClose | __dtxFlush | __dtxForceRel | __dtxGoBottom |
| __dtxGoCold | __dtxGoHot | __dtxGoto | __dtxGotoId |
| __dtxGoTop | __dtxNew | __dtxOrderCondition | |
| __dtxOrderCreate | __dtxOrderInfo | __dtxOrderListAdd | |
| __dtxOrderListClear | | __dtxOrderListFocus | |
| __dtxOrderListRebuild | | __dtxPack | __dtxPlaceKey |
| __dtxSeek | __dtxSkipRaw | __dtxSort | __dtxSuper |
| __dtxSysName | __dtxZap | | |

Object Module Name: DTX0

    _DTXINIT    __DTXGETFUNCTABLE    __dtxPlaceKeyP
    __DTXWEP

Object Module Name: DTXDYN

    _VDBFNTX

Object Module Name: NTXLOCK1

    NEWLOCKS    __NewIndexLock

Object Module Name: NTXERR

    _NTXERR

Object Module Name: BRIG

    __IndexLockExit      __IndexLockInit       __IndexReadLock        __IndexReadUnlock
    __IndexWriteLock     __IndexWriteUnlock

Object Module Name: _DBFNTX

    DBFNTX

## DBFNDX.LIB

Object Module Name: _DBFNDX

    DBFNDX

Object Module Name: NDX0

    _NDXINIT             __NDXGETFUNCTABLE                            __NDXWEP

Object Module Name: NDX1

    __ndxClose           __ndxFlush            __ndxForceRel          __ndxGoBottom
    __ndxGoCold          __ndxGoHot            __ndxGoto              __ndxGotoId
    __ndxGoTop           __ndxNew              __ndxOrderCondition
    __ndxOrderCreate     __ndxOrderInfo        __ndxOrderListAdd
    __ndxOrderListClear                        __ndxOrderListFocus
    __ndxOrderListRebuild                      __ndxPack              __ndxSeek
    __ndxSkipRaw         __ndxSort             __ndxSuper             __ndxSysName
    __ndxZap

Object Module Name: NDXDYN

    _VDBFNDX

## DBFMDX.LIB

Object Module Name: dbf40

    _MDBFINIT            __MDBFGETFUNCTABLE                           __mdbfPlaceRecP

Object Module Name: dbf41

    __mdbfAddField       __mdbfAppend          __mdbfBlank            __mdbfBof
    __mdbfChange         __mdbfChildEnd        __mdbfChildStart       __mdbfChildSync
    __mdbfClose          __mdbfCreate          __mdbfDelete           __mdbfDeleted
    __mdbfEof            __mdbfFlush           __mdbfForceRel         __mdbfFound
    __mdbfGetRaw         __mdbfGetValue        __mdbfGetVarLen        __mdbfGoBottom
    __mdbfGoCold         __mdbfGoHot           __mdbfGoto             __mdbfGotoId
    __mdbfGoTop          __mdbfHeaderSize      __mdbfInfo             __mdbfLock
    __mdbfLupdate        __mdbfNew             __mdbfOpen             __mdbfPack
    __mdbfPlaceRec       __mdbfPutRaw          __mdbfPutRec           __mdbfPutValue
    __mdbfRecall         __mdbfReccount        __mdbfRecno            __mdbfRecSize
    __mdbfSetFieldExtent                       __mdbfSetFilter        __mdbfSkip
    __mdbfSkipRaw        __mdbfSort            __mdbfStructSize       __mdbfSuper

| | | | |
|---|---|---|---|
| __mdbfSysName | __mdbfTrans | __mdbfTransRec | __mdbfUnlock |
| __mdbfZap | ___db_memo_block_size | | |

### Object Module Name: mdx0

| | | | |
|---|---|---|---|
| _MDXINIT | __MDXGETFUNCTABLE | | __MDXWEP |

### Object Module Name: mdx1

| | | | |
|---|---|---|---|
| __mdxClose | __mdxFlush | __mdxForceRel | __mdxGoBottom |
| __mdxGoCold | __mdxGoHot | __mdxGoto | __mdxGotoId |
| __mdxGoTop | __mdxIndexExt | __mdxNew | __mdxOrderCondition |
| __mdxOrderCreate | __mdxOrderDelete | __mdxOrderInfo | __mdxOrderListAdd |
| __mdxOrderListClear | | __mdxOrderListFocus | |
| __mdxOrderListRebuild | | __mdxPack | __mdxSeek |
| __mdxSkipRaw | __mdxSort | __mdxSuper | __mdxSysName |
| __mdxZap | ___TagFind | | |

### Object Module Name: net

| | | | |
|---|---|---|---|
| _D4APPLK | _D4APPUNLK | __netMDXalck | __netMDXapplck |
| __netMDXappunlk | __netMDXaunl | __netMDXblck | __netMDXbunl |
| __netMDXflck | __netMDXfunl | __netMDXrlck | __netMDXrunl |
| __netMDXwho | | | |

### Object Module Name: dbf4dyn

_VDBFIV

### Object Module Name: mdxdyn

_VDBFMDX

### Object Module Name: _dbfmdx

| | |
|---|---|
| DBFMDX | _DBFMDX |

### Object Module Name: mdcmd

| | | |
|---|---|---|
| DB4DBTBLK | RDDDBFINFO | RDDORDINFO |

## DBFCDX.LIB

### Object Module Name: fox0

| | | | |
|---|---|---|---|
| _FOXINIT | __FOXGETFUNCTABLE | | __FOXWEP |
| __SEXfunctable | __sexNew | __sexPlaceKeyP | |

### Object Module Name: fox1

| | | | |
|---|---|---|---|
| ISREINDEX | _MasterIsStructural | | _sexDirtyRead |
| _sexEmpty | _sexSortOption | _sLocalErr | _SysName |
| __sexClose | __sexError | __sexFlush | __sexForceRel |
| __sexfpath | __sexGoBottom | __sexGoCold | __sexGoHot |
| __sexGoto | __sexGotoID | __sexGoTop | __sexIndexExpr |
| __sexOpen | __sexOrderBagCreate | | __sexOrderBagExt |

```
__sexOrderCreate    __sexOrderInfo      __sexOrderListAdd
__sexOrderListClear                     __sexOrderListFocus
__sexOrderListRebuild                   __sexPack           __sexSeek
__sexSkipRaw        __sexSort           __sexSysName        __sexZapTable
__sxCopyright       __sxdoError         __sxIsReindex       __sxOrderAsNumber
```

## Object Module Name: sxblock

```
_blkCalcBlanks      _blkCalcDupes       _blkGo              _blkInitLeaf
_blkIsLeaf          _blkKey             _blkKeyInsert       _blkKeyValue
_blkLastKeyNo       _blkPutInfo         _blkRecNo           _blkSpaceInfo
_blkStuffKey
```

## Object Module Name: sxcreate

```
_indexCreate        _indexReindex       _indexReindexTag    _sexPlaceKey
```

## Object Module Name: sxindex

```
_indexClose         _indexFlush         _indexGrow          _indexOpen
_indexShrink
```

## Object Module Name: sxmemo

```
__sxMemoLength      __sxReadMemo        __sxWriteMemo
```

## Object Module Name: sxtag

```
_tagCompare         _tagCompareInit     _tagDeleteKey       _tagEof
_tagFlush           _tagFreeBlocks      _tagGoBottom        _tagGoto
_tagGoTop           _tagGotoParent      _tagInit            _tagInsertKey
_tagKey             _tagRecNo           _tagSeek            _tagSkip
_tagThisBlock       _tagTrueBottom      _tagTrueTop         __sexGoSelf
__sexKeyPosition    __sexKeyUpdate
```

## Object Module Name: sxutil

```
_caHexNums          _listadd            _listadd_after      _listadd_before
_listfirst          _listlast           _listnext           _listpop
_listprev           _listremove         _sexParm2Type       _sexAliasXlate
__sextrim_n         __sxAlert           __sxBaseLen         __sxGetExt
__sxNameExt         __sxParseName       __sxSmartUpper      __sxSwapBytes
___ltoax
```

## Object Module Name: sxfile

```
_sexfbuf_finish     _sexfbuf_init       _sexfbuf_reset      _sexfbuf_write
_sexfclose          _sexfcommit         _sexfcreate         _sexflength
_sexflength_set     _sexfopen           _sexfopen_test      _sexfread
_sexfread_all       _sexfwrite          _sexfwrite_repeat
__sexOpener         ___sxPageRead       ___sxPageReadLock
```

## Object Module Name: sxsetopt

```
__sexOrderCondition                     __sxCondClear
```

**Object Module Name: sxkillta**

    \_\_sexOrderDestroy

**Object Module Name: sxnation**

    \_sexmBADDBSTRUCT    \_sexmBADINDEXEXPR   \_sexmBUFFPUFF
    \_sexmCANTFINDKEY    \_sexmCORRUPTED      \_sexmINVALIDKEYLEN
    \_sexmKEYTOOLONG     \_sexmNOBUFFMEM       \_sexmNONCOMPACT   \_\_sxNextChar
    \_\_sxPrevChar

**Object Module Name: sxexpr**

    \_\_sexChkExpr        \_\_sexKillExpr

**Object Module Name: sxmisc**

    \_\_ClipAlloc         \_\_ClipFree         \_\_sexOurDriver

**Object Module Name: sxcnvrt**

    \_tagDbl2Fox        \_tagFox2Dbl       \_\_sexValToFox

**Object Module Name: sxmemuti**

    \_sxMemoBlock      \_sxPutMemoBlock

**Object Module Name: sxxmemo**

    \_\_sxFindFreeBlock    \_\_sxFlushMemoRoot
    \_\_sxInsertFreeBlock  \_\_sxIsFreeBlock      \_\_sxKillMemoRoot
    \_\_sxMemoSignature    \_\_sxReadMemoRoot

**Object Module Name: sxinfuti**

    \_\_sxBlankCount     \_\_sxDupeCount     \_\_sxKeyRecNo

**Object Module Name: sxnet**

    \_sexlock          \_sexunlock        \_\_sexalck         \_sexaunl
    \_\_sexflck         \_\_sexfunl         \_\_sexilck         \_\_sexiunl
    \_\_sexrlck         \_\_sexrunl

**Object Module Name: sxlock**

    \_tagLock          \_tagUnlock         \_\_sxUpdateTag

**Object Module Name: sxilock**

    \_\_sxIndexLock     \_\_sxIndexUnlock

**Object Module Name: sxifind**

    \_indexActivateStructural       \_indexFindIndex     \_indexFindOrder
    \_indexFindTag      \_indexFindTagNo     \_indexOrderNo      \_indexOrderPos

**Object Module Name:** sxtryo

`_sexFindKeyByRecno`

**Object Module Name:** sxbskip

`_blkEof`　　`_blkGoBottom`　　`_blkGoTop`　　`_blkSkip`

**Object Module Name:** sxbseek

`_blkBranchSeekRec`　　`_blkSeek`

**Object Module Name:** sxdelkey

`_blkKeyDelete`

**Object Module Name:** foxdyn

`_VDBFCDX`

**Object Module Name:** fxdbf0

`_FXDBFINIT`　　`__FXDBFGETFUNCTABLE`　　`__FXDBFWEP`
`__sxdbfPlaceRecP`

**Object Module Name:** fxdbf1

`__MemoExt`　　`__sexMemoSize`　　`__sxdbfAddField`　　`__sxdbfClose`
`__sxdbfCreate`　　`__sxdbfFlush`　　`__sxdbfGetValue`　　`__sxdbfGetVarLen`
`__sxdbfOpen`　　`__sxdbfPlaceRec`　　`__sxdbfPutValue`　　`__sxdbfStructSize`
`__sxdbfSysName`　　`__sxdbfZap`

**Object Module Name:** fxdbfdyn

`_VFXDBF`

**Object Module Name:** csupport

`__aFulshr`　　`__xmemcmp`

**Object Module Name:** cdxinit

`DBFCDX`

# ANSITERM.LIB

**Object Module Name:** BEEPANSI

`__beep_`

**Object Module Name:** DISPANSI

`_VDISPLAY`

**Object Module Name:** KBDPCDOS

`_VKEYBOARD`

Object Module Name: MOUSEIBM

  _VMOUSE

## DBPX.LIB

 Object Module Name: dbhandle

  ___pdxKTable

 Object Module Name: dbpxreg

  DBPX    DBPXREG

 Object Module Name: _decode

  ___pdxReadDWord8 ___pdxReadWord8 ___pdxWriteDWord8
  ___pdxWriteWord8

 Object Module Name: fldinfo

  ___pdxFieldInfo

 Object Module Name: getsort

  ___pdxGetSortOrder

 Object Module Name: keycommi

  ___pdxCommitKeyed  ___pdxFlushKeyed

 Object Module Name: keycopy

  ___pdxCopyKeyedTable

 Object Module Name: keycreat

  ___pdxCreateKeyed

 Object Module Name: keydel

  ___pdxDeleteKeyedRec  ___pdxKillKeyedRec

 Object Module Name: keylck

  ___pdxRecLockKeyed

 Object Module Name: keyopen

  ___pdxCloseKeyedTable  ___pdxOpenKeyedTable
  ___pdxPXBuffSize  ___pdxCloseKeyed

 Object Module Name: keyread

  ___pdxKeyRecGet ___pdxSeekKeyed ___pdxSeekKeyed

Object Module Name: keyskip

    `___pdxSkipKeyed`

Object Module Name: keyupdat

    `___pdxUpdateKeyed`

Object Module Name: keywrite

    `___pdxKeyPut`    `___pdxPutKeyed`

Object Module Name: moresort

    `___pxSortOrder`

Object Module Name: noncommi

    `___pdxCommitNonKeyed`

Object Module Name: noncopy

    `___pdxCopyNonKeyedTable`

Object Module Name: noncrea

    `___pdxCreateNonKeyed`

Object Module Name: nondel

    `___pdxDeleteNonKeyedRec`

Object Module Name: nonflen

    `___pdxResetBuffer`    `___pdxTableLength`
    `___pdxTableRecs`

Object Module Name: nongoto

    `___pdxGotoNonKeyed`    `___pdxTopBottomNonKeyed`

Object Module Name: nonlck

    `___pdxRecLockNonKeyed`

Object Module Name: nonopen

    `___pdxCloseNonKeyedTable`    `___pdxDBBuffSize`    `___pdxOpenNonKeyedTable`
    `___pdxCloseNonKeyed`

Object Module Name: nonread

    `___pdxGetNonKeyed`

Object Module Name: nonrec

    `___pdxSkipNonKeyed`

**Object Module Name: nonupdat**

    \_\_pdxUpdateNonKeyed

**Object Module Name: nonwrite**

    \_\_pdxAppendNonKeyed               \_\_pdxInsertNonKeyed

**Object Module Name: pdx0**

    \_PDBINIT           \_\_PDBGETFUNCTABLE           \_\_pdxPlaceRecP

**Object Module Name: pdx1**

| | | | |
|---|---|---|---|
| \_CurrDbStruct | \_CurrSortParm | \_\_goSelf | \_\_NOTSUPP |
| \_\_pdxAddField | \_\_pdxAppend | \_\_pdxBof | \_\_pdxChildEnd |
| \_\_pdxChildStart | \_\_pdxChildSync | \_\_pdxClose | \_\_pdxCreate |
| \_\_pdxdbfinfo | \_\_pdxDelete | \_\_pdxDeleted | \_\_pdxEof |
| \_\_pdxFieldSub | \_\_pdxFLock | \_\_pdxFlush | \_\_pdxForceRel |
| \_\_pdxFound | \_\_pdxGetValue | \_\_pdxGetVarLen | \_\_pdxGoBottom |
| \_\_pdxGoCold | \_\_pdxGoHot | \_\_pdxGotoID | \_\_pdxGoTop |
| \_\_pdxGotoRec | \_\_pdxHeaderSize | \_\_pdxInsertFields | |
| \_\_pdxKillFields | \_\_pdxLock | \_\_pdxLupdate | \_\_pdxNew |
| \_\_pdxOpen | \_\_pdxorderc | \_\_pdxPack | \_\_pdxPlaceRec |
| \_\_pdxPutRec | \_\_pdxPutValue | \_\_pdxReccount | \_\_pdxRecno |
| \_\_pdxRecordSize | \_\_pdxRLock | \_\_pdxSetFieldExtent | |
| \_\_pdxSetFilter | \_\_pdxSkipRaw | \_\_pdxSkipRec | \_\_pdxSort |
| \_\_pdxStructSize | \_\_pdxSysName | \_\_pdxTrans | \_\_pdxTransRec |
| \_\_pdxUnlock | \_\_pdxZapTable | | |

**Object Module Name: pdxappdb**

    \_\_pdxAppendBlank

**Object Module Name: pdxclose**

    \_\_pdxClose

**Object Module Name: pdxcommi**

    \_\_pdxCommit

**Object Module Name: pdxconv**

| | | | |
|---|---|---|---|
| \_\_pdxdblton | \_\_pdxitosn | \_\_pdxntodbl | \_\_pdxsntoi |
| \_\_pdxstrtoa | \_\_pdxstrtodate | | |

**Object Module Name: pdxcopyt**

    \_\_pdxCopyStruct

**Object Module Name: pdxdata**

| | | | |
|---|---|---|---|
| \_\_pxBlankNum | \_\_pxBlockSize | \_\_pxCurrRecno | \_\_pxInternalErr |
| \_\_pxSetBlankNum | \_\_pxTempBuff | \_\_pxTempDir | |

**Object Module Name: pdxfldda**

    \_\_atostr        \_\_datetostr        \_pdxJulian        \_pxDays

**Object Module Name: pdxgoto**

    \_pdxGoto

**Object Module Name: pdxgotop**

    \_pdxTopBottom      \_pdxTopBottomKeyed      \_pdxTopBottomSec

**Object Module Name: pdxinit**

| \_ClipMem | \_InitFlag | \_pdxError | \_pdxLockMode |
| --- | --- | --- | --- |
| \_pdxParent | \_pdxPassFlag | \_pdxPassHigh | \_pdxPassLow |
| \_pdxRelations | \_pdxSelected | \_pdxSoftSeek | \_strbuf |
| \_pdxInit | \_pxNetMode | | |

**Object Module Name: pdxlogin**

    \_pdxLogin

**Object Module Name: pdxlogou**

    \_pdxLogout      \_pdxlogout

**Object Module Name: pdxlupda**

    \_pdxLastUpdate

**Object Module Name: pdxsndxc**

    \_pdxSNdxCreate

**Object Module Name: pdxsndxs**

    \_pdxSNdxSet

**Object Module Name: pdxrecde**

    \_pdxRecDel

**Object Module Name: pdxskip**

    \_pdxSkip      \_pdxSkipAdjust

**Object Module Name: pdxtbllo**

    \_pdxTblLockMode

**Object Module Name: pdxuse**

| \_PDbufnum | \_PPbufnum | \_PXbufnum | \_PYbufnum |
| --- | --- | --- | --- |
| \_pdxIUse | \_pdxUse | \_pdxOpen | |

### Object Module Name: pdxutil

```
_MovedRecNo        __copyustr         __trimstr          ___pdxChkTable
___pdxClearBuffer                     ___pdxENetName     ___pdxFieldNo
___pdxHomeDir      ___pdxNetDir       ___pdxRecFlush     ___pdxRefresh
___pdxWorkArea     ___xatoi
```

### Object Module Name: pdxzap

```
__pdxZap
```

### Object Module Name: pfcreate

```
___pdxCreateFile
```

### Object Module Name: pfrename

```
___pdxRename
```

### Object Module Name: pfseek

```
__aLseekrd         __aLseekwt         ___pdxReadNode     ___pdxWriteNode
___pxminibuf
```

### Object Module Name: pfutil

```
___pdxNextName     ___pdxSecIdxNum
```

### Object Module Name: ppx0

```
_PDXINIT           __PDXGETFUNCTABLE                     __PDXWEP
__ppxPlaceKeyP
```

### Object Module Name: ppx1

```
_ClipperMem        _dbpxCopyright     __ppxClearIndex    __ppxClose
__ppxCreateIndex   __ppxFlush         __ppxForceRel      __ppxGoBottom
__ppxGoCold        __ppxGoHot         __ppxGotoID        __ppxGoTop
__ppxGotoRec       __ppxIndexExpr     __ppxIndexExt      __ppxIndexOrder
__ppxNew           __ppxOrderInfo     __ppxOrderListFocus
__ppxPack          __ppxPlaceKey      __ppxReindex       __ppxSeek
__ppxSetIndex      __ppxSkipRaw       __ppxSort          __ppxSysName
__ppxZapTable      ___dbpxDb
```

### Object Module Name: ptxclose

```
___pdxCloseSecondary
```

### Object Module Name: ptxcreat

```
___pdxCreateSecondary
```

### Object Module Name: ptxkskip

```
___pdxNextSecKey
```

Object Module Name: ptxmakky

    ___pdxFmtIndexKey                    ___pdxFmtNonIndexKey

Object Module Name: ptxpopen

    ___pdxOpenIncSecondary

Object Module Name: ptxread

    ___pdxSeekSecIndex

Object Module Name: ptxseek

    ___pdxSeekSecKey

Object Module Name: ptxskip

    ___pdxSkipSecIndex                 ___pdxSkipSecNext
    ___pdxSkipSecPrev

Object Module Name: ptxsopen

    ___pdxOpenNonSecondary

Object Module Name: ptxutil

    ___pdxFindOrder    ___pdxGetIncIndexList    ___pdxGetNonIndexList
    ___pdxIncIndexCount               ___pdxNonIndexCount

Object Module Name: ptxwrite

    ___pdxPutSecondaryKey

Object Module Name: pxsortda

    _leafs           _nextfile        _nonleafs       _pxcombuf
    _temp1nm       _temp2nm        _tempnm

Object Module Name: pxsortfu

    _DBPXopen       ___pdxSortFunc

Object Module Name: setsort

    ___pdxSetSortOrder               ___pdxSortOrder

Object Module Name: tbllock

    ___pdxTblLockKeyed              ___pdxTblLockNonKeyed

Object Module Name: tempdir

    ___pdxSetTempDir   ___pdxTempName

Object Module Name: tempname

    _basename       _cropext        ___pdxExpandName

Object Module Name: token
    __SCANSCOP

Object Module Name: _copyptx
    ___pdxCopySecIndex

Object Module Name: _fndbuff
    ___pdxFindBuff

Object Module Name: _fndnode
    ___pdxFindNode

Object Module Name: _frebuff
    ___pdxFreeAll        ___pdxFreeIMem

Object Module Name: _getbuff
    ___pdxGetBuff

Object Module Name: _getnode
    ___pdxGrabNode

Object Module Name: _keyopen
    ___pdxNewPXNode   ___pdxResetIndex   ___pdxSaveKGNode   ___pdxOpenKeyed

Object Module Name: _misc
    ___pdxReadDWord   ___pdxReadWord    ___pdxStuffDWord   ___pdxStuffWord

Object Module Name: _netutil
    _itisme           ___pdxIsLocked    ___pdxSleep

Object Module Name: _ptxback
    _howmany          ___pdxRewindIndex

Object Module Name: _ptxforw
    ___pdxForwardIndex

Object Module Name: _ptxnew
    ___pdxMakeSecondary

Object Module Name: _pxchang
    ___pdxCheckChg

Object Module Name: _pxcreat
    ___pdxCreateObject

Object Module Name: _pxdel

    ___pdxDelRec

Object Module Name: _pxfopen

    ___pdxFClose    ___pdxFOpen

Object Module Name: _pxintl

    ___pdxIntlCompare

Object Module Name: _pxlock

| | | | |
|---|---|---|---|
| ___pdxAddRecLock | ___pdxAddTblLock | ___pdxAddWS | ___pdxCanRead |
| ___pdxCanWrite | ___pdxCheckLock | ___pdxChkKey | ___pdxCloseLock |
| ___pdxDelTblLock | ___pdxLockClose | ___pdxLockOpen | ___pdxOpenLock |
| ___pdxUpdateLock | ___pdxUpdateRecLock | | ___pdxUpdateTblLock |
| ___pdxUpdateWS | ___pxRecnoChange | | |

Object Module Name: _pxmulti

| | | | |
|---|---|---|---|
| _MultiUser | ___pdxUser | ___pxLockBuffer | ___pxLockSlot |
| ___pxMaxRecLocks | ___pxNetHandle | ___pxOpenLocks | ___pxSessionID |
| ___pxUserName | ___pxWorkDir | | |

Object Module Name: _pxnew

    ___pdxNewRec

Object Module Name: _pxnode

    ___pdxCycleNodes    ___pdxGetPNode

Object Module Name: _pxopen

    ___pdxDBChanged    ___pdxNewDBNode    ___pdxSaveGNode    ___pdxOpenNonKeyed

Object Module Name: _pxskip

    ___pdxNextPrev

Object Module Name: _pxtop

    ___pdxRewFwd

Object Module Name: _pxwrite

    ___pdxPutRec

Object Module Name: _reclck

    ___pdxreclock

Object Module Name: fdate

    ___pdxFDate

**Object Module Name:** name

```
___pdxNetName
```

**Object Module Name:** pdxdyn

```
_DEF_RDDNAME     _VPDB
```

**Object Module Name:** ppxdyn

```
_VDBPX
```

**Object Module Name:** _doslock

```
_doslock          _dosunlk
```

**Object Module Name:** rename

```
_rename
```

**Object Module Name:** d_creat

```
__dos_creat       __dos_creatnew
```

**Object Module Name:** strrchr

```
_strrchr
```

**Object Module Name:** ftime

```
_ftime
```

**Object Module Name:** d_find

```
__dos_findfirst   __dos_findnext
```

**Object Module Name:** stricmp

```
_strcmpi          _stricmp
```

**Object Module Name:** read

```
_read
```

**Object Module Name:** lseek

```
_lseek
```

**Object Module Name:** sopen

```
_sopen
```

**Object Module Name:** unlink

```
_remove           _unlink
```

**Object Module Name:** memcmp

```
_memcmp
```

Object Module Name: write
```
_write
```

Object Module Name: ctype
```
__ctype            __ctype_
```

Object Module Name: atoi
```
_atoi
```

Object Module Name: memset
```
_memset
```

Object Module Name: tmpfile
```
_tmpfile           _tmpnam
```

Object Module Name: itoa
```
_itoa
```

Object Module Name: open
```
_open              __copensub         __cXENIXtoDOSmode
```

Object Module Name: memcpy
```
_memcpy
```

Object Module Name: dup
```
_dup               _dup2
```

Object Module Name: close
```
_close
```

Object Module Name: strcmp
```
_strcmp
```

Object Module Name: creat
```
_creat
```

Object Module Name: memmove
```
_memmove
```

Object Module Name: toupper
```
_toupper
```

Object Module Name: dosret
```
__dosret0          __dosretax         __dosreturn        __maperror
```

**Object Module Name: fopen**

```
_fopen
```

**Object Module Name: timeset**

```
_daylight       _timezone        _tzname         ___dnames
___mnames
```

**Object Module Name: access**

```
_access
```

**Object Module Name: txtmode**

```
__fmode         __iomode
```

**Object Module Name: xtoa**

```
__cltoasub      __cxtoa
```

**Object Module Name: days**

```
__days          __lpdays
```

**Object Module Name: _tmpoff**

```
__old_pfxlen    __tempoff        __tmpoff
```

**Object Module Name: _file**

```
__buferr        __bufin          __bufout        __iob
__iob2          __lastiob
```

**Object Module Name: stackava**

```
_stackavail
```

**Object Module Name: intdos**

```
_intdos
```

**Object Module Name: tzset**

```
_tzset          __isindst        __tzset
```

**Object Module Name: dtoxtime**

```
__dtoxtime
```

**Object Module Name: atox**

```
__catox
```

**Object Module Name: stream**

```
__getstream
```

**Object Module Name: chkstk**
```
 STKHQQ              __aaltstkovr        __chkstk
```

**Object Module Name: rmtmp**
```
 _rmtmp
```

**Object Module Name: atol**
```
 _atol
```

**Object Module Name: getenv**
```
 _getenv
```

**Object Module Name: _open**
```
 __openfile
```

**Object Module Name: strncmp**
```
 _strncmp
```

**Object Module Name: _cflush**
```
 __cflush
```

**Object Module Name: fclose**
```
 _fclose
```

**Object Module Name: fflush**
```
 _fflush
```

**Object Module Name: flushall**
```
 _flushall
```

**Object Module Name: _freebuf**
```
 __freebuf
```

**Object Module Name: ltoa**
```
 _ltoa
```

**Object Module Name: flength**
```
 _filelength
```

**Object Module Name: strchr**
```
 _strchr
```

**Object Module Name: strnicmp**
```
 _strnicmp
```

Object Module Name: str2dbl
```
_atof
```

## PCBIOS.LIB

Object Module Name: BEEP
```
__beep_
```

Object Module Name: DISPPCB
```
_VDISPLAY
```

Object Module Name: KBDIBM
```
_VKEYBOARD
```

Object Module Name: MOUSEIBM
```
_VMOUSE
```

## NOVTERM.LIB

Object Module Name: BEEP
```
__beep_
```

Object Module Name: DISPIBM
```
_VDISPLAY
```

Object Module Name: KBDPCDOS
```
_VKEYBOARD
```

Object Module Name: MOUSEIBM
```
_VMOUSE
```

## SAMPLES.LIB

Object Module Name: ARRAY
```
ABLOCK          ABROWSE         ACOMP           AMAX
AMIN            DIMENSIONS
```

Object Module Name: BOX
```
BOXMENU         BOXSHADOW
```

Object Module Name: DATE
```
ADDMONTH        ARRAYASDAT      DATEASAGE       DATEASARRA
DATEISLEAP      DMY             MDY             NTOD
```

### Object Module Name: DICT

| DICTAT | DICTEVAL | DICTNEW | DICTPUT |
| DICTPUTPAI | DICTREMOVE | | |

### Object Module Name: ENVIRON

| FILEBASE | FILEDRIVE | FILEEXT | FILEPATH |
| FULLPATH | GETPATH | SETALL | |

### Object Module Name: FILEIO

| DIREVAL | FEOF | FGETS | FILEBOTTOM |
| FILEEVAL | FILEPOS | FILESIZE | FILETOP |
| FPUTS | FREADLN | FWRITELN | |

### Object Module Name: FILEMAN

| FILEMAN | MEMOUDF | PROCESSKEY |

### Object Module Name: GAUGE

| GAUGEDISPL | GAUGENEW | GAUGEUPDAT |

### Object Module Name: ITERATOR

| COLLECT | EXTRACT | IEVAL |

### Object Module Name: KEYBOARD

INKEYWAIT

### Object Module Name: LOCKS

| ADDREC | FILLOCK | NETUSE | RECLOCK |

### Object Module Name: NUM

| BASETOBASE | CEILING | DTOR | FLOOR |
| NUMASCURRE | NUMASLOG10 | NUMGETDECI | NUMGETLEN |
| RTOD | SIGN | | |

### Object Module Name: PRINT

PRINTCODES

### Object Module Name: SCROLBAR

| SCROLLBARD | SCROLLBARN | SCROLLBARU |

### Object Module Name: STACK

| STACKISEMP | STACKNEW | STACKPOP | STACKPUSH |
| STACKTOP | | | |

### Object Module Name: STATUS

| STATUSNEW | STATUSUPDA |

Object Module Name: **STRING**

| CITYSTATE | LISTASARRA | OCCURS | PROPER |

Object Module Name: **TBDEMO**

| DOGET | TBDEMO |

Object Module Name: **TIME**

| SECONDSASD | TIMEASAMPM | TIMEASSECO | TIMEASSTRI |
| TIMEDIFF   | TIMEISVALI |            |            |

Object Module Name: **VALEDIT**

VALEDIT

## Other Linkers

Three other linkers are available for Clipper 5.2: Blinker; Warplink, which is similar to Blinker; and Microsoft's linker, which works with Clipper 5.0 files. Each has its own algorithm for managing dynamic overlays, C, and ASM subroutines, incremental linking, and speeding performance (both while linking and at run time). Because of its unique feature set and its differences from RTLink, we will focus our attention on Blinker in this discussion of other linkers for Clipper 5.2.

The biggest advantage of Blinker is speed. An incremental link with Blinker is faster than a link with RTLink using a .PLL (prelink library). In addition, Blinker compacts the symbol table. This means that you are not required to batch program modules together in a .CLP file in order to allow the compiler to combine like symbols (e.g., memory variables). Finally, Blinker will handle overlaying C and ASM code, as well as EXTEND.LIB. One thing to note, however, is that the only EXTEND.LIB that may be overlaid is one that has not been modified. Taking out the EXAMPLEP.OBJ or replacing it with your own granulated version of the equivalent will cause problems.

One notable Blinker feature is its ability to "burn in" the needed variables and environment (SET CLIPPER=vXXX;fXXX) to the executable file. This allows the program to modify its own file and variable tables without needing a preexecution configuration at the DOS level. In addition to these possibilities is the added benefit of burning in an execution timer, an idea that can be used for demonstration purposes. Finally, Blinker taps into VMM via Clipper's API and allows such things as disk swapping, support for expanded memory, and, as standardization increases, extended memory.

## Linking Ideas

Sometimes, a simple coding change will result in a savings in memory; sometimes, an equally simple compiling switch (e.g., /L) will save on memory as well. In addition, the way we link has an impact on our final product. No one linking scheme or technique is universally correct: different linking schemes are needed for different linking requirements. Know your environment and know the result you want to see before attempting to find the correct linking pattern to achieve that goal.

# Virtual Memory Manager (VMM)

## WHAT IS VMM?

In the past, Clipper handled memory through Microsoft's MALLOC( ) function, which partitioned off pseudosegments of memory in 4K contiguous blocks. Once strings and data lapped over from one segment partition to another, memory fragmentation became a problem. Reclaiming the memory space gobbled up by memory fragmentation was impossible. Blinker and other third-party products helped, but the real solution had to come from within Clipper.

With Clipper 5.0, the memory management system is known as VMM; it pools used memory that is not being accessed out to disk, allowing the free memory pool to hold more information and data. *Real* memory is the memory that is actually available to an application at the time of program execution. *Virtual* memory is the use of a disk, RAM drive, or expanded memory as a means of expanding real memory. This entire structure—including management of real and virtual memory—is handled by the software package and emulates many hardware-related functions and features; however, it does not make direct use of Intel's 386 and 486 protected mode virtual memory model.

In essence, VMM is a traffic cop, managing traffic as it flows through an application. This manager looks at traffic in terms of *segments* that range from 1 to 64K of data. When the traffic in real memory becomes full, the manager looks at the current flow of traffic (data) and decides what is not currently active or needed. That data is then swapped out to disk to make way for data that needs to be processed at that particular moment. This is similar to the operation of a normal memory manager, but it has one advantage. While managing the flow of data, VMM can reorganize the data segments to best fit in the available memory space. This means that during a Clipper wait state (a moment when the application is sitting idle, waiting for the end-user to enter data), the VMM system will repool memory and remove any memory fragments that may exist. (While this is advantageous under most circumstances, there are cases when C-language routines will no longer work if this is done.) In the past, a Clipper "wait" state was defined by the following commands: WAIT, ACCEPT, INPUT, MENU TO, or READ. Since the INKEY(0) function is now used in the READ command and can be used in a similar manner in all of the other functions, it is safe to say now that a Clipper "wait" state occurs when the Clipper environment detects no active movement of code, no keyboard input, or no database processing. Basically, if nothing is taking place, Clipper considers that a "wait" state.

As data needs to be recalled from a swapped-out area, the manager again looks at the traffic, determines what segments of memory are no longer active, and displaces them in a similar fashion. The maximum amount of theoretical virtual address space is 64 MB.

VMM may swap out to three places: EMS (LIM 3.2 Expanded Memory), a RAM drive, or conventional disk storage. VMM can use up to 8 MB of expanded memory. However, the amount of EMS space available is controlled by the E environmental switch setting in the Clipper environmental variable, which is defined at the DOS prompt as follows:

```
SET CLIPPER=Exxxx
```

Here *xxxx* is the number of kilobytes Clipper can use with its expanded memory manager (EMM): The range for *xxxx* is from 0 TO 8192K. If the E switch is set to 0, EMM is disabled and Clipper VMM's manager will not use expanded memory to assist with memory management. One thing to note with the use of expanded memory: While it will speed the performance of an application, some disk caching routines use it as well. If this is the case on the machine running a Clipper-compiled application, an optional environmental switch may be used:

```
SET CLIPPER=BADCACHE
```

This environmental setting causes VMM to preserve the integrity and state of the *page frame* in expanded memory and to refresh it and restore it before and after each access of expanded memory. In essence, the area of expanded memory used by the caching routine is temporarily removed, intact, during EMM use and is restored once the operation is completed. It should, however, be noted that this environmental switch should be used only as a last resort. If performance is still an issue, simply remove the disk-caching program from memory and allow the Clipper application and VMM to have complete access to EMS.

If there is not enough EMS space available for the VMM system to swap out unused memory segments, or if it has been turned off, a temporary disk file may be created to hold memory segments. This disk file will, by default, be a maximum of 8 MB and will be used only if needed. If the upper limit of this amount is exceeded, the VMM system will shut down the application. This disk file, known as the *swap file*, may be controlled to a certain degree through two environmental switches:

```
SET CLIPPER=SWAPK:<expN1>
SET CLIPPER=SWAPPATH:<expC1>
```

In these examples, <expN1> is the maximum size of the swap file, ranging from 256 to 64,000; <expC1> is the disk drive and/or directory path to be used to store the swap file. This may be a RAM disk. By default, the current DOS directory will be used.

VMM may *never* be turned off; it is always executing within an application. Therefore, any C or ASM routine requiring a predefined or fixed location in memory will not work unless the C or ASM routine goes through the VMM system. This can be accomplished through the VM.API file, which is part of the Clipper 5.2 package and is discussed at length in the book *Object-Oriented Clipper 5.2*.

In addition to controlling swap files, an additional DOS environmental variable may be used to control the placement of temporary files created during sorting and indexing operations. This variable can be created as follows:

```
SET TEMPPATH=<directory path>
```

The default for this will be the current DOS directory.

## SEGMENTED VIRTUAL OBJECT STORE (SVOS)

Within the VMM system, there are basically two areas of memory that an application will use (other than the area of memory used for dynamic overlays, discussed below). SVOS is that portion of the VMM system that works on character strings, arrays, macro-compiled code blocks, and objects, to mention a few. This system allows VMM to compact memory, which in turn reduces the need for memory swapping. In addition, SVOS allows for "memory garbage collection." This basically means that some values within a Clipper-compiled application may refer to several other values, such as arrays and the elements within them. This garbage collection algorithm automatically reclaims space previously occupied by values no longer accessible through any variable or array. In essence, by eliminating the name of the array, all its elements are also released. When this happens, the garbage collection routine not only frees up the memory for the main array reference, but also the individual references and pointers associated with individual subscripts or elements. Both routines within the SVOS system are dynamic: The amount of repooled space and the garbage collection routines are based on available free-pool at start-up and on the data types being manipulated in an application. Because it is a dynamic function of the language and/or compiler, the theoretical minimum space is 1 MB, and the maximum is 16 MB.

### WORKING WITH DYNAMIC OVERLAYS AND VMM

If an application uses a dynamic overlay section of Clipper-compiled code (by default), the code within this overlay area is broken down into fixed-size memory *pages*. Similar in nature to an index page (in dBASE an index page is 512 bytes, while in Clipper an index page is 2K), these pages reside either within the executable file or within an overlay file. In a way that is similar to an indexing algorithm, large code fragments may take up multiple pages of memory, while several smaller code fragments may be grouped together to take up a single page.

These pages are processed by VMM and are seen as segments of data as well. This means that unused sections of code segments or data segments will be swapped out for newly requested code segments. To handle all of this swapping, a fixed amount of real memory is needed to cache in and out the most active dynamic overlay page. These dynamic overlay pages are now managed on a competitive basis with other memory allocations. However, VMM can be told how many file handles to keep active for the disk file containing the virtual pages. If a file is closed, the pages of memory are discarded from "virtual memory" and VMM reorganizes the system. The range for this is from 1 to 8, with a default setting of 2. To control the number of file handles controlled by VMM, use the following DOS environmental setting:

```
SET CLIPPER=DNYF:x
```

In this example, $x$ ranges from 1 to 8.

## Summary

Linking an application can be just as complicated as programming and compiling. The options available give you greater flexibility in designing the right application for your client and/or customer. However, along with this added flexibility, the available choices also require careful planning. Know your environment, know your client's environments, and do what you can to solve all of the related issues up-front. Choose one linking option and stick to it; do not change in the middle.

# 3

# The Preprocessor and UDCs

## The Preprocessor: An Overview

Starting with Clipper 5.0, a preprocessor was introduced to complement the Clipper compiler. This new feature creates endless new possibilities for changing the way we code with Clipper and the way we solve problems with Clipper. It helps to make code more maintainable, and makes it easier to implement standards not only for a single application, but for all applications written in Clipper 5.2. Yet, as often as not, misconceptions about the preprocessor abound.

So what is the Clipper preprocessor? Although it is often seen as a separate entity ("the preprocessor"), it is in fact a part of the compiler. The preprocessor parses and modifies source code before the compiler goes to work to generate an object file. And in reality, the preprocessor is nothing more than an intelligent translator.

The preprocessor begins by reading designated header files (generally indicated with a .CH file extension, which stands for "Clipper header"). You may notice, for example, that a number of these .CH files are included with your distribution disks (and are generally written to the \CLIPPER52\INCLUDE directory on your hard disk). Once all necessary header files are read, Clipper begins to scan the source code in a particular .PRG file to find code that matches patterns in the header files. For the most part, this amounts to Clipper's finding commands in source code and translating them into their equivalent statements and functions which are found in the header files. And that, in a nutshell, summarizes the operation of the Clipper preprocessor.

There are, however, a number of important details to keep in mind when working with the preprocessor. First, the central file to the preprocessor is STD.CH. It is a special header file (STD.CH stands for "standard Clipper header") that contains all of the command definitions for the Clipper language; we will examine it later in this chapter. It is unique in that it is the only header file that the preprocessor will read automatically; the preprocessor must be explicitly instructed to read all other header files. Because of its importance, it is a good idea to keep a backup copy of STD.CH that you will not modify, as well as a second copy that you can modify. If at any time your working copy of STD.CH is destroyed, use this backup copy. In addition, never work with the STD.CH file directly. If you want to modify any standard Clipper command, do so in your copy of this header file and not in the original STD.CH.

Second, the process of compiling an application always includes the preprocessing step. It cannot be shut off or disabled. This step is transparent, and the translated version of the original program (.PRG) file is lost when the object (.OBJ) file is generated. You can, however, force Clipper to save this translated version in a file by using the /P compiling switch (discussed in Chapter 1, "Clipper, the Compiler.") This creates a preprocessed output (or .PPO) file, which is an intermediate file that is actually used to the Clipper compiler to generate object code. To make this more understandable, think of the internals of the Clipper language as being a library of functions. All commands, such as CLEAR SCREEN, must be translated into their equivalent internal functions. The preprocessor takes what you code as CLEAR SCREEN, finds the functional equivalent in the STD.CH template file, and produces an intermediate (.PPO) file in which the command CLEAR SCREEN is replaced by SCROLL( ); SETPOS(0,0). The intermediate file containing these two function calls is then compiled and linked with the Clipper library.

Third, it is important to understand the exact nature of the preprocessing. For example, some inexperienced programmers try to use the preprocessor as a means of implementing macros and variable substitution. But the preprocessor makes translations, and these translations are issued at compile-time (in fact, *before* the actual compilation). But because macros and macro substitution occur at run time, the preprocessor is simply not an appropriate tool.

Fourth, it is important to understand the exact sequence and operation of the preprocessor. A single program (.PRG) file can be translated against one file (STD.CH) or many. If multiple header files are to be read, the preprocessor begins by loading the last file designated and using it to translate source code. It will then successively load each file and use it to translate source code until it reaches the first header file. Finally, once it has finished with the translations contained in the first header file, it loads STD.CH. So the processor loads header files and performs their translations in reverse order. This means that any command from your own header file that has the same name or syntax as one in STD.CH will take precedence over the definition in STD.CH.

In addition, the preprocessor will read a single header file from the end of the file to its top (or beginning). This can be a problem, however, if a header file contains both general and specific versions of a single command. In that case, make sure that the commands are organized from the most generic form at the top of the file to the most specific at the end. That will insure that all specific commands will be correctly translated into their specific functions rather than into the more generic functions, while the more general commands will also be correctly translated.

Fifth, do not just start coding for the preprocessor. Take your time and gradually work into its style and conventions. Try to code routines as typical functions first; then make the proper preprocessor conversions, using the #define, #translate, #command, #xtranslate, or #xcommand directives. If you try to code a preprocessor statement directly without checking the logic of your basic function, you may spend long hours trying to figure out which part is wrong—your use of the preprocessor commands, or the basic function itself.

Finally, two characters have special meaning to the preprocessor and conflict with typical Clipper coding conventions. These are the < and the [ characters. Whenever you want to use literal values within the preprocessor, these characters must be preceded by the backslash character (\). A further detailed explanation is included in the discussion of the #translate/#xtranslate and the #command/#xcommand preprocessor directives later in this chapter.

## Syntax

Various preprocessor commands may be placed directly into your Clipper code. These commands are preprocessor directives and are indicated by the # character directly in front of them:

```
#define
#undef
#ifdef, #else, #endif
#ifndef, #else, #endif
#include
#translate, #xtranslate
#command, #xcommand
#stdout
#error
```

Each command may be placed anywhere in a file that is to be read by the preprocessor. However, except for special purposes that will be discussed later, most preprocessor directives should be placed at the beginning of a compilation cycle. This makes for easier program maintenance.

## #define

**Syntax**         `#define <pCONSTANT> [<value>]`

The #define preprocessor directive defines a manifest constant, <pCONSTANT>, and optionally associates <value> with it. During the preprocessing phase, Clipper will replace each occurrence of the manifest constant in a program file with <value>, assuming that <value> is specified. Note that the identifier specified as <pCONSTANT> is case-sensitive. Also note that <value> is optional. However, if it is not present, the manifest constant <pCONSTANT> remains defined. The significance of this will become apparent when we examine the #ifdef and #ifndef preprocessor directives.

This preprocessing directive allows you to predefine keywords, known as *manifest constants*, to have specific values. This not only adds meaning to code but makes it easier to modify that code for future enhancements, inevitable "bug" fixes, and minor alterations. Using #define statements gives more flexibility in maintaining the code, enhances the language to fit the individual style of the developer, and reduces the symbol table, which in turn lowers the amount of memory needed to load a Clipper-compiled program module.

In the past, developers would assign a variable name to a value and then evaluate it. For example,

```
PUBLIC ESC := 27

if lastkey() == ESC
   * Do something
endif
```

In this example, a numeric variable named *ESC* is assigned the value of 27. This is then compared with the value of LASTKEY( ) in the next command line. Since this is a PUBLIC variable, *ESC* may be used throughout the application. Doing so, however, takes up space in the symbol table. Using a #define preprocessor statement instead will allow Clipper to literally replace each occurrence of *ESC* with its value. This means that the constant ESC would not appear in the symbol table, yet the code would be translated correctly. This is demonstrated in the examples that follow.

Consider a code fragment that initializes the screen to have white lettering on a blue background.

```
SETCOLOR( "1/7, 7/1" )
```

Taking this one step further, you could do the following:

```
cNormal := "1/7, 7/1"
setcolor( cNormal )
```

This is the equivalent of a simple #define in previous versions of Clipper. The trouble, however, is that, in looking at the code, there is no way to know specifically what *cNormal* means. In contrast, in Clipper 5.2, you would do the following:

```
#define pNORMAL "1/7, 7/1"
setcolor( pNORMAL)
```

or, to help give meaning to the numbers, try the following:

```
#define pBLUE "1"
#define pWHITE "7"
SETCOLOR( pBLUE + "/" + pWHITE )
```

Another excellent use for a manifest constant is in referring to specific keyboard values. Remembering the value of each key is sometimes impossible. So having a special header file with these values in it is clearly advantageous. Consider the old style of coding:

```
nNumber := 1
read
@ 10,10 get nNumber
if lastkey() == 27
   * Perform an update
endif
```

With the #DEFINE preprocessor directive we can give meaning to the code fragment:

```
#define pESC 27
nNumber := 1
```

```
read
@ 10,10 get nNumber
if lastkey() == pESC
   * Perform an update
endif
```

Or we can carry this one step further:

```
#define pABORT (lastkey() == 27)
nNumber := 1
read
@ 10,10 get nNumber
if pABORT
   * Perform an update
endif
```

Since #define substitutes values for text in our source code, it is important that we adopt a consistent convention for naming manifest constants which makes unintended changes to source code unlikely. For example, in most of the Clipper header files supplied by Computer Associates, all letters in manifest constants are in upper case, and a prefix is followed by an underscore character ("_"), which is followed by a root name. But it is also important that this convention result in manifest constant names that are easy to remember, since this is frequently why a manifest constant is used in the first place. And here, the convention used in the header files does not produce particularly memorable manifest constant names. In contrast, the convention used throughout this book is to place a lower case "p" in front of the root name of the manifest constant.

A good practice to follow is to group your #define statements together and place them at the top of the program file or #include file (a topic that we will look at in a moment).

Ordinarily, once you #define a manifest constant, you then use it throughout a program file to represent key coding phrases that are likely to repeat themselves. But you can also make multiple definitions of a single keyword throughout an application; however, keep in mind that Clipper will replace the code fragment with the current definition of the keyword. For example, consider the following code fragment:

```
#define ONE "1"
? ONE
#define ONE "Hello"
? ONE
```

Looking at the output file from the preprocessor, we would see the following:

```
QOut( "1" )
QOut( "Hello" )
```

As you can see, the keyword ONE was altered in the second #define statement, and any code compiled after that redefinition shows the new value.

In addition, #define is case sensitive. For an example of this, consider the following:

```
#define ONE "Hello"
? one
? ONE
```

Looking at the output file, we would see the following:

```
QOut( one )
QOut( "Hello" )
```

In the second output statement, the keyword ONE was replaced by the string "Hello." However, in the first example, no translation occurred, since the variable *one* is in lowercase. Be careful of this: Simple statements may not act properly because of inconsistent coding styles. For help on this, please see Appendix 1.

You should also remember that #define statements apply only to the file in which they occur; they are not visible to any other file. It is not necessary, however, to place the #define statements in the program file itself. Instead, an entire file of #define statements can be applied to a particular program file by using the #include directive, which will be discussed later. The key point is that, whether #define directives are included in the source code or whether an #include directive is used to load a file containing the #define directives, the manifest constants nevertheless are visible only to the file containing the #define or the #include.

You may also generate a manifest constant at compile time with the /D switch. This will become more meaningful once we discuss the #ifdef and #ifndef preprocessor statements. (See Chapter 1 for more information about this compiler switch.)

The following examples best illustrates the point of a manifest constant:

```
 1 : * File:      Define1.prg
 2 :
 3 : memvar GETLIST   // This is to avoid a warning message
 4 :
 5 : #define pESC 27
 6 : #define pABORT() (LASTKEY() = 27 .OR. !UPDATED())
 7 :
 8 : function Main()
 9 :
10 :    local nNumber := 0
11 :
12 :    scroll()    // No need to CLS since there is an @ command
13 :
14 :    @ 10,10 get nNumber
15 :    read
16 :    if !(lastkey() == pESC )
17 :       // Perform some sort of an update
18 :    endif
19 :
20 :    @ 12,10 get nNumber
21 :    read
22 :    if !pABORT()
23 :       @ 14,10 say "Perform the update!"
24 :       inkey(0)
25 :    endif
26 :
```

```
27 :     return( NIL )
28 :
29 : // End of File: Define1.prg
```

On line 5, we associate the keyword pESC with the value of 27, and on line 6, we associate the string pABORT( ) with the expression that tests the value of LASTKEY( ) as well as UPDATED( ). In essence, the code is now easier to read without increasing memory consumption (because memory variables have been avoided) and we have not increased the number of references in the symbol table.

Again, looking at the intermediate file generated by the compiler, the above coding extract would look like this:

```
memvar GETLIST

function Main()

  local nNumber := 0

  scroll()

  SetPos( 10, 10 ) ; AAdd( GetList, _GET_( nNumber, "nNumber",,, ):display() )
  ReadModal(GetList) ; GetList := {}
  if !(lastkey() == 27 )

  endif

  SetPos( 12, 10 ) ; AAdd( GetList, _GET_( nNumber, "nNumber",,, ):display() )
  ReadModal(GetList) ; GetList := {}
  if !(LASTKEY() = 27 .OR. !UPDATED())
    DevPos( 14, 10 ) ; DevOut( "Perform the update!" )
    inkey(0)
  endif

  return( NIL )
```

Note that the replacements for the pESC and pABORT( ) definitions have been properly made in the intermediate file.

Our example program also illustrates an occasional side-effect of using the preprocessor. On line 3, we initialize a memory variable which, as far as we can see, is never used in the program; this line of code, it would appear, is certainly superfluous. Yet, if we omit line 3, Clipper will display a warning message if we compile with the /W switch. This is because a preprocessor translation makes use of a variable which does not exist in our original source code. And if we compare our original source code with the .PPO file that is produced when we compile it, we can identify the command whose translation has created this. On lines 14–15 and 20–21, we create a typical data entry screen by using a combination of the @...GET and READ commands. Yet, if we look at the preprocessor output (.PPO) file, we can see that each of these commands translates into one or more functions that make use of an array named *GetList[ ]*. The @...GET command, for instance, uses AADD( ) to add an element to the *GetList[ ]* array. And READ first passes *GetList[ ]* as a parameter to the READMODAL( ) function and then reinitializes it.

One of the greatest challenges the preprocessor poses for the programmer is knowing when to define a symbol or when to simply make it a memory variable. Understanding this difference could mean the difference between cluttered, kludgy code and effective, clean code. Looking back to our color schemes example, we could do the following:

```
 1 : * File:      Define2.prg
 2 :
 3 : #define pBLUE "1"
 4 : #define pBLACK "0"
 5 : #define pWHITE "7"
 6 :
 7 : function Main()
 8 :
 9 :    local cScreen := Color(pBLUE, pWHITE, pWHITE, pBLACK)
10 :
11 :    setcolor( cScreen )
12 :    cls
13 :    ? "This is a test.  Press any key...."
14 :    inkey(0)
15 :
16 :    return( NIL )
17 :
18 : *******************
19 :
20 : static function Color( cFirst, cSecond, cThird, cFourth )
21 :
22 :    return(cFirst + "/" + cSecond + ", " + cThird + "/" + cFourth)
23 :
24 : // End of File: Define2.prg
```

Since the screen color can vary throughout an application, memory variables should be used to handle colors. In our example, the function Color( ) is passed the color constants and converts them into a memory variable string.

Up until this point, we have been looking at #define statements that define manifest constants, some of which appear to be functions (as in the case of the pABORT( ) reference in DEFINE1.PRG). These latter are known as pseudofunctions, which represent attempts to assign a name reference to an expression without placing a symbol for it in the symbol table. In DEFINE1.PRG, a reference to pABORT( ) cannot be found in the program's symbol table, and yet it works, since it is nothing more than a word representation of an expression that includes the LASTKEY( ) and UPDATED( ) functions.

Pseudofunctions are resolved at compile time—not at run time. As with a manifest constant, the advantage of a pseudofunction is that it will give more meaning to your code and make it easier to modify in the future. However, keep in mind that the typical type-checking that is common in many functions is not possible with simple pseudofunction translations. This implies that you should not try to trick your pseudofunctions. A good rule to follow is that if the routine is to be distributed to a general user base with varying skill levels, it may be best to keep simple functions as they are rather than to convert them to pseudofunctions.

Although we have used the #define directive to create pseudofunctions, ordinarily the #translate and #xtranslate directives are used for this purpose. Although they will be discussed later, DEFINE3.PRG illustrates this method of creating a pseudofunction.

```
 1 : * File:     Define3.prg
 2 :
 3 : #define pBLUE  "1"
 4 : #define pBLACK "0"
 5 : #define pWHITE "7"
 6 : #xtranslate COLOR(<exp1>, <exp2>) => <exp1>+"/"+<exp2>
 7 :
 8 : function Main()
 9 :
10 :    local cScreen := COLOR(pBLUE,pWHITE)
11 :
12 :    setcolor( cScreen )
13 :    cls
14 :    ? "Press any key to continue..."
15 :    inkey(0)
16 :
17 :    return( NIL )
18 :
19 : // End of File: Define3.prg
```

In this example, what was the Color( ) function in DEFINE2.PRG is now the COLOR( ) preprocessor pseudofunction. We will look at how this translation really works in a few moments.

## #undef

**Syntax**     #undef [pCONSTANT]

This preprocessing statement allows you to undefine those manifest constants or pseudo-functions previously defined via the #define preprocessor directive. Only the name of the manifest constant or the pseudofunction need be provided to the #undef command statement. Undefining a manifest constant or pseudofunction gives you the ability to turn off identifiers, especially those used in large coding sections or those used for setting up a demonstration program.

In many cases, the repetitive use of a variable indicates the need for a #define command; however, in some cases, the scope of this command is very limited. It may therefore be necessary to undefine the constant that has been defined earlier. Consider the following:

```
 1 : * File:     Define4.prg
 2 :
 3 : function Main()
 4 :
 5 : #define HARDCR  chr(13)+chr(10)
 6 :
 7 :    local cString1 := "Pressing the ESC Key will abort " + HARDCR
 8 :    local cString2 := "the window of PROMPTS and return " + HARDCR
 9 :    local cString3 := "you to the main DBEDIT() window  " + HARDCR
10 :
11 : #undef HARDCR
12 :
13 :    local hardcr := "This is a test"  // Though this violates the notation
14 :
15 :    memowrit("HELPTEXT.TXT", cString1 + cString2 + cString3)
```

```
16 :
17 :    cls
18 :    ? hardcr
19 :    wait
20 :    type( "Helptext.txt" )
21 :    wait
22 :
23 :    return( NIL )
24 :
25 : // End of File: Define4.prg
```

In the Clipper intermediate file DEFINE4.PPO, which is shown below, you can see that some of the HARDCR references were properly replaced with the CHR(13)+CHR(10) character combination, while the specific reference on line 18 remains as a variable: This happens since *hardcr* is a manifest constant on lines 7 through 9, since it was defined on line 5. But since the #undef directive is used to undefine the manifest constant, *hardcr* on lines 13 and 18 remains a memory variable.

```
function Main()

   local cString1 := "Pressing the ESC Key will abort " + chr(13)+chr(10)
   local cString2 := "the window of PROMPTS and return " + chr(13)+chr(10)
   local cString3 := "you to the main DBEDIT() window  " + chr(13)+chr(10)

   local hardcr := "This is a test"

   memowrit("HELPTEXT.TXT", cString1 + cString2 + cString3)

   Scroll() ; SetPos(0,0)
   QOut( hardcr )
   __Wait( )
   __TypeFile( ( "Helptext.txt" ), .F. )
   __Wait( )

   return( NIL )
```

## #ifdef/ #else/ #endif and #ifndef/ #else/ #endif

**Syntax**
```
#ifdef <pCONSTANT>
   <code statements>
[#else]
   <code statements>
[#endif]

#ifndef <pCONSTANT>
   <code statements>
[#else]
   <code statements>
[#endif]
```

These preprocessor directives allow you to set up applications for conditional compilation. If the manifest constant specified in the #ifdef condition is previously defined via the #define command, the following <code statements> will be compiled. If it is not, these code statements will not be compiled; and if there is a corresponding #else preprocessor command, that code set will be compiled instead.

On the other hand, if a manifest constant is not defined via the #define preprocessor command statement and the #ifndef statement is issued, those <code statements> following #ifndef will be compiled. If the manifest constant is defined, the #else condition in the #ifndef preprocessor directive will be executed and the code that follows it will be compiled.

Depending on the nature of your programming needs, you may wish to conditionally compile something if a manifest constant is defined (e.g., for testing code fragments) or, conversely, you may wish to conditionally compile something if no manifest constant is defined (e.g., to not add restraining variables to a demonstration package and set those variables to specific values). In either case, there are two ways manifest constants may be defined: directly using the preprocessor directives #define and #undefine; or using a compiling switch (the /D switch) that sets up a global definition. (See Chapter 1, "Clipper, The Compiler," for more information on this.)

The #ifdef/#ifndef preprocessor directive works just like the IF ... ELSE ... ENDIF command within the language, but it works prior to compilation.

Keep in mind that these preprocessor statements are examined prior to compiling the code. In essence, they replace, alter, or add code to an application before the source code is converted to an object file. A pseudocode example of #ifdef/#else might look like the following:

```
#ifdef <defined keyword>
   * add code section
#else
   * add this code section
#endif
```

The inverse of this logic would be:

```
#ifndef <undefined keyword>
   * add code section
#else
   * add this code block
#endif
```

An actual coded program might look like the following:

```
 1 : * File:     Ifdef1.prg
 2 :
 3 : #define pDEMO        // This is just defined with no value
 4 :
 5 : function Main()
 6 :
 7 :    cls
 8 :
 9 :    #ifdef pDEMO
10 :       ? "This code line will be added because this is a DEMO program."
11 :    #endif
12 :
13 :    ?
14 :    ? "This is a test program"
15 :
```

```
16 :    return( NIL )
17 :
18 : // End of File: ifdef1.prg
```

The intermediate file IFDEF1.PPO contains the following:

```
function Main()

  Scroll() ; SetPos(0,0)
    QOut( "This code line will be added because this is a DEMO program." )

  QOut( )
  QOut( "This is a test program" )

  return( NIL )
```

As you can see, since the keyword pDEMO is defined by the #define statement on line 3, the code within the #ifdef/#endif construct on line 10 will be added to the compiled program. Looking at the intermediate file, we can see that this line of output is indeed added to the compiled program. Two key points to keep in mind here are that the word pDEMO must be defined prior to the #ifdef/#endif statements, and that the test on the manifest constant pDEMO is case sensitive.

Of course, the #else preprocessor statement could be added to handle a code fragment that needs to be added in case the #ifdef construct fails. For that purpose, here is an expansion of the previous coding example:

```
 1 : * File:    Ifdef2.prg
 2 :
 3 : #define pDEMO
 4 :
 5 : function Main()
 6 :
 7 :    cls
 8 :
 9 :    #ifdef pdemo
10 :       ? "This code line will be added because this is a DEMO program."
11 :    #else
12 :       ? "No, this code section will be added to the program instead"
13 :       ? "of the other two lines...."
14 :    #endif
15 :
16 :    ?
17 :    ? "This is a test program"
18 :
19 :    return( NIL )
20 :
21 : // End of File: Ifdef2.prg
```

Since the symbol pDEMO is defined on line 3 and the #ifdef statement tests a manifest constant named *pdemo*, the code on lines 12 and 13 will be added to the application instead of line 10. Remember, all preprocessing statements are case sensitive; therefore, the test against a lowercase *pdemo* on line 9 fails, since the #define creates an uppercase pDEMO.

It is worth stressing again that the #ifdef/#else/#endif construct does not add a conditional statement to the compiled program. Instead, it adds a particular block of code, depending on whether a particular manifest constant has or has not been defined. The .PPO file generated when compiling IFDEF2.PRG graphically illustrates this:

```
function Main()

  Scroll() ; SetPos(0,0)

    QOut( "No, this code section will be added to the program instead" )
    QOut( "of the other two lines...." )

  QOut( )
  QOut( "This is a test program" )

  return( NIL )
```

Because *pdemo* has not been defined, line 10 has not been included in the compiled program.
The following example illustrates the #ifndef/#endif preprocessor directives:

```
 1 : * File:     Ifndef1.prg
 2 :
 3 : #define pTEST
 4 :
 5 : function Main()
 6 :
 7 :   cls
 8 :
 9 :   #ifndef pDEMO
10 :     ? "This code line will be added because this is a DEMO program."
11 :   #else
12 :     ? "No, this code section will be added to the program instead"
13 :     ? "of the other two lines...."
14 :   #endif
15 :
16 :   ?
17 :   ? "This is a test program"
18 :
19 :   return( NIL )
20 :
21 : // End of File: Ifndef1.prg
```

The intermediate file that is generated by the preprocessor using the /P switch appears as follows:

```
function Main()

  Scroll() ; SetPos(0,0)

    QOut( "This code line will be added because this is a DEMO program." )

  QOut( )
  QOut( "This is a test program" )

  return( NIL )
```

Since pDEMO is not defined, the code within the #ifndef clause on line 10, rather than the code following the #else command, is added to the program. Again, it is important to understand that these directives are evaluated BEFORE the actual compilation. They do not direct program flow; rather, they add the proper code to the application based on simple symbolic definitions.

As another example, #ifdef or #ifndef can be used to create code branches for fully functional applications as well as for those applications that are limited to demonstration purposes. A perfect example of this would be the following:

```
 1 : * File:      Ifndef2.prg
 2 :
 3 : #define pTRUE .T.
 4 : #xtranslate STUBB() => Announce("In the " + procname() + " Module")
 5 :
 6 : function Main()
 7 :
 8 :    local nChoice := 1
 9 :
10 :    cls
11 :
12 :    #ifndef pDEMO
13 :       dispbox(2,29,8,51,2)   // Give me a double line!
14 :    #else
15 :       dispbox(2,29,6,51,2)
16 :    #endif
17 :
18 :    while pTRUE
19 :       @ 3,30 prompt " 1: Chart of Account "
20 :       @ 4,30 prompt " 2: Transactions       "
21 :       @ 5,30 prompt " 3: Reports / Lists    "
22 :
23 :       #ifndef pDEMO
24 :          @ 6,30 prompt " 4: Posting            "
25 :          @ 7,30 prompt " 5: Closing Period     "
26 :       #endif
27 :
28 :       menu to nChoice
29 :       do case
30 :       case nChoice == 0
31 :          exit
32 :       case nChoice == 1
33 :          AddAcct()
34 :       case nChoice == 2
35 :          TransAct()
36 :       case nChoice == 3
37 :          Reports()
38 :
39 :       #ifndef pDEMO
40 :          case nChoice == 4
41 :             Posting()
42 :          case nChoice == 5
43 :             Closing()
44 :       #endif
45 :
46 :       endcase
47 :    enddo
48 :
49 :    return( NIL )
50 :
51 : *******************
52 :
53 : static procedure AddAcct()
```

```
54 :
55 :      STUBB()
56 :
57 : *******************
58 :
59 : static procedure TransAct()
60 :
61 :      STUBB()
62 :
63 : *******************
64 :
65 : static procedure Reports()
66 :
67 :      STUBB()
68 :
69 : #ifndef pDEMO      // Again, it's defined!
70 :
71 : *******************
72 :
73 : static procedure Posting()
74 :
75 :      STUBB()
76 :
77 : *******************
78 :
79 : static procedure Closing()
80 :
81 :      STUBB()
82 :
83 : #endif
84 :
85 : *******************
86 :
87 : static procedure Announce( cVerb )    // The saying passed as a parm
88 :
89 :      local cScreen := savescreen()   // save the entire screen!
90 :
91 :      devpos(maxrow(), 00 )
92 :      devout( cVerb )
93 :      devout( space(5) )
94 :      devout( "Any key to continue..." )
95 :      inkey(0)
96 :
97 :      restscreen(,,,,cScreen)   // Skip parameters for default values!
98 :
99 : // End of File: Ifndef2.prg
```

From this program, the fourth and fifth menu prompts (on lines 24 and 25) as well as their associated calls to supporting routines (on lines 40 through 43) are included in the compiled program. To create the demo version, we could, of course, insert the following line after line 4 of the program:

```
#define pDEMO
```

But to make things simpler, we could add the definition of the desired manifest constant directly to our command line when we call Clipper. The command would look something like this:

```
Clipper Ifndef2 /M /V /P /DpDEMO
```

The switches are not case sensitive. pDEMO, the token defined immediately after the /D switch, is the manifest constant for the program to be compiled; it is case-sensitive. In this case, pDEMO will be defined in IFNDEF2.PRG.

Regardless of the method, if pDEMO is defined, neither menu options four and five nor the routines called by them would be included in the program. As a result, a demo program can be quickly built as a subset of a regular application; and you, the developer, need only to focus on the total picture, going back later to surround those sections of code that may be omitted for demonstrational purposes with a manifest constant.

Once again, do not confuse the operation of the preprocessor with that of the compiled application. For example, this command construct would not work:

```
IF DOSERROR() != 0
   #define DEMO
ENDIF
```

This code would, presumably, initialize a manifest constant, DEMO, that can be used to set off a series of #ifdef or #ifndef statements throughout an application. But the reason this command set is not valid is that the call to the DOSERROR( ) function is made while the application is running; however, the #define directive is evaluated before the application is linked. Therefore, the preprocessor does not interpret an environment or condition; it merely acts on those symbols that are defined.

In a real-world environment, this support for conditional compilation can be very useful. In building the library in *Clipper 5.2 Power Tools*®, each of the stand-alone functions was contained in a separate program file. Each file also contained an example that tested the function. Whenever a function needed work, the test program could be compiled and run, in effect turning the function into a stand-alone executable. To see this more clearly, consider this program module.

```
/*         Name:  Parse.prg
         Author:  Steve Straley
         Notice:  Copyright(c) - 1991 by
                  Sirius Software Development, Inc.
                  All Rights Reserved
                  415-399-9810
           Date:  July 1, 1991
        Compile:  Clipper Parse /m /p /v /w /a /n
        Version:  Clipper 5.01
   Include Path:  \PTools\Include
    Environment:  f051;
           Link:  N/A
   Library Path:  \Clipper\501
           Note:  This is a generic parsing function that can go
                  from right to left as well as left to right.  In
                  addition, this function can perform iterations
                  within the string before returning a value.  The
                  first parameter to the function should be passed
                  by reference.
*/

#include "PTVALUE.CH"
#include "PTVERBS.CH"
#include "PTCOLOR.CH"
#include "PTINKEY.CH"
```

```
#ifdef pTEST
                          *******************

                          function Main()

                            local cString := "Now is the time"
                            local aValues := {"who", "is"}

                            cls

                            ? Parse( cString, "ASD")   // Item NOT found!
                            inkey(0)

                            ? Parse( cString, aValues )
                            inkey(0)

                            ? Parse( cString, {"who", "isn't", "and"})
                            inkey(0)

                            while !empty( cString )
                              qout( Parse( @cString, " " ) )
                            enddo

                            VOID

#endif

*******************

function Parse( cMainString, xSubString, lLeft2Right, nIterations )

  local nCounter          // number of passes through string
  local nLoop             // For/Next loop in case xSubString is array
  local cRetValue := ""   // return value
  local cItem             // Individual character in the array

  //   cMainString    = the string to be parsed
  //   xSubString     = the character to parse by or array of chars
  //   lLeft2Right    = a logical toggle to decide if the function is to parse
  //                    from right-to-left or from left-to-right (default)
  //   nIterations    = a numeric parameter telling how many iterations to
  //                    be performed.  The default number is 1

  if valtype(cMainString) == pCHARACTER .or. ;
     valtype(cMainString) == pMEMO

    if !( (xSubString IS pARRAY) .or. (xSubString IS pCHARACTER) )
      xSubString := ""
    endif

    DEFAULT lLeft2Right TO pTRUE, ;
            nIterations TO 1

    for nCounter := 1 TO nIterations

      IF xSubString IS pCHARACTER
        cRetValue := ParseIt( @cMainString, @xSubString, lLeft2Right )

      else
        // xSubString is really an array of string to look for
        // the concept here is that we can parse on any one of the
        // string elements in the array so long as it appears
```

```
            // in the main string.  Here, a range of things can be the
            // "parsing" character

            cRetValue := cMainString  // Default return value

            for nLoop := 1 to len( xSubString )   // do the entire array!

              // check to see if the element in the array is character

              IF xSubString[nLoop] IS pCHARACTER
                cItem := xSubString[nLoop]

                // The item to look for is in the string
                if !(ParseIt( cMainString, cItem, lLeft2Right ) == cMainString)
                  cRetValue := ParseIt( @cMainString, cItem, lLeft2Right )
                  exit
                endif

              ENDIF

           next

         endif

      next

   else
     cRetValue := ""

   endif

   return( cRetValue )

*********************

static function ParseIt( cMainString, xSubString, lLeft2Right )

   // offset position in string
   local nOffset := if( lLeft2Right, at(xSubString, cMainString), ;
                                     rat(xSubString, cMainString) )

   // width of string delimiter
   local nWidth  := len( xSubString )

   local cTempBack := ""        // temporary holding string

   if lLeft2Right
     cTempBack    := if( !empty(nOffset), ;
                         substr(cMainString, 1, nOffset - nWidth), cMainString)
     cMainString := if( !empty(nOffset), ;
                         substr(cMainString, nOffset+nWidth), "")
   else
     cTempBack    := if( !empty(nOffset), ;
                         substr( cMainString, nOffset + nWidth), cMainString)
     cMainString := if( !empty(nOffset), ;
                         substr( cMainString, 1, nOffset-nWidth), "")
   endif

   return( cTempBack )

* End of File
```

We can then compile PARSE.PRG as follows:

```
Clipper Parse /m /n /v /a /w /p /dpTEST
```

In this case, the first function in this object module is Main( ), which contains several tests of the Parse( ) function. This object module could then be linked with the appropriate libraries to generate PARSE.EXE. Once our test of the Main( ) function indicates that the Parse( ) function is working properly, we can then generate a new object file, as follows:

```
Clipper Parse /m /n /v /a /w /p
```

Now, the Main( ) function is no longer included in the object (.OBJ) file, and the module is ready for inclusion in a library. This also helps for internal documentation: It is clear how the function might be used. In addition, if changes to the function ever need to be issued, the previous tests are still available for conditional compilation.

## #include

**Syntax**       `#include "<filename>"`

The #include file is one of the critical features supported by Clipper 5.2's preprocessor. An #include statement instructs the preprocessor to insert the contents of another file at the specified location within a program. This file, specified here as <filename>, should focus on other preprocessor statements that may be common to many program modules. In other words, rather than placing the same set of #define's or #xtranslate's in each .PRG file, an #include file can be used to hold these directives.

Basically, the #include directive "drops" in the contents of the file <filename> at the location listed in the .PRG file. And while the #include file generally consists exclusively of more preprocessor directives, it is also possible for the #include file to contain actual code fragments. This, however, is not recommended; any program file that depends on this technique to load additional source code will not be in sync with the debugger.

Another point to keep in mind is that while the exact path of the #include file can be specified along with the <filename>, this is not recommended. The path for all #include files should be specified either in an RMAKE script file, discussed in Chapter 8, "Clipper Utilities and Debugging," or specified via the DOS INCLUDE environmental variable, which can be defined like this:

```
set include=\clipper\52;\random\ptools
```

Here, two directories are specified that may contain the #include file <filename>. For further information regarding this DOS environmental variable, see Chapter 1, "Clipper, The Compiler."

As we noted above, while the #include directive can be used to insert blocks of code into a program file, it is much more commonly used to "load" a series of preprocessor definitions into a program. Here, the Clipper preprocessor is clearly inspired by the C language. The following code fragment, for example, can be found at the beginning of almost every main module of source code written in C:

```
#include "stdio.h"
#include "dos.h"
```

These two files contain the standard input/output definitions and common DOS interface definitions.

Using the #include directive in this way, we could, for example, remove all #define directives from our program and place them in an #include file. For example, consider the following:

```
 1 : * File:     Include1.prg
 2 :
 3 : #include "Newdefs.inc"
 4 :
 5 : function Main()
 6 :
 7 :    cls
 8 :    PAUSE()           // Pseudo-function defined in Newdefs.inc
 9 :
10 :    if lastkey() == pESC
11 :       ? "You pressed the ESC key."
12 :    endif
13 :
14 :    return( NIL )
15 :
16 : // End of File: Include1.prg
```

When this program is preprocessed, the information within the file NEWDEFS.INC is included within the program starting at line 3. Looking at NEWDEFS.INC, we would see the following:

```
1 : * File:     Newdefs.inc
2 :
3 : #define pESC 27
4 :
5 : #xtranslate PAUSE() => ( qout("Press any key..."), inkey(0) )
6 :
7 : memvar getlist    // In case any GET is used!
8 :
9 : // End of File: Newdefs.inc
```

Within the NEWDEFS.INC file are the directives that define the constants and pseudo-functions used on lines 8 and 10 of INCLUDE1.PRG. Be careful when doing this type of manifest constant construction—the #include directive must precede the use of any manifest constants and pseudofunctions that are defined in the #include file. Looking at the intermediate file INCLUDE1.PPO, we see the following:

```
#line 1 "Newdefs.inc"
memvar getlist
#line 5 "INCLUDE1.PRG"
function Main()

   Scroll() ; SetPos(0,0)
   ( qout("Press any key..."), inkey(0) )

   if lastkey() == 27
     QOut( "You pressed the ESC key." )
   endif

   return( NIL )
```

Here it is obvious that the directives within NEWDEFS.INC are properly set up before the main file, INCLUDE1.PRG, is compiled. We can tell this because the references to PAUSE( ) and pESC are replaced with their respective definitions. Therefore, one use for #include files is to hold a series of #define statements for an application. Instead of cluttering up the beginning of a code fragment with a series of #define statements, they may reside in another file that may be simply included within an application at the designated point.

Keep in mind that #include files may contain references to other #include files. In addition, #include files may contain conditional directives that may help give further instructions to the preprocessor and to the compiler. Also it is important to note that #include files are processed in the order that they are seen within the .PRG file; however, individual translations within the #include file occur from the bottom to the top.

This is an example to show how an #include file might contain a reference to another, more encompassing #include file.

```
 1 : * File:     Include2.prg
 2 :
 3 : #include "Moredefs.inc"
 4 :
 5 : function Main()
 6 :
 7 :    local cDrive := "c"
 8 :
 9 :    cls
10 :    @ 10,10 say "Drive: " get cDrive pict "!:"
11 :    read
12 :
13 :    if ABORTED()
14 :       ? "You pressed the ESC key."
15 :    endif
16 :
17 :    return( NIL )
18 :
19 : // End of File: Include2.prg
```

And for the corresponding INCLUDE file, we have the following:

```
 1 : * File:     Moredefs.inc
 2 :
 3 : #include "newdefs.inc"
 4 :
 5 : // First the extra definitions
 6 :
 7 : #define pF10 -9
 8 : #define pBLACK N
 9 : #define pWHITE W
10 : #define pBLUE B
11 :
12 : #xtranslate ABORTED() => (lastkey() == 27)
13 : #xtranslate COLOR( <exp,...> ) => (#<exp>)
14 :
15 : // End of File: Moredefs.inc
```

In this example, the GET command, through its translation in STD.CH, defines a variable *GETLIST[ ]*. To prevent a warning message from appearing, the header file named NEWDEFS.INC on line 7 contains the MEMVAR statement, which explicitly refers to *GETLIST[ ]*. With this header file in place, no warning messages will be displayed should the /W switch be used. This header file is brought by the secondary #include directive on line 3 of MOREDEFS.INC. This means that while INCLUDE2.PRG explicitly includes only MOREDEFS.INC, that header file in turn specifies NEWDEFS.INC. This means that header files can be nested. This next example reiterates that point:

```
 1 : * File:     Include3.prg
 2 :
 3 : #include "moredefs.inc"
 4 :
 5 : function Main()
 6 :
 7 :    local cProgLetter := " "
 8 :    local cDataLetter := " "
 9 :
10 :    set key pF10 to ShowHelp
11 :    setcolor( COLOR( pWHITE/pBLACK, pBLUE/pWHITE ) )
12 :
13 :    cls
14 :    @ 10,10 say "Program Drive: " get cProgLetter pict "!"
15 :    @ 12,10 say "   Data Drive: " get cDataLetter pict "!"
16 :
17 :    read
18 :    if ABORTED()
19 :       ? "You pressed the ESC key."
20 :    endif
21 :
22 :    return( NIL )
23 :
24 : *******************
25 :
26 : static procedure ShowHelp( cProg, nLine, cVar )
27 :
28 :    local cScreen := savescreen()    // Instead of the SAVE SCREEN command
29 :
30 :    @ 20,30 say "The F10 key was pressed..."
31 :
32 :    PAUSE()
33 :
34 :    restscreen(,,,,cScreen)    // Use all of the coordinates for the screen
35 :
36 : // End of File: Include3.prg
```

Again on line 3, the MOREDEFS.INC file is specified as an #include file, and it in turn uses the NEWDEFS.INC file. This means that INCLUDE3.PRG has access to the definitions in both files as we can see when it correctly translates manifest constants and pseudofunctions on lines 10, 11, 18, and 32.

Typically, for ease of identification, header files for Clipper have a ".CH" file extension. In addition, for clarity, header files should focus on one specific purpose. In other words, it is preferable to define all of the possible color manifest constants in one file, while defining all of the ASCII key values in another.

*The Preprocessor and UDCs* 115

Even if header files are devoted to specific purposes, however, the use of the #include directive to read in multiple header files, as well as the use of nested #include statements, creates the possibility of defining the same manifest constant, pseudofunction, or user-defined command more than once. If the same symbolic reference is found in more than one preprocessor directive, a warning message will result. A technique for circumventing this problem can be found in the following example:

```
/*
   Program ..........: HELIOS.CH
   Notice ....... ...: Copyright (c) 1992 Sirius Software Development, Inc.
   Author(s) ........: Steve Straley
   Date Started .....: 09/23/92
   Application Name .: HELIOS
   Compile ..........: n/a
   Link .............: n/a
   Version ..........: 1.12
   Purpose ..........: Helios Global Header File

*/

// Colors
#define pCLR_LEN        7
#define pCLR_NORMAL     1
#define pCLR_BOLD       2
#define pCLR_INVERSE    3
#define pCLR_BLINKINV   4
#define pCLR_ALERT      5
#define pCLR_UNAVAIL    6
#define pCLR_SHADOW     7

// General Values
#define pYES        .t.
#define pNO         .f.
#define pON         .t.
#define pOFF        .f.
#define pTRUE       .t.
#define pFALSE      .f.
#define pCRLF       chr(13)+chr(10)
#define pTOP        1
#define pLEFT       2
#define pBOTTOM     3
#define pRIGHT      4

#define pCHARACTER  "C"
#define pOBJECT     "O"
#define pNULL       " "
#define pARRAY          "A"
#define pNUMERIC        "N"
#define pDATE           "D"
#define pUNDEFINED      "U"
#define pBLOCK      "B"
```

```
// Commands and Functions
#ifndef NO_HELIOS_COMMANDS
  #include "HELCOMM.ch"
#endif

// Mouse functions
#ifndef NO_HELIOS_MOUSE
  #include "HELMSE.ch"
#endif

// Networking defines
#ifndef NO_HELIOS_NETWORK
  #include "HELNET.ch"
#endif

// Keys
// The following is the basic function key listing
#ifndef NO_HELIOS_KEYS
  #include "HELKEYS.ch"
#endif
```

This is the header file for a package called Helios produced by Sirius Software Development. Among its directives are several #include directives that are nested within #ifndef directives. For example, if a .PRG file which uses this header file has previously defined key definitions, the definitions found in HELKEYS.CH might conflict. Therefore, the directive to include that file is nested within a #ifndef directive. Now, if in the original .PRG file which uses this file, the following lines appeared:

```
#define NO_HELIOS_KEYS
#include "Helios.ch"
```

When the file HELIOS.CH is included in the compiling process, the manifest constant NO_HELIOS_KEYS will be defined and thus, instruct the preprocessor to *not* include the HELKEYS.CH header file. It is this type of nesting that makes the preprocessor a powerful and useful tool to master.

### #translate, #xtranslate, #command, and #xcommand

**Syntax**         #translate <source pattern> => <output pattern>
                   #command <source pattern> => <output pattern>
                   #xtranslate <source pattern> => <output pattern>
                   #xcommand <source pattern> => <output pattern>

These four preprocessor directives all define the syntax that allows a command or a function to be translated into either a user-defined function or a function that is native to Clipper. Its most obvious application is in translating the command set currently supported by Clipper into the functions that are actually native to Clipper. If we examine STD.CH, it becomes clear that the entire Clipper command language is not "native" to Clipper, but is merely translated into the functions that Clipper can understand. But this use of the preprocessor suggests some other applications for these four directives. The creation of user-defined commands and pseudofunctions to simplify the syntax of Clipper functions is an obvious possibility. But in addition, these preprocessor directives allow us to customize Clipper to more closely resemble the functions that we find in other languages, like C or Pascal, or the commands that are available in other language products, like the various dialects of dBASE.

The rules for translation are the same for all four directives. There are, however, subtle differences. For example, the #translate and #xtranslate directives can make translations anywhere in a line, while the #xcommand and #command directives can make translations only on lines that stand alone. In addition, the difference between the #xtranslate and #xcommand versus the #command and #translate is that the #x... directives require an exact match, while the other two need only match on the first four letters of each word. These latter directives are intended to make Clipper commands compatible with the various versions of dBASE, all of which allow any command to be abbreviated by using its first four letters. Hence, the #command and #translate directives are pervasive in STD.CH. But while it is necessary for STD.CH to use the #command and #translate directives, our commands and pseudofunctions need not adhere to these conventions. This means that we will be using the #xtranslate and #xcommand directives almost exclusively.

The rules for reading these directives are simple. Any translation defined to the left of the "=>" symbol constitutes the <source pattern>. This defines the syntax of the code found in a .PRG file. The patterns defined on the right side of the "=>" symbol define the code into which the <source pattern> is translated. These translations, if the /P compiler switch is used, can be seen in the .PPO file generated when the .PRG file is compiled. The rules for the text found in the <source pattern> (.PRG file) are as follows:

<source pattern>   The source pattern—the pattern that is to be matched with the input source code—may consist of the following components:

- **Literals** are defined as *literal tokens* or literal values. These literals must appear exactly as in the source pattern in order for #translate/#command to work properly.

- **Keywords** are identifiers that are compared according to dBASE coding conventions (only the first four letters of the input text must match; comparisons are case insensitive).

- **Match tokens** are known as *match markers*, and they assign a name to a fragment of the input text that serves to identify it and aid in translating it. This marker or token may also be used in the <out pattern> portion of #translate/#command/#xtranslate/#xcommand. Match tokens must be delimited by angle brackets (<>), and the first letter of the token itself must be either an underscore character (_) or any alphabetic character. Examples of tokens are

| | |
|---|---|
| <token> | This is considered a *regular match marker* and will match the next legal expression in the input text. |
| <token,...> | This is a *list match marker*. It will match a comma-separated list of legal expressions found in the input text. |
| <token:words> | This is a *restricted match marker*. It will match the input text to one of the words in a comma-separated word list. If the token does not match at least one of the words, the match will fail. |

&lt;*token*&gt;	This is a *wild match marker*. It matches any input text from the current byte position to the end of the statement.

- **Optional Clauses** are portions of the &lt;source pattern&gt; that are surrounded by a set of brackets ([ ]). They are used to specify a portion of the pattern that may be absent from the input text. Optional clauses may contain any of the elements allowed within a &lt;source pattern&gt;, including other optional clauses.

**&lt;output pattern&gt;**   The output pattern—the text the preprocessor outputs if it is able to match the input source code with the source pattern—consists of the following components:

- **Literals** are defined as *literal tokens* and are written directly to the output text to be compiled.
- **Words** are defined as *keywords* and *identifiers* and are written directly to the output text to be compiled.
- **Result tokens** are defined as *result markers* and refer directly to the match tokens specified. If the input text matches the pattern specified by the match marker, the result marker defines how this matching text will be written to the output text. There are several types of result tokens, and they are independent of the corresponding match tokens. They are:

&lt;token&gt;	This is a regular result token. It writes the matched input text to the result text. If nothing is matched, no text is written.

#&lt;token&gt;	This is a dumb stringify result token. To *stringify* means to take the literal input text and surround it with quotation marks. The matched input text is enclosed in quotation marks (or stringified) and written and compiled. If no input text was matched, a NULL byte will be written in its place and compiled. If the matched input text is a list that matches a list token, each element in that list is surrounded by quotation marks and written and compiled.

&lt;"token"&gt;	This is a normal stringify result token. This operation will attempt to surround each listed item that is separated by spaces and commas with a separate set of quotation marks. This token writes the NIL keyword to the output text if no input text matches the source pattern markers. If a match does occur, it operates just like the #&lt;token&gt; result token.

&lt;(token)&gt;	This is a smart stringify result token. The difference between this stringify operation and the previous one is that a dumb stringify will surround the entire expression with quotation marks as one large entity. Matched input text is stringified only if the input does not make up a complex expression. If no input text is matched, the NIL keyword will be written to the output text and compiled.

<[token]>    This is a blockify result token. To *blockify* means to take the input text and attempt to write it out in code block format. Input text is written in code block format and compiled. If no input text is matched, the NIL keyword will be written to the output text and compiled.

<.token.>   This is a logify result token. To *logify* means to take the input text and attempt to write it out in a logical data format. Matched input text will cause a .T. to be written to the output text. If no input text is matched, a logical false (.F.) will be written to the output text.

- **Repeating clauses** are a portion of the output text surrounded by square brackets ([ ]). The text within the brackets will be written to the output zero or more times, depending on how many times the input was matched by any result marker within the repeating clause.

Again, the difference between the #translate and #xtranslate directives, as well as between the #command and #xcommand directives, is that the traditional dBASE-like ability to abbreviate a command to its first four letters is supported by #translate and #command, whereas it is not supported by either of the #x... directives. In essence, the #x... directives require exact matches on all keywords in the input text pattern. Therefore, the following command

```
#xcommand DELETION => something else
```

will not get confused with the following

```
#command DELET => something else
```

This can be extremely useful when similar user-defined commands and pseudofunctions match previously defined expressions.

**WARNING** Because the character for an array subscript conflicts with the preprocessor's optional clause character, the \ character must precede the array subscript marker. This tells the preprocessor that the following character is a literal and not a preprocessor identifier. In addition, because the character for the <source pattern> conflicts with the less-than operator, the \ character must also precede the less-than character. Otherwise, the preprocessor will consider the following text to be either a <source pattern> token or an <out pattern> token.

To begin our examination of #xcommand and #xtranslate, let us look at a simple translate operation. Here is the function that obtains the system environment:

```
? GETENV()
```

In some other versions of the dBASE dialect, this function is expressed as follows:

```
? GETENVE()
```

Assuming that our source code uses the non-Clipper version of the function, by using the #xtranslate preprocessing directive, we can simply alter the syntax of the language without changing all of the coding statements throughout our application:

```
#xtranslate GETENVE() => GETENV()
```

As another example, in versions of Clipper prior to Clipper 5.0, the ALLTRIM( ) function was, in fact, a call to two other Clipper functions, LTRIM( ) and TRIM( ). In actual code, this is what ALLTRIM( ) used to look like:

```
function AllTrim( cString )
  return( ltrim(trim( cString )) )
```

Now, we can simply tell the preprocessor to translate the contents of a function into two other functions. So the Alltrim( ) function could be defined as follows:

```
#xtranslate Alltrim(<c>) => Ltrim(Trim( <c> ))
```

Clipper's preprocessor will pass the contents of the character parameter, remove the reference to the ALLTRIM( ) function, and replace it with the LTRIM(TRIM( )) combination. Similarly, in the past, numeric output sometimes required multiple calls to the LTRIM(TRIM(STR( ))) functions. Now, a simple translation directive will simplify our code and rid us of the worry of unbalanced parentheses.

```
#xtranslate NumberStr( <n> ) => Ltrim(trim(str( <n> )))
i := 1
? "The value is " + NumberStr( i )
```

It is also possible to include conditional operators within the translation. For example, assuming that the Isdigit( ) function were not already part of the language, we could create it as follows using the #xtranslate preprocessor directive.

```
#xtranslate Isdigit( <c> ) => ( (<c>) >= "0" .and. (<c>) <= "9" )
```

Here, the character parameter (<c>) is compared with the strings "0" and "9," and if the ASCII value of the first byte in string <c> is between those two ranges, the value of the Isdigit( ) function will be a logical true. Without having to program an actual function, we can tell the preprocessor to translate all occurrences of the Isdigit( ) function into the expression to the right of the => characters. As another example, Isalpha( ) could be a preprocessor translation of the ISUPPER( ) .OR. ISLOWER( ) function combination. In essence, we can make new functions by combining other functions. We can also pass multiple parameters; each parameter is passed by a letter representing the parameter.

It is critical to remember that the parameter representations on both sides of the translation must be equal. For example, if a function took multiple data types, we could translate the following:

```
#xtranslate Strval( <e> ) => Newval( <e> )
? STRVAL( date() )
? STRVAL( 10 )
```

\* \* \* \* \* \* \* \* \* \* \* \* \* \* \* \* \* \* \* \*

```
function NewVal( xData )

  local cRetValue := ""

  do case
  case valtype( xData ) == "D"
    cRetValue := dtoc(xData)
  case valtype( xData ) == "N"
    cRetValue := alltrim(str(xData))
  endcase

  return( cRetValue )
```

In this code fragment, we simply translated STRVAL( ) into a user-defined function named Newval( ); the parameter is represented by the letter <e> on both sides of the translation.

Again as a reminder, it is important to understand that the preprocessor will match items in an include/header file from the bottom to the top. For example, assume the following command was found in a .PRG file:

```
CLEAR SCREEN
```

The definition for this command in STD.CH looks like this:

```
#command CLS
;
        => Scroll()
;
          ; SetPos(0,0)

#command CLEAR SCREEN
;
        => CLS
```

By translating from the bottom to the top, the CLEAR SCREEN command first is translated into the CLS command. Then, processing up toward the top of the file, the CLS command is in turn translated into the double function call of SCROLL( ) and SETPOS( ).

Up to this point, we have looked at examples of a regular input token being matched and translated into the code specified as a regular output token. The following example will demonstrate how an input list token can be translated into a regular output token.

```
 1 : * File:      Trans1.prg
 2 :
 3 : #define pTRUE .T.
 4 : #define pWHITE "W"
 5 : #define pBLACK "N"
 6 : #define pBLUE "B"
 7 :
 8 : #xcommand MAKE FRAME => dispbox(0,0,maxrow(),maxcol(), 2)
 9 : #xtranslate COLOR( <exp,...> ) => #<exp>
10 :
```

```
11 :  function Main()
12 :
13 :     if ( One(), Two(), Three(), pTRUE )
14 :        inkey(0)
15 :        if ( One(), pTRUE )
16 :           setcolor( COLOR( pWHITE/pBLACK ) )
17 :           scroll()
18 :        endif
19 :     endif
20 :
21 :     return( NIL )
22 :
23 :  *******************
24 :
25 :  static procedure One()
26 :
27 :     setcolor( COLOR( pBLUE/pWHITE ) )
28 :     scroll()
29 :
30 :  *******************
31 :
32 :  static procedure Two()
33 :
34 :     MAKE FRAME
35 :
36 :  ******************
37 :
38 :  static procedure Three()
39 :
40 :     @ 10,20 SAY "Hi there... press any key"
41 :
42 :  // End of File: Trans1.prg
```

The value of the expression on line 13 is a logical true (.T.). In deriving that value, the functions One( ), Two( ), and Three( ) are called in that order. The values of those functions are not important: Only the last value in the expression (pTRUE) is important.

On line 34, the user-defined command MAKE FRAME is used. Since it is defined by the #xcommand directive on line 8, it must appear on a line by itself, unlike the COLOR( ) pseudofunction.

Both on line 16 and on line 27 within the One( ) function, the COLOR( ) pseudofunction is used. It is defined on line 9 by an #xtranslate directive, which means that COLOR( ) may appear anywhere in a line, either by itself or with other text, and will still be correctly translated. So on line 27, the COLOR( ) pseudofunction is a parameter to the SETCOLOR( ) function, and within the COLOR( ) function are two manifest constants. This ability to mix and match various preprocessor components enables us to create a very powerful and customizable language to suit our needs.

The form of the preprocessor translation for the COLOR( ) parameter on line 9 is worth noting in greater detail. The list match marker is used in the source pattern, indicating that the COLOR( ) pseudofunction accepts a comma-delimited list of color strings. The dumb stringify marker is used in the result pattern to delimit the color string with quotation marks.

In our next example, a piece of input text is converted into a code block:

```
#command RECALL [FOR <for>] [WHILE <while>] ;
    [NEXT <next>] [RECORD <rec>] [<rest:REST>] [ALL] ;
    => ;
    DBEval( {|| DBRecall()}, ;
    <{for}>, <{while}>, <next>, <rec>, <.rest.> )
```

Here, the internal Clipper function DBEVAL( ) is called. This function will work on every record in a database. If the following command was given:

```
RECALL FOR RECNO() > 10
```

the output text compiled would be the following:

```
DBEval( {|| DBRecall()}, {|| RECNO() > 10},,,, .F. )
```

The second parameter of the DBEVAL( ) function must be a code block. The blockify result token generates this code block. It is also important to note the use of option clauses with this command. The text that is specified in these clauses may appear in any order, yet when they are translated, they are in the correct order for the function. In other words, if we opted for

```
RECALL FOR recno() > 50 WHILE !(lastkey() == pESC)
```

or if we coded:

```
RECALL WHILE !(lastkey() == pESC) FOR recno() > 50
```

the preprocessor would translate both into the following:

```
dbeval( {|| dbrecall()}, {|| recno() > 50}, {|| !(lastkey() == pESC)},,,.F.)
```

As we will see later in this chapter, it is in this way that the preprocessor allows us to build commands that will correctly supply parameters to our functions. This is, in fact, a very substantial advantage that the preprocessor offers—it automatically handles the translation of a command into a complex user-defined function, thus freeing us from having to know the formal order of parameters to the function.

This #command directive also includes a restricted match marker that corresponds to a logify result marker. Here, if the word REST is found in the input text, a logical true will be placed as the sixth parameter to the DBEVAL( ) function. Otherwise, a logical false would be written.

Take a look at a few variations of the RECALL command to see the differences:

```
RECALL FOR RECNO() > 10
RECALL
RECALL ALL
RECALL rest
RECALL Rest
RECALL REST
RECALL rEST
```

The above source code generates the following Clipper intermediate file:

```
DBEval( {|| dbRecall()}, {|| RECNO() > 10},,,,, .F. )
dbRecall()
DBEval( {|| dbRecall()},,,,,, .F. )
DBEval( {|| dbRecall()},,,,,, .T. )
DBEval( {|| dbRecall()},,,,,, .T. )
DBEval( {|| dbRecall()},,,,,, .T. )
DBEval( {|| dbRecall()},,,,,, .T. )
```

Repeating clauses are also handled by the preprocessor. For example, the STORE command can take several variables in a list and store a single value to all of them. This is similar to chaining several := operations together. But in looking at STD.CH, we can see how Clipper uses the preprocessor to build this chain appropriately.

```
#command STORE <value> TO <var1> [, <varN> ] => ;
         <var1> := [ <varN> := ] <value>
```

Here, every new variable added to the STORE variable list will be comma-separated. Whenever this should occur, a translation is made to replace the comma with a := in the appropriate location. Here are a few commands with this syntax:

```
STORE 1 TO x
STORE 1 TO x, y
STORE 1 TO x, y, z
```

And looking at the intermediate .PPO file, we have the following:

```
x := 1
x := y := 1
x := y := z := 1
```

Often literal translations in quotations are necessary. For example, when we work with colors, we can do any of the following:

```
SET COLOR TO 7/0
SET COLOR TO &memvar.
SET COLOR TO "7/0"
```

Looking at the preprocessor statement for SET COLOR TO, we see the following:

```
#command   SET COLOR TO <*spec*>  =>  SetColor( #<spec> )
#command   SET COLOR TO ( <c> )   =>  SetColor( <c> )
#command   SET COLOR TO           =>  SetColor( "W/N,N/W,N,N,N/W" )
```

In the first case, the parameter 7/0 looks like a mathematical operation because 7/0 are not strings—they are numbers. The preprocessor would match this with the first #command statement and surround the color settings with quotation marks. In the second and third instances, those settings would be translated as is. Here is the output generated for compilation:

```
SetColor( "7/0" )
SetColor( "&memvar." )
SetColor( '"7/0"' )
```

Notice that in the last example, Clipper knew that the double quotation marks were used in the code fragment, and the preprocessor stepped down to the next set of string delimiters, the single quotation. In all of these cases, the compiler "stringified" the input text in the output text. The SetColor( ) function must have a string data type passed to it, yet in some command statements (e.g., SET COLOR TO 7/0 ) the input text is not surrounded by quotation marks. The dumb stringify result marker is used. The smart stringify marker is avoided, since a legitimate color string (e.g., SET COLOR TO 7/0, 0/7 ) could look like a list and needs only to be surrounded once with a set of quotation marks.

Using the #xcommand preprocessor directive, we can see in this next example how a user-defined command could be used to build a new stringify result token:

```
#xcommand TITLE <*words*> => ;
         CLS ;;
         @ 0,0 SAY #<words>
TITLE Hello there...
```

In this case, if the command verb called TITLE is used, any text on that line would be replaced with quotation marks surrounding the expression in an @ SAY command. If we were to compile this, we would see the following:

```
Scroll(); SetPos(0,0) ; DevPos( 0,0 ) ; Devout( "Hello there..." )
```

This brings up one more feature of Clipper: its support for multiple commands. In Clipper 5.2, multiple commands on a single command line could be coded as follows:

```
DO CASE
CASE option = 1;   One()
CASE option = 2;   Two()
OTHERWISE;    EXIT
ENDCASE
```

This should not be used extensively; yet, if it is used, it can make code more readable, especially if there is a one-to-one relationship between a value and a function or procedure call. In this example, every option has one clause, and this relationship is denoted by the semicolon (;) operator, which starts a second Clipper instruction on the same line of source code. To do this with the preprocessor, a double semicolon is needed for the #command and #translate preprocessor statements only. In the previous example, the TITLE user-defined command equates to two Clipper instructions: Clear the screen first, and then display the title at the appropriate coordinates.

## #error

**Syntax**        `#error [<output text to screen>]`

This preprocessor command will generate a compiling error and display the specified optional message to the output device. This allows for in-line compiling tests to be completed before an actual compiling process is to take place. For example:

```
#define pDEMO

#ifndef pDEMO
  #error The demonstration mode is not yet established
#endif
```

Here, if the definition of a manifest constant pDEMO is forgotten, either in a program file or by using the /D compiling switch, the compiling process will stop and the string "The demonstration mode is not yet established" will be displayed to the screen.

## #stdout

**Syntax**          #stdout <expression>

This directive allows for the contents of <expression> to be displayed to the screen during the compiling process. To help evaluate the significance of this directive, consider the following example program:

```
 1 : * File:   Stdtest.prg
 2 :
 3 : function Main()
 4 :
 5 :    local nAmount
 6 :
 7 :    #ifdef pDEMO
 8 :       #stdout ****************************************
 9 :       #stdout Compiling for a demo: 10 Records maximum
10 :       #stdout ****************************************
11 :       nAmount := 10
12 :    #else
13 :       nAmount := 99999999999999
14 :    #endif
15 :
16 :    cls
17 :    ? "Number of allowed records:", nAmount
18 :
19 :    return( NIL )
20 :
21 : // End of File: Stdtest.prg
```

Now, if this file were compiled via the following DOS command:

```
clipper stdtest /n /m /b /v /a /w /p
```

then this file would compile with the value of 99999999999999 stored to the variable *nAmount*. However, if the following DOS command was issued:

```
clipper stdtest /n /m /b /v /a /w /p /dpDEMO
```

then, directly under the Computer Associates log-on message for the compiler, the following would appear:

```
*******************************************
Compiling for a demo: 10 Records maximum
*******************************************
```

and the value of *nAmount* would be set to 10. This directive is useful to provide information about the compiling process and what is happening within the files.

Sometimes, when working with many header files, an error in a preprocessor directive generates a message and halts the compilation process. Often, these errors may only appear when one translation goes into another, and if that is the case, finding the problem can be a chore. The #stdout directive, however, allows us to track the progress of the header files as they are loaded into an application, as the following code fragment illustrates:

```
/*         Name:    PTInkey.ch
         Author:    Steve Straley
         Notice:    Copyright(c) 1991-1993 - Sirius Software Development,
Inc.
                    All Rights Reserved     - 415-399-9810
           Date:    July 1, 1991
        Compile:    N/A
        Version:    Clipper 5.01
   Include Path:    \PTools\Include
    Environment:    f051;
           Link:    N/A
   Library Path:    \Clipper\501
           Note:    This header file contains all of the manifest constants
                    for the inkey values within the Clipper environment for
                    the Power Tools Library

*/

#stdout Using PTInkey.ch
```

Placed at strategic locations within each header file, a message can be generated as the file is brought into the compiling process. In addition to helping detect errors within the header files themselves, this can be useful if preprocessor memory space is suddenly exhausted.

## Making Your Own Language

In real life, there are two types of programmers: those who like to write functions (who are typically called "tool makers") and those who like to write applications, typically using those tools. For example, consider the following header file that is a part of the Helios library file:

```
/*
    Program ............: SSDGET.CH
    Notice .............: Copyright (c) 1992 Sirius Software Development, Inc.
    Author(s) ..........: Steve Straley
    Date Started .......: 09/23/92
    Application Name ...: HELIOS
    Compile ............: n/a
    Link ...............: n/a
```

```
               Version ............: 1.12
               Purpose ............: Helios Get System Core

*/

// GET Alone
#command @ <row>, <col> GET <var> [COLOR <getcolor>]        ;
                       [PICTURE <pic>] [VALID <valid>] [WHEN <when>] ;
                       [SEND <msg>] [MESSAGE <Getmsg> ;
                          [MSGCOLOR <msgcolor>] [AT <mRow>, <mCol>] ] ;
                       [NAME <name>] [TIMEOUT <time> [EXECUTE <func>]] ;
                       [KEYSET <key> TO <block>]   ;
      => SetPos( <row>, <col> )                                         ;
         ;AAdd( GetList, _GET_( <var>, <(var)>, <pic>, <{valid}>, <{when}> ));
         [; ATail(GetList):colorDisp(<getcolor>)]                    ;
         [; ATail(GetList):<msg>]                                    ;
         ;atail(getlist):cargo := GetCargoBuild({<Getmsg>,;
                                        <msgcolor>, <mRow>,<mCol>,<name>,;
                                        <time>,<{func}>,<key>,<{block}>}) ;;
               if !(atail(getlist):cargo\[pCARGOGETNAME] == NIL) ;;
                   atail(getlist):name := upper(atail(getlist):cargo\[pCARGOGETNAME]) ;;
                   atail(getlist):cargo\[pCARGOGETNAME] := NIL;;
               end

// GET & SAY
#command @ <row>, <col> SAY <sayxpr>                       ;
                       [<sayClauses>,...>] GET <var> [<getClauses>,...>] ;
       => @ <row>, <col> SAY <sayxpr> [<sayClauses>]         ;;
          @ Row(), Col()+1 GET <var>   [<getClauses>]

#command READ [STARTING WITH <pos>] ;
              [PRIOR EXECUTE <preblock>] ;
              [DURING EXECUTE <durblock>] ;
              [POST EXECUTE <postblock>] ;
              [TIMEOUT <timeout> [EXECUTE <func>]];
=>;
          ReadModal(getlist, <pos>, <{preblock}>, <{durblock}>,;
          <{postblock}>, <timeout>, <{func}>) ;
          getlist := {}

#xcommand INIT DATA TO <aInfo> => <aInfo> := { {}, {} }

#xcommand DEFINE DATA IN <array> GET <get> ;
                AT <Grow>, <Gcol> [COLOR <Gcolor>] ;
                [PICTURE <Gpict>] ;
                [MESSAGE <message> [MSGCOLOR <msgcolor>][AT <mRow>, <mCol>] ] ;
                [NAME <name> ] [TIMEOUT <time> [EXECUTE <func>]] ;
                [KEYSET <key> TO <block>] [READER <reader> ] ;
                [WHEN <when>] [VALID <valid>] ;
      => BuildGet(<array>, , ;
             {<get>, {|a| if(a=nil, <get>, <get>:=a)}, <(get)>, <Grow>, ;
             <Gcol>, <Gcolor>, <Gpict>, <message>, <msgcolor>,<mRow>,;
              <mCol>, <name>, <reader>, <{when}>, <{valid}>, <time>, ;
              <{func}>, <key>,<{block}>   } )

#xcommand DEFINE DATA IN <array> SAY <say> ;
                AT <row>, <col> ;
                [PICTURE <pict>] [COLOR <color>] ;
                [GET <get> [AT <gRow>, <gCol>] ;
                [COLOR <gColor>] [PICTURE <gPict>] ;
                [MESSAGE <message> [MSGCOLOR <newcolor>][AT <mRow>, <mCol>] ] ;
```

```
                        [NAME <name>] [TIMEOUT <time> [EXECUTE <func>]] ;
                        [KEYSET <key> TO <block>] [READER <reader> ] ;
                        [WHEN <when>] [VALID <valid>] ] => ;
           BuildGet( <array>, {<row>, <col>, <say>, <pict>, <color>, ;
                   {|cPict, cColor| setpos(<row>, <col>), ;
                    if(cPict == NIL, devout(<say>, <color> ), ;
                        devoutpict( <say>, cPict, <color> ) ) } } ;
                [, {<get>, {|a| if(a=nil, <get>, <get>:=a)}, <(get)>, ;
                    <gRow>, <gCol>, <gColor>, <gPict>, ;
                    <message>, <newcolor>, <mRow>, ;
                    <mCol>,<name>,<reader>, <{when}>, <{valid}>,;
                    <time>, <{func}>, <key>,<{block}> } ] )

#xcommand READ DATA <aInfo> [STARTING WITH <pos>] ;
                    [PRIOR EXECUTE <preblock>] ;
                    [DURING EXECUTE <durblock>] ;
                    [POST EXECUTE <postblock>] ;
                    [TIMEOUT <timeout> [EXECUTE <func>]] ;
    =>;
            ReadModal(<aInfo>, <pos>, <{preblock}>, <{durblock}>,;
                      <{postblock}>, <timeout>, <{func}>)
```

In this header file the simple @...SAY...GET commands translate into a series of complex function calls and instance variable assignments. In the case of the DEFINE DATA IN command that translates into the BuildGet( ) function, the complexity of the parameters for that function can be staggering. The tool makers of a company think in terms of the complex function calls: The application builders of a company just want to use those function calls with ease. The preprocessor is the tool that makes Clipper the language of inclusion, not exclusion.

Now, in the pure sense of the Clipper language, there is no such thing as a user-defined command, nor are there any real *pseudofunctions*. These are terms given to the process by which the preprocessor takes commands and functions and converts them into function calls (either to internal Clipper functions or to personal, user-defined functions) or grouped expressions.

The only real difference between a user-defined command and a pseudofunction is in the preprocessor statement. A user-defined command requires the #command directive, while a pseudofunction requires the #translate directive. The process for translating input and output text for both the #command and the #translate directives is the same. The only difference to Clipper between the two is in the location of what is to be preprocessed. That is to say, where does the statement that will be preprocessed appear in a command line? Is it the complete line (a command) or is it in-line, appearing anywhere in a command line (a function)? The choice is up to the programmer. If a programmer's background is more C and Pascal-oriented, converting the Clipper command dialect to a more function-oriented base may be preferred. On the other hand, if the background is in BASIC or COBOL, a more verb-oriented command set is the preferred method to solve programming problems. Regardless of the choice, the preprocessor is the answer.

## USER-DEFINED COMMANDS VS. USER-DEFINED FUNCTIONS

While many programmers feel that function-based languages offer a syntactical consistency that makes it easier to code, there is also a large contingency that advocates the use of commands over the use of functions. But each style of coding in fact has numerous advantages. Commands can free the programmer from the need to worry about the order in which parameters are passed to a function, since the optional clauses to a command may appear in any order. With the aid of the preprocessor and Clipper 5.2, user-defined commands also allow the programmer to define a set of operations that alter the language's underlying functionality without affecting its base code (as in changing database drivers and the like). And of course, a large number of people simply find commands to be more "intuitive" than functions.

On the other hand, many programmers, and particularly those with backgrounds in C, find functions to be more "intuitive" than commands. In addition, functions can be used in a number of situations in which commands cannot. For example, commands cannot be used in a code block, nor can they be used in extended expressions.

Some of the limitations of commands, however, can be overcome with the aid of the preprocessor. For example, it is possible to build a series of user-defined commands that will directly use the extended expression abilities within Clipper. For example, the following code fragment could be applied to all of the other database-oriented commands:

```
#command SKIP ALIAS <a>          => <a> -> ( dbSkip(1) )
#command SKIP <n> ALIAS <a>      => <a> -> ( dbSkip(<n>) )
```

The choice between function-based and command-based programming should fit the styles and experience levels of individual programmers or the programmers in a particular environment. And in some cases, a compromise between the two may be necessary. For instance, it is preferable to adopt function-based programming to build generic routines and comprehensive subsystems, and to complement these with a series of commands that make implementation of those functions and subsystems easier.

## PSEUDOFUNCTIONS

A pseudofunction is merely the word representation of an expression. For example, if we want to calculate the number of occurrences of one string in another, we could build a complex expression using the STRTRAN( ) function. However, we could, for the sake of clarity, build that expression using what appears to be a function but is, in fact, merely a textual string which is translated into the expression. Consider the following:

```
#xtranslate OCCURRENCE( <a>, <b> )      => ;
            ( INT(LEN( <b> )-LEN(STRTRAN(<b>, <a>, ""))) / LEN(<a>) )
```

These translational matches are not case sensitive. Looking back to the rules of the preprocessor, text on the left of the "=>" characters is the input text, and text to the right is the output text. The "<>" characters symbolize either input or output chunk markers, depending on which side of the "=>" characters we are looking. Although there are a number of different types of input and output chunk markers, in the OCCURRENCE( ) pseudofunction, both the input and output chunk markers (<c>) are regular chunk markers. That is to say, whatever appears between the left and the right parentheses of the OCCURRENCE( ) function is placed as is between the parentheses of the embedded LEN(STRTRAN( ) function. The match is made based on the name of the match marker on the left of the "=>" with that on the right. This is how the preprocessor knows what piece of text in a .PRG file goes where in the output text.

Again, one of the key things to remember is to use the #xtranslate and #xcommand directives to force an exact match. Consider this translation:

```
#xtranslate UPPERLOWER(<exp>)
=>(upper(substr(<exp>,1,1))+lower(substr(<exp>,2)) )
```

If #translate is used instead of #xtranslate for this preprocessor directive, the string UPPE in the input text would be output as UPPE. Having translated the line, the preprocessor would then attempt another pass, and would translate the string UPPE into UPPE. This would continue until, fairly quickly, the preprocessor would run out of memory. The preprocessor would then display the error message, "Fatal C3002 Input buffer overflow."

Before writing your first pseudofunction, try writing the function as you normally would have in the past—as a user-defined function. In other words, get the process to work properly before attempting to use the preprocessor to save memory and processing speed.

In addition, you must understand Clipper expressions. In other words, the following has a value:

```
( FOUND(), DATE(), EOF() )
```

Each function within the expression is called individually from left to right. The value of the expression is the last function called—in this case, the EOF( ) function. Many Clipper internal operations can be batched in this fashion to make programming for Clipper 5.2 more useful, creative, and extensible.

We can begin to tap the power of Clipper's expressions by examining the APPEND BLANK command and its preprocessor:

```
#command APPEND BLANK         =>   dbAppend()
```

Using the preprocessor to create a somewhat more mnemonic pseudofunction, we can build the following:

```
#xtranslate Append() => dbAppend()
```

But now that we have defined a new pseudofunction, we can modify it somewhat. In particular, we can combine functions to give the expression ( Append( ) ) more meaning. For example, let us add a call to NETERR( ) to the dbAppend( ) function. This preprocessor statement would look like this:

```
#translate Append() => ( dbAppend(), !NETERR() )
```

The expression now has the value of NETERR( ), and a blank record has been added if the function returns a logical true (.T.) value. We have extended the range of possible uses for the Append( ) pseudofunction. Now, in our programs, we could do the following:

```
if Clients->( Append() )
   // A blank record has been added to the Clients database
   // and there is no NETERROR().
endif
```

In addition to their flexibility, pseudofunctions offer a number of advantages. Since they are simple preprocessor translations, they are generally easier to read and maintain than functions. And since they do not occupy space in the symbol table, they take up less memory than formal functions. Finally, pseudofunctions possess all the extended capabilities that are common to all functions, such as the ability to return a value and the ability to be called in unselected work areas.

At the same time, it is important to note the disadvantages of pseudofunctions. There are in fact two major areas in which pseudofunctions are inferior to functions: data initialization, and parameter validation. In terms of data initialization, a LOCAL or STATIC memory variable cannot be declared within the output portion of a pseudofunction; these data storage types may only be defined at the top of a formal procedure or function. But since a pseudofunction is really just an expanded expression, it does not fall into this category. Second, parameter validation is reserved for formal functions and procedures; they are impossible in pseudofunctions, which again are nothing more than translated expressions. As a result, the programmer must make certain that the correct parameters are passed to the pseudofunction before calling it; otherwise erroneous results may occur.

A final disadvantage of pseudofunctions is also worth noting. In cases in which the pseudofunction produces a run-time error, the problem can be difficult to detect and diagnose, since the name of the pseudofunction will not be included in the run-time stack that is displayed to the screen. This might be confusing if one were to search on a specified line for an error in which the function listed does not appear. However, this limitation can be easily circumvented by working with the .PPO file, which shows how Clipper expands and handles all pseudofunctions.

In order to better appreciate the power and flexibility of pseudofunctions, let's examine a number of concrete examples. What follows is PTFUNCS.CH, one of the header files found in *Clipper 5.2 Power Tools*.

```
/*       Name:      PTFuncs.ch
       Author:      Steve Straley
       Notice:      Copyright(c) - 1991 by
                    Sirius Software Development, Inc.
                    All Rights Reserved
                    415-399-9810
         Date:      July 1, 1991
      Compile:      N/A
      Version:      Clipper 5.01
 Include Path:      \PTools\Include
  Environment:      f051;
         Link:      N/A
 Library Path:      \Clipper\501
         Note:      This is a header file for the Clipper Power Tools Library
                    and includes all pseudo-functions and expressions
*/

#xtranslate DBZAP()                                               => ;
            ( if( !empty(alias()), (__dbzap(), (lastrec()==0)), .f. ) )

#xtranslate DBCONTINUE()                                          => ;
            ( __dbContinue(), found() )

#xtranslate DBLOCATE( <for> [, <while> [, <next> [, <rec> [, <rest:REST>]]]] ) =>;
            ( __dbLocate( <{for}>, <{while}>, <next>, <rec>, <.rest.> ), found() )
```

```
#xtranslate NOFERROR()                                          => ;
            ( FERROR() == 0 )

#xtranslate SETFILTER( <exp>, <move> )                          => ;
            ( dbSetFilter( <{exp}>, <"exp"> ), dbGotop(), dbfilter() )

#xtranslate SETFILTER( <exp> )                                  => ;
            ( dbSetFilter( <{exp}>, <"exp"> ), dbfilter() )

#xtranslate SETFILTER()                                         => ;
            ( dbClearFilter( NIL ), dbfilter() )

#xtranslate ISWRAP()                                            => ;
            ( SET( _SET_WRAP ) )

#xtranslate WHATAREA(<x>)                                       => ;
            <x>->(SELECT())

#xtranslate APPEND()                                            => ;
            ( IF( !EMPTY(ALIAS()), ( dbAppend(), .T.), .F.) )

#xtranslate EJECT()                                             => ;
            ( __Eject(), .T. )

#xtranslate UPPERLOWER(<exp>)                                   => ;
            ( upper(substr(<exp>,1,1))+lower(substr(<exp>,2)) )

#xtranslate FILECOPY( <source>, <destination> )                 => ;
            ( __CopyFile( <(source)>, <(destination)> ) )

#xtranslate KEYBOARD([<exp>])                                   => ;
            ( __Keyboard(<exp>), .T. )

#xtranslate SAY( <row>, <col>, <exp> [, <color> ] )                         => ;
            ( setpos(<row>, <col>), devout( <exp>, <color> ) )

#xtranslate SAYPICT( <row>, <col>, <exp>, <pict> [, <color> ] )             => ;
            ( setpos(<row>, <col>), devoutpict( <exp>, <pict>, <color> ) )

#xtranslate GET( <var> [, <pict>, <bValid>, <bWhen>] )          => aadd( getlist, ;
            _get_( <var>, <(var)>, <pict>, <bValid>, <bWhen> ) )
#xtranslate GET( <var> [, <pict>, <bValid>] )                   => aadd( getlist, ;
            _get_( <var>, <(var)>, <pict>, <bValid>, ) )
#xtranslate GET( <var> [, <pict>, , <bWhen>] )                  => aadd( getlist, ;
            _get_( <var>, <(var)>, <pict>,, <bWhen> ) )
#xtranslate GET( <var> [, <pict> ] )                            => aadd( getlist, ;
            _get_( <var>, <(var)>, <pict>,, ) )
#xtranslate GET( <var>, [,<bValid> [, <bWhen>]] )               => aadd( getlist, ;
            _get_( <var>, <(var)>,, <bValid>, <bWhen> ) )
#xtranslate GET( <var>, ,[, <bWhen>] )                          => aadd( getlist, ;
            _get_( <var>, <(var)>, , , <bWhen> ) )

#xtranslate WAIT( [<c>] )                                       => ;
            ( WaitKey( <c> ) )

#xtranslate VALIDPARM(<x>, <y>)                                 => ;
            ( IF( <x> == NIL, <y>, IF( VALTYPE(<x>) != VALTYPE(<y>), <y>, <x> )))

#xtranslate CLS()                                               => ;
            ( scroll(), setpos(0,0) )
```

```
#xtranslate OCCURRENCE( <a>, <b> )                                      => ;
            ( INT(LEN( <b> )-LEN(STRTRAN(<b>, <a>, ""))) / LEN(<a>) )

#xtranslate DAYS( <secs> )                                              => ;
            ( int( <secs> ) / 86400 )

#xtranslate DBF()                                                       => ;
            alias()

#xtranslate TSTRING( <secs> )                                           => ;
            ( StringZeros( int( Modulus( <secs>/3600, 24)), 2, 0 ) + ":" + ;
              StringZeros( int( Modulus( <secs>/  60, 60)), 2, 0 ) + ":" + ;
              StringZeros( int( Modulus( <secs>,      60)), 2, 0 ) )

#xtranslate SECS( <time> )                                              => ;
            ( val( <time> ) * 3600 + val( substr( <time>, 4 ) ) ;
            * 60 + val( substr( <time>, 7 ) ) )

#xtranslate LENNUM( <number> )                                          => ;
            ( len( alltrim( str( <number> ) ) ) )

#xtranslate ODD( <number> )                                             => ;
            ( !empty( <number> % 2 ) )

#xtranslate EVEN( <number> )                                            => ;
            ( empty( <number> % 2 ) )

#xtranslate FORCEBETWEEN(<x>,<y>,<z>)   => ;
            (if(<x>\>=<y>.and.<x>\<=<z>, <x>, max(min(<y>, <z>), <x>)))

#xtranslate LOWBYTE( <byte> ) => ( int( <byte> % 256 ) )
#xtranslate HIGHBYTE( <byte> ) => ( int( <byte> / 256 ) )
#xtranslate HIGHBIT( <number> ) => (<number> * ( 2**8 ) )

#xtranslate COLDBOOT() => ReBoot(0)
#xtranslate WARMBOOT() => ReBoot(1)

#xtranslate MAKECOLOR( <c,...> ) => #<c>

#xtranslate CLEARESC() => ( __keyboard(chr(0)), inkey() )

#xtranslate SETCENTURY( [<x>] )  => __SetCentury( <x> )

#xtranslate PTREAD() => ( setcursor(1), ptreadmodal( getlist ), getlist := {}, ;
                         setcursor(0), lastkey() != 27 )

#xtranslate DOSFILEPATH(<c>) => substr( <c>, 1, rat("\", <c>) )
#xtranslate DOSFILENAME(<c>) => substr( <c>, rat("\",<c>)+1 )
#xtranslate DOSFILEEXT( <exp> ) => substr( <exp>, rat(".", <exp>) + 1 )

#xtranslate DATEREADR()        => ;
            {|oGet, nTime, lTimeOut, bExceptions, aList, nPos| ;
             DateReader(oGet,nTime, lTimeOut, bExceptions, aList, nPos)}

#xtranslate RLREADER()         => ;
            {|oGet, nTime, lTimeOut, bExceptions, aList, nPos| ;
             R2LReader(oGet,nTime, lTimeOut, bExceptions, aList, nPos)}

#xtranslate MEMBLOCK(<x>)      => { {|a| if(a=nil, <x>, <x>:=a)}, <(x)> }
#xtranslate MEMPACK()          => memory(-1)
```

```
#xtranslate MEMSEGS()              => memory(101)
#xtranslate MEMHEAP()              => memory(102)
#xtranslate MEMREAL()              => memory(104)

#xtranslate SOFTFOUND()            => ( !found() .and. !eof() )

#xtranslate CalcOnGet([<row>,<col>,<color>]) => ;
            {|cName,nLine,cVar,oGet,aList,nPos| oGet:varput(
Calculator(,{<row>,<col>,<color>}) )}

#xtranslate SetPrinter()           => set( 23 )
#xtranslate SetConsole()           => set( 17 )
#xtranslate SetDevice()            => set( 20 )
#xtranslate SetConfirm()           => set( 27 )
#xtranslate SetAlternate()         => set( 18 )
#xtranslate SetDeleted()           => set( 11 )
#xtranslate SetMargin()            => set( 25 )
#xtranslate SetWrap()              => set( 35 )

#xtranslate MAKEDATE( <cDate> ) => ctod( #<cDate> )
```

Two major threads run through all of the pseudofunctions presented above. First, they free us from the need to remember precisely what parameter needs to be passed to a function. Second, pseudofunctions make it possible to pay less attention to syntax and to coding conventions, and instead to focus our attention on building an application. Finally, they frequently make code easier to read and, as a result, easier to maintain.

For example, we can test the status of the printer by using either of the following two function calls:

```
#include "SET.CH"

lPrStatus := SET(_SET_PRINTER)
lPrStatus := SET(23)
```

But rather than having to remember the numeric value that must be passed to the SET( ) function in order to determine the status of the printer or the number and position of the underscore characters that are found in the _SET_PRINTER manifest constant, we can instead define the SETPRINTER( ) pseudofunction:

```
#xtranslate SetPrinter() => set(23)
```

This frees us, of course, from the need to remember arcane syntax. But it also produces a line of code that clearly illustrates the intent of the function.

Incidentally, as this pseudofunction shows, it is not necessary for a pseudofunction to contain either a match marker (a chunk marker on the left side of the => symbol) or a result marker (a chunk marker on the right side of the => symbol). Where this is the case, the input text is simply translated to the literal output text.

Similarly, the following is a fairly typical code fragment that creates an empty date variable:

```
dDate := ctod("  /  /  ")
```

We can make initializing a date easier, however, by using this pseudofunction:

```
dDate := MAKEDATE()
```

where MAKEDATE( ) is defined as follows:

```
#xtranslate MAKEDATE( <cDate> ) = ctod( #<cDate> )
```

Similarly, the use of color in applications can be made significantly easier by using manifest constants in conjunction with pseudofunctions. PTCOLOR.CH, for instance, assigns a series of manifest constants to the various valid colors. But even when the colors have been assigned descriptive words for the letter or numeric representations (like pBLUE for "B"), these strings may still be too cumbersome to use with the SETCOLOR( ) function. For example:

```
SETCOLOR( pWHITE +"/" + pBLUE )
```

It would be nice to do something like this:

```
SETCOLOR(pWHITE/pBLUE)
```

This makes more sense and is easier to program. The preprocessor has an output chunk marker directive that can take the above example and place the proper number of quotation marks around it; this is the dumb-stringify chunk marker. Now, the preprocessor statement would look something like this:

```
#xtranslate MAKECOLOR( <c,...> ) => #<c>

#xtranslate MakeColor( <c,...> ) => SETCOLOR( #<c> )
```

This preprocessor statement says to take in a list of items as the input text (<c,...>) and to output that list with quotation marks around each individual item. Therefore, quotation marks will surround strings that are separated by commas. Commas delineate a list. So we can now define our colors as shown below:

```
#define pWHITE "W"
#define pBLUE  "B"
#xtranslate MAKECOLOR( <c,...> ) => #<c>

setcolor( MAKECOLOR( pWHITE/pBLUE ))
setcolor( MAKECOLOR( pWHITE/pBLUE, pBLUE/pWHITE ))
setcolor( MAKECOLOR( pWHITE/pBLUE, pBLUE/pWHITE,,,pWHITE/pBLUE ))
```

Since we used the list match marker, we must use commas to separate all color pairs. Because we have used the dumb stringify result marker to output the color pairs, the preprocessor output file appears as follows:

```
SETCOLOR( '"W"/"B"' )
SETCOLOR( '"W"/"B", "B"/"W"' )
SETCOLOR( '"W"/"B", "B"/"W",,,"W"/"B"' )
```

The individual color settings are translated in accordance with their respective #define statements, only to be retranslated with the MAKECOLOR( ) pseudofunction.

Note that, should there be any confusion on what the various preprocessor translations are, the .PPO files are useful tools that should be looked at closely. This means that the /P compiling switch should be used as often as necessary. This file, the .PPO file, can be an additional learning tool for the Clipper language. Seeing how your code gets translated means understanding STD.CH, the preprocessor, and how new combinations can benefit you.

Combining several conventional commands and/or functions together to make one generic pseudofunction can make programming simpler and more readable. For example, many times at the end of a READ command, the programmer will want to include the following code:

```
@ 10,10 Get xVariable
read
if !( lastkey() == pESC )   // ASCII 27
    // perform update of record
ENDIF
```

By using the preprocessor and a pseudofunction, we can combine the internal function ReadModal( ) (which is the READ command in function form) and the expression (LASTKEY( ) != pESC) into one single expression.

```
#xtranslate PTREAD() => ( setcursor(1), ptreadmodal( getlist ),
getlist := {}, setcursor(0), lastkey() != 27 )
```

And inside of an application, the code making use of this pseudofunction would look something like this:

```
@ 10,10 Get xVariable
if PTREAD()
   // perform update of record
endif
```

We have enhanced the standard Clipper READ command or READMODAL( ) function to turn the cursor on, perform the READ, reinitialize the array of GETs in *GetList[ ]*, and turn the cursor off. Finally, the value of the pseudofunction becomes the value of the expression LASTKEY( ) != 27.

In building pseudofunctions, it is important to use STD.CH, the standard Clipper header file, as a guide. In fact, that is what we have done in defining the PTREAD( ) pseudofunction. Here, for example, is the definition of the READ command in STD.CH:

```
#command READ                              ;
       = ReadModal(GetList)                ;
       ; GetList := {}
```

We have preserved the basic meaning of the READ command by including code to call ReadModal( ) and then clear out the *GetList[ ]* array within our PTREAD( ) pseudofunction.

Enhancements may be made to other Clipper functions as well. For example, several low-level file functions deal with manipulating bytes within files. However, there is no FEOF( ) function. Like the EOF( ) function for a database, FEOF( ) might return a logical true (.T.) if the end-of-file marker in a low-level file has been reached. In the past, this function had to be written as a regular user-defined function. But a user-defined function normally takes up space in the symbol table and is slower to process than a regular expression. Now the preprocessor can be used to combine several Clipper 5.2 features in order to convert the function FEOF( ) to the new pseudofunction FEOF( ).

```
#xtranslate Fskip( <file>, <number> ) => ;
           FSEEK( <file>, <number>, 1 )

#xtranslate Feof( <file> ) => ;
           ( ( _at  := FSEEK( <file>, 0, 1 ) ), ;
             ( _ret := FSEEK( <file>, 0, 2 ) ), ;
             ( FSEEK( <file>, _at, 0 ) ), ;
             ( _ret \< _at ) )
```

The key here is that the last expression in the FEOF( ) pseudofunction is (_ret \< _at). The preprocessor has two special characters that conflict with the standard Clipper symbol set. Optional lists are delineated with the "[" character, which Clipper uses to delineate arrays. The "<" character is used to start a chunk marker, but Clipper uses it as the less-than symbol. In this case, the "<" character represents a less-than symbol rather than a chunk marker. We have to tell the preprocessor that, while it is translating the FEOF( ) call, it should interpret the "<" character as a literal string and not as the start of a chunk marker. To do this, the "\" character must precede the "<" (and the "[" character as well). Without the "\" character, Clipper would give the following compiling error:

```
A.PRG
A.PRG(5)    Error C2061   Label error in #translate/#command
1 error
```

Again, it is a good idea to get a user-defined FEOF( ) function to work properly before attempting to work with pseudofunctions and the preprocessor. Without understanding that getting the function to work in the first place and getting the concept to translate to the preprocessor are separate operations, hours may be spent looking in the wrong place for an error that may not be present.

## USER-DEFINED COMMANDS

STD.CH, the standard Clipper header file, serves to illustrate the user-defined command. This file serves as the template file to implement the Clipper command set, which has its origins in dBASE III and even, in the case of some commands, dBASE II. In fact, there is no difference between a user-defined command and those commands defined in STD.CH. The same techniques used in that file can be used in creating a private set of user-defined commands. Once we have mastered these techniques, we can build a subset of the commands we would normally use, or we can enhance existing commands to work better with the needs of our applications. Typically, we take the concepts found in STD.CH, learn how those concepts are implemented, and then judge whether those individual elements are sound enough to stand without modification or whether they need improvement.

For example, the CLS command translates into a pair of functions: SCROLL( ) and SETPOS( ). We know that the SCROLL( ) function is what actually clears the screen, while the SETPOS( ) function places the cursor at the top left screen coordinate. Now, if in our applications we more often than not clear the screen and then perform some direct cursor manipulation, either via the @...BOX, @...SAY, or @...PROMPT commands, why should the CLS command place the cursor at the top left corner of the screen only for it to be repositioned by the next instruction? It should not, and yet, we accept this as "the way it ought to be" simply because it has been the way we have grown accustomed to programming. Some programmers may opt to use the SCROLL( ) function directly, but this misses the purpose of the preprocessor. By changing the behavior of the command to better fit how our applications work, we can leave the language intact, keep it verb-based, and allow more people to stay in touch with the language. It is a learning process between us and the way the language is constructed. While Clipper is a function-based language, the commands allow us to look at how things have been and allow us the opportunity to make alterations for the better.

This focus is not just on the commands exclusively: It can be on the functions that underlay those commands. For example, at the conclusion of every COUNT TO command, the record pointer remains at the bottom of the data set. Since the COUNT TO command translates into the DBEVAL( ) function, we can safely assume that the DBEVAL( ) function is responsible for keeping the record pointer at the bottom. We can then write a new function that optionally returns the record pointer back to the original position. Once that is finished, we could then alter the COUNT TO command to take on an optional clause, called for example STAY PUT.

Again, the advantages of user-defined commands are threefold. First, if your programming background comes from a command-driven language rather than a function-oriented one, commands are preferred. Second, if you desire to bring more end users into the programming picture, words and phrases can be used to prototype and model an application. These commands and words can be adapted by the end-user. Bringing the end-user into the development cycle has several benefits: fewer changes, easy acceptance, greater ability to zero in on the problems experienced by end-users. User-defined commands and the Clipper preprocessor can be used to quickly bring these types of people, as well as beginning programmers, into the application development cycle. Finally, user-defined commands can be used to reprogram the dialect and modify the way certain commands typically work.

Again, the main difference between user-defined commands and pseudofunctions is that the commands must appear on a line by themselves. For example, we would never see the following:

```
IF APPEND BLANK
```

However, this does not mean that the APPEND BLANK words may never appear in the middle of a command; it does mean that those commands initialized with the #xcommand directive can only appear on a command line by themselves. Commands may also be defined with the #xtranslate option; however, only #xcommand statements may have multiple command lines symbolized by the double semicolon (;;).

## THE BASICS

Let's start by looking at some typical programming techniques used in an application. For example, consider the following command set:

```
WHILE .T.
ENDDO
```

This marks off a programming loop that will be performed continuously until an EXIT command (or a QUIT) is encountered within these two command statements. That command set, however, is different from this one:

```
WHILE !EOF()
ENDDO
```

Other than the value of the expression in the WHILE command, there is no difference between these two statements. However, the first example implies something totally different from the second. There is an implicit ending to the second programming example that is missing in the first. A beginning programmer may be confused. A user-defined command may help clear up this confusion. By using some other command verb, the WHILE .T. command set can be given more meaning than just a simple WHILE .T.

```
#xcommand PROCESS => WHILE .T.
#xcommand END PROCESS => ENDDO
#xcommand TERMINATE => EXIT
```

Now, in a practical programming environment, we could see the following:

```
PROCESS

   cls            // Clear the screen
   DrawBorder()   // Draws the main menu's border

   if empty( xVar := MakeMenu() ) // Draw a menu and if ESC is pressed....
      TERMINATE
   else
      // process other menu commands
   endif

END PROCESS
```

Although the internal operation is still WHILE .T., EXIT, and ENDDO, the programmer sees something different, something that means more than giving an expression to the WHILE command.

Expanding on this, we can redirect the way code is processed. Many times in the course of an application command statements like the following one appear:

```
WHILE !( lastkey() == pESC )
   // Process something
ENDDO
```

The trouble here is that the programmer must ensure that the last key pressed prior to the WHILE command line must never be the ESC key, or the WHILE... ENDDO loop will never execute. However, this programming restraint is virtually impossible to overcome. There are two ways of getting around this problem. First, by making certain that the keyboard buffer is cleared of any key and, specifically, by making certain that the last key pressed prior to this command line is not the ESC key. To do this, extra programming steps need to be taken; for example,

```
keyboard chr(1)
inkey(0)
```

```
while !( lastkey() == pESC )
  // Process something
enddo
```

In this code fragment, the keyboard is stuffed with a keyboard value that will be immediately processed by the INKEY(0) function. This in turn will set the value of the LASTKEY( ) function to something other than 27. Another possible way to program this is

```
WHILE .T.
  // Process something
  IF LASTKEY() =pESC
     EXIT
  ENDIF
ENDDO
```

Here, the programmer has to remember to test for the last key pressed; however, this condition is not part of the loop, nor is it clear by looking at the code commands what the escape condition is. Programming should be made as clear, intuitive, and concise as possible within each module. Reading a large piece of code requires time; a code line should be interpreted quickly and spontaneously. Therefore, we could use the preprocessor to help eliminate the extra code we do not need, to read:

```
#xcommand REPEAT => WHILE .T.
#xcommand UNTIL <exp> => IF <exp> ; EXIT ; END ; END
```

Here, the REPEAT command is introduced. It is nothing more than a WHILE .T. command; however, this WHILE .T. is different in meaning from the PROCESS command. The difference is in the escape routine. The UNTIL command takes an expression which, in essence, builds the above IF ... EXIT ... END command condition. Now the programming loop makes more practical sense, and the programmer should be able to look at the code and know what is about to take place. Using this command we might have the following:

```
REPEAT
  DataEntry()    // Do the data entry thing
UNTIL  lastkey() == pESC
```

If it were allowed, we could even get our Clipper 5.2 code ready for Visual Objects for Clipper by issuing some potentially new commands and options that may appear in the Windows version of the compiler. For example, it has been widely held that the FOR ... NEXT command is too limiting: It requires the macro compiler within Clipper to work on each iteration of the loop in order to know the values of the variables involved as well as the stepping value. With this in mind, it has been suggested that a new option called "DOWN TO" will be implemented to help speed up the application that uses a FOR...NEXT loop in reverse order. This would make the Clipper language of today compatible with the language of tomorrow:

```
1 : * File:   Testfor.prg
2 :
3 : #xcommand FOR <x> := <nStart> DOWN TO <nEnd> STEP <value> => ;
4 :              for <x> := <nStart> to <nEnd> step (-1 * <value>)
5 :
6 : #xcommand FOR <x> := <nStart> DOWN TO <nEnd> => ;
```

```
 7 :                    for <x> := <nStart> to <nEnd> step -1
 8 :
 9 : ********************
10 :
11 : function Main()
12 :
13 :    local nCounter
14 :
15 :    cls
16 :
17 :    FOR nCounter := 10 DOWN TO 1
18 :        ? nCounter
19 :    NEXT
20 :
21 :    return( NIL )
22 :
23 : // End of File: Testfor.prg
```

Here, the FOR...DOWN TO commands defined on lines 3 through 7 translate into the FOR statement. Remember, statements are those parts of the language which are defined within the language and, thus, are intrinsic to it. The FOR statement is known by the compiler as a loop processor, much like the WHILE statement is seen in the following extract from STD.CH:

```
#command do while <exp> => while <exp>
```

Here, the DO WHILE command translates into the WHILE statement. This is the technique used with the above FOR ... DOWN TO command, which is translated into the FOR ... NEXT statement.

## INTERMEDIATE USES

Adding to the command set to make more sense of some of the programming nuances can be easily handled by the preprocessor—as can extending the basic command set by either including new phrases and key words or simply taking what is implied in STD.CH and making a formal command declaration. For example, the difference between the single ? character command and the double ?? character command is important. The ? command translates to the QOUT( ) function, while the ?? command translates to the QQOUT( ) function. The QOUT( ) function issues a CHR(13)+CHR(10) character combination before the expression is printed to the output device. The QQOUT( ) function (and the ?? command) does not issue any CHR(13)+CHR(10) combination. This means that a linefeed occurs before the output is displayed. In using a generic report writer, this difference is important to know and allow for in line calculations. What may be better is a new command, one that issues the CHR(13)+CHR(10) at the end of the line and not at the beginning:

```
#xcommand ??? [ <list,...> ] => QQOUT( CHR(13) ) ;;
                                QQOUT( <list> ) ;;
                                QQOUT( CHR(13)+CHR(10) )
```

Here, CHR(13) is used to make sure that the output is flush left, which is the original intent of the QOUT( ) function and the ? command. After the expression is displayed, an additional call to QQOUT( ) is made, but this time with the CHR(13)+CHR(10) combination.

Looking to STD.CH, additional ideas quickly come to mind. For example, the READ command contains the following translation:

```
#command READ => ;
    ReadModal(GetList) ; GetList := {}
```

Here, several ideas appear. First, it is possible to take the READ command and redirect it to call a modified GETSYS.PRG file such as the one discussed in Chapter 18, "Data Entry Options." That would then appear something like this:

```
#command READ => ;
             MyReadMod( M->GetList ) ; M->GetList := {}
```

The preprocessor translation also implies that the information for an active GET is stored in an array named *GetList[ ]*. Looking to the preprocessor translation for the GET command, we can see that the array *GetList[ ]* is built dynamically:

```
#command @ <row>, <col> GET <var> [PICTURE <pic>] ;
           [VALID <valid>] [WHEN <when>] [SEND <msg>] => ;
    SetPos( <row>, <col> ) ;;
    AAdd( GetList, GET_( <var>, <(var)>, ;
          <pic>, <{valid}>, <{when}> ):display() ) ;
    [; ATail(GetList):<msg>]
```

How much effort would it be to take that array variable and store it to a NEW array variable, at the same time freeing the *GetList[ ]* array in order to dynamically build a new set of GETs? This is at the heart of nested GETs. Being able to create them lies in your ability to look through, think through, and plan through the standard header file, STD.CH. Taking this to a practical level, here is the preprocessor command line:

```
#xcommand SAVE GET TO <var> => ;
          <var> := ACLONE(M->GetList) ; M->GetList := {}
```

Again, the input and output chunk markers are both regular, and the matching text will be replaced as is. The variable named in <var> will contain the original set of GETs stored in the *GetList[ ]* array. Once they are stored, the current *GetList[ ]* array is reinitialized to a length of 0. This, in effect, clears the current GET if this command should be called from a SET KEY command or a SETKEY( ) function. On the other side of the ledger, bringing back a nested GET is just as easy:

```
#xcommand RESTORE GET FROM <var> => M->GetList := ACLONE(<var>)
```

But saving and restoring GETs affects just one aspect of the Clipper environment. Saving other items in an application is just as important. It should be easy to see the potential of saving the SET environment: The SET( ) function gives us all of the values, and those values could be dynamically stored to a memory variable that is an array pointer:

```
#command SAVE ENVIRONMENT TO <var> => ;
         <var> := {} ;;
         AADD( <var>, SET(1) ) ;;
         AADD( <var>, SET(2) ) ;;
              .
         etc.
```

In essence, we have applied what we have learned about the *GetList[ ]* array in order to build a similar structure with the SET commands. The single semicolon means a line continuation; the #command that is being defined is not yet finished and is continued onto the next line. On the next line is a double semicolon. This tells the preprocessor that the #command is still being defined (the first semicolon) and that the output should contain a semicolon as well. This, in essence, is a multiple command line. The variable named in the input regular chunk marker as <var> is initialized to an empty array, only to be filled, one at a time, with the values from multiple SET( ) calls.

We could also build the following:

```
#command SAVE ROW <n> TO <var> => ;
         <var> := SaveScreen( <n>, 0, <n>, Maxcol() )

#command RESTORE ROW <n> FROM <var> => ;
         RestScreen( <n>, 0, <n>, Maxcol(), <var> )
```

As a final example of enhancements that slightly but significantly alter the Clipper language, here is a standard Clipper command that is used in almost every application:

```
#command SET INDEX TO [ <(index1)> [, <(indexn)>]] => ;
         dbClearIndex() ;
         [; dbSetIndex( <(index1)> )] ;
         [; dbSetIndex( <(indexn)> )]
```

This command clears all indexes whenever it is invoked. But frequently, we may merely want to add an index to the index list, rather than closing all open indexes only to have them reopened. Looking at the header file, new possibilities should seem evident, such as

```
#command ADD INDEX <name> TO <alias> => ;
         <alias>->( dbSetIndex( <(name)> ) )
```

Here, the input chunk marker labeled <alias> is used in an extended expression call, and the input chunk marker <name> is encapsulated with a set of parentheses around the name of the index file <name>.

Along with using the preprocessor to increase the flexibility of the Clipper language and to mold it so that it operates in the way we want, we can also use the preprocessor as a tool to make our applications run more efficiently. The possibilities here are endless, although taking full advantage of the preprocessor to optimize the performance of our applications requires a thorough understanding of STD.CH and the operation of the preprocessor. For example, some variation on the following line of code is found repeatedly in all applications:

```
@ 10,10 Say "Steve's Birthday is: " + dtoc( Names->bdate )
```

We have to convert the *bdate* field in the Names work area from a date data type to a character string if we are to concatenate it with the string "Steve's Birthday is: ". When this is translated, we have the following:

```
devpos(10,10);devout("Steve's Birthday is: " + ;
dtoc(Names->bdate))
```

Three functions are involved. We also know that the cursor is positioned at the proper location because of the DEVPOS( ) function. We also know that the behavior of the SAY command and, thus, the DEVOUT( ) function, is that the expression will be displayed to the current device and that the cursor will be positioned to the right, one column after the end of the expression. And finally, we also know that we can SAY a character string or SAY a date or SAY a number—that the DEVOUT( ) function accepts any data type. Would it not then be possible to make direct function calls to do the following:

```
devpos(10,10)
devout("Steve's Birthday is: " )
devout( Names->bdate )
```

Here, three functions are still used and the contents of Names->bdate are displayed directly after the end of the expression "Steve's Birthday is: ". However, in this example, there is not a conversion of a date to a string nor is that string concatenated with another string. Both of these operations require memory and extra processing. In any real-world application, this is detrimental to optimal performance.

We can now retrofit our new discoveries back into the core language. It is apparent that the DEVOUT( ) function repeats, and within the preprocessor, we have such a thing as a REPEATING CLAUSE. We can then reprogram the basic @...SAY command to now work for us rather than against us:

```
#xcommand @ <row>, <col> [ SAY <exp> [COLOR <color>] ] => ;
          devpos( <row>, <col> ) ;
          [; devout( <exp>, <color> ) ]
```

We can then call this enhanced @...SAY command as follows:

```
@ 10,10 Say "Steve's Birthday is: " SAY Names->bdate
```

## ADVANCED USES

The ability to implement new commands is now part of the Clipper philosophy. Customizing the language to fit personal programming needs has extended the power of the language. However, this power has some drawbacks. First of all, if a command set is too personalized or not standardized from application to application, supporting any extended command or pseudofunction set is virtually impossible. Second, it will be even harder for Computer Associates to support the language adequately without supporting the core internal functions. Finally, there will be a growing desire to pick up other header files from other people, bulletin boards, books, and so on. A word of extreme caution is in order because it would take very little effort to place the following command in a header file:

```
#command APPEND BLANK => __dbZap()
```

Depending on the order in which the header files are included in the application, this command may or may not be in effect to make the fatal substitution. But the problem is still there; all header files should be thoroughly read and understood before being used in any application. Arbitrary use of another header file without carefully examining it first is as foolish as blindly receiving and loading an executable program without any knowledge of what it may or may not do to the operating system, hard disk, or both.

Now, we have a limited amount of memory available in the preprocessor. Some of it is used for STD.CH, while the rest, nearly 96K, is available for all of the other header files that we may opt to use. Whether or not we make extensive use of other header files, we can speed up the compiling process by removing those commands in STD.CH which are rarely used, sort of like a STUB.CH file. Then, using the /U compiler switch, we could tell the compiler to not use STD.CH but use the STUB.CH file in its place. Fewer translations mean faster compilations. Appendix 2 contains STUBSTD.CH, a proposed minimal header file that can be substituted for STD.CH.

Finally, simple mathematical operations can be given words, which in turn can be given to end-users to help build a program. For example, consider this command set:

```
* File:     Words.ch

#xtranslate PRE-INCREMENT <n>           => ++<n>
#xtranslate POST-INCREMENT <n>          => <n>++
#xtranslate PRE-DECREMENT <n>           => --<n>
#xtranslate POST-DECREMENT <n>          => <n>--
#xtranslate ADD <n> TO <y>              => <y>+=<n>
#xtranslate SUBTRACT <n> FROM <y>       => <y>-=<n>
#xtranslate MULTIPLY <n> TO <y>         => <y>*=<n>
#xtranslate DIVIDE <n> FROM <y>         => <y>/=<n>
#xtranslate REMAINDER <n> OF <y>        => IF(<n> = 0, 0, <y>%=<n>)
#xtranslate RAISE <y> TO POWER OF <n>   => <y>^=<n>
#xtranslate WHAT IS <n,...>             => Qout( <n> )

// End of File: Words.ch
```

The code that uses this set might look like this:

```
* File:     Usewords.prg

#include "Words.ch"

// A command just for this file
#xcommand ASSIGN <value> TO <var1> [AND <var2>] => ;
          <var1> := [ <var2> := ] <value>

function Main

   local nAmount1
   local nAmount2
   local nTemp

   // And now for the commands

   ASSIGN 2 TO nAmount1 AND nAmount2
   WHAT IS (MULTIPLY 3 TO nAmount2)
   WHAT IS (ADD 2 TO nAmount1)

   ASSIGN 1 TO nTemp

   PRE-INCREMENT nTemp

   WHAT IS nTemp
   WHAT IS (ADD 1 TO nTemp)
   WHAT IS (REMAINDER 0 OF 2)
```

```
            WHAT IS (RAISE nTemp TO POWER OF 4)

        return( NIL )

    // End of File: UseWords.prg
```

In this form, the flow of the program can be easily understood by an end-user. The preprocessor output file (.PPO) would look like this:

```
#line 1 "Words.ch"
#line 5 "USEWORDS.PRG"

function Main

   local nAmount1
   local nAmount2
   local nTemp

   nAmount1 := nAmount2 := 2
   Qout( (nAmount2*=3) )
   Qout( (nAmount1+=2) )

   nTemp := 1

   ++nTemp

   Qout( nTemp )
   Qout( (nTemp+=1) )
   Qout( (IF(0 = 0, 0, 2%=0)) )
   Qout( (nTemp^=4) )

   return( NIL )
```

It is possible to conceive of an environment in which a Clipper-compiled application uses the Clipper preprocessor to interface with an end-user to help design an application, to specify user needs more clearly, and to give the programmer a clear indication of the direction in which the end-user would like to go. Using Clipper and the preprocessor to build on this fundamental relationship is not only evolutionary but revolutionary as well.

## OTHER POSSIBILITIES

Sometimes, a picture is worth a thousand words. The picture here rests in the next two command extensions:

```
#xcommand ON KEY <label> DO <program> => ;
          SETKEY( <label>, {|p,l,v| <program>(p,l,v)} )

#xcommand ENVIRONMENT PROCEDURE =>
```

The ON KEY command is a dBASE IV command, and the ENVIRONMENT PROCEDURE is a COBOL command. In the first example, the ON KEY command is translated to the

Clipper SETKEY( ) function. In the second example, the ENVIRONMENT PROCEDURE command is simply ignored; it is similar to the SET ECHO command and others seen in STD.CH.

This means that Clipper's preprocessor can be set up, with special header files, to take programs in other languages and dialects and get them to work in Clipper 5.2. As a matter of fact, STD.CH is the file that makes old Clipper code work with the new, and that explains how COBOL, Pascal, C, FoxBASE, and dBASE code can all be translated to Clipper 5.2. This is one more reason why Clipper 5.2 is not an upgrade—it is different. The preprocessor and the header files we choose to use are what makes it possible to upgrade into Clipper 5.2.

## Summary

The preprocessor gives us the flexibility to make Clipper unique for us and our programming environment. That environment may mean the inclusion, not exclusion, of end users and beginning programmers. The environment may be personal and unique, may use private commands and personal programming techniques. And finally, other languages may be brought into the programming fold. Other dialects and languages can now contribute directly to a product's development cycle. Clipper can act like a translator or a bridge to other people, other ideas, other solutions. Clipper can take other languages and dialects not known for their power and give them speed, power, and punch.

# 4

# Operators and Conditions

CA-Clipper 5.2 supports a large number of programming operators and conditional statements that will make your programming easier. Some of these operators have their roots in other languages, especially Pascal or C. But with the new approach to Clipper as an "open" language, and with some of the new operators that appear in Clipper 5.x, what may appear to be a handy operator may be dangerous. However, the danger lies only in assumptions made by the programmer that are based on faulty information. Therefore the way to avoid the potential danger is to have a clear understanding of the functionality of these operators, their placement in your code, and their resulting values.

## Basic Symbols

Below is a list of the valid Clipper operators, symbols, and conditional statements:

| | |
|---|---|
| & | Macro substitution |
| && | In-line notation or comment |
| @ | Variable passed by reference |
| /* | Begin notation or comment |
| */ | End notation or comment |
| . | Macro terminator |
| ; | Continuation of command to the next line |
| ;; | Preprocessor multiple command statements (#translate, #xtranslate, #xcommand, and #command only) |
| ( ) | Expression delimiter |
| { } | Array delimiter |

*(continued)*

| | |
|---|---|
| [ ] | Array subscript delimiter, or Preprocessor optional string delimiter |
| " | String delimiter |
| "" | String delimiter |
| {\|\|} | Code block delimiter |
| : | Send operator |
| $ | Substring operator |
| = | Assignment or Comparison |
| == | Exact comparison |
| := | In-line assignment |
| + | Addition, Positive expression, or Concatenation |
| – | Subtraction, Negative expression, or Concatenate and remove intervening blanks |
| / | Division |
| * | Multiplication, or Preprocessor stringify |
| ** | Exponentiate |
| ^ | Exponentiate |
| % | Modulus |
| ! | NOT Expression (*Note*: If there is a trailing blank space, then this equates to the RUN command) |
| != | Not equal comparison |
| < > | Not equal comparison |
| # | Not equal comparison, or Preprocessor directive |
| < | Less than comparison, or Preprocessor chunk marker |
| > | Greater than comparison, or Preprocessor chunk marker |
| <= | Less than or equal to comparison |
| >= | Greater than or equal to comparison |
| => | Preprocessor directive (#translate, #xtranslate, #xcommand, and #command only) |
| -> | Alias pointer |
| += | In-line add and assign |
| –= | In-line subtract and assign |
| *= | In-line multiply and assign |
| /= | In-line divide and assign |
| **= or ^= | In-line exponentiation and assignment |
| %= | In-line modulus and assignment |
| ++ | Pre-increment or post-increment |

| | |
|---|---|
| -- | Pre-decrement or post-decrement |
| .OR. | Logical OR |
| .NOT. | Logical NOT |
| .AND. | Logical AND |

Because of Clipper's evolution in the direction of an "open" application development language by adding the preprocessor and by attempting to make the language's syntax more "C-like," a number of symbols and symbol patterns now have multiple meanings, while other symbols are new to the language. And in some instances, the programmer can choose from among two or more symbols to accomplish the same result. For example, the in-line notation symbol, traditionally represented by the && characters, now is represented as well by the /* and */ symbols, the symbols typically used by C programmers to document their code.

The following program demonstrates some of these new operators.

```
 1 : * File:     Oper1.prg
 2 :
 3 : function Main()
 4 :
 5 :    local aNewArray := {}
 6 :
 7 :    private cString1 := "Hello"
 8 :    private cString2 := "cString1"
 9 :
10 :    ? &cString2.
11 :
12 :    * This is a notation so long as the first character is the "*"
13 :    * symbol.  In addition:
14 :
15 :    /* This is also a symbol pattern for a note provided that it is
16 :       terminated with the appropriate closing symbol.  It should be
17 :       noted that these types of notational symbols CANNOT be nested
18 :       one within another */
19 :
20 :    ? cString1      && In-line notations can also be made
21 :    ? cString1      // with the && characters or....
22 :    ? cString2      /* these character as well as the end characters
23 :                       can appear later, even on another line just
24 :                       like C */
25 :
26 :    ? &( cString2 )
27 :
28 :    ? type("aNewArray"), valtype( aNewArray )
29 :
30 :    aNewArray := array(10)
31 :    afill( aNewArray, 1 )
32 :
33 :    ? aNewArray[1]    // which is different from the following...
34 :
```

```
35 :    ? [This is a test]
36 :
37 :    use Clients new
38 :
39 :    ? Clients->account, Clients->( recno() ), Field->account
40 :
41 :    return( NIL )
42 :
43 :    // End of File: Oper1.prg
```

In this example, the array *aNewArray[ ]* is initialized on line 5, and the type of the variable is displayed by both the TYPE( ) function and the VALTYPE( ) function on line 28. (Remember, the TYPE( ) function uses a macro to expand the parameter; VALTYPE( ) does not. This means that if a LOCAL variable is used, it is inappropriate to use the TYPE( ) function. A LOCAL variable is not available in the symbol table; therefore the TYPE( ) function, when it attempts macro-expansion of the specified variable name, will return a "U". However, the VALTYPE( ) function will return the appropriate letter for each data type regardless of the data storage class.) The length of the array at this point is 0; however, after the array is reinitialized with the ARRAY( ) function on line 30, it has a length of 10. Then, after each of the elements in *aNewArray[ ]* is filled with the numeric value of 1, the first subscript is displayed. The hard brackets look like the characters that are used on line 35 to delineate the character string "This is a test." Hard brackets can be used both as character string delimiters and as array subscript indicators.

In addition, this example uses both the alias of the work area and the FIELD statement. Both of these aliases on line 39 use the -> operator. The first expression tells Clipper to get the field in the designated work area (the name of the work area appears to the left of the operator). In the third expression on line 39, the FIELD expression refers to the contents of the specified field in the current work area.

## STRINGS AND DATES

Some of the operators work with dates and strings. For example, many times we take it for granted that the expressions X – Y, X + Y, and X = Y are numeric; but for string operations, some of these basic operations take on new meaning.

Clipper 5.2 has a rule about strings being compared to other strings: Assuming that EXACT is OFF, Clipper will compare the string on the right of the comparison to the string on the left until it runs out of character positions. If the two strings are equal at that point, even though the string on the left might be longer, Clipper would consider the strings to be equivalent. This means that the following expression would yield a logical true (.T.) value:

```
x = ""
y = "Hello World"
? y = x
```

Again, Clipper evaluates the expression by doing a character-by-character comparison of the right side with the left side until no characters remain on the right side; because of this, the NULL byte value for the variable X equals Y. If the order of this comparison were reversed (? y = x ), this would no longer be true, and the comparison would yield a logical false. However, to force Clipper to evaluate both sides of the equation, we use a new operator:

```
x = ""
y = "Hello World"
? x == y
```

This tells Clipper to evaluate the string both left-to-right and right-to-left. In essence, the == operator does the following:

```
? ( (x = y) .AND. (y = x) )
```

The double equal comparison operator works on all data types. Below is a program that demonstrates some of these operations, with a special emphasis on string data types.

```
 1 : * Name:      Oper2.prg
 2 :
 3 : function Main()
 4 :
 5 :   local cString := "Now for a test"
 6 :   local cTemp1  := "This is the first one        "
 7 :   local cTemp2  := ", while this is the second   "
 8 :   local dDate   := date()
 9 :
10 :   cls
11 :
12 :   @ 0,0 say "Working with '$', '=', '()', '!', '!=', and '==' "
13 :
14 :   @ 2,0 say "cString is equal to:  " + cString
15 :
16 :   @ 4,0 say [       "a" $ cString : ] + ;
17 :        if( ("a" $ cString), "True", "False" )
18 :   @ 5,0 say [       "A" $ cString : ] + ;
19 :        if( ("A" $ cString), "True", "False" )
20 :   @ 6,0 say [ "A" $ UPPER(cString) : ] + ;
21 :        if( ("A" $ UPPER(cString) ), "True", "False" )
22 :   @ 7,0 say [     !("A" $ cString) : ] + ;
23 :        if( !("A" $ cString), "True", "False" )
24 :   @ 8,0 say [       ("" = cString) : ] + ;
25 :        if( ("" = cString), "True", "False" )
26 :   @ 9,0 say [      ("" == cString) : ] + ;
27 :        if( ("" == cString), "True", "False" )
28 :   @ 10,0 say [    !("" == cString) : ] + ;
29 :        if( !("" == cString), "True", "False" )
30 :   @ 11,0 say [        (cString != "") : ] + ;
31 :        if( (cString != ""), "True", "False" )
32 :   @ 12,0 say [         (cString = "") : ] + ;
33 :        if( (cString = ""), "True", "False" )
34 :   @ 13,0 say [        (cString == "") : ] + ;
35 :        if( (cString == ""), "True", "False" )
36 :   @ 14,0 say [        (cString <> "") : ] + ;
37 :        if( (cString <> ""), "True", "False" )
38 :   @ 15,0 say [         (cString # "") : ] + ;
39 :        if( (cString # ""), "True", "False" )
40 :
```

```
41 :     @ 24,00 say "Press any key for next screen.."
42 :     inkey(0)
43 :
44 :     cls
45 :
46 :     ? cTemp1, cTemp2
47 :     ? len(cTemp1), len(cTemp2)
48 :     ? cTemp1 + cTemp2
49 :     ? len( cTemp1 + cTemp2 )
50 :     ? cTemp1 - cTemp2
51 :     ? len( cTemp1 - cTemp2 )
52 :
53 :     @ 24,00 say "Press any key for next screen.."
54 :     inkey(0)
55 :
56 :     cls
57 :     ? "    Today is " + DTOC(dDate)
58 :     ? " Tomorrow is " + DTOC(dDate + 1)
59 :     ? "Yesterday was " + DTOC(dDate - 1)
60 :     ?
61 :     wait
62 :
63 :     return( NIL )
64 :
65 : // End of File: Oper2.prg
```

In lines 16 through 39, a series of string comparisons are made using either the substring operator, the equal operator, the exact equal operator, or the not equal operator. The key thing to remember in these lines is how string comparisons are made. For example, the only difference between lines 25 and 33 is on which side of the equal sign operator the null byte is located. Whenever the shorter string is on the right side of the equal sign, there is a greater chance of having a match. In line 33, the variable *cString* is being compared to a NULL byte; this yields a logical TRUE. If we reverse the order, as on line 25, the expression now yields a logical FALSE. Carrying this further, the following expressions all yield logical TRUE values.

```
? "AMERICA" = "A"
? "AMERICA" = "AM"
? "AMERICA" = "AME"
```

On the other hand, the following do *not* give us logical TRUE values:

```
? "A" = "AMERICA"
? " " = "AMERICA"
? "AMERICA" = "A "
? "AM" = "AMERICA"
```

Order is important. If you wish to check the length of the string on both sides of the operator, use the double-equal (==) operator. All of the single-equal expressions used above would yield a logical FALSE if the double-equal operator were used instead.

The minus operator is demonstrated on the string in line 50. String concatenation occurs in every program; however, there are times when string concatenation will leave blank spaces between the concatenated strings (on lines 6 and 7, for example). In line 50, using the minus operator to join the two strings tells Clipper to move the blank spaces at the end of the first string (in this case the variable *cTemp1*) to the back end of the entire expression. This in turn moves the value of *cTemp2* up against the last noncharacter value in *cTemp1*. The length of the two strings remains the same as if they were simply joined with the + operator, as lines 49 and 51 show.

## MATHEMATICS

Perhaps one of the greatest enhancements to the language is its addition of in-line variable operations. These include operators common to other languages, as in-line add and assign, in-line subtract and assign, pre-increment, and post-decrement. The following example shows four of the more common in-line assignment operators: add, subtract, divide, and multiply. These examples may also be applied to the in-line assignment operators for exponentiation and modulus.

```
 1 : * File:       Oper3.prg
 2 :
 3 : #include "PTVerbs.ch"
 4 :
 5 : function Main()
 6 :
 7 :    local dDate := date()
 8 :    local nNumber1
 9 :    local nNumber2
10 :    local nNumber3
11 :    local nNumber4
12 :    local cString1
13 :    local cString2
14 :    local cString3
15 :
16 :    cString1 := cString3 := "This is the first one          "
17 :    cString2 := ", while this is the second     "
18 :    nNumber1 := nNumber2 := nNumber3 := nNumber4 := 1
19 :
20 :    scroll()
21 :
22 :    @  0, 0 SAY "Working with the += operator "
23 :    ? "   nNumber1 += nNumber3  : ", ( nNumber1 += nNumber3 )
24 :    ? "nNumber1 += nNumber2++ : ", ( nNumber1 += nNumber2++ )
25 :    ? "               nNumber4 : ", nNumber4
26 :    ? "nNumber1 += --nNumber4 : ", ( nNumber1 += --nNumber4 )
27 :    ? "               nNumber4 : ", nNumber4
28 :    ? "nNumber1 += nNumber4-- : ", ( nNumber1 += nNumber4-- )
29 :    ? "             ++nNumber4 : ", ++nNumber4
30 :    ? "               nNumber3 : ", nNumber3
31 :    ? "               nNumber2 : ", nNumber2
```

```
32 :      ? "             nNumber1 : ", nNumber1
33 :      @ 24,00 SAY "Press any key..."
34 :      inkey(0)
35 :      scroll()
36 :
37 :      nNumber1 := nNumber2 := nNumber3 := nNumber4 := 1
38 :      @ 0, 0 SAY "Working with the -= operator "
39 :      ? "  nNumber1 -= nNumber3 : " , ( nNumber1 -= nNumber3 )
40 :      ? "nNumber1 -= nNumber2++ : " , ( nNumber1 -= nNumber2++ )
41 :      ? "              nNumber4 : " , ( nNumber4 )
42 :      ? "nNumber1 -= --nNumber4 : " , ( nNumber1 -= --nNumber4 )
43 :      ? "              nNumber4 : " , ( nNumber4 )
44 :      ? "nNumber1 -= nNumber4-- : " , ( nNumber1 -= nNumber4-- )
45 :      ? "            ++nNumber4 : " , ( ++nNumber4 )
46 :      ? "              nNumber3 : " , ( nNumber3 )
47 :      ? "              nNumber2 : " , ( nNumber2 )
48 :      ? "              nNumber1 : " , ( nNumber1 )
49 :      @ 24,00 SAY "Press any key..."
50 :      inkey(0)
51 :      scroll()
52 :
53 :      nNumber1 := nNumber2 := nNumber3 := nNumber4 := 2
54 :      @ 0, 0 SAY "Working with the *= operator "
55 :      ? "  nNumber1 *= nNumber3 : " , ( nNumber1 *= nNumber3 )
56 :      ? "nNumber1 *= nNumber2++ : " , ( nNumber1 *= nNumber2++ )
57 :      ? "              nNumber4 : " , ( nNumber4 )
58 :      ? "nNumber1 *= --nNumber4 : " , ( nNumber1 *= --nNumber4 )
59 :      ? "              nNumber4 : " , ( nNumber4 )
60 :      ? "nNumber1 *= nNumber4-- : " , ( nNumber1 *= nNumber4-- )
61 :      ? "            ++nNumber4 : " , ( ++nNumber4 )
62 :      ? "              nNumber3 : " , ( nNumber3 )
63 :      ? "              nNumber2 : " , ( nNumber2 )
64 :      ? "              nNumber1 : " , ( nNumber1 )
65 :      @ 24,00 SAY "Press any key..."
66 :      inkey(0)
67 :      scroll()
68 :
69 :      nNumber1 := nNumber2 := nNumber3 := nNumber4 := 2
70 :      @ 0, 0 SAY "Working with the /= operator "
71 :      ? "  nNumber1 /= nNumber3 : " , ( nNumber1 /= nNumber3 )
72 :      ? "nNumber1 /= nNumber2++ : " , ( nNumber1 /= nNumber2++ )
73 :      ? "              nNumber4 : " , ( nNumber4 )
74 :      ? "nNumber1 /= --nNumber4 : " , ( nNumber1 /= --nNumber4 )
75 :      ? "              nNumber4 : " , ( nNumber4 )
76 :      ? "nNumber1 /= nNumber4-- : " , ( nNumber1 /= nNumber4-- )
77 :      ? "            ++nNumber4 : " , ( ++nNumber4 )
78 :      ? "              nNumber3 : " , ( nNumber3 )
79 :      ? "              nNumber2 : " , ( nNumber2 )
80 :      ? "              nNumber1 : " , ( nNumber1 )
81 :      @ 24,00 SAY "Press any key..."
82 :      inkey(0)
83 :      scroll()
84 :
```

```
 85 :    @ 0,0 SAY "Now, let's work some strings...."
 86 :    ? cString1
 87 :    ? cString2
 88 :    ? len(cString1)
 89 :    ? len(cString2)
 90 :    ? cString1 += cString2
 91 :    ? len( cString1 )
 92 :    ? (cString1 := cString3) - cString2
 93 :    ? len( cString1 )
 94 :    ? cString1
 95 :    ? len( cString1 )
 96 :    ? cString2
 97 :    ? len( cString2 )
 98 :    ? cString3
 99 :    ? len( cString3 )
100 :
101 :    @ 24,00 SAY "Press any key..."
102 :    inkey(0)
103 :    scroll()
104 :
105 :    @ 0,0 SAY "Finally, back to dates...."
106 :
107 :    ? "    Today is ", dtoc(dDate++)
108 :    ? " Tomorrow is ", dtoc(dDate--)
109 :    ? "Yesterday is ", dtoc(--dDate)
110 :    ?
111 :    inkey(0)
112 :
113 :    return( NIL )
114 :
115 : // End of File: Oper3.prg
```

As you can see, the in-line assignment operators are not used only for numeric values. On lines 86 through 99, some in-line operations are performed on the strings that were also used in the previous programming example. And finally, the pre- and post-increment/decrement operators may work with dates as well as with numeric expressions.

Serious problems can result if you do not fully understand how the pre- and post-increment or decrement operators work. In many cases, we can make the wrong assumptions and end up with the wrong values. In addition, many in-line assignments can be made within other in-line assignments. With some of these new in-line operators, programming can be reduced to a few simple instructions. However, especially with the pre- and post-increment and decrement operators, not only the location of the variables but the position of the operators is important. Some of the following examples will point out how a simple positional error can develop wrong answers:

```
1 : * File:      Oper4.prg
2 :
3 : function Main()
4 :
5 :    local nPointer := 0
6 :    local aArray   := array(10)
```

```
 7 :    local nCounter
 8 :    local nNum1, nNum2, nNum3, nNum4, nNum5, nNum6
 9 :
10 :    private cExt     // because this is macro-expanded
11 :
12 :    cls
13 :
14 :    for nCounter := 1 to len( aArray )
15 :       aArray[nCounter] := nPointer++
16 :    next
17 :
18 :    ? "With a POST INCREMENT operation"
19 :    ?
20 :    ? "The length of the array is ", len( aArray )
21 :    ?
22 :
23 :    for nCounter := 1 to len( aArray )
24 :       cExt := transform( nCounter, "99" )
25 :       ? "The value of subscript &cExt. is: ", aArray[nCounter]
26 :    next
27 :
28 :    ?
29 :    ? "Press any key for next array..."
30 :    inkey(0)
31 :
32 :    cls
33 :    nPointer := 0
34 :    aArray   := array(10)
35 :
36 :    for nCounter := 1 to len( aArray )
37 :       aArray[nCounter] := ++nPointer
38 :    next
39 :
40 :    ? "With a PRE INCREMENT operation"
41 :    ?
42 :    ? "The length of the array is ", len( aArray )
43 :    ?
44 :    for nCounter := 1 to len( aArray )
45 :       cExt := transform(nCounter, "99")
46 :       ? "The value of subscript &cExt. is: ", aArray[nCounter]
47 :    next
48 :
49 :    ?
50 :    ? "Press any key for more in-line assignments..."
51 :    inkey(0)
52 :
53 :    cls
54 :    ? "Here are 6 values...."
55 :    nNum1 := nNum2 := nNum3 := nNum4 := nNum5 := nNum6 := 2
56 :    ?
57 :    ? nNum1, nNum2, nNum3, nNum4, nNum5, nNum6
58 :    ?
59 :    ? "And now the in-line equation"
60 :    ?
```

```
61 :    ? "nNum1 %= (nNum2 -= (nNum3 += (nNum4 /= (nNum5 *= nNum6)))) = ", ;
62 :      nNum1 %= (nNum2 -= (nNum3 += (nNum4 /= (nNum5 *= nNum6))))
63 :    ?
64 :    ? "And now the 6 values again...."
65 :    ?
66 :
67 :    ? nNum1, nNum2, nNum3, nNum4, nNum5, nNum6
68 :
69 :    return( NIL )
70 :
71 : // End of File: Oper4.prg
```

In this example, the array initialized on line 6 will be processed through the FOR...NEXT statements on lines 14 through 16, giving the array elements in *aArray[ ]* the values 0 through 9. When the array is reinitialized on line 34 and assigned values by the FOR...NEXT loop on lines 36 to 38, however, its elements now have the values 1 through 10. The only difference between the two is the position of the increment operator. The value of the variable *nPointer*, which starts off with a value of 0 on line 5, is assigned to the subscript before the incrementation occurs on line 15. This means that the values of *nPointer*, and therefore the values assigned to the array elements, range from 0 to 9. However, on line 37 the increment operator is in front of the variable *nPointer*. This is known as a pre-increment operator. The value of *nPointer* will be incremented before its value is assigned to the array's subscript position. Therefore the values of *nPointer* will now range from 0 to 10, and the values assigned to the array elements will range from 1 to 10. This simple difference can affect not only array positions, but values of variables as well. Confusing the pre-increment or pre-decrement operator with the post-increment or post-decrement operator may have staggering ripple effects in your applications.

In-line assignments can also be made within in-line assignments. Each value will retain the new in-line value assigned. It may be advantageous to start with simple in-line assignments, gradually building to a complex expression, as on lines 61 and 62.

## Rules of Precedence

Another potential pitfall is the order of operations. Depending on the types of in-line assignments, mathematical operations, and/or logical expressions, values may be different because of the order in which Clipper evaluates these types of operations. Without carefully considering Clipper's rules of precedence, unexpected results may occur.

Clipper considers all equations in terms of levels. A level is that part of an equation that is to be considered on its own. For example, the following equation has two levels:

```
x := (1 * 5) + (5 / 2)
```

The first level is the two halves of the equation segregated by the parentheses. The second level is the equation that evaluates the results of the preceding level. In some cases, many of our coding styles make use of only one level:

```
x := 1 + 3 - 4 * 6 / 2 ^3
```

When there are multiple operations on the same level, the order of precedence for mathematical operations is the following:

| | |
|---|---|
| First: | Any unary positive or negative |
| Second: | Any exponentiation |
| Third: | Any multiplication, division, or modulus |
| Fourth: | Any addition or subtraction |

Where operators at the same level have the same precedence, mathematical operations are performed from left to right.

As with mathematical operations, any logical operation follows the same basic rules of precedence. When two or more logical expressions appear on the same level, the order of precedence will be

| | |
|---|---|
| First: | Any .NOT. (unary negate) |
| Second: | Any .AND. (logical and) |
| Third: | Any .OR. (logical or) |

Again, where operators at the same level have the same order of precedence, operations are performed from left to right.

To get a better feel for this, here are a few examples of common situations in which the order of precedence might arise:

```
 1 : * File:     Oper5.prg
 2 :
 3 : function Main()
 4 :
 5 :    local nNum1 := 1
 6 :    local nNum2 := 2
 7 :    local nNum3 := 3
 8 :    local nNum4 := 5
 9 :    local nNum5, nNum6, nNum7, nNum8
10 :
11 :    nNum5 := nNum6 := nNum7 := nNum8 := 4
12 :
13 :    ? nNum1 + nNum2 + nNum3 - nNum4 / nNum5 * nNum6 + nNum7 ** nNum8
14 :    ? nNum1 + nNum2 + (nNum3 - nNum4) / (nNum5 * nNum6 + nNum7) ;
15 :             ** nNum8
16 :    ? (nNum1 + (nNum2 + (nNum3 - nNum4))) / (nNum5 * ;
17 :             ((nNum6 + nNum7) ** nNum8))
18 :    ? (nNum1 + nNum2) + (nNum3 - nNum4) / (nNum5 * nNum6) + nNum7 ;
19 :             ** nNum8
20 :
21 :    ? nNum1 + ((nNum2 + nNum3 - (nNum4 / nNum5)) * nNum6) + ;
22 :             (nNum7 ** nNum8)
23 :    ? nNum1 + (nNum2 + (nNum3 - nNum4)) / (nNum5 * ((nNum6 + nNum7)) ;
24 :             ** nNum8)
25 :    ? nNum1 + nNum2 + nNum3 - nNum4 / (nNum5 * nNum6) + (nNum7 ;
26 :             ** nNum8)
```

```
27 :      return( NIL )
28 :
29 : // End of File: Oper5.prg
```

In this example, which expression will give us a value of 1? Each pair of parentheses sets a new level of precedence that needs to be evaluated before all others. The deeper the parentheses are embedded, the greater the potential for different values. The expression that evaluates to a 1 is the one on lines 23 and 24. Using the expression on line 13 as an example, and referring to the order in which Clipper *naturally* evaluates a complex expression, we start with the exponential, move to the multiplication/division portion, and end with the simple addition/subtraction. Breaking it down, we start by taking *nNum7* ** *nNum8* and evaluating it: This is 4 ** 4, which is 256. Now the line should look like this:

```
nNum1 + nNum2 + nNum3 - nNum4 / nNum5 * nNum6 + 256
```

Moving to the next level, let us evaluate *nNum4 / nNum5 * nNum6* which is 5 / 4 * 4. This equates to 5. Now our equation looks like this:

```
nNum1 + nNum2 + nNum3 - 5 + 256  = 1 + 2 + 3 - 5 + 256
                                 = 6 - 5 + 256
                                 = 1 + 256
                                 = 257
```

Moving to the next expression on line 14 we have the following:

```
1 + 2 + (3 - 5) / (4 * 4 + 4) ** 4
```

Within this expression, there are two subexpressions at the lowest level that must be evaluated before the rest of the expression can be solved. Within the second subexpression, the order of precedence still applies, which means that 4 * 4 will be evaluated before the 4 is added. Once evaluated, the expression will look like this:

```
1 + 2 + ( -2 ) / (20) ** 4
```

Having evaluated those expressions on the lowest level, we must now evaluate the exponentiation. Now our expression looks like this:

```
1 + 2 + ( -2 ) / 160000 = 1 + 2 =.0000125
                        = 3 - .0000125
                        = 2.9999875
```

Since decimals are not set, the default decimal position will be 2, which means the number displayed will be 3.00.

Now, we will take the third expression, on lines 16 and 17. At first it will look like this:

```
(1 + (2 + (3 - 5))) / (4 * ((4 + 4) ** 4 ))
```

Basically, the point here is that both the denominator and numerator are on the same level, which means that the expressions within them must be expanded and evaluated before the simple division can occur. Breaking this down step by step, we will have the following:

```
(1 + (2 + (-2))) / (4 * (8) ** 4 ) = (1 + 0) / (4 * 4096)
                                   = 1 / 16384
                                   = 0.00
```

Our fourth expression, on lines 18 and 19, looks like this:

```
(1 + 2) + (3 - 5) / (4 * 4) + 4 ** 4 = (3) + (-2) / (16) + 4 ** 4
```

We have to evaluate all of the expressions on the same level in order of operation. This means we take the 4 ** 4 first, followed by the -2 / 16 in order to complete this level. Continuing, we will have the following:

```
(1 + 2) + (3 - 5) / (4 * 4) + 4 ** 4 = (3) + (-2) / (16) + 256
                                     = (3) + (-.12) + 256
                                     = 2.88 + 256
                                     = 258.88
```

Moving on to the fifth expression, on lines 21 and 22, we start with the following:

```
nNum1 + ((nNum2 + nNum3 - (nNum4 / nNum5)) * nNum6) + (nNum7 ** nNum8)
```

which is translated to

```
1 + ((2 + 3 - (5 / 4)) * 4) + (4 ** 4)
```

Looking at this we have

```
1 + ((2 + 3 - (1.25)) * 4) + (4 ** 4) = 1 + ((5 - 1.25) * 4) + (256)
                                      = 1 + ((3.75) * 4) + (256)
                                      = 1 + (15) + (256)
                                      = 1 + 271
                                      = 272.00
```

Our sixth expression is the only expression that evaluates to a numeric 1.00. To get it, let's expand the original expression

```
nNum1 + (nNum2 + (nNum3 - nNum4)) / (nNum5 * ((nNum6 + nNum7)) ** nNum8)
```

to the following:

```
1 + (2 + (3 - 5)) / (4 * ((4 + 4)) ** 4)
```

Stepping through this, taking each level and evaluating it within the parentheses, then matching operators on the same level and working our way downward, we get the following:

```
1+(2+(3-5)) / (4*((4+4)) ** 4) = 1 + (2 + (-2)) / (4 * ((8)) ** 4)
                               = 1 + (0) / (4 * (4096))
                               = 1 + (0) / (16384)
                               = 1 + 0
                               = 1
```

And finally, taking the last expression, we would have the following breakdown:

```
nNum1+nNum2+nNum3-nNum4 / (nNum5 * nNum6) + (nNum7 ** nNum8)
                        = 1 + 2 + 3 - 5 / (4 * 4) + (4 ** 4)
                        = 1 + 2 + 3 - 5 / 16 + 256
                        = 1 + 2 + 3 - .31 + 256
                        = 6 - .31 + 256
                        = 5.69 + 256
                        = 261.69
```

*Operators and Conditions* 163

However, the rules of precedence extend to the evaluation of all expressions and not just those containing the traditional mathematical operators. Clipper's overall order of precedence follows these rules:

| | |
|---|---|
| First: | Pre-increment/decrement |
| Second: | String operations |
| Third: | Date operations |
| Fourth: | Mathematical operations |
| Fifth: | Relational operations |
| Sixth: | Logical operations |
| Seventh: | Assignment operations |
| Eighth: | Post-increment/decrement |

## Tips on Expressions and Operators

### CONCISE BOOLEAN EXPRESSIONS

Sometimes with logical operators, we have a tendency to overuse the .OR., .AND., and .NOT. operators to get a particular condition. For example, how often have you seen code like the following?

```
 1 : * File:      Oper8.prg
 2 :
 3 : function Main()
 4 :
 5 :    local nNum1 := 0
 6 :    local nNum2 := 1
 7 :    local nNum3 := 2
 8 :
 9 :    ? (nNum1 = 0 .and. nNum2 = 0 .and. nNum3 = 0) .or. ;
10 :      (nNum1 = 0 .and. nNum2 != 0 .and. nNum3 = 0) .or. ;
11 :      (nNum1 = 0 .and. nNum2 = 0 .and. nNum3 != 0) .or. ;
12 :      (nNum1 = 0 .and. nNum2 != 0 .and. nNum3 != 0)
13 :
14 :    ? (nNum1 = 0)
15 :
16 :    return( NIL )
17 :
18 : // End of File: Oper8.prg
```

In this example, picture the expression on lines 9 to 12 used instead in a SET FILTER TO expression. Using Boolean logic, this SET FILTER TO command can be reduced to a single simple expression:

```
SET FILTER TO (a = 0)
```

or

```
SET FILTER TO EMPTY( a )
```

You can use a Venn diagram to graphically show the distinct areas of each expression, or you may use Boolean algebra in Clipper to reduce large indexing and filter expressions into simple and compact ones. To accomplish this, we have to begin with some key definitions. These definitions, or postulates, will be given without proof.

In the following example, A*A will mean A .AND. A, A+A will mean A .OR. A; != or .NOT. will be equated with a set of parentheses ( ) and will have the normal distributive connotation. 0 is the null set and U is the universe.

```
Y*Y=Y and Y+Y=Y
Y*Z=Z*Y and Y+Z=Z+Y
Y*(Z*W)=(Y*Z)*W and Y+(Z+W)=(Y+Z)+W
Y*(Z+W)=(Y*Z)+(Y*W)
0*W=0 and U*Y=U
0+Y=Y and U+Y=U
Y*!Y=0 and Y+!Y=U
!(Y*Z)=!Y+!Z and !(Y+Z)=!Y*!Z
!(!Y)=Y
```

Now, referring to the expression in the previous programming example, we can substitute the variable *a* for A=0 and !A for A!=0. The logical expression is then:

```
A*B*C+A*!B*C+A*B*!C+A*!B*!C => (factor out the variable A)
A*[ B*C+!B*C+B*!C+!B*!C ]
A*[ (B+!B)*C+(B+!B)*!C ]
A*[ U*C+U*!C ]
A*[ C+!C ]
A*[ U ]
A
```

Remember, knowing and applying simple Boolean logic will save on memory allocation and increase execution speed.

## ALIASED MEMORY VARIABLES OR ALIASED FIELDS?

In any database development environment, it is important to be able to differentiate database fields from memory variables. In the Xbase family of languages, developing a means of distinguishing the two is generally left to the programmer; a common convention with which most of us are probably familiar, for example, is to precede the root name of memory variables with a prefix (like m or m_) to differentiate them from database field names.

Clipper, on the other hand, requires that the programmer apply a uniform system for differentiating field names from memory variable names. Memory variables can be indicated by using the M-> or MEMVAR-> statements; database fields can be indicated by using <alias>-> or FIELD->). But if we cannot apply this method of aliasing both memory variables and database fields consistently, it should be abandoned. And in fact this rule breaks down because this method of aliasing memory variables cannot handle passing a memory variable by reference (using the @ symbol). Therefore, memory variables should be used without any alias pointer; fields, which cannot be passed by reference to a subroutine, should explicitly contain their alias pointer or the FIELD-> pointer. In addition, to resolve any confusion on Clipper's part, all program modules should be compiled with the /V compiler switch. This switch tells the compiler to assume that any ambiguous references are variables.

## MULTIPLE COMMANDS FOR THE PREPROCESSOR AND LINE CONTINUATIONS

For program files and the preprocessor, the semicolon is used to continue a Clipper command onto the next line. Often, for the sake of clarity, we limit the width of a command line. For example, some expressions, especially those nested within an IF command that is, in turn, within a DO CASE, which is within a WHILE command, start at the 30th column. By the time they have concluded, the line length could easily exceed 130 columns. To make the code for the application more readable, semicolons are used to break up the line to continue onto the next one.

```
? VAL(SUBSTR(newstring, 1, 10)
? RESTSCREEN(0,0,MAXROW(),MAXCOL(), Dulling( ;
  SAVESCREEN(0,0,MAXROW(),MAXCOL())))
? SET FILTER TO Clients->account = "2" .AND. ;
                Clients->due  1.00
* or *
? Clients->due + Clients->amount + ;
  VAL(Clients->account)
```

Insert the semicolon either after the comma in a parameter list, after the opening call to a nested function, or after the operator in a complex expression. Never use the semicolon between the alias of a work area and the pointing operator (->), before a comma separator, or before an expression operator.

In Clipper 5.2, semicolons can also be used to put multiple commands on a single line. For example,

```
? "Press any key to move on" ; INKEY(0)
```

The INKEY(0) operation will be preprocessed onto the next line. Sometimes, for clarity, using the semicolon operator can be helpful when concatenating two operations onto the same line. In the example above, the INKEY(0) pertains only to the ? (QOUT( )) operation. Another example of semicolons to clarify program code is

```
DO CASE
CASE option = 1 ; Addrec()
CASE option = 2 ; Editrec()
CASE option = 3 ; Deleterec()
CASE option = 4 ; Printrec()
OTHERWISE       ; EXIT
ENDCASE
```

Again, this is a matter of style, but the point is clear: The code visually tells the story of the operations and coding branches.

Unlike the semicolon operator, the double-semicolon operator can only be used on lines that are to be read by the preprocessor and that contain a #command, #xcommand, #xtranslate, or #translate directive. This tells Clipper that the command or translated statement consists of more than one operation. For example, looking at the definition of the CLEAR ALL command in STD.CH, the standard Clipper header file, we see the following:

```
#command CLEAR ALL => ;
    CLOSE DATABASES;
    ;CLOSE FORMAT;
    ;CLEAR MEMORY;
    ;CLEAR GETS;
    ;SET ALTERNATE OFF;
    ;SET ALTERNATE TO
```

In essence, the first semicolon tells Clipper that the command is to continue; the second states this is an additional command line. Similarly, the SUM command is defined in STD.CH as follows:

```
#command SUM [ <x1> [, <xn>]  TO  <v1> [, <vn>] ]            ;
         [FOR <for>]                                         ;
         [WHILE <while>]                                     ;
         [NEXT <next>]                                       ;
         [RECORD <rec>]                                      ;
         [<rest:REST>]                                       ;
         [ALL]                                               ;
                                                             ;
      => <v1> := [ <vn> := ] 0                               ;
         ; DBEval(                                           ;
                 {|| <v1> := <v1> + <x1> [, <vn> := <vn> + <xn> ]}, ;
                 <{for}>, <{while}>, <next>, <rec>, <.rest.> ;
               )
```

Each single semicolon indicates that the preprocessor #command continues onto the next line. The double semicolon operator between the line that assigns 0 to a variable and the DBEVAL( ) function tells Clipper that the variable assignment is a separate operation from the call to DBEVAL( ).

## FIELDS AND IN-LINE ASSIGNMENTS

It is possible to assign values to a field with the in-line operators in the same fashion as for variables. To do this, be sure to use the /V switch to declare ambiguous references as memory variables. Then make sure that the fields being assigned values have either the name of the alias with the -> symbol or the FIELD-> statement.

```
1 : * File:      Oper6.prg
2 :
3 : function Main()
4 :
5 :    if file( "CLIENTS.DBF" )
6 :       use Clients new
7 :       Clients->current := Clients->due := 0   // Yes, this replaces!
8 :
```

```
 9 :        cls
10 :        ShowValues("Fields set to Zero...")
11 :
12 :        ? "CLIENTS POST-INCREMENT IS: ", Clients->current++
13 :
14 :        ShowValues("After the incrementing")
15 :
16 :        Clients->due += (++Clients->current * 2)
17 :
18 :        ShowValues("DUE is set with CURRENT being set")
19 :
20 :        Clients->current *= Clients->due / 3
21 :
22 :        ShowValues("CURRENT is set with DUE being set")
23 :    endif
24 :    wait
25 :    scroll()
26 :
27 :    return( NIL )
28 :
29 : ********************
30 :
31 : static function ShowValues( cSaying )
32 :
33 :    ?
34 :    ? cSaying
35 :    ?
36 :    ? "CURRENT IS", Clients->current
37 :    ? "DUE IS", Clients->due
38 :    ?
39 :
40 :    return( NIL )
41 :
42 : // End of File: Oper6.prg
```

In-line assignments are equivalent to the REPLACE <field> WITH <value> command statement. And as program OPER6.PRG shows, pre-incrementors/decrementors, post-incrementors/decrementors, and all in-line assignments work on fields in the same manner as they do on variables.

## WORKING WITH == AND !

Variables sometimes need to be compared from left to right as well as from right to left. To accomplish this directly in the code, use the double-equal operator, ==. However, when working with the == operator, its negation is

```
!( <exp1> == <exp2> )
```

not

```
<exp1> !== <exp2>
```

Make sure that the evaluation of the == is performed first and the results obtained. Then take those results and negate them with the ! operator.

## WORKING WITH ZEROS, %, AND /

Many languages will return a division by 0 error when you attempt to use a zero as the denominator in an expression that involves division. Clipper 5.2, however, does not. If the numerator is 0, Clipper 5.2 will return a 0 for division both with the division operator and the modulus operator. For example, both the following expressions return 0:

```
qout( 2 % 0 )
qout( 2 / 0 )
```

Note that, in Summer '87 and prior versions of Clipper, division by zero would produce a run-time error.

This handling of division by zero makes Clipper 5.2 more robust. On the other hand, it also means that mathematical operations can more easily yield inaccurate results if division by zero occurs and goes undetected. As always in the case of division by zero, the solution to this problem is to check for division by zero errors beforehand, rather than depending on Clipper to do it.

## USING THE MINUS OPERATOR ON STRINGS IN INDEXES

Using the minus sign to build an index may at first appear to solve many indexing problems; however, it will also cause additional problems with similar records. Concatenating two character fields by removing trailing spaces between the two fields and adding them to the end of the string concatenation, making the index key a consistent length, often has unintended consequences. Consider the following expression:

```
INDEX ON <expC1> - <expC2> TO <filename>
```

Now consider the following three records:

```
<expC1>       <expC2>

Smith         Emerson
Smithe        Bill
Smithelon     Alice
```

Normally, this is what the index should look like with the records in the proper order; however, if the index were built on the expression UPPER( <expC1> - <expC2> ), then the order would look like this:

```
UPPER( <expC1> - <expC2> )

SMITHEBILL
SMITHELONALICE
SMITHEMERSON
```

Obviously, this is not in the proper order. Using the minus operator to concatenate strings in an index expression may not be the best programming solution.

## EVALUATING EXPRESSIONS

We will cover this topic in depth in Chapter 9, "Macros and Expressions." In the meantime, a quick look is in order, since expressions can be assigned to memory variables by most of the operators listed above. Evaluating expressions is not only critical in understanding the values assigned to variables, but also in setting up the proper programming environment within an application.

```
 1 : * File:     Oper7.prg
 2 :
 3 : function Main()
 4 :
 5 :    local nNumber1 := 1
 6 :    local nNumber2 := ( One(), Two(), nNumber1++, nNumber1 := ;
 7 :                      (nNumber1 / 34) * 2 ) + 2
 8 :
 9 :    ? nNumber1, nNumber2
10 :
11 :    return( NIL )
12 :
13 : *******************
14 :
15 : static function One()
16 :
17 :    cls
18 :    ? procname()
19 :    wait
20 :
21 :    return( NIL )
22 :
23 : *******************
24 :
25 : static function Two
26 :
27 :    cls
28 :    ? "And now... ", procname(), procname(1)
29 :    wait
30 :
31 :    return( NIL )
32 :
33 : // End of File: Oper7.prg
```

Here, the value of the last operation within the expression will be assigned to the variable *nNumber2*, and the value of the variable *nNumber1* will be post-incremented as well.

# 5

# Data Types, Parameters, Statements, and UDFs

In the past, we were concerned only with character (or string), numeric, date, and logical data types. In the case of a database, an additional data type was added to the language: a memo field. This is a contiguous block of information stored in an ancillary file (known as a .DBT file), which has a beginning block pointer in the original database.

As the language grew, one more data type was added: the array.

Now, with Clipper 5.x, two more data types have been added: code blocks and NIL. A code block is nothing more than a pointer to compiled code. This pointer can be passed and treated as data that is used by subroutines, procedures, and functions. (Code blocks are discussed further in Chapter 15, "Code Blocks."). All variables (except for PUBLIC variables, which start off as a logical false (.F.) when initialized) are initialized to a NIL data type. In the past, procedures had a default return value of a logical false (.F.); now, they have a default return value of NIL. NIL values are also automatically passed to a function or procedure if the parameter is skipped:

```
? Myfunc(x, y,,,,z)
```

All of the parameters between y and z in the function Myfunc( ) will have a data type of NIL.

All of these data types can be tested by the TYPE( ) function. The return value from each of these is as follows:

| Code | Returns | Meaning |
| --- | --- | --- |
| TYPE("array") | "A" | Array data type |
| TYPE("block") | "B" | Code block data type |
| TYPE("string") | "C" | Character data type |
| TYPE("date") | "D" | Date data type |

*(continued)*

| Code | Returns | Meaning |
| --- | --- | --- |
| TYPE("logical") | "L" | Logical data type |
| TYPE("Clients->memo") | "M" | Memo field |
| TYPE("number") | "N" | Numeric data type |
| TYPE("object") | "O" | Object data type |
| TYPE("unknown") | "U" | NIL data type or undefined |

Two other values, UE and UI, may also be returned from the TYPE( ) function. They are discussed in Chapter 7, "CA-Clipper Function Reference," under TYPE( ). Additionally, in Clipper 5.2, the TYPE( ) function has a superset function, the VALTYPE( ) function. It is similar to the TYPE( ) function, except that it evaluates the expression passed to it rather than using macro expansion of the parameter, as does the TYPE( ) function. The values returned by the VALTYPE( ) function are as follows:

| Code | Returns | Meaning |
| --- | --- | --- |
| VALTYPE(aArray) | "A" | Array data type |
| VALTYPE(block) | "B" | Code block data type |
| VALTYPE(string) | "C" | Character data type |
| VALTYPE(date) | "D" | Date data type |
| VALTYPE(logical) | "L" | Logical data type |
| VALTYPE(Clients->memo) | "M" | Memo field |
| VALTYPE(number) | "N" | Numeric data type |
| VALTYPE(object) | "O" | Object data type |
| VALTYPE(unknown) | "U" | NIL data type or undefined |

## Variable Initialization and Storage Class

Each memory variable data type (with the exception of the memo field, which belongs to a database and follows all its rules) has a data storage class. The data type and data storage class are the two characteristics that define a memory variable. The data storage class is the signature byte for that variable: It tells Clipper what rules this memory variable must adhere to. In Clipper 5.2 there are four storage classes for memory variables—PUBLIC, PRIVATE, LOCAL, and STATIC; they are discussed below. Note that, although we have included PUBLIC, PRIVATE, LOCAL, and STATIC, as well as the related PARAMETERS statement in the command reference section of this book, technically they all are "statements" rather than commands. The main difference between these two is that a statement is a native part of the Clipper language, while a command is defined in STD.CH and is translated by the preprocessor into Clipper's native command set.

## PUBLIC

```
PUBLIC <memvar> [, <memvar>...]
```

The PUBLIC statement declares the memory variables specified as *memvar* within an application. These variables are initialized to a logical false (.F.) value until they are assigned specific values. These variables remain defined for the duration of the application and may be seen (as well as used, altered, manipulated, and evaluated) by any subroutine, procedure, or function. A PUBLIC memory variable may be released from the system by either the CLEAR ALL, CLEAR MEMORY, or RELEASE <memvar> command.

There is one PUBLIC variable—*clipper*—that has a default value of logical true (.T.), not logical false, when it is initialized. This gives Clipper applications the ability to run under any interpreted environment.

Here is an example program that demonstrates these various items:

```
 1 :   * File:        Public.prg
 2 :
 3 :   function Main()
 4 :
 5 :      public clipper, xVal1, xVal2, xVal3 := "Hello"
 6 :
 7 :      ? clipper
 8 :      ? xVal1
 9 :      ? xVal2
10 :      ? xVal3
11 :
12 :      wait "Press any key to adjust values"
13 :
14 :      AdjustValues()
15 :      wait "Now, press any key to see them"
16 :
17 :      ? clipper
18 :      ? xVal1
19 :      ? xVal2
20 :      ? xVal3
21 :
22 :      wait
23 :      clear memory
24 :
25 :      ? valtype( clipper )
26 :      ? valtype( xVal1 )
27 :      ? valtype( xVal2 )
28 :      ? valtype( xVal3 )
29 :
30 :      return( NIL )
31 :
32 :   *******************
```

```
33 :
34 : static procedure AdjustValues()
35 :
36 :    xVal1 := 39
37 :    xVal2 := "This is a test"
38 :    xVal3 := date()
39 :
40 : // End of File: Public.prg
```

While the four variables on line 5 are assigned a storage class, only one is also assigned a value. Two of the remaining variables are automatically assigned a logical false (.F.) value and will be seen on the screen on lines 8 and 9.

However, the special memory variable *clipper* by default is assigned a value of logical true (.T.). The reason for this stems from the history of Clipper as a "dBASE compiler." This memory variable could be used to segregate code that was unique to Clipper from code that could execute under a dBASE-compatible interpreter. This was the case because dBASE would initialize the public variable *clipper* to a logical false (.F.) value. An IF...ELSE...ENDIF construct could then be used to execute the relevant block of code, or an IF...ENDIF statement could be used to make sure that Clipper code was not executed in an interpreted environment. This is shown in the following pseudocode example:

```
IF clipper
      < execute Clipper code >
ELSE
      < execute dBASE code >
ENDIF

IF clipper
      < execute Clipper code >
ENDIF
```

## PRIVATE

```
PRIVATE <memvar> [, <memvar>...]
```

There are three ways to initialize a private memory variable: with the PRIVATE statement, with the PARAMETERS statement, or through normal variable assignment. With either the PRIVATE or PARAMETERS statement, the variables declared are initially set to a NIL data type.

Note that the DECLARE statement also provides a fourth way to initialize a PRIVATE memory variable. However, because DECLARE is a "compatibility command" that will not necessarily be supported in future versions of CA-Clipper, it should be avoided in favor of the PRIVATE statement.

Once any variable with the PRIVATE data storage class has been declared, it remains for the duration of the program flow, until the application returns to the procedure or function above the subroutine making the original variable declaration. In essence, a PRIVATE memory variable initialized at the very top of an application will act like a PUBLIC memory variable. A PRIVATE memory variable can be viewed by a subroutine and modified accordingly. However, a memory variable initialized as PRIVATE within a function or a procedure that has the same name as another previously declared memory variable will hide and protect the other memory variable from any assignment and manipulation within that procedure or function and also within subsequent subroutines. Consider the following coding example:

```
 1 : * Name:      Private.prg     // This has to be compiled w/o the /E
 2 :
 3 : function Main()
 4 :
 5 :    private xData1 := 1
 6 :
 7 :    cls
 8 :
 9 :    xData2 := "This is it"
10 :    xData3 := date()
11 :    ? "The values are set first to...."
12 :    ?
13 :    ? xData1, xData2, xData3
14 :
15 :    DoFunc( xData3 )
16 :
17 :    ?
18 :    ? "And now they are..."
19 :    ?
20 :    ? xData1, xData2, xData3
21 :
22 : ****************
23 :
24 : static function DoFunc
25 :
26 :    parameters xNewData
27 :
28 :    private xData2 := 0
29 :
30 :    xNewData := .t.
31 :
32 :    ?
33 :    ? "The value of the variables inside the function are as follows:"
34 :    ?
35 :    ? ++xData1, xData2, xNewData
36 :    ?
37 :    wait
38 :
39 :    return( NIL )
40 :
41 : // End of File: Private.prg
```

In this example, the variables *xData1*, *xData2*, and *xData3* are initialized and have a data storage class of PRIVATE. Notice that the variables *xData2* and *xData3* are made private by simply assigning them values. The program shows their values, and then passes the value of *xData3* to the routine DoFunc( ). In this routine, on lines 24 and following, the parameter *xNewData* assumes the value of a logical true (.T.), and a new PRIVATE variable, *xData2*, is initialized. Then the variables *xNewData*, *xData2*, and *xData1*, having been increased by one, are displayed on line 35. It would be possible to branch off from this routine at this point and manipulate these three variables directly. Their current values will remain in effect as long as the application does not return to the original point in the program that called the DoFunc( ) subroutine. Finally, once the RETURN on line 39 is issued, the variable *xNewData* and the second variable *xData1* are discarded and the original value of *xData2* is restored. The value of *xData1* reflects the increase because that variable was visible within the subroutine.

## LOCAL

```
LOCAL <memvar> [, <memvar>...]
```

LOCAL memory variables are really what some C programmers envision as PRIVATE memory variables. There are several things to keep in mind with this data storage class.

First, these memory variables are visible only within the subroutine that initializes them, although they exist within the routine that creates them and within the subroutines that may in turn be invoked by it. Once the subroutine in which the LOCAL variable was declared finishes execution, the LOCAL variable is released.

Second, LOCAL memory variables do not generate a token within the symbol table; only PRIVATE and PUBLIC data variables do. This means that the main load module will not contain symbols for those memory variables, which in turn makes more free pool memory available. However, be careful to not succumb to the theory that memory savings can be obtained by changing any PRIVATE reference to a LOCAL reference. If you do, applications may not work properly under Clipper 5.2 as they did under earlier versions of the compiler. For example, if there is no symbol in the symbol table for a variable, then the SAVE command will not be able to find it when a variable skeleton is provided. As a result, variables that are expected to be saved and restored from a file will not be.

Third, Clipper evaluates LOCAL and STATIC variables faster than PUBLIC and PRIVATE variables. This is because LOCAL and STATIC variables are defined on the current memory stack; the definition of a PUBLIC or PRIVATE variable is stored within the symbol table. This means that the latter symbols need to be evaluated and placed on the stack, which requires an additional processing step.

Fourth, there are two ways to initialize a LOCAL variable. The first is with the LOCAL command statement, like this:

```
LOCAL memvar
```

The second is to pass it as a local parameter to a procedure or function. A LOCAL parameter is one that is identified on the same command line as the FUNCTION or PROCEDURE declaration. For example,

```
FUNCTION Myfunc(memvar)
```

or

```
PROCEDURE Subroutine(memvar)
```

In each case, the variable *memvar* is a variable with a LOCAL data storage class.

And finally, a LOCAL (and STATIC) variable must be initialized *before* any command or function statement within the code. In other words, LOCAL variables may not be initialized in the midst of an operating routine; they must be initialized in the topmost section of the procedure or function. A coding extract like the following would produce a compiling error, "LOCAL declaration follows executable statement:"

```
Function Myfunc
    parameter nValue
    nValue++
    local nCounter := nValue++
    return( nCounter )
```

Here the LOCAL command statement came after post-incrementing the variable *nValue*. The following small program demonstrates the power of a LOCAL variable.

```
 1 : * Name:      Local.prg
 2 :
 3 : function Main()
 4 :
 5 :   cls
 6 :
 7 :   xData1 := 1
 8 :   ? "The value of XDAT1 is now PRIVATE and set..."
 9 :   ? xData1
10 :   ?
11 :   ? "And now a call to a subroutine..."
12 :   First(xData1)
13 :
14 :   ? xData1
15 :   ? type( "xValue" ) // The VALTYPE() function would yield an error
16 :
17 :   return( NIL )
18 :
19 : *******************
20 :
21 : static function First(xValue)
22 :
23 :   local xData1 := "Testing"
24 :
25 :   ? "Now, pass this and a LOCAL parameter to a secondary subroutine"
26 :   ? "just to be looked at..."
27 :   ?
28 :   ? xValue
29 :   ? xData1
30 :   ?
31 :   ? "Any key..."
32 :   inkey(0)
33 :   cls
34 :
35 :   SecondCall()
36 :   ?
```

```
37 :    ? "Back from the subroutine.  Any key.."
38 :    inkey(0)
39 :
40 :    return( NIL )
41 :
42 : *******************
43 :
44 : static function SecondCall()
45 :
46 :    ? "And now the values of the variables from the other routines are"
47 :    ? "as follows:"
48 :    ?
49 :    ? type("xData1")
50 :    ? type("xValue")   // The VALTYPE() function would yield an error
51 :    ?
52 :    ? "Press any key to return to secondary routine..."
53 :    inkey(0)
54 :
55 :    return( NIL )
56 :
57 : // End of File: Local.prg
```

To begin with, the variable *xData1* on line 7 defaults to a PRIVATE data storage class since no formal data storage class is given to the variable. This is then passed to the routine called First( ), which accepts it as a parameter named *xValue*. This is known as a "formal parameter," as opposed to a regular parameter, which is more common in older applications. This parameter is declared on the command line along with the name of the subroutine; therefore, it is a LOCAL parameter rather than a PRIVATE one. Remember, the PARAMETERS statement creates PRIVATE data variables.

On line 23, a new LOCAL variable *xData1* is defined and assigned a string value. This new LOCAL *xData1* variable will not conflict with the PRIVATE memory variable *xData1* initialized in the calling routine: LOCAL variables are only visible within the routine that declares them and hide all PRIVATE or PUBLIC variables with the same name. Also, the new LOCAL parameter named *xValue* is displayed on line 28 along with the new value of *xData1* on the following line.

A call to yet another subroutine named SecondCall( ) is made in which the data types of both LOCAL variables of First( ) are displayed using the TYPE( ) function (in lines 49 and 50). Since the variable *xData1* was originally declared PRIVATE in the main routine, only that variable is visible to the SecondCall( ) function. Therefore, the value from the TYPE( ) function on line 49 will be an "N" for numeric; the assigned value of *xData1* on line 7 was a numeric data type. However, the TYPE( ) of the variable named *xValue* is "U" or Undefined: LOCAL parameters and variables are not visible to subroutines. Eventually, the value of *xData1* as well as U for undefined—the data type of the variable *xValue*—is displayed after all of the subroutines have completed their operation (lines 14 and 15) .

The key here is that LOCAL variables and parameters do not step on PRIVATE or PUBLIC variables; LOCAL variables and parameters can only be seen (or are visible) by the routine in which they were initialized; LOCAL variables and parameters have a lifespan equal to the operation of the procedure or function in which they were initialized.

## STATIC

```
STATIC <memvar> [, <memvar>...]
```

The STATIC variable is identical to the LOCAL storage class with one exception. A STATIC variable is retained within the creating procedure or function, even after program flow has left it. This is particularly useful for independent "black-box" functions, which must contain their own set of unique variables and must maintain those values from iteration to iteration. A good example of this would be a report-writing routine: Each record of a database is fed to this routine, and the routine maintains a separate line-counter variable. This variable is updated and maintained as a STATIC variable no matter how many times program flow returns back to a higher-level procedure. Here is an example not only of a STATIC variable, but of the difference between it and a LOCAL memory variable.

```
 1 : * File:      Static.prg
 2 :
 3 : function Main()
 4 :
 5 :    use Clients new
 6 :    cls
 7 :
 8 :    ?? padc( "Press any key for next line...", maxcol() )
 9 :    ?  "Account........Status......."
10 :    ?? "LOCAL:internal    STATIC:linecount"
11 :    ?
12 :    while Clients-( !eof() )
13 :        Clients-( Reporter( Clients-account, Clients-status ), dbskip() )
14 :    enddo
15 :
16 :    return( NIL )
17 :
18 : **********************
19 :
20 : static function Reporter( xData1, xData2 )
21 :
22 :    static nLineCount
23 :    local  nInternal := 0
24 :
25 :    if nLineCount == NIL
26 :       nLineCount = 0
27 :    endif
28 :    if empty( nLineCount++ )
29 :       scroll(2,0)
30 :    endif
31 :
32 :    ?? Data1, xData2, ++nInternal, nLineCount
33 :    ?? chr(13) + chr(10)
34 :
35 :    inkey(0)
36 :
37 :    nLineCount %= 22      // Why not...
38 :
39 :    return( NIL )
40 :
41 : // End of File: Static.prg
```

In this example, the main thrust of the program rests on lines 22 and 23. While the variable *nInternal* is initialized to a LOCAL data type with a value of 0, the variable *nLineCount* is initialized as STATIC. This means that while the visibility of *nLineCount* will remain confined to the Reporter( ) subroutine, the value of *nLineCount* will be retained when the routine ends, making it available whenever the routine is called again. On the first pass through the loop on lines 12 through 14, the Reporter( ) function is called and the STATIC variable *nLineCount* is initialized; its beginning value will be NIL. Lines 25 through 27 test this and either assign a value of 0 to the variable or leave its value unchanged.

STATIC variables cannot be released. This means that if a procedure uses STATIC variables, other routines later on in the execution of a program may in turn call that same routine and its STATIC variables will remain accessible. In those cases, it may be necessary to pass additional parameters to the subroutines using STATIC variables to set those variables to beginning values in case their value is not NIL.

The following table shows the differences among these four data storage classes; it lays out the lifespan and visibility of the LOCAL, STATIC, PRIVATE, and PUBLIC data classes:

|  | Lifespan: Duration for which variable exists | Visibility: Which routines can see them |
| --- | --- | --- |
| **LOCAL** | Initializing routine and subroutines | Initializing routine only |
| **STATIC** | Duration of program execution | Initializing routine only |
| **PRIVATE** | Initializing routine and subroutines | Initializing routine and subroutine |
| **PUBLIC** | Duration of program execution | Duration of program execution |

Although the PUBLIC and PRIVATE statements are in many ways superseded by the LOCAL and STATIC variable statements, this is not to say that they should be done away with. First, for those values that are systemwide and which may be reset, toggled, or changed at any of a number of places throughout a program, and for those values that must be retained between application sessions, the PUBLIC statement is ideal. These variables are generally stored to a memory variable file (.MEM) and help control generic system default values for an application. The PRIVATE variable may also be used to save and restore values from a memory variable file. Both PRIVATE and PUBLIC data declarations are also ideal for those values that need to be macro-expanded. LOCAL and STATIC variables cannot be macro-expanded. Additionally, the PRIVATE command is important if you want to mask out a higher-level PRIVATE or PUBLIC variable from a lower-level procedure or function.

The LOCAL and STATIC variables are ideal for holding values within the routine exclusively. There are no symbolic references for LOCAL and STATIC variables; they are created in memory at the time they are called. PRIVATE and PUBLIC variables, on the other hand, are referenced within the symbol table and are allocated space within the main load module of an application prior to execution. The only difference between a LOCAL and a STATIC variable is the STATIC variable's ability to remember a value. On the surface this may seem very powerful, and indeed it is; however, this can cause some program dilemmas. Sometimes, STATIC variables need to be reset to initial values; however, since they are only visible to the routine that created them, that routine needs to be programmed in such a way either to use the STATIC variables or to reset them.

All four data storage classes are important, and all four require careful planning and diligent observation of programming style to be used effectively. There is a time and a place for each of them; design your application accordingly!

## FILEWIDE STATIC VARIABLES

Clipper also supports a small but significant variation on the STATIC statement. If a program file (.PRG) is compiled with the /N switch, no symbol for the file is generated. To clarify the significance of this for STATIC variables, let's examine what happens when we do compile a .PRG file with the /N switch. Without the /N switch, Clipper automatically assumes that there is a starting module within the .PRG file whose name is the same as the .PRG filename; accordingly, Clipper generates a reference in the symbol table to the .PRG file itself. However, with the /N switch, Clipper does not assume that there is a module within the .PRG file whose name is the same as the program filename, and does not generate a reference to it in the symbol table. As a result, if a STATIC variable is initialized at the topmost level of the file, that variable will not be visible to any single subroutine within the .PRG file; instead, its visibility will extend to all routines within the program file, but it will not be visible to other program files.

This kind of file-wide STATIC variable is significant, since it allows the programmer to define individual .PRG files that will serve particular purposes, and to define "publiclike" variables that are important to that program file and to all of the functions and procedures within it. This allows the developer to pass only those parameters from function to function and from procedure to procedure that are necessary, and to hide them from the view of other modules and program files. In fact, this is how GETSYS.PRG, the basic data entry module that defines the operation of the GET object, operates.

At the same time, filewide STATIC variables should be used with caution. The excessive use of the STATIC statement for filewide scoping can slow down the performance of an application.

To see filewide scoping in action, consider the following example:

```
 1 : * File:      Param3.prg
 2 :
 3 : static nNumber1 := 0
 4 :
 5 : function Main()
 6 :
 7 :    cls
 8 :
 9 :    ? "Initial value of nNumber1", nNumber1++
10 :    FirstCall()
11 :
12 :    return( NIL )
13 :
14 : *******************
```

```
15 :
16 : static function FirstCall()
17 :
18 :    ? "And now the value of the variable is:", nNumber1
19 :    ?
20 :    ? "Name on the subroutine stack is: ", procname(0), procname(1)
21 :
22 :    SecondCall()
23 :
24 :    return( NIL )
25 :
26 : *********************
27 :
28 : static function SecondCall()
29 :
30 :    ? "And finally, the value of the variable is: ", ++nNumber1
31 :
32 :    return( NIL )
33 :
34 : // End of file: Parm3.prg
```

In this example, the variable *nNumber1* is defined as a STATIC variable on line 3, outside of the formal function named Main( ) on line 5. If this module was not compiled with the /N switch, then the static variable would belong to the subroutine named Param3( ) which, if executed, would simply return to DOS. If, on the other hand, this file were to be compiled with the /N switch, then the symbol for Param3( ) would not be available for the STATIC variable to "cling" to; rather, it would be available throughout the file. As seen within the Main( ) routine on line 9, the variable is displayed and post-incremented. Then the FirstCall( ) function is called, and the value of *nNumber1* again is displayed on line 18. Along with the variable, the names of the various subroutines are also displayed to the screen using the PROCNAME( ) function. This is how the subroutine stack can be traced and how run-time errors which show the exact order of subroutines are displayed to the screen. Finally, on line 30, the variable *nNumber* is pre-incremented and displayed to the screen.

## Declaration Statements

### MEMVAR AND FIELD

Two new declaration statements in Clipper 5.x, the MEMVAR and the FIELD statements, are used to resolve potential conflicts between memory variables and database fields.

The MEMVAR command statement is implemented in Clipper 5.2 to resolve unaliased references within an application by assuming that the reference is a PUBLIC or PRIVATE memory variable. To create an implicit memory variable list in Clipper 5.2, use the following coding convention:

```
MEMVAR <memvar> [, <memvar> ...]
```

This does not create the memory variable—it simply forces Clipper to assume that an unaliased reference using that name is a reference to a memory variable. Note that any

MEMVAR declaration MUST appear before any other executable Clipper code, similar to the LOCAL and STATIC statements; otherwise, a compiling error message will be generated.

```
 1 : * File:      Memvar.prg
 2 :
 3 : memvar account     // This variable will be used in the program!
 4 :
 5 : function Main()
 6 :
 7 :   account := 1    // assign the variable a value
 8 :
 9 :   use Clients new
10 :
11 :   while Clients->( !eof() )
12 :     ? Clients->account, account++
13 :     Clients->( dbskip() )           // This is the SKIP command
14 :   enddo
15 :
16 :   return(NIL)
17 :
18 : // End of File: Memvar.prg
```

In this brief example, we have told the compiler that there will be at least one explicit memory variable with the name of *Account*. On line 9, a new database is used—Clients. Within this database there is a field named Clients->account, yet in the loop that follows, there is no mistaken identity between the two. Typically in the past, with a memory variable having the same name as a field, the field would take precedence. Here, since the field has an alias associated with it, there is no confusion.

The use of the FIELD or MEMVAR statements provides an *explicit* means of identifying unaliased references. In addition, however, Clipper provides an *implicit* means of identifying unaliased references. If a module is compiled with the /V switch, the unaliased reference is assumed to be a memory variable. If the module is compiled with the /W switch, the Clipper compiler will display a warning message similar to the following:

```
Warning C1004 Ambiguous reference, assuming memvar: <memvar>.
```

However, if the module is compiled with the /ES2 switch, which informs Clipper to not generate an object (.OBJ) file if any warnings are encountered, ambiguous references will effectively block the compiling process. In this case, use of either the MEMVAR or FIELD statement is necessary to explicitly resolve unaliased references.

Perhaps the major use of the MEMVAR declaration is to define the array *GetList[ ]*, the internal array that is created by the @...GET command, as the following preprocessor translation from STD.CH shows:

```
SetPos( <row>, <col> )                                    ;
  ; AAdd( GetList,                                        ;
    _GET_( <var>, <(var)>, <pic>, <{valid}>, <{when}> ):display() ) ;
  [; ATail(GetList):<msg>]
```

If the /W switch is used when compiling, a warning message will be generated, since the variable *GetList[ ]* is otherwise undefined. If the MEMVAR statement that defines *GetList[ ]* is placed at the topmost part of the program module that uses the @...GET command, the reference to *GetList[ ]* will no longer be ambiguous and a warning message will no longer appear.

The FIELD statement is used to declare the names of database fields to the application and optionally supplies the implicit alias for each name listed. The syntax is similar to the MEMVAR command:

```
FIELD <fieldname> [, <fieldname> ...] [IN <database>]
```

Like the MEMVAR statement, FIELD simply makes the assumption that unaliased references to the names contained in the list are references to database fields. And like the MEMVAR, STATIC, and LOCAL commands, the FIELD command must appear in a subroutine, procedure, or function before any executable code. Here is an example of the FIELD statement:

```
 1 : * Name:      Field.prg
 2 :
 3 : // List the fields that will be used in this file
 4 :
 5 : field files, sizes, subdrive, per_used in Notap
 6 :
 7 : function Main()
 8 :
 9 :    cls
10 :    use Notap new
11 :    use Clients new
12 :
13 :    while Clients->( !eof() )
14 :       ? Clients->status, Clients->account
15 :
16 :       if Notap->( !eof() )
17 :          ? "   ", files, sizes, left(subdrive, 25), per_used
18 :          Notap->( dbskip() )
19 :       endif
20 :
21 :       Clients->( dbskip() )     // This is the SKIP command
22 :
23 :       if row() == 22
24 :          wait
25 :          cls
26 :       endif
27 :    enddo
28 :
29 :    return( NIL )
30 :
31 : // End of File: Field.prg
```

This example is similar to the MEMVAR program except here we are working with fields in databases rather than with memory variables. However, the same rules apply. Declaring to the compiler in advance which unaliased symbols in an application are fields and which are memory variables will resolve any potential ambiguity. Additionally, in the case of the FIELDS declaration, fields are not only declared, but they are also linked with their alias work area. In this example, the four fields listed on line 5 all point to the Notap work area. By using the FIELD command, all three versions of the following calling conventions are identical:

| Using FIELD Declaration | Using Field-> alias pointer | Using ALIAS( ) area pointer |
|---|---|---|
| FIELD files, sizes,; subdrive, per_used | USE Notap NEW SELECT Notap | USE Notap NEW |
| files | Field->files | Notap->files |
| sizes | Field->sizes | Notap->sizes |
| subdrive | Field->subdrive | Notap->subdrive |
| per_used | Field->per_used | Notap->per_used |

## EXTERNAL

This command is used to tell the compiler in advance of any external subroutine that may need to be linked into the application. For example, sometimes the name of a function or a procedure will be part of a macro-expansion or a string, such as

```
for nCounter := 1 to 3
   cExt := alltrim(str(nCounter))
   do Proc&cExt.
next
```

or

```
cBranch = "Listchoice"
&cBranch.()
```

In either example, the procedures or functions that may be called when each of these coding examples is executed would probably produce a run-time error telling you that there is a "missing external." Because the name of a routine is not explicitly declared to the linker, it does not know what subroutines may be executed, namely Proc1 through Proc3 and Listchoice( ). All of these routines are within macro expansions or string definitions. This means that since neither the linker nor the compiler is able to determine the name of the routine that may be executed, you must tell it in advance that you may need these routines and that they need to be included in the symbol table at linking time. To do this you need to add the EXTERNAL command statement with the name of each routine that may be executed. For example, the EXTERNAL command using the above examples would appear as follows:

```
EXTERNAL Proc1, Proc2, Proc3
```

```
for nCounter := 1 TO 3
  cExt := alltrim(str(nCounter))
  do Proc&cExt.
next
```

or

```
EXTERNAL Listchoice

branch = "Listchoice"
&branch.( )
```

As with the LOCAL, STATIC, FIELD, and MEMVAR declarations, the EXTERNAL statement must appear before any executable command statement and before any PARAMETERS command. It may, however, appear in any order within the above set of four statements.

Note that the EXTERNAL statement may not be supported in future versions of CA-Clipper and should be replaced by the REQUEST statement.

## REQUEST

Although the REQUEST statement is to be supported in future versions of CA-Clipper and is to be preferred over the EXTERNAL statement, an examination of STD.CH, the standard Clipper header file, yields a surprising find: REQUEST simply translates into the EXTERNAL statement. Therefore, at the moment at least, REQUEST is nothing more than a command that is identical to the EXTERNAL statement; it is not an intrinsic part of the Clipper language. However, for future compatibility, it should nevertheless be used instead of EXTERNAL.

## The Order of Variable and Field Statements

The exact placement of the statements defining data storage classes and unaliased references in a program module is particularly important. If a statement is in the wrong place, Clipper will display an error message, "<type> declaration follows executable statement", and abort the compilation process. The table below shows the order in which each statement must appear in order to not cause a compiling error. Statements at the same level can appear in any order.

| Level | Statement |
| --- | --- |
| 1 | File-wide STATIC variables |
| 2 | LOCAL parameters (e.g., FUNCTION Main(<xLocal1>,<xLocal2>) |
| 3 | FIELD, MEMVAR, LOCAL, or STATIC |
| 4 | PUBLIC or PRIVATE |

The REQUEST, EXTERNAL, and PARAMETERS statements can be placed anywhere without producing a syntax error. Note, however, that the PARAMETERS statement must precede the use of the parameters that are passed to a particular routine.

## Parameter Passing

The parameter is one of the most fundamental aspects of any language, including Clipper. There are many different ways in which a variable may be passed from one subroutine to another, and each way has a different meaning; that is, the value of that memory variable is different and is coded differently as well. A parameter can come from the DOS environment, from the command line, or from the normal sources—a procedure or a function. In addition, the method in which a memory variable is passed is as important as its type or storage class. How well you understand and control parameters will dictate the effectiveness of your programs.

To begin with the very basics, keep in mind that parameter passing normally works with LOCAL, STATIC, or PRIVATE memory variables. Normally, PUBLIC memory variables are manipulated directly—they can be accessed throughout an application without being passed as parameters; a direct reference to their individual names is sufficient to alter their values. For the remaining types of data storage classes, parameters are generally passed by value or by reference. Parameters can also be passed from DOS and via the DOS environment.

Clipper will allow you to pass up to 255 parameters to a function or procedure. Keep in mind that there is a limit to the length of the command line in Clipper 5.2. The old limitation of 255 characters to a command line has been lifted in Clipper 5.2. However, use tight, compact code; exaggerated lengths of command lines can make an application too unwieldy to debug. Try to use the features of Clipper as you need to, but do not overextend yourself to the point of unmaintainability. You may find some features convenient in the front-end of the development cycle, but you will ultimately pay for them on the back-end.

In Clipper, information can be passed from routine to routine in four ways, with the calling convention and syntax depending on the nature of the call and the type of routine being called. All of these points will become obvious in one moment. For now, let us look at each of these four ways in which a parameter may be passed from routine to routine and at how arrays are passed.

### PARAMETERS BY VALUE

The format of a parameter that is passed by value differs depending on whether it is passed to a function or to a procedure. However, in each case, the result is the same. In essence, when a parameter is passed by value, only a copy of the memory variable is passed and not the actual variable (*actual variable* means the internal address pointer to that variable). When a variable is passed by value, the address pointer is shielded from direct manipulation. When something is passed by value, the value stored at that address (or, if you choose to view it as such, a copy of the variable) is passed. In essence, it would look something like Figure 5.1.

*188  Straley's Programming with Clipper 5.2*

```
┌─────────────────────────┐                          ┌──────────────────┐
│ PROCEDURE Main          │                          │   Clipper's      │
│                         │                          │  Memory Stack    │
│ PRIVATE x, y, z         │                          │                  │
│ x := y := z := 1        │      Value of variables  │                  │
│                         │ ◄──────────────────────  │  Address for x   │
│ DO Subroutine WITH ;    │                          │  Address for y   │
│   (x), (y), (z)         │ ─────────┐               │  Address for z   │
│                         │          │               │                  │
│ Subroutine (x, y, z)    │          │               │                  │
│                         │          │               │  Address for a   │
└─────────────────────────┘          │               │  Address for b   │
                                     │               │  Address for c   │
   Function or Procedure             │               │                  │
┌─────────────────────────┐          │               └──────────────────┘
│ ... Subroutine          │          ▼
│                         │    Call by value
│ PARAMETERS a, b, c      │◄── to subroutine
│                         │
│ DO Another WITH;        │
│   (a), (b), (c)         │
│                         │
│ Another (a, b, c)       │
└─────────────────────────┘
```

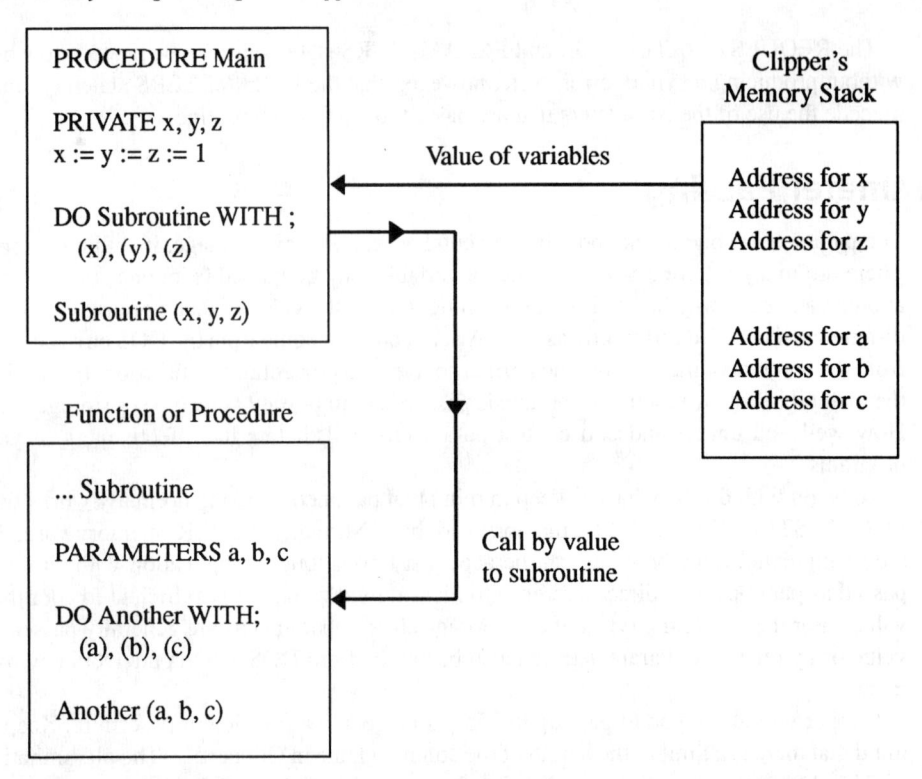

**Figure 5.1  Parameters passed by value**

In this case, manipulation of the parameter in the called subroutine will not change the value of the variable/parameter once control has returned to the calling routine.

There are two methods to pass a parameter by value. The first is typical of the way a parameter might be passed to a procedure, while the second is typical of the way a parameter might be passed to a function:

```
DO Subroutine WITH (x)
Subroutine(x)
```

Actually, either method will in fact work with both procedures and functions. But since the return value of the subroutine is lost when it is invoked with the DO statement, the first method is more appropriate for calling procedures. On the other hand, since DO has been designated as a compatibility statement that may not be retained in future versions of Clipper, the second is the preferred method for calling all subroutines and passing them parameters by value.

To see this in action, here is a program with both types of calling conventions:

```
   1 : * Name:      Parm1.prg // Do not compile this with any warning switch!
   2 :
   3 : function Main()
   4 :
```

```
 5 :    cls
 6 :
 7 :    nNum1 := nNum2 := nNum3 := 1
 8 :
 9 :    ? "These are the values of the variables before the call is made "
10 :    ? "to the first subroutine which will be a PROCEDURE"
11 :    ?
12 :    ? nNum1, nNum2, nNum3
13 :    ?
14 :    ? "Press any key to go on..."
15 :    inkey(0)
16 :
17 :    do ProcRoutine with (nNum1), (nNum2)
18 :
19 :    ?
20 :    ? "And now, looking at nNum1, nNum2, and nNum3 we have"
21 :    ? "the following values:"
22 :    ?
23 :    ? nNum1, nNum2, nNum3
24 :    ?
25 :    ? "Press any key for next example..."
26 :    inkey(0)
27 :
28 :    cls
29 :
30 :    ? "These are the values, once again, of the three variables "
31 :    ? "before they are passed by value to a FUNCTION"
32 :    ?
33 :    ? nNum1, nNum2, nNum3
34 :    ?
35 :    ? "Press any key to go on..."
36 :    inkey(0)
37 :
38 :    FuncRoutine( nNum1, nNum2 )
39 :
40 :    ?
41 :    ? "And now, the values of the variables nNum1, nNum2,"
42 :    ? "and nNum3 are: "
43 :    ?
44 :    ? nNum1, nNum2, nNum3
45 :    ?
46 :    ? "Any key to end..."
47 :    inkey(0)
48 :    cls
49 :
50 :    return( NIL )
51 :
52 : ********************
53 :
54 : static procedure ProcRoutine( nNum1, nNum2 )
55 :
56 :    nNum1 := ++nNum3      // Adjust the private variable
57 :    nNum2 := nNum3--      // as well as assigning variables
58 :
```

```
59 :      ?
60 :      ? "And now, the values of the variables nNum1, nNum2,"
61 :      ? "and nNum3 are: "
62 :      ?
63 :      ? nNum1, space(10), nNum2, space(10), nNum3
64 :      ?
65 :      ? "Press any key to return..."
66 :      inkey(0)
67 :
68 :   *********************
69 :
70 :   static function FuncRoutine( nNum1, nNum2 )
71 :
72 :      nNum1 := "Hello, a data change"
73 :      nNum2 := date() + nNum3++
74 :
75 :      ?
76 :      ? "And now, the values of the variables nNum1, nNum2,"
77 :      ? "and nNum3 are: "
78 :      ?
79 :      ? nNum1, space(10), nNum2, space(10), nNum3
80 :      ?
81 :      ? "Press any key to return..."
82 :      inkey(0)
83 :
84 :   // End of File: Parm1.prg
```

In this example, three variables are initialized on line 7. After being displayed, two of the three parameters are passed to the procedure ProcRoutine. The variables are passed by value on line 17, since the names of the variables are each surrounded by a set of parentheses, which means that only the variables' values will be passed to the subroutine and not the address pointers to the variables' values.

Inside the procedure ProcRoutine( ) on line 54, the two variables *nNum1* and *nNum2* are now LOCAL parameters. The value of a preincremented variable *nNum3* is stored to the variable *nNum1* on line 56, and the value of the postdecremented variable *nNum3* is stored to the variable *nNum2* on line 57.

One of the disadvantages of a PRIVATE memory variable (which includes a variable not given an explicit storage class, as on line 7) is that subroutines can access private variables defined "higher" in the program without their being explicitly passed to the subroutine. This is not good modular programming. In addition, it does not lend itself to code reusability. In this case, if the procedure ProcRoutine were needed in some other program, it would not work "as-is" unless there was a private variable named *nNum3* available for it to manipulate. One alternative is to use filewide STATIC variables, while a second is to explicitly pass all variables that may be needed to the subroutine. This example, although it violates these common rules, is created to emulate the way xBase programming "used" to look like and not what it should look like now.

Back to the example, on line 56, the variable *nNum3* is incremented to 2 before its value is stored to *nNum1*. On the next line, *nNum3*'s value of 2 is stored to *nNum2* before *nNum3* is decremented to a value of 1. Again, this manipulation of the variable *nNum3* is allowed, although not recommended, since *nNum3* is a PRIVATE memory variable. After the manipulations, program control is returned to the calling program, which shows the values of the three variables one more time on line 23. Since the variable *nNum3* was incremented and decremented only once, the value will once again be 1. The other two variables will also be 1, since they were passed to the subroutine by value.

After this, the same two variables are passed by value to the function FuncRoutine( ) on line 38. Inside this function, the two LOCAL parameters, *nNum1* and *nNum2*, are not only assigned new values but also new data types. However, in this subroutine, the value of *nNum3* is manipulated as well. Again, this is allowed, since *nNum3* is a PRIVATE variable that is visible to all lower-level routines, even though it was not passed as a parameter to the function. However, manipulating a straggling variable inside of a dependent subroutine in this way will one day cause havoc if you ever have to trace down that one variable as being the source of your woes.

As was the case when program control returned from the called subroutine ProcRoutine( ), the variables *nNum1* and *nNum2* retain their original values once FuncRoutine( ) has returned control to Main( ). However, the variable *nNum3* has changed.

## PARAMETERS BY REFERENCE

When a parameter is passed by reference, the address pointer for that variable is passed, which grants the called subroutines access to alter those values. Figure 5.2 shows how that looks internally to Clipper.

By passing the address pointer that points to the actual value of the passed variable, you are giving the keys to unlock the door to a subroutine. Any manipulation performed on the parameter within the subroutine will be reflected once program control is returned to the calling routine. This manipulation means that both the values and data types of those passed memory variables can be altered.

Two methods can be used to pass a parameter by reference. As is the case when passing a parameter by value, the first is typical of the way a parameter is passed to a procedure, while the second is typical of the way a parameter is passed to a function:

```
DO Subroutine WITH x
Subroutine(@x)
```

Actually, either method will in fact work with both procedures and functions. But since the return value of the subroutine is lost when it is invoked with the DO statement, the first method is more appropriate for calling procedures. On the other hand, since DO has been designated as a compatibility statement that may not be retained in future versions of Clipper, the second is the preferred method for calling all subroutines and passing them parameters by reference.

To see this in action, here is a sample program:

```
1 : * Name:      Parm2.prg    // Make sure that this is NOT compiled
2 :                           // with the /W warning switch
3 : function Main()
4 :
5 :    cls
6 :
```

## Straley's Programming with Clipper 5.2

```
PROCEDURE Main

PRIVATE x, y, z
x := y := z := 1

DO Subroutine WITH ;
   x, y, z

Subroutine (@x, @y, @z)
```

Call by ref.
to routine

Clipper's
Memory Stack

Address for x
Address for y
Address for z

Address for a
Address for b
Address for c

Function or Procedure

```
... Subroutine

PARAMETERS a, b, c

DO Another WITH;
   a, b, c

Another (@a, @b, @c)
```

Manipulates the
address pointer
in stack directly

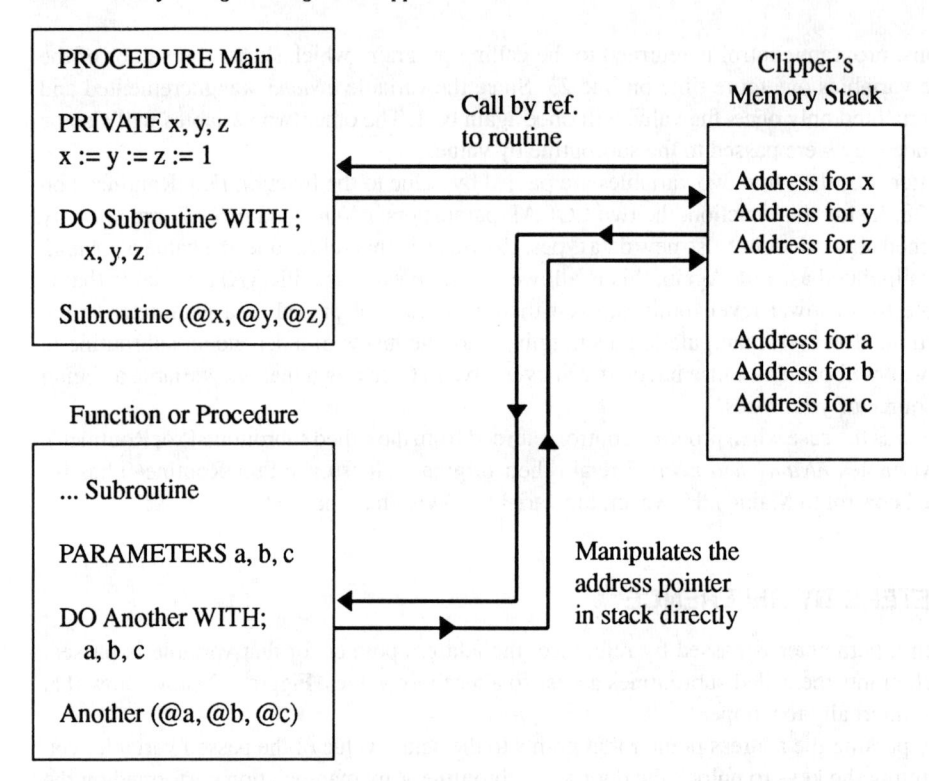

**Figure 5.2  Parameters passed by reference**

```
 7 :    nNum1 := nNum2 := nNum3 := 1
 8 :
 9 :    ? "These are the values of the variables before the call is made "
10 :    ? "to the first subroutine, which will be a PROCEDURE"
11 :    ?
12 :    ? nNum1, nNum2, nNum3
13 :    ?
14 :    ? "Press any key to go on..."
15 :    inkey(0)
16 :
17 :    do ProcRoutine with nNum1, nNum2, (nNum3)
18 :    ?
19 :    ? "And now, the values of the variables nNum1, nNum2, and "
20 :    ? "nNum3 are: "
21 :    ?
22 :    ? nNum1, nNum2, nNum3
23 :    ?
24 :    ? "Press any key for next example..."
25 :    inkey(0)
26 :
27 :    cls
28 :
29 :    ? "These are the values, once again, of the three variables "
30 :    ? "before they are passed by value to a FUNCTION"
```

```
31 :     ?
32 :     ? nNum1, nNum2, nNum3
33 :     ?
34 :     ? "Press any key to go on..."
35 :     inkey(0)
36 :
37 :     FuncRoutine(@nNum1, @nNum2, nNum3)
38 :
39 :     ?
40 :     ? "And now, the values of the variables nNum1, nNum2, and "
41 :     ? "nNum3 are: "
42 :     ?
43 :     ? nNum1, nNum2, nNum3
44 :     ?
45 :     ? "Any key to end..."
46 :     inkey(0)
47 :     cls
48 :
49 :     return( NIL )
50 :
51 : *********************
52 :
53 : static procedure ProcRoutine( nNum1, nNum2, nNum3 )
54 :
55 :     nNum1 := ++nNum3
56 :     nNum2 := nNum3++
57 :
58 :     ?
59 :     ? "And now, the values of the variables nNum1, nNum2, and "
60 :     ? "nNum3 are now: "
61 :     ?
62 :     ? nNum1, nNum2, nNum3
63 :     ?
64 :     ? "Press any key to return..."
65 :     inkey(0)
66 :
67 : *********************
68 :
69 : static function FuncRoutine( nNum1, nNum2, nNum3 )
70 :
71 :     nNum1 := "Hello, a data change"
72 :     nNum2 := date() + nNum3++
73 :
74 :     ?
75 :     ? "And now, the values of the variables nNum1, nNum2, and "
76 :     ? "nNum3 are now: "
77 :     ?
78 :     ? nNum1, space(10), nNum2, space(10), nNum3
79 :     ?
80 :     ? "Press any key to return..."
81 :     inkey(0)
82 :
83 :     return( NIL )
84 :
85 : // End of File: Parm2.prg
```

This program is similar to PARM1.PRG, but in this example parameters are passed both by reference and by value to a procedure and a function. In both cases, the variable *nNum3* is protected from being manipulated in the lower subroutines called by Main( ) because it is passed by value; the remaining two variables, *nNum1* and *nNum2*, are passed by reference.

A further examination of the two methods of passing parameters for procedures and functions is in order. Visually, consider the similarities among these four examples:

```
DO Subroutine WITH x      <--->   Subroutine(@x)
DO Subroutine WITH (x)    <--->   Subroutine(x)
```

In the latter of the two pairs, if you were to remove the literals DO and WITH (as well as the blank spaces) on the left side, you would have the function call on the right side. This shows that symbolically a function and a procedure are the same to Clipper 5.2. The default return value of a procedure is a NIL data type (in pre-Clipper 5.0 versions it was a logical false (.F.)). This further shows why a symbol redefinition error would occur if there was a function and a procedure with the same name: In essence, they are the same to Clipper.

The @ symbol is the added command character that allows a function to pass a variable by reference, which is the default method of passing a parameter to a procedure. In other words, we commonly code the following:

```
DO Subroutine WITH xItem
```

This passes the variable *xItem* by reference. Notice that there are no parentheses surrounding the variable; parentheses would look like a function call but would pass the variable by VALUE and not by REFERENCE. To implement this in a function, the character @ was added to change the way the parameter is passed. As a matter of fact, the following is permissible, though not practical, in Clipper 5.2:

```
DO Subroutine WITH (@xItem)
```

The set of parentheses passes the value of *xItem* to the Subroutine routine, and the @ character toggles it to be passed by reference. If you remove the DO and WITH command statements as well as the blank characters, this looks like a direct function call.

## PASSING ARRAYS AS PARAMETERS

Since arrays are valid data types, they fit the same pattern as typical character, numeric, or date variables. However, some of the behavior of passing an array around may seem a bit awkward. Rest assured, they work just like any other data type. This means that if the name of the array is passed to a subroutine, it is passed by value. Because an array is a collection of pointers as well, this means that the subroutine has access to any of the variables in that array. It also means that the subroutine may attach other items to the array via the AADD( ) function or the ASIZE( ) function. In essence, an array in Clipper is a union of structures. What this means is that if an array is passed by value, the subroutine does not have direct access to the pointer to that array structure. It may have access to join items to it, or it may have access to individual pieces within the structure, but it does not have direct access to the memory pointer for that structure. Another way to look at this is that the value of an array consists of the individual pieces that make up the array. This definition works well with the theory that everything in Clipper has a value, including an array.

Now, this also should mean that arrays can be passed by reference as well by simply using an "@" symbol in front of the name. This means, just like the other data types, that the pointer to the array reference is available for change. It also means that the array reference can now "point" to an entirely NEW array structure. This will be seen in the following example program. Many of the new concepts pertaining to array technology are explored in depth in Chapter 10, "Arrays."

```
 1 : * File:        Parmar1.prg
 2 :
 3 : function Main()
 4 :
 5 :    local aValue := {3,23,13,55}
 6 :
 7 :    cls
 8 :
 9 :    qout( "Array elements..." )    // A simple display
10 :    aeval( aValue, {|xItem| qout( xItem )} )
11 :    setpos(0,0)
12 :
13 :    ModiElement( aValue )
14 :    scroll(0,0,maxrow(),maxcol(),,-20)
15 :    qout( "Modified Elements..." ) // Display after an element is added
16 :    aeval( aValue, {|xItem| qout(xItem)} )
17 :    setpos(0,0)
18 :
19 :    ModiArray( aValue )
20 :    scroll(0,0,maxrow(),maxcol(),,-20)
21 :    qout( "Passed by value..." )    // Display elements after value
22 :    aeval( aValue, {|xItem| qout(xItem)} )
23 :    setpos(0,0)
24 :
25 :    ModiArray( @aValue )
26 :    scroll(0,0,maxrow(),maxcol(),,-20)
27 :    qout( "Passed by ref..." )   // Display elements after reference
28 :    aeval( aValue, {|xItem| qout(xItem)} )
29 :    setpos(10,0)
30 :
31 :    return( NIL )
32 :
33 : *******************
34 :
35 : static function ModiElement( aArray )
36 :
37 :    // This function will modify an element of the array passed to
38 :    // it as well as add an element to the end of the array:
39 :
40 :    aArray[len(aArray)] := "This is a test"
41 :    aadd( aArray, date() )
42 :
43 :    return( NIL )
44 :
```

```
45 :   ********************
46 :
47 :   static function ModiArray( aArray )
48 :
49 :      // This function will attempt to make a new array reference and
50 :      // will store it to the array passed to the function.
51 :
52 :      local aLiteral := {"Pleiades", "DocBase", "Helios", "Hermes", ;
53 :                                                    "Sirius Products"}
54 :
55 :      aArray := aLiteral
56 :
57 :      return( NIL )
58 :
59 :   // End of File: Paramar1.prg
```

The original array is defined on line 5. The variable *aValue[ ]* is nothing more than a reference to that array. Line 10 displays the contents of this array to the screen. On line 14, the enhanced SCROLL( ) function is used to move the screen contents to the right by 20 columns. This means that all of the array elements and the literal expression on line 9 will be 20 columns over to the right. Prior to that, the ModiElement( ) function is called, with the variable *aValue[ ]* passed to it by value. On line 35, this function accepts the parameter as a local variable named *aArray[ ]*. On line 40 the last element in the array *aArray[ ]* is modified to be the literal string, and an additional element is stored to the array on line 41. Keep in mind that while individual array elements may be modified and new items stored to an array, it does not alter the basic structure, which is still protected since the original array *aValue[ ]* was passed by value and not by reference. Therefore, when this function on line 35 terminates and control is returned to the Main( ) function, the elements in the array *aValue[ ]*, as seen on line 16, will have an additional element, and the next to last element in this array will be a string data type.

Up to this point in the example program, we have focused on the individual array elements and not on the array pointer itself. On line 19, the array *aValue[ ]* is passed to the function ModiArray( ) by value. Within this function which is defined on lines 47 and following there is a new LOCAL variable called *aLiteral[ ]* which has a series of product names: string data types. Look at this as a new array being defined on line 52. Then on line 55, that array pointer, or structure, is stored to the local parameter *aArray[ ]*, which is the value of the variable *aValue[ ]*. Since the original array is passed by value and not by reference, this array structure defined on line 52 cannot take the place of the original array created on line 5. This is the significant difference and a major point to grasp. Since the array *aValue[ ]* is not passed by reference, the pointer to the structure of that array is protected and thus cannot be overwritten with a pointer to a new structure, as seen on line 55. When this function terminates and control is returned to the Main( ) function, the individual elements in *aValue[ ]* will be displayed once again to the screen (line 22), and the values in that array will be the same as they were in the previous display.

The situation is different on line 25, in which the array *aValue[ ]* is passed by reference since the "@" symbol is used. When the literal array on line 52 is assigned to the local parameter on line 55, that array reference now replaces the original array reference on line 5. This means that all of the values and the original structure of the array will be lost and replaced by a new structure, namely, the array called *aLiteral[ ]*. So when the ModiArray( )

function returns control to the Main() function and the individual items in *aValue[ ]* are displayed to the screen on line 28, the strings of the second array will be seen on the screen, and none of the previous values will be available.

This is an important feature of Clipper. Since arrays follow the same rules as any other data type, they can be used in a conventional manner. Functions can return an array since a function has a value and now an array has a value. In addition, we can create programs that initialize arrays to be empty and pass them to more specialized functions by reference and allow them to create the appropriate array at the appropriate time. In other words, a code fragment might look like this:

```
local aSystemData := {}

if LoadData( @aSystemData, "DOCBASE.INI" )
   MainMen(aSystemData)
else
   ErrorMessage( "Unable to load system parameters" )
endif
```

Here, the array is created as an empty structure. Since it is passed by reference to the function LoadData( ), the function can build a new array structure based on the contents of the file DOCBASE.INI. If the creation of this new array is successful, then the function will return a logical true (.T.) value and we can then in turn call MainMenu( ), passing the array of new values to it. If, on the other hand, an error occurs in the process of creating an array, then the ErrorMessage( ) function will be called.

It is important to stress that this has nothing to do with passing individual array elements. They can only be passed by value, since using the "@" symbol in conjunction with an array element causes a compiler error, "Invalid use of @ (pass by reference) operator." In essence,

```
@aArray[1]
```

is not allowed by the compiler.

One way to pass an array element is to pass a function along the entire array with a numeric value that serves as a pointer to a particular element. The trouble with this is that the function has access to not only the one element in question, but to the other elements as well. Another way to simulate passing an array element by reference is to pass a code block to which the array subscript in question is stored. The following program illustrates this:

```
 1 : * File:      Parmar2.prg
 2 :
 3 : #include "PTValue.ch"    // Power Tools header file
 4 : #include "PTVerbs.ch"    // User defined header file
 5 :
 6 : // User-defined command for a GET/SET code block
 7 :
 8 : #xtranslate @@<exp> => {|xItem| IF( xItem == NIL, <exp>, <exp> := xItem)}
 9 :
10 : function Main()
11 :
12 :    local aArray := {1, 2, 3}
13 :    local nTemp  := 23
14 :
15 :    cls
16 :    ? "Before the call"
```

```
17 :        ? aArray[1], aArray[2], aArray[3]
18 :
19 :        PassDown( @@aArray[1] )
20 :
21 :        ? "After the call"
22 :        ? aArray[1], aArray[2], aArray[3]
23 :        ?
24 :        ?
25 :
26 :        // And now, call the same routine with only a variable
27 :        ? "And now the value of the nTemp variable is: ", nTemp
28 :        PassDown( @nTemp ) // Typical pass by reference
29 :        ? "Finally, the value of the variable is now: ", nTemp
30 :
31 :        return( NIL )
32 :
33 : **********************
34 :
35 : static function PassDown( xData ) // Could be a code block
36 :
37 :        ? "Inside of the function, the value is: "
38 :
39 :        if valtype( xData ) == pBLOCK    // just in case it is NOT a
40 :           ?? eval( xData )              // code block
41 :        else
42 :           ?? xData
43 :        endif
44 :
45 :        // And now use the user-defined command that is the same as the
46 :        // call to the VALTYPE() function
47 :
48 :        IF xData IS pBLOCK
49 :           eval( xData, 40 )    // Assign the value to the code block
50 :        else
51 :           xData := 40          // Just assign the variable directly
52 :        endif
53 :
54 :        return( pTRUE )
55 :
56 : // End of File: Parmar2.prg
```

In this example program, the preprocessor is used to convert the @@ symbols on line 8 to a code block expression. This code block actually takes a parameter named *xItem* (since we do not really know what data type might be assigned to an array element) and stores it to the array element at the specified subscript position. If no value is passed to the code block, as seen on line 40 with the call to the EVAL( ) function, the IF( ) function within the code block simply returns the value of the array element. This serves a dual purpose: The value of the array element may be used to seek items in databases prior to storing a new value to it, as well as simply to store a new value.

It is critical to keep in mind that the array on line 12 is declared LOCAL; the code block passed to the function PassDown( ) is created on line 19, which is within the same subroutine as the array declaration. This means that the array and all its elements are visible to the code block, even once the code block is passed to the subroutine. It is vital to visualize the fact that the operation specified in the code block is created within the same procedure/function as *aArray[ ]*, which allows all elements to be visible and manipulated at lower levels through the code block.

This type of code block, one which may be used to get a value or to set a value, is called a *Get/Set Code Block*. For additional information on code blocks and expressions, please refer to Chapter 15, "Code Blocks."

Another item to note is the flexibility of the PassDown( ) function. It checks the data type of the parameter passed to it. Therefore, in the case of using the "@@" symbol to simulate passing an array element by reference, the function on lines 38 and 39 makes the appropriate determination and follows it with a call to EVAL( ). However, if some other data type is passed to the function, as happens on line 28, the function does not make a call to EVAL( ) but rather simply gets the value of the parameter or sets the value of the parameter. This takes place on lines 42 and 51 and makes this function robust and extensible: It may be used in a variety of applications. Expanding on this function, we can quickly see that a generic lookup/list-box function may be built that could be used in conjunction with the WHEN clause or even the VALID clause.

## OBTAINING VALUES FROM THE DOS COMMAND LINE

In all of the previous examples, the discussion has centered around the formal methods of passing parameters from within an application. But there are two additional types of parameters that are external to an application. The first is a parameter passed from the DOS command line directly to the Clipper application. Since procedures and functions are, for the most part, the same thing to Clipper, so are the program files that house these subroutines. Therefore the following command line can appear as the first executable command statement in the main program:

```
PARAMETERS <expC1> [, <expC2>...]
```

This allows one or more parameters on the DOS command line immediately after the name of the program to be passed to that program. All parameters on the command line are separated by blank spaces. Each parameter passed from the DOS command line to the program will be of a string data type. If an entire substring is passed as a single parameter, a special string manipulation function is needed to convert a single parameter into what may become a collection of words. If the program needs to have a parameter of a data type other than a character string, the necessary data type conversion must be performed within the program. Finally, as with functions and procedures, the PCOUNT( ) function will work with parameters accepted from the DOS command line.

To get a good understanding of the possibilities of using DOS command line parameters, try the following command statements to launch PARM4:

```
Parm4
Parm4 *.EXE
Parm4 *.* All.files.in.directory
Parm4 *.exe All.files.after.01/01/80 01/01/80
```

In the first example, all files will be displayed, and the default title "All Files" will appear at the top of the screen. The second example will have the same title; however, only executable files will be displayed. The titles in the third and fourth examples contain the "." character, which will be removed and replaced by the space character. This is done because the space character is the parameter delimiter for DOS. And in the fourth example, the third parameter passed to the program is a date string, which is converted to a date data type within the program itself.

```
 1 : * Name:      Parm4.prg
 2 :
 3 : #include "PTVerbs.ch"
 4 :
 5 : function Main( cSkeleton, cTitle, cDate )
 6 :
 7 :    local aFiles          // Array of files to be obtained
 8 :    local dDate           // Date variable
 9 :
10 :    DEFAULT cSkeleton TO "*.*", ;
11 :            cTitle    TO "All Files", ;
12 :            cDate     TO "01/01/10"
13 :
14 :    dDate := ctod( cDate )    // Now, convert character date to a REAL date
15 :
16 :    cTitle := strtran( cTitle, ".", " ")    // strip file of "." chars
17 :
18 :    aFiles := directory( cSkeleton )
19 :
20 :    cls
21 :    @ 0,0 say padc(cTitle, maxcol()+1)
22 :    devpos(2,0)
23 :
24 :    aeval( aFiles, {|aFile| if( aFile[3] >= dDate, ;
25 :       ShowItem(aFile[1]), NIL )} )
26 :
27 :    return( NIL )
28 :
29 : *******************
30 :
31 : static function ShowItem( cFileName )   // Name of passed file
32 :
33 :    qqout( padr( cFileName, 20 ) )
34 :    if row() == maxrow() - 2
35 :      @ maxrow(), 00 say "Press any key for next screen"
36 :      inkey(0)
37 :      scroll(2,0)
38 :    endif
39 :
40 :    return( NIL )
41 :
42 : // End of File: Parm4.prg
```

On line 26, the parameter that contains the title (*cTitle*) is passed to the STRTRAN( ) function. This function will convert all occurrences of the "." character to the " " character. And on line 14, the parameter that will contain the date-checking variable is converted to the proper data type. The directory will be obtained based on the skeleton passed as the first parameter: The DIRECTORY( ) function will return a pointer to a multidimensional array that will contain the names, sizes, date stamps, time stamps, and file attribute bytes for those files matching the skeleton. The AEVAL( ) function will simply evaluate each element in the array named *aFiles[ ]*. Both the DIRECTORY( ) and AEVAL( ) functions have extended explanations and samples of code within separate chapters. For now, this routine simply displays the names of the files that match the specifications passed from the DOS command line.

## OBTAINING VALUES FROM ENVIRONMENTAL VALUES

The second way to pass a parameter to a Clipper application from outside of the application itself is via a DOS environmental variable. Many generic applications, specifically programming tools and utilities (including compilers and linkers), use these variables to control conditions within the program. With Clipper 5.2, they are used to control compiling options. Other possible environmental variables that may be evaluated by the program are the PATH and COMSPEC, which defines the location of COMMAND.COM. Clipper 5.2 has a function, GETE( ), that retrieves specified environmental strings. A call to the function to get the computer's path would look like this:

```
cPath := GETE("PATH")
```

The function will return the string that matches the environmental variable name which is passed to it as a parameter string. If the environmental variable has not been defined, the function will return a NULL byte.

An environmental variable may be created using the SET command in DOS similar to this:

```
SET CLIPPERCMD=C:\CLIPPER
```

Note that the amount of space allocated to the DOS environment is initially limited and may be increased to accommodate additional SET commands. In some versions of DOS, a special program must be run to patch the DOS BIOS after the machine has booted up. However, in most environments today, additional space is allocated to the DOS environment by placing the SHELL command in the CONFIG.SYS file. That command would look something like this:

```
SHELL=C:\COMMAND.COM /P: /E:nnnn
```

In this example, *nnnn* is a number between 160 and 32768; it stands for the number of characters reserved for environmental variables in a special area of memory reserved by DOS. Keep in mind that the more SET commands in the AUTOEXEC.BAT file (not to mention those added directly at the DOS command level), the more the free environmental space will decrease. Normally, the default paths and number of available file handles are set as part of the environment.

```
 1 : * Name:      Parm5.prg
 2 :
 3 : #include "PTVerbs.ch"    // Power Tools header file
 4 :
 5 : function Main( cSkeleton )  // DOS file skeleton!
 6 :
 7 :    local aFiles            // Array obtained from the directory
 8 :    local cTitle
 9 :    local cPath    := if( empty( gete("DIRPATH")), curdir(), ;
10 :                                           gete("DIRPATH") )
11 :
```

```
12 :      DEFAULT cSkeleton TO "*.*"
13 :
14 :      cPath := strtran( "\" + cPath + "\", "\\", "\")
15 :      aFiles := directory( cPath + cSkeleton )
16 :      cTitle := "File Listing for " + cPath + cSkeleton
17 :
18 :      scroll()
19 :      @ 0,0 say padc( cTitle, maxcol()+1)
20 :      devpos(2,0)
21 :
22 :      aeval( aFiles, {|aFile| ShowName(aFile[1]) } )
23 :
24 :      return( NIL )
25 :
26 : ********************
27 :
28 : static function ShowName( cFileName )
29 :
30 :      ?? padr(cFileName, 20)
31 :      if row() == maxrow() - 2
32 :        @ maxrow(), 00 say "Press any key for next screen"
33 :        inkey(0)
34 :        scroll(2,0)
35 :      endif
36 :
37 :      return( NIL )
38 :
39 : // End of File: Param5.prg
```

To fully see this program in action, you must set a DOS environmental variable that will be the search path for the directory skeleton passed as a DOS command parameter. The special SET command to use is

```
SET DIRPATH=<path>
```

<cPath> may be something like \DOS\ or DOS. The directory separator character is added to both ends of the environmental parameter within the program (line 14). Additionally, any duplication of the backslash characters is removed on the same line via the STRTRAN( ) function. This makes the operation robust enough to handle abnormal situations. It is absolutely unpredictable whether or not the end-user will place the final "\" character in the path string. This way, the possibility of a bad path is less likely.

The *cPath* variable is based on the return value from the GETE( ) function on lines 9 and 10. If no environmental variable is used or if DIRPATH is misspelled, the function GETE( ) will return a NULL byte, which in turn will be evaluated as EMPTY( ). If this is the case, the current directory will be used because of the call to CURDIR( ) function (line 9); if not, the value of the GETE( ) function is used as the path. This variable's value is then used in conjunction with the value of the *cSkeleton* variable. This variable is obtained directly from the DOS command line and is the directory skeleton to be used; if none is passed as a parameter, it will be a NIL data type, and by default all files (line 12) will be displayed. As in the previous example, AEVAL( ) is used to print out the names of those files.

It is interesting to note that the function Main( ) is the first function called in this routine since the file is compiled with the /N switch. In addition, since it is defined as a function, it contains a formal parameter which is automatically assigned a LOCAL data storage class.

## Statements

Several other statements can help in the development of an application. Most pertain to functions rather than to variables; however, some of the similarities between the two can be quickly seen.

### STATIC FUNCTION AND STATIC PROCEDURE

Very much like the STATIC statement defines a memory variable that is visible only within the routine in which it was defined, the STATIC FUNCTION or STATIC PROCEDURE statement defines a subroutine that is visible only within the individual .PRG file in which it is located. This has several advantages. First, because Clipper does not have to generate a symbol for the subroutine within the symbol table, execution of the module will be somewhat faster; Clipper will not have to search the symbol table for a reference to the location of the routine, but instead can access the routine directly. Second, since the procedure or function is visible only to the .PRG file within which it is located and is not represented by a symbol in the symbol table, it is possible for a static routine in one .PRG file to have the same name as a static routine or even a public function or procedure in another .PRG file. Finally, it represents a way of hiding a subroutine or limiting access to it to those routines (located in the same program file) that need to call it directly. Similarly, if object modules were collected and formatted to create a .LIB file, these static functions and procedures within each object module would not appear in a listing of the .LIB file.

Basically, the rule for using a STATIC FUNCTION or STATIC PROCEDURE is simple: If a function or procedure is written specifically for the use of a particular .PRG file and will never be called directly outside of that .PRG file, it should be defined as a STATIC routine.

### INIT PROCEDURE

INIT PROCEDURE defines a subroutine that will be automatically executed at program startup as long as the module containing it is linked into the application. To take an extreme case, let's imagine that we generate an .EXE file from three object files, as follows:

```
RTLINK FI example, one, two PLL base52
```

If each object module (EXAMPLE.OBJ, ONE.OBJ, and TWO.OBJ) contained an INIT PROCEDURE routine, they would be executed one at a time, in the order in which the modules were linked into the application, before the first public routine in EXAMPLE.EXE is executed.

Like STATIC subroutines, routines defined by the INIT PROCEDURE statement do not generate symbols in the symbol table. Because of this, they are not considered public, and cannot be called by any other procedure or function in an application. Their sole purpose is to execute once, at program startup.

The power of the INIT statement, then, lies in its ability to define an initialization routine that will execute at the start of an application. In terms of program management, this means that the developer can focus on the function of individual modules while leaving the procedures to initialize them—like initializing STATIC variables or opening databases and indexes—to a module that will automatically execute at startup. This is particularly important for the development of reusable subsystems that can simply be included as plug-and-play modules in an application. For example, a customized error system, like the one in this book, or a third-party help library, like Sirius Software's Helios, can be linked into an application and can independently set up their environment to ensure proper behavior before the first routine in the application is executed.

## EXIT PROCEDURE

The EXIT PROCEDURE statement is virtually identical to INIT PROCEDURE, except that it defines a routine that is to be performed automatically during the normal termination of an application. The subroutine defined by EXIT PROCEDURE is a perfect candidate to close special database files or to write data to a special log file.

## ANNOUNCE

The ANNOUNCE statement allows a name—i.e., a public reference—to be assigned to an object module that might otherwise not have one. Using the REQUEST statement (which was discussed earlier in this chapter), it can then be linked into an application. The major rationale underlying ANNOUNCE is that it can be used to assign an identifier to program modules that consist exclusively of INIT or EXIT routines. The module can then be REQUESTED using this identifier so that it can be linked into the application.

What follows is an example of how ANNOUNCE and REQUEST might fit together in an application. Both the DOCBASE.PRG and DOCSYSTEM.PRG modules should be compiled with the following switches:

```
/m /n /a /w /p /v /es2
```

The object modules can then be linked as follows:

```
rtlink fi docbase, docsyste pll base52

 1 : * File:     Docbase.prg
 2 :
 3 : function Main()
 4 :
 5 :    // This is the formal DOCBASE program module.  Now to make the
 6 :    // formal request of the module needed for initialization
 7 :
 8 :    request DocSys   // This will match with the ANNOUNCE
 9 :
10 :    cls
11 :    ? "And the values of the various components are: "
12 :
```

```
13 :    aeval( SystemIni(), {|xItem| qout( xItem )} )
14 :
15 :    ?
16 :    ? "Press any key for the shutdown process to take place..."
17 :    inkey(0)
18 :
19 :    return( NIL )
20 :
21 : // End of File: DocBase.prg


 1 : * File:     DocSystem.prg
 2 :
 3 : static aSystem
 4 :
 5 : Announce DocSys   // This is the DocBase System Initialization Stuff
 6 :
 7 : init procedure StartUp
 8 :
 9 :    aSystem := array(4)     // This will be an array to contain the
10 :                            // system information
11 :
12 :    aSystem[1] := setcolor()    // assign the color screen
13 :    aSystem[2] := "\" + curdir() + "\"
14 :    aSystem[3] := .t.
15 :    aSystem[4] := date()
16 :
17 :    // The system array has been initialized
18 :
19 : exit procedure ShutDown
20 :
21 :    cls
22 :    close all
23 :    ? "Normal shutdown experienced"
24 :
25 : function SystemIni()     // This function will simply return the
26 :                          // contents of the filewide static array
27 :
28 :    return( aSystem )
29 :
30 : // End of File: DocSystem.prg
```

The DocSys module contains one public function, one INIT function, and one EXIT function. The INIT function initializes the filewide STATIC variable *aSystem[ ]* to the appropriate values. Since the array is a filewide static variable, only those routines within the object module have access to it. Within the DocBase module, there may be a need to obtain these values; therefore a PUBLIC function called SystemIni( ) is created only to return the array *aSystem[ ]*.

## User-Defined Functions

Practically every example in this book uses a function in one form or another. But Clipper has never really differentiated between a procedure and a function: They both were symbols in the symbol table that when called would be referenced and executed. This is why a function and a procedure cannot share the same name, and why a function or a procedure cannot have the same name as a .PRG file. But several other similarities, some of them somewhat surprising to many Clipper programmers, can in turn be drawn from this fact. Since there is no difference between a function and a procedure, we can call a procedure as if it were a function:

```
function Main()

  cls
  SubRoutine()

procedure SubRoutine()

   // rest of code
```

Even though SubRoutine( ) is defined as a "procedure," it can be called like a function. This is why the "DO" command is no longer necessary: A function call can be used in its place. We can also see this identity of procedures and functions in the definition of the SET KEY command. This command typically is used like this:

```
SET KEY pF10 TO PopList
```

in which the routine PopList is defined like this:

```
procedure PopList( cProgram, nLineNumber, cVariable )
```

Now, if we were to look at the SET KEY definition in STD.CH, it would show us the following:

```
#command SET KEY <n> TO <proc>                                              ;
     => SetKey( <n>, {|p, l, v| <proc>(p, l, v)} )
```

Here we can see that the name of the routine, PopList, is placed in a code block and passed to the SETKEY( ) function; however, within that code block, the preprocessor adds a pair of parentheses, making the procedure look like a function. So our code defines the routine as a procedure, yet Clipper converts it to a function. Why? There is no difference.

Since there is no difference between a function and a procedure, it must be seen that a procedure has a value, since functions "return" values. In the past, the value of a procedure was a logical false (.F.); now, the value is a NIL, which is a valid data type. The point to this is one of the most fundamental concepts in the Clipper language: **Everything has a value!** Even an expression has a value (the last item listed in the expression). The only difference between an expression and a function is that there is a public name associated with a function while an expression just "is" when it is executed. However, if it was possible to store an expression to a variable, then the expression's value would be the value of the variable. In addition, if this were possible, then the expression (or variable) could be passed from subroutine to subroutine, and the expression would have a name: the name of the variable. This is precisely the definition of a code block.

## Summary

Only a few key areas of the Clipper language demand strict attention; the rest may be mastered in the course of the development cycle. The material in this chapter is one of those areas. Without careful attention to such concepts as data types, storage class, and parameter passing, without the discipline to know the impact each point has on an application, and without the confidence to know when and where to use these various features, the application will die without having the chance to live. It is that important. Give yourself time to go over this chapter again fully before pressing on into any of the other "technical" areas of the language.

# 6

# Clipper Command Reference

This chapter contains a complete listing of standard commands in Clipper 5.2. The basic way to read these commands is as follows. The <exp> symbol represents the expression that is passed to the command. If the expression doesn't require a specific data type—meaning any data type may be used in the command—the symbol will be <expX>. Use the following table as a guide:

| | |
|---|---|
| <expC> | Character expression |
| <expN> | Numeric expression |
| <expL> | Logical expression |
| <expB> | Block expression |
| <expD> | Date expression |
| <expA> | Array expression |
| <expX> | Mixed data type expression |

A number after any of the capitalized letters (e.g., <expC1>) represents the parameter position in the argument list (e.g., <expL5> is a logical expression that is the fifth parameter); if the expression accepts multiple data types, the position value will appear immediately after the <exp> characters (e.g., <exp6>).

If a pair of brackets ([ ]) appears in the command syntax, that portion of the command is optional. Any repeating parameters, options, or expressions will be symbolized with a "..." character set. If a semicolon character (;) is used, the line in question will continue onto the next.

Keep in mind that all of the commands have functional translations and one can see what those functional equivalents are by turning to STD.CH and reading the preprocessor translations. For more information on the preprocessor, please see Chapter 3.

For information on functions that appear in the "See Also" section, see Chapter 7.

Both commands and statements are included in this chapter. In those cases where the item is a command, it will be entitled "COMMAND" as opposed to being entitled "STATEMENT."

# !

| | |
|---|---|
| **COMMAND** | Runs a DOS command, an executable program, or a batch file. |
| **SYNTAX** | `! <expC1>` |
| **PARAMETER** | `<expC1>`   DOS command, program, or batch file to execute |
| **DESCRIPTION** | Execute the specified DOS command or program from the Clipper application.<br><br>For this command to execute properly, there must be enough memory to load both an additional copy of COMMAND.COM as well as the operation or program that is being called. For internal DOS commands, only the amount of memory required by COMMAND.COM needs to be allotted.<br><br>COMMAND.COM must be available on the path specified in COMSPEC, which may be set in CONFIG.SYS.<br><br>COMMAND.COM has a different memory footprint in each version of DOS, which must be calculated accordingly. |
| **NOTE** | The ! <expC1> command syntax is a compatibility command and may not be supported in future versions. Use the RUN command instead. |
| **SEE ALSO** | RUN |

# ?

| | |
|---|---|
| **COMMAND** | Outputs an expression. |
| **SYNTAX** | `? [ <expX1>] [, <expX2> ...]` |
| **PARAMETERS** | Any expression |
| **DESCRIPTION** | This operator evaluates and displays the value of the given expression. Assuming that output is being sent to the screen, the placement of expressions listed with this command will be dependent on the value of MAXCOL( ). If the current column position exceeds MAXCOL( ), the expression will wrap to the next line and an internal row counter will be incremented. If the value of this counter exceeds MAXROW( ), the screen will scroll up one line. If the device is set to the printer and it has been activated via the SET PRINTER ON command, the row and column position of the printer head (PROW( ) and PCOL( )) will be updated as the expression is displayed. Otherwise, the ROW( ), COL( ) functions are updated instead. If the output device has been redirected to an alternate file via the SET ALTERNATE TO <filename> and SET ALTERNATE ON commands, neither ROW( ), COL( ), PROW( ), or PCOL( ) will be updated. |

| | |
|---|---|
| **NOTE** | The command causes a carriage return/line feed character combination to be issued BEFORE the expression(s) contained in the parameter list is displayed. |
| **SEE ALSO** | ??, @ ... SAY |
| **EXAMPLE** | See the CLEAR MEMORY command. |

## ??

| | |
|---|---|
| **COMMAND** | Outputs an expression. |
| **SYNTAX** | `?? [ <expX1>] [, <expX2> ...]` |
| **PARAMETERS** | Any expression |
| **DESCRIPTION** | This operator evaluates and displays the value of the given expression. Assuming that output is being sent to the screen, the placement of expressions listed with this command will be dependent on the value of MAXCOL( ). If the current column position exceeds MAXCOL( ), the expression will wrap to the next line and an internal row counter will be incremented. If the value of this counter exceeds MAXROW( ), the screen will scroll up one line. If the device is set to the printer and it has been activated via the SET PRINTER ON command, the row and column position of the printer head (PROW( ) and PCOL( )) will be updated as the expression is displayed. Otherwise, the ROW( ), COL( ) functions are updated instead. If the output device has been redirected to an alternate file via the SET ALTERNATE TO <filename> and SET ALTERNATE ON commands, neither ROW( ), COL( ), PROW( ), or PCOL( ) will be updated. |
| **NOTE** | This command differs from the ? command in that no carriage return/line feed character combination will be issued unless it is specifically identified in the expression list. |
| **SEE ALSO** | ?, @ ... SAY |
| **EXAMPLE** | See the CLEAR MEMORY command. |

## @ ... BOX

| | |
|---|---|
| **COMMAND** | Displays a box with given string borders and fill characters. |
| **SYNTAX** | `@ <expN1>, <expN2>, <expN3>, <expN4> BOX <expC5> [COLOR <expC6>]` |

| | | |
|---|---|---|
| **PARAMETERS** | <expN1> | Top row coordinate |
| | <expN2> | Left column coordinate |
| | <expN3> | Bottom row coordinate |
| | <expN4> | Right column coordinate |
| | <expC5> | Border string with optional fill character |
| | <expC6> | Color string |

**DESCRIPTION** This command draws a box on the screen at the specified top, left, bottom, and right coordinates. The border string may be either eight or nine characters in length. The first eight characters refer to the eight different characters that make up the border of a box, starting with the upper left corner. The ninth character, if specified, represents the character that will be used to fill the entire boxed region that is WITHIN the specified bordered area. If a color string is specified, then that color will be used when the boxed area is created. The system color will not be set to this color value, however.

**NOTE** The cursor is placed at the <expN1> + 1, <expN2> + 1 coordinate. In addition, since graphic characters are explicitly used in <expC5>, this command may not be appropriate for code that will be ported to other video monitors on other platforms.

**SEE ALSO** @ ... TO, @ ... CLEAR ... TO

**EXAMPLE** See the CLEAR MEMORY command.

## @ ... CLEAR ... TO

**COMMAND** Clears and/or draws a frame in a given box area.

**SYNTAX** `@ <expN1>, <expN2> [CLEAR [TO] <expN3>, <expN4>]`

| | | |
|---|---|---|
| **PARAMETERS** | <expN1> | Top row coordinate |
| | <expN2> | Left column coordinate |
| | <expN3> | Bottom row coordinate |
| | <expN4> | Right column coordinate |

**DESCRIPTION** This command clears a region of the screen. That region is determined by the number of coordinates specified in the command. If only two parameters are used, a rectangular region of the screen is cleared from those coordinate points down to the value of MAXROW( ) and over to the value of MAXCOL( ). If all four coordinates are used, the region of the screen that is cleared begins at <expN1>, <expN2> and ends at <expN3>, <expN4>. In either case, the value of ROW( ) and COL( ) after the screen has been cleared will be the value of <expN1>, <expN2> and the cursor will be placed at those coordinates.

If the CLEAR command is NOT specified, the region that will be cleared will begin at the specified coordinates of <expN1>, <expN2>; however, the screen will be cleared only for the line. The line will be cleared up to the position indicated by the value of <expN1>, MAX-COL( ).

**SEE ALSO**  @ ... BOX, CLEAR, SCROLL( )

**EXAMPLE**  See the CLEAR MEMORY command.

# @ ... GET

**COMMAND**  Creates a GET object and displays it to the screen.

**SYNTAX**  @ <expN1>, <expN2>, [SAY <expC3> [PICTURE <expC4>] COLOR <expC5> ] GET <expX6> [PICTURE <expC7>] [WHEN <expL8>] [VALID <expL9> / RANGE <expX10>, <expX11>] [COLOR <expC12>]

**PARAMETERS**
| | |
|---|---|
| <expN1> | Row coordinate |
| <expN2> | Column coordinate |
| <expC3> | Message to display |
| <expC4> | Character expression of PICTURE displayed |
| <expC5> | Color to be used for the SAY expression |
| <expX6> | Variable/field name |
| <expC7> | Character expression of PICTURE to get |
| <expL8> | Logical expression to allow GET |
| <expL9> | Logical expression to validate GET input |
| <expX10> | Lower RANGE value |
| <expX11> | Upper RANGE value |
| <expC12> | Color string to be used for the GET expression |

**DESCRIPTION**  This command adds a GET object to the reserved array variable named GETLIST[ ] and displays it to the screen. The field or variable to be added to the GET object is specified in <expX6> and is displayed at row, column coordinate <expN1>, <expN2>.

If the SAY clause is used, <expC3> will be displayed starting at <expN1>, <expN2>, with the field variable <expX6> displayed at ROW( ), COL( ) + 1. If <expC4>, the picture template for the SAY expression <expC3>, is used, all formatting rules contained will apply. See the TRANSFORM( ) function for further information.

If <expC7> is specified, the PICTURE clause of <expC7> will be used for the GET object and all formatting rules will apply. See the table below for GET formatting rules.

If the WHEN clause is specified, when <expL8> evaluates to a logical true (.T.) condition, the GET object will be activated; otherwise, the

GET object will be skipped and no information will be obtained via the screen. The name of a user-defined function returning a logical true (.T.) or false (.F.) or a code block may be specified in <expL8>. This clause is not activated until a READ command or READMODAL( ) function call is issued.

If the VALID clause is specified and <expL9> evaluates to a logical true (.T.) condition, the current GET will be considered valid and the get operation will continue onto the next active GET object. If not, the cursor will remain on this GET object until aborted or until the condition in <expL9> evaluates to true (.T.). The name of a user-defined function returning a logical true (.T.) or false (.F.) or a code block may be specified in <expL9>. This clause is not activated until a READ command or READMODAL( ) function call is issued.

If the RANGE clause is specified instead of the VALID clause, the two inclusive range values for <expX6> must be specified in <expX10> and <expX11>. If <expX6> is a date data type, <expX10> and <expX11> must also be date data types; if <expX6> is a numeric data type, <expX10> and <expX11> must also be numeric data types. If a value fails the RANGE test, a message of OUT OF RANGE will appear in the SCOREBOARD area (row = 0, col = 60). The RANGE message may be turned off if the SET SCOREBOARD command or SET( ) function is appropriately toggled.

**NOTE**  GET functions/formatting rules:

| | |
|---|---|
| @A | Allows only alphabetic characters. |
| @B | Numbers will be left-justified. |
| @C | All positive numbers will be followed by CR. |
| @D | All dates will be in the SET DATE format. |
| @E | Dates will be in British format; numbers in European format. |
| @K | Allows a suggested value to be seen within the GET area but clears it if any noncursor key is pressed when the cursor is in the first position in the GET area. |
| @R | Nontemplate characters will be inserted. |
| @S<expN> | Allows horizontal scrolling of a field or variable that is <expN> characters wide. |
| @X | All negative numbers will be followed by DB. |
| @Z | Displays zero values as blanks. |
| @! | Forces uppercase lettering. |
| @( | Displays negative numbers in parentheses with leading spaces. |
| @) | Displays negative numbers in parentheses without leading spaces. |

GET templates/formatting rules:

| | |
|---|---|
| A | Only alphabetic characters allowed. |
| N | Only alphabetic and numeric characters allowed. |
| X | Any character allowed. |
| L | Only T or F allowed for logical data. |
| Y | Only Y or N allowed for logical data. |
| 9 | Only digits, including signs, will be allowed. |
| # | Only digits, signs, and spaces will be allowed. |
| ! | Alphabetic characters are converted to uppercase. |
| $ | Dollar signs will be displayed in place of leading spaces for numeric data types. |
| * | Asterisks will be displayed in place of leading spaces for numeric data types. |
| . | Position of decimal point. |
| , | Position of comma. |

Format PICTURE functions may be grouped together as well as used in conjunction with a PICTURE template; however, a blank space must be included in the PICTURE string if there are both functions and templates.

**SEE ALSO** @ ... SAY, READ, TRANSFORM( ), Chapter 16, "CA-Clipper Objects."

**EXAMPLE** See the READ command or Chapter 18, "Data Entry Options."

## @ ... PROMPT

**COMMAND** Activates a light-bar menu selection at the given coordinates.

**SYNTAX** `@ <expN1>, <expN2> PROMPT <expC3> [MESSAGE <expC4>]`

**PARAMETERS**
    <expN1> Row coordinate to begin PROMPT item
    <expN2> Column coordinate to begin PROMPT item
    <expC3> Actual prompt string
    <expC4> Associated message string

**DESCRIPTION** This command generates a single light-bar menu item and places its position into the internal menu item stack. This stack is used to report which menu item was selected. The stack counter is independent of the contents of the string <expC3> as well as the values of <expN1> and <expN2>.

The menu item is drawn in the current standard color or in the unselected color, whichever is used. The current menu item is depicted by the color specified by the enhanced color set.

All prompt items are activated by a call to the MENU TO command. You can have up to 32 PROMPT commands in a single MENU TO activation stack.

As each PROMPT is displayed on the screen, the values of ROW( ) and COL( ) are updated accordingly.

If used, the MESSAGE string in <expC4> is displayed for each PROMPT item. The location of the string is determined by the setting of the SET MESSAGE TO command.

Color bytes in between PROMPT and/or MESSAGE strings will not individually control the color of certain characters within either <expC3> or <expC4>.

**SEE ALSO**     MENU TO, SET MESSAGE, SET WRAP

**EXAMPLE**      See the MENU TO command or Chapter 17.

## @ ... SAY

**COMMAND**      Displays data to specified coordinates of the current device.

**SYNTAX**
```
@ <expN1>, <expN2> SAY <expX3> [PICTURE <expC4>]
    [COLOR <expC5>]
```

**PARAMETERS**
| | |
|---|---|
| <expN1> | Row coordinate |
| <expN2> | Column coordinate |
| <expX3> | Value to display |
| <expC4> | PICTURE format |
| <expC5> | Color string |

**DESCRIPTION**  This command displays the contents of <expX3> at row, column coordinates <expN1>, <expN2>. A PICTURE clause may be specified in <expC4>. If the current device is set to the printer, the output will go to the printer; the default is for all output to go to the screen.

**NOTE**         For a complete list of PICTURE templates and functions, see the TRANSFORM( ) function.

**SEE ALSO**     @ ... GET, SET DEVICE, TRANSFORM( )

**EXAMPLE**      See the READ command or Chapter 18.

# @ ... TO

| | |
|---|---|
| **COMMAND** | Draws a border. |
| **SYNTAX** | `@ <expN1>, <expN2> TO <expN3>, <expN4> [DOUBLE] [COLOR <expC5>]` |
| **PARAMETERS** | <expN1>   Top row coordinate<br><expN2>   Left column coordinate<br><expN3>   Bottom row coordinate<br><expN4>   Right column coordinate<br><expC5>   Color expression |
| **DESCRIPTION** | This command draws either a single-lined or double-lined border at the specified coordinates. If the DOUBLE command option is not used, the default is a single-lined border. There is no SINGLE command option.<br><br>Once finished, the value of ROW( ) and COL( ) will be <expN1> + 1 and <expN2> + 1, respectively. In addition, the cursor will be positioned on those coordinates. |
| **SEE ALSO** | @ ... BOX, @ ... CLEAR |
| **EXAMPLE** | See the CLEAR MEMORY command. |

# ACCEPT

| | |
|---|---|
| **COMMAND** | Waits for user input and assigns it to a character variable. |
| **SYNTAX** | `ACCEPT [<expC1>] TO <expC2>` |
| **PARAMETERS** | <expC1>   option prompting string<br><expC2>   name of character variable to contain user input |
| **DESCRIPTION** | This command waits for user input. If specified in <expC1>, a prompt message will be displayed at the current ROW( ) + 1 position; the message will always start at column 0. This means that the ACCEPT command is similar to ? or the QOUT( ) function in that a carriage return/line feed combination is issued prior to the command's operation.<br><br>The input string can be up to 255 characters long. If the cursor position within the input string exceeds the value of MAXCOL( ), the input will continue onto the next line.<br><br>The input variable, regardless of the intended contents, will be a character data type memory variable. |
| **NOTE** | The ACCEPT command generates a Clipper wait state; therefore, the SET KEY TO command will have an effect on it. In addition, the ESC |

key is not supported; however, the BACKSPACE, LEFT ARROW, and ENTER/RETURN keys are. The ENTER key terminates the input string. If no input is given, the default value for <expC2> will be a NULL byte.

**SEE ALSO**   @ ... SAY, @ ... GET, INPUT, WAIT

**EXAMPLE**   See the WAIT command.

## ANNOUNCE

**STATEMENT**   Declares a module identifier.

**SYNTAX**   ANNOUNCE <expC1>

**PARAMETER**   <expC1>   Name of module to be identified

**DESCRIPTION**   This statement defines a module identifier which means that the linker will recognize this module <expC1> when it is REQUESTED. An ANNOUNCE can represent a collection of routines and therefore can only appear once in a .PRG file. In addition, only unique names can be used for <expC1>. If <expC1> is the same name as a function or a .PRG file, an error message will be generated.

**SEE ALSO**   INIT PROCEDURE, EXIT PROCEDURE, REQUEST, EXTERNAL

**EXAMPLE**   Please see Chapter 5.

## APPEND BLANK

**COMMAND**   Appends a blank record to a database file.

**SYNTAX**   APPEND BLANK

**PARAMETER**   None

**DESCRIPTION**   This command adds a new record to the end of the database in the currently selected work area. All fields in that database will be given empty data values. That is to say character fields will be filled with blank spaces, date fields will be filled with CTOD(" / / "), numeric fields with 0, logical fields with .F., and memo fields with NULL bytes. The header of the database is not updated until the record is flushed from the buffer and the contents are written to the disk.

Under a networking environment, APPEND BLANK performs an additional operation; it also attempts to lock the newly added record. If the database file is currently exclusively locked or if a locking assignment is made to LASTREC( ) + 1, NETERR( ), the testing for failure of a network function, will return a logical true (.T.) immediately after the APPEND BLANK command. The NETERR( ) function does not unlock the locked record.

**SEE ALSO**  APPEND FROM, FLOCK( ), RLOCK( ), UNLOCK, NETERR( ), ADDREC( )

**EXAMPLE**  See the APPEND FROM command.

## APPEND FROM

**COMMAND**  Adds records to a database from another database file or an ASCII file.

**SYNTAX**
```
APPEND FROM <expC1> [FIELDS <expC2>] [<expC3>]
[WHILE <expL4>] [FOR <expL5>] [SDF / DELIMITED
[WITH BLANK] <expC6> ] [VIA <expC7>]
```

**PARAMETERS**
- \<expC1\>  Source file to append from
- \<expC2\>  Listing of fields to be copied
- \<expC3\>  Scope of operation: NEXT, RECORD, or ALL
- \<expL4\>  Logical condition for WHILE condition
- \<expL5\>  Logical condition for FOR condition
- \<expC6\>  Field delimiter used in source file
- \<expC7\>  Name of RDD

**DESCRIPTION**  The APPEND FROM command copies records to the current database from the ASCII file or .DBF file specified in <expC1>. If you don't wish to include all of the fields, from the source database in the target database, use the FIELD command line verb along with the <expC2> parameter to select the field(s) that you want APPENDed to the target. The fields that are being APPENDed must correspond to existing fields in the target database.

The <expC3> parameter defines the scope condition for the APPEND FROM command. Acceptable values for <expC3> are NEXT<expn> (where <expN> represents a group of records starting at the current record), RECORD<expn> (where <expN> is the record number), REST that extend the scope from the current record to the end of the database, and ALL the default scope condition, that selects all of the records in the database for processing. The selected record(s) is APPENDed as long as the WHILE condition <expL4> remains a logical true (.T.), and the record(s) meet the FOR condition specified in <expL5>.

There are three types of acceptable ASCII source files, SDF, DELIMITED and DELIMITED [WITH BLANK]. The DELIMITED command verb identifies the source file as a text file in which the length of the fields and records are variable and the character fields are surrounded by the default delimiter, double quotation marks. If the Delimiter is not a double quotation mark, use the <expC6> parameter to change the default entry. DELIMITED [WITH BLANK] also refers to variable length fields and records. It is different from DELIMITED inasmuch as the character fields are free of quotes and the fields in general are separated by a space. SDF files have fixed length records and fields

**NOTE**  If a field has the same name in the target database as in the source but is of a different data type, a run-time error will occur. Also, if a field in the target database is of greater length than the source database, the data coming into the target file will be padded to the appropriate length. On the other hand, if the target field is shorter than the source, the field will be truncated. If both fields are numeric in data type but the source field is greater in width than the target, another run-time error will take place. The date field(s) in the source file must follow the YYYYMMDD format to avoid unpredictable results.

On a network, this command does not require that the target database be used exclusively or that the file be completely locked. When called, the source database/file is opened in read-only mode. If access to the source file is denied, a run-time error will be displayed.

If the DELIMITED WITH clause is specified, that portion of the command line MUST appear as the last clause.

If SET DELETED ON is in effect and there are records marked for deletion in the source database, those records will not be added. Records in the target database marked for deletion will not be affected.

The VIA clause specifies the name of the RDD <expC7> to be used to input the data. If it is not specified, then the RDD in the current work area will be used.

**SEE ALSO**  APPEND BLANK, COPY TO, Chapter 13

**EXAMPLE**

```
 1 * File       Appbdemo.prg
 2 * Compile    Rmake sample /dFILE:appbdemo
 3
 4 #Command SET LASTKEY TO <VALUE> => Keyboard(<Value>) ; INKEY(0)
 5 #define pTRUE .T.
 6
 7 procedure Main()
 8
 9   if file( "Ontap.dbf" )
10     use Ontap new         // Open up a database
11     copy to Temp          // Copy all fields to file TEMP
12     use Temp              // No NEW clause can use same area!
13     Temp->( ShowVals() )  // Just look at current record values
14     append blank          // Append a blank record to the bottom
15     Temp->( ShowVals() )  // Just look at current record values
16     AddRec()              // Appends a blank record to the bottom
```

```
17     Temp->(showVals() )  // Just look at the current record values
18
19     qout( "Press any key to remove all records!" )
20     inkey(0)
21     zap        // This removes all of the records!
22
23     append from Notap // A standard APPEND FROM
24     cls               // Since cursor is in position, no need for function
25     go top            // The record pointer needs to be re-wound after an
26                       // APPEND FROM command
27     devout( "Press ESC when finished looking!" )
28     while   !lastkey() = 27
29       dbedit( 1,0,maxrow(),maxcol() )    // Show the records!
30     enddo
31
32     // The following uses the FIELDS clause in the COPY TO command to
33     // generate a new database with only the specified fields.
34     // In addition to this, the user-defined function Showrec() will
35     // simply display the current record at the specified coordinates.
36     // Since the return value of this function is always a logical true,
37     // the operation will work on all records.
38
39     @ maxrow()-1, 0 clear
40     devpos( maxrow(), 0 )
41     devout( "Record: " )
42
43     use Ontap
44     copy fields Ontap->files, Ontap->sizes to Temp ;
45         while ShowRec( maxrow(), 9 )
46     use Temp
47     cls
48     devout( "Press ENTER when finished looking!" )
49     SET LASTKEY TO CHR(13)    // Removes Esc from the buffer
50     while   !lastkey() = 27
51       dbedit( 1,0, maxrow(), maxcol() ) // Show records & only 2 fields
52     enddo
53     cls
54     ferase( "Temp.dbf" )
55   endif
56
57 *********************
58
59 static procedure Showvals()
60
61   local nCount    // This is for the FOR...NEXT loop
62
63   cls     // No need to position cursor... it is with this command
64   devout( "Record Number:" )
65   devout( recno() )
66   for nCount := 1 to fcount()
67     devpos( nCount, 0 )
68     devout( "Field Name: " )
69     devout( field(nCount) )      // This is the same as FIELDNAME()
70     devpos( nCount, 30)
71     devout( "Value: " )
72     devout( fieldget( nCount ) ) // Value of field!
73   next
```

```
74    wait
75
76 *********************
77
78 static function Showrec( nRow, nCol )
79
80    @ nRow, nCol say recno()
81
82    return( pTRUE )
83
84 // End of File: Appbdemo.prg
```

# AVERAGE

| | |
|---|---|
| **COMMAND** | Calculates the mean value of numeric fields in the currently selected database. |
| **SYNTAX** | AVERAGE <expN1> TO <expN2> [<expC3>] [FOR <expL4>] [WHILE <expL5>] |
| **PARAMETERS** | <expN1>    List of the numeric fields that are to be averaged for each record processed |
| | <expN2>    List of the numeric variables that are to receive the results of the calculations |
| | <expC3>    Scope of the operation |
| | <expL4>    Logical FOR condition |
| | <expL5>    Logical WHILE condition |
| **DESCRIPTION** | The AVERAGE command averages the values in one or more numeric fields <expN1> and stores the result(s) to a numeric variable(s) <expN2>. Each variable in the receiving variable list <expN2> must correspond to a field in the field list <expN1>. The <expC3> parameter is used to define the scope of the calculation. Acceptable values for <expC3> are NEXT <expN> (where <expN> represents a group of records starting at the current record), RECORD <expN> (where <expn> is the record number), REST which extend the scope from the current record to the end of the database, and ALL the default scope condition, that selects all of the records in the database for processing. The selected records must meet the FOR condition specified in <expL4> and the AVERAGE function will continue processing as long as the WHILE condition <expL5> remains a logical true (.T.). |
| **NOTE** | Fields with values of zero will still be included in calculating the averages. To avoid this, specifically rule out those fields with zero balances by using a FOR conditional expression. |
| **SEE ALSO** | COUNT, SUM, TOTAL |
| **EXAMPLE** | See the TOTAL command. |

## BEGIN SEQUENCE

| | |
|---|---|
| **COMMAND** | Creates a sequence of commands for BREAK. |
| **SYNTAX** | ```
BEGIN SEQUENCE
  <command statements>
  [BREAK [<exp1>]]
  <command statements>
  [RECOVER [USING <expC2>] ]
  <command statements>
END [SEQUENCE]
``` |
| **PARAMETERS** | <expX1>   Any expression passed to <expC2> |
| | <expC2>   The name of a variable to contain a value from BREAK |
| **DESCRIPTION** | This command structure can be used for various program control, branching, and exception and error handling routines. If the BREAK <expX1> statement is encountered, program control is given to the RECOVER statement (if there is one) at the same level of nesting, or to the statement immediately following the END statement of the same level. If a value is specified in the BREAK command structure, that value will be passed to the variable listed in the <expC2> statement within the RECOVER USING command construct. |
| **NOTE** | A BREAK command may be placed within lower-level subroutines, thereby allowing a RETURN (explicit or assumed) to be performed between a BEGIN SEQUENCE and RECOVER command. |
| | Any DO WHILE, ENDDO, FOR, or NEXT statement outside the control of a BEGIN SEQUENCE, RECOVER, BREAK, or END SEQUENCE must have the ending control outside as well. A LOOP command WITHIN a RECOVER statement is permitted as long as the BEGIN SEQUENCE control is surrounded by the DO WHILE construct. |
| | You may nest up to 15 sets of BEGIN ... END SEQUENCE operations. If nested, each set should relate to one specific task or operation within the application. |
| **SEE ALSO** | RETURN, ERRORBLOCK( ), Chapter 19 |
| **EXAMPLE** | See Chapter 19. |

## CALL

| | |
|---|---|
| **COMMAND** | Executes an assembly language or C subroutine. |
| **SYNTAX** | `CALL <expC1> [WITH <expC2>]` |
```

**PARAMETERS**  &lt;expC1&gt;   Name of the subroutine to execute
&lt;expC2&gt;   Name of the variables passed to the subroutine

**DESCRIPTION**   This command executes a program module that has been compiled or assembled separately. All modules should follow these rules:

1. The procedure must be defined as a FAR routine and must end with a FAR return instruction.

2. All parameters passed to the subroutine are placed on the stack following C conventions.

3. Each parameter is a FAR (4-byte) pointer to the actual parameter value. Using the WORD( ) function allows a 2-byte binary value to be passed instead.

4. The DX:BX as well as the ES:BX registers contain a copy of the first 4 bytes of information from the parameter list.

5. All subroutines must preserve the BP, SS, SI, DI, ES, and DS registers and must clear the direction flag.

6. Any supporting library for the subroutine must be linked into the application as well.

7. Character strings are passed by reference and are null-terminated.

8. Data item lengths must be preserved.

9. All subroutines must be in the "Intel 8086 relocatable object file format" and must have the .OBJ file extension.

10. Numeric parameters follow IEEE floating-point logic. To pass a parameter as an integer, the WORD( ) function is needed. Note that values passed using the WORD( ) function are restricted to a range of 32,767.

11. Date parameters are passed as a 4-byte (long) FAR value containing the Julian day number.

12. Logical values are passed as 2-byte binary integer FAR values containing either a 0 (for a logical false (.F.)) or a 1 (or nonzero) (for a logical true (.T.)).

13. You may pass only up to seven expressions of any data type to the specified subroutine.

**NOTE**   This command is considered a compatibility command and is not recommended for future use. Instead, use of the Extend System and its calling conventions are the prescribed method for calling outside subroutines.

**SEE ALSO**   WORD( )

## CANCEL

| | |
|---|---|
| **COMMAND** | Terminates program execution. |
| **SYNTAX** | CANCEL |
| **PARAMETER** | None |
| **DESCRIPTION** | This command terminates the Clipper application. In doing so, it will close all open files after attempting to write information from buffers, and return control to the operating system.<br><br>When an application terminates successfully, a DOS error level of 0 is set. If, however, a run-time error is experienced, the value of the DOS error level is set to 1 or to the value of ERRORLEVEL( ) last recorded within the application. |
| **NOTE** | This is a compatibility command and may not be supported in future versions. |
| **SEE ALSO** | RETURN, QUIT |
| **EXAMPLE** | See the QUIT command. |

## CLEAR

| | |
|---|---|
| **COMMAND** | Clears the screen and pending GETs. |
| **SYNTAX** | CLEAR |
| **PARAMETER** | None |
| **DESCRIPTION** | This command clears the screen, cancels any pending GETs, and reinitializes the GET object to an empty array. |
| **NOTE** | Do not use the CLEAR command within a subroutine called by the SET KEY TO command or by a subroutine called by a WHEN or VALID clause in a data entry stream. This command will cancel the pending environment. |
| **SEE ALSO** | CLEAR SCREEN / CLS, CLEAR GETs |

## CLEAR ALL

| | |
|---|---|
| **COMMAND** | Resets the entire environment. |
| **SYNTAX** | CLEAR ALL |

| | |
|---|---|
| **PARAMETER** | None |
| **DESCRIPTION** | This command clears all public and private memory variables, closes all open databases and their associated indexes and memo files, selects the first work area, closes any open FORMAT and ALTERNATE files, clears any pending READ command, and releases the GET object. |
| **NOTE** | This is a compatibility command and may not be supported in future versions. |
| **SEE ALSO** | CLEAR GETs, CLEAR MEMORY, CLOSE, SET( ), RELEASE |

## CLEAR GETS

| | |
|---|---|
| **COMMAND** | Clears a pending GET/READ stack. |
| **SYNTAX** | `CLEAR GETS` |
| **PARAMETER** | None |
| **DESCRIPTION** | This command clears the pending READ command and reinitializes the GET stack to an empty GET object model. |
| **SEE ALSO** | READ, CLEAR, CLOSE, RELEASE, @...GET, SET TYPEAHEAD |
| **EXAMPLE** | See the READ command or Chapter 18. |

## CLEAR MEMORY

| | |
|---|---|
| **COMMAND** | Clears out all private and public memory variables. |
| **SYNTAX** | `CLEAR MEMORY` |
| **PARAMETER** | None |
| **DESCRIPTION** | This command releases all memory variables from the system. If a memory variable is CLEARED rather than RELEASED, it needs to be reinitialized before being used in the application. LOCAL and STATIC variables are unaffected by this command because these variables do not have any symbolic token associated with them in the main load of an application. The CLEAR MEMORY command, in other words, refers to all symbolically defined variables and clears their address locations in memory. |

**SEE ALSO**     RELEASE, CLEAR

**EXAMPLE**

```
 1 :  * File       Dispdemo.prg
 2 :  * Compile    Rmake sample /dFILE:dispdemo
 3 :
 4 :  #define pPAUSE INKEY(4)
 5 :
 6 :  procedure Main()
 7 :
 8 :     local cVar1
 9 :     local cVar2
10 :     local cVar3
11 :
12 :     private cVar4
13 :     cVar4 := 'space'
14 :     cVar1 := cVar2 := replicate( "*", 9 )
15 :     cVar2 := replicate( chr(219), 8 ) + " "
16 :     cVar3 := replicate( chr(178), 9 )
17 :
18 :     cls                      // This clears the screen
19 :     run dir *.* /w           // This gets the directory!
20 :     @ 10,10 clear to 20,70   // This clears the screen at
21 :                              // the specified coordinates
22 :     pPAUSE                   // This pauses four seconds
23 :     @ 10,10 to 20,70 double  // This now draws a double line
24 :     @ 11,11 say ""           // Places the cursor at coordinates
25 :     ?? "Any key ...."        // The output is displayed
26 :     inkey(0)                 // This is the pause!
27 :     @ 11,11,19,69 box cVar1  // A box of **** w/o space
28 :     pPAUSE
29 :     @ 12,12,18,68 box cVar2  // A box of CHR(219) w/space
30 :     pPAUSE
31 :     @ 13,13,17,67 box cVar3  // A box of CHR(178) w/o space
32 :     pPAUSE
33 :     @ 15,40 clear            // This clears a rectangular region
34 :     wait
35 :     clear screen             // This clears the screen
36 :     ? "The TYPE of cVar1 is: "        // Single ? command
37 :     ?? valtype( cVar1 )               // Data TYPE of C
38 :     ? "The TYPE of cVar4 is: "        // Double ?? command
39 :     ?? valtype( cVar4 )               // Data TYPE of VAR
40 :     clear memory                      // Clears memory
41 :     ? "The TYPE of cVar1 is: ", valtype( cVar1 )
42 :     ? "The TYPE of cVar4 is: ", valtype( "cVar4" )
43 :
44 :  // Since CVAR1 is a local variable, CLEAR MEMORY does not affect it, but
45 :  // CVAR4 is a private variable and the command DOES affect it.  Since the
46 :  // variable is released, a RUN-TIME error should be generated when the
47 :  // VALTYPE() of VAR is displayed.  Unfortunately, there is really no other
48 :  // way to show this.
49 :
50 :  // End of File: Dispdemo.prg
```

## CLEAR SCREEN | CLS

| | |
|---|---|
| **COMMAND** | Clears the video screen. |
| **SYNTAX** | `CLEAR SCREEN | CLS` |
| **PARAMETER** | None |
| **DESCRIPTION** | This command clears the screen. Any pending GETs or active memory variables are NOT cleared. |
| **SEE ALSO** | @ ... CLEAR TO, CLEAR GETs, CLEAR |
| **EXAMPLE** | See the CLEAR MEMORY command. |

## CLEAR TYPEAHEAD

| | |
|---|---|
| **COMMAND** | Clears the keyboard buffer. |
| **SYNTAX** | `CLEAR TYPEAHEAD` |
| **PARAMETER** | None |
| **DESCRIPTION** | This command clears the keyboard buffer of any pending character(s). |
| **SEE ALSO** | KEYBOARD, SET TYPEAHEAD |
| **EXAMPLE** | See the KEYBOARD command. |

## CLOSE

| | |
|---|---|
| **COMMAND** | Closes a database or other open files. |
| **SYNTAX** | `CLOSE <expC1>` |
| **PARAMETER** | <expC1>   File type |
| **DESCRIPTION** | The CLOSE command closes a database in the current work area.<br>    The CLOSE <alias> command closes a database in the work area with the specified alias name.<br>    The CLOSE ALTERNATE command closes an open alternate file.<br>    The CLOSE DATABASES command closes all open databases and their associated index files.<br>    The CLOSE ALL command closes all open databases and all associated indexes. In addition, it closes all format files, and it also moves the selected work area pointer to the 1st position. |

The CLOSE FORMAT command closes all open FORMAT files.

The CLOSE INDEXES command closes all open index files that are currently active. This command only works in the currently active work area.

**SEE ALSO** USE, QUIT, SET( ), RETURN, SET ALTERNATE, SET INDEX

**EXAMPLE** See the USE command.

## COMMIT

**COMMAND** Flushes the memory buffer and performs a hard-disk write.

**SYNTAX** COMMIT

**PARAMETER** None

**DESCRIPTION** This command performs a hard-disk write for all work areas. Before the disk write is performed, all buffers are flushed to DOS. The files remain open during the disk write.

**NOTE** The disk write feature will only work with versions of DOS 3.3 or higher. Otherwise this command only empties the buffer.

**SEE ALSO** SKIP 0

## CONTINUE

**COMMAND** Resumes a pending LOCATE.

**SYNTAX** CONTINUE

**PARAMETER** None

**DESCRIPTION** This command resumes a search initiated by a LOCATE FOR command by continuing to search for records that meet the search criterion. If a CONTINUE is successful in its search, the record pointer moves to that record; otherwise, the EOF( ) marker is set to a logical true (.T.) and the record pointer jumps to the last record.

**SEE ALSO** LOCATE

**EXAMPLE** See the LOCATE command.

## COPY FILE

| | |
|---|---|
| **COMMAND** | Copies a file. |
| **SYNTAX** | COPY FILE <expC1> TO <expC2>[< >] |
| **PARAMETERS** | <expC1>    Filename of source file<br><expC2>    Filename of target file |
| **DESCRIPTION** | This command makes an exact copy of <expC1> and names it <expC2>. Both files must have the file extension included; the drive and the directory names must also be specified if they are different from the default drive and/or directory. <expC2> can also refer to a DOS device (e.g., LPT1). This command does not observe the SET PATH TO or the SET DEFAULT TO settings. The COPY FILE command resides in the EXTEND Library. |
| **SEE ALSO** | ERASE, COPY TO, RENAME, FRENAME( ), FERASE( ) |
| **EXAMPLE** | See the ERASE command. |

## COPY STRUCTURE

| | |
|---|---|
| **COMMAND** | Copies a database structure to a new database. |
| **SYNTAX** | COPY STRUCTURE [FIELDS <expC1>... TO <expC2> |
| **PARAMETERS** | <expC1>    Field name<br><expC2>    Target file name |
| **DESCRIPTION** | This command copies only the structure of the currently selected database to the file named <expC2>. All fields are copied unless the FIELDS clause is used, in which case the names of the fields will be specified in <expC1> separated by commas.<br>    The names of the fields to be copied cannot be in a macro substitution. The fields must be defined in separate variables or coded as literals in the program or procedure file. The name of the file specified as <expC2> must include the drive and directory designator if the file is to be created in a directory other than the default drive or directory. If no file extension is given to <expC2>, the file will contain a .DBF extension. If <expC2> exists, the file will be overwritten. |
| **SEE ALSO** | COPY TO, COPY STRUCTURE EXTENDED, CREATE, DBCREATE( ) |
| **EXAMPLE** | See the CREATE command. |

## COPY STRUCTURE EXTENDED

**COMMAND**  Copies field names and definitions to a database file.

**SYNTAX**  `COPY STRUCTURE EXTENDED TO <expC1>`

**PARAMETER**  <expC1>    Target filename

**DESCRIPTION**  This command creates a new database consisting of only four fields: FIELD_NAME, FIELD_TYPE, FIELD_LEN, and FIELD_DEC. Each record contains the field information for one field in the currently selected database. The new database, <expC1>, therefore contains the structural information for a new database file that can be created with the CREATE FROM command.

The format for a STRUCTURE EXTENDED database is

| Name | Type | Length | Decimals |
|---|---|---|---|
| FIELD_NAME | C | 10 | 0 |
| FIELD_TYPE | C | 1 | 0 |
| FIELD_LEN | N | 3 | 0 |
| FIELD_DEC | N | 4 | 0 |

**NOTE**  Because Clipper supports character fields of up to 64K, the length of a character field can exceed the maximum value of the FIELD_LEN field. Therefore, a formula is used to determine the lengths of character fields greater than 255 bytes. The FIELD_DEC field is used to store the number of 256-byte increments that are used in the field to-be-created, with the remainder being stored in the FIELD_LEN field. In other words, if a field to-be-created will have a length of 512, a 2 would be stored in the FIELD_DEC field and a 0 in the FIELD_LEN field. Then, when the database is created, the following calculation will automatically take place:

`FIELD_LEN = (FIELD_DEC * 256) + FIELD_LEN`

**SEE ALSO**  COPY STRUCTURE, CREATE, CREATE FROM, DBSTRUCT( ), DBCREATE( )

**EXAMPLE**  See the CREATE command.

## COPY TO

**COMMAND**  Copies records from one database to another database file or an ASCII file.

**SYNTAX**  COPY [FIELDS <expC1>] TO <expC2> [<expC3>]
[WHILE <expL4>] [FOR <expL5>] [SDF / DELIMITED
[WITH BLANK] <expC6> ] [VIA <expC7>]

**PARAMETERS**
<expC1>   Listing of fields to be copied
<expC2>   Target/receiving file
<expC3>   Scope of operation: NEXT, RECORD, or ALL
<expL4>   Logical condition for WHILE condition
<expL5>   Logical condition for FOR condition
<expC6>   Field delimiter used in source file
<expC7>   Name of Replaceable Database Driver (RDD)

**DESCRIPTION**   The COPY TO command copies records from the current database to the ASCII (.txt) file or database (.dbf) file specified in <expC2>. If you don't wish to include all of the fields, from the source database in the target database, use the FIELD command line verb along with the <expC1> parameter to select the field(s) that you want copied to the target. The fields that are being copied must correspond to existing fields in the target database.

The <expC3> parameter defines the scope condition for the COPY TO command. Acceptable values for <expC3> are NEXT<expN> (where <expN> represents a group of records starting at the current record), RECORD<expN> (where <expN> is the record number), REST that extend the scope from the current record to the end of the database, and ALL the default scope condition, that selects all of the records in the database for processing. The selected record(s) is copied as long as the WHILE condition <expL4> remains a logical true (.T.), and the record(s) meet the FOR condition specified in <expL5>.

There are three types of acceptable ASCII target files, SDF, DELIMITED and DELIMITED [WITH BLANK]. The DELIMITED command verb identifies the recipient file as a text file in which the lengths of the fields and records are variable and the character fields are surrounded by the default delimiter—double quotation marks. If the Delimiter is not a double quotation mark, use the <expC6> parameter to change the default entry. DELIMITED [WITH BLANK] also refers to variable length fields and records. It is different from DELIMITED inasmuch as the character fields are free of quotes and the fields in general are separated by a space. SDF files have fixed length records and fields.

**NOTE**   If a field with the same name in the target database is of a different data type in the source database, a run-time error will occur. Also, if a field in the target database is of greater length than the source database, the data coming into the target file will be padded to the appropriate length. On the other hand, if the target field is shorter than the source, the field will be truncated. If both fields are numeric in data type but the source field is greater in width than the target, another run-time error will take place. The date field(s) in the source file must follow the YYYYMMDD format to avoid unpredictable results.

At the time of the COPY TO command, if there is an open index in the selected work area and SET ORDER is other than 0, the records will be copied based on the controlling index key as oppose to the the order they were entered in.

On a network, this command does require that the target database be used exclusively or that the file be completely locked.

If the DELIMITED WITH clause is specified, that portion of the command line MUST appear as the last clause.

If SET DELETED ON is in effect and there are records marked for deletion in the source database, those records will not be added. Records in the target database marked for deletion will not be affected.

The VIA clause specifies the name of the RDD <expC7> to be used to input the data. If it is not specified, then the RDD in the current work area will be used.

**SEE ALSO** APPEND FROM, COPY FILE, COPY STRUCTURE, SET DELETED, Chapter 13

**EXAMPLE** See the APPEND FROM command.

# COUNT

**COMMAND** Totals the number of records in a database to a memory variable or a field.

**SYNTAX**
```
COUNT TO <expN1> [<expC2>] [WHILE <expL3>]
[FOR <expL4>]
```

**PARAMETERS**
- <expN1>  Name of a memory variable
- <expC2>  Scoping condition
- <expL3>  WHILE condition
- <expL4>  FOR condition

**DESCRIPTION** This command counts how many records in the currently active database meet a specific condition and stores that value to a memory variable or a field named <expN1>.

The command's scope is defined by <expC2>. Possible scopes are ALL, RECORD <expN>, NEXT <expN>, or REST; the default is ALL if <expC2> is not specified.

The command will perform the operation WHILE <expL3> remains a logical true (.T.). Once it is a logical false, the operation will stop.

234  Straley's Programming with Clipper 5.2

The command will perform the operation FOR all records matching the condition in <expL4>. Only those records matching the condition will be processed.

**SEE ALSO** AVERAGE, SUM, TOTAL, DBEVAL( )

**EXAMPLE** See the TOTAL command.

## CREATE

**COMMAND** Creates a STRUCTURE EXTENDED database file.

**SYNTAX** `CREATE <expC1>`

**PARAMETER** `<expC1>` Filename

**DESCRIPTION** This command creates an empty database file with four fields: FIELD_NAME, FIELD_TYPE, FIELD_LEN, and FIELD_DEC.

| Name | Type | Length | Decimals |
| --- | --- | --- | --- |
| FIELD_NAME | C | 10 | 0 |
| FIELD_TYPE | C | 1 | 0 |
| FIELD_LEN | N | 3 | 0 |
| FIELD_DEC | N | 4 | 0 |

Since character fields may be greater than 255 bytes, a formula is used to define the length of character fields greater than 255 bytes. Because of this, the field length information will be stored in the following manner:

```
FIELD_LEN := INT( length % 256 ); FIELD_DEC := INT( length / 256 )
```

If <expC1> already exists, it will be overwritten.

**NOTE** The CREATE command automatically USES the database that it creates. Issue a CLOSE DATABASE or a USE command immediately following this command in order to flush the buffers and update the database.

**SEE ALSO** COPY STRUCTURE EXTENDED, CREATE FROM, DBCREATE( ), DBSTRUCT( )

**EXAMPLE**

```
1 : * File       Creademo.prg
2 : * Compile    RMake sample /dFILE:creademo
3 : #command SET LASTKEY TO <value> => KEYBOARD(<VALUE>); INKEY(0)
4 : #xtranslate SHOWVALUES() => ;    // Substitute a UDF!
5 :    cls
```

```
 6 :    devout("Press ESC to move on....")
 7 :    while !lastkey=27
 8 :    dbedit(1,0,maxrow(),maxcol())
 9 :    ENDDO
10 :    SET LASTKEY to chr(0)
11 :    cls
12 :
13 : procedure Main()
14 :
15 :    use Notap new      // Regular database
16 :    SHOWVALUES()       // Show the values via DBEDIT()
17 :    Showfields()       // Show the fields of NOTAP
18 :
19 :    cls
20 :    copy structure extended to Newfile    // STR Extend the Notap file
21 :    use Newfile new                       // Use this file in old area
22 :    SHOWVALUES()                          // Show the values via DBEDIT()
23 :
24 :    devout("Working...")
25 :    append blank    // Add a new record to structure extended file
26 :    Newfile->field_name := "DEMO"
27 :    Newfile->field_type := "C"
28 :    Newfile->field_len  := 10
29 :    Newfile->field_dec  := 0
30 :
31 :    // And now, we simply recreate the NOTAP file using the new structure,
32 :    // but be aware that the records within NOTAP must be saved first and
33 :    // APPEND INTO the new file
34 :
35 :    close databases           // This closes ALL databases
36 :    create Temp from Newfile  // This converts the 4-fielded database in
37 :                              // use to TEMP.
38 :    close databases           // The database must be closed
39 :
40 :    use Temp new
41 :    Showfields()
42 :    append from Notap
43 :    use                       // Closes the file in current use
44 :    delete file Notap.dbf     // This deletes the file NOTAP
45 :    rename Temp.dbf to Notap.dbf    // And this renames the file
46 :
47 :    close databases    // Just to be sure!
48 :    use Notap new      // Once again, open the NOTAP file
49 :    SHOWVALUES()       // Show the values via DBEDIT()
50 :    Showfields()       // Show the fields of NOTAP
51 :
52 :    close databases    // Close all files
53 :    erase Newfile.dbf
54 :
55 :    create Template    // An empty structure extended database
56 :    Template->( Addvalue( {"LASTNAME", "C", 10, 0} ) )
57 :    Template->( Addvalue( {"FIRSTNAME", "C", 15, 0} ) )
58 :    Template->( Addvalue( {"AGE", "N", 2, 0} ) )
59 :    Template->( Addvalue( {"BDATE", "D", 8, 0} ) )
60 :    Template->( Addvalue( {"AMOUNT", "N", 10, 2} ) )
61 :
62 :    go top
```

```
63 :    Showfields()      // Potential field values from new database
64 :    use
65 :    create Demo from Template   // Demo from TEMPLATE Structure
66 :    close database              // The database must be closed
67 :    erase Template
68 :    use Demo new
69 :    SHOWVALUES()                // What were fields are now records
70 :
71 : ********************
72 :
73 : static procedure Showfields() // Could be a preprocessor translation!
74 :
75 :    aeval( dbstruct(), ;
76 :           {|aField| qout(aField[1],aField[2],aField[3],aField[4])} )
77 :    wait
78 :
79 : ********************
80 :
81 : static procedure AddValue( aData )
82 :
83 :    append blank
84 :    field->field_name := aData[1]
85 :    field->field_type := aData[2]
86 :    field->field_len  := aData[3]
87 :    field->field_dec  := aData[4]
88 :
89 : // End of File: Creademo.prg
```

# CREATE FROM

| | |
|---|---|
| **COMMAND** | Creates a new database from a STRUCTURE EXTENDED database. |
| **SYNTAX** | CREATE <expC1> FROM [<expC2>] [NEW] [ALIAS <expC3>] [VIA <expC4>] |
| **PARAMETERS** | <expC1>   Target Filename |
| | <expC2>   Source Filename |
| | <expC3>   Alias name of the file being created |
| | <expC4>   Name of Replaceable Database Driver to use in creating <expC1> |
| **DESCRIPTION** | This command creates a new database file named <expC1> from a STRUCTURE EXTENDED database named <expC2>. The records in <expC2> become the fields in <expC1>. |

If the NEW clause is specified, then the file <expC1> will be immediately opened in a new work area; otherwise, when the file <expC1> is created, it will be immediately opened in the current work area.

If <expC3> is specified, then that will be the ALIAS name of the file <expC1> when it is opened. If this is not specified, then the root name of <expC1> will be the alias name used.

The VIA clause allows for the name of a Replaceable Database Driver <expC4> to be used in the creation of the file <expC1>. It is important to keep in mind that the structure of the structure extended file <expC2> is of the same database drive type when creating <expC1>.

**SEE ALSO** COPY STRUCTURE, COPY STRUCTURE EXTENDED, CREATE, DBCREATE( ), DBSTRUCT( )

**EXAMPLE** See the CREATE command.

---

# DECLARE

---

**COMMAND** Initializes an array to a specified size.

**SYNTAX**

```
DECLARE <expA1>[<expN2>] [, <expA3>[<expN4>]...]
```

**PARAMETERS**

| | |
|---|---|
| <expA1> | Array name |
| <expN2> | Array size |
| <expA3> | Array name |
| <expN4> | Array size |

**DESCRIPTION** This command establishes a PRIVATE array named <expA1> of <expN2> elements. Additional arrays may be DECLAREd on the same command line by separating each declaration with a comma. The brackets ([ ]) around <expN2> and <expN4> must be included when working with arrays.

Once initialized, each data element within the array is set to a NIL data type. Keep in mind that an empty array will have 0 elements, the LEN( ) function returns 0, and the EMPTY( ) function will return logical true (.T.). The VALTYPE( ) function will return a letter "A" for even an empty array.

**NOTE** This is a compatibility command and may not be supported in future versions.

**SEE ALSO** PRIVATE, PUBLIC, ARRAY ( ), Chapter 10, "Arrays"

**EXAMPLE**

```
* File       Decldemo.prg
* Compile    RMake sample /dFILE:decldemo

memvar getlist

procedure Main()

   local aData := {}   // The new way to create an array
   local aTemp4
   local aTemp5
   local aTemp6
```

```
12 :  //   private aTemp1    // These variables CAN NOT BE assigned a data
13 :  //   private aTemp2    // storage class because we are using the DECLARE
14 :  //   private aTemp3    // statement
15 :
16 :  clear                                          // This needs GETLIST!!!!
17 :  declare aTemp1[10], aTemp2[4], aTemp3[1]  // The command way
18 :  aTemp4 := array(5)                             // The function way
19 :  aTemp5 := aTemp6 := array(3)
20 :
21 :  qout( "Name      Length     Data Type" )
22 :
23 :  qout( "aData",  len(aData ), space(6), valtype(aData ) ) // a  0   A
24 :  qout( "aTemp1", len(aTemp1), space(6), valtype(aTemp1) ) // b  10  A
25 :  qout( "aTemp2", len(aTemp1), space(6), valtype(aTemp1) ) // c  4   A
26 :  qout( "aTemp3", len(aTemp1), space(6), valtype(aTemp1) ) // d  1   A
27 :  qout( "aTemp4", len(aTemp1), space(6), valtype(aTemp1) ) // e  5   A
28 :  qout( "aTemp5", len(aTemp1), space(6), valtype(aTemp1) ) // f  3   A
29 :  qout( "aTemp6", len(aTemp1), space(6), valtype(aTemp1) ) // g  3   A
30 :
31 :  // End of File: Decldemo.prg
```

# DELETE

**COMMAND**       Marks records in a database for deletion.

**SYNTAX**        DELETE [<expC1>] [WHILE <expL2>] [FOR <expL3>]

**PARAMETERS**    <expC1>   Scoping statement
                  <expL2>   Logical condition for WHILE condition
                  <expL3>   Logical condition for FOR condition

**DESCRIPTION**   This command marks a record(s) for deletion in the selected work area. Without any conditional or scoping clause, only the current record is marked for deletion. Both the WHILE and FOR conditions may exist simultaneously. The FOR condition will take precedence.

If SET DELETED is ON and the current record is marked for deletion, it will still be visible, since deleted records are only visible at the time they are marked for deletion. Once the record pointer is moved to another record, they are no longer acknowledged or visible on the screen.

If SET DELETED is OFF, deleted records will be distinguished by an asterisk in the first position when the DISPLAY or LIST command displays them on a screen, or sends them to a printer or file.

In a networking situation, this command requires that if only one record is to be deleted, that record must be locked prior to issuing the DELETE command. If, on the other hand, several records are to be

|   |   |
|---|---|
|   | deleted, the file must be locked or used exclusively before the records may be marked for deletion. |
| **NOTE** | Deleted records are not visible when set deleted is on. But they are part of the database and can be recalled via use of the RECALL command. Use the PACK command to permanently remove them. |
| **SEE ALSO** | PACK, RECALL, SET DELETED, RLOCK( ), FLOCK( ) |
| **EXAMPLE** | See the PACK command. |

## DELETE FILE

| | |
|---|---|
| **COMMAND** | Deletes a file from the disk. |
| **SYNTAX** | `DELETE FILE <expC1>` |
| **PARAMETER** | `<expC1>`   Name of file to remove |
| **DESCRIPTION** | This command removes a file from the disk. The use of a drive, directory, and wild-card skeleton operator is allowed. The file extension is required. The SET DEFAULT and SET PATH commands do not affect this command.<br>The file must be considered closed by the operating system before it may be deleted. |
| **SEE ALSO** | ERASE |
| **EXAMPLE** | See the ERASE command. |

## DELETE TAG

| | |
|---|---|
| **COMMAND** | Removes an Order from an Order Bag. |
| **SYNTAX** | `DELETE TAG <expC1> [IN <expC2>],`<br>`[ <expC3>[ IN <expC4>]]` |
| **PARAMETERS** | `<expC1>`   Name of Order to be removed<br>`<expC2>`   Name of the Order Bag file<br>`<expC3>`   Name of other Orders to be removed<br>`<expC4>`   Name of additional Order Bag file |
| **DESCRIPTION** | This command removes the Order `<expC1>` from the disk file Order Bag `<expC2>`. If `<expC2>` is not specified, every Order Bag in the current or specified work area will be searched. Additional pairs of |

Order tags and Order Bags may be included in <expC3> and <expC4> respectively as long as the pairs are separated by a comma and reside in the selected or current work area. If <expC2> isn't specified and the Order Tag <expC1> isn't unique, DELETE TAG removes the first occurrence of the Order Tag <expC1> it encounters. The selected work area needs to be indexed in order for the DELETE TAG command to work. In the event that the Order tag to be deleted is the controlling index tag, when it is deleted, the records will revert to their entry order.

**NOTE** If the Order Tag or Order Bag doesn't exist in the current work area, a run-time error will be generated.

**SEE ALSO** SET FILTER, SET ORDER

**EXAMPLE** Please see Chapter 12.

# DIR

**COMMAND** Displays directory names and file information.

**SYNTAX** DIR [<expC1>]

**PARAMETER** <expC1>    DOS file specification including, but not requiring, drive, path, and DOS file skeleton

**DESCRIPTION** This command displays the filenames, number of records, size of the files in bytes, and the date of the last update for all databases on the designated drive and/or path.

If <expC1> is not specified, a search of "*.DBF" will be made. Other files may be displayed by using DOS wild cards in the <expC1> expression as in a DOS DIR command.

**NOTE** This is a compatibility command and may not be supported in future versions.

**SEE ALSO** DIRECTORY( ) function

**EXAMPLE**

```
1 : * File      Ddirdemo.prg
2 : * Compile   Rmake sample /dFILE:ddirdemo
3 :
4 : procedure Main()
5 :
6 :    cls
7 :    devout( "Press any key for the database files!" )
8 :    inkey(0)
9 :    dir         // This has a different LOOK-AND-FEEL
```

```
10 :    wait "Now, how about the .PRG files!"
11 :    cls
12 :    dir *.PRG    // than THIS command!
13 :
14 : // End of File: Ddirdemo.prg
```

# DISPLAY

**COMMAND**  Displays the records of a database file.

**SYNTAX**  DISPLAY <expX1> [TO PRINTER] [TO FILE <expC2>] [<expC3>] [FOR <expL4>] [WHILE <expL5>] [OFF]

**PARAMETERS**
- <expX1>   List of fields to display
- <expC2>   Filename to port to
- <expC3>   Scope
- <expL4>   Logical expression for FOR condition
- <expL5>   Logical expression for WHILE condition

**DESCRIPTION**  This command allows the contents of selected fields to be displayed by placing the field names in a character expression list <expX1>. Each field must be separated by a comma.

If the TO PRINT option is specified, the output of this command will be echoed to the printer as they are displayed on the screen.

If the TO FILE option is specified, the output of this command will be echoed to an alternate file named <expC2> as well as to the screen. If a file extension is not specified, a .TXT extension will be added.

<expC3> is the scope condition for this command. Valid scopes include NEXT <expN> (number of records to be displayed, where <expN> is the number of records), REST (all records from the current record position), and ALL (all records). The default is ALL.

The two logical expressions (<expL3> and <expL4>) may work in conjunction with one another, where <expL4> is the logical expression for the FOR condition (for records to be displayed within a given range) and <expL5> for the WHILE condition (for records to be displayed, meeting the condition until it fails).

The OFF clause turns off the display of the record number when records are being displayed.

**SEE ALSO**  LIST, DBEVAL( )

**EXAMPLE**  See the LIST command.

## DO

| | |
|---|---|
| **COMMAND** | Begins execution of a procedural subroutine. |
| **SYNTAX** | `DO <expC1> [WITH <expX2> [, ...] ]` |
| **PARAMETERS** | `<expC1>` Filename or subroutine name <br> `<expX2>` Parameter list |
| **DESCRIPTION** | This command begins execution of a program file or a subroutine. If specified, the WITH clause passes a parameter list to the called subroutine. Up to 128 arguments may be passed, each separated by a comma. The parameter list passed to the subroutine need not match the number of parameters accepted within the subroutine. <br><br> Since procedures and functions are referred to internally as the same entity, the value of a procedure is a NIL data type. The execution of a called procedural subroutine is terminated with the RETURN command, the end-of-file marker, or the beginning of a new function or procedure. |
| **NOTE** | This is a compatibility command and may not be supported in future versions. |
| **SEE ALSO** | EVAL( ), FUNCTION, PROCEDURE |

## DO CASE...ENDCASE

| | |
|---|---|
| **STATEMENT** | Executes branch operations for structured program control. |
| **SYNTAX** | ```
DO CASE
CASE <expL1>
   <commands>
[CASE <expL2>]
   <commands>
[OTHERWISE]
   <commands>
ENDCASE
``` |
| **PARAMETERS** | `<expL1>` Logical expression for first CASE test <br> `<expL2>` Logical expression for subsequent CASE tests |
| **DESCRIPTION** | This command allows for structured program control by selecting a specified set of commands to be performed based on the evaluation of a set of logical expressions. Once a CASE structured condition has been evaluated to be logically true (.T.), those command statements within |
```

the CASE branch will be executed. Once completed, program flow will begin at the line immediately following the ENDCASE command.

This command is identical to the IF command construct where the beginning CASE command relates to the initial IF condition and each subsequent CASE command relates to a subsequent ELSEIF command, the OTHERWISE command relates to the ELSE command, and the ENDCASE command relates to the ENDIF command.

Since the DO CASE and IF commands are identical, an appropriate use is in programming situations where nested branching controls are needed. In these cases, alternating between a DO CASE and a nested IF, or an IF command and a nested DO CASE, may help maintain the program flow.

**SEE ALSO**     DO WHILE, FOR, IF, IF( )

**EXAMPLE**     See the MENU TO command.

# DO WHILE...ENDDO

**STATEMENT**     Executes a programming loop.

**SYNTAX**
```
DO WHILE <expL1>
    <commands>
ENDDO
```

**PARAMETER**     <expL1>     Logical expression evaluating to true or false

**DESCRIPTION**     This command allows statements within the DO WHILE and associated ENDDO structure to be repeated as long as the expression <expL1> evaluates to a logical true. The beginning of the loop will be evaluated and reexecuted when either the ENDDO command or the LOOP statement is encountered. If the condition is no longer true, execution of commands within the loop will terminate and the line immediately following the ENDDO command will be processed. If the EXIT command is encountered within the loop, the loop will be terminated, and program flow will continue to the command statements immediately after the ENDDO command.

The DO keyword is not needed: WHILE <expL1> alone is acceptable.

**SEE ALSO**     FOR ... NEXT, DBEVAL( ), LOOP, EXIT

## EJECT

| | |
|---|---|
| **COMMAND** | Issues a command to advance the printer to the top of the form. |
| **SYNTAX** | EJECT |
| **PARAMETER** | None |
| **DESCRIPTION** | This command issues a form-feed command to the printer. If the printer is not properly hooked up to the computer, an error will NOT be generated and the command will be ignored.<br><br>Once completed, the values of PROW( ) and PCOL( ), the row and column indicators for the printer, will be set to 0. Their values, however, may be manipulated before or after issuing an EJECT by using the DEVPOS( ) function. |
| **SEE ALSO** | DEVPOS( ), SET PRINTER, PROW( ), PCOL( ) |

## ERASE

| | |
|---|---|
| **COMMAND** | Removes a file from the disk. |
| **SYNTAX** | ERASE <expC1> |
| **PARAMETER** | <expC1>    Name of file to remove |
| **DESCRIPTION** | This command removes a file from the disk. The use of a drive, directory, and wild-card skeleton operator is allowed for the root of the filename. The file extension is required. The SET DEFAULT and SET PATH commands do not affect this command.<br><br>The file must be considered closed by the operating system before it may be deleted. |
| **SEE ALSO** | DELETE FILE, FERASE( ) |

**EXAMPLE**

```
1  * File       Erasdemo.prg
2  * Compile    RMake sample /dFILE:erasdemo
3
4  procedure Main()
5
6     local cOutfile := "BADTAP.DBF"
7     local cInfile  := "NOTAP.DBF"
8
9     cls
10    qout( "Before the COPY FILE command" )
11    ShowExist( cInfile )
12    ShowExist( cOutfile )
```

```
13    qout()
14    QOUT()
15
16    copy file (cInfile) to (cOutfile)
17    qout( "After the COPY FILE command" )
18    ShowExist( cInfile )
19    ShowExist( cOutfile )
20    qout()
21    qout()
22    wait
23
24    rename (cOutfile) to "Tempfile.dbf"
25    qout( "And now AFTER the RENAME command..." )
26    ShowExist( cInfile )
27    ShowExist( cOutfile )
28    ShowExist( "Tempfile.dbf" )
29    qout()
30    qout()
31
32    erase Tempfile.dbf
33    qout( "After the ERASE command." )
34    ShowExist( cInfile )
35    ShowExist( cOutfile )
36    ShowExist( "Tempfile.dbf" )
37    qout()
38    qout()
39    wait
40
41    cls
42    qout( "Before the COPY FILE command" )
43    ShowExist( cInfile )
44    ShowExist( cOutfile )
45    qout()
46    qout()
47
48    copy file (cInfile) to (cOutfile)
49    qout( "After the COPY FILE command" )
50    ShowExist( cInfile )
51    ShowExist( cOutfile )
52    qout()
53    qout()
54
55    delete file (cOutfile)
56    qout( "After the DELETE command." )
57    ShowExist( cInfile )
58    ShowExist( cOutfile )
59    qout()
60    qout()
61    wait
62    cls
63
64 *******************
65
66 static procedure ShowExist( cFile )
67
68    // The STATIC command means that this procedure will only be called by a
69    // routine within this program file.  There is no symbolic reference to
```

```
70      // this routine in the symbol table
71
72      qout( "Name of file:" )
73      qqout( padr( cFile,15) )
74      qqout( "Does the file exist? " )
75      qqout( if( file(cFile), "Yes", "No, it doesn't" ) )
76
77 // End of File: Erasdemo.prg
```

# EXIT

**STATEMENT**   Aborts a programming loop.

**SYNTAX**   EXIT

**PARAMETER**   None

**DESCRIPTION**   This command causes program flow to immediately jump out of a controlling DO WHILE ... ENDDO or FOR ... NEXT loop and process the line immediately after the ENDDO or NEXT.

**SEE ALSO**   DO WHILE ... ENDDO, FOR ... NEXT, LOOP

**EXAMPLE**

```
Procedure Main
  local Ncount
  for nCount := 1 TO 10
    wait
    if lastkey() == 27    // The ESC key
      exit                // Get out of the loop
    endif
  next
return NIL
```

# EXTERNAL

**STATEMENT**   Specifies external routines that may be used by a program.

**SYNTAX**   EXTERNAL <expC1>

**PARAMETER**   <expC1>   List of subroutines that may be called from within the application

**DESCRIPTION**   This statement is used to declare a symbol during the compiling stage to be used later by the linker for resolution purposes. This allows a procedure or function to be called by a macro, a code block, a REPORT FORM or LABEL FORM command, an indexing routine or expression, or by the ACHOICE( ), MEMOEDIT( ), and DBEDIT( ) functions at

*Clipper Command Reference* 247

|  |  |
|---|---|
| | run time, although that subroutine may not be visible and recognized at compile time.
This command tells the linker to be sure to bring in the definitions of these external routines. |
| **NOTE** | Clipper functions may not be made EXTERNAL. If they are required and are not directly called, a dummy call to them must be made for a proper external reference to be created.
In addition, this statement may not be supported in future versions of Clipper and is replaced by the REQUEST command. |
| **SEE ALSO** | DO, REQUEST, ANNOUNCE |

## FIELD

| | |
|---|---|
| **STATEMENT** | Declares a list of database field names. |
| **SYNTAX** | `FIELD <expX1> [, <expX2>...] [IN <expC3>]` |
| **PARAMETERS** | `<expX1>` A field name
`<expX2>` Additional field names
`<expC3>` An alias name |
| **DESCRIPTION** | This command declares the names of fields <expX1> (and <expX2> and following) with an optional alias identifier as <expC3> for each. This allows Clipper to resolve any reference to a field specified in the field list by viewing it as a field when it is not explicitly referenced by an alias. If a field is not listed in this list and it is not explicitly tagged with an alias identifier, it may be viewed as a memory variable, which may cause run-time errors. This command has no effect on memory variables or on field references buried within a macro expansion. |
| **SEE ALSO** | MEMVAR, LOCAL, STATIC, FUNCTION, PROCEDURE, Chapter 1 on "Compiler Switches." |
| **EXAMPLE** | See the CREATE command. |

## FIND

| | |
|---|---|
| **COMMAND** | Searches for a value in a database whose order is based on a controlling index. |
| **SYNTAX** | `FIND <expC1>` |
| **PARAMETER** | `<expC1>` Character expression |

| | |
|---|---|
| **DESCRIPTION** | This command searches the active indexed database for the first record that matches the character expression <expC1>, which must be a literal string or a variable enclosed in parentheses.
If <expC1> is found, the value of FOUND( ) will be a logical true (.T.) and the value for EOF( ) will be a logical false (.F.). If the expression is not found, FOUND( ) will return a logical false (.F.) and EOF(<N>) will return a logical true (.T.). |
| **NOTE** | This is a compatibility command and may not be supported in future versions. |
| **SEE ALSO** | SEEK, SET SOFTSEEK, SET( ), FIYBD( ), EOF( ) |
| **EXAMPLE** | See the SEEK command. |

## FOR...NEXT

| | |
|---|---|
| **STATEMENT** | Executes a programming loop for a specified number of iterations. |
| **SYNTAX** | ```
FOR <expN1> := <expN2> TO <expN3> [STEP <expN4>]
   <commands>
   [EXIT]
   [LOOP]
NEXT
``` |
| **PARAMETERS** | <expN1>  Loop control counter
<expN2>  Starting value of loop counter
<expN3>  Ending value of loop counter
<expN4>  Amount to increment loop counter |
| **DESCRIPTION** | This command allows the repeated execution of a series of commands while a numeric variable, <expN1>, takes on values ranging from <expN2> to <expN3>. Upon entering the loop, the memory variable <expN1> will be initialized to <expN2>. Thereafter, with each iteration of the loop, the value of <expN1> may increment or decrement by the amount of the STEP expression <expN4>.
While the memory variable and expressions are mandatory, the STEP operator is optional. It may increment or decrement the value of <expN1>. If the STEP clause is not used, a STEP of +1 is the default.
The EXIT statement will unconditionally terminate the loop and execute the statement immediately following the NEXT statement.
The LOOP statement will unconditionally jump to the top of the FOR ... NEXT loop, perform the necessary increment or decrement to <expC1>, and continue processing as expected. |
| **SEE ALSO** | DO WHILE, DBEVAL( ), AEVAL( ) |
```

# FUNCTION

**STATEMENT**  Declares a subroutine as a user-defined function.

**SYNTAX**
```
[INIT] [EXIT] [STATIC] FUNCTION <expC1>
[( <expX2>... )]
<commands>
RETURN( <expX> )
```

**PARAMETERS**  
&lt;expC1&gt;  Function name  
&lt;expX2&gt;  LOCAL (formal) parameters  
&lt;expX&gt;  The return value of the function

**DESCRIPTION**  This command initializes a user-defined function named &lt;expC1&gt;. The name of the subroutine may be of any length, with the first 10 bytes being significant. If specified, &lt;expX2&gt; and following will contain a list of LOCAL parameters to be accepted by this function. This is identical to the parameters command, except for a difference in data storage class (the parameters command creates private memory variables).

If the STATIC clause is specified, the function &lt;expC1&gt; may only be called by those procedures or functions declared in the same source file.

If the INIT clause is specified, then the specified function will be called when the compiled application is initially executed; there is no need for a formal reference to it. In addition, the INIT clause acts like a STATIC in that there is no formal symbolic reference to it in the symbol table. Multiple program files may contain INIT FUNCTIONS with the same name. The order in which all of the INIT routines are called is based on the linking order of the application.

If the EXIT clause is specified, then the specified function will be called when the application is about to stop being processed. There is no need for a formal reference to it. In addition, the EXIT clause acts like a STATIC in that there is no formal symbolic reference to it in the symbol table. Multiple program files may contain the EXIT FUNCTIONs with the same name. The order in which all of the EXIT routines are called is based on the linking order of the application.

The return value of the function is expressed as &lt;expX&gt; and may be of any data type, including an array or code block.

**NOTE**  For additional information on user-defined functions, see Chapter 5.

**SEE ALSO**  PROCEDURE, PARAMETERS, LOCAL, STATIC, VALTYPE( ), NIL, PCOUNT( )

**EXAMPLE**  Please see Chapter 5.

# GO

| | |
|---|---|
| **COMMAND** | Positions the record pointer at a specific location. |
| **SYNTAX** | `GO[TO] <expN1> / [BOTTOM][TOP]` |
| **PARAMETER** | `<expN1>`   If used, it is the record number or record identifier |
| **DESCRIPTION** | This command moves the record pointer <expN1> in the currently selected area to the specified record. Typically, <expN1> is the number of a database; however, it can be a record identifier specific to the structure of the data set in the current and active work area. BOTTOM, if used, positions the record pointer at the bottom of the database and TOP positions the record pointer on the first record in the database.

The BOTTOM, TOP, and record number options may not coexist; only one may be issued at a time.

If an index is in use with the database in the active work area, the record moved to as a result of the BOTTOM and TOP clauses is affected by the index key or an active FILTER condition. Otherwise, if no index is active or if no filter condition is present, TOP will move the record pointer to record number 1 and BOTTOM will move it to LASTREC( ).

The GO <expN1> explicit command is not affected by an active index, SET DELETED ON, or the condition in a SET FILTER command. |
| **NOTE** | Issuing a GOTO RECNO( ) command in a network environment will refresh the database and index buffers. This is the same as a SKIP 0 command. |
| **SEE ALSO** | SKIP, RECNO( ), LASTREC( ), EOF( ), BOF( ) |
| **EXAMPLE** | |

```
 1 : * File      Godemo.prg
 2 : * Compile   Rmake sample /dFILE:godemo
 3 : * Note      This shows the commands GO, GO TOP, GO BOTTOM, SKIP, and SKIP
 4 : *          with an ALIAS, as well as the use of the header file EXTCOM.CH
 5 : *          which calls the Clipper internals for these commands and
 6 : *          converts them into function form. This example also touches on
 7 : *          the possibility of working in unselected work areas by simply
 8 : *          calling the function with an alias pointer.
 9 :
10 : procedure Main()
11 :
12 :    use Clients new index Client1
13 :    use Notap new
14 :    go 4
15 :
16 :    cls
17 :    ShowStuff( "4 Records in NOTAP" )
18 :    go top
19 :    ShowStuff( "TOP of NOTAP" )
```

```
20 :    skip -1
21 :    ShowStuff( "Skipped past TOP of NOTAP" )
22 :    go bottom
23 :    ShowStuff( "BOTTOM of NOTAP" )
24 :    skip +1
25 :    ShowStuff( "Skipped past BOTTOM of NOTAP" )
26 :    wait
27 :
28 :    skip 5 alias Clients
29 :
30 :    // The next few command lines are expressions to be performed in the
31 :    // CLIENTS work area.  First the Showstuff() expression will be called,
32 :    // followed by a functionalized form of the commands being talked about
33 :    // in this example.
34 :
35 :    cls
36 :    Clients->( ShowStuff( "6 Records in CLIENTS" ), dbgotop() )
37 :    Clients->( ShowStuff( "TOP of CLIENTS" ), dbskip(-1) )
38 :    Clients->( ShowStuff( "Skipped past TOP of CLIENTS" ), dbgobottom())
39 :    Clients->( ShowStuff( "BOTTOM of CLIENTS" ), dbskip(1) )
40 :    Clients->( ShowStuff( "Skipped past BOTTOM of CLIENTS" ) )
41 :    wait
42 :
43 : *******************
44 :
45 : procedure Showstuff( xExp )
46 :
47 :    qout( padr( xExp, 35) )
48 :    qqout("Record Number: ", recno() )
49 :    qout( space(35) )
50 :    qqout("  Top of file: ", bof() )
51 :    qout( space(35) )
52 :    qqout("  End of file: ", eof() )
53 :    qout()
54 :
55 : // End of File:Godemo.prg
```

# IF...ENDIF

**STATEMENT**    Conditional command branching.

**SYNTAX**       IF <expL1>
                 [ELSEIF] <expL2>
                 [ELSE]
                 ENDIF

**PARAMETERS**   <expL1>   Any logical expression to be evaluated as a primary condition

                 <expL2>   A subsequent logical expression to be evaluated as a possible branching condition

**DESCRIPTION** This command statement allows conditional branching based on the logical expression <expL1> in a structured programming environment.

Nested IF command statements are allowed within the same procedure, function, or program file. All IF command statements must terminate with a corresponding local ENDIF.

The steps that are performed are sequential among the IF and/or ELSEIF conditions. Once a condition is met sequentially in the execution of the program, the following commands are performed until either an ELSEIF, ELSE, or ENDIF command statement is encountered. Once a command branch has finished executing, the command statement immediately following the controlling ENDIF will be executed.

**NOTE** To assist in making code more readable, mix this command within nested DO CASE commands and vice versa.

**SEE ALSO** IF( ), DO CASE ... END CASE, DO WHILE...END DO, FOR..NEXT

**EXAMPLE** See the MENU TO command.

## INDEX

**COMMAND** Creates an index file for a database.

**SYNTAX**
```
INDEX ON <expX1> TO <expC2> [UNIQUE] [<expC3>]
[ FOR <expL4>] [WHILE <expL5>] [ [ EVAL <expL6>]
[ EVERY <expN7>] ] [ASCENDING | DESCENDING]
```

**PARAMETERS**
- <expX1>  Expression to be indexed on
- <expC2>  A filename
- <expC3>  Character string of scope
- <expL4>  Logical condition for the FOR condition
- <expL5>  Logical condition for the WHILE condition
- <expL6>  Logical expression to evaluate on records
- <expN7>  Number of records to perform an evaluation

**DESCRIPTION** This command creates a file <expC2> whose file header contains the key structure specified in <expX1>. This key structure is associated with the database that was open at the time the INDEX command was called. The length of <expX1> may be up to 250 characters, and it may be of a character, date, numeric, or logical data type; only memo fields may not be indexed. If <expX1> is to be a concatenation of items, all items within the expression must be of the same data type to avoid a run-time type conflict error. The order of the index algorithm is the ASCII value of the characters for character data types, numeric order for numeric data types, chronological order for date data types (with blank dates as the lowest date), and logical order for logical data types (with .F. values as the lowest).

If not specified in <expC2>, the default .NTX file extension is used. If other index drivers are used in place of the .NTX drivers within the DBFNTX.LIB file, the extension will vary. For example, for dBASE III or dBASE IV compatible indexes, the default index file extension, if <expC2> does not contain one, is .NDX.

If specified, the UNIQUE clause indicates that only those unique keys for <expX1> will be added to <expC2>.

This command indexes all records in the database, starting with the first record regardless of the state of SET DELETED or the presence or absence of a filtered condition. At the end of the operation, the record pointer will be positioned at the first record in the database.

When the index file is created, it is done exclusively. If in a network environment this should fail, a run-time error would be generated.

The parameter <expC3> determines the scope of the index expression as in the keywords of "NEXT <expN>", "REST", "RECORD <expN>" or ALL, the default scope. The inclusion of a keyword other than ALL means that only a portion of the current database is involved in the index process. It is important to note the indexing scope is not stored in the header of the index file and must be maintained by the programmer.

If specified, the FOR clause allows for a conditional set of records on which the index is created. Only those records meeting the FOR condition in <expL4> are included in the index file. Just like the index expression, up to 250 characters are allowed as part of the FOR condition. Additionally, the expression used in this clause is stored to the index header and may be seen by such global commands as REINDEX.

If specified, the WHILE clause allows for another condition to be tested on each record. As long as <expL5> evaluates to a logical .T., the indexing process will continue. As soon as the expression <expL5> fails, the indexing process will terminate. Keep in mind that this clause and condition is not stored in the index header and must be maintained by the programmer.

If the EVAL clause is specified, then the expression <expL6> will be evaluated either for each record being indexed in the database or in the scope, or every <expN7> record should the EVERY clause be specified as well. Similar to the WHILE condition, when the expression <expL6> returns a logical false (.F.), the indexing operation will stop. Additionally, the expression is not stored in the index header and must be maintained by the programmer.

The ASCENDING clause allows the index keys to be sorted/created in increasing order. This is the default condition of the index; it is not stored in the header of the index file and is understood by the REINDEX operation. If, on the other hand, the DESCENDING clause is specified, then the index is created in decreasing order.

| | |
|---|---|
| **NOTE** | Clipper builds a key based on a blank record and requires that the index key be of a fixed length. If a TRIM( ) is performed in an index expression, a NULL byte will be the size of the index (based on an empty database). Therefore, if a TRIM( ) is necessary, allowance must be made for the largest possible data that might be in the key field. To help facilitate this, the PADR( ) or PADL( ) function should be used in conjunction with the index expression.
| | Indexes may be generated in descending order, but to accomplish this, the key expression must be indexed on the DESCEND( ) of the expression. See the DESCEND( ) function for further information or use the DESCENDING clause as part of the INDEX command. Keep in mind that an index created with the DESCENDING clause does not need the DESCEND( ) function as part of the index expression <expX1> nor does it need to be used with the SEEK or FIND commands (including the DBSEEK( ) function). |
| | User-defined functions may be used within the key expression of the index file. Keep in mind that the function's name will remain in the header of the index file. |
| **SEE ALSO** | DESCEND( ), SET INDEX, SET( ), REINDEX, SET ORDER |
| **EXAMPLE** | See Chapter 12. |

## INPUT

| | |
|---|---|
| **COMMAND** | Enters a value into a variable. |
| **SYNTAX** | `INPUT [<expC1>] TO <expC2>` |
| **PARAMETERS** | <expC1>    Message to be displayed |
| | <expC2>    Name of a variable to receive the input |
| **DESCRIPTION** | This command accepts user input from the keyboard and stores it to the variable named <expC2>. If used, a message will be displayed starting at the leftmost column of the screen at ROW( ) + 1 of the cursor position; the contents of this message are stored within <expC1>. |
| | If <expC2> does not exist or is not a visible LOCAL or STATIC memory variable, the command will treat the variable as a PRIVATE variable. Mathematical expressions are allowed, and up to 255 characters may be entered into the data stream. If the input exceeds MAXCOL( ), the input stream will continue onto the next row. Pressing the Enter key terminates the user input. If no value other than the Enter key has been input, and <expC2> had not been assigned a value previously, a NIL is stored to <expC2>. |

**SEE ALSO**  ACCEPT, READ, @ ... SAY, @ ... GET

**EXAMPLE**  See the WAIT command.

# JOIN

**COMMAND**  Joins two database files to generate a new database file.

**SYNTAX**  JOIN WITH <expC1> TO <expC2> FOR <expL3> [FIELDS <expX4>...]

**PARAMETERS**  
<expC1>  The alias work area or the database filename  
<expC2>  The database file to be created  
<expL3>  Logical expression for FOR condition  
<expX4>  List of field names to be created in the output database

**DESCRIPTION**  This command creates a new database named <expC2> based on two open databases—one in the current work area and the other in the work area specified by the alias of <expC1>—for all records meeting the criteria specified by <expL3>.

The FIELDS command verb singles out fields to be included in the resulting database <expC2>. If the FIELDS command verb is specified, only those fields listed in <expX4> will be created in the target database. Fields from the secondary work area must have their alias name explicitly used in conjunction with this clause. If the FIELDS command verb followed by <expX4> is not used, all fields from the current work area are created in the target database, but no fields from the secondary database will be included.

**NOTE**  For each record in the primary work area, JOIN scans each record in <expC1> and creates a new record whenever the FOR condition specified by <expL3> is satisfied. If there is no FOR condition, the number of records in the new database will equal the product of the number of records in the two open database files. In other words, if four records appear in the secondary work area and 10 records exist in the primary work area, 40 records will be generated in the target database, regardless of what fields are specified.

**SEE ALSO**  COPY TO, APPEND FROM

**EXAMPLE**

```
1 *File      Joindemo.prg
2 * Compile  RMake sample /dFILE:joindemo
3
4 #Command SET LASTKEY TO <Value> => Keyboard(<Value>) ; INKEY(0)
```

```
 5
 6 procedure Main()
 7
 8    cls
 9    use Clients new
10    use Notap new
11
12    Clients->( Showvals() )
13    Notap->( Showvals() )
14
15    cls
16
17    qout("Working on the JOIN command!")
18    join with Clients to Join1 for .t.
19    wait
20    join with Clients to Join2 for Notap->sizes > 5000
21    join with Clients to Join3 for Notap->sizes > 5000 ;
22        fields sizes, files
23
24    use Join1 new
25    use Join2 new
26    use Join3 new
27
28    Join1->( Showvals() )
29    Join2->( Showvals() )
30    Join3->( Showvals() )
31
32 *******************
33
34 static procedure Showvals
35
36    cls
37    devout("Press ESC when finished looking!")
38    devout(space(10))
39    devout("Alias:")
40    devout(alias())
41    devpos(1,0)
42    devout("Fields:")
43    devout(padr(fcount(), 20))
44    devout("Records:")
45    devout(lastrec())
46    set lastkey to chr(13)
47    while !lastkey() = 27
48       dbedit(2,0,maxrow(),maxcol())
49    enddo
50 // End of File: Joindemo.prg
```

# KEYBOARD

**COMMAND**    Stuffs the keyboard with a string.

**SYNTAX**    KEYBOARD <expC1>

**PARAMETER**     <expC1>    String to be processed, one character at a time, by the keyboard processor

**DESCRIPTION**    This command stuffs the input buffer with <expC1>. The number of characters that can be stuffed into the keyboard buffer is controlled by the SET TYPEAHEAD command and may range from 0 to 32,655, with each character appearing in the ASCII range of 0 to 255. None of the extended keys may be stuffed into the keyboard buffer.

Issuing a KEYBOARD(" ") will clear the keyboard buffer.

**SEE ALSO**     SET TYPEAHEAD, SET( ), INKEY( ), CLEAR, LASTKEY ( )

**EXAMPLE**

```
 1 : * File       Keybdemo.prg
 2 : * Compile    RMake sample /dFILE:keybdemo
 3 :
 4 : procedure Main()
 5 :
 6 :    cls
 7 :    keyboard "New"
 8 :    inkey(0)
 9 :    qout ( "LastKey ", chr(LastKey()), "NextKey ", Chr(NextKey()))
10 :    inkey(0)                  // take out the value of the NEXTKEY()
11 :    qqout( chr(inkey()) )
12 :
13 :    keyboard "New"
14 :    inkey(0)
15 :    qout ( "LastKey ", chr(LastKey()), "NextKey ", Chr(NextKey()))
16 :    clear typeahead
17 :    qqout( chr(inkey()) )
18 :
19 :    wait
20 :
21 :    set typeahead to 2
22 :    keyboard "New"
23 :    inkey(0)
24 :    qout ( "LastKey ", chr(LastKey()), "NextKey ", Chr(NextKey()))
25 :    inkey(0)                  // take out the value of the NEXTKEY()
26 :    qqout( chr(inkey()) )
27 :
28 : // End of File: Keybdemo.prg
```

# LABEL FORM

**COMMAND**     Displays labels to the screen or an alternate device.

**SYNTAX**       LABEL FORM <expC1> [TO PRINTER] [TO FILE <expC2>] [<expC3>] [WHILE <expL4>] [FOR <expL5>] [SAMPLE] [NOCONSOLE]

| | |
|---|---|
| **PARAMETERS** | <expC1>　Name of label file |
| | <expC2>　Name of an alternate file |
| | <expC3>　Expression of a scoping condition |
| | <expL4>　WHILE condition |
| | <expL5>　FOR condition |

**DESCRIPTION**　This command allows labels to be printed based on the format outlined in a .LBL file specified as <expC1>. By default, output will go to the screen; however, this output may be rerouted with either the TO PRINTER or the TO FILE clause.

If the TO FILE clause is specified, the name of the ASCII text file containing the generated labels will be <expC2>. If no file extension is specified, a .TXT extension is added.

<expC3> is the scope condition for this command. Valid scopes include NEXT <expN> (number of records to be displayed, where <expN> is the number of records), RECORD <expN> (a specific record to be printed), REST (all records starting from the current record position), and ALL (all records). The default is ALL.

Both logical expressions may work in conjunction with one another, where <expL5> is the logical expression for the FOR condition (for records to be displayed within a given value range) and <expL4> for the WHILE condition (for records to be displayed until they fail to meet the condition).

If the SAMPLE clause is specified, test labels will be generated.

If the NOCONSOLE clause is specified, the console will be turned off while this command is being executed.

This command follows the search criteria outlined in the SET PATH TO command. The path may be specified, along with the drive letter, in <expC1>.

**NOTE**　The NOCONSOLE is not a supported clause but may be in future versions.

**SEE ALSO**　REPORT FORM, SET PRINTER, SET CONSOLE, SET( )

**EXAMPLE**

```
 1 : * File      Label1.prg
 2 : * Compile   Rmake sample /dFILE:Label1
 3 :
 4 : procedure Main()
 5 :
 6 :    use Ontap new
 7 :    cls
 8 :    if alias() == "ONTAP"          // Check to see if file is in USE
 9 :      if file( "ONTAP1.LBL" )      // Check to see if it is there
10 :        label form Ontap1
11 :        wait
12 :        cls
13 :        label form Ontap1 to file "ONTAP1.TXT"
```

```
14 :        wait
15 :        cls
16 :        label form Ontap1 for Ontap->sizes > 2000
17 :        wait
18 :        cls
19 :        label form Ontap1 sample
20 :        wait
21 :        cls
22 :     endif
23 :  endif
24 :
25 : // End of File: Label1.prg
```

# LIST

**COMMAND**  Lists records to the screen or to an alternate device.

**SYNTAX**  LIST [<expX1>...] [TO PRINTER] [TO FILE <expC2>] [<expC3>] [WHILE <expL4>] [FOR <expL5>] [OFF]

**PARAMETERS**
<expX1>   List of field names(s)
<expC2>   Filename
<expC3>   Scope of the command
<expL4>   Logical expression of WHILE condition
<expL5>   Logical expression of FOR condition

**DESCRIPTION**  This command displays the contents of a database to the screen or the specified output device. Specifically displayed will be those fields listed in <expX1>. If the output is to be sent to an alternate file, the name of that file needs to be specified in <expC2>. If no file extension is given, the default file extension will be .TXT.

<expC3> is the scope condition for this command. Valid scopes include NEXT <expN> (number of records to be displayed, where <expN> is the number of records), RECORD <expN> (represents a particular record), REST (all records from current record position to the end of the file), and ALL (all records). The default is ALL.

Both FOR and WHILE expressions may work in conjunction with one another, where <expL5> is the logical expression for the FOR condition (for records to be displayed within a given value range), and <expL4>, for the WHILE condition (for records to be displayed that meet a condition until it fails).

If the OFF clause is specified, no record numbers will be displayed. The default is to display record numbers.

**NOTE**  This command will indent the number of character positions specified by the SET MARGIN TO command when the output is sent to the printer.

**SEE ALSO**     DISPLAY, DBEVAL( ), DBEDIT( )

**EXAMPLE**

```
 1 : * File      Listdemo.prg
 2 : * Compile   RMake sample /dFILE:listdemo
 3 :
 4 : /* This first example shows several ways in which the LIST
 5 :    command may be used.
 6 :
 7 :    The structure of the file used is:
 8 :
 9 :    FILES       CHARACTER    12    0
10 :    SIZES       NUMERIC      12    0
11 :    DATESTAMP   DATE          8    0
12 :    TIMES       CHARACTER     8    0
13 :    COMMENT     MEMO         10    0
14 :    FILE_USE    CHARACTER    40    0
15 :    SUBDRIVE    CHARACTER    50    0
16 :    PER_USED    NUMERIC       8    4   */
17 :
18 : field files, sizes, datestamp in Notap
19 :
20 : procedure Main()
21 :
22 :    USE Notap NEW
23 :
24 :    cls
25 :    list  // Nothing prints but record numbers.  Also, the record pointer is
26 :          // rewound at the conclusion of the command
27 :    wait
28 :    cls
29 :    list files, sizes, datestamp
30 :    wait
31 :    cls
32 :    list files, sizes, datestamp FOR Notap->sizes > 5000
33 :    wait
34 :    cls
35 :    list files, sizes, datestamp FOR Notap->sizes > 5000 OFF
36 :    wait
37 :    cls
38 :    qout(" Printing to file... listout1.txt..." )
39 :
40 :    // When printing to an alternate file, the output is echoed; therefore,
41 :    // in order to suppress the output to the screen, the SET CONSOLE OFF
42 :    // command or the appropriate SET() function should be issued.
43 :
44 :    list files, sizes, datestamp for Notap->sizes > 5000 ;
45 :                    to file "listout1.txt"
46 :
47 :    wait "Press any key to work with the DISPLAY command..."
48 :
49 :    // The record pointer is rewound when the list command is called, not at
50 :    // the conclusion of the list command.  So, in order for the DISPLAY
51 :    // command to work, we need to reposition the record pointer to some
52 :    // position.
```

```
53 :
54 :     go 4
55 :
56 :     cls
57 :     display
58 :     wait
59 :     cls
60 :     display files, sizes, datestamp
61 :     wait
62 :     cls
63 :     display files, sizes, datestamp NEXT 15
64 :     wait
65 :     cls
66 :
67 :     // With the addition of the ALL scope clause, the display command acts
68 :     // identically to the list command
69 :
70 :     display files, sizes, datestamp all
71 :     wait
72 :     cls
73 :     display files, sizes, datestamp all off
74 :     wait
75 :     cls
76 :     display files, sizes, datestamp all for Notap->sizes > 5000
77 :     wait  "And now for the final test"
78 :
79 :
80 :
81 :     cls
82 :     qout(" Printing to file... listout2.txt..." )
83 :     display files, sizes, datestamp all for Notap->sizes > 5000 ;
84 :            to file "listout2.txt"
85 :     wait "Press any key to exit"
86 :     cls
87 :
88 : // End of File: listdemo.prg
```

# LOCAL

**STATEMENT**  Initializes a local memory variable or array.

**SYNTAX**  LOCAL <expC1> [:= <expX2>]

**PARAMETERS**  &lt;expC1&gt;  Name of a memory variable or array
&lt;expX2&gt;  Value to be assigned to a variable or array

**DESCRIPTION**  This command initializes a LOCAL memory variable or array. The name of either is specified in <expC1>. If more than one variable is being initialized with the LOCAL command, separate each entry with a comma. If a variable or an array is to be assigned a start-up value, that expression may be specified in <expX2> and following.

LOCAL variables are symbols generated at run time and are resolved at compile time. The visibility and life span of a LOCAL variable or array is limited to the function or procedure in which it is defined.

No macro expansions are allowed in the LOCAL declaration statement.

No Clipper command other than FUNCTION, PROCEDURE, PUBLIC, PRIVATE, PARAMETERS, MEMVAR, STATIC, and FIELD, may precede the LOCAL command.

LOCAL array references may not be initialized (i.e., assigned values) on the same command line as the LOCAL command statement. This can be done later in the program.

LOCAL variables and arrays are not affected by the RELEASE command.

**NOTE** For further information on this command, see Chapter 5.

**SEE ALSO** STATIC, FIELD, MEMVAR, FUNCTION, PROCEDURE, PARAMETERS, RELEASE

## LOCATE

**COMMAND** Sequentially searches for a record.

**SYNTAX** `LOCATE [<expC1>] FOR <expL2> [WHILE <expL3>]`

**PARAMETERS**
&lt;expC1&gt;    Scoping condition
&lt;expL2&gt;    Expression for FOR condition
&lt;expL3&gt;    Expression for WHILE condition

**DESCRIPTION** This command searches the selected database for the first record that matches the expression in <expL2>.

If used, <expC1> specifies the scope of this command. Valid scopes include NEXT <expN> (where <expN> is the number of records), REST (all records from the current record position), RECORD <expN>, and ALL (all records). The default is ALL.

This command will search for and position the record pointer at the first record meeting the FOR condition <expL2>. This option is similar to filtering only those records meeting the condition <expL2>.

If the WHILE clause is specified, the program will search for the first record meeting the FOR condition WHILE <expL3> remains a logical true (.T.). Once <expL3> is a logical false (.F.), the operation is terminated.

Once an item is located, the FOUND( ) flag is toggled to a logical true (.T.) and the record meeting the selection criteria becomes the current record. If no item is found, the FOUND( ) flag is toggled to a logical false (.F.) and the record pointer may be repositioned to its original location, based on the scope criteria.

To search further without moving back to the top of the file, the CONTINUE command may be invoked. The CONTINUE command requires its own scope expression since it does not recognize the scoping expression or the WHILE clause condition used in the original LOCATE command.

**SEE ALSO**     SEEK, FIND, CONTINUE, SKIP

**EXAMPLE**

```
 1 : * File       Locademo.prg
 2 : * Compile    RMake sample /dFILE:Locademo
 3 :
 4 : #define pESC 27
 5 : #xtranslate DISPVALS() => qout( recno(), found(), field->file_name )
 6 :
 7 : procedure Main()
 8 :
 9 :    use Filenos new
10 :    DISPVALS()            // Displays RECNO(), FOUND(), and file_name
11 :    qout()
12 :    // Now, do the first locate
13 :    locate for "C" == left( field->file_name, 1 )
14 :    DISPVALS()
15 :
16 :    // Position the database and then locate to show that LOCATE does not
17 :    // rewind the record pointer
18 :
19 :    go 40
20 :    locate for "C" == left( field->file_name, 1 ) next 20
21 :    DISPVALS()
22 :
23 :    continue       // Continue a locate based on last condition
24 :    DISPVALS()
25 :
26 :    wait
27 :    cls
28 :    go top
29 :    devout("Press ESC to abort search.   ")
30 :    devout("Dots represents scan in operation")
31 :
32 :    // No records should be found for the FOR condition of this command;
33 :    // however, the WHILE condition will be performed on every record which
34 :    // will display a series of "."'s until the EOF() marker has been
35 :    // reached, the FOR condition met (which will not happen), or until the
36 :    // ESC key is pressed, causing the value of the WHILE expression (namely
37 :    // the call to Conditional()) to be a logical false (.F.).
38 :
39 :    locate for ".,5321W"$left( field->file_name, 1) while Conditional()
40 :    DISPVALS()
41 :    wait
42 :    cls
43 :
44 : *******************
```

```
45 :
46 : static function Conditional
47 :
48 :    local lRetValue := !(inkey() == pESC)
49 :
50 :    qqout(".")
51 :
52 :    return( lRetValue )
53 :
54 : // End of File: Locademo.prg
```

# LOOP

| | |
|---|---|
| **STATEMENT** | Goes to the top of a loop and proceeds with program execution. |
| **SYNTAX** | LOOP |
| **PARAMETER** | None |
| **DESCRIPTION** | This command immediately jumps to the beginning of the current DO WHILE ... ENDDO loop or the current FOR ... NEXT loop. If the structure being executed is a FOR ... NEXT loop, the variable specified in the FOR condition (the loop counter) is incremented or decremented accordingly. |
| **SEE ALSO** | DO WHILE ... ENDDO, FOR ... NEXT, EXIT, BEGIN SEQUENCE |

# MEMVAR

| | | |
|---|---|---|
| **STATEMENT** | Declares private and public memory variables and arrays. | |
| **SYNTAX** | MEMVAR <expC1> [, <expC2>...] | |
| **PARAMETERS** | <expC1> | Memory variable name |
| | <expC2> | Continued variable list |
| **DESCRIPTION** | This command tells the compiler to resolve any reference to a memory variable designated within this list as if it possessed an explicit memory variable alias with either the M-> or MEMVAR-> prefix. Only those memory variables that do not contain any such explicit alias are affected by this command. Those memory variables within macro expansions are not affected by this command. | |
| **NOTE** | The MEMVAR declaration must appear before any executable command; it is similar to the LOCAL, STATIC, FIELD, PARAMETERS, FUNCTION, and PROCEDURE command statements. | |

**SEE ALSO**      LOCAL, STATIC, FIELD, PARAMETERS, FUNCTION, PROCEDURE

**EXAMPLE**      Please see Chapter 5.

# MENU TO

**COMMAND**      Executes a menu bar for active PROMPT statements.

**SYNTAX**      `MENU TO <expN1>`

**PARAMETER**      <expN1>     Variable name

**DESCRIPTION**      This command allows the creation of a menu system and stores the result of the menu selection to the variable <expN1>.

This command highlights the first @ PROMPT menu item (or the @ PROMPT menu item in the <expN1>th position) and will allow the cursor to move from one @ PROMPT menu item to the next. MENU TO also places in <expN1> the numeric value of the menu item that was selected. If the ESC key is pressed, the value of <expN1> will be 0.

There can be up to 32 PROMPT commands for any one active MENU TO command.

Cursor movement within the MENU TO command follows the following table:

| UP ARROW | Previous PROMPT |
| --- | --- |
| DOWN ARROW | Next PROMPT |
| HOME | First PROMPT |
| END | Last PROMPT |
| LEFT ARROW | Previous PROMPT |
| RIGHT ARROW | Next PROMPT |
| PgUp | Select PROMPT |
| PgDn | Select PROMPT |
| ENTER | Select PROMPT |
| ESC | Abort MENU TO |

The first character in the PROMPT display, Select PROMPT, returns PROMPT position.

**SEE ALSO**      @ ... PROMPT, SET MESSAGE, SET WRAP, SET( )

**EXAMPLE**

```
1 : * File      Menudemo.prg
2 : * Compile   Rmake sample /dFILE:menudemo
3 :
4 : #define pTRUE .T.
5 : #define pMESSAGE 36 // The parameter for the SET() function
6 :
```

```
 7 : procedure Main()
 8 :
 9 :    local nOption
10 :
11 :    cls
12 :    while pTRUE
13 :
14 :       @ 4,25 to 10,55
15 :       @ 5,26 prompt padr(" 1> Overlapping Menus",  29)
16 :       @ 6,26 prompt padr(" 2> Menus with Messages", 29)
17 :       @ 7,26 prompt padr(" 3> Pull Down Menus",    29)
18 :       @ 8,26 prompt padr(" 4> Spread Sheet Menus", 29)
19 :       @ 9,26 prompt padr(" 5> Quit Program",       29)
20 :       menu to nOption
21 :
22 :       do case
23 :       case nOption == 1
24 :          Overlap()    // Overlapping Menus...
25 :
26 :       case nOption == 2
27 :          Messages()   // Menus with MESSAGES
28 :
29 :       case nOption == 3
30 :          PullDown()   // Pull Down Menus
31 :
32 :       case nOption == 4
33 :          Lotus()      // Lotus spread sheets
34 :
35 :       otherwise
36 :          exit
37 :
38 :       endcase
39 :    enddo
40 :
41 :    cls
42 :
43 : ******************
44 :
45 : static procedure Overlap()
46 :
47 :    local nOption
48 :
49 :    set wrap on
50 :    save screen
51 :
52 :    while pTRUE
53 :       CLS
54 :       @ 0,0 say "Overlapping Menus...  WRAP AROUND IS ON"
55 :       @ 1,0 to 5,17 double
56 :       @ 2,1 prompt " 1> Over Lap #1 "
57 :       @ 3,1 prompt " 2> Over Lap #2 "
58 :       @ 4,1 prompt " 3> over lap #3 "
59 :       menu to nOption
60 :       if empty(nOption)    // It's equal to 0
61 :          EXIT
62 :       else
63 :          Overlap1(nOption, 1)
```

```
 64 :      endif
 65 :   enddo
 66 :
 67 :   restore screen
 68 :   set wrap off
 69 :
 70 : *********************
 71 :
 72 : static procedure Overlap1( nOption, nBase )
 73 :
 74 :   local nChoice
 75 :   local nPosition := ++nBase + nOption
 76 :   local cScreen   := savescreen(nPosition, nBase+1, nPosition+5, nBase+21)
 77 :
 78 :   while pTRUE
 79 :      @ nPosition, nBase+1 to nPosition+5, nBase+21
 80 :      @ nPosition+1,nBase+2 prompt " 1> First Overlap  "
 81 :      @ nPosition+2,nBase+2 prompt " 2> Second Overlap "
 82 :      @ nPosition+3,nBase+2 prompt " 3> Third Overlap  "
 83 :      @ nPosition+4,nBase+2 prompt " 4> Fourth Overlap "
 84 :      menu to nChoice
 85 :
 86 :      if nChoice == 0
 87 :         exit
 88 :      else
 89 :         if !(procname(2) == "OVERLAP1")   // Prevents OVER recursion!
 90 :            Overlap1( nPosition+nChoice, nBase )
 91 :         else
 92 :            @ 20,0 say "You selected: "
 93 :            @ row(), col() say nChoice
 94 :            @ 21,0 say "Any key..."
 95 :            inkey(0)
 96 :            @ 20,0 clear
 97 :         endif
 98 :      endif
 99 :   enddo
100 :
101 :   restscreen(nPosition, nBase+1, nPosition+5, nBase+21, cScreen)
102 :
103 : *******************
104 :
105 : static procedure Messages
106 :
107 :   local nChoice
108 :   local nLine := maxrow()
109 :
110 :   save screen
111 :   @ 12,30 to 18,50 double
112 :   set wrap on
113 :
114 :   while pTRUE
115 :      // The following statement first POST DECREMENTS the value of LINE.
116 :      // If the current value of LINE is less than 20, the value of LINE is
117 :      // assigned the value of MAXROW() and that expression becomes the new
118 :      // row number for the SET MESSAGE TO command; otherwise, the value of
119 :      // line is used.  Once evaluated, LINE is decremented.
120 :
```

```
121 :       set message to if( nLine-- < 20, (nLine := maxrow()),nLine ) center
122 :
123 :       @ 13,31 prompt padc("Chart of Accounts", 19) ;
124 :               message "COA Account Numbers"
125 :       @ 14,31 prompt padc("Transactions", 19) ;
126 :               message "Journal Transactions for COA"
127 :       @ 15,31 prompt padc("Posting", 19) ;
128 :               message "Post Batch Transactions to General Ledger Accounts"
129 :       @ 16,31 prompt padc("End of Period", 19) ;
130 :               message "EOP Processing"
131 :       @ 17,31 prompt padc("Reports", 19)
132 :       menu to nChoice
133 :
134 :       if nChoice == 1          // HEAD 2 = COMMANDs
135 :       elseif nChoice ==  2     // HEAD 2 = COMMANDs
136 :       elseif nChoice ==  3     // HEAD 2 = COMMANDs
137 :       elseif nChoice ==  4     // HEAD 2 = COMMANDs
138 :       else
139 :          exit
140 :       endif
141 :
142 :       @ set(pMESSAGE), 0   // Clears the line !!
143 :
144 :    enddo
145 :    set wrap off
146 :    set message to 0
147 :    restore screen
148 :
149 : *******************
150 :
151 : static procedure Lotus()
152 :
153 :    local nChoice
154 :
155 :    save screen
156 :    cls
157 :    set wrap on
158 :    set message to 1
159 :    while pTRUE
160 :       @ 0,0  prompt "Files"    message "Work with a file"
161 :       @ 0,8  prompt "Compile"  message "Compile an existing spread sheet"
162 :       @ 0,18 prompt "Graph"    message "Graph a spread sheet"
163 :       @ 0,26 prompt "Save"     message "Save your work!"
164 :       @ 0,33 prompt "Quit"     message "Return to Main Menu"
165 :       menu to nChoice
166 :
167 :       if nChoice == 0 .or. nChoice == 5
168 :          exit
169 :       endif
170 :
171 :    enddo
172 :
173 :    set message to 0
174 :    set wrap off
175 :    restore screen
176 :
177 : *******************
```

```
178 :
179 : static procedure PullDown()
180 :
181 :    @ maxrow()-2, 0 say "This topic is handled EXTENSIVELY in"
182 :    @ maxrow()-1, 0 say "the Chapter on Windows, Screens,and Menus"
183 :    @ maxrow(),   0 say "Any key...."
184 :    inkey(0)
185 :    @ maxrow()-2,0 clear
186 :
187 : // End of File: Menudemo.prg
```

## NOTE

| | |
|---|---|
| **STATEMENT** | Creates a single-line notation in source code. |
| **SYNTAX** | NOTE [<expC1>] |
| **PARAMETER** | <expC1>   Character expression |
| **DESCRIPTION** | This command allows text to be entered into the program to describe the operation being taken by the command. |
| **NOTE** | This is a compatibility command and may not be supported in future versions. |
| **SEE ALSO** | Chapter 4, *, //, /* ... */, && |

## PACK

| | |
|---|---|
| **COMMAND** | Removes records marked for deletion from a database. |
| **SYNTAX** | PACK |
| **PARAMETER** | None |
| **DESCRIPTION** | This command removes records that were marked for deletion from the currently selected database. This command does not pack the contents of a memo field; those files must be packed via low-level file functions.<br><br>All open index files will be automatically reindexed once the PACK command has completed its operation. On completion, the record pointer is placed on the first record in the database. |
| **SEE ALSO** | ZAP, DELETED( ), DELETE, RECALL, DBEVAL( ) |
| **EXAMPLE** | |

```
1 : * File      Showpack.prg
2 : * Compile   Rmake sample /dFILE:showpack
```

```
  3 :
  4 : #define pTRUE .T.
  5 : #xtranslate EVEN( <number> ) => ( int(<number> / 2) == <number> / 2 )
  6 : #xtranslate MULTIPLEOF( <number>, <base> ) =>;
  7 :            ( INT(<number> / <base>) == <number> / <base> )
  8 :
  9 : memvar getlist
 10 :
 11 : procedure Main()
 12 :
 13 :   local nOldRec
 14 :
 15 :   cls
 16 :   ? "Copying the file... One moment..."
 17 :   copy file Filenos.dbf to Showpack.dbf
 18 :   use Showpack new
 19 :   nOldRec := lastrec()
 20 :   ?? chr(13)              // This uses the same line by issuing a CR only!
 21 :   ?? "Number of records are: "
 22 :   ?? padr( lastrec(), 40) // This should clear the rest of the line
 23 :   ? "Deleting records: "
 24 :   delete for EVEN( recno() ) while ShowRec(2,24)
 25 :   wait
 26 :   cls
 27 :   list Showpack->disk_no, Showpack->sub_no, Showpack->sub_name for ;
 28 :        deleted()
 29 :   wait "And now, a partial RECALL...."
 30 :   go top  // This is necessary in order to get the RECALL to work!
 31 :
 32 :   cls
 33 :   ? "Record Number: "
 34 :   recall all for MULTIPLEOF( recno(), 3 ) while ShowRec(1, 24)
 35 :   wait "Any key for the current listing..."
 36 :
 37 :   list Showpack->disk_no, Showpack->sub_no, Showpack->sub_name ;
 38 :        for deleted()
 39 :   wait "And now... any key for the PACK!"
 40 :
 41 :   pack  // All records marked for deletion are removed!
 42 :
 43 :   cls
 44 :   ? "The old LASTREC() value was :", nOldRec
 45 :   ? "The new LASTREC() value is...", lastrec()
 46 :   wait
 47 :   clear all            // This makes reference to GETLIST
 48 :   erase Showpack.dbf
 49 :   cls
 50 :
 51 : *******************
 52 :
 53 : static function ShowRec( nRow, nCol )
 54 :
 55 :   // This function is used strictly for the purpose of displaying the
 56 :   // current record number that is being processed by a global command
 57 :   // such as DELETE and RECALL.  This function always returns TRUE and
 58 :   // therefore may be used exclusively in a WHILE condition
 59 :
```

```
60 :      @ nRow, nCol say recno()
61 :
62 :      return( pTRUE )
63 :
64 : // End of File: Showpack.prg
```

## PARAMETERS

**STATEMENT**   Declares private parameter variables.

**SYNTAX**   `PARAMETERS <expX1>...`

**PARAMETER**   `<expX1>`   Variable name(s)

**DESCRIPTION**   This command declares PRIVATE data storage positions for the variables named in <expX1>. The values for these variables will be passed to them, either by value or by reference, from a calling procedure or function.

The number of parameters defined in the PARAMETER statement does not have to match the number of parameters passed to the routine.

Parameters accepted into a function or procedure via the PARAMETER command may not have a formal LOCAL parameter list included with them.

Parameters may be skipped when called by simply including a comma in the calling command line; those PARAMETERS skipped will have a NIL value. There may be up to 128 variables listed in a PARAMETER command.

The PARAMETERS declaration must appear before any executable command; it is similar to the LOCAL, STATIC, FIELD, MEMVAR, FUNCTION, and PROCEDURE command statements.

**SEE ALSO**   FUNCTION, PROCEDURE, LOCAL, PRIVATE, PCOUNT( ), MEMVAR, FIELD, PUBLIC

**EXAMPLE**   Please see Chapter 5.

## PRIVATE

**STATEMENT**   Creates private memory variables and/or arrays.

**SYNTAX**   `PRIVATE <expX1> [, <expX2>...]`

**PARAMETER**   `<expX1>`   Variable or array name(s)

**DESCRIPTION** This command creates memory variables that are hidden from either higher-level variables, previously PUBLIC declared variables, or other variables within the same function or procedure. The name of the variable is expressed as <expX1>; if a PRIVATE array is to be created, the convention would be <expX1> [<expN>], where <expN> is the number of subscripts allowed in that array.

PRIVATE is the default storage class of any memory variable created by itself (without this command) or via the PARAMETERS command. PRIVATE variables are tokenized, which means a symbolic token is generated for each PRIVATE variable and stored in the symbol table in the main load of the application. PRIVATE variables are different from LOCAL or STATIC memory variables.

**NOTE** For additional information, see Chapter 5.

**SEE ALSO** FIELD, LOCAL, PARAMETERS, PROCEDURE, FUNCTION, STATIC, PUBLIC

**EXAMPLE** See Chapter 5.

## PROCEDURE

**STATEMENT** Declares a user-defined procedure.

**SYNTAX**
```
[INIT] [EXIT] [STATIC] PROCEDURE <expC1>
[( <expX2>... )]
 <commands>
[RETURN]
```

**PARAMETERS**    <expC1>   Name of the procedure
                       <expX2>   Parameter list

**DESCRIPTION** This command declares a subroutine with the name of <expC1>. The name of the subroutine may be of any length, with the first 10 bytes being significant. If specified, <expX2> and following will contain a list of LOCAL parameters to be accepted by this procedure. This is identical to the PARAMETERS command except for the data storage class.

If the STATIC clause is specified, the procedure <expC1> may only be called by those procedures or functions declared in the same source file.

If the INIT clause is used, then the specified procedure will be called when the compiled application is initially executed. There is no need for an explicit call to it. Otherwise the INIT clause acts like a STATIC in that there is no formal symbolic reference to it in the symbol table. Multiple program files may contain INIT PROCEDUREs with the same name. The order in which all of the INIT routines are called is based on the linking order of the application.

If the EXIT clause is specified, then the specified function will be called when the application is about to stop being processed. There is no need for a formal reference to it. The EXIT clause acts like a STATIC in that there is no formal symbolic reference to it in the symbol table. Multiple program files may contain the EXIT PROCEDUREs with the same name. The order in which all of the EXIT routines are called is based on the linking order of the application.

A procedure will terminate operation if a CANCEL, QUIT, or RETURN statement is executed. The procedure will also RETURN by default when either the end-of-file marker is found or when the beginning of another PROCEDURE or FUNCTION is encountered.

The default RETURN value of a procedure is a NIL data type. Except for this, a procedure is the same as a user-defined function.

**SEE ALSO**  FUNCTION, LOCAL, PRIVATE, RETURN, STATIC, PCOUNT( ), ANNOUNCE, REQUEST

# PUBLIC

**STATEMENT**  Creates public memory variables and/or arrays.

**SYNTAX**  `PUBLIC <expX1...>`

**PARAMETER**  <expX1>  Variable or array name(s)

**DESCRIPTION**  This command creates memory variables that are visible to all programming routines, procedures, and/or functions. The name of the variable is expressed as <expX1> and following. If a PUBLIC array is to be created, the convention would be <expX1> [<expN>], where <expN> is the number of subscripts allowed in that array.

PUBLIC variables are tokenized, which means that a symbolic token is generated for each PUBLIC variable and stored in the symbol table in the main load of the application. PUBLIC variables are different from LOCAL or STATIC memory variables.

Variables that are defined as PUBLIC and are not initialized to a value have a default value of logical false (.F.). The one exception is a variable named CLIPPER. This variable is used to toggle sections of code reserved for dBASE III compatibility. If used, this variable is initialized to a default value of logical true (.T.).

If any array is made PUBLIC when a previous PRIVATE or PUBLIC variable or array of the same name exists, the PUBLIC array will be created on top of the previous variable declaration.

| | |
|---|---|
| **NOTE** | For additional information, see Chapter 5. |
| **SEE ALSO** | PRIVATE, DECLARE, LOCAL, STATIC |
| **EXAMPLE** | See Chapter 5. |

# QUIT

| | |
|---|---|
| **COMMAND** | Terminates program execution. |
| **SYNTAX** | QUIT |
| **PARAMETER** | None |
| **DESCRIPTION** | This command terminates the Clipper application. In doing so, it closes all open files after attempting to write information from buffers, and returns control to the operating system.<br><br>When an application terminates successfully, a DOS error level of 1 is set. If, however, a run-time error is experienced, the value of the DOS error level is set to 0 or the value of the ERRORLEVEL( ) last executed within the application. |
| **SEE ALSO** | RETURN, CANCEL |

**EXAMPLE**

```
 1 : * File      Quitdemo.prg
 2 : * Compile   Rmake sample /dFILE:quitdemo
 3 :
 4 : procedure Main()
 5 :
 6 :    while .t.          // This loop will only be performed once since
 7 :       cls             // there is a QUIT command within it; however,
 8 :       Subroutine()    // there is a CANCEL within Subroutine()
 9 :       qout( "We NEVER get here!!!" )
10 :       inkey(0)
11 :       quit
12 :    enddo
13 :
14 : ********************
15 :
16 : static procedure Subroutine
17 :
18 :    qout( "Press any key to cancel this routine" )
19 :    inkey(0)
20 :    cancel   // This terminates the program as well
21 :
22 :    // The following commands will never be executed! because the CANCEL
23 :    // command is in the way!
24 :
```

```
25 :    qout( "This is a second line that will not be printed" )
26 :
27 : // End of File: Quitdemo.prg
```

# READ

**COMMAND**  Activates the current GET system.

**SYNTAX**  READ [SAVE]

**PARAMETER**  None

**DESCRIPTION**  This command activates all current @ ... GETs stored within the GETLIST[ ] array. If used, the SAVE clause does not clear out the GETLIST[ ] array, whereas the READ command without the SAVE clause does.

When the READ command is activated, Clipper begins processing each of the GetList arrays. Each programmed WHEN clause is then evaluated before that particular @ ... GET is activated; once activated, each programmed VALID clause is then evaluated before that particular @ ... GET is resolved and the program moves onto the next command or GET statement.

Following is a table of the accepted key movements within the READ command.

| *Key* | *Operation* |
| --- | --- |
| Left Arrow | Character left. Remain in current GET. |
| Ctrl-S | Character left. Remain in current GET. |
| Right Arrow | Character right. Remain in current GET. |
| Ctrl-D | Character right. Remain in current GET. |
| Ctrl-Left Arrow | Word left |
| Ctrl-A | Word left |
| Ctrl-Right Arrow | Word right |
| Ctrl-F | Word right |
| Up Arrow | Previous GET |
| Ctrl-E | Previous GET |
| Down Arrow | Next GET |
| Ctrl-X | Next GET |
| ENTER | Next GET |

*(continued)*

| Key | Operation |
|---|---|
| Ctrl-M | Next GET |
| Home | First character of current GET |
| End | Last character of current GET |
| Ctrl-Home | Beginning of first GET |
| Ctrl-End | Beginning of last GET |
| Ctrl-U | Restore previous GET value provided that ENTER key has yet to be pressed. |
| Ctrl-Y | Delete from cursor position to end of GET. |
| Ctrl-T | Delete word right. |
| BACKSPACE | Delete character left and drag characters accordingly. |
| Ctrl-H | Delete character left and drag character accordingly. |
| DEL | Delete character at cursor position and drag remaining characters accordingly. |
| Ctrl-G | Delete character at cursor position and drag remaining characters accordingly. |
| INS | Toggle the insert character. |
| Ctrl-V | Toggle the insert character. |
| Ctrl-W | Complete and save all the GETs. |
| Ctrl-C | Complete and save all the GETs. |
| PgUp | Complete and save all the GETs. |
| PgDn | Complete and save all the GETs. |

**NOTE**  See the chapter on GET object system and GETSYS.PRG for additional information on the READ command and READMODAL( ) function.

**SEE ALSO**  @ ... GET, CLEAR GETS, READMODAL( ), UPDATED( ), Chapter 16

**EXAMPLE**

```
1 : * File       Getdemo.prg
2 : * Compile    RMake sample /dFILE:getdemo
3 :
4 : #include "PTColor.ch"   // Power Tools Header file of color settings
5 : #include "PTValue.ch"   // Power Tools Header file of misc values
6 : #include "PTFuncs.ch"   // Power Tools Header file of pseudofunctions
7 :
8 : memvar name, address, city, state, zip, amount, member, joined
9 :
```

```
10 :    procedure Main()
11 :
12 :       local getlist := {}      // This is for the GET stuff
13 :
14 :       name    := space(40)    // Name of person
15 :       address := space(24)    // Address of person
16 :       city    := space(15)    // City of address
17 :       state   := space(2)     // State
18 :       zip     := space(10)    // Zip Code + 4
19 :       amount  := 0.00         // Amount paid to club
20 :       member  := pTRUE        // Member in good standing
21 :       joined  := ctod("")     // Date joined
22 :
23 :       if iscolor()
24 :          setcolor( MAKECOLOR(pWHITE/pBLUE, pBLACK/pWHITE,"","",pWHITE/pBLUE))
25 :       endif
26 :
27 :       cls
28 :
29 :       @ 3,0 say "Enter the Club Member"
30 :       @ 5,5 say "   Name: " get name    picture "@!"
31 :       @ 6,5 say "Address: " get address picture "@X@S15"
32 :       @ 7,5 say "   City: " get city    picture "@X"
33 :       @ 8,5 say "  State: " get state   picture "!!"
34 :       @ 9,5 say "    Zip: " get zip     picture "99999-9999"
35 :       @ 10,5 say " Amount: " get amount  picture "$ #####.##"
36 :       @ 11,5 say " Member: " get member  picture "Y"
37 :       @ 12,5 say " Joined: " get joined  picture "99/99/99"
38 :       read save
39 :
40 :       cls
41 :       @ 0,0 say "With the PREVIOUS READ SAVE command, the @ SAY logic"
42 :       @ 1,0 say "is not saved, only the GET.  Press the ENTER key to"
43 :       @ 2,0 say "find this out!"
44 :       read
45 :       if iscolor()
46 :          setcolor(MAKECOLOR(pBLUE/pWHITE, pBLACK/pWHITE, ;
47 :                   "", "", pBLUE/pWHITE) )
48 :       endif
49 :       cls
50 :       @ 0,0 say "And now, reverse the SETCOLOR() screen and display!"
51 :       @ 5,5 say "   Name: " get name    picture "@!"
52 :       @ 6,5 say "Address: " get address // Default to show entire string
53 :       @ 7,5 say "   City: " get city    picture "@X"
54 :       @ 8,5 say "  State: " get state   picture "!!"
55 :       @ 9,5 say "    Zip: " get zip     picture "99999-9999"
56 :       @ 10,5 say " Amount: " get amount  picture "$ #####.##"
57 :       @ 11,5 say " Member: " get member  picture "Y"
58 :       @ 12,5 say " Joined: " get joined  picture "99/99/99"
59 :       clear gets
60 :       wait
61 :       cls
62 :
63 : // End of File: Getdemo.prg
```

## RECALL

| | |
|---|---|
| **COMMAND** | Unmarks records previously marked for deletion. |
| **SYNTAX** | `RECALL [<expC1>] [FOR <expL2>] [WHILE <expL3>]` |
| **PARAMETERS** | `<expC1>` Scope of the command |
| | `<expL2>` Logical expression for FOR condition |
| | `<expL3>` Logical expression for WHILE condition |
| **DESCRIPTION** | This command unmarks one or more records marked for deletion and reactivates them in the current database. If specified, the scope for this operation may be specified in `<expC1>`. Valid scopes are ALL, NEXT `<expN>` (records), RECORD `<expN>` (a specific record number), and REST (all remaining records). The default scope is ALL. |
| | If the FOR clause is specified, only those records meeting the FOR condition `<expL2>` will be reactivated. This option is similar to filtering only those records meeting the condition `<expL2>`. |
| | If the WHILE clause is specified, all records meeting the FOR condition will be searched while `<expL3>` remains a logical true (.T.). Once `<expL3>` is a logical false (.F.), the operation will be terminated. |
| | If a record is DELETED and SET DELETED ON is specified, the record will still be visible for a RECALL provided that the database record pointed to has not been skipped. Once a record marked for deletion with a SET DELETED ON condition has been skipped, it no longer can be RECALLed until the SET DELETED ON condition has been removed. |
| **SEE ALSO** | DELETE, PACK, SET DELETED, DELETED( ), DBEVAL( ) |
| **EXAMPLE** | See the DELETE command. |

## REINDEX

| | |
|---|---|
| **COMMAND** | Rebuilds open indexes. |
| **SYNTAX** | `REINDEX [EVAL <expL1>] [EVERY <expN2>]` |
| **PARAMETERS** | `<expL1>` Logical expression to evaluate |
| | `<expN2>` Number of records to move |
| **DESCRIPTION** | This command rebuilds all of the active index files in the current work area. When rebuilding is completed, the record pointer is placed at the first record of the controlling index. If this command is issued in a networked environment, the database file must be used EXCLUSIVE to avoid a run-time error. |

This command does not rebuild the header of any of the index files regenerated. In fact, the successful operation of this command assumes that the index header is valid. If there is a corrupted index header, this command will not ensure that a proper index is being built. For this reason, use the INDEX ON command.

If the EVAL clause is specified, then the expression <expL1> will be evaluated either for each record being indexed in the database or in the scope, or every <expN2> record should the EVERY clause be specified as well. Similar to the WHILE condition, when the expression <expL1> returns a logical false (.F.), the indexing operation will stop. Additionally, the expression is not stored in the index header and must be maintained by the programmer.

**SEE ALSO**  INDEX, PACK, SET INDEX, USE, SET ORDER

# RELEASE

**COMMAND**  Releases public and private memory variables.

**SYNTAX**
```
RELEASE <expX1>...
RELEASE ALL [LIKE / EXCEPT <expX2>]
```

**PARAMETERS**  <expX1>   A variable name(s)
<expX2>   Variable skeleton

**DESCRIPTION**  This command deletes a public or private memory variable from memory and reallocates that memory space for future use. Individual memory variables and/or arrays may be specified in <expX1> and following. If a group of variables meeting certain criteria needs to be RELEASEd, that criteria may be specified in the RELEASE ALL LIKE, or RELEASE ALL EXCEPT command. In this case, <expX2> is a skeleton clause. A question mark (?) and an asterisk (*) are treated just as they are in DOS: A question mark will mask a single character in <expX2>; an asterisk will mark one or more characters in <expX2>.

**SEE ALSO**  CLEAR MEMORY, LOCAL, STATIC, PRIVATE, PUBLIC

**EXAMPLE**

```
 1 : * File      Realdemo.prg
 2 : * Compile   RMake sample /dFILE:realdemo
 3 :
 4 : procedure Main()
 5 :
 6 :    local   nVar1
 7 :    public  nVar2
 8 :    private nVar3
 9 :
10 :    nVar1 := nVar2 := nVar3 := 0
```

```
11 :
12 :    ? valtype( nVar2 )     // Output will be N
13 :    ? valtype( nVar3 )     // Output will be N
14 :    ? valtype( nVar1 )     // Output will be N
15 :    ? nVar2                // Output will be 0
16 :    ? nVar3                // Output will be 0
17 :    ? nVar1                // Output will be 0
18 :
19 :    release nVar3, nVar1   // The RELEASE command doesn't work on LOCALs
20 :
21 :    ? valtype( nVar2 )     // Output will be N
22 :    ? valtype( nVar3 )     // Output will be U
23 :    ? valtype( nVar1 )     // Output will be N
24 :    ? nVar2                // Output will be 0
25 :    ? nVar3                // Output will be NIL
26 :    ? nVar1                // 0
27 :
28 : // End of File: Realdemo.prg
```

# RENAME

| | |
|---|---|
| **COMMAND** | Changes the name of a specified file. |
| **SYNTAX** | `RENAME <expC1> TO <expC2>` |
| **PARAMETERS** | `<expC1>`   Old filename<br>`<expC2>`   New filename |
| **DESCRIPTION** | This command changes the name of <expC1> to <expC2>. Both <expC1> and <expC2> must include a file extension. This command is not affected by the SET PATH TO or SET DEFAULT TO commands; drive and directory designators must be specified if either file is in a directory other than the default drive and directory.<br><br>If <expC2> is currently open or if it previously exists, this command will not perform the desired operation. |
| **SEE ALSO** | COPY FILE, ERASE, FILE( ), FRENAME( ), FERASE( ) |
| **EXAMPLE** | See the ERASE command. |

# REPLACE

| | |
|---|---|
| **COMMAND** | Assigns values to fields. |
| **SYNTAX** | `REPLACE <expX1> WITH <expX2> [, <expX3> WITH <expX4>...] [<expC5>] [FOR <expL6>] [WHILE <expL7>]` |

**PARAMETERS**   <expX1>   Field name
                          <expX2>   Expression to place in <expX1>
                          <expX3>   Additional field name(s)
                          <expX4>   Expression to place in <expX3>
                          <expC5>   Expression of scope
                          <expL6>   Logical expression for FOR condition
                          <expL7>   Logical expression for WHILE condition

**DESCRIPTION**   This command takes the field specified as <expX1> and replaces it with the value of <expX2>. Additional fields may be specified if each REPLACE WITH iteration is separated with a comma, where <expX3> is the name of another field to be replaced by the value of <expX4>.

<expC5> is the scope for this command. Valid scopes include NEXT <expN> (where <expN> is the number of records), RECORD <expN> (a specific record), REST (all records from current record position), and ALL (all records). The default is the current record only.

Both logical expressions may work in conjunction with one another, where <expL6> is the logical expression for the FOR condition (for records to be replaced within a given range) and <expL7> for the WHILE condition (for records meeting the condition until it fails).

**NOTE**   This command is identical to FIELD-><expX1> := <expX2> or ALIAS-><expX1> := <expX2>

**SEE ALSO**   In-line assignments in Chapter 4, "Operators and Conditions," FIELD, STORE

**EXAMPLE**

```
 1 : * File       Repldemo.prg
 2 : * Compile    Rmake sample /dFILE:repldemo
 3 :
 4 : memvar files, sizes, datestamp
 5 :
 6 : procedure Main()
 7 :
 8 :     ?
 9 :     ? "Copying files.  One moment..."
10 :
11 :     copy file Ontap.dbf to Badtap.dbf
12 :     copy file Ontap.dbt to Badtap.dbt
13 :     use Badtap new
14 :
15 :     cls
16 :     files     := Badtap->files
17 :     sizes     := Badtap->sizes
18 :     datestamp := Badtap->datestamp
19 :
20 :     ? "Here are the values of the three variables"
21 :     ? files, sizes, datestamp
22 :     ?
23 :     replace Badtap->files with "Noname", Badtap->sizes with 0, ;
24 :             Badtap->datestamp with date()
```

```
25 :
26 :    skip 0    // Flush the buffer
27 :    commit    // Perform a hard-disk write
28 :
29 :    ?  "And after the REPLACE and restore of the values, "
30 :    ?? "here they are again..."
31 :
32 :    files     := Badtap->files
33 :    sizes     := Badtap->sizes
34 :    datestamp := Badtap->datestamp
35 :
36 :    ? files, sizes, datestamp
37 :    ?
38 :    Badtap->files     := "NewName!"  // This is the same as a REPLACE
39 :    field->sizes      := 999999      // Either the ALIAS() name or
40 :    field->datestamp := ctod("")     // FIELD declaration must be included!
41 :
42 :    skip 0    // Flush the buffer
43 :    commit    // Perform a hard-disk write
44 :
45 :    ? "And now, after the final REPLACEment...."
46 :
47 :    files     := Badtap->files
48 :    sizes     := Badtap->sizes
49 :    datestamp := Badtap->datestamp
50 :
51 :    skip 0    // Flush the buffer
52 :    commit    // Perform a hard-disk write
53 :
54 :    ? files, sizes, datestamp
55 :    ?
56 :    wait
57 :    erase Badtap.*   // ERASE command may take wild card skeletons!
58 :    cls
59 :
60 : // End of File: Repldemo.prg
```

# REPORT

**COMMAND**       Displays a report.

**SYNTAX**        REPORT FORM <expC1> [TO PRINTER] [TO FILE <expC2>]
                  [<expC3>] [WHILE <expL4>] [FOR <expL5>] [PLAIN |
                  HEADING <expC6>] [NOEJECT] [SUMMARY] [NOCONSOLE]

**PARAMETERS**   <expC1>   Name of label file

                  <expC2>   Name of alternate file

                  <expC3>   Scope

                  <expL4>   Logical expression of WHILE condition

                  <expL5>   Logical expression of FOR condition

                  <expC6>   Report heading

**DESCRIPTION** This command prints out the report named <expC1>, which is a standard .FRM file. The file extension is not required because .FRM will be assumed. The SET PATH TO and SET DEFAULT TO commands affect the search for the file <expC1>; unless a drive and path are specified in <expC1>, REPORT will search the path specified in the SET PATH command if it cannot find the report form in the current directory.

The output of the report will be offset based on the setting of the SET MARGIN TO value.

By default, output will go to the console; however, it may be controlled via either the TO PRINTER or TO FILE clause. If the output is to go to the file, the name of the alternate file is specified in <expC2>. Unless specified in <expC2>, the default file extension will be .TXT.

<expC3> is the scope for this command. Valid scopes include NEXT <expN> (where <expN> is the number of records), RECORD <expN> (a specific record to be displayed), REST (all records from the current record position), and ALL (all records). The default is ALL.

Both logical expressions may work in conjunction with one another, where <expL5> is the logical expression for the FOR condition (for records to be displayed within a given range) and <expL4> for the WHILE condition (for records to be displayed until the condition fails).

If the PLAIN clause is specified, date and page numbers are suppressed. In addition, there is no automatic page breaking, and the report title and column headings appear only once at the top of the form.

If the HEADING clause is used, <expC6> is displayed on the first line of each report page. The value of <expC6> is evaluated only once before executing the report; varying the values of <expC6> is not allowed. The PLAIN clause will take precedence over the HEADING clause if both are included.

If the NOEJECT clause is used, the initial page eject on the report will not be issued when the output clause TO PRINTER is specified. Otherwise, this clause has no effect.

If the SUMMARY clause is specified, the report will contain only groups, subgroups, and grand total information. The detailed line item information will be ignored.

If the NOCONSOLE clause is specified, output to the console will be turned off while this command is being executed.

**SEE ALSO** LABEL FORM, DISPLAY, LIST

**EXAMPLE**

```
1 : * File       Reptdemo.prg
2 : * Compile    Rmake sample /dFILE:reptdemo
3 :
4 : #define pTRUE .T.
5 :
6 : procedure Main()
7 :
8 :    if file( "Ontap.dbf" )
```

```
 9 :        if file( "Ontap1.frm" )
10 :           use Ontap new
11 :           cls
12 :           report form Ontap1
13 :           wait
14 :           cls
15 :           report form Ontap1 for Ontap->sizes > 2000
16 :           wait
17 :           cls
18 :           report form Ontap1 for Ontap->sizes > 2000 ;
19 :                  heading "This is an example!" to file "Output2.txt"
20 :           wait
21 :           cls
22 :           report form Ontap1 summary
23 :           wait
24 :           if setmode(43,80)
25 :              cls
26 :              report form Ontap1 for Ontap->sizes > 2000 to file "Output3.txt"
27 :              wait
28 :              setmode(25,80)
29 :           endif
30 :           cls
31 :        endif
32 :     endif
33 :
34 : // End of File: Reptdemo.prg
```

# REQUEST

| | |
|---|---|
| **COMMAND** | Specifies external routines that may be used by a program. |
| **SYNTAX** | REQUEST <expC1> |
| **PARAMETER** | <expC1>  List of subroutines that may be called from within the application |
| **DESCRIPTION** | This statement is used to declare a symbol during the compiling stage to be used later by the linker for resolution purposes. This allows a procedure or function to be called by a macro, a code block, a REPORT FORM or LABEL FORM command, an indexing routine or expression, or by the ACHOICE( ), MEMOEDIT( ), and DBEDIT( ) functions, when that subroutine may not be visible and recognized at compile time but will be called at run-time. This command tells the linker to be sure to bring in the definitions of these external routines. |
| **NOTE** | This command is designed to take precedence over the EXTERNAL statement. Since the REQUEST command is nothing more than a literal translation into the EXTERNAL request, it behaves the same way. However, in future versions of Clipper (DOS or WINDOWS), the REQUEST command is preferred due to syntactical relevance. |

| | |
|---|---|
| **SEE ALSO** | ANNOUNCE, EXTERNAL |
| **EXAMPLE** | See Chapter 13. |

## RESTORE FROM

| | |
|---|---|
| **COMMAND** | Restores the contents of a memory file. |
| **SYNTAX** | `RESTORE FROM <expC1> [ADDITIVE]` |
| **PARAMETER** | <expC1>    Filename of a memory variable file |
| **DESCRIPTION** | This command retrieves from disk the contents of the memory variable file <expC1> and activates all of the memory variables stored in that file. The file extension of .MEM is assumed, but a different extension may be specified. The drive and directory path may be additionally specified in <expC1>.<br><br>Without the ADDITIVE clause, those variables in the memory file <expC1> will be loaded into the system and will occupy the free pool of memory, thus removing all previous values. If the ADDITIVE clause is specified, the values of the variables within the file <expC1> are either added to the free pool or replace previous values of the same name found. |
| **SEE ALSO** | SAVE TO |
| **EXAMPLE** | See the SAVE TO command. |

## RESTORE SCREEN

| | |
|---|---|
| **COMMAND** | Restores a previously saved screen. |
| **SYNTAX** | `RESTORE SCREEN [FROM <expC1>]` |
| **PARAMETER** | <expC1>    Any variable name of character data type |
| **DESCRIPTION** | This command restores a screen previously saved by the SAVE SCREEN command. If no clause is specified, an internal memory variable contains the screen when the SAVE SCREEN command is executed.<br><br>If the contents of the screen were saved to a variable <expC1> with the SAVE SCREEN TO <expC1> command, the FROM clause must use the variable name <expC1>. The contents of <expC1> are then restored to the screen. |

| | |
|---|---|
| | The length of the string variable <expC1> is determined by the following equation: (MAXROW( ) * MAXCOL( ) * 2). For each character saved from the screen there is an associated attribute byte. |
| **NOTE** | This is a compatibility command and may not be supported in future versions. |
| **SEE ALSO** | SAVE SCREEN, SAVESCREEN( ), RESTSCREEN( ) |
| **EXAMPLE** | See the SAVE SCREEN command. |

## RETURN

| | |
|---|---|
| **STATEMENT** | Terminates the execution of a subroutine. |
| **SYNTAX** | `RETURN [<expX1>]` |
| **PARAMETER** | <expX1>    Any valid data expression or value, including an array reference, code block pointer, or NIL |
| **DESCRIPTION** | This command restores control to the routine that originally called the current procedure or function. If there is no routine to return control to, control is returned to DOS.

If the routine is a FUNCTION, the value of the function is determined by the value expressed in <expX1>. Any valid data type is allowed to be RETURNed to the calling routine: dates, numbers, characters, logicals, code blocks, NIL, and arrays.

The default RETURN value of a PROCEDURE is a NIL data type. |
| **SEE ALSO** | PROCEDURE, FUNCTION |

## RUN

| | |
|---|---|
| **COMMAND** | Executes an external program or DOS command. |
| **SYNTAX** | `RUN <expC1> | ! <expC1>` |
| **PARAMETER** | <expC1>    A command or program name |
| **DESCRIPTION** | This command executes a program or DOS command from within a currently running Clipper program. When the RUN command has completed execution of the specified DOS command or program, program control is given to the command line immediately following the RUN command. Additionally, launching a memory resident program from WITHIN a Clipper application will affect the amount of available memory for the application. |

Clipper loads an extra copy of COMMAND.COM whenever the RUN command is encountered. The size of this file depends on the version of the operating system. Generally speaking, the higher the DOS version number, the larger the COMMAND.COM file and thus it imposes a greater demand on available memory. In addition, COMMAND.COM must be available on the drive and directory path specified by the COMSPEC environment variable; by default, this is the root directory of the drive from which DOS is booted.

**NOTE** The SET DEFAULT and SET PATH commands have no effect on the command.

The RUN command is similar to the ! command. ! is a compatibility command and is NOT recommended. Therefore, always use the RUN command.

**SEE ALSO** !

**EXAMPLE**

```
 1 : * File      Rundemo.prg
 2 : * Compile   Rmake sample /dFILE:rundemo
 3 :
 4 : procedure Main()
 5 :
 6 :    cls
 7 :    run dir /w
 8 :    wait
 9 :    ! ver  // this gets the version number of the operating system
10 :    wait
11 :    run ver getver
12 :    cls
13 :    ? memoread( "Getver." )
14 :    wait
15 :    erase Getver.
16 :
17 : // End of File: Rundemo.prg
```

# SAVE SCREEN

**COMMAND** Saves the screen to a variable or an internal variable.

**SYNTAX** SAVE SCREEN [TO <expC1>]

**PARAMETER** <expC1>    Screen variable name

**DESCRIPTION** This command saves the screen to either an internal memory variable or to an external memory variable named <expC1>. The length of the string saved is MAXROW( ) * MAXCOL( ) * 2.

| | | |
|---|---|---|
| **NOTE** | | This is a compatibility command and may not be supported in future versions. |
| **SEE ALSO** | | SAVESCREEN( ), RESTSCREEN( ), RESTORE SCREEN |

**EXAMPLE**

```
 1 : * File       Sdemo.prg
 2 : * Compile    RMake sample /dFILE:sdemo
 3 :
 4 : #include "PTInkey.ch"
 5 : #include "PTValue.ch"
 6 :
 7 : procedure Main()
 8 :
 9 :    local nTop        := 7
10 :    local nLeft       := 20
11 :    local nBottom     := 12
12 :    local nRight      := 60
13 :    local cMidscreen  := savescreen( nTop, nLeft, nBottom, nRight )
14 :
15 :    run dir *.* /w
16 :    save screen
17 :    cls
18 :    wait "Press any key to get entire screen..."
19 :    restore screen
20 :    wait "And now press any key to start something new..."
21 :
22 :    if setmode(25,80)
23 :      Dragit(nTop, nLeft, nBottom, nRight, cMidscreen)
24 :      if setmode(43,80)
25 :        Dragit(nTop, nLeft, nBottom, nRight, cMidscreen)
26 :      endif
27 :    endif
28 :    cls
29 :    setmode(25,80)
30 :    cls
31 :    restore screen
32 :
33 : *********************
34 :
35 : static procedure Dragit(nTop, nLeft, nBottom, nRight, cScr)
36 :
37 :    local nKey
38 :
39 :    cls
40 :    @ 0,0 say "Use the cursor keys to DRAG the saved screen!"
41 :    keyboard chr( pENTER )
42 :
43 :    while pTRUE
44 :      nKey := inkey(0)
45 :      do case
46 :      case nKey == pUP_ARROW .and. !(nTop == 1)
47 :        scroll(nTop--, nLeft, nBottom--,nRight)
48 :
49 :      case nKey == pDOWN_ARROW .and. !(nBottom == maxrow())
50 :        scroll(nTop++, nLeft, nBottom++, nRight)
```

```
51 :
52 :        case nKey == pLEFT_ARROW .and. !(nLeft == 0)
53 :          scroll(nTop,nLeft--,nBottom,nRight--)
54 :
55 :        case nKey == pRIGHT_ARROW .and. !(nRight == maxcol())
56 :          scroll(nTop, nLeft++, nBottom, nRight++)
57 :
58 :        case nKey == pESC
59 :          exit
60 :
61 :      endcase
62 :
63 :      restscreen(nTop, nLeft, nBottom, nRight, cScr)
64 :
65 :    enddo
66 :
67 : // End of File: Sdemo.prg
```

## SAVE TO

**COMMAND**      Saves all or part of a set of memory variables to a file.

**SYNTAX**      SAVE TO <expC1> [ALL [LIKE | EXCEPT <expC2>] ]

**PARAMETERS**      <expC1>    A filename
    <expC2>    Skeleton pattern

**DESCRIPTION**      This command stores all or part of the current set of memory variables to a designated file <expC1>. Without any parameters specified, all PUBLIC and PRIVATE memory variables will be stored to the <expC1> file. The file <expC1> will have a default file extension of .MEM.

Several kinds of variables will not be saved: variables declared as STATIC or LOCAL; arrays; previously defined variables now hidden by a PRIVATE or LOCAL declaration; and PRIVATE or PUBLIC variables with array pointers or code block data types.

If the ALL LIKE | EXCEPT clause is specified, a memory variable skeleton is required. The skeleton clause <expC2> allows the use of a question mark (?) or an asterisk (*) as part of the skeleton pattern. A question mark represents a single character, while an asterisk represents one or more characters.

**SEE ALSO**      RESTORE FROM, LOCAL, PRIVATE, PUBLIC, STATIC

**EXAMPLE**

```
1 : * File       Savedemo.prg
2 : * Compile    RMake sample /dFILE:savedemo
3 :
4 : procedure Main()
5 :
6 :   local   dTemp1      := date()
```

```
 7 :      private dVar1      := date()
 8 :      private dVar2      := date()
 9 :      private dVar3      := date()
10 :      private dVar4      := date()
11 :      private cScrcolor  := setcolor()
12 :      private cScrdata   := "C"
13 :      private cScrprog   := "C"
14 :      private cScrpath   := curdir()
15 :      private nTemp1     := 1
16 :      private cTemp2     := "Demo Program"
17 :
18 :      cls
19 :      ? "The variables..."
20 :      ?
21 :      ? dVar1, dVar2, dVar3, dVar4
22 :      ? cScrcolor, cScrdata, cScrprog, cScrpath
23 :      ? nTemp1, cTemp2, dTemp1
24 :      wait
25 :
26 :      save to "Memfile1"
27 :      save all like dVar* to "Memfile2"
28 :      save all except nTemp1 to "Memfile3"
29 :
30 :      restore from "Memfile2"  // Only dVar* variables will be seen
31 :
32 :      ?
33 :      ? "The variables after a general RESTORE FROM!"
34 :      ?
35 :      ? dVar1, dVar2, dVar3, dVar4
36 :
37 :    * ? valtype(scrcolor), valtype(scrdata), ;
38 :    *   valtype(scrprog), valtype(scrpath)   // Don't print unless
39 :                                             // want a run-time error!
40 :    * ? valtype(nTemp1), valtype(cTemp2)     // Same thing for these!
41 :      ? valtype(dTemp1)                      // A LOCAL is unaffected!
42 :
43 :      wait
44 :      restore from "Memfile3" additive
45 :      cls
46 :      ? "The variables after a RESTORE FROM ADDITIVE..."
47 :      ?
48 :      ? dVar1, dVar2, dVar3, dVar4
49 :      ? cScrcolor, cScrdata, cScrprog, cScrpath
50 :
51 :      // ? valtype(nTemp1)           // This is still NOT around!
52 :
53 :      ? valtype(cTemp2), valtype(dTemp1)
54 :      wait
55 :      restore from "Memfile1"
56 :      cls
57 :      ? "All variables are restored!"
58 :      ?
59 :      ? dVar1, dVar2, dVar3, dVar4
60 :      ? cScrcolor, cScrdata, cScrprog, cScrpath
61 :      ? nTemp1, cTemp2, dTemp1
62 :      wait
```

```
63 :    cls
64 :
65 : // End of File:Savedemo.prg
```

## SEEK

**COMMAND**      Searches for a value based on an active index.

**SYNTAX**       SEEK <expX1> [SOFTSEEK]

**PARAMETER**    <expX1>    Any expression

**DESCRIPTION**  This command searches for the first record that matches <expX1> in a database file with an active index file. If the record is found, the value of FOUND( ) is a logical true (.T.) while the value of EOF( ) is a logical false (.F.). If no item is found, the value of FOUND( ) is a logical false (.F.) and the value of EOF( ) is a logical true (.T.).

This command always *rewinds* the database pointer and starts the search from the top of the file.

If the SOFTSEEK clause is specified, then the search will be made as if the global setting of SET SOFTSEEK ON was in existence. If SOFTSEEK is not specified, then it will default to the internal setting of SET SOFTSEEK.

If SOFTSEEK is ON, the values of FOUND( ) and EOF( ) will both be a logical false if there is a record with a greater index key value than the key expression <expX1>; the record pointer will also position itself on that record. However, if there is no greater key in the index, EOF( ) will return a logical true (.T.) value.

The SET EXACT command has no effect on the operation of this command.

**SEE ALSO**     SET SOFTSEEK, SET( ), EOF( ), FOUND( )

**EXAMPLE**
```
 1 : * File      Seekdemo.prg
 2 : * Compile   Rmake sample /dFILE:seekdemo
 3 :
 4 : #define pTRUE .T.
 5 : #define pESC 27
 6 :
 7 : memvar files, datestamp, getlist
 8 :
 9 : procedure Main()
10 :
11 :    use Ontap new
12 :
13 :    // Because of the formal MEMVAR declaration, the reference to the field
```

```
14 :    // DATESTAMP must be preceded by alias in order for it to work properly.
15 :
16 :    index on dtos(field->datestamp) to Ontap2
17 :    set index to Ontap, Ontap2
18 :
19 :    files     := space(12)
20 :    datestamp := ctod( "" )
21 :
22 :    while pTRUE
23 :      cls
24 :      @ 0,0 say "Press ESC to quit!"
25 :      @ 4,4 say "Enter name: " get files
26 :      @ 5,4 say "      date: " get datestamp
27 :      read
28 :
29 :      if (lastkey() == pESC)
30 :        exit
31 :      else
32 :        @ 8,4 say "Can a NULL byte be found? "
33 :        find ""
34 :        ?? if( found(), "Yes", "No" )
35 :        @ 9,4 say " Can the NAME be found? "
36 :        seek trim( files )
37 :        ?? if( found(), "Yes", "No" )
38 :
39 :        set order to 2
40 :        set softseek on
41 :        seek dtos( datestamp )
42 :
43 :        @ 10,4 say " Can the DATE be found? "
44 :        ?? if( found(), "Yes", "No" )
45 :        if found()
46 :          @ 11,4 say "The date we are positioned on is: "
47 :          ?? Ontap->datestamp
48 :        endif
49 :        set order to 1    // Set the order back to ONTAP.NTX
50 :        set softseek off  // Make for exact matches!
51 :        ?
52 :        wait
53 :      endif
54 :    enddo
55 :
56 : // End of File: Seekdemo
```

# SELECT

**COMMAND**      Changes to another work area.

**SYNTAX**       SELECT <expX1>

**PARAMETER**    <expX1>    Character expression for alias or numeric expression for work area

**DESCRIPTION** This command moves Clippers internal primary focus to the designated work area of <expN1> or the alias name of <expC1>.

A SELECT 0 will select the next unused work area.

Up to 255 work areas are supported. Each work area has its own alias and record pointer and its own FOUND( ), DBFILTER( ), DBRSELECT( ), and DBRELATION( ) function values. Information from another previously SELECTED or USED work area may be obtained, provided that the alias of that work area precedes the expression to be obtained. This is also true for user-defined functions and commands to be performed in unselected work areas.

**NOTE** In some cases, due to memory fragmentation, a run-time error expressing a type conflict may occur when an existing alias is reselected with the SELECT command. In this event, a SELECT SELECT("alias") dual operation may be in order.

**SEE ALSO** SET INDEX, USE, ALIAS, SELECT( )

**EXAMPLE** See the USE command.

# SET ALTERNATE

**COMMAND** Toggles and echoes output to an alternate file.

**SYNTAX**
```
SET ALTERNATE TO <expC1> [ADDITIVE]
SET ALTERNATE [ON / OFF] [(<expL2>)]
```

**PARAMETERS** <expC1>   Filename
<expL2>   Logical expression to toggle command

**DESCRIPTION** This command toggles and outputs console information to the alternate file <expC1>, provided that the command is toggled on or the condition <expL2> is set to a logical true (.T.). If <expC1> does not have a file extension, .TXT will be assumed. The filename may optionally have a drive letter and/or directory path. If none is specified, the current drive and directory will be used.

If the ALTERNATE file is created but no ALTERNATE ON command is issued, nothing will be echoed to the file.

If the ADDITIVE clause is used, then the information will be appended to the existing alternate file. Otherwise, a new file will be created with the specified name (or an existing one will be overwritten) and the information will then be appended to the file. The default is to create a new file.

A SET ALTERNATE TO command will close an alternate file.

**NOTE** This command may be called via the SET(18) (toggle the alternate status) and the SET(19) (create the alternate file) function calls.

**SEE ALSO** CLOSE, SET CONSOLE, SET PRINTER, SET( )

---

## SET BELL

---

**COMMAND** Toggles the bell to sound once a GET has been completed.

**SYNTAX** `SET BELL [ON / OFF] [(<expL1>)]`

**PARAMETER** <expL1> Logical expression to toggle command

**DESCRIPTION** This command toggles the bell to sound whenever a character is entered into the last character position of a GET, or if an invalid data type is entered into a GET. If the value of <expL1> is a logical true (.T.), the bell will be turned ON; otherwise, the bell will be turned OFF.

**NOTE** This command may be called via the SET(26) function call.

**SEE ALSO** SET CONFIRM, @ ... GET, SET( ), READ, READMODAL( )

---

## SET CENTURY

---

**COMMAND** Toggles the century digits in all date displays.

**SYNTAX** `SET CENTURY [ON / OFF] [(<expL1>)]`

**PARAMETER** <expL1> Logical expression to toggle command

**DESCRIPTION** This command allows the input and display of dates with the century prefix. It will be in standard MM/DD/YYYY format unless specified by the SET DATE command or SET( ) function. If <expL1> is a logical true (.T.), the command will be set ON; otherwise, the command will be set OFF.

**SEE ALSO** SET DATE, SET EPOCH, CTOD( ), DATE( ), DTOC( ), SET( )

---

## SET COLOR

---

**COMMAND** Establishes a system color.

**SYNTAX**

```
SET COLOR TO [[<expC1>] [, <expC2>] [, <expC3>]
[, <expC4>] [, <expC5>]]
```

| | | |
|---|---|---|
| **PARAMETERS** | <expC1> | Standard color |
| | <expC2> | Enhanced color |
| | <expC3> | Border color |
| | <expC4> | Background color |
| | <expC5> | Unselected color |

**DESCRIPTION** This command sets the screen colors. If there is no parameter with this command, the color of the system is set to "W/N,N/W,N,N,N/W".

<expC1> is the string for the standard colors; these are the colors that are used with many of the console, full-screen, and interface commands and functions.

<expC2> is the string for the enhanced colors. This color set is used for highlighted displays, such as GETs (with INTENSITY set on), PROMPTs, ACHOICE( ), and DBEDIT( ).

<expC3> is the string for the border color. This area of the screen surrounds the normal display area and cannot be written to.

<expC4> is the string for the background color. Currently, it is not supported on any platform and is used only as a compatibility parameter slot.

<expC5> is the string for the unselected color. This allows the current GET or current PROMPT to be a different color from all of the other active GETs and/or PROMPTs.

**NOTE** This is a compatibility command and may not be supported in future versions.

This command may also be called via the SET(15) function call.

**SEE ALSO** SETCOLOR( ), SET( ), ISCOLOR( ), Appendix 6.

## SET CONFIRM

**COMMAND** Determines whether or not an exit key must be pressed to end a GET.

**SYNTAX** `SET CONFIRM [ON / OFF] [(<expL1>)]`

**PARAMETER** <expL1>  Logical expression to toggle command

**DESCRIPTION** If set ON, this command requires that the ENTER key (or any other recognized exit key) be pressed to end each GET. If turned OFF, any key may exit the GET once the GET space or buffer has been filled with values. If <expL1> is a logical true (.T.), the command will be turned on; otherwise, the command will turned off.

**NOTE** This command may be called via the SET(27) function call.

**SEE ALSO** READ, @ ... GET, SET BELL, SET( ), READMODAL( )

## SET CONSOLE

| | |
|---|---|
| **COMMAND** | Toggles the console display. |
| **SYNTAX** | `SET CONSOLE [ON / OFF] [(<expL1>)]` |
| **PARAMETER** | <expL1>   Logical expression to toggle command |
| **DESCRIPTION** | This command turns the screen either off or on for all screen displays other than direct output via the @ ... SAY commands or the <->DEVOUT( ) function. If <expL1> is a logical true (.T.), the console will be turned ON; otherwise, the console will be turned OFF. |
| **NOTE** | This command may be called via the SET(17) function call. |
| **SEE ALSO** | SET DEVICE, SET( ) |

## SET CURSOR

| | |
|---|---|
| **COMMAND** | Toggles the cursor on or off. |
| **SYNTAX** | `SET CURSOR [ON / OFF] [(<expL1>)]` |
| **PARAMETER** | <expL1>   Logical expression to toggle command |
| **DESCRIPTION** | This command toggles the cursor on or off. If the value of <expL1> is a logical true (.T.), the cursor will be visible; otherwise the cursor will be hidden. |
| **NOTE** | This command may be called via the SET(16) function call. |
| **SEE ALSO** | SET( ), SETCURSOR( ) |

## SET DATE

| | |
|---|---|
| **COMMAND** | Assigns a date format or chooses a predefined date data set. |
| **SYNTAX** | `SET DATE FORMAT [TO] <expC1>`<br>`SET DATE [TO] [ ANSI / BRITISH / FRENCH /GERMAN / ITALIAN / JAPAN / USA / AMERICAN ]` |
| **PARAMETER** | <expC1>   Keyword for date format |
| **DESCRIPTION** | This command sets the date format for function display purposes. If specified, <expC1> may be a customized date format in which the letters d, m, and y may be used to design a date format. The default is an |

AMERICAN date format; specifying no parameters will set the date format to AMERICAN. Below is a table of the various predefined date formats:

| Syntax | Date Format |
|--------|-------------|
| ANSI | yy.mm.dd |
| BRITISH | dd/mm/yy |
| FRENCH | dd/mm/yy |
| GERMAN | dd.mm.yy |
| ITALIAN | dd-mm-yy |
| JAPAN | yy/mm/dd |
| USA | mm-dd-yy |
| AMERICAN | mm/dd/yy |

**NOTE** This command may be called via the SET(4) function call.

**SEE ALSO** SET CENTURY, SET EPOCH, SET( ), CTOD( ), DATE( ), DTOC( )

## SET DECIMALS

**COMMAND** Sets the number of decimal places to be displayed.

**SYNTAX** `SET DECIMALS TO [<expN1>]`

**PARAMETER** <expN1>   Number of decimals

**DESCRIPTION** This command establishes the number of decimal places that Clipper will display in mathematical calculations, functions, memory variables, and fields. Issuing no parameters with this command will default the number of decimals to 0. For the decimals to be seen, the SET FIXED ON command must be activated.

**NOTE** This command may be called via the SET(3) function call.

**SEE ALSO** SET FIXED, SET( )

## SET DEFAULT

**COMMAND** Establishes the Clipper search drive and directory.

**SYNTAX** `SET DEFAULT TO [<expC1>]`

**PARAMETER** <expC1>   Drive and/or path

| | |
|---|---|
| **DESCRIPTION** | This command changes the drive and directory used for reading and writing database, index, memory, and alternate files. Specifying no parameters with this command will default the operations to the current logged drive and directory. |
| **NOTE** | This command may be called via the SET(7) function call. |
| **SEE ALSO** | SET PATH, CURDIR( ), SET( ) |

## SET DELETED

| | |
|---|---|
| **COMMAND** | Toggles the visibility of records marked for deletion. |
| **SYNTAX** | `SET DELETED [ON / OFF] [(<expL1>)]` |
| **PARAMETER** | <expL1>    Logical expression to toggle command |
| **DESCRIPTION** | This command is, in essence, a filter placed on all databases in all work areas to mask out those records marked for deletion. If <expL1> is set to a logical true (.T.), the deleted mask will be turned ON; otherwise, the deleted mask will be turned OFF.<br><br>The RECALL ALL command does not recall any records if the SET DELETED command is active. On an INDEX or REINDEX command, all records will be included regardless of the status of the SET DELETED command.<br><br>To exclusively mask out those records marked for deletion within one particular work area, the SET FILTER TO !DELETED( ) command is available. |
| **NOTE** | This command may be called via the SET(11) function call. |
| **SEE ALSO** | SET FILTER, SET( ), DELETED( ), DELETE, RECALL |

## SET DELIMITERS

| | |
|---|---|
| **COMMAND** | Defines and toggles field delimiters. |
| **SYNTAX** | `SET DELIMITERS [ON / OFF] [(<expL1>)]`<br>`SET DELIMITERS TO [<expC2>][DEFAULT]` |
| **PARAMETERS** | <expL1>    Logical expression for a toggle<br><expC2>    Pair of delimiter characters |
| **DESCRIPTION** | This dual command allows the delimiters surrounding a GET to be toggled ON or OFF and to set the default character used as a delimiter. By default, the delimiters are turned OFF, and the characters surround- |

ing GETs, if turned ON, would be "::". If <expL1> is a logical true (.T.) expression, the command would be toggled ON; if the expression is a logical false (.F.), the command would be turned off.

If <expC2> is specified, the two characters surrounding a GET may be changed. Regardless of the length of <expC2>, only the first two bytes are used; the first byte is the left delimiter and the next byte is the right delimiter. If the DEFAULT clause is specified, the default characters are reset to be the delimiters for a GET.

No matter what the delimiters are set to, they will not show unless the delimiters are toggled ON.

**NOTE** Both of these commands may also be called via the SET(33) (to toggle the delimiters on and off) and SET(34) (to set the delimiters) functions.

**SEE ALSO** @ ... GET, SET INTENSITY, SET( )

## SET DEVICE

**COMMAND** Directs all @ .. SAY output to a device.

**SYNTAX** `SET DEVICE TO [PRINTER / SCREEN]`

**PARAMETER** None

**DESCRIPTION** This command determines whether the output from the @ ... SAY command and the DEVPOS( ) and DEVOUT( ) functions will be displayed to the printer or to the screen.

When the device is set to the PRINTER, the SET MARGIN value adjusts the position of the column values accordingly. Also, an automatic page eject will be issued when the current printhead position is less than the last printed row. Finally, if used in conjunction with the @...GET commands, the values for the GETs will all be ignored.

**NOTE** This command may also be called via the SET(20) function.

**SEE ALSO** @ ... SAY, SET PRINTER, SETPRC( ), SET( )

## SET EPOCH

**COMMAND** Specifies a base year for interpreting dates.

**SYNTAX** `SET EPOCH TO <expN1>`

**PARAMETER** <expN1>     Base century

| | |
|---|---|
| **DESCRIPTION** | This command sets the base year value for dates that have only two digits. The default setting is 1900. Dates between 01/01/0100 and 12/31/2999 are fully supported. |
| **NOTE** | This command may also be called via the SET(5) function. |
| **SEE ALSO** | SET CENTURY, SET DATE, CTOD( ), DATE( ), DTOC( ), SET( ) |

## SET ESCAPE

| | |
|---|---|
| **COMMAND** | Toggles ESC as an exit key for a READ command or READMODAL function. |
| **SYNTAX** | `SET ESCAPE [ON / OFF] [(<expL1>)]` |
| **PARAMETER** | <expL1>   Logical expression for a toggle |
| **DESCRIPTION** | This command allows an ESC key to abort out of a READ command or READMODAL( ) function. If turned on, any active WHEN, VALID, or RANGE clause is ignored and the READ is completed. If turned OFF, the ESC key will not be allowed to exit out of a READ condition. If the value of <expL1> is a logical true (.T.), the ESC key will be turned ON; otherwise, a logical false (.F.) will turn it OFF. |
| **NOTE** | This command may also be called via the SET(28) function. |
| **SEE ALSO** | SET KEY, READ, SETCANCEL( ), SET( ) |

## SET EXACT

| | |
|---|---|
| **COMMAND** | Toggles an exact match for character string comparisons. |
| **SYNTAX** | `SET EXACT [ON / OFF] [(<expL1>)]` |
| **PARAMETER** | <expL1>   Logical expression for a toggle |
| **DESCRIPTION** | This command determines how character strings are compared. If toggled ON, any character expressions being compared must match exactly; if toggled OFF, the match is based on string length and position within the comparison expression. If <expL1> is a logical true (.T.), the toggle will be considered ON, and a logical false (.F.) will toggle the command off. |
| | This command is equivalent to the == operator for string evaluations, which is preferred for most numeric evaluations. |

| | |
|---|---|
| **NOTE** | This is a compatibility command and may not be supported in future versions. This command may also be called via the SET(1) function. |
| **SEE ALSO** | SEEK, SET( ) |

## SET EXCLUSIVE

| | |
|---|---|
| **COMMAND** | Toggles the shared or exclusive use of a database. |
| **SYNTAX** | `SET EXCLUSIVE [ON / OFF] [(<expL1>)]` |
| **PARAMETER** | <expL1>    Logical expression for a toggle |
| **DESCRIPTION** | This command determines the way in which a database and related memo and index files are opened. If set ON, the files are in EXCLUSIVE use only—only that user may have access to them. If OFF, the files are in SHARED mode. If <expL1> is a logical true (.T.), the command is turned ON; if <expL1> is a logical false (.F.), the command is turned off. |
| **NOTE** | This is a compatibility command and may not be supported in future versions. This command also may be called with the SET(8) function. |
| **SEE ALSO** | USE, FLOCK( ), NETERR( ), SET( ) |

## SET FILTER

| | |
|---|---|
| **COMMAND** | Establishes a filter condition for an active work area. |
| **SYNTAX** | `SET FILTER TO [<expL1>]` |
| **PARAMETER** | <expL1>    Logical expression for condition to be met |
| **DESCRIPTION** | This command masks a database so that only those records that meet the condition prescribed by the logical expression in <expL1> will be shown. The expression <expL1> may contain field names, variable names, or other expressions and conditions.<br><br>If no parameter is specified with the SET FILTER command, any filter condition on the active work area is turned off. This is the default condition.<br><br>If any filter condition is set in a work area with active indexes, performance when traversing through the database will be considerably slower than it would if all active indexes were closed and the filter were allowed to work on the database in its natural order. If an index is needed, |

the filter should be a subset of the controlling index key, and all other nonessential indexes should be closed.

Each work area can maintain a separate and unique filter condition.

If this command is active, a GO TOP command should be issued immediately in order to position the record pointer to the top record meeting the filter condition. Otherwise, an unwanted record may appear in the filtered subset.

**SEE ALSO**     SET DELETED, DBFILTER( ), TBROWSENEW( )

## SET FIXED

**COMMAND**     Sets the number of decimal positions to be displayed.

**SYNTAX**     `SET FIXED [ON / OFF] [(<expL1>)]`

**PARAMETER**     <expL1>     Logical expression for a toggle

**DESCRIPTION**     This command activates a systemwide fixed placement of the decimal places shown for all numeric output. If the value of <expL1> is a logical true (.T.), FIXED will be turned ON; otherwise, it will be turned OFF.

When SET DECIMALS OFF is used, the following rules apply to the number of decimal places displayed:

| | |
|---|---|
| Addition/Subtraction | Same as the operand with the greatest number of decimal digits |
| Multiplication | Sum of the operand decimal digits |
| Division | Determined by SET DECIMAL TO |
| Exponentiation | Determined by SET DECIMAL TO |
| LOG( ) | Determined by SET DECIMAL TO |
| EXP( ) | Determined by SET DECIMAL TO |
| SQRT( ) | Determined by SET DECIMAL TO |
| VAL( ) | Determined by SET DECIMAL TO |

**NOTE**     This command may also be called via the SET(2) function.

**SEE ALSO**     SET DECIMALS, EXP( ), LOG( ), SQRT( ), VAL( ), SET( )

## SET FORMAT

**COMMAND**     Activates a format file when a READ is called.

**SYNTAX**     `SET FORMAT TO [<expC1>]`

| | |
|---|---|
| **PARAMETER** | <expC1>　　Filename |
| **DESCRIPTION** | This command selects a custom format that has been previously stored in file <expC1>. If no file extension is specified in <expC1>, the default extension will be .FMT. Files with a .FMT extension will not be recognized in a compiling script file. |
| **NOTE** | This is a compatibility command and may not be supported in future versions. |
| **SEE ALSO** | @ ... GET, @ ... SAY, READ, READMODAL( ) |

## SET FUNCTION

| | |
|---|---|
| **COMMAND** | Assigns a character string to a function key. |
| **SYNTAX** | `SET FUNCTION <expN1> TO <expC2>` |
| **PARAMETERS** | <expN1>　　Number of the function key<br><expC2>　　Character expression |
| **DESCRIPTION** | This command allows a character string <expC2> to be stored to 40 possible function keys <expN1>, listed as 1 through 40. The values of <expC2> may conflict with previously SET KEY commands. Below is a table of the 40 keys. |

| Function Key | Keyboard Mapping |
|---|---|
| 1 – 10 | F1 -> F10 |
| 11 – 20 | Shift-F1 -> Shift-F10 |
| 21 – 30 | Ctrl-F1 -> Ctrl-F10 |
| 31 – 40 | Alt-F1 -> Alt-F10 |

| | |
|---|---|
| **SEE ALSO** | SET KEY, KEYBOARD |

## SET INDEX

| | |
|---|---|
| **COMMAND** | Opens an index file or files in the current work area. |
| **SYNTAX** | `SET INDEX TO [<expC1> [, <expC2>...]] [ADDITIVE]` |
| **PARAMETERS** | <expC1>　　An index filename<br><expC2>　　An index filename(s) |
| **DESCRIPTION** | This command opens an index file named <expC1> (and following) for use with the current database. If there is more than one file in the list, the order of the database will be determined by the key in the first index |

file listed. All file operations will be based on the first index file; however, all index files in the index list will be updated if the key values in the database are updated.

Issuing this command without any file parameters will close all active indexes. Any active index previously in use will also be closed if additional index files are specified. Up to 15 index files may be active in any one work area.

If the ADDITIVE clause is specified, then any file specified in <expC1> will be added to the index list without closing the active indexes. If the ADDITIVE clause is not specified, then all indexes will be closed before the index file <expC1> will be opened.

**SEE ALSO**     SET ORDER, SET( ), CLOSE, INDEX, USE

## SET INTENSITY

| | |
|---|---|
| **COMMAND** | Toggles the enhanced display of PROMPTs and GETs. |
| **SYNTAX** | `SET INTENSITY [ON / OFF] [(<expL1>)]` |
| **PARAMETER** | <expL1>    Logical expression for a toggle |
| **DESCRIPTION** | This command sets the field input color and the @ ... PROMPT menu color to either highlighted (inverse video) or normal color. The default condition is ON (highlighted). |
| **NOTE** | This command may also be called via the SET(31) function. |
| **SEE ALSO** | @ ... GET, @ ... PROMPT, @ ... SAY, SET( ) |

## SET KEY

| | |
|---|---|
| **COMMAND** | Assigns a procedure or a function to a key. |
| **SYNTAX** | `SET KEY <expN1> TO [<expC2>]` |
| **PARAMETERS** | <expN1>    Number of the scan code of a key<br><expC2>    A subroutine name |
| **DESCRIPTION** | This command is used to assign the subroutine named <expC2> to the key expressed as <expN1>. The value of <expN1> is determined by a key's return value from INKEY(0); not specifying a value for <expC2> will de-assign the subroutine previously assigned to the key.<br><br>The connection between the routines specified in <expC2> and the keys expressed in <expN1> is activated only at a Clipper wait state. A |

wait state is any normal pausing operation other than the INKEY(0) function. These commands are ACCEPT, INPUT, MENU TO, READ, WAIT, ACHOICE( ), DBEDIT( ), and MEMOEDIT( ).

When an assigned key is pressed during a wait state, three parameters are automatically passed to <expC2>: PROCNAME( ), PROCLINE( ), and READVAR( ). These parameters need not be explicitly passed to <expC2>.

Key conflicts may occur when a new procedure is assigned to a key that has been previously assigned a character string by the SET FUNCTION TO command or the SET( ) function or has been involved in a user-defined function within ACHOICE( ), DBEDIT( ), or MEMOEDIT( ).

A maximum of 32 keys may be assigned at any one time. The F1 key, at the startup of an application, is assigned to a routine named Help.

SET KEY operations take precedence over the SET ESCAPE and SETCANCEL( ) operations.

**SEE ALSO**         KEYBOARD, READ, INKEY( ), SETKEY( )

## SET MARGIN

**COMMAND**         Sets the left margin offset for all printed output.

**SYNTAX**          `SET MARGIN TO [<expN1>]`

**PARAMETER**       <expN1>    Numerical value of offset

**DESCRIPTION**     This command adjusts the left-hand margin for all printed output according to the value of <expN1>. If no parameter is specified, the default left-hand margin will be 0.

**NOTE**            This command may also be invoked with the SET(25) function call.

**SEE ALSO**        SET( ), @ ... SAY, SET DEVICE, SET PRINTER

## SET MESSAGE

**COMMAND**         Establishes a message row for @ ... PROMPT commands.

**SYNTAX**          `SET MESSAGE TO [<expN1> [CENTER]]`

**PARAMETER**       <expN1>    Row number

**DESCRIPTION**     This command is designed to work in conjunction with the MENU TO and @ ... PROMPT commands. With this command, a row number between 0 and MAXROW( ) may be specified in <expN1>. This establishes the row on which any message associated with an @ ... PROMPT command will appear. If the value of <expN1> is 0, all messages will be suppressed.

All messages will be left-justified unless the CENTER clause is used. In this case, the individual messages in each @ ... PROMPT command will be centered at the designated row (unless <expN1> is 0). All messages are independent; therefore, the screen area cleared out by the centered message will vary based on the length of each individual message.

Specifying no parameters with this command sets the row value to 0, which suppresses all message output.

The British spelling of CENTRE is also supported.

**NOTE** This command may also be invoked with the SET(36) (specify the row for the message) and SET(37) (toggle the CENTER clause) function calls.

**SEE ALSO** SET( ), SET WRAP, MENU TO, @ ... PROMPT

## SET ORDER

**COMMAND** Sets a controlling index order.

**SYNTAX** SET ORDER TO [<expN1> | TAG <expC2> [IN <epxX3>] ]

**PARAMETER** <expN1>   Position of controlling index

**DESCRIPTION** This command selects a new active index from the list of open index files. If <expN1> is 0, the natural order of the database is in control. This is suggested for adding records to a database with active indexes; altering the controlling index to 0 allows the keys in all other indexes to be maintained properly. The range of values may be from 0 to 15.

Passing no parameters to this command sets the natural order to 0.

The optional TAG clause allows access to multiple-order Order Bags in which the name of the order is specified as <expC2>.

The optional IN clause is the name of a file <expX3> containing one or more Orders.

**SEE ALSO** INDEX, INDEXORD( ), SET INDEX

**EXAMPLE** See Chapter 12.

## SET PATH

**COMMAND** Specifies a search path for opening files.

**SYNTAX** `SET PATH TO [<expC1>]`

**PARAMETER** <expC1>  Search path

**DESCRIPTION** This command specifies the search path for files required by most commands and functions not found in the current drive and directory. This pertains primarily, but not exclusively, to databases, indexes, and memo files, as well as to memory, label, and report files. The search hierarchy is

1. Current drive and directory
2. The SET DEFAULT path
3. The SET PATH path

**NOTE** This command is the same as SET(6).

**SEE ALSO** SET DEFAULT, CURDIR( ), SET( )

## SET PRINTER

**COMMAND** Toggles the printer and controls the printer device.

**SYNTAX**
```
SET PRINTER ON / OFF
SET PRINTER (<expL1>)
SET PRINTER TO [ <expC2> ] [ADDITIVE]
```

**PARAMETERS** <expL1>  Logical condition by which to toggle the printer
<expC2>  A device name or an alternate filename

**DESCRIPTION** This command can direct all output that is not controlled by the @ ... SAY command and the DEVPOS( ) and DEVOUT( ) functions to the printer. If specified, the condition <expL1> toggles the printer ON if logical true (.T.) and OFF if logical false (.F.). If no argument is specified in the command, the alternate file (if one is open) is closed, or the device is reselected and the PRINTER option is turned OFF.

If a device is specified in <expC2>, the output will be directed to that device instead of to the PRINTER. A specified device may be a literal string or a variable, as long as the variable is enclosed in parentheses. For a network, do not use a trailing colon when redirecting to a device.

If an alternate file is specified, <expC2> becomes the name of a file that will contain the output. If no file extension is specified, an extension of .PRN will be defaulted to.

|  |  |
|---|---|
| | If the ADDITIVE clause is specified, the information will be appended to the end of the specified output file. Otherwise, a new file will be created with the specified name (or an existing file will first be cleared) and the information will then be appended to the file. The default is to create a new file. |
| **NOTE** | This command is the same as SET(23, .T.), which turns the printer on in the SET( ) function. |
| **SEE ALSO** | SET DEVICE, SET CONSOLE, DEVOUT( ), SET( ) |

## SET PROCEDURE

|  |  |
|---|---|
| **COMMAND** | Specifies a file to be included in the compilation process. |
| **SYNTAX** | `SET PROCEDURE TO [<expC1>]` |
| **PARAMETER** | <expC1>  A filename |
| **DESCRIPTION** | This command allows a series of routines that are contained in the file <expC1> to be included in a compiled program. If one is not specified, a .PRG file extension will be assumed. |
| **NOTE** | This is a compatibility command that may not be supported in future versions. |
| **SEE ALSO** | DO, EVAL( ), FUNCTION, PROCEDURE, Chapter 1, #include. |

## SET RELATION

|  |  |
|---|---|
| **COMMAND** | Relates two active work areas together by a common key field or record number. |
| **SYNTAX** | `SET RELATION [TO <expX1> INTO <expC2> [, <expX3> INTO <expC4>...]] [ADDITIVE]` |
| **PARAMETERS** | <expX1>  Expression to be tied to<br><expC2>  Work area alias<br><expX3>  Expression to be tied to<br><expC4>  Work area alias |
| **DESCRIPTION** | This command links the expression <expX1> in the currently selected work area to the work area named <expC2>. If <expX1> is the name of a field or fields in the current work area, the value of that field will be SEEKed in alias area <expC2>. For this to work properly, the controlling index in <expC2> must be of the same type as the expression found |

in <expX1>. Whenever the active file's record pointer is repositioned, the linked file is searched for the first record matching the key expression from the active file.

If <expX1> is a record number, a simple GOTO command will be issued in the alias work area <expC2>. Additional key fields or expressions (<expX3> and following) may be tied to other work areas (<expC4> and following). Up to eight child RELATIONS are supported from one mother file. Cyclical relations are not supported.

If the ADDITIVE clause is specified, the relations previously set in the current work area are not removed, and the relation being set is added to existing ones. If not specified, all active relations in the current work area will be removed prior to being reestablished.

If there are no arguments with this command, all relations are removed in the currently selected work area.

**SEE ALSO** DBRELATION( ), DBRSELECT( ), SEEK

## SET SCOREBOARD

**COMMAND** Toggles the display area for READ and MEMOEDIT( ) operations.

**SYNTAX** `SET SCOREBOARD [ON/OFF] [(<expL1>)]`

**PARAMETER** <expL1> Logical expression to toggle command

**DESCRIPTION** This command toggles the display area in the upper-right corner of the screen for the READ command and MEMOEDIT( ) function. If in a GET and a value is outside of a RANGE clause, the INS key is pressed (for a READ), or the ESC key is pressed in MEMOEDIT( ) during an edit condition, appropriate messages will appear in this area. To turn off this display, toggle SCOREBOARD to OFF. The default is to turn ON the SCOREBOARD.

If <expL1> is a logical true (.T.), the SCOREBOARD area will be active; a logical false (.F.) will turn off the SCOREBOARD area.

**SEE ALSO** READ, MEMOEDIT( ), @ ... GET, SET( )

## SET SOFTSEEK

**COMMAND** Toggles relative seek conditions.

**SYNTAX** `SET SOFTSEEK [ON/OFF] [(<expL1>)]`

**PARAMETER** <expL1> Logical expression to toggle command

| | |
|---|---|
| **DESCRIPTION** | This command determines whether *relative* seeking will be used in searching a database.
If the SET SOFTSEEK command is ON, a SEEK or FIND command is issued, and no match is found, the record pointer will be set to the next record in the index that has a higher key value than the expression in the SEEK or FIND command. The FOUND( ) and EOF( ) will both return a logical false (.F.). If <expL1> is a logical true (.T.), SET SOFTSEEK will be ON; a logical false (.F.) value will SET SOFTSEEK OFF.
Specifying no parameters with this command will turn OFF the SOFTSEEK operation. |
| **NOTE** | This command is the same as making a SET(9) call. |
| **SEE ALSO** | SEEK, SET ORDER, SET INDEX, FOUND( ), EOF( ), SET( ) |
| **EXAMPLE** | See the SEEK command. |

## SET TYPEAHEAD

| | |
|---|---|
| **COMMAND** | Sets the size of the typeahead buffer. |
| **SYNTAX** | `SET TYPEAHEAD TO <expN1>` |
| **PARAMETER** | <expN1>   Size of the keyboard buffer |
| **DESCRIPTION** | This command sets the size of the keyboard buffer. The buffer can be as small as 0 (no keys allowed in the keyboard buffer) to a maximum of 32,768. |
| **SEE ALSO** | CLEAR TYPEAHEAD, KEYBOARD, INKEY( ), NEXTKEY( ) |

## SET UNIQUE

| | |
|---|---|
| **COMMAND** | Toggles the inclusion of nonunique keys in an index file. |
| **SYNTAX** | `SET UNIQUE [ON/OFF] [(<expL1>)]` |
| **PARAMETER** | <expL1>   Logical expression to toggle command |
| **DESCRIPTION** | This command determines whether all records with the same value on a key expression will be included in the index file. An index created with SET UNIQUE ON will create an index based solely on each unique value within the database. An attribute byte within the index header file (position 277) will be set to a 1. Only the first record of those with duplicate keys will be included in the index file. |

Issuing no arguments with this command will toggle the SET UNIQUE command off.

A logical expression may be used to toggle this command. If <expL1> is a logical true (.T.), the SET UNIQUE command will be turned on; otherwise it will be turned off.

**NOTE** This is a compatibility command and may not be supported in future versions.

This command is the same as making a call to SET(10).

**SEE ALSO** SET( ), INDEX, SEEK, PACK

## SET WRAP

| | |
|---|---|
| **COMMAND** | Toggles wrapping the PROMPTs in a menu. |
| **SYNTAX** | `SET WRAP ON/OFF`<br>`SET WRAP (<expL1>)` |
| **PARAMETER** | <expL1>   Logical expression for toggle |
| **DESCRIPTION** | This command toggles the highlighted bars in an @ ... PROMPT command to wrap around in a bottom-to-top and top-to-bottom manner. If the value of the logical expression <expL1> is a logical false (.F.), the wrapping mode is set OFF; otherwise, it is set ON. |
| **NOTE** | This command is the same as making a call to SET(35). |
| **SEE ALSO** | @ ... PROMPT, MENU TO |
| **EXAMPLE** | See the MENU TO command. |

## SKIP

| | |
|---|---|
| **COMMAND** | Moves the record pointer in the current or an aliased work area. |
| **SYNTAX** | `SKIP [<expN1>] [ALIAS <expX2>]` |
| **PARAMETERS** | <expN1>   Number of records to skip<br><expX2>   Numeric or character expression |
| **DESCRIPTION** | This command moves the record pointer <expN1> records in the active work area or in an unselected area specified as numeric expression <expX2> or as alias character expression <expX2>.<br><br>If no record argument is specified in <expN1>, the default SKIP will be 1 record. |

A SKIP 0 will flush and refresh the internal database buffer and make any change made to the record visible without moving the record pointer in either direction.

**SEE ALSO** COMMIT, GO, LOCATE, SEEK, FIND, RECNO( )

**EXAMPLE** See the GO command.

# SORT

**COMMAND** Generates a new database in sorted order.

**SYNTAX**
```
SORT TO <expC1> ON <expX2> [/A /D /C] [, <expX3>
[/A /D /C ]...] [<expC4>] [WHILE <expL5>]
[FOR <expL6>]
```

**PARAMETERS**
- <expC1>   Filename
- <expX2>   A field name
- <expX3>   A field name list
- <expC4>   Expression of the scope
- <expL5>   Logical expression of WHILE condition
- <expL6>   Logical expression of FOR condition

**DESCRIPTION** This command sorts the contents of the currently active database on field <expX2> to file <expC1>. Additional sort fields may be specified in <expX3> and following. The default operation will sort records in alphabetical, chronological, or numerical order as specified by the ON <expX2> clause.

Optionally for each field specified, a sorting switch may be toggled as follows:

- /A   ASCENDING order
- /D   DESCENDING order
- /C   Ignore CASE

Combining switches is valid: /AC or /CD, and so on.

Memo fields may not be sorted, and multiple sort fields must be separated by commas. Field sorting criteria may not be specified in a macro-expansion call.

Three file handles must be available for this command to work properly. In addition, the file being sorted must be locked or used exclusively if this command is to work in a network environment.

<expC4> is the scope for this command. Valid scopes include NEXT <expN> (where <expN> is the number of records), RECORD <expN>

(a specific record number), REST (all records from the current record position), and ALL (all records). The default is ALL.

Both logical expressions may work in conjunction with one another, where <expL6> is the logical expression for the FOR condition (for records to be sorted within a given range) and <expL5> is the logical expression for the WHILE condition (for records meeting the condition to be sorted until it fails).

**SEE ALSO**  INDEX, DBEVAL( ), USE

**EXAMPLE**

```
 1 : * File      Sortdemo.prg
 2 : * Compile   RMake sample /dFILE:sortdemo
 3 : * Note      This shows how the SORT command will work with a condition
 4 : *           and in descending order.  Do not use an alias name along with
 5 : *           the field that is to be sorted.  Run-time errors may occur if
 6 : *           called using an alias along with a field to be sorted.
 7 :
 8 : procedure Main()
 9 :
10 :    use Ontap new
11 :    sort to Sort1 on files
12 :    wait "First sort completed...Any key"
13 :    sort to Sort2 on files for Ontap->sizes > 3000
14 :    wait "Second sort completed...Any key"
15 :    sort to Sort3 on files /D
16 :    wait "Final sort completed...Any key"
17 :
18 :    close databases
19 :    use Sort1 new
20 :    use Sort2 new
21 :    use Sort3 new
22 :
23 :    Sort1->( ShowRecords("Sorted by File Name") )
24 :    Sort2->( ShowRecords("Sorted by Files Name for Sizes > 3000"))
25 :    Sort3->( ShowRecords("Inverse Sorted by File Name") )
26 :
27 :    close all
28 :    erase Sort1.dbf
29 :    erase Sort2.dbf
30 :    erase Sort3.dbf
31 :
32 :    cls
33 :
34 : *********************
35 :
36 : static procedure ShowRecords( cSaying )
37 :
38 :    cls
39 :    devout( 0,0 )
40 :    devout("Press ESC to continue...")
41 :    devout( padc( cSaying, 40) )
42 :    dbedit()
43 :
44 : // End of File: Sortdemo.prg
```

## STATIC

| | |
|---|---|
| **STATEMENT** | Initializes a static memory variable or array. |
| **SYNTAX** | `STATIC <expX1> [, <expX2>...] [:= <expX3>]` |
| **PARAMETERS** | `<expX1>` A memory variable name |
| | `<expX2>` A memory variable list |
| | `<expX3>` Expression to be assigned to the variable |
| **DESCRIPTION** | This command initializes a STATIC memory variable or array. The name of either is specified in <expX1> and following. If a variable or an array is to be assigned a start-up value, that expression may be specified in <expX3> and following. |
| | STATIC variables are generated symbols at run time and are resolved at compile time. The visibility of a STATIC variable or array is limited to the function or procedure in which it is defined. The life span of a STATIC variable or array is the duration of the program's execution. |
| | No macro expansions are allowed in the STATIC declaration statement. |
| | The only Clipper commands that may precede the STATIC command are FUNCTION, PROCEDURE, PUBLIC, PRIVATE, PARAMETERS, MEMVAR, LOCAL, and FIELD. |
| | STATIC variables and arrays are not affected by the RELEASE command. |
| **NOTE** | For further information on this command, see Chapter 5. |
| **SEE ALSO** | LOCAL, FIELD, MEMVAR, FUNCTION, PROCEDURE, PARAMETERS |

## STORE

| | |
|---|---|
| **COMMAND** | Stores a value to a variable or a list of variables. |
| **SYNTAX** | `STORE <expX1> TO <expC2> [, <expC3>...]` |
| **PARAMETERS** | `<expX1>` Value to be assigned to variable(s) |
| | `<expC2>` Variable name |
| | `<expC3>` Variable name(s) |
| **DESCRIPTION** | This command initializes a memory variable <expC2> or variables <expC3> and following to the value of <expX1>. |
| **NOTE** | This is a compatibility command and may not be supported in future versions. |

**SEE ALSO**    Chapter 4, :=, PRIVATE, PUBLIC, STATIC, LOCAL

**EXAMPLE**

```
STORE 1 TO a, b, c
? a  // Display of 1
? b  // Display of 1
? c  // Display of 1
a := b:= c := 45
? a  // Display of 45
? b  // Display of 45
? c  // Display of 45
```

# SUM

**COMMAND**    Sums the field values in a database to a memory variable.

**SYNTAX**    SUM <expN1> TO <expN2> [<expC3>] [WHILE <expL4>] [FOR <expL5>]

**PARAMETERS**
<expN1>   Numeric expression to sum
<expN2>   Variable name
<expC3>   Scope condition
<expL4>   Logical expression of WHILE condition
<expL5>   Logical expression of FOR condition

**DESCRIPTION**    This command sums the numeric field(s) listed in expressions <expN1> to the memory variable(s) listed in <expN3>. The numeric expressions may represent the values of numeric fields and/or numeric calculations derived from formulas that are based on numeric fields. For this command to function properly, there must be an equal number of numeric fields or calculations and memory variables.

<expC3> is the scope for this command. Valid scopes include NEXT <expN> (where <expN> is the number of records), RECORD <expN> (a specific record number), REST (all records from the current record position), and ALL (all records). The default is ALL.

Both logical expressions may work in conjunction with one another, where <expL5> is the logical expression for the FOR condition (for records to be summed within a given range) and <expL4> is the logical expression for the WHILE condition (for records to be summed until the condition no longer holds).

**SEE ALSO**    AVERAGE, TOTAL, COUNT, DELETE, RECALL, DBEVAL( )

**EXAMPLE**    See the TOTAL command.

# TEXT

**COMMAND**  Displays a block of text as literals to an output device.

**SYNTAX**
```
TEXT [TO PRINTER] [TO FILE <expC1>]
    <text>
ENDTEXT
```

**PARAMETER**  <expC1>   A filename

**DESCRIPTION**  This command outputs a block of text specified as <text> to the current device.

If the TO PRINTER clause is specified, the output will go to the printer.

If the TO FILE clause is specified, the name of the alternate file to contain the output is specified as <expC1>. If no file extension is given to <expC1>, an extension of .TXT will be used.

If either the TO FILE or the TO PRINTER command clause is used, the output will still be displayed to the screen as well as to the designated output device. To toggle this feature off, the SET CONSOLE OFF command or SET( ) function needs to be called.

**NOTE**  This is a compatibility command and may not be supported in future versions.

**SEE ALSO**  DEVPOS( ), DEVOUT( ), QOUT( ), QQOUT( ), SET CONSOLE( ), ?, ??

**EXAMPLE**

```
 1 : * File      Textdemo.prg
 2 : * Compile   RMake sample /dFILE:textdemo
 3 :
 4 : procedure Main()
 5 :
 6 :    cls
 7 :    text
 8 :    This to show that text can be generated on the screen without
 9 :    worrying about the beginning and ending quotation marks.  The
10 :    trouble with this command is that it is rarely used in an
11 :    application.  Most output to the screen, to the printer, or even
12 :    to a file, is formatted in a way that is acceptable to the
13 :    customer or to the client.  This can only be accomplished via
14 :
15 :    DEVPOS(), DEVOUT() and @ SAY logic in Clipper.
16 :
17 :    Press any key to move on...
18 :    endtext
19 :    inkey(0)
20 :    cls
21 :    text to file "Showtext.txt"
22 :    Remember, this is a compatibility command and may not be supported in
23 :    future versions of the compiler.  It is only in the command set in
```

```
24 :    order to be more compatible with previous versions of the compiler.
25 :
26 :    Any key...
27 :    inkey(0)
28 :    endtext
29 :    cls
30 :    devout("Remember to look at SHOWTEXT.TXT to see the output...")
31 :
32 : // End of File:Textdemo.prg
```

# TOTAL

**COMMAND**  Totals values in records of a database based on the key value.

**SYNTAX**  TOTAL ON <expX1> [FIELDS <expN2> ] TO <expC3> [<expC4>] [WHILE <expL5>] [FOR <expL6>]

**PARAMETERS**
- <expX1>  Expression of key value
- <expN2>  Numeric field(s) to be totaled
- <expC3>  Filename
- <expC4>  Expression of scope condition
- <expL5>  Logical expression of WHILE condition
- <expL6>  Logical expression of FOR condition

**DESCRIPTION**  This command is used to total numeric fields in the currently selected work area based on expression <expX1> to a new database named <expC3>. For this command to have the desired effect, <expX1> should correspond to the way in which the database is ordered (either indexed or sorted). The numeric fields to be TOTALed in the output database need to be specified in <expN2>. If the FIELDS command verb is excluded from the parameter list, the numeric fields in the output database will only contain the numeric values of the first unique record that matched the key. In other word, the numeric fields are not totaled and only unique occurrences of the key and accompanying fields are copied to the new database <expC3>.

<expC4> is the scope for this command. Valid scopes include NEXT <expN> (where <expN> is the number of records), RECORD <expN> (a specific record to be printed), REST (all records from the current record position), and ALL (all records). The default is ALL.

Both logical expressions may work in conjunction with one another, where <expL6> is the logical expression for the FOR condition (for records to be totaled within a given range) and <expL5> is the logical condition for the WHILE condition (for records meeting the condition to be totaled until it fails).

318   *Straley's Programming with Clipper 5.2*

If SET DELETED is off, records marked for deletion in the source database are totaled in the new database and they also maintain their DELETED status.

**NOTE**   A run-time error is generated when the numeric field(s) that is being summed isn't large enough to accommodate the resulting totals.

**SEE ALSO**   AVERAGE, INDEX, SORT, SUM

**EXAMPLE**

```
 1: * File      Totdemo.prg
 2: * Compile   RMake sample /dFILE:totdemo
 3:
 4: #define pTRUE .T.
 5:
 6:procedure Main()
 7:
 8:    local nVar1
 9:    local nVar2
10:    local nVar3
11:    local nVar4
12:    local nVar5
13:    local nVar6
14:    local nVar7
15:    local nVar8
16:
17:    cls
18:    use Ontap new
19:    index on Ontap->datestamp to ontap3
20:
21:    SayAndWait("Any key for first AVERAGE...")
22:    average Ontap->sizes to nVar1  while ShowRec()
23:    inkey(0)
24:
25:    go top
26:    SayAndWait("Any key for second AVERAGE...")
27:    average Ontap->sizes to nVar2 for Ontap->sizes > 2000 while ShowRec()
28:    inkey(0)
29:
30:    go top
31:    SayAndWait("Any key for first SUM")
32:    sum Ontap->sizes to nVar3  while ShowRec()
33:    inkey(0)
34:
35:    go top
36:    SayAndWait("Any key for second SUM")
37:    sum Ontap->sizes to nVar4 for Ontap->sizes > 2000 while ShowRec()
38:    inkey(0)
39:
40:    go top
41:    SayAndWait("Any key for first COUNT")
42:    count to nVar5 while ShowRec()
43:    inkey(0)
44:
45:    go top
```

```
 46:    SayAndWait("Any key for second COUNT")
 47:    count to nVar6 for Ontap->sizes > 2000 while ShowRec()
 48:    inkey(0)
 49:
 50:    go top
 51:    wait "Any key for next screen...."
 52:    cls
 53:    devout( space(15) )
 54:    devout("Average")
 55:    devout( space(20) )
 56:    devout("Sum")
 57:    devout( space(15) )
 58:    devout("Count")
 59:    devout( space(20) )
 60:    ?
 61:    ? nVar1, nVar2, nVar3, nVar4, nVar5, nVar6
 62:
 63:    wait "Any key for TOTAL ON"
 64:
 65:    total on Ontap->datestamp fields sizes to Totvals
 66:    wait "Any key to see the output!"
 67:    close ontap
 68:    use Totvals new
 69:    dbedit()
 70:    cls
 71:
 72: *******************
 73:
 74: static function Showrec()
 75:
 76:    devpos(maxrow(),0)
 77:    devout("Record: ")
 78:    devout( recno() )
 79:
 80:    return( pTRUE )
 81:
 82: *******************
 83:
 84: static procedure SayAndWait( cSaying )
 85:
 86:    static nRow
 87:    static nCol
 88:
 89:    if nRow == NIL
 90:       nRow := nCol := 0   // If initialized, start at top of screen
 91:    endif
 92:
 93:    // The ROW and COL variables are STATIC because they are to be
 94:    // remembered.  In addition, they are post incremented, which means that
 95:    // the variables are incremented AFTER they are evaluated. This means
 96:    // that although they start at 0,0, at the conclusion of the call to
 97:    // DEVPOS(), the ROW and values will be 1,1
 98:
 99:    @ nRow++, nCol++ say cSaying
100:    *inkey(0)
101:
102: // End of File:Totdemo.prg
```

## TYPE

**COMMAND**     Types out the contents of a file to the printer or another file.

**SYNTAX**      `TYPE <expC1> [TO PRINT]/[TO FILE <expC2>]`

**PARAMETERS**  &lt;expC1&gt;    Filename
&lt;expC2&gt;    Alternate filename

**DESCRIPTION** This command types out the contents of &lt;expC1&gt; to the screen unless the printer or an alternate file is specified. If the FILE clause is specified, the name of the alternate file is expressed as &lt;expC2&gt;.

**NOTE**        The DOS redirection option is not supported. In order to get output to a printer, use the TO PRINT option; and use the TO FILE option rather than setting an alternate file.

**SEE ALSO**    COPY FILE, SET ALTERNATE

**EXAMPLE**

```
 1 : * File      Typedemo.prg
 2 : * Compile   RMake sample /dFILE:Typedemo
 3 :
 4 : procedure Main()
 5 :
 6 :    local cFile := "TESTOUT.TXT"
 7 :
 8 :    if file( "\AUTOEXEC.BAT" )
 9 :       cls
10 :       type "\AUTOEXEC.BAT"
11 :       wait
12 :       if file( "\CONFIG.SYS" )
13 :          cls
14 :          type "\CONFIG.SYS" to file(cFile)
15 :          wait
16 :          cls
17 :          type ( cFile )    // This is "TESTOUT.TXT"
18 :          wait
19 :       endif
20 :    endif
21 :
22 : // End of File: Typedemo.prg
```

## UNLOCK

**COMMAND**    Releases a record or file lock.

**SYNTAX**     `UNLOCK [ALL]`

**PARAMETER**  None

**DESCRIPTION** This command releases the file or record lock in the selected work area. If the [ALL] clause is used, all locks in all work areas will be removed.

**NOTE** The UNLOCK command does not unlock an associated lock in a RELATED database.

**SEE ALSO** FLOCK( ), RLOCK( ), USE, SET EXCLUSIVE

## UPDATE

**COMMAND** Updates information from one .DBF file to another.

**SYNTAX** UPDATE FROM <expC1> ON <expX2> [RANDOM] REPLACE <expX3> WITH <expX4> [, <expX5> WITH <expX6> ...]

**PARAMETERS**
<expC1> Alias name
<expX2> Key expression
<expX3> Field name
<expX4> Expression to be replaced
<expX5> Field name
<expX6> Expression to be replaced

**DESCRIPTION** This command uses data from an existing database expressed as <expC1> and changes the records in the current work area by matching records based on a common expression, <expX2>.

If the RANDOM clause is NOT specified, both the current database and the FROM database must be indexed or sorted in the order indicated by <expX2>. If RANDOM is used, the current database must still be indexed on <expX2>, but the FROM database can be in any order. If on a network, the current database must be used exclusively, the FROM database can be shared.

The fields that are altered and the value of the fields or expressions that are to replace them are specified in the REPLACE clause, expressed as <expX3> with <expX4>, <expX5> with <expX6>, and so on.

**NOTE** Deleted records are also updated if SET DELETED is off.

**SEE ALSO** INDEX, JOIN, REPLACE, SORT, TOTAL

**EXAMPLE**

```
1 : * File      Upddemo.prg
2 : * Compile   RMake sample /dFILE:Upddemo
3 :
4 : procedure Main()
5 :
6 :    use Ontap new
7 :    copy to Showit for recno() < 150
8 :    close Ontap
9 :    use Notap   // Use the same work area!
```

```
10 :    dbedit()
11 :    use Showit new
12 :    dbedit()
13 :    cls
14 :    ? Notap->( lastrec() ), Notap->( alias() )
15 :    wait
16 :    ? Showit->( lastrec() ), Showit->( alias() )
17 :    wait
18 :    update from Notap on Notap->files replace ;
19 :         Showit->sizes with Notap->sizes * 1000
20 :    dbedit()
21 :    cls
22 :
23 :    // End of File:Upddemo.prg
```

# USE

**COMMAND**  Opens a work area and uses a database file.

**SYNTAX**  USE [<expC1>] [INDEX <expC2>,...] [ALIAS <expC3>]
[EXCLUSIVE / SHARED] [NEW] [READONLY] [VIA <expC4>]

**PARAMETERS**
<expC1>  Name of the database file to use
<expC2>  Index file/index list to be used with the file
<expC3>  Alias name for work area
<expC4>  Replaceable Database Driver Name

**DESCRIPTION**  This command opens an existing database in the current work area if <expC1> is specified; otherwise, it closes the database in the current work area.

If the NEW clause is specified, the next available work area will be selected before the database is used. If the database file specified by <expC1> has an associated memo file, that file will be opened automatically.

Up to 15 index files may be opened for the current database. However, this limit may be reduced based on the number of previously open files or the number of files available to the application. Index files to be opened are listed by name in <expC2> following the INDEX clause.

If used, <expC3> contains the alias name for the database. If not specified, the root name of the database specified in <expC1> will be used.

If the EXCLUSIVE clause is used, the database named in <expC1> will be opened by the user exclusively, thus locking it from all other nodes or users on the network. If the SHARED clause is specified, this will open the database for shared use and override the current EXCLUSIVE setting specified by that user or node.

If the READONLY clause is specified, the file attribute will be set to be READONLY. If it is not specified, the file is opened in normal read-write mode.

If used, <expC4> contains the name of the replaceable database driver to be used in a given work area. The VIA clause must be followed by a character expression, with constant values surrounded by quotation marks.

**NOTE**  The EXCLUSIVE clause does not allow any other user to have access to that file until the file is closed. The SHARED clause allows other users to have access to the database. The default condition of the USE command if neither clause is specified is based on the setting of the SET EXCLUSIVE command. If set on, the file will be USEd exclusively; if not, the file will be SHARED.

The number of files that may be opened by a Clipper application is based on either the number specified in the CONFIG.SYS file of the operating machine or the value of the SET CLIPPER F:xxx switch. If both are specified, the application will use the smaller of the two values. If the F:xxx value or the FILES command in CONFIG.SYS is to be greater than 5, the number should be an odd number.

The same database file may be opened in more than one work area using different aliases. This is practical for look-up purposes only and should be avoided as much as possible in a network environment.

**SEE ALSO**  SET INDEX, USED( ), NETERR( ), CLOSE, ALIAS( ), SELECT, dbSETDRIVER( )

**EXAMPLE**

```
 1 : * File       Usedemo.prg
 2 : * Compile    RMake sample /dFILE:Usedemo
 3 :
 4 : procedure Main()
 5 :
 6 :    use Notap    new alias Cons
 7 :    use Ontap    new index Ontap
 8 :    use Filenos  new index Filenos1, Filenos2 exclusive
 9 :    use Clients  new readonly
10 :
11 :    cls
12 :    ? Cons->( lastrec() )     // NOT Notap... It's Cons!
13 :    ? Ontap->( lastrec() )
14 :    ? Filenos->( lastrec() )
15 :    ? Clients->( lastrec() )
16 :    wait
17 :
18 :    select Ontap
19 :    use                       // Close the file!
20 :    ShowAlias()
21 :    close Filenos             // Close the file as well
22 :    ShowAlias()
23 :    close databases           // Close all databases!
```

```
24 :      ShowAlias()
25 :
26 :   *********************
27 :
28 :   static procedure ShowAlias()
29 :
30 :      local nCount
31 :
32 :      for nCount := 1 to 10
33 :         devpos( nCount, 0 )
34 :         devout( "Work Area " )
35 :         devoutpict( nCount, "99" )
36 :         devout( "   Alias-> " )
37 :         devout( if( empty(alias(nCount)), space(10), alias(nCount) ) )
38 :      next
39 :      wait
40 :
41 :   // End of File: Usedemo.prg
```

# WAIT

| | |
|---|---|
| **COMMAND** | Pauses program execution until a key is pressed. |
| **SYNTAX** | WAIT [<expC1>] [TO <expC2>] |
| **PARAMETERS** | <expC1>   Character expression to be displayed |
| | <expC2>   Memory variable name |
| **DESCRIPTION** | This command stops all processing until a key is pressed. |
| |     The expression <expC1> is a string to be used as a prompt message. If none is used, the default prompt message of "Press any key to continue..." will be displayed. The message, in either case, is displayed starting at ROW( ) + 1, 0. If the position of ROW( ) is equal to MAXROW( ), the screen will scroll up one line and the WAIT prompt will be displayed. |
| |     If the TO clause is added, the value of the key pressed is stored to the memory variable named in <expC2>. This is a character variable that does not need to be initialized prior to issuing this command. |
| **NOTE** | This is a compatibility command and may not be supported in future versions. |
| **SEE ALSO** | ACCEPT, INPUT, INKEY(0) |

**EXAMPLE**

```
1 : * File      Waitdemo.prg
2 : * Compile   RMake sample /dFILE:Waitdemo
3 :
4 : procedure Main()
5 :
```

```
 6 :    local xTemp1, xTemp2, xTemp3, xTemp4
 7 :
 8 :    cls
 9 :    accept "Enter something: " to xTemp1
10 :    input  "Enter some mathematical expression..." to xTemp2
11 :    input  "Now, enter a DATE() expression... " to xTemp3
12 :    wait   "And now for the WAIT..." to xTemp4
13 :    wait
14 :
15 :    ?
16 :    ? valtype( xTemp1 ), xTemp1
17 :    ? valtype( xTemp2 ), xTemp2
18 :    ? valtype( xTemp3 ), xTemp3
19 :    ? valtype( xTemp4 ), xTemp4
20 :
21 : // End of File:Waitdemo.prg
```

# ZAP

**COMMAND**    Removes all records from a database.

**SYNTAX**     ZAP

**PARAMETER**  None

**DESCRIPTION** This command removes all of the records from the database in the current work area. This operation also updates any index files in use at the time of this operation. In addition, this command removes all items within an associated memo file.

In a network environment, any file that is about to be ZAPped must be used exclusively.

**SEE ALSO**   DELETE, PACK, USE

**EXAMPLE**    See the APPEND FROM command.

# 7

# Clipper Function Reference

This chapter contains a complete listing of the standard functions in Clipper 5.2. The listing also includes those functions found in the sample source code and are now included in a library. The basic way to read these functions is as follows. The <exp> symbols represent the expression that is passed to the function. Use the following table as a data type expression guide:

| | |
|---|---|
| <expC> | Character expression |
| <expN> | Numeric expression |
| <expL> | Logical expression |
| <expB> | Block expression |
| <expD> | Date expression |
| <expA> | Array expression |
| <expO> | Object data type |
| <expX> | Mixed on unknown expression |
| <nIndex> | Ordinal expression |

A number after any of the capitalized letters (e.g., <expC1>) represents the numerical position in the parameter list (e.g., <expL5> is a logical expression that is the fifth parameter); if the expression accepts multiple data types, the positional value will appear immediately after the <expX> characters (e.g., <expX6>).

If a pair of brackets ([ ]) appears in the command syntax, that portion of the command is optional. Any repeating parameters, options, or expressions will be symbolized with a "..." character set. If a semicolon character (;) is used, the line in question continues onto the next.

Most functions will work on the currently selected database by default, and on any open database if the command is preceded by the database alias or work area number. Hence, RECNO( ) returns the current record number of the currently selected database, while Orders->( recno( ) ) returns the record number in the ORDERS database. The key to using the alias is the extended expression facility in Clipper. Simply calling the function from within an expression with the alias in front will make the function be performed in the alias work area. In addition, alias referencing can stand on a line by itself. Throughout this function reference, the ability of a database function to operate on databases in this way is generally expressed as "the current or designated database."

While reading this section of the book there are a couple of rules to keep in mind:

1. If a function does not specify a RETURN value, then it will be assumed that the return value of the function will be a NIL value.

2. In some cases, no example is provided when there is one in a chapter exclusively dedicated to that particular topic. For example, most of the array functions in this section will not have an example for they will appear in Chapter 10.

In addition, all of the public functions used in application development and found in any of the Clipper libraries that come with the package are documented.

## The Functions, Pseudofunctions, and Expressions

## AADD( )

| | |
|---|---|
| **FUNCTION** | Dynamically adds an element to an array. |
| **SYNTAX** | `AADD( <expA1> [, <expX2>] )` |
| **PARAMETERS** | <expA1>　　The name of an array<br><expX2>　　Element to add to array <expA1> |
| **RETURNS** | <expX>　　The value of <expX2> if specified, otherwise this function returns a NIL value |
| **LIBRARY** | CLIPPER.LIB |
| **DESCRIPTION** | This function dynamically increases the length of the array named <expA1> by one element and stores the value of <expX2> to that newly created element.<br>　　<expX2> may be an array reference pointer, which in turn may be stored to an array's subscript position. This is discussed further in Chapter 10. |
| **NOTE** | This function is similar to the ASIZE( ) function, except that it will dynamically increase the size of an array only one element at a time; it also fills the new element with a value. |
| **SEE ALSO** | ASIZE( ), ADEL( ), AINS( ) |

# ABLOCK( )

| | |
|---|---|
| **FUNCTION** | Creates a GET/SET code block for array element. |
| **SYNTAX** | ABLOCK( <expC1>, <expN2> ) |
| **PARAMETERS** | <expC1>  String representation of an array that is to be considered |
| | <expN2>  Subscript position of array element to be blockified |
| **RETURNS** | <expB>  GET/SET code block |
| **LIBRARY** | SAMPLES.LIB |
| **DESCRIPTION** | This function takes the string representation of an array expressed as <expC1> at the element position of <expN2> and creates a code block value for it. It will work if &(<expC1>)[ <expN2> ] is an array reference as well. |
| **NOTE** | This function will not work if the array is stored as a LOCAL or a STATIC variable. In addition, the array must be "visible" anywhere that the code block is to be evaluated. |

**EXAMPLE**

```
 1 : * File     Ablodemo.prg
 2 : * Compile RMake sampmore /dFILE:ablodemo
 3 :
 4 : procedure Main()
 5 :
 6 :    private aValues := {2, 4, 6, 8, 10}
 7 :    private bCode   := ABlock( "aValues", 3 )
 8 :
 9 :    ? valtype( bCode )     // "B"
10 :    ? eval( bCode )        // 6
11 :
12 :    PassOn( bCode )
13 :
14 : static procedure PassOn( bCode )
15 :
16 :    ? eval( bCode )        // 6 since AVALUE is a PRIVATE var, it's visible
17 :
18 : // End of File: Ablodemo.prg
```

# ABROWSE( )

| | |
|---|---|
| **FUNCTION** | Browses the contents of a 2-dimensional array. |
| **SYNTAX** | ABROWSE( <expA1> [, <expN2>] [, <expN3>] [, <expN4>], [<expN5>] ) |

| | | |
|---|---|---|
| **PARAMETERS** | <expA1> | Array to be browsed (2-dimensional) |
| | <expN2> | Top row coordinate of window region |
| | <expN3> | Left column coordinate of window region |
| | <expN4> | Bottom row coordinate of window region |
| | <expN5> | Right column coordinate of window region |
| **RETURNS** | <expX> | Selected value within array element or NIL if no value is selected |
| **LIBRARY** | SAMPLES.LIB | |
| **DESCRIPTION** | This function will browse the contents of the 2-dimensional array <expA1> in the window coordinates beginning at <expN2>, <expN3> through to <expN4>, <expN5>. The default values for these parameters are 0, 0, MAXROW( ), and MAXCOL( ), respectively. | |
| | All typical cursor movement is allowed with the ENTER key used to select the highlighted array element. If the ESC key is pressed, then no element is selected and the function will return a NIL value. | |
| **SEE ALSO** | TBROWSENEW( ), BROWSE( ), DBEDIT( ), ACHOICE( ) | |

**EXAMPLE**

```
 1 : * File     Abrodemo.prg
 2 : * Compile RMake sampmore /dFILE:abrodemo
 3 :
 4 : procedure Main()
 5 :
 6 :    local xValue
 7 :
 8 :    scroll()
 9 :    if !( (xValue := ABrowse( directory(), 10,10,20,60 ) ) == NIL )
10 :      devpos(0,0)
11 :      ?? "The value selected was: "
12 :      ?? xValue
13 :    else
14 :      devpos(0,0)
15 :      ?? "No value was selected!"
16 :    endif
17 :
18 : // End of File: Abrodemo.prg
```

# ABS( )

| | |
|---|---|
| **FUNCTION** | Returns the absolute value of a number. |
| **SYNTAX** | ABS( <expN1> ) |
| **PARAMETER** | <expN1>   Any number |
| **RETURNS** | <expN>   Numeric value |

| | |
|---|---|
| **LIBRARY** | CLIPPER.LIB |
| **DESCRIPTION** | This function yields the absolute value of the numeric value or expression <expN1>. |

**EXAMPLE**

```
 1 : * File:     Absdemo.prg
 2 : * Compile:  RMake Sample /dFILE=ABSDEMO
 3 :
 4 : procedure Main()
 5 :
 6 :    local nNumber1 := 50
 7 :    local nNumber2 := 27
 8 :
 9 :    cls
10 :
11 :    qout( nNumber1 - nNumber2 )           // Shows 23
12 :    qout( nNumber2 - nNumber1 )           // Shows -23
13 :    qout( abs( nNumber1 - nNumber2 ) )    // Shows 23
14 :    qout( abs( nNumber2 - nNumber1 ) )    // Shows 23
15 :    qout( abs( -1 * 345 ) )               // Shows 345
16 :
17 : // End of File: Absdemo.prg
```

In this example, the order of the two variables *nNumber1* and *nNumber2* is important only when their sign is considered, as shown in lines 11 and 12. The ABS( ) function takes the absolute value of the expressions and returns the same value (lines 13 and 14) regardless of which value, *nNumber1* or *nNumber2*, is larger than the other.

# ACHOICE( )

| | |
|---|---|
| **FUNCTION** | Displays a window list box of array items. |
| **SYNTAX** | ACHOICE( <expN1>, <expN2>, <expN3>, <expN4>, <expA5> [, <expX6>] [, <expC7>] [, <expN8>] [, <expN9>] ) |
| **PARAMETERS** | <expN1>  Top row coordinate of the window |
| | <expN2>  Left column coordinate of the window |
| | <expN3>  Bottom row coordinate of the window |
| | <expN4>  Right column coordinate of the window |
| | <expA5>  Array of items to be viewed |
| | <expX6>  Array of logical values or a single logical value |
| | <expC7>  Name of user-defined function to process keystroke exceptions |
| | <expN8>  Subscript value where highlight bar is to initially be displayed |
| | <expN9>  Beginning row position to display highlight bar |

| | | |
|---|---|---|
| **RETURNS** | <expN> | Array subscript position of selected item |
| **LIBRARY** | EXTEND.LIB | |

**DESCRIPTION** This function displays a list-box window with top left and bottom right coordinates of <expN1> through <expN4>. It will return the numeric subscript position of the item selected in <expN>. If no item is selected, the function will return a 0.

The array <expA5> contains the items to be displayed within the windowed area.

The argument <expX6> can take one of two forms. The first is a parallel array of logical values, <expA6>, (or string expressions that evaluate to a logical value when it is macro expanded) one for each of the menu choices specified in <expA5>. The logical value in the parallel array <expA6> determines whether the corresponding item in <expA5> is available for selection. Alternatively, <expX6> may be a single logical variable value, representing a global condition: logical true (.T.) for all items to be selected, or logical false (.F.) for no items not to be selected.

If used, <expC7> is the name of a user-defined function (UDF) that will be executed whenever a key other than the allowable action keys (listed below) is pressed. This function does not have parentheses or arguments.

If used, <expN8> will contain the element of the array that will be highlighted when the ACHOICE( ) function is called. If this parameter isn't included, the first element in <expA5> will be highlighted.

If used, <expN9> will contain the initial relative window row position for the first available choice in the window. The default value is 0.

If a user-defined function is not specified, the action keys in the following table are automatically processed:

| *Key* | *Action* |
|---|---|
| Home | First element |
| End | Last element |
| Return | Select element, return subscript position |
| ESC | Abort function, return 0 |
| Left Arrow | Abort function, return 0 |
| Right Arrow | Abort function, return 0 |
| Any Alphanumeric Character | Next element in array with the same first letter |

The following keystrokes are always processed:

| *Key* | *Action* |
|---|---|
| Up Arrow | Up one element |
| Down Arrow | Down one element |

| Key | Action |
|---|---|
| PgUp | Up the number of elements defined for the menu window to the same relative row position |
| PgDn | Down the number of elements defined for the menu window to the same relative row position |
| Ctrl-PgDn | Last element in the array |
| Ctrl-PgUp | First element in the array |
| Ctrl-Home | First item in the windowed area |
| Ctrl-End | Last item in the windowed area |

When a user-defined function is specified in the ACHOICE( ) call, three parameters are automatically passed to the user-defined function and may be used within the function. These three parameters are:

| UDF Parameter | | |
|---|---|---|
| | #1: | Mode of ACHOICE( ) |
| | #2: | Array subscript position on which highlighted bar rests |
| | #3: | Relative row position of item within window coordinates |

The potential values for the ACHOICE( ) mode [the first parameter to the UDF( )] are as follows:

| Passed Mode | Meaning |
|---|---|
| 0 | ACHOICE( ) is idle |
| 1 | Attempt to cursor past top of array list |
| 2 | Attempt to cursor past bottom of array list |
| 3 | Keystroke exception |
| 4 | No item is available for selection |

Once the user-defined function has finished executing, it must return a value to ACHOICE( ) that tells the ACHOICE( ) function what to do. The following table lists the values that can be returned by the UDF called by the ACHOICE( ) function.

| Return Mode | Meaning |
|---|---|
| 0 | Abort selection, return 0 |
| 1 | Make selection, return subscript position |
| 2 | Continue processing ACHOICE( ) |
| 3 | Go to next element whose first character matches the last key pressed |

| | |
|---|---|
| **NOTE** | If a user-defined function is used, the definition of that function may not be STATIC. If it is, the user-defined function will be ignored. |
| **SEE ALSO** | MENU TO |

## ACLONE( )

| | | |
|---|---|---|
| **FUNCTION** | Duplicates a multidimensional array. | |
| **SYNTAX** | ACLONE( <expA1> ) | |
| **PARAMETER** | <expA1> | Name of array to be cloned |
| **RETURNS** | <expA> | A new array pointer reference complete with nested array values |
| **LIBRARY** | EXTEND.LIB | |
| **DESCRIPTION** | This function makes a complete copy of the array expressed as <expA1> and returns a cloned set of array values. This provides a complete set of array values for all dimensions within the original array <expA1>. | |
| **SEE ALSO** | ACOPY( ) | |

## ACOMP( )

| | | |
|---|---|---|
| **FUNCTION** | Compares the elements in one array with those in another. | |
| **SYNTAX** | ACOMP( <expA1>, <expB2>, <expN3>, <expN4> ) | |
| **PARAMETERS** | <expA1> | Array to be compared |
| | <expB2> | Code block that contains expression of comparison |
| | <expN3> | Numeric subscript starting position |
| | <expN4> | Numeric subscript ending position |
| **RETURNS** | <expX> | Results of the expression in the block |
| **LIBRARY** | SAMPLES.LIB | |
| **DESCRIPTION** | This function will compare all of the elements in <expA1> from element position <expN3> through to the <expN4>th element, evaluating each element to the code block <expB2>.<br><br>Two values are passed to the <expB2>: First, the contents of each element in <expA1> and then the running evaluation, starting with the first element's value. | |
| **SEE ALSO** | AEVAL( ), EVAL( ), DBEVAL( ) | |

## EXAMPLE

```
 1 : * File     Acomdemo.prg
 2 : * Compile Rmake sampmore /dFILE:Acomdemo
 3 :
 4 : procedure Main()
 5 :
 6 :    local aData := array(20)
 7 :    local nCount
 8 :
 9 :    for nCount := 1 to 20
10 :       aData[nCount] := nCount * 23
11 :    next
12 :
13 :    cls
14 :    ? "Selected value was: "
15 :    ?? AComp( aData, ;
16 :             {|nFirst, nSecond| nFirst > 200 .and. nSecond < 300 }, ;
17 :             1, ;
18 :             len( aData ) )
19 :    ? "Values in the array are:"
20 :    aeval( aData, ;
21 :             {|nValue, nPosition| qout( nValue, "At position", nPosition )} )
22 :    inkey(0)
23 :
24 : // End of File: Acomdemo.prg
```

# ACOPY( )

**FUNCTION**        Copies elements from one array to another.

**SYNTAX**          ACOPY( <expA1>, <expA2> [, <expN3>] [, <expN4>] [,<expN5>])

**PARAMETERS**  <expA1>   Name of array to be copied
                <expA2>   Name of array to copy to
                <expN3>   Beginning subscript position to copy from <expA1>
                <expN4>   The number of subscript elements to copy from <expA1>
                <expN5>   The starting subscript position in <expA2> to copy elements to

**RETURNS**         <expA>    An array pointer reference

**LIBRARY**         CLIPPER.LIB

**DESCRIPTION**    This function copies array elements from <expA1> to <expA2>.
    <expN3> is the beginning element to be copied from <expA1>; the default is 1.
    <expN4> is the number of elements to be copied from <expA1>; the default is the entire array.

&lt;expN5&gt; is the subscript number in the target array, &lt;expA2&gt; , to which array elements are to be copied; the default is 1.

This function will copy all data types in &lt;expA1&gt; to &lt;expA2&gt;. If an array element in &lt;expA1&gt; is a pointer reference to another array, that array pointer will be copied to &lt;expA2&gt;; not all subdimensions will be copied from one array to the next. This must be accomplished via the ACLONE( ) function.

**NOTE** If array &lt;expA1&gt; is larger than &lt;expA2&gt;, array elements will start copying at &lt;expN5&gt; and continue copying until the end of array &lt;expA2&gt; is reached. The ACOPY( ) function doesn't append subscript positions to the target array, the size of the target array &lt;expA2&gt; remains constant.

**SEE ALSO** ACLONE( )

# ADEL( )

| | |
|---|---|
| **FUNCTION** | Deletes an element from an array. |
| **SYNTAX** | ADEL( &lt;expA1&gt;, &lt;expN2&gt; ) |
| **PARAMETERS** | &lt;expA1&gt;    Name of array from which an element is to be removed |
| | &lt;expN2&gt;    Subscript of the element to be removed |
| **RETURNS** | &lt;expA&gt;    An array pointer reference |
| **LIBRARY** | CLIPPER.LIB |
| **DESCRIPTION** | This function deletes the element found at the &lt;expN2&gt; subscript position in the array specified in &lt;expA1&gt;. All array elements in the array &lt;expA1&gt; below the given subscript position &lt;expN2&gt; will move up one position in the array. In other words, what was formerly the sixth subscript position will become the fifth subscript position. The length of the array &lt;expA1&gt; will remain unchanged, as the last element of the array becomes a NIL data type. |
| **SEE ALSO** | AINS( ), ASIZE( ), AADD( ) |

# ADIR( )

**FUNCTION**    Obtains directory information and fills corresponding arrays with directory information.

**SYNTAX**    ADIR( &lt;expC1&gt; [, &lt;expA2&gt; [, &lt;expA3&gt; [, &lt;expA4&gt; [, &lt;expA5&gt; [, &lt;expA6&gt;]]]]] )

| | | |
|---|---|---|
| **PARAMETERS** | <expC1> | A directory skeleton |
| | <expA2> | Array of filenames |
| | <expA3> | Array of file sizes |
| | <expA4> | Array of file date stamps |
| | <expA5> | Array of file time stamps |
| | <expA6> | Array of file attribute bytes |
| **RETURNS** | <expN> | Number of files on disk |
| **LIBRARY** | EXTEND.LIB | |

**DESCRIPTION** This function returns the number of files that match a pattern specified by the directory skeleton of <expC1>. This skeleton will accept drive and path names, as well as wild-card characters.

<expA2> is the name of a previously declared array. If used, the names of all files matching the specified pattern in <expC1> will be inserted into it.

<expA3> is the name of a previously declared array. If used, the sizes of all files matching the specified pattern in <expC1> will be inserted into it.

<expA4> is the name of a previously declared array. If used, the date stamps of all files matching the specified pattern in <expC1> will be inserted into the array.

<expA5> is the name of a previously declared array. If used, the time stamps of all files matching the specified pattern in <expC1> will be inserted into this array.

<expA6> is the name of a previously declared array. If used, the file attribute bytes of all files matching the specified pattern in <expC1> will be inserted into it.

If <expA6> is specified, the values inserted are as follows:

| | |
|---|---|
| A | Archive File |
| D | Directory |
| H | Hidden file |
| R | Read Only file |
| S | System file |

It should be noted that the return value of the ADIR( ) function will yield different results depending on which parameters have been passed to the function. In particular, specifying the sixth parameter along with a directory skeleton of *.* will cause the return value to be larger than if the sixth parameter is omitted. In this case, the size of the array should not be declared by using the sixth parameter.

**NOTE** This is a compatibility function and should be replaced by the DIRECTORY( ) function.

**SEE ALSO** DIRECTORY( ), AFIELDS( ), DBSTRUCT( )

## ADDMONTH( )

| | |
|---|---|
| **FUNCTION** | Generates a new date based on a beginning date and the number of months to add to it. |
| **SYNTAX** | ADDMONTH( <expD1>, <expN2> ) |
| **PARAMETERS** | <expD1>   Beginning date to consider<br><expN2>   Number of months to add to beginning date |
| **RETURNS** | <expD>   Calculated new date |
| **LIBRARY** | SAMPLES.LIB |
| **DESCRIPTION** | This function takes the date <expD1> and adds <expN2> months to it and returns a new date value. The function will adjust the year value of the returned date should the number of months to be added to the date push the year counter into a new year. |
| **SEE ALSO** | DATE( ) |
| **EXAMPLE** | See the YEAR( ) function |

## ADDREC( )

| | |
|---|---|
| **FUNCTION** | Attempts to append a blank record. |
| **SYNTAX** | ADDREC( [<expN1>] ) |
| **PARAMETER** | <expN1>   Number of seconds to wait |
| **RETURNS** | <expL>   Success value |
| **LIBRARY** | SAMPLES.LIB |
| **DESCRIPTION** | This function will attempt to append a blank record to the selected work area and return a logical true (.T.) if it was successful; otherwise, a logical false (.F.) will be returned.<br>    Should the database file be locked, ADDREC( ) will wait <expN2> seconds before again attempting to append the blank record. If <expN2> isn't specified, the default value of 2 will be assigned to the parameter. |
| **NOTE** | There is no error checking with this function, therefore if this function is used without an active database present, an error message will be generated. |
| **SEE ALSO** | APPEND BLANK, COPY TO, APPEND FROM |
| **EXAMPLE** | See the APPEND FROM command. |

## AEVAL( )

| | |
|---|---|
| **FUNCTION** | Evaluates the subscript elements of an array. |
| **SYNTAX** | `AEVAL( <expA1>, <expB2> [, <expN3>] [,<expN4>])` |
| **PARAMETERS** | `<expA1>` Array to be evaluated |
| | `<expB2>` Code block to evaluate each element processed |
| | `<expN3>` The beginning array element to evaluate |
| | `<expN4>` The number of elements to process |
| **RETURNS** | `<expA>` An array pointer reference |
| **LIBRARY** | CLIPPER.LIB |
| **DESCRIPTION** | This function will evaluate and process the subscript elements in `<expA1>`. A code block passed as `<expB2>` defines the operations to be executed on each element of the array. All elements in `<expA1>` will be evaluated unless specified by a beginning subscript position in `<expN3>` for `<expN4>` elements. |
| | Two parameters are passed to the code block `<expB2>`. The individual elements in an array are the first parameter and the subscript position is the second. |
| | AEVAL( ) does not replace a FOR...NEXT loop for processing arrays. If an array is an autonomous unit, AEVAL( ) is appropriate. If the array is to be altered or if elements are to be reevaluated, a FOR...NEXT loop is more appropriate. |
| **SEE ALSO** | EVAL( ), DBEVAL( ) |
| **EXAMPLE** | See Chapters 10 and 14. |

## AFIELDS( )

| | |
|---|---|
| **FUNCTION** | Fills referenced arrays with database field information |
| **SYNTAX** | `AFIELDS( <expA1> [, <expA2> [, <expA3> [,<expA4>]]])` |
| **PARAMETERS** | `<expA1>` Array of field names |
| | `<expA2>` Array of field data types |
| | `<expA3>` Array of field lengths |
| | `<expA4>` Array of field decimal positions |
| **RETURNS** | `<expN>` Number of fields in a database or work area |
| **LIBRARY** | CLIPPER.LIB |

| | |
|---|---|
| **DESCRIPTION** | This function will fill a series of arrays with the field names, field types, field lengths, and number of field decimal positions for the currently selected or designated database. Each array parallels the different descriptors of a file's structure. The first array will consist of the names of the fields in the current work area. All other arrays are optional and will be filled with the corresponding data.<br><br>This function will return a zero if no parameters are specified or if no database is available in the current work area. Otherwise, the number of fields or the length of the shortest array argument, whichever is smaller, will be returned. |
| **NOTE** | This is a compatibility function and should be replaced by the DBSTRUCT( ) function. |
| **SEE ALSO** | ADIR( ), DBSTRUCT( ), DIRECTORY( ), DBCREATE( ) |

# AFILL( )

| | |
|---|---|
| **FUNCTION** | Fills an entire array dimension with a value. |
| **SYNTAX** | `AFILL( <expA1>, <expX2> [, <expN3>] [, <expN4>] )` |
| **PARAMETERS** | `<expA1>`   Name of array to be filled<br>`<expX2>`   Expression to be globally filled in `<expA1>`<br>`<expN3>`   Subscript starting position<br>`<expN4>`   Number of subscripts to be filled |
| **RETURNS** | `<expA>`   An array pointer |
| **LIBRARY** | EXTEND.LIB |
| **DESCRIPTION** | This function fills each element of an array named `<expA1>` with the value `<expX2>`. If specified, `<expN3>` denotes the beginning element to be filled and array elements will continue to be filled for `<expN4>` positions. If NOT specified, the value of `<expN3>` will be 1 and the value of `<expN4>` will be the value of LEN( `<expA1>` ); thus, all subscript positions in the array `<expA1>` will be filled with the value of `<expX2>`.<br><br>This function will work on only a single dimension of `<expA1>`. If there are array pointer references within a subscript of `<expA1>`, those values will be lost, since this function will overwrite those values with new values. |
| **SEE ALSO** | AINS( ), ADEL( ), AADD( ), ASIZE( ) |

# AINS( )

| | |
|---|---|
| **FUNCTION** | Inserts a NIL value at an array subscript position. |
| **SYNTAX** | `AINS( <expA1>, <expN2> )` |
| **PARAMETERS** | `<expA1>` Array name<br>`<expN2>` Subscript position in `<expA1>` |
| **RETURNS** | `<expA>` Array pointer |
| **LIBRARY** | CLIPPER.LIB |
| **DESCRIPTION** | This function inserts a NIL value in the array named `<expA1>` at the `<expN2>`th position.<br><br>All array elements starting with the `<expN2>`th position will be shifted down one subscript position in the array list and the last item in the array will be removed completely. In other words, if an array element were to be inserted at the fifth subscript position, the element previously in the fifth position would now be located at the sixth position.<br><br>The length of the array will remain unaffected. |
| **SEE ALSO** | AADD( ), ASIZE( ), ADEL( ), ARRAY( ), AFILL( ) |

# ALERT( )

| | |
|---|---|
| **FUNCTION** | Creates a simple modal dialog. |
| **SYNTAX** | `ALERT( <expC1> [, <expA2> ] [, <expC3> ] )` |
| **PARAMETERS** | `<expC1>` Message<br>`<expA2>` Array of options<br>`<expC3>` Color string |
| **RETURNS** | `<expN>` Numeric value of choice selected |
| **LIBRARY** | CLIPPER.LIB |
| **DESCRIPTION** | This function displays a message-filled dialog box to the screen and returns a numeric value based on an option selected by the user. The ESC key has a value of 0. A message to the user is placed in the character expression `<expC1>`. If multiple lines are needed for the display message, then a semicolon must be used to indicate where new lines begin within the single message string. The center area of the screen will be used for the dialog box generated by this function. |

If no array of options <expA2> is used, the default message "OK" will be displayed. The left and right cursor keys may move the highlighted option, and the options will wrap around.

If used, <expC3> will contain the color string to be used by the function. This setting does not affect the overall color setting of the system.

**NOTE**  This function is sensitive to the full-screen I/O system. If it is not present, this function will use TTY-style-based I/O handling methods to display the messages.

**SEE ALSO**  @ ... PROMPT, MENU TO

**EXAMPLE**

```
 1 : * File:       Alrtdemo.prg
 2 : * Compile:    Rmake Sample /dFILE:alrtdemo
 3 :
 4 : procedure Main()
 5 :
 6 :    local aYesNo   := {"Yes", "No"}    // One set of options
 7 :    local aOutput := {"Screen", "Printer", "Alternate File"} // Another set
 8 :    local nOption
 9 :    local cSaying
10 :
11 :    scroll()
12 :
13 :    if !empty( alert( "Want the next test?" ) )   // Default options appear
14 :       if alert( "Are you sure you want to quit?", aYesNo ) == 2
15 :          if !empty( nOption := alert( "Print to...", aOutput, "W+/B" ) )
16 :             dispout( "You selected output to: " )
17 :             dispout( aOutput[ nOption ] )
18 :             qout()
19 :             dispout( "Any key..." )
20 :             inkey(0)
21 :             scroll()
22 :          endif
23 :          cSaying := "This is just to see what would happen;"
24 :          cSaying += "if this were to append in this fashion?"
25 :          alert( cSaying )
26 :       endif
27 :    endif
28 :
29 : // End of File: Alrtdemo.prg
```

# ALIAS( )

**FUNCTION**  Returns the alias name of a work area.

**SYNTAX**  ALIAS( [<expN1>] )

| | |
|---|---|
| **PARAMETER** | <expN1>  Number of a work area |
| **RETURNS** | <expC>  Name of alias |
| **LIBRARY** | CLIPPER.LIB |
| **DESCRIPTION** | This function returns the alias of the work area indicated by <expN1>; if <expN1> is not provided, the alias of the current work area is returned. This function does not differ from the Clipper function DBF( ), which is strictly a compatibility function. |
| **SEE ALSO** | DBF( ), USED( ) |

**EXAMPLE**

```
 1 : * File:     Aliasdem.prg
 2 : * Compile:  Rmake sample /dFILE=aliasdem
 3 :
 4 : procedure Main()
 5 :
 6 :    cls
 7 :    if file( "CLIENTS.*" ) .and. file( "NOTAP.*" )
 8 :       use Clients new
 9 :       use Notap new
10 :       select 0         // Select an un-opened work area: same as NEW
11 :       qout( if( alias() == "", "No Name!", alias() ) )
12 :       Clients->( qout( alias() ) )   // Aliases can appear in front of line
13 :       qout( alias(1) )               // Alias of work area number 1
14 :       qout( Notap->( alias() ) )
15 :       qout( alias(2) )
16 :    endif
17 :
18 : // End of File: Aliasdem.prg
```

# ALLTRIM( )

| | |
|---|---|
| **FUNCTION** | Removes leading and trailing blank spaces from a string. |
| **SYNTAX** | ALLTRIM( <expC1> ) |
| **PARAMETER** | <expC1>  Any character expression |
| **RETURNS** | <expC>  Character expression |
| **LIBRARY** | EXTEND.LIB |
| **DESCRIPTION** | This function returns the string <expC1> with all leading and trailing blank spaces removed. |
| **SEE ALSO** | LTRIM( ), TRIM( ), SUBSTR( ) |

## EXAMPLE

```
qout( alltrim( padr( "Hello", 20 ) ) )
qout( alltrim( padl( "Hello", 20 ) ) )
qout( alltrim( padc( "Hello", 20 ) ) )

// All 3 yield the five characters "Hello" on 3 separate lines.
```

# ALTD( )

| | |
|---|---|
| **FUNCTION** | Invokes the Clipper Debugger. |
| **SYNTAX** | ALTD( [<expN1>] ) |
| **PARAMETER** | <expN1>  Numeric value to toggle the debugger |
| **LIBRARY** | CLIPPER.LIB |
| **DESCRIPTION** | This function executes or toggles the status of the Clipper debugger. If no parameters are passed and if the Debugger is considered invoked, it will be called. The optional parameters mean the following: |

| *<expN1>* | *Meaning* |
|---|---|
| None | Invoke Debugger if enabled |
| 0 | Disable the Debugger (ALT-D Key) |
| 1 | Enable the Debugger (ALT-D Key) |
| All others | No Action |

Turning off the ALT-D key activates the INKEY(0) function to return an ASCII value of 288.

| | |
|---|---|
| **NOTE** | Additional information on the Clipper Debugger may be found in Chapter 8. |
| **SEE ALSO** | SETCANCEL( ) |

# AMAX( )

| | |
|---|---|
| **FUNCTION** | Returns the maximum numeric value in an array. |
| **SYNTAX** | AMAX( <expA1> ) |
| **PARAMETER** | <expA1>  Array to be searched |
| **RETURNS** | <expN>  Element position of highest value |

*Clipper Function Reference* 345

| | |
|---|---|
| **LIBRARY** | SAMPLES.LIB |
| **DESCRIPTION** | This function will search through the array <expA1> evaluating the numeric data contained within the subscripts and will return the numeric subscript position that holds the highest numeric value. If there is an error, the function will return a numeric 0. It makes the assumption that all elements within <expA1> are of numeric data type; otherwise, a run-time error will be generated. |
| **SEE ALSO** | AMIN( ), MAX( ), MIN( ) |

## AMIN( )

| | |
|---|---|
| **FUNCTION** | Returns the minimum numeric value in an array. |
| **SYNTAX** | `AMIN( <expA1> )` |
| **PARAMETER** | <expA1>   Array to be searched |
| **RETURNS** | <expN>    Element position of lowest value |
| **LIBRARY** | SAMPLES.LIB |
| **DESCRIPTION** | This function will search through the array <expA1> evaluating the numeric data contained within the subscripts and will return the numeric subscript position that holds the lowest value. If there is an error, the function will return a numeric 0. It makes the assumption that all elements within <expA1> are of numeric data type. If they're not, a run-time error will be generated. |
| **SEE ALSO** | AMAX( ), MAX( ). MIN( ) |

## AMPM( )

| | |
|---|---|
| **FUNCTION** | Returns a time string in AM/PM format. |
| **SYNTAX** | `AMPM( <expC1> )` |
| **PARAMETER** | <expC1>   Character expression in time string format |
| **RETURNS** | <expC>    Character expression |
| **LIBRARY** | EXTEND.LIB |
| **DESCRIPTION** | This function accepts the formatted 24-hour time string <expC1> and returns an 11-byte character string in 12-hour a.m./p.m. format. |

| | |
|---|---|
| **NOTE** | This is a compatibility function and may not be supported in future releases. |
| **SEE ALSO** | TSTRING( ), SECONDS( ), SECS( ) |

# ARRAY( )

| | | |
|---|---|---|
| **FUNCTION** | Declares an array of a given size. | |
| **SYNTAX** | `ARRAY ( <expN1> [, <expN2> [,...] ] )` | |
| **PARAMETERS** | <expN1> | Number of elements in first dimension |
| | <expN2> | Number of elements in second dimension |
| | <...> | Number of elements in respective dimensions |
| **RETURNS** | <expA> | Array reference pointer |
| **LIBRARY** | CLIPPER.LIB | |
| **DESCRIPTION** | This function returns an uninitialized array with a length of <expN1>. Nested arrays are uninitialized within the same array pointer reference if additional parameters are specified. The maximum value for <expN1> (and following) is 4096. | |

The LEN( ) function will return the number of elements in the array if the array name is the only parameter used or if the subscript used is an array reference.

The TYPE( ) and VALTYPE( ) functions will return an "A" for an array data type if the array name without element numbers is passed to either function or if the array subscript contains an array reference.

Establishing a memory variable with the same name as the array may destroy the original array and release the entire contents of the array. This is, of course, contingent on the data storage type of either the array or the variable with the same name as the array.

Arrays cannot be saved to an external file via the SAVE TO command.
Arrays cannot be passed as parameters with the CALL command.
This function is similar to the DECLARE, PRIVATE, and PUBLIC commands.

| | |
|---|---|
| **SEE ALSO** | Chapter 10 |
| **EXAMPLE** | See Chapter 10. |

## ARRAYASDATE( )

| | |
|---|---|
| **FUNCTION** | Converts an array with date information into a date |
| **SYNTAX** | ARRAYASDATE( <expA1> ) |
| **PARAMETER** | <expA1>   Array of three elements |
| **RETURNS** | <expD>   Converted date information |
| **LIBRARY** | SAMPLES.LIB |
| **SYNTAX** | This function takes the three elements in the array <expA1> and attempts to convert the items into a working date value. The array elements must be in the following format: |

```
<expA1>[1] -> nYear
<expA1>[2] -> nMonth
<expA1>[3] -> nDay
```

| | |
|---|---|
| **SEE ALSO** | DATE( ), CTOD( ), DTOS( ), DATEASARRAY( ) |
| **EXAMPLE** | See DATEASAGE. |

## ASC( )

| | |
|---|---|
| **FUNCTION** | Returns the ASCII value of a character. |
| **SYNTAX** | ASC( <expC1> ) |
| **PARAMETER** | <expC1>   Any character expression |
| **RETURNS** | <expN>   ASCII value |
| **LIBRARY** | CLIPPER.LIB |
| **DESCRIPTION** | This function returns the ASCII value of the leftmost character of any character expression passed as <expC1>. |
| **NOTE** | For a chart of the ASCII characters, refer to Appendix 5. |
| **SEE ALSO** | CHR( ) |

## ASCAN( )

| | |
|---|---|
| **FUNCTION** | Scans array elements for a specific expression. |
| **SYNTAX** | `ASCAN( <expA1>, <expX2> [, <expN3>] [, <expN4>] )` |
| **PARAMETERS** | <expA1>   Name of array to be scanned <br> <expX2>   Expression to search for within <expA1> <br> <expN3>   Beginning subscript position at which to start the search <br> <expN4>   Number of elements to scan within <expA1> |
| **RETURNS** | <expN>   Numeric value of subscript position where <expX2> was found |
| **LIBRARY** | EXTEND.LIB |
| **DESCRIPTION** | This function scans the contents of the array named <expA1> for the value of <expX2>. The returned value is the position in the array <expA1> in which <expX2> was found. If it was not found, the value of the function will be 0. <br><br> If specified, the beginning subscript position at which to start scanning may be set with the value passed as <expN3>. The default is 1. <br><br> If specified, the number of array elements to scan may be set with the value passed as <expN4>. The default is the number of elements in the array <expA1>. <br><br> The condition of SET EXACT ON/OFF does affect how this function compares strings. <br><br> If <expX2> is a code block, the operation of the function is slightly different. Each array subscript pointer reference is passed to the code block to be evaluated. The scanning routine will continue until the value obtained from the code block is a logical true (.T.) or until the end of the array has been reached. |
| **SEE ALSO** | AEVAL( ), ACOMP( ) |

## ASIZE( )

| | |
|---|---|
| **FUNCTION** | Adjusts the size of an array. |
| **SYNTAX** | `ASIZE( <expA1>, <expN2> )` |

| | | |
|---|---|---|
| **PARAMETERS** | <expA1> | Name of array to be dynamically altered |
| | <expN2> | Numeric value representing the new size of <expA1> |
| **RETURNS** | <expA> | An array pointer reference |
| **LIBRARY** | CLIPPER.LIB | |

**DESCRIPTION** This function will dynamically increase or decrease the size of <expA1> by adjusting the length of the array to <expN2> subscript positions.

If the length of the array <expA1> is shortened, those former subscript positions are lost. If the length of the array is lengthened, a NIL data value is assigned to new subscript positions.

**SEE ALSO** ADEL( ), AINS( ), AADD( )

---

# ASORT( )

**FUNCTION** Sorts the contents of an array.

**SYNTAX** ASORT( <expA1> [, <expN2>] [, <expN3>] [,<expB4>] )

| | | |
|---|---|---|
| **PARAMETERS** | <expA1> | Name of array to be sorted |
| | <expN2> | First element to sort |
| | <expN3> | Number of elements to sort |
| | <expB4> | Code block to alter sorting parameters |
| **RETURNS** | <expA> | An array pointer reference |
| **LIBRARY** | EXTEND.LIB | |

**DESCRIPTION** This function sorts the contents of array <expA1> beginning at subscript position <expN2> and continuing for <expN3> elements. The default is an ascending sort of the entire array <expA1> beginning with the first element.

If specified, <expB4> may be used to alter the sorting condition and criteria. The function passes two array elements to the block to test if they are in sorted order, as specified in the code block. The values passed to the code block will be based on the current and following array elements.

| | | |
|---|---|---|
| **NOTE** | The sorting criteria is as follows: | |
| | Characters | Sorted by the ASCII value of each character |
| | Dates | Sorted in chronological order |
| | Logicals | Sorted by logical false as lowest value |
| | Numerics | Sorted by order of magnitude |
| **SEE ALSO** | AEVAL( ), ASCAN( ) | |

## AT( )

| | |
|---|---|
| **FUNCTION** | Locates the position of a substring in a main string. |
| **SYNTAX** | AT( <expC1>, <expC2> ) |
| **PARAMETERS** | <expC1>   Substring to search for |
| | <expC2>   Main string to search |
| **RETURNS** | <expN>   Starting position of the first occurrence of the substring in the main string |
| **LIBRARY** | CLIPPER.LIB |
| **DESCRIPTION** | This function searches the string <expC2> for the characters in the first string <expC1>. If the substring is not contained within the second expression, this function will return a zero (0) value. |
| **NOTE** | This search operation performs a left-to-right scan. The RAT( ) function is identical to this function, except that it performs a right-to-left operation. |
| **SEE ALSO** | $, RAT( ) |

**EXAMPLE**

```
 1 : * File:     Atdemo.prg
 2 : * Compile:  Rmake sample /dFILE=atdemo
 3 :
 4 : procedure Main()
 5 :
 6 :    local cString := "This is a test"
 7 :
 8 :    cls
 9 :    qout( "is" $ cString )          // is .T.
10 :    qout( at("is", cString) )       // is 3
11 :    qout( rat("is", cString) )      // is 6
12 :
13 :    qout( "IS" $ cString )          // is .F.
14 :    qout( at("IS", cString) )       // is 0
15 :    qout( rat("IS", cString) )      // is 0
16 :
17 : // End of File: Atdemo.prg
```

## ATAIL( )

| | |
|---|---|
| **FUNCTION** | Returns the rightmost element of an array. |
| **SYNTAX** | ATAIL( <expA1> ) |
| **PARAMETER** | <expA1>    Name of an array |
| **RETURNS** | <expX>    Expression of the last element in the array |
| **LIBRARY** | CLIPPER.LIB |
| **DESCRIPTION** | This function returns the value of the last element in the array named <expA1>. This function does not alter the size of the array or any of the subscript values. |
| **SEE ALSO** | LEN( ), ARRAY( ), ASIZE( ), AADD( ) |

## BASETOBASE( )

| | |
|---|---|
| **FUNCTION** | Converts a string of a number from one base to another. |
| **SYNTAX** | BASETOBASE( <expC1>, <expN2>, <expN3> ) |
| **PARAMETERS** | <expC1>    Character string of a number to be converted<br><expN2>    Numeric value of beginning base of <expC1><br><expN3>    Numeric value of ending base of <expC1> |
| **RETURNS** | <expC>    Character string of number in new base |
| **LIBRARY** | SAMPLES.LIB |
| **DESCRIPTION** | This function takes the character representation of a number found in <expC1> which is noted in a base of <expN2> and attempts to convert it to a base <expN3>. The value of the function will be the converted value of <expC1> in the new base format.<br><br>If there is an error with any of the parameters, the return value of the function will be a NIL value. |
| **SEE ALSO** | CEILING( ), FLOOR( ), DTON( ) |

**EXAMPLE**

```
1 : * File      B2bdemo.prg
2 : * Compile Rmake sampmore /dFILE:b2bdemo
3 :
4 : procedure Main()
5 :
6 :    cls
7 :    ? "100 from base 10 to base 2 is: ", BaseToBase( "100", 10, 2 )
8 :    ? "100 from base 10 to base 3 is: ", BaseToBase( "100", 10, 3 )
```

```
 9 :      ? "100 from base 10 to base 4 is: ", BaseToBase( "100", 10, 4 )
10 :      ? "100 from base 10 to base 5 is: ", BaseToBase( "100", 10, 5 )
11 :      ? "100 from base 10 to base 6 is: ", BaseToBase( "100", 10, 6 )
12 :
13 : // End of File: B2bdemo.prg
```

## BIN2I( )

| | |
|---|---|
| **FUNCTION** | Converts binary to integer. |
| **SYNTAX** | BIN2I( <expC1> ) |
| **PARAMETER** | <expC1>    Binary character |
| **RETURNS** | <expN>    Integer value |
| **LIBRARY** | EXTEND.LIB |
| **DESCRIPTION** | This function converts a character string <expC1> that is formatted as a 16-bit signed integer to a Clipper numeric value. |
| **SEE ALSO** | BIN2L( ), BIN2W( ), I2BIN( ), L2BIN( ) |

## BIN2L( )

| | |
|---|---|
| **FUNCTION** | Converts binary 32-bit to integer. |
| **SYNTAX** | BIN2L( <expC1> ) |
| **PARAMETER** | <expC1>    Binary character |
| **RETURNS** | <expN>    Integer value |
| **LIBRARY** | EXTEND.LIB |
| **DESCRIPTION** | This function converts a character string <expC1> formatted as a 32-bit signed long integer into a Clipper numeric value. |
| **SEE ALSO** | BIN2I( ), BIN2W( ), I2BIN( ), L2BIN( ) |

## BIN2W( )

| | |
|---|---|
| **FUNCTION** | Converts binary 16-bit to integer. |
| **SYNTAX** | BIN2W( <expC1> ) |

| | | |
|---|---|---|
| **PARAMETER** | <expC1> | Binary character |
| **RETURNS** | <expN> | Integer value |
| **LIBRARY** | EXTEND.LIB | |
| **DESCRIPTION** | This function converts a character string expressed as <expC1> formatted as a 16-bit unsigned integer to a Clipper numeric value. | |
| **SEE ALSO** | BIN2I( ), BIN2L( ), I2BIN( ), L2BIN( ) | |

## BOF( )

| | |
|---|---|
| **FUNCTION** | Tests for the beginning-of-file condition. |
| **SYNTAX** | BOF ( ) |
| **PARAMETER** | None |
| **RETURNS** | <expL>   Logical true (.T.) or false (.F.) |
| **LIBRARY** | CLIPPER.LIB |
| **DESCRIPTION** | This function determines if the beginning of file marker has been reached. If so, the function will return a logical true (.T.); otherwise, a logical false (.F.) will be returned.<br><br>By default, BOF( ) will apply to the currently selected database unless the function is preceded by an alias. |
| **SEE ALSO** | GO, SKIP, EOF( ) |

**EXAMPLE**

```
 1 : * File:      Bofdemo.prg
 2 : * Compile:   Rmake Sample /dFILE=BOFDEMO
 3 :
 4 : procedure Main()
 5 :
 6 :    cls
 7 :
 8 :    use Clients new    // O.k.  Use this database
 9 :    use Notap new      // and use this one as well
10 :
11 :    // Obtain the values of BOF() and RECNO() in the current work area and
12 :    // in the Clients work area as well
13 :
14 :    qout( bof(), recno() )                                 // .f.     1
15 :    qout( Clients->( bof() ), Clients->( recno() ) )       // .f.     1
16 :    wait
17 :
18 :    // Skip one record in the Clients work area and reevaluate
19 :
20 :    skip -1 alias Clients
```

```
 21 :    qout( bof(), recno() )                              // .f.      1
 22 :    qout( Clients->( bof() ), Clients->( recno() ) )  // .t.      1
 23 :    wait
 24 :
 25 :    // Position the record pointer in the current work area at the last
 26 :    // record and test for the EOF() condition.  It is important to remember
 27 :    // that the value of RECNO() will be one greater than the value of
 28 :    // LASTREC() if an EOF() condition is true.  This is NOT the case with
 29 :    // the BOF() condition.
 30 :
 31 :    dbgobottom()     // GO BOTTOM in current area
 32 :
 33 :    qout( eof(), recno() )                  // .f.
 34 :    qout( Clients->( eof() ), Clients->( recno() ), ;
 35 :          Clients->( bof() ) )        // .f.  1 .t.
 36 :    wait
 37 :    // Now skip in both work areas, one beyond the end of file marker in the
 38 :    // current work area and to the last record in the Clients work area
 39 :
 40 :    skip
 41 :    Clients->( Dbgobottom(), lastrec() )
 42 :    qout( eof(), recno() )                              // .t.
 43 :    Clients->( qout( eof(), recno(), bof() ) )  // .f.     29     .f.
 44 :    wait
 45 :
 46 : // End of File: Bofdemo.prg
```

# BOXMENU( )

| | |
|---|---|
| **FUNCTION** | Paints quick menu inside a boxed region. |
| **SYNTAX** | BOXMENU( <expA1> [, <expN2>] [, <expN3>] [, <expN4>] [, <expN5>] [, <expC6>] [, <expN7>] [, <expC8>] [, <expC9>] ) |

**PARAMETERS**  
<expA1>  Array of menu items to be displayed  
<expN2>  Top row coordinate of window region  
<expN3>  Left column coordinate of window region  
<expN4>  Bottom row coordinate of window region  
<expN5>  Right column coordinate of window region  
<expC6>  Character string of menu title  
<expN7>  Numeric position of starting menu item  
<expC8>  Character string of frame format  
<expC9>  Character string of color for region  

**RETURNS**  <expN>  Numeric element position of selected menu item or NIL if an error has occurred

**LIBRARY**  SAMPLES.LIB

**DESCRIPTION** This function will attempt to display a pop-up menu of items found in <expA1> within the shadowed window region of <expN2>, <expN3> through to <expN4>, <expN5>. This function will return the numeric subscript position of the element selected; 0 if the ESC key was pressed and NIL if there is an array with any of the base parameters. The default values for the window coordinates are 0,0 to MAXROW( ), MAXCOL( ). The starting position of the menu prompt to highlight will be expressed in <expN7> while the title for the menu will be expressed in <expC6>. If not specified, the starting menu prompt will be the first prompt in the window region and the title of the menu will be a NULL string: no title. The default frame of 8 characters will be a double barred frame while the color setting, passed as <expC9> defaults to the current value of the SETCOLOR( ) function.

**SEE ALSO** BOXSHADOW( )

**EXAMPLE**

```
 1:*File     Boxdemo.prg
 2:* Compile Rmake sampmore /dFILE:boxdemo
 3:
 4: procedure Main
 5:
 6:    local aMenu    := {}
 7:    local nChoice := 1
 8:
 9:    aadd( aMenu, " General Ledger " )
10:    aadd( aMenu, " Accounts Payable " )
11:    aadd( aMenu, " Inventory " )
12:    aadd( aMenu, " Payroll " )
13:    aadd( aMenu, " Point of Sale " )
14:
15: setcolor("W/R","W/BG","W/R")
16:    cls
17:
18:    while !( nChoice == 0 )
19:
20:     dispbox(0,0,maxrow()-3,maxcol()-3,replicate(chr(178),9))
21:
22:     BoxShadow(0,0,maxrow()-3,maxcol()-3)
23:
24:      nChoice := BoxMenu( aMenu, 5, 25, 5+len(aMenu), 50, ;
25:        " Accounting ", nChoice,,"W/B" )
26:     devpos(maxrow()-3,0)
27:     devout( "Selection was: " )
28:     devout( nChoice )
29:     inkey(2)
30:    enddo
31:
32:    scroll()
33:
34: // End of File: Boxdemo.prg
```

## BOXSHADOW( )

| | |
|---|---|
| **FUNCTION** | Builds a boxed shadow based on window coordinates. |
| **SYNTAX** | BOXSHADOW(<expN1>, <expN2>, <expN3>, <expN4>) |
| **PARAMETERS** | <expN1>　Top row coordinate<br><expN2>　Left column coordinate<br><expN3>　Bottom row coordinate<br><expN4>　Right column coordinate |
| **LIBRARY** | SAMPLES.LIB |
| **DESCRIPTION** | This function will draw a shadowed box within the top coordinates of <expN1>, <expN2> through <expN3>, <expN4>. |
| **SEE ALSO** | BOXMENU( ) |
| **EXAMPLE** | Please see BOXMENU( ) for an example. |

## BREAK( )

| | |
|---|---|
| **FUNCTION** | Allows controlled break-out from the BEGIN SEQUENCE command. |
| **SYNTAX** | BREAK( <expX1> ) |
| **PARAMETER** | <expX1>　Any expression, including NIL, to be passed to the RECOVER USING command |
| **LIBRARY** | CLIPPER.LIB |
| **DESCRIPTION** | This function allows the value of an expression <expX1> to be passed to the respective RECOVER USING command statement within a controlling BEGIN SEQUENCE ... END SEQUENCE command construct. If there is no RECOVER USING command within the BEGIN SEQUENCE ... END SEQUENCE construct, program flow will jump to the respective END SEQUENCE statement.<br><br>This function is the same as the BREAK command. |
| **SEE ALSO** | BEGIN SEQUENCE, Chapter 19 |
| **EXAMPLE** | See Chapter 19. |

## BROWSE( )

| | |
|---|---|
| **FUNCTION** | Permits generic browsing of data. |
| **SYNTAX** | BROWSE([<expN1> [, <expN2> [, <expN3> [,<expN4>]]]]) |

| | | |
|---|---|---|
| **PARAMETERS** | <expN1> | Top row coordinate, default of 0 |
| | <expN2> | Left column coordinate, default of 0 |
| | <expN3> | Bottom row coordinate, default of MAXROW( ) |
| | <expN4> | Right column coordinate, default of MAXCOL( ) |
| **LIBRARY** | EXTEND.LIB | |
| **DESCRIPTION** | This is a simple browsing function that simulates the use of DBEDIT( ). | |
| **NOTE** | This function is not recommended for use because of its excessive and unnecessary coding overhead. In addition, it is considered a "compatibility" function and should be replaced by the TBROWSE class. | |
| **SEE ALSO** | DBEDIT( ) | |

## CDOW( )

| | | |
|---|---|---|
| **FUNCTION** | Converts a date to the day of the week. | |
| **SYNTAX** | `CDOW( <expD1> )` | |
| **PARAMETER** | <expD1> | Any date expression |
| **RETURNS** | <expC> | Character expression |
| **LIBRARY** | CLIPPER.LIB | |
| **DESCRIPTION** | This function returns a character string of the day of the week (Monday, Tuesday, etc.) from a date expression <expD1> passed to it. | |
| | If a NULL date is passed to the function, the value of the function will be a NULL byte. | |
| **SEE ALSO** | DAY( ), DOW( ), DATE( ), CMONTH( ) | |
| **EXAMPLE** | See the YEAR( ) function. | |

## CEILING( )

| | | |
|---|---|---|
| **FUNCTION** | Returns the smallest integer near passed a given boundary. | |
| **SYNTAX** | `CEILING( <expN1> )` | |
| **PARAMETER** | <expN1> | Any numeric value |
| **RETURNS** | <expN> | Integer near boundary |
| **LIBRARY** | SAMPLES.LIB | |
| **DESCRIPTION** | This function will return the smallest integer that is greater than or equal to the passed parameter of <expN1>. | |

**SEE ALSO**  DTOR( ), BASETOBASE( ), FLOOR( )

**EXAMPLE**

```
 1 : * File     Ceildemo.prg
 2 : * Compile Rmake sampmore /dFILE:Ceildemo
 3 :
 4 : procedure Main()
 5 :
 6 :   local nCount
 7 :
 8 :   cls
 9 :   for nCount := 1 to 11 step .7
10 :      ? "The base: ", nCount, ;
11 :        " [ Ceiling is:", Ceiling(nCount), ;
12 :        " ][ Floor is:", Floor(nCount)
13 :   next
14 :
15 : // End of File: Ceildemo.prg
```

# CHR( )

| | |
|---|---|
| **FUNCTION** | Converts an ASCII value to its character value. |
| **SYNTAX** | CHR( <expN1> ) |
| **PARAMETER** | <expN1>   Any ASCII character code |
| **RETURNS** | <expC>   Character expression of that ASCII code |
| **LIBRARY** | CLIPPER.LIB |
| **DESCRIPTION** | This function returns the ASCII character code for <expN1>. The number expressed *must* be an integer within the range of 0 to 255, inclusive. The CHR( ) function will send the character returned to whatever device is presently set. |
| | The CHR( ) function may be used for printing special codes as well as normal and graphic character codes. For a complete list of character values, see the ASCII chart in Appendix 5. |
| **NOTE** | CHR(0) will yield a character byte with a length of 1, and the result will be treated as any other character. However, a null byte symbolized as (" ") will continue to have a length of 0. |
| **SEE ALSO** | ASC( ), INKEY( ) |

**EXAMPLE**

```
 1 : * File:     Chrdemo.prg
 2 : * Compile:  RMake sample /dFILE:chrdemo
 3 :
 4 : #define pCRLF chr(13)+chr(10)
 5 :
 6 : procedure Main()
```

```
 7 :
 8 :    local nCount
 9 :
10 :    cls
11 :
12 :    for nCount := 65 to 127
13 :       qqout( chr(nCount), space(2) )
14 :       if col()+4 > maxcol()
15 :          qqout( pCRLF )
16 :       endif
17 :    next
18 :
19 :    wait "Those are the CHR() values... "
20 :    qout()
21 :
22 :    for nCount := 65 to 127
23 :       qqout( asc(chr( nCount )), space(2) )
24 :       if col()+4 > maxcol()
25 :          qqout( pCRLF )
26 :       endif
27 :    next
28 :
29 :    qout( "And these are the ASC() values..." )
30 :
31 : // End of File: Chrdemo.prg
```

# CITYSTATE( )

| | |
|---|---|
| **FUNCTION** | Converts city, state, and zip-code information into string format. |
| **SYNTAX** | CITYSTATE( <expC1>, <expC2>, <expC3> ) |
| **PARAMETERS** | <expC1>　Character string of city information<br><expC2>　Character string of state information<br><expC3>　Character string of zip-code information |
| **RETURNS** | <expC>　Converted string of address information |
| **LIBRARY** | SAMPLES.LIB |
| **DESCRIPTION** | This function simply attempts to take the information of the address and format it with the proper placement of the "," between <expC1> and <expC2> as well as the placement of an extra space between <expC2> and <expC3>, and returns that string. |

# CMONTH( )

| | |
|---|---|
| **FUNCTION** | Returns the name of the month. |
| **SYNTAX** | CMONTH( <expD1> ) |

| | | |
|---|---|---|
| **PARAMETER** | <expD1> | Any date expression |
| **RETURNS** | <expC> | Character expression |
| **LIBRARY** | CLIPPER.LIB | |
| **DESCRIPTION** | This function returns the name of the month (January, February, March, etc.) from a date expression <expD1> passed to it. | |
| | If a NULL date is passed to the function, the return value will be a NULL byte. | |
| **SEE ALSO** | CDOW( ), DATE( ), MONTH( ), YEAR( ), DOW( ), DTOC( ) | |
| **EXAMPLE** | See the YEAR( ) function. | |

## COL( )

| | | |
|---|---|---|
| **FUNCTION** | Returns the current screen column position. | |
| **SYNTAX** | COL ( ) | |
| **PARAMETER** | None | |
| **RETURNS** | <expN> | Current column position |
| **LIBRARY** | CLIPPER.LIB | |
| **DESCRIPTION** | This function returns the current cursor column position. The value for this function can range between 0 and MAXCOL( ). In addition, the beginning value for this function, whenever the screen is cleared, is 0. | |
| **SEE ALSO** | ROW( ), PCOL( ), CLS, PROW( ) | |
| **EXAMPLE** | See the ROW( ) function. | |

## COLLECT( )

| | | |
|---|---|---|
| **FUNCTION** | Collects information stored in an array | |
| **SYNTAX** | COLLECT ( <expA1>, <expB2> ) | |
| **PARAMETERS** | <expA1> | Array of information to be processed |
| | <expB2> | Code block of collection |
| **RETURNS** | <expA> | Array of results |
| **LIBRARY** | SAMPLES.LIB | |

**DESCRIPTION** This function takes the contents of <expA1> and evaluates the code block <expB2> against each element in the passed array and stores the results to an array that will be the return value of the function.

**SEE ALSO** AEVAL( ), EVAL( ), LEVAL( ), EXTRACT( )

**EXAMPLE**

```
 1 : * File     Colldemo.prg
 2 : * Compile Rmake sampmore /dFILE:colldemo
 3 :
 4 : procedure Main()
 5 :
 6 :   local aData    := {2,3,44,1,2,66,45,90}
 7 :   local aResults
 8 :   local nCount
 9 :
10 :   cls
11 :   aResults := Collect(aData, {|nValue| nValue*23} )
12 :
13 :   for nCount := 1 to len( aData )
14 :     ? "Seed value is:", aData[nCount], "[  Collected value is:", ;
15 :                         aResults[nCount]
16 :   next
17 :
18 : // End of File: Colldemo.prg
```

# COLORSELECT( )

**FUNCTION** Activates the attribute in the current color setting.

**SYNTAX** COLORSELECT(<nIndex>)

**PARAMETER** <nIndex>   Ordinal position corresponding to the current list of color attributes set by the SETCOLOR( ) function

**LIBRARY** CLIPPER.LIB

**DESCRIPTION** This function will activate the <nIndex> color pair found in SETCOLOR( ) based on the following table:

| <nIndex> | *Meaning* |
|---|---|
| 0 | Standard color pair |
| 1 | Enhanced color pair |
| 2 | Border color |
| 3 | Background color |
| 4 | Unselected color pair |

**SEE ALSO** SETCOLOR( )

## CTOD( )

| | |
|---|---|
| **FUNCTION** | Converts a character string to a date expression. |
| **SYNTAX** | `CTOD( <expC1> )` |
| **PARAMETER** | <expC1>   A character date in the format "mm/dd/yy" |
| **RETURNS** | <expD>   Date expression |
| **LIBRARY** | CLIPPER.LIB |
| **DESCRIPTION** | This function converts a date that has been entered as a character expression to a date expression. The character expression will be in the form "MM/DD/YY" (based on the default value in SET DATE) or in the appropriate format specified by the SET DATE TO command. If an improper character string is passed to the function, an empty date value will be returned. |
| **SEE ALSO** | SET DATE, DATE( ), DTOS( ) |
| **EXAMPLE** | See the YEAR( ) or DATE( ) function. |

## CURDIR( )

| | |
|---|---|
| **FUNCTION** | Returns the current DOS directory name. |
| **SYNTAX** | `CURDIR( [<expC1>] )` |
| **PARAMETER** | <expC1>   DOS drive letter |
| **RETURNS** | <expC>   Name of directory |
| **LIBRARY** | EXTEND.LIB |
| **DESCRIPTION** | This function yields the name of the current DOS directory on a specified drive. If <expC1> is not specified, the currently logged drive will be used.<br>This function will not return leading or trailing backslash characters.<br>If an error has been detected by the function or if the current DOS directory is the root, the value of the function will be a NULL byte. |
| **SEE ALSO** | FILE( ) |

**EXAMPLE**

```
1 : * File:      Curdemo.prg
2 : * Compile:   RMake sample /dFILE:curdemo
3 :
4 : procedure Main()
```

```
 5 :
 6 :    local getlist := {}    // This is for the READ/@...GET command
 7 :    local cDrive   := "C"
 8 :    local cPath    := "\" + curdir() + "\"
 9 :
10 :    // Just in case the "\\" appear together if CURDIR() returns a NULL
11 :    // byte, let's remove it with the STRTRAN() function
12 :
13 :    DoLook( cPath )
14 :    scroll()    // Need only this since there is an @...command to follow
15 :
16 :    @ 1,0 say "Enter drive letter: " get cDrive pict "!"
17 :    read
18 :    DoLook("\" + curdir(cDrive) + "\")
19 :
20 :    scroll()
21 :
22 : ******************
23 :
24 : static procedure DoLook( cThePath )
25 :
26 :    cThePath := strtran( cThePath, "\\", "\" )
27 :
28 :    if !file( cThePath + "*.DBF" )
29 :       qqout( "There are no database files in the directory! " )
30 :    else
31 :       qout( "There are " )
32 :       qqout( len( directory(cThePath + "*.dbf") ) )
33 :       qqout( "database files that may be USED" )
34 :       qout()
35 :       qout( "The path of those files is: " + cThePath )
36 :    endif
37 :    wait
38 :
39 : // End of File: Curdemo.prg
```

# DATE( )

| | |
|---|---|
| **FUNCTION** | Yields the DOS system date. |
| **SYNTAX** | DATE() |
| **PARAMETER** | None |
| **RETURNS** | <expD>    DOS system date |
| **LIBRARY** | CLIPPER.LIB |
| **DESCRIPTION** | This function returns the current system date. |
| **SEE ALSO** | CTOD( ), DTOS( ), DTOC( ), DAY( ), MONTH( ), CMONTH( ), ADDMONTH( ) |

## EXAMPLE

```
1 : * File:     D1demo.prg
2 : * Compile:  Rmake sample /dFILE:d1demo
3 :
4 : procedure Main()
5 :
6 :    SET DATE TO ANSI
7 :    ShowDate( "Ansi" )
8 :    SET DATE TO BRITISH
9 :    ShowDate( "British" )
10 :   SET DATE TO FRENCH
11 :   ShowDate( "French" )
12 :   SET DATE TO GERMAN
13 :   ShowDate( "German" )
14 :   SET DATE TO ITALIAN
15 :   ShowDate( "Italian" )
16 :   SET DATE TO JAPAN
17 :   ShowDate( "Japan" )
18 :   SET DATE TO USA
19 :   ShowDate( "USA" )
20 :   SET DATE FORMAT TO "YYYY*MM*DD"
21 :   ShowDate("YYYY*MM*DD")
22 :
23 :   scroll()
24 :
25 : *******************
26 :
27 : static procedure ShowDate( cSay )
28 :
29 :    cls
30 :    qout( "The format is: " + cSay )
31 :    qout()
32 :    qout( " Date is normally: ", date()  )
33 :    qout( "    DTOS() is then: ", dtos( date() ) )
34 :    qout( "    DTOC() is then: ", dtoc( date() ) )
35 :    qout( "          of DTOS(): ", valtype( dtos( date() ) ) )
36 :    qout( "          of DTOC(): ", valtype( dtoc( date() ) ) )
37 :    qout()
38 :    wait
39 :
40 : // End of File: D1Demo.prg
```

## DATEASAGE( )

| | |
|---|---|
| **FUNCTION** | Converts a date of birth to a specific age. |
| **SYNTAX** | DATEASAGE( <expD1> ) |
| **PARAMETER** | <expD1>   Any valid date |
| **RETURNS** | <expN>   Numeric date as age |

**LIBRARY**      SAMPLES.LIB

**DESCRIPTION**    This function takes the date expressed as <expD1>, considering it as a birthdate and compares it against the system date, converts it into a numeric response as an age in years.

**SEE ALSO**      DMY( ), ADDMONTH( ) DATEASARRAY( ), ARRAYASDATE( )

**EXAMPLE**

```
 1: *File dateuse.prg
 2:
 3: Procedure main()
 4:
 5: local getlist:={} // required for the Get / Say operation
 6: local dArray:={}
 7: local aDate:=ctod("  /  /  ")
 8: local sDate:=ctod("  /  /  ")
 9:
10: local Lcount:=0, ncount:=0
11: cls
12:
13: @8,20 Say "Enter your date of birth" GET aDate Picture "  /  /   "
14:
15: READ
16:
17: @10,20 Say "Your are " + str(DATEASAGE(aDate))+ " years old"
18:
19: devpos(13,20)
20: Text
21:   I'm testing for the number of leap years between your
22:   your date of birth and today.
23: endtext
24: qout()
25: sDate:=aDate
26:
27: For nCount = 1 to DATEASAGE(aDate)
28:
29:   If DATEISLEAP(sDate)
30:     ? sDate," was a leap year"
31:     lCount := lCount + 1
32:   endif
33:   dArray:=DATEASARRAY(sDate)
34:   dArray[1]:=(dArray[1]+1)
35:    sDate:=ARRAYASDATE(dArray)
36:
37: Next
38: wait
39: cls
40: @14,20 Say "There have been " +alltrim(str(Lcount)) + " leap years "
41:
42: inkey(0)
43: cls
44: return
45: // End of file: dateuse.prg
```

## DATEASARRAY( )

| | |
|---|---|
| **FUNCTION** | Converts a date to an array. |
| **SYNTAX** | `DATEASARRAY( <expD1> )` |
| **PARAMETER** | <expD1>    Any valid date data type |
| **RETURNS** | <expA>    Array of date information |
| **LIBRARY** | SAMPLES.LIB |
| **DESCRIPTION** | This function takes the date expressed as <expD1> and converts it into an array where the first element is the year, the second element is the month, and the third element is the day. |
| **SEE ALSO** | DMY( ), ARRAYASDATE( ), DATEASAGE( ) |
| **EXAMPLE** | See DATEASAGE( ) |

## DATEISLEAP( )

| | |
|---|---|
| **FUNCTION** | Tests to see if given date is in a leap year. |
| **SYNTAX** | `DATEISLEAP( <expD1> )` |
| **PARAMETER** | <expD1>    Any valid date data type |
| **RETURNS** | <expL>    Logical true (.T.) or logical false (.F.) |
| **LIBRARY** | SAMPLES.LIB |
| **DESCRIPTION** | This function takes the date <expD1> and sees if it falls within a leap year; if it does, the function will return a logical true (.T.); otherwise, a logical false (.F.) will be returned. |
| **SEE ALSO** | DATE( ), DMY( ), DATEASARRAY( ), ARRAYASDATE( ), YEAR( ) |
| **EXAMPLE** | See DATEASAGE( ) |

## DAY( )

| | |
|---|---|
| **FUNCTION** | Returns the numeric day of the month. |
| **SYNTAX** | `DAY( <expD1> )` |
| **PARAMETER** | <expD1>    Any date expression |

| | |
|---|---|
| **RETURNS** | <expN> Numeric day of the month |
| **LIBRARY** | CLIPPER.LIB |
| **DESCRIPTION** | This function returns the numeric value of the day of the month from a date. |
| **SEE ALSO** | CTOD( ), DTOS( ), DTOC( ), DATE( ), MONTH( ), CMONTH( ) |
| **EXAMPLE** | See the YEAR( ) function. |

## DAYS( )

| | |
|---|---|
| **FUNCTION** | Converts elapsed seconds into days. |
| **SYNTAX** | DAYS ( <expN1> ) |
| **PARAMETER** | <expN1> The number of seconds |
| **RETURNS** | <expN> The number of days |
| **LIBRARY** | EXTEND.LIB |
| **DESCRIPTION** | This function converts <expN1> seconds to the equivalent number of days; 86,399 seconds represents one day, 0 seconds being midnight. |
| **NOTE** | This is a compatibility function and may not be supported in future versions. |
| **SEE ALSO** | SECONDS( ), SECS( ), ELAPTIME( ) |
| **EXAMPLE** | See the TSTRING( ) function. |

## DBAPPEND( )

| | |
|---|---|
| **FUNCTION** | Appends a new record to a database file. |
| **SYNTAX** | DBAPPEND ( [<expL1>] ) |
| **PARAMETER** | <expL1> Toggle to release record locks |
| **LIBRARY** | CLIPPER.LIB |
| **DESCRIPTION** | This function adds a new record to the end of the database in the selected or aliased work area. All fields in that database will be given empty data values—character fields will be filled with blank spaces, date fields with CTOD(" / / "), numeric fields with 0, logical fields with .F., and memo fields with NULL bytes. The header of the database is not updated until |

the record is flushed from the buffer and the contents are written to the disk.

Under a networking environment, DBAPPEND( ) performs an additional operation: It attempts to lock the newly added record. If the database file is currently exclusively locked or if a locking assignment is made to LASTREC( ) + 1, NETERR( ) will return a logical true (.T.) immediately after the DBAPPEND( ) function. This function does not unlock the locked record.

If <expL1> is passed as a logical true (.T.) value, it will release the record locks, which allows the application to maintain multiple record locks during an appending operation. The default for this parameter is a logical false (.F.).

**SEE ALSO** APPEND BLANK, DBUNLOCK( ), DBUNLOCKALL( ), ADDREC( )

## DBCLEARFILTER( )

**FUNCTION** Clears the current filter condition in a work area.

**SYNTAX** DBCLEARFILTER( )

**PARAMETER** None

**LIBRARY** CLIPPER.LIB

**DESCRIPTION** This function clears any active filter condition for the current or selected work area.

**SEE ALSO** DBSETFILTER( ), DBFILTER( )

## DBCLEARINDEX( )

**FUNCTION** Closes all open index files in a work area

**SYNTAX** DBCLEARINDEX( )

**PARAMETER** None

**LIBRARY** CLIPPER.LIB

**DESCRIPTION** This function removes all open indexes in a selected or aliased work area.

**SEE ALSO** DBCREATEINDEX( ), DBSETINDEX( )

## DBCLEARRELATION( )

**FUNCTION** Clears any existing database relation in a work area.

**SYNTAX** `DBCLEARRELATION( )`

**PARAMETER** None

**LIBRARY** CLIPPER.LIB

**DESCRIPTION** This function clears any existing database relation in the selected or aliased work area.

**SEE ALSO** DBSETRELATION( ), DBRELATION( ), DBRSELECT( )

## DBCLOSEALL( )

**FUNCTION** Closes all open files in all work areas.

**SYNTAX** `DBCLOSEALL( )`

**PARAMETER** None

**LIBRARY** CLIPPER.LIB

**DESCRIPTION** This function closes all open databases and all associated indexes. In addition, it closes all format files and moves the work area pointer to the first position.

**SEE ALSO** DBUSEAREA( ), DBCLOSEAREA( ), DBCLEARINDEX( )

## DBCLOSEAREA( )

**FUNCTION** Closes a database file in a work area.

**SYNTAX** `DBCLOSEAREA( )`

**PARAMETER** None

**LIBRARY** CLIPPER.LIB

**DESCRIPTION** This function will close any database open in the selected or aliased work area.

**SEE ALSO** DBUSEAREA( ), DBCLOSEALL( )

## DBCOMMIT( )

| | |
|---|---|
| **FUNCTION** | Updates all index and database buffers for a given work area. |
| **SYNTAX** | `DBCOMMIT( )` |
| **PARAMETER** | None |
| **LIBRARY** | CLIPPER.LIB |
| **DESCRIPTION** | This function updates all of the information for a given, selected, or active work area. This operation includes all database and index buffers for that work area only. This function does not globally update all open work areas. |
| **SEE ALSO** | DBCOMMITALL( ), DBCLOSEAREA( ) |

## DBCOMMITALL( )

| | |
|---|---|
| **FUNCTION** | Flushes the memory buffer and performs a hard-disk write. |
| **SYNTAX** | `DBCOMMITALL()` |
| **PARAMETER** | None |
| **LIBRARY** | CLIPPER.LIB |
| **DESCRIPTION** | This function performs a hard-disk write for all work areas. Before the disk write is performed, all buffers are flushed to DOS. This function will only work with versions of DOS 3.3 or higher. |
| **SEE ALSO** | DBSKIP( ), COMMIT |

## DBCREATE( )

| | | |
|---|---|---|
| **FUNCTION** | Creates an empty database from an array. | |
| **SYNTAX** | `DBCREATE( <expC1>, <expA2> [, <expC3>] )` | |
| **PARAMETERS** | <expC1> | Name of a database to be created |
| | <expA2> | Name of a multidimensional array that contains a database structure |
| | <expC3> | Name of the Replaceable Database Driver |
| **LIBRARY** | CLIPPER.LIB | |

**DESCRIPTION** This function creates the database file specified as <expC1> from the multidimensional array named <expA2>. If no file extension is used with <expC1>, the .DBF extension will be assumed.

The array specified in <expA2> must follow a few guidelines when being built prior to a call to DBCREATE( ):

- All subscript values in the second dimension must be set to proper values.

- The fourth subscript value in the second dimension—which contains the decimal value—must be specified, even for nonnumeric fields.

- The second subscript value in the second dimension—which contains the field data type—must contain a proper value: C, D, L, M, or N. It is possible to use additional letters for clarity (e.g., "Numeric" for "N"); however, the first letter of this array element must be a proper value.

- The DBCREATE( ) function does not use the decimal field to calculate the length of a character field longer than 256. Values up to the maximum length of a character field (which is 65,519 bytes) are stored directly in the database in the length attribute if that database was created via this function. However, a file containing fields longer than 256 bytes is not compatible with any interpreter.

The <expC3> parameter specifies the name of the Replaceable Database Driver to use to create the database. If it is not specified, then the Replaceable Database Driver in the current work area is used.

**SEE ALSO** CREATE FROM, DBSTRUCT( ), COPY STRUCTURE EXTENDED

**EXAMPLE**

```
 1 : * File:      Dbcdemo.prg
 2 : * Compile:   RMake sample /dFILE:dbcdemo
 3 :
 4 : procedure Main()
 5 :
 6 :    local aStru    := {}   /// This is an empty array!
 7 :    local bDisplay := {|aRec| qout(aRec[1], aRec[2], aRec[3], aRec[4])}
 8 :
 9 :    aadd( aStru, {"LNAME",    "C", 25, 0} )
10 :    aadd( aStru, {"FNAME",    "C", 20, 0} )
11 :    aadd( aStru, {"MNAME",    "C",  1, 0} )
12 :    aadd( aStru, {"HIREDATE", "D",  8, 0} )
13 :    aadd( aStru, {"MARRIED",  "L",  1, 0} )
14 :    aadd( aStru, {"SALARY",   "N", 10, 2} )
15 :
16 :    qout( "Here is the structure..." )
17 :    qout()
18 :
19 :    aeval( aStru, bDisplay )
20 :    wait
```

```
21 :
22 :    qout()
23 :    if !file( "CREATED.DBF" )
24 :      qout( "File does not yet exist!" )
25 :      dbcreate( "CREATED", aStru )
26 :      inkey(1)                        // This is strictly a pause!
27 :
28 :      if file( "CREATED.DBF" )
29 :        qout( "And now it IS created!" )
30 :        use Created new
31 :        if !empty( alias() )   // Yes, there is a database open
32 :          qout( "And now it is even USED!" )
33 :          qout()
34 :          aeval( dbstruct(), bDisplay )
35 :          wait
36 :          dbcloseall()  // We have to close before we can erase
37 :        endif
38 :      endif
39 :    endif
40 :
41 :    ferase( "Created.dbf" )
42 :
43 : // End of File: Dbcdemo.prg
```

## DBCREATEINDEX( )

**FUNCTION**      Creates an index file for a database.

**SYNTAX**        DBCREATEINDEX( <expC1>, <expX2>, <expB3> [, <expL4>] )

**PARAMETERS**    <expC1>    Filename
                  <expX2>    Key value
                  <expN3>    Code block to produce index keys
                  <expL4>    Unique status flag

**LIBRARY**       CLIPPER.LIB

**DESCRIPTION**   This function creates an index file <expC1> with a key expression of <expX2>. The value of <expX2> is placed in the header of the index file <expC1>. The evaluation of key values for creating keys in the index file is stored to a code block expression as <expB3>. The length of <expX2> may be up to 250 characters and may be of character, date, numeric, or logical data type. Memo fields may not be indexed.

The order of the index algorithm is the ASCII value of the characters for character data types, numeric order for numeric data values, chronological order for date data types (with blank dates as the lowest date), and logical order for logical data types (with .F. values as the lower values).

If <expL4> is a logical true (.T.), only those records with unique keys will be added to the index file. The default value for this will be a logical false (.F.).

This function indexes all records in the database starting with the first record, regardless of whether a deleted or filtered condition is present. At the end of the operation, the record pointer will be positioned at the first record in the database. When the index file is created, it is done EXCLUSIVEly. If this should fail in a network environment, a run-time error will be generated.

**SEE ALSO**   DBSETINDEX( ), DBREINDEX( ), DBCLEARINDEX( )

## DBDELETE( )

**FUNCTION**   Marks records for deletion in a database.

**SYNTAX**   DBDELETE ( )

**PARAMETER**   None

**LIBRARY**   CLIPPER.LIB

**DESCRIPTION**   This function marks a record for deletion in the selected or aliased work area. If the DELETED setting is on, the record will still be visible until the record pointer in that work area is moved to another record.

Records are marked as DELETEd by an asterisk located in the first position on the screen, printer, or file if shown by the DISPLAY or LIST command, provided that SET DELETED is OFF.

In a networking situation, this function requires that the record be locked prior to issuing the DBDELETE( ) function.

**SEE ALSO**   DBRECALL( )

## DBEDIT( )

**FUNCTION**   Browses a database or work area.

**SYNTAX**   DBEDIT( [<expN1>] [, <expN2>] [, <expN3>] [,<expN4>] [, <expA5>] [, <expC6>] [, <expA7>] [, <expA8>] [,<expA9>] [, <expA10>] [, <expA11> ] )

**PARAMETERS**   
<expN1>   Top row coordinate
<expN2>   Left column coordinate
<expN3>   Bottom row coordinate
<expN4>   Right column coordinate

|  |  |  |
|--|--|--|
| | &lt;expA5&gt; | List of values to be displayed |
| | &lt;expC6&gt; | UDF to control keystrokes during DBEDIT( ) |
| | &lt;expA7&gt; | List of picture strings |
| | &lt;expA8&gt; | List of heading strings |
| | &lt;expA9&gt; | List of heading separators |
| | &lt;expA10&gt; | List of column separators |
| | &lt;expA11&gt; | List of footing separators |
| **RETURNS** | &lt;expL&gt; | Logical true (.T.) or false (.F.) |
| **LIBRARY** | EXTEND.LIB | |

**DESCRIPTION** This function displays and edits records from one or more work areas. The area displayed is in a window with the top, left, bottom, and right coordinates listed in &lt;expN1&gt;, &lt;expN2&gt;, &lt;expN3&gt;, and &lt;expN4&gt;, respectively. If not used, the default values for these four parameters are 0,0, MAXROW( ), and MAXCOL( ). The function will return a logical true (.T.) or false (.F.) based on the final key pressed and whether there is a specified user-defined function that controls the keystrokes and the operation of this function.

&lt;expA5&gt; is the name of an array containing the names of fields or calculated expressions to be displayed for every record in the database. If it is not used, DBEDIT( ) will display all of the fields in the currently selected work area.

&lt;expC6&gt; is the name of a user-defined function that will execute when a key is pressed. Only the root name of the function, without parameters or parentheses, is allowed. If none is used, the default keys specified in the active key table below will control the DBEDIT( ) function. These keys, with the exception of the ESC, RETURN, and any additional key that doesn't appear in the table, will continue to control the DBEDIT( ) function when a UDF &lt;expC6&gt; is included.

If a user-defined function is not specified, the action keys in the following table are automatically processed by DBEDIT:

| *Key* | *Action* |
|---|---|
| Home | First column of the current screen |
| End | Last column of the current screen |
| Left Arrow | Move one column to the left |
| Right Arrow | Move one column to the right |
| Up Arrow | Up one column |
| Down Arrow | Down one column |
| PgUp | Move up one screen to the same relative row position |
| PgDn | Forward one screen to the same relative row position |
| Ctrl-PgDn | Last row of the column |

| Key | Action |
|---|---|
| Ctrl-PgUp | First row of the column |
| Ctrl-Home | First column in the windowed area |
| Ctrl-End | Last column in the windowed area |
| Ctrl-Right Arrow | Move one column to the right |
| Ctrl-Left Arrow | Move one column to the left |
| Return | Abort function |
| ESC | Abort function |

<expA7> is the name of an array that contains the PICTURE expressions for formatting the column defined by each corresponding array element in <expA5>.

<expA8> is the name of an array that contains the headings for each column defined in <expA5>. If no headings are specified, the name of the expression evaluated in each subscript position in <expA5> is displayed. If only a single character string is used as the value of this parameter, that string will be used as the header for each column displayed.

<expA9> is the name of an array containing the characters used to draw lines that separate the headings and the field area. If a single character string is used instead as the value of this parameter, that string will be used for each column displayed.

<expA10> is the name of an array containing the characters used to draw lines that separate the columns. If only a single character string is used as the value of this parameter, that string will be used for each column.

<expA11> is the name of an array containing the footers for each column array defined in <expA5>. If no parameter is specified, footers will not be displayed. If only a single character string is used as the value of this parameter, that string will be used for each column displayed.

When a user-defined function is used to process all keystrokes during the operation of DBEDIT( ), two parameters are automatically passed to the function, which in turn may or may not make use of these parameters. These parameters are:

| | |
|---|---|
| Mode | The status of DBEDIT( ) |
| Column | The column that is currently being processed by DBEDIT( ) |

The following table lists the possible values for the MODE variable:

| Mode | Meaning |
|---|---|
| 0 | DBEDIT( ) is idle: Any cursor movement keys have been handled and no keys are pending. |
| 1 | Attempt to cursor past BOF( ). |

*(continued)*

| Mode | Meaning | (continued) |
|---|---|---|
| 2 | Attempt to cursor past EOF( ). | |
| 3 | Database file / work area is empty. | |
| 4 | Keystroke exception. | |

The user-defined function specified in DBEDIT( ) has a return value, and the value of the function tells DBEDIT( ) what action to take. Following is a table of possible return values from the user-defined function and the associated response.

| RETURN | Meaning |
|---|---|
| 0 | Quit DBEDIT( ). |
| 1 | Continue DBEDIT( ). |
| 2 | Force data to be reread and the screen refreshed accordingly, and continue processing. |

**NOTE** This is a compatibility function and may not be supported in future versions.

If a user-defined function is used, that function may not be defined as a STATIC function; if it is, the function will be ignored.

**SEE ALSO** DBEVAL( ), TBROWSEDB( ), TBCOLUMNNEW( )

**EXAMPLE** See Chapter 12.

# DBEVAL( )

**FUNCTION** Evaluates records in a database or work area.

**SYNTAX** DBEVAL( <expB1> [, <expB2>] [, <expB3>] [,<expN4>] [, <expN5>] [, <expL6>] )

**PARAMETERS**
<expB1>  Code block expression for each record processed
<expB2>  Code block expression of FOR condition
<expB3>  Code block expression of WHILE condition
<expN4>  Number of records to process
<expN5>  Record number to process
<expL6>  Logical indication of scope

**LIBRARY** CLIPPER.LIB

**DESCRIPTION** This function processes the code block expressed as <expB1> for every record in the current or designated work area. If no other parameters are specified, every record will be processed by the function.

| | |
|---|---|
| **NOTE** | If you are working with a WHILE code block, the database is not rewound to the top of the file. If working without a WHILE code block, an internal GO TOP will be performed. |
| **SEE ALSO** | AEVAL( ), EVAL( ) |
| **EXAMPLE** | Please see Chapter 12. |

## DBF( )

| | |
|---|---|
| **FUNCTION** | Alias name of a work area. |
| **SYNTAX** | DBF ( ) |
| **PARAMETER** | None |
| **RETURNS** | <expC>     Name of alias |
| **LIBRARY** | CLIPPER.LIB |
| **DESCRIPTION** | This function returns the alias name of the currently selected work area. This function is the same as the Clipper function ALIAS( ). |
| **NOTE** | This is a compatibility function and may not be supported in future versions. |
| **SEE ALSO** | ALIAS( ), USED( ) |

## DBFILTER( )

| | |
|---|---|
| **FUNCTION** | Returns the filter expression in a work area. |
| **SYNTAX** | DBFILTER ( ) |
| **PARAMETER** | None |
| **RETURNS** | <expX>     Filter expression |
| **LIBRARY** | CLIPPER.LIB |
| **DESCRIPTION** | This function returns the expression of the SET FILTER TO command for the current or designated work area. If no filter condition is present, a NULL string will be returned. |
| **NOTE** | If the value of <expX> uses local or static variables created during the execution of an application when setting the filter, that expression may not work properly when reused at other times or in other locations within the application. |

| | |
|---|---|
| **SEE ALSO** | SET FILTER TO, DBRELATION( ), DBRSELECT( ), DBSETFILTER( ), DBCLEARFILTER( ) |
| **EXAMPLE** | See the DBRSELECT( ) function. |

## DBGOBOTTOM( )

| | |
|---|---|
| **FUNCTION** | Moves the record pointer to the bottom of the database. |
| **SYNTAX** | DBGOBOTTOM( ) |
| **PARAMETER** | None |
| **LIBRARY** | CLIPPER.LIB |
| **DESCRIPTION** | This function moves the record pointer in the selected or aliased work area to the end of the file. The position of the record pointer is affected by the values in the index key or by an active FILTER condition. Otherwise, if no index is active or if no filter condition is present, the value of the record pointer will be LASTREC( ). |
| **SEE ALSO** | DBGOTOP( ), DBGOTO( ) |

## DBGOTO( )

| | |
|---|---|
| **FUNCTION** | Positions the record pointer to a specific location. |
| **SYNTAX** | DBGOTO( <expX1> ) |
| **PARAMETER** | <expX1>   Record number or unique identity |
| **LIBRARY** | CLIPPER.LIB |
| **DESCRIPTION** | This function places the record pointer, if working with a .DBF file, in the selected or aliased work area at the record number specified by <expX1>. The position is not affected by an active index or by any environmental SET condition.

Issuing a DBGOTO( RECNO( ) ) call in a network environment will refresh the database and index buffers. This is the same as a DBSKIP(0) call.

The parameter <expX1> may be something other than a record number. In some data formats, for example, the value of <expX1> is a unique primary key while in other formats, <expX1> could be an array offset if the data set was an array. |
| **SEE ALSO** | DBSKIP( ), DBGOTOP( ), DBGOBOTTOM( ), GO |

## DBGOTOP( )

| | |
|---|---|
| **FUNCTION** | Moves the record pointer to the top of the database. |
| **SYNTAX** | `DBGOTOP()` |
| **PARAMETER** | None |
| **LIBRARY** | CLIPPER.LIB |
| **DESCRIPTION** | This function moves the record pointer in the selected or aliased work area to the top of the file. The position of the record pointer is affected by the values in the index key or by an active FILTER condition. Otherwise, if no index is active or if no filter condition is present, the value of RECNO( ) will be 1. |
| **SEE ALSO** | DBGOBOTTOM( ), DBGOTO( ) |

## DBRECALL( )

| | |
|---|---|
| **FUNCTION** | Recalls a record previously marked for deletion. |
| **SYNTAX** | `DBRECALL()` |
| **PARAMETER** | None |
| **LIBRARY** | CLIPPER.LIB |
| **DESCRIPTION** | This function unmarks those records marked for deletion and reactivates them in the aliased or selected work area. If a record is DELETED and the DELETED setting is on, the record will still be visible for a DBRECALL( ) provided that the database record pointed to has not been skipped. Once a record marked for deletion with the DELETED setting ON has been skipped, it no longer can be brought back with DBRECALL( ). |
| **SEE ALSO** | DBDELETE( ), PACK |

## DBREINDEX( )

| | |
|---|---|
| **FUNCTION** | Rebuilds open indexes. |
| **SYNTAX** | `DBREINDEX()` |
| **PARAMETER** | None |

| | |
|---|---|
| **LIBRARY** | CLIPPER.LIB |
| **DESCRIPTION** | This function rebuilds all of the active index files in the selected or aliased work area. When completed, the record pointer is placed at the first record of the controlling index. If this command is issued in a networked environment, the database file must be used EXCLUSIVEly to avoid a run-time error.

This function does not rebuild the header of any of the index files re-generated. In fact, this function uses the existing index header in its operation. If there is a corrupted index header, this function will not ensure that a proper index is built. |
| **SEE ALSO** | DBCREATEINDEX), DBSETINDEX( ), DBUSEAREA( ), DBCLEARINDEX( ) |

# DBRELATION( )

| | | |
|---|---|---|
| **FUNCTION** | Returns the expression used in a SET RELATION TO command for the current or designated work area. | |
| **SYNTAX** | `DBRELATION( <expN1> )` | |
| **PARAMETER** | <expN1> | Order of the relation in the SET RELATION TO command |
| **RETURNS** | <expX> | The relation key |
| **LIBRARY** | CLIPPER.LIB | |
| **DESCRIPTION** | This function returns the character expression used by the SET RELATION TO command to relate the database in the current or designated work area to other open databases in other work areas. <expN1> designates the particular ordinal relation desired for that database.

If no relation is set in the specified work area, a NULL string will be returned.

If a relation is built with Clipper's macro expansion capabilities by using the & symbol, this function may not return correct results if recompiled and used. | |
| **SEE ALSO** | DBFILTER( ), DBRSELECT( ), DBSETRELATION( ), DBCLEARRELATION( ) | |
| **EXAMPLE** | See the DBRSELECT( ) function. | |

## DBRLOCK( )

| | |
|---|---|
| **FUNCTION** | This function locks the record based on identifier. |
| **SYNTAX** | DBRLOCK( [<expX1>] ) |
| **PARAMETER** | <expX1>  Record identifier |
| **RETURNS** | <expL>  Logical true (.T.) if lock was successful |
| **LIBRARY** | CLIPPER.LIB |
| **DESCRIPTION** | This function attempts to lock a record which is identified by <expX1> in the active data set. (In a .DBF file, <expX1> would be a record number.) If the lock was successful, the function will return a logical true (.T.) value; otherwise, a logical false (.F.) will be returned. If <expX1> is not passed it will be assumed to lock the currently active record/data item. |
| **SEE ALSO** | RLOCK( ), FLOCK( ), DBLOCKLIST( ), DBUNLOCK( ) |
| **EXAMPLE** | Please see Chapter 12. |

## DBRLOCKLIST( )

| | |
|---|---|
| **FUNCTION** | This function returns a list of locked records in the database work area. |
| **SYNTAX** | DBRLOCKLIST( ) |
| **PARAMETER** | None |
| **RETURNS** | <expA>  Array of locked records |
| **LIBRARY** | CLIPPER.LIB |
| **DESCRIPTION** | This function will return an array of locked records in a given and active work area. If the returned array is an empty array (meaning no elements in it), then there are no locked records in that work area. |
| **SEE ALSO** | RLOCK( ), FLOCK( ), DBRLOCK( ), DBRUNLOCK( ) |
| **EXAMPLE** | Please see Chapter 12. |

## DBRSELECT( )

| | |
|---|---|
| **FUNCTION** | Shows dependent work areas in a relation. |
| **SYNTAX** | DBRSELECT( <expN1> ) |

**PARAMETER** &lt;expN1&gt;  Numeric expression for a work area

**RETURNS** &lt;expN&gt;  Numeric expression

**LIBRARY** CLIPPER.LIB

**DESCRIPTION** This function returns the work area number that is tied via the SET RELATION TO command to the current or designated database. &lt;expN1&gt; indicates the order of the relation as defined in the SET RELATION TO command. If no relation is set, the function will return a 0.

**SEE ALSO** SET RELATION, DBFILTER( ), DBRELATION( )

**EXAMPLE**

```
 1 : * File:      Dbrfdemo.prg
 2 : * Compile:   RMake sample /dFILE:dbrfdemo
 3 :
 4 : procedure Main()
 5 :
 6 :    local nCount
 7 :
 8 :    use Clients new
 9 :    set filter to recno() > 15
10 :    use Notap new index Notap
11 :    use Ontap new index Ontap
12 :    set relation to Ontap->files into Notap
13 :
14 :    for nCount := 1 to 10
15 :      if !empty( alias(nCount) )
16 :        (nCount)->( ShowStuff() )   // &(alias(nCount))->( ShowStuff() )
17 :      endif
18 :    next
19 :    scroll()
20 :
21 : ******************
22 :
23 : static procedure ShowStuff()
24 :
25 :    cls
26 :    qout( "       Name of area: " + alias() )
27 :    qout( "Number of records: " + str(lastrec()) )
28 :    qout( "    Current record: " + str(recno()) )
29 :    qout( "  Filter condition: " + dbfilter() )
30 :    qout( "       Related Key: " + dbrelation() )
31 :    qout( "    Related area #: " + str(dbrselect()) )
32 :    if !( alias( dbrselect() ) == alias() )
33 :      qout( "Related area name: " + alias( dbrselect() ) )
34 :    endif
35 :    qout()
36 :    wait
37 :
38 : // End of File: Dbrfdemo.prg
```

# DBRUNLOCK

| | |
|---|---|
| **FUNCTION** | Unlocks a record based on its identifier. |
| **SYNTAX** | DBRUNLOCK( [<expX1>] ) |
| **PARAMETER** | <expX1>   Record identifier, typically the record number |
| **LIBRARY** | CLIPPER.LIB |
| **DESCRIPTION** | This function will attempt to unlock the record specified as <expX1>, which in a .DBF file format is the record number. If not specified, then the current active record/data item will be unlocked. In some cases where the data source is not a .DBF file, the value of <expX1> may be a unique primary key value which is dependent on the structure of the data file that it is referencing. |
| **SEE ALSO** | DBRLOCK( ), DBRLOCKLIST( ), FLOCK( ), RLOCK( ) |
| **EXAMPLE** | Please see Chapter 12. |

# DBSEEK( )

| | |
|---|---|
| **FUNCTION** | Searches for a value based on an active index. |
| **SYNTAX** | DBSEEK( <expX1> [, <expL2>] ) |
| **PARAMETERS** | <expX1>   Any expression<br><expL2>   Toggle SOFTSEEK condition |
| **RETURNS** | <expL>   Logical true if found, otherwise false |
| **LIBRARY** | CLIPPER.LIB |
| **DESCRIPTION** | This function searches for the first record in a database file whose index key matches <expX1>. If the item is found, the function will return a logical true (.T.), the value of FOUND( ) will be a logical true (.T.), and the value of EOF( ) will be a logical false (.F.). If no item is found, then the function will return a logical false, the value of FOUND( ) will be a logical false (.F.), and the value of EOF( ) will be a logical true (.T.).<br>This function always "rewinds" the database pointer and starts the search from the top of the file.<br>If the SOFTSEEK flag is on or if <expL2> is set to a logical true (.T.), the value of FOUND( ) will be a logical false and EOF( ) will be a logical false if there is an item in the index key with a greater value than the key expression <expX1>; at this point the record pointer will position itself on that record. However, if there is no greater key in the index, |

EOF( ) will return a logical true (.T.) value. If <expL2> is not passed, then the function will look to the internal status of SOFTSEEK before performing the operation. The default of <expL2> is a logical false (.F.).

**SEE ALSO**   DBGOTO( ), FOUND( ), EOF( )

# DBSELECTAREA( )

**FUNCTION**   Changes to another work area.

**SYNTAX**   DBSELECTAREA( <expX1> )

**PARAMETER**   <expX1>   Alias or work area

**LIBRARY**   CLIPPER.LIB

**DESCRIPTION**   This function moves Clipper's internal primary focus to the work area designated by <expX1>. If <expX1> is numeric, then it will select the numeric work area; if <expX1> is a character, then it will select the work area with the alias name.

DBSELECTAREA(0) will select the next available and unused work area.

Up to 255 work areas are supported. Each work area has its own alias and record pointer, as well as its own FOUND( ), DBFILTER( ), DBRSELECT( ), and DBRELATION( ) function values. Information from another previously SELECTED or USED work area may be obtained, provided that the alias of that work area precedes the expression to be obtained. This is also true for user-defined functions and commands to be performed in unselected work areas.

**SEE ALSO**   DBSETINDEX( ), DBUSEAREA( ), DBCLEARINDEX( )

# DBSETDRIVER( )

**FUNCTION**   Establishes the name of a replaceable database driver for a selected work area.

**SYNTAX**   DBSETDRIVER( [<expC1>] )

**PARAMETER**   <expC1>   Database Driver Name

**RETURNS**   <expC>   Active driver name

**LIBRARY**   CLIPPER.LIB

**DESCRIPTION**   This function returns the name of the current database driver for the selected work area. The default will be "DBFNTX". If specified,

&lt;expC1&gt; contains the name of the database driver that should be used to activate and manage the work area. If the specified driver is not available, this function will have no effect.

**SEE ALSO** DBUSEAREA( ), DBCLOSEAREA( )

**EXAMPLE** Please see Chapter 13.

## DBSETFILTER( )

**FUNCTION** Establishes a filter condition for a work area.

**SYNTAX** DBSETFILTER( &lt;expB1&gt; [, &lt;expC2&gt;] )

**PARAMETERS** &lt;expB1&gt;  Code block expression for filtered evaluation
&lt;expC2&gt;  Character expression of code block

**LIBRARY** CLIPPER.LIB

**DESCRIPTION** This function masks a database so that only those records that meet the condition prescribed by the expression in the code block &lt;expB1&gt; and literally expressed as &lt;expC2&gt; are visible.

If &lt;expC2&gt; is not passed to this function, then the DBFILTER( ) function will return an empty string showing no filter in that work area which in fact, would not be correct.

**SEE ALSO** DBFILTER( ), SET( ), TBROWSENEW( ), DBCLEARFILTER( )

## DBSETINDEX( )

**FUNCTION** Adds indexes to an open work area.

**SYNTAX** DBSETINDEX( &lt;expC1&gt; )

**PARAMETER** &lt;expC1&gt;  Filename

**LIBRARY** CLIPPER.LIB

**DESCRIPTION** This function opens an index file named &lt;expC1&gt; in the selected or aliased work area. There may be up to 15 index files active in any one work area. Index files are added to an internal stack in such a way that the last index file added will be the controlling index.

**NOTE** This function is for compatibility and should be replaced by the ORDLISTADD( ) function.

**SEE ALSO** DBCLEARINDEX( ), DBCREATEINDEX( ), ORDLISTADD( ), SET ORDER TO

## DBSETORDER( )

| | |
|---|---|
| **FUNCTION** | Sets a controlling index order. |
| **SYNTAX** | `DBSETORDER( <expN1> )` |
| **PARAMETER** | <expN1>   Numeric expression of controlling index order |
| **LIBRARY** | CLIPPER.LIB |
| **DESCRIPTION** | This function selects a new active index from the index list. If <expN1> is 0, the natural order of the database is in control. This is suggested for adding records to a database with active indexes; altering the controlling index to 0 allows the keys in all other indexes to be maintained properly. The range of values for <expN1> may be from 0 to 15. |
| **SEE ALSO** | DBSETINDEX( ), DBCREATEINDEX( ), DBCLEARINDEX( ) |

## DBSETRELATION( )

| | |
|---|---|
| **FUNCTION** | Relates two active work areas together by a common key or record number. |
| **SYNTAX** | `DBSETRELATION( <expX1>, <expB2>, <expC3> )` |
| **PARAMETERS** | <expX1>   Alias work area or numeric work area value<br><expB2>   Code block expression for evaluation<br><expC3>   Related key |
| **LIBRARY** | CLIPPER.LIB |
| **DESCRIPTION** | This function links the aliased or selected work area to the work area named <expX1> (either by the alias name or the numeric work area number) by means of a common expression <expC3>. The expression in <expC3> is also passed in code block format expressed as <expB2> that will be evaluated each time the record pointer in the selected work area is moved. |
| **SEE ALSO** | DBCLEARREL( ), DBRELATION( ), DBRSELECT( ) |

## DBSKIP( )

| | |
|---|---|
| **FUNCTION** | Moves the record pointer in the selected work area. |
| **SYNTAX** | `DBSKIP( [<expN1>] )` |

| | |
|---|---|
| **PARAMETER** | <expN1> Number of records to move record pointer |
| **LIBRARY** | CLIPPER.LIB |
| **DESCRIPTION** | This function moves the record pointer <expN1> records in the selected or aliased work area. The default value of <expN1> will be 1.<br><br>A DBSKIP(0) will flush and refresh the internal database buffer and make any changes made to the record visible without moving the record pointer in either direction. |
| **SEE ALSO** | DBCOMMITALL( ), DBSEEK( ), DBGOTO( ) |

## DBSTRUCT( )

| | |
|---|---|
| **FUNCTION** | Creates a multidimensional array of a database structure. |
| **SYNTAX** | DBSTRUCT() |
| **PARAMETER** | None |
| **RETURNS** | <expA> Array pointers to database structure |
| **LIBRARY** | CLIPPER.LIB |
| **DESCRIPTION** | This function returns a multidimensional array. This array has array pointers to other arrays, each of which contains the characteristic of a field in the active work area. The length of this array is based on the number of fields in that particular work area. In other words, LEN(DBSTRUCT( )) is equal to the value obtained from FCOUNT( ).<br><br>Each subscript position in the second dimension of this array follows the following structure table:<br><br>array[x, 1]  Field name<br>array[x, 2]  Field type<br>array[x, 3]  Field length<br>array[x, 4]  Field decimals<br><br>The value of *x* will be the particular field number being evaluated.<br>This function will return an empty array if it is called in a work area without an active database. |
| **NOTE** | This function replaces the AFIELDS( ) function. |
| **SEE ALSO** | DBCREATE( ), AFIELDS( ), COPY STRUCTURE EXTENDED |
| **EXAMPLE** | |

```
1 : * File:      Dbstdemo.prg
2 : * Compile:   Rmake sample /dFILE:dbstdemo
3 :
4 : procedure Main()
```

```
  5 :
  6 :    use Clients new
  7 :    use Notap new
  8 :    use Ontap new
  9 :
 10 :    Clients->( Showstru( dbstruct() ) )
 11 :    Notap->( Showstru( dbstruct() ) )
 12 :    Ontap->( Showstru( dbstruct() ) )
 13 :
 14 : *******************
 15 :
 16 : static procedure ShowStru( aStru )
 17 :
 18 :    cls
 19 :    aeval( aStru, {|aField| qout( padr(aField[1], 15) ), ;
 20 :                            qqout( padr(aField[2], 15) ), ;
 21 :                            qqout( padr(aField[3], 15) ), ;
 22 :                            qqout( padr(aField[4], 4) )} )
 23 :    wait
 24 :
 25 : // End of File: Dbstdemo.prg
```

# DBUNLOCK( )

| | |
|---|---|
| **FUNCTION** | Unlocks a record or releases a file lock. |
| **SYNTAX** | DBUNLOCK() |
| **PARAMETER** | None |
| **LIBRARY** | CLIPPER.LIB |
| **DESCRIPTION** | This function releases the file or record lock in the currently selected or aliased work area. It will not unlock an associated lock in related databases. |
| **SEE ALSO** | DBUNLOCKALL( ), DBCLOSE( ), DBUSEAREA( ), DBCLOSEALL( ), DBRLOCK( ), DBRUNLOCK( ) |

# DBUNLOCKALL( )

| | |
|---|---|
| **FUNCTION** | Unlocks all records and releases all file locks in all work areas. |
| **SYNTAX** | DBUNLOCKALL() |
| **PARAMETER** | None |
| **LIBRARY** | CLIPPER.LIB |

**DESCRIPTION** This function will remove all file and record locks in all work areas.

**SEE ALSO** DBUNLOCK( ), DBCLOSEAREA( ), DBUSEAREA( ), DBCLOSEALL( ), DBRLOCK( ), DBRUNLOCK( )

# DBUSEAREA( )

**FUNCTION** Opens a work area and uses a database file.

**SYNTAX** DBUSEAREA( [<expL1>] [, <expC2>], <expC3> [, <expC4>] [, <expL5>] [,<expL6>])

**PARAMETERS**
<expL1>   A logical expression for the new work area
<expC2>   Database driver name
<expC3>   File name
<expC4>   Alias name
<expL5>   Shared/exclusive status flag
<expL6>   Read-write status flag

**LIBRARY** CLIPPER.LIB

**DESCRIPTION** This function opens an existing database named <expC3> in the current work area. If <expL1> is set to a logical true (.T.) value, then the database <expC3> will be opened in the next available and unused work area. The default value of <expL1> is a logical false (.F.).

If used, <expC2> is the name of the database driver associated with the file <expC3> that is opened. The default for this will be the value of DBSETDRIVER( ).

If used, <expC4> contains the alias name for that work area. If not specified, the root name of the database specified in <expC3> will be used.

If <expL5> is set to a logical true (.T.) value, the database that is specified in <expC3> will be opened by the user EXCLUSIVEly, thus locking it from all other nodes or users on the network. If <expL5> is set to a logical false (.F.) value, then the database will be in SHARED mode. If <expL5> is not passed, then the function will turn to the internal setting of SET EXCLUSIVE to determine a setting.

If <expL6> is specified, the file will be set to READ ONLY mode. If it is not specified, the file will be opened in normal read-write mode.

**SEE ALSO** USE, DBCLOSEAREA( ), DBSETINDEX( ), DBCREATEINDEX( ), DBSELECTAREA( )

## DELETED( )

| | |
|---|---|
| **FUNCTION** | Tests if a record's deletion flag is set. |
| **SYNTAX** | `DELETED()` |
| **PARAMETER** | None |
| **RETURNS** | &lt;expL&gt;    Logical true (.T.) or false (.F.) |
| **LIBRARY** | CLIPPER.LIB |
| **DESCRIPTION** | This function returns a logical true (.T.) if the current record in the selected or designated work area has been marked for deletion. If not, the function will return a logical false (.F.). |
| **SEE ALSO** | SET DELETED, RECALL, DELETE, DBDELETE( ) |

## DESCEND( )

| | |
|---|---|
| **FUNCTION** | Yields an index key pointer in descending order. |
| **SYNTAX** | `DESCEND( <expX1> )` |
| **PARAMETER** | &lt;expX1&gt;    Any expression that would normally be indexed |
| **RETURNS** | &lt;expX&gt;    Key expression |
| **LIBRARY** | EXTEND.LIB |
| **DESCRIPTION** | This function is used to create indexes in descending order. It creates an index of the same data type as &lt;expX1&gt;.<br><br>To SEEK or FIND an expression in an index created with the DESCEND( ) function, the SEEK or FIND expression must be used with the DESCEND( ) function. |
| **SEE ALSO** | INDEX, SEEK, FIND |

**EXAMPLE**

```
 1 : * File:      Descdemo.prg
 2 : * Compile:   RMake sample /dFILE:descdemo
 3 :
 4 : #xtranslate SHOWSTUFF() => (qout(fieldget(2), fieldget(1), fieldget(3)))
 5 :
 6 : procedure Main()
 7 :
 8 :    use Clients new
 9 :    index on Clients->account to Order1
10 :
11 :    cls
12 :    dbeval( {|| SHOWSTUFF()} )
```

```
13 :    wait
14 :
15 :    index on descend( Clients->account) to Order2
16 :    cls
17 :    dbeval( {|| SHOWSTUFF()} )
18 :    wait
19 :
20 :    set index to Order1, Order2
21 :
22 :    if dbseek("40")
23 :       cls
24 :       dbeval( {|| SHOWSTUFF()},,,recno() )
25 :    endif
26 :    wait
27 :
28 :    wait Clients->( dbsetorder(2), dbseek("40") )
29 :
30 :    if Clients->( dbseek( descend( "40" ) ) )
31 :       cls
32 :       qout("Descend")
33 :       dbeval( {|| SHOWSTUFF()},,,recno() )
34 :    endif
35 :
36 :    // End of File: Descdemo.prg
```

# DEVOUT( )

**FUNCTION**   Displays values to a device.

**SYNTAX**   DEVOUT( <expX1> [, <expC2>] )

**PARAMETERS**   <expX1>   Any expression to be displayed
<expC2>   Color string

**LIBRARY**   CLIPPER.LIB

**DESCRIPTION**   This function outputs the expression <expX1> to the device at coordinates preassigned via the DEVPOS( ) function. This function, in conjunction with the DEVPOS( ) and DEVOUTPICT( ) functions, is used by the preprocessor to replace the command-oriented @. . .SAY <expX1> syntax with a more function-oriented equivalent.

If used, the string value of <expC2> is used to set the color of the screen prior to displaying the contents of <expX1>. This does not affect the system's overall color setting.

**NOTE**   It is possible to have several DEVOUT( ) function calls replace string concatenations on output statements. Rather than issuing a QOUT( a + b + c ), where a, b, and c are string variables, it is more efficient to issue consecutive DEVOUT( ) calls for each variable. This will save memory.

**SEE ALSO**   DEVPOS( ), DEVOUTPICT( ), @ ... SAY

## DEVOUTPICT( )

| | |
|---|---|
| **FUNCTION** | Displays a value to a device using a picture template. |
| **SYNTAX** | DEVOUTPICT( <expX1>, <expC2> [, <expC3>] ) |
| **PARAMETERS** | <expX1>  Any expression to be displayed<br><expC2>  A picture template<br><expC3>  Color string |
| **LIBRARY** | CLIPPER.LIB |
| **DESCRIPTION** | This function outputs the expression <expX1> to the device with a picture template specified by <expC2> at coordinates preassigned via the DEVPOS( ) function. This function, in conjunction with the DEVPOS( ) and DEVOUT( ) functions, is used by the preprocessor to replace the command-oriented @ ... SAY <expX1> syntax with a more function-oriented equivalent.<br><br>If used, the string value of <expC3> is used to set the color of the screen prior to displaying the contents of <expX1>. This does not affect the system's overall color setting. |
| **SEE ALSO** | DEVOUT( ), DEVPOS( ), @ ... SAY ... PICTURE |

## DEVPOS( )

| | |
|---|---|
| **FUNCTION** | Positions a device at specified coordinates. |
| **SYNTAX** | DEVPOS( <expN1>, <expN2> ) |
| **PARAMETERS** | <expN1>  Row coordinate<br><expN2>  Column coordinate |
| **LIBRARY** | CLIPPER.LIB |
| **DESCRIPTION** | This function positions the cursor or printhead at the specified row and column coordinates of <expN1>, <expN2>.<br><br>If the current device is set to the SCREEN, this function is similar to SETPOS( ) and updates the values of ROW( ) and COL( ), respectively.<br><br>If the current device is set to the PRINTER, this function will move the printhead. The movement is accomplished by issuing enough CHR(10)s (line feeds) to reset the value of PROW( ) and PCOL( ). It may be necessary to issue a SETPRC( ) function prior to calling this function. |
| **SEE ALSO** | SETPOS( ), DEVOUT( ), DEVOUTPICT( ) |

## EXAMPLE

```
 1 : * File:      Devdemo.prg
 2 : * Compile:   Rmake sample /dFILE:devdemo
 3 :
 4 : procedure Main()
 5 :
 6 :    local nCount
 7 :
 8 :    cls
 9 :    devpos(3,10)
10 :    devout("This is an example")
11 :    devpos(10,30)
12 :    devoutpict("This is an example", "@!")
13 :    devout( " of how this can continue!!!" )
14 :    wait
15 :
16 :    cls
17 :    for nCount := 1 to 10
18 :       devpos(nCount, nCount)
19 :       devoutpict( nCount * 3000, "999,999")
20 :    next
21 :    wait
22 :
23 : // End of File: Devdemo.prg
```

# DICTAT( )

| | |
|---|---|
| **FUNCTION** | Returns associated value tied to data dictionary key word. |
| **SYNTAX** | DICTAT( <expA1>, <expC2> ) |
| **PARAMETERS** | <expA1>  Array holding data dictionary |
| | <expC2>  Character name of key word |
| **RETURNS** | <expX>  Associated value to key word in dictionary |
| **LIBRARY** | SAMPLES.LIB |
| **DESCRIPTION** | This function searches through the data dictionary <expA1> for the key word <expC2> and returns the associated value with that key entry. The array <expA1> should have been created via the DICTNEW( ) function and maintained by one of the other dictionary functions. |
| **SEE ALSO** | DICTEVAL( ), DICTNEW( ), DICTPUT( ), DICTPUTPAIR( ), DICTREMOVE( ) |
| **EXAMPLE** | Please see Chapter 16. |

## DICTEVAL( )

| | |
|---|---|
| **FUNCTION** | Evaluates a code block against a data dictionary array. |
| **SYNTAX** | `DICTEVAL( <expA1>, <expB2> )` |
| **PARAMETERS** | <expA1>  Array holding data dictionary<br><expB2>  Code block for processing |
| **RETURNS** | <expA>  Data dictionary array reference |
| **LIBRARY** | SAMPLES.LIB |
| **DESCRIPTION** | This function evaluates the contents of the code block <expB2> against each key and value contained in the data dictionary array <expA1>. When the code block is evaluated, one element is passed to the code block which is an array containing two elements: 1) the key word; and 2) the value associated with that key word. When completed, this function will return a reference to the array <expA1>. |
| **SEE ALSO** | DICTAT( ), DICTNEW( ), DICTPUT( ), DICTPUTPAIR( ), DICTREMOVE( ) |
| **EXAMPLE** | Please see Chapter 16. |

## DICTNEW( )

| | |
|---|---|
| **FUNCTION** | Creates an array used for the data dictionary functions. |
| **SYNTAX** | `DICTNEW()` |
| **RETURNS** | <expA>  Array to be used for the data dictionary routines |
| **LIBRARY** | SAMPLES.LIB |
| **DESCRIPTION** | This function will simply return an array that is to be used by the other data dictionary functions. This array will hold up to 4096 elements, one for each data dictionary item. An item consists of an array based on the following structure:<br><br><expA>[x]      Array of key item<br><expA>[x, 1]   Key word associated with dictionary item<br><expA>[x, 2]   Any data type associated with key word in data dictionary |

| | |
|---|---|
| **SEE ALSO** | DICTAT( ), DICTEVAL( ), DICTPUT( ), DICTPUTPAIR( ), DICTREMOVE( ) |
| **EXAMPLE** | Please see Chapter 16. |

## DICTPUT( )

| | | |
|---|---|---|
| **FUNCTION** | Enters/replaces a data dictionary key word and item. | |
| **SYNTAX** | `DICTPUT( <expA1>, <expC2>, <expX3> )` | |
| **PARAMETERS** | <expA1> | Array holding data dictionary |
| | <expC2> | Key words associated with data item |
| | <expX3> | Any valid data type tied to key word in dictionary |
| **RETURNS** | <expX> | The value of <expX3> |
| **LIBRARY** | SAMPLES.LIB | |
| **DESCRIPTION** | This function takes the key word expressed as <expC2> and the associated value/item <expX3> and attempts to place them into the data dictionary <expA1>. If the item exists, then the function will replace the old <expX3> value with the new value; otherwise, it will simply add the pair to the data dictionary. When it is finished, the function will return the value of <expX3>. | |
| **SEE ALSO** | DICTAT( ), DICTEVAL( ), DICTNEW( ), DICTPUTPAIR( ), DICTREMOVE( ) | |
| **EXAMPLE** | Please see Chapter 16. | |

## DICTPUTPAIR( )

| | | |
|---|---|---|
| **FUNCTION** | Adds an item and key word pair to data dictionary. | |
| **SYNTAX** | `DICTPUTPAIR( <expA1>, <expA2> )` | |
| **PARAMETERS** | <expA1> | Array holding data dictionary |
| | <expA2> | Array holding key word and data item for dictionary |
| **RETURNS** | <expA> | A reference back to <expA2> |
| **LIBRARY** | SAMPLES.LIB | |
| **DESCRIPTION** | This function takes an array <expA2> and either adds it to the data dictionary <expA1> or, if it is found in the data list, simply replaces the | |

old values with the new values. The structure of the array <expA2> is a two element array in which the first element is the key word for the pairing and the second is the data item associated with the key word to be kept by the data dictionary. In graphical terms, the structure of <expA2> is the following:

| | |
|---|---|
| <expA2>[1] | Key word associated with dictionary item |
| <expA2>[2] | Any data type associated with key word in data dictionary |

It is the contents of <expA2>[1] that makes the entry into the data dictionary unique. When this function has completed its operation it will return a reference to <expA2>.

**SEE ALSO**  DICTAT( ), DICTEVAL( ), DICTNEW( ), DICTPUT( ), DICTREMOVE( )

**EXAMPLE**  Please see Chapter 16.

## DICTREMOVE( )

**FUNCTION**  Removes a data item from the data dictionary.

**SYNTAX**  `DICTREMOVE( <expA1>, <expC2> )`

**PARAMETERS**
<expA1>   Array holding data dictionary
<expC2>   Unique key word to be found in dictionary

**RETURNS**  <expA>   Reference to modified <expA1>

**LIBRARY**  SAMPLES.LIB

**DESCRIPTION**  This function attempts to remove the dictionary pair within the data dictionary <expA1> for a key word of <expC2>. It will return a reference to the modified data dictionary value of <expA1>.

**SEE ALSO**  DICTAT( ), DICTEVAL( ), DICTNEW( ), DICTPUT( ), DICTPUTPAIR( )

**EXAMPLE**  Please see Chapter 16.

## DIMENSIONS( )

**FUNCTION**  Calculates the dimensions of an array.

**SYNTAX**  `DIMENSIONS( <expA1> )`

| | | |
|---|---|---|
| **PARAMETER** | <expA1> | Any array data type |
| **RETURNS** | <expA> | Array describing dimensions of parameter |
| **LIBRARY** | SAMPLES.LIB | |

**DESCRIPTION** This function will return an array describing the dimensions of the array <expA1>. It will attempt to traverse down through all of the dimensions of an array and assumes that all of the elements in the array are uniform. Therefore, if the array <expA1> contains mixed data types and may be ragged in nature, the values returned from this function would be as if the array <expA1> were a matrix filled out to the largest possible dimension.

**SEE ALSO** ACOMP( ), ARRAY( ), AMIN( ), AMAX( )

**EXAMPLE**

```
 1 : * File     Dimcalc.prg
 2 : * Compile RMake sampmore /dFILE:dimcalc
 3 :
 4 : procedure Main()
 5 :
 6 :    local aCalc
 7 :    local aData := {}  // start off as an empty array
 8 :
 9 :    cls
10 :    aCalc := dimensions( directory() )
11 :    ? aCalc[1]    // Number of files on the disk
12 :    ? aCalc[2]    // 5: file name, size, date, time, and attribute
13 :
14 :    aCalc := dimensions( array(20) )
15 :    ? aCalc[1]    // should be 20
16 :
17 :    aadd( aData, directory() )
18 :    aCalc := dimensions( aData )
19 :    ? aCalc[1] // Should be 1
20 :    ? aCalc[2] // Number of files on the disk
21 :    ? aCalc[3] // 5: file name, size, date, time, and attribute
22 :
23 :    aadd( aData, "Hello" )
24 :    aCalc := dimensions( aData )
25 :    ? aCalc[1] // Should now be 2
26 :    ? aCalc[2] // Number of files on the disk
27 :    ? aCalc[3] // 5: file name, size, date, time, and attribute
28 :
29 : // End of File: Dimcalc.prg
```

# DIRECTORY( )

**FUNCTION** Creates a multidimensional array of directory information.

**SYNTAX** DIRECTORY( <expC1> [, <expC2> ] )

**PARAMETERS**     &lt;expC1&gt;     A directory skeleton
&lt;expC2&gt;     File attribute bytes

**RETURNS**     &lt;expA&gt;     Multidimensional array pointer

**LIBRARY**     CLIPPER.LIB

**DESCRIPTION**     This function returns a multidimensional array of directory information based on the directory skeleton in &lt;expC1&gt;. If &lt;expC1&gt; is omitted, it defaults to all normal and archive files (*.*). If used, &lt;expC2&gt; contains a string designating special files that are to be included in the directory array if they posses a particular file attribute. Valid characters in the string &lt;expC2&gt; are:

- H   Hidden files
- S   System files
- D   Directories, including parent and children
- V   Include the DOS volume label, exclude all files

The directory skeleton in &lt;expC1&gt; may contain a directory name as well as a path. If not specified, the currently logged drive and subdirectory will be used.

The second dimension of this array contains individual file information based on the directory skeleton. The function returns an array of single-dimensional arrays; LEN(DIRECTORY(&lt;expC1&gt;)) is the same as the value obtained from ADIR(&lt;expC1&gt;), which is the number of files that match the specified skeleton. The structure of the second dimension is based on the following format:

- array[x, 1]   Filename
- array[x, 2]   File size
- array[x, 3]   File date stamp
- array[x, 4]   File time stamp
- array[x, 5]   File attribute byte

If D, H, or S is specified in &lt;expC2&gt;, the order is not critical. One, two, or all three characters may be used together to make up the value of &lt;expC2&gt;. Keep in mind that normal archive files that match the directory skeleton in &lt;expC1&gt; will also be included in the array returned from this function.

If no files match the specified DOS skeleton pattern, this function will return an EMPTY( ) array with a LEN( ) of 0. If the V character is specified in &lt;expC2&gt;, no other characters need to be specified, and ONLY the volume label will be looked at. If a volume label exists, the LEN( ) of the DIRECTORY( ) function will be 1, with the second dimension still containing the five structured elements. If no volume label is specified, the value returned from this function will be an EMPTY( ) array with a LEN( ) of 0.

**NOTE** This function replaces the ADIR( ) function in previous versions of the compiler.

**SEE ALSO** ADIR( ), DBSTRUCT( ), DBCREATE( ), AEVAL( )

**EXAMPLE**

```
 1 : * File:     Dirdemo.prg
 2 : * Compile:  RMake sample /dFILE:dirdemo
 3 :
 4 : #xtranslate DirEval( <mask>, <block> ) => ;
 5 :               aeval( directory("\*.*", <mask>), <block> )
 6 :
 7 : procedure Main()
 8 :
 9 :    cls
10 :    DIREVAL( "", { |xParm| Show( xParm, "" ) } )
11 :    wait
12 :    cls
13 :    DIREVAL( "D", {|xParm| Show( xParm, "D" ) } )
14 :    wait
15 :    cls
16 :    DIREVAL("H", { |xParm| Show( xParm, "H" ) } )
17 :    wait
18 :    cls
19 :    DIREVAL("S", { |xParm| Show( xParm, "S" ) } )
20 :
21 : *******************
22 :
23 : static procedure Show( aRec, cExcept )
24 :
25 :    if empty(cExcept) .or. ;
26 :       (!empty(cExcept) .and. aRec[5] != "A")
27 :       aeval( aRec, {|xData| qqout( padr(xData, 14) )} )
28 :       qout()
29 :    endif
30 :
31 : // End of File: DirDemo.prg
```

# DISKSPACE( )

**FUNCTION** Calculates the number of available bytes on a drive.

**SYNTAX** DISKSPACE( [<expN1>] )

**PARAMETER** <expN1>   Optional drive designator in numeric format

**RETURNS** <expN>   The number of bytes available on the specified drive

**LIBRARY** EXTEND.LIB

**DESCRIPTION** This function returns the number of bytes available on the specified disk drive. The disk drive is designated by the value of <expN1>, where 1

represents drive A; 2, drive B; 3, C; etc. If no value is given for <expN1>, the function returns the space available on the currently logged drive.

**SEE ALSO**  RECSIZE( ), LUPDATE( ), HEADER( ), LASTREC( )

## DISPBEGIN( )

**FUNCTION**     Begins virtual screen.

**SYNTAX**       `DISPBEGIN()`

**PARAMETER**    None

**LIBRARY**      CLIPPER.LIB

**DESCRIPTION**  This function begins the definition of a virtual screen. All direct video output will be captured in the virtual screen and will be displayed after being terminated with the DISPEND( ) function.

DISPBEGIN( ) may be nested by several calls to DISPBEGIN( ) before a call to DISPEND( ). An internal stack counter is maintained and keeps track of the appropriate virtual screen buffer. To keep track of the levels of saved screens, the DISPCOUNT( ) function may be used.

**SEE ALSO**     DISPEND( ), DISPCOUNT( )

**EXAMPLE**      See Chapter 17.

## DISPBOX( )

**FUNCTION**     Draws a box at the specified coordinates.

**SYNTAX**       `DISPBOX( <expN1>, <expN2>, <expN3>, <expN4> [, <expX5>] [, <expC6>] )`

**PARAMETERS**
| | |
|---|---|
| <expN1> | Top row coordinate |
| <expN2> | Left column coordinate |
| <expN3> | Bottom row coordinate |
| <expN4> | Right column coordinate |
| <expX5> | Box string or numeric flag |
| <expC6> | Color expression |

**LIBRARY**      CLIPPER.LIB

**DESCRIPTION**  This function draws a box at the coordinates <expN1> through <expN4>. If <exp5> is set to a numeric 1, a single border box string will be used at the coordinates; if a numeric 2 is used, a double border box will be used. If <expX5> is a string of 9 characters, those characters will be used at each of the 9 positions that are required to draw and fill the box coordinates.

Optionally, <expC6> is a color string that will be used when the box is drawn. The color setting does not affect the overall color settings of a system/application.

**SEE ALSO**     DISPOUT( ), @ ... BOX

## DISPCOUNT( )

| | |
|---|---|
| **FUNCTION** | Returns the number of stacked DISPBEGIN( ) calls requiring a DISPEND( ) call to clear the stack. |
| **SYNTAX** | `DISPCOUNT()` |
| **PARAMETER** | None |
| **RETURNS** | <expN>    The number of DISPEND( ) function calls required |
| **LIBRARY** | CLIPPER.LIB |
| **SEE ALSO** | DISPEND( ), DISPBEGIN( ) |
| **EXAMPLE** | See Chapter 17. |

## DISPEND( )

| | |
|---|---|
| **FUNCTION** | Terminates and displays a virtual screen. |
| **SYNTAX** | `DISPEND()` |
| **PARAMETER** | None |
| **LIBRARY** | CLIPPER.LIB |
| **DESCRIPTION** | This function terminates and displays the contents of the virtual screen as established with a DISPBEGIN( ) function call. All direct video output is captured to the virtual screen and is immediately displayed with the DISPEND( ) call. |
| **SEE ALSO** | DISPBEGIN( ), DISPCOUNT( ) |
| **EXAMPLE** | See Chapter 17. |

## DISPOUT( )

| | |
|---|---|
| **FUNCTION** | Displays a value. |
| **SYNTAX** | `DISPOUT( <expX1> [, <expC2>] )` |
| **PARAMETERS** | `<expX1>` Expression to be displayed |
| | `<expC2>` Color string |
| **LIBRARY** | CLIPPER.LIB |
| **DESCRIPTION** | This function displays the expression <expX1> to the screen at the current location of the cursor. This function does not adhere to the settings in the SET DEVICE TO command. |
| | If used, the string value of <expC2> is used to set the color of the screen prior to displaying the contents of <expX1>. This does not affect the system's overall color setting. |
| **SEE ALSO** | DEVOUT( ), SETPOS( ), DEVPOS( ) |

## DMY( )

| | |
|---|---|
| **FUNCTION** | Converts a date to a string format |
| **SYNTAX** | `DMY( <expD1> )` |
| **PARAMETER** | `<expD1>` Any date data type |
| **RETURNS** | `<expC>` Formatted character string of date |
| **LIBRARY** | SAMPLES.LIB |
| **DESCRIPTION** | This function takes the date <expD1> and converts it into a string that is formatted as "DD MONTH YYYY" and returns that value. |
| **SEE ALSO** | DATE( ), MDY( ), DATEASARRAY( ), ARRAYASDATE( ) |

## DOSERROR( )

| | |
|---|---|
| **FUNCTION** | Returns the last DOS error encountered. |
| **SYNTAX** | `DOSERROR( [<expN1>] )` |
| **PARAMETER** | `<expN1>` Any numeric value |
| **RETURNS** | `<expN>` Numeric value that represents the DOS error |

| | |
|---|---|
| **LIBRARY** | CLIPPER.LIB |
| **DESCRIPTION** | This function returns the number of the last DOS error encountered. A complete list of DOS errors may be found in Appendix 7.
The value returned from this function may be set by the value passed to the function via <expN1>. This value should coincide with the listing of error values found in Appendix 7.
This function is the same as the FERROR( ) function used with low-level file functions. |
| **NOTE** | The DOSERROR( ) value is set whenever there is a run-time error. This error is associated with the activation of the run-time error block. |
| **SEE ALSO** | ERRORBLOCK( ), ERRORLEVEL( ), FERROR( ) |

# DOW( )

| | |
|---|---|
| **FUNCTION** | Value for the day of the week. |
| **SYNTAX** | DOW ( <expD1> ) |
| **PARAMETER** | <expD1>   Any date |
| **RETURNS** | <expN>   Numeric value representing the day of the week |
| **LIBRARY** | CLIPPER.LIB |
| **DESCRIPTION** | This function returns the number representing the day of the week for the date expressed as <expD1>. These values are as follows:

1 = Sunday
2 = Monday
3 = Tuesday
4 = Wednesday
5 = Thursday
6 = Friday
7 = Saturday |
| **SEE ALSO** | DTOC( ), CDOW( ), DATE( ), DTOS( ), DAY( ) |
| **EXAMPLE** | See the DATE( ) function. |

# DTOC( )

| | |
|---|---|
| **FUNCTION** | Date to character conversion. |
| **SYNTAX** | DTOC ( <expD1> ) |

| | |
|---|---|
| **PARAMETER** | <expD1>   Any date |
| **RETURNS** | <expC>   Character representation of a date |
| **LIBRARY** | CLIPPER.LIB |
| **DESCRIPTION** | This function converts any date expression (a field or variable) expressed as <expD1> to a character expression in the default format "mm/dd/yy". The date format that is expressed by this function is controlled in part by the date format specified in the SET DATE command. |
| **SEE ALSO** | DATE( ), DTOS( ), SET DATE |
| **EXAMPLE** | See the DATE( ) function. |

## DTOR( )

| | |
|---|---|
| **FUNCTION** | Converts degrees into radians. |
| **SYNTAX** | DTOR( <expN1> ) |
| **PARAMETER** | <expN1>   An angle's degrees |
| **RETURNS** | <expN>   A number expressed in radians |
| **LIBRARY** | SAMPLES.LIB |
| **DESCRIPTION** | This function takes the size of an angle expressed in degrees, <expN1>, and converts it into radians, and returns that value. |
| **SEE ALSO** | BASETOBASE( ), NUMASLOG10( ), SIGN( ) |

## DTOS( )

| | |
|---|---|
| **FUNCTION** | Date-to-string conversion. |
| **SYNTAX** | DTOS( <expD1> ) |
| **PARAMETER** | <expD1>   Any date expression |
| **RETURNS** | <expC>   String notation of the date |
| **LIBRARY** | CLIPPER.LIB |
| **DESCRIPTION** | This function returns the value of <expD1> as a character string in the format of YYYYMMDD. If the value of <expD1> is an empty date (i.e., CTOD(" ")), this function will return eight blank spaces. |

| | |
|---|---|
| **NOTE** | This function is extremely useful for indexing on date and character expressions because it preserves the date order of the original date. |
| **SEE ALSO** | DTOC( ), DATE( ), CTOD( ) |
| **EXAMPLE** | See the DATE( ) function. |

# ELAPTIME( )

| | | |
|---|---|---|
| **FUNCTION** | Calculates elapsed time. | |
| **SYNTAX** | ELAPTIME( <expC1>, <expC2> ) | |
| **PARAMETERS** | <expC1> | Character expression in time string format |
| | <expC2> | Character expression in time string format |
| **RETURNS** | <expC> | Character expression |
| **LIBRARY** | EXTEND.LIB | |
| **DESCRIPTION** | This function returns a string that shows the difference between the starting time represented as <expC1> and the ending time as <expC2>. If the starting time is greater than the ending time, the function will assume that the day changed once. | |
| **NOTE** | This is a compatibility function and may not be supported in future versions. | |
| **SEE ALSO** | SECS( ), SECONDS( ), TIME( ), DAYS( ) | |
| **EXAMPLE** | See the SECONDS( ) function. | |

# EMPTY( )

| | | |
|---|---|---|
| **FUNCTION** | Evaluates an expression for an empty condition. | |
| **SYNTAX** | EMPTY( <expX1> ) | |
| **PARAMETER** | <expX1> | Any expression other than a code block |
| **RETURNS** | <expL> | Logical true (.T.) or false (.F.). |
| **LIBRARY** | CLIPPER.LIB | |
| **DESCRIPTION** | This function is used to evaluate the expression in <expX1> to see if an EMPTY( ) condition exists. If so, a logical true (.T.) will be returned; otherwise, a logical false (.F.) will be returned. | |

An EMPTY( ) condition varies for different data types. Below is a table that lists each data type and the cause for an EMPTY( ) condition.

| Data Type | Condition |
|---|---|
| Array | An array with 0 length |
| Character | Any string with only spaces, tabs, carriage return/line feed, or a NULL byte |
| Date | CTOD(" ") |
| Numeric | 0 |
| Logical | A false (.F.) value |
| Memo | Same as Character |

**SEE ALSO**  ALLTRIM( ), LEN( ), IF( )

# EOF( )

| | |
|---|---|
| **FUNCTION** | Tests for the end-of-file condition. |
| **SYNTAX** | EOF ( ) |
| **PARAMETER** | None |
| **RETURNS** | <expL>  Logical true (.T.) or false (.F.) |
| **LIBRARY** | CLIPPER.LIB |
| **DESCRIPTION** | This function determines if the end-of-file marker has been reached. If it has, the function will return a logical true (.T.); otherwise, a logical false (.F.) will be returned. |
| **SEE ALSO** | GO BOTTOM, BOF( ), GO TOP |
| **EXAMPLE** | See the BOF( ) function. |

# ERRORINHANDLER( )

| | |
|---|---|
| **FUNCTION** | Assures a clean exit from an application. |
| **SYNTAX** | ERRORINHANDLER ( ) |
| **PARAMETER** | None |
| **LIBRARY** | SAMPLES.LIB |

**DESCRIPTION** This function makes certain of a clean and prompt exit from an application. When called, it creates an "Error recovery failure" which may be interrogated from within a customized Error System. It will also indicate the name of the subroutine executing the function as well as the line number.

**SEE ALSO** ERRORNEW( ), ERRORBLOCK( )

**EXAMPLE** Please see Chapter 19.

## ERRORBLOCK( )

| | |
|---|---|
| **FUNCTION** | Posts an executable code block for run-time errors. |
| **SYNTAX** | ERRORBLOCK( [<expB1>] ) |
| **PARAMETER** | <expB1>    Code block expression |
| **RETURNS** | <expB>    Code block expression |
| **LIBRARY** | CLIPPER.LIB |
| **DESCRIPTION** | This function returns the current error-handling code block for the specified error code block in <expB1>. If no code block is passed to the function, this function will return a default error handle block for the run-time error system. |
| **SEE ALSO** | BEGIN SEQUENCE, BREAK( ) |
| **EXAMPLE** | For a complete discussion of this function, see Chapter 19. |

## ERRORLEVEL( )

| | |
|---|---|
| **FUNCTION** | Sets and evaluates the current error-level status. |
| **SYNTAX** | ERRORLEVEL( [<expN1>] ) |
| **PARAMETER** | <expN1>    New error-level value |
| **RETURNS** | <expN>    Numeric expression |
| **LIBRARY** | CLIPPER.LIB |
| **DESCRIPTION** | This function returns the current Clipper error-level code and optionally sets that code to a value of <expN1>. This code, if used, becomes the exit value of the Clipper application. The acceptable value for <expN1> is between 0 and 255, inclusive. |

If a Clipper application does not exit properly, the return code to DOS for the application will be 1, regardless of the setting of this function. If, however, the application completes processing normally, the DOS return code will be either a 0 or the value set by this function.

**SEE ALSO** DOSERROR( ), QUIT

**EXAMPLE** For a detailed explanation of this function, see Chapter 16.

## ERRORNEW( )

**FUNCTION** Generates a Clipper error object.

**SYNTAX** ERRORNEW ( )

**PARAMETER** None

**RETURNS** <expO>   Clipper object structure

**LIBRARY** CLIPPER.LIB

**DESCRIPTION** This function returns a Clipper error object that may be used to develop a complex and sophisticated error-handling system.

The following is a list of the Instance Variables that make up the structure of the returned error object:

| | |
|---|---|
| ARGS | Array of functions or operator arguments |
| CANDEFAULT | Toggles default recovery availability |
| CANRETY | Toggles retry possibility after an error |
| CANSUBSTITUTE | Toggles if new result may be substituted after error |
| CARGO | User-definable slot |
| DESCRIPTION | Character description of error |
| FILENAME | Name of file associated with error |
| GENCODE | Clipper error code |
| OPERATION | Character description of failed operation |
| OSCODE | Operating system error code |
| SEVERITY | Numeric value of error's severity |
| SUBCODE | Subsystem-specific error code |
| SUBSYSTEM | Character description of subsystem generating error |
| TRIES | Number of failed attempts at operation |

*Clipper Function Reference* 409

| | |
|---|---|
| **SEE ALSO** | GETNEW( ), TBROWSEDB( ), TBROWSENEW( ), TBCOLUMNNEW( ) |
| **EXAMPLE** | For a detailed explanation of this function, see Chapter 16. |

## EVAL( )

| | | |
|---|---|---|
| **FUNCTION** | Evaluates code block. | |
| **SYNTAX** | EVAL( <expB1> [, <expX2> [, ... ]] ) | |
| **PARAMETERS** | <expB1> | Code block expression to be evaluated |
| | <expX2> | Argument to be passed to the code block expression |
| | <expX...> | Argument list to be passed to the code block expression |
| **RETURNS** | <exp> | Any expression |
| **LIBRARY** | CLIPPER.LIB | |
| **DESCRIPTION** | This function evaluates the code block expressed as <expB1> and returns its evaluated value. If there are multiple expressions within the code block, the last expression will be the value of this function. |
| | If the code block requires parameters to be passed to it, they are specified in the parameter list <expX2> and following. Each parameter is separated by a comma within the expression list. |
| **SEE ALSO** | AEVAL( ), DBEVAL( ) |
| **EXAMPLE** | See Chapter 15. |

## EXP( )

| | | |
|---|---|---|
| **FUNCTION** | Calculates the exponential of a real number. | |
| **SYNTAX** | EXP( <expN1> ) | |
| **PARAMETER** | <expN1> | Any real number |
| **RETURNS** | <expN> | Numeric value |
| **LIBRARY** | CLIPPER.LIB | |
| **DESCRIPTION** | This function returns the exponential of any given real number <expN1>. |

**NOTE** For a more accurate exponential of any number, the SET DECIMAL TO command must be invoked to carry the results out to the desired number of places. The default setting is 2.

**SEE ALSO** LOG( ), SET DECIMAL

## EXTRACT( )

**FUNCTION** Returns an array of elements matching a criteria.

**SYNTAX** EXTRACT( <expA1>, <expB2> )

**PARAMETERS**    <expA1>  Array of items to search through and extract
   <expB2>  Code block with extracting condition

**RETURNS** <expA>   Array of extracted items

**LIBRARY** SAMPLES.LIB

**DESCRIPTION** This function takes the array <expA1> and attempts to extract items from it based on a criteria specified in <expB2>. Each element in <expA1> is evaluated and passed to the code block and if that item matches the criteria within the code block <expB2>, the item is added to an array which, at the end of the process, will be returned by the function. If no items can be found that match the criteria within <expB2>, then the function will return an EMPTY( ) array.

**SEE ALSO** ARRAY( ), AEVAL( ), AADD( )

**EXAMPLE**

```
 1 : * File    Extrdemo.prg
 2 : * Compile RMake sampmore /dFILE:extrdemo
 3 :
 4 : procedure Main()
 5 :
 6 :    local aResults
 7 :
 8 :    cls
 9 :    aResults := extract( directory(), {|aItem| "E"$upper(aItem[1])} )
10 :
11 :    ? "And now, a listing of all the files with the letter 'E' in them..."
12 :    ? len( aResults )
13 :    inkey(0)
14 :    aeval( aResults, {|aFile| qout(aFile[1]) } )
15 :
16 : // End of File: Extrdemo.prg
```

## FCLOSE( )

| | |
|---|---|
| **FUNCTION** | Closes an open file. |
| **SYNTAX** | `FCLOSE( <expN1> )` |
| **PARAMETER** | <expN1>   DOS file handle |
| **RETURNS** | <expL>   Logical true (.T.) or false (.F.) |
| **LIBRARY** | CLIPPER.LIB |
| **DESCRIPTION** | This function closes an open file with a DOS file handle of <expN1> and writes the associated DOS buffer to disk. The <expN1> value is derived from the FOPEN( ) or FCREATE( ) functions. |
| **SEE ALSO** | FOPEN( ), FCREATE( ), FREAD( ), FWRITE( ), FERROR( ) |
| **EXAMPLE** | See Chapter 14. |

## FCOUNT( )

| | |
|---|---|
| **FUNCTION** | Counts the number of fields in an active database. |
| **SYNTAX** | `FCOUNT()` |
| **PARAMETER** | None |
| **RETURNS** | <expN>   Numeric expression |
| **LIBRARY** | CLIPPER.LIB |
| **DESCRIPTION** | This function returns the number of fields in the current or designated work area. If no database is open in this work area, the function will return 0. |
| **SEE ALSO** | DBSTRUCT( ), AFIELDS( ), DBCREATE( ) |

## FCREATE( )

| | |
|---|---|
| **FUNCTION** | Creates a file. |
| **SYNTAX** | `FCREATE( <expC1> [, <expN2> ] )` |
| **PARAMETERS** | <expC1>   Name of the file to create<br><expN2>   Numeric code for the DOS file attribute |
| **RETURNS** | <expN>   Numeric expression |

| | |
|---|---|
| **LIBRARY** | CLIPPER.LIB |
| **DESCRIPTION** | This function creates a new file with a filename of <expC1>. The default value of <expN2> is 0 and is used to set the DOS attribute byte for the file being created by this function.

The return value will be the DOS file handle that is associated with the new file. This number will be between 0 and 65,535, inclusive. If an error occurs, the return value of this function will be -1.

If the file <expC1> already exists, the existing file will be truncated to a file length of 0 bytes.

If specified, the following table shows the values for <expN2> and their related meanings to the file <expC1> being created by this function. |

| Value of <expN2> | File Attribute |
|---|---|
| 0 | Normal/Default, Read/Write |
| 1 | Read only, Attempting to open for output returns an error |
| 2 | Hidden, Excluded from normal DIR search |
| 3 | System, Excluded from normal DIR search |

This function does not adhere to the default values set by the SET DEFAULT TO or SET PATH TO commands; if the drive and/or directory path is necessary, it must be explicitly stated in <expC1>.

| | |
|---|---|
| **SEE ALSO** | FCLOSE( ), FOPEN( ), FWRITE( ), FREAD( ), FERROR( ) |
| **EXAMPLE** | See Chapter 14. |

## FERASE( )

| | | |
|---|---|---|
| **FUNCTION** | Erases a file. | |
| **SYNTAX** | `FERASE( <expC1> )` | |
| **PARAMETER** | <expC1> | Name of file to erase |
| **RETURNS** | <expN> | 0 if successful, −1 if not |
| **LIBRARY** | CLIPPER.LIB | |
| **DESCRIPTION** | This function deletes the file specified in <expC1> from the disk. No extensions are assumed. The drive and path may be included in <expC1>; neither the SET DEFAULT nor the SET PATH command controls the performance of this function. If the drive or path is not used, the function will look for the file only on the currently selected directory on the logged drive. | |

If the function is able to successfully delete the file from the disk, the value of the function will be 0; otherwise a -1 will be returned. If not successful, additional information may be obtained by calling the FERROR( ) function.

**NOTE** Any file that is to be removed by FERASE( ) must still be closed.

**SEE ALSO** ERASE, FRENAME( ), CLOSE

**EXAMPLE** See the FRENAME( ) function.

## FERROR( )

**FUNCTION** Reports the error status of low-level file functions.

**SYNTAX** FERROR ( )

**PARAMETER** None

**RETURNS** &lt;expN&gt;   Value of the DOS error last encountered by a low-level file function

**LIBRARY** CLIPPER.LIB

**DESCRIPTION** After every low-level file function, this function will return a value that provides additional information on the status of the last low-level file function's performance. If the FERROR( ) function returns a 0, no error was detected. Below is a table of possible values returned by the FERROR( ) function.

| FERROR( ) Value | Reason |
| --- | --- |
| 0 | Successful |
| 2 | File not found |
| 3 | Path not found |
| 4 | Too many files open |
| 5 | Access denied |
| 6 | Invalid handle |
| 8 | Insufficient memory |
| 15 | Invalid drive specified |
| 19 | Attempt to write to a write-protected disk |
| 21 | Drive not ready |
| 23 | Data CRC error |
| 29 | Write fault |
| 30 | Read fault |
| 32 | Sharing violation |
| 33 | Lock violation |

| | |
|---|---|
| **NOTE** | The low-level file functions include FERROR( ), FCLOSE( ), FCREATE( ), FERASE( ), FRENAME( ), FOPEN( ), FREAD( ), and FREADSTR( ). |
| **SEE ALSO** | DOSERROR( ) |
| **EXAMPLE** | See Chapter 14. |

# FIELD( )

| | | |
|---|---|---|
| **FUNCTION** | Returns the name of a field at a numeric field location. | |
| **SYNTAX** | `FIELD( <expN1> )` | |
| **PARAMETER** | <expN1> | Field order |
| **RETURNS** | <expC> | Field name |
| **LIBRARY** | CLIPPER.LIB | |
| **DESCRIPTION** | This function returns the name of the field at the <expN>th position. If the numeric value passed to this function does not correspond to an existing field in the designated or selected work area, this function will return a NULL byte. | |
| | The FIELD( ) function is synonymous with the FIELDNAME( ) function, although the latter function is no longer documented within Clipper 5.2. | |
| **SEE ALSO** | AFIELDS( ), FCOUNT( ) | |
| **EXAMPLE** | See the FIELDPUT( ) function. | |

# FIELDBLOCK( )

| | | |
|---|---|---|
| **FUNCTION** | Generates a code block for a specific field. | |
| **SYNTAX** | `FIELDBLOCK( <expC1> )` | |
| **PARAMETER** | <expC1> | A field name |
| **RETURNS** | <expB> | Code block expression |
| **LIBRARY** | CLIPPER.LIB | |
| **DESCRIPTION** | This function returns a code block that, when evaluated, either obtains or places a value for the given field named <expC1>. If the field named in <expC1> does not exist, the function will return a NIL data type. | |
| **SEE ALSO** | FIELDWBLOCK( ), MEMVARBLOCK( ) | |

**EXAMPLE**

```
 1 : * File:      Fbdemo.prg
 2 : * Compile:   RMake sample /dFILE:Fbdemo
 3 :
 4 : procedure Main()
 5 :
 6 :    local bCode1
 7 :    local bCode2
 8 :
 9 :    use Statcode new
10 :    bCode1 := fieldblock( field(1) )
11 :    bCode2 := fieldblock( "descript" )
12 :
13 :    cls
14 :    qqout( "Listing for: " + alias() )
15 :    dbeval( {|| qout( eval(bCode1), eval(bCode2) )} )
16 :    wait
17 :    cls
18 :
19 : // End of File: FBDemo.prg
```

# FIELDGET( )

| | |
|---|---|
| **FUNCTION** | Obtains the value of a specific field in a specific record. |
| **SYNTAX** | FIELDGET( <expN1> ) |
| **PARAMETER** | <expN1>    Field position |
| **RETURNS** | <expX>    Any expression |
| **LIBRARY** | CLIPPER.LIB |
| **DESCRIPTION** | This function returns the value of the field at the <expN1>th location in the selected or designated work area. If the value in <expN1> does not correspond to an available field position in this work area, the function will return a NIL data type. |
| **SEE ALSO** | FIELDPUT( ), FIELDPOS( ) |
| **EXAMPLE** | See the FIELDPUT( ) function. |

# FIELDNAME( )

| | |
|---|---|
| **FUNCTION** | Returns the name of a field at a numeric field location. |
| **SYNTAX** | FIELDNAME( <expN1> ) |
| **PARAMETER** | <expN1>    Field order |

| | |
|---|---|
| **RETURNS** | <expC>    Field name |
| **LIBRARY** | CLIPPER.LIB |
| **DESCRIPTION** | This function returns the name of the field at the <expN>th position. If the numeric value passed to this function does not correspond to an existing field in the designated or selected work area, this function will return a NULL byte.<br><br>    The FIELDNAME( ) function is synonymous with the FIELD( ) function, although the latter function is no longer documented within Clipper 5.2. |
| **SEE ALSO** | AFIELDS( ), FCOUNT( ) |
| **EXAMPLE** | See the FIELDPUT( ) function. |

## FIELDPOS( )

| | |
|---|---|
| **FUNCTION** | Returns the ordinal position of a field. |
| **SYNTAX** | `FIELDPOS( <expC1> )` |
| **PARAMETER** | <expC1>    Name of a field |
| **RETURNS** | <expN>    Ordinal position of the field |
| **LIBRARY** | CLIPPER.LIB |
| **DESCRIPTION** | This function returns the ordinal position of the specified field <expC1> in the current or aliased work area. If there isn't a field under the name of <expC1> or if no database is open in the selected work area, the function will return a 0. |
| **SEE ALSO** | FIELDGET( ), FIELDNAME( ), FIELD( ), FIELDPUT( ) |

## FIELDPUT( )

| | |
|---|---|
| **FUNCTION** | Places a value in a specific field in a specific record. |
| **SYNTAX** | `FIELDPUT( <expN1>, <expX2> )` |
| **PARAMETERS** | <expN1>    The field position<br><expX2>    Expression to be assigned to the specified field |
| **RETURNS** | <expX>    Any expression |
| **LIBRARY** | CLIPPER.LIB |

**DESCRIPTION** This function assigns the value in <expX2> to the <expN1>th field in the current or designated work area. If the operation is successful, the return value of the function will be the same as the value assigned to the specified field. If the operation is not successful, the function will return a NIL data type.

**SEE ALSO** FIELDGET( )

**EXAMPLE**

```
 1 : * File:      Flddemo.prg
 2 : * Compile:   RMake sample /dFILE:flddemo
 3 :
 4 : procedure Main()
 5 :
 6 :    cls
 7 :    use clients new
 8 :    Copy to Temp
 9 :    Use Temp
10 :    Temp ->(dbeval({||ShowField( )}))
11 : ********************
12 :
13 : static procedure ShowField()
14 :
15 :    if row() == 0
16 :       qqout( "Record #    Field Name    Former Value    New Value" )
17 :    endif
18 :
19 :    qout ( padr( recno(), 15) )
20 :    qqout( padr( field( 13 ), 15) )
21 :    qqout( padr( fieldget( 13 ), 15 ) )
22 :    qqout( padr( fieldput(13, date()+recno()), 15) )
23 :
24 :    if row() > 20
25 :       qout()
26 :       qout( "Press any key for next screen..." )
27 :       inkey(0)
28 :       cls
29 :    endif
30 :
31 : // End of File: Flddemo.prg
```

# FIELDWBLOCK( )

| | | |
|---|---|---|
| **FUNCTION** | | Generates a code block for a specific field value in a specific work area. |
| **SYNTAX** | | FIELDWBLOCK( <expC1>, <expN2> ) |
| **PARAMETERS** | <expC1> | The name of the field |
| | <expN2> | A work area |
| **RETURNS** | <expB> | Code block expression |

| | |
|---|---|
| **LIBRARY** | CLIPPER.LIB |
| **DESCRIPTION** | This function returns a code block that evaluates the field <expC1> in the <expN2> work area. This code block, when evaluated, either places values in or obtains values from the designated field. If the field specified in <expC1> does not exist or if the work area <expN2> does not exist, the function will return a NIL data type. |
| **SEE ALSO** | FIELDBLOCK( ), MEMVARBLOCK( ) |

# FILE( )

| | | |
|---|---|---|
| **FUNCTION** | Tests for the existence of file(s). | |
| **SYNTAX** | `FILE( <expC1> )` | |
| **PARAMETER** | <expC1> | DOS skeleton or filename to find |
| **RETURNS** | <expL> | Logical true (.T.) or false (.F.) |
| **LIBRARY** | CLIPPER.LIB | |
| **DESCRIPTION** | This function returns a logical true (.T.) if the given filename <expC1> exists.<br><br>DOS skeleton symbols may be used in the filename in <expC1>, as may the drive and/or path name. If a drive and directory are not explicitly specified, FILE( ) will first search the current drive and directory, and will then look for the file in the directories specified by the SET PATH TO and SET DEFAULT TO commands. However, this command does not look at the values set in the DOS PATH command. | |
| **SEE ALSO** | SET PATH, SET DEFAULT, SET( ) | |
| **EXAMPLE** | See the FRENAME( ) function. | |

# FILEBASE( )

| | | |
|---|---|---|
| **FUNCTION** | Returns the root name of a given file. | |
| **SYNTAX** | `FILEBASE( <expC1> )` | |
| **PARAMETER** | <expC1> | Character string of filename |
| **RETURNS** | <expC> | Eight-letter root name of the file |
| **LIBRARY** | SAMPLES.LIB | |

| | |
|---|---|
| **DESCRIPTION** | This function takes the file named <expC1> which may or may not contain a drive designator, path, and file extension, and extracts from that the up-to eight-character root name of the file and returns that string. |
| **SEE ALSO** | FILE( ), FILEDRIVE( ), FILEEXT( ), FILEPATH( ) |
| **EXAMPLE** | See the FULLPATH( ) function. |

## FILEDRIVE( )

| | | |
|---|---|---|
| **FUNCTION** | Returns the drive letter associated with a filename. | |
| **SYNTAX** | `FILEDRIVE( <expC1> )` | |
| **PARAMETER** | <expC1> | Character string of a filename |
| **RETURNS** | <expC> | Drive designator |
| **LIBRARY** | SAMPLES.LIB | |
| **DESCRIPTION** | This function takes the filename expressed as <expC1> that may or may not contain a file extension and/or search path and extracts the drive designator that may be associated with the file name. The function returns the one-letter drive name. If no drive letter appears in the string <expC1>, then a NULL string will be returned. | |
| **SEE ALSO** | FILE( ), FILEBASE( ), FILEEXT( ), FILEPATH( ), FULLPATH( ) | |
| **EXAMPLE** | Please see the FULLPATH( ) function. | |

## FILEEXT( )

| | | |
|---|---|---|
| **FUNCTION** | Returns the three-letter file extension of a file. | |
| **SYNTAX** | `FILEEXT( <expC1> )` | |
| **PARAMETER** | <expC1> | Character string with filename |
| **RETURNS** | <expC> | Three-letter file extension |
| **LIBRARY** | SAMPLES.LIB | |
| **DESCRIPTION** | This function takes the file named <expC1>, which may or may not contain a drive designator, path, and file extension, and extracts from that the up-to three-character file extension of the file and returns that string. If the file <expC1> does not contain a file extension, then a NULL byte will be returned. | |

| | |
|---|---|
| **SEE ALSO** | FILE( ), FILEBASE( ), FILEDRIVE( ), FILEPATH( ), FULLPATH( ) |
| **EXAMPLE** | See the FULLPATH( ) function. |

## FILEPATH( )

| | | |
|---|---|---|
| **FUNCTION** | Extracts the path of a file based on name. | |
| **SYNTAX** | `FILEPATH( <expC1> )` | |
| **PARAMETER** | <expC1> | Character string of filename |
| **RETURNS** | <expC> | Path name of the file |
| **LIBRARY** | SAMPLES.LIB | |
| **DESCRIPTION** | This function takes the file named <expC1>, which may or may not contain a drive designator, path, and file extension, and extracts from that the path, excluding the drive designator and filename. If the file <expC1> does not contain a file path, then a NULL byte will be returned. | |
| **SEE ALSO** | FILE( ), FILEBASE( ), FILEDRIVE( ), FILEEXT( ), FULLPATH( ) | |
| **EXAMPLE** | See the FULLPATH( ) function. | |

## FILLOCK( )

| | | |
|---|---|---|
| **FUNCTION** | Attempts to lock a file. | |
| **SYNTAX** | `FILLOCK( [<expN1>] )` | |
| **PARAMETER** | <expN1> | Number of seconds for retry operation |
| **RETURNS** | <expL> | Logical true (.T.) or a logical false (.F.) |
| **LIBRARY** | SAMPLES.LIB | |
| **DESCRIPTION** | This function attempts to lock a file and returns a logical true (.T.) if it was successful; otherwise, a logical false (.F.) is returned. The number of seconds to retry should an attempt fail is specified via the <expN1> parameter. The default value for <expN1> is 2 seconds. | |
| **SEE ALSO** | FLOCK( ), RLOCK( ), DBUNLOCKALL( ), ADDREC( ) | |

## FKLABEL( )

| | |
|---|---|
| **FUNCTION** | Returns the name of a function key. |
| **SYNTAX** | `FKLABEL( <expN1> )` |
| **PARAMETER** | <expN1>   Any number between 0 and 40, inclusive |
| **RETURNS** | <expC>   Name of key |
| **LIBRARY** | EXTEND.LIB |
| **DESCRIPTION** | This function returns the name assigned to the function key specified by <expN1>. If <expN1> is less than 0 or greater than 40, a NULL byte will be returned. |
| **NOTE** | This is a compatibility function that may not be supported in future releases. |
| **SEE ALSO** | FKMAX( ), SET FUNCTION |

## FKMAX( )

| | |
|---|---|
| **FUNCTION** | Sets the maximum number of function keys. |
| **SYNTAX** | `FKMAX()` |
| **PARAMETER** | None |
| **RETURNS** | <expN>   Number of function keys on keyboard |
| **LIBRARY** | EXTEND.LIB |
| **DESCRIPTION** | This function will always return 40, which is the number of standard function keys available for the IBM PC/XT/AT. |
| **NOTE** | This is a compatibility function that may not be supported in future releases. |
| **SEE ALSO** | FKLABEL( ) |

## FLOCK( )

| | |
|---|---|
| **FUNCTION** | Locks a file. |
| **SYNTAX** | `FLOCK()` |
| **PARAMETER** | None |

| | | |
|---|---|---|
| **RETURNS** | <expL> | Logical true (.T.) or false (.F.) |
| **LIBRARY** | CLIPPER.LIB | |
| **DESCRIPTION** | This function returns a logical true (.T.) if a file lock is attempted and is successfully placed on the current or designated database. This function will also unlock all record locks placed by the same network station. | |
| **SEE ALSO** | USE <EXCLUSIVE>, UNLOCK, RLOCK( ) | |

## FLOOR( )

| | | |
|---|---|---|
| **FUNCTION** | Returns largest integer in a base range. | |
| **SYNTAX** | FLOOR( <expN1> ) | |
| **PARAMETER** | <expN1> | Any numeric value |
| **RETURNS** | <expN> | Largest integer in range |
| **LIBRARY** | SAMPLES.LIB | |
| **DESCRIPTION** | This function will return the largest integer that is less than or equal to the value <expN1>. | |
| **SEE ALSO** | INT( ), CEILING( ) | |
| **EXAMPLE** | Please see the CEILING( ) function. | |

## FOPEN( )

| | | |
|---|---|---|
| **FUNCTION** | Opens a file. | |
| **SYNTAX** | FOPEN( <expC1> [, <expN2>] ) | |
| **PARAMETERS** | <expC1> | Name of the file to open |
| | <expN2> | DOS file open mode |
| **RETURNS** | <expN> | DOS file handle |
| **LIBRARY** | CLIPPER.LIB | |
| **DESCRIPTION** | This function opens the file expressed as <expC1> and returns a DOS file handle to be used with other low-level file functions. The value of <expN2> represents the status of the file that is to be opened; the default value is 0. The DOS file open modes are as follows: | |

| <expN2> | Mode |
|---|---|
| 0 | Read Only |
| 1 | Write Only |

| <expN2> | Mode |
|---|---|
| 2 | Read/write |
| 16 | Exclusive Read Only |
| 17 | Exclusive Write Only |
| 18 | Exclusive Read/Write |
| 32 | Prevent other read only |
| 33 | Prevent other write only |
| 34 | Prevent read/write only |
| 48 | Deny Read Only |
| 49 | Deny Write Only |
| 50 | Deny Read/Write |
| 64 | Share Read Only |
| 65 | Share Write Only |
| 66 | Share Read/Write |

If there is an error in opening the file, a -1 will be returned by the function. File handles may be in the range of 0 to 65,535. The status of the SET DEFAULT TO and SET PATH TO commands has no effect on this function. Directory names and paths must be specified along with the file that is to be opened.

If an error has occurred, see the return values from FERROR( ) for possible reasons for the error.

**SEE ALSO**     FCLOSE( ), FCREATE( ), FREAD( ), FWRITE( ), FERROR( )

**EXAMPLE**      See Chapter 14.

# FOUND( )

**FUNCTION**     Determines the success of a previous search operation.

**SYNTAX**       FOUND ( )

**PARAMETER**    None

**RETURNS**      <expL>     Logical true (.T.) or false (.F.)

**LIBRARY**      CLIPPER.LIB

**DESCRIPTION**  This function is used to test if the previous SEEK, LOCATE, CONTINUE, or FIND operation was successful. Each work area has its own FOUND( ) flag, so that a FOUND( ) condition may be tested in unselected work areas by using an alias.

**SEE ALSO**     SEEK, EOF( ), FIND

**EXAMPLE**      See the DESCEND( ) function.

## FREAD( )

| | |
|---|---|
| **FUNCTION** | Reads a specified number of bytes from a file. |
| **SYNTAX** | FREAD( <expN1>, @<expC2>, <expN3> ) |
| **PARAMETERS** | <expN1>   DOS file handle<br>@<expC2>  Character expression passed by reference<br><expN3>   Number of bytes to read |
| **RETURNS** | <expN>    Numeric expression |
| **LIBRARY** | CLIPPER.LIB |
| **DESCRIPTION** | This function reads the characters from a DOS file whose file handle is <expN1> into a character memory variable expressed as <expC2>. The function returns the number of bytes successfully read into <expC2>.<br><br>The value of <expN1> is obtained from either a call to the FOPEN( ) or the FCREATE( ) function.<br><br>The <expC2> expression is passed by reference and must be defined before this function is called. It also must be at least the same length as <expN3>.<br><br><expN3> is the number of bytes to read, starting at the current DOS file pointer position. If this function is successful in reading the characters from the file, the length of <expC2> or the number of bytes specified in <expN3> will be the value returned. The current DOS file pointer advances the number of bytes read with each successive read.<br><br>The return value is the number of bytes successfully read from the file <expN1>. If a 0 is returned, or if the number of bytes read matches neither the length of <expC2> nor the specified value in <expN3>, an end-of-file condition has been reached. |
| **SEE ALSO** | FWRITE( ), FREADSTR( ), FOPEN( ), FCLOSE( ), FERROR( ) |
| **EXAMPLE** | See Chapter 14. |

## FREADSTR( )

| | |
|---|---|
| **FUNCTION** | Reads a string from a file. |
| **SYNTAX** | FREADSTR( <expN1>, <expN2> ) |
| **PARAMETERS** | <expN1>   DOS file handle number<br><expN2>   Number of bytes to read |
| **RETURNS** | <expC>    Character expression |

| | |
|---|---|
| **LIBRARY** | CLIPPER.LIB |
| **DESCRIPTION** | This function returns a character string of <expN2> bytes from a file whose DOS file handle is <expN1>.
The value of the file handle <expN1> is obtained from either the FOPEN( ) or FCREATE( ) functions.
The value of <expN2> is the number of bytes to read from the file.
The returned string will be the number of characters specified in <expN2> or the number of bytes read before an end-of-file character (ASCII 26) is found. |
| **NOTE** | This function is similar to the FREAD( ) function, except that it will not read binary characters that may be required as part of a header of a file construct. Characters such as CHR(0) and CHR(26) may keep this function from performing its intended operation. In this event, the FREAD( ) function should be used in place of the FREADSTR( ) function. |
| **SEE ALSO** | FREAD( ), FWRITE( ), FCLOSE( ), FOPEN( ), FCREATE( ), FERROR( ) |
| **EXAMPLE** | See Chapter 14. |

# FRENAME( )

| | | |
|---|---|---|
| **FUNCTION** | Renames a file. | |
| **SYNTAX** | `FRENAME( <expC1>, <expC2> )` | |
| **PARAMETERS** | <expC1> | Old filename to be changed |
| | <expC2> | New filename |
| **RETURNS** | <expN> | If successful, a 0 will be returned; otherwise, a -1 will be returned. |
| **LIBRARY** | CLIPPER.LIB | |
| **DESCRIPTION** | This function renames the specified file <expC1> to <expC2>. A filename and/or directory name may be specified for either parameter. However, if a path is supplied as part of <expC2> and this path is different from either the path specified in <expC1> or (if none is used) the current drive and directory, the function will not execute successfully.
Neither parameter is subject to the control of the SET PATH TO or SET DEFAULT TO commands. In attempting to locate the file to be renamed, this function will search the default drive and directory or the drive and path specified in <expC1>. It will not search directories named | |

by the SET PATH TO and SET DEFAULT TO commands or by the DOS PATH statement.

If the file specified in <expC2> exists or if the file is open, the function will be unable to rename the file. If the function is unable to complete its operation, it will return a value of -1. If it is able to rename the file, the return value for the function will be 0. A call to the FERROR( ) function will give additional information about any error found.

If <expC1> is a database (.DBF) file, any accompanying .DBT file (memo file) will not be automatically renamed. An additional function call for this file must be made.

**SEE ALSO**        FERASE( ), FERROR( ), RENAME

**EXAMPLE**

```
 1 : * File:      Filedemo.prg
 2 : * Compile:   RMake sample /dFILE:filedemo
 3 :
 4 : #xtranslate FCOPY(<a>, <b>) => __CopyFile( <(a)>, <(b)> )
 5 :
 6 : procedure Main()
 7 :
 8 :    cls
 9 :    if file( "HELP*.TXT" )
10 :      qout( " Some, or all, of the help files exist." )
11 :      if file( "HELPTXT1.TXT" )
12 :        qout( "Changing HELPTXT1.TXT to HELPTXT1.BAD" )
13 :        qout( "Using the FRENAME() function!")
14 :
15 :        frename( "HELPTXT1.TXT", "HELPTXT1.BAD" )
16 :
17 :        qout( " Is it with .TXT extension? ", file("HELPTXT1.TXT") )
18 :        qout( " Is it with .BAD extension? ", file("HELPTXT1.BAD") )
19 :
20 :        // the following function is a preprocessor translation that calls
21 :        // a Clipper internal and is a direct replacement for the COPY
22 :        // FILE <a> TO <b> command in function form
23 :
24 :        FCOPY( Helptxt1.bad, Helptxt1.txt )
25 :        FCOPY( Helptxt2.txt, Helptxt2.bad )
26 :        FCOPY( Helptxt3.txt, Helptxt3.bad )
27 :
28 :        if file( "HELP*.BAD" )
29 :          // Calling the DIRECTORY() function to get a multidimensional
30 :          // array with the names of the files that are to be erased one at
31 :          // a time.
32 :          aeval( directory("HELP*.BAD"), {|aFile| ;
33 :                 ferase( aFile[1] ), qout( aFile[1], " is now erased!" )} )
34 :        endif
35 :      endif
36 :    endif
37 :
38 : // End of File: FileDemo.prg
```

## FSEEK( )

**FUNCTION**  Positions the file pointer in a file.

**SYNTAX**  FSEEK( <expN1>, <expN2> [, <expN3> ] )

**PARAMETERS**
<expN1>  The DOS file handle
<expN2>  The number of bytes to move
<expN3>  The relative position in the file

**RETURNS**  <expN>  Numeric value

**LIBRARY**  CLIPPER.LIB

**DESCRIPTION**  This function sets the file pointer in the file whose DOS file handle is <expN1> and moves the file pointer by <expN2> bytes from the file position designated by <expN3>. The returned value is the relative position of the file pointer to the beginning-of-file marker once the operation has been completed.

<expN1> is the file handle number. It is obtained from the FOPEN( ) or FCREATE( ) function.

The value of <expN2> is the number of bytes to move the file pointer from the position determined by <expN3>. The value of <expN2> may be a negative number, suggesting backward movement.

The value of <expN3> designates the starting point from which the file pointer should be moved, as shown in the following table:

| <expN3> | File position |
|---|---|
| 0 | Beginning of file |
| 1 | Current file pointer position |
| 2 | End of file |

If a value is not provided for <expN3>, it defaults to 0 and moves the file pointer from the beginning of the file.

**SEE ALSO**  FREAD( ), FWRITE( ), FCLOSE( ), FOPEN( ), FCREATE( ), FERROR( )

**EXAMPLE**  Please see Chapter 14.

## FULLPATH( )

**FUNCTION**  Returns the full path of a file.

**SYNTAX**  FULLPATH( <expC1> [, <expL2>] )

**PARAMETERS**  &lt;expC1&gt;   Filename
&lt;expL2&gt;   Toggle to use SET PATH or SET DEFAULT

**RETURNS**  &lt;expC&gt;   Path name

**LIBRARY**  SAMPLES.LIB

**DESCRIPTION**  This function takes the filename expressed as &lt;expC1&gt; and either searches the file on the currently logged drive, the paths specified from the DOS PATH statement, or the internal settings for SET PATH or SET DEFAULT. If the file is found on the logged directory, the return value will be that directory's name. If not and if &lt;expL2&gt; is not specified or is set to a logical false (.F.) value, then the function will look to the internal setting for SET PATH TO, if specified. If &lt;expL2&gt; is set to a logical true, the function will use the DOS PATH environmental setting and will search for the file &lt;expC1&gt;.

If the function cannot find the file &lt;expC1&gt; in any of these paths, the function will return a NULL string.

**SEE ALSO**  FILE( ), FILEBASE( ), FILEEXT( ), FILEPATH( ), FILEDRIVE( )

**EXAMPLE**

```
 1 : * File      FStfdemo.prg
 2 : * Compile Rmake sampmore /DFILE:FStfdemo
 3 :
 4 : procedure Main()
 5 :
 6 :    local cFile := "c:\dos\command.com"   // This is our base file
 7 :
 8 :    cls
 9 :    ? "Does the file exist? ", file( cFile )
10 :    if file( cFile )
11 :      ? " Now, the base name? ", filebase( cFile )    // COMMAND
12 :      ? "      On what drive? ", filedrive( cFile )   // C
13 :      ? " And with what ext.? ", fileext( cFile )     // COM
14 :      ? "    With what path? ", filepath( cFile )     // C:\DOS\
15 :      ?
16 :      ? "It's important to see that neither the ':' nor the '.' are carried"
17 :      ? "with the results from some of these functions.  And now...."
18 :      ?
19 :      cFile := "CHKDSK.*"
20 :      ? fullpath( cFile, .f.)   // use SET PATH TO criteria
21 :      set path to c:\dos\       // now set the path
22 :
23 :      ? fullpath( cFile, .f.)   // use SET PATH TO criteria
24 :      ? fullpath( cFile, .t.)   // use DOS PATH criteria
25 :    endif
26 :
27 : // End of File: Fstfdemo.prg
```

## FWRITE( )

| | |
|---|---|
| **FUNCTION** | Writes characters to a file. |
| **SYNTAX** | `FWRITE( <expN1>, <expC2> [, <expN3>] )` |
| **PARAMETERS** | <expN1>   DOS file handle number<br><expC2>   Character expression to be written<br><expN3>   The number of bytes to write |
| **RETURNS** | <expN>   Numeric value |
| **LIBRARY** | CLIPPER.LIB |
| **DESCRIPTION** | This function writes the contents of <expC2> to the file designated by its file handle <expN1>. If used, <expN3> is the number of bytes in <expC2> to write.<br><br>The returned value is the number of bytes successfully written to the DOS file. If the returned value is 0, an error has occurred (unless this is intended). A successful write occurs when the number returned by FWRITE( ) is equal to either LEN( <expC2>) or <expC3>.<br><br>The value of <expC2> is the string or variable to be written to the open DOS file <expN1>.<br><br>The value of <expN3> is the number of bytes to write out to the file. The disk write begins with the current file position in <expN1>. If this variable is not used, the entire contents of <expC2> is written to the file.<br><br>To truncate a file, a call of FWRITE( nHandle, " ", 0 ) is needed. |
| **SEE ALSO** | FREAD( ), FCLOSE( ), FOPEN( ), FCREATE( ), FERROR( ) |
| **EXAMPLE** | Please see Chapter 14. |

## GAUGEDISP( )

| | |
|---|---|
| **FUNCTION** | Displays a gauge to the screen. |
| **SYNTAX** | `GAUGEDISP( <expA1> )` |
| **PARAMETER** | <expA1>   Array holding gauge information |
| **RETURNS** | <expA>   Reference to gauge array |
| **LIBRARY** | SAMPLES.LIB |

| | |
|---|---|
| **DESCRIPTION** | This function displays the contents of the gauge array <expA1> that was created by the GAUGENEW( ) function. It is used to simulate a gas-gauge indicator. |
| **SEE ALSO** | GAUGENEW( ), GAUGEUPDAT( ) |
| **EXAMPLE** | See the GAUGEUPDAT( ) function. |

## GAUGENEW( )

| | | |
|---|---|---|
| **FUNCTION** | Creates a new gauge array. | |
| **SYNTAX** | GAUGENEW( <expN1>, <expN2>, <expN3>, <expN4> [, <expC5>] [, <expC6>] [, <expC7>] ) | |
| **PARAMETERS** | <expN1> | Top row coordinate of gauge region |
| | <expN2> | Left column coordinate of gauge region |
| | <expN3> | Bottom row coordinate of gauge region |
| | <expN4> | Right column coordinate of gauge region |
| | <expC5> | Background color setting of gauge region |
| | <expC6> | Color of gauge indicator |
| | <expC7> | Character symbol for gauge indicator |
| **RETURNS** | <expA> | A gauge array |
| **LIBRARY** | SAMPLES.LIB | |
| **DESCRIPTION** | This function builds and returns an array that holds display information that will display a gas-gauge indicator. The coordinate of the window region for the gauge begins at <expN1>, <expN2> and continues through to <expN3>, <expN4>.<br><br>The color of the gauge region may be assigned by <expC5>. The default color for <expC5> will be "W/N". The color of the gauge indicator may be specified to <expC6> which will have a default color setting of "W+/N". The character used as the gauge indicator may be specified as <expC7> with a default of CHR(219). | |
| **SEE ALSO** | GAUGEDISP( ), GAUGEUPDAT( ) | |
| **EXAMPLE** | Please see the GAUGEUPDAT( ) function. | |

## GAUGEUPDAT( )

| | |
|---|---|
| **FUNCTION** | Updates internal gauge information and displays to the screen. |
| **SYNTAX** | GAUGEUPDAT( <expA1>, <expN2> ) |

**PARAMETERS** &lt;expA1&gt;  Array of gauge information created by GAUGENEW( )
&lt;expN2&gt;  Numeric value representing percent completed

**RETURNS** &lt;expA&gt;  A reference to updated gauge array

**LIBRARY** SAMPLES.LIB

**DESCRIPTION** This function takes the gauge array &lt;expA1&gt; created by the GAUGENEW( ) function, displays the gauge to the screen, and calculates the percentage based on the value &lt;expN2&gt;.

**SEE ALSO** GAUGEDISP( ), GAUGENEW( )

**EXAMPLE**

```
 1 : * File       Gaugdemo.prg
 2 : * Compile    RMake sampmore /dFILE:gaugdemo
 3 :
 4 : procedure Main()
 5 :
 6 :    local aGauge
 7 :    local nStart
 8 :
 9 :    cls
10 :    ? "First, let's create a Gauge Array:"
11 :
12 :    aGauge := gaugenew(maxrow()-3, 0, maxrow()-1, maxcol())
13 :
14 :    ? "This beast has the following number of elements to it:", ;
15 :       len( aGauge )
16 :
17 :    inkey(2)
18 :
19 :    ? "Now, let's draw it to the screen..."
20 :    GaugeDisplay( aGauge )
21 :
22 :    setpos(4,0)   // Must re-position the cursor
23 :    inkey(2)
24 :
25 :    ? "Now, let's just engage it for 60 seconds..."
26 :    nStart := seconds()
27 :
28 :    while seconds() <= nStart+60
29 :       GaugeUpdate( aGauge, (seconds()-nStart) / 60 )
30 :    enddo
31 :    setpos(5,0)
32 :    ? "Press any key for indexing with the Gauge!"
33 :    inkey(0)
34 :    cls
35 :    ? "Indexing a file... one moment...."
36 :
37 :    if file( "Filenos.dbf" )   // there is a file
38 :       GaugeDisplay( aGauge )  // Must do this one.....
39 :       use Filenos new
40 :       index on Filenos->sub_no to temp ;
41 :           eval (GaugeUpdate( aGauge, recno()/lastrec() ), .t.)
42 :       dbcloseall()
```

```
43 :      ferase( "Temp.ntx" )
44 :    endif
45 :    setpos(0,0)
46 :    ? "Index file created.  Press any key to terminate program..."
47 :    inkey(0)
48 :    scroll()
49 :
50 : // End of File: GuagDemo.prg
```

## GETACTIVE( )

| | |
|---|---|
| **FUNCTION** | Obtains the currently active GET object. |
| **SYNTAX** | GETACTIVE() |
| **PARAMETER** | None |
| **RETURNS** | <expO>    Clipper GET object |
| **LIBRARY** | CLIPPER.LIB |
| **DESCRIPTION** | This function returns the currently active GET object that is being processed by the READMODAL( ) function or the READ command. If no GET object is active, the function will return a NIL data type. |
| **SEE ALSO** | READMODAL( ), GETNEW( ) |
| **EXAMPLE** | See Chapter 16. |

## GETAPPLYKEY( )

| | | |
|---|---|---|
| **FUNCTION** | Applies the ASCII value of a key to a GET object. | |
| **SYNTAX** | GETAPPLYKEY( <expO1>, <expN2> ) | |
| **PARAMETERS** | <expO1> | GET object to be used in READ |
| | <expN2> | ASCII value from INKEY(0) |
| **LIBRARY** | CLIPPER.LIB | |
| **DESCRIPTION** | This function takes the value from <expN2> and applies it to the GET object in <expO1>. Cursor key values are applied to cursor movement methods; data keys are entered into the GET system by default. If the value of <expN2> is set to a SETKEY( ) procedure, this function will execute the code block/procedure assigned to that key. | |

| | |
|---|---|
| | The GET object in <expO1> must be considered "in focus" before any keystroke is applied. |
| **SEE ALSO** | SETKEY( ), GETREADER( ), READMODAL( ) |

## GETDOSETKEY( )

| | |
|---|---|
| **FUNCTION** | Executes a code block in SETKEY( ) while preserving the context of the passed GET object. |
| **SYNTAX** | `GETDOSETKEY( <expO1> )` |
| **PARAMETER** | <expO1>   GET object to be used in READ |
| **LIBRARY** | CLIPPER.LIB |
| **DESCRIPTION** | This function executes a code block found in a SETKEY( ) stack and preserves the context of the passed GET object. The procedure name, line number, and variable name are automatically passed to the code block for evaluation. |
| **SEE ALSO** | GETREADER( ), GETPREVALIDATE( ), GETPOSTVALIDATE( ) |

## GETENV( )

| | |
|---|---|
| **FUNCTION** | Obtains DOS environmental settings. |
| **SYNTAX** | `GETENV( <expC1> )` |
| **PARAMETER** | <expC1>   Environmental variable to obtain |
| **RETURNS** | <expC>   Value of that variable |
| **LIBRARY** | EXTEND.LIB |
| **DESCRIPTION** | This function yields a string that is the value of the environmental variable <expC1>, which is stored at the DOS level with the SET command. If no environmental variable can be found, the value of the function will be a NULL byte. |
| **NOTE** | In previous versions, the GETE( ) function was used in place of the GETENV( ) function. In Clipper 5.2, the GETE( ) function continues to be supported although it is no longer documented. |

## EXAMPLE

```
 1 : * File:      Getedemo.prg
 2 : * Compile:   Rmake sample /dFILE:Getedemo
 3 :
 4 : procedure Main()
 5 :
 6 :   cls
 7 :   qout( getenv("COMSPEC") )
 8 :   qout( getenv("NOSPEC") )    // This should be blank!
 9 :   qout( getenv("PATH") )
10 :
11 :   if empty( getenv("PROCOUNT") )
12 :     qout( "Try entering 'SET PROCOUNT=b1;f2;r4' at DOS prompt" )
13 :   else
14 :     qout( "The PROCOUNT environment is set to:", GETENV("PROCOUNT") )
15 :   endif
16 :
17 : // End of File: Getedemo.prg
```

# GETNEW( )

| | |
|---|---|
| **FUNCTION** | Generates a GET object. |
| **SYNTAX** | GETNEW( [<expN1>] [, <expN2>] [, <expB3>] [,<expC4> [, <expC5>] [, <expC6>] ) |
| **PARAMETERS** | <expN1>   Numeric row position. |
| | <expN2>   Numeric column position. |
| | <expB3>   Code block for SET/GET variable in GET object. Do not use MEMVARBLOCK for arrays in a GET. |
| | <expC4>   Character expression of the variable in the SET/GET code block. |
| | <expC5>   Character expression of GET picture clause. |
| | <expC6>   Character expression of GET color string. |
| **RETURNS** | <expO>   Clipper GET object |
| **LIBRARY** | CLIPPER.LIB |
| **DESCRIPTION** | This function generates a Clipper GET object with the following object structure: |

| Instance Variables | Description |
|---|---|
| BADDATE | Indicates if the edit buffer has an invalid date. |
| BLOCK | Code block associated with a GET variable. |

| Instance Variables | Description |
| --- | --- |
| BUFFER | Character value defining the edit buffer. |
| CARGO | A user-definable slot. |
| CHANGED | A toggle indicating if GET:BUFFER has changed. |
| CLEAR | A toggle indicating whether the editing buffer should be cleared. |
| COL | The GET column number. |
| COLORSPEC | The GET object's display attributes. |
| DECPOS | The decimal point location within the edit buffer. |
| EXITSTATE | A system value to record the means used by the GET object to exit. |
| HASFOCUS | A flag that indicates whether the GET object has the input focus. |
| MINUS | Toggle indicating whether or not the GET object has input focus. |
| NAME | The GET variable name. |
| ORIGINAL | Character string containing original value of GET variable. For updating the buffer, use the varGet( ) and varPut( ) methods for the GET object. |
| PICTURE | A picture string for the GET variable. |
| POS | The current cursor location within the edit buffer. |
| POSTBLOCK | A code block to validate a newly entered value. |
| PREBLOCK | A code block to decide if an edit condition is permitted. |
| READER | A code block used to implement special read behaviors. |
| REJECTED | A toggle that indicates if the last inserted or overwritten character was rejected. |
| ROW | The GET row number. |
| SUBSCRIPT | An array of element positions if the data source is an array element. |
| TYPE | The GET variable data type. |
| TYPEOUT | A logical flag that indicates an attempt to move the cursor out of the edit buffer. |

| Methods | Description |
| --- | --- |
| ASSIGN( ) | Assigns the edit buffer to a GET variable. |
| COLORDISP( ) | Changes a GET object's color and then redisplays it. |
| DISPLAY( ) | Displays the GET on screen. |
| KILLFOCUS( ) | Takes the input focus away from the GET object. |
| RESET( ) | Resets internal state information on GET. |
| SETFOCUS( ) | Gives the input focus to the GET object. |
| UNDO( ) | Sets the GET variable back to GET:ORIGINAL. |
| UNTRANSFORM( ) | Converts character values to original data type. |
| UPDATEBUFFER( ) | Updates the edit buffer and redisplays the GET. |
| VARGET( ) | Returns the current value of the GET variable. |
| VARPUT( ) | Places the GET variable into a passed value. |

| Cursor Methods | Description |
| --- | --- |
| END( ) | Moves the cursor to the rightmost position. |
| HOME( ) | Moves the cursor to the leftmost position. |
| LEFT( ) | Moves the cursor left 1 position. |
| RIGHT( ) | Moves the cursor right 1 position. |
| TODECPOS( ) | Moves the cursor right of GET:DECPOS. |
| WORDLEFT( ) | Moves the cursor left one word. |
| WORDRIGHT( ) | Moves the cursor right one word. |

| Editing Methods | Description |
| --- | --- |
| BACKSPACE( ) | Moves the cursor left and deletes one character. |
| DELETE( ) | Deletes the character directly under the cursor. |
| DELEND( ) | Deletes characters from current cursor position to end of GET buffer. |
| DELLEFT( ) | Deletes the character left of the cursor. |
| DELRIGHT( ) | Deletes the character right of the cursor. |
| DELWORDLEFT( ) | Deletes the word left of the cursor. |
| DELWORDRIGHT( ) | Deletes the word right of the cursor. |

|  | Entry Methods | Description |
|---|---|---|
|  | INSERT( ) | Allows characters to be inserted. |
|  | OVERSTRIKE( ) | Allows characters to be overwritten. |

**SEE ALSO** READMODAL( ), GETACTIVE( ), READ

**EXAMPLE** See Chapter 16.

## GETPATH( )

**FUNCTION** Returns location of file found in search path.

**SYNTAX** `GETPATH( <expC1>, <expC2> )`

**PARAMETERS**
- \<expC1\> File name to search for
- \<expC2\> DOS search path

**RETURNS** \<expX\> NIL or directory in which file was found

**LIBRARY** SAMPLES.LIB

**DESCRIPTION** This function will attempt to search for the file \<expC1\> in the path specified as \<expC2\>; if it is found, it will return the directory name containing the file. If the file is not found in the search path (typically the DOS PATH environmental string), then the function will return a NIL value.

**SEE ALSO** FULLPATH( ), FILEBASE( ), GETENV( ), SET( ), FILE( )

## GETPREVALIDATE( )

**FUNCTION** Validates a GET object prior to giving it focus.

**SYNTAX** `GETPREVALIDATE( <expO1> )`

**PARAMETER** \<expO1\> GET object to be used in READ

**RETURNS** \<expL\> Logical expression

**LIBRARY** CLIPPER.LIB

**DESCRIPTION** This function takes the GET object in \<expO1\> and attempts to evaluate the code block used in the WHEN condition, if present. If the function returns a logical true (.T.), the GET object has been prevalidated successfully.

**SEE ALSO** GETREADER( ), GETPOSTVALIDATE( ), GETDOSETKEY( )

## GETPOSTVALIDATE( )

**FUNCTION**  Validates a GET object after giving it focus.

**SYNTAX**  `GETPOSTVALIDATE( <expO1> )`

**PARAMETER**  <expO1>  GET object to be used in READ

**RETURNS**  <expL>  Logical expression

**LIBRARY**  CLIPPER.LIB

**DESCRIPTION**  This function takes the GET object in <expO1> and attempts to evaluate the code block used in the VALID condition, if present. If the function returns a logical true (.T.), the GET object has been postvalidated successfully.

**SEE ALSO**  GETREADER( ), GETPREVALIDATE( ), GETDOSETKEY( )

## GETREADER( )

**FUNCTION**  Implements the standard read behavior for active GETS.

**SYNTAX**  `GETREADER( <expO1> )`

**PARAMETER**  <expO1>  GET object to be used in READ

**LIBRARY**  CLIPPER.LIB

**DESCRIPTION**  This function actually READs the specified GET object in <expO1>. This function is called by the READMODAL( ) function.

**SEE ALSO**  READMODAL( ), GETAPPLYKEY( ), GETNEW( )

## HARDCR( )

**FUNCTION**  Globally replaces all soft carriage returns with hard carriage returns.

**SYNTAX**  `HARDCR( <expC1> )`

**PARAMETER**  <expC1>  Any character string

**RETURNS**  <expC>  Formatted character string

**LIBRARY**  EXTEND.LIB

| | |
|---|---|
| **DESCRIPTION** | This function replaces all soft carriage returns [ CHR(141) ] found in the character expression<expC1> with the hard carriage return [CHR(13) ].<br><br>This function will only work for CHR(141)+CHR(10) combinations. If a CHR(141) character exists by itself, without a following CHR(10) character, the function will not replace it with a CHR(13). |
| **SEE ALSO** | MEMOTRAN( ), STRTRAN( ), MEMOEDIT( ) |
| **EXAMPLE** | Please see Chapter 11. |

# HEADER( )

| | |
|---|---|
| **FUNCTION** | Returns the length of a database file header. |
| **SYNTAX** | HEADER() |
| **PARAMETER** | None |
| **RETURNS** | <expN>   The numeric size of a database file header in bytes |
| **LIBRARY** | EXTEND.LIB |
| **DESCRIPTION** | This function returns the number of bytes in the header of the selected database or the database in the designated work area. |
| **NOTE** | If used in conjunction with the LASTREC( ), RECSIZE( ), and DISKSPACE( ) functions, this function is capable of implementing a backup and restore routine. |
| **SEE ALSO** | LASTREC( ), RECSIZE( ), DISKSPACE( ) |
| **EXAMPLE** | See the RECSIZE( ) function. |

# I2BIN( )

| | |
|---|---|
| **FUNCTION** | Converts numeric integer to 16-bit binary string |
| **SYNTAX** | I2BIN( <expN1> ) |
| **PARAMETER** | <expN1>   Numeric integer |
| **RETURNS** | <expC>   16-bit binary character |
| **LIBRARY** | EXTEND.LIB |

| | |
|---|---|
| **DESCRIPTION** | This function converts the integer <expN1> to a 16-bit binary integer in character format, in which the least significant byte is first. If there are decimal values in <expN1> they will be truncated. |
| **SEE ALSO** | BIN2I( ), BIN2L( ), BIN2W( ), CHR( ), L2BIN( ), FWRITE( ), FREAD( ) |
| **EXAMPLE** | Please see Chapter 14. |

## IEVAL( )

| | | |
|---|---|---|
| **FUNCTION** | Evaluates a code block a specified number of times. | |
| **SYNTAX** | `IEVAL( <expN1>, <expB2> )` | |
| **PARAMETERS** | <expN1> | Numeric top range for the code block iterations |
| | <expB2> | Code block to be evaluated |
| **RETURNS** | <expX> | The value of the last iteration within the code block |
| **LIBRARY** | SAMPLES.LIB | |
| **DESCRIPTION** | This function will evaluate the code block <expB2>, <expN1> times. The starting position of the internal incrementation starts at 1 and increments in whole steps through to the value of <expN1>. If <expN1> is not an integer, the decimal values will be truncated. The function will return the value of the code block on the last iteration. | |
| **SEE ALSO** | AEVAL( ), EVAL( ), DBEVAL( ) | |

**EXAMPLE**

```
 1 : * File     IEval.prg
 2 : * Compile Rmake sampmore /dFILE:ievaldemo
 3 :
 4 : procedure Main()
 5 :
 6 :    cls
 7 :
 8 :    // The following will print out 100 through 2300 to the screen
 9 :    // and then wait for a key to be pressed
10 :    ieval( 23, {|nItem| qout(nItem * 100)} )
11 :    inkey(0)
12 :
13 :    cls
14 :    ? "And now the value of the function is: ", ;
15 :       ieval( 23, {|nItem| nItem*100} )          // should be 2300
16 :
17 : // End of File: Ievademo.prg
```

# IF( )

**FUNCTION**  Tests a condition and returns results.

**SYNTAX**  IF( <expL1>, <expX2>, <expX3> ) | IIF( <expL1>, <expX2>, <expX3> )

**PARAMETERS**
<expL1>  Any expression that results in a logical evaluation
<expX2>  Any expression to be executed if the condition is true
<expX3>  Any expression to be executed if the condition is false

**RETURNS**  <expX>  Any expression

**LIBRARY**  CLIPPER.LIB

**DESCRIPTION**  This function returns <expX2> if the evaluation of <expL1> is a logical true (.T.); otherwise, the function will return <expX3> if <expL1> evaluates to logical false (.F.).

**SEE ALSO**  DO CASE, IF

**EXAMPLE**

```
 1 : * File:     Ifdemo.prg
 2 : * Compile:  RMake Sample /DFILE:IFDEMO
 3 :
 4 : procedure Main()
 5 :
 6 :    local nVal1 := 0
 7 :    local nVal2 := 23
 8 :    local nVal3 := 16
 9 :
10 :
11 :    cls
12 :    // The IF() function can be very straightforward.  In this first
13 :    // example, a simple comparison is made and a string becomes the value
14 :    // of the IF() function.  This string is printed to the console.
15 :
16 :    qout( if( date() == date(),     ; // Condition
17 :         "The date equals itself", ; // TRUE output
18 :         "ERROR" ) )                  // FALSE output
19 :
20 :    // Sometimes, especially when numerics are involved, run-time errors may
21 :    // be avoided.  Here, since nVal1 is 0, a division on it would be fatal.
22 :    // Since only one side of the IF() function is compared at any one time,
23 :    // all is well.
24 :
25 :    qout( if( empty(nVal1), ;        // Condition
26 :              0, ;                   // TRUE value
27 :              nVal2 / nVal1 ) )      // FALSE value
28 :
29 :    // Nested and complex IF() functions may be built, with the value of one
30 :    // IF() being compared or expressed in an option or parameter of the other.
31 :
32 :    qout( if( nVal3 < nVal2 .and. EMPTY( nVal1 ), ;  // Condition
```

```
33 :            if( !empty(nVal2 % nVal3), ;      // TRUE value #1
34 :                "Value1", ;                    // TRUE value #2
35 :                "Value2" ), ;                  // FALSE value #2
36 :            "Value3" ) )                       // FALSE value #1
37 :
38 : // End of File: Ifdemo.prg
```

# INDEXEXT( )

| | |
|---|---|
| **FUNCTION** | Returns the file extension of the index module used in an application. |
| **SYNTAX** | INDEXEXT() |
| **PARAMETER** | None |
| **RETURNS** | <expC>    Character expression |
| **LIBRARY** | CLIPPER.LIB |
| **DESCRIPTION** | This function returns a string that tells what indexes are to be used or will be created in the compiled application. The default value is ".NTX". This is controlled by the particular database driver that is linked with the application. |
| **SEE ALSO** | INDEX ON, INDEXKEY( ), INDEXORD( ) |

# INDEXKEY( )

| | |
|---|---|
| **FUNCTION** | Yields the key expression of a specified index file. |
| **SYNTAX** | INDEXKEY( <expN1> ) |
| **PARAMETER** | <expN1>   Order of the index file in the USE...INDEX or SET INDEX TO command |
| **RETURNS** | <expC>    The index key |
| **LIBRARY** | CLIPPER.LIB |
| **DESCRIPTION** | This function returns the character string stored in the header of an index file.<br><br>The index key is displayed for an index file that is designated by <expN1>, its position in the USE...INDEX or SET INDEX TO command in the currently selected or designated work area. If there is no corresponding index key at the specified order position, a NULL byte will be returned. |
| **SEE ALSO** | INDEX ON, SET ORDER TO, INDEXORD( ) |

## INDEXORD( )

| | |
|---|---|
| **FUNCTION** | Returns the numeric position of the controlling index. |
| **SYNTAX** | INDEXORD() |
| **PARAMETER** | None |
| **RETURNS** | <expN>   Ordinal position of a controlling index |
| **LIBRARY** | EXTEND.LIB |
| **DESCRIPTION** | The INDEXORD( ) function returns the numeric position of the current controlling index in the selected or designated work area.

A returned value of 0 indicates that no active index is controlling the database, which therefore is in its natural order. |
| **SEE ALSO** | INDEXKEY( ), SET ORDER TO |

## INKEY( )

| | |
|---|---|
| **FUNCTION** | Returns a numeric value for the key currently pressed. |
| **SYNTAX** | INKEY( [<expN1>] ) |
| **PARAMETER** | <expN1>   Seconds to wait for a keypress |
| **RETURNS** | <expN>   Code value for the key pressed |
| **LIBRARY** | CLIPPER.LIB |
| **DESCRIPTION** | This function allows direct input from the keyboard at specified times during an operation.

If <expN1> is specified and its value is greater than 0, this function will wait <expN1> seconds for a key to be pressed. If a key is pressed within that time frame, the value of the key pressed will be the value of the function. If no key is pressed, the value of the function will be 0.

If <expN1> is 0, the function will wait indefinitely for a key to be pressed. If <expN1> is not specified, the function will return the value of the key pressed at the very moment the function is called.

INKEY( ) will return the ASCII value of all printable characters. Nonprintable characters have been assigned special values, however, so that the value of the function can range from –39 to 387. |
| **SEE ALSO** | LASTKEY( ), NEXTKEY( ), CHR( ), ASC( ), SET KEY |
| **EXAMPLE** | See the LASTKEY( ) function. |

## INKEYWAIT( )

| | |
|---|---|
| **FUNCTION** | Identical to INKEY( ) except that it observes any SET KEY stack operation/assignment. |
| **SYNTAX** | INKEYWAIT( <expN1> ) |
| **PARAMETER** | <expN1>   Number of seconds to wait |
| **RETURNS** | <expN>   ASCII value of the key pressed |
| **LIBRARY** | SAMPLES.LIB |
| **DESCRIPTION** | This function is almost identical to the INKEY( ) function except that if a key is pressed and if that key has been previously assigned to a SET KEY operation, this function will perform the SET KEY operation before returning control to the calling subroutine.<br><br>The function will pass to the SET KEY code block two parameters: the name of the calling subroutine and the line number of execution. Please note that unlike the INKEY( ) function, the parameter to this function is required: The lowest value for <expN1> is .01 second. |
| **SEE ALSO** | INKEY( ), SETKEY( ), WAIT, MENU TO, READ |

## INT( )

| | |
|---|---|
| **FUNCTION** | Returns the integer portion of a numeric value. |
| **SYNTAX** | INT( <expN1> ) |
| **PARAMETER** | <expN1>   Any numeric value |
| **RETURNS** | <expN>   Integer portion of the numeric value |
| **LIBRARY** | CLIPPER.LIB |
| **DESCRIPTION** | This function converts a numeric expression to an integer. All decimal digits are truncated. This function does not round a value upward or downward; it merely truncates a numeric expression. |
| **SEE ALSO** | ROUND( ), STRZERO( ). |

## ISALPHA( )

| | |
|---|---|
| **FUNCTION** | Determines whether the leftmost character in a string is an alphabetic character. |
| **SYNTAX** | ISALPHA( <expC1> ) |
| **PARAMETER** | <expC1>   Any character string |
| **RETURNS** | <expL>   Logical true (.T.) or false (.F.) |
| **LIBRARY** | EXTEND.LIB |
| **DESCRIPTION** | This function returns a logical true (.T.) if the first character in <expC1> is an alphabetic character. If not, the function will return a logical false (.F.). |
| **SEE ALSO** | ISDIGIT( ), ISLOWER( ), UPPER( ), LOWER( ) |
| **EXAMPLE** | See the UPPER( ) function. |

## ISCOLOR( )

| | |
|---|---|
| **FUNCTION** | Tests for a color monitor or color adapter card. |
| **SYNTAX** | ISCOLOR() |
| **PARAMETER** | None |
| **RETURNS** | <expL>   Logical true (.T.) or false (.F.) |
| **LIBRARY** | CLIPPER.LIB |
| **DESCRIPTION** | This function returns a logical true (.T.) if a color graphics card has been installed on the computer executing the Clipper application. If no card is present, the function will return a logical false (.F.). |
| **SEE ALSO** | SET COLOR, SETCOLOR( ) |

## ISDIGIT( )

| | |
|---|---|
| **FUNCTION** | Checks if leftmost character is a digit character. |
| **SYNTAX** | ISDIGIT( <expC1> ) |

| | |
|---|---|
| **PARAMETER** | <expC1>   Any character string |
| **RETURNS** | <expL>   Logical true (.T.) or logical false (.F.) |
| **LIBRARY** | EXTEND.LIB |
| **DESCRIPTION** | This function takes the character string <expC1> and checks to see if the leftmost character is a digit, from 1 to 9. If so, the function will return a logical true (.T.) value; otherwise, it will return a logical false (.F.) |
| **SEE ALSO** | ISALPHA( ), ISUPPER( ), ISLOWER( ), UPPER( ), LOWER( ) |

## ISLOWER( )

| | |
|---|---|
| **FUNCTION** | Checks to see if the leftmost character is a lowercased letter. |
| **SYNTAX** | `ISLOWER( <expC1> )` |
| **PARAMETER** | <expC1>   Any character expression |
| **RETURNS** | <expL>   Logical true (.T.) or a logical false (.F.) |
| **LIBRARY** | EXTEND.LIB |
| **DESCRIPTION** | This function takes the character string <expC1> and checks to see if the leftmost character is a lowercased letter. If so, the function will return a logical true (.T.) value; otherwise, it will return a logical false (.F.) |
| **SEE ALSO** | ISALPHA( ), ISDIGIT( ), ISUPPER( ), UPPER( ), LOWER( ) |

## ISPRINTER( )

| | |
|---|---|
| **FUNCTION** | Checks to see if the LPT1 port is ready. |
| **SYNTAX** | `ISPRINTER()` |
| **PARAMETER** | None |
| **RETURNS** | <expL>   Logical true (.T.) or logical false (.F.) |
| **LIBRARY** | EXTEND.LIB |
| **DESCRIPTION** | This function will return a logical true (.T.) if the LPT1 port is ready; otherwise, it will return a logical false (.F.) value.<br><br>It is important to keep in mind that this function is hardware-dependent and may work only on some machines. |
| **SEE ALSO** | ISCOLOR( ), SET( ) |

## ISUPPER( )

**FUNCTION**  Checks to see if the leftmost character is an uppercased letter.

**SYNTAX**  `ISUPPER( <expC1> )`

**PARAMETER**  <expC1>   Any character expression

**RETURNS**  Logical true (.T.) or a logical false (.F.)

**LIBRARY**  EXTEND.LIB

**DESCRIPTION**  This function takes the character string <expC1> and checks to see if the leftmost character is a lowercased letter. If so, the function will return a logical true (.T.) value; otherwise, it will return a logical false (.F.)

**SEE ALSO**  ISALPHA( ), ISDIGIT( ), ISLOWER( ), LOWER( ), UPPER( )

## LASTKEY( )

**FUNCTION**  Returns the value of the last key processed.

**SYNTAX**  `LASTKEY( )`

**PARAMETER**  None

**RETURNS**  <expN>   ASCII character code of last key pressed

**LIBRARY**  CLIPPER.LIB

**DESCRIPTION**  This function returns the ASCII character code of the last key pressed and held by Clipper's keyboard buffer. As keys are processed during a Clipper wait state (i.e., ACCEPT, INKEY(0), INPUT, DBEDIT( ), ACHOICE( ), MEMOEDIT( ), READ, or WAIT), each key pressed is given to this function. This function will only hold one key value at a time; the current key processed will replace the previous value of LASTKEY( ).

**NOTE**  In some cases, the ESC key, which aborts some functions, needs to be cleared from the I/O buffer before the next operation is processed. For further examples of this, see Chapter 5.

**SEE ALSO**  INKEY(0), NEXTKEY( ), INKEYWAIT( ), KEYBOARD, TYPEAHEAD

## EXAMPLE

```
 1 : * File      Keysdemo.prg
 2 : * Compile Rmake sample /dFILE:keysdemo
 3 :
 4 : #include "PTVerbs.ch"   // Power Tools Header file of commands/statements
 5 : #include "PTInkey.ch"   // Power Tools header file of ASCII values
 6 :
 7 : procedure Main()
 8 :
 9 :   local cTemp            // A temporary string
10 :   local getlist := {}    // This is for the GET and the READ command
11 :
12 :   PROCESS    // Similar to the WHILE .t.
13 :
14 :     cTemp := space(10)
15 :     cls
16 :
17 :     devpos(8,10)
18 :     devout("Press ESC to abort...")
19 :
20 :     @ 10,10 say "Enter something more than 3 characters! " GET cTemp
21 :     read
22 :
23 :     if lastkey() == pESC
24 :        exit
25 :     endif
26 :
27 :     keyboard alltrim( cTemp )   // O.k... stuff the keyboard
28 :     inkey(0)                    // remove first one in from stack
29 :
30 :     devpos(12,10)
31 :     devout("The lastkey processed was")
32 :     devpos(12,55)
33 :     devout( chr( lastkey() ) )
34 :
35 :     devpos(13,10)
36 :     devout("The value of the key being processed is")
37 :     devpos(13,55)
38 :     devout( chr( inkey(0) ) )
39 :
40 :     devpos(14,10)
41 :     devout("The next key to BE processed is")
42 :     devpos(14,55)
43 :     devout( chr( nextkey() ) )
44 :
45 :     devpos(20,10)
46 :     devout("Please press any key to continue...")
47 :     clear typeahead
48 :
49 :     INKEY(0)
50 :
51 :   END PROCESS    // Similar to the ENDDO statement
52 :
53 : // End of File: Keysdemo.prg
```

## LASTREC( )

| | |
|---|---|
| **FUNCTION** | Returns the number of records in an active work area or database. |
| **SYNTAX** | LASTREC() |
| **PARAMETER** | None |
| **RETURNS** | <expN>   Numeric expression |
| **LIBRARY** | CLIPPER.LIB |
| **DESCRIPTION** | This function returns the number of records present in the database in the selected or designated work area. If no records are present, the value of this function will be 0. Additionally, if no database is in use in the selected or designated work area, this function will return a 0 value as well.<br><br>The SET FILTER TO and SET DELETED TO command have no effect on the value obtained from this function. |
| **SEE ALSO** | RECCOUNT( ), EOF( ), GO BOTTOM, RECNO( ), DBGOBOTTOM( ) |

## LEFT( )

| | |
|---|---|
| **FUNCTION** | Extracts the leftmost substring of a character expression. |
| **SYNTAX** | LEFT( <expC1>, <expN2> ) |
| **PARAMETERS** | <expC1>   Main character expression to be parsed<br><expN2>   Number of bytes to return beginning at the leftmost position |
| **RETURNS** | <expC>   Substring of evaluation |
| **LIBRARY** | CLIPPER.LIB |
| **DESCRIPTION** | This function returns the leftmost <expN2> characters of <expC1>. It is equivalent to the following programming expression:<br><br>    = SUBSTR( <expC1>, 1,<expN2> ) |
| **SEE ALSO** | SUBSTR( ), RIGHT( ), AT( ), RAT( ) |
| **EXAMPLE** | See the SUBSTR( ) function. |

# LEN( )

**FUNCTION**  Evaluates the length of a character expression or array.

**SYNTAX**  LEN( <expX1> )

**PARAMETER**  <expX1>  Any character expression, or the name of an array

**RETURNS**  <expN>  Numeric value

**LIBRARY**  CLIPPER.LIB

**DESCRIPTION**  If <expX1> is a character expression, this function returns the number of characters in <expX1>. If the character expression contains any CHR(0) characters, they will be added to the value obtained from this function. NULL bytes, by contrast, have no length.

If <expX1> is the name of an array, this function will return the number of initialized positions in the first dimension of that array. If the array <expX1> has no initialized subscript position in it, the value from this function will be 0.

**SEE ALSO**  TRIM( ), ALLTRIM( ), LTRIM( ), TRIM( )

**EXAMPLE**

```
 1 : * File     Lendemo.prg
 2 : * Compile Rmake sample /dFILE:Lendemo
 3 :
 4 : procedure Main()
 5 :
 6 :    local aTemp1 := {}
 7 :    local aTemp2 := { 1, 2, 3 }
 8 :    local cTemp3 := "This is a test!"
 9 :    local nTemp4 := 0
10 :    local nTemp5 := 1.23
11 :    local nTemp6 := 43243324123423
12 :
13 :    cls
14 :    qout( "            First, an empty array has length of: ", ;
15 :          len(aTemp1) )
16 :    qout( "Second, an array with 3 subscripts has length of: ", ;
17 :          len(aTemp2) )
18 :    qout( "                    The length of the string is: ", ;
19 :          len(cTemp3) )
20 :    wait
21 :
22 :    qout()
23 :    qout()
24 :    qout(" The length of the first number is: ", lennum( nTemp4 ) )
25 :    qout("The length of the second number is: ", lennum( nTemp5 ) )
26 :    qout("                 The final number is: ", lennum( nTemp6 ) )
27 :
28 : // End of File: Lendemo.prg
```

# LENNUM( )

| | |
|---|---|
| **FUNCTION** | Determines the length of a given number. |
| **SYNTAX** | LENNUM( <expN1> ) |
| **PARAMETER** | <expN1>   Numeric expression |
| **RETURNS** | <expN>   Numeric expression |
| **LIBRARY** | EXTEND.LIB |
| **DESCRIPTION** | This function returns the length of <expN1>. It is useful in determining relative column positions for numeric values. The TRANSFORM( ) function may be used as well. |
| **NOTE** | This is a compatibility function and may not be supported in future versions. |
| **SEE ALSO** | LEN( ), TRANSFORM( ), STR( ) |
| **EXAMPLE** | See the LEN( ) function. |

# LISTASARRAY( )

| | |
|---|---|
| **FUNCTION** | Converts a delimited string to an array. |
| **SYNTAX** | LISTASARRAY( <expC1> [, <expC2>] ) |
| **PARAMETERS** | <expC1>   String to be converted<br><expC2>   Optional delimiting character |
| **RETURNS** | <expA>   Array of items from string |
| **LIBRARY** | SAMPLES.LIB |
| **DESCRIPTION** | This function takes the string <expC1> and attempts to convert it into an array. Elements in the array are determined by the string delimiter <expC2> which, if not passed, defaults to the "," character. |
| **SEE ALSO** | SUBSTR( ), AT( ), RAT( ) |

**EXAMPLE**

```
1 : * File     LaaDemo.prg
2 : * Compile RMake sampmore /dFILE:laademo
3 :
4 : procedure Main()
5 :
6 :    local aColors := listasarray( setcolor() )
7 :    local nCount
8 :
```

```
 9 :     scroll()
10 :     @ 10,10 say "This will be in reverse coloring" color aColors[2]
11 :
12 :     if iscolor()
13 :        setcolor( "W/B,B/W,,,GR+/B" )    // First, we have to make a setting
14 :        aColors := listasarray( setcolor() )
15 :        @ 13,10 say "The color setting is now..."
16 :        devout( setcolor() )
17 :        qout( "And the individually parsed values are: " )
18 :        for nCount := 1 to len( aColors )
19 :           qout( "Item number", nCount )
20 :           qqout( "  ==  ", aColors[nCount] )
21 :        next
22 :     endif
23 :
24 : // End of File: Laademo.prg
```

## LOG( )

| | |
|---|---|
| **FUNCTION** | Returns the natural logarithm of a number. |
| **SYNTAX** | LOG( <expN1> ) |
| **PARAMETER** | <expN1>    Any numeric expression |
| **RETURNS** | <expN>    Numeric value |
| **LIBRARY** | CLIPPER.LIB |
| **DESCRIPTION** | This function will return the natural logarithm of the number <expN1>.<br>If <expN1> is 0 or is less than 0, a numeric overflow condition exists, which is depicted on the display device as a series of asterisks.<br>This function is the inverse of EXP( ); however, due to rounding problems within Clipper, the LOG( ) of an EXP( ) of a number may not always return that number. |
| **SEE ALSO** | EXP( ) |

## LOWER( )

| | |
|---|---|
| **FUNCTION** | Universally lowercases a character string expression. |
| **SYNTAX** | LOWER( <expC1> ) |
| **PARAMETER** | <expC1>    Any character expression |
| **RETURNS** | <expC>    Lowercased value of <expC1> |
| **LIBRARY** | CLIPPER.LIB |

| | |
|---|---|
| **DESCRIPTION** | This function converts any character expression passed as <expC1> to its lowercase representation. Any nonalphabetic character within <expC1> will remain unchanged. |
| **SEE ALSO** | UPPER( ), ISLOWER( ), ISUPPER( ) |
| **EXAMPLE** | See the UPPER( ) function. |

## LTRIM( )

| | | |
|---|---|---|
| **FUNCTION** | Removes leading spaces from a string. | |
| **SYNTAX** | `LTRIM( <expC1> )` | |
| **PARAMETER** | <expC1> | Any character expression |
| **RETURNS** | <expC> | The same character expression with leading spaces removed |
| **LIBRARY** | CLIPPER.LIB | |
| **DESCRIPTION** | This function trims the leading blanks from the character string <expC1>. If <expC1> is a NULL byte, the function will simply return a NULL byte. | |
| **SEE ALSO** | TRIM( ), RTRIM( ), PADC( ), PADR( ), PADL( ) | |
| **EXAMPLE** | See the SUBSTR( ) function. | |

## LUPDATE( )

| | | |
|---|---|---|
| **FUNCTION** | Yields the date the database was last updated. | |
| **SYNTAX** | `LUPDATE()` | |
| **RETURNS** | <expD> | Date of last update |
| **LIBRARY** | EXTEND.LIB | |
| **DESCRIPTION** | This function returns the date recorded by DOS when the selected or designated database was last written to disk. This function will only work for those database files in USE. | |
| **SEE ALSO** | USE, DBUSEAREA( ), REPLACE, COMMIT | |

## L2BIN( )

| | |
|---|---|
| **FUNCTION** | Converts a numeric value to a 32-bit binary integer. |
| **SYNTAX** | `L2BIN( <expN1> )` |
| **PARAMETER** | <expN1>    Any numeric value |
| **RETURNS** | <expC>    Character string of conversion |
| **LIBRARY** | EXTEND.LIB |
| **DESCRIPTION** | This function takes a numeric integer expressed as <expN1> and converts it to a character string formatted as a 32-bit signed integer. |
| **SEE ALSO** | I2BIN( ), BIN2I( ), BIN2L( ), BIN2W( ) |
| **EXAMPLE** | Please see Chapter 14. |

## MAX( )

| | |
|---|---|
| **FUNCTION** | Returns the maximum of either two numbers or two dates. |
| **SYNTAX** | `MAX( <expX1>, <expX2> )` |
| **PARAMETERS** | <expX1>    Any numeric value, or any date value<br><expX2>    Any numeric value, or any date value |
| **RETURNS** | <expX>    Either a numeric or date value |
| **LIBRARY** | CLIPPER.LIB |
| **DESCRIPTION** | This function returns the larger of the two passed expressions. If <expX1> and <expX2> are numeric data types, the value returned by this function will be a numeric data type as well and will be the larger of the two numbers passed to it. If <expX1> and <expX2> are date data types, the returned value for this function will be a date data type as well; it will be the latest of the two dates passed to it. |
| **SEE ALSO** | MIN( ) |
| **EXAMPLE** | See the MAXROW( ) function. |

## MAXCOL( )

| | |
|---|---|
| **FUNCTION** | Determines the maximum number of columns in the present video mode. |

| | |
|---|---|
| **SYNTAX** | MAXCOL ( ) |
| **PARAMETER** | None |
| **RETURNS** | <expN>    Numeric expression |
| **LIBRARY** | CLIPPER.LIB |
| **DESCRIPTION** | This function returns the maximum number of columns available in the present mode of the video screen. Since the beginning column position is always 0, the default return value for this function is 79 in 80-column mode.<br><br>The value of this function may be altered by successfully calling the SETMODE( ) function. |
| **SEE ALSO** | ROW( ), COL( ), MAXROW( ), SETMODE( ) |
| **EXAMPLE** | See the MAXROW( ) function. |

## MAXROW( )

| | |
|---|---|
| **FUNCTION** | Determines the maximum number of rows in the present video mode. |
| **SYNTAX** | MAXROW ( ) |
| **PARAMETER** | None |
| **RETURNS** | <expN>    Numeric expression |
| **LIBRARY** | CLIPPER.LIB |
| **DESCRIPTION** | This function returns the maximum number of rows available in the present mode of the video screen. Since the beginning row position is always 0, the default return value for this function is 24 for a 25-column video display.<br><br>The value of this function may be altered by successfully calling the SETMODE( ) function. |
| **SEE ALSO** | ROW( ), COL( ), MAXCOL( ), SETMODE( ) |

**EXAMPLE**

```
 1 : * File       Maxdemo.prg
 2 : * Compile    Rmake sample /dFILE:maxdemo
 3 :
 4 : procedure Main()
 5 :
 6 :    local nTemp1 := 10
 7 :    local dTemp2 := date() - nTemp1
 8 :
 9 :    cls
10 :    ? "And now for some tests..."
```

```
11 :    ? max(nTemp1, 200), min(nTemp1, 200)
12 :    ? max(dTemp2, date()), min(dTemp2, date() )
13 :    wait
14 :
15 :    ? maxrow(), maxcol()
16 :
17 :    if setmode(43,80)
18 :       ? maxrow(), maxcol()
19 :       wait
20 :    endif
21 :
22 :    setmode(25,80)
23 :    cls
24 :
25 : // End of File: Maxdemo.prg
```

# MDY( )

| FUNCTION | Converts a date into a string. |
|---|---|
| SYNTAX | MDY( <expD1> ) |
| PARAMETER | <expD1>   Any date data type |
| RETURNS | <expC>   Converted string value |
| LIBRARY | SAMPLES.LIB |
| DESCRIPTION | This function takes the date expressed as <expD1> and converts it into a string that is formatted as: "MONTH DD, YYYY". |
| SEE ALSO | DMY( ), YEAR( ), DATE( ) |

# MEMOEDIT( )

| FUNCTION | Provides a basic string and memo editor. |
|---|---|
| SYNTAX | MEMOEDIT( [<expC1>] [, <expN2>] [, <expN3> ]<br>[,<expN4> ] [, <expN5>] [, <expL6>] [, <expC7>]<br>[, <expN8>] [,<expN9>] [, <expN10>] [, <expN11>]<br>[, <expN12>] [,<expN13>] ) |
| PARAMETERS | <expC1>   Character expression to edit/display |
|  | <expN2>   Top row coordinate |
|  | <expN3>   Left column coordinate |
|  | <expN4>   Bottom row coordinate |
|  | <expN5>   Right column coordinate |
|  | <expN6>   Logical true (.T.) or false (.F.) |

|          |           |                                  |
|----------|-----------|----------------------------------|
|          | <expC7>   | UDF to process keystrokes        |
|          | <expN8>   | Line length                      |
|          | <expN9>   | Tab size                         |
|          | <expN10>  | Number of the line with cursor   |
|          | <expN11>  | Column location of cursor        |
|          | <expN12>  | Numeric expression               |
|          | <expN13>  | Numeric expression               |
| **RETURNS**  | <expC>    | Character expression         |
| **LIBRARY**  | EXTEND.LIB |                              |

**DESCRIPTION** This function expands the ability to display, browse, or edit a memo field or a character string in a windowed area. It returns the displayed or edited string. The string or memo to be displayed or edited is specified as <expC1>, and the browsing area is specified as <expN2>, <expN3> for the top row, column coordinates to <expN4>, <expN5> for the bottom row, column coordinates. If not specified, the default values of these four parameters are 0, 0, MAXROW( ), and MAXCOL(<N>), respectively.

If the string or memo is to be edited, the value of <expL6> should be set to a logical true (.T.). To display it only, a value of logical false (.F.) should be used instead. The default value for this parameter is true (.T.)

The name of a Clipper user-defined function that processes keystrokes within the MEMOEDIT( ) function may be specified as <expC7>. Only the root name of the function is allowed to be passed without either parameter arguments or parentheses. If used, the name of the function must be within quotes. It will not be seen by the compiler and a symbolic token will not be generated for it. Therefore, unless the function is defined within the routine that calls it, make sure that the user-defined function is linked in with the application and is available at run time. To ensure this, an added EXTERNAL command line may be needed. If this parameter is not specified, the default routine for keystroke processing will be used.

The line length for the MEMOEDIT( ) function may be specified as well. If <expN8> is greater than the equation (<expN5> - <expN3> - 1), the window area will scroll horizontally until the maximum line length is reached.

The value of <expN9> is the tab size: The default value is 4.

The initial line for the MEMOEDIT( ) function to place the cursor on is specified in <expN10>: The default is 1.

The initial column in the line for the MEMOEDIT( ) function to place the cursor on is specified in <expN11>; the default is 0.

The initial row to place the cursor relative to the current window position of the MEMOEDIT( ) function is specified in parameter <expN12>; the default is 0.

The initial column to place the cursor relative to the current window position of the MEMOEDIT( ) function is specified in parameter <expN13>; the default is 0.

Three parameters may be passed to the user-defined function specified in <expC7>. These parameters are automatically passed to the subroutine and need to be specified in the parameter list within the function <expC7>. All, some, or none of the parameters can be accepted by the function. The three parameters, in order they are passed, are: (1) the mode of MEMOEDIT( ), (2) the current row in the edit, and (3) the current column in the edit.

The values for the mode of MEMOEDIT( ) are as follows:

| Modes | Description |
| --- | --- |
| 0 | Idle. |
| 1 | Reconfigurable or unknown keystroke; <expC1> remains unaltered. |
| 2 | Reconfigurable or unknown keystroke; <expC1> is altered. |
| 3 | Start-up condition. |

Since the routine that is called by MEMOEDIT( ) is a function, the value returned by the function tells MEMOEDIT( ) what to do. The values passed back from the user-defined function to MEMOEDIT( ) follow these guidelines:

| Return Value | Action in MEMOEDIT( ) |
| --- | --- |
| 0 | Performs the default action. |
| 1-31 | Performs the action that corresponds to a key value. |
| 32 | Ignores the current key pressed. |
| 33 | Processes the current key and toggles the insert control key. |
| 34 | Toggles the word-wrap control. |
| 35 | Toggles the scrolling control. |
| 100 | Moves to the next word. Resolves key value collisions. |
| 101 | Moves to the bottom right of the window area. Resolves key value collisions. |

By default, the action of cursor movement is as follows:

| | |
| --- | --- |
| Ctrl-E / Up Arrow | Up one line |
| Ctrl-C / Down Arrow | Down one line |
| Ctrl-S / Left Arrow | Left one line |

Command Function Reference 459

| | |
|---|---|
| Ctrl-D / Right Arrow | Right one line |
| Ctrl-A / Ctrl-Left Arrow | Left one word |
| Ctrl-F / Ctrl-Right Arrow | Right one word |
| HOME | Beginning of current line |
| END | End of current line |
| Ctrl-HOME | Beginning of memo/string |
| Ctrl-END | End of memo/string |
| PgUp | Window Up |
| PgDn | Window Down |
| Ctrl-PgUp | Beginning of current window |
| Ctrl-PgDn | End of current window |
| Ctrl-W | Conclude and write |
| ESC | Aborts editing/keep old memo |
| Ctrl-Y | Deletes current line |
| Ctrl-T | Deletes word right |
| Ctrl-B | Reformats memo/string in window |
| Ctrl-V / Ins | Turns Insert on/off |
| Return | Beginning of next line |
| Delete | Delete character |
| Backspace | Delete previous character |
| Tab | Adds spaces or characters |

When a user-defined function is used, the keys noted in the table below are configurable. The default action of these keys can be altered and another user specified action can be slated to occur. This is accomplished by assigning a RETURN value other than 0 to the key. For example, allocating the Ctrl-B key a return value of 32 causes MEMOEDIT to ignore the key and cancel the default operation (reformat the memo).

| *Key* | *Default Value* |
|---|---|
| Ctrl-W | Conclude and write |
| ESC | Aborts editing/keep old memo |
| Ctrl-Y | Deletes current line |
| Ctrl-T | Deletes word right |
| Ctrl-B | Reformats memo/string in window |
| Ctrl-V | Turns Insert on/off |

**NOTE** If only viewing a memo or string, the cursor will remain in the top left corner of the window area and the text will scroll accordingly.

If a user-defined function is used, it should not be defined as a STATIC function. If it is, the function will be ignored by MEMOEDIT( ).

**SEE ALSO** MEMOTRAN( ), MEMOREAD( ), MEMOWRIT( )

**EXAMPLE** Please see Chapter 11.

# MEMOLINE( )

| | |
|---|---|
| **FUNCTION** | Extracts a substring or line from a string or memo. |
| **SYNTAX** | MEMOLINE( <expC1> [, <expN2>] [, <expN3>] [,<expN4>] [, <expL5>] ) |
| **PARAMETERS** | <expC1>   A string or memo field |
| | <expN2>   Line length |
| | <expN3>   Line to be extracted |
| | <expN4>   Tab size |
| | <expL5>   Toggle for word wrap |
| **RETURNS** | <expC>   Character expression |
| **LIBRARY** | EXTEND.LIB |

**DESCRIPTION**  This function extracts a formatted line from <expC1> based on the number of characters per line expressed as <expN2>. With a line width of <expN2>, <expN3> defines the line to be extracted from <expC1>.

The number of columns to indent the tab character—CHR(9)—may be specified in <expN4>; the default tab size is 4. However, if the tab size defined in <expN4> exceeds the line length in <expN2>, the value of <expN4> will be <expN2> – 1.

It is also possible to specify whether lines should be formed based on character count only, or based on the inclusion of complete words on a line. By default, word wrap is off, which means that lines can be formed based on character count alone. But word wrap can be toggled on with <expL5>, which prevents a single word from being broken up onto two lines.

If <expN2> is not specified, the default line length will be 79. And if <expN3> is not specified, the first line will be extracted from the string.

If the line number specified in <expN3> is greater than the total number of formatted lines in <expC1>, the function will return a NULL byte.

**NOTE**  If the tab spacing value <expN4> and/or the word-wrap toggle <expL5> is used in conjunction with previous function calls in MEMOEDIT( ) and/or MLCOUNT( ), be sure to maintain consistency for these values.

**SEE ALSO**  MEMOEDIT( ), MLCOUNT( ), MLPOS( )

**EXAMPLE**  Please see Chapter 11.

# MEMOREAD( )

| | |
|---|---|
| **FUNCTION** | Converts a disk file to a character string. |
| **SYNTAX** | `MEMOREAD( <expC1> )` |
| **PARAMETER** | <expC1>　　The name of a file. |
| **RETURNS** | <expC>　　Character expression |
| **LIBRARY** | EXTEND.LIB |
| **DESCRIPTION** | This function retrieves the contents of <expC1> from the disk and returns the contents as a contiguous string.

If the file specified in <expC1> cannot be found, the function will return a NULL byte.

The maximum file size that a Clipper application can read using this function is 65,519 bytes. This maximum may actually be lower based on the amount of available memory at the time of the function call. A check of the MEMORY( ) function may be implemented to test beforehand.

This function does not follow the path criteria specified in the SET PATH TO or SET DEFAULT TO commands. It does, however, adhere to the DOS search path.

This function attempts to open the file <expC1> in shared, read-only mode. If the file <expC1> is opened exclusively before this function attempts to open it, a NULL string will be returned. |
| **SEE ALSO** | MEMOWRIT( ), MEMOEDIT( ) |
| **EXAMPLE** | Please see Chapter 11. |

# MEMORY( )

| | |
|---|---|
| **FUNCTION** | Calculates available free memory. |
| **SYNTAX** | `MEMORY( <expN1> )` |
| **PARAMETER** | <expN1>　　Numeric indicator of the type of free memory |
| **RETURNS** | <expN>　　Amount of memory available in 1K blocks |
| **LIBRARY** | CLIPPER.LIB |

| | |
|---|---|
| **DESCRIPTION** | The value of this function is the amount of available memory in free pool, calculated based on the value of the passed parameter. Below is a table of what the values of the passed parameter may be: |

    0  Total space for character variables
    1  Largest contiguous block of space for character variables
    2  Space available for a RUN command

All values are estimates.

Free pool is a dynamic area of memory used in part to execute external operations and programs and to store character string values.

| | |
|---|---|
| **NOTE** | Since Clipper will load an additional copy of COMMAND.COM whenever a RUN command is executed, and since different machines will operate with different versions of DOS, it is possible to have an application RUN another program on some machines and not on others. |

Use this function to help control and monitor the amount of memory used by an application that is used across two or more machines.

| | |
|---|---|
| **SEE ALSO** | RUN, ! |
| **EXAMPLE** | |

```
qout( memory(0) )
qout( memory(1) )
qout( memory(2) )

if memory(0) > 40
    // Execute a DBEDIT() call
endif
```

## MEMOTRAN( )

| | | |
|---|---|---|
| **FUNCTION** | Formats a string from hard/soft carriage return/line feed characters. | |
| **SYNTAX** | MEMOTRAN( <expC1> [, <expC2>] [, <expC3>] ) | |
| **PARAMETERS** | <expC1> | Character expression |
| | <expC2> | Character expression to replace hard carriage return |
| | <expC3> | Character expression to replace soft carriage return |
| **RETURNS** | <expC> | Character expression - formatted |
| **LIBRARY** | EXTEND.LIB | |
| **DESCRIPTION** | This function returns <expC1> with the hard carriage returns and the soft carriage returns replaced with <expC2> and <expC3>, respectively. | |

Hard carriage returns with line feed characters ( CHR(13) + CHR(10) ) will be replaced with a semicolon unless a different character is specified by the value of <expC2>.

|  |  |
|---|---|
|  | Soft carriage returns with line feed characters ( CHR(141) + CHR(10) ) will be replaced with a space unless a different character is specified by the value of <expC3>. |
| **NOTE** | To strip all formatting characters from a memo field or from a character string returned by the MEMOEDIT( ) function, a MEMOTRAN ( <expC1>, " ", " " ) should be used. |
| **SEE ALSO** | MEMOEDIT( ), HARDCR( ), STRTRAN( ) |
| **EXAMPLE** | Please see Chapter 11. |

## MEMOWRIT( )

|  |  |  |
|---|---|---|
| **FUNCTION** | Writes the contents of a string or memo field to a disk file. | |
| **SYNTAX** | `MEMOWRIT( <expC1>, <expC2> )` | |
| **PARAMETERS** | <expC1> | Filename |
|  | <expC2> | String or memo field |
| **RETURNS** | <expL> | Logical expression (true or false) |
| **LIBRARY** | EXTEND.LIB | |
| **DESCRIPTION** | This function writes <expC2> to a disk file named <expC1>. If no drive designator or path is given with <expC1>, the currently logged drive and directory will be used. | |
|  | If the write operation is successful, the function will return a logical true (.T.); otherwise, a logical false (.F.) will be returned. | |
| **SEE ALSO** | MEMOEDIT( ), HARDCR( ), STRTRAN( ) | |
| **EXAMPLE** | Please see Chapter 11. | |

## MEMVARBLOCK( )

|  |  |  |
|---|---|---|
| **FUNCTION** | Generates a code block for a memory variable. | |
| **SYNTAX** | `MEMVARBLOCK( <expC1> )` | |
| **PARAMETER** | <expC1> | The name of a variable |
| **RETURNS** | <expB> | Code block expression |
| **LIBRARY** | CLIPPER.LIB | |

| | |
|---|---|
| **DESCRIPTION** | This function returns a code block that, when evaluated, either places or obtains a value for the variable named <expC1>. If the name of the variable in <expC1> does not exist, this function will return a NIL data type. |
| **NOTE** | If the variable <expC1> is NOT a PRIVATE or a PUBLIC memory variable, this function will not work properly. The variable has to have a symbol in the symbol table in order for this function to macro-expand properly and to build the code block. |
| **SEE ALSO** | FIELDBLOCK( ), FIELDWBLOCK( ) |

# MIN( )

| | | |
|---|---|---|
| **FUNCTION** | Determines a minimum value or date. | |
| **SYNTAX** | MIN( <expX1>, <expX2> ) | |
| **PARAMETERS** | <expX1> | Either a numeric expression or a date expression |
| | <expX2> | Either a numeric expression or a date expression |
| **RETURNS** | <expX> | Either a numeric expression or a date expression |
| **LIBRARY** | CLIPPER.LIB | |
| **DESCRIPTION** | This function determines the smaller of two numeric or date values. The value of the function will be the result of this comparison. If <expX1> is a numeric data type, <expX2> must also be a numeric date type. The same may be said if <expX1> is a date data type. | |
| **SEE ALSO** | MAX( ) | |
| **EXAMPLE** | See the MAXROW( ) function. | |

# MLCOUNT( )

| | | |
|---|---|---|
| **FUNCTION** | Counts the number of formatted lines in a string or memo. | |
| **SYNTAX** | MLCOUNT( <expC1> [, <expN2>] [, <expN3> ] [,<expL4>] ) | |
| **PARAMETERS** | <expC1> | A string or memo field |
| | <expN2> | Line width |
| | <expN3> | Tab width |
| | <expL4> | Word-wrap toggle |

| | | |
|---|---|---|
| **RETURNS** | <expN> | Number of lines |
| **LIBRARY** | EXTEND.LIB | |

**DESCRIPTION** This function returns the number of lines in <expC1> based on a line length of <expN2> characters, a tab size of <expN3> spaces, and a toggle <expL4> that determines whether or not words are to be wrapped.

If not specified, the value of <expN2> will be 79. The length of a line may be up to 254 characters, with 4 being the minimum.

If not specified, the default tab size <expN3> will be 4. If the value of <expN3> is greater than or equal to the value of <expN2>, the default value of <expN3> will be <expN2> − 1.

The default value for <expL4> is a logical true (.T.).

**NOTE** If the tab spacing value <expN4> and/or the word-wrap toggle <expL5> is used in conjunction with previous function calls in MEMOEDIT( ) and/or MLCOUNT( ), be sure to maintain consistency for these values.

**SEE ALSO** MLPOS( ), MEMOLINE( ), MEMOTRAN( )

**EXAMPLE** Please see Chapter 11.

## MLCTOPOS( )

**FUNCTION** Returns the character position of a row/column coordinate in a memo or string.

**SYNTAX** MLCTOPOS(<expC1>, <expN2>, <expN3>, <expN4> [, <expN5>] [, <expL6>])

| **PARAMETERS** | <expC1> | A string or memo field |
|---|---|---|
| | <expN2> | Line width |
| | <expN3> | Line number |
| | <expN4> | Column coordinate |
| | <expN5> | Tab width |
| | <expL6> | Word-wrap toggle |
| **RETURNS** | <expN> | Numeric expression |
| **LIBRARY** | EXTEND.LIB | |

**DESCRIPTION** This function returns the character position in the string or memo field expressed as <expC1>. The width of each line is expressed as <expN2>, with the row/column coordinates to look to expressed as <expN3>,<expN4>, respectively, starting at 1 for the line number and 0 for the column. In addition, the tab width value must be expressed as

<expN5>, with the word-wrap toggle expressed as the logical expression <expL6>.

This function works in conjunction with MEMOEDIT( ). The row and column position of a string or memo expressed in MEMOEDIT( ) is used to return the character position of that string.

**SEE ALSO**     MLCOUNT( ), MLPOS( ), MEMOEDIT( ), MPOSTOLCR( )

**EXAMPLE**

```
 1 : * File       Mlctdemo.prg
 2 : * Compile    RMake sample /DFILE:Mlctdemo
 3 :
 4 : #define pFALSE .f.
 5 : #define pTRUE .t.
 6 :
 7 : procedure Main()
 8 :
 9 :    local cTemp := "This is a test to see if this will work"
10 :
11 :    cTemp += chr(13)+chr(10)
12 :    cTemp += "and if I can figure the rest of this"
13 :    cTemp += chr(13)+chr(10)
14 :    cTemp += "out..."
15 :
16 :    cls
17 :    memoedit( cTemp, 0,0,10,70, pFALSE, "",70,4)
18 :    qout()
19 :
20 :    qout( mlctopos(cTemp, 70, 0, 0, 4, pTRUE ) )
21 :    qout( mlctopos(cTemp, 70, 1, 5, 4, pTRUE ) )
22 :    qout( mlctopos(cTemp, 70, 2, 0, 4, pTRUE ) )
23 :    qout( mlctopos(cTemp, 70, 3, 1, 4, pTRUE ) )
24 :    wait
25 :
26 :    cls
27 :    qout( "The beginning character at 0,0 is...")
28 :    qout()
29 :    qout( substr( cTemp, mlctopos(cTemp, 70, 0, 0, 4, pTRUE ) ) )
30 :    wait
31 :    qout( "The beginning character at 1, 5 is..." )
32 :    qout()
33 :    qout( substr( cTemp, mlctopos(cTemp, 70, 1, 5, 4, pTRUE ) ) )
34 :    wait
35 :    qout( "The beginning character at 2,0 is..." )
36 :    qout()
37 :    qout( substr(cTemp, mlctopos(cTemp, 70, 2, 0, 4, pTRUE ) ) )
38 :    wait
39 :    qout( "The beginning character at 3, 1 is..." )
40 :    qout()
41 :    qout( substr(cTemp, mlctopos(cTemp, 70, 3, 1, 4, pTRUE ) ) )
42 :
43 : // End of File: Mlctdemo.prg
```

# MLPOS( )

| | |
|---|---|
| **FUNCTION** | Determines the position of a line in a string. |
| **SYNTAX** | `MLPOS( <expC1>, <expN2>, <expN3> [, <expN4>] [,<expL5>])` |
| **PARAMETERS** | `<expC1>`    A string or memo field<br>`<expN2>`    The line length<br>`<expN3>`    The line number<br>`<expN4>`    The tab width<br>`<expL5>`    Logical true (.T.) or false (.F.) to word-wrap toggle |
| **RETURNS** | `<expN>`    Numeric expression |
| **LIBRARY** | EXTEND.LIB |
| **DESCRIPTION** | This function determines the character position of a specified line number `<expN3>` in a string or memo field expressed as `<expC1>` with `<expN2>` as the number of characters per line. `<expN4>` is the size of the tab spacing used in `<expC1>`, while `<expL4>` is a toggle for word wrap.<br><br>If not specified, the default tab size `<expN4>` will be 4. The default value for `<expL5>` is a logical true (.T.). |
| **NOTE** | If the tab spacing value `<expN4>` and/or the word-wrap toggle `<expL5>` is to be used in conjunction with previous function calls in MEMOEDIT( ) and/or MLCOUNT( ), be sure to maintain consistency for these values. |
| **SEE ALSO** | MEMOLINE( ), MEMOEDIT( ), MLCOUNT( ) |
| **EXAMPLE** | Please see Chapter 11. |

# MOD( )

| | |
|---|---|
| **FUNCTION** | Returns the modulus of two numbers. |
| **SYNTAX** | `MOD( <expN1>, <expN2> )` |
| **PARAMETERS** | `<expN1>`    Numerator in a divisional expression<br>`<expN2>`    Denominator in a divisional expression |
| **RETURNS** | `<expN>`    Remainder from the division |

| | |
|---|---|
| **LIBRARY** | EXTEND.LIB |
| **DESCRIPTION** | This function will return a value that corresponds to the value that dBASE III Plus yields for expressing the remainder of one number divided by another.

Since Clipper has the modulus operator (%), the MOD( ) function may provide results different from those expected. In some cases, run-time errors will be suppressed and numeric zeros returned for division involving a zero value. |
| **NOTE** | This is a compatibility function between past versions of Clipper or dBASE III Plus and may not be kept in the language in future versions. |
| **EXAMPLE** | Please see Chapter 4. |

# MONTH( )

| | |
|---|---|
| **FUNCTION** | Converts a date expression to a numeric month value. |
| **SYNTAX** | `MONTH( <expD1> )` |
| **PARAMETER** | <expD1>   Any date value |
| **RETURNS** | <expN>   Corresponding number of the month in the year, ranging from 0 to 12. |
| **LIBRARY** | CLIPPER.LIB |
| **DESCRIPTION** | This function returns a number that represents the month of the given date expression <expD1>. If a NULL date ( CTOD(" ") ) is passed to this function, the value of the function will be 0. |
| **SEE ALSO** | CDOW( ), DOW( ), CMONTH( ) |
| **EXAMPLE** | See the YEAR( ) function. |

# MPOSTOLC( )

| | |
|---|---|
| **FUNCTION** | Cursor position of an element in a memo or string. |
| **SYNTAX** | `MPOSTOLC(<expC1>, <expN2>, <expN3> [, <expN4>] [,<expL5>])` |
| **PARAMETERS** | <expC1>   Character expression or memo
<expN2>   Line width
<expN3>   Offset position |

|  |  |  |
|---|---|---|
|  | <expN4> | Tab width in the memo |
|  | <expL5> | Word-wrap condition in the memo |
| **RETURNS** | <expA> | Array expression |
| **LIBRARY** | EXTEND.LIB |  |

**DESCRIPTION** This function returns an array with two elements: The first is the row number, and the second is the column number. These values are used in positioning the cursor at a specified row and column position within a MEMOEDIT( ) function for the given string <expC1> with a line width of <expN2>, a tab width of <expN4>, and a word-wrap toggle expressed as <expL5>. The value of <expN3> is the byte offset of the item to be searched for in <expC1>.

**NOTE** This may be best used in conjunction with the MLCTOPOS( ) function.

**SEE ALSO** MEMOEDIT( ), MLPOS( ), MLCTOPOS( ), MLCOUNT( )

**EXAMPLE**

```
 1 : * File     Mlpodemo.prg
 2 : * Compile  RMake sample /dFILE:Mlpodemo
 3 :
 4 : #define pTRUE .t.   // Here are a couple of manifest constants
 5 : #define pFALSE .f.  // specifically for this file
 6 :
 7 : procedure Main()
 8 :
 9 :    local cTemp := "This is a test to see if this will work"
10 :    local nOffset1
11 :    local nOffset2
12 :    local nOffset3
13 :    local nOffset4
14 :
15 :    cTemp += chr(13)+chr(10)
16 :    cTemp += "and if I can figure the rest of this"
17 :    cTemp += chr(13)+chr(10)
18 :    cTemp += "out..."
19 :
20 :    keyboard chr(27)
21 :    cls
22 :    memoedit(cTemp, 0,0,10,70, pFALSE, "",70,4)
23 :
24 :    qout()
25 :    qout()
26 :    qout()
27 :
28 :    nOffset1 := at( "if",   cTemp )
29 :    nOffset2 := at( "will", cTemp )
30 :    nOffset3 := at( "of",   cTemp )
31 :    nOffset4 := at( "out",  cTemp )
32 :
33 :    qout()
34 :    qout("The row, column position in MEMOEDIT() for each element..")
```

```
35 :    qout()
36 :    qout( "Text           Condition          ROW         COLUMN")
37 :    qout()
38 :    qout( "IF          From top of file ")
39 :    qqout( mpostolc(cTemp, 70, nOffset1, 4, pTRUE)[1] )
40 :    qqout( mpostolc(cTemp, 70, nOffset1, 4, pTRUE)[2] )
41 :    qout( "WILL        From top of file ")
42 :    qqout( mpostolc(cTemp, 70, nOffset2, 4, pTRUE)[1] )
43 :    qqout( mpostolc(cTemp, 70, nOffset2, 4, pTRUE)[2] )
44 :    qout( "OF          From top of file ")
45 :    qqout( mpostolc(cTemp, 70, nOffset3, 4, pTRUE)[1] )
46 :    qqout( mpostolc(cTemp, 70, nOffset3, 4, pTRUE)[2] )
47 :    qout( "OUT...      From top of file ")
48 :    qqout( mpostolc(cTemp, 70, nOffset4, 4, pTRUE)[1] )
49 :    qqout( mpostolc(cTemp, 70, nOffset4, 4, pTRUE)[2] )
50 :
51 : // End of File: Mlpodemo.prg
```

# NETERR( )

| | |
|---|---|
| **FUNCTION** | Tests for the success of a network function. |
| **SYNTAX** | NETERR( [<expL1>] ) |
| **PARAMETER** | <expL1>   Logical expression |
| **RETURNS** | <expL>   Logical value based on the success of a network operation or function |
| **LIBRARY** | CLIPPER.LIB |
| **DESCRIPTION** | This function returns a logical true (.T.) if a USE, APPEND BLANK, or a USE...EXCLUSIVE command is issued and fails in a network environment.<br><br>In the case of the USE and USE...EXCLUSIVE commands, a NETERR( ) value of .T. would be returned if another node of the network has exclusive use of a file. And in the case of the APPEND BLANK command, NETERR( ) will return a logical true (.T.) if the file or record is locked by another node or if the value of LASTREC( ) has been advanced.<br><br>The value of NETERR( ) may be changed via the value of <expL1>. This will allow the run-time error-handling system to control the way certain errors are handled. |
| **SEE ALSO** | FLOCK( ), RLOCK( ), NETNAME( ) |

# NETNAME( )

| | |
|---|---|
| **FUNCTION** | Returns the network station name. |
| **SYNTAX** | NETNAME( ) |
| **PARAMETER** | None |
| **RETURNS** | <expC>     Name of the network station |
| **LIBRARY** | CLIPPER.LIB |
| **DESCRIPTION** | This function returns the name of the network station in a 15-character string. If no station name is present, the value of the function will be a NULL byte. For this function to work properly, the IBM PC Local Area Network Program must be loaded. |
| **SEE ALSO** | NETERR( ) |

# NETUSE( )

| | |
|---|---|
| **FUNCTION** | Attempts to USE a database with optional retry. |
| **SYNTAX** | NETUSE( <expC1>, <expL2> [, <expN3> ] ) |
| **PARAMETERS** | <expC1>     Name of database to open<br><expL2>     Toggle of open mode<br><expN3>     Number of seconds to wait between retry efforts |
| **RETURNS** | <expL>     Logical true (.T.) or a logical false (.F.) |
| **LIBRARY** | SAMPLES.LIB |
| **DESCRIPTION** | This function will attempt to open and use the file <expC1> and if it is successful, it will return a logical true (.T.) value; otherwise, a logical false (.F.) will be returned. The mode in which the file is opened is controlled by <expL2>. If <expL2> is set to a logical true (.T.) value, then the file will be opened in EXCLUSIVE mode; if <expL2> is a logical false (.F.), it will be opened in SHARED mode. The number of seconds to wait for a retry is passed as <expN3>. The default value of <expN3> is 2 representing 2 seconds between retry options. |
| **SEE ALSO** | DBUSEAREA( ), USE, FLOCK( ), SET EXCLUSIVE |

## NEXTKEY( )

| | |
|---|---|
| **FUNCTION** | Returns the ASCII value of the next key in the keyboard buffer. |
| **SYNTAX** | `NEXTKEY()` |
| **PARAMETER** | None |
| **RETURNS** | <expN>    ASCII key value |
| **LIBRARY** | CLIPPER.LIB |
| **DESCRIPTION** | This function reads the next keystroke from the keyboard buffer without removing it and returns the ASCII value of that key. It therefore may be used to process pending and future keystrokes. If the keyboard buffer is empty, the function will return 0. |
| **SEE ALSO** | SET KEY, LASTKEY( ), INKEY( ) |
| **EXAMPLE** | See the LASTKEY( ) function. |

## NOSNOW( )

| | |
|---|---|
| **FUNCTION** | Toggles the snow condition in an application. |
| **SYNTAX** | `NOSNOW( <expL> )` |
| **PARAMETER** | <expL>    Logical true (.T.) or false (.F.) |
| **LIBRARY** | CLIPPER.LIB |
| **DESCRIPTION** | This function toggles the snow suppression state of an application by passing it either a logical true (.T.) for snow suppression or a logical false (.F.). |

## NTOD( )

| | |
|---|---|
| **FUNCTION** | Converts numeric values to a date data type. |
| **SYNTAX** | `NTOD( <expN1>, <expN2>, <expN3> )` |
| **PARAMETERS** | <expN1>    Numeric value for a month<br><expN2>    Numeric value for a day<br><expN3>    Numeric value for a year |
| **RETURNS** | <expD>    Formatted date data type |

| | |
|---|---|
| **LIBRARY** | SAMPLES.LIB |
| **DESCRIPTION** | This function takes the values of <expN1>, <expN2>, and <expN3> and attempts to return a date data type which adheres to the internal setting of SET DATE FORMAT. |
| **SEE ALSO** | DATE( ), DAY( ), MONTH( ), YEAR( ) |

## NUMASCURRENCY( )

| | | |
|---|---|---|
| **FUNCTION** | Converts a number to currency format. | |
| **SYNTAX** | NUMASCURRENCY( <expN1>, <expC2>, <expN3> ) | |
| **PARAMETERS** | <expN1> | Numeric value to be converted |
| | <expC2> | Character string of currency format |
| | <expN3> | Numeric toggle to determine side |
| **RETURNS** | <expC> | Formatted currency string |
| **LIBRARY** | SAMPLES.LIB | |
| **DESCRIPTION** | This function will take the number <expN1> and attempt to convert it to represent a currency format with a currency symbol expressed as <expC2>. The function will return the formatted string. If <expN3> is a negative number, then the currency symbol <expC2> will be placed on the left side of the amount; otherwise, it will be placed on the right side of the currency amount. | |
| **SEE ALSO** | NUMASLOG10( ) | |

## NUMASLOG10( )

| | | |
|---|---|---|
| **FUNCTION** | Converts a number to a log base 10. | |
| **SYNTAX** | NUMASLOG10( <expN1> ) | |
| **PARAMETER** | <expN1> | Any positive number |
| **RETURNS** | <expX> | NIL or a numeric conversion |
| **LIBRARY** | SAMPLES.LIB | |
| **DESCRIPTION** | This function will take the positive number <expN1> and return the log base 10 of that number. If the number <expN1> is not a positive number, then the function will return a NIL value. | |
| **SEE ALSO** | NUMASCURRENCY( ) | |

## NUMGETDECIMALS( )

| | |
|---|---|
| **FUNCTION** | Determines the number of decimal places in a number. |
| **SYNTAX** | NUMGETDECIMALS( <expN1> ) |
| **PARAMETER** | <expN1>   Any numeric value |
| **RETURNS** | <expN>   Number of decimal places |
| **LIBRARY** | SAMPLES.LIB |
| **DESCRIPTION** | This function takes the number <expN1>, attempts to determine the number of decimal places found in the number, and returns that value. If 0 is returned, then there are no decimal places found in <expN1>. |
| **SEE ALSO** | LENNUM( ), NUMGETLEN( ) |

## NUMGETLEN( )

| | |
|---|---|
| **FUNCTION** | Determines the number of whole numbers in a value. |
| **SYNTAX** | NUMGETLEN( <expN1> ) |
| **PARAMETER** | <expN1>   Any numeric value |
| **RETURNS** | <expN>   A numeric length |
| **LIBRARY** | SAMPLES.LIB |
| **DESCRIPTION** | This function will take any numeric value in <expN1> and attempt to determine the number of whole digits found in it. |
| **SEE ALSO** | LENNUM( ), NUMGETDECIMALS( ) |

## OCCURS( )

| | |
|---|---|
| **FUNCTION** | Determines the number of occurrences of a string in another string. |
| **SYNTAX** | OCCURS( <expC1>, <expC2> ) |
| **PARAMETERS** | <expC1>   Search string<br><expC2>   Target string |
| **RETURNS** | <expN>   Number of occurrences |
| **LIBRARY** | SAMPLES.LIB |

| | |
|---|---|
| **DESCRIPTION** | This function returns the number of times <expC1> appears in <expC2>. |
| **SEE ALSO** | STRTRAN( ), LEN( ), SUBSTR( ) |

## ORDBAGEXT( )

| | | |
|---|---|---|
| **FUNCTION** | Yields the Order Bag extension. | |
| **SYNTAX** | ORDBAGEXT( ) | |
| **PARAMETER** | None | |
| **RETURNS** | <expC> | RDD Extension name |
| **LIBRARY** | CLIPPER.LIB | |
| **DESCRIPTION** | This function returns the character name of the RDD extension for the Order Bag. This is determined by the active RDD for the selected work area.<br><br>This function, due to the RDD technology in Clipper 5.2, replaces the INDEXEXT( ) function. | |
| **SEE ALSO** | INDEXEXT( ), ORDBAGNAME( ) | |
| **EXAMPLE** | Please see Chapter 12. | |

## ORDBAGNAME( )

| | | |
|---|---|---|
| **FUNCTION** | Yields the Order Bag name. | |
| **SYNTAX** | ORDBAGNAME( <expX1> ) | |
| **PARAMETER** | <expX1> | Character name of Order Bag or number representing Order Bag |
| **RETURNS** | <expC> | Order Bag name |
| **LIBRARY** | CLIPPER.LIB | |
| **DESCRIPTION** | This function returns the name of the Order Bag for the specified work area. If <expX1> is a numeric data type, it will represent the position in the Order List of the target order. If <expX1> is a character data type, it will represent the name of the target order. In essence, it will tell the name of the database (if that RDD is in use) for the given index name or index order number. | |

**SEE ALSO** INDEXORD( ), ORDBAGEXT( ), ALIAS( )

**EXAMPLE** Please see Chapter 12.

# ORDCREATE( )

**FUNCTION** Creates an order in an Order Bag.

**SYNTAX**
```
ORDCREATE( <expC1> [, <expC2>], <expX3>
[, <expB4>] [, <expL5>] )
```

**PARAMETERS**
- \<expC1> Name of the file that contains one or more Orders.
- \<expC2> Name of the order to be created
- \<expX3> Key value for order for each record in current work area
- \<expB4> Code block that evaluates to a key for the Order for each record in the work area
- \<expL5> Toggles the unique status of the index

**LIBRARY** CLIPPER.LIB

**DESCRIPTION** This function creates an order for the current work area. It is similar to the DBCREATEINDEX( ) except that this function allows different Orders based on the RDD in effect. The name of the file <expC1> or the name of the Order <expC2> are technically both considered to be "optional" except that at least one of the two must exist in order to create the order.

The parameter <expX3> is the index key expression; typically in a .DBF driver, the maximum length of the key is 255 characters.

If <expB4> is not specified, then the code block is created via macro-expanding the value of <expX3>.

If <expL5> is not specified, then the current internal setting of SET UNIQUE ON or OFF will be observed.

The active RDD driver determines the capacity in the order for a specific Order Bag.

If the name <expC1> is found in the Order Bag can contain only a single order, then the name <expC1> is erased and the new Order is added to the Order List in the current or specified work area. On the other hand, if it can contain multiple Tags and if <expC1> does not already exist in the Order List, then it is added. If it does exist, then the <expC1> replaces the former name in the Order List in the current or specified work area.

**SEE ALSO** ORDSETFOCUS( ), ORDNAME( ), DBCREATEINDEX( ), INDEX ON, USE

**EXAMPLE** Please see Chapter 12.

## ORDDESTROY( )

| | |
|---|---|
| **FUNCTION** | Removes an order from an Order Bag. |
| **SYNTAX** | `ORDDESTROY( <expC1> [, <expC2>] )` |
| **PARAMETERS** | <expC1>  Name of the order to remove <br> <expC2>  Name of the Order Bag from which order is to be removed |
| **LIBRARY** | CLIPPER.LIB |
| **DESCRIPTION** | This function attempts to remove the order named <expC1> from the file containing the Order Bag named <expC2>. If <expC2> is not specified, then the name of the file will be based on the value of the ORDNAME( ) function. If the extension is not included with the name of the order file, then the extension will be obtained from the default extension of the current and active RDD. <br><br> The DBFNTX and DBFNDX drivers do not support multi-Order Bags; therefore, there cannot be an order to "destroy" from a bag. This function works only for those drivers which support multiple-Order Bags (e.g., DBFPX and DBFCDX drivers). |
| **SEE ALSO** | ORDCREATE( ), DELETE TAG |
| **EXAMPLE** | Please see Chapter 12. |

## ORDFOR( )

| | |
|---|---|
| **FUNCTION** | Returns FOR expression of an order. |
| **SYNTAX** | `ORDFOR( <expX1> [, <expC2>] )` |
| **PARAMETERS** | <expX1>  Order name of the target order or the numeric order position in the Order List. <br> <expC2>  Name of an Order Bag |
| **RETURNS** | <expC>  Expression containing FOR condition for an order |
| **LIBRARY** | CLIPPER.LIB |
| **DESCRIPTION** | This function returns a character string that is the expression for the FOR condition for the specified order. The order may be specified if <expX1> is the name of the order. However, <expX1> may be a numeric which represents the position in the Order List of the desired Order. <br><br> If the order was not created using the FOR clause or if the RDD does not support the FOR condition, the value of this function will be a NULL byte. |

| | |
|---|---|
| **SEE ALSO** | ORDERKEY( ), ORDCREATE( ), ORDNAME( ), ORDLIST( ), ORDNUMBER( ), INDEX ON |
| **EXAMPLE** | Please see Chapter 12. |

# ORDKEY( )

| | | |
|---|---|---|
| **FUNCTION** | Yields key expression of an order. | |
| **SYNTAX** | `ORDKEY( <expX1> [, <expC2>] )` | |
| **PARAMETERS** | <expX1> | Order name or order index number |
| | <expC2> | Name of Order Bag |
| **RETURNS** | <expC> | |
| **LIBRARY** | CLIPPER.LIB | |
| **DESCRIPTION** | This function returns the name of the index key expression based on the name of the order passed as <expX1> or the position in the Order List of the desired order expressed as an integer in <expX1>. Optionally, the name of the Order Bag in a file on disk may be specified as <expC2>. | |
| **SEE ALSO** | ORDFOR( ), ORDKEY( ), ORDNAME( ), ORDNUMBER( ) | |
| **EXAMPLE** | Please see Chapter 12. | |

# ORDLISTADD( )

| | | |
|---|---|---|
| **FUNCTION** | Adds an order to the Order List. | |
| **SYNTAX** | `ORDLISTADD( <expC1> [, <expC2>] )` | |
| **PARAMETERS** | <expC1> | Name of Order Bag |
| | <expC2> | Name of order |
| **LIBRARY** | CLIPPER.LIB | |
| **DESCRIPTION** | This function adds the specific order <expC2> from the Order Bag expressed as <expC1> to the Order List of the current work area. If <expC2> is not specified, then all of the orders found in the Order Bag <expC2> will be added to the Order List. | |
| | The parameter <expC1> is the name of a file that contains one or more orders. | |
| | Any orders previously associated with the active work area will continue to be active. However, if the current Order Bag contains only | |

one order associated with it, then it will become the controlling order; otherwise, the controlling order will remain unchanged.

After the new orders are opened, the record pointer is positioned to the first logical record in the controlling order.

**SEE ALSO**    DBSETINDEX( ), DBUSEAREA( )

**EXAMPLE**    Please see Chapter 12.

## ORDLISTCLEAR( )

**FUNCTION**    Clears the current Order List.

**SYNTAX**    ORDLISTCLEAR( )

**PARAMETER**    None

**LIBRARY**    CLIPPER.LIB

**DESCRIPTION**    This function clears all orders from the Order List for the current or selected work area.

**SEE ALSO**    DBCLEARINDEX( ), ORDLISTADD( )

**EXAMPLE**    Please see Chapter 12.

## ORDLISTREBUILD( )

**FUNCTION**    Rebuilds all orders in selected and active Order List.

**SYNTAX**    ORDLISTREBUILD( )

**PARAMETER**    None

**LIBRARY**    CLIPPER.LIB

**DESCRIPTION**    This function attempts to rebuild all of the orders in the Order List in the current and selected work area.

**SEE ALSO**    REINDEX, ORDCREATE( ), INDEX, DBCREATEINDEX( )

**EXAMPLE**    Please see Chapter 12.

## ORDNAME( )

| | |
|---|---|
| **FUNCTION** | Yields the name of an order in the Order List. |
| **SYNTAX** | `ORDNAME( <expN1> [, <expC2>] )` |
| **PARAMETERS** | `<expN1>` Position in the Order List of the desired order<br>`<expC2>` Name of file containing order |
| **RETURNS** | `<expC>` Order name |
| **LIBRARY** | CLIPPER.LIB |
| **DESCRIPTION** | This function returns the name of the order identified by position `<expN1>` in the Order List. If specified, the name of a disk file containing an order may be offered in `<expC2>`. |
| **SEE ALSO** | ORDFOR( ), ORDKEY( ), ORDNUMBER( ) |
| **EXAMPLE** | Please see Chapter 12. |

## ORDNUMBER( )

| | |
|---|---|
| **FUNCTION** | Yields the position of an order in an Order List. |
| **SYNTAX** | `ORDNUMBER( <expC1> [, <expC2>] )` |
| **PARAMETERS** | `<expC1>` Name of the order in question<br>`<expC2>` Name of a disk file containing the Order Bag |
| **RETURNS** | `<expN>` Position of `<expC1>` in `<expC2>` |
| **LIBRARY** | CLIPPER.LIB |
| **DESCRIPTION** | This function returns the position of an order expressed as `<expC1>` in an Order Bag, optionally expressed as `<expC2>`. This will search the Order List in order to find a match of `<expC1>`. If the name of the order `<expC1>` cannot be found in the Order List, a run-time, recoverable error will be generated. This should be kept in mind when building a custom error system.<br><br>The disk file `<expC1>` will contain one or more orders. If not specified, then the current Order Bag for an active work area will be used. |
| **SEE ALSO** | SET INDEX TO, DBSETORDER( ), INDEXORD( ), INDEX ON |
| **EXAMPLE** | Please see Chapter 12. |

## ORDSETFOCUS( )

| | |
|---|---|
| **FUNCTION** | Sets focus to an order and an Order List. |
| **SYNTAX** | `ORDSETFOCUS( [ <expX1> ] [, <expC2> ] )` |
| **PARAMETERS** | <expX1>  Name of the order in the Order List or the position of the order in the Order List |
| | <expC2>  Name of disk file containing the orders |
| **RETURNS** | <expC>  Name of previous order in focus |
| **LIBRARY** | CLIPPER.LIB |
| **DESCRIPTION** | This function returns the name of the order in the Order List that is "in focus" or in control of the data set. If a new order is specified either by name or position in the Order List via <expX1>, then the function will assign that order to be the controlling order yet return the name of the order that was previously in control. When a controlling order is changed, the record pointer remains where it is in the data set. |
| | You may specify a disk file containing one or more orders. If this is not specified, then the current Order List in the active and selected work area will be used. |
| **NOTE** | This function superseded the INDEXORD( ) function and should be used in its place. |
| **SEE ALSO** | SET INDEX, DBSETORDER( ), INDEXORD( ) |
| **EXAMPLE** | Please see Chapter 12. |

## OS( )

| | |
|---|---|
| **FUNCTION** | Returns the name of the operating system. |
| **SYNTAX** | `OS( )` |
| **PARAMETER** | None |
| **RETURNS** | <expC>  Operating system name |
| **LIBRARY** | CLIPPER.LIB |
| **DESCRIPTION** | This function returns the name and version of the operating system that is in use. |
| **NOTE** | This is a compatibility function and may not be supported in future versions. |
| **SEE ALSO** | VERSION( ), GETENV( ) |

## OUTERR( )

| | |
|---|---|
| **FUNCTION** | Outputs a list to the standard error device. |
| **SYNTAX** | OUTERR( <expX1> ) |
| **PARAMETER** | <expX1>    Any expression list |
| **LIBRARY** | CLIPPER.LIB |
| **DESCRIPTION** | This function writes the contents of the expression list passed as <expX1> to the standard error device. This output does not disturb the printer or the console device. |
| **SEE ALSO** | OUTSTD( ), DISPOUT( ) |
| **EXAMPLE** | See the OUTSTD( ) function. |

## OUTSTD( )

| | |
|---|---|
| **FUNCTION** | Outputs a list to the standard device. |
| **SYNTAX** | OUTSTD( <expX1> ) |
| **PARAMETER** | <expX1>    Any expression list |
| **LIBRARY** | CLIPPER.LIB |
| **DESCRIPTION** | This function sends the contents of <expX1> to the standard output device. This output may be redirected using the conventional DOS redirection symbols. |
| **SEE ALSO** | DISPOUT( ), OUTERR( ), QOUT( ), QQOUT( ) |

**EXAMPLE**

```
 1 : * File       Outsdemo.prg
 2 : * Compile    RMake sample /dFILE:Outsdemo
 3 :
 4 : procedure Main()
 5 :
 6 :    local nRow := 0
 7 :    local cField1
 8 :    local cField2
 9 :    local cField3
10 :
11 :    if file( "Clients.dbf" )
12 :       cls
13 :       use Clients new
14 :       cField1 := fieldblock( field(1) )
15 :       cField2 := fieldblock( field(2) )
16 :       cField3 := fieldwblock( field(3), select() )
```

```
17 :
18 :      Clients->( dbeval( {|| outstd( eval(cField1), ;
19 :                                     eval(cField2), ;
20 :                                     eval(cField3) + chr(13)+chr(10) )} ) )
21 :      wait
22 :
23 :      cls
24 :      Clients->( dbeval( {|| outerr( eval(cField1), ;
25 :                                     eval(cField2), ;
26 :                                     eval(cField3) + chr(13)+chr(10) )} ) )
27 :
28 :      wait
29 :      cls
30 :
31 :      dbeval( {|| setpos(nRow++,0), dispout( padr( eval(cField1),15) + ;
32 :                  eval(cField2) )},{|| !(nRow == 20)})
33 :      wait
34 :   endif
35 :
36 : // End of File: Outsdemo.prg
```

# PADC( )

| | |
|---|---|
| **FUNCTION** | Centers an expression for a given width. |
| **SYNTAX** | PADC( <expX1>, <expN2> [, <expC3> ] ) |
| **PARAMETERS** | <expX1>    Number, Character, or date to pad <br> <expN2>    Width of the output string <br> <expC3>    Fill character |
| **RETURNS** | <expC>    A Character expression |
| **LIBRARY** | EXTEND.LIB |
| **DESCRIPTION** | This function takes a date, number, or character expression <expX1> and attempts to center the expression within a string of a given width expressed as <expN2>. The default character used to pad either side of <expX1> will be a blank space; however, this character may be explicitly specified via the value of <expC3>. <br><br> If the length of <expX1> is longer than <expN2>, this function will truncate the string <expX1> from the leftmost side to the length of <expN2>. |
| **SEE ALSO** | ALLTRIM( ), PADL( ), PADR( ) |

**EXAMPLE**

```
1 : * File       Paddemo.prg
2 : * Compile    RMake sample /dFILE:Paddemo
3 :
4 : procedure Main()
```

```
 5 :
 6 :    cls
 7 :
 8 :    DispPads( date(), 20 )
 9 :    wait
10 :
11 :    cls
12 :    DispPads( 34.455, 20 )
13 :    wait
14 :
15 :    cls
16 :    DispPads( "Clipper 5.2", 20 )
17 :    wait
18 :
19 :    cls
20 :    DispPads( date(), 20, chr(178) )
21 :    wait
22 :
23 : static procedure DispPads( xData, nWidth, cChar )
24 :
25 :    local nCount
26 :
27 :    for nCount := 19 to maxcol() step 20
28 :       qout( replicate( ".", maxcol() ) )
29 :       qqout( chr(13) )
30 :       qqout( "..Width of" )
31 :       qqout( alltrim(str( nCount ) ) )
32 :       qqout( "..." )
33 :       qout( padc( xData, nCount, cChar ) )   // Center Justified
34 :       qout( padl( xData, nCount, cChar ) )   // Right Justified
35 :       qout( padr( xData, nCount, cChar ) )   // Left Justified
36 :       qout()
37 :    next
38 :
39 : // End of File: Paddemo.prg
```

# PADL( )

| | |
|---|---|
| **FUNCTION** | Left-justifies an expression for a given width. |
| **SYNTAX** | PADL( <expX1>, <expN2> [, <expC3> ] ) |
| **PARAMETERS** | <expX1>   Character, date, or number to work with |
| | <expN2>   Width of the output string |
| | <expC3>   Fill character |
| **RETURNS** | <expC>   A Character expression |
| **LIBRARY** | EXTEND.LIB |
| **DESCRIPTION** | This function takes a character, date, or numeric expression <expX1> and attempts to left-justify it within a string of a given width expressed as <expN2>. The default character used to pad the right side of <expX1> |

will be a blank space; however, this character may be changed via the value of <expC3>. If the length of <expX1> is longer than <expN2>, this function will truncate the expression <expX1> from the leftmost side to the length of <expN2>.

**SEE ALSO**  ALLTRIM( ), PADC( ), PADR( )

**EXAMPLE**  See the PADC( ) function.

## PADR( )

**FUNCTION**  Right-justifies an expression for a given width.

**SYNTAX**  `PADR( <expX1>, <expN2> [, <expC3> ] )`

**PARAMETERS**
- <expX1>  Character, date, or number to work with
- <expN2>  Width of the output string
- <expC3>  Fill character

**RETURNS**  <expC>  A Character expression

**LIBRARY**  EXTEND.LIB

**DESCRIPTION**  This function takes a string, date, or numeric expression <expX1> and attempts to right-justify it within a string of a given width expressed as <expN2>. The default character to pad the left side of <expX1> will be a blank space; however, this character may be modified via the value of <expC3>. If the length of <expX1> is longer than <expN2>, this function will truncate the expression <expX1> from the leftmost side to the length of <expN2>.

**SEE ALSO**  ALLTRIM( ), PADC( ), PADL( )

**EXAMPLE**  See the PADC( ) function.

## PCOL( )

**FUNCTION**  Returns the relative column position of the printer head.

**SYNTAX**  `PCOL()`

**PARAMETER**  None

**RETURNS**  <expN>  Printhead column position

**LIBRARY**  CLIPPER.LIB

| | |
|---|---|
| **DESCRIPTION** | This function returns the current column position plus one of the print-head. The beginning value of this function for a printer set at the top-of-form will be 0. |
| **SEE ALSO** | ROW( ), COL( ), PROW( ), SETPRC( ) |

# PCOUNT( )

| | |
|---|---|
| **FUNCTION** | Counts the number of parameters passed to a routine. |
| **SYNTAX** | PCOUNT ( ) |
| **PARAMETER** | None |
| **RETURNS** | <expN>     Number of parameters passed |
| **LIBRARY** | CLIPPER.LIB |
| **DESCRIPTION** | This function returns the number of successful parameter matches. If a parameter is skipped, this function will still consider it as a match, even though the value of a skipped parameter will be NIL. If no parameters are passed to a function or a procedure, the value of this function will be 0 or EMPTY( ). |
| **SEE ALSO** | Chapter 5, NIL VALTYPE( ); FUNCTION; PROCEDURE; PARAMETERS |

**EXAMPLE**

```
 1 : * File       Pardemo.prg
 2 : * Compile    RMake sample /dFILE:pardemo
 3 :
 4 : procedure Main()
 5 :
 6 :    local nCount
 7 :
 8 :    cls
 9 :    for nCount := 1 to 10
10 :       ShowStuf( nCount )
11 :    next
12 :    wait
13 :
14 :    cls
15 :    for nCount := 1 to 10
16 :       ShowStuf( nCount )
17 :    next
18 :    wait
19 :
20 :    ShowStuf()    // No parameters... clear the STATIC vars
21 :    cls
22 :    for nCount := 1 to 10
23 :       ShowStuf( nCount )
```

```
24 :    next
25 :    wait
26 :
27 :    scroll()              // Just clear the screen!
28 :    ShowStuf()            // No parameters... clear the STATIC vars
29 :    ShowStuf( ,.t. )      // Skip the first parameter, but it is still a NIL
30 :                          // value and can be checked as such
31 :
32 : ********************
33 :
34 : static function ShowStuf( xValue, xAnother )
35 :
36 :    static nRow := 0
37 :    static nCol := 0
38 :
39 :    if !empty( pcount() )  // A parameter was passed!
40 :       if xAnother == NIL   // It wasn't passed
41 :          devpos( nRow++, nCol )
42 :          devout( xValue )
43 :       else
44 :          devpos( nRow++, 0 )
45 :          devout( "The first parameter was skipped and the second was passed" )
46 :          devpos( nRow++, 0 )
47 :          devout( "which means that the value of PCOUNT is: " )
48 :          devout( pcount() )
49 :          devpos( nRow++, 0 )
50 :          devout( "and the value of XVALUE is: " )
51 :          devout( xValue )
52 :       endif
53 :
54 :    else  // When using STATIC variables in an application, one way to
55 :          // re-set their values to beginning default values is to use
56 :          // the PCOUNT() function to toggle these variables to be
57 :          // changed.
58 :
59 :       nRow := nCol := 0
60 :    endif
61 :
62 :    return( NIL )
63 :
64 : // End of File: Pardemo.prg
```

# PRINTCODES( )

**FUNCTION**   Sends printer codes to the printer.

**SYNTAX**     PRINTCODES( <expC1> )

**PARAMETER**  <expC1>   String of printer codes

**LIBRARY**    SAMPLES.LIB

| | |
|---|---|
| **DESCRIPTION** | This function takes the string <expC1> that may have embedded control codes for the printer and attempts to send the codes to that printer. It will maintain the old printer position should the codes shift the printhead. |
| **SEE ALSO** | PROW( ), PCOL( ), SETPRC( ) |

# PROCLINE( )

| | | |
|---|---|---|
| **FUNCTION** | Returns the line number of a function or procedure. | |
| **SYNTAX** | PROCLINE( [<expN1>] ) | |
| **PARAMETER** | <expN1> | Subroutine depth level |
| **RETURNS** | <expN> | Corresponding line number |
| **LIBRARY** | CLIPPER.LIB | |
| **DESCRIPTION** | This function returns the source code line number of the application. If the application or program module was compiled with the /L (no line numbers) switch, the value for this function will always be 0. If not specified, the line number returned will be for the currently active procedure, function, or code block. If specified, <expN1> is the depth pointer that refers to Clipper's activation stack. A value of 0 represents the current routine, a value of 1 refers to the previous calling routine, a value of 2 refers to the second previous calling routine, and so on. | |
| | If you are working from a code block routine, the value returned from this function will be the line number in which the code block was originally defined. | |
| **SEE ALSO** | PROCNAME( ), READVAR( ) | |
| **EXAMPLE** | See the example in the PROCNAME( ) function. | |

# PROCNAME( )

| | | |
|---|---|---|
| **FUNCTION** | Returns the name of a current or previous function, procedure or subroutine. | |
| **SYNTAX** | PROCNAME( [<expN1>] ) | |
| **PARAMETER** | <expN1> | Subroutine depth level |
| **RETURNS** | <expC> | Name of the subroutine at the specified activation level |
| **LIBRARY** | CLIPPER.LIB | |

**DESCRIPTION**  This function returns the name of an application's subroutine. If the value of this function is a NULL byte, the activation stack pointer is beyond the topmost program module level. If <expN1> is not specified, the subroutine name returned by this function will be the currently active procedure, function, or code block. If specified, <expN1> is the depth pointer that refers to Clipper's activation stack. A value of 0 represents the current routine; a value of 1 refers to the previous calling routine, a value of 2 refers to the second previous calling routine, and so on.

If you are working from a code block routine, the value returned from this function will be the name of the subroutine in which the code block was originally defined.

**SEE ALSO**  PROCLINE( ), READVAR( )

**EXAMPLE**

```
 1 : * File      Procdemo.prg
 2 : * Compile   Rmake sample /dFILE:procdemo
 3 :
 4 : procedure Main()
 5 :
 6 :    One()
 7 :
 8 : *******************
 9 :
10 : procedure One()    // Even though it is called like a function, it can be
11 :                    // a proc.
12 :
13 :    Two()
14 :
15 : *******************
16 :
17 : function Two()     // The difference between the two is that there needs to
18 :                    // be a RETURN statement on a function
19 :
20 :    Three()
21 :
22 :    return( NIL )
23 :
24 : *******************
25 :
26 : procedure Three()
27 :
28 :    Four()
29 :
30 : *******************
31 :
32 : procedure Four     // Doesn't have to have the closing paren's
33 :
34 :    eval( {|| Five()} )   // Acts like a function/procedure call!
35 :
36 : *******************
37 :
38 : function Five      // Could have been a procedure!
39 :
```

```
40 :    Six()
41 :
42 :    return( NIL )
43 :
44 : *******************
45 :
46 : procedure Six
47 :
48 :    local nLevel := 0  // Start with the current procedure/level
49 :
50 :    // This little loop will go through and post-increment the level pointer
51 :    // which will force it to the next level at the top of each iteration
52 :
53 :    cls
54 :    while !empty( procname( nLevel ) )
55 :      qout( padr( procname(nLevel), 20 ), procline(nLevel++) )
56 :    enddo
57 :
58 : // End of File: Procdemo.prg
```

## PROPER( )

| | |
|---|---|
| **FUNCTION** | Capitalizes each word in a given string. |
| **SYNTAX** | PROPER( <expC1> ) |
| **PARAMETER** | <expC1>   Any character string |
| **RETURNS** | <expC>   Formatted character string |
| **LIBRARY** | SAMPLES.LIB |
| **DESCRIPTION** | This function will take the string <expC1> and capitalize each word found in it and return the formatted string. |
| **SEE ALSO** | UPPER( ), LOWER( ), SUBSTR( ) |

## PROW( )

| | |
|---|---|
| **FUNCTION** | Returns the relative row position of the printhead. |
| **SYNTAX** | PROW( ) |
| **PARAMETER** | None |
| **RETURNS** | <expN>   Row position |
| **LIBRARY** | CLIPPER.LIB |

| | |
|---|---|
| **DESCRIPTION** | This function returns the current row position of the printhead. The beginning value of this function for a printer set at the top of the form will be 0. |
| **SEE ALSO** | ROW( ), COL( ), SETPRC( ), PCOL( ) |

## QOUT( )

| | |
|---|---|
| **FUNCTION** | Displays an expression to a device. |
| **SYNTAX** | `QOUT( [<expX1> [, <expX2>...]] )` |
| **PARAMETERS** | <expX1> Any expression <br> <expX2> Any expression, and so on |
| **LIBRARY** | CLIPPER.LIB |
| **DESCRIPTION** | This function is the standard replacement for the "?" command. It will issue a carriage return/line feed combination before the first expression <expX1> is displayed. <br><br> If the device is set to the printer, the function will update PROW( ) and PCOL( ). <br><br> If a multiple expression list is specified, a single blank space will be issued to separate each expression. |
| **SEE ALSO** | ?, ??, QQOUT( ) |

## QQOUT( )

| | |
|---|---|
| **FUNCTION** | Displays an expression to a device. |
| **SYNTAX** | `QQOUT( [<expX1> [, <expX2>...]] )` |
| **PARAMETERS** | <expX1> Any expression <br> <expX2> Any expression, and so on |
| **LIBRARY** | CLIPPER.LIB |
| **DESCRIPTION** | This function is the standard replacement for the "??" command. No carriage return/line feed combination will be issued in conjunction with this function. <br><br> If the device is set to the printer, the function will update PROW( ) and PCOL( ). <br><br> If a multiple expression list is specified, a single blank space will separate each expression. |
| **SEE ALSO** | ?, ??, QOUT( ) |

## RANGECHECK( )

| | |
|---|---|
| **FUNCTION** | Checks the value of a GET variable in a range. |
| **SYNTAX** | `RANGECHECK( <expO1>, <expX2>, <expX3>, <expX4> )` |
| **PARAMETERS** | <expO1>  Any GET object<br><expX2>  Unused parameter<br><expX3>  Date, character, or numeric value for "low" range<br><expX4>  Date, character, or numeric value for "high" range |
| **RETURNS** | <expL>  Logical true (.T.) or false (.F.) value |
| **LIBRARY** | CLIPPER.LIB |
| **DESCRIPTION** | This function takes the value found in the GET object <expO1> and tests to see if it is in the range beginning at <expX3> and ending at <expX4>. The data type of <expX3> and <expX4> must be the same data type as the value found in the GET object <expO1>. The parameter <expX2> is not used in this function and may be skipped with a NIL value.<br><br>If the value of the variable in the GET object <expO1> is within the range inclusively, then the function will return a logical true (.T.). If not, then the function will return a logical false (.F.) value and will display a message to the SCOREBOARD region, should it be turned on, indicating the "high" and "low" values. |
| **SEE ALSO** | VALID clause, WHEN clause, SET( ) |

## RAT( )

| | |
|---|---|
| **FUNCTION** | Searches for a substring from the right side of a string. |
| **SYNTAX** | `RAT(<expC1>, <expC2>)` |
| **PARAMETERS** | <expC1>  Character string to locate<br><expC2>  Main string to be searched |
| **RETURNS** | <expN>  Location of beginning position |
| **LIBRARY** | EXTEND.LIB |
| **DESCRIPTION** | This function [ RIGHT AT( ) ] searches through <expC2> for the first existence of <expC1>. The search operation is performed from the right side of <expC2> to the left. If the function is unable to find any occurrence of <expC1> in <expC2>, the value of the function will be 0. |
| **SEE ALSO** | AT( ), $, SUBSTR( ), RIGHT( ), OCCURS |
| **EXAMPLE** | See the AT( ) function. |

## RDDLIST( )

| | |
|---|---|
| **FUNCTION** | Yields an array of available RDDs in an application. |
| **SYNTAX** | `RDDLIST( [<expN1>] )` |
| **PARAMETER** | <expN1>   RDD Type |
| **RETURNS** | <expA>   Array of active RDDs |
| **LIBRARY** | CLIPPER.LIB |
| **DESCRIPTION** | This function will return an array of active RDDs in an application. If <expN1> is not supplied, then all active RDDs will be listed in the array. The following table shows the potential values for <expN1>. |

| Value | Meaning |
|---|---|
| 1 | Full RDD implementation |
| 2 | Import/Export only |

| | |
|---|---|
| **SEE ALSO** | DBSETDRIVER( ), RDDNAME( ), RDDSETDEFAULT( ) |
| **EXAMPLE** | Please see Chapter 12. |

## RDDNAME( )

| | |
|---|---|
| **FUNCTION** | Returns the name of the currently active RDD. |
| **SYNTAX** | `RDDNAME( )` |
| **PARAMETER** | None |
| **RETURNS** | <expC>   RDD name |
| **LIBRARY** | CLIPPER.LIB |
| **DESCRIPTION** | This function will return the name of the RDD active in the currently selected work area. |
| **SEE ALSO** | DBSETDRIVER( ), RDDLIST( ), RDDSETDEFAULT( ) |
| **EXAMPLE** | Please see Chapter 12. |

## RDDSETDEFAULT( )

| | |
|---|---|
| **FUNCTION** | Sets/Gets the default RDD driver in an application. |
| **SYNTAX** | `RDDSETDEFAULT( [<expC1>] )` |

| | |
|---|---|
| **PARAMETER** | <expC1>   RDD name |
| **RETURNS** | <expC>   Old driver name |
| **LIBRARY** | CLIPPER.LIB |
| **DESCRIPTION** | This function returns the name of the default replaceable database driver (RDD) in the application. If specified, <expC1> is the name of a new driver to be used as the "default" driver. The function will still return the name of the old default driver prior to establishing a new one. |
| **NOTE** | This function is to replace the DBSETDRIVER( ) function. |
| **SEE ALSO** | DBSETDRIVER( ), RDDNAME( ) |
| **EXAMPLE** | Please see Chapter 12. |

# READEXIT( )

| | |
|---|---|
| **FUNCTION** | Toggles the use of the UP and DOWN arrow keys to exit a READ. |
| **SYNTAX** | `READEXIT( [<expL1>] )` |
| **PARAMETER** | <expL1>   Logical true (.T.) or false (.F.) |
| **RETURNS** | <expL>   Logical true (.T.) or false (.F.) |
| **LIBRARY** | CLIPPER.LIB |
| **DESCRIPTION** | This function toggles the UP and DOWN arrow keys as exit keys to a READ command or READMODAL( ) function. If no parameter is specified, the function will return the current setting.<br><br>The default setting for the UP and DOWN arrow keys is a logical false (.F.). |
| **SEE ALSO** | READINSERT( ), READ |
| **EXAMPLE** | See to the READINSERT( ) function. |

# READFORMAT( )

| | |
|---|---|
| **FUNCTION** | SETS/GETS code block for FORMAT file. |
| **SYNTAX** | `READFORMAT( [<expB1>] )` |
| **PARAMETER** | <expB1>   Code block representing .PRG file for a FORMAT |
| **RETURNS** | <expB>   Code block pointing to FORMAT file |

**LIBRARY** CLIPPER.LIB

**DESCRIPTION** This function accesses the current format file in its internal code block and returns that code block. A new format file could be assigned to the internal value by passing it as <expB1>.

**SEE ALSO** READUPDATED( ), SET FORMAT TO, READ

# READINSERT( )

**FUNCTION** Toggles the status of the INS key in a READ or MEMOEDIT( ).

**SYNTAX** READINSERT( [<expL1>] )

**PARAMETER** <expL1>   Logical true (.T.) or false (.F.)

**RETURNS** <expL>   Logical true (.T.) or false (.F.)

**LIBRARY** CLIPPER.LIB

**DESCRIPTION** This function checks or toggles the status of the INSERT key for all READs and MEMOEDIT( ) functions.
 The default setting is a logical false (.F.).

**SEE ALSO** READEXIT( )

**EXAMPLE**

```
 1 : * File       Readdemo.prg
 2 : * Compile    Rmake sample /dFILE:readdemo
 3 :
 4 : #include "PTVerbs.ch"   // Power Tools Header file of commands/statements
 5 : #include "PTInkey.ch"   // Power Tools Header file of ASCII keystrokes
 6 :
 7 : procedure Main()
 8 :
 9 :    local cTemp    := space(10)
10 :    local getlist := {}          // This is for the READ command and prevents
11 :                                 // a warning message ASSUMING MEMVAR
12 :
13 :    PROCESS    // This is a used-defined command
14 :       cls
15 :
16 :       devpos( 10,10 )
17 :       devout( "Insert status: " )
18 :       devout( if( readinsert(), "<On>", "<Overstrike>" ) )
19 :
20 :       devpos(11,10)
21 :       devout( "UP/DOWN keys: " )
22 :       devout( if( readexit(), "Exit a get", "DO NOT EXIT" ) )
23 :
24 :       devpos(15,20)
25 :       devout("Press ESC to quit")
```

```
26 :
27 :      @ 16,20 say "Enter value for X" get cTemp
28 :      read
29 :
30 :      if lastkey() == pESC
31 :         exit
32 :      endif
33 :
34 :      devpos(20,20)
35 :      devout("The value of the last key pressed was" )
36 :      devout( lastkey() )
37 :
38 :      devpos(22,20)
39 :      devout("Press any key to continue....")
40 :
41 :      inkey(0)
42 :      cTemp:=space(10)
43 :      readinsert( !readinsert() )
44 :      readexit( !readexit() )
45 :
46 :   enddo
47 :
48 :   cls
49 :   @ 0,0 say "And now... build the screen and use the READKILL() function"
50 :   @ 1,0 say "to turn off the active GET list..."
51 :
52 :   @ 3,10 say "Enter value for X" get cTemp when (readkill(.t.), .t.)
53 :   read
54 :
55 :   @ 6,0 say "Press any key...."
56 :
57 :   inkey(0)
58 :
59 :   ? "And now two sets of calls to check the status of the last GET"
60 :   ?
61 :   ? readupdated(), updated()    // current value of these two functions
62 :   ? readupdated(!readupdated()), updated()   // and now the toggled value
63 :
64 : // End of File: Readdemo.prg
```

# READKEY( )

**FUNCTION**      Returns the key value for the key used to exit from a READ.

**SYNTAX**        READKEY()

**PARAMETER**     None

**RETURNS**       <expN>    Numeric expression

**LIBRARY**       EXTEND.LIB

| | | |
|---|---|---|
| **DESCRIPTION** | This function returns a number representing the key pressed to exit from any full-screen editing mode. Some of the values returned from this function simulate the key values obtained from other interpreters. These key values, shown in the following table, are different from the LASTKEY( ) function: | |

| Exit Key | Simulated Value |
|---|---|
| Up Arrow | 5 |
| Down Arrow | 2 |
| PgUp | 6 |
| PgDn | 7 |
| CTRL-pgup | 31 |
| CTRL-pgdn | 30 |
| ESC | 12 |
| Ctrl-END | 14 |
| Ctrl-W | 14 |
| TYPE PAST END | 15 |
| ENTER | 15 |

**NOTE**  This is a compatibility function and may not be supported in future versions.

**SEE ALSO**  LASTKEY( ), INKEY( ), NEXTKEY( )

## READKILL( )

**FUNCTION**  Kills the active GETLIST array and all active GET objects.

**SYNTAX**  `READKILL( [<expL1>] )`

**PARAMETER**  <expL1>   Toggle status of active read

**RETURNS**  <expL>   Logical true (.T.) or logical false (.F.)

**LIBRARY**  CLIPPER.LIB

**DESCRIPTION**  This function returns the status of the internal variable keeping track of the active GETLIST of GET objects being processed by the READMODAL( ) function. If <expL1> is assigned to a logical true (.T.) value, it will attempt, while processing the READMODAL( ) function, to kill the active READ.

**SEE ALSO**  READINSERT( ), READEXIT( )

**EXAMPLE**  Please see the READINSERT( ) function.

## READMODAL( )

| | |
|---|---|
| **FUNCTION** | Activates a READ on the current GETLIST. |
| **SYNTAX** | READMODAL( <expA1>  [, <expN2> ] ) |
| **PARAMETERS** | <expA1>   Array expression with GET information<br><expN2>   Ordinal position to start at in the GET list |
| **LIBRARY** | CLIPPER.LIB |
| **DESCRIPTION** | This function implements a full-screen editing mode for the GETs assigned in the array specified as <expA1>.<br>The starting position for the GET list may be specified as <expN2>. If not specified or if out of range, the default value for <expN2> will be 1, which means that the data entry will start with the first GET in the list. |
| **NOTE** | This function is slightly different from the READ command in that it will not clear out the specified GET array. |
| **SEE ALSO** | GETACTIVE( ), GETNEW( ), READ |
| **EXAMPLE** | Please see Chapter 18. |

## READUPDATED( )

| | |
|---|---|
| **FUNCTION** | GETS/SETS the internal updated status of an active READ process. |
| **SYNTAX** | READUPDATED( [<expL1>] ) |
| **PARAMETER** | <expL1>   Toggle the internal updated status of an active GETLIST |
| **RETURNS** | <expL>   Original status of the updated value in the active READMODAL( ) function |
| **LIBRARY** | CLIPPER.LIB |
| **DESCRIPTION** | This function is similar to the UPDATED( ) function except that it can set the status of the internal variable reporting the updated status of a GET variable. The function will return the original status of the internal UPDATED value. If <expL1> is passed, then that value will be assigned to the internal UPDATED variable. |
| **SEE ALSO** | UPDATED( ), READEXIT( ), READINSERT( ), READKILL( ) |
| **EXAMPLE** | Please see the READINSERT( ) function. |

## READVAR( )

| | |
|---|---|
| **FUNCTION** | Returns the name of the current variable from a MENU TO or READ command. |
| **SYNTAX** | `READVAR( [<expC1>] )` |
| **PARAMETER** | <expC1>  Name of variable to be used in the SETKEY( ) function and other global operations |
| **RETURNS** | <expC>  Name of a variable or field |
| **LIBRARY** | CLIPPER.LIB |
| **DESCRIPTION** | This function returns the name of the variable pending in the current GET/MENU system. If none is pending, a NULL byte will be returned.<br><br>If the variable found by this function is in a READ command or a READMODAL( ) function, and if that variable is a field name, the value from this function will be either the name of the field with the alias name or the work area. If the variable is an array subscript, this function will return the name of the array as well as the subscript value.<br><br>The value returned by this function may be set by passing the name of the variable to the function in <expC1>. |
| **SEE ALSO** | PROCLINE( ), PROCNAME( ), SET KEY, SETKEY( ) |

## RECCOUNT( )

| | |
|---|---|
| **FUNCTION** | Counts the number of records in a database. |
| **SYNTAX** | `RECCOUNT( )` |
| **PARAMETER** | None |
| **RETURNS** | <expN>  Number of records |
| **LIBRARY** | CLIPPER.LIB |
| **DESCRIPTION** | This function returns the number of records present in the database in the selected or designated work area. If no records are present, the value of this function will be 0. Additionally, if no database is in use in the work area, this function will return a 0 value as well.<br><br>The SET FILTER TO and SET DELETED TO commands have no effect on the value obtained from this function. |
| **NOTE** | This function is a compatibility function and may not be supported in future versions. |
| **SEE ALSO** | LASTREC( ), EOF( ), GO, RECNO( ), DBGOBOTTOM( ) |

## RECLOCK( )

**FUNCTION**      Attempts to lock a record with optional retry.

**SYNTAX**        RECLOCK( [<expN1>] )

**PARAMETER**     <expN1>     Number of seconds to attempt a retry

**RETURNS**       <expL>      Logical true (.T.) or a logical false (.F.)

**LIBRARY**       SAMPLES.LIB

**DESCRIPTION**   This function will return a logical true (.T.) value if it is able to lock the current record in the active and/or selected work area. If a logical false (.F.) is returned, then the record was not locked. Optionally, a value representing the number of seconds to attempt a retry <expN1> may be included. If not passed, the default value of <expN1> is 2, meaning 2 seconds to wait before re-attempting to lock the record.

**SEE ALSO**      ADDREC( ), FILLOCK( )

## RECNO( )

**FUNCTION**      Returns the current record number or identity.

**SYNTAX**        RECNO( )

**PARAMETER**     None

**RETURNS**       <expX>      Record number or identity

**LIBRARY**       CLIPPER.LIB

**DESCRIPTION**   This function returns the position of the record pointer or record identity in the currently selected or designated work area.
    If the database is empty and if the RDD is the traditional .DBF file, the value of this function will be 1. Otherwise, the value of RECNO( ) will be based on the structure of the type of data file currently active in the work area.

**SEE ALSO**      LASTREC( ), EOF( ), BOF( ), GO TOP, GO BOTTOM, DBGOTOP( ), DBGOBOTTOM( )

**EXAMPLE**       Please see Chapter 12.

# RECSIZE( )

**FUNCTION** Returns the size of a single record in an active database.

**SYNTAX** RECSIZE()

**PARAMETER** None

**RETURNS** &lt;expN&gt;   Record size

**LIBRARY** EXTEND.LIB

**DESCRIPTION** This function returns the number of bytes used by a single record in the currently selected or designated database file. If no database is in use in this work area, the return value from this function will be zero.

**SEE ALSO** HEADER( ), LASTREC( ), DISKSPACE( )

**EXAMPLE**

```
 1 : * File       Recsdemo.prg
 2 : * Compile    Rmake sample /dFILE:recsdemo.prg
 3 :
 4 : // For convenience, here is a pseudofunction
 5 : #xtranslate FSIZE() => header() + (recsize() * lastrec() + 1)
 6 :
 7 : procedure Main()
 8 :
 9 :    use Clients new
10 :    use Ontap new
11 :    use Notap new
12 :
13 :    cls
14 :    qout( Clients->(header()),  Ontap->(header()),  Notap->(header()) )
15 :    qout( Clients->(recsize()), Ontap->(recsize()), Notap->(recsize()) )
16 :    qout( Clients->(lastrec()), Ontap->(lastrec()), Notap->(lastrec()) )
17 :
18 :    qout( Clients->(FSIZE()), Ontap->(FSIZE()), Notap->(FSIZE()) )
19 :    qout( diskspace() )
20 :
21 : // End of File: Recsdemo.prg
```

# REPLICATE( )

**FUNCTION** Repeats a single character expression.

**SYNTAX** REPLICATE( &lt;expC1&gt;, &lt;expN2&gt; )

**PARAMETERS** &lt;expC1&gt;   Any character expression to be repeated
&lt;expN2&gt;   Number of times to duplicate &lt;expC1&gt;

**RETURNS** &lt;expC&gt;   Character expression

| | |
|---|---|
| **LIBRARY** | CLIPPER.LIB |
| **DESCRIPTION** | This function returns a string composed of <expN2> repetitions of <expC1>. The length of the character string returned from this function may not exceed 64K. A value of 0 for <expN2> will yield a NULL string. |
| **SEE ALSO** | SPACE( ), PADR( ), PADC( ), PADL( ) |
| **EXAMPLE** | See the examples for PADR( ) or SAVESCREEN( ). |

## RESTSCREEN( )

| | |
|---|---|
| **FUNCTION** | Restores a specified area of the screen. |
| **SYNTAX** | `RESTSCREEN( [<expN1>] [, <expN2>] [, <expN3>] [, <expN4>], <expC5>)` |
| **PARAMETERS** | <expN1>　Top row position<br><expN2>　Left column position<br><expN3>　Bottom row position<br><expN4>　Right column position<br><expC5>　String to be restored to the screen |
| **LIBRARY** | EXTEND.LIB |
| **DESCRIPTION** | This function restores the screen contents of the string <expC5> at the window coordinate beginning at <expN1>, <expN2> down through to <expN3>, <expN4>.<br>　　The default value of <expN1>, <expN2> will be 0,0 and the default values for <expN3>, <expN4> will be the value of maxrow( ), maxcol( ). |
| **NOTE** | This function is specifically associated with the IBM-PC and may not be supported with other screen drivers. |
| **SEE ALSO** | SAVE SCREEN, RESTORE SCREEN, SAVESCREEN( ) |
| **EXAMPLE** | Please see the SAVESCREEN( ) function. |

## RIGHT( )

| | |
|---|---|
| **FUNCTION** | Returns the rightmost substring of a character expression. |
| **SYNTAX** | `RIGHT( <expC1>, <expN2> )` |
| **PARAMETERS** | <expC1>　Character expression to be processed<br><expN2>　The number of characters to be parsed from <expC1> |

| | |
|---|---|
| **RETURNS** | <expC>    Substring character expression |
| **LIBRARY** | EXTEND.LIB |
| **DESCRIPTION** | This function returns the rightmost <expN2> characters of <expC1>. If the value of <expN2> is zero or a negative number, the value returned by this function is a NULL byte. |
| **SEE ALSO** | LEFT( ), SUBSTR( ) |
| **EXAMPLE** | Please refer to the SUBSTR( ) function. |

## RLOCK( )

| | |
|---|---|
| **FUNCTION** | Locks a record in a work area. |
| **SYNTAX** | RLOCK( ) |
| **PARAMETER** | None |
| **RETURNS** | <expL>    Logical true (.T.) or false (.F.) |
| **LIBRARY** | CLIPPER.LIB |
| **DESCRIPTION** | This function returns a logical true (.T.) if an attempt to lock a specific record in the selected or designated work area is successful. It will yield a false (.F.) if either the file or the desired record is currently locked.<br><br>A record that is locked remains locked until another RLOCK( ) is issued or until an UNLOCK command is executed. |
| **SEE ALSO** | FLOCK( ), USE <EXCLUSIVE>, SET EXCLUSIVE |

## ROUND( )

| | |
|---|---|
| **FUNCTION** | Rounds off a numeric expression. |
| **SYNTAX** | ROUND( <expN1>, <expN2> ) |
| **PARAMETERS** | <expN1>    Numeric expression to be rounded<br><expN2>    The number of places to round to |
| **RETURNS** | <expN>    Numeric expression |
| **LIBRARY** | CLIPPER.LIB |
| **DESCRIPTION** | This function rounds off the value of <expN1> to the number of decimal places specified by <expN2>. If the value of <expN2> is a negative number, the function will attempt to round <expN1> in whole numbers; |

numbers from 5 through 9 will be rounded up, and all others will be rounded down.

**SEE ALSO**  INT( ), STR( ), VAL( ), SET FIXED

**EXAMPLE**  See the STRZERO( ) function.

# ROW( )

**FUNCTION**  Returns the current row position.

**SYNTAX**  ROW()

**PARAMETER**  None

**RETURNS**  <expN>   The screen's row position

**LIBRARY**  CLIPPER.LIB

**DESCRIPTION**  This function returns the current cursor row location. The return value of this function is between 0 and MAXROW( ).

**SEE ALSO**  COL( ), PROW( ), PCOL( ), SETMODE( )

**EXAMPLE**

```
 1 : * File       Rowdemo.prg
 2 : * Compile    Rmake sample /dFILE:rowdemo
 3 :
 4 : procedure Main()
 5 :
 6 :    local aDir := directory()   // Take all normal, archive files
 7 :    local nCount
 8 :
 9 :    cls
10 :    // What this program will try to demonstrate is that the value of the
11 :    // CLS command as well as the QQOUT() and QOUT() function have a direct
12 :    // impact on the display and value of the ROW() and COL() functions.
13 :    // Each item is displayed to the screen, and if the current COL()
14 :    // position is close to MAXCOL() and ROW() is close to the value of in
15 :    // relation to MAXROW(), the display is cleared and the items are then
16 :    // displayed.
17 :
18 :    for nCount := 1 to len( aDir )
19 :       qqout( padr( "Row #" + alltrim(str( row() ) ), 15) )
20 :       qqout( padr( aDir[nCount, 1], 12 ) )
21 :       qqout( padc( aDir[nCount, 2], 25 ) )
22 :       qqout( padr( aDir[nCount, 3], 10 ) )
23 :       qqout( padr( aDir[nCount, 4], 10 ) )
24 :       qqout( aDir[nCount, 5], chr(13)+chr(10) )
25 :       if row() == 21
26 :          qout()
27 :          wait "Press any key for next screen!!!"
28 :          cls
```

```
29 :      endif
30 :    next
31 :    qout()
32 :    wait "Press any key for COL() test!"
33 :
34 :    cls
35 :    for nCount := 1 to len( aDir )
36 :      qqout( padr( aDir[nCount, 1], 20 ) )
37 :
38 :      if col() > 60   // This adjusts the column position
39 :        qqout()
40 :      endif
41 :
42 :      if row() == 21  // And this tests the row position
43 :        qout()
44 :        wait "And now, any key for more..."
45 :        cls
46 :      endif
47 :    next
48 :
49 : // End of File: Rowdemo.prg
```

# RTOD( )

| | |
|---|---|
| **FUNCTION** | Converts radians to degrees. |
| **SYNTAX** | RTOD( <expN1> ) |
| **PARAMETER** | <expN1>   Number of radians to be converted |
| **RETURNS** | <expN>   Number of equivalent degrees |
| **LIBRARY** | SAMPLES.LIB |
| **DESCRIPTION** | This function takes the value <expN1> which should be a number in radians, and converts it to a value in degrees. |
| **SEE ALSO** | DTOR( ) |

# RTRIM( )

| | |
|---|---|
| **FUNCTION** | Removes trailing spaces from a string. |
| **SYNTAX** | RTRIM( <expC1> ) |
| **PARAMETER** | <expC1>   Any character expression |
| **RETURNS** | <expC>   The formatted character expression |
| **LIBRARY** | CLIPPER.LIB |

| | |
|---|---|
| **DESCRIPTION** | This function returns the value of <expC1> with trailing blank spaces removed. |
| **NOTE** | This function is identical to TRIM( ) and is the opposite of LTRIM( ). |
| **SEE ALSO** | TRIM( ), LTRIM( ), ALLTRIM( ) |
| **EXAMPLE** | See the SUBSTR( ) function. |

## SAVESCREEN( )

| | | |
|---|---|---|
| **FUNCTION** | Saves the screen at specified window coordinates. | |
| **SYNTAX** | SAVESCREEN( [<expN1>] [, <expN2>] [, <expN3>] [, <expN4>] ) | |
| **PARAMETERS** | <expN1> | Top row coordinate |
| | <expN2> | Left column coordinate |
| | <expN3> | Bottom row coordinate |
| | <expN4> | Right column coordinate |
| **RETURNS** | <expC> | Character expression |
| **LIBRARY** | EXTEND.LIB | |
| **DESCRIPTION** | This function saves the screen contents in the windowed area beginning at top-left coordinates <expN1>, <expN2> down through to bottom-right coordinates expressed as <expN3>, <expN4>. The length of the character string returned by the function will be twice the area specified by the window coordinates because of the individual attributes associated with each screen character.<br><br>The default values for <expN1>, <expN2> will be 0,0 and the default values for <expN3>, <expN4> will be MAXROW( ), MAXCOL( ). | |
| **SEE ALSO** | SAVE SCREEN, RESTORE SCREEN, SAVESCREEN( ) | |
| **EXAMPLE** | | |

```
 1 : * File       Sscrdemo.prg
 2 : * Compile    RMake sample /dFILE:sscrdemo
 3 :
 4 : #include "PTInkey.ch"    // Power Tools Header file of ASCII values
 5 : #include "PTVerbs.ch"    // Power Tools Header file of commands/statements
 6 : #include "PTValue.ch"    // Power Tools Header file of misc values.
 7 :
 8 : procedure Main()
 9 :
10 :    local cScreen          // Will hold the image of the screen of the window
11 :    local cBackground      // Background screen image for shifting purposes
12 :    local nRow             // Row value for the display
13 :    local nKey             // ASCII value of key pressed
```

```
14 :    local nCol     := 0  // starts off with this value
15 :    local nTop     := 10 // Top coordinate of window region
16 :    local nLeft    := 10 // Left column coordinate of window region
17 :    local nBottom  := 15 // Bottom row coordinate of window region
18 :    local nRight   := 30 // Right column coordinate of window region
19 :
20 :    scroll()                        // Why use CLS when there is direct cursor
21 :    dispbox( 10,10,15,30,pDBAR) // positioning with this function?
22 :    cScreen := savescreen(10,10,15,30)
23 :
24 :    ? "Press any key..."
25 :    inkey(0)
26 :
27 :    restscreen(10,10,15,30,cScreen)
28 :    for nRow := 0 to 10
29 :       restscreen(nRow, nCol, nRow+5, nCol+20, cScreen )
30 :       inkey(1)
31 :       nCol += 3  // Increment the value of the column
32 :    next
33 :
34 :    @ nRow, nCol say "Any key..."
35 :    inkey(0)
36 :
37 :    scroll()
38 :    @ maxrow(), 0 say "Use the cursor keys to drag the frame!"
39 :
40 :    setcursor( 0 ) // Turn cursor off!
41 :
42 :    PROCESS
43 :       // This also shows the use of the REPLICATE() function in conjunction
44 :       // with the Box() translation. In this, 8 CHR(177)'s will be the
45 :       // frame  of the window that is about to be dragged!
46 :       cBackground := savescreen( nTop, nLeft, nBottom, nRight )
47 :       dispbox( nTop, nLeft, nBottom, nRight, replicate( chr(177), 8 ) )
48 :
49 :       nKey := inkey(0)    // Wait for a key and assign!
50 :       restscreen( nTop, nLeft, nBottom, nRight, cBackground )
51 :
52 :       // Now, process the keystroke!
53 :       do case
54 :       case nKey == pESC .or. nKey == pENTER
55 :          exit
56 :
57 :       case nKey == pUP_ARROW
58 :          if nTop - 1 >= 0
59 :             nTop--
60 :             nBottom--
61 :          endif
62 :
63 :       case nKey == pDOWN_ARROW
64 :          if nBottom + 1 <= maxrow()
65 :             nTop++
66 :             nBottom++
67 :          endif
68 :
69 :       case nKey == pLEFT_ARROW
70 :          if nLeft - 1 >= 0
```

```
 71 :           nLeft--
 72 :           nRight--
 73 :         endif
 74 :
 75 :      case nKey ==pRIGHT_ARROW
 76 :        if nRight + 1 <= maxcol()
 77 :          nRight++
 78 :          nLeft++
 79 :        endif
 80 :
 81 :      case nKey == pTAB
 82 :        setmode(43,80)
 83 :
 84 :      case nKey == pBKSP    // because the values for the box may have been
 85 :        setmode(25,00)      // extended beyond the border of the new window,
 86 :                            // we will just go back to the defaults!
 87 :        nTop := nLeft := 10
 88 :        nBottom := 15
 89 :        nRight  := 30
 90 :
 91 :      endcase
 92 :
 93 :   END PROCESS
 94 :
 95 :   if nKey == pENTER
 96 :     scroll()
 97 :     dispbox( nTop, nLeft, nBottom, nRight, pDBAR)
 98 :     @ maxrow(), 00 say "And here is the final box!"
 99 :   endif
100 :
101 : // End of File: Sscrdemo.prg
```

## SCROLL( )

**FUNCTION**    Manipulates a windowed area.

**SYNTAX**      SCROLL( [<expN1>] [, <expN2>] [, <expN3> ]
                [, <expN4>] [,<expN5>] [, <expN6>] )

**PARAMETERS**  <expN1>   Top row coordinate
                <expN2>   Left column coordinate
                <expN3>   Bottom row coordinate
                <expN4>   Right column coordinate
                <expN5>   Number of rows to scroll
                <expN6>   Number of columns to scroll

**LIBRARY**     CLIPPER.LIB

**DESCRIPTION** This function either scrolls the screen up or down from the top-left coordinates of <expN1>, <expN2> to the bottom-right coordinates <expN3>,<expN4>. Based on the value of <expN5>, this function may also clear the specified windowed area. The values of <expN5> and their operation are as follows:

| <expN5> | Operation |
|---|---|
| 0 | Clears the windowed area |
| – <number> | Scrolls down <number> rows |
| + <number> | Scrolls up <number> rows |

Optionally, the number of columns to scroll may be specified by <expN6>. The values of <expN6> and their operation are as follows:

| <expN6> | Operation |
|---|---|
| – <number> | Scrolls left <number> of columns |
| + <number> | Scrolls right <number> of columns |

Passing no parameters to this function clears the entire screen.

**SEE ALSO**      @ ... CLEAR

**EXAMPLE**

```
 1 : * File       Scrodemo.prg
 2 : * Compile    Rmake sample /dFILE:scrodemo
 3 :
 4 : procedure Main()
 5 :
 6 :    local nTop      := 11
 7 :    local nBottom   := 12
 8 :    local nLeft     := 20
 9 :    local nRight    := 60
10 :    local cScreen
11 :    local nCount
12 :
13 :    scroll()
14 :    run dir /w
15 :    cScreen := savescreen()   // the entire screen
16 :    wait
17 :
18 :    for nCount := 1 to 5
19 :      scroll( nTop, nLeft, nBottom, nRight, 0 )  // The entire region
20 :      inkey(1)
21 :      nTop    -= 2
22 :      nBottom += 2
23 :      nLeft   -= 5
24 :      nRight  += 5
25 :    next
26 :    wait
27 :
28 :    restscreen(,,,,cScreen)   // +1Restore the screen
29 :    for nCount := 1 to maxrow()
30 :      scroll(,,,,-1)          // scroll the entire screen
31 :      inkey(1)
32 :    next
33 :    wait
34 :
```

```
35 :    restscreen(,,,,cScreen)   // +1Restore the screen
36 :    for nCount := 1 to maxrow()
37 :       scroll(,,,,1)          // scroll the entire screen
38 :       inkey(1)
39 :    next
40 :    wait
41 :
42 :    // And now, to show the use of the vertical scroll parameter!
43 :    restscreen(,,,,cScreen)   // +1Restore the screen
44 :    for nCount := 1 to maxcol()
45 :       scroll(,,,,,1)         // scroll the entire screen
46 :       inkey(1)
47 :    next
48 :    wait
49 :
50 :    restscreen(,,,,cScreen)   // +1Restore the screen
51 :    for nCount := 1 to maxcol()
52 :       scroll(,,,,,-1)        // scroll the entire screen
53 :       inkey(1)
54 :    next
55 :    wait
56 :
57 :    scroll()
58 :
59 : // End of File: Scrodemo.prg
```

# SCROLLBARDISPLAY( )

**FUNCTION**    Displays a scrollbar to the screen.

**SYNTAX**      SCROLLBARDISPLAY( <expA1> )

**PARAMETER**   <expA1>   Array of scrollbar information

**RETURNS**     <expA>    A reference to the scrollbar array

**LIBRARY**     SAMPLES.LIB

**DESCRIPTION** This function takes the information contained in the array <expA1> and displays it to the screen. The contents of <expA1> must be created via the SCROLLBARNEW( ) function and updated via the SCROLLBARUPDATE( ) function.

**SEE ALSO**    SCROLLBARNEW( ), SCROLLBARUPDATE( )

**EXAMPLE**     Please see the SCROLLBARUPDATE( ) function.

# SCROLLBARNEW( )

| | |
|---|---|
| **FUNCTION** | Creates a scroll bar array with given information. |
| **SYNTAX** | SCROLLBARNEW( <expN1>, <expN2>, <expN3> [, <expC4>] [, <expN5>] ) |
| **PARAMETERS** | <expN1> Top row coordinate of scrollbar region<br><expN2> Left column coordinate of scrollbar region<br><expN3> Bottom row coordinate of scrollbar region<br><expC4> Colors string of scrollbar region<br><expN5> Starting position within scrollbar |
| **RETURNS** | <expA> |
| **LIBRARY** | SAMPLES.LIB |
| **DESCRIPTION** | This function builds and returns a scrollbar array that is to be used by the SCROLLBARDISPLAY( ) and SCROLLBARUPDATE( ) functions. The top row and column coordinates of the scrollbar region are specified as <expN1>, <expN2> while the bottom row, column coordinates will be <expN3>, <expN2>. The color of the scrollbar region is specified as <expC4>. If not passed it will default to a color of "W/N": white lettering on black background. The initial position within the scrollbar is defined as <expN5> and if it is not passed, it will default to 1.<br><br>This function sets up an array that may be used in conjunction with any TBROWSE object, ACHOICE( ), DBEDIT( ) or MEMOEDIT( ) function to generate a scrollbar as the cursor moves. |
| **SEE ALSO** | SCROLLBARDISPLAY( ), SCROLLBARUPDATE( ) |
| **EXAMPLE** | Please see the SCROLLBARUPDATE( ) function. |

# SCROLLBARUPDATE( )

| | |
|---|---|
| **FUNCTION** | Updates internal information in the SCROLLBAR array and displays it to the screen. |
| **SYNTAX** | SCROLLBARUPDATE( <expA1>, <expN2>, <expN3>, <expL4> ) |
| **PARAMETERS** | <expA1> Scrollbar array to be updated and displayed<br><expN2> Current position |

|  |  |
|---|---|
| <expN3> | Total number of positions |
| <expL4> | Toggle to force a re-paint/update |

**RETURNS**  <expA>  A reference to the updated SCROLLBAR array

**LIBRARY**  SAMPLES.LIB

**DESCRIPTION**  This function updates and displays the SCROLLBAR Array <expA1>, previously created with the SCROLLBARNEW( ) function. SCROLL-BARUPDATE( ) allows you to move either up or down the scrollbar, scrolling the number of positions specified in <expN3>, starting at position <expN2>. The decision to scroll/update the status of the SROLLBAR Array is determined by the <expL4> parameter. If <expL4> evaluates to a logical true (.T.) the update will occur, otherwise, if <expL4> evaluates to a logical false (.F.), the array won't be updated.

**SEE ALSO**  SCROLLBARNEW( ), SCROLLBARDISPLAY( )

**EXAMPLE**

```
 1 : *File      Sbardemo.prg
 2 : * Compile  RMake sampmore /dFILE:Sbardemo.prg
 3 :
 4 : #INCLUDE "PTFUNCS.CH"
 5 : #INCLUDE "PTVALUE.CH"
 6 : #INCLUDE "PTCOLOR.CH"
 7 :
 8 : procedure Main()
 9 :
10 :    local ascrollbar
11 :    local nStart
12 :
13 :    setcolor(MAKECOLOR(pWHITE/pMAGENTA, ;
14 :            pWHITE/pBLACK,pWHITE/pMAGENTA))
15 :
16 :    cls
17 :
18 :    ? "First, let's create a scrollbar Array:"
19 :
20 :    ascrollbar := scrollbarnew(5,20, maxrow()-5,;
21 :            MAKECOLOR(pWHITE/pBLUE,pWHITE/pBLACK,pWHITE/pBLUE))
22 :    ?
23 :    ? "The Scrollbar Array has the following number of elements to it:", ;
24 :       len( ascrollbar )
25 :
26 :    inkey(2)
27 :    ?
28 :    ? "Now, let's draw the bar to the screen..."
29 :
30 :    scrollbardisplay( scrollbarnew(8,20, maxrow()-5,;
31 :            MAKECOLOR(pWHITE/pBLUE,pWHITE/pBLACK,pWHITE/pBLUE)) )
32 :
33 :    inkey(3)
34 :    SETPOS(MAXROW(),MAXCOL())
35 :
```

```
36 :     WAIT
37 :
38 : cls
39 :     ? "Now, let's just engage it for 15 rows..."
40 :
41 :     *setpos(5,20)
42 :     for nstart = row() to 15
43 :         scrollbardisplay( scrollbarnew(5,20, maxrow()-5,;
44 :             MAKECOLOR(pWHITE/pBLUE,pWHITE/pBLACK,pWHITE/pBLUE)) )
45 :         scrollbarUpdate(ascrollbar,nstart,15,.t.)
46 :         inkey(1)
47 :
48 :     next
49 :
50 :     devpos(maxrow(),maxcol())
51 :
52 : wait
53 :
54 :     // end of file :Sbardemo.prg
```

# SECONDS( )

| | |
|---|---|
| **FUNCTION** | Returns the number of elapsed seconds past midnight. |
| **SYNTAX** | SECONDS() |
| **PARAMETER** | None |
| **RETURNS** | \<expN\>    Number of seconds |
| **LIBRARY** | EXTEND.LIB |
| **DESCRIPTION** | This function returns a numeric value representing the number of elapsed seconds based on the current system time.<br><br>The system time is considered to start at 0 (midnight); it continues up to 86,399 seconds. The value of the return expression is displayed in both seconds and hundredths of seconds. |
| **SEE ALSO** | TIME( ) |
| **EXAMPLE** | See the TSTRING( ) function. |

# SECONDSASDAYS( )

| | |
|---|---|
| **FUNCTION** | Converts numeric seconds to days. |
| **SYNTAX** | SECONDASDAYS( \<expN1\> ) |
| **PARAMETER** | \<expN1\>    Number of seconds |

| | |
|---|---|
| **RETURNS** | <expN> Number of elapsed days |
| **LIBRARY** | SAMPLES.LIB |
| **DESCRIPTION** | This function is a replacement of the DAYS( ) function and will return the number of days given the total number of elapsed seconds expressed as <expN1>. |
| **SEE ALSO** | SECS( ), TIME( ), SECONDS( ), DAYS( ) |

## SECS( )

| | |
|---|---|
| **FUNCTION** | Returns the number of seconds from the system time. |
| **SYNTAX** | `SECS( <expC1> )` |
| **PARAMETER** | <expC1> Character expression in a time string format |
| **RETURNS** | <expN> Number of seconds |
| **LIBRARY** | EXTEND.LIB |
| **DESCRIPTION** | This function returns a numeric value that is the number of elapsed seconds from midnight based on a time string given in <expC1>. |
| **NOTE** | This is a compatibility function and may not be supported in future versions. |
| **SEE ALSO** | SECONDS( ), ELAPTIME( ), TIME( ) |
| **EXAMPLE** | See the TSTRING( ) function. |

## SELECT( )

| | |
|---|---|
| **FUNCTION** | Returns the work area number for a specified alias. |
| **SYNTAX** | `SELECT( [<expC1>] )` |
| **PARAMETER** | <expC1> Alias/work area name |
| **RETURNS** | <expN> Work area number |
| **LIBRARY** | CLIPPER.LIB |
| **DESCRIPTION** | This function returns the work area number for the specified alias name <expC1>. If no parameter is specified, the current work area will be the return value of the function. |
| **SEE ALSO** | ALIAS( ), SELECT, USE |

# SET( )

**FUNCTION**   Changes or evaluates environmental settings.

**SYNTAX**   `SET( <expN1> [, <expX2>] [, <expL3>] )`

**PARAMETERS**
&lt;expN1&gt;   Numeric code for the setting
&lt;expX2&gt;   Any expression to assign a value to the setting
&lt;expL3&gt;   Logical Expression

**RETURNS**   &lt;exp&gt;   Any expression

**LIBRARY**   CLIPPER.LIB

**DESCRIPTION**   This function assigns the value in &lt;expN2&gt; to the SET environment that corresponds to the value of &lt;expN1&gt;. The value of the function will be the current value of the particular global setting.

If needed, the third parameter is used to toggle the appropriate SET( ) switch to be in append mode or create mode. The default is a logical false (.F.)—do not append, re-create the files as needed. This is used in conjunction with the SET ALTERNATE TO and SET PRINTER TO commands.

Following is a table of values for &lt;expN1&gt;, possible values for &lt;expX2&gt;, and the corresponding SET command or toggle that is associated with &lt;expN1&gt;:

| &lt;expN1&gt; | Data type of &lt;expX2&gt; | Values of &lt;expX2&gt; | Command |
|---|---|---|---|
| 1 | Logical | .T./.F. | SET EXACT ON/OFF |
| 2 | Logical | .T./.F. | SET FIXED ON/OFF |
| 3 | Numeric | 0 – 18 | SET DECIMALS TO 0 – 18 |
| 4 | Character | YYYYMMDD | SET DATE FORMAT TO YYYYMMDD |
| 5 | Numeric | &lt;base year&gt; | SET EPOCH &lt;base year&gt; |
| 6 | Character | &lt;path&gt; | SET PATH &lt;path&gt; |
| 7 | Character | &lt;default&gt; | SET DEFAULT TO &lt;default&gt; |
| 8 | Logical | .T./.F. | SET EXCLUSIVE TO ON/OFF |
| 9 | Logical | .T./.F. | SET SOFTSEEK ON/OFF |
| 10 | Logical | .T./.F. | SET UNIQUE ON/OFF |
| 11 | Logical | .T./.F. | SET DELETED ON/OFF |
| 12 | Logical | .T./.F. | SETCANCEL( ) |
| 13 | Logical | .T./.F. | ALTD( ) |

*(continued)*

| <expN1> | Data type of <expX2> | Values of <expX2> | Command |
|---|---|---|---|
| 14 | Numeric | 0 – 32767 | SET TYPEAHEAD TO 0 – 32767 |
| 15 | Character | X/X,X/X,X,X,X/X | SETCOLOR(X/X,X/X,X,X,X/X) |
| 16 | Numeric | 0–4 | SETCURSOR(0–4) |
| 17 | Logical | .T./.F. | SET CONSOLE ON/OFF |
| 18 | Logical | .T./.F. | SET ALTERNATE ON/OFF |
| 19 | Character | <file> | SET ALTERNATE TO <file> |
| 20 | Character | <device> | SET DEVICE TO <device> |
| 21 | Logical | .T./.F. | SET EXTRA ON/OFF |
| 22 | Character | <device> | SET EXTRA TO <device> |
| 23 | Logical | .T./.F. | SET PRINTER ON/OFF |
| 24 | Character | <file> | SET PRINTER TO <file> |
| 25 | Numeric | <0–MAXCOL( )> | SET MARGIN TO <0–MAXCO( )> |
| 26 | Logical | .T./.F. | SET BELL ON/OFF |
| 27 | Logical | .T./.F. | SET CONFIRM ON/OFF |
| 28 | Logical | .T./.F. | SET ESCAPE ON/OFF |
| 29 | Logical | .T./.F. | READINSERT( ) |
| 30 | Logical | .T./.F. | READEXIT( ) |
| 31 | Logical | .T./.F. | SET INTENSITY ON/OFF |
| 32 | Logical | .T./.F. | SET SCOREBOARD ON/OFF |
| 33 | Logical | .T./.F. | SET DELIMITERS ON/OFF |
| 34 | Character | <char char> | SET DELIMITERS TO <char char> |
| 35 | Logical | .T./.F. | SET WRAP ON/OFF |
| 36 | Numeric | <0-MAXROW( )> | SET MESSAGE TO <0-MAXROW( )> |
| 37 | Logical | .T./.F. | SET MESSAGE . . . CENTER |
| 38 | Numeric | <number> | COUNT <number> |
| 38 | Logical | .T./.F. | PAUSING WITH CTRL-S |

**NOTE** The following table lists preprocessor constants that are used to initialize the SET commands in the Clipper environment. These are listed in the SET.CH.

```
_SET_EXACT          1
_SET_FIXED          2
_SET_DECIMALS       3
_SET_DATEFORMAT     4
_SET_EPOCH          5
_SET_PATH           6
```

|              |    |
|--------------|----|
| _SET_DEFAULT | 7  |
| _SET_EXCLUSIVE | 8 |
| _SET_SOFTSEEK | 9 |
| _SET_UNIQUE, | 10 |
| _SET_DELETED | 11 |
| _SET_CANCEL | 12 |
| _SET_DEBUG | 13 |
| _SET_TYPEAHEAD | 14 |
| _SET_COLOR | 15 |
| _SET_CURSOR | 16 |
| _SET_CONSOLE | 17 |
| _SET_ALTERNATE | 18 |
| _SET_ALTFILE | 19 |
| _SET_DEVICE | 20 |
| _SET_EXTRA | 21 |
| _SET_EXTRAFILE | 22 |
| _SET_PRINTER | 23 |
| _SET_PRINTFILE | 24 |
| _SET_MARGIN | 25 |
| _SET_BELL | 26 |
| _SET_CONFIRM | 27 |
| _SET_ESCAPE | 28 |
| _SET_INSERT | 29 |
| _SET_EXIT | 30 |
| _SET_INTENSITY | 31 |
| _SET_SCOREBOARD | 32 |
| _SET_DELIMITERS | 33 |
| _SET_DELIMCHARS | 34 |
| _SET_WRAP | 35 |
| _SET_MESSAGE | 36 |
| _SET_MCENTER | 37 |
| _SET_COUNT | 38 |
| _SET_SCROLLBREAK | 38 |

**SEE ALSO**   SET commands, ALTD( ) SETCANCEL( ), READINSERT( ), READEXIT( )

**EXAMPLE**

```
 1 : * File       Setsdemo.prg
 2 : * Compile    Rmake sampmore /dFILE:setsdemo
 3 :
 4 : #include "PTValue.ch"   // Power Tools Header file of misc. values
 5 :
 6 : //#define pCURSOR 16
 7 : //#define pDELIM_TOGGLE 33
 8 : //#define pDELIMITERS 34
 9 : //#define pESC 28
10 : //#define pCOLOR 15
```

```
 11 :   //#define pON  .T.
 12 :   //#define pOFF .F.
 13 :
 14 :   procedure Main()
 15 :
 16 :      local nTemp    := 0
 17 :      local getlist := {}    // This is to prevent a warning message
 18 :      local aData            // This is for the SETALL() function
 19 :
 20 :      cls
 21 :      set( pCURSOR, pCURSOR_OFF )  // turn the cursor off
 22 :      qout( "The cursor is off" )
 23 :      inkey(0)
 24 :      set( pCURSOR, pCURSOR_ON )   // Cursor is now on...
 25 :      qout( "The cursor is on..." )
 26 :      inkey(0)
 27 :      set( pCURSOR, pCURSOR_LOWER )
 28 :      qout( "The cursor is a lower block.." )
 29 :      inkey(0)
 30 :      set( pCURSOR, pCURSOR_BLOCK )
 31 :      qout( "The cursor now is a full cursor" )
 32 :      inkey(0)
 33 :
 34 :      scroll()
 35 :      set( pDELIMITERS, pON )  // Turn on the delimiters
 36 :
 37 :      @ 10,10 say "Enter something" get nTemp
 38 :      read
 39 :      set( pDELIMCHARS, "{}")  // Change the delimiters
 40 :      scroll()
 41 :      @ 10,10 say "Enter something" get nTemp
 42 :      read
 43 :
 44 :      scroll()
 45 :      set( pDELIMITERS, pOFF )    // Turn the delimiters off
 46 :      @ 10,10 say "Enter something" get nTemp
 47 :      read
 48 :
 49 :      scroll()
 50 :      set( pESCAPE, pOFF )     // ESC key is turned off
 51 :      @ 10,10 say "Try pressing ESC..." get nTemp
 52 :      read
 53 :
 54 :      setcolor( "W/N, N/W" )
 55 :      scroll()
 56 :      @ 10,10 say "Here are the colors..." get nTemp
 57 :      clear gets
 58 :      wait
 59 :
 60 :      setcolor( "N/W, W/N" )
 61 :      scroll()
 62 :      @ 10,10 say "And now here they are..." get nTemp
 63 :      clear gets
 64 :      wait
 65 :
 66 :      setcolor( "W/N, N/W" )
 67 :
```

```
68 :    aData := setall()            // Get the entire array of SET() information
69 :    set( pCURSOR, pCURSOR_ON )   // Cursor is now on...
70 :    cls
71 :    qout( "And here is the information of the SET" )
72 :    aeval( aData, {|xItem, nPosition| qout( "Position", nPosition ), ;
73 :                                      qqout( " || Value is: ", xItem ), ;
74 :                                      inkey(2) } )
75 :
76 : * End of File
```

## SETALL( )

| | |
|---|---|
| **FUNCTION** | GET/SET environment SET( ) values. |
| **SYNTAX** | SETALL( [<expA1>] ) |
| **PARAMETER** | <expA1>   Array of new environmental settings |
| **RETURNS** | <expA>    Array of old environmental settings |
| **LIBRARY** | SAMPLES.LIB |
| **DESCRIPTION** | This function will take an array expressed in <expA1>, which contains new individual settings for the SET( ) function, and assign these new SET( ) values to the environment variables. It will return an array of the original SET( ) values. Each subscript position in the array returned from this function and passed to this function must adhere to the ordinal position found in the table of the SET( ) function and in the header file called SET.CH. |
| **NOTE** | When issued without the optional <expA1> parameter, the SETALL( ) function returns an array of the current environmental settings. |
| **SEE ALSO** | SET( ), SET commands |
| **EXAMPLE** | Please see the SET( ) function. |

## SETBLINK( )

| | |
|---|---|
| **FUNCTION** | Toggles the blinking condition on displays. |
| **SYNTAX** | SETBLINK( [<expL1>] ) |
| **PARAMETER** | <expL1>   Logical true (.T.) or false (.F.) |
| **RETURNS** | <expL>    Logical true (.T.) or false (.F.) |
| **LIBRARY** | CLIPPER.LIB |

| | |
|---|---|
| **DESCRIPTION** | This function modifies the interpretation of the asterisk character in a SET COLOR TO string. If SETBLINK( ) is set on, the asterisk indicates a blink condition; if the function is set off, the intensity is set on rather than blinking. The return value of the function is the current setting. If specified, the setting may be toggled by passing logical true (.T.) or false (.F.) to <expL1>.
The default value of this function is a logical true (.T.). |
| **NOTE** | Blinking and background intensity attributes are not available at the same time.
Since it is hardware specific, this function applies only to IBM-PC compatible computers with CGA, EGA, or VGA video adapters. |
| **SEE ALSO** | SETCOLOR( ) |

**EXAMPLE**

```
 1 : * File       Blindemo.prg
 2 : * Compile    RMake sample /dFILE:blindemo
 3 :
 4 : #define pFALSE .F.
 5 : #define pTRUE .T.
 6 :
 7 : procedure Main()
 8 :
 9 :   local nVar    := 0
10 :   local cColor  := "W/N, N/W"
11 :   local cBright := "W*/N, N*/W"
12 :   local getlist := {}
13 :
14 :   cls
15 :   setcolor( cColor )
16 :   @ 10,10 say "Hello" get nVar
17 :   read
18 :
19 :   setblink( pTRUE )
20 :   setcolor( cBright )
21 :   @ 12,10 say "This should blink.." get nVar
22 :   read
23 :
24 :   setblink( !setblink() )
25 :   @ 14,10 say "And now it should not..." get nVar
26 :   read
27 :
28 :   cls
29 : // End of File: Blindemo.prg
```

# SETCANCEL( )

| | |
|---|---|
| **FUNCTION** | Toggles ALT-C as a termination key. |
| **SYNTAX** | SETCANCEL( [<expL1>] ) |

| | | |
|---|---|---|
| **PARAMETER** | <expL1> | Logical true (.T.) or false (.F.) |
| **RETURNS** | <expL> | Logical true (.T.) or false (.F.) |
| **LIBRARY** | CLIPPER.LIB | |
| **DESCRIPTION** | This function toggles the termination key ALT-C in a Clipper application. If <expL1> is set to a logical true (.T.), ALT-C will interrupt a Clipper application and terminate to the operating system. If the ALT-C key is to be disabled, the value of <expL1> should be a logical false (.F.). Turning off the ALT-C causes INKEY(0) to return an ASCII value of 302. The default setting is a logical true (.T.). | |
| | This function returns the current status of ALT-C. | |
| **SEE ALSO** | ALTD( ), SET( ), SET ESCAPE | |

## SETCOLOR( )

| | |
|---|---|
| **FUNCTION** | Sets or evaluates the current screen color. |
| **SYNTAX** | `SETCOLOR( [<expC1>] )` |
| **PARAMETER** | <expC1>    A color string |
| **RETURNS** | <expC>    The current color setting |
| **LIBRARY** | CLIPPER.LIB |
| **DESCRIPTION** | This function returns the current color setting as a character expression. |
| | If <expC1> is passed to this function, that character expression must contain the standard SET COLOR TO expression for the function to properly set the application's color. |
| | If a parameter is passed, this function returns the previous color setting; otherwise, the function returns the current color setting. |
| | Only color–letter combinations are supported with the SETCOLOR( ) function. The color string is made up of five components, with each component separated by a comma. A slash separates the individual colors (foreground / background) within each of the five components. The five components are |

| | |
|---|---|
| Standard | All output to the screen |
| Enhanced | GET and PROMPT selections |
| Border | Not supported on EGA and VGA |
| Background | Not Supported |
| Unselected | Unselected GETS and items tagged in ACHOICE( ) |

For a complete chart of supported colors, see Appendix 6.

| | |
|---|---|
| **SEE ALSO** | SET COLOR, SETBLINK( ), ISCOLOR( ), SET INTENSITY |
| **EXAMPLE** | See the SETMODE( ) function. |

## SETCURSOR( )

| | |
|---|---|
| **FUNCTION** | Defines the cursor shape. |
| **SYNTAX** | `SETCURSOR( [<expN1>] )` |
| **PARAMETER** | <expN1>    Value of the cursor shape |
| **RETURNS** | <expN>    Value of the current cursor shape |
| **LIBRARY** | CLIPPER.LIB |
| **DESCRIPTION** | This function returns the current shape of the cursor. If specified, <expN1> modifies the shape of the cursor. Below is a table of the values for <expN1> and the resulting shape of the cursor. |

| <expN1> | Shape |
|---|---|
| 0 | No cursor |
| 1 | Underlined cursor |
| 2 | Lower-half block cursor |
| 3 | Full block cursor |
| 4 | Upper-half block cursor |

The SET CURSOR OFF command is similar to a SETCURSOR(0) function call; the SET CURSOR ON command is similar to a SETCURSOR(1) function call.

| | |
|---|---|
| **SEE ALSO** | SET CURSOR |
| **EXAMPLE** | See the SETMODE( ) function. |

## SETKEY( )

| | |
|---|---|
| **FUNCTION** | Assigns a key to a subroutine. |
| **SYNTAX** | `SETKEY( <expN1> [, <expB2>] )` |
| **PARAMETERS** | <expN1>    The ASCII code for a key<br><expB2>    Subroutine to be activated when the key is pressed |
| **RETURNS** | <expX>    Code block assigned to the specified key on a NIL value |
| **LIBRARY** | CLIPPER.LIB |
| **DESCRIPTION** | This function takes the ASCII scan code key value expressed as <expN1> and assigns the code block <expB2> to that key. If no value for <expB2> is expressed, the key is no longer assigned to a subroutine; this works the same as SET KEY TO. The function returns the code |

block currently assigned to the key <expN1>; if no key is assigned to it, a NIL data type is returned.

**SEE ALSO**          SET KEY, EVAL( ), INKEY( )

**EXAMPLE**           See the SETMODE( ) function.

## SETMODE( )

| | |
|---|---|
| **FUNCTION** | Sets the display mode for row depth and column width. |
| **SYNTAX** | SETMODE( <expN1>, <expN2> ) |
| **PARAMETERS** | <expN1>   Bottom row coordinate |
| | <expN2>   Right column coordinate |
| **RETURNS** | <expL>   Logical true (.T.) or false (.F.) |
| **LIBRARY** | CLIPPER.LIB |
| **DESCRIPTION** | This function sets the video display mode and alters the values of MAXROW( ) and MAXCOL( ). The settings for the mode are determined by passing the values for MAXROW( ) and MAXCOL( ) as the values of <expN1> and <expN2>, respectively. If the function is able to set the video mode accordingly, it will return a logical true (.T.); otherwise, no mode will be set, the values of MAXROW( ) and MAXCOL( ) will be retained, and the function will return a logical false (.F.). |
| **NOTE** | Some video monitors and cards have different mode settings. See your appropriate manuals for the appropriate values. |
| **SEE ALSO** | MAXROW( ), MAXCOL( ) |

**EXAMPLE**

```
 1 : * File       Setmdemo.prg
 2 : * Compile    Rmake sample /dFILE:setmdemo
 3 :
 4 : #define pTAB 9
 5 :
 6 : procedure Main()
 7 :
 8 :    local getlist := {}
 9 :    local nTemp   := 0
10 :    local nCount
11 :
12 :    if file( "Notap.dbf" )
13 :       use Notap new    // Just open the database
14 :       select(0)        // Move off to a new area
15 :
16 :    cls
17 :    wait "Press any key to test the MODE via SETMODE()"
```

```
18 :      if setmode(43,80)
19 :        qout( maxrow(), maxcol() )
20 :        wait
21 :        if setmode(25,80)
22 :          qout( maxrow(), maxcol() )
23 :          wait
24 :        endif
25 :      endif
26 :
27 :      cls
28 :      wait "Press any key to show the SETCOLOR() function"
29 :      setcolor( "W/N, N/W" )
30 :      wait "This is the normal color..."
31 :      setcolor( "N/W, W/N" )
32 :      wait "And this is the color reversed..."
33 :      setcolor( "W/N, N/W" )
34 :
35 :      for nCount := 0 to 4
36 :        setcursor( nCount )
37 :        qout( "Press any key with SETCURSOR() value of ", nCount )
38 :        inkey(0)
39 :      next
40 :
41 :      cls
42 :      setkey( pTAB, {|| Notap->( Branch() )} )
43 :
44 :      @ 10,10 say "Press TAB for SETKEY() branch" get nTemp
45 :      read
46 :
47 :    endif
48 :
49 : *******************
50 :
51 : static function Branch()
52 :
53 :    devpos(maxrow()-1, 00 )
54 :    devout( "We have branched out to this routine..." )
55 :    devout( "... any key to continue..." )
56 :    devpos(maxrow(), 00 )
57 :    devout( "And the alias we're in is: " )
58 :    devout( alias() )
59 :    inkey(0)
60 :    scroll( maxrow()-1, 00 )
61 :
62 :    return( NIL )
63 :
64 : // End of File: Setmdemo.prg
```

# SETPOS( )

**FUNCTION**    Moves the cursor to a position.

**SYNTAX**     SETPOS( <expN1>, <expN2> )

| | |
|---|---|
| **PARAMETERS** | <expN1> Row coordinate |
| | <expN2> Column coordinate |
| **LIBRARY** | CLIPPER.LIB |
| **DESCRIPTION** | This function moves the cursor to the specified row, column coordinates of <expN1>, <expN2>. The values for these parameters range for <expN1> from 0 to MAXROW( ) and for <expN2> from 0 to MAX-COL( ).
After the cursor has been positioned, the values for ROW( ) and COL( ) are updated accordingly. |
| **SEE ALSO** | DEVPOS( ), ROW( ), COL( ) |
| **EXAMPLE** | See the OUTSTD( ) function. |

# SETPRC( )

| | |
|---|---|
| **FUNCTION** | Sets the printer's row and column position. |
| **SYNTAX** | `SETPRC( <expN1>, <expN2> )` |
| **PARAMETERS** | <expN1> Top row coordinate |
| | <expN2> Top column coordinate |
| **LIBRARY** | CLIPPER.LIB |
| **DESCRIPTION** | This function sets the internal PROW( ) and PCOL( ) values to the specified numeric values passed to this function as <expN1> and <expN2>. It is especially useful when issuing printer control codes without altering the values of PROW( ) and PCOL( ). |
| **SEE ALSO** | SET DEVICE, SET PRINTER, PROW( ), PCOL( ) |

# SETTYPEAHEAD( )

| | |
|---|---|
| **FUNCTION** | Sets the typeahead buffer. |
| **SYNTAX** | `SETTYPEAHEAD( <expN1> )` |
| **PARAMETER** | <expN1> Typeahead buffer size |
| **LIBRARY** | CLIPPER.LIB |
| **DESCRIPTION** | This function sets the typeahead buffer to <expN1> characters. |
| **SEE ALSO** | SET TYPEAHEAD, SET( ) |

## SIGN( )

| | |
|---|---|
| **FUNCTION** | Returns the sign of a number. |
| **SYNTAX** | `SIGN( <expN1> )` |
| **PARAMETER** | <expN1>   Any number |
| **RETURNS** | <expN>   Numeric code for the sign of a number |
| **LIBRARY** | SAMPLES.LIB |
| **DESCRIPTION** | This function will test the value of <expN1> and return a code that represents the possible sign of that number: |

| Return Value | Meaning |
|---|---|
| 0 | <expN1> is zero |
| 1 | <expN1> is a positive number |
| −1 | <expN1> is a negative number |

**SEE ALSO**   ABS( )

## SOUNDEX( )

| | |
|---|---|
| **FUNCTION** | Yields a sounds-like calculation. |
| **SYNTAX** | `SOUNDEX( <expC1> )` |
| **PARAMETER** | <expC1>   Character expression |
| **RETURNS** | <expC>   Character expression |
| **LIBRARY** | EXTEND.LIB |
| **DESCRIPTION** | This function yields a character expression that is derived from the string <expC1>. This new expression will be a sounds-like calculation based on the string passed to it. A code or simulation string will be returned. |
| **NOTE** | If an index algorithm is based on this function, any SEEK or FIND call must contain this function in the search expression. |
| **SEE ALSO** | INDEX, SEEK, FIND |

**EXAMPLE**

```
1 : * File      Soundemo.prg
2 : * Compile   Rmake sample /dFILE:soundemo
3 :
4 : procedure Main()
5 :
6 :    cls
```

```
 7 :    use Clients new
 8 :    index on Clients->name to Sound1
 9 :    Clients->( dbgotop(), ShowItems(1, "Normal Order!") )
10 :
11 :    index on soundex(Clients->name) to Sound2
12 :    Clients->( dbgotop(), ShowItems(12, "SOUNDEX() order!" ) )
13 :
14 : *******************
15 :
16 : static function ShowItems( nRow, ;      // Row to start off on
17 :                            cString )    // String to display for a header
18 :
19 :    local nShowCol := 0
20 :    local nShowRow := nRow
21 :
22 :    @ nRow-1, 0 say cString
23 :
24 :    while !eof() .and. !(nRow == nRow + 10)
25 :       devpos( nShowRow, nShowCol )
26 :       devoutpict( recno(), "99 ")
27 :       devout( left(Clients->name, 16) )
28 :
29 :       if (nShowCol += 20) > 60
30 :          nShowCol := 0
31 :          nShowRow += 1
32 :       endif
33 :       dbskip()
34 :    enddo
35 :
36 :    return( NIL )
37 :
38 : // End of File: Soundemo.prg
```

# SPACE( )

| | |
|---|---|
| **FUNCTION** | Returns a string of blank spaces. |
| **SYNTAX** | SPACE( <expN1> ) |
| **PARAMETER** | <expN1>　　Length of the string |
| **RETURNS** | <expC>　　A string of blank spaces |
| **LIBRARY** | CLIPPER.LIB |
| **DESCRIPTION** | This function returns a string consisting of <expN1> blank spaces. If the value of <expN1> is 0, a NULL string will be returned. |
| **SEE ALSO** | PADC( ), PADR( ), PADL( ), REPLICATE( ) |

## SQRT( )

| | |
|---|---|
| **FUNCTION** | Calculates the square root of a number. |
| **SYNTAX** | `SQRT( <expN1> )` |
| **PARAMETER** | <expN1>   Numeric expression |
| **RETURNS** | <expN>   Numeric expression |
| **LIBRARY** | CLIPPER.LIB |
| **DESCRIPTION** | This function returns the square root of <expN1>. The precision of this evaluation is based solely on the setting of the SET DECIMALS TO command. Any negative number passed as <expN1> will always return a 0. |
| **SEE ALSO** | SET DECIMALS |

## STACKISEMPTY( )

| | |
|---|---|
| **FUNCTION** | Tests to see if the stack array is empty. |
| **SYNTAX** | `STACKISEMPTY( <expA1> )` |
| **PARAMETER** | <expA1>   Array stack |
| **RETURNS** | <expL>   Logical true (.T.) or a logical false (.F.) |
| **LIBRARY** | SAMPLES.LIB |
| **DESCRIPTION** | This function will return a logical true (.T.) if the stack array <expA1> is considered empty containing no element of any value. NIL value elements do not fall into this consideration. A logical false (.F.) will be returned if the array <expA1> is not empty. |
| **SEE ALSO** | STACKNEW( ), STACKPUSH( ), STACKPOP( ) |
| **EXAMPLE** | Please see the STACKTOP( ) function. |

## STACKNEW( )

| | |
|---|---|
| **FUNCTION** | Generates a new stack array. |
| **SYNTAX** | `STACKNEW()` |
| **PARAMETER** | None |

| | |
|---|---|
| **RETURNS** | <expA>   Stack array |
| **LIBRARY** | SAMPLES.LIB |
| **DESCRIPTION** | This function returns an array that will be used as a stack. A stack is a data structure that follows a Last-In-First-Out (LIFO) mechanism. Items being added to the stack are considered to be "pushed" onto the stack while items being removed are considered to be "popped" off of the stack. |
| **SEE ALSO** | STACKTOP( ), STACKPUSH( ), STACKPOP( ), STACKISEMPTY( ) |
| **EXAMPLE** | Please see the STACKTOP( ) function. |

## STACKPUSH( )

| | |
|---|---|
| **FUNCTION** | Adds an element to the stack array. |
| **SYNTAX** | STACKPUSH( <expA1>, <expX2> ) |
| **PARAMETERS** | <expA1>   A stack array<br><expX2>   Any item being added to the stack array |
| **RETURNS** | <expA>   A reference to the modified stack array |
| **LIBRARY** | SAMPLES.LIB |
| **DESCRIPTION** | This function will take the data item <expX2> of any valid data type, add it to the stack array <expA1>, and will return a reference to the modified array structure. |
| **SEE ALSO** | STACKNEW( ), STACKPOP( ), STACKISEMPTY( ) |
| **EXAMPLE** | Please see the STACKTOP( ) function. |

## STACKPOP( )

| | |
|---|---|
| **FUNCTION** | Removes an element from a stack array. |
| **SYNTAX** | STACKPOP( <expA1> ) |
| **PARAMETER** | <expA1>   A stack array |
| **RETURNS** | <expX>   Any value data type |
| **LIBRARY** | SAMPLES.LIB |

| | |
|---|---|
| **DESCRIPTION** | This function will return and remove the last item stored to the stack array <expA1>. If there are no items in the stack array <expA1>, then the function will return a NIL value. However, keep in mind that NIL is a valid data type and thus, the function might return a NIL value which does not represent that the array is empty. |
| **SEE ALSO** | STACKNEW( ), STACKPUSH( ), STACKISEMPTY( ), STACKTOP( ) |
| **EXAMPLE** | Please see the STACKTOP( ) function. |

## STACKTOP( )

| | |
|---|---|
| **FUNCTION** | Returns the first item in the stack array. |
| **SYNTAX** | STACKTOP( <expA1> ) |
| **PARAMETER** | <expA1>    A stack array |
| **RETURNS** | <expX>    Any valid data type |
| **LIBRARY** | SAMPLES.LIB |
| **DESCRIPTION** | This function simply returns the value of the first element stored to the stack array <expA1> and does not remove it from the stack array. |
| **SEE ALSO** | STACKNEW( ), STACKPUSH( ), STACKPOP( ), STACKISEMPTY( ) |
| **EXAMPLE** | |

```
 1 : * File       Stakdemo.prg
 2 : * Compiler   Rmake sampmore /dFILE:stakdemo
 3 :
 4 : procedure Main()
 5 :
 6 :    local aStack := stacknew()    // Create a new stack
 7 :
 8 :    cls
 9 :    ? " Length of the stack is now: ", len( aStack )
10 :    ? "           Is the stack empty? ", stackisempty( aStack )
11 :    stackpush( aStack, date() )   // Add the date to the stack
12 :    stackpush( aStack, time() )   // Add the time to the stack
13 :    ? "        And now the length is: ", len( aStack )
14 :    ? "The first value in stack is: ", stacktop( aStack )
15 :    stackpop( aStack )            // Removes the last value in stack
16 :    ? "        And now the length is: ", len( aStack )
17 :    ? "And the value of the top is: " , stackpop( aStack )
18 :    ? "And now, is the stack empty? ", stackisempty( aStack )
19 :
20 : // End of File: Stakdemo.prg
```

## STATUSNEW( )

| | |
|---|---|
| **FUNCTION** | Creates a new moving status indicator. |
| **SYNTAX** | STATUSNEW( [<expN1>] [, <expN2>] [, <expC3>] ) |
| **PARAMETERS** | <expN1>   Row position of status indicator<br><expN2>   Column position of status indicator<br><expC3>   Color of status characters |
| **RETURNS** | <expA>   An array of status indicator information |
| **LIBRARY** | SAMPLES.LIB |
| **DESCRIPTION** | This function will build and return an array that may be used to display a moving indicator while some process is taking place in an application. The row of the status indicator is passed as <expN1> with a default value of 0. The column of the status indicator is passed as <expN2> with a default value of 0. The color of the status character is passed as <expC3> with a default value of "W+/N": bright white letters on black background. |
| **SEE ALSO** | STATUSUPDATE( ) |
| **EXAMPLE** | Please see the STATUSUPDATE( ) function. |

## STATUSUPDATE( )

| | |
|---|---|
| **FUNCTION** | Updates the screen and indicator for a given status array indicator. |
| **SYNTAX** | STATUSUPDATE( <expA1> ) |
| **PARAMETER** | <expA1>   A status indicator array |
| **LIBRARY** | SAMPLES.LIB |
| **DESCRIPTION** | This function will take the array of information passed as <expA1>, which is a status indicator array created by the STATUSNEW( ) function. This function will display the status characters to the screen and increment the internal counter. |
| **SEE ALSO** | STATUSNEW( ) |

**EXAMPLE**

```
1 : * File       Statdemo.prg
2 : * Compile    Rmake sampmore /dFILE:statdemo
3 :
4 : procedure Main()
5 :
```

```
 6 :    local cStartTime := time()   // Hold the starting time
 7 :    local aStatus := statusnew( 10,30,"W+/N" ) // Array holding the status
 8 :
 9 :    cls
10 :    ? "This will show a status indicator for 60 seconds..."
11 :
12 :    @ 10,10 say "Processing....."
13 :    @ 10,29 say "[ ]"
14 :    setcursor( 0 )                // Turn off the cursor
15 :    while timeasseconds(timediff( cStartTime, time() ))  < 60
16 :       statusupdate( aStatus )
17 :       inkey(.02)     // Otherwise, it would be too fast!
18 :    enddo
19 :    setcursor( 1 )    // re-set the cursor
20 :
21 : // End of File: Statdemo.prg
```

# STR( )

| | |
|---|---|
| **FUNCTION** | Converts a numeric value to a string. |
| **SYNTAX** | STR( <expN1> [, <expN2>] [, <expN3>] ) |
| **PARAMETERS** | <expN1>  Numeric expression to be converted |
| | <expN2>  Length of the string |
| | <expN3>  Number of decimal places |
| **RETURNS** | <expC>  Character expression |
| **LIBRARY** | CLIPPER.LIB |
| **DESCRIPTION** | This function converts any numeric expression <expN1> into a character string. The second parameter <expN2> sets the length of the string, while the value of <expN3> sets the number of decimal places to be included. |

If the value of <expN2> is less than the length of <expN1>, an overflow condition exists and the return value of the function will be a string of asterisks.

If <expN2> is less than the required value for <expN3>, the function rounds off to the nearest decimal place.

If no value for <expN3> is given while <expN2> has a value, the function rounds off to the nearest integer.

The function returns a character string based in part on the type source of the data in <expN1>. This source is based on the following table:

| *Data Source of <expN1>* | *Return Length* |
|---|---|
| Database Field | Length of field with decimal places |
| Variables / Constants | Minimum length of 10 with decimal places |

| Data Source of <expN1> | Return Length |
|---|---|
| MONTH( )/DAY( ) | Minimum of 3 |
| YEAR( ) | Minimum of 5 |
| RECNO( ) | Minimum of 7 |

**SEE ALSO** TRANSFORM( ), VAL( )

**EXAMPLE** See the STRZERO( ) function.

# STRTRAN( )

**FUNCTION** Translates substring values within a main string.

**SYNTAX** STRTRAN( <expC1>, <expC2> [, <expC3>] [,<expN4>] [, <expN5>] )

**PARAMETERS**
<expC1>  The string to search
<expC2>  The string to locate
<expC3>  The replacement string
<expN4>  The first occurrence to be replaced
<expN5>  Number of occurrences to replace

**RETURNS** <expC>  Character expression

**LIBRARY** EXTEND.LIB

**DESCRIPTION** This function searches for any occurrence of <expC2> in <expC1> and replaces it with <expC3>. If <expC3> is not specified, a NULL byte will replace <expC2>.

If <expN4> is used, its value defines the first occurrence to be replaced. The default value is 1. Additionally, if used, the value of <expN5> tells the function how many occurrences of <expC2> in <expC1> are to be replaced. The default of <expN5> is all occurrences.

**SEE ALSO** MEMOTRAN( ), SUBSTR( ), AT( ), STUFF( )

**EXAMPLE** See the STUFF( ) function.

# STRZERO( )

**FUNCTION** Converts a number to a string with leading zeros.

**SYNTAX** STRZERO( <expN1> [, <expN2>] [, <expN3> ] )

| | | |
|---|---|---|
| **PARAMETERS** | <expN1> | Numeric expression |
| | <expN2> | Length of string |
| | <expN3> | Number of decimal positions in string |
| **RETURNS** | <expC> | Character expression |
| **LIBRARY** | EXTEND.LIB | |

**DESCRIPTION** This function converts a number <expN1> into a string with leading zeros instead of blank spaces. <expN2> sets the desired length of the return string, while <expN3> is the number of additional decimal positions to be included.

**NOTE** This is a compatibility function and may not be supported in future versions.

**SEE ALSO** STR( )

**EXAMPLE**

```
 1 : * File      Roundemo.prg
 2 : * Compile   Rmake sample /dFILE:roundemo
 3 :
 4 : procedure Main()
 5 :
 6 :    local nTemp1 := 3.1414926
 7 :    local nTemp2 := 23
 8 :    local nTemp3 := 6.76
 9 :
10 :    cls
11 :    qout( "Working with the STR() function..." )
12 :    qout()
13 :    qout( str( nTemp1 ) )
14 :    qout( str( nTemp1, 1) )
15 :    qout( str( nTemp1, 1, 3) )
16 :    qout( str( nTemp1, 1, 1) )
17 :    qout( str( nTemp2, 2, 2) )
18 :    qout( str( nTemp2, 5) )
19 :    qout()
20 :    wait
21 :
22 :    cls
23 :    qout( "Working with the ROUND() function...." )
24 :    qout()
25 :    qout( round(nTemp1, 1) )
26 :    qout( round(nTemp1, 2) )
27 :    qout( round(nTemp1, 3) )
28 :    qout( round(nTemp1, 4) )
29 :    qout( round(nTemp3, 1) )
30 :    qout( round(nTemp3, 2) )
31 :    qout( round(nTemp3, 3) )
32 :    qout( round(nTemp3, 4) )
33 :    qout( round(nTemp2, 2) )
34 :    qout()
```

```
35 :    wait
36 :
37 :    cls
38 :    qout("Working with the STR() function...." )
39 :    qout()
40 :    qout( int( nTemp1 ) )
41 :    qout( int( nTemp2 ) )
42 :    qout( int( nTemp3 ) )
43 :    qout()
44 :    wait
45 :
46 :    nTemp1 := 3.1414926
47 :    nTemp2 := 23
48 :    nTemp3 := 6.76
49 :    cls
50 :
51 :    qout("Working with the STRZERO() function..." )
52 :    qout()
53 :    qout( strzero( nTemp1, 10, 2 ) )
54 :    qout( strzero( nTemp1 ) )
55 :    qout( strzero( nTemp2, 3 ) )
56 :    qout( strzero( nTemp2, 4 ) )
57 :    qout( strzero( nTemp2, 5 ) )
58 :    qout( strzero( nTemp3, 1 ) )
59 :    qout( strzero( nTemp3, 5, 1 ) )
60 :    qout( strzero( -nTemp3, 5, 1) )
61 :    qout( strzero( nTemp3, 5, 2 ) )
62 :    qout( strzero( nTemp3, 6, 2 ) )
63 :    qout( strzero( nTemp3, 7, 2 ) )
64 :    qout( strzero( nTemp3, 7, 3 ) )
65 :    qout()
66 :    wait
67 :
68 :    cls
69 :    qout("This shows a rounding problem...")
70 :    qout()
71 :    qout( 3 == round( 2.00 - .0001, 1) )
72 :    qout( 3 )
73 :    qout( round( 3.00 - .0001, 1 ) )
74 :    qout( transform(3,"99") == transform(3.00 - .0001, "99") )
75 :
76 : // End of File: Roundemo.prg
```

# STUFF( )

| | |
|---|---|
| **FUNCTION** | Stuffs a string into another string. |
| **SYNTAX** | STUFF( <expC1>, <expN2>, <expN3>, <expC4> ) |
| **PARAMETERS** | <expC1>  Character expression |
| | <expN2>  Starting position of deletion/insertion |

|   |   |   |
|---|---|---|
|   | <expN3> | Number of characters to delete |
|   | <expC4> | String to insert |
| **RETURNS** | <expC> | Character expression |
| **LIBRARY** | EXTEND.LIB | |

**DESCRIPTION** This function places a character string, <expC4>, inside the character expression <expC1>. <expN2> determines the character position in <expC1> at which <expC4> will be inserted. <expN3> determines how many characters in <expC1> will be deleted to form the new string.

The basic thing to remember about this function is that the delete operation specified in <expN3> is performed BEFORE the insert operation specified by the value of <expN2> and the string <expC4>.

It is important to remember that no parameter may be skipped. If the number of characters to be deleted is 0, a 0 is required for the third parameter. If no characters are to be added to the string, a NULL byte should be the fourth parameter.

**SEE ALSO** STRTRAN( ), SUBSTR( )

**EXAMPLE**

```
 1 : * File       Strtdemo.prg
 2 : * Compile    Rmake sample /dFILE:strtdemo
 3 :
 4 : procedure Main()
 5 :
 6 :    local cTemp := "This is a string to use for this"
 7 :
 8 :    cls
 9 :    devout("String: ")
10 :    devout( cTemp )
11 :
12 :    devpos(4,0)
13 :    devout("The number of words in the STRING is: ")
14 :    devout( Occurrence( " ", cTemp )+1 )
15 :
16 :    @ 7,0 say stuff( cTemp,21, 0,"BE ")
17 :    @ 8,0 say stuff(cTemp,17,16,"")
18 :    @ 9,0 say stuff( stuff(cTemp,17,16,""), 9,0, "TO BE ")
19 :
20 : ********************
21 :
22 : static function Occurrence( cString, ; // This is a faster function than
23 :                             cSub )     // the OCCURS function
24 :
25 :
26 :    return( int( (len(cSub) - ;
27 :           len(strtran(cSub, cString, "")) ) / len( cString ) ) )
28 :
29 : // End of File: Strtdemo.prg
```

# SUBSTR( )

| | |
|---|---|
| **FUNCTION** | Returns a substring from a main string. |
| **SYNTAX** | SUBSTR( <expC1>, <expN2> [, <expN3> ] ) |
| **PARAMETERS** | <expC1>   Character expression |
| | <expN2>   Starting position |
| | <expN3>   Number of characters |
| **RETURNS** | <expC>    Character expression |
| **LIBRARY** | CLIPPER.LIB |
| **DESCRIPTION** | This function returns a character string formed from <expC1>, starting at the position of <expN2> and continuing on for a length of <expN3> characters. If <expN3> is not specified, the value will be all remaining characters from the position of <expN2>. |

The value of <expN2> may be negative. If it is, the direction of operation is reversed from a default of left-to-right to right-to-left for the number of characters specified in <expN2>.

The length of <expC1> may be a maximum of 65,519 bytes.

**SEE ALSO**    STUFF( ), AT( ), LEFT( ), RIGHT( )

**EXAMPLE**

```
 1 :  * File      Subsdemo.prg
 2 :  * Compile   Rmake sample /dFILE:subsdemo
 3 :
 4 :  procedure Main()
 5 :
 6 :     local cString := padc("This is a test", 40)
 7 :
 8 :     cls
 9 :
10 :     qout( len(cString) )
11 :     qout( cString )
12 :
13 :     qout( substr( cString, 1, 17 ) )
14 :     qout( substr( cString, 15, 5 ) )
15 :     qout( substr( cString, 20, -5 ) )
16 :     qout( substr( cString, 30 ) )
17 :
18 :     qout()
19 :     qout( left( cString, 24 ) )
20 :     qout( right( cString, 24 ) )
21 :     qout()
22 :
23 :     qout( len( trim( cString ) ) )
24 :     qout( len( ltrim( cString ) ) )
```

```
25 :    qout( len( rtrim( cString ) ) )
26 :    qout( len( alltrim( cString ) ) )
27 :
28 : // End of File: Subsdemo.prg
```

# TBROWSEDB( )

| | |
|---|---|
| **FUNCTION** | Generates a Clipper Browse Object with defaults. |
| **SYNTAX** | TBROWSEDB(<expN1>, <expN2>, <expN3>, <expN4>) |
| **PARAMETERS** | <expN1>  Top row coordinate |
| | <expN2>  Left column coordinate |
| | <expN3>  Bottom row coordinate |
| | <expN4>  Right column coordinate |
| **RETURNS** | <expO>   Clipper TBROWSE object |
| **LIBRARY** | CLIPPER.LIB |
| **DESCRIPTION** | This function sets up a browsing window at top-left coordinates of <expN1>, <expN2> to bottom-right coordinates of <expN3>, <expN4>. The function returns a BROWSE object with default code blocks for the GO TOP, SKIP, and GO BOTTOM operations. The table below lists the structure of a BROWSE object. |

| *Instance Variables* | |
|---|---|
| AUTOLITE | Logical value to control highlighting |
| CARGO | User-definable slot |
| COLCOUNT | Number of BROWSE columns |
| COLORSPEC | Index color table for BROWSE object |
| COLPOS | Current cursor column position |
| COLSEP | Character for column separator |
| FREEZE | Number of columns to freeze |
| FOOTSEP | Character for footing separator |
| GOBOTTOMBLOCK | Code block to go bottom |
| GOTOPBLOCK | Code block to go top |
| HEADSEP | Character for heading separator |
| HITBOTTOM | Logical toggle if end of data |
| HITTOP | Logical toggle if top of data |
| LEFTVISIBLE( ) | Indicates if a leftmost unfrozen column is visible |
| NBOTTOM | Bottom row of BROWSE screen area |

### Instance Variables

| | |
|---|---|
| NLEFT | Left column of BROWSE screen area |
| NRIGHT | Right column of BROWSE screen area |
| NTOP | Top row of BROWSE screen area |
| RIGHTVISIBLE | Indicates if a rightmost unfrozen column is visible |
| ROWCOUNT | Number of visible data rows in BROWSE |
| ROWPOS | Current cursor row position |
| SKIPBLOCK | Code block to skip data source |
| STABLE | Flag indicating stable BROWSE object |

### Methods

| | |
|---|---|
| ADDCOLUMN( ) | Adds TBCOLUMN object to BROWSE area. |
| COLORRECT( ) | Alters color of rectangular group of cells. |
| COLWIDTH | Returns the width of a given column. |
| CONFIGURE( ) | Reconfigures internal setting of BROWSE object/area. |
| DEHILITE( ) | De-highlights current cell. |
| DELCOLUMN( ) | Removes an existing column object from TBROWSE object. |
| DOWN( ) | Moves cursor down one row. |
| END( ) | Moves cursor to rightmost visible data column. |
| FORCESTABLE( ) | Performs a full stabilization. |
| GETCOLUMN( ) | Gets a specific TBCOLUMN object. |
| GOBOTTOM( ) | Positions data source to bottom of file. |
| GOTOP( ) | Positions data source to top of file. |
| HILITE( ) | Highlights current cell. |
| HOME( ) | Moves cursor to leftmost visible data column. |
| INSCOLUMN( ) | Adds a new column object to existing TBROWSE object. |
| INVALIDATE( ) | Redraws display in TBROWSE object without refreshing underlying data source. |
| LEFT( ) | Moves cursor left one column. |

*(continued)*

*Methods*

| | |
|---|---|
| PAGEDOWN( ) | Moves cursor down one BROWSE page. |
| PAGEUP( ) | Moves cursor up one BROWSE page. |
| PANEND( ) | Moves cursor to rightmost data column. |
| PANHOME( ) | Moves cursor to leftmost data column. |
| PANLEFT( ) | Moves cursor left one BROWSE page. |
| PANRIGHT( ) | Moves cursor right one BROWSE page. |
| REFRESHALL( ) | All data in BROWSE area to be refreshed at next stabilize. |
| REFRESHCURRENT( ) | All data in current row in BROWSE area to refreshed at next stabilize. |
| RIGHT( ) | Moves cursor right one column. |
| SETCOLUMN( ) | Replaces one TBCOLUMN object with another. |
| STABILIZE( ) | Performs BROWSE stabilization. |
| UP( ) | Moves cursor up one row. |

**SEE ALSO**     TBROWSENEW( ), TBCOLUMNNEW( )

**EXAMPLE**     See Chapter 16.

# TBROWSENEW( )

**FUNCTION**     Generates a Clipper Browse object without defaults.

**SYNTAX**     TBROWSENEW( <expN1>, <expN2>, <expN3>, <expN4> )

**PARAMETERS**
<expN1>     Top row coordinate
<expN2>     Left column coordinate
<expN3>     Bottom row coordinate
<expN4>     Right column coordinate

**RETURNS**     <expO>     Clipper BROWSE object

**LIBRARY**     CLIPPER.LIB

**DESCRIPTION**     This function sets up a browsing window at top left coordinates of <expN1>, <expN2> to bottom right coordinates of <expN3>, <expN4>. The function returns a TBROWSE object with default code blocks for GO TOP, SKIP, and GO BOTTOM operations. Below is the structure of a BROWSE object.

Command Function Reference   541

### Instance Variables

| | |
|---|---|
| AUTOLITE | Logical value to control highlighting |
| CARGO | User-definable slot |
| COLCOUNT | Number of BROWSE columns |
| COLORSPEC | Index color table for BROWSE object |
| COLPOS | Current cursor column position |
| COLSEP | Character for column separator |
| FREEZE | Number of columns to freeze |
| FOOTSEP | Character for footing separator |
| GOBOTTOMBLOCK | Code block to go bottom |
| GOTOPBLOCK | Code block to go top |
| HEADSEP | Character for heading separator |
| HITBOTTOM | Logical toggle if end of data |
| HITTOP | Logical toggle if top of data |
| LEFTVISIBLE( ) | Indicates if a leftmost unfrozen column is visible |
| NBOTTOM | Bottom row of BROWSE screen area |
| NLEFT | Left column of BROWSE screen area |
| NRIGHT | Right column of BROWSE screen area |
| NTOP | Top row of BROWSE screen area |
| RIGHTVISIBLE | Indicates if a rightmost unfrozen column is visible |
| ROWCOUNT | Number of visible data rows in BROWSE |
| ROWPOS | Current cursor row position |
| SKIPBLOCK | Code block to skip data source |
| STABLE | Flag indicating stable BROWSE object |

### Methods

| | |
|---|---|
| ADDCOLUMN( ) | Adds TBCOLUMN object to BROWSE area. |
| COLORRECT( ) | Alters color of rectangular group of cells. |
| COLWIDTH | Returns the width of a given column. |
| CONFIGURE( ) | Reconfigures internal setting of BROWSE object/area. |
| DEHILITE( ) | De-highlights current cell. |

*(continued)*

*Methods*

| | | |
|---|---|---|
| | DELCOLUMN( ) | Removes an existing column object from TBROWSE object. |
| | DOWN( ) | Moves cursor down one row. |
| | END( ) | Moves cursor to rightmost visible data column. |
| | FORCESTABLE( ) | Performs a full stabilization. |
| | GETCOLUMN( ) | Gets a specific TBCOLUMN object. |
| | GOBOTTOM( ) | Positions data source to bottom of file. |
| | GOTOP( ) | Positions data source to top of file. |
| | HILITE( ) | Highlights current cell. |
| | HOME( ) | Moves cursor to leftmost visible data column. |
| | INSCOLUMN( ) | Adds a new column object to existing TBROWSE object. |
| | INVALIDATE( ) | Redraws display in TBROWSE object without refreshing underlying data source. |
| | LEFT( ) | Moves cursor left one column. |
| | PAGEDOWN( ) | Moves cursor down one BROWSE page. |
| | PAGEUP( ) | Moves cursor up one BROWSE page. |
| | PANEND( ) | Moves cursor to rightmost data column. |
| | PANHOME( ) | Moves cursor to leftmost data column. |
| | PANLEFT( ) | Moves cursor left one BROWSE page. |
| | PANRIGHT( ) | Moves cursor right one BROWSE page. |
| | REFRESHALL( ) | All data in BROWSE area to be refreshed at next stabilize. |
| | REFRESHCURRENT( ) | All data in current row in BROWSE area to refreshed at next stabilize. |
| | RIGHT( ) | Moves cursor right one column. |
| | SETCOLUMN( ) | Replaces one TBCOLUMN object with another. |
| | STABILIZE( ) | Performs BROWSE stabilization. |
| | UP( ) | Moves cursor up one row. |

**SEE ALSO**   TBROWSEDB( ), TBCOLUMNNEW( )

**EXAMPLE**   See Chapter 16.

## TBCOLUMNNEW( )

| | |
|---|---|
| **FUNCTION** | Creates a Clipper Column object. |
| **SYNTAX** | `TBCOLUMNNEW( <expC1>, <expB2> )` |
| **PARAMETERS** | `<expC1>`  Column heading |
| | `<expB2>`  Code block expression used for data retrieval |
| **RETURNS** | `<expO>`  Clipper TBColumn object |
| **LIBRARY** | CLIPPER.LIB |
| **DESCRIPTION** | This function is used to generate a Clipper TBColumn object that is to be stored to a Clipper TBROWSE (Browsing) object. To create this object, the header of the object must be specified in `<expC1>` and the data retrieval code block specified in `<expB2>`. The table below shows the structure of the Clipper TBColumn object. |

*Instance Variables*

| | |
|---|---|
| BLOCK | Code block to retrieve data in column |
| CARGO | User-definable slot |
| COLORBLOCK | Code block determines color of data |
| COLSEP | Character for column separator |
| DEFCOLOR | Index definition of colors |
| FOOTING | Column footing |
| FOOTSEP | Character for footing separator |
| HEADING | Column heading |
| HEADSEP | Character for heading separator |
| PICTURE | Character string for picture template to display information with |
| WIDTH | Column display width |

| | |
|---|---|
| **SEE ALSO** | TBROWSEDB( ), TBROWSENEW( ) |
| **EXAMPLE** | Please see Chapter 16. |

## TIME( )

| | |
|---|---|
| **FUNCTION** | Returns the system time as a string. |
| **SYNTAX** | `TIME()` |

| | |
|---|---|
| **PARAMETER** | None |
| **RETURNS** | <expC>   Character string representing time |
| **LIBRARY** | CLIPPER.LIB |
| **DESCRIPTION** | This function returns the system time represented as a character expression in the format of HH:MM:SS. |
| **SEE ALSO** | DATE( ), SECONDS( ) |
| **EXAMPLE** | See the TSECONDS( ) function. |

## TIMEASAMPM( )

| | |
|---|---|
| **FUNCTION** | Converts time string to 12-hour format. |
| **SYNTAX** | `TIMEASAMPM( <expC1> )` |
| **PARAMETER** | <expC1>   Any time string |
| **RETURNS** | <expC>   Formatted 12-hour time string |
| **LIBRARY** | SAMPLES.LIB |
| **DESCRIPTION** | This function is identical to the AMPM( ) function in that it will take the time string <expC1> and return a string to a 12-hour format with the letters " am" or " pm" attached. |
| **SEE ALSO** | TIME( ), AMPM( ) |

## TIMEASSECONDS( )

| | |
|---|---|
| **FUNCTION** | Converts a time string into number of seconds. |
| **SYNTAX** | `TIMEASSECONDS( <expC1> )` |
| **PARAMETER** | <expC1>   Any time string |
| **RETURNS** | <expN>   Number of seconds since midnight |
| **LIBRARY** | SAMPLES.LIB |
| **DESCRIPTION** | This function is identical to the SECS( ) function in that it will convert a time string <expC1> to the number of seconds since midnight. |
| **SEE ALSO** | TIME( ), SECONDS( ), SECS( ) |
| **EXAMPLE** | Please see the STATUSUPDATE( ) function. |

## TIMEASSTRING( )

| | |
|---|---|
| **FUNCTION** | Converts number of seconds to a time string. |
| **SYNTAX** | `TIMEASSTRING( <expN1> )` |
| **PARAMETER** | <expN1>   Number of seconds |
| **RETURNS** | <expC>   Formatted time string |
| **LIBRARY** | SAMPLES.LIB |
| **DESCRIPTION** | This function takes the number of seconds passed as <expN1> and returns a formatted time string. This is identical to the TSTRING( ) function. |
| **SEE ALSO** | TIME( ), TSTRING( ) |

## TIMEDIFF( )

| | |
|---|---|
| **FUNCTION** | Returns the difference between two time strings. |
| **SYNTAX** | `TIMEDIFF( <expC1>, <expC2> )` |
| **PARAMETERS** | <expC1>   Beginning time string<br><expC2>   Ending time string |
| **RETURNS** | <expC>   Difference between the two in time string format |
| **LIBRARY** | SAMPLES.LIB |
| **DESCRIPTION** | This function is identical to the ELAPTIME( ) function in that it will return a time string which is the difference between the beginning time of <expC1> and the ending time of <expC2>. |
| **SEE ALSO** | TIME( ), TSTRING( ), ELAPTIME( ) |
| **EXAMPLE** | Please see the STATUSUPDATE( ) function. |

## TIMEISVALID( )

| | |
|---|---|
| **FUNCTION** | Validates a string as a "time" string. |
| **SYNTAX** | `TIMEISVALID( <expC1> )` |
| **PARAMETER** | <expC1>   String in a time format |
| **RETURNS** | <expL>   Logical true (.T.) or a logical false (.F.) |

| | |
|---|---|
| **LIBRARY** | SAMPLES.LIB |
| **DESCRIPTION** | This function will return a logical true (.T.) value if the string <expC1> is seen to be a valid time string formatted as "HH:MM:SS". If <expC1> is not a valid time string, then the function will return a false (.F.) value. |
| **SEE ALSO** | TIME( ), TSTRING( ) |

## TONE( )

| | | |
|---|---|---|
| **FUNCTION** | Generates a tone through the computer's speaker. | |
| **SYNTAX** | TONE( <expN1>, <expN2> ) | |
| **PARAMETERS** | <expN1> | Frequency of tone |
| | <expN2> | Duration of tone |
| **LIBRARY** | EXTEND.LIB | |
| **DESCRIPTION** | This function generates a computer tone based on the frequency of the sound expressed as <expN1> and on the duration of the tone expressed as <expN2>. | |
| | The value of <expN1> must be a positive number and is evaluated only as an integer; all other numbers are truncated. The frequency specified is based in hertz, or cycles per second. Any value below 20 is too low to be heard. | |
| | The value of <expN2> must also be a positive number and is evaluated only as an integer; all other numbers are truncated. The time of the duration is expressed in 1/18 increments per second. Therefore, 1 second of sound is expressed as an 18. | |
| | See Appendix 8 for a complete tonal chart of the notes generated by this function. | |
| **NOTE** | This function is designed to work only with 100% IBM-PC compatible machines. | |
| **SEE ALSO** | SET BELL, SET( ) | |
| **EXAMPLE** | | |

```
 1 : * File       Tonedemo.prg
 2 : * Compile    Rmake sample /dFILE:tonedemo
 3 :
 4 : #include "PTValue.ch"      // Power Tools Header file of values
 5 : #include "PTVerbs.ch"      // Power Tools Header file of commands/statements
 6 : #include "PTInkey.ch"      // Power Tools Header file of ASCII values
 7 :
 8 : #xtranslate BADTONE() => ( tone(164.80, 4), tone(130, 1) )
 9 :
10 : procedure Main()
11 :
```

```
12 :    local nTemp    := 0
13 :    local getlist := {}    // Prevents a warning message!
14 :
15 :    PROCESS              // A user-defined command for WHILE .T.
16 :      scroll()           // Don't need CLS since there is an @...SAY
17 :      @ 10,10 say "Enter a value...: " get nTemp
18 :      read
19 :      if !( lastkey() == pESC )    // ESC wasn't pressed
20 :        do case
21 :        case nTemp == 0              // could have used EMPTY(nTemp)
22 :          Charge()
23 :        case nTemp > 0
24 :          GoodTone()
25 :        otherwise
26 :          BADTONE()        // Calls the pseudofunction
27 :        endcase
28 :        @ maxrow(), 00 say "Press any key to go again!"
29 :        inkey(0)
30 :      else
31 :        exit
32 :      endif
33 :    END PROCESS
34 :
35 : *******************
36 :
37 : static function Charge
38 :
39 :    tone(261.70, 3)
40 :    tone(329.60, 3)
41 :    tone(349.20, 3)
42 :    tone(392.00, 3)
43 :    tone(349.20, 3)
44 :    tone(392.00, 10)
45 :
46 :    return( NIL )
47 :
48 : *******************
49 :
50 : static function GoodTone
51 :
52 :    local nCount     // This is for the FOR ... NEXT loop
53 :
54 :    for nCount := 1 to 6
55 :      tone(523.00, 1)
56 :    next
57 :
58 :    return( NIL )
59 :
60 : // End of File: Tonedemo.prg
```

# TRANSFORM( )

**FUNCTION**  Formats a value based on a specified picture template.

**SYNTAX**  TRANSFORM( <expX1>, <expC2> )

548    *Straley's Programming with Clipper 5.2*

| PARAMETERS | <expX1> | Any expression to be formatted |
|---|---|---|
|  | <expC2> | Character string with picture template |
| RETURNS | <expC> | Formatted expression in character format |
| LIBRARY | CLIPPER.LIB | |

**DESCRIPTION**   This function returns <expX1> in the format of the picture expression passed to the function as <expC2>.

There are two components that can make up <expC2>: a function string and a template string. Function strings are those functions that globally tell what the format of <expX1> should be. These functions are represented by a single character preceded by the @ symbol.

There are a couple of rules to follow when using function strings and template strings:

- First, a single space must fall between the function template and the template string if they are used in conjunction with one another.
- Second, if both components make up the value of <expC2>, the function string must precede the template string. Otherwise, the function string may appear without the template string and vice versa.

The table below shows the possible function strings available with the TRANSFORM( ) function:

| @B | Left-justify the string within the format. |
|---|---|
| @C | Issue a CR after format if numbers are positive. |
| @D | Put date in SET DATE format. |
| @E | Put date in British format. |
| @R | Insert nontemplate characters. |
| @X | Issue a DB after format if numbers are negative. |
| @Z | Display any zero as blank space. |
| @( | Enclose negative numbers in parentheses. |
| @! | Convert alpha characters to uppercased format. |
| @) | Enclose negative numbers in parentheses and remove leading blank spaces. |

The second part of <expC2> consists of the format string. Each character in the string may be formatted based on using the following characters as template markers for the string:

| A,N,X,9,# | Any data type |
|---|---|
| L | Show logicals as "T" or "F" |
| Y | Show logicals as "Y" or "N" |
| ! | Convert to uppercase |
| $ | Dollar sign in place of leading spaces in numeric expressions |

|   |   |
|---|---|
| * | Asterisks in place of leading spaces in numeric expressions |
| , | Commas position |
| . | Decimal point position |

**SEE ALSO**  @ ... SAY, DEVOUTPICT( ), VALEDIT( )

**EXAMPLE**

```
 1 :  * File      Trandemo.prg
 2 :  * Compile   Rmake sample /dFILE:trandemo
 3 :
 4 :  #xtranslate DEVSPACE() => devout(space(3))
 5 :
 6 :  procedure Main()
 7 :
 8 :     local cString  := "This is a test"
 9 :     local nNumber1 := 99231.34
10 :     local nNumber2 := -82312.00
11 :     local nNumber3 := 0
12 :     local lValue   := .T.
13 :     local dDate    := date()
14 :
15 :     cls
16 :     outstd("Working with STRINGS and transform()")
17 :     devpos(4,1)
18 :     devout("String is set to -> ")
19 :     devout( cString )
20 :     devpos(5,1)
21 :     devout("  All uppercased -> ")
22 :     devout( transform( cString, "@!" ) )
23 :     qout()
24 :     qout()
25 :     wait
26 :     cls
27 :     outstd("Working with DATES and transform()" )
28 :     set date to ansi
29 :     devpos(4,1)
30 :     devout("Format of date is-> ")
31 :     devout( transform( dDate, "@D" ) )
32 :     devout(" <- ANSI format")
33 :     set date to german
34 :     devpos(5,1)
35 :     devout("Format of date is-> ")
36 :     devout( transform( dDate, "@D" ) )
37 :     devout(" <- GERMAN format")
38 :     set date to japan
39 :     devpos(6,1)
40 :     devout("Format of date is-> ")
41 :     devout( transform( dDate, "@D" ) )
42 :     devout(" <- JAPAN format")
43 :     set date to italian
44 :     devpos(7,1)
45 :     devout("Format of date is-> ")
46 :     devout( transform( dDate, "@D" ) )
47 :     devout(" <- ITALIAN format")
```

```
 48 :    set date to french
 49 :    devpos(8,1)
 50 :    devout("Format of date is-> ")
 51 :    devout( transform( dDate, "@D" ) )
 52 :    devout(" <- FRENCH format")
 53 :    set date to usa
 54 :    devpos(9,1)
 55 :    devout("Format of date is-> ")
 56 :    devout( transform( dDate, "@D" ) )
 57 :    devout(" <- USA format")
 58 :    qout()
 59 :    qout()
 60 :    wait
 61 :    cls
 62 :    outstd("Working with NUMBERS and transform()" )
 63 :
 64 :    devpos(4,1)
 65 :    devout(" Working with the @B template -> " )
 66 :    devout(transform(nNumber1, "@B"))
 67 :    DEVSPACE()
 68 :    devout(transform(nNumber2, "@B"))
 69 :    DEVSPACE()
 70 :    devout(transform(nNumber3, "@B"))
 71 :    devpos(5,1)
 72 :    devout(" Working with the @C template -> " )
 73 :    devout(transform(nNumber1, "@C"))
 74 :    DEVSPACE()
 75 :    devout(transform(nNumber2, "@C"))
 76 :    DEVSPACE()
 77 :    devout(transform(nNumber3, "@C"))
 78 :    devpos(6,1)
 79 :    devout(" Working with the @X template -> " )
 80 :    devout(transform(nNumber1, "@X"))
 81 :    DEVSPACE()
 82 :    devout(transform(nNumber2, "@X"))
 83 :    DEVSPACE()
 84 :    devout(transform(nNumber3, "@X"))
 85 :    devpos(7,1)
 86 :    devout(" Working with the @Z template -> " )
 87 :    devout(transform(nNumber1, "@Z"))
 88 :    DEVSPACE()
 89 :    devout(transform(nNumber2, "@Z"))
 90 :    DEVSPACE()
 91 :    devout(transform(nNumber3, "@Z"))
 92 :    devpos(8,1)
 93 :    devout(" Working with the @( template -> " )
 94 :    devout(transform(nNumber1, "@("))
 95 :    DEVSPACE()
 96 :    devout(transform(nNumber2, "@("))
 97 :    DEVSPACE()
 98 :    devout(transform(nNumber3, "@("))
 99 :    devpos(9,1)
100 :    devout(" Working with the @) template -> " )
101 :    devout(transform(nNumber1, "@)"))
102 :    DEVSPACE()
103 :    devout(transform(nNumber2, "@)"))
104 :    DEVSPACE()
```

```
105 :     devout(transform(nNumber3, "@)"))
106 :     qout()
107 :     qout()
108 :     wait
109 :
110 : // End of File: Trandemo.prg
```

## TRIM( )

| | |
|---|---|
| **FUNCTION** | Removes trailing spaces from a string. |
| **SYNTAX** | TRIM( <expC1> ) |
| **PARAMETER** | <expC1>   Any character expression |
| **RETURNS** | <expC>   The formatted character expression |
| **LIBRARY** | CLIPPER.LIB |
| **DESCRIPTION** | This function returns the value of <expC1> with any trailing blank spaces removed. |
| **NOTE** | This function is identical to RTRIM( ) and is the opposite of LTRIM( ). Together with LTRIM( ), this function equates to the ALLTRIM( ) function. |
| **SEE ALSO** | RTRIM( ), LTRIM( ), ALLTRIM( ) |
| **EXAMPLE** | See the SUBSTR( ) function. |

## TSTRING( )

| | |
|---|---|
| **FUNCTION** | Converts seconds into a time string. |
| **SYNTAX** | TSTRING( <expN1> ) |
| **PARAMETER** | <expN1>   Numeric expression |
| **RETURNS** | <expC>   Character expression |
| **LIBRARY** | EXTEND.LIB |
| **DESCRIPTION** | This function converts <expN1> seconds into a time string. |
| **NOTE** | This is a compatibility function and may not be supported in future versions. |
| **SEE ALSO** | SECS( ), SECONDS( ), TIME( ) |

**EXAMPLE**

```
 1 : * File       D3demo.prg
 2 : * Compile    Rmake sample /dFILE:d3demo
 3 :
 4 : #include "PTVerbs.ch"
 5 : #include "PTInkey.ch"
 6 :
 7 : #xtranslate DEVSPACE() => devout(space(3))
 8 :
 9 : procedure Main()
10 :
11 :    local getlist   := {}
12 :    local nSeconds  := seconds()
13 :    local cTime     := time()
14 :    local nDays
15 :
16 :    PROCESS                  // User defined command
17 :       scroll()              // Just clear the screen
18 :       nDays := 0
19 :       @ 5,5 say "Enter number of seconds to test for " get nDays
20 :       @ 7,5 say "Make sure you enter something > 86399"
21 :       read
22 :       if ( lastkey() == pESC )
23 :          exit
24 :       else
25 :          devpos(9,5)
26 :          devout( "The number of days equal to that is: " )
27 :          devout( str( days( nDays ) ) )   // Or SecondsAsDays()
28 :          devpos(10,5)
29 :          devout( "The current number of elapsed seconds " )
30 :          devout( "since midnight is: " )
31 :          devout( str( secs( time() ) ) )
32 :          devpos(11,5)
33 :          devout( "The current time is: " )
34 :          devout( time() )
35 :          devpos(12,5)
36 :          devout("The number of elapsed seconds in " )
37 :          devout("TIME() format is ")
38 :          devout( tstring( seconds() - nSeconds ) )
39 :          devpos(13,5)
40 :          devout("And the elapsed time is :")
41 :          devout( elaptime( time(), cTime ) )
42 :
43 :          devpos(17,5)
44 :          devout("Press the ESC key to stop the time")
45 :          while !( inkey() == pESC )
46 :             devpos(18,5)
47 :             devout( time() )
48 :             DEVSPACE()
49 :             devout( seconds() )
50 :             DEVSPACE()
51 :             devout( tstring( seconds() - nSeconds ) )
52 :             DEVSPACE()
53 :             devout( elaptime( time(), cTime ) )
54 :          enddo
55 :       endif
```

```
56 :    END PROCESS
57 :
58 : // End of File: D3demo.prg
```

# TYPE( )

| | |
|---|---|
| **FUNCTION** | Returns the data type of an expression. |
| **SYNTAX** | TYPE ( <expC1> ) |
| **PARAMETER** | <expC1>    The expression whose type is to be determined |
| **RETURNS** | <expC>    Code for the data type |
| **LIBRARY** | CLIPPER.LIB |
| **DESCRIPTION** | This function returns a character expression that serves as a code to represent the data type of <expC1>. This function uses macro expansions within the language to test data types, including function names, for their data values. Consequently, it will not return accurate results for a LOCAL or STATIC variable. Below is a code list of data type characters. |

| Value of TYPE( ) | Data Type |
|---|---|
| A | Array |
| B | Code Block |
| C | Character |
| D | Date |
| L | Logical |
| M | Memo |
| N | Numeric |
| O | Object |
| U | NIL, Local, Static |
| UE | Syntactical error |
| UI | Indeterminate error |
| U | Internal error |

This function cannot obtain the return data type of a function; refer to VALTYPE( ). If the name of a function is not directly in the table for CLIPPER.LIB (e.g., a UDF or a function in EXTEND.LIB), the type function will return a UI. or a U. value. Additionally, if a parameter that is declared on the FUNCTION or PROCEDURE command line along with the name of the subroutine is tested using the TYPE( ) function, a return code of U. will be generated.

| | |
|---|---|
| **SEE ALSO** | VALTYPE( ) |
| **EXAMPLE** | See the VALTYPE( ) function. |

## UPDATED( )

| | |
|---|---|
| **FUNCTION** | Determines if the last active READ changed data. |
| **SYNTAX** | UPDATED() |
| **PARAMETER** | None |
| **RETURNS** | <expL>   Logical true (.T.) or false (.F.) |
| **LIBRARY** | CLIPPER.LIB |
| **DESCRIPTION** | This function tests whether the last READ command changed any of the data associated with the appropriate GETs. If so, this function will return a logical true (.T.); otherwise, a logical false (.F.) will be returned.<br><br>The update status of any GET is only altered if information is processed through the GET via the KEYBOARD system. If a GET is altered directly (e.g., a variable is altered by a user-defined function), the update flag is not altered. |
| **SEE ALSO** | READ, READUPDATED( ) |
| **EXAMPLE** | Please see the READINSERT( ) function. |

## UPPER( )

| | |
|---|---|
| **FUNCTION** | Converts a character expression to uppercase format. |
| **SYNTAX** | UPPER( <expC1> ) |
| **PARAMETER** | <expC1>   Any character expression |
| **RETURNS** | <expC>   Formatted character expression |
| **LIBRARY** | CLIPPER.LIB |
| **DESCRIPTION** | This function converts all alpha characters in <expC1> to uppercase values and returns that formatted character expression. |
| **SEE ALSO** | LOWER( ), ISUPPER( ), ISLOWER( ) |

**EXAMPLE**

```
1 : * File      Updemo.prg
2 : * Compile   Rmake sample /dFILE:updemo
3 :
4 : procedure Main()
5 :
6 :    local cString1 := "This is a test"
7 :    local cString2 := "5.2 is the newest release"
8 :
```

```
 9 : cls
10 : qout( "Value of CSTRING1 is:", cString1 )
11 : qout( "Value of CSTRING2 is:", cString2 )
12 : qout()
13 : qout( "UPPER(cString1):", upper(cString1) )
14 : qout( "UPPER(cString2):", upper(cString2) )
15 : qout( "LOWER(cString1):", lower(cString1) )
16 : qout( "LOWER(cString2):", lower(cString2) )
17 : qout()
18 : qout( "Is first character of CSTRING1 a digit?", isdigit(cString1))
19 : qout( "Is first character of CSTRING2 a digit?", isdigit(cString2))
20 : qout( "Is first character of CSTRING1 a character?", isalpha(cString1))
21 : qout( "Is first character of CSTRING2 a character?", isalpha(cString2))
22 : qout()
23 : qout( "Is first character of CSTRING1 a uppercased?", isupper(cString1))
24 : qout( "Is first character of CSTRING2 a uppercased?", isupper(cString2))
25 : qout( "Is first character of CSTRING1 a lowercased?", islower(cString1))
26 : qout( "Is first character of CSTRING2 a lowercased?", islower(cString2))
27 : qout()
28 : wait
29 : cls
30 :
31 : // End of File: Updemo.prg
```

# USED( )

| | |
|---|---|
| **FUNCTION** | Checks whether a database is in use in a work area. |
| **SYNTAX** | USED( ) |
| **PARAMETER** | None |
| **RETURNS** | <expL>    Logical true (.T.) or false (.F.) |
| **LIBRARY** | CLIPPER.LIB |
| **DESCRIPTION** | This function returns a logical true (.T.) if a database file is in USE in the current or designated work area. If no alias is specified along with this function, it will default to the currently selected work area. |
| **SEE ALSO** | ALIAS( ), SELECT( ), SELECT |

# VAL( )

| | |
|---|---|
| **FUNCTION** | Converts a number from a character type to numeric. |
| **SYNTAX** | VAL( <expC1> ) |
| **PARAMETER** | <expC1>    Any character expression |

| | | |
|---|---|---|
| **RETURNS** | <expN> | Numeric value of that character expression |
| **LIBRARY** | CLIPPER.LIB | |
| **DESCRIPTION** | This function converts any number previously defined as a character expression <expC1> into a numeric expression. | |
| **SEE ALSO** | STR( ), TRANSFORM( ) | |

# VALEDIT( )

| | |
|---|---|
| **FUNCTION** | One-time editing of value |
| **SYNTAX** | VALEDIT( <expN1>, <expN2>, <expX3> [, <expC4>] [, <expC5>] ) |
| **PARAMETERS** | <expN1>   Numeric value for row position<br><expN2>   Numeric value for column position<br><expX3>   Any valid data type/variable name<br><expC4>   Character string of PICTURE clause<br><expC5>   Character string of COLOR |
| **RETURNS** | <expX>   Modified value of <expX3> |
| **LIBRARY** | SAMPLES.LIB |
| **DESCRIPTION** | This function is a one-time edit of the variable <expX3> at the screen location of <expN1>, <expN2>. Optionally, a picture string may be specified as <expC4> as well as a color string <expC5>. If <expC4> is not specified, then no picture string will be used. If <expC5> is not specified, then the current value of SETCOLOR( ) will be used. The function will return the modified value of <expX3>. Keep in mind that this function does not recognize any SET KEY operation, unlike the READMODAL( ) function. |
| **SEE ALSO** | READMODAL( ), READ |

**EXAMPLE**

```
 1 : * File      ValEDemo.prg
 2 : * Compile   RMake sampmore /dFILE:valedemo
 3 :
 4 : procedure Main()
 5 :
 6 :    local cTemp := space(10)
 7 :    local nTemp := 23321
 8 :
 9 :    scroll()
10 :    @ 0,0 say "This shows the use of the VALEDIT() function."
11 :    @ 5,20 say "Enter a value..."
12 :
```

```
13 :     cTemp := valedit( 10,10, cTemp )
14 :     scroll(5,0)
15 :     @ 5,20 say "And now, a new value (enter something!)"
16 :
17 :     nTemp := valedit(8,35,nTemp, "@K", "N*+/W" )
18 :
19 :     scroll()
20 :     devpos(2,0)
21 :     devout( "The value of the first VALEDIT() call was: " )
22 :     devout( cTemp )
23 :     devpos(4,0)
24 :     devout( "And the value of the second call was: " )
25 :     devout( nTemp )
26 :
27 : // End of File: Valedemo.prg
```

# VALTYPE( )

**FUNCTION** Validates the data type of an expression.

**SYNTAX** VALTYPE( <expX1> )

**PARAMETER** <expX1>  Any expression

**RETURNS** <expC>  Character expression

**LIBRARY** CLIPPER.LIB

**DESCRIPTION** This function returns a single-character value representing the data type of <expX1>. Below is a table of the possible return codes for VALTYPE( )

| Value of VALTYPE( ) | Meaning |
| --- | --- |
| A | Array |
| B | Code Block |
| C | Character |
| D | Date |
| L | Logical |
| M | Memo |
| N | Numeric |
| O | Object |
| U | NIL |

This function is considered to be a system function in that it evaluates the expression <expX1> and returns a character code for that expression's data type. This function will evaluate the data type of a STATIC and LOCAL memory variable as well as a user-defined function and functions within EXTEND.LIB.

**SEE ALSO**      TYPE( )

**EXAMPLE**

```
 1 : * File      Valtdemo.prg
 2 : * Compile   Rmake sample /dFILE:valtdemo
 3 :
 4 : procedure Main()
 5 :
 6 :    private cString1 := "Hello"
 7 :    private cString2 := "RECNO()"
 8 :    private cString3 := "DBEDIT()"
 9 :    private nTemp1   := 0
10 :    private lTemp1   := .T.
11 :    private bTemp1   := {|| Try()}
12 :    private dTemp1   := DATE()
13 :    private cString4 := "User()"
14 :
15 :    cls
16 :    devpos(2,10)
17 :    qqout("Values for TYPE()", Padl("VALTYPE,"1b))
18 :    qout()
19 :    qout("Variable cString1")
20 :    qout("         cString2")
21 :    qout("         cString3")
22 :    qout("         nTemp1")
23 :    qout("         lTemp1")
24 :    qout("         bTemp1")
25 :    qout("         dTemp1")
26 :    qout("         cString4")
27 :    devpos(4,20)
28 :    devout(type("cString1"))
29 :    devout(space(17))
30 :    devout(valtype(cString1))
31 :    devpos(5,20)
32 :    devout(type("cString2"))
33 :    devout(space(17))
34 :    devout(valtype(cString2))
35 :    devpos(6,20)
36 :    devout(type(cString3))
37 :    devout(space(17))
38 :    devout(valtype(cString3))
39 :    devpos(7,20)
40 :    devout(type("nTemp1"))
41 :    devout(space(17))
42 :    devout(valtype(nTemp1))
43 :    devpos(8,20)
44 :    devout(type("lTemp1"))
45 :    devout(space(17))
46 :    devout(valtype(lTemp1))
47 :    devpos(9,20)
48 :    devout(type("bTemp1"))
49 :    devout(space(17))
50 :    devout(valtype(bTemp1))
51 :    devpos(10,20)
52 :    devout(type("dTemp1"))
53 :    devout(space(17))
```

```
54 :     devout(valtype(dTemp1))
55 :     devpos(11,20)
56 :     devout(type(cString4))
57 :     devout(space(17))
58 :     devout(valtype(cString4))
59 :
60 : ***************
61 :
62 : static function User()
63 :
64 :     return( .f. )
65 :
66 : ****************
67 :
68 : static procedure Try() // This is dummy proc to avoid a linking error
69 :
70 : // End of File: Valtdemo.prg
```

## VERSION( )

**FUNCTION**    Returns the Clipper version.

**SYNTAX**      VERSION()

**PARAMETER**   None

**RETURNS**     &lt;expC&gt;    Character expression

**LIBRARY**     EXTEND.LIB

**DESCRIPTION** This function returns the version number of the Clipper compiler/library.

**NOTE**        This is a compatibility function and may not be supported in future versions.

**SEE ALSO**    OS( )

## WORD( )

**FUNCTION**    Converts CALL numeric parameters.

**SYNTAX**      WORD(&lt;expN1&gt;)

**PARAMETER**   &lt;expN1&gt;    Numeric expression to be converted

**LIBRARY**     CLIPPER.LIB

**560** *Straley's Programming with Clipper 5.2*

| | |
|---|---|
| **DESCRIPTION** | This function converts <expN1> to an integer ranging between plus or minus 32,767. It is used in conjunction with the CALL command to take double parameters and convert them into integer values. |
| **NOTE** | This is a compatibility function and may not be supported in future versions. |
| **SEE ALSO** | Extend System |

## YEAR( )

| | |
|---|---|
| **FUNCTION** | Converts the year portion of a date into a numeric value. |
| **SYNTAX** | YEAR ( <expD1> ) |
| **PARAMETER** | <expD1>    Any date expression |
| **RETURNS** | <expN>    The year portion of the date |
| **LIBRARY** | CLIPPER.LIB |
| **DESCRIPTION** | This function returns the numeric value for the year in <expD1>. This value will always be a four-digit number and is not affected by the settings of the SET CENTURY and SET DATE commands. Additionally, an empty date expression passed to this function will yield a zero value. |
| **SEE ALSO** | DAY( ), MONTH( ) |

**EXAMPLE**

```
 1 : * File      D2demo.prg
 2 : * Compile   Rmake sample /dFILE:d2demo
 3 :
 4 : #xtranslate NULLDATE() => CTOD("")
 5 :
 6 : procedure Main()
 7 :
 8 :    cls
 9 :    qout( "  The day of the week is ", cdow(date()) )
10 :    qout( "The month of the year is ", cmonth(date()) )
11 :    qout()
12 :    qout( "Passing a NULL date to either function" )
13 :    qout( "gives a string with NO length: ", len(cdow(NULLDATE())) )
14 :    qqout( " and ", len(cmonth( NULLDATE() )) )
15 :    wait
16 :
17 :    cls
18 :    setcursor(0)
19 :    Calendar()
20 :    setcursor(1)
21 :    inkey(0)
22 :    cls
```

```
23 :
24 : *******************
25 :
26 : static procedure Calendar()
27 :
28 :    local dDate
29 :    local nCount
30 :    local nTemp
31 :    local nRow
32 :    local nCol
33 :
34 :    for nCount := 1 to 12
35 :       dDate := ctod( str(nCount,2) + "/01/1993" )
36 :       nTemp := 0
37 :       nRow  := 6
38 :       nCol  := dow(dDate) * 5
39 :
40 :       CalenScr()
41 :       @ 3, 6 say dDate
42 :       @ 4, 6 say ( cmonth(dDate) + " - " + str(year(dDate)) )
43 :
44 :       while month(dDate) == month( dDate + nTemp )
45 :         @ nRow, nCol say day( dDate + nTemp++ )
46 :         if (nCol += 5) > 36
47 :            nRow += 2
48 :            nCol := 5
49 :         endif
50 :       enddo
51 :       inkey(3)
52 :    next
53 :
54 : *******************
55 :
56 : static procedure CalenScr
57 :
58 : setpos(0,0)
59 : text
60 :
61 :
62 :
63 :
64 :
65 :
66 :
67 :
68 :
69 :
70 :
71 :
72 :
73 :
74 :
75 :
76 :
77 :
78 : endtext
79 :
80 : // End of File: D2demo.prg
```

# Part II

*Clipper Concepts*

# 8

# Clipper Utilities and Debugging

In this chapter we will cover the various utility programs that come with Clipper 5.2. Some of these utilities make programming easier; some are simple utilities to view data, indexes, and variables; and others help generate report and label files as well as source code files. In this chapter, we will be looking at the following utilities:

| | |
|---|---|
| RMAKE.EXE | Program maintenance |
| PE.EXE | Program editor |
| DBU.EXE | Database utility program |
| RL.EXE | Report and label generator |
| NG.EXE | Norton Guide's engine |
| CLD.EXE | Clipper debugger |

## RMAKE.EXE

This utility program is designed to build applications without the hassle of batch files. It may also be used for maintaining the integrity of a corporate library of functions, procedures, or header files. The operation of the RMAKE.EXE program is based on a comparison of date and time stamps of source files in relation to the destination file—an object file (.OBJ), a library file (.LIB), or an executable file (.EXE). Whenever the date and time stamp of a source file is later than the date and time stamp of the destination file, RMAKE detects an out-of-sequence condition and refers to the command template for the source file to rebuild the destination file. After this has been accomplished, the destination file will have a later date and time stamp value than the source file.

### COMMANDS

Two types of commands can be used with RMAKE.EXE. The first set is composed of those optional switches that may be issued from the DOS command line when RMAKE is called.

The other set of commands are the statements used in an RMAKE script file (.RMK by default), which tell RMAKE what operations are to be called, the order of operations, and the relationship of source files to destination file.

## RMAKE OPTIONAL SWITCHES

| | |
|---|---|
| /B | Display debugging information. |
| /D | Define a macro. |
| /D<expC1>:<exp> | <expC1>: Name of the macro.<br><exp>: Value of the macro. |
| /I | Ignore execution errors: Forces the utility to continue executing even if a line within the file causes an error. |
| /N | Null Make: Causes the program to display all of the commands that would be performed from the make file without executing them. |
| /S | Search Subdirectories: Causes the program to search all of the subdirectories from the current directory (unless the subdirectory is explicitly named) for files that are not found. |
| /U | Enable Comments: Ordinarily, RMAKE recognizes C-style comments (/* and */ or //). However, this switch forces the utility program to treat the "#" character as a comment indicator. If used, all make file directives must be preceded by the "!" character instead of the "#" character. |
| /W | Show Warnings: Displays warning messages that may occur while processing the make file. |
| /XS | Establish the maximum symbol table size. |
| /XS<expN1> | <expN1>: Number of symbols in the table. This option alters the default size of the symbol table from 500 symbols to a size of <expN1> symbols. This affects the amount of memory needed to run the application. |
| /XW | Establish internal workspace size. |
| /XW<expN1> | <expN1>: Number of bytes for the internal workspace for the application being built. The default size is 2048 bytes. |

## RMAKE COMMAND STATEMENTS

| | |
|---|---|
| $* | Macro without path or extension. This macro will expand to the targeted filename without a path or extension. |
| $@ | Macro with path or extension. This macro will expand to the targeted filename with a path or extension. |

| | |
|---|---|
| $** | Macro with full dependency. This macro will expand to the complete list of full-dependency filenames. |
| $< | Macro with full name. This macro will expand to the full name of the dependency file that triggered the action. |
| $? | Macro with full dependency, date triggered. This macro will expand to the complete list of full-dependency filenames that have a more recent date and time stamp than the target file. |
| #! | Execute an action. |
|    #!<expC1> | <expC1>: Any action or command. This directive executes <expC1> during the first phase of the RMAKE.EXE parsing operation. Any valid DOS command can be used with this directive. |
| #ifeq | Process two equal words. |
|    #ifeq <expC1> <expC2> | <expC1>: Character/macro expression.<br><expC2>: Character/macro expression.<br>This directive will process the subsequent RMAKE directives and statements if the expression in <expC1> is identical to the expression in <expC2>. Both expressions must be enclosed in quotation marks if they contain spaces. In addition, the match is NOT case-sensitive. |
| #ifndef | Process if the macro does not exist. |
|    #ifndef <expC1> | <expC1>: Macro name. This directive will process the subsequent RMAKE directives and statements if the macro named <expC1> is not defined. All statements that follow until either the #ENDIF or #ELSE statement will be processed. |
| #ifdef | Process if the macro exists. |
|    #ifdef <expC1> | <expC1>: Macro name. This directive will process the subsequent RMAKE directives and statements if the macro named <expC1> is defined. All statements that follow until either the #ENDIF or #ELSE statement will be processed. |
| #else | Conditional directive. This is a conditional RMAKE directive that will work with the #ifdef, #ifndef, and #iffile statements. |
| #end[if] | End process. This ends any of the following conditional RMAKE directives: #ifdef, #ifndef, and #iffile. |
| #iffile | Process if a file exists. |
|    #iffile <expC1> | <expC1> Filename. This directive will process the subsequent RMAKE directives and statements if the file named in <expC1> exists. All statements that follow until either the #ENDIF or #ELSE statement will be processed. |

*(continued)*

#include                     Include file.

    #include "<expC1>"         <expC1>: Filename. This directive tells the RMAKE.EXE program to include the directives listed in the file named <expC1> as part of the operation. RMAKE will not search for the file in directories specified by the INCLUDE environment variable. A subdirectory path must be explicitly mentioned as part of the filename if the file is located outside the current directory.

#undef                     Undefine a macro.

    #undef <expC1>           <expC1>: Name of macro. This directive removes any previously defined macro, including those macros defined on the command line or in RMAKE environmental settings. An environmental variable may not be undefined; however, it may be hidden by defining a macro with the same name.

#stderr                    Display an error message.

    #stderr "<expC1>"         <expC1>: Text of the message. This directive will write the string <expC1> to the standard error device or file.

#stdout                    Display a message.

    #stdout "<expC1>"         <expC1>: Text of the message. This directive will write the string <expC1> to the standard output device or file.

## INVOKING RMAKE.EXE

The syntax to call RMAKE is the following:

```
RMAKE [<expC1>] [<expC2>] [<expC3>]
```

<expC1>:    A filename that contains the directives and commands to be executed by RMAKE. This expression may be a file list as long as the files are separated by spaces. If no file extension is given, .RMK will be assumed. Any other extension should be specified along with the name of the script file being processed, as should the drive and directory path if the file is not located in the current directory. When RMAKE.EXE finishes processing the script file(s) <expC1>, it will set a DOS return code indicating the final state of the operation.

<expC2>:    A list of macro definitions. Each macro definition should be separated by a space and takes the syntax:

    ```
<Macro Name>=<value>
```

<expC3>:    Option list. Options are not case-sensitive and must be preceded with either the "/" or "-" character. No extra space is needed between options.

## ENVIRONMENTAL VARIABLES

Command-line arguments and options may instead be supplied to RMAKE via a DOS environmental variable:

```
SET RMAKE=[[<expC1>][<expC2>]]
```

&lt;expC1&gt;:   Make file list
&lt;expC2&gt;:   RMAKE command options and directives

Those options or files specified in the environmental variable are scanned before any command-line options or filenames. Therefore, the command-line setting can override any setting previously defined in the environmental variable.

## RMAKE OPERATION AND RULES

Central to the operation of the RMAKE script file is the concept of target files and dependent files. Normally, the dependent files, based on some rule, will generate or create a new target file. In application development, the .PRG files will eventually generate an .OBJ file (when compiled); in turn, the .OBJ files will eventually generate an .EXE file (when linked).

The operation of RMAKE is subject to two rules. The first rule is the dependency rule. The second rule is the inference rule. Each rule and method has a direct impact on what, when, and why a dependent file will generate a target file.

During the second of RMAKE's two passes through the script file, the dependencies of a target file are gathered and an internal listing is made of the dependent files that make up that specified target file. Along with this internal listing, the necessary actions to be taken are determined. No blank line can be present between a listing of dependencies and the commands that generate the target file from the dependent file(s). For example, here is a simple dependency statement with both dependent and target files, as well as an action statement:

```
Gendata.exe:       Gendata.obj
    Rtlink Fi Gendata
```

The date and time stamp on GENDATA.EXE (the target or destination file) is compared to the date and time stamp of GENDATA.OBJ (the dependent file). The action to be taken if the date and/or time stamp of GENDATA.OBJ is later than GENDATA.EXE is to call RTLINK.EXE.

Dependencies may include multiple dependent files and may spill over onto the next line in the script file by using the "\" character:

```
udf.lib: CheckAmount.obj NumericWord.obj MakeEmpty.obj \
         Attribute.obj ColorString.obj Dulling.obj Sin.obj \
         Cosin.obj EggTimer.obj Fordinal.obj Eom.obj Parse.obj \
         YesNo.obj DosStru.obj ListBox.obj MakeArra.obj
    lib @udf.lst
```

In this example, if the date and/or time stamps of any of the object files listed in the dependent file section is later than the destination file (UDF.LIB), the library manager (named LIB.EXE) will be called with the script file UDF.LST.

Along with dependency rules, an inference rule may also be applied. An inference rule defines a series of actions to be taken when those actions are not explicitly specified following the dependency rule. The syntax for an inference is as follows:

```
.<expC1>.<expC2>:
   [<expC3>]...
```

<expC1>:   File extension of the dependent files
<expC2>:   File extension of the destination file
<expC3>:   Commands and actions to be taken

When no action statement follows a dependency rule, RMAKE will search for an inference rule whose file extensions match those of the dependent and target files. We can modify the above example to show how an inference rule would work along with a dependency rule:

```
.obj.lib:
   if not errorlevel 1 lib @udf.lst

udf.lib:  CheckAmount.obj NumericWord.obj MakeEmpty.obj \
          Attribute.obj ColorString.obj Dulling.obj Sin.obj \
          Cosin.obj EggTimer.obj Fordinal.obj Eom.obj Parse.obj \
          YesNo.obj DosStru.obj ListBox.obj MakeArra.obj
```

Since no action is to be taken following the dependency rule, RMAKE will search through the file for the appropriate inference and take the necessary action.

So far, the trouble with these examples is that the files listed on both the target and the destination side of the equation are hard-coded; as a result, the script file needs to be modified to change with the growing needs of the application. As an application grows, the information needed for putting together that application should also change easily and, if possible, automatically. Sometimes, the methods used to make an application may vary as well. To help with variable information, either in the inference rule or dependency rule section, support for macros is included in the RMAKE.EXE utility program.

To define a macro, use the following syntax:

```
<expC1>=<expC2>
where <expC1> Macro being defined
      <expC2> Value of macro
```

Once a macro is defined, the macro may be referred to as follows:

```
$(<expC1>)  <expC1>: Macro name
```

Whenever this pattern is found within the script file, RMAKE will replace the name of the macro with its associated value. If that macro is not defined, a null string will be substituted. Along with the basic macro, there are five predefined macros that help match patterns and macros with values. These are discussed at the beginning of the section entitled "RMAKE Command Statements."

To help see this, here is a predefined macro in an inference rule:

```
.prg.obj:
   Clipper $* /N
```

This tells RMAKE that if it encounters an .OBJ target file and a .PRG dependent file in a dependency rule that lacks an action statement, it should call Clipper using the target filename and the /N compiling switch without an associated path or file extension. This means that the dependency rule may contain a file extension and/or path associated with the destination files, but they will not be used when Clipper is called. To see this in action, consider the following RMAKE script file:

```
.prg.obj:
   Clipper $* /N
.obj.lib:
   if not errorlevel 1 lib @udf.lst

CheckAmount.obj    :   CheckAmount.prg
NumericWord.obj    :   NumericWord.prg
MakeEmpty.obj      :   MakeEmpty.prg
Attribute.obj      :   Attribute.prg
ColorString.obj    :   ColorString.prg
Dulling.obj        :   Dulling.prg
Sin.obj            :   Sin.prg
Cosin.obj          :   Cosin.prg
EggTimer.obj       :   EggTimer.prg
Fordinal.obj       :   Fordinal.prg
Eom.obj            :   Eom.prg
Parse.obj          :   Parse.prg
YesNo.obj          :   YesNo.prg
DosStru.obj        :   DosStru.prg
ListBox.obj        :   ListBox.prg
MakeArra.obj       :   MakeArra.prg

udf.lib:   CheckAmount.obj NumericWord.obj MakeEmpty.obj \
           Attribute.obj ColorString.obj Dulling.obj Sin.obj \
           Cosin.obj EggTimer.obj Fordinal.obj Eom.obj Parse.obj \
           YesNo.obj DosStru.obj ListBox.obj MakeArra.obj
```

Each one of the .PRG files listed is a dependent file for an associated .OBJ file. Since there is no action following any of the dependency rules, the inference rule for .PRG.OBJ is used. This inference will call Clipper, replacing the macro with the root name of the target files (all of the .OBJ files). This means that if any of the .PRG files on the right side of the dependency rule has a later date and time stamp, the appropriate .OBJ file on the left will be generated using the inference rule previously defined. As RMAKE examines all of the dependency rules, the dependencies for the destination file UDF.LIB will be checked. This in turn will invoke the inference rule for that dependency rule, and a new .LIB file will be generated if necessary.

To further understand the various rules and the use of macros, here is a make file for the RL.EXE program. The name of the file is RL.RMK; it is a part of the distribution set.

```
//
//   Rl.rmk
//
//   Make file for RL, Clipper REPORT and LABEL FORM design program.
//
//   Copyright (c) 1990-1993, Computer Associates International, Inc.
//   All rights reserved.
//

.prg.obj:
    clipper $< /m /n

.obj.exe:
    set rtlinkcmd=/posi
    rtlink $**, $@ ;

rlfront.obj:    rlfront.prg
rlback.obj:     rlback.prg
rldialg.obj:    rldialg.prg

rl.exe:         rlfront.obj  rlback.obj  rldialg.obj
```

RL.RMK specifies that the three .PRG files will be used to make the destination files based on the inference rule pertaining to .PRG and .OBJ files. That rule contains two macros. The first macro tells RMAKE to call Clipper with the full name of the dependent file that triggered the rule. When Clipper is called, two switches will be used: /m for single module only and /o to specify the .OBJ file's locations and names. This is followed by another macro that creates a new target file of the same name and in the same directory as the target file specified in the dependency rule. Since both dependent and target files have the same root name, however, the effect will be the same as if the command did not use a macro.

Once all destination .OBJ files are checked with their dependent files, the dependency rule for RL.EXE is checked. Here, the three .OBJ files now become the dependent files for the target file RL.EXE. Since there is no action within this dependency rule, the appropriate inference rule is then sought and used. In this rule, a new macro is used. Prior to calling RTLINK, a DOS environmental variable is set to place RTLINK into POSITIONAL mode. The first macro is expanded into the complete list of dependent files specified in the dependency rule. This means that RMAKE will call RTLINK using each of the .OBJ filenames in the dependency rule as input to RTLINK's FI statement. Following this, the full name of the target file is used as the output for the RTLINK program. In essence, this is how RMAKE would expand the macro:

```
set rtlinkcmd=/posi
rtlink rlfront.obj, rlback.obj, rldialg.obj, rl.exe;
```

Several .RMK files are included in the Clipper distribution package, each with a unique set of macros, directives, and switches. These are excellent sources of additional examples and templates to be mimicked.

## More Complex Use of RMAKE

Making use of these various options allows for a more flexible programming environment. For example, the following sample RMAKE file is used to create a screen editor called SE.EXE.

```
//  SE.rmk

// There are two ways to control output of the .exe & .obj files.
// First, call this make file with the /D command.  For example, to
// have the .exe output be contained in the \PLEIADES directory, type:
//
//         rmake se /DEXE:\PLEIADES
//
// The lines below instruct RMAKE to test for the existence of this
// variable and act accordingly.  This method does not take up
// DOS environmental space.

#ifdef OUTPUTOBJ
    makepath[.obj] := "$(OUTPUTOBJ)"
    #stdout ""
    #stdout "PATH FOR .OBJ FILES IS: '$(OUTPUTOBJ)'"

#else
    #stdout ""
    #stdout "WRITING .OBJ FILES TO CURRENT DIRECTORY"

#end

#ifdef OUTPUTEXE
    makepath[.exe] := "$(OUTPUTEXE)"
    #stdout ""
    #stdout "PATH FOR THE .EXE FILE IS: '$(OUTPUTEXE)'"

#else
    #stdout "WRITING .EXE FILE TO THE CURRENT DIRECTORY"

#end

// Alternatively, the technique used in Nantucket's examples,
// sets environmental variables to the directories
// where the output should go.
//
// The following lines would cause the same result as above, but use
// DOS environmental space.

// !ifeq "$(OUTPUTOBJ)" ""
//      !stdout "WRITING .OBJ FILES TO CURRENT DIRECTORY"
```

```
//  !else
//      makepath[.obj] := "$(OUTPUTOBJ)"
//      !stdout "PATH FOR .OBJ FILES IS: '$(OUTPUTOBJ)'"

//  !end

// Create a macro we will use in the link cycle
se_objs:=se.obj seenv.obj sefunc.obj semove.obj sebox.obj segtext.obj

// Inference rule - expand to full name of dependency file triggering rule
// Assumes CLIPPERCMD variable is appropriately set
.prg.obj:
    clipper $<

.obj.exe:
    set rtlinkcmd=/posi /PLL:BASE50
    rtlink $** ssddict.obj genfunc.obj sirius.obj, $@ ;
    // Assume RTLINKCMD is appropriately set
    // file $** expands to full list of dependency file names

// Dependency statements for .obj's
se.obj:         se.prg
seenv.obj:      seenv.prg
sefunc.obj:     sefunc.prg
semove.obj:     semove.prg
sebox.obj:      sebox.prg
segtext.obj:    segtext.prg

// Dependency rule for linking into the .exe
se.exe:         $(se_objs)
```

Notice the use of the macros from within the file and the detailed level of comments. The script files for the RMAKE utility can be just as detailed in annotating code as the program files being compiled.

### The Ultimate Use of RMAKE

Our final example uses a text file to define the various macros that will be used to not only compile the various modules of the Hermes library, but to build the library as well. The text file, named LOCALE.TXT, is used to specify the directory path for the various components needed to make the library. Rather than redefining these macros from within the actual HERMES.RMK file, the text file is used as a simple definition base. First, here are the contents of the LOCALE.TXT file:

```
// Path to various pieces required by the .mak file
libpath    = \clipper5\lib
objpath    = \hermes\source
srcpath    = \hermes\source
cl5        = \clipper5\bin\clipper.exe
libmgr     = \clipper5\bin\lib.exe
```

And now, here is the HERMES.RMK file that uses these macros:

```
/*
                    The HERMES RMake Make File
    ----------------------------------------------------------------

    This file is used to perform upkeep on the HERMES.LIB file, that
    accompanies the HERMES package.

    Background
    ----------
    Hermes is a collection of subsystems that can be used in application
    development.  Many of these subsystems use the same function primitives,
    such as PressKeyMsg(), which displays a message and waits for the user
    to press a key.

    The general functions used by all the subsystems have been collected into
    a general library.  This file is the MAKE file for that library.

    Files you will need
    -------------------
    The library contains routines written in Assembly and Clipper.  The
    source for the assembly routines is not provided at this time.  However,
    the object code is provided, and is only referred to in the final
    action line that creates the library.  Therefore, to rebuild
    the Hermes library, you must have:

        Nantucket Clipper v5.01 or later
        Nantucket RMake
        A "compatible" Library utility


    Library Utility
    ---------------
    We use LIB.EXE from Microsoft, and so its commands are what is contained
    in the inference rules below.  You don't have to use LIB.EXE, but either
    your library program must support the ability to manage Intel 8086
    relocatable object code using the following command for replacing
    object modules:

        lib <libname> -+objname

    or you must change that line below to the appropriate command.  Note that
    Microsoft has made LIB available on CompuServe in the MSOFT and MSLANG forums.

    Environment
    -----------
    We assume:
    1.  That the proper path to the INCLUDE files that shipped
        with Clipper is contained in a variable called INCLUDE.

    2.  That the Clipper compiler is called CLIPPER, and has not been renamed.

    3.  Macros
        Certain macro variables contain the paths to the files that are
        used to build this lib.  The macros should be created in a separate
        file called "LOCALE.TXT".  "LOCALE.TXT" contains one line for each
        macro used in the make file.  The macros are:
```

```
libpath    Path to the resulting library (i.e., \clipper5)
objpath    Path to where .obj files should be put (i.e., \clipper5\obj)
srcpath    Path to where the source code is found (i.e., \clipper5\source)
cl5        Path and name of Clipper 5.0 compiler
libmgr     Path and name of library utility (i.e. \clipper5\bin\lib)
```

```
Functions In Library
--------------------
```

Each function is contained in its own .obj file. The matching .prg file
is named by an underscore character and the first seven characters of
the function name. For example, PressKeyMsg() becomes "_presske.prg".

The general functions in the library are as follows:

```
AcceptTo        Provides an ACCEPT TO replacement
AltLetter       Gives the ALT equivalent for a letter key, or
                the letter equivalent for an ALT-letter key.
AttrSub         Substitutes an attribute character in a string
                constructed with SaveScreen()
ColorAttribute  Returns ASCII number for a color attribute byte given
                the color string
ColorConvert    Converts a Clipper color to its stringified equivalent
ColorTran       Translates a string to include attribute bytes
CurDrive        Returns the currently logged drive, i.e. "C:"
Errorbeep       Sounds a beep
LFill           Left fills a string with a character
Hermesrt        Hermes/Class(y) runtime CRC module
SSDMouse.obj:
  Mse_status    Returns and optionally sets current mouse status (on/off)
  Mse_reset     Performs a reset of the mouse
  Mse_show      Turns the mouse cursor on
  Mse_hide      Turns the mouse cursor off
  Mse_getpos    Gets row/col coordinate information for mouse cursor
  Mse_setpos    Sets row/col coordinate information for mouse cursor
  Mse_butprs    Determines which mouse button was last pressed
  Mse_butrel    Determines which mouse button was last released
RestBox         Restores a screen image saved with SaveBox()
SaveBox         Saves a screen image, including coordinates
SetKey          SetKey replacement, adds more functionality
SetKeySeek      Looks up a setkey based on a tag
SetKeyList      Lists all setkeys in effect
SetMouse        Creates a mouse "hot spot" stack, which works much like
                SETKEY() for keys
WaitKey         Sirius WAIT replacement
ShowGenError    General message display for an error object
```

Objects are stored in filenames without a leading underscore.  They are:

```
Abstract objects
================
BaseBox         Inherited by all non-Clipper objects
ScrlBox         Inherited from BaseBox, and by all those box type
                objects that have vertical or horizontal scrollbars
```

```
Utility Objects
===============
ScrollBar       Implements horizontal or vertical scroll bars
```

```
Dialog objects
==============
Dialog          Inherited by all Dialog objects
Filebox         Dialog to maneuver around disks/directories/files
MsgBox          Displays a message, "OK" button
YNBox           Displays a message, user ansers "Yes","No","Cancel"
AbortBox        Displays a message, user ansers "Abort","Retry","Cancel"
SaveFile        File box for saving files
BrowBox         Dialog for browsing a single TBrowse object

Dialog Member Objects
=====================
Basebrowse      Basic TBrowse-in-a-Dialog object
Baselist        Basic list box object
Dirlist         List box for directories
Drvlist         List box for drives
Filelist        List box for files
Basechk         Basic check box
Baseget         Basic GET object
Basepush        Basic Push Button object
Basetext        Basic text display object
Boxtext         Text box display object
Entryget        Basic GET for data entry
Baserad         Basic radio buttons object
Basespin        Basic spin button object
CombBox         Combination EntryGet and ListBox/Browse
DropList        Dropdown Listbox
MemoDisp        Displays long/wide strings with scroll bars

*/

makepath[.ch] = "C:\clipper5\ssdinc"
// Get the location macros
#include "locale.txt"

// Get rid of the library response file
#iffile $(srcpath)\Hermes.rsp
    #! del $(srcpath)\Hermes.rsp
#endif
#! echo -+$(objpath)\ptoolsa1 & >> $(srcpath)\Hermes.rsp
#! echo -+$(objpath)\ptoolsc & >> $(srcpath)\Hermes.rsp
#! echo -+$(objpath)\attrsub & >> $(srcpath)\Hermes.rsp
#! echo -+$(objpath)\hermesrt & >> $(srcpath)\Hermes.rsp

#iffile $(srcpath)\Hermes.err
   #! del $(srcpath)\Hermes.err
#endif

// Inference rule for compiling
.prg.obj:
        $(c15) $(srcpath)\$* /a /m /n /w /o$(objpath)\$* >> $(srcpath)\Hermes.err
        echo -+$(objpath)\$* & >> $(srcpath)\Hermes.rsp

// Inference rule for creating library
.rsp.lib:
        echo ,$(srcpath)\Hermes.lst; >> $(srcpath)\Hermes.rsp
        if not exist $(libpath)\Hermes.lib $(libmgr) $(libpath)\Hermes.lib;
        $(libmgr) $(libpath)\Hermes.lib @$(srcpath)\Hermes.rsp
```

```
// General library
$(objpath)\_accepto.obj    :    $(srcpath)\_accepto.prg    hermes.ch
$(objpath)\_altlett.obj    :    $(srcpath)\_altlett.prg    hermes.ch
$(objpath)\_colorat.obj    :    $(srcpath)\_colorat.prg    hermes.ch
$(objpath)\_colorco.obj    :    $(srcpath)\_colorco.prg    hermes.ch
$(objpath)\_colortr.obj    :    $(srcpath)\_colortr.prg    hermes.ch
$(objpath)\_curdriv.obj    :    $(srcpath)\_curdriv.prg    hermes.ch
$(objpath)\_errorbe.obj    :    $(srcpath)\_errorbe.prg    hermes.ch
$(objpath)\_lfill.obj      :    $(srcpath)\_lfill.prg      hermes.ch
$(objpath)\ssdmouse.obj    :    $(srcpath)\ssdmouse.prg    hermes.ch
$(objpath)\_restbox.obj    :    $(srcpath)\_restbox.prg    hermes.ch
$(objpath)\_savebox.obj    :    $(srcpath)\_savebox.prg    hermes.ch
$(objpath)\_setkey.obj     :    $(srcpath)\_setkey.prg     hermes.ch
$(objpath)\_skseek.obj     :    $(srcpath)\_skseek.prg     hermes.ch
$(objpath)\_sklist.obj     :    $(srcpath)\_sklist.prg     hermes.ch
$(objpath)\_setmous.obj    :    $(srcpath)\_setmous.prg    hermes.ch
$(objpath)\_showgen.obj    :    $(srcpath)\_showgen.prg    hermes.ch
$(objpath)\_waitkey.obj    :    $(srcpath)\_waitkey.prg    hermes.ch

// Miscellaneous objects
$(objpath)\scrlbar.obj     :    $(srcpath)\scrlbar.prg     hermes.ch

// Abstract Dialog objects
$(objpath)\basebox.obj     :    $(srcpath)\basebox.prg     hermes.ch
$(objpath)\scrlbox.obj     :    $(srcpath)\scrlbox.prg     hermes.ch

// Turnkey Dialog objects
$(objpath)\basediag.obj    :    $(srcpath)\basediag.prg    hermes.ch
$(objpath)\filebox.obj     :    $(srcpath)\filebox.prg     hermes.ch
$(objpath)\savefile.obj    :    $(srcpath)\savefile.prg    hermes.ch
$(objpath)\msgbox.obj      :    $(srcpath)\msgbox.prg      hermes.ch
$(objpath)\ynbox.obj       :    $(srcpath)\ynbox.prg       hermes.ch
$(objpath)\abortbox.obj    :    $(srcpath)\abortbox.prg    hermes.ch
$(objpath)\browbox.obj     :    $(srcpath)\browbox.prg     hermes.ch

// Dialog Member objects
$(objpath)\basebrow.obj    :    $(srcpath)\basebrow.prg    hermes.ch
$(objpath)\baselist.obj    :    $(srcpath)\baselist.prg    hermes.ch
$(objpath)\dirlist.obj     :    $(srcpath)\dirlist.prg     hermes.ch
$(objpath)\drvlist.obj     :    $(srcpath)\drvlist.prg     hermes.ch
$(objpath)\filelist.obj    :    $(srcpath)\filelist.prg    hermes.ch
$(objpath)\basechk.obj     :    $(srcpath)\basechk.prg     hermes.ch
$(objpath)\baseget.obj     :    $(srcpath)\baseget.prg     hermes.ch
$(objpath)\entryget.obj    :    $(srcpath)\entryget.prg    hermes.ch
$(objpath)\basepush.obj    :    $(srcpath)\basepush.prg    hermes.ch
$(objpath)\basetext.obj    :    $(srcpath)\basetext.prg    hermes.ch
$(objpath)\boxtext.obj     :    $(srcpath)\boxtext.prg     hermes.ch
$(objpath)\memodisp.obj    :    $(srcpath)\memodisp.prg    hermes.ch
$(objpath)\baserad.obj     :    $(srcpath)\baserad.prg     hermes.ch
$(objpath)\basespin.obj    :    $(srcpath)\basespin.prg    hermes.ch
$(objpath)\combbox.obj     :    $(srcpath)\combbox.prg     hermes.ch
$(objpath)\droplist.obj    :    $(srcpath)\droplist.prg    hermes.ch

// Build the library
$(libpath)\Hermes.LIB      :    $(srcpath)\Hermes.RSP
```

## PE.EXE

This is a simple program editor that uses MEMOEDIT( ) and various support functions to perform simple program changes. It can be used as a module for future text editors for the Clipper environment. The program needs to be compiled and linked before executing.

## DBU.EXE

This is a simple database generation and maintenance program with complete menus and a help system. It can be used as an environmental object or subsystem in a future application. The program needs to be compiled and linked before executing.

## RL.EXE

This is a report and label generator written purely in Clipper code that can be used to create and maintain all of an application's .RPT and .LBL files. This program needs to be compiled and linked before executing.

## NG.EXE

This is the Norton Instant Access engine. Once invoked, it will stay in memory and provide instant access to all Clipper help files. However, this uses approximately 70K of the memory that might otherwise be used for compiling, linking, and executing an application. If a file is specified as an argument to NG, the Norton Instant Access engine will be called in a "pass-through" mode: The designated file will be loaded with NG, and once the operation with the specified file is completed, NG will automatically unload itself from memory.

There are a couple of utilities like DOCBASE.EXE, listed in the back of this book, which are designed to help maintain libraries and the .NG files for those libraries and applications.

## The Clipper Debugger

Once a module or a subroutine has been completed, testing and debugging it is the next step. This is an arduous but necessary chore. Each developer has his or her own unique techniques for tracking down and resolving bugs that were formed when the programmer was first introduced to the language and the tools that were available at that time. For example, many developers today simply insert the WAIT command in key areas of the application rather than work with the debugger to track down values. Even though the debugger in Clipper 5.2 is powerful, to some, the simple WAIT command is sufficient. This is due, in large part, to the history of each programmer's exposure to the language. If they learned to program and debug without a debugger and with only the WAIT command, that may still be the generally preferred method. Even today, the value of a particular memory variable, the type of the variable, or the precise location of a program's execution path often requires a simple WAIT. However, for those to whom the concepts of debugging are new or for those familiar with products such as Microsoft's CodeView, working with Clipper 5.2's debugger will be easy, and the debugging challenge will be easier to conquer.

## PREPARING CODE AND RESTRICTIONS

Before Clipper 5.x, whenever an application was running and the debugger was needed, the ALT-D keys would invoke the debugger from within the application. In contrast, in Clipper 5.0 and 5.2, the application executes through the debugger, with various commands, options, keystrokes, and window options available from the debugger. In essence, the Debugger runs the program; the program does not call the debugger.

To prepare for this, the application needs to be told in advance that the compilation process must include hooks for the debugger library. To do this, the following switch must be used when compiling the modules for a program that will be running through the debugger:

```
Clipper <expC1> /B

    <expC1> Filename to compile
```

If a Clipper script file (.CLP or Clip file) is used, the /B option will be used for every file. Any module that is compiled without the /B switch and is executed through the debugger will be ignored. Keep in mind that if the /L option is used during the compilation stage, all line numbers will be lost and there will not be any specific reference back to the source code from the debugger, and thus, no debugging is possible.

Several observations should be made prior to using the debugger. These focus on false expectations that may arise from false assumptions. For example, in many applications developed with Clipper 5.2, the use of header files will be extensive. These files tell the compiler to make in-line translations of all #defines (manifest constants) or #translates (pseudofunctions) before compiling the .PRG file and creating the .OBJ file. Since this translation takes place before the actual object file is generated, the debugger will not be able to refer back to the original source of a problem in the same manner that it could for a standard Clipper command or function, or even a user-defined function or procedure. Using the .PPO (preprocessor output) file will help cross-reference the source code to the actual reference while executing the program in the debugger.

Another consideration concerns source code in header files. In these cases, the line-numbering scheme will be thrown off, thus affecting the ability of the debugger to yield an accurate line number. In addition, multiple commands may be placed on a single line; while an error may occur in any expression, the debugger will point to an entire line of code at a time. Therefore, the entire line is treated as a single entity regardless of the number of individual operations that are present within it.

Code blocks and macro substitutions are also handled in a special fashion when viewed with the debugger. For example, in the case of a code block, the line of code that originally initialized the code block will be viewed, as will the actual line of code that evaluates the code block. This may be seen as a two-step process when in reality it is only one step, and the second line is displayed as nothing more than a reference tool. And macro substitutions will be seen as character strings of the reference containing the macro substitution.

## CALLING THE DEBUGGER

In order to call the debugger directly from DOS, the following command should be issued:

```
CLD <expC1>
```

<expC1> Executable filename

Additional parameters may be passed to the debugger when invoked, as follows:

```
CLD /Q /S /43 /50 @<script file> <application> [Parameters]
```

Unlike the compiler, the switches for the debugger must appear before the application's name. They stand for the following:

| | |
|---|---|
| /Q | Quiet Mode. Run the application directly and invoke the debugger if the ALT-D key is pressed. |
| /S | Split Screen. Split the video screen in half, running the application in the upper half of the screen and the debugger menu in the lower half. |
| /43 | 43-Line Mode. Run the debugger and the application in 43-line mode. |
| /50 | 50-Line Mode. Run the debugger and the application in 50-line mode. |
| @<script file> | Execute debugging commands prior to the execution of the application. |
| <application> | Name of the program that is to be debugged. |
| [Parameters] | The parameter list that is passed to the application. |

When this has been done, the screen shown in Figure 8.1 should appear.

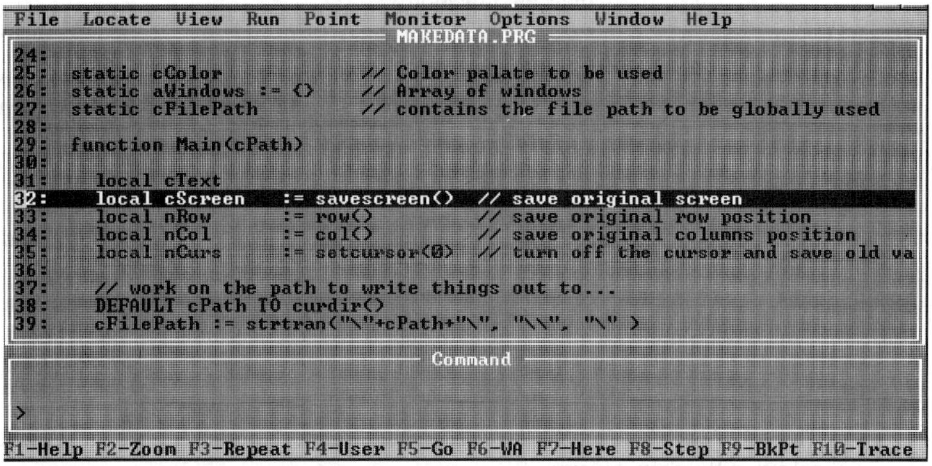

**Figure 8.1 The Clipper Debugger**

Normally, there are two screens to the debugging system. The top screen contains the source code that is being processed by the debugger in the application. This is the *Code Window*. The bottom screen contains an area for issuing commands to view specific parameters, to control program flow, and to give special instructions to the debugger. This is the *Command Window*. Within the Code window, the highlighted bar indicates the line of source code that is about to be processed, while a block character represents the cursor and can be used to mark lines of code. The top center of the Code window shows the name of the source code file currently being executed. If a source code file is not available for the debugger, the Code window will be blank and an appropriate message indicating the name of the file that is missing will be displayed.

An active window is characterized by a highlighted border—a border consisting of double lines—surrounding the window. Inactive windows have only a single border. In this example, the Code window is active. You can navigate among the open windows, and make an inactive window active, by pressing Tab to navigate forward or Shift-Tab to navigate backward.

Seven additional windows may appear in the debugging system. They are

| | |
|---|---|
| Watch Window | This window will display any watchpoints or tracepoints that may be set. A watchpoint or tracepoint is established in the Command window or from the menu bar. |
| Callstack Window | This window displays the Callstack. Again, the Callstack is controlled from the Command window or from the menu bar. |
| Monitor Window | This window displays the value of monitored variables. |
| View Work Area Window | This window displays information on work areas and open database files. |
| View Sets Window | This window displays all the SET values and permits their modification. |
| Set Color Window | This window displays the debugger's color settings and permits their modification. |
| Help Window | The Help window, which is shown in Figure 8.2, is actually two windows. The left window lists topics for which help is available, while the right window provides the text to accompany the topic highlighted in the left window. |

The attributes of open windows can be modified in a variety of ways:

- The active window can be *sized* by selecting Window: Size from the menu bar and using the cursor keys to resize it. An alternate method is to press ALT-G to increase the active window by one line and to press ALT-S to shrink it. ALT-U and ALT-D will have the same effect on the Command window specifically. For example, Figure 8.3 shows a smaller Code window (after pressing ALT-U several times) and a larger Command window.

- The active window can be *iconized* (shrunk almost to the point of invisibility) by selecting Window: Iconize.

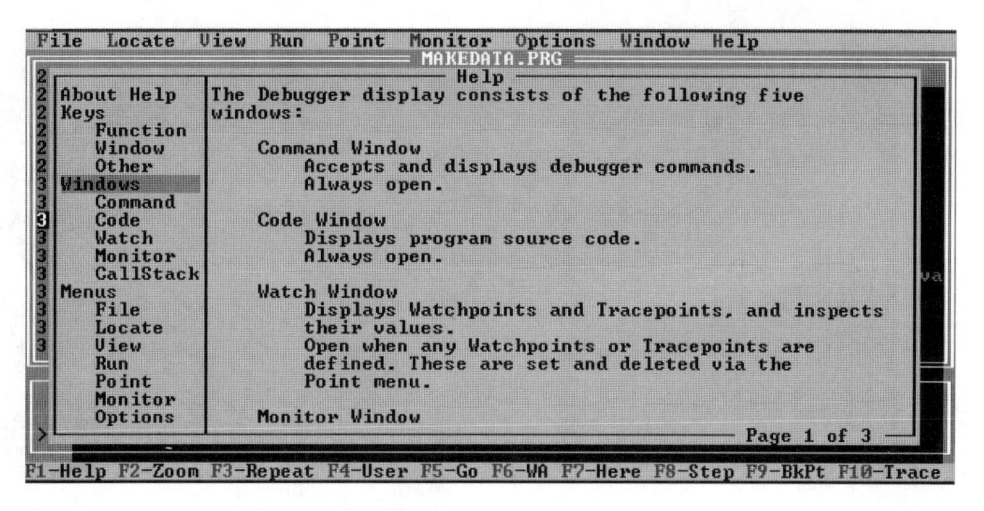

```
File  Locate  View  Run  Point  Monitor  Options  Window  Help
                              MAKEDATA.PRG
 2                              Help
 2 About Help  The Debugger display consists of the following five
 2 Keys        windows:
 2    Function
 2    Window         Command Window
 2    Other              Accepts and displays debugger commands.
 3 Windows            Always open.
 3    Command
 3    Code        Code Window
 3    Watch          Displays program source code.
 3    Monitor        Always open.
 3    CallStack
 3 Menus         Watch Window
 3    File           Displays Watchpoints and Tracepoints, and inspects
 3    Locate         their values.
 3    View           Open when any Watchpoints or Tracepoints are
      Run            defined. These are set and deleted via the
      Point          Point menu.
      Monitor
      Options     Monitor Window
                                                  Page 1 of 3
F1-Help  F2-Zoom  F3-Repeat  F4-User  F5-Go  F6-WA  F7-Here  F8-Step  F9-BkPt  F10-Trace
```

**Figure 8.2**   The Debugger Help Window

- The active window can be *zoomed* (enlarged to full screen) by selecting Window: Zoom or pressing F2. Pressing F2 once more will restore the original display.
- The active window can be *moved* by selecting Window: Move and using the cursor keys.
- All open windows can be *restored* to their default sizes and locations by selecting Window: Tile.

Along with these nine basic windows, two additional window-like areas are controlled by the debugger. First, during the operation of the application, *Dialog Boxes* may appear.

```
File  Locate  View  Run  Point  Monitor  Options  Window  Help
                              MAKEDATA.PRG
24:
25:   static cColor               // Color palate to be used
26:   static aWindows := {}       // Array of windows
27:   static cFilePath             // contains the file path to be globally used
28:
29:   function Main(cPath)
30:
31:       local cText
32:       local cScreen    := savescreen()  // save original screen
33:       local nRow       := row()         // save original row position
34:       local nCol       := col()         // save original columns position
35:       local nCurs      := setcursor(0)  // turn off the cursor and save old va
                                      Command
 >
F1-Help  F2-Zoom  F3-Repeat  F4-User  F5-Go  F6-WA  F7-Here  F8-Step  F9-BkPt  F10-Trace
```

**Figure 8.3**   Changing the size of the Command and Code windows

**584** Straley's Programming with Clipper 5.2

**Figure 8.4** Dialog Boxes

These areas of the screen are usually centered within the debugger's general screen area and may look something like Figure 8.4.

In addition, various *menu options* (Figure 8.5) may be selected by pressing the first letter of the menu item (the menu is displayed across the top of the Code window) and the ALT key. Once a menu item is active, adjacent menu items may be selected instead by moving either the left or the right arrow keys. The menus will wrap around, and the ESC key will deactivate a menu.

Options within menus may also be selected by moving the highlighted bar up or down with the appropriate cursor keys or by pressing the highlighted letter of the option within the menu. Once an option is selected from a menu, such as LINE NUMBERS in the View menu, the operation will be performed and the menu will disappear.

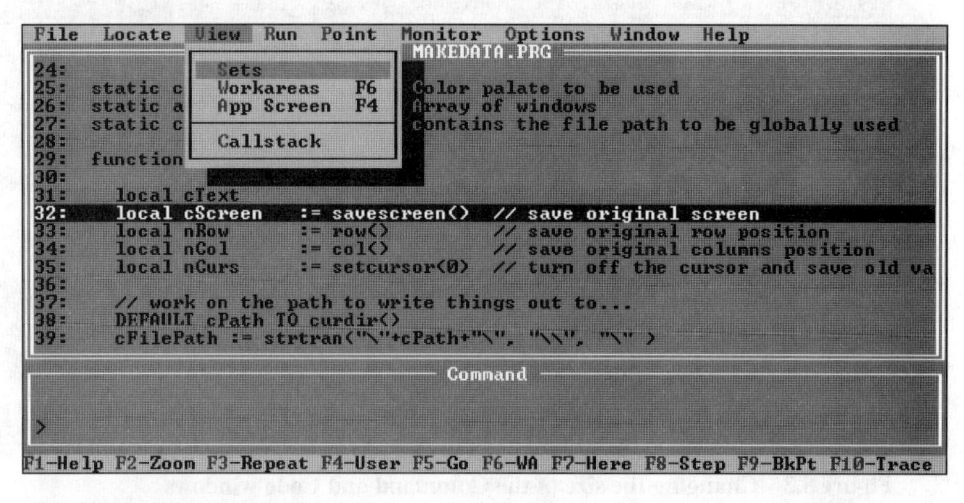

**Figure 8.5** Menu options

Following are the options available from the debugger's menus:

### File Menu

| | |
|---|---|
| OPEN | Displays a file in the Code window. The name of the file to display is entered in a dialog box that appears in the center of the screen. The current debugging session is saved and, once the file has been viewed, the debugging session can be reactivated by selecting the File Resume option. |
| RESUME | Clears the file currently being viewed and redisplays the application originally being debugged. |
| DOS ACCESS | Activates a DOS shell. This will load another copy of COMMAND.COM into memory. To leave the DOS shell and return to the debugger, the word "exit" must be typed in at the DOS prompt. |
| EXIT | Exits the debugging session and returns to DOS. |

### Locate Menu

| | |
|---|---|
| FIND | Searches through the application's source code for a specific character string when the Code window is active. The character string to search for is entered into a dialog box that appears in the center of the screen. The search will always start at the first line of code. If the character expression is found, the cursor stops on the appropriate line; otherwise, the cursor remains in its current location. |
| NEXT | Searches for the next occurrence of the character string found by the previously executed FIND command. If the string is not found, the cursor will remain in its current location. |
| PREVIOUS | Searches for the previous occurrence of the character expression last found either with the FIND command or the NEXT command. If no character string was found, the cursor will not move. |
| GOTO LINE | This command moves the cursor from its current position to the specified line number, which is entered when a dialog box appears in the center of the screen. If the number entered is greater than the total number of lines in the application, the cursor will remain in place. |
| CASE SENSITIVE | This is a toggle that tells the debugger whether searches for character strings are case-sensitive or not. By default, searches are not case-sensitive; this is indicated by the normal appearance of the Case Sensitive menu option. However, when the Case Sensitive option is selected, a check appears next to the menu option to indicate that the option is active, and the search for any string will be case-sensitive. |

### View Menu

| | |
|---|---|
| SETS | This option opens the View Sets window, which displays the Clipper System Settings and allows them to be modified. |
| WORKAREAS | This option opens the View Workareas window, which displays information on all open database files. |
| APP SCREEN | This temporarily erases the debugger screen and displays the application's screen. Once any key is pressed, the debugger screen is restored. |
| CALLSTACK | This is a toggle that determines whether or not the Callstack window will be open. |

### Run Menu

| | |
|---|---|
| RESTART | Reloads the current application in the debugger. All debugger settings remain unchanged. |
| ANIMATE | Executes an application in Animate mode, which means that each line of source code will be executed, the highlighted bar will be moved to the next line, and the process repeated. |
| STEP | Executes the application in Single Step Mode. After a highlighted line of source code is executed, the debugger will move the highlight to the next line and stop. Code for functions and procedures called by the current program are also displayed in the Code window. |
| TRACE | Like Step, Trace executes the application in Single Step Mode. Unlike Step, it does not display the code for functions called by the current program. |
| GO | Causes the debugger to display the application screen and execute the application at normal speed. Execution continues until the debugger is invoked again with ALT-D. |
| TO CURSOR | Executes in Run mode only those lines of code between the highlighted bar and the cursor. |
| NEXT ROUTINE | Executes the application from the highlighted line to the next procedure or function call. |
| SPEED | Sets the speed in which Animate mode will operate. The range of SPEED is a number between 0 (the default) and 9. The lower the number, the faster Animate mode will operate. |

### Point Menu

| | |
|---|---|
| WATCHPOINT | Allows you to add a watchpoint. Selecting this menu option opens a dialog box in the center of the screen where you can enter a memory |

*Clipper Utilities and Debugging* 587

| | |
|---|---|
| WATCHPOINT *(continued)* | variable, a field, or an expression whose value will be traced during program execution. If it is not already open, the Watch window is opened, and the name of the watchpoint is displayed there. |
| TRACEPOINT | Allows you to trace a value in the Watch window. When you select this menu option, you can enter the value of a memory variable, a field, or an expression in the dialog box that opens in the center of the screen. If it is not already open, the Watch window is opened and the name of the tracepoint is displayed there. |
| BREAKPOINT | Designates the line on which the cursor is positioned as a breakpoint. The debugger will then change the line's color to distinguish it as a breakpoint. This option is actually a toggle; if the cursor is on a line that has already been defined as a breakpoint, selecting this option will delete it. |
| DELETE | Opens a dialog box that prompts for the number of the WatchPoint or TracePoint that is to be deleted. Once the number is entered, that item is removed from the Watch window. Note that unnecessary or duplicate tracepoints or watchpoints can also be removed by selecting the Watch window, moving the cursor to the line containing the tracepoint or watchpoint, and pressing the DEL key. |

## *Monitor Menu*

| | |
|---|---|
| PUBLIC | Toggles the display of PUBLIC variables in the Watch window. |
| PRIVATE | Toggles the display of PRIVATE variables in the Watch window. |
| STATIC | Toggles the display of STATIC variables in the Watch window. |
| LOCAL | Toggles the display of LOCAL variables in the Watch window. |
| ALL | Toggles the display of all variables, including PUBLIC, PRIVATE, STATIC, and LOCAL. |
| SORT | Toggles whether items displayed in the Watch window are to be displayed in alphabetical order or by storage class (the default). |

## *Options Menu*

| | |
|---|---|
| PREPROCESSED CODE | This is a toggle that determines whether the Code window will display source code from a .PRG file or preprocessed code from a .PPO file; the default is OFF to display source code. |
| LINE NUMBERS | This is a toggle that determines whether line numbers will appear to the left of each line in the Code window. By default, it is ON. |

| | |
|---|---|
| EXCHANGE SCREENS | A toggle that defines how the debugger will handle the application screen in Animate mode. If Exchange Screens is ON (the default), the screen will be shown for each line of code executed; if OFF, it will be shown only when input is required. |
| SWAP ON INPUT | If Exchange Screens is OFF, this option acts as a toggle to determine whether the application screen will be displayed in Animate mode when input is required. |
| CODEBLOCK TRACE | This option controls the debugger's display of code blocks. If ON (the default), whenever a code block is evaluated, the debugger will move the highlighted bar to the line on which it was defined. |
| MENU BAR | This toggle controls whether the menu bar is displayed at all times (the default) or only when the ALT key is pressed. |
| MONO DISPLAY | This option controls whether the debugger's display is color (when Mono Display is off) or monochrome. |
| COLORS | Activates the debugger Colors window, where you can view and modify the debugger's color settings for selected interface elements. |
| TAB WIDTH | This option allows you to set the tab width in the Code window. |
| SAVE SETTINGS | Opens a dialog box and prompts for the name of a scriptfile file in which all debugger settings will be saved. By default, the file will be given a .CLD extension. |
| RESTORE SETTINGS | Opens a dialog box and prompts for the name of a debugger Script file from which to restore the debugger's settings to execute. |

### Window Menu

For these options, see our discussion of the debugger's windowing interface earlier in this section.

### Help Menu

Selecting one of the four menu options listed here (Keys, Windows, Menus, Commands) will open the Help window and display information about that topic. Selecting About Help will open the debugger's general Help window.

## DEBUGGING POINTS

Before going through the various screens, commands, settings, and keystroke options, three items that are central to working with the debugger to isolate problems must be defined. These are

| | |
|---|---|
| WatchPoints | Show the value of a variable, a field, or an expression in the Watch window. This does not pause the execution of an application being debugged. |
| TracePoints | Show the value of a variable, a field, or an expression in the Watch window. Whenever a value set as a TracePoint changes, the application pauses. |
| BreakPoints | Specific locations in the source code that will cause the application to pause and return control to the debugger. |

# The Keyboard Interface

Each window has unique keystroke assignments, although some of the key movements are the same from window to window. In addition, the function keys are universal to the debugging system. These keys are

| | | |
|---|---|---|
| F1 | Help | A complete listing of keys and commands. |
| F2 | Zoom mode | Expands the active window to the full size of the screen. Pressing F2 again restores the window to its original size. |
| F3 | Retype last command | Retypes the last command that was entered in the Command window. The ENTER key must be pressed to issue the command. |
| F4 | Go to app. screen | Temporarily suspends the debugger screen and displays the application's screen. |
| F5 | Run the application | Tells the debugger to execute the application in Run mode. |
| F6 | Show View Work Area | Displays the View Work Area window, which contains information on open databases. |
| F7 | Run the application | Runs the application up to the point indicated by the cursor. |
| F8 | Step through application | Executes the line of code indicated by the highlighted bar. Once the action is completed, the process will stop and the highlighted bar will advance one line. |

| F9 | Set/delete BreakPoint | Marks the line of code indicated by the cursor as a BreakPoint. Pressing this key with the cursor on a line of code previously marked as a BreakPoint will unmark it as a BreakPoint. |
| F10 | Trace | Steps through code in a manner similar to the F8 key; however, no code for the functions called by the current program that are located in separate files will be displayed. |

Keystroke assignments for each window or type of display object are as follows:

### Code Window

| Key | Function |
| --- | --- |
| Up Arrow | Move the cursor up one line. |
| Down Arrow | Move the cursor down one line. |
| Left Arrow | Pan left one character. |
| Right Arrow | Pan right one character. |
| Ctrl-Page Up | Move the cursor to the top of the file. |
| Ctrl-Page Down | Move the cursor to the bottom of the file. |
| Home | Scroll the cursor to the beginning of the line. |
| END | Pans a screen to the right. |
| Page Up | Scroll up one screen. |
| Page Down | Scroll down one screen. |

### Command Window

| Key | Function |
| --- | --- |
| Left Arrow | Move the cursor one character left on the command line. |
| Right Arrow | Move the cursor one character right on the command line. |
| Home | Move the cursor to the beginning of the line. |
| End | Move the cursor to the end of the line. |
| DEL | Delete the current character. |
| Backspace | Delete the previous character and drag. |
| INS | Toggle insert mode. |
| ESC | Clear the command line. |
| F3 | Retype the previous command (no ENTER key issued). |
| Up Arrow | Move the cursor to the previous line in the command history buffer. |
| Down Arrow | Move the cursor to the next line in the command history buffer. |

## Watch Window and Monitor Window

| Key | Function |
| --- | --- |
| Up Arrow | Move the highlighted bar up one line. |
| Down Arrow | Move the highlighted bar down one line. |
| Ctrl-Page Up | Move the highlighted bar to the first line. |
| Ctrl-Page Down | Move the highlighted bar to the last line. |
| Page Up | Scroll up one screen. |
| Page Down | Scroll down one screen. |
| DEL | Remove the WatchPoint or TracePoint (Watch window only). |
| ENTER/RETURN | Inspect or change the value of the selected item. |

## Callstack Window

| Key | Function |
| --- | --- |
| Up Arrow | Move the highlighted bar up one line. |
| Down Arrow | Move the highlighted bar down one line. |
| Page Up | Scroll up one screen. |
| Page Down | Scroll down one screen. |
| Ctrl-Page Up | Move highlighted bar to the first line. |
| Ctrl-Page Down | Move highlighted bar to the last line. |

## Help Window

| Key | Function |
| --- | --- |
| Up Arrow | Move the highlighted bar up one line. |
| Down Arrow | Move the highlighted bar down one line. |
| Page Up | Scroll up one screen. |
| Page Down | Scroll down one screen. |
| ESC | Close the window. |

## View Work Area Window

| Key | Function |
| --- | --- |
| Tab | Cycle forward to next group box. |
| Shift-Tab | Cycle backward to previous group box. |

*(continued)*

### View Work Area Window (continued)

| Key | Function |
|---|---|
| Up Arrow | Move up one item within group box. |
| Down Arrow | Move down one item within group box. |
| ENTER | Expand/shrink the heading in the highlighted database's group box. |

### Dialog Boxes

| Key | Function |
|---|---|
| Left Arrow | Move the cursor one character left in the text box. |
| Right Arrow | Move the cursor one character right in the text box. |
| Home | Move the cursor to the beginning of the line. |
| End | Move the cursor to the end of the line. |
| Ins | Toggle between insert and overstrike mode. |
| DEL | Delete the current character. |
| Backspace | Delete the previous character and drag. |
| ENTER/RETURN | Save changes and exit the dialog box. |
| ESC | Close the dialog box. |

## DEBUGGING COMMANDS

The following commands are accepted in the Command window.

| Command | Action |
|---|---|
| ?/?? | View a variable or expression. |
| ANIMATE | Begin Animate mode and run the application. |
| BP | Set a BreakPoint. |
| CALLSTACK | Toggle the Callstack window open. |
| DELETE | Remove one or more debugger settings. |
| DOS | Execute a DOS shell. |
| FIND | Find a character string. |
| GO | Begin the application in Run mode. |
| GOTO | Move the cursor to a specific line. |
| HELP | Display the Help window. |
| INPUT | Input commands from a script file. |
| LIST | View WatchPoints, TracePoints, and BreakPoints. |
| NEXT | Go to the next occurrence of a character string. |
| NUM | Toggle the display of line numbers in the Code window. |

## DEBUGGING COMMANDS *(continued)*

| Command | Action |
|---|---|
| OUTPUT | Display the application screen. |
| PREV | Go to the previous occurrence of a character string. |
| QUIT | Exit the debugger. |
| RESTART | Reload the current application. |
| RESUME | Return from viewing a file. |
| SPEED | Control the step speed in Animate mode. |
| STEP | Execute the application in single step mode. |
| TP | Specify a variable or expression as a TracePoint. |
| VIEW | View a file. |
| WP | Specify a variable or expression as a WatchPoint. |

Some of these commands may also be executed from the menus or with the function keys. These commands are

| Command | Menu | Option | Function Key |
|---|---|---|---|
| ANIMATE | Run | Animate | |
| BP | Point | BreakPoint | F9 |
| CALLSTACK | View | Callstack | |
| DELETE | Point | Delete | |
| DOS | File | DOS Access | |
| FIND | Locate | Find | |
| GO | Run | Go | F5 |
| GOTO | Locate | Goto Line | |
| HELP | Help | | F1 |
| INPUT | Options | Restore Settings | |
| NEXT | Locate | Next | |
| NUM | Options | Line numbers | |
| OUTPUT | View | App. screen | F4 |
| PREV | Locate | Previous | |
| QUIT | File | Exit | |
| RESTART | Run | Restart | |
| RESUME | File | Resume | |
| SPEED | Run | Speed | |
| STEP | Run | Step, F8 | |
| TP | Point | TracePoint | |
| VIEW | File | Open | |
| WP | Point | WatchPoint | |

## DEBUGGER COMMAND REFERENCE

### ?

**SYNTAX**         ? <exp1>

**PARAMETER**     <exp1>: Any expression to be viewed

**DESCRIPTION**    This command displays the specified variable or expression specified as <exp1>. If <exp1> is a function or an expression, the value of the function or expression will be displayed. In-line assignments may be used along with this command. ? will display the value of the variable or expression on the next line of the Command window, while ?? will display the value in a popup window.

### ANIMATE

**SYNTAX**         ANIMATE

**PARAMETER**     None

**DESCRIPTION**    This command executes an application in Animate mode, which means that each line of source code will be executed, the highlighted bar will be moved to the next line, and the process repeated.

### BP

**SYNTAX**         BP [AT] <expN1> [[IN] <expC2> ]

**PARAMETERS**    <expN1>: Line number where the program is to stop.
<expC2>: Filename or subroutine. If <expC2> is the name of a program, then the BreakPoint will be set in that program; otherwise, the current program file will be used. If <expC2> is a subroutine, the BreakPoint will be set in that routine.

**DESCRIPTION**    This command sets a BreakPoint at a designated line of a program file or subroutine.

## CALLSTACK

**SYNTAX**     CALLSTACK <expC1>

**ARGUMENTS**     <expC1>: ON or OFF

**DESCRIPTION**     This command toggles the display of the Callstack window. If <expC1> is ON, the Code window will be reduced to fit the Callstack window on the right-hand side of the screen. If <expC1> is OFF, the Callstack window is removed and the Code window is returned to its original size.

## DELETE

**SYNTAX**     DELETE [ALL [WP|TP|BP]] [WP|TP|BP <expN1>]

**PARAMETERS**     ALL: Removes all debugger settings.
WP: WatchPoints
TP: TracePoints
BP: BreakPoints
<expN1>: Line number of each individual WP, TP, or BP to remove.

**DESCRIPTION**     This command deletes WatchPoints, TracePoints, or BreakPoints. If the ALL clause is used with a type, all elements of any one type will be removed. Note, however, that using either the DELETE ALL TP command or the DELETE ALL WP command will remove both all WatchPoints and all TracePoints and will close the Watch window. If no type is specified, then all types will be removed.

## DOS

**SYNTAX**     DOS

**PARAMETER**     None

**DESCRIPTION**     This command loads an extra copy of COMMAND.COM and allows temporary access to DOS. To exit the DOS shell, the word "exit" must be entered. The debugger retains control of the application.

## FIND

**SYNTAX**    FIND <expC1>

**PARAMETER**    <expC1>: Character expression to search for

**DESCRIPTION**    This command searches through the application for a specific character string expressed as <expC1>. The search will always start at the first line of code. If the character expression is found, the cursor moves to the appropriate line; otherwise, an error message is displayed in the Command window. The FIND command will observe the Case Sensitive toggle in the Locate menu.

## GO

**SYNTAX**    GO

**PARAMETER**    None

**DESCRIPTION**    This command executes the application in Run mode until a BreakPoint or a TracePoint is reached. If the ALT-D key is pressed, the debugger's main screen will be displayed and the execution of the application will be temporarily halted.

## GOTO

**SYNTAX**    GOTO <expN1>

**PARAMETER**    <expN1>: Line number

**DESCRIPTION**    This command moves the cursor from its current position to the specified line number expressed as <expN1>. If <expN1> is greater than the total number of lines in the application, the cursor will remain in place.

## HELP

**SYNTAX**    HELP

**PARAMETER**    None

**DESCRIPTION**    This command displays the Help window.

## INPUT

**SYNTAX**      `INPUT <expC1>`

**PARAMETER**      <expC1>: filename

**DESCRIPTION**      This command reads the commands in the script file named <expC1> into the debugging system. If no file extension is used with <expC1>, a .TXT extension is assumed.

         The debugger will suspend keyboard input and execute the commands listed within the <expC1> file. Once all of the commands within the file have been executed, the debugger will regain control.

## LIST

**SYNTAX**      `LIST WP|TP|BP`

**ARGUMENTS**      WP: List all WatchPoints
         TP: List all TracePoints
         BP: List all BreakPoints

**DESCRIPTION**      This command lists all WatchPoints, TracePoints, or BreakPoints.

## NEXT

**SYNTAX**      `NEXT`

**PARAMETER**      None

**DESCRIPTION**      This command searches for the next occurrence of the character string found by the previous FIND command. If the string is not found, the cursor will not move.

## NUM

**SYNTAX**      `NUM <expC1>`

**ARGUMENTS**      <expC1>: ON or OFF

**DESCRIPTION**      This command toggles the display of line numbers in the source code listing in the Code window.

## OUTPUT

| | |
|---|---|
| **SYNTAX** | OUTPUT |
| **PARAMETER** | None |
| **DESCRIPTION** | This command temporarily removes the debugging screen and displays the application screen. Once any key is pressed, the application screen is cleared and the debugging screen is restored. |

## PREV

| | |
|---|---|
| **SYNTAX** | PREV |
| **PARAMETER** | None |
| **DESCRIPTION** | This command searches for the previous occurrence of the last character expression found either with the FIND command or the NEXT command. If no character string is found, the cursor will remain on the current line. |

## QUIT

| | |
|---|---|
| **SYNTAX** | QUIT |
| **PARAMETER** | None |
| **DESCRIPTION** | This command terminates the debugging session and returns control to DOS. |

## RESTART

| | |
|---|---|
| **SYNTAX** | RESTART |
| **PARAMETER** | None |
| **DESCRIPTION** | This command reloads the current application in the debugger. All debugger settings remain in effect. |

# RESUME

| | |
|---|---|
| **SYNTAX** | `RESUME` |
| **PARAMETER** | None |
| **DESCRIPTION** | This command clears the file that is currently being viewed with the VIEW command and redisplays the original source code in the Code window. This command does not affect any BreakPoints, TracePoints, or WatchPoints. |

# SPEED

| | |
|---|---|
| **SYNTAX** | `SPEED [<expN1>]` |
| **PARAMETER** | <expN1>: Speed value |
| **DESCRIPTION** | This command sets the speed at which Animate mode will operate. If no value is provided, the current setting will be displayed. The range of <expN1> may be any number from 0 to 9, inclusive. The lower the number, the faster Animate mode will operate. |

# STEP

| | |
|---|---|
| **SYNTAX** | `STEP` |
| **PARAMETER** | None |
| **DESCRIPTION** | This command will execute the current application in single step mode. It will execute the line indicated by the highlighted bar, move the bar to the following line, and stop. |

# TP

| | |
|---|---|
| **SYNTAX** | `TP <exp1>` |
| **PARAMETER** | <exp1>: Any expression to be traced |
| **DESCRIPTION** | This command will trace the value of any memory variable, field, or expression that is expressed as <exp1>. As a TracePoint is added to the Watch window, the top of the screen is adjusted to accommodate this new expression. |

## VIEW

| | |
|---|---|
| **SYNTAX** | `VIEW <expC1>` |
| **PARAMETER** | <expC1>: Filename |
| **DESCRIPTION** | This command will display the file <expC1> in the Code window. The current debugging session is saved, and once the file has been viewed, the debugging session is reactivated. |

## WP

| | |
|---|---|
| **SYNTAX** | `WP <exp1>` |
| **PARAMETER** | <exp1>: Any expression to be watched |
| **DESCRIPTION** | This command opens the Watch window and displays the value of the memory variable, field, or expression <exp1>. |

# 9

# Macros and Expressions

## What Is a Macro?

The concept of a macro is simple: It is a symbolic representation of a greater entity. In most languages, a macro is something that, when expanded, will tell the compiler to look for an associated definition and act accordingly. For example,

```
cString1 := "Hello World"
cString2 := "cString1"

? cString2
? &cString2.
```

The character used to symbolize a macro is the ampersand character (&). The dot character (".") at the end of the macro expression terminates the macro; it quickly identifies the end of the macro for the compiler. In this example, the string "Hello World" is assigned to the variable *cString1*. The string form of *cString1* is then assigned to the variable *cString2*. When displayed the first time, the value of *cString2* is simply the string "cString1"; however, if we macro-expand the variable *cString2*, the compiler will display the value underneath the apparent value of *cString2*, which in this case is the value of *cString1*. Thus, the string "Hello World" will appear. Internally, when a macro command is executed, each character within the macro expression is looked at individually. The macro is therefore expanded from left to right, and the true representation of the macro is then evaluated.

## ILLEGAL SUBSTITUTIONS

In Clipper, some command verbs and clauses cannot be put into a macro. That is to say, a variable representation of an expanded command line must be known to the compiler during the compilation process and not at run time. For example, consider the following:

```
cVerb := "Clients->age, Clients->first_name, Clients->last_name"
LIST &cVerb.
cVerb := "Clients->last_name"
LIST &cVerb.
```

The intent is to have three fields LISTed to the console in the first command and to have only one field LISTed in the second, which might allow the end-user to choose which field values to show and to build the LIST string by concatenating choices. However, this will not work. One rule on macro substitutions in Clipper is that syntactical parts of a command line must not appear in a macro. In this example, the comma separating each field is part of the syntactical structure of the LIST command. The compiler must know in advance how many items are to be involved with each LIST command. Here, in both cases, the only thing that would be displayed would be the contents of the Clients->last_name field. Since the compiler allotted only one item in the first LIST call, when the macro is expanded, only the single symbolic token that is logically expanded will be displayed. To get three fields of information onto the screen and still allow the end-user to choose those values, the required form would be

```
cVerb1 := "Clients->last_name"
cVerb2 := "Clients->first_name"
cVerb3 := "Clients->age"
LIST &cVerb1., &cVerb2., &cVerb3.
```

There are a few more guidelines to follow in dealing with macro substitution. One of the most common errors that will occur is a macro involving a LOCAL variable. Consider the following:

```
local cString1 := "Hello World"
local cString2 := "cString1"

? cString2
? &cString2.
```

Although this coding extract looks the same as our initial macro example, the difference is staggering. The variables that were initialized in the previous example as PRIVATE memory variables (which is the default state) are here initialized as LOCAL variables. Remember, LOCAL variables are not included in the symbol table. This means that while Clipper will be able to display the contents of the variable *cString2*, it will not be able to expand and display the contents of the variable *cString1*. A run-time error will be generated. This error is more commonly found in the following format:

```
? Macro("Hello world")

function Macro( cMacro )
```

```
local cString := "cMacro"
? &cString.
```

In this example, the parameter *cMacro* is also a LOCAL memory variable: It is initialized on the command line with the FUNCTION declaration, which makes it a LOCAL parameter. It, too, cannot be properly expanded because the definition for the variable *cMacro* is not in the symbol table.

But Clipper's inability to find a variable in the symbol table is not the only reason that a macro might fail. If we try to use a macro to define a PUBLIC variable and we are compiling with the /A switch, Clipper will produce an error message informing us of an illegal declaration. This, for example, occurs when we attempt to define the following PUBLIC variable:

```
PUBLIC cVar&cString.
```

This occurs because the /A switch implies that all variables must be known to the compiler. But since we are trying to build a new variable by macro-expanding an existing one, Clipper does not know of the new variable (in the case of our example, named "cVar&cString") and therefore generates an error message.

## MACROS AND ARRAY DECLARATIONS AND DEFINITIONS

Another point about macros concerns array declarations and definitions. For example, the following is not allowed:

```
cVar := "array[10]"
DECLARE &cVar.
```

Since the hard brackets are a syntactical part of the DECLARE command, they cannot be part of the macro expansion. However, this is legal:

```
cVar     := "99"
cNew     := "array"
nCount   := 15

local me&cVar.[10]
local &cNew.[nCount]
```

In the first array declaration, the array *me99[ ]* is initialized with 10 elements; in the second LOCAL statement (which can declare an array as well), the array *array[ ]* is declared to have 15 elements. Additionally, you can declare an array in the following way:

```
cArray := "array"
&cArray := array(15)
? valtype( &cArray )
```

Here, the name of the array that will be declared via a call to the ARRAY( ) function is stored in a string to the variable *cArray*; this is then macro-expanded and the array is initialized to 15 subscript positions. The VALTYPE( ) function is used to macro-expand the *cArray* variable to see if in fact the array named *array[ ]* is properly established.

All of this could be duplicated by the following:

```
cVar := "{,,,,,,,,,,,,,,,}"
aArray := &cVar
```

Here, the variable *aArray[ ]* will be an array with 15 elements in it, all of them having a NIL value.

## MACROS AND CODE BLOCKS

The concept of a code block has yet to be thoroughly explained; however, a quick look at it in relation to macros is in order. First, code blocks may be embedded in string variables and macro-expanded at the appropriate times. In developing an application, there are cases when macro expansions are used to call actual subroutines. For example,

```
 1 : * File:     Macro1.prg
 2 :
 3 : function Main()
 4 :
 5 :    local nChoice := 1  // Menu option selection
 6 :    private cExt        // results of the stringify.. this MUST be
 7 :                        // a PRIVATE variable in order to macro-expand
 8 :
 9 :    while !empty( nChoice )
10 :      scroll()                  // clear the screen w/o positioning
11 :
12 :      @ 10,38 prompt " 1> Enter  "
13 :      @ 11,38 prompt " 2> Modify "
14 :      @ 12,38 prompt " 3> Scan   "
15 :      @ 13,38 prompt " 4> Quit   "
16 :      menu to nChoice
17 :
18 :      if nChoice >= 1 .and. nChoice <= 3
19 :        cExt := str( nChoice, 1 )
20 :        Sub&cExt()                  // instead of the DO command
21 :      else
22 :        exit
23 :      endif
24 :
25 :    enddo
26 :
27 :    return( NIL )
28 :
29 : *********************
30 :
31 : procedure Sub1
32 :
33 :    @ 24,00 say "Inside ENTER module.  Any key..."
34 :    inkey(0)
35 :
36 : *********************
37 :
38 : procedure Sub2
39 :
```

```
40 :        @ 24,00 say "Inside MODIFY module.  Any key..."
41 :        inkey(0)
42 :
43 : *******************
44 :
45 : procedure Sub3
46 :
47 :        @ 24,00 say "Inside SCAN module.  Any key..."
48 :        inkey(0)
49 :
50 : // End of File: Macro1.prg
```

In this example, the variable *cExt* is built from the STR( ) of the MENU TO variable, *nChoice*. *cExt* is then used in conjunction with the function call on line 20 to make a call to any one of the three subroutines. This function call replaces the need to include a DO command which should be avoided since it may not be supported in future versions. In essence, each menu item picks which subroutine may be performed.

Code blocks can be used to achieve the same thing, as shown in the following example:

```
 1 : * File:      Macro2.prg
 2 :
 3 : *******************
 4 :
 5 : function Main()
 6 :
 7 :     local nChoice := 1
 8 :     local bOperation       // Code block to do things!
 9 :
10 :     while !empty( nChoice )
11 :       scroll()
12 :       @ 10,38 prompt " 1> Enter    "
13 :       @ 11,38 prompt " 2> Modify   "
14 :       @ 12,38 prompt " 3> Scan     "
15 :       @ 13,38 prompt " 4> Quit     "
16 :       menu to nChoice
17 :
18 :       if nChoice >= 1 .and. nChoice <= 3
19 :         do case
20 :         case nChoice == 1
21 :            bOperation := {|| Sub1()}
22 :
23 :         case nChoice == 2
24 :            bOperation := {|| Sub2()}
25 :
26 :         otherwise
27 :            bOperation := {|| Sub3()}
28 :
29 :         endcase
30 :
31 :         eval( bOperation )
32 :
33 :       else
34 :         exit
35 :       endif
```

```
36 :     enddo
37 :
38 :     return( NIL)
39 :
40 : ********************
41 :
42 : static procedure Sub1
43 :
44 :     @ 24,00 say "Inside ENTER module.  Any key..."
45 :     inkey(0)
46 :
47 : ********************
48 :
49 : static procedure Sub2
50 :
51 :     @ 24,00 say "Inside MODIFY module.  Any key..."
52 :     inkey(0)
53 :
54 : ********************
55 :
56 : static procedure Sub3
57 :
58 :     @ 24,00 say "Inside SCAN module.  Any key..."
59 :     inkey(0)
60 :
61 : // End of File: Macro2.prg
```

Here, the variable *bOperation* is built within a massive CASE statement, which may be seen as a replacement for a conditional CASE statement with branching calls to the various subroutines for each menu item selected. The execution of that code block, which performs the various functions built by the DO CASE statement, is issued on line 31 through the EVAL( ) function. This will be elaborated upon in the chapter on code blocks.

The next example shows how code blocks may work along with the macro capabilities in Clipper 5.2; it macro-expands a code block.

```
 1 : * File:     Macro3.prg
 2 :
 3 : ********************
 4 :
 5 : function Main()
 6 :
 7 :     local nChoice := 1         // Result of the MENU operation
 8 :     local cOperation           // character string of a code block
 9 :
10 :     while !empty( nChoice )
11 :        scroll()
12 :        @ 10,38 prompt " 1> Enter  "
13 :        @ 11,38 prompt " 2> Modify "
14 :        @ 12,38 prompt " 3> Scan   "
15 :        @ 13,38 prompt " 4> Quit   "
16 :        menu to nChoice
17 :
18 :        if nChoice >= 1 .and. nChoice <= 3
```

```
19 :
20 :            ? (cOperation := "{|| Sub" + str(nChoice,1) + "()}")
21 :            inkey(0)
22 :
23 :            eval( &cOperation. )
24 :         else
25 :            exit
26 :         endif
27 :
28 :      enddo
29 :
30 :      return( NIL )
31 :
32 : *********************
33 :
34 : procedure Sub1
35 :
36 :      @ 24,00 say "Inside ENTER module.   Any key..."
37 :      inkey(0)
38 :
39 : *********************
40 :
41 : procedure Sub2
42 :
43 :      @ 24,00 say "Inside MODIFY module.   Any key..."
44 :      inkey(0)
45 :
46 : *********************
47 :
48 : procedure Sub3
49 :
50 :      @ 24,00 say "Inside SCAN module.   Any key..."
51 :      inkey(0)
52 :
53 : // End of File: Macro3.prg
```

Here, the variable *cOperation* is a string that is conditionally built based on the STR( ) value of the MENU TO variable *nChoice*. Then, when the call to the EVAL( ) function—which actually executes the code block—is made, the variable *cOperation* is macro-expanded. In this case, code block technology is being employed; however, the advantages here may be nebulous because the code block will be evaluated only AFTER the macro expansion takes place. In other words, the call will be as slow as a regular macro expansion, as seen in the very first example.

There are other possibilities with macro substitution. For example, we could use a macro to point to the work area we want to work with, or we could use it to work with expressions. Both topics will be touched on in a moment.

Remember one rule in general: Macros are slower than code blocks; code blocks, however, are not the answer to all macro woes. Code blocks are significantly different in theory from macro substitution. However, macro substitution, with the advent of code blocks, is not needed extensively in an application. Proper use of the two will give your application the balance, power, and performance that you and your clients will require and expect.

Keep in mind that in a good and maintainable structured programming environment, you should try to use macro substitutions as little as possible. Additionally, for the integrity of the memory system, avoid macro expansions; they are not cleanly dealt with within the free pool memory of the system.

# Expressions and Parentheses

## THE CONCEPT

Expressions in Clipper are defined by a set of parentheses ( ). An expression, like a function, has a value and can be assigned to a variable, displayed to the screen, or even compared to a previous variable, condition, or expression. Normally, expressions look something like this:

```
x := (y ** 5) / 6
```

In this equation, the expression "y ** 5" is evaluated first. Its value is then passed to the rest of the equation to be eventually assigned to the variable *x*.

Carrying this further, a set of parentheses can surround a series of values, including function calls, and the value of the expression will be the last value evaluated. To see this in action, consider this coding example:

```
 1 : * File:      Express1.prg
 2 :
 3 : *******************
 4 :
 5 : function Main()
 6 :
 7 :    local nExpress1, ;       // First expression
 8 :          nExpress2, ;       // Second expression
 9 :          nExpress3          // Third expression
10 :
11 :    use Clients new
12 :
13 :    cls
14 :
15 :    nExpress1 := Clients->( recno(), lastrec(), 5 )
16 :    nExpress2 := ( 5, lastrec(), recno() )
17 :    nExpress3 := ( 5, recno(), lastrec() )
18 :
19 :    qout( nExpress1, nExpress2, nExpress3 )
20 :
21 :    ? nExpress1 += ( Saying(), nExpress2 )
22 :    ? nExpress3 += ( nExpress1 /= nExpress1 )
23 :    ? nExpress1
24 :
25 :    return( NIL )
26 :
27 : *******************
28 :
29 : static procedure Saying
```

```
30 :
31 :    ? "This just displays a message, and the default return value"
32 :    ? "for the procedure will be a NIL data type, which will have"
33 :    ? "no bearing on the value of the variables"
34 :    ?
35 :    ? "Any key..."
36 :    inkey(0)
37 :    ?
38 :
39 : // End of File: Express1.prg
```

In this example, three variables are assigned the values of the three corresponding expressions on lines 15 through 17. Remember, the last value of the expression will be the value that will be assigned to the respective variable. In this case, the variable *nExpress1* will have the value of 5; the variable *nExpress2* will have the value of RECNO( ); the variable *nExpress3* will have the value of LASTREC( ). Eventually, those values will be displayed on line 19.

Line 21 is an in-line assignment and adds the value of the variable *nExpress2* to the value of the variable *nExpress1*, which is assigned back to the variable *nExpress1*. This is how the "+=" operator works. In the process of actually assigning a value, a call to the Saying procedure is made. The default return value for this procedure is NIL, and it has no effect on the value of the expression on line 21.

*Note:* It is important to remember that the value of the expression is the last item in the expression, regardless of the values encountered along the way.

After the INKEY(0) call on line 36 is executed, the value of *nExpress2* is added to the value of *nExpress1*. Then, on line 22, the value of the expression is added to the value of *nExpress3* and the value of *nExpress3* is displayed. This expression is an in-line assignment as well. The value of the expression "nExpress1 /= nExpress1" is 1, which is added to the value of *nExpress3*—in other words, 1 is added to the value of *nExpress3*, which is displayed on line 23.

## MACRO-EXPANDED EXPRESSIONS

The values of expressions can be macro-expanded as well. This is particularly useful if a coding scenario is built that relies on the value of Clipper's internal functions. Those functions, when macro-expanded, have added meaning and value.

```
 1 : * File:      Express2.prg
 2 :
 3 : *******************
 4 :
 5 : function Main()
 6 :
 7 :    local nCounter
 8 :
 9 :    use Clients new
10 :
11 :    while Clients->( !eof() )
12 :       cls
```

```
13 :        for nCounter := 1 to Clients->( fcount() )
14 :           ? &( fieldname(nCounter) ), Clients->( fieldget(nCounter) )
15 :        next
16 :
17 :        wait
18 :
19 :        skip
20 :
21 :     enddo
22 :
23 :     return( NIL )
24 :
25 : // End of File: Express2.prg
```

Here, the database CLIENTS is open, with the record pointer at the top of the database. The loop beginning on line 11 will execute until the end-of-file marker is reached. Within this loop, a new FOR ... NEXT loop is executed. This loop reads the name of the field at each field position. The FIELDNAME( ) function on line 14 will return a character string containing the name of the field at that position; however, our goal is to acquire the field's value, not its name. To do this, the expression on line 14, which surrounds the call to the FIELDNAME( ) function, is macro-expanded. The field's value is then displayed to the screen. (However, after saying all of this, it is important to note that this is the same operation as a direct call to the FIELDGET( ) function, which obtains the value of a particular field. The opposite operation, storing a field value rather than obtaining it, is handled by the FIELDPUT( ) function.) After values for all fields are displayed, the record is skipped and the process repeats itself. The point here is clear: Expressions can be macro-expanded.

## EXTENDED USE OF EXPRESSIONS

Expressions may house functions and/or procedures, as previously seen. Expressions are similar to functions: They return a value. Fields, like functions, have a value as well, and expressions take on some of the attributes of fields. From this stems Clipper's extended use of expressions. Expressions may be "pointed to" with the desired work area alias, which will instruct the expression to perform its operation in the prescribed work area; therefore, any subroutine called within a "pointed-to" expression need not concern itself with the previous work area or with the current work area. This means that such techniques as working in unselected work areas and seeking elements in unselected work areas become programming tools for your toolbox. To see this in action, consider this coding extract:

```
use Trans new
use Clients new
? Trans->( lastrec() )
? Clients->( lastrec() )
```

Each call to the LASTREC( ) function will return a value: The value returned will be based on the number of records in the pointed-to work area. Clipper will automatically jump to the Trans work area, find the value of LASTREC( ), assign it to the expression, and jump back to the original work area. To expand on this, here is a program that makes multiple calls to the DBEDIT( ) function and allows the end-user to step through the available indexing possibilities. But the program never selects an alias work area.

```
 1 : * File:      Express3.prg
 2 :
 3 : #include "PTInkey.ch"    // Clipper Power Tools Header File
 4 :
 5 : ********************
 6 :
 7 : function Main()
 8 :
 9 :    use Clients   new index Clients
10 :    use Notap     new index Notap
11 :    use Ontap     new index Ontap
12 :    use Trans     new index Trans
13 :    use Statcode  new
14 :    use Disknos   new index Disknos
15 :    use Filenos   new index Filenos, Filesub, Filetype
16 :    use Statbase  new
17 :
18 :    scroll()   // clear the entire screen
19 :
20 :    Clients->( dbedit(,,,,,"Keys") )
21 :    Notap->( dbedit(,,,,,"Keys") )
22 :    Ontap->( dbedit(,,,,,"Keys") )
23 :    Trans->( dbedit(,,,,,"Keys") )
24 :    Statcode->( dbedit(,,,,,"Keys") )
25 :    Disknos->( dbedit(,,,,,"Keys") )
26 :    Filenos->( dbedit(,,,,,"Keys") )
27 :    Statbase->( dbedit(,,,,,"Keys") )
28 :
29 :    scroll()
30 :
31 :    return( NIL )
32 :
33 : ********************
34 :
35 : function Keys( nMode )
36 :
37 :    local nRetValue := 1    // Default return value
38 :
39 :    if nMode == 4           // Keystroke exceptions
40 :      do case
41 :      case chr( lastkey() ) == "+"
42 :        set order to ( if ( empty( indexkey(indexord()+1)), 1, ;
43 :                            indexord()+1) )
44 :        nRetValue := 2
45 :
46 :      case lastkey() == pESC
47 :        nRetValue := 0
48 :
49 :      endcase
50 :
51 :    endif
```

```
52 :
53 :       return( nRetValue )
54 :
55 : // End of File: Express3.prg
```

In this example, a series of files is opened along with their corresponding indexes. In the case of the Filenos work area, three indexes are opened. From lines 20 to 27, the DBEDIT( ) function is sequentially active in each of the pointed-to work areas. DBEDIT( )'s default positioning and values are used, except that keystroke exceptions are handled by the Keys( ) function. As this program works through each work area, notice that there is no SELECT command or DBSELECTAREA( ) function to either change to the new work area or to return from the old one. This is due to the extended capabilities of an expression. In Clipper, functions and operations within expressions can be told where they are to operate; this is accomplished via an alias pointer in front of the expression.

Note that when DBEDIT( ) is operating within the Filenos work area, you can press the "+" character to change the index order. This is handled by the Keys( ) function, which is a keystroke handling routine called by DBEDIT( ) in each of the work areas. For further information on how a user-defined function can manipulate the DBEDIT( ) function, see Chapter 12.

Of course, there is the extended possibility of macro-expanding the alias work area that points to the DBEDIT( ) function. This allows one generic function or routine to work from an area that may be selected by the end-user.

```
 1 : * File:      Express4.prg
 2 :
 3 : #include "PTInkey.ch"        // Power Tools Header File
 4 :
 5 : ******************
 6 :
 7 : function Main()
 8 :
 9 :    local aItems := {}        // Array of items collected
10 :    local nChoice := 1        // Variable collecting the choice
11 :
12 :    use Clients new index Clients
13 :    aadd( aItems, alias() )
14 :    use Notap new index Notap
15 :    aadd( aItems, alias() )
16 :    use Ontap new index Ontap
17 :    aadd( aItems, alias() )
18 :    use Trans new index Trans
19 :    aadd( aItems, alias() )
20 :    use Statcode new
21 :    aadd( aItems, alias() )
22 :    use Disknos new index Disknos
23 :    aadd( aItems, alias() )
24 :    use Filenos new index Filenos, Filesub, Filetype
25 :    aadd( aItems, alias() )
26 :    use Statbase new
27 :    aadd( aItems, alias() )
28 :
```

```
29 :    while !( nChoice == 0 )    // the same as "!empty(nChoice)"
30 :       scroll()                // use this function due to the DEVPOS()
31 :       @ 1,0 say "Pick an area to view..."
32 :
33 :       nChoice := achoice(3,5,15,20,aItems)
34 :
35 :       if nChoice > 0
36 :          (nChoice)->( dbedit(,,,,,"Keys") )
37 :       endif
38 :    enddo
39 :    scroll()
40 :
41 :    return( NIL )
42 :
43 : ********************
44 :
45 : function Keys( nMode )
46 :
47 :    local nRetValue := 1
48 :
49 :    if nMode == 4          // Keystroke exceptions
50 :       do case
51 :       case chr(lastkey()) == "+"
52 :          set order to ( if( empty( indexkey(indexord()+1)), 1, ;
53 :                                     indexord()+1) )
54 :          nRetValue := 2
55 :
56 :       case lastkey() == pESC
57 :          nRetValue := 0
58 :
59 :       endcase
60 :    endif
61 :
62 :    return( nRetValue )
63 :
64 : // End of File: Express4.prg
```

In this example program, the array *aItems[ ]* is dynamically built, with each element representing a database opened in a NEW work area. Once all of the areas are opened, the loop begins on line 29. Since each ALIAS( ) name was placed in an array, that array is used as a pseudo-menu of options. If an area is picked, the value from ACHOICE( ) on line 33 will not be .NOT. EMPTY( ), and thus it will be greater than 0. Once the choice is made, the value of *nChoice* points to the work area we selected, and the alias of that area is obtained through the ALIAS( ) function. Embedding this value in an expression and then macro-expanding that expression, we have the alias area which is used to "point to" the area we want the real expression to be performed in, namely the call to DBEDIT( ).

Once the DBEDIT( ) function has completed its operation, the loop will start over, the work areas will be redisplayed through the ACHOICE( ) function, and the program will wait for a new choice.

The implications of working in unselected work areas should be easy to appreciate. List boxes and validation routines should now work in any data entry screen, regardless of the arrangement of the work areas involved. Pointer logic and the concept of function-oriented programming should now also be clear.

```
 1 : * File:      Express5.prg
 2 :
 3 : #include "PTInkey.ch"    // Power Tools Header files for key values
 4 : #include "PTValue.ch"    // Misc. values
 5 : #include "PTVerbs.ch"    // And all user-defined commands!
 6 :
 7 : *********************
 8 :
 9 : function Main()
10 :
11 :    local getlist := {}    // For the @...GET commands
12 :    local xVar1
13 :    local xVar2
14 :    local xVar3
15 :
16 :    use Clients new
17 :    use Ontap    new
18 :    use Trans    new index Trans
19 :
20 :    xVar1 := Clients->( MakeEmpty(2) )
21 :    xVar2 := Ontap->( MakeEmpty(3) )
22 :    xVar3 := Trans->( MakeEmpty( fieldpos( "NOW_DUE" ) ) )
23 :
24 :    while pTRUE
25 :      scroll()
26 :
27 :      @ 10,10 get xVar1 valid Clients->( Listbox(@xVar1, 2, 10, 35, 20, 55) )
28 :      @ 11,10 get xVar2 valid Ontap->( Listbox(@xVar2,3,,,,,{field(3), ;
29 :                 field(4)} ) )
30 :      @ 12,10 get xVar3
31 :      read
32 :
33 :      if lastkey() == pESC
34 :         exit
35 :      endif
36 :
37 :    enddo
38 :
39 :    return( NIL )
40 :
41 : *********************
42 :
43 : function Listbox(xValue, nField, nTop, nLeft, nBottom, nRight, ;
44 :                  aArray, bLookUp, bStoreBlock, bAfterBlock )
45 :
46 :    local cScreen    := savescreen(nTop,nLeft,nBottom,nRight)
47 :    local xRetValue := pTRUE
48 :
49 :    // bStoreBlock --> tells the function what to store to the
50 :    //                 variable if an item is selected.
51 :
52 :    // bAfterBlock --> tells the function what to do after the
53 :    //                 selection is made and the value is stored.
54 :
55 :    // bLookUp     --> tells the function if a condition is NOT
56 :    //                 present to perform a look-up list. Normally,
57 :    //                 this will be the dbseek() function, though is
```

```
 58 :   //                  not limited to it.
 59 :
 60 :
 61 :   if !empty( alias() )   // we are in a work area!
 62 :
 63 :      DEFAULT nField   TO 1, ;
 64 :              nTop     TO 5, ;
 65 :              nLeft    TO 40, ;
 66 :              nBottom  TO 20, ;
 67 :              nRight   TO 70, ;
 68 :              bLookUp TO {|| pFALSE }, ;
 69 :              bStoreBlock TO {|| fieldget( nField ) }, ;
 70 :              bAfterBlock TO {|| pTRUE }
 71 :
 72 :
 73 :      if aArray == NIL
 74 :        aArray := { field( nField ) }  // could have used FIELDNAME()
 75 :      endif
 76 :
 77 :      // Allow the UP ARROW to be a .T. condition in order for the
 78 :      // end user to UP-THROUGH a data list w/o being forced to enter
 79 :      // in items.
 80 :
 81 :      if !( lastkey() == pUP_ARROW )
 82 :
 83 :         if !eval( bLookUp )      //  Failed condition
 84 :
 85 :            dispbox( nTop, nLeft, nBottom, nRight, pDBAR )
 86 :            dbedit( nTop+1, nLeft+1, nBottom-1, nRight-1, ;
 87 :                    aArray, "LISTKEYS" )
 88 :
 89 :            if lastkey() == pENTER   // a selection was made!
 90 :              xValue := eval( bStoreBlock )
 91 :            endif
 92 :
 93 :         endif
 94 :
 95 :         xRetValue := eval( bAfterBlock )
 96 :
 97 :      endif
 98 :
 99 :   endif
100 :
101 :   restscreen(nTop,nLeft,nBottom,nRight,cScreen)
102 :
103 :   return( xRetValue )
104 :
105 : *********************
106 :
107 : function Listkeys( nMode )   // keystroke function for DBEVAL()
108 :
109 :    local nRetValue := 1
110 :
111 :    if nMode == 4
112 :      if lastkey() == pENTER .or. lastkey() == pESC
113 :        nRetValue := 0
114 :      endif
115 :    endif
116 :
117 :    return( nRetValue )
118 :
```

```
119 : *********************
120 :
121 : function MakeEmpty( nNumber )
122 :
123 :    local nRecordNumber          // Contains old record number!
124 :    local xRetValue              // Unknown return value... NIL is default
125 :
126 :    DEFAULT nNumber TO 1         // Get the first field!
127 :
128 :    if nNumber < 1 .or. nNumber > fcount()  // Out of field range!
129 :       nNumber := 1    // Still use field #1
130 :    endif
131 :
132 :    if !empty( alias() )          // Make function Robust Enough!
133 :       nRecordNumber := recno()   // save old record number!
134 :
135 :       // Use the PHANTOM RECORD (a blank record of the structure)
136 :       // as a template of blank values for all field items
137 :
138 :       dbgoto(0)
139 :
140 :       xRetValue := fieldget( nNumber )   // Get the contents!
141 :
142 :       // return to the original record number
143 :
144 :       dbgoto( nRecordNumber )
145 :
146 :    endif
147 :
148 :    return( xRetValue )
149 :
150 : // End of File: Express5.prg
```

In this example, the use of alias pointers with functions is pushed to its extreme. On lines 16 through 18, three databases are opened, including one index. On lines 20 through 22, three memory variables are initialized to "empty" values, based on the pointed-to work areas. The variable *xVar1* is assigned a blank value based on the structure of the second field in the Clients work area; the variable *xVar2* is assigned a blank value based on the structure of the third field in the Ontap work area; and the variable *xVar3* is assigned a blank value based on the ordinal position of the "NOW_DUE" field in the Trans work area. This is obtained from the FIELDPOS( ) function, which also works in the Trans work area. Keep in mind that we use the "x" *meta symbol* to denote that the variable *xVar3* is either an unknown data type or a mixed data type.

At this point, a closer look at the MakeEmpty( ) function beginning on line 121 is in order. This function takes the numeric parameter *nNumber* and obtains the value of that field using the FIELDGET( ) function. In order to get a blank field value, the "phantom record" is used. In order to get to this record, which is nothing more than a blank record of the structure of the database in memory, we go either to record number 0 or to the end of the file and skip beyond it. Since that requires two operations, the call to DBGOTO(0) on line 138 is more efficient. Once the record pointer is positioned on the "phantom record," the FIELDGET( ) function on line 140 gets the appropriate value, and the function returns the record pointer to the original record number on line 144. All of this will not take place if the function is called without having an alias available (line 132). This means that the function is more robust and works in abnormal situations. Should there be no alias, the return value of the function will be a NIL, since the variable *xRetValue* is initialized on line 124 but not given a value. This means that the default value for this variable, until properly assigned a value, will be NIL.

When all values have been obtained, the actual loop beginning on line 24 takes over. Here, each of the three variables is within a GET; two of them have an associated VALID clause. This clause uses an alias pointer to tell the Listbox( ) function which work areas to work in.

The Listbox( ) function beginning on line 43 is a first step toward building a generic lookup function, which will be expanded upon in Chapter 18. The key to this function is that it will work in the pointed-to work area, as did the MakeEmpty( ) function. Within this function, a preprocessor command, DEFAULT ... TO, is used heavily. This user-defined command actually tests to see if the data type of the variable corresponds to the data type of its default value. If they are the same, then the variable is not assigned the default value. Otherwise, if the two items are of different data types, then the default value will be assigned to the memory variable. Therefore, if no parameter is passed to the MakeEmpty( ) function on line 121, the variable *nNumber* will have a NIL value. This value does not match the value of the number 1, which means that the command will store the value of 1 to the variable *nNumber* on line 126. Keep in mind that this does not test to see if the number, if passed, is within a specified range. For example, the value of *nNumber* may be a –1, which is numeric but invalid, since there cannot be a field whose ordinal position is –1. So, the DEFAULT ... TO command does not handle all situations.

In this simple example, the expression used in the VALID clauses of the GET statements on lines 27–29 may be used in WHEN clauses as well. We could even apply this to other programming situations. The key is the fact that functions are expressions and can, therefore, be pointed to with the necessary alias, as in the previous case of MakeEmpty( ) and Listbox( ). We could take some commonly used database operations found in Clipper's standard header file (STD.CH) and convert them to function calls. This would allow us to point to them as well whenever we needed to perform an operation like setting a database filter or an index order, skipping a record, deleting or recalling a record, and, with additional support from user-defined functions, performing a seek operation. Remember, the internal function calls within STD.CH may change; therefore it is a good idea to make clear Clipper-like function calls using the preprocessor's #xtranslate command to, in turn, call the internal functions. For example, we may want to use the PACK or the ZAP commands in their function forms. We could build the following:

```
#xtranslate Pack()              =>  __dbPack()
#xtranslate Zap()               =>  __dbZap()
```

To see how all of this is put together, consider the following expressions, using the ALIAS( ) function in conjunction with the macro operator to "point" to the appropriate work area for some of the functions we commonly use:

```
1 : * File:      Express6.prg
2 :
3 : #include "PTValue.ch"       // Power Tools header file of values
4 : #include "PTInkey.ch"       // Power Tools header file of keys
5 : #include "PTVerbs.ch"
6 :
7 : ********************
```

```
  8 :
  9 : function Main()
 10 :
 11 :    OpenFiles()       // Open the files!
 12 :    scroll()          // clear the screen
 13 :    DispStats()       // display file statistics!
 14 :
 15 :    Filenos->( dbsetorder(3) )
 16 :    Trans->( dbskip() )
 17 :    Statcode->( dbgobottom() )
 18 :
 19 :    Disknos->( dbsetfilter( {|| recno() > 4}, "recno() > 4" ) )
 20 :
 21 :    DispStats()
 22 :
 23 :    dbcloseall()   // close all work areas!
 24 :
 25 :    DispStats()
 26 :    scroll()
 27 :    OpenFiles()
 28 :
 29 :    // Now, we will perform a loop without concern to the selected
 30 :    // work area and seek in yet another unselected work area!
 31 :
 32 :    while Disknos->( !eof() )
 33 :      if Filenos->( SeekIt( Disknos->sub_no, 1 ) )
 34 :        DispItems()
 35 :      endif
 36 :      Disknos->( dbskip() )
 37 :    enddo
 38 :
 39 :    scroll()
 40 :
 41 :    return( NIL )
 42 :
 43 : *******************
 44 :
 45 : static function Dispitems()
 46 :
 47 :    @ 0,0 say "    Name:"
 48 :    @ 2,0 say "   Rec #:"
 49 :    @ 3,0 say "   Disk #"
 50 :    @ 4,0 say "    Sub #"
 51 :    @ 5,0 say " Sub Name"
 52 :    @ 6,0 say "File Name"
 53 :
 54 :    @ 0,20 say Disknos->( alias() )
 55 :    @ 0,60 say Filenos->( alias() )
 56 :    @ 2,20 say Disknos->( recno() )
 57 :    @ 2,60 say Filenos->( recno() )
 58 :    @ 3,20 say Disknos->disk_no
 59 :    @ 3,60 say Filenos->disk_no
 60 :    @ 4,20 say Disknos->sub_no
 61 :    @ 4,60 say Filenos->sub_no
```

```
 62 :      @ 5,60 say Filenos->sub_name
 63 :      @ 6,60 say Filenos->file_name
 64 :      inkey(1)
 65 :
 66 :      return( NIL )
 67 :
 68 : *********************
 69 :
 70 : function DispStats()
 71 :
 72 :      local nColumn  := 15
 73 :      local nRow     := 1
 74 :      local nCounter        // for the FOR loop
 75 :
 76 :      dispbegin()           // turn on the virtual screen!
 77 :
 78 :      @ 1,0 say "     Alias"
 79 :      @ 2,0 say "     Recno()"
 80 :      @ 3,0 say "Lastrec()"
 81 :      @ 4,0 say "    Filter"
 82 :      @ 5,0 say "Index Ord"
 83 :
 84 :      for nCounter := 1 to 4
 85 :         @ nRow++, nColumn say alias( nCounter )
 86 :         if !empty( alias( nCounter ) )
 87 :            @ nRow++, nColumn say (nCounter)->( recno() )
 88 :            @ nRow++, nColumn say (nCounter)->( lastrec() )
 89 :            @ nRow++, nColumn say (nCounter)->( dbfilter() )
 90 :            @ nRow,   nColumn say (nCounter)->( indexord() )
 91 :         endif
 92 :         nRow      := 1
 93 :         nColumn  += 15
 94 :      next
 95 :
 96 :      dispend()      // turn off the virtual screen!
 97 :
 98 :      @ maxrow() - 1, 00 say "Any key...."
 99 :      inkey(0)
100 :
101 :      return( NIL )
102 :
103 : *******************
104 :
105 : static function OpenFiles()
106 :
107 :      use Trans     new index Trans
108 :      use Statcode new
109 :      use Disknos   new index Disknos
110 :      use Filenos   new index Filenos, Filesub, Filetype
111 :
112 :      return( NIL )
113 :
114 : *******************
115 :
```

```
116 : function Seekit( xItem, nOrder, lKeep )
117 :
118 :    local lRetValue := pFALSE // The return value of the function
119 :    local nCurrentOrder        // Current set order for the indexing!
120 :
121 :    DEFAULT nOrder TO 1, ;     // Default to SET ORDER OF 1
122 :            lKeep TO pFALSE    // stay put in the index order
123 :
124 :    if !empty( alias() )       // ONLY if a database is open!
125 :       nCurrentOrder := indexord()  // Current index order
126 :
127 :       if !( xItem == NIL )
128 :          dbsetorder( nOrder )
129 :          lRetValue := dbseek( xItem )
130 :          if !lKeep                  // don't keep index order
131 :             dbsetorder( nCurrentOrder )
132 :          endif
133 :       endif
134 :    endif
135 :
136 :    return( lRetValue )
137 :
138 : // End of File: Express6.prg
```

Here, the use of functions instead of commands is pushed to the limits. Function-oriented programming is a way of life in other languages. While the roots of Clipper are set firmly in a verb-oriented command language, the future rests in functions and objects. To illustrate this better, all of the file-opening commands are within the OpenFiles( ) procedure called on lines 11 and 27, with the definition of the routine appearing on lines 105 through 110. After the files have been opened and the screen cleared on line 12, the status of all of the files is displayed in the DispStats( ) routine. On lines 15 through 19, four separate calls are made to various functions, each pointed to with various alias pointers. Then the DispStats( ) routine is called again, this time showing new values for each of the work areas.

On line 23, the files are closed, and the values are once again displayed. The files are then reopened. Beginning on line 32, a WHILE loop works from the Disknos work area. The conditional statement on line 33 performs the SeekIt( ) function in the Filenos work area while passing the value of the field Disknos->sub_no to that function. If the item is found, the value of SeekIt( ) will be true (.T.), causing the function DispItems( ) to be called on line 34. After this test, the record pointer in the Disknos work area is moved via the DBSKIP( ) function. If no parameter is passed to the DBSKIP( ) function, the default skip will be one record.

The SeekIt( ) function starting on line 116 is an enhancement of the DBSEEK( ) function. This function allows for an index order, passed as the second parameter to the function, to be set prior to the seeking operation. Optionally, a third parameter may be passed to the function which tells the function to not restore the original index order after the seeking operation. All of this could have been handled by the following:

```
Area->( (dbsetorder(3), lTemp := dbseek(xValue), dbsetorder(1), lTemp ) )
```

Here, the variable *lTemp* needs to be initialized in advance since it is being used in this expression. The value of the expression will be the value of *lTemp*. However, in the process of handling the expression, the index order is set to 3, the value *xValue* is SEEKed, and the value of the DBSEEK( ) function is stored to *lTemp*. The index order is then returned to 1, and the value of the expression in the AREA work area is the value of the variable *lTemp*... or the value of the DBSEEK( ) function. The thing to keep in mind is that the SeekIt( ) function could be used, the above code sample could be used, or even a preprocessor pseudofunction or command could be constructed to do the same thing. It is important to fit the language to the style of coding that is more appropriate to the individual style of the programmer.

The point of all of this is simple: By reducing the Clipper command set to a series of independent functions or expressions, the versatility to work with each command in several locations within your code will greatly increase. By taking several typical commands and joining them together, you can get more power out of the Clipper language. In this example, we have taken what commonly would have been two or three operations that are usually called individually, and we have embedded them in our own function, which we can call and evaluate immediately and use in an unselected work area as well. That is just one of the advantages of function-oriented programming: pushing the expressions in other areas to yield positive results.

# 10

# Arrays

## Arrays in Clipper 5.2

An array is nothing more than a stack-like structure in memory that holds a category of memory variables. Before Clipper 5.0, simple memory variables held supremacy over array-based logic for two reasons. First, array subscript information was lost when working with a help system or a procedure called from a SET KEY TO command. Second, memory variables can be easily saved to disk to a special .MEM file via the SAVE TO command, while arrays cannot be easily saved to a disk file. And as a side note, array technology in the past was only one-dimensional. To build a matrix, special user-defined functions were needed to find the correct subscript in a one-dimensional array, thus simulating a multidimensional approach in coding style and convention.

In Clipper 5.2 array technology is handled in a different manner. First, array subscript information can be passed to a customized help system or to any procedure or function called by the SET KEY TO command. Second, the biggest difference in array technology is the multidimensional approach. Arrays in Clipper 5.2 are not truly multidimensional; they still are single-dimensional. However, arrays may contain other arrays, and the compiler accepts two forms of syntax to address those subarrays.

There is still no enhancement that supports saving arrays to disk, as seen in Chapter 13. This can only be done by using low-level file functions or your own user-defined functions.

In Clipper 5.2, arrays are still one-dimensional; however, an array element may contain a pointer to another one-dimensional array. Let's use this to help us out:

```
X  1  2  3   4
1  1  2  3   4
2  2  4  6   8
3  3  6  9  12
4  4  8  12 16
```

The column starting down from the X is our original array. It contains references for the 1's strip, the 2's strip, the 3's strip, and finally, the 4's strip. Because we have arrays embedded inside an array, the original array will have not only length but depth as well. This is considered "multidimensional," although it is not the same type of array as is a matrix that may be found in other languages. For example, in C, the thirteenth array element of a 12 by 2 array would be the same as 2,1 (noted as [2][0] in C) of that same array. Not so in Clipper: You would get an "out of bounds" error.

Although it is not quite the same, there are some new C-like concepts that we can begin to give to our new array logic. In essence, Clipper 5.2 arrays will have structure; our coding examples and applications will, as a result, have structure as well.

Many things in an application can have structure. Windows have structure. An application may have X number of windows, and each window will have several components that make up its unique characteristics. Similarly, Clipper objects have a structure. Each object is unique and can be looked at individually; each component may be looked at as well, or they may be linked or grouped together to form one large object-oriented system. The work areas involved in a particular application may have structure as well—each work area has a unique component. Together, they make up the application.

In Clipper 5.2, arrays are an accumulation of memory variable address pointers and are collected under a single memory address pointer known as an array reference. This pointer, or reference, is addressed by using the name of the array. An array reference in turn may contain other references. In essence, a one-dimensional array may be stored to an element of another array. This union of information means that a multidimensional array is an array reference that has in it elements that contain the references to other one-dimensional arrays. This type of branching may be expanded, with the only real restriction being the amount of available memory. Technically, arrays may have up to 4096 elements in a single dimension, a theoretical limit that may never be reached in live applications. To better illustrate this, Figure 10.1 graphically depicts how arrays are stored and embedded in one another.

In this example, the main array named *array[ ]* is a three-dimensional array; its fourth element is an array reference to a two-dimensional array. In that array, the first and sixth elements are also references to other arrays. The two methods for pointing to a single dimension of a multidimensional array are the following:

```
x := aArray[6][6][2]  // The C construct
x := aArray[6, 6, 2]  //The Pascal construct
```

Even though the arrays have mixed data types, including objects, an array is multidimensional so long as one element is a reference to another array. This should imply that array references can be changed and manipulated by reference: You have the address pointer that either directs you to another pointer or to the element itself. The accumulation of individual array elements that point to specific addresses is considered the array reference. Therefore, since a subscript position can contain another array reference, passing that subscript value to a subroutine means an array reference is passed to the subroutine. This can be confusing, but it is extremely important to understand this topic. In other words, if the sixth subscript element contained another array reference, the values in that array—the one stored in the array subscript—can be manipulated by a subroutine.

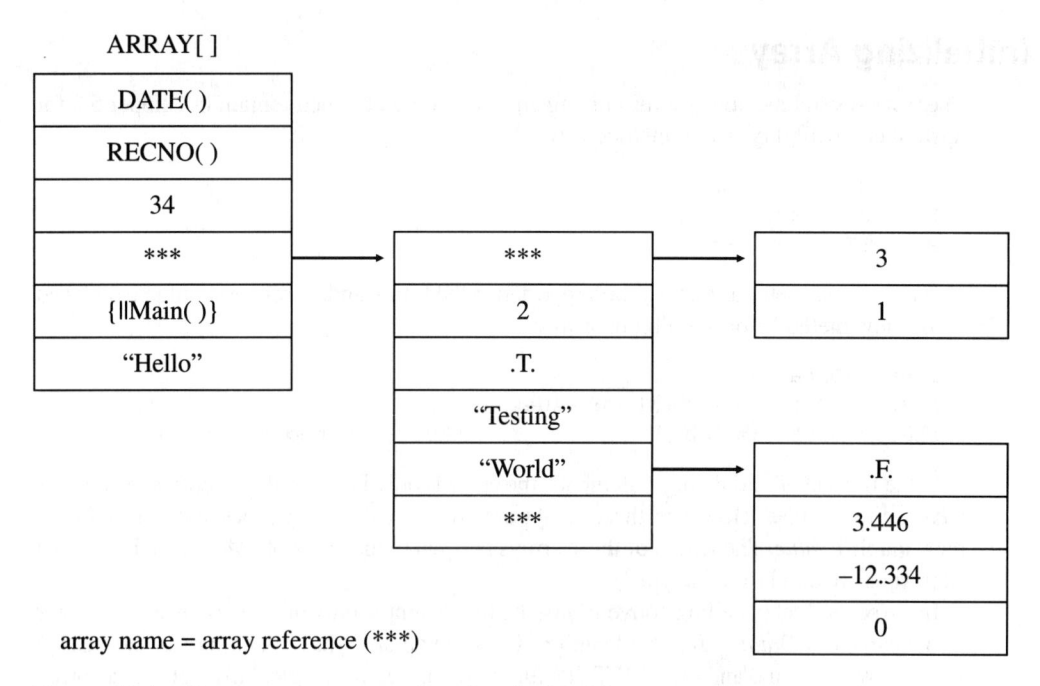

```
        ARRAY[ ]
      ┌──────────┐
      │  DATE( ) │
      ├──────────┤
      │ RECNO( ) │
      ├──────────┤
      │    34    │
      ├──────────┤        ┌──────────┐        ┌──────────┐
      │   ***    │───────▶│   ***    │───────▶│    3     │
      ├──────────┤        ├──────────┤        ├──────────┤
      │{||Main( )}│        │    2     │        │    1     │
      ├──────────┤        ├──────────┤        └──────────┘
      │ "Hello"  │        │    .T.   │
      └──────────┘        ├──────────┤
                          │"Testing" │
                          ├──────────┤        ┌──────────┐
                          │ "World"  │───────▶│    .F.   │
                          ├──────────┤        ├──────────┤
                          │   ***    │        │  3.446   │
                          └──────────┘        ├──────────┤
                                              │ −12.334  │
                                              ├──────────┤
 array name = array reference (***)           │    0     │
                                              └──────────┘
```

**Figure 10.1  How arrays are stored and embedded in one another**

For example,

`Changeit( aArray[6] )`

Any element in the array stored in *aArray[6]* will be altered in the Changeit( ) subroutine. In this particular case, even though a specific array element is being passed to the Changeit( ) routine, that element is an array reference, complete with a set of subscript values of its own. In this case, the array within *aArray[6]* can be manipulated from within the Changeit( ) routine.

Other points worth noting about how Clipper 5.2 handles arrays include the following:

- Arrays in Clipper 5.2 are 1-based. In other languages, particularly in C, arrays are 0-based, meaning that the first element of an array has a zero subscript. Clipper starts all array subscript positions at 1.
- The default data storage class for an array is private; however, it can take any other storage class upon initialization.
- Arrays may not have an alias pointer when they are referred to.
- A single dimension of an array may have up to 4096 elements in it, although, practically, a more frequent limitation will be the amount of available memory rather than internal stack limitations.
- An array is not required to contain the same data type for each of its elements.

## Initializing Arrays

There are several methods for initializing an array, some of which remain in Clipper 5.2 for upward compatibility. These methods are

```
DECLARE array[ <nValue> ]
PUBLIC  array[ <nValue> ]
PRIVATE array[ <nValue> ]
```

However, these methods may not be supported in the future and therefore should be replaced by the new methods for initializing arrays:

```
local  aData := {}
static aData := array( <nValue> )
static aData := Udf()            // A user-defined function
```

In the first set of initializing statements, the array is only initialized; its depth and contents have yet to be filled. However, these arrays are created with a length based on the value of the variable *nValue*. The length of these arrays is equal to the value of *nValue*; the individual subscripts are of a NIL data type.

In the second set of calling conventions, the first example only initializes the array pointer to the name of *aData[ ]*. It has a length of 0. When an array has a length of 0, the LEN( ) function will return 0 and the EMPTY( ) function will return a logical true (.T.). If an array contains element positions yet no value is associated with them, the array is no longer considered empty, since unused elements have a NIL value. Elements can only be added to an array via the AADD( ) or ASIZE( ) functions, or by reinitializing *aData[ ]* through one of the other methods listed here. The ARRAY( ) function is similar to any of the first three initializing methods; it creates the pointer for the array and allocates memory "slots" for the number of subscript elements specified by the value of the variable passed to the function. Finally, the last method allows a user-defined function to pass the main pointer back to an array created, initialized, and set within the definition of that function. All of these methods are shown in the following example:

```
 1 :  * File:      Array1.prg
 2 :
 3 :  function Main()
 4 :
 5 :     local nCounter      // for the FOR ... NEXT loop
 6 :
 7 :     local aArray1   := array(10)
 8 :     local aArray4   := {}
 9 :     local aArray5   := {,,,,,,,,,,,,,,}
10 :     local aArray6   := MakeArray()
11 :
12 :     private aArray2 := array(11)
13 :     public  aArray3 := array(12)
14 :
15 :     cls
16 :     qout( len( aArray1 ), valtype( aArray1[1] ) )
17 :     qout( len( aArray2 ), valtype( aArray2[1] ) )
18 :     qout( len( aArray3 ), valtype( aArray3[1] ) )
```

```
19 :    qout( len( aArray4 ) )
20 :    qout( len( aArray5 ), valtype( aArray5[1] ) )
21 :    qout( len( aArray6 ), valtype( aArray6[1] ) )
22 :
23 :    AddVal( aArray1 )    // Pass the value of aArray1[]
24 :
25 :    qout()
26 :    qout( "Press any key for the new values..." )
27 :    inkey(0)
28 :
29 :    cls
30 :    for nCounter := 1 to len( aArray1 )
31 :       qout( aArray1[nCounter], aArray3[nCounter] )
32 :    next
33 :
34 :    wait
35 :    scroll()
36 :
37 :    return( NIL )
38 :
39 : *******************
40 :
41 : static function AddVal( aArray )
42 :
43 :    memvar aArray2    // This is the private variable and should be
44 :                     // here to prevent a warning message
45 :
46 :    afill( aArray, date() ) // fill all elements of the passed array!
47 :    afill( aArray2, 1 )   // fill all of the elements of PUBLIC array
48 :
49 :    return( NIL )
50 :
51 : *******************
52 :
53 : static function MakeArray()
54 :
55 :    local aRetValue := array(4)
56 :
57 :    afill( aRetValue, 32 )
58 :
59 :    return( aRetValue )
60 :
61 : // End of File: Array1.prg
```

This example initializes six different arrays that vary in size and in data storage class. For example, the arrays declared on lines 7 through 10 are all different and are created in different ways. The array on line 7 is created via the ARRAY( ) function, while the array on line 9 is a literal array. Both of these examples show how an array can be created with a specific size yet with no values assigned to any of the element positions. In both of these cases, they are .NOT. EMPTY( ). On the other hand, the array *aArray4[ ]* created on line 8 is an EMPTY( ) array: It has no length. And the array created on line 10 has the value of the MakeArray( ) function. Since arrays are valid data types, user-defined functions can return arrays just as easily as they return characters, dates, etc. The arrays created on lines 7–10 are all initialized as LOCAL memory variables. On the other hand, the arrays created on lines 12 and 13, although they are created using the same ARRAY( ) function used on line 7, belong to different data storage classes, since one is initialized as PRIVATE and the other is initialized as PUBLIC.

It is important not to confuse a NIL value with the data type symbol for it: "U." On lines 16 through 20 the results from the VALTYPE( ) function for each of the first elements of each array are displayed to the screen. Those arrays have first elements with NIL values; however, the data type symbol for NIL is "U." Since the array created by the MakeArray( ) function on line 10 returns an array filled with numeric 32s (line 57 and 59), the data type of the first element of the array on line 21 will be "N," representing "numeric."

On line 23, the array *aArray1[ ]* is passed by value to the subroutine AddVal( ), which starts on line 41. Within this subroutine, all the elements of the PRIVATE array *aArray2[ ]* are filled with numeric 1s while the passed array *aArray[ ]* is filled with dates. This is equivalent to filling each element of *aArray1[ ]* with dates, since *aArray1[ ]* is passed to the AddVal( ) subroutine and is known as *aArray[ ]* within the subroutine. When AddVal( ) terminates, the values of *aArray[1]* have been changed.

Looking further at how arrays may be coded, initialized, assigned, and more important, copied and altered is in order. The most important thing to recognize is that a variable and an array are NOT the same. The pointers to either data type follow different rules. For example, assigning a single value to three separate variables, altering one of those values, and printing out the results would show that the single altered variable now has a different value than the other two.

```
a := b := c := 1
b := 3
? a, b, c
```

The assignment to a memory variable makes three separate variable pointers, and altering one has no effect on the other two. However, array declaration is different. When an array is initialized, the pointer, or reference, for it can be shared by multiple variables. When any one of those array references is manipulated, the change is reflected in all other variable references throughout an application. Using the above logic in an array example, we have

```
a := b := {1, 2, 3}
b[2] := 9
? a[1], a[2], a[3]
? b[1], b[2], b[3]
```

In this example, the second subscript of the array reference assigned to *b[ ]* is altered to have a value of 9; the second subscript to the reference *a[ ]*, which is assigned to the same array, will be altered as well.

We can also initialize a reference to a multidimensional array. In the above example, the arrays are initialized to a single dimension, each with three elements. Since individual array subscript positions can contain pointers to other arrays, we can initialize a multidimensional array in the following manner:

```
a := {1, {date(), date()+1}, {"A", "B", "C"}}
```

If we were to print this out, the output would look (graphically) something like this:

```
1

date()           date+1

A                B                C
```

Functions can return the references, or pointers, to arrays and multidimensional arrays. Therefore, these two statements are equivalent to one another:

```
a := {1, {DATE(), DATE()+1}, {"A", "B", "C"}}
a := Myfunc()

function Myfunc

    return( {1, {DATE(), DATE()+1}, {"A", "B", "C"}} )
```

An individual element of an array may be obtained in the following manner:

```
b := a[1]
```

This would assign the value 1 to the variable *b*.

Pushing Clipper 5.2 further, since the pointer named *a[ ]* is the same as the array itself, the individual element from the array may be obtained in the following fashion:

```
b := {1, {DATE(), DATE()+1}, {"A", "B", "C"}}[1]
```

Pushing Clipper 5.2 a little further, we can embed the subscript in the return value from a user-defined function like this:

```
b := Myfunc()

function Myfunc

    return( {1, {date(), date()+1}, {"A", "B", "C"}}[1] )
```

And going even further, since functions may return the address reference to an initialized array, and since subscript positions may sit next to the array reference (whatever form it may take) without generating a compiling error and/or warning message, we could code the following:

```
b := Myfunc(1)

function Myfunc(x)

    return( Arrays()[x] )

function arrays

    return( {1, {date(), date()+1}, {"A", "B", "C"}} )
```

All three scenarios are possible in Clipper 5.2. Here is some sample code to help illustrate our discussion so far.

```
 1 : * File:     Array2.prg
 2 :
 3 : ******************
 4 :
 5 : function Main()
 6 :
 7 :    local nCounter    // counter for a FOR...NEXT loop
 8 :    local aFirst
 9 :    local aSecond
10 :
11 :    cls
12 :    qout( "First, initialize two arrays" )
13 :
14 :    // Make a literal array shared by 2 vars!
15 :
16 :    aFirst := aSecond := {33, 23, 11}
17 :
18 :    qout( "Assign one value to one subscript" )
19 :
20 :    aSecond[2] := 5
21 :
22 :    qout( "And here are the results..." )
23 :
24 :    qout( aFirst[1], aFirst[2], aFirst[3] )
25 :    qout( aSecond[1], aSecond[2], aSecond[3] )
26 :
27 :    qout()
28 :    qout( "Press any key to continue" )
29 :    inkey(0)
30 :    qout()
31 :    qout( "Now filling the aFirst[] array with dates...")
32 :
33 :    afill( aFirst, date() )
34 :    qout()
35 :    qout( "And the values of the two arrays are now..." )
36 :    qout()
37 :
38 :    qout( aFirst[1], aFirst[2], aFirst[3] )
39 :    qout( aSecond[1], aSecond[2], aSecond[3] )
40 :    qout()
41 :    qout( "Press any key to move on..." )
42 :    inkey(0)
43 :
44 :    cls
45 :    qout( NewList(2) )
46 :    qout( OldList(2) )
47 :    qout()
48 :
49 :    for nCounter := 1 to len( DayList() )
50 :       qout( space(3), DayList()[ nCounter ] )
```

```
51 :     next
52 :
53 :     return( NIL )
54 :
55 : *******************
56 :
57 : static function NewList( nElement )
58 :
59 :     return( {"sunday", "monday", "tuesday"}[nElement] )
60 :
61 : *******************
62 :
63 : static function OldList( nElement )
64 :
65 :     return( DayList()[nElement] )
66 :
67 : *******************
68 :
69 : static function Daylist()
70 :
71 :     return( {"Sunday", "Monday", "Tuesday", "Wednesday", "Thursday", ;
72 :             "Friday", "Saturday"} )
73 :
74 : // End of File: Array2.prg
```

On line 16, the same array reference is assigned to two variables: *aFirst[ ]* and *aSecond[ ]*. While we manipulate only one subscript value in the *aSecond[ ]* array, on lines 24 and 25 you can see that values at the second subscript position of both arrays have been changed. In essence, you do not change an array as you would expect: You are changing the value that the particular memory address is pointing to. In this case, both *aFirst[ ]* and *aSecond[ ]* point to the same address. If you do not intend for two (or more) variables to share the same array reference, separate initializing statements must be used for each array.

The interesting point to note is that array address pointers are similar to the address pointers that functions return. On line 57, the function NewList( ) builds an array within the RETURN( ) statement, and the array element whose subscript equals the value of *nElement* is returned as the function's value. Since this is nothing more than a memory pointer, we could, as on line 65, have the value of the DayList( ) function be an array, take the array element directly from it, and pass it back as the OldList( ) function's value. Of course, we could express it directly, as shown in the QOUT( ) function on line 50.

## Parameter Passing

Since arrays are now valid data types, they have some of the same properties as the other data types—and in particular, they can be passed around from subroutine to subroutine.

Like any other data type, when we pass the name of the variable to the subroutine, we are passing it by value and not by reference. But how can that be true, if array elements are still susceptible to modification? The value of the array is the individual elements within the array and not the actual pointer to the reference of the array itself. In other words, arrays are typically passed by value, and the values of an array are the individual pointers to the elements of that array. This is, however, far different from the actual pointer to the array: to pass that, we must pass the array by reference by using the @ symbol. To see this illustrated, please see Chapter 5, "Data Types, Parameter Passing, Statements, and UDFs."

## Supporting Functions and AEVAL( )

Clipper 5.2 supports the new array technology with an assortment of powerful array-based functions. But in working with these functions, it must be understood that arrays in Clipper 5.2 are not matrices. Therefore, any function designed to work with an entire array will only work with the first dimension of that array. Any pointer to another array within an individual subscript will not work with the function unless otherwise noted. And one function, AFILL( ), can destroy any subarray, since it will replace the beginning dimension's elements with new values, in the process overwriting those array elements that contain other array references within them.

Below is a list of functions that work in conjunction with Clipper 5.2 arrays:

| Function | Description |
| --- | --- |
| AADD( ) | Dynamically adds elements to an array. |
| ACHOICE( ) | Executes a popup menu. |
| ACLONE( ) | Duplicates a nested or multidimensional array. |
| ACOPY( ) | Copies elements from one array to another. |
| ADEL( ) | Deletes an array element. |
| ADIR( ) | Builds an array containing directory information. |
| AEVAL( ) | Executes a code block on each array element. |
| AFIELDS( ) | Builds an array containing information on a database structure. |
| AFILL( ) | Fills an array with specified values. |
| AINS( ) | Inserts a NULL element in an array. |
| ARRAY( ) | Creates an uninitialized array with a given length. |
| ASCAN( ) | Scans an array for a value or code block. |
| ASIZE( ) | Dynamically grows or shrinks an array. |
| ASORT( ) | Sorts an array. |
| ATAIL( ) | Returns the last element of array. |
| DBSTRUCT( ) | Returns a multidimensional array containing information on the database structure of a specified work area. |
| DIRECTORY( ) | Returns either an array or a multidimensional array with either the volume label or the contents of a directory. |

Of course, additional user-defined functions may be built to give Clipper 5.2 arrays the full arsenal of tools needed for developing applications.

## AADD( )

The AADD( ) function dynamically increases the size of an array and stores values to it. For example, we could create an array with 10 elements and store the values 1 through 10 to each subsequent subscript of that array. One of the ways we might code that would be

```
local aArray[10]
for nCounter := 1 to len( aArray )    // In this case, 10
   aArray[nCounter] := nCounter
next
```

By initializing an empty array and dynamically increasing its size, we can achieve the same effect:

```
local aArray := {}
for nCounter := 1 to 10
   aadd( aArray, nCounter )    // Adding an element and a value!
next
```

The variable *aArray[ ]* is defined as an EMPTY( ) array. Each time the FOR ... NEXT loop is executed, a call is made to the AADD( ) function, which increases the size of *aArray[ ]* by one element and stores the value of *nCounter* to that new subscript position.

The AADD( ) function can dynamically increase the size of an array and store the contents of another array pointer to it at the same time. For example, here are three variations of the same technique:

```
aFirst := {3, 2, 1}
aSecond := {}
aadd(aFirst, aSecond)
aadd(aFirst, {4, 3, 2})
aadd(aFirst, MyFunc() )

*******************

function `MyFunc()

   return( {date(), time(), 35} )
```

The point is that in Clipper 5.2, you do not need to know in advance the maximum possible size of an array before initializing it. The AADD( ) function will let you "grow" an array as you need to, and it will assign a value to each new subscript position.

## ACHOICE( )

Clipper 5.2's ACHOICE( ) function is similar to pre-Clipper 5.x versions. Below is an example of a simple ACHOICE( ) function call:

```
1 : * File:     Array3.prg
2 :
3 : #include "PTValue.ch"      // Power Tools Header file
4 : #include "PTVerbs.ch"      // Power Tools user defined commands!
```

```
 5 : #include "PTInkey.ch"      // ASCII key values....
 6 :
 7 : *******************
 8 :
 9 : function Main()
10 :
11 :    local aFiles := asort( FileNames() )
12 :    local nChoice
13 :
14 :    scroll()
15 :
16 :    dispbox(2,10,14,26, pDBAR)
17 :
18 :    // call the ACHOICE() function and assign the value
19 :    // as well as evaluate it to continue or not
20 :
21 :    while !( ( nChoice := aChoice(3,11,13,25,aFiles,,,nChoice) ) == 0 )
22 :      if !( lastkey() == pESC )
23 :        @ 21,10 SAY "The file you picked was : " + aFiles[nChoice]
24 :        @ 23,10 say "Any key to pick another..."
25 :        inkey(0)
26 :        scroll(21,00)
27 :      endif
28 :    enddo
29 :
30 :    scroll()
31 :
32 :    VOID   // User-Defined Command: RETURN(NIL)
33 :
34 : *******************
35 :
36 : static function FileNames()
37 :
38 :    #define pFILE_NAME 1
39 :
40 :    local aDir       := directory()
41 :    local aRetValue  := array( len( aDir ) )
42 :    local nCounter
43 :
44 :    for nCounter := 1 to len( aDir )
45 :      aRetValue[nCounter] := padr( aDir[nCounter, pFILE_NAME], 20 )
46 :    next
47 :
48 :    return( aRetValue )
49 :
50 :    #undef pFILE_NAME
51 :
52 : // End of File: Array3.prg
```

Since array references can be created and initialized in a user-defined function, a call is first made to the FileNames( ) function, which returns an array that is then sorted by the ASORT( ) function on line 11. The complex and nested expression on line 21 first calls the ACHOICE( ) function and, if the ENTER key is pressed from within it, returns the subscript of the selected array element. This value is then immediately stored to the *nChoice* variable, and if that variable's value is not equal to 0, the WHILE statement will be satisfied and we will move onto line 22. Since we know that the value of *nChoice* is not 0, we can then use it to refer to a position in the array used by ACHOICE( ). The value of the array element in this position represents the file that we selected with the ACHOICE( ) function. The filename is displayed to the screen via the @...SAY command on line 23.

If no item is picked within the ACHOICE( ) function, the value of the variable *nChoice* will be 0 and the WHILE statement will stop processing. The ACHOICE( ) function will display a scrollable list box at the coordinates 3,11 and 13,25. The value of *nChoice* is passed as the 8th parameter to the ACHOICE( ) function to tell it which position in the array to highlight and from which to start the operation.

ACHOICE( ) generates a list box in which navigation is controlled by the cursor keys and/or a user-definable keystroke function. This program will show each item as it is selected from the array by the ACHOICE( ) function.

Along with an array to be used by the ACHOICE( ) function, it is possible to specify an ancillary array which determines whether elements in the first array will be selectable. This can be used to prevent items in the array from being selected. The following program illustrates this:

```
 1 : * File:      Array4.prg
 2 :
 3 : #include "PTValue.ch"
 4 : #include "PTVerbs.ch"
 5 : #include "PTInkey.ch"
 6 :
 7 : *******************
 8 :
 9 : function Main()
10 :
11 :    local aFiles    := asort( FileNames() )
12 :    local aToggles  := array( len(aFiles) )  // Parallel array of logics!
13 :    local nChoice := 1
14 :
15 :    setcolor( "W/B,N/W,,,GR+*/B" )
16 :    cls
17 :
18 :    afill( aToggles, pTRUE )   // Assign a .t. to all elements
19 :
20 :    dispbox(2,10,14,26,pDBAR)   // Make a frame
21 :
22 :    while !( ( nChoice := achoice(3,11,13,25,aFiles, aToggles) ) == 0 )
23 :
24 :       if !( lastkey() == pESC )
25 :
26 :          @ 21,10 SAY "The file you picked was: " + aFiles[nChoice]
27 :          @ 32,10 say "Any key to pick another..."
28 :
29 :          inkey(0)
30 :          aToggles[nChoice] := !aToggles[nChoice]   // Acts as a toggle!
31 :
32 :          scroll(21,00)
33 :       endif
34 :    enddo
35 :
36 :    cls
37 :    qqout( padc( "Items picked from the list", maxcol() ) )
```

```
38 :       qout()
39 :
40 :       for nChoice := 1 to len( aFiles )
41 :          if !aToggles[ nChoice ]
42 :             qqout( padr( aFiles[nChoice], 20 ) )
43 :             if row() > 20
44 :                scroll(1,0,21,maxcol(),1)
45 :                qqout( chr(pENTER) )
46 :             else
47 :                qout()
48 :             endif
49 :             inkey(.4)
50 :          endif
51 :       next
52 :
53 :       qout("Press any key...")
54 :       inkey()
55 :       scroll()
56 :
57 :       VOID
58 :
59 : *******************
60 :
61 : static function FileNames()
62 :
63 :    #define pFILE_NAME 1
64 :
65 :    local aDir      := directory()
66 :    local aRetValue := array( len( aDir ) )
67 :    local nCounter
68 :
69 :    for nCounter := 1 to len( aDir )
70 :       aRetValue[nCounter] := padr( aDir[nCounter, pFILE_NAME], 20 )
71 :    next
72 :
73 :    return( aRetValue )
74 :
75 :    #undef pFILE_NAME
76 :
77 : // End of File: Array4.prg
```

Remember, a function can return the reference to the array that was initialized within that function. Such is the case on line 11, where the value of the function FileNames( ) is passed directly to the ASORT( ) function, which obviously sorts the array and assigns that value to the variable *aFiles[ ]*.

This example of the ACHOICE( ) function uses a secondary array of logical values to determine which elements of the primary array will be selectable. Each item in *aFiles[ ]* has a corresponding logical value in the parallel array, *aToggles[ ]*. If the logical value for any particular subscript is set to true (.T.), the item in the array that is being displayed through ACHOICE( ) at that particular subscript position is displayed and can be selected by the ACHOICE( ) function. If, however, the logical value in the parallel array is set to false (.F.), the item at that same subscript position is displayed but cannot be selected. In addition, those items which are marked by *aToggles[ ]* as unselectable will appear in the "unselected" color setting established on line 15. This means that those items which cannot be picked will appear in flashing yellow letters with a blue background (GR+*/B). All other items within the array passed to ACHOICE( ) will appear in white letters on a blue background (W/B) unless the cursor is positioned on the element—in which case the element will appear in black letters on a white background (N/W).

To illustrate this in our program, a parallel array needs to be created (line 12) and set to a default value. In this case, the default value is to have all items in ACHOICE( ) selectable (line 18). Lines 22 through 34 are dedicated to the ACHOICE( ) function and displaying the selection. The loop will continue so long as the ESC key is not pressed inside of the ACHOICE( ) function. Pressing the ESC key will force the value of ACHOICE( ) to be 0, a value which in turn will be assigned to the variable *nChoice*, which will cause the loop to be aborted. If an item is selected, however, the value of *nChoice* will not be 0, the loop will not be aborted, and the name of the file will be displayed. Additionally, on line 30, the value of the element in the secondary array *aToggles[ ]* will be set to its opposite condition, which will be a logical false (.F.) after its associated file has been selected. Then, when the ACHOICE( ) function is called again in the loop, that item which was selected will no longer be selectable from the ACHOICE( ) function.

Once the WHILE loop is exited, the second half of this example (lines 36–57) prints out those filenames that have been selected by the ACHOICE( ) function. In this particular example, the QOUT( ) function (which is the Clipper 5.2 equivalent of the ? command) is called if the value of the subscript in the *aToggles[ ]* array is set to a logical false (.F.), which marks it as a tagged item. As the items in the array *aFiles[ ]* are displayed to the screen for those tagged in the parallel array *aToggles[ ]*, the value of the ROW( ) function will increment. At some point, if there are enough items tagged to display, the value of ROW( ) will be greater than 20, as tested on line 43. If this is the case, the SCROLL( ) function will move up all of the items in the screen region from 1,0 to 21,MAXROW( ) by one row. Then the cursor needs to be positioned in the proper place for the next filename to be displayed; therefore, on line 45, the QQOUT( ) function is called using only the CHR( ) value for the ENTER key. Since this is not the line-feed character, the cursor will be positioned at the left-most column on the same line, ready for the next item to be displayed. As items are displayed to the screen, the routine pauses 0.4 of a second (line 49) until the next item is processed by this FOR...NEXT loop.

The FileNames( ) function on line 61 and following uses several Clipper 5.2 features. The value of the DIRECTORY( ) function is stored to the array *aDir[ ]* on line 65, and the LEN( ) of that array is then used in the call to the ARRAY( ) function on line 66. The value of the ARRAY( ) function is then stored to the *aRetValue[ ]* variable. The FOR ... NEXT loop on lines 69 through 71 takes the name of the file located at the 1 position (which is the manifest constant pFILE_NAME) of the subarray found in the *nCounter* position of the *aDir[ ]* array and stores it to the *nCounter* position of the *aRetValue[ ]* array. Since the DIRECTORY( ) function returns a multidimensional array, this routine converts it to a single-dimensional array containing only the filenames. Once all filenames from the *aDir[ ]* array are stored to *aRetValue[ ]*, the array reference *aRetValue[ ]* is the return value of the FileNames( ) function.

One of the things to keep in mind is that the array that is passed to the ACHOICE( ) function may not contain pointers to code blocks or to other arrays. Any element that contains such an address pointer will not be expressed by the ACHOICE( ) function. For example, the following set of program instructions will only cause the ACHOICE( ) function to terminate immediately:

```
nChoice := ACHOICE(10,10,20,40,DIRECTORY())
```

Since the DIRECTORY( ) function returns an array of array references to other arrays, those subarrays will not be expressed by the ACHOICE( ) function and will cause the value of the variable *nChoice* to be 0.

The ACHOICE( ) function (along with MEMOEDIT( ) and DBEDIT( )) also allows the use of a user-defined function to handle keystroke exceptions and special conditions. To see this in action, consider the following example:

```
 1 : * File:     Array5.prg
 2 :
 3 : #include "PTValue.ch"
 4 : #include "PTInkey.ch"
 5 : #include "PTVerbs.ch"
 6 :
 7 : #xtranslate STUFFKEY( <key> ) => keyboard chr(<key>)
 8 :
 9 : *******************
10 :
11 : function Main()
12 :
13 :    local aFiles  := asort( FIleNames() )
14 :    local nChoice
15 :
16 :    scroll()
17 :    dispbox( 2,10,14,29, pDBAR )
18 :
19 :    Keys(pTRUE, aFiles)    // Establish the data set!
20 :    StartPosition()        // Create the static variable for starting pos
21 :
22 :    while pTRUE
23 :
24 :       nChoice := achoice( 3,11,13,28, aFiles,, "Keys", StartPosition() )
25 :
26 :       if lastkey() == pESC
27 :          exit
28 :
29 :       else
30 :          if !( nChoice == 0 )
31 :
32 :             aFiles := Keys( pTRUE )  // Obtain the data set!
33 :
34 :             @ 5,35 SAY "Ok... you selected: " + aFiles[nChoice]
35 :             @ 7,35 SAY "       The item is: " ;
36 :                   + if( chr(16) $ aFiles[nChoice], "", "NOT" ) ;
37 :                   + " deleted."
38 :             @ 9,35 say "Any key to go on..."
39 :             inkey(0)
40 :
41 :             Keys(pTRUE, aFiles)    // Reset the data set!
42 :             scroll(5,35)
43 :          endif
44 :       endif
45 :    enddo
46 :    scroll()
47 :
48 : VOID
49 :
50 : *******************
51 :
```

```
 52 : FUNCTION Keys( xMode, xItem, nPosition)
 53 :
 54 :    // If xMode is a logical true, then the array that is to be
 55 :    // manipulated will be passed to xItem and the value of xRetValue
 56 :    // will be the array... this way we can get back the values in the
 57 :    // array once we are finished with it.  xItem will either be the
 58 :    // element position/item or the actual array
 59 :
 60 :    #define pIDLE       0
 61 :    #define pTOP        1
 62 :    #define pBOTTOM     2
 63 :    #define pEXCEPTION  3
 64 :    #define pNONE       4
 65 :    #define pQUIT       0
 66 :    #define pSELECTION  1
 67 :    #define pCONTINUE   2
 68 :    #define pGOTO       3
 69 :
 70 :    static aData                   // The data set to be worked on!
 71 :
 72 :    local xRetValue := 2           // Default return value
 73 :    local nKey      := lastkey()   // value of the key pressed
 74 :
 75 :    IF xMode IS pLOGICAL           // User-defined command!
 76 :      IF xItem IS pARRAY
 77 :         aData := xItem            // set the array up for future use!
 78 :      else
 79 :         xRetValue := aData
 80 :         aData := NIL
 81 :      endif
 82 :
 83 :    else                           // It is numeric... standard func. call.
 84 :
 85 :      do case
 86 :      case xMode == pTOP
 87 :         STUFFKEY( pCTRL_PGDN )
 88 :
 89 :      case xMode == pBOTTOM
 90 :         STUFFKEY( pCTRL_PGUP )
 91 :
 92 :      case xMode == pEXCEPTION
 93 :
 94 :         do case
 95 :         case nKey == pENTER       // a selection was made
 96 :            xRetValue := pSELECTION
 97 :
 98 :         case nKey == pESC         // abort the selection
 99 :            xRetValue := pQUIT
100 :
101 :         case nKey == pDEL         // toggle the delete flag
102 :            aData[xItem] := if( (chr(16) $ aData[xItem]),,;
103 :                               space(3), ;
104 :                               " " + chr(16) + " ") + ;
105 :                               substr(aData[xItem], 4)
106 :
107 :            StartPosition(xItem)   // Assign the starting position
108 :
109 :         STUFFKEY( pDOWN_ARROW )
110 :            xRetValue := pQUIT
111 :         endcase
```

```
112 :      endcase
113 :    endif
114 :
115 :    return( xRetValue )
116 :
117 :    #undef pIDLE
118 :    #undef pTOP
119 :    #undef pBOTTOM
120 :    #undef pEXCEPTION
121 :    #undef pNONE
122 :    #undef pQUIT
123 :    #undef pSELECTION
124 :    #undef pCONTINUE
125 :    #undef pGOTO
126 :
127 : *******************
128 :
129 : static function StartPosition( nValue )
130 :
131 :    static nStartAt
132 :
133 :    local nRetValue
134 :
135 :    IF nValue IS pNUMERIC
136 :       nStartAt := nValue
137 :    else
138 :       if nStartAt == NIL    // Not yet established!
139 :          nStartAt := 1
140 :       endif
141 :       nRetValue := nStartAt
142 :    endif
143 :
144 :    return( nRetValue )
145 :
146 : *******************
147 :
148 : static function FileNames()
149 :
150 :    #define pFILE_NAME 1
151 :
152 :    local aDir      := directory()
153 :    local aRetValue := array( len( aDir ) )
154 :    local nCounter
155 :
156 :    for nCounter := 1 to len( aDir )
157 :       aRetValue[nCounter] := padl( aDir[nCounter, pFILE_NAME], 18 )
158 :    next
159 :
160 :    return( aRetValue )
161 :
162 :    #undef pFILE_NAME
163 :
164 : // End of File: Array5.prg
```

The only significant difference between this example and the previous one is the implementation of the user-defined function to process keystrokes within the ACHOICE( ) function. On line 24, the seventh parameter, KEYS( ), is the name of the function that is to be called by the ACHOICE( ) function. Only the name of the function is passed as a character string, without the matching opening and closing parentheses. In addition to this function, a function called StartPosition( ) is used to maintain the starting position for the ACHOICE( )

function. A memory variable could have been used; however, the reasons for using this method will be explained in a moment.

When the function Keys( ) is called by the ACHOICE( ) function, three parameters will always be passed to the user-defined routine. These parameters will always be passed, but they may not be accepted. For a parameter to be not accepted within the user-defined function, the LOCAL or PRIVATE PARAMETER list must not be included or must be limited to either one or two variable names. In other words, if there is no PARAMETER within the user-defined function, either on the declaration line with the name of the function (thus making it a LOCAL PARAMETER) or no PARAMETER command line (making it a PRIVATE PARAMETER), the three variables passed from ACHOICE( ) to the function will not be visible. If only one value is accepted from the ACHOICE( ) function, the last two values will not be seen within the user-defined function. (It should be noted that, with the advent of the LOCAL parameter, there is virtually no reason not to accept all three parameters from the ACHOICE( ) function call.)

The three values passed from ACHOICE( ) to the user-defined function (in this case, Keys( )) are

- PARAMETER #1: the mode of ACHOICE( ). The value of this parameter may be the following:

    | 0 | Idle |
    | 1 | Cursor beyond top of list |
    | 2 | Cursor beyond bottom of list |
    | 3 | Keystroke exception |
    | 4 | No selectable items |

- PARAMETER #2: current element in the array of items the cursor is positioned on.

- PARAMETER #3: relative row position of the item within the windowed area.

However, even though we are developing Keys( ) as a keystroke exception routine for ACHOICE( ), this does not mean that the function that will be called by ACHOICE( ) cannot be used in other places for other reasons. The data type of the first parameter will always be a numeric if called from ACHOICE( ); but we could use that same parameter as something other than a numeric to extend the use of the function called by ACHOICE( ) in other areas.

The example above touches on this concept. On line 19, the Keys( ) function is called with a logical true (.T.) as the first parameter. As the second parameter, the array of filenames created and sorted on line 13 is passed. Since the array *aFiles[ ]* is a local variable, the Keys( ) function ordinarily cannot see it: The scope of the *aFiles[ ]* variable is restricted, and it is not visible to the Keys( ) function. However, the Keys( ) function needs to manipulate the contents of that array. The logical true (.T.) tells the Keys( ) function that the second parameter is an array. This means that the *xMode* parameter on line 52 will be logical and *xItem* will be an array. On line 70, a STATIC variable named *aData[ ]* is established with no value yet assigned. On line 75, if the parameter *xMode* is a logical data type and if the *xItem[ ]* parameter is of array data type, then *xItem[ ]* is assigned to the static variable *aData[ ]*. This now makes the LOCAL variable *aFiles[ ]* visible within the Keys( ) function.

It also means that the contents of *aFiles[ ]* at the time Keys( ) is first called will be remembered as the *aData[ ]* array whenever the function is called again. On the other hand, if the data type of *xMode* is numeric, then the Keys( ) function, as seen for example on lines

102 through 104, uses the *aData[ ]* array created by the previous call to Keys( ). Of course, once ACHOICE( ) concludes processing (line 24), the ability to get back the values of *aData[ ]* which could have been altered by the Keys( ) function is essential. On line 32, the Keys( ) function is called without a second parameter but with a logical true (.T.) as the first. This tells the Keys( ) function on lines 79 and 80 to return the reference of the *aData[ ]* array, which is then stored back to the variable *aFiles[ ]*. Of course, it should be obvious that the value of the *xMode* variable, the first parameter passed to Keys( ), does not have to be a logical true (.T.); it merely needs to be a logical data type—true or false.

Since the ACHOICE( ) function is making a call to a specific function, the value of that function is important. The return value of the function to ACHOICE( ) tells ACHOICE( ) what to do. These values may be one of the following:

0   Abort selection.
1   Make selection.
2   Continue processing ACHOICE( ).
3   Go to the next item that has the same first character as that of the last key pressed.

Lines 52 and following contain the Keys( ) function. The preprocessor was used to include the values passed to and returned by KEYS( ) directly in the code in lines 60 through 68. A special header file with these #defines listed may also be created and included (using #include), or the Clipper 5.2 header file ACHOICE.CH may be specified.

The default return value for Keys( ), a 2 representing the code for continued processing, is stored to a LOCAL variable *xRetValue* on line 72. In addition, the value of LASTKEY( ) is stored to the variable *nKey*. If the Keys( ) function is called by ACHOICE( ), then the data type of *xMode* will NOT be logical, causing the Keys( ) function to examine the values of *xMode*, *xItem*, and *nPosition* more carefully through a series of DO CASE...ENDCASE statements on lines 85 through 112. For example, on line 87, if an attempt is made to move the cursor beyond the top of the ACHOICE( ) list, the keyboard is stuffed with the value of pCTRL_PGDN; this actually puts the cursor at the bottom of the ACHOICE( ) list. The opposite is true if an attempt is made to move the cursor beyond the bottom of the ACHOICE( ) list; in line 90, the keyboard is stuffed with pCTRL_PGUP. This combination achieves a wraparound effect, similar to that with SET WRAP ON in a MENU TO command. If there is a keystroke exception, then *xMode* will be the value of the pEXCEPTION manifest constant, and line 92 and following will be processed. In this case, the program looks at the ASCII value of the last key pressed, which is stored in the variable *nKey*. The three keys that make up an acceptable exception condition are pENTER, pESC, and pDEL. The preprocessor definitions for these three keys are found in PTINKEY.CH.

Of course, the real power of Keys( ) lies in its ability to greatly expand on the processing of keystrokes while inside of the ACHOICE( ) function.

## ACLONE( )

Unlike ACOPY( ), which we look at in the next example, the ACLONE( ) function will not only copy the first dimension of an array but will copy all subarrays stored to array elements.

This means that the ACLONE( ) function is used to copy a multidimensional array. It is illustrated in the following sample program:

```
 1 : * File:      Array6.prg
 2 :
 3 : ********************
 4 :
 5 : function Main()
 6 :
 7 :    local aData   := { {1,2,3}, {4,5,6}, {7,8,9} }
 8 :    local aClone
 9 :
10 :    cls
11 :
12 :    ShowValues( aData, 5 )   // Show the contents of the array!
13 :
14 :    wait
15 :
16 :    aClone := aclone( aData )
17 :    ShowValues( aClone, 10 )
18 :
19 :    aClone[1] := "Hello"
20 :
21 :    qout()
22 :    qout( valtype( aClone[1] ), valtype( aData[1] ) )
23 :    inkey(0)
24 :
25 :    return( NIL )
26 :
27 : ********************
28 :
29 : static function ShowValues( aArray, nRow )
30 :
31 :    local nXCounter
32 :    local nYCounter
33 :
34 :    for nXCounter := 1 to len( aArray )
35 :       for nYCounter := 1 to len( aArray[ nXCounter ] )
36 :          @ nRow + nYCounter, (nXCounter * 15) say aArray[nXCounter, nYCounter]
37 :       next
38 :    next
39 :
40 :    return( NIL )
41 :
42 : // End of File: Array6.prg
```

# ACOPY( )

The ACOPY( ) function is slightly different from the ACLONE( ) function and is different from just assigning a new variable with the contents of another array reference. Unlike ACLONE( ), the ACOPY( ) function copies only the values within a single dimension of an array to another array. The references to other arrays within array subscripts are assigned NIL values when copied. Unlike simply assigning one array to another with a statement like *aArray2:=aArray1*, it creates a new array whose values can be modified independently of the original array. However, the one powerful feature of the ACOPY( ) function is its ability to copy a range of subscripts within the source array.

```
 1 : * File:      Array7.prg
 2 :
 3 : #include "PTValue.ch"    // Power Tools header file of values
 4 : #include "PTVerbs.ch"    // and a header file of user-defined commands
 5 :
 6 : *******************
 7 :
 8 : function Main()
 9 :
10 :    local aData := { {1,2,3}, {4,5,6}, {7,8,9} }
11 :    local aCopy := array( 3 )
12 :
13 :    cls
14 :
15 :    ShowValues( aData, 4 ) // Show the contents beginning on 4
16 :
17 :    acopy( aData, aCopy )
18 :
19 :    ShowValues( aCopy, 10 )
20 :
21 :    aCopy[2,1] := 0
22 :
23 :    qout( aCopy[2,1], aData[2,1] )  // Show both elements!
24 :    inkey(0)
25 :
26 :    VOID   // User defined command for RETURN(NIL)
27 :
28 : *******************
29 :
30 : static function ShowValues( aArray, nRow )
31 :
32 :    local nCounter    // This is for the first level FOR...NEXT loop
33 :    local nScan       // This is for the second level FOR...NEXT loop
34 :
35 :    for nCounter := 1 to len( aArray )
36 :       IF aArray[nCounter] IS pARRAY      // User-defined command!
37 :          for nScan := 1 to len( aArray[nCounter] )
38 :
39 :             @ nScan+nRow, (nCounter*15) say aArray[nCounter, nScan]
40 :
41 :          next
42 :       else
43 :          @ (nCounter/4), ((1%4)*10) say aArray[nCounter]
44 :       ENDIF
45 :    next
46 :
47 :    qout()
48 :    qout("Press any key for next screen..." )
49 :    inkey(0)
50 :
51 :    VOID
52 :
53 : // End of File: Array7.prg
```

In this example, the array initialized on line 10 is copied to the array *aCopy[ ]* on line 17. Note that the array that will receive the copy from ACOPY( ) must be declared to the proper

*Arrays* 645

size prior to the call. In this particular example, line 11 sets up the *aCopy[ ]* array to the proper size, using the ARRAY( ) function just prior to the call to the ACOPY( ) function.

## ADEL( )

The ADEL( ) function removes an element from an array and moves all elements from the point of the deletion to the end of the array forward one subscript position. The last element in the array is set to a NIL data type. This is shown in the following:

```
 1 : * File:      Array8.prg
 2 :
 3 : *******************
 4 :
 5 : function Main()
 6 :
 7 :   local aData := {}
 8 :   local nCounter
 9 :
10 :   for nCounter := 1 to 20
11 :      aadd( aData, nCounter )
12 :   next
13 :
14 :   cls
15 :   aeval( aData, {|xItem| qout(xItem)} )   // display all of the elements
16 :   qout()
17 :   qout( "Any key for the ADEL() function..." )
18 :   inkey(0)
19 :
20 :   adel( aData, 11 )   // Remove the 11th element and move up!
21 :
22 :   cls
23 :   aeval( aData, {|xItem| qout(xItem)} )   // display all of the elements
24 :   qout()
25 :   qout( "The 20th data element is now NIL" )
26 :   inkey(0)
27 :
28 :   aData[20] := date()
29 :
30 :   cls
31 :   aeval( aData, {|xItem| qout(xItem)} )   // display all of the elements
32 :   qout()
33 :   qout( "The 20th data element is now a date" )
34 :   inkey(0)
35 :
36 :   return( NIL )
37 :
38 : // End of File: Array8.prg
```

After the empty array *aData[ ]* is created, AADD( ) dynamically increases the size of the array and adds the value of *nCounter* to each newly added subscript. Remember, AADD( ) adds only one element of an array at a time, yet, unlike the ASIZE( ) function, a value can be immediately assigned to the new subscript position. Once all 10 elements have been allocated to the array named *aData[ ]* and their values have been displayed, a call to the ADEL( ) function is made on line 20. Here, the eleventh subscript position in *aData[ ]* is removed, and all subsequent values are moved up. In other words, what was the twelfth subscript value is now the eleventh, the thirteenth is now the twelfth, and so on up to the length of *aData[ ]*. ADEL( ) works from one dimension of an array only. The twentieth position of *aData[ ]* is then assigned a NIL value. The length of the array is still 20; however, only the first 19 elements have non-NIL values. Eventually, on line 28, the last value of the array is reassigned the computer's current date.

## AEVAL( )

This is one of the most powerful functions in the arsenal of array-based functions. It is similar to DBEVAL( ) and EVAL( ), except that it executes a code block for every element in an array. Additionally, it acts like a massive FOR ... NEXT loop; however, at the conclusion of its operation, it will return a value. The AEVAL( ) function requires two parameters: an array to work with, and a code block to tell it what to do to each element in the array. This type of coding is just one more example of the future of Clipper, where parameters will tell generic functions what to do and when.

The AEVAL( ) function will work with every element in an array or with a limited number of array elements if range parameters are supplied to the AEVAL( ) call. For now, let's work with every element in the array in this coding extract:

```
aData := {}
for nCounter := 1 to 10
    AADD(aData, nCounter)
next
```

Now, to display each of those elements, we could code a FOR ... NEXT loop, or we could use the AEVAL( ) function in the following manner:

```
aeval( aData, {|xItem| qout(xItem)} )
```

Let's break apart this function in terms of the two parameters passed to it. First, each element in the array named *aData[ ]* will be evaluated in the AEVAL( ) function. The operation that will be performed on each element is described in the code block (the second parameter). Looking at the code block, we see that every element (now referred to as *xItem*) passed from the AEVAL( ) function to the code block will be passed to the QOUT( ) function. The QOUT( ) function is equivalent to the "?" command—it displays a value. Bringing all this together, you could say that the value of every element in the array named *aData[ ]* will be passed to the code block in the form of a LOCAL variable named *xItem* and will be displayed to the console via the QOUT( ) function. If you are not yet comfortable with code block technology, see Chapter 15.

The AEVAL( ) function can work with multidimensional arrays. Remember, the first dimension of this type of array simply contains a reference to another array. What is therefore passed to the code block if AEVAL( ) is to evaluate a multidimensional array is nothing more than the array reference to an array that is a subarray within the original array. Again, this array reference is a local variable. Looking back to our earlier discussion, the AEVAL( ) function simply passes one "strip" to the code block; the code block needs to look at each element within that array. To better see this, the following example uses the previous coding example to reduce to a single statement the lines of code needed for displaying a directory.

```
  1 : * File:      Array9.prg
  2 :
  3 : #include "PTValue.ch"    // Power Tools Values
  4 :
  5 : *******************
  6 :
  7 : function Main()
  8 :
  9 :    cls
 10 :
 11 :    aeval( directory(), {|aFiles| qqout( padr( aFiles[1], 15 ), aFiles[2], ;
 12 :                                   aFiles[3], aFiles[4], pCRLF ), ;
 13 :                                   BreakPoint() } )
 14 :
 15 :    qout( "And now for a nested AEVAL() call..." )
 16 :    inkey(0)
 17 :
 18 :    cls
 19 :
 20 :    aeval( directory(), {|aFiles| aeval( aFiles, ;
 21 :                                   {|xItem| qqout( padr( xItem, 15) )}), ;
 22 :                                   qqout( pCRLF ), ;
 23 :                                   BreakPoint() } )
 24 :
 25 :    return( NIL )
 26 :
 27 : *******************
 28 :
 29 : static function BreakPoint()
 30 :
 31 :    if row() == 20
 32 :       @ 22,00 say "Any key for next screen...."
 33 :       inkey(0)
 34 :       cls
 35 :    endif
 36 :
 37 :    return( NIL )
 38 :
 39 : // End of File: Array9.prg
```

The DIRECTORY( ) function on line 11 returns an array reference to a multidimensional array. This means that each element of the array will contain a subarray. The length of the array will be the number of files on the disk matching the specified file skeleton. In this example, no skeleton was specified. The width of the array will always be five elements: the filename, the file size, the file date stamp, the file time stamp, and the file's attribute byte. When AEVAL( ) gets this array reference, each element in the first dimension will be passed to the code block within AEVAL( ). This means that the code block is looking at a single-dimensional array, each element of which is itself a five-element array. This makes up, in essence, the second dimension.

The code block in lines 11 through 13 prints out all of the elements of the subarray contained within the element passed to it. Keep in mind that the notation is of array elements of a single-dimensional array. After all of the elements are printed out via the QQOUT( ) function (which is the ?? command in function form), a call to the BreakPoint( ) function is made for every element in the DIRECTORY( ) array. It simply checks the current row on the screen and, if the screen is full of information, line 32 prompts the user to press any key to continue and then clears the screen.

In the second call to AEVAL( ) on line 20, the array reference in each subscript position in the DIRECTORY( ) function is passed to a nested AEVAL( ) function call. This in turn prints out each element on the screen. In the second call, the LOCAL parameter *xItem* will contain the filename, the file size, the file date stamp, the file time stamp, and the file attribute byte, respectively: These are the elements of the arrays in the second dimension. The PADR( ) function on line 21 is used to convert the passed data type—whether it be date, numeric, or logical—to the appropriate string representation. The additional QQOUT( ) call at the end of line 22 is used to send the carriage return/line feed combination after the line is printed.

The QOUT( ) (or ? command) actually prints out a carriage return/line feed before printing the values specified in the function call. This may throw off the display's line count. Since the screen was cleared on line 18, the cursor is at the top left position of the screen; there is no need to issue a QOUT( ), which would put the cursor at the leftmost margin, since we are already there.

In the next example, the code block for the AEVAL( ) call is first assigned to a variable before it is used. Additionally, the concept of a function returning the reference to an array is used to its fullest.

```
 1 : * File:      Array10.prg
 2 :
 3 : #include "PTValue.ch"      // Power Tools Header file of values
 4 :
 5 : *******************
 6 :
 7 : function Main()
 8 :
 9 :    local bCode := {|xItem| qqout( padr( xItem,15 ) ), BreakPoint() }
10 :
11 :    cls
12 :    aeval( OnlyNames( directory() ), bCode )
13 :
14 :    return( NIL )
15 :
16 : *******************
17 :
18 : static function OnlyNames( aDir )
19 :
20 :    local aNames := {}
21 :
22 :    aeval( aDir, {|aFiles| aadd( aNames, aFiles[1] )} )
23 :
24 :    return( asort( aNames ) )
25 :
26 : *******************
27 :
28 : static function BreakPoint()
29 :
30 :    if col() > 60
31 :       qqout( pCRLF )
32 :    endif
```

```
33 :
34 :    if row() == 20
35 :       @ 22,00 say "Any key for next screen...."
36 :       inkey(0)
37 :       cls
38 :    endif
39 :
40 :    return( NIL )
41 :
42 : // End of File: Array10.prg
```

The main point of this example is not so much the call to AEVAL( ) on line 12 but the call to AEVAL( ) on line 22. This call is inside the user-defined function named OnlyNames( ). This function first initializes a LOCAL array on line 20. The value of the LOCAL parameter *aDir[ ]* on line 18 is the value of the DIRECTORY( ) function called on line 12. The AEVAL( ) on line 22 will take each array element in *aDir[ ]* and pass it to the code block, where this element is known as the LOCAL parameter *aFiles[ ]*. The element in the first position of *aFiles[ ]* will be the name of the file. This in turn is passed to the AADD( ) function, which dynamically increases the size of *aNames[ ]* and adds the value of *aFiles[1]* to it. This continues for each element in *aDir[ ]* until there is a new single-dimensional array named *aNames[ ]* containing only the filenames from the DIRECTORY( ) function. This array reference, which is a single-dimensional array, becomes the value returned by Only-Names( ) and is then passed to the code block on line 12.

Finally, using the AEVAL( ) function in conjunction with the DIRECTORY( ) function gives new potential and advanced capabilities.

```
 1 : * Name:      Array11.prg
 2 :
 3 : #include "PTValue.ch"
 4 : #include "PTVerbs.ch"
 5 :
 6 : ********************
 7 :
 8 : function Main()
 9 :
10 :    local nChoice
11 :    local aDir        := {"\"}
12 :    local nCounter    := 0
13 :    local bDisplay
14 :    local aSubDirs
15 :
16 :    while ++nCounter <= len( aDir )
17 :
18 :       if !empty( aSubDirs := GetDirs( aDir[nCounter] ) )
19 :          aeval( aSubDirs, {|cName| aadd( aDir, cName )} )
20 :       endif
21 :
22 :    enddo
23 :
24 :    asort( aDir )   // Sort the directory names!
25 :
26 :    PROCESS    // User-Defined command to do a loop!
27 :       cls
28 :       dispbox(0,0,18,61,pDBAR)
29 :       @ 0,1 say " Directory Tree "
```

```
30 :
31 :        if empty( nChoice := achoice( 1,1,17,60, aDir ) )
32 :           exit
33 :        endif
34 :
35 :        @ 22,0 say aDir[ nChoice ]
36 :        inkey(0)
37 :     END PROCESS
38 :
39 :     scroll()
40 :
41 :     // one more time to show the new display mechanism!
42 :     nCounter := 0
43 :     aDir     := {"\"}
44 :     bDisplay := {|cName| devpos(maxrow(), 0 ), ;
45 :                          devout( padr(cName, maxcol() ) ) }
46 :
47 :     while ++nCounter <= len( aDir )
48 :
49 :        if !empty( aSubDirs := GetDirs( aDir[nCounter], bDisplay ) )
50 :           aeval( aSubDirs, {|cName| aadd( aDir, cName )} )
51 :        endif
52 :
53 :     enddo
54 :
55 :
56 :     VOID     // User defined command of RETURN NIL
57 :
58 :  ********************
59 :
60 :  static function GetDirs( cPattern, bShow )
61 :
62 :     local aSubs := {}
63 :
64 :     DEFAULT bShow TO {|cName| qqout(".")}   // Default display item
65 :
66 :     // the following is a complex AEVAL() with nested functions and
67 :     // evaluations.
68 :
69 :     aeval( directory(cPattern + "*.", "D"), ;
70 :            {|aFile| if( aFile[5] == "D" .and. ;
71 :                        !( "." == aFile[1] .or. ".." == aFile[1]), ;
72 :                        ( aadd( aSubs, cPattern + aFile[1] + "\"), ;
73 :                          eval( bShow, cPattern + aFile[1] + "\" ) ), ;
74 :                        NIL ) } )
75 :
76 :     return( aSubs )
77 :
78 :  // End of File: Array11.prg
```

In this program, we start with an array named *aDir[ ]* on line 11 that contains a single element. In addition to this, we initialize counting variable *nCounter* and assign it a value of 0 on line 12. On lines 16 through 20, the variable *nCounter* is pre-incremented and compared with the length of the array named *aDir[ ]*. This means that the value of *nCounter* is increased by one before the comparison. If *nCounter* were not pre-incremented, the program would not execute, since it would attempt to pass the zeroth (0th) position in *aDir[ ]* to the GetDirs( ) function on line 18. We could also have post-incremented this variable, provided the starting value of the variable was 1. Therefore, the loop beginning on line 16 will continue to process as long as the value of *nCounter* does not exceed the number of elements in the array named *aDir[ ]*. If the condition on line 16 is true, the compound expression on line 18 is evaluated.

Looking at the innermost expression first, the value of the element at the *nCounter* position in the array *aDir[ ]* is passed to the function GetDirs( ), and the value returned by GetDirs( ), which will be discussed below, is in turn assigned to the array *aSubDirs[ ]*. If the *aSubDirs[ ]* array is not EMPTY( ), the AEVAL( ) on line 19 will execute. (An array is considered "empty" when there are no element positions in it: In essence, the array will have a length of 0.) The value of the *aDir[nCounter]* for the first pass will be the string "\"; this is the value first passed to the GetDirs( ) function.

The GetDirs( ) function begins on line 60. It is passed the LOCAL parameter *cPattern*, which represents the name of the directory to use for the DIRECTORY( ) function; as we have seen, the first time GetDirs( ) is called, this is represented by the variable *aDir[nCounter]*, whose value is "\", in the calling program. *cPattern* is the directory to use for the DIRECTORY( ) function. If there are any subdirectories in the given directory, the LOCAL array named *aSubs[ ]* on line 62 will be built using the AADD( ) function on line 72 in conjunction with the AEVAL( ) on line 69. The DIRECTORY( ) function on line 69 returns a multidimensional array of file and directory names (the "D" parameter to the DIRECTORY( ) function provides for this) whose file specification is formed by the concatenated string cPattern + "*.". The code block determines whether each element of this array is a directory and, if "." or ".." is not part of that directory's name, adds a string containing *cPattern* and the directory name to the *aSubs[ ]* array on line 72. The test for a "." or ".." character excludes the current and parent subdirectory; they should have been found previously in the *aDir[ ]*. If no subdirectory exists, *aSubs[ ]* will be an empty array, which in turn is assigned to the *aSubDirs[ ]* variable on line 49.

Before going forward, further study of the GetDirs( ) function is in order. On line 64, a user-defined command found in the PTVERBS.CH header file and included on line 4 forces a code block to be assigned to the *bShow* parameter. If the second parameter to the GetDirs( ) function is not passed, then a default code block will be created. This code block appears in the EVAL( ) function on line 73, which is used along with the AADD( ) function to build the list of subdirectories. This complex expression is executed should the IF( ) condition on line 71 be met; otherwise, the expression simply returns a NIL value. But if the condition is true, the directory names are added to the *aSubs[ ]* array and the code block *bShow* is evaluated. The current directory name (stored in *aFile[1]*) and the value of *cPattern*, along with the literal "\" string, are passed to the code block *bShow*. This then becomes the value of the LOCAL parameter *cName* shown on line 64. But regardless of the value of this parameter, the QQOUT( ) function is called, displaying a "." to the screen. This means that while elements are being dynamically added to the *aSubs[ ]* array, a "." will appear on the screen, telling the end-user that something is happening.

Implementing *bShow* as a parameter and a variable in this manner gives us considerable flexibility in customizing our program and determining how much information is shown to the user. Consider the following code blocks as potential values for the *bShow* parameter:

```
bShow := {|| NIL}
bShow := {|cName| devpos(maxrow(), 0), devout(padr(cName, ;
   maxcol()))}
```

When the EVAL( ) on line 73 evaluates the first code block, nothing will take place. In essence, nothing is displayed while the elements are being added. However, in the second example, the value of *cName* is passed to the DEVOUT( ) function, which displays it after the position of the cursor is set via the DEVPOS( ) function. The PADR( ) function is used to allow for different lengths for the value of *cName*. This code block is actually used on the second test example beginning on lines 39 and following. The code block *bDisplay* is created on lines 44 and 45, and it is passed to the GetDirs( ) function on line 49.

Once the value of *aSubDirs[ ]* on line 18 is successfully assigned and tested, the AEVAL( ) function processes that array and adds each element, passed to the code block as *cName*, to the array *aDir[ ]*. This is the main array of directory names. In essence, this loop between lines 16 through 22 builds a directory tree that will be sorted (line 24) and eventually used in the ACHOICE( ) function on line 31.

## AFILL( )

The AFILL( ) function fills an entire array with a default value. This value will be stored to every element of an array, but only to its first dimension. If a multidimensional array is passed to the AFILL( ) function, any subarrays contained within the main array will be lost, thus destroying the multidimensional array. However, any single element of an array that contains a reference to another array (and is thus a multidimensional array) can be passed to the AFILL( ) function to fill that array reference with default values. For example,

```
aTest := {}
aadd(aTest, {1,2,3})
aadd(aTest, {4,5,6})
aadd(aTest, {7,8,9})

aeval(aTest, {|xItem| qout( xItem[1], xItem[2], xItem[3])} )

afill(aTest[1], 1)

aeval(aTest, {|xItem| qout(xitem[1], xItem[2], xItem[3])} )
```

In the first call of AEVAL( ), the output would be:

```
1  2  3
4  5  6
7  8  9
```

The first element of *aTest* is passed to the AFILL( ) function, and then the second call to AEVAL( ) produces the following output:

```
1  1  1
4  5  6
7  8  9
```

For another look at the AFILL( ) function using a variety of data types, here is a simple example:

```
 1 : * Name:      Array12.prg
 2 :
 3 : *******************
 4 :
 5 : function Main()
 6 :
 7 :    local aData := array(10)
 8 :
 9 :    afill( aData, 1 )
10 :    ShowValues( aData, "With 1's" )
11 :
12 :    afill( aData, date() )
13 :    ShowValues( aData, "With dates" )
14 :
15 :    afill( aData, .t. )
16 :    ShowValues( aData, "With logicals" )
17 :
18 :    afill( aData, "Straley's Programming with Clipper 5.2" )
19 :    ShowValues( aData, "With Book Titles" )
20 :
21 :    afill( aData, {|| inkey(0)} )
22 :    ShowValues( aData, "With code blocks" )
23 :
24 :    return( NIL )
25 :
26 : *******************
27 :
28 : static function ShowValues( aData, cSaying )
29 :
30 :    scroll()           // No need to CLS since direct cursor position
31 :    @ 0,0 say cSaying  // immediately follows the clearing of the screen
32 :    qout()
33 :
34 :    aeval( aData, {|xItem, nSub| ;
35 :                     qout( "Element Number: " ), ;
36 :                     qqout( padr(nSub, 4) ), ;
37 :                     qqout( " => " ), ;
38 :                     qqout( if( valtype(xItem) == "B", "CODE BLOCK", xItem ) )} )
39 :
40 :    qout()
41 :    qout( "Press any key to continue" )
42 :    inkey(0)
43 :
44 :    return( NIL )
45 :
46 : // End of File: Array12.prg
```

In this example, the array named *aData[ ]* is filled with five different data types, and each is then displayed to the screen within the ShowValues( ) routine by using AEVAL( ).

## AINS( )

As a counter-function to ADEL( ), AINS( ) is used to insert an element in an array at the specified subscript location. Keep in mind that the values and array references within the array at that position and after are shifted down one subscript position. This means that the last subscript value will be lost when AINS( ) completes its task.

```
 1 : * File:     Array13.prg
 2 :
 3 : #include "PTInkey.ch"
 4 : #include "PTValue.ch"
 5 :
 6 : *******************
 7 :
 8 : function Main()
 9 :
10 :   local aData := array(10)
11 :   local nCounter
12 :   local aStruct
13 :
14 :   for nCounter := 1 to 10
15 :      aData[nCounter] := nCounter
16 :   next
17 :
18 :   ShowTypes(aData)
19 :
20 :   ains( aData, 4 )
21 :   ShowTypes(aData)
22 :
23 :   cls
24 :
25 :   use Clients new
26 :
27 :   aeval( Clients->( dbstruct() ), {|aField| qout( aField[1], aField[2], ;
28 :                                                   aField[3], aField[4] )} )
29 :   qout()
30 :   qout( "And that's the structure of the CLIENTS database" )
31 :   inkey(0)
32 :
33 :   cls
34 :   aStruct := Clients->( JustNames( dbstruct() ) )
35 :
36 :   Clients->( dbedit(1,1,20,60, aStruct, "Keys" ) )
37 :
38 :   aadd( aStruct, NIL )    // Open up another slot
39 :   ains( aStruct, 1   )    // Move everything down the stack
40 :
41 :   aStruct[1] := "RECNO()"
42 :
43 :   Clients->( dbedit(1,1,20,60, aStruct, "Keys" ) )
44 :
45 :   scroll()
46 :
47 :   return( NIL )
48 :
49 : *******************
50 :
51 : static function ShowTypes( aValues )
52 :
53 :   cls
54 :   aeval( aValues, {|xItem| qout( if( xItem == NIL, "Undefined", xItem ) )} )
55 :   ?
56 :   wait
57 :
58 :   return( NIL )
```

```
59 :
60 : *******************
61 :
62 : static function JustNames( aStructure )
63 :
64 :    local aRetValue := array( len( aStructure ) )
65 :
66 :    aeval( aStructure, {|aField, nPos| aRetValue[nPos] := aField[1]} )
67 :
68 :    return( aRetValue )
69 :
70 : *******************
71 :
72 : function Keys( nMode )
73 :
74 :    local nRetValue := 1
75 :
76 :    if nMode == 4
77 :       if lastkey() == pESC .or. lastkey() == pENTER
78 :          nRetValue := 0                              // QUIT the dbedit!
79 :       endif
80 :    endif
81 :
82 :    return( nRetValue )
83 :
84 : // End of file: Array13.prg
```

The thing to remember about the AINS( ) function is that it will insert an element into an array by moving all elements after the inserted element down one position. For example, we start with an array named *aData[ ]*. It has a length of 10, and each element contains the value of its subscript position (lines 14 through 16). After these values are displayed by the ShowTypes( ) routine called on line 18, a call to AINS( ) is made, passing the main array named *aData[ ]* and the number 4. This tells AINS( ) to take *aData[ ]* and move all subscript values from positions 4 to 10 down one position, thus opening subscript position 4 to be filled with a value. The value that was stored in subscript position 10 (10) will be dropped from the array. Additionally, a NIL value is stored to the newly inserted subscript position in *aData[ ]*; it will be undefined, as can be seen in the output produced by the second call to ShowTypes( ) on line 21.

Due to the nature of AINS( ), we sometimes need to keep items from falling out of the structure of the array; therefore, we can increase the size of the array prior to calling AINS( ). Prior to the second call to AINS( ) on line 39, we increase the size of the array *aStruct[ ]* by one, and simultaneously store a NIL value to the last subscript position. Then, when the AINS( ) function is called on the next line, all values are shifted down one subscript position. Then on line 39, the expression "RECNO( )" is stored to the first subscript position to be evaluated by the DBEDIT( ) function.

## ARRAY( )

The ARRAY( ) function simply declares and initializes the specified array. This is identical to the DECLARE statement, except it is in function form. In other words, the following two Clipper statements are identical:

```
aData := array(10)
DECLARE aData[10]
```

As with the DECLARE command, the ARRAY( ) function only initializes the specified array; it does not assign a value to any of its subscript positions.

## ASCAN( )

This function allows you to "seek" an expression in an array. As with most of the array-based functions, this operation will only work in the current (or single) dimension of the specified array. However, there are some new twists. First, the elements that can be scanned are sensitive to the condition of the SET EXACT flag. In other words, if SET EXACT is ON, the search element must exactly match an item within the array specified. Second, the search order will always be from the top of the array to the end. To reverse the search, the array must be reversed in order. Third, the search item does not need to be of the same data type as those in the array. Clipper will not produce a run-time error; if no match is found, it will return a 0 as the value of the ASCAN( ) function.

There is a special condition when the search item is a code block. In this case, the ASCAN( ) function will pass the current element of the array as a parameter. Inside the code block, any operation may be performed. If the code block returns a logical true (.T.) value, the operation will stop and ASCAN( ) will return the subscript position of that element. If the code block returns a logical false (.F.), ASCAN( ) will automatically process the next array element. This will continue until the code block returns a logical true (.T.) or until the last element in the array has been processed.

```
 1 : * Name:      Array14.prg
 2 :
 3 : #include "PTInkey.ch"
 4 : #include "PTValue.ch"
 5 :
 6 : *******************
 7 :
 8 : function Main()
 9 :
10 :     local aArray   := array(200)
11 :     local nStart   := 1
12 :     local cFile    := space(13)
13 :     local getlist  := {}
14 :     local nCounter
15 :
16 :     set( pSCOREBOARD, pOFF )    // This shuts off the scoreboard!
17 :
18 :     for nCounter := 1 to 200
19 :        aArray[nCounter] := nCounter
20 :     next
21 :
22 :     cls
23 :
24 :     qout( ascan( aArray, 5 ) )
25 :     qout( ascan( aArray, 112, 100 ) )
26 :     qout( ascan( aArray, "Hello there" ) )
27 :     qout()
28 :
29 :     qout( "Press any key for scan..." )
30 :     inkey(0)
31 :
```

```
32 :    aArray := {}      // Build up the file names
33 :    aeval( directory(), {|aFile| aadd( aArray, aFile[1] )} )
34 :
35 :    while pTRUE
36 :       scroll(5,0)
37 :       setpos(5,0)
38 :       ShowItems( aArray, nStart )
39 :
40 :       if !empty( cFile )
41 :          keyboard chr( pEND )
42 :       endif
43 :       scroll(20,00)
44 :
45 :       @ maxrow(), 00 say "Enter name :" GET cFile PICT "@K@!@X"
46 :       read
47 :
48 :       if !( lastkey() == pESC )
49 :          nStart := ascan( aArray, {|cItem| upper(cItem) == alltrim(cFile)} )
50 :          nStart := if( nStart == 0, 1, nStart )
51 :       else
52 :          exit
53 :
54 :       endif
55 :
56 :    enddo
57 :    scroll()
58 :
59 :    return( NIL )
60 :
61 : ********************
62 :
63 : static function ShowItems( aData, nWhich )
64 :
65 :    aeval( aData, {|xItem| qqout( padr(xItem,20)), BreakPoint()}, nWhich )
66 :
67 :    return( NIL )
68 :
69 : ********************
70 :
71 : static function BreakPoint()
72 :
73 :    local lRetValue := !( inkey() == pESC )
74 :
75 :    if lRetValue
76 :       if row() == 20
77 :          @ maxrow(), 0 say "Any key for next screen...."
78 :          inkey(0)
79 :          cls
80 :          lRetValue := ( lastkey() == pESC )
81 :       endif
82 :    endif
83 :
84 :    return( lRetValue )
85 :
86 : // End of File: Array14.prg
```

Once *aArray[ ]* has been filled with 200 elements whose values range from 1 to 200, the ASCAN( ) function on line 24 returns the subscript position at which the value 5 is found in the array *aArray[ ]*. Then ASCAN( ) is used to search for the position where the value

112 can be found, beginning with the 100th element. Finally, on line 26, ASCAN( ) searches for the character expression "Hello there," which returns a 0.

Next, a new array reference is created and stored to *aArray[ ]* on lines 32 and 33. Using the AEVAL( ) function in conjunction with the DIRECTORY( ) function, the filenames found in the DIRECTORY( ) function are individually processed and stored to the *aArray[ ]* array.

The main loop on line 35 finally calls ShowItems( ) on line 38, which displays the values of *aArray[ ]* starting with subscript value *nStart* (initialized on line 11). As long as the value of LASTKEY( ) is not 27 (a value derived by the preprocessor from pESC in the PTINKEY.CH file included on line 3), the program prompts the user to enter a filename on lines 45 and 46. If one is entered, ASCAN( ) will be called on line 49. Each element of the array *aArray[ ]* is passed to the code block, with each value individually being stored to the LOCAL parameter named *cItem*. This value is then compared to the value of the ALLTRIM( ) of *cFile*, which is the variable holding the results of the user input. If a match is made, the value of the code block becomes a logical true (.T.), which tells ASCAN( ) to return the positional value that was currently being processed by the code block. If the code block never evaluates to a logical true (.T.), the value of ASCAN( ) will be 0. In this case, the value of *nStart* is reset to 1; otherwise, its value reflects the position of the filename that matches the string input by the user. In the next call to ShowItems( ), this new value of *nStart* is then used to indicate the array element at which the display should begin.

## ASIZE( )

The ASIZE( ) function allows you to dynamically increase or decrease the size of an array. It will only work with one dimension of an array. Additionally, while ASIZE( ) can increase or decrease the size (or length) of an array, it does not initialize the elements in newly created positions, nor does it keep those subscripts in a shrunken array. The initial value of an element that has been added by the ASIZE( ) function is a NIL.

```
 1 : * File:     Array15.prg
 2 :
 3 : *******************
 4 :
 5 : function Main()
 6 :
 7 :    local aArray := {}
 8 :    local nCounter
 9 :
10 :    for nCounter := 1 to 10
11 :       aadd( aArray, nCounter )
12 :    next
13 :
14 :    ShowValues( aArray )
15 :
16 :    asize( aArray, 9 )
17 :
18 :    ShowValues( aArray )
19 :
20 :    asize( aArray, len( aArray ) + 1 )   // Similar to an AADD(aArray,NIL)
21 :
22 :    ShowValues( aArray )
```

```
23 :
24 :    return( NIL )
25 :
26 : *******************
27 :
28 : static function ShowValues( aData )
29 :
30 :    local nRow := 3
31 :
32 :    scroll()
33 :    devpos(1,0)
34 :    devout( "Length is: " )
35 :    devout( len( aData ) )
36 :
37 :    devpos(3,0)
38 :    devout( "Values are:" )
39 :    aeval( aData, {|xItem| devpos( nRow++, 15 ), devout( xItem )} )
40 :
41 :    wait
42 :
43 :    return( NIL )
44 :
45 : // End of File: Array15.prg
```

Here, *aArray[ ]* is initialized on line 7. The array length is 0, but it can be resized with the ASIZE( ) or AADD( ) function. After being initialized, *aArray[ ]* is then passed to the AADD( ) function within the FOR ... NEXT loop on lines 10 through 12. This means that the eventual length of *aArray[ ]* will be 10, with the value of *nCounter* being stored to each element in *aArray[ ]* as each new subscript is added. After the values are all displayed by the ShowValues( ) function on line 14, the array is resized down to 9. The last value in the array is lost, as can be seen when the values of the subscripts are displayed in ShowValues( ). Then, on line 20, *aArray[ ]* is resized back to 10 positions; but the new subscript position is set to a NIL value, which is seen when the call to ShowValues( ) on line 22 is made.

## ASORT( )

This function sorts the contents of an array; it does not, however, sort the references to other arrays contained within an array's single dimension. The ASORT( ) function will only sort on a single dimension; each dimension MUST be sorted independently. A feature added to the ASORT( ) function is the optional code block parameter that can tell the function "how" to sort. Here is a sample program that demonstrates the ASORT( ) function.

```
 1 : * File:     Array16.prg
 2 :
 3 : #define pFILE_NAME 1
 4 : #define pFILE_SIZE 2
 5 : #define pFILE_DATE 3
 6 :
 7 : *******************
 8 :
 9 : function Main()
10 :
11 :    local aData := Alphabet()
12 :
13 :    cls
```

```
 14 :
 15 :    ShowStuff( aData, "The array" )
 16 :
 17 :    ShowStuff( asort(aData), "Alphabetical" )
 18 :
 19 :    aData := Alphabet()    // Need to make it again!
 20 :    ShowStuff( asort(aData,3), "Starting at #3" )
 21 :
 22 :    aData := Alphabet()
 23 :    ShowStuff( asort(aData, 10, 5), "Sorted at 10, for 5")
 24 :
 25 :    aData := Alphabet()
 26 :    ShowStuff( asort(aData,,,{|cFirst, cSecond| cFirst > cSecond}), ;
 27 :               "Reverse Order" )
 28 :
 29 :    aData := Alphabet()
 30 :
 31 :    cls
 32 :    ShowVals( asort(directory(),,,;
 33 :              {|aFile1, aFile2| aFile1[pFILE_NAME] < aFile2[pFILE_NAME]}))
 34 :    inkey(0)
 35 :
 36 :    cls
 37 :    ShowVals( asort(directory(),,,;
 38 :              {|aFile1, aFile2| aFile1[pFILE_SIZE] < aFile2[pFILE_SIZE]}))
 39 :    inkey(0)
 40 :
 41 :    cls
 42 :    ShowVals( asort(directory(),,,;
 43 :              {|aFile1, aFile2| aFile1[pFILE_DATE] < aFile2[pFILE_DATE]}))
 44 :    inkey(0)
 45 :
 46 :    return( NIL )
 47 :
 48 :
 49 : *******************
 50 :
 51 : static function Alphabet()
 52 :
 53 :    local cString  := "QWERTYUIOPASDFGHJKLZXCVBNM"
 54 :    local aData    := {}
 55 :    local nCounter
 56 :
 57 :    for nCounter := 1 to 26
 58 :       aadd( aData, substr( cString, nCounter, 1 ) )
 59 :    next
 60 :
 61 :    return( aData )
 62 :
 63 : ******************
 64 :
 65 : static function ShowStuff( aData, cSaying )
 66 :
 67 :    aeval( aData, {|cItem| qqout( padr(cItem, 2 ) )} )
 68 :    qqout( "   " )
 69 :    qqout( cSaying )   // Why concatenate a string... save memory!
 70 :    inkey(0)
 71 :    qout()
 72 :
 73 :    return( NIL )
 74 :
```

```
 75 : *******************
 76 :
 77 : static function ShowVals( aData )
 78 :
 79 :   cls
 80 :   aeval( aData, {|xItem| qout( MakeString(xItem) ), ;
 81 :                          BreakPoint() } )
 82 :
 83 :   return( NIL )
 84 :
 85 : *******************
 86 :
 87 : static function MakeString( aDir )
 88 :
 89 :   local cRetValue := ""
 90 :
 91 :   aeval( aDir, {|xItem| cRetValue += padr(xItem, 15)} )
 92 :
 93 :   return( cRetValue )
 94 :
 95 : *******************
 96 :
 97 : static function BreakPoint()
 98 :
 99 :   if row() == 20
100 :     @ maxrow(), 0 say "Any key for next screen..."
101 :     inkey(0)
102 :     cls
103 :   endif
104 :
105 :   return( NIL )
106 :
107 : // End of File: Array16.prg
```

This example illustrates the possibilities of the ASORT( ) function. To begin with, the Alphabet( ) function called on lines 11, 19, 22, 25, and 29 basically builds an array with the various letters from the alphabet in each subscript position. On each of these lines, the value of the array from Alphabet( ) is stored to a LOCAL variable named *aData[ ]* which is manipulated by the ASORT( ) function and then passed to the ShowStuff( ) routine, which displays the sorted value. A special sort criteria is given to the ASORT( ) function each time it is called. For example, in the first call on line 17, the elements in *aData[ ]* are alphabetically sorted; in the second call to ASORT( ), the elements are alphabetically sorted beginning with the third subscript position; in the third call to the ASORT( ) function, five elements of *aData[ ]* are sorted beginning with the tenth element.

On line 26, ASORT( ) is used with the *aData[ ]* variable along with a code block. When used in this way, ASORT( ) passes two array elements at a time to the code block. The value returned by the code block indicates whether they are in sorted order. If the code block returns a logical true (.T.) value because the expression within the code block is satisfied, the two elements will be considered in the correct order; if the code block returns a logical false, the two elements will be reversed in the final sorted array. For example, in any array sorted in ascending order, the value of the first element will be less than the value of the second element. Hence, the code block to reflect this is:

```
{ |xExp1,xExp2| xExp1 < xExp2 }
```

In an array sorted in descending order, the value of the first array element will be greater than subsequent elements. The code block for this is:

```
{ |xExp1,xExp2| xExp1 > xExp2 }
```

It is also possible to allow for a variety of other enhancements in determining how data in an array is sorted. But suffice it to say that, in the case of our code block used on line 26, the letter Z stored in subscript position 20 will float to the top, and eventually the letter A at position 11 will float to the bottom. The ASORT( ) function will evaluate this code block until all of the elements in the *aData[ ]* array will meet the condition: a condition where the elements will be in reverse alphabetical order.

The sort criteria that is used in the ASORT( ) on line 33 is slightly different. In these examples from line 33 and following, the array element that is passed to the code block is itself an array. Remember, the DIRECTORY( ) function returns a multidimensional array in which the filename is in the first position, file size is in the second position, the date and time stamps are in the third and fourth positions, and the file attribute resides in the fifth position. The block initialized on line 33 takes the names from the first position of this multidimensional array and sorts them alphabetically when called by the ASORT( ) function on line 33. The sorting criteria specified in the code block on line 38 are based on the file sizes returned from the DIRECTORY( ) function on line 37. Files will be sorted and displayed from the smallest to the largest. Finally, the last sorting criteria specified on line 43 works on the date stamps of each file: This means that the files will be sorted and displayed from the earliest date stamp to the newest.

Using ASORT( ) to work with arrays of various dimensions, with various sorting criteria, and with a range of elements within an array, adds new possibilities on how to approach daily application-based problems.

## Arrays and User Entry Possibilities

Along with the standard array support functions, several independent functions have been enhanced to support the use of arrays and array subscripts as data entry solutions. One is the READVAR( ) function, which returns the name of the current GET variable. For example, the following procedure is commonly used to create a context-sensitive help system for a data entry routine:

```
procedure Help( cProgram, nLineNumber, cVariable )
```

In the past, the *cVariable* variable would only contain the root name of the array if the F1 key was pressed during a GET of an array variable. For example, if the command line looked like this:

```
@ 10,10 SAY "Enter Name: " GET array[1] PICT "@!"
```

The value of the *cVariable* variable when the F1 key was pressed on this particular GET would be "array." In Clipper 5.2, the value of the *cVariable* variable, and the value of the READVAR( ) function as well, will contain the subscript position along with the root name of the variable. In other words, if the F1 key was pressed on this same GET in Clipper 5.2, the value of the *cVariable* variable would be "array[1]."

Along with the improvements made in the return value from the READVAR( ) function, additional enhancements have been made to the PROCNAME( ) and PROCLINE( ) functions. These functions now take an optional parameter: the depth of the procedure or function count. In other words, Clipper will allow you to trace backward from the current program's path. For example,

```
PROCEDURE One

   Two()

*******************

PROCEDURE Two

   ? PROCNAME(), PROCLINE()
   ? PROCNAME(1), PROCLINE(1)
```

In this example, the first return value for both PROCNAME( ) and PROCLINE( ) will be the current line number and the name of the Two( ) procedure. It would be the same as calling **PROCNAME(0) and PROCLINE(0)**. However, in the second call to these functions, the return value of PROCNAME(1) will be ONE and the value for PROCLINE(1) (provided the application was not compiled with the /L switch to suppress line numbers) will be the line number that made the call to the Two( ) subroutine.

Because of these two new features of the language, array-based data entry routines are even easier to implement. To help with data entry, the ability to initialize an array in the same way that one might APPEND BLANK to a database to quickly gather up a record's worth of information and store it to an array, and to quickly store the contents of an array to a database can be easily performed in a few lines of Clipper code.

```
 1 : * Name:      Array17.prg
 2 :
 3 : #include "PTValue.ch"
 4 : #include "PTVerbs.ch"
 5 :
 6 : *******************
 7 :
 8 : function Main()
 9 :
10 :    local aClients
11 :    local aTrans
12 :
13 :    use Clients new
14 :    use Trans new
15 :
16 :    aClients := Clients->( InitArray() )
17 :    aTrans   := Trans->( InitArray(1) )
18 :
19 :    DisplayArray( aClients )
20 :    qout()
21 :    qout( "Any key..." )
22 :    inkey(0)
23 :
24 :    DisplayArray( aTrans )
```

```
 25 :      qout()
 26 :      qout( "Any key..." )
 27 :      inkey(0)
 28 :
 29 :      Clients->( StoreArray() )
 30 :      Trans->( StoreArray(1) )
 31 :
 32 :      Clients->( DisplayArray( lastrec() ) )
 33 :      qout()
 34 :      qout( "Any key..." )
 35 :      inkey(0)
 36 :
 37 :      Trans->( DisplayArray( 1 ) )
 38 :      qout()
 39 :      qout( "Any key..." )
 40 :      inkey(0)
 41 :      scroll()
 42 :
 43 :      return( NIL )
 44 :
 45 : *******************
 46 :
 47 : static function DisplayArray( aData )
 48 :
 49 :      local nRow       := 0
 50 :      local nCol       := 0
 51 :      local cGetColor := AColor()[2]
 52 :      local nCounter
 53 :
 54 :      cls
 55 :
 56 :      IF aData IS pARRAY                   // User-defined command!
 57 :         for nCounter := 1 to len( aData )
 58 :
 59 :            @ nRow++, nCol say aData[nCounter] color cGetColor
 60 :
 61 :            if nRow > 20
 62 :               if nCol += 40 > 60
 63 :                  @ maxrow(), 0 say "Any key..."
 64 :                  inkey(0)
 65 :                  cls
 66 :                  nRow := nCol := 0
 67 :               endif
 68 :            endif
 69 :         next
 70 :      else
 71 :
 72 :         for nCounter := 1 to fcount()
 73 :
 74 :            @ nRow++, nCol say fieldget( nCounter ) color cGetColor
 75 :
 76 :            if nRow > 20
 77 :               if nCol += 40 > 60
 78 :                  @ maxrow(), 0 say "Any key...."
 79 :                  inkey(0)
 80 :                  cls
 81 :                  nRow := nCol := 0
 82 :               endif
 83 :            endif
 84 :         next
```

```
 85 :      endif
 86 :
 87 :      return( NIL )
 88 :
 89 : ******************
 90 :
 91 : static function StoreArray( aRecord, nRecord, nAtField, nEndField )
 92 :
 93 :      local nCounter
 94 :      local lRetValue := pFALSE
 95 :
 96 :      if !empty( alias() )
 97 :         IF aRecord IS pARRAY
 98 :
 99 :            DEFAULT nRecord TO 0, nAtField TO 1, nEndField TO fcount()
100 :
101 :            if( nRecord == 0, dbappend(), dbgoto( nRecord ) )
102 :
103 :            for nCounter := nAtField to nEndField
104 :
105 :               fieldput( nCounter, aRecord[nCounter])
106 :
107 :            next
108 :
109 :            lRetValue := pTRUE
110 :         endif
111 :      endif
112 :
113 :      return( lRetValue )
114 :
115 : ******************
116 :
117 : static function InitArray( nRecord, nAtField, nEndField )
118 :
119 :      local aRetValue := {}
120 :      local nCounter
121 :
122 :      if !empty( alias() )
123 :
124 :         DEFAULT nRecord TO 0, ;             // use this record number
125 :                 nAtField TO 1, ;            // start at this field position
126 :                 nEndField TO fcount()       // go to the end of this list
127 :
128 :         if !empty( nRecord )
129 :            dbgoto( nRecord )
130 :         endif
131 :
132 :         for nCounter := nAtField to nEndField
133 :           aadd( aRetValue, if( empty(nRecord), ;
134 :                                MakeEmpty( nCounter ), ;
135 :                                fieldget(nCounter) ) )
136 :         next
137 :      endif
138 :
139 :      return( aRetValue )
140 :
141 : ******************
142 :
143 : static function MakeEmpty( xField )
144 :
```

```
145 :    local nRecord             // Hold the original record number!
146 :    local xRetValue           // Unknown return value... start w/ NIL
147 :
148 :    if !empty( alias() )      // There is a work area
149 :
150 :       nRecord := recno()
151 :       dbgoto(0)              // Go to the phantom record
152 :
153 :       IF xField IS pCHARACTER    // the name of the field was used!
154 :
155 :          // scan the structure of the array for the specified field
156 :          // and if found, then store it to the variable.
157 :
158 :          xField := ascan( dbstruct(), ;
159 :                           {|aFields| aFields[1] == upper(xField)} )
160 :
161 :       else
162 :          DEFAULT xField TO 0        // Make sure it's numeric
163 :
164 :          if xField < 1 .or. xField > fcount()   // field number out of range
165 :             xField := 0
166 :          endif
167 :
168 :       endif
169 :
170 :       if !( xField == 0 )   // There is a field position
171 :          xRetValue := fieldget( xField )
172 :       endif
173 :
174 :       dbgoto( nRecord )
175 :    endif
176 :
177 :    return( xRetValue )
178 :
179 : // The following is a part of the Clipper 5.2 Power Tools Book!
180 :
181 : *******************
182 :
183 : function AColor( cColor )
184 :
185 :    local aRetValue := {}     // Default return array
186 :    local cTemp      := ""    // Temporary variable
187 :    local cLocation           // Parsing location finder
188 :    local nCounter            // Local variable for the FOR...NEXT loop
189 :
190 :    DEFAULT cColor TO setcolor()
191 :
192 :    for nCounter := 1 to 5
193 :
194 :       cLocation := at( ",", cColor )
195 :       cTemp     := left( cColor, cLocation-1 )
196 :       cColor    := substr( cColor, cLocation+1 )
197 :
198 :       if nCounter == 5 .and. empty( cTemp )
199 :          aadd( aRetValue, aRetValue[2] )       // Add the original GET value!
200 :       else
201 :          aadd( aRetValue, cTemp )
202 :       endif
203 :
204 :       cTemp := ""
205 :
```

```
206 :    next
207 :
208 :    return( aRetValue )
209 :
210 : // End of File: Array17.prg
```

After two databases are opened in separate work areas on lines 13 and 14, the arrays *aClients[ ]* and *aTrans[ ]* are initialized by the InitArray( ) function. This function is told to work in a specific work area by placing it in an expression (a pair of parentheses) using the alias pointer. The InitArray( ) function is defined on lines 117 through 139. Up to three parameters may be passed to it, and all have default values should any one be skipped. So long as the InitArray( ) function is working in a work area, the default values will be set if necessary (lines 124 through 126). If the record number requested is not 0, the position of the record pointer is adjusted. Then the FOR ... NEXT loop on lines 132 through 136 is executed. It dynamically builds the array *aRetValue[ ]* using either the MakeEmpty( ) function or the FIELDGET( ) function. If a record number is specified to InitArray( ), then the values obtained from FIELDGET( ) will be stored to *aRetValue[ ]* from the fields from the *nAtField* position to the field at the *nEndField* position. If no record is specified, the MakeEmpty( ) will return a blank field value for the field at the *nCounter* position. Two functions in this example are taken from the Clipper 5.2 Power Tools Library. The first one is the MakeEmpty( ) function, and the other is the AColor( ) function. The MakeEmpty( ) function will return a blank field value for a field specified either by a numeric position or a name. The AColor( ) function takes the color attributes passed to it (or the current setting returned by the SETCOLOR( ) function) and converts the string to an array. This makes working with specific colors in the color index string easier. In other words, the "SAY" color is the first element returned from AColor( ) while the "unselected GET color" is the last.

The MakeEmpty( ) function takes advantage of the DBSTRUCT( ) function along with the ASCAN( ) function. Here, if a field name is specified, then the function needs to obtain the ordinal position of the field in the structure. If the parameter *xField* is a character data type, then the condition on line 153 will be a logical true (.T.) and lines 158 and 159 will be executed. Since DBSTRUCT( ) returns a multidimensional array, the contents of *aFields[ ]* will be the array of each field's definition. The first element of this field will be the name of the field; it is tested against the UPPER( ) of the parameter *xField*. If there is a match, the ASCAN( ) function will return the position within the array returned from DBSTRUCT( ) where the match takes place. This value is then stored back to the *xField* variable, and program flow proceeds to lines 170 through 172. If the value of *xField* cannot be found within the structure of the database, then the value returned from ASCAN( ) will be 0. If any invalid data type (i.e., not a character or a numeric parameter) is passed to the function as the value of xField, it will be assigned a value of 0. Lines 164, 165, and 166 make the function even more robust should a numeric parameter be passed to this function that is out of the range of possible field positions. Finally, if the value of *xField* is not 0, then the FIELDGET( ) function is called and stores a value to *xRetValue*.

The MakeEmpty( ) function is based on the premise of getting blank field values from record 0. The original record position is stored to a temporary variable named *nRecord*, and the record pointer is then moved to record 0—the "phantom record." This record comes into play under a variety of conditions. For example, in traversing a database, if you skip beyond the end of the file, a blank record will appear on the screen. The same occurs when skipping beyond the top of the file. In indexing, if an index is created using a blank database, the indexing algorithms use the phantom record. The "phantom record" is a copy of the structure of the database in memory, and we can use that to our advantage because all of the fields will be of the proper length and data type. In essence, since this record is just a blank record in memory, getting a value from it is no different than getting a value from any other field.

The FIELDGET( ) function is a special function that supersedes the archaic way of doing the following:

```
temp := FIELDNAME( x )
retval := &temp.
```

or simply put:

```
retval := &( FIELDNAME( x ) )
```

In either example, whether the variable *temp*, which contains the name of the field in question, is macro-expanded to get the value of the field, or the expression within the FIELDNAME( ) function is macro-expanded, the point is still the same: The macro parser rather than a direct function call is used to obtain a value. The FIELDGET( ) function replaces the need to use the macro-expansion facilities in Clipper to obtain the value of any particular field. The opposite of the FIELDGET( ) function is the FIELDPUT( ) function; it places a value in the specified field. It is used on line 105.

The point of this example is to show the power and ease with which arrays and array subscripts can be used to quickly obtain or store a complete record of information. This avoids the hassle of parallel naming conventions for memory variables, which are used in data entry screens to represent their field counterparts. In essence, FIELDPUT( ) and FIELDGET( ), Clipper's equivalents of Gather( ) and Scatter( ), are quick, efficient, and elegant programming means to a desired end.

## Data Caching and Transaction Rollback

The ability of the STATIC storage class to hold the value of an array as well as to return an array structure adds additional potential not only to our array-based technology but to our approach to problem-solving with arrays as well. Building on the previous example that actually grabs data from a database and returns a record in an array, we can build a data-caching system. And going one step farther, using that collection of data records held in memory, we can reverse the process and restore a group of records from an array of arrays. This is one form of transaction rollback.

```
 1 : * File:      Array18.prg
 2 :
 3 : #include "PTValue.ch"    // Power Tools Header file
 4 : #include "PTVerbs.ch"    // Header file for the verbs/UDC's
 5 :
 6 : #xcommand ROLLBACK AT <recno> WITH <array> => GO <recno> ;;
 7 :    aeval( <array>, {|x| StoreArray(x, recno()), dbskip() } ) ;;
 8 :    Cache(,,pTRUE)
 9 :
10 : ********************
11 :
12 : function Main()
13 :
```

```
14 :    local aData
15 :
16 :    use Clients new
17 :
18 :    aData := Clients->( Cache( 10 ) )
19 :
20 :    dispbox( 0,0,21,51, pDBAR )
21 :    aeval( aData, {|aRecord| achoice(1,1,20,50,aRecord)} )
22 :
23 :    scroll()
24 :    aData := Clients->( Cache( 3,15 ) )
25 :
26 :    dispbox( 0,0,21,51, pDBAR )
27 :    aeval( aData, {|aRecord, nElement| devpos(0,1), ;
28 :                                       devout( nElement ), ;
29 :                                       achoice(1,1,20,50,aRecord)} )
30 :
31 :    qout( "Any key...." )
32 :    inkey(0)
33 :
34 :    ROLLBACK AT 1 WITH aData
35 :
36 :    Clients->( dbgotop() )    // Same as the GO TOP command
37 :    keyboard chr(0)           // These two functions will clear the buffer
38 :    inkey()                   // and set the value of LASTKEY()
39 :
40 :    Clients->( dbedit() )
41 :
42 :    scroll()
43 :
44 :    return( NIL )
45 :
46 : *******************
47 :
48 : static function Cache( nRecsToCache, nBaseRec, lReInit )
49 :
50 :    static aArray
51 :
52 :    local nCounter
53 :
54 :    DEFAULT lReInit TO pFALSE, nRecsToCache TO 1
55 :
56 :    if aArray == NIL .or. lReInit
57 :       aArray := {}
58 :    endif
59 :
60 :    if !empty( alias() )   // there is a work area for this function
61 :
62 :       DEFAULT nBaseRec TO recno()
63 :
64 :       if nBaseRec <= lastrec() .and. nBaseRec > 0
65 :
66 :          for nCounter := nBaseRec to ( nBaseRec + nRecsToCache ) - 1
67 :             aadd( aArray, InitArray( nCounter ) )
68 :          next
69 :
70 :          dbgoto( nBaseRec )
71 :
72 :       endif
73 :
74 :    endif
75 :
```

```
 76 :    return( aArray )
 77 :
 78 : ********************
 79 :
 80 : static function InitArray( nRecord, nAtField, nEndField )
 81 :
 82 :    local aRetValue := {}
 83 :    local nCounter
 84 :
 85 :    if !empty( alias() )
 86 :
 87 :       DEFAULT nRecord TO 0, ;              // use this record number
 88 :               nAtField TO 1, ;             // start at this field position
 89 :               nEndField TO fcount()        // go to the end of this list
 90 :
 91 :       if !empty( nRecord )
 92 :          dbgoto( nRecord )
 93 :       endif
 94 :
 95 :       for nCounter := nAtField to nEndField
 96 :
 97 :          aadd( aRetValue, if( empty( nRecord ), MakeEmpty( nCounter ), ;
 98 :                                                fieldget( nCounter ) ) )
 99 :
100 :       next
101 :    endif
102 :
103 :    return( aRetValue )
104 :
105 : ********************
106 :
107 : static function MakeEmpty( xField )
108 :
109 :    local nRecord              // Hold the original record number!
110 :    local xRetValue            // Unknown return value... start w/ NIL
111 :
112 :    if !empty( alias() )    // There is a work area
113 :
114 :       nRecord := recno()
115 :       dbgoto(0)               // Go to the phantom record
116 :
117 :       IF xField IS pCHARACTER    // the name of the field was used!
118 :
119 :          // scan the structure of the array for the specified field
120 :          // and if found, then store it to the variable.
121 :
122 :          xField := ascan( dbstruct(), ;
123 :                           {|aFields| aFields[1] == upper(xField)} )
124 :
125 :       else
126 :          DEFAULT xField TO 0            // Make sure it's numeric
127 :
128 :          if xField < 1 .or. xField > fcount()  // field number out of range
129 :             xField := 0
130 :          endif
131 :
132 :       endif
133 :
134 :       if !( xField == 0 )   // There is a field position
135 :          xRetValue := fieldget( xField )
136 :       endif
```

```
137 :
138 :        dbgoto( nRecord )
139 :     endif
140 :
141 :     return( xRetValue )
142 :
143 : *******************
144 :
145 : static function StoreArray( aRecord, nRecord, nAtField, nEndField )
146 :
147 :     local nCounter
148 :     local lRetValue := pFALSE
149 :
150 :     if !empty( alias() )
151 :        IF aRecord IS pARRAY
152 :
153 :           DEFAULT nRecord TO 0, nAtField TO 1, nEndField TO fcount()
154 :
155 :           if( nRecord == 0, dbappend(), dbgoto( nRecord ) )
156 :
157 :           for nCounter := nAtField to nEndField
158 :
159 :              fieldput( nCounter, aRecord[nCounter])
160 :
161 :           next
162 :
163 :           lRetValue := pTRUE
164 :        endif
165 :     endif
166 :
167 :     return( lRetValue )
168 :
169 : // End of File: Array18.prg
```

A user-defined command is defined on lines 6 through 8. The new command ROLLBACK AT <recno> WITH <array> refers to a user-defined function named Cache( ). This is a very good example of extending and customizing the language to fit our needs. Once the Clients database is opened on line 16, the Cache( ) function is called in the Clients work area. The value 10 is passed to this function; line 48 shows us that this value is stored to a LOCAL parameter named *nRecsToCache*. The user-defined DEFAULT ... TO command, defined in the PTVERBS.CH header file, makes sure that default values are assigned to the various parameters, as on lines 54 and 62. This command sets a default value of *lReInit* to a logical false (.F.), and the number of records to cache to 1. Should it be appropriate, the starting record, stored in the *nBaseRec* parameter, will be the current value of the RECNO( ) function. So in this first call to the Cache( ) function, the number of records to cache will be 10, starting at the current record position.

One of the major things to note about this function is its use of a STATIC data storage variable. The array that is dynamically built will be held by the Cache( ) function until it is told to release the array by the *lReInit* parameter, which must be a logical true (.T.). On the first call, when the variable *aArray[ ]* is initialized as STATIC, its value will be NIL, regardless of the value of *lReInit* on line 48. If *nBaseRec* is not specified, the default value will be the current record number. So long as this value is less than or equal to LASTREC( ) and greater than 0, the loop on lines 66 through 68 will execute. This loop works starting with the specified record number up through the specified number of records to cache. If 10 records are to be cached and we start at record number 1, records 1 through 10 will be dynamically added to the array specified in the AADD( ) call on line 67. Note that the FOR ... NEXT loop subtracts 1 from the expression. In this example 1 plus 10 will be 11, which is one more than we need; therefore we must back off one record. The InitArray( ) is carried over from the previous example; it basically returns an array of record values. If this array is added via AADD( ) to *aArray[ ]*, we will be building a structure of records that are cached in memory. The depth of this array will be the number of records that are cached, and the width is the number of fields in the database being used at the time of the call to InitArray( ) on line 66. This multidimensional array is stored to the variable *aData[ ]* on line 18.

Each record is then displayed by the ACHOICE( ) on line 21. Remember, ACHOICE( ) is within a code block called from AEVAL( ); therefore the value of the LOCAL parameter *aRecord[ ]* on line 21 is an array reference to each record cached. On line 24, three more records are cached and added to the STATIC array on line 50. These three records are 15, 16, and 17, as specified by the second parameter passed to the Cache( ) function on line 24. After these have been collected, all 13 records are displayed again by the ACHOICE( ) and AEVAL( ) functions on line 27. In addition, a second parameter is passed to the code block called by the AEVAL( ) function. This parameter, named *nElement*, is a numeric value for the numeric element being worked on in the *aData[ ]* array. This value is in turn displayed to the screen via the DEVPOS( ) and DEVOUT( ) function calls within the associated code block. Finally, on line 34, the user-defined command ROLLBACK AT 1 WITH *aData* is issued, and all of the records that are kept in the array *aData[ ]* are restored to the database beginning at record number 1.

# Environmental Control: SET KEYs, the SET Environment, SET RELATION

A constant problem for the Clipper programmer is that changes in the Clipper environment are often unintentional and therefore difficult to detect, while the original Clipper environment is often difficult to restore. Yet, the Clipper environment is a kind of structure, and arrays are particularly conducive to representing structures. Clearly, management of the Clipper environment is an excellent application for arrays.

The Clipper environment consists of three major components: the SETKEY stack, in which hot keys are assigned activation routines; the SET environment, which represents a variety of customizable system-level variables that control how Clipper as a system operates; and the database environment. Of these, using arrays to handle the SETKEY stack is the most difficult, primarily because the SETKEY( ) function, given a "hot key," returns its associated code block, and this code block cannot be printed or viewed.

ARRAY19.PRG suggests some of the power that arrays offer in controlling the Clipper environment:

```
1 : * File:    Array19.prg
2 :
3 : #include "PTValue.ch"
4 : #include "PTVerbs.ch"
5 : #include "PTInkey.ch"
6 :
```

```
 7 : *******************
 8 :
 9 : function Main()
10 :
11 :    local aData
12 :
13 :    use Statcode new
14 :    index on Statcode->status to Statcode
15 :
16 :    use Trans new
17 :    index on Trans->adate to Tdate
18 :    index on Trans->account to Trans
19 :    set index to Tdate, Trans
20 :    Trans->( dbsetorder(2) )
21 :
22 :    use Clients new
23 :    index on Clients->account to Clients
24 :    set filter to recno() > 13
25 :    Clients->( dbgotop() )
26 :
27 :    set relation to Clients->account into Trans, ;
28 :                    Clients->status  into Statcode
29 :
30 :    use Filenos new
31 :    index on Filenos->disk_no to Files
32 :
33 :    use Disknos new
34 :    index on Disknos->disk_no to Disks
35 :    set relation to Disknos->disk_no into Filenos
36 :
37 :    ShowAreas()
38 :
39 :    aData := SetAreas()
40 :
41 :    cls
42 :    aeval( aData, {|aItem| qout( aItem[1] )} )
43 :
44 :    inkey(0)
45 :    aeval( aData, {|aItem| ReSet( aItem[1] )} )
46 :
47 :    ShowAreas()
48 :
49 :    aeval( aData, {|aItem| PopDBF( aItem, pFALSE )} )
50 :
51 :    ShowAreas()
52 :
53 :    return( NIL )
54 :
55 : *******************
56 :
57 : static function ReSet( cWorkArea )
58 :
59 :    (cWorkArea)->( dbsetOrder(1) )
60 :    (cWorkArea)->( dbclearFilter() )
61 :    (cWorkArea)->( dbclearRelation() )
62 :    (cWorkArea)->( dbgotop() )
63 :
64 :    return( NIL )
65 :
66 : *******************
```

```
 67 :
 68 : static function PopDBF( aData, lRemove )
 69 :
 70 :    local lAddition := pFALSE
 71 :    local bTemp
 72 :
 73 :    DEFAULT lRemove to pTRUE
 74 :
 75 :    ( aData[1] )->( dbgoto( aData[2] ) )
 76 :
 77 :    if !empty( aData[3] )
 78 :       bTemp := &("{||" + aData[3] + "}")
 79 :       ( aData[1] )->( dbsetfilter( bTemp, aData[3] ) )
 80 :       ( aData[1] )->( dbgotop() )
 81 :    endif
 82 :
 83 :    (aData[1])->( aeval( aData[4], {|xItem| SetRelate(xItem, @lAddition)} ) )
 84 :
 85 :    (aData[1])->( dbsetorder( aData[5] ) )
 86 :
 87 :    return( NIL )
 88 :
 89 : ********************
 90 :
 91 : static function Setrelate( aData, lAddit )
 92 :
 93 :    private  cRelate := aData[1]
 94 :    private  cInto   := alias(aData[2])
 95 :
 96 :    if !empty( cRelate )
 97 :       if !empty( cInto )
 98 :          if !lAddit
 99 :             set relation to &cRelate. into &cInto.
100 :             lAddit := pTRUE
101 :          else
102 :             set relation additive to &cRelate into &cInto.
103 :          endif
104 :       endif
105 :    endif
106 :
107 :    return( NIL )
108 :
109 : ********************
110 :
111 : static function ShowAreas()
112 :
113 :    local nCounter
114 :    local nInCount
115 :
116 :    for nCounter := 1 to 20
117 :       if empty( alias(nCounter) )
118 :          exit
119 :       endif
120 :
121 :       cls
122 :
123 :       qout( "    Alias is: " )
124 :       qqout( alias( nCounter ) )
125 :
126 :       qout( "    Recno() is: " )
127 :       qqout( (nCounter)->( recno() ) )
```

```
128 :
129 :       qout( "   Filter is: " )
130 :       qqout( (nCounter)->( dbfilter() ) )
131 :
132 :       for nInCount := 1 to 8
133 :         qout( "Relation #" )
134 :         qqout( padr(nInCount, 1) )
135 :         qqout( " is: " )
136 :         (nCounter)->( qqout( if( empty( dbrelation(nInCount) ), ;
137 :                                 "None Set", dbrelation(nInCount) ) ) )
138 :
139 :         qqout("   field to work area: " )
140 :         (nCounter)->( qqout( if(empty(dbrelation(nInCount)), "None", ;
141 :                              alias( dbrselect(nInCount) )) ) )
142 :       next
143 :
144 :       qout( "Index Ord is: " )
145 :       qqout( (nCounter)->( indexord() ) )
146 :
147 :       for nInCount := 1 to 8
148 :         qout( "  Key #" )
149 :         qqout( padr(nInCount, 1) )
150 :         qqout( " is: " )
151 :         qqout( (nCounter)->( indexkey(nInCount) ) )
152 :       next
153 :       qout()
154 :       inkey(0)
155 :
156 :    next
157 :
158 :    return( NIL )
159 :
160 : *******************
161 :
162 : static function PushDbf()
163 :
164 :    local aData := {}     // Collects information about the work area
165 :
166 :    aadd( aData, alias()      )
167 :    aadd( aData, recno()      )
168 :    aadd( aData, dbfilter()   )
169 :    aadd( aData, Related()    )
170 :    aadd( aData, indexord()   )
171 :    aadd( aData, IndexExpressions() )
172 :
173 :    return( aData )
174 :
175 : *************************
176 :
177 : static function IndexExpressions()
178 :
179 :    local aData := {}
180 :    local nCounter
181 :
182 :    for nCounter := 1 to 8
183 :      if !empty( indexkey( nCounter ) )
184 :        aadd( aData, indexkey( nCounter ) )
185 :      endif
186 :    next
187 :
188 :    return( aData )
```

```
189 :
190 : *********************
191 :
192 : static function Related()
193 :
194 :    local aData      := {}
195 :    local nCounter
196 :
197 :    for nCounter := 1 to 8
198 :       if !empty( dbrelation( nCounter ) )
199 :          aadd( aData, { dbrelation( nCounter ), dbrselect( nCounter ) } )
200 :       endif
201 :    next
202 :
203 :    return( aData )
204 :
205 : *******************
206 :
207 : function SetAreas()
208 :
209 :    local aData := {}
210 :    local nCounter
211 :
212 :    for nCounter := 1 to 250
213 :       if !empty( alias(nCounter) )
214 :          aadd( aData, (nCounter)->( PushDbf() ) )
215 :       endif
216 :    next
217 :
218 :    return( aData )
219 :
220 : // End of File: Array19.prg
```

## Passing an Array Element by Reference

In true modular programming environments, it is ideal to keep the name of a function the same whether it is working with a memory variable or with an array element. The function should be programmed to know the difference. However, for all practical purposes, an array element may only be passed by value, whereas a variable may be passed either by value or by reference. Passing an entire array along with a pointer to the appropriate subscript position does not provide an optimal programming solution: The variable requires only one parameter, while the array requires two (one for the base name of the array and the other for the subscript position). In addition to this, if the name of the array is passed to the subroutine, regardless of the value of the subscript position, the subroutine has complete access to any of the elements in the passed array. This may become a problem, especially when working in a team environment. By using the preprocessor to convert a "@@" character into a code block expression, which in turn is passed to a user-defined function, we can overcome these difficulties and pass an array element by reference. The code block will instruct the function what operation to perform, in this case to store a value to a particular array element. For an example of this, here is a sample program that will work only with Clipper 5.2:

```
1 : * File:     Array20.prg
2 :
3 : #include "PTValue.ch"
4 : #include "PTVerbs.ch"
```

```
 5 :
 6 : *********************
 7 :
 8 : function Main()
 9 :
10 :    local getlist   := {}           // Making a LOCAL data list for GETs
11 :    local aData     := {1,2,3}
12 :    local nValue    := 0
13 :    local bDisplay := {|| qout( "This values of the elements are:" ), ;
14 :                         qqout( aData[1], aData[2], aData[3] ), ;
15 :                         qout( "And the value of the variable is:" ), ;
16 :                         qqout( nValue ) }
17 :
18 :    cls
19 :
20 :    eval( bDisplay )    // Show the stuff!
21 :
22 :    // Now perform the data entry on the Stuff!
23 :
24 :    @ 10,10 get aData[1] when Lookup( @@aData[1] )
25 :    @ 11,10 get nValue   when Lookup( @nValue )
26 :    read
27 :
28 :    scroll(4,0)
29 :    setpos(4,0)
30 :    qout( "And now, the values after the GET..." )
31 :    eval( bDisplay )    // Show the stuff again!
32 :    qout()
33 :
34 :    return( NIL )
35 :
36 : *********************
37 :
38 : static function Lookup( xVar )
39 :
40 :    @ maxrow()-1,00 SAY "The simple display would be: " ;
41 :                   SAY if( valtype(xVar)==pBLOCK, eval(xVar), xVar )
42 :
43 :    @ maxrow(),00 say "Press any key to continue!"
44 :    inkey(0)
45 :
46 :    scroll(23,00)
47 :
48 :    IF xVar IS pBLOCK       // Array element by reference!
49 :       eval( xVar, 200 )
50 :    else                    // Typical variable passed by reference!
51 :       xVar := 200
52 :    endif
53 :
54 :    return( pTRUE )
55 :
56 : // End of File: Array20.prg
```

In this example, the preprocessor is used to convert the array element to an array element in a code block. In essence, this line of code

```
Lookup( @@aData[1] )
```

is translated into this:

```
Lookup( {|x| IF(x == NIL, aData[1], aData[1] := x)} )
```

Inside the STATIC function Lookup( ), if the parameter passed to the function is a code block, line 41 simply evaluates it; otherwise, the value of the parameter is displayed. The code block translation shows that if no parameter is passed to the code block, then the variable *X* will be NIL and the value of the code block will be the value of *aData[1]*. This is useful for seeking records in a database off of either the array element or the actual memory variable. Even though the array *aData[ ]* on line 11 is declared as a LOCAL variable, the code block is created within the confines of the same procedure/function, which means that the array and the elements of the array are visible at the time the code block is created. This visibility allows the code block to pass down to the Lookup( ) function the instructions to either show the value of the array element (line 41) or to actually store a value (line 49). The function is made robust enough to know the difference between a regular parameter, regardless how it is passed (by value or by reference), and an array element.

The point is that we can use several different features of the language to achieve a very special and important effect. Remember, no one aspect of the language is more important than another. By mixing the preprocessor, code blocks, rules about LOCAL variables, and array elements, a new programming paradigm has been derived. The language is filled with these possibilities.

## The QU Program: A Look at Nested Arrays

This next example program attempts to graphically display the way nested arrays work in Clipper.

```
 1 : * File:     QuArray.prg
 2 :
 3 : #include "PTValue.ch"
 4 : #include "PTInkey.ch"
 5 : #include "PTColor.ch"
 6 : #include "PTVerbs.ch"
 7 :
 8 : // #include "extcom.ch"
 9 :
10 : ********************
11 :
12 : function Main( cColor )
13 :
14 :    // This is a test module for the QuArray() function.  That function and
15 :    // all of the following functions make up the QuArray() example
16 :
17 :    local aData
18 :
19 :    DEFAULT cColor TO "GR+/B"
20 :
21 :    setcolor( cColor )
22 :
23 :    cls
24 :
25 :    QuArray( directory() )
26 :    qout( pCRLF, "Any key to continue...." )
27 :    inkey(0)
28 :
29 :    QuArray( {} )
```

```
30 :    qout( pCRLF, "Any key to continue...." )
31 :    inkey(0)
32 :
33 :    aData := {}
34 :    aadd( aData, {1, 2,,3, {"Test", date(), directory()}} )
35 :    aadd( aData, date() )
36 :    aadd( aData, {|| Main()} ) // A code block pointing to this routine
37 :    aadd( aData, tbrowsenew(1,1,23,40) )
38 :    aadd( aData, pTRUE )
39 :    aadd( aData, "Hello world!" )
40 :
41 :    QuArray( aData )
42 :    qout( pCRLF, "Any key to continue...." )
43 :    inkey(0)
44 :
45 :    return( NIL )
46 :
47 : *******************
48 :
49 : function QuArray( aData, nDepth )  // The array to be looked at...
50 :
51 :    local nChoice := 1
52 :    local nTop
53 :    local nLeft
54 :    local nBottom
55 :    local nRight
56 :    local cScreen
57 :
58 :    if nDepth == NIL   // Nothing was passed to it!
59 :       cls
60 :       @ 0,0 say "QuArray()"
61 :       nDepth := 0
62 :    endif
63 :
64 :    nTop    := 1
65 :    nLeft   := ((++nDepth - 1) * 1)
66 :    nBottom := maxrow() - 1
67 :    nRight  := maxcol()
68 :
69 :    cScreen := savescreen( nTop, nLeft, nBottom, nRight )
70 :
71 :    dispbox( nTop, nLeft, nBottom, nRight, pDBAR )
72 :
73 :    @ nTop, nLeft+1 SAY " Array length = " ;
74 :                    SAY len( aData )
75 :
76 :    PROCESS
77 :
78 :       keyboard chr( pLEFT_ARROW )
79 :
80 :       if empty( aData )   // No elements are in the array
81 :
82 :          @ maxrow(), 0 SAY "There are no elements in this array " ;
83 :                        SAY "to process.  Any key to continue..."
84 :
85 :          keyboard ""    // Clear the keyboard that's stuffed!
86 :          inkey(0)
87 :          exit
88 :
89 :       else
```

```
 90 :
 91 :          nChoice := achoice( nTop+1, nLeft+1, nBottom-1, nRight-1, ;
 92 :                              DefineArray(aData),, "MarkArray", nChoice )
 93 :
 94 :       if !empty( nChoice )
 95 :          if valtype(aData[nChoice]) $ "AO"   // Allow objects to be seen
 96 :
 97 :             SaySub( nChoice, pTRUE )
 98 :             QuArray( aData[nChoice], nDepth )
 99 :             SaySub()
100 :
101 :          endif
102 :       else
103 :          exit
104 :       endif
105 :    endif
106 :  END PROCESS
107 :
108 :    restscreen( nTop, nLeft, nBottom, nRight, cScreen )
109 :
110 :    if nDepth == 1
111 :       SaySub()
112 :       cls
113 :    endif
114 :
115 :    return( pTRUE )
116 :
117 : ********************
118 :
119 : static function DefineArray( aData )
120 :
121 :    local aRetValue := {}
122 :
123 :    // Get the array named ARRAY[] and build one large array for the
124 :    // ACHOICE() function in which all of the items are of the same
125 :    // data type
126 :
127 :    aeval( aData, {|xItem| aadd( aRetValue, ;
128 :                    if( valtype(xItem) == pARRAY, "Array Pointer", ;
129 :                    if( valtype(xItem) == pBLOCK, "Code Block Pointer", ;
130 :                    if( valtype(xItem) == pOBJECT, "Object", ;
131 :                    StrVal(xItem))))} )
132 :
133 :    return( aRetValue )
134 :
135 : ********************
136 :
137 : static function StrVal(xItem)   // Convert X to string of X
138 :
139 :    local cRetValue
140 :
141 :    do case
142 :    case valtype(xItem) == pCHARACTER
143 :       cRetValue := xItem
144 :
145 :    case valtype(xItem) == pNUMERIC
146 :       cRetValue := str( xItem )
147 :
148 :    case valtype(xItem) == pDATE
149 :       cRetValue := dtoc( xItem )
```

```
150 :
151 :      case valtype(xItem) == pLOGICAL
152 :         cRetValue := if( xItem, "TRUE", "FALSE" )
153 :
154 :      otherwise
155 :         cRetValue := "Unknown Value"
156 :
157 :      endcase
158 :
159 :      return( cRetValue )
160 :
161 : *******************
162 :
163 : function MarkArray( nMode, nPointer, nRow )
164 :
165 :    // User-defined keystroke function to be processed within the
166 :    // ACHOICE() function.  This function can NOT be a STATIC function!
167 :
168 :    #define pCONTINUE 2
169 :    #define pSELECT 1
170 :    #define pSTOP_ACHOICE 0
171 :
172 :    local nRetValue := pCONTINUE
173 :
174 :    SaySub(nPointer)
175 :
176 :    if nMode == 3   // Key exception
177 :       do case
178 :       case lastkey() == pESC
179 :          nRetValue := pSTOP_ACHOICE
180 :
181 :       case lastkey() == pENTER
182 :          nRetValue := pSELECT
183 :
184 :       endcase
185 :    endif
186 :
187 :    #undef pCONTINUE
188 :    #undef pSELECT
189 :    #undef pSTOP_ACHOICE
190 :
191 :    return( nRetValue )
192 :
193 : *******************
194 :
195 : static function SaySub( nPointer, lAddThis )
196 :
197 :    static cOutput
198 :
199 :    if nPointer == NIL .and. lAddThis == NIL
200 :       if !( cOutput == NIL )
201 :          cOutput := left( cOutput, len(cOutput) - 4 )
202 :          if "pt:" $ cOutput
203 :             @ maxrow(), 0 say padr(cOutput, maxcol()-len(cOutput))
204 :          else
205 :             cOutput := NIL
206 :          endif
207 :       endif
208 :    else
209 :       if cOutput == NIL
```

```
210 :        cOutput := "SubScript: "
211 :     endif
212 :
213 :     if lAddThis == NIL
214 :        devpos( maxrow(), 0 )
215 :        devout( cOutput )
216 :        devoutpict( nPointer, "999" )
217 :     else
218 :        cOutput += transform(nPointer, "999,")
219 :     endif
220 :
221 :  endif
222 :
223 :  return( NIL )
224 :
225 : // End of File: Qu.prg
```

The key to this example is that the arrays that are being tested within the Main( ) routine could be any array in any application. In a beta cycle, the QuArray( ) function could be used to examine the contents of any specific array by inserting the following code:

```
setkey( pTAB, {|| QuArray( aArray )} )
```

In this particular code fragment, the array within the application would be *aArray[ ]*, and the QuArray( ) function would be called by pressing the TAB key at any Clipper "wait" state. However, in the case of QUARRAY.PRG, direct function calls to QuArray( ) are made. On line 25, the QuArray( ) will display the multidimensional array returned from the DIRECTORY( ) function. The length of this array should be the number of files found in the directory. The length of each array nested within this array will be 5, with an element devoted to the filename, file size, file date, file time, and file attribute, respectively.

On line 29, the QuArray( ) function will attempt to show an empty array, and as a result, the appropriate message will appear at the bottom of the screen. Finally, on line 33, a new array named *aData[ ]* is initialized, and on the following lines through to line 39, new elements are added to this array. The first element in *aData[ ]* will be an array data type with five elements in it; the third element will be NIL, and the fifth will be an array. The fourth element in *aData[ ]* will be the value returned from the TBROWSENEW( ) function. This function is called a constructor, as discussed in Chapter 16, "Clipper Objects," and it returns an object of a particular class. In this case, this function is designed to return an object from the TBROWSE class; however, the point is that the fourth element will be an object data type, and it will be interesting to note that, in processing this data type on line 41. QuArray( ) treats objects as if they have a length similar to an array (e.g., a definite number of elements, which is the value returned by the LEN( ) function). From this, a plausible conclusion can be drawn that objects are like arrays, except with predefined structure and attached code that controls their behavior.

The key to the QuArray( ) function is the same as the key to saving arrays to a disk file: recursion. Since array elements may have other array references within them, and since the QuArray( ) function is designed to work with the single dimension of an array, if an element is an array, the QuArray( ) function should be recursively called to show nested levels within the array. If the data type of the highlighted element as selected from the ACHOICE( ) function on line 91 is of array or object data type, the condition on lines 94 and 95 will be true and the QuArray( ) function will be called again, with the element in question as well as a depth counter. Since all of the important variables that hold position, screen images, and coordinates are stored to LOCAL variables, each recursive call to the same function will create new memory variables with the same names yet will not mix their values with those from preceding calls. In essence the *cScreen* variable on line 69 will be unique for each call to the QuArray( ) function.

Through using LOCAL variables in conjunction with recursive programming, a graphical image of an array structure can be easily constructed and viewed. This function can be used in a variety of ways, as a debugging tool, as an aid to help understand the meaning of a ragged array, as a means of simulating a matrix, or as a way of depicting other data types, like objects, that behave similar to arrays.

# 11

# Memos: Memo Fields and Large Strings

## The Basics of Memo Handling

The basic purpose of a memo field is to provide some sort of notepad-like field tied not only to a database, but to a record as well. In a way, it is like a permanently related secondary database: When a note is added to a record, regardless of the size of the note, the size of the master record in the main database does not change. Memo files are dynamic: They will grow every time that the memo field is modified; however, they will not grow with a call to the APPEND BLANK command.

There are two parts to a memo: a memo pointer, which is kept in the record of the main database, and the actual memo, which is stored in the memo file. A memo file has the same root name as its associated database, but it has a .DBT extension that cannot be altered. If a database has an associated .DBT file, the first byte in the header of the .DBF file will be HEX 83. Normally, the first byte in the header of a .DBF file is HEX 03. The pointer in the record is a 10-byte numeric value. It contains the pointer to the beginning block in the memo file for that particular memo. Memos in the memo file itself are broken down into 512-byte blocks, with the first 512 bytes reserved for the memo file header. If a memo is 514 characters long, it would require two blocks in the memo file to store the necessary string, with the beginning block pointer stored to the actual memo field in the main database. The remaining 510 bytes in the second block of this memo would not be used. Memos must start at the beginning byte position in a 512-byte block, and each block of a memo field must be contiguous.

All of this should raise some interesting possibilities, since memo fields are nothing more than large strings. As a matter of fact, Clipper can handle strings up to 64K long. (This length may be smaller based on the amount of available memory, which could be determined by making a call to the MEMORY(1) function. For example, in the case of the MEMOEDIT( ) function, Clipper will make a copy of the string, or memo, once the function is called. This allows MEMOEDIT( ) to return the original string if an abort condition should be present. Therefore, if the string were 60K in size, Clipper would require 120K from the free pool of the application in order to handle the MEMOEDIT( ) call.) Additionally, text files—or any file for that matter—may be seen as one large string and handled accordingly. In essence, there is a large body of ancillary functions and commands that may be used to help work with large strings, text files, and memo fields.

Keep in mind that a memo field is nothing more than a large string, which means that the string-based functions in Clipper can work with a memo field. These functions include AT( ), $, and SUBSTR( ). Additionally, Clipper 5.2 has several functions that will help in working with, manipulating, and evaluating large strings:

| | |
|---|---|
| HARDCR( ) | Globally replaces all occurrences of a soft carriage-return character in a string with a hard carriage return. |
| MEMOEDIT( ) | Edits or displays the contents of a memo field or string. |
| MEMOLINE( ) | Extracts a line from a memo field or string. |
| MEMOREAD( ) | Reads the contents of a disk file and returns a character string. |
| MEMOTRAN( ) | Replaces all occurrences of soft and hard carriage returns with new characters. |
| MEMOWRIT( ) | Writes a memo field or a character string to disk. |
| MLCOUNT( ) | Counts the number of lines in a memo field or character string. |
| MLCTOPOS( ) | Returns the line and column of a particular byte position of text in MEMOEDIT( ). |
| MLPOS( ) | Determines the position of a line in a memo field or a character string. |
| MPOSTOL( ) | Calculates the relative row and column position of a particular byte in MEMOEDIT( ). |
| STRTRAN( ) | Globally replaces all occurrences of a specified string in a character string with a new string. |
| STUFF( ) | Deletes or inserts characters in a character string. |

For the most part, handling memo fields and large strings centers around one function: MEMOEDIT( ). Most functions discussed in the chapter center around its capabilities and return value.

## Individual Functions for Memo Handling

To start this discussion off, the following program demonstrates a few string-oriented and memo-handling functions and shows the potential of memo technology in Clipper 5.2.

```
1 : * File:      Memo1.prg
2 :
3 : #include "PTValue.ch"    // Header file from Power Tools 5.2
4 : #include "PTVerbs.ch"    // Header file from Power Tools 5.2
5 :
6 : #define pFLASH "W+*/N" // Color for flashing titles
7 :
```

```
 8 :  function Main()
 9 :
10 :     local cString  // Initialize the variable for the file
11 :     local nCounter // variable for the FOR...NEXT loop
12 :
13 :     cString := "Hello there, this is a "
14 :     cString += CHR(141) + CHR(10)
15 :     cString += "wonderful compiler!"
16 :
17 :     scroll()
18 :     // pad the string to be centered in output
19 :     devpos(0,0)
20 :     devout( padc("The string with soft carriage returns", maxcol()), ;
21 :             pFLASH )
22 :
23 :     qout( cString )   // This is the ? command
24 :     qout( )
25 :
26 :     devout( padc("The value of HARDCR()", maxcol()), pFLASH )
27 :
28 :     qout( hardcr( cString ) )
29 :     qout()
30 :
31 :     devout( padc("The value of MEMOTRAN()", maxcol()), pFLASH )
32 :
33 :     qout( memotran(cString, chr(141), "" ) )
34 :
35 :     devpos(maxrow(),0)
36 :     devout( "Press any key...." )
37 :     inkey(0)
38 :
39 :     cls
40 :     cString := hardcr( cString )
41 :
42 :     devout( padc( "The string with hard-carriage returns", maxcol() ), ;
43 :             pFLASH )
44 :
45 :     qout( cString )
46 :     qout()
47 :
48 :     devout( padc("The value of MEMOTRAN()", maxcol()), pFLASH )
49 :     qout( memotran(cString, "|", space(1)) )
50 :     qout()
51 :
52 :     devout( padc("The value of STRTRAN()", maxcol() ), pFLASH )
53 :     qout( strtran( cString, "t", "(T)") )
54 :
55 :     devpos(maxrow(),0)
56 :     devout( "Press any key...." )
57 :     inkey(0)
58 :
59 :     scroll()     // Both of these functions make up
60 :     setpos(0,0)  // the CLS command
61 :
62 :     qout( Expand( "This is a wonderful compiler!" ) )
63 :
64 :     devpos(maxrow(),0)
65 :     devout( "Press any key...." )
66 :     inkey(0)
```

```
 67 :
 68 :    cString := "This is a wonderful compiler!"
 69 :
 70 :    for nCounter := 2 to len( cString ) step 2
 71 :      cString := stuff(cString, nCounter, 1, "" )
 72 :    next
 73 :    qout()
 74 :    qout( cString )
 75 :    qout()
 76 :
 77 :    qout( stuff( stuff( "This is a wonderful compiler!", 1, 4, ;
 78 :             "CA-Clipper 5.2"), 31, 8, "program") )
 79 :
 80 :    qout()
 81 :    devout( "Press any key...." )
 82 :    inkey(0)
 83 :
 84 :    cls
 85 :
 86 :    return( NIL )
 87 :
 88 : *******************
 89 :
 90 : static function Expand( cString, cChar )
 91 :
 92 :    local nCounter    // Counter for the FOR...NEXT loop
 93 :
 94 :    DEFAULT cString TO "", ;   // Insure that the parameters
 95 :            cChar   TO " "     // are correct
 96 :
 97 :    if !empty( cString )
 98 :
 99 :      for nCounter := len( cString ) to 1 step 1
100 :        cString := stuff( cString, nCounter, 0, cChar )
101 :      next
102 :
103 :    endif
104 :
105 :    return( cString )
106 :
107 : // End of File: Memo1.prg
```

In this first program example of memos and large-string control in Clipper 5.2, the HARDCR( ), MEMOTRAN( ), STRTRAN( ), and STUFF( ) functions are used. To begin with, the variable *cString* contains a soft carriage-return character, or CHR(141). This character, with its seventh bit set high, tells MEMOEDIT( ) to attempt a reformat at that character position. (The normal carriage-return character is ASCII 13. By taking the seventh bit of a byte and toggling it on, in essence we have 2 to the seventh power, or 128, added to 13, giving us a new ASCII value of 141. Those characters with the seventh bit set high are normally used for special text formatting and as graphical characters.)

After the string is initialized on lines 13 through 15, it is displayed on line 23 and then passed to the HARDCR( ) function on line 28. This function, and MEMOTRAN( ) as well, will manipulate the variable passed to it. It is as if the strings are passed by reference because the functions will manipulate and modify the strings according to the options specified in the parameters passed to the functions. Here, the HARDCR( ) function in line 28 will remove all CHR(141) characters and replace them with CHR(13)—the "hard" carriage-return character. After this is displayed, a call to the MEMOTRAN( ) function is made on line 33. This function replaces the double-character combinations (either hard or soft carriage return plus line-feed character patterns) globally with single-character values. The MEMOTRAN( ) function is the same as the following nested function call:

```
cVar := strtran( strtran( cString, chr(13)+chr(10), " " ), chr(141)+chr(10), " " )
```

The MEMOTRAN( ) function can be seen again on line 49, this time working with the second character parameter, which is the hard carriage-return character replacement. Finally on line 53, the STRTRAN( ) function is used to globally replace the single character "t" with "(T)" in the variable *cString*. This function can produce very powerful results, and will be looked at in depth in the next programming example.

On line 62, the user-defined function Expand( ) uses the STUFF( ) function to stuff a blank character between each character in the variable *cString*. Next, on line 71, the STUFF( ) function is used to delete characters, similar to the STRTRAN( ) function. The difference is that the STRTRAN( ) function will globally replace a character in a string with another character (or a NULL). However, the STUFF( ) function will work on only the particular characters that are specified within a particular range of text. Additionally, the STUFF( ) function deletes characters first, then replaces them with the new characters. On lines 70 through 72, every second character in the variable *cString* is removed. Finally, an actual delete-and-replace scenario has been built in this multiple function call on lines 77 and 78. Taking the inner-most function first, the STUFF( ) function will replace the first four characters of the string "This is a wonderful compiler!" with the string "CA-Clipper 5.2" The value of the first call to STUFF( ) will be "CA-Clipper 5.2 is a wonderful compiler!" This string is then passed to the outside STUFF( ) function, which deletes eight characters starting from the 31st position and replaces them with the string "program." The ending value of this double function call will be "CA-Clipper 5.2 is a wonderful program!"

As previously mentioned, the STRTRAN( ) function can be used in unique ways. For example, the function can determine the number of desired elements in a string, provided the delimiting characters are specified. To show this better, here is an example:

```
 1 : * File:     Memo2.prg
 2 :
 3 : #include "PTValue.ch"    // Header files also found in the
 4 : #include "PTFuncs.ch"    // CA-Clipper 5.2 Power Tools Book
 5 :
 6 : #xtranslate NUMBERSTR(<numb>) => alltrim(transform(<numb>, "9999"))
 7 :
 8 : function Main()
 9 :
10 :    local cString := "Chart of Accounts/"  // Init the variable
11 :    local nValue                           // Number of items in string
12 :    local nWords                           // Individual words
13 :
14 :    cls
15 :
16 :    qout( "Here is the string: " )
17 :
18 :    cString += "Journal Entry/Reports/Utilities"
19 :
20 :    qout()             // This is the ? command
21 :    qout( cString )
```

```
22 :      qout()
23 :      qout()
24 :
25 :      nValue := OCCURRENCE( "/", cString )      // Pseudofunction!
26 :
27 :      qout( "There are " + NUMBERSTR( nValue ) + " occurrences of " + ;
28 :            "the '/' character " )
29 :      qout( "        which means that there are " + NUMBERSTR( nValue+1 ) + ;
30 :            " menu items." )
31 :
32 :      qout()
33 :      qout( "Press any key..." )
34 :      inkey(0)
35 :
36 :      cls
37 :
38 :      if file( "HELPTXT3.TXT" )
39 :         cString := strtran( memotran( memoread ( "HELPTXT3.TXT"), ;
40 :                   " ", " "), "  ", " " )
41 :         qout( cString )
42 :         qout()
43 :
44 :         nWords := OCCURRENCE( " ", cString ) + 1
45 :
46 :         qout( "There are " + NUMBERSTR( nWords ) + " words in " + ;
47 :               "HELPTXT3.TXT." )
48 :      endif
49 :
50 :      return( NIL )
51 :
52 : // End of File: Memo2.prg
```

The OCCURRENCE( ) pseudofunction on line 25 is simply a preprocessor translation found in the include file PTFUNCS.CH. It is defined as follows:

```
#xtranslate OCCURRENCE( <a>, <b> ) => ;
 ( INT(LEN( <b> )-LEN(STRTRAN(<b>, <a>, ""))) / LEN(<a>) )
```

It takes the length of the main string, here expressed as *cString*, and weeds out all occurrences of the first string, expressed here as "/". Then the pseudofunction compares the length of the original string, *cString*, with that of the results. The difference will be the number of "occurrences" of one string in the other. If the string being sought is greater than 1, then the results must be divided by the length of the first parameter. This allows this function to be used for a variety of purposes, including calculating the number of lines in a text file, or in the case of this example program, the number of menu items in a string.

This demonstration also uses the MEMOREAD( ) function. If the file HELPTXT3.TXT can be found in the current directory (it should have been created by the MAKEDATA.PRG program found in Appendix 1), a call to the MEMOREAD( ) function is made on line 39. This function simply goes out to the disk and obtains the specified file. The return value of the function is the file represented as one large string, carriage returns included. The nested MEMOTRAN( ) function removes those extra characters and replaces them with blank spaces. If in this process there should be a double space combination, it is replaced by a single blank space by the STRTRAN( ) function. The point demonstrated in this small example is that string manipulation is easy in Clipper 5.2. It should be tackled and understood as any other Clipper topic.

# MEMOEDIT( )

## MEMOEDIT( ) BASICS

MEMOEDIT( ) has two modes, edit and view. The mode is controlled by the function's sixth parameter, a logical toggle. MEMOEDIT( ) will work on string variables as well as on memo fields. Moreover, if you apply the concept that a function's value, if it is of a character data type, can be passed to the MEMOEDIT( ) function, new possibilities unfold. To begin with, here is the basic format for calling the MEMOEDIT( ) function with the first six parameters:

```
MEMOEDIT( <cString>, <nTop>, <nLeft>, <nBottom>, <nRight>, <lEdit> )
```

In this first example, the value of <lEdit> will be a logical true (.T.), which opens the MEMOEDIT( ) window in edit mode and allows the user to enter as much text as possible. To terminate the session, press the CTRL-W keys to save the value of MEMOEDIT( ) to the prescribed variable.

```
 1 : * File:     Memo3.prg
 2 :
 3 : #include "Sirius.inc"   // Master include file for all header files
 4 :
 5 : function Main()
 6 :
 7 :    local cText
 8 :
 9 :    set( pSCOREBOARD, pOFF )
10 :    scroll()
11 :    dispbox( 2,10,20,70, pDBAR )
12 :    devpos(2,11)
13 :    devout( " Press CTRL-W to save " )
14 :
15 :    cText := memoedit( "", 3,11,19,69,pTRUE)
16 :    ShowMemo( cText )
17 :
18 :    if file("ONTAP.DB?")  // see if DBF or the DBT file is there
19 :
20 :       use Ontap new
21 :       scroll()
22 :       dispbox(5,17,17,63,pSBAR)
23 :       devpos(5,18)
24 :       devout( " Press CTRL-W to save " )
25 :
26 :       Ontap->notes := memoedit(Ontap->notes, 6,18,16,62,pTRUE)
27 :
28 :       ShowMemo( Ontap->notes )
29 :    endif
30 :
31 :    if file("HELPTXT2.TXT")
32 :
33 :       cls
34 :       dispbox(1,30,24,50,pDBAR)
35 :
36 :       memowrit( "HELPTXT2.TXT", memoedit( memoread( "HELPTXT2.TXT" ), ;
37 :                 2,31,23,49,pTRUE) )
38 :
39 :       ShowMemo( memoread( "HELPTXT2.TXT" ) )
40 :
41 :    endif
```

```
42 :
43 :    cls
44 :
45 :    VOID    // This is a RETURN(NIL) to avoid a warning!
46 :
47 : ********************
48 :
49 : static function ShowMemo( cString )
50 :
51 :    cls
52 :    qout( cString )
53 :    qout()
54 :    qout( "Press any key...." )
55 :    inkey(0)
56 :    cls
57 :    qout( hardcr( cString ) )
58 :    qout()
59 :    qout( "Press any key..." )
60 :    inkey(0)
61 :
62 : return( NIL )
63 :
64 : // End of File: Memo3.prg
```

In these three quick examples of the MEMOEDIT( ) function, the various kinds of data that can work with it should be apparent. In the first example on line 15, the variable *cText* will be assigned the value of MEMOEDIT( ) after the operation is complete. The initial value passed to the function will be a null byte. In the second example on line 26, the initial value will be a memo field from the Ontap database. Again, the value of the MEMOEDIT( ) function will be stored back to the field and, in turn, the field will be passed to the ShowMemo( ) procedure to be displayed, first with soft carriage returns present, then without them. In the final call to the MEMOEDIT( ) function on lines 36 and 37, the value of the MEMOREAD( ) function is passed to the MEMOEDIT( ) function. This function actually reads the file HELPTXT2.TXT and returns a character string of that file's contents. This is then passed to the MEMOEDIT( ) function to be edited as the user sees fit.

Next, the value of MEMOEDIT( ) is passed to the MEMOWRIT( ) function to simply write the contents of the string to the assigned file; in this case, it is the same file read by the MEMOREAD( ) function. Finally, keep in mind that in this example, the windowed area for the three MEMOEDIT( ) calls is drawn by the DISPBOX( ) function (which is the @...DOUBLE, @...TO, and @...BOX commands on lines 11, 22, and 34). The MEMOEDIT( ) function by itself does not clearly delineate the editing region.

It is a stylistic point whether to use the functions rather than the commands. It is important to know both in order to make the proper decision on when one might be used in lieu of the other, especially when working with code blocks.

In all three calls to MEMOEDIT( ), the upper right corner of the video screen has been turned off. This area, also used for the RANGE clause in a GET, is known as the SCOREBOARD area. The function call on line 9 could be replaced with the following command:

```
SET SCOREBOARD OFF
```

By doing this, if the insert key is toggled on, no "<insert>" message would clutter up the screen (especially if a border should appear in that area). Additionally, if the ESC key is pressed during editing with MEMOEDIT( ) (if the sixth parameter is set to a logical true

## Memos: Memo Fields and Large Strings 693

(.T.) value), the message "Abort Edit (Y/N)" would typically appear, requiring the user to press either letter before continuing with the application. All of this is suppressed if the scoreboard area is turned off.

Another possibility is to use the MEMOEDIT( ) function as a display routine, especially for reports that may extend beyond the 80 columns of the screen. Again, the thing to keep in mind here is the size of the report being ported in from the disk and passed to the MEMOEDIT( ) function. Although the maximum is 64K, the lower limit is still largely based on the amount of memory available for MEMOEDIT( ).

```
 1 :  * File:      Memo4.prg
 2 :
 3 :  #include "Sirius.inc"    // Sirius master include file
 4 :  #include "SET.CH"        // CA-Clipper's SET header file
 5 :
 6 :  function Main()
 7 :
 8 :     set(_SET_CONSOLE, pOFF )
 9 :     set(_SET_ALTERNATE, pON )
10 :     set(_SET_ALTFILE, "SPECIAL.TXT" )
11 :
12 :     cls
13 :     use Filenos new via "DbfNtx"
14 :
15 :     while Filenos->( recno() ) <= 100
16 :        @ maxrow(), 00 say Filenos->( recno() )
17 :        qout( Filenos->disk_no, Filenos->sub_no, Filenos->sub_name, ;
18 :              Filenos->file_name, Filenos->file_type, ;
19 :              str( Filenos->file_size ), dtoc( Filenos->file_date ), ;
20 :              Filenos->file_time )
21 :        qout()
22 :
23 :        Filenos->( dbskip() )    // This is the SKIP command
24 :     enddo
25 :
26 :     set(_SET_ALTERNATE, pOFF )
27 :     set(_SET_ALTFILE, "" )
28 :
29 :     setkey( pF10, {|| ShowMemory() } )   // SET KEY function
30 :
31 :     cls
32 :     if memory(2) > 30
33 :        dispbox(3,3,20,75,pDBAR)
34 :        devpos( 3, 5)
35 :        devout( " ESC when finished.  F10 for Memory ")
36 :        memoedit( memoread( "SPECIAL.TXT"),4,4,19,74, pFALSE,"",200)
37 :     endif
38 :     scroll()
39 :
40 :     VOID      // Terminate the function Main()
41 :
42 :  *******************
43 :
44 :  static function ShowMemory()
45 :
46 :     local cScreen  := savescreen(5,25,14,65)   // save the screen
47 :     local nRow     := row()                    // current row position
48 :     local nCol     := col()                    // current column position
49 :
50 :     dispbox(5,25,14,65,pSBAR)
```

```
51 :        // use the preprocessor combine the DEVPOS() and DEVOUT()
52 :        // functions, similar to the @...SAY command
53 :
54 :        SAY( 6,26, "   Available Memory: " + str(memory(0)) )
55 :        SAY( 7,26, "     Largest Block: " + str(memory(1)) )
56 :
57 :        // However, to save on unnecessary string copies and bloated
58 :        // memory use, the DEVOUT() function should be used in place
59 :        // of the string concatenation
60 :
61 :        devpos( 8,26 )
62 :        devout("        RUN Memory: " )
63 :        devout( memory(2) )
64 :
65 :        devpos( 10,26 )
66 :        devout( "Last ROW() position: " )
67 :        devout( nRow )
68 :
69 :        devpos(11,26)
70 :        devout("Last COL() position: ")
71 :        devout( nCol )
72 :
73 :        devpos(13,26)
74 :        devout( "Any key...")
75 :
76 :        inkey(0)
77 :        restscreen( 5,25,14,65, cScreen )
78 :        devpos( nRow, nCol )                    // just position the cursor!
79 :
80 :        VOID
81 :
82 : // End of File: Memo4.prg
```

A special elongated report is created using the Filenos database and written to a file named SPECIAL.TXT. This report consists of the first 100 records in the database, with the output being the first few fields of the database. Again, using the SET( ) function instead of the command-based syntax of the past, ALTERNATE is set ON on line 9, the CONSOLE is turned OFF on line 8, and the alternate file SPECIAL.TXT is created and opened on line 10. After closing the alternate file and setting ALTERNATE OFF on lines 26 and 27, a test is made on line 32 to see if there is enough memory to show the report. If there is, a call to MEMOREAD( ) in conjunction with MEMOEDIT( ) is made on line 36. In this particular call to MEMOEDIT( ), the sixth parameter is set to a logical false (.F.), which tells the function that this operation will be in view mode only.

The seventh parameter is for the name of the user-defined function that will handle the keystroke exceptions; none is named here.

The eighth parameter sets the line length at 200. Since this is longer than the windowed area defined by the left and right screen coordinates, the MEMOEDIT( ) function will automatically scroll horizontally as the cursor approaches the rightmost edge of the window. The MEMOEDIT( ) function automatically provides this ability to scroll if the column width specified is greater than the windowed area.

Finally, the program illustrates a SETKEY( ) function call (equivalent to the SET KEY TO command). If the F10 key is pressed while the report is displayed, a call is made to the ShowMemory( ) function. This routine simply shows the last coordinates for the cursor within the MEMOEDIT( ) as well as the amount of available memory. The cursor's positional values are used to reposition the cursor to the appropriate location on the screen once the ShowMemory( ) routine has finished its operation (line 78).

## USING THE KEYSTROKE FUNCTION FOR MEMOEDIT( )

The MEMOEDIT( ) function allows the programmer to create and define a user-defined function that will handle the keys as they are entered and processed by the function. To specify a user-defined function, simply issue the name of the function in quotation marks without the associated parentheses as the seventh parameter to MEMOEDIT( ). For example, if the keystroke-handling function is named Keys( ), the call to MEMOEDIT( ) might look something like this:

```
MEMOEDIT( cString, 1, 1, 20, 78, pTRUE, "KEYS" )
```

Since the specified function can handle all keystrokes within the MEMOEDIT( ) function, it is recommended that all SET KEY TO keys be turned off prior to the call to MEMOEDIT( ). This is to ensure stability and performance within MEMOEDIT( ) and the user-defined function. If a key evaluated within the user-defined function is programmed to perform one operation or task but has been previously assigned to perform some SET KEY TO operation, the task within the user-defined function may never be reached. The SET KEY TO condition may take over the operation and thus control MEMOEDIT( ).

It is important to note that this keystroke handling routine must be defined as a public rather than a STATIC function. A function defined as STATIC can only be seen within the routines that are contained within the source file. The sole exception is that a STATIC function can remain visible to other functions if its name is passed in a code block. But since MEMOEDIT( ) does not accept code blocks, the name of the function must be passed to the macro parser. When the name of a STATIC function is macro-expanded, Clipper will search for it within the symbol table. But because the function is STATIC, it does not generate a reference in the symbol table. Therefore, the MEMOEDIT( ) function will simply ignore the reference to the function and perform all default keystroke operations.

To fully understand the keystroke handling function, we need to break it down into two separate parts—the parameters passed to it by MEMOEDIT( ), and the value it returns to MEMOEDIT( ). First, Clipper will automatically pass three parameters to the specified function. Every time a key is pressed or MEMOEDIT( ) is at an "idle" condition, Clipper will send to the named function the *mode* of MEMOEDIT( ), the current *line* position within the MEMOEDIT( ) windowed area, and the current *column* position within the MEMOEDIT( ) area. The mode of MEMOEDIT( ), the first parameter, can take one of four values:

0    Idle MEMOEDIT( ) condition.
1    Reconfigurable or unknown keystroke (edit buffer unchanged).
2    Reconfigurable or unknown keystroke (edit buffer altered).
3    Start-up condition.

The value returned by the function tells MEMOEDIT( ) what to do. The possible values for the user-defined function are as follows:

| | |
|---|---|
| 0 | Perform the default action. |
| 1–31 | Perform the action as requested, based on the key value. |
| 32 | Ignore the key (disable). |
| 33 | Process the keystroke as data. |
| 34 | Toggle word-wrap condition. |
| 35 | Toggle scrolling state. |
| 100 | Move to the next word. |
| 101 | Move to the bottom right of the MEMOEDIT( ) window. |

To see this in action, consider the following example:

```
 1 : * File:    Memo5.prg
 2 :
 3 : #include "Sirius.inc"  // Master include file
 4 :
 5 : #xtranslate SAVEROW( <row> ) => savescreen(<row>,0,<row>,maxcol())
 6 : #xtranslate RESTROW( <row>, <temp> ) => ;
 7 :                      restscreen(<row>, 0, <row>, maxcol(), <temp>)
 8 :
 9 : function Main()
10 :
11 :    local cWord   // Initialize a variable
12 :
13 :    cls
14 :    set( pSCOREBOARD, pOFF )
15 :
16 :    dispbox(0,0,23,79,pDBAR)    // draw a border
17 :
18 :    cWord := hardcr( memoedit( "", 1,1,22,78, pTRUE,"Keys") )
19 :
20 :    cls
21 :    qqout( cWord ) // The double the ?? command!
22 :    inkey(0)
23 :
24 : return( NIL )
25 :
26 : ********************
27 :
28 : function Keys( nMode, nRow, nCol )  // This can not be a STATIC
29 :
30 :    local nRetValue  := 0           // default return value
31 :    local cTemp                     // temporary character variable
32 :    local nKey       := lastkey()   // value of LASTKEY() pressed
33 :
34 :    @ 24,00 say "Lastkey: "
35 :    @ 24,09 say nKey         picture "###"
36 :    @ 24,42 say if( readinsert(), "<ins>", "<ovr>" )
37 :    @ 24,50 say "Line: "
38 :    @ 24,56 say nRow         picture "###"
39 :    @ 24,62 say "Col: "
40 :    @ 24,67 say nCol         picture "###"
41 :    @ 24,72 say time()
42 :
43 :    if nMode == 1 .or. nMode == 2
```

```
44 :
45 :        do case
46 :        case nKey == pINS
47 :           readinsert( !readinsert() )          // This is a toggle
48 :           keyboard chr( pRIGHT_ARROW ) + ;
49 :                   chr( pLEFT_ARROW )
50 :           setcursor( if( readinsert(), 1, 3) )
51 :           nRetValue := 32
52 :
53 :        case nKey == pCTRL_END          // or CTRL_W
54 :           cTemp := SAVEROW(maxrow())    // save the last row
55 :           @ maxrow(), 0 say padr("That key is now ALT_W", maxcol()+1)
56 :           inkey(0)
57 :           RESTROW(maxrow(), cTemp)      // restore the row
58 :           nRetValue := 32
59 :
60 :        case nKey == pALT_W
61 :           cTemp := SAVEROW( maxrow() )
62 :           @ maxrow(), 0 say padr( "Ready to save? ", maxcol() + 1)
63 :           inkey(0)
64 :           RESTROW( maxrow(), cTemp )
65 :           if chr( lastkey() ) $ "Yy"    // was the questioned affirmed
66 :              nRetValue := 23
67 :           endif
68 :
69 :        endcase
70 :
71 :     endif
72 :
73 :     return( nRetValue )
74 :
75 : // End of File: Memo5.prg
```

In this example, the main thing to keep track of is the return value of the Keys( ) function, which is the user-defined function called by MEMOEDIT( ) on line 18. Every time MEMOEDIT( ) makes a call to this function, which begins on line 28, three LOCAL or "formal" parameters are passed to it. Following this are three more LOCAL variables; one is the return value for the Keys( ) function, which tells MEMOEDIT( ) what to do. This variable is named *nRetValue*, and it defaults to 0; as the table before this programming example shows, 0 tells MEMOEDIT( ) to take the default action of the key pressed. The variable *nKey*, which is assigned on line 32, will contain the ASCII value of the last key pressed. The mode of MEMOEDIT( ) is evaluated based on the case structured DO CASE statements on lines 45 through 69. In this section of code, three different values for *nKey* are evaluated if the value of the MEMOEDIT( ) mode is either a 1 or a 2. If the last key pressed was the insert key (line 46) or CTRL-W (line 60), different operations will be performed; however, the value of *nRetValue* will be 32. This disables the operation of the key within MEMOEDIT( ); in essence the key is internally ignored. The point to note here is that CTRL-W, which typically saves a memo, has been turned off. In this example, the ALT-W key, tested on line 60, actually saves the memo being worked on in MEMOEDIT( ), since the value of the *nRetValue* variable will be 23. This is in the range of key values telling MEMOEDIT( ) to perform the action as requested based on the ASCII value. Since the ASCII value 23 is CTRL-W, we have in essence reconfigured the default key sequence for saving a memo in MEMOEDIT( ) from CTRL-W to ALT-W.

## RESTRICTING THE SIZE OF MEMOEDIT( )

Because MEMOEDIT( ) is a free-form editor of sorts, there is no direct way of limiting the number of characters to be entered into the function. Counting characters, adding for normal operations and subtracting when certain keys are pressed, can be not only cumbersome to code for but awkward to maintain and slow to execute. There are some ways, however, to use MEMOEDIT( ) in conjunction with the KEYBOARD command to achieve the desired effect.

```
 1 : * File:      Memo6.prg
 2 :
 3 : #include "PTInkey.ch"     // Power Tools header file
 4 : #include "PTValue.ch"     // Power Tools header file
 5 :
 6 : function Main()
 7 :
 8 :    local nRestrict := 4
 9 :    local cString
10 :
11 :    cls
12 :
13 :    dispbox(7,20,20,60,pDBAR)
14 :
15 :    Keys(pTRUE, nRestrict)
16 :    cString := hardcr( memoedit( "", 8,21,19,59, pTRUE,"Keys"))
17 :    Keys(pFALSE)
18 :
19 :    cls
20 :    qout( cString )
21 :
22 :    return( NIL )
23 :
24 : *********************
25 :
26 : function Keys( xMode, nRow, nCol )
27 :
28 :    static nRestriction
29 :
30 :    local nKey      := lastkey()
31 :    local nRetValue := 0
32 :
33 :    if valtype( xMode ) == pLOGICAL    // a logical was passed first
34 :       if xMode                        // accept the second parameter
35 :          nRestriction := nRow
36 :       else
37 :          nRestriction := NIL
38 :       endif
39 :    else                               // this is the standard call
40 :
41 :       if !( nRestriction == NIL )     // the value has been set!
42 :          if nRow > nRestriction
43 :             keyboard replicate(chr(8), nCol) + chr( pUP_ARROW ) + ;
44 :                      chr( pEND )
45 :          endif
46 :       endif
47 :
48 :    endif
49 :
50 :    return( nRetValue )
```

```
51 :
52 : // End of File: Memo6.prg
```

Two major events are happening within this example: the MEMOEDIT( ) buffer is restricted to a specific size, and the function Keys( ) will be programmed in advance of the call by MEMOEDIT( ) and will hold the number of lines of text allowed within the MEMOEDIT( ) window. The number of lines that will be allowed is initially assigned to the variable *nRestrict*. This could have been a literal value used in the function call to Keys( ) on line 15. It also could have been a manifest constant in place of a LOCAL memory variable. In either case, the use of the Keys( ) function on lines 15 and 17 remains unchanged. To get the value of *nRestriction* into the Keys( ) function, we need to have the Keys( ) function accept parameters of different data types. Since Clipper's default method for passing parameters from MEMOEDIT( ) follow the numeric, numeric, numeric pattern, we can use this to our advantage. On line 15, the first call to Keys( ) is made, passing a logical true (.T.) as the first parameter and the value of *nRestrict* as the second. Since MEMOEDIT( ) will always pass a numeric data type as the first parameter to the Keys( ) function, this logical true (.T.) will act as a "setup" parameter, telling the function to handle the second value, the one holding the value of *nRestrict*, specially. Within the Keys( ) function on line 33, the test is made to see if the parameter *xMode* is a logical data type and if so, and if it is set to a logical true (.T.), then the static variable *nRestriction* on line 28 will be "set". Since this is a STATIC variable, it will be remembered by the Keys( ) function when it is called by the MEMOEDIT( ) function.

In case this Keys( ) function should be used elsewhere, the restriction is turned off by another call on line 17, immediately after the MEMOEDIT( ) call on line 16. This call simply passes a logical false (.F.) to the function, which is seen on line 36 as a signal to reassign the value of *nRestriction* as NIL. If the value of *nRestriction* is NIL, the logic to test for a line length on lines 41 through 46 is ignored.

The other point to this sample is the technique used for restricting MEMOEDIT( ) to a specified number of lines. As MEMOEDIT( ) calls the Keys( ) function at the conclusion of each keystroke, the value of *xMode* now is a numeric data type. This means that the value passed to *nRow* contains the row number and not the restriction number. If the current value of *nRow* is greater than the value of the statically defined variable *nRestriction*, we delete all of the characters that may have wrapped around to this line by issuing enough CHR(8)s (backspace characters) to clear the column, followed by an up arrow and one end-of-line character. This means that restricting input will remove the characters that spill over onto the unwanted line and place the cursor back on the last character of the last line (in this case that will be line 4).

The main thing to note is that you must make the windowed area in the MEMOEDIT( ) call GREATER than the number of lines you are limiting output to. If the number of rows in MEMOEDIT( ) is only equal to or less than the number of lines to which text is restricted, this technique will not work because the value of *nRow* is based on the relative window area inside of MEMOEDIT( ). If the window area is equal to or less than the value of *nRestriction*, the value of *nRow* inside of the Keys( ) function can never be greater than the value of *nRestriction*.

This technique could be modified to allow the keyboard to be stuffed with the proper characters that would place the cursor at the end of a line should the BKSP key be pressed when the value of *nCol* is a 0.

# Form( ) Function for Output

Some of the supporting functions for MEMOEDIT( ) can be helpful in formatting text for the printer, especially text that needs to be put into columns. Fortunately, Clipper 5.2 comes with a cast of supporting functions that makes this string manipulation much easier. Below is an example of a large string being formatted in a varying-sized column. The calls to MLCOUNT( ) and MEMOLINE( ) make this example work.

```
 1 : * File:      Memo7.prg
 2 :
 3 : #include "PTValue.ch"    // Header file from Power Tools
 4 : #include "PTInkey.ch"
 5 :
 6 : function Main()
 7 :
 8 :    local getlist := {}    // This is optional
 9 :    local nWidth  := 10
10 :    local cString := "Now is the time for all good men to come "
11 :
12 :    cString += "to the aid of their country regardless of the "
13 :    cString += "word-processor they happen to be using at the time "
14 :    cString += "of this demonstration."
15 :
16 :    while pTRUE
17 :       cls
18 :
19 :       @ 0,0 say  "Enter the width of the column: " get nWidth ;
20 :           valid nWidth > 9 .and. nWidth < 41
21 :       read
22 :
23 :       if lastkey() == pESC
24 :          exit
25 :       endif
26 :
27 :       @ 2,0 say "This is the way it should look: "
28 :       Form( cString, nWidth, 32 )
29 :
30 :       qout()              // The ? command for spacing
31 :       qout( "Press any key...." )
32 :       inkey(0)
33 :
34 :    enddo
35 :
36 :    while pTRUE
37 :       cls
38 :       @ 0,0 say   "Enter NEW width of the column: " get nWidth ;
39 :           valid nWidth > 9 .and. nWidth < 51
40 :       read
41 :
42 :       if lastkey() == pESC
43 :          exit
44 :       endif
45 :
46 :       @ 2,0 say "Before...-> "
47 :       Form( cString, nWidth, 12, " <- and after" )
48 :
49 :       qout()
50 :       qout( "Press any key...." )
```

```
51 :      inkey(0)
52 :
53 :    enddo
54 :
55 :    return( NIL )
56 :
57 : *********************
58 :
59 : static function Form( cString, nWide, nAnchor, cSay )
60 :
61 :    // cString    --> String to columnize
62 :    // nWide      --> Width of the column
63 :    // nAnchor    --> Beginning position of the column to work in
64 :    // cSay       --> String to say on the first line only of form()
65 :
66 :    local cPadding := space( nAnchor )
67 :    local nCounter
68 :    local nHowMany := mlcount( cString, nWide, ,pTRUE )
69 :
70 :    for nCounter := 1 to nHowMany
71 :      if !( nCounter == 1 )
72 :        qqout( cPadding )
73 :      endif
74 :
75 :      qqout( memoline( cString, nWide, nCounter, , pTRUE ) + ;
76 :             if( (cSay != NIL .and. nCounter = 1), cSay, "" ) + ;
77 :             CHR(13) + CHR(10) )
78 :    next
79 :
80 :    return( "" )
81 :
82 : // End of File: Memo7.prg
```

The object of the program is to take the large string named *cString* built on lines 10 through 14 and form columnized output. The specified column width is determined by the user on line 21; the value of *nWidth* cannot be less than 9 nor greater than 40. When evaluating ranges, avoid the less than equal and greater than equal symbols if an alternative expression may be used. In this case, the VALID expression on line 20 could have read: VALID width >= 10 .AND. width <= 40. While this may be somewhat easier to read than the expression on line 20, it is slower to execute. To Clipper, both operations take one additional step to evaluate because of the use of the equal sign. Individually, this may not seem significant; however, compounded over the lifetime of an application, the savings could be noticeable. In addition, remember that a compromise is made in performance for the sake of clarity. Clearing the screen using the CLS command, which places the cursor at the top, left corner of the screen, only to be followed by code that positions the cursor somewhere else for a display is just another example. The CA-Clipper language is riddled with these options, largely due to our xBASE approach to problem solving.

Once the column width is determined, the string and the width are passed to the Form( ) function. This function, beginning on line 59 and following, first tries to calculate the number of lines that will be printed based on the size of the *cString* variable and the value of *nWide* (line 68). The value of *nAnchor* tells the function the beginning position for the printout. The point is that the function Form( ) will return a formatted string. The first line of the string will print out immediately at the cursor position. Every line thereafter needs to be padded with enough blank spaces so that each line lines up under the initial line. The value of *nAnchor* tells the function how many spaces to pad, which is stored to a variable named *cPadding* on line 66. The MLCOUNT( ) function is used to calculate the number of lines that will be involved in the printing. The logical pTRUE on line 68 tells the MLCOUNT( ) to calculate based on a word-wrap condition; that same toggle is used in the MEMOLINE( ) function in line 75 for the MEMOLINE( ) function. Remember to keep these consistent: It does not pay to have a calculation of lines based on one condition without using the same scenario when actually printing out the string.

Once the number of lines has been stored to the LOCAL variable *nHowMany*, the FOR ... NEXT loop beginning on line 70 actually prints out the columns using the MEMOLINE( ) function to parse out each line from the variable *cString*. Note that if the function Form( ) is working from the first line, the condition on line 72 is skipped. This is the padding operation; all subsequent lines will have a padded space. The QQOUT( ) function (or the ?? command) is used in place of the QOUT( ) function (the ? command) because QOUT( ) issues a CHR(13)+CHR(10) character combination *before* printing the expression while QQOUT( ) does not.

In the second call to the Form( ) function on line 47, we pass a fourth parameter, which is a continuation string. If the parameter *cSay* on line 59 is passed a value, that string will print out after the columnized string on lines 75 through 77. This string will print out on only the first line, leaving the rest of the column to be printed out in a normal fashion. This function could be modified to accept an array as the value for *cSay*, printing out each element of the array after each columnized element is printed via the MEMOLINE( ) function. There are endless possibilities using these two functions in conjunction with one another to produce the desired effect.

## A Major Text Editor

Extending Clipper is what this language deserves. By adding direct key processing within the user-defined function called by MEMOEDIT( ) and combining that with DBSTRUCT( ), EVAL( ), DBEDIT( ), PROMPT, arrays and AEVAL( ), and even a secondary call to another MEMOEDIT( ), a powerful program editor can be built for the Clipper developer—an editor written in Clipper to understand the Clipper environment. Note that, in order for the program to execute successfully, it must be passed the name of the file to edit as a parameter when the program is executed. For example:

```
 1 : * File:      Memo8.prg
 2 :
 3 : #include "Sirius.inc"      // Major include
 4 :
 5 : #xtranslate NumberStr(<x>) => alltrim(transform(<x>, "99999"))
 6 :
 7 : function Main( cFile )
 8 :
 9 :     local cDrive      // The drive letter to work on
10 :     local cFileText   // The contents of the file edited
11 :
12 :     cls
13 :
```

```
 14 :    if cFile == NIL    // no parameter is passed
 15 :       @ maxrow(), 00 say "Filename required"
 16 :
 17 :    else
 18 :
 19 :       FileName( cFile )   // Tell the function the file name!
 20 :
 21 :       cDrive    := Drive()
 22 :       cFileText := Wp( if( !file( cFile ), "", ;
 23 :                            memoread( cFile ) ), 1, 0,23, 79 )
 24 :
 25 :       if !( lastkey() == pESC )
 26 :          memowrit( cFile, hardcr( cFileText ) )
 27 :       endif
 28 :
 29 :    endif
 30 :
 31 :    scroll()
 32 :
 33 :    return( NIL )   // just like a procedure
 34 :
 35 : *******************
 36 :
 37 : static function Wp( cText, nTop, nLeft, nBottom, nRight )
 38 :
 39 :    dispbox( nTop, nLeft, nBottom, nRight, pSBAR )
 40 :    set( pSCOREBOARD, pOFF )
 41 :
 42 :    return( memoedit( cText, nTop+1, nLeft+1, nBottom-1, ;
 43 :                      nRight-1, pTRUE, "WP_KEYS", 250) )
 44 :
 45 :    return( NIL )
 46 :
 47 : *******************
 48 :
 49 : function Wp_keys( nMode, nRow, nCol )   // Keystroke processing
 50 :
 51 :    #define pGETCOLOR   "N/W"
 52 :    #define pSAYCOLOR   "W/N"
 53 :
 54 :    static cWord := ""
 55 :
 56 :    local cInsSay                    // Saying for the INS keys
 57 :    local nRetValue := 0             // Default return value
 58 :    local nKey      := lastkey()     // ASCII key pressed
 59 :
 60 :    #ifdef pTEST
 61 :       @ maxrow(),20 say nKey
 62 :       @ maxrow(),31 say nRetValue
 63 :       @ maxrow(),42 say nMode
 64 :    #endif
 65 :
 66 :    do case
 67 :    case nMode == 0
 68 :       cInsSay := if( readinsert(), " Ins ", " Ovr ")
 69 :
 70 :       devpos( 0,0 )
 71 :       devout( FileName(), pGETCOLOR )
 72 :
 73 :       devpos(maxrow(),0)
```

```
 74 :        devout( "Row: ",                pSAYCOLOR )
 75 :        devoutpict( nRow, "###,###",    pGETCOLOR )
 76 :        devout( "   Col: ",             pSAYCOLOR )
 77 :        devoutpict( nCol, "###",        pGETCOLOR )
 78 :        devout( "   ",                  pSAYCOLOR )
 79 :        devout( cInsSay,                pGETCOLOR )
 80 :
 81 :     case nMode == 1 .or. nMode == 2
 82 :        // This processes all of the keystrokes for this editor.
 83 :        // Some of the planned features are the following:
 84 :        // Insert mode: toggles, Load files, Modify structure
 85 :        //              Call field name, Load Memory variables
 86 :
 87 :        do case
 88 :        case nKey == pINS
 89 :           setcursor( if( readinsert(!readinsert()), 1, 3 ) )
 90 :           keyboard chr(pRIGHT_ARROW) + chr(pLEFT_ARROW)
 91 :           nRetValue := 0
 92 :
 93 :        case nKey == pALT_L      // Load a file
 94 :           WpLoadFile()
 95 :
 96 :        case nKey == pALT_S      // Show files
 97 :           ShowAlias(2,1,10,25, ;
 98 :                    {|nTop, nLeft, nChoice| ;
 99 :                     ShowStru(nTop+nChoice, nLeft, nChoice)})
100 :
101 :        case nKey == pALT_M      // Modify Structure
102 :           ShowAlias(2,1,15,25, ;
103 :                    {|nTop, nLeft, nChoice| ;
104 :                       ModiStru(nTop, nLeft, nChoice)} )
105 :
106 :        case nKey == pALT_R      // Show Records
107 :           ShowAlias(2,1,10,25, ;
108 :                    {|nTop, nLeft, nChoice| ;
109 :                       ShowRecord(nTop, nLeft, nChoice)} )
110 :
111 :        case nKey == pALT_G      // Generate files
112 :           WpGenFile()
113 :
114 :        case nKey == pALT_U      // Un-use all files
115 :           WpCloseFiles()
116 :
117 :        case nKey == pALT_F      // Files on DIR
118 :           WpDirFile()
119 :
120 :        case nKey == pF1         // Help on System
121 :           WpHelp()
122 :
123 :        case nKey == pALT_W      // Save a File
124 :           nRetValue := 23
125 :
126 :        endcase
127 :
128 :     endcase
129 :
130 :     return( nRetValue )
131 :
132 : ******************
133 :
```

```
134 : static function WpLoadFile()
135 :
136 :    local cScreen   := savescreen(1,0,23,79)
137 :    local cFile     := space(13)
138 :    local getlist   := {}
139 :
140 :    PROCESS          // User-Defined Command: DO WHILE .T
141 :
142 :       dispbox( 2,1,4,78, pDBAR )
143 :       @ 3, 2 say    "Enter File Name: " get cFile ;
144 :              picture "@K XXXXXXXXXXXX"
145 :
146 :       if SSDRead(getlist)
147 :          if !file( trim( cFile ) + ".DBF" )
148 :             @ 3,40 say "Not available."
149 :          else
150 :             @ 3,40 say "File now USEd.  Any key"
151 :             inkey(0)
152 :             use (cFile) new
153 :          endif
154 :       else
155 :          exit
156 :       endif
157 :
158 :    END PROCESS      // User-Defined Command: ENDDO
159 :
160 :    restscreen(1,0,23,79, cScreen)
161 :
162 :    VOID             // Typically, return( NIL )
163 :
164 : *********************
165 :
166 : static function WpGenFile()
167 :
168 :    local cScreen := savescreen(2,1,10,78)
169 :    local getlist := {}
170 :    local cFile              // file name
171 :    local aArray
172 :    local nTempNum           // Temporary number to keep track
173 :    local nRow               // Numeric position of the row
174 :    local nCol               // Numeric position of the column
175 :    local cFName             // Contains the field name
176 :    local cFType             // Contains the field type generated
177 :    local nFLength           // Contains the field length
178 :    local nFDecimal          // Contains the field decimal
179 :
180 :    PROCESS
181 :
182 :       cFile   := space(12)       // Initialize the variable
183 :       dispbox(2, 1, 10, 78, pDBAR)
184 :
185 :       @ 3,2 say "New File: " get cFile picture "@X"
186 :
187 :       if SSDRead(getlist)
188 :
189 :          if file( trim( cFile ) + ".DBF" )
190 :             @ 3,27 say "File Exists.  Any key"
191 :          else
192 :             nTempNum := 0
193 :             nRow     := 4
```

```
194 :          nCol    := 3
195 :          aArray  := {}
196 :
197 :          PROCESS      // get field descriptors
198 :
199 :            getlist  := {}
200 :            cFName   := space(10)
201 :            cFType   := space(1)
202 :            nFLength := nFDecimal := 0
203 :
204 :            @ nRow, nCol say "Field # " + transform( ++nTempNum, "999" ) ;
205 :                    get cFName picture "@!" valid !empty( cFName )
206 :
207 :            @ nRow, col()+1 get cFType picture "!" ;
208 :                    valid ( cFType $ "MDCLN" .or. ;
209 :                            lastkey() == pUP_ARROW )
210 :
211 :            @ nRow, col()+1 get nFLength picture "####" ;
212 :                    valid nFLength > 0 ;
213 :                    when Goodfield(@nFLength, cFType)
214 :
215 :            @ nRow, col()+1 get nFDecimal picture "##" ;
216 :                    valid ( lastkey() == pUP_ARROW ) .or. ;
217 :                    if( !empty(nFDecimal), ;
218 :                        (nFDecimal + 1 < nFLength), pTRUE)
219 :
220 :          if SSDRead(getlist)
221 :            devpos(nRow, nCol)
222 :            devout( "Field # " )
223 :            devoutpict( nTempNum, "999" )
224 :            devout( " " + cFName + " " )
225 :            devout( cFType + " " )
226 :            devoutpict( nFLength, "9999" )
227 :            devoutpict( nFDecimal, "99")
228 :
229 :            aadd( aArray, {cFName, cFType, nFLength, nFDecimal} )
230 :
231 :            if ++nRow > 9
232 :              nRow := 4
233 :              if (nCol += 36) > 70
234 :                inkey(0)
235 :                scroll( 4, 3, 9, 77)   // clear the area
236 :                nCol := 3
237 :              endif
238 :            endif
239 :
240 :          else
241 :
242 :            if !empty( aArray )   // There are elements
243 :              if YesNo(3,27, "Generate the File? ")
244 :                dbcreate( trim( cFile ), aArray )
245 :                ReadKill()
246 :                getlist := {}
247 :              endif
248 :              exit
249 :            endif
250 :
251 :          endif
252 :
253 :          END PROCESS
```

```
254 :
255 :         endif
256 :      else
257 :         exit
258 :      endif
259 :
260 :   END PROCESS
261 :
262 :   restscreen(2,1,10,78, cScreen)
263 :
264 :   return( NIL )
265 :
266 : *********************
267 :
268 : static function Showalias( nTop,      ; // top row for window
269 :                            nLeft,    ; // left column for window
270 :                            nBottom,  ; // bottom row for window
271 :                            nRight,   ; // right column for window
272 :                            bBlock )
273 :
274 : // block    --> the code block for additional operations should
275 : //              an alias area be picked.
276 :
277 :   local nCounter
278 :   local cScreen := savescreen(nTop, nLeft, nBottom, nRight)
279 :   local nChoice := 1
280 :   local aArray  := {}
281 :
282 :   for nCounter := 1 to 50
283 :      if !empty( alias(nCounter) )
284 :         aadd(aArray, alias(nCounter) )
285 :      endif
286 :   next
287 :
288 :   if !empty( aArray )
289 :      dispbox(nTop, nLeft, nBottom, nRight, pDBAR)
290 :
291 :      while !empty( nChoice )
292 :        nChoice := achoice(nTop+1, nLeft+1, nBottom-1, ;
293 :                           nRight-1, aArray)  // select an area
294 :        if !empty( nChoice ) .and. bBlock != NIL    // if selection
295 :
296 :           nChoice := &( alias(nChoice) )->( ;
297 :                      eval( bBlock, nTop, nLeft, nChoice ) )
298 :        endif
299 :      enddo
300 :
301 :   endif
302 :
303 :   restscreen(nTop, nLeft, nBottom, nRight, cScreen)
304 :
305 :   return( nChoice )
306 :
307 : *********************
308 :
309 : static function ShowStru( nTop,    ; // top row coordinate
310 :                           nLeft,   ; // top col coordinate
311 :                           nChoice  ; // value of CHOICE from func()
312 :                         )
313 :
```

```
314 :      local nStarting := 0
315 :      local cScreen    := savescreen(nTop, nLeft+2, nTop+16, 33)
316 :      local bBlock
317 :
318 :      dispbox(nTop, nLeft+2, nTop+16, 33, pDBAR)
319 :      devpos(nTop, 19 )
320 :      devout( " [ " )
321 :      devout( alias() )
322 :      devout( " ] ")
323 :
324 :      bBlock := {|aField| padr(aField[1], 12) + aField[2] + ;
325 :                          transform(aField[3], " 9999") + ;
326 :                          transform(aField[4], "99") }
327 :
328 :      aeval( dbstruct(), {|aField| DispItem( aField, nTop+1, 4, ;
329 :                         nTop+15, 32, bBlock, empty(nStarting++))} )
330 :
331 :      devpos(nTop+16, nLeft+3)
332 :      devout( " Finished ")
333 :      inkey(0)
334 :      restscreen(nTop, 3, nTop+16, 33, cScreen)
335 :
336 :      return( nChoice )
337 :
338 : *********************
339 :
340 : static function ModiStru( nRow, ;    // row coordinate of area
341 :                           nCol, ;    // column coordinate of area
342 :                           nChoice ;  // numeric value of CHOICE
343 :                         )
344 :
345 :      local cScreen    := savescreen( nRow, nCol, nRow + 15, nCol + 29 )
346 :      local nRetValue := nChoice
347 :      local lModified := pFALSE
348 :      local aArray     := {}
349 :      local getlist    := {}
350 :      local nExtra
351 :      local cFName         // Name of the field
352 :      local cFType         // Data type of the field
353 :      local nFLength       // Length of the field
354 :      local nFDecimal      // Number of decimals for the field
355 :      local cFileName
356 :      local nCounter
357 :
358 :      aeval( dbstruct(), {|aFields| aadd(aArray, ;
359 :                         padr(aFields[1], 12) + aFields[2] + ;
360 :                             transform(aFields[3], " 9999") + ;
361 :                             transform(aFields[4], " 99")) } )
362 :
363 :      while !empty( nChoice )
364 :        dispbox( nRow, nCol, nRow + 15, nCol + 29, pDBAR )
365 :        devpos( nRow, nCol+2 )
366 :        devout( " [ " + alias() + " ] " )
367 :
368 :        nExtra := 0
369 :        nChoice := achoice( nRow+1, nCol+1, nRow+12, nCol+28, ;
370 :                           aArray,, "ModiKeys", nChoice)
371 :
372 :        if !empty( nChoice )
373 :
```

```
374 :       do case
375 :       case  lastkey() == pDOWN_ARROW
376 :         // wants to add a new item to the list...
377 :         if YesNo(nRow+14, nCol+1, " New Field?" )
378 :           nExtra := 1
379 :         endif
380 :
381 :       case lastkey() == pENTER
382 :         // wants to modify a field value...
383 :         if YesNo(nRow+14, nCol+1, " Modify Field? " )
384 :           nExtra := 2
385 :         endif
386 :
387 :       case lastkey() == pDEL
388 :         if YesNo(nRow+14, nCol+1, "Delete this field?" )
389 :           lModified := pTRUE
390 :           adel(aArray, nChoice)
391 :           asize(aArray, len(aArray)-1)
392 :         endif
393 :
394 :       endcase
395 :
396 :       if !empty( nExtra )
397 :         if nExtra == 1
398 :           cFName := space(10)
399 :           cFType := space(1)
400 :           nFLength  := nFDecimal := 0
401 :         else
402 :           cFName     := padr( dbstruct()[nChoice, 1],10)
403 :           cFType     :=       dbstruct()[nChoice, 2]
404 :           nFLength   :=       dbstruct()[nChoice, 3]
405 :           nFDecimal  :=       dbstruct()[nChoice, 4]
406 :         endif
407 :
408 :         @ nRow+14, nCol+1  say "=> "
409 :         @ nRow+14, col()+1 get cFName picture "!!!!!!!!!!" ;
410 :                        valid !empty( cFName )
411 :         @ nRow+14, col()+1 get cFType picture "!" ;
412 :                        valid (cFType $ "MDCLN" .or. ;
413 :                               lastkey() == pUP_ARROW )
414 :         @ nRow+14, col()+1 get nFLength picture "####" ;
415 :                        valid nFLength > 0    ;
416 :                        when Goodfield(@nFLength, cFType)
417 :         @ nRow+14, col()+1 get fdec PICT "##" ;
418 :                        valid ( lastkey() == pUP_ARROW ) .OR. ;
419 :                              if(!empty(nFDecimal), ;
420 :                                 (nFDecimal + 1 < nFLength), ;
421 :                                 pTRUE)
422 :
423 :         if SSDRead(getlist)
424 :           if nExtra == 1
425 :             aadd(aArray, padr(cFName, 12) + cFType + ;
426 :                      transform(nFLength, " 9999") + ;
427 :                      transform(nFDecimal, " 99"))
428 :           else
429 :             aArray[nChoice] := padr(cFName, 12) + cFType + ;
430 :                         transform(nFLength, " 9999") + ;
431 :                         transform(nFDecimal, " 99")
432 :           endif
433 :           lModified := pTRUE
```

```
434 :            endif
435 :
436 :         endif
437 :
438 :      else
439 :        if lModified
440 :          if YesNo(nRow+14, nCol+1, "Alter Structure?")
441 :             cFileName := alias()
442 :             frename( cFileName + ".DBF", cFileName + ".$$$" )
443 :             dbcreate( cFileName+ ".DBF", ModiArray( aArray ) )
444 :             append from ( cFileName + ".$$$")
445 :             ferase( cFileName + ".$$$" )
446 :
447 :             nRetValue := 0
448 :
449 :             for nCounter := 1 to 20
450 :                &( alias(nCounter) )->( dbclosearea() )   // close the area!
451 :             next
452 :             select(1)
453 :             @ nRow+14, nCol+1 say "All Files Closed!  Any key."
454 :             inkey(0)
455 :          endif
456 :        endif
457 :
458 :      endif
459 :
460 :   enddo
461 :
462 :   restscreen( nRow, nCol, nRow + 15, nCol + 29, cScreen )
463 :
464 :   return( nRetValue )
465 :
466 : *******************
467 :
468 : function ModiKeys( nMode, nItem, nWRow )
469 :
470 :   local nRetValue := 2
471 :   local nKey      := lastkey()
472 :
473 :   do case
474 :   case nMode == 3
475 :     do case
476 :     case nKey == pESC
477 :        nRetValue := 0
478 :     case nKey == pENTER
479 :        nRetValue := 1
480 :     case nKey == pDEL
481 :        nRetValue := 1
482 :     endcase
483 :
484 :   case nMode == 2
485 :     nRetValue := 1
486 :
487 :   endcase
488 :
489 :   return( nRetValue )
490 :
491 : *******************
492 :
493 : function ModiArray( aArray )   // this is strictly for ModiStru()
```

```
494 :
495 :    local aRetValue := {}
496 :
497 :    aeval( aArray, {|aItem| aadd( aRetValue, ;
498 :                         {left(aItem, 10), substr(aItem, 13, 1), ;
499 :                          val(substr(aItem, 14, 5)), ;
500 :                          val(substr(aItem, 19, 3))} ) } )
501 :
502 :    return( aRetValue )
503 :
504 : ********************
505 :
506 : function Goodfield( nLength,  ;   // default length of the field
507 :                     lDataType ;   // data type of the field.
508 :                   )
509 :
510 :    local lRetValue := pTRUE
511 :
512 :    do case
513 :    case lDataType  == pMEMO
514 :      nLength      := 10
515 :      lRetValue := pFALSE
516 :
517 :    case lDataType == pLOGICAL
518 :      nLength      := 1
519 :      lRetValue := pFALSE
520 :
521 :    case lDataType == pDATE
522 :      nLength      := 8
523 :      lRetValue := pFALSE
524 :
525 :    endcase
526 :
527 :    return( lRetValue )
528 :
529 : // The following routines all deal with displaying the directory
530 : // on the screen while editing.  The hot key was ALT_F for FILES.
531 :
532 : ********************
533 :
534 : static function WpDirFile() // called from WP_keys()
535 :
536 :    local screen := savescreen(2,1,22,78)
537 :
538 :    dispbox(2,1,22,78,pDBAR)
539 :    files( 4, 1, 21, 77, Drive() + curdir() )
540 :    restscreen(2,1,22,78,screen)
541 :
542 :    return( NIL )
543 :
544 : ********************
545 :
546 : static function Files( nTop, nLeft, nBottom, nRight, cWhere )
547 :
548 :    local nStarting   := 0
549 :    local getlist     := {}
550 :    local cSkeleton   := space(13)
551 :    local bBlock      := { |aItem| padr(aItem[1], 14) + ;
552 :                         transform(aItem[2], ;
553 :                         "9,999,999") + " " + dtoc( aItem[3] ) }
```

```
554 :
555 :
556 :     @ nTop-1, nLeft+1 say "Pattern:" get cSkeleton
557 :
558 :     if SSDRead(getlist)
559 :        devpos( nTop1, nLeft+1 )
560 :        devout( "Files of: " )
561 :        devout( cWhere )
562 :        devout( "\" )
563 :        devout( trim( cSkeleton ) )
564 :
565 :        aeval( directory( cWhere + "\" + trim(cSkeleton)), ;
566 :              {|aFile| Dispitem(aFile, nTop, nLeft, nBottom, nRight, ;
567 :                     bBlock, empty( nStarting++ ) )} )
568 :
569 :        @ nTop-1, 50 say "Finished..."
570 :        inkey(0)
571 :
572 :     endif
573 :
574 :     return( NIL )
575 :
576 : ******************
577 :
578 : static procedure WpHelp()
579 :
580 :     local cScreen := savescreen(2, 2,6,19)
581 :     local nOption := 1
582 :
583 :     dispbox( 2,2,6,19, pDBAR )
584 :
585 :     PROCESS
586 :
587 :        @ 3,3 prompt "Keystrokes       "
588 :        @ 4,3 prompt "General Help     "
589 :        @ 5,3 prompt "Available Memory"
590 :        menu to nOption
591 :
592 :        if !HelpText( nOption )
593 :           exit
594 :        endif
595 :
596 :     END PROCESS
597 :
598 :     restscreen( 2, 2,6,19, cScreen )
599 :
600 : ******************
601 :
602 : static function HelpText( nChoice )
603 :
604 :     local cText       := ""
605 :     local lRetValue := ( !empty(nChoice) )
606 :
607 :     do case
608 :     case nChoice == 1
609 :        cText += "F1    -> Help System"        + pCRLF
610 :        cText += "INS   -> Toggle Insert"      + pCRLF
611 :        cText += "ALT X -> Save and Exit"      + pCRLF
612 :        cText += "ALT L -> Load a Database"    + pCRLF
613 :        cText += "ALT S -> Show Files in Use"  + pCRLF
```

```
614 :      cText += "ALT G -> Generate a Database" + pCRLF
615 :      cText += "ALT M -> Modify a Database"   + pCRLF
616 :      cText += "ALT F -> Directory of Files"  + pCRLF
617 :      cText += "ALT U -> Unuse files in use"  + pCRLF
618 :      cText += "ALT R -> Show Records"        + pCRLF
619 :      cText += "ALT W -> Save File"
620 :
621 :   case nChoice == 2
622 :      cText += "This utility is designed to simply "
623 :      cText += "allow some general program editing "
624 :      cText += "to the specified file from DOS.  It "
625 :      cText += "may be expanded upon to provide more "
626 :      cText += "power, which may be useful in the "
627 :      cText += "development of an application in "
628 :      cText += "CA-Clipper 5.2."
629 :
630 :   case nChoice == 3
631 :      cText += "Available space for character" + pCRLF
632 :      cText += "         values: "
633 :      cText += NumberStr( memory(0) ) + pCRLF
634 :      cText += "Largest contiguous block for" + pCRLF
635 :      cText += "         character value: "
636 :      cText += NumberStr( memory(1) ) + pCRLF
637 :      cText += "Area for a RUN command: "
638 :      cText += NumberStr( memory(2) )
639 :
640 :   endcase
641 :
642 :   if lRetValue
643 :      Showtext(3, 20, 15, 60, cText )
644 :   endif
645 :
646 :   return( lRetValue )
647 :
648 : *******************
649 :
650 : static procedure WpCloseFiles()
651 :
652 :   // This is used to quickly close all of the databases in
653 :   // use and to start with a CLEAN slate.
654 :
655 :   local nCounter      // FOR ... NEXT counter
656 :   local cTemp         // screen image of row
657 :
658 :   for nCounter := 1 to 20
659 :      &( alias(nCounter) )->( dbclosearea() )
660 :   next
661 :
662 :   select(1)
663 :
664 :   cTemp := savescreen(maxrow(), 0, maxrow(), maxcol())
665 :
666 :   scroll(maxrow(), 0, maxrow(), maxcol() )
667 :   @ maxrow(),00 say "All Files Closed.  Any key..."
668 :   inkey(0)
669 :
670 :   restscreen(maxrow(), 0, maxrow(), maxcol(), cTemp )
671 :
672 : *******************
673 :
```

```
674 : function ShowRecord( nRow, nColumn, nChoice )
675 :
676 :    local cScreen := savescreen( nRow, nColumn, nRow+17, nColumn+50 )
677 :
678 :    dispbox( nRow, nColumn, nRow+17, nColumn+50, pSBAR )
679 :
680 :    @ nRow, nColumn+2 say " [ " + alias() + " ] "
681 :
682 :    if empty( lastrec() )
683 :      @ nRow+15, nColumn+1 say "No Records in database.  Any key..."
684 :      inkey(0)
685 :
686 :    else
687 :      CLEARESC()    // clear the keyboard buffer and remove LASTKEY()
688 :      dbedit( nRow+1, nColumn+1, nRow+16, nColumn+49 )
689 :
690 :    endif
691 :
692 :    restscreen( nRow, nColumn, nRow+17, nColumn+50, cScreen )
693 :
694 :    return( nChoice )
695 :
696 : // The following routines/functions are generic functions that may
697 : // be used for other purposes and utilities
698 :
699 : *********************
700 :
701 : function SSDRead(getlist)    // Sirius Software Develop's READ
702 :
703 :    local nOldCursor := setcursor(3)   // Large, full cursor
704 :
705 :    read
706 :    setcursor( nOldCursor )
707 :    return( !(lastkey() == pESC) )
708 :
709 : *********************
710 :
711 : static function Drive()
712 :
713 :    local cRetValue := "C:"
714 :
715 :    if memory(2) > 40
716 :      run vol > vfile.$$$
717 :      cRetValue := substr( memoread( "vfile.$$$" ), 20, 1) + ":\"
718 :      ferase( "vfile.$$$" )
719 :    endif
720 :
721 :    return( cRetValue )
722 :
723 : *********************
724 :
725 : function Dispitem( aData, nTop, nLeft, nBottom, nRight, ;
726 :                   bBlock, lAtTop )
727 :
728 :    local cScreen
729 :
730 :    static nCol
731 :    static nRow
732 :    static nSkipLen
733 :
```

```
734 :    if nSkipLen == NIL    // Not initialized yet!
735 :       nSkipLen := len( eval(bBlock, aData) ) + 2
736 :    endif
737 :
738 :    if nCol == NIL .or. lAtTop
739 :       nCol := nLeft + 2
740 :       nRow := nTop
741 :    endif
742 :
743 :    if nRow > nBottom
744 :       nRow := nTop
745 :       nCol += nSkipLen
746 :    endif
747 :
748 :    if nCol > nRight - nSkipLen
749 :       cScreen := savescreen( nBottom+1, nLeft+2, nBottom+1, nLeft+14 )
750 :       @ nBottom+1, nLeft+2 say " Any key... "
751 :       inkey(0)
752 :       restscreen( nBottom+1, nLeft+2, nBottom+1, nLeft+14, cScreen)
753 :       scroll( nTop+1, nLeft+2, nBottom, nRight-1)
754 :       nRow := nTop
755 :       nCol := nLeft + 2
756 :    endif
757 :
758 :    @  nRow++, nCol say eval( bBlock, aData )
759 :
760 :    return( pTRUE )
761 :
762 : *********************
763 :
764 : function YesNo( nRow, nCol, cSaying )
765 :
766 :    local lRetValue
767 :
768 :    @ nRow, nCol say cSaying
769 :
770 :    PROCESS
771 :
772 :       while !( chr(inkey(0)) $ "YyNn" )
773 :       enddo
774 :
775 :       lRetValue := chr(lastkey())$"Yy"
776 :
777 :       @ nRow, nCol + len(cSaying)+1 ;
778 :             say if( lRetValue, "Yes", "No " )
779 :
780 :       if inkey(0) == pENTER
781 :          exit
782 :       else
783 :          keyboard chr(lastkey())
784 :       endif
785 :
786 :    END PROCESS
787 :
788 :    @ nRow, nCol say space( len(cSaying) + 4)
789 :
790 :    return( lRetValue )
791 :
792 : ******************
793 :
```

```
794 :  procedure Showtext( nTop, nLeft, nBottom, nRight, cText, cKeys )
795 :
796 :     local cScreen := savescreen(nTop, nLeft, nBottom, nRight)
797 :
798 :     DEFAULT cKeys TO ""
799 :
800 :     dispbox(nTop, nLeft, nBottom, nRight, pDBAR)
801 :
802 :     @ nBottom, nLeft+2 say " Esc to Exit "
803 :
804 :     memoedit( cText, nTop+1, nLeft+1, nBottom-1, nRight-1,pFALSE, cKeys)
805 :     restscreen(nTop, nLeft, nBottom, nRight, cScreen)
806 :
807 :  *******************
808 :
809 :  static function FileName(cFile)
810 :
811 :     // This function will keep the name of file name for other
812 :     // purposes.
813 :
814 :     static cFIleName
815 :
816 :     if !( cFile == NIL )     // the file name was passed
817 :        cFileName := cFile
818 :     endif
819 :
820 :     return( cFileName )
821 :
822 :  // End of File: Memo8.prg
```

In essence, this program makes extended use of the ability to program the user-defined function called by the MEMOEDIT( ) nestled in the Wp( ) function on line 37. All operations are handled in the Wp_keys( ) function passed to the MEMOEDIT( ) function on line 43 and defined on lines 49 and following. Several operations take place in this area of the code. Take a few minutes to go over each keystroke operation and coding possibility.

On lines 97, 102, and 107, the essence of Clipper 5.2 comes through. In these three lines of code, three calls to the ShowAlias( ) function are made; however, on each of those lines, the fifth parameter is a code block. This code block tells the ShowAlias( ) function what to do; it is a user-defined equivalent of DBEVAL( ). The power of Clipper 5.2 lies in the fact that the parameter, in this case the code block, tells ShowAlias( ) what to do. Without the code block, it is a very dull and dry function: In the windowed area on the screen, ShowAlias( ) will simply show the alias names of the work areas. However, in one case, if an area is selected, the database structure for that work area can be shown (line 98); in another case, the structure can be modified (line 103); and in the final call to ShowAlias( ), the records in the database can be seen (line 103).

Going one step farther: You can even have MEMOEDIT( ) work within MEMOEDIT( ), as in the case of the help text displayed when the HelpText( ) function on line 602 is called. This shows the extended power and the possibilities of the MEMOEDIT( ) function.

## Summary

Many other possibilities have not been touched on. For example, the various string functions, combined with the array functions, could be used to generate three-across labels without skipping three records at a time. The screen attribute bytes could be parsed out and used for screen shots for documentation or for the error system. All of these possibilities are discussed in the book *The Steve Straley Seminars: Clipper 5.0*. Memos, strings, and the functions that support these two items stretch the language to handle any demand made by a user, add punch to an application, and give the creative flexibility to consider other utility-based operations. MEMOEDIT( ) is just one function in the Clipper arsenal, but the fundamental question of "what if" that this function may raise should open the door to possibilities in other areas as well.

# 12

# *Database Management*

Clipper is in part a database management system. Manipulating data within the Clipper language is fundamental to application development, and special consideration of a few concepts is required. Within the Clipper environment, several functions and commands address these issues.

Setting up a database is always the most difficult aspect of an application. If the database is not properly created in terms of fields and indexes, the application will not work properly. When you set up a database, keep this concept in mind: Program for change. The end-user always wants a field name changed, a data type altered, an index key added or subtracted, a field lengthened.

One technique in application development is to build from the known reports (or planned reports). The proper database cannot be built without knowing what the output should look like; the proper data entry screen cannot be planned until the database has been built. While programming may be either modular or linear, application development comes from a desire to get at information, to see information in a variety of ways. Without knowing how information is related, how the needs of the end-user must be expressed on the screen or on a piece of paper, planning the structure of the database and the index keys becomes futile.

## The Files

Three files are related to database management in the standard Clipper database management system. They have .DBF, .DBT, and .NTX file extensions. The .DBT file will have the same root name as the .DBF file; it contains the memo field information for the .DBF file.

### THE DATABASE FILE

The database file normally has a .DBF file extension. Character fields may be up to 64K in size, and there may be up to 1024 fields in a database file. If a database file has an associated memo file (.DBT), the first byte of its file header will be 83 hex; otherwise, a normal database file will have an 03 hex byte as the initial signature byte in the file header. Currently, there is some incompatibility between Clipper and dBASE IV files, particularly because of this first header byte. Here is the basic structure of a Clipper .DBF file:

### Structure of the Header of the .DBF File

| Byte Offset | Format | Contents |
|---|---|---|
| 0 | 03 or 083h | Signature byte: 03—.DBF with no memo .DBT file or 131 (083h—.DBF with memo .DBT file |
| 1 | Year | Last update year, without century (1991 = 91) |
| 2 | 01 to 12 | Month of last update |
| 3 | 01 to 31 | Day of last update |
| 4–7 | long | Number of records |
| 8–9 | word | Location in file where data begins (START) |
| 10–11 | word | Record length (field size plus 1) |
| 12–31 | N/A | Reserved |

Field definitions begin at byte offset 32 and are 32 bytes long. The last field structure is followed by a constant 13 (0Dh) and a constant 0 (00h), indicating the end of the field structures.

### Field Definition Structure (Repeat for each field)

| Byte Offset | Format | Contents |
|---|---|---|
| 0–10 | Character | Field name (printable string; no spaces; null terminated; null padded) |
| 11 | Character | Field type (Character, Logical, Memo, Numeric, or Date) |
| 12–15 | N/A | Reserved |
| 16 | Unsigned integer | Total length, including decimal for numerics (referred to in text as LENGTH) |
| 17 | Unsigned integer | Number of decimal places |
| 18–31 | N/A | Reserved |

At offset START (defined above in the header of the file), the first data record begins. Each field is stored sequentially according to the order in the header. Before each record is a deleted flag that is either a space or an asterisk ("*"). If the deleted flag is an asterisk, the record is tagged for deletion. The field length specified in the header includes the deleted flag. Below is a brief definition of each field type, and the method of storage employed.

Character (field type = "C")
: Character fields may contain any ASCII character from 0 to 255, and are always of a fixed length (defined by LENGTH in the field structure definition). Note that the string is not null terminated. An empty character field contains all spaces (32, 20h).

Numeric (field type = "N")
: Numerics are stored as their character equivalents with the decimal included. There is no decimal character if the number of decimal places is zero. Empty numerics are padded with leading spaces, have a zero before the decimal point, and zero padding after the decimal point to the end of the field. An empty numeric of length 9 with two decimals would look like this: "     0.00".

Logical (field type = "L")
: Logical fields are stored as a single character. "T" is stored for true. All other characters are assumed to equate to a false value (though "F" is most likely to be used). An empty logical contains an "F" character.

Date (field type = "D")
: Date fields are exactly eight characters in length. A date field is stored in the format YYYYMMDD where YYYY = Year with century, MM = Month, and DD = Day. 10/20/82 would be stored as "19821020".

Memo (field type = "M")
: Memo fields are always 10 bytes in length. The 10 bytes hold a pointer to the first 512-byte block in a .DBT file that contains the memo text. The pointer is in ASCII—all spaces indicates that there is no memo text for that field.

## THE MEMO FILE

The structure of a memo file is simple. The first 512 bytes are reserved for the header of the file. The first four bytes form a 32-bit integer that indicates the number of 512-byte blocks (including the block occupied by the header) in the file. The remainder of the header in the memo file is normally filled with garbage from the free pool buffer; this may be used for internal information for an application. Following this comes 512-byte blocks containing the memo fields belonging to individual records. Clipper requires that each memo field be stored in contiguous 512-byte blocks if more than one block is required.

The Clipper memo (.DBT) file is treated as an integral part of the database (.DBF) file. For example, if the COPY TO command is used to copy a database file, the memo file is copied as well.

Memo files are organized in 512-byte blocks, the first of which is the file header. It has the following simple format:

### Header File Structure of .DBT

| Byte Offset | Format | Contents |
| --- | --- | --- |
| 0–3 | Long | Number of 512-byte blocks in the file, including the header |
| 4–511 | Unused | Reserved |

The data blocks also have a simple format: They simply contain the data, terminated by a Ctrl-Z (01Ah, 26 decimal). Memos may be up to 64K in length. If the memo field does not contain an even multiple of 512 bytes, the unused remainder of the block is padded with spaces to 512 bytes.

Although the size of the memo file header is 512 bytes, the subsequent 512-byte block is not used to store memo fields in memo files that contain records; hence, this space is unused.

The minimum size of a memo is 512 bytes, which equals one block; the number of bytes occupied by any memo is also a multiple of 512, the Clipper memo field block size. If a memo is, for example, 600 bytes long, it will take up two contiguous blocks in the memo file beyond the header (which is also 512 bytes long) and the empty 512-byte block that is adjacent to the header.

The operation of reading a memo field is simple. The numeric value stored in the .DBF file's memo field for a particular record points to the particular 512-byte block after the header at which its accompanying memo starts. Each memo is terminated with the end-of-file character, 1Ah or ASCII 26. Since memos are contiguous, everything from the beginning of this block and, if necessary, continuing into subsequent blocks will be read until Clipper encounters the end-of-file character. If a memo is edited with MEMOEDIT( ) or a similar operation, a copy of the memo is placed in memory. If the memory is expanded beyond its last free, contiguous 512-byte block, the original block pointer in the .DBF file is altered, and the memo is placed at the end of the .DBT file—the only place where a memo may grow or shrink and still be continuous.

Packing a database will remove only those records marked for deletion within the .DBF file. It will not alter the block pointer in the associated memo field and, consequently, will not "pack" the .DBT file. A Clipper utility program called DBT50.EXE may also be used to "pack" the .DBT file.

## THE INDEX FILE

Although Clipper can "link in" a variety of other index file types (a topic discussed in Chapter 13, "Indexes and RDDs"), we will focus on the standard Clipper .NTX index file. These are built on a balanced B-tree algorithm with two 1024-page buffers that keep track of the key information. The minimum size of a Clipper .NTX file is therefore 2048 bytes. A B-tree algorithm is one based on a binary search structure. Consider picking a number between 1 and 100. To find the number quickly, start at the middle (50) and ask whether the number is greater than or less than the midpoint. If the number is greater than the midpoint, the midpoint becomes the bottom range, a new midpoint is found, and the process is repeated. If the number is less than the midpoint, the midpoint becomes the top range, a new midpoint is found, and the process is again repeated. Eventually, the number will be found. If the range of numbers to be selected is from 1 to 200 rather than from 1 to 100, the binary search will have to include only one additional step—the step that places 100 as the first midpoint.

When an index is created, Clipper places the midpoint value at the top of the file so that any item either to the left or to the right of the midpoint (or seed node) can be quickly found. Keeping this value as the midpoint value at all times in the life span of an application is vital for optimum performance. If you do not have to keep the internal keys and structure in the memory of the environment (which is the method used by most interpreters), the integrity of the index file is elevated. In addition, by keeping the tree balanced at all times, even in an ADD, EDIT, or DELETE mode, the tree does not get lopsided. In some cases, a lopsided index tree will slow up traversing the database when that index is active. What once appeared to be an acceptable LOCATE or LIST command may no longer process efficiently. Rebuilding the indexes from scratch will remove this problem; however, this takes additional time and disk space. In Clipper, both integrity and optimum speed are handled automatically.

The value of the index expression (keys) and a record pointer are stored in the .NTX file. This can be seen by examining a piece of the .NTX file named TRANS.NTX, generated from the GENDATA.PRG program and shown in Figure 12.1. The account number in the Trans work area is visible, as is a pointer to the record number. The pointer is typically 5 bytes away from the end of a particular key.

One position in the header of the .NTX file tells whether or not the index file was created with SET UNIQUE ON or OFF. This byte is at decimal position 278 (if we begin counting from one from the beginning of the file); it is 00 hex if the UNIQUE flag was off when the file was created, and 01 hex for SET UNIQUE ON.

## Rules and Tips for Database Management

Do not simply issue a REINDEX command in order to rebuild an index file. This function looks at the header of the index file and attempts to rebuild it based on its ability to interpret the expression stored there. If the header of the index file is corrupted, the file will not be rebuilt and a run-time error will be generated. Always refer to the original INDEX ON command whenever rebuilding an index expression.

Be aware of the phantom record. Clipper maintains a blank record in memory that contains the structure of the database in that work area. If you skip through a database and an EOF( ) or BOF( ) condition is experienced, the phantom record will appear. To avoid this, always reposition the record pointer to either the end of the file (GO BOTTOM) or the top of the file (GO TOP).

Try to build from string indexes as much as possible. Data, including dates and numbers, are stored to the database in a string-based format. Converting this to either a number or a date on which to index is an additional step that may not be needed.

Build filters for databases that match at least the preexisting primary key of an index expression. If a filter is built that does not match the primary key of an index expression, turn off any controlling index. SEEKing the first item in a filter condition that matches an index expression is faster than issuing a GO TOP command.

724  Straley's Programming with Clipper 5.2

```
                    Browser - TRANS.NTX
 File  Hide&Seek  ClipCopy  ClipAppend  Options                  Help=F1
 0480: 00 00 00 00 8e 00 00 00 - 32 30 30 30 30 00 00      .......-200000..
 0490: 00 00 01 00 00 00 31 30 - 30 30 30 30 00 00 00 00   ......10-0000....
 04a0: 02 00 00 00 32 30 30 30 - 30 30 00 00 00 00 03 00   ....2000-00......
 04b0: 00 00 32 30 30 30 30 31 - 00 00 00 00 04 00 00 00   ..200001-.......
 04c0: 32 30 30 30 31 30 00 00 - 00 00 05 00 00 00 33 30   200010..-.....30
 04d0: 30 30 30 30 00 00 00 00 - 06 00 00 00 33 32 33 33   0000....-...3233
 04e0: 33 33 00 00 00 00 90 00 - 00 00 32 30 30 30 31 30   33.....-..200010
 04f0: 00 00 00 00 ac 00 00 00 - 32 30 30 30 31 30 00 00   ........,-200010..
 0500: 00 00 c8 00 00 00 32 30 - 30 30 31 30 00 00 00 00   ..H...20-0010....
 0510: 0a 00 00 00 36 31 30 30 - 30 30 00 00 00 0b 00      ....6100-00.....
 0520: 00 00 37 31 34 34 34 32 - 00 00 00 00 0c 00 00 00   ..714442-.......
 0530: 37 34 30 30 30 30 00 00 - 00 00 a9 00 00 00 31 30   740000..-..)...10
 0540: 30 30 30 30 00 00 00 00 - c5 00 00 00 31 30 30 30   0000....-E..1000
 0550: 30 30 00 00 00 00 42 00 - 00 00 36 31 30 30 30 30   00....B.-.610000
 0560: 00 00 00 00 44 00 00 00 - 37 34 30 30 30 30 00 00   ....D...-740000..
 0570: 00 00 56 00 00 00 32 30 - 30 30 30 30 00 00 00 00   ..V...20-0000....
 0580: 58 00 00 00 32 30 30 30 - 31 30 00 00 00 00 8f 00   X...2000-10.....
 0590: 00 00 32 30 30 30 30 31 - 00 00 00 00 c6 00 00 00   ..200001-....F...
 05a0: 32 30 30 30 30 30 00 00 - 00 00 5e 00 00 00 36 31   200000..-..^...61
 05b0: 30 30 30 30 00 00 00 00 - 60 00 00 00 37 34 30 30   0000....-`...7400
 05c0: 30 30 00 00 00 00 72 00 - 00 00 32 30 30 30 30 30   00....r.-..200000
 05d0: 00 00 00 00 74 00 00 00 - 32 30 30 30 31 30 00 00   ....t...-200010..
 05e0: 00 00 76 00 00 00 33 32 - 33 33 33 33 00 00 00 00   ..v...32-3333....
 05f0: c7 00 00 00 32 30 30 30 - 30 31 00 00 00 00 7a 00   G...2000-01....z.
 0600: 00 00 36 31 30 30 30 30 - 00 00 00 00 7c 00 00 00   ..610000-....|...
 0610: 37 34 30 30 30 30 00 00 - 00 00 1d 00 00 00 31 30   740000..-....10
 0620: 30 30 30 30 00 00 00 00 - 1e 00 00 00 32 30 30 30   0000....-...2000
 0630: 30 30 00 00 00 00 1f 00 - 00 00 32 30 30 30 30 31   00.....-..200001
 0640: 00 00 00 00 20 00 00 00 - 32 30 30 30 31 30 00 00   .... ...-200010..
 0650: 00 00 21 00 00 00 33 30 - 30 30 30 30 00 00 00 00   ..!...30-0000....
 0660: 22 00 00 00 33 32 33 33 - 33 33 00 00 00 00 91 00   "...3233-33.....
 0670: 00 00 33 30 30 30 30 30 - 00 00 00 00 ad 00 00 00   ..300000-....-...
 0680: 33 30 30 30 30 30 00 00 - 00 00 c9 00 00 00 33 30   300000..-..I...30
 0690: 30 30 30 30 00 00 00 00 - 26 00 00 00 36 31 30 30   0000....-&...6100
 06a0: 30 30 00 00 00 00 27 00 - 00 00 37 31 34 34 34 32   00....'.-..714442
```

**Figure 12.1 A hex dump of TRANS.NTX showing account numbers and pointers to the record number**

When file maintenance involves modifying field values that are contained in key expressions, the SET ORDER TO 0 command or the DBSETORDER( ) function must be issued. Particularly when multiple records containing the same key or portion of an index key are needed, this will prevent the record pointer from jumping abruptly, thus forcing the program to overlook all similar records. For example, imagine our database contains the records with the following index keys, which have been generated based on area code and telephone number:

```
212    374-9000
212    555-1212
212    582-0001
212    852-3333
212    976-1212
```

Further imagine that the controlling index is AREA_CODE + TELEPHONE, and we now want to change all 212 area codes to 718 using a DO WHILE loop within a program. When we attempt this, the first record's area code will be changed successfully. The record will be immediately repositioned with the index file, however, and the record pointer will continue to point to it. In short, the record pointer will jump, and will now point to a record with a

718 area code. Since the DO WHILE condition is now false, the loop will terminate. We would have succeeded in updating only one of our records, while we failed to update an additional four. All five records will be modified, however, if we SET ORDER TO 0 before attempting the update.

Never index from a TRIM( ) expression or from the <expC1> – <expC2> construct. If field concatenation or truncation is needed, use any expression in conjunction with PADR( ).

In designing a database application, use the concept of a master database—an extra database that maintains the unique key field values for all relations and indexes. Most developers build index keys from account numbers and/or codes that in turn relate to other child databases. For example, "order number 1" will tie to the parts-on-order database, and the order number will be the key value that ties the two together. However, while this may seem logically sound, many unnecessary restrictions are now in place. First, the integrity of the key field needs to be verified across all related databases. A change in length to any of these fields disrupts the validity of a good relation. Second, the order entry number normally is involved with the data entry portion of the application. Giving the end user (customer) access to a key field can be hazardous, especially if the end user should want to change that field in any way. Moving the key relations away from a data entry item to an internal "pointer" is ideal. The use of a master database is discussed in depth in *Clipper 5.2 Power Tools*.

## Creating a Database File

There are two basic ways to create a database file. One is with DBU.EXE, a program on your distribution diskettes that needs to be compiled and linked. This method provides a simplistic interactive system in which you can create database structures on the fly. However, it is external to the application you are building. Some applications need to have a start-up procedure—one that actually creates all of the databases and indexes automatically. Testing to see if certain files are available and, if they are not, moving to a procedure that creates the databases is handy when you are developing "canned" software applications such as an accounting program. The second way to create a database achieves this goal by using a basic command or a function: the CREATE command and the DBCREATE( ) function.

### CREATE

The CREATE command creates a STRUCTURE EXTENDED database, which will have only four fields in it: FIELD_NAME, FIELD_TYPE, FIELD_LEN, and FIELD_DEC. Appending blank records to this database and filling in each field with the appropriate information builds the structure of a to-be-created database. Each record in this database will eventually be the field of a newly created database. Therefore, if there are 20 records in the STRUCTURE EXTENDED database, there will be 20 fields in a database created from this structure. Keep in mind when building any database that character strings in Clipper may be longer than 255 bytes. Yet, the FIELD_LEN field of the STRUCTURE EXTENDED database will only hold a number up to 255. In Clipper, the field structure of a character string larger than 255 bytes is held in both the FIELD_LEN and FIELD_DEC fields. The FIELD_LEN field is used for the modulus of 256 and the actual field length, and the

FIELD_DEC field contains the number of 256-byte units in the field length. In other words, if we wanted to create a field 300 bytes long, the FIELD_LEN field would contain 44 and the FIELD_DEC field would contain 1. This means that there is one 256-byte block plus an additional 44 bytes: (1 * 256) + 44 = 300.

Once the structure is built, the CREATE FROM command is needed to build a typical .DBF file from this STRUCTURE EXTENDED database. The CREATE FROM command takes the records in the STRUCTURE EXTENDED database and creates the fields of a new database. A word of caution: Make certain that the STRUCTURE EXTENDED database is closed before creating a new database. Once the new database is created, make sure again that the buffers in that work area are closed. One way to handle this is with the USE command. Here is an example program that builds a database but uses DBSTRUCT( ) to help show the final output.

```
 1 : // File      Dbf1.prg
 2 : // Compile   Rmake sample /dFILE:dbf1
 3 :
 4 : #include "PTValue.ch"    // Power Tools Header file of values
 5 : #include "PTVerbs.ch"    // Power Tools Header file of commands/statements
 6 :
 7 : procedure Main()
 8 :
 9 :    create Temp
10 :    use Temp
11 :
12 :    Temp->( AppendIt( "lname",   "c", 15 ) )
13 :    Temp->( AppendIt( "fname",   "c", 10 ) )
14 :    Temp->( AppendIt( "notes",   "m", 10 ) )
15 :    Temp->( AppendIt( "bdate",   "d", 8 ) )
16 :    Temp->( AppendIt( "age",     "n", 2 ) )
17 :    Temp->( AppendIt( "balance", "n", 10, 2 ) )
18 :    Temp->( AppendIt( "active",  "l", 1 ) )
19 :    Temp->( AppendIt( "picture", "c", 300 ) )
20 :
21 :    close database              // Close it before CREATing
22 :    create Newdata from Temp
23 :    close                       // Close the file
24 :    use Newdata
25 :    cls
26 :    aeval( dbstruct(), {|aFile| qout( padr(aFile[1],15), padr(aFile[2], 3), ;
27 :                                 padr(aFile[3],10), padr(aFile[4],10))})
28 :
29 :    wait
30 :    cls
31 :    dir Temp.dbf
32 :    wait
33 :    dir Newdata.*
34 :    wait
35 :    erase Temp.dbf
36 :    erase Newdata.DBF
37 :    erase Newdata.dbt
38 :    cls
39 :
40 : *********************
41 :
42 : static function AppendIt( cFieldName, cFieldType, nFieldSize, nFieldDec )
43 :
44 :    // cFieldName -- the field name to be created
45 :    // cFieldType -- the field data type
```

```
46 :    // nFieldSize -- the size of the field
47 :    // nFieldDec  -- the decimal position
48 :
49 :    local nRetValue := 0
50 :
51 :    DEFAULT nFieldDec TO 0    // default value
52 :
53 :    if !empty( alias() )
54 :       if valtype( cFieldName ) + valtype( cFieldType ) + ;
55 :                                valtype( nFieldSize ) == "CCN"
56 :          append blank
57 :
58 :          FIELD->field_name := cFieldName    // The name
59 :          FIELD->field_type := cFieldType    // The type
60 :
61 :          if nFieldSize > 255 .and. cFieldType == pCHARACTER
62 :             FIELD->field_len := int(nFieldSize % 256)
63 :             FIELD->field_dec := int(nFieldSize / 256)
64 :          else
65 :             FIELD->field_len := nFieldSize
66 :             FIELD->field_dec := nFieldDec
67 :          endif
68 :
69 :          nRetValue := recno()
70 :
71 :       endif
72 :    endif
73 :
74 :    return( nRetValue )
75 :
76 : // End of File: Dbf1.prg
```

In this example, the STRUCTURE EXTENDED database is created with the CREATE command on line 9 and is then USEd on the following line. Once used, records are added to the database. These records will eventually become fields in a database that will be created from this structure-extended database. To help place the information into the proper fields, the AppendIt( ) function takes each parameter and works within the Temp work area. Within the AppendIt( ) function beginning on line 42, the only default parameter allowed is the field decimal value stored in *nFieldDec*. Additional parameter checking could be implemented to test the value of *cFieldType* and automatically place the proper value for the field size in *nFieldSize* (e.g., "D" as a data type would always have a length of 8). On lines 61 through 67, the size of the field in *nFieldSize* is checked; if the field to be created is a character field (line 61) and the size of the field is larger than 255 bytes, the special algorithm previously described is implemented.

After all the records have been added, the Temp database is closed and a new database called Newdata is created from the structure-extended database named Temp. After the newly created database is closed and then reopened, AEVAL( ) processes the array returned from the DBSTRUCT( ) function to show that the structure of the newly created database indeed corresponds to the contents of the records added to the Temp database.

The CREATE command automatically creates a STRUCTURE EXTENDED database and allows that database to be filled with values. However, this method is extremely disk intensive—all data is passed to and from the disk drive, whether it is for the STRUCTURE EXTENDED database or the database to be created. Working from the disk drive can slow down the operation of an application.

## DBCREATE( )

The other way to create a database is with the DBCREATE( ) function. This function uses a multidimensional array built in memory to create a new database. The length of this array will be the number of fields in the database to be created. The width of this array (the number of elements in each subarray) is four: field name, field type, field length, and field decimal. Building a database structure with DBCREATE( ) is far faster than the previous method using the CREATE command. To show this in action, the DBSTRUCT( ) function is used as well in the following example.

```
 1 : // File      Dbf2.prg
 2 : // Compile   RMake sample /dFILE:dbf2
 3 :
 4 : #include "PTValue.ch"
 5 : #include "PTVerbs.ch"
 6 :
 7 : procedure Main()
 8 :
 9 :    local aTemp := {} as array
10 :
11 :    aadd( aTemp, { "lname", "c", 15, 0 } )
12 :    aadd( aTemp, { "fname", "c", 10, 0 } )
13 :    aadd( aTemp, { "notes", "m", 10, 0 } )
14 :    aadd( aTemp, { "bdate", "d", 8, 0 } )
15 :    aadd( aTemp, { "age", "n", 2, 0 } )
16 :    aadd( aTemp, { "balance", "n", 10, 2 } )
17 :    aadd( aTemp, { "active", "l", 1, 0 } )
18 :    aadd( aTemp, { "picture", "c", 300, 0 } )
19 :
20 :    dbcreate( "NEWDATA", aTemp )
21 :    use Newdata new
22 :    cls
23 :    aeval( dbstruct(), {|aFile| qout( padr(aFile[1],15), padr(aFile[2], 3), ;
24 :                              padr(aFile[3],10), padr(aFile[4],10) ) } )
25 :
26 :    wait
27 :    dir Newdata.*
28 :    wait
29 :    erase Newdata.dbf
30 :    erase Newdata.dbt
31 :    cls
32 :
33 : // End of File: Dbf2.prg
```

In this example, the structure of the database that is to be created is stored in the array called *aTemp[ ]*. This array is built dynamically through continuous AADD( ) calls beginning on line 11 and ending on line 18. The array *aTemp[ ]* is made up of individual arrays; each holds the structure of the individual fields that will make up the database when it is created. In other words, the length of the array *aTemp[ ]* will be the number of fields that database will contain; the structure of each field (the name, data type, length, and decimal position) is stored in individual arrays as well. These individual arrays are stored in the subscript elements of *aTemp[ ]* as it is being dynamically built. The array { "lname", "C", 25, 0 } is an array with a length of 4; the pointer to this array is stored in the first element of the array *aTemp[ ]*. A*Temp[ ]* becomes a multidimensional array of a database structure.

Once the array is built, the call to DBCREATE( ) is made, passing to it the name of the new database to be created and the array containing that database's eventual structure. As in the previous example, this new database is opened and a call is made to both AEVAL( ) and DBSTRUCT( ), which shows the structure of the newly created database. One thing to note in this example is that it is not necessary to USE an additional database (the STRUCTURE EXTENDED database), nor is there a need to close any other database or work area. The structure is built in memory and the file is created.

## Using a Database, Index, and Relations

Using a database, setting up index files, setting index orders, and establishing relations between them is the heart of an application. Indeed, like a human body, an application requires precise performance from all of its vital organs: database creation, database relations, underlying interface, data entry, data validation, and finally, reports. An application is like a wall made from bricks, laid on a solid foundation, one brick at a time. And like a brick wall, each brick needs straw. Without the straw, without a careful foundation, without a plan of what is to be built, one brick at a time, the wall, or the application, will crumble.

We start with the USE command. It can open a file in the current work area or in an unselected work area, it permits a file to be used exclusively or shared on a network, and it can be used to close a file in a particular work area. A database may be opened in more than one work area at the same time; however, extreme care should be taken if this is done. The database should be used only for lookup purposes, and the two work areas should never write data back to the database.

In an application, the order of data in the work area is important. In addition, the ability to look up certain pieces of data quickly is just as vital. Both are handled with an index file, which is a separate file that contains the expression on which the file is ordered. The expression used in the INDEX ON command is called the key expression and is stored in the header of the index file. The maximum length of an index expression is 250 characters. In addition, the keys within the expression must be of the same data type.

Note that in prior versions of Clipper, extra blank spaces between keys in the index expressions were removed. In Clipper 5.2 they are maintained. For example,

```
INDEX ON Clients->account + STR( RECNO() ) TO Newfile
```

The blank spaces between Clients->account and the + character and the STR( ) function, as well as the blank spaces within the STR( ) function, previously were removed before the expression was placed into the header of the index file. These blank spaces are maintained in Clipper 5.2.

When an index is created with the INDEX ON command, the record pointer is repositioned at the top of the file and the index file is active.

Once index files have been created, it is possible to open more than one index at a time. This is accomplished with the SET INDEX command. Up to 15 index files per .DBF file may be maintained (opened at the same time). This, of course, is also limited by the number of files that may be opened at any one time on a given computer. When the SET INDEX command is used, all previously open and active indexes are closed and the index listed first in the command becomes the controlling index. Consider this code extract:

```
SET INDEX TO Name, Account, City, Zip
```

Looking at the preprocessor output file, that expression is translated to the following:

```
if !.F. ; ordListClear() ; end;;
ordListAdd( "Name" ); ordListAdd( "Account"); ordListAdd( "City" );;
ordListAdd( "Zip" )
```

First, the ordListClear( ) call closes all open index files. Second, each index filename is passed to the ordListAdd( ) function, with the Name index file the first file opened and made active.

With the ADDITIVE clause in Clipper 5.2, it is now possible to open a new set of indexes using the SET INDEX TO command without closing existing indexes. Using this new feature, our previous code extract looks like this:

```
SET INDEX TO Name, Account, City, Zip ADDITIVE
```

The preprocessor translates this as follows:

```
if !.T. ; ordListClear() ; end; ordListAdd( "Name" ), ;
ordListAdd( "Account" ), ordListAdd( "City" ), ordListAdd( "Zip" )
```

Since the IF command always evaluates to a logical false (.F.), the ordListClear() function is never executed. The indexes, therefore, are simply added to the existing list of index files. The controlling index before the new SET INDEX command was issued continues to be the controlling index.

The controlling order of the indexes may be altered without reissuing a new SET INDEX command. This is done with the SET ORDER TO command. For example, if the controlling index needed to be shifted from the NAME.NTX file to the ACCOUNT.NTX file, the following command would have to be issued:

```
SET ORDER TO 2
```

The numeric parameter represents the ordinal position in which the index files were opened. Even though the Account file is now the controlling index, the NAME.NTX file is still in position 1. All operations involving a SEEK, FIND, or SET RELATION command work from the controlling index of a database or work area. In addition, setting the order of a work area to 0 (e.g., SET ORDER TO 0) sets the natural order for that database, which is in record number order. The index files are still active, although they do not control the actual order in which the database will be traversed.

Once databases are opened and indexes created and in use, setting up relations between files is critical. The concept of a relation is simple—it ties two (or more) work areas together by means of a common field or expression. For example, consider a database of customers and another of invoices. Rather than copying customer information for each invoice, only a related field is added to the invoice database. This field ties each invoice record to the original customer record that the invoice is made out against. To set up a relation between files, the SET RELATION command is used. To relate two files together, the related file must be ordered by an index file that contains the key field that defines the relation. As a record in the main (or parent) database moves, the value from a field is related to the key field of the second (or child) database. In essence, the value from the field in the first database is SEEKed in the second, thus causing the record pointer in the second database to move as the record pointer in the first moves. To get a basic understanding of this concept, here is a simple example program.

```
 1 : // File       Dbf3.prg
 2 : // Compile    Rmake sample /dFILE:dbf3
 3 :
 4 : procedure Main()
 5 :
 6 :    use Statcode new
 7 :    index on Statcode->status to Statcode
 8 :
 9 :    use Clients new         // "INDEX Clients" is the same thing!
10 :    set index to Client1
11 :
12 :    ShowHeader()
13 :    Clients->( dbeval( {|| ShowStuff()} ) )   // work on all records
14 :
15 :    wait
16 :
17 :    set relation to FIELD->status into Statcode
18 :
19 :    ShowHeader()
20 :    Clients->( dbeval( {|| ShowStuff()} ) )   // work on all records
21 :    wait
22 :    cls
23 :
24 : *******************
25 :
26 : static procedure ShowStuff
27 :
28 :    if row() > 21
29 :       scroll(3,0,22,79,1)    // Scrolls up the screen one row
30 :       devpos(21,0)           // set the cursor position
31 :    endif
32 :    qqout( chr(13) )          // Just in case, carriage return to left
33 :
34 :    qqout( padr(Clients->status, 3) )
35 :    qqout( padr(Statcode->status,3) )
36 :    qqout( padr(Statcode->descript,25) )
37 :    qqout( padr(Clients->account,20) )
38 :    qqout( padr(Clients->name,20) )
39 :
40 :    qqout( chr(10) )   // issue the line feed at end. the CR+LF
41 :                       // characters MAY be broken up.
42 :    inkey(.5) // the smallest number seen by INKEY(), will be a
43 :              // 2-digit number, e.g., .01.
44 :
45 : *******************
46 :
47 : static procedure ShowHeader
48 :
49 :    cls
50 :    devout(" Codes    Description " )
51 :    @ 1,0 say "In Files   (in Statcode)     Account         Name"
```

```
52 :    @ 2,0 say replicate( "=", maxcol() )
53 :    devpos( 3,0 )
54 :
55 : // End of File: Dbf3.prg
```

Two databases are used, with the index in the Statcode work area built on the Statcode->Status field, and the index in the Clients work area built on the Clients->Account field. On the first call to DBEVAL( ), the record pointer in the Clients work area moves down through the file without affecting the Statcode work area. Then, once that has finished, on line 17, the two databases are tied together based on the value of the status field in the Clients work area. As the record pointer in the Clients work area moves, the value in the Clients->Status field is SEEKed in the Statcode work area. This moves the file pointer automatically in the Statcode work area.

Relations between two files may also be based on the record number in the primary, or parent, database. In this case, an active index file in the child work area is not needed.

So far we have discussed instances in which a single "child" database is related to a single "parent" database. However, many applications require a one-to-many relationship, which is similar to the one-to-one relationship discussed here, except that more databases and indexes are involved. There may be up to eight child relations to a single parent database. (This does not mean that there may be only eight; multiple relations are possible, including nesting from a child database to create subsequent grandchild relations.) For a one-to-many relationship, the ADDITIVE clause can be used to define new relations while preserving the relations already in place in that work area. Be careful, however—a SET RELATION command without an ADDITIVE clause will remove any existing relations in preference to the new relation. If this is not the effect desired, the ADDITIVE clause should be used.

In addition to a relation or an index, a database can be manipulated based on the existence of a filter. A filter acts like a cloak and masks records from being seen or considered. In essence a filter creates a temporary subset of a database. This is similar to a FOR clause on some functions; or to the SET DELETED flag, which is a filter that causes only those records not marked for deletion to be viewed by the programming operation. Each work area has its own filter condition. A filter is established with the SET FILTER command. A filter expression can be stored to a memory variable and macro-expanded. This will take more processing time than working with a code block from DBEVAL( ); however, if a filter is necessary, make certain that the variable that is to be expanded in the SET FILTER command is not a LOCAL or a STATIC variable. Since there is no symbolic representation for a LOCAL or a STATIC memory variable, it cannot be macro-expanded and will cause a run-time error.

## Looking at Internal Information

When a file is opened in a work area, that work area has a name associated with it. Normally, the root name of the file that is being used is the name of the work area. This name is known as the alias. Sometimes, a work area may have an alias name that is different from the root name of the file, especially if the filename has a confusing sound and a more generic, mnemonic name is given as the name of the work area. In any event, Clipper can have up to 250 work areas open at any one time, provided the computer on which the application is running is DOS 3.3 or higher, the proper Clipper environmental switch (F) has been set, and the DOS CONFIG.SYS file has the proper values for FILES.

Each work area has a unique set of values, independent of all the other work areas. For example, each work area has a unique name known as the alias, and the ALIAS( ) function returns a different value based on which work area is being referred to. In addition, other functions have different values depending on which work area is being referred to. These functions include, but are not limited to, HEADER( ), RECNO( ), LASTREC( ), RECSIZE( ), FOUND( ), INDEXORD( ), INDEXKEY( ), DBFITLER( ), DBRSELECT( ), EOF( ), BOF( ), and, of course, ALIAS( ). In this next example, a few databases are opened along with a few indexes and relations. Each of these functions will be tested.

```
 1 : // File       Dbf4.prg
 2 : // Compile    Rmake sample /dFILE:dbf4
 3 :
 4 : #include "PTValue.ch"    // Power Tools of misc values
 5 : #include "PTVerbs.ch"    // Power Tools of commands/statements
 6 : #include "PTFuncs.ch"    // Power Tools pseudofunctions
 7 :
 8 : procedure Main()
 9 :
10 :    local nCount as int
11 :
12 :    use Statcode new
13 :    index on Statcode->status to Statcode    // The Statcode Area
14 :
15 :    use Trans new
16 :    index on Trans->adate to Tdate
17 :    set index to Tdate, Trans               // The Trans Area
18 :    set order to 2
19 :
20 :    use Clients new index Client1
21 :    set relation to FIELD->status into Statcode, FIELD->account into Trans
22 :
23 :    use Disknos new
24 :    use Filenos new
25 :
26 :    Clients->( dbseek( "1" ) )
27 :    Trans->( SETFILTER( Trans->account == Clients->account ) )
28 :    Disknos->( dbgotop(), dbskip(-1) )
29 :    Filenos->( dbgobottom(), dbskip() )
30 :    Filenos->( SETFILTER( ODD( recno() ) ) )
31 :
32 :    scroll()
33 :    @ 2,0 say replicate( "=", maxcol() )
34 :
35 :    for nCount := 1 to 12
36 :      @ nCount+2, 78 say if(len(alltrim(str(nCount)))==2, ;
37 :                            alltrim(str(nCount)), +alltrim(str(nCount)))
38 :    next
39 :
40 :    while Clients->( !eof() )
41 :      for nCount := 1 to 5
42 :        ShowThem( nCount )
43 :      next
44 :      inkey(.5)
45 :      Clients->( dbskip() )
46 :      Disknos->( dbskip() )
47 :      Filenos->( dbskip(-1) )
48 :    enddo
49 :
50 :    wait
```

```
51 :    cls
52 :    devpos (2,0)
53 :
54 :    *******************
55 :
56 : static procedure ShowThem( nArea )
57 :
58 :    #xtranslate PADITEM( <row>, <exp> ) => ;
59 :                devpos( <row>, (nArea*15)-14 ) ;;
60 :                devout( padr( <exp>, 15 ) )
61 :
62 :    #xtranslate THEITEM( <row>, <exp> ) => ;
63 :                devpos( <row>, (nArea*15)-14 ) ;;
64 :                devout( padr( if(<exp>, "True", "False"), 15 ) )
65 :
66 :    select (nArea)
67 :
68 :    PADITEM(  1, alias() )
69 :    PADITEM(  3, lastrec() )
70 :    PADITEM(  4, header() )
71 :    PADITEM(  5, recsize() )
72 :    THEITEM(  6, bof() )
73 :    THEITEM(  7, eof() )
74 :    THEITEM(  8, found() )
75 :    PADITEM(  9, dbfilter() )
76 :    PADITEM( 10, recno() )
77 :    PADITEM( 11, indexord() )
78 :    PADITEM( 12, indexkey( indexord() ) )
79 :    PADITEM( 13, dbrelation() )
80 :    PADITEM( 14, if( !empty(dbrelation()), alias(dbrselect()), "") )
81 :
82 :    @ 16, 8 say " 1 = LAST RECORD"
83 :    @ 17, 8 say " 2 = HEADER RECORD"
84 :    @ 18, 8 say " 3 = RECORD SIZE"
85 :    @ 19, 8 say " 4 = BEGINNING OF FILE"
86 :    @ 20, 8 say " 5 = END OF FILE"
87 :    @ 21, 8 say " 6 = FOUND"
88 :    @ 16,40 say " 7 = FILTER"
89 :    @ 17,40 say " 8 = CURRENT RECORD NUMBER"
90 :    @ 18,40 say " 9 = INDEX ORDER"
91 :    @ 19,40 say "10 = INDEX KEY"
92 :    @ 20,40 say "11 = DBRELATION"
93 :    @ 21,40 say "12 = IF EMPTY(DBRELATION)"
94 :
95 : // End of File: Dbf4.prg
```

In this example, five databases are used. Some have indexes built and some do not. Some have multiple indexes, index orders altered, multiple relations, and filters. Once all of the files and indexes have been opened and the relations established, filters are set in the Filenos (line 30) and the Trans (line 27) work areas, the BOF( ) and EOF( ) markers are tripped in the Disknos and Filenos work areas, and a SEEK is performed in the Clients work area, thus setting the value of FOUND( ). In the WHILE loop on lines 40 to 48, each of the five work areas is scanned when the ShowThem( ) procedure is called with the numeric value of *nCount*, a number ranging from 1 to 5 and representing the work area in use. Inside this function, the work area for *nArea* is selected and the various functions are called. The output shows that each of these functions has a different value in each work area; they are independent of one another. The preprocessor is used (lines 58 through 64) to help arrange the output in columns. Once the ShowThem( ) procedure is finished and the FOR ... NEXT loop has scanned through the first five work areas, the program sits idle for .5 second (line 44). If no key is pressed in that time, the next three operations are performed before the loop on line 41 starts all over again. Keep in mind that on the last call to the ShowThem( ) procedure, the current work area is 5; however, all three of the dbskip( ) operations will be performed in separate work areas (Clients, Disknos, and Filenos) regardless of which work area is the active one. The expression dbskip( ) is performed in the "pointed-to" work area.

## Working with the Fields

Most database functions deal with database information in general. There is a group of functions that deal with individual fields and the values within those field locations; these functions are FCOUNT( ), FIELDGET( ), FIELDPUT( ), and FIELD( ). The FIELD( ) function is a shortened version of the FIELDNAME( ) function, which is still supported in Clipper 5.2. In addition to these functions, a second group—FIELDBLOCK( ) and FIELDWBLOCK( )—deals with field values and code blocks. While these latter functions can be used on an individual basis, they have greater impact when used with the TBROWSE( ) object.

The FCOUNT( ) function is similar to LEN( ) when working with an array or to the PCOUNT( ) function when working with parameters in a procedure or function—the FCOUNT( ) function yields the number of fields in a given work area.

The FIELD( ) (or FIELDNAME( ) ) function gives the name of a field at the given ordinal position. Sometimes, in programming situations, it was necessary to do the following:

```
x = FIELDNAME( 1 )
value = &x.
* manipulate the value of VALUE
&x = value
```

In this example, the value of the function FIELDNAME( ) tells us the name of the first field. This name is then stored to the variable "x". By macro-expanding the variable we are in essence getting the value of that field for the current record. After we manipulate its value, we try to REPLACE it with the value of VALUE, which is to be stored to "&x.", the name of the first field that was macro-expanded. All of this is slow and inefficient. Macro expansions consume time and memory.

Now in Clipper 5.2 we have two new solutions that get us away from this type of programming—FIELDGET( ) and FIELDPUT( ). To get an overall perspective on these functions and their interrelationship, look at this programming example, which uses these functions along with FIELDBLOCK( ).

```
1 : // File      Dbf5.prg
2 : // Compile   RMake sample /dFILE:dbf5
3 :
4 : #include "PTValue.ch"
5 : #include "PTInkey.ch"
6 : #include "PTVerbs.ch"
7 :
8 : procedure Main()
```

```
 9 :
10 :    local nCount                as int
11 :    local aArrayFields := {}    as array // We do not want the same array pointer
12 :    local aFarFields   := {}    as array // going to both of these variables!
13 :    local nChar                 as int
14 :
15 :    cls
16 :
17 :    // The key to remember is that the array for the code block for a
18 :    // particular work area needs to be built in that work area in order to
19 :    // avoid an internal error 612.
20 :
21 :    use Filenos new index Filenos1
22 :    for nCount := 3 to 10
23 :       aadd( aFarFields, fieldblock( fieldname(nCount), select() ) )
24 :    next
25 :
26 :    use clients new
27 :    for nCount := 1 to 8
28 :       aadd( aArrayFields, fieldblock( fieldname( nCount ) ) )
29 :    next
30 :
31 :    cls
32 :    for nCount := 1 to Clients->( fcount() )
33 :       Clients->( qout( padr(fieldname(nCount),15), padr(field(nCount),15) ) )
34 :    next
35 :
36 :    wait "And now for the other work area!"
37 :
38 :    cls
39 :    for nCount := 1 to Filenos->( fcount() )
40 :       Filenos->( qout( padr(field(nCount),15), padr(fieldname(nCount),15)))
41 :    next
42 :    wait "Any key for a simple replacement!"
43 :
44 :    // Since the FIELD() and/or FIELDNAME() functions return the name of a
45 :    // field at a certain ordinal position in the database, this value is
46 :    // necessary for the FIELDGET() and FIELDPUT() functions. However, there
47 :    // are times when the name is known but not the ordinal position. In
48 :    // this case, the FIELDPUT() function is used.
49 :
50 :    cls
51 :
52 :    Filenos->( qout( fieldget(3), fieldget( fieldpos("sub_name")), ;
53 :                     "Name is =>" + field(3) ) )
54 :
55 :    Clients->( qout( fieldget(1), fieldget( fieldpos("Status") ),;
56 :                     "Name is =>" + field(1) ) )
57 :
58 :    wait "And now after a new value has been placed back..."
59 :
60 :    nChar := asc( Clients->( fieldget(1) ) )
61 :
62 :    Clients->( fieldput(1, chr(++nChar)) )
63 :    Clients->( qout( fieldget(1), fieldget( fieldpos("Status") ),;
64 :                     "Name is =>" + field(1) ) )
65 :
66 :    wait "Any key for the listings!"
67 :    cls
68 :
```

```
69 :    while !eof()
70 :       qout()
71 :       aeval( aArrayFields, {|bData| qqout( padr(eval(bData), 8 ) + chr(186))} )
72 :       skip
73 :       inkey(.5)
74 :    enddo
75 :    wait
76 :
77 :    cls
78 :
79 :    REPEAT     // User-Defined Command!
80 :       qout()
81 :       Filenos->( aeval( aFarFields, {|bData| qqout( padr( eval( bData ), ;
82 :                                               8 ) + chr(186) ) } ) )
83 :       Filenos->( dbskip() )
84 :       inkey(.1)
85 :    UNTIL Filenos->( eof() ) .or. lastkey() == pESC
86 :
87 : // End of File: Dbf5.prg
```

Two arrays are initialized as separate variables; each array is to work from a separate work area. Once the Filenos database is opened, eight code blocks (on lines 22 through 24) are created and dynamically stored to the *aFarFields[ ]* array. A similar scenario takes place for the Clients database and *aArrayFields[ ]* on lines 27 through 29. Before these two arrays are evaluated, a comparison of the FIELD( ) and FIELDNAME( ) functions is made for both work areas to ensure that both functions return identical results. The extended use of alias pointers for the work areas is used throughout this example.

On lines 52 through 64, the FIELDGET( ) and FIELDPUT( ) functions are used. When working with arrays, specifically with data entry screens and databases, a one-to-one relationship is made between the subscript position of an array element and the ordinal position of a field in a database. Where the value of 1 is used on the FIELDGET( ) and FIELDPUT( ) functions on lines 63 and 64, this could just as easily have been a variable containing a value or a subscript position in an array. Generic data entry routines can be quickly and easily programmed without regard to the name of the field, just using its ordinal position. The counterpart to the FIELD( ) function (which yields the name of a field based on the ordinal position of that field) is the function FIELDPOS( ); this function returns the ordinal position of a field based on its name.

Lines 69 through 74 traverse the database in a conventional way using the AEVAL( ) function to process each of the code blocks within the *aArrayFields[ ]* array and to evaluate them with the EVAL( ) function. The results of the evaluation, or the actual field values, are then displayed to the screen. For this array, code blocks for only eight fields were obtained; therefore, only the values of each record for those eight fields are displayed to the screen. On the next loop—which is the same type of loop except that the exit condition is evaluated at the bottom of the REPEAT loop (this is a user-defined command)—the same traversing and evaluating of field values takes place, but this time in the Filenos work area. In both of these cases, the code blocks used to display the field values are created with the FIELD-BLOCK( ) function. Briefly, these are known as GET/SET code blocks; alternately, they might be called gather/scatter code blocks or FIELDGET/FIELDPUT code blocks. In other words, the FIELDBLOCK( ) function, as well as the FIELDWBLOCK( ) function, returns a code block that can be used either to get the value of a particular field from a record or to store the value of a particular field to a record. For example, we can define the following code block:

```
use Clients new
bGetSet := FIELDBLOCK("Name")
```

We can then use our code block to get the contents of the Name field, as follows:

```
cName := eval( bGetSet)
```

Similarly, we can use the same code block to modify the value of the field, as follows:

```
eval(bGetSet,"A-One Consulting")
```

The use of the FIELDBLOCK( ) and FIELDWBLOCK( ) function will be discussed at length in Chapter 18, "Clipper Objects."

## Traversing the Database

Traversing a database is a daily exercise, one that can be either dreaded or anticipated with pleasure. Of course, many outside environmental factors can come into play when one is skipping through a database—open indexes, existing filters, relations to other work areas—and all influence how one can pass through a database as well as the time it takes to do this.

Starting with the basics, the simple method used to skip through a database is something like the following:

```
use <file>

while !eof()
  // perform an operation
  skip
enddo
```

In Clipper 5.2, a new function—DBEVAL—automatically walks through a database. For the above operation, here is how the code might look:

```
use <file>

bCode := {|| <perform an operation>}

dbeval( bCode )
```

This function might be used to take six standard Clipper commands—REPLACE, DELETE, RECALL, AVERAGE, SUM, and COUNT—and reduce them to the same function: DBEVAL( ). This is at the heart of modular, object-oriented, and data-driven programming.

Two points in particular are worth emphasizing regarding DBEVAL( ). First, every record in the database will be processed automatically without a SKIP command. Second, we must make sure that a code block that works on the database performs the operations we want. The key point is that the operations we would normally place between a WHILE !EOF( ) and its respective ENDDO should be placed in functions, and those functions placed within code blocks; these code blocks will be evaluated for every record in the database processed by DBEVAL( ). If this is not clear to you, please reread that last sentence! The code block passed to DBEVAL( ) is evaluated for every record processed by DBEVAL( ). In other words, if we were to code a pseudo-DBEVAL( ), the code might look something like this:

```
function Dbeval( bOperation )

  if !empty( alias() )  // We have a work area
    while !eof()
      eval( bOperation )
      skip
    enddo
  endif

return( NIL )
```

The power of this approach is that we may take advantage of this way of thinking and expand on it with our applications. We will be programming code blocks and passing them to more generic functions that in turn evaluate and process. We will program, in essence, the data and not the function. And the function—in this case DBEVAL( )—will look and act differently based on how we call it—not on the number of parameters that are passed to it but on the instruction set stored in a code block. Consider the fact that DELETE ALL, REPLACE ALL, and AVERAGE do different things yet in reality are the same function. Programming in Clipper 5.2 and for the future means understanding this major shift in how we program.

## Simple DBEVAL( )

In most of the examples in this chapter we have looked at scanning through a database based on various conditions. Now here is an example of a couple of DBEVAL( ) function calls, each with different operations.

```
 1 : // File      Dbf6.prg
 2 : // Compile   RMake sample /dFILE:dbf6
 3 :
 4 : #include "PTValue.ch"
 5 : #include "PTFuncs.ch"
 6 : #include "PTVerbs.ch"   // Power Tools Header file of commands/statements
 7 :
 8 : procedure Main()
 9 :
10 :   local bOp1     := {|| qout(padr(fieldget(1),15), ;
11 :                               padr(fieldget(2),15))}         as block
12 :   local bOp2     := {|| MyFunc() }                           as block
13 :   local nTotDue  := 0.00                                     as int
14 :   local bOp3     := {|| (nTotDue += FIELD->due), qqout(".") } as block
15 :
16 :   use Clients new
17 :   cls
18 :   Clients->( dbeval( bOp1 ) )
19 :   wait
20 :   cls
21 :   Clients->( dbeval( bOp2 ) )
22 :   wait
23 :   cls
24 :   Clients->( dbeval( bOp3 ) )
```

```
25 :      wait "The total due is " + alltrim(str(nTotDue))
26 :      nTotDue := 0.00
27 :
28 :      set index to Client2 additive
29 :      Clients->( dbgotop() )
30 :
31 :      cls
32 :      Clients->( dbeval( bOp1 ) )
33 :      wait
34 :      cls
35 :      Clients->( dbeval( bOp2 ) )
36 :      wait
37 :      cls
38 :      Clients->( dbeval( bOp3 ) )
39 :      wait "The total due is " + alltrim(str(nTotDue))
40 :      nTotDue := 0.00
41 :
42 :      Clients->( SETFILTER( !empty( FIELD->due ) ), dbgotop() )
43 :
44 :      cls
45 :      Clients->( dbeval( bOp1 ) )
46 :      wait
47 :      cls
48 :      Clients->( dbeval( bOp2 ) )
49 :      wait
50 :      cls
51 :      Clients->( dbeval( bOp3 ) )
52 :      wait "The total due is " + alltrim(str(nTotDue))
53 :      nTotDue := 0.00
54 :      cls
55 :
56 :   ********************
57 :
58 :   static procedure MyFunc()
59 :
60 :      if row() == 0
61 :         qqout("Working with MyFunc!")
62 :         qout()
63 :         qout( "Record    No    Status    #5    Name              #7    Account " )
64 :         qout( replicate("=", maxcol() ) )
65 :      endif
66 :
67 :      qout( padl(recno(), 3) )
68 :      qqout( padc( FIELD->status, 11 ) )
69 :      qqout( padr( FIELD->name, 28 ) )
70 :      qqout( FIELD->account )
71 :
72 :      if row() >= 21
73 :         qout()
74 :         qqout( "Any key for next screen" )
75 :         inkey(0)
76 :         scroll( 5,0,23,maxcol(), 0 )   // Clear the screen!
77 :         devpos( 4,0 )
78 :      endif
79 :
80 :   // End of File: Dbf6.prg
```

The tasks that will be performed are stored in the code blocks on lines 10, 12, and 14. Each of these code blocks are LOCAL variables. The first code block says that the first and second field values will be displayed to the screen (or printer or file) by the QOUT( )

function. Nestled in this are two separate calls to the PADR( ) function as well. There is no reference to the names of the fields being displayed, only that the first and second fields will be displayed. In addition, there is no reference to what database this operation will work from, only that the QOUT( ) function will be called with two values. The second code block contains a call to the MyFunc( ) procedure. The third code block makes an in-line assignment to the variable *nTotDue*. This variable is accumulated with the value from the FIELD->Due field being stored to this variable. This is the only reference to a specific field, yet there is no reference to a work area. The expression also calls the QQOUT( ) function, which will display a "." character every time the complete expression is evaluated.

Finally, a database is opened and the DBEVAL( ) function is called three different times, each time passing to it a different code block to operate on each record processed by the DBEVAL( ) function. As DBEVAL( ) on line 18 works on each record in the Clients work area, the first code block, named *bOp1*, will display the contents of the fields in ordinal positions 1 and 2. On the second DBEVAL( ) on line 21, the MyFunc( ) procedure is called as each record is evaluated. This function, defined on line 58, simply displays additional field values to the screen. As the record pointer in the Clients work area moves, the field values displayed by the MyFunc( ) procedure change. Finally, in the third call, each record is evaluated by DBEVAL( ) again, this time accumulating the value of FIELD->Due to the LOCAL memory variable *nTotDue*.

Once the value of *nTotDue* is displayed on the screen on line 25, the value of *nTotDue* must be cleared out (line 26); otherwise, if the code block *bOp3* should be called again, the value of *nTotDue* would continue to be accumulated.

Each time the DBEVAL( ) function is called, the record pointer in the Clients work area is rewound to the top of the file. This happens since there are no additional parameters (no FOR conditional block and no WHILE conditional block) to tell the record pointer not to rewind.

When additional conditions are added to the equation—an additional index file in line 28 and a FILTER condition in line 42—DBEVAL( ) will continue to operate on every record that meets the new criteria. The concept of modular programming allows the DBEVAL( ) function to work differently because of the calls made by code blocks automatically take account of environmental conditions.

One thing should be noted when looking at this example. Not only is the amount of coding significantly smaller and the programming more modular in style and approach when working with DBEVAL( ), but it also performs faster than the conventional WHILE !EOF( ) ... SKIP ... ENDDO programming technique.

## WORKING WITH THE FOR AND WHILE CONDITIONS

Determining what records are to be processed by DBEVAL( ) (a FOR condition) and how long the process will continue (a WHILE condition) are both handled by code blocks. Again, the operations that meet the FOR and WHILE conditions of DBEVAL( ) must be expressed as, or preprocessed to, code block parameters. Looking to the STD.CH file we can see that a typical command such as

```
RECALL ALL FOR RECNO() > 5 WHILE ShowRecs()
```

is preprocessed to the following:

```
DBEval( {|| dbRecall()}, {|| recno() = 5}, {|| ShowRecs()},,, .F. )
```

The ALL clause is ignored. Each expression, both for the FOR and the WHILE conditions, is preprocessed into a code block that is passed as a parameter directly to the DBEVAL( ) function. These values may be stored, in advance of a call to the DBEVAL( ) function, as formal variables. Consider the following sample program that extends this approach:

```
 1 : // File       Dbf7.prg
 2 : // Compile    Rmake sample /dFILE:db7
 3 :
 4 : #include "PTValue.ch"
 5 : #include "PTFuncs.ch"
 6 : #include "PTVerbs.ch"  // Power Tools header file commands/statements
 7 :
 8 : procedure Main()
 9 :
10 :    local nTotDue := 0.00                              as int
11 :    local bOp1   := {|| qout( padr( fieldget(1), 15 ), ;
12 :                               padr(fieldget(2), 15))}    as block
13 :    local bOp2   := {|| MyFunc() }                     as block
14 :    local bOp3   := {|| (nTotDue += FIELD->due), qqout(".") } as block
15 :    local bFor   := {|| !empty( FIELD->due ) }         as block
16 :
17 :    use Clients new
18 :    cls
19 :    Clients->( dbeval( bOp1, bFor) )
20 :    wait
21 :    cls
22 :    Clients->( dbeval( bOp2, bFor) )
23 :    wait
24 :    cls
25 :    Clients->( dbeval( bOp3, bFor) )
26 :    wait "The total due is " + alltrim(str( nTotDue ))
27 :    nTotDue := 0.00
28 :
29 :    cls
30 :    use Trans new
31 :    Trans->( dbeval( bOp1,, {|| !Timer(.01)} ) )
32 :    wait
33 :    Timer()  // This clears out the STATIC variable!
34 :
35 : *********************
36 :
37 : static procedure MyFunc
38 :
39 :    if row() == 0
40 :       qqout("Working with MyFunc!")
41 :       qout()
42 :       qout( "Record ")
43 :       qout( "  No   Status #5 Name                #7 Account " )
44 :       qout( replicate("=", maxcol) ) )
45 :    endif
46 :
47 :    qout( padl(recno(), 3) )
48 :    qqout( padc( FIELD->status, 11 ) )
49 :    qqout( padr( FIELD->name, 28 ) )
50 :    qqout( FIELD->account )
```

```
51 :
52 :    if row() >= 21
53 :       qout()
54 :       qqout( "Any key for next screen" )
55 :       inkey(0)
56 :       scroll( 5,0,23,maxcol(), 0 ) // Clear the screen!
57 :       devpos( 4,0 )
58 :    endif
59 :
60 : ********************
61 :
62 : static function Timer( nElapsed )
63 :
64 :    local lRetValue
65 :
66 :    static nStartAt
67 :
68 :    if nElapsed != NIL       // A parameter was passed
69 :       if nStartAt == NIL    // Not yet set!
70 :          nStartAt := seconds()
71 :       endif
72 :
73 :       lRetValue := ( ( seconds() - nStartAt ) >= nElapsed )
74 :
75 :    else
76 :       nStartAt  := NIL
77 :       lRetValue := pTRUE
78 :
79 :    endif
80 :
81 :    return( lRetValue )
82 :
83 : // End of File: Dbf7.prg
```

In this example, the same three code-block variables with the same operations as in the last example are initialized on lines 11 through 14. The code block that will contain the FOR clause is stored to the LOCAL variable named *bFor* (line 15). Looking to that code block, those records that do not have an empty value for the FIELD->Due field will be processed by DBEVAL( ). As in the previous example, three calls to the DBEVAL( ) function are made within the Clients work area, with the results being similar to the previous ones but limited to only those records meeting the FOR condition. On the final call to the DBEVAL( ) function, the FOR condition is skipped and the WHILE condition is passed to the function. No variable is involved, and the function called within this code block is the Timer( ) function. Remember, the WHILE conditional code block stipulates that the DBEVAL( ) function will continue to process so long as the expression within the WHILE condition remains a logical true (.T.). A better way of looking at the expression is that the DBEVAL( ) function will continue to process WHILE the condition within it remains a logical true (.T.).

The Timer( ) function is unique. It uses the STATIC memory variable storage class to remember the initial setting of the SECONDS( ) function (line 70). In essence, this function sets the elapsed time to allow the function to be a logical true (.T.). Once the allowed elapsed time has expired as set by the parameter *nElapsed*, the function returns a logical false (.F.) because the expression on line 73 is false. This value makes the WHILE condition false, which in turn stops DBEVAL( ) from processing. The second call to the Timer( ) function, a call without a value passed to it (line 33), resets the STATIC variable within the Timer( )

function (*nStartAt*) to a NIL value. If the Timer( ) function is called again, the value of *nStartAt* would be NIL, as it was on the initial call. Therefore, the call to the Timer( ) function on line 33 is similar in nature to resetting the variable *nTotDue* to a beginning value, as seen on line 31.

## Building a Database of Another Data Format

This topic will be examined in greater detail in Chapter 13, which deals with all of the issues surrounding the other database drivers and indexing considerations. However, in this next example, we take a quick look at how Clipper can handle data formats other than the default DBFNTX.

```
 1 : // File       Dbf8.prg
 2 : // Compile    RMake sampndx /dFILE:dbf8
 3 :
 4 : REQUEST Dbfndx
 5 :
 6 : procedure Main()
 7 :
 8 :    local nCount
 9 :
10 :    use Clients new
11 :
12 :    dbcreate( "DBClient", Clients->( dbstruct() ), "DBFNDX" )
13 :
14 :    use DBClient new via "dbfndx"
15 :    index on DBClient->account to DBClient
16 :
17 :    while Clients->( !eof() )
18 :       DBClient->( dbappend() )
19 :       for nCount := 1 to Clients->( fcount() - 2 )
20 :          DBClient->( fieldput( nCount, Clients->( fieldget(nCount) ) ) )
21 :       next
22 :       Clients->( dbskip() )
23 :    enddo
24 :
25 :    wait
26 :
27 : // End of File: Dbf8.prg
```

To make this work, a special RMAKE file was used that looks like this:

```
.prg.obj:
        clipper $(FILE) /m /n /p /w /a /v /es2 /b

.obj.exe:
        if not errorlevel 1 rtlink fi $(FILE) lib dbfndx, dbfntx

$(FILE).obj       :      $(FILE).prg
$(FILE).exe       :      $(FILE).obj

// End of File
```

To start, the REQUEST command is used. This tells Clipper to make sure that more than just the default DBFNTX database driver will be needed. In this case, the DBFNDX drive will be used in some of the following operations. Once this program has finished its operation, the data and the index should be checked in dBASE III just to make sure that the data is now in a new file format.

On line 12, a new database is created using the DBCREATE( ) function. This function uses the array structure obtained from the DBSTRUCT( ) function to build a new database using the DBFNDX database driver. To accomplish this, the Clients database needs to be opened first (line 10) in the standard DBFNTX data format. Once the new file called DBClient is created, it is brought into use on line 14 using the DBFNTX data driver to tell Clipper how information is to be read in that work area. Once open, an index is created. Remember, since the work area uses the DBFNDX database driver, the index created on line 15 will be in dBASE III's NDX file format. Lines 17 through 23 simply take information from the Clients work area and place it into the DBClients work area, showing that Clipper can allow multiple database drivers in different work areas at the same time. To double check this, when browsing the DBClient database and the DBClient index file in dBASE III, see if the last two fields in the DBClient database have information in them: line 19 purposely avoided using those last two fields.

## Summary

This chapter deals with the basics of database and record manipulation. With Clipper 5.2, this also encompasses using other data formats through the RDD technology. In the next chapter (Chapter 13) we will be looking at those drivers more intently.

# 13

# *Indexes and RDDs*

In previous versions of Clipper, the treatment of databases and index files was either limited to a discussion dealing only with .DBF files and their companion .NTX files, or to a discussion of using .NDX files, which allow Clipper to be compatible with dBASE III. With Clipper 5.2, we must instead focus on how these and other data formats can coexist in a Clipper application. Rather than having to choose which of the two index file formats we will use in a particular application as a whole, Clipper now allows us to tie the data format to the data in a specific work area. One consequence of this is that the precise format of the data becomes transparent to us (and, of course, to the user). We can still manipulate a particular database by referring to its alias or work area name and invoking a standard set of commands or functions, even though internally the mechanics of working with that database are completely different.

## The NTX File Format

Clipper uses a modified B+-tree style index structure. Each file consists of pages that are 1024 bytes long. The first page is the index file header, which has the following structure:

| Bytes | Byte Format | Contents |
| --- | --- | --- |
| 0–1 | Word | Signature Byte (03 = Index file) |
| 2–3 | Word | Clipper index version number |
| 4–7 | Long | Offset in file for first index page |
| 8–11 | Long | Offset to an unused key page |
| 12–13 | Word | Key size + 8 bytes (distance between key pages) |

*(continued)*

*(continued)*

| Bytes | Byte Format | Contents |
|---|---|---|
| 14–15 | Word | Key size |
| 16–17 | Word | Number of decimals in key (if numeric) |
| 18–19 | Word | Maximum entries per page |
| 20–21 | Word | Minimum entries per page or half page (The first, or root page of an index has a minimum of 1 entry regardless of this value.) |
| 22–277 | Char | Key expression, followed by CHR(0) bytes (for a total of 256 bytes) |
| 278 | Byte | 1 if index is unique, 0 if not |
| 279–1023 | Char | 745 Filler bytes (pads to 1024) |

Index key pages have the following structure:

| Bytes | Byte Format | Contents |
|---|---|---|
| 0–1 | Word | Number of used entries on this page. (This number will be between the minimum and maximums defined in the header unless it is the root page.) |
| 2 | Unsigned pointers | An array of unsigned longs begins here. The array length is equal to the maximum number of key entries per page +1. They contain offsets onto the page where the key values (ITEMS) are located. |
| Remainder of page | | ITEM entries (described below) |

Following the array of unsigned pointers to offsets in the page are the key value entries. These so-called ITEM entries describe a key value and its record's position in the database. The key value is always stored as a character string, regardless of its type.

### ITEM Entry Structure

| Bytes | Byte Format | Contents |
|---|---|---|
| 0–1 | Long | Pointer to a page in the index file, containing keys that are prior to this key. |
| 2–3 | Long | Record number in controlling database file. |
| 4 | Character Key | This field begins at offset 4 and continues for the length of the key. Numerics are padded with leading zeros. |

## Basics of the RDDs

Until Clipper 5.2, we perceived the Clipper database management system as a component that worked in tandem and was intimately associated with the Clipper programming language. Even the introduction of replaceable database drivers (RDDs) in Clipper 5.0 did not break this close association, since Nantucket's attempt to support RDDs was confined to providing the traditional drivers for both .NDX and .NTX index files.

With Clipper 5.2's more ambitious support for replaceable database drivers, we must now begin to think of a layered approach to database management. In addition, rather than viewing Clipper databases in their totality, we must now begin to focus on the individual work area, since a particular RDD is applied to a particular work area, rather than to the entire database management system as a whole.

This layered approach also means that the overall set of database commands, functions, and operations will behave the same way in each work area, regardless of the database drive that is active at the time. This is critical for the developer; it allows an application to work as a single unit, without explicit regard for the type of data file format actually in place in each work area. SKIP, for example, means the same thing, regardless of whether the file is a .DBF file or a Paradox file. In other words, the SKIP command applies to a particular work area; and Clipper, in managing the information between hard disk, database driver, and work area, takes care of the rest. Once the replaceable database driver is defined, the format of the file that is open in a particular work area becomes completely transparent to us.

As we have said, the introduction of replaceable database drivers forces us to think of the entire database management system as a layered entity. Sitting on top are the commands and functions we typically use to get things done. For the most part, this deals with the work area. All three of the following examples do the same thing:

Example 1

```
select Clients
skip
```

Example 2

```
skip 1 alias clients
```

Example 3

```
Clients->( dbskip() )
```

In each case, the operation of skipping is performed in the Clients work area. The latter two examples are the preferred methods of skipping, since they perform the operation directly with the work area alias. The initial example is not preferable because if the SELECT command is not close to the SKIP operation, there is no way of knowing whether the SKIP operation is actually being performed in the proper work area. Removing the guesswork from programming is critical when trying to develop an application on time and hopefully either under budget or for a profit. Deciding between the command-based example (#2) or the function-based example (#3) is then a matter of personal taste.

Directly underneath the command and function interface is the RDD layer or the database driver layer. It is this layer that relates the work area alias with the file format assigned to it. So when we want to SKIP in the clients work area, we do not care about its data format, just that a record pointer will move in the right direction. The format of that file and what constitutes a record or an index structure is all handled by the RDD layer. This layer then interprets the operation given to it in relation to the file format and then sends that information down to the stored data layer which is a fixed mechanism handled by the operating system's file system. It is within this layer that the actual operation is performed.

These last two layers are not important to us. What is important about RDDs is that they allow us to treat these last two layers as unimportant, and instead to focus on what we want to do, when, and with what—issues that are typically dealt with on the command and function level.

Now, the question arises, how can we alter the RDD layer without affecting the other layers on top or on bottom? To answer that question, let us first take a look at a series of indexing operations that can be performed using the default DBFNTX driver (.DBF file as the database file format and .NTX as the index file format). The file should be compiled and linked using SAMPNDX.RMK, which is shown in Appendix 3.

```
 1 : // File      Ind1.prg
 2 : // Compile   RMake sampndx /dFILE:ind1
 3 :
 4 : // Note      Please be certain to make this file with the RMAKE script
 5 : //           file that includes the lib DBFNDX as part of the link list
 6 :
 7 : #include "PTValue.ch"   // Power Tools Header file of msc. values.
 8 : #include "PTVerbs.ch"   // Power Tools Header file of commands/statements
 9 : #include "PTInkey.ch"   // Power Tools Header file of ASCII key strokes
10 : #include "PTFuncs.ch"   // Power Tools Header of pseudofunctions
11 :
12 : procedure Main()
13 :
14 :    local aGas       as array    // Visual Objects compatible
15 :    local nCount := 0 as int     // found in the PTVERBS.CH header file
16 :
17 :
18 :    if file( "filenos.dbf" )    // O.k... there is the value...
19 :
20 :       cls
21 :       ? "Using the file and building the first index"
22 :       use Filenos new
23 :       set filter to recno() > 50
24 :       go top
25 :       index on str(recno()) + Filenos->file_name to FIn1
26 :       wait
27 :       close all
28 :       use Filenos new index Fin1
29 :       @ 0,0 say padr("Records should be in STR() of RECNO() order...",maxcol())
30 :       browse()
31 :       close all
32 :       cls
33 :       ? "Working on second index"
34 :       use Filenos new
35 :       index on str(recno()) + Filenos->file_name to Fin2 for recno() > 50
36 :       close all
```

```
37 :       use Filenos new index Fin2
38 :       @ 0,0 say padr("Records should be in RECNO() order but only those >
50...",maxcol())
39 :       browse()
40 :       cls
41 :       ? "Working on third index, a complex FOR condition (range of items)..."
42 :       close all
43 :       use Filenos new
44 :       index on str(recno()) + Filenos->file_name to Fin3 ;
45 :           for recno() > 50 .and. recno() <= 58
46 :       @ 0,0 say padr("Now, here are records 50 to 58....",maxcol())
47 :       browse()
48 :       cls
49 :       close all
50 :       use Filenos new index Fin1, Fin2, Fin3
51 :       Filenos->( dbsetorder(1), dbgotop(), browse() )
52 :       wait
53 :       Filenos->( dbsetorder(2), dbgotop(), browse() )
54 :       wait
55 :       Filenos->( dbsetorder(3), dbgotop(), browse() )
56 :       wait
57 :
58 :       cls
59 :       // now use the indexes again and this time, show a gas gauge
60 :       // after showing the gas gauge, use the WHILE condition to separate
61 :       // or break out of an index
62 :
63 :       ? "This next example builds a Gas Gauge from SAMPLES.LIB and is used"
64 :       ? "In an EVAL of the index.  Keep in mind that the EVAL of the index"
65 :       ? "is NOT a code block!"
66 :
67 :       aGas := gaugenew(10,0,13,maxcol())
68 :       close all
69 :       use Filenos new
70 :       gaugedisplay( aGas )
71 :       index on Filenos->file_name to FIn4 ;
72 :           eval (gaugeupdate(aGas, recno()/lastrec()), pTRUE )
73 :
74 :       devpos(maxrow()-1,00)
75 :       wait
76 :
77 :       scroll()
78 :       @ 8,0 say "Press the ESC key to abort the index!"
79 :
80 :       gaugedisplay( aGas := gaugenew(10,0,13,maxcol()) )
81 :       index on Filenos->file_name to FIn5 ;
82 :           for recno() < lastrec()/2 ;
83 :           while ( inkey() != pESC ) ;
84 :           eval (gaugeupdate(aGas, recno()/lastrec()), pTRUE )
85 :
86 :       // And now, let's look at using some of the other clauses with the
87 :       // INDEX command
88 :
89 :       devpos( maxrow()-1,00)
90 :       wait if( lastkey() == pESC, "Index not completely built!", ;
91 :                                   "Index fine and ready for action..." )
92 :
93 :       ? file("Fin5.ntx" )
94 :       wait
95 :
```

```
 96 :    // The following example is a problem discovered by Troy Henikoff
 97 :    // along with the solution he gave me.
 98 :
 99 :    close all
100 :    use Filenos new
101 :    index on str(recno()) to FIn6 for ODD(recno()) ;
102 :                            eval (nCount := nCount + 1, pTRUE)
103 :    browse()
104 :    cls
105 :    ? "And here are the respective values....(press any key to move on...)"
106 :    Filenos->( qout( lastrec(), lastrec()/2, nCount ) )
107 :
108 :    set index to              // Clear the index list
109 :    nCount := 0               // Reset the index counter
110 :
111 :    index on str(recno()) to FIn6 ;
112 :          for odd(recno()) .and. (nCount++,pTRUE)
113 :
114 :    @ 0,0 say "Now, here are the ODD records and ESC to see the values..."
115 :    browse()
116 :    ?
117 :    ? "And now, these are the values .... "
118 :    Filenos->( qout( lastrec(), lastrec()/2, nCount ) )
119 :
120 :    wait
121 :
122 :    cls
123 :    ? "And now for a descending index..."
124 :    close all
125 :    use filenos new                                  // This time use the file
126 :    index on padr(recno(),10) to FInd7 descending   // and index in reverse
127 :    go top                                           // order and go to the top
128 :    ? recno(), Filenos->file_name, eof()
129 :    skip
130 :    ? recno(), Filenos->file_name, eof()
131 :
132 :    seek padr(lastrec()/2,10)        // an item in the middle w/o
133 :    browse()                         // using the DESCEND() func.
134 :    cls
135 :    close all
136 :    erase Fin?.ntx
137 :    ?? "All finished!!!"
138 :
139 :    endif
140 :
141 : // End of File: Ind1.prg
```

The function to display a gas gauge is used in the indexing commands in several places. On line 14, the array *aGas[ ]* is declared, and on line 67 it is assigned values. That array is then used to display the gauge to the screen on line 70, and to update the gauge to display the progress of the indexing operation on lines 72 and 84. Note that this latter operation makes use of the EVAL clause of the INDEX ON command. The expression used in the EVAL clause on line 72 must conclude with a logical true (.T.) value; otherwise, the indexing operation would no longer continue.

The EVAL clause is just one of the new clauses available in some of the replaceable database drivers. Another clause is the FOR clause, as seen on line 35. Here, the index is built in Filenos->file_name order for the first 49 records. This condition is stored along with the index file, so if the REINDEX command is called, the FOR condition will be remembered and the index will again be properly built. In addition to the FOR clause, Clipper allows you to specify a WHILE clause for an indexing operation as well. This can be seen on line 83 of the INDEX ON command beginning on line 81. Here, the index will be built in Filenos ->file_name order for the first half of the records in the database. However, while Clipper attempts to build that index file, the INKEY( ) function in the WHILE clause on line 83 will poll the keyboard. If the ESC key is not pressed, the value of the expression in that clause will be a logical true, allowing the index to continue processing. Once the expression on line 83 returns a logical false (.F.) value, the indexing operation will stop regardless of its progress and of the number of records that have been indexed. Therefore it is important to make certain that the index is totally built if the WHILE clause is used; otherwise, erroneous and partial data may appear in the index file.

Another new feature is the ability to index in descending order without using the DESCEND( ) function in either the index key expression or in the SEEK expression. On lines 125 and following, the index FIND7 is built in descending order, and on line 132, the midway point is "SEEKed" without using the DESCEND( ) function to coincide with the index key. This saves two function calls and allows the programmer to not worry about remembering whether or not the index was created with the DESCEND( ) function—it will be remembered automatically.

But while the new clauses substantially enhance the power, flexibility, and ease of generating Clipper index files, they also have introduced some new problems. For example, consider a conditional index in which only the ODD records will be included in the scope of the index file. When generating the index file, we want to count how many records actually get into the index file. As seen on lines 101 and 102, the FOR condition is based on the value of the pseudofunction ODD( ), and the EVAL clause attempts to increment the value of *nCount* for each record that matches the scope of the FOR condition. However, that is not what takes place. The EVAL clause will work on every record regardless of whether that record matches the FOR condition or not. Therefore, the value of the *nCount* variable on line 103, after the INDEX command completes processing, will equal the value of LASTREC( ) for this particular database.

However, if we adjust our thinking and consider how the FOR clause in lines 111 and 112 addresses this problem, we see new possibilities. Since Clipper's default state is to enable shortcutting optimization, the FOR condition on line 112 says that if the record being indexed is not ODD( ), then the expression ODD(RECNO( )) will be a logical false (.F.). Consequently, there will be no need to look at the second part of the .AND. condition which is the part that actually increments the variable *nCount*. However, if the value of RECNO( ) is an ODD( ) value, then that expression will be a logical true (.T.) and Clipper will process the second half of the .AND. condition, thus incrementing the variable *nCount*.

In that previous example we used the DBFNTX replaceable database driver, which is used by default unless we explicitly specify otherwise. If we do wish to use other RDDs, however, we must be sure that they are linked into the application as well. So the first step in using a new database driver in a Clipper application is to "request" it. This can be accomplished with the REQUEST command:

```
REQUEST DBFNDX
```

This tells Clipper to link in the DBFNDX driver from the DBFNDX.LIB file. This means that we must make certain that that file is a part of the link list. To see this, here is the make file that is used for most of the remaining example programs in this chapter:

```
// File            Samprdd.rmk
// Purpose         To be a general script file for the SAMPLES library
//                 as well as the RDD libraries

.prg.obj:
    clipper $(FILE) /m /n /p /w /a /v /es2 /b

.obj.exe:
    if not errorlevel 1 rtlink fi $(FILE) lib dbfndx, \
dbfntx, samples, dbfcdx, dbfmdx, dbpx, samples

$(FILE).obj         :       $(FILE).prg
$(FILE).exe         :       $(FILE).obj

// End of file: Samprdd.rmk
```

These two steps—of issuing the REQUEST statement to define the driver whose code is to be linked into the application and of defining the root name of the .LIB file containing the driver in the file link list—are always necessary in order to ensure that the code for the replaceable database driver will be present when an application needs it.

The next step is to actually define the RDD that will control particular database and indexing operations. Clipper 5.2 provides two methods of doing this, the first global and the second more specific.

As we noted above, Clipper by default uses the DBFNTX driver to control database and indexing operations. The RDDSETDEFAULT( ) function and the DBSETDRIVER( ) function return the name of the replaceable database driver that is currently the default, and optionally allows a new default database driver to be designated. This driver will then control all database operations unless a different driver is explicitly specified in a particular work area or until a new default driver is defined.

The following line of code returns the name of the RDD currently in control of an application as a whole:

```
cName := rddsetdefault()    // Just get the name of the current driver
```

To define a new default RDD for an application, simply pass the driver's name to the RDDSETDEFAULT( ) function. For example, the following line of code sets the RDD to DBFNDX:

```
rddsetdefault( "dbfndx" )
```

While RDDSETDEFAULT( ) controls the overall "default" RDD for an application at a given time, it is also possible to set the RDD for a particular work area. This is accomplished with the VIA clause of the USE command:

```
use Clients new via "dbfndx"
```

Regardless of the value of RDDSETDEFAULT( ), the driver to be used for all data manipulation for the Clients work area will be the DBFNDX driver.

*Indexes and RDDs* 755

We should note at the outset, however, that the full complex of database and indexing operations supported by the DBFNTX driver is not necessarily supported by the other replaceable database drivers. For example, this next application uses the same code as the previous example but uses the DBFNDX database driver. With this slight change in database and index format, some of the DBFNTX driver's indexing possibilities are lost:

```
 1 : // File      Ind2.prg
 2 : // Compile   RMake samprdd /dFILE:ind2
 3 :
 4 : #include "PTValue.ch"   // Power Tools Header file of msc. values.
 5 : #include "PTVerbs.ch"   // Power Tools Header file of commands/statements
 6 : #include "PTInkey.ch"   // Power Tools Header file of ASCII key strokes
 7 : #include "PTFuncs.ch"   // Power Tools Header of pseudofunctions
 8 :
 9 : request dbfndx
10 :
11 : procedure Main()
12 :
13 :    local aGas        as array   // Visual Objects compatible
14 :    local nCount := 0 as int     // found in the PTVERBS.CH header file
15 :
16 :    if file( "filenos.dbf" )  // O.k... there is the value...
17 :
18 :       dbsetdriver( "DBFNDX" )
19 :
20 :       cls
21 :       ? "Using the file and building the first index"
22 :       use Filenos new
23 :       set filter to recno() > 50
24 :       go top
25 :        index on str(recno()) + Filenos->file_name to FIn1
26 :       wait
27 :       close all
28 :       use Filenos new index Fin1
29 :       @ 0,0 say padr("Records should be in STR() of RECNO() order...",maxcol())
30 :       browse()
31 :       close all
32 :       cls
33 :
34 :       // The commented code comes from IND1.prg and is NOT supported in this
35 :       // program simply because of the default data driver
36 :
37 :       /*
38 :
39 :       ? "Working on second index"
40 :       use Filenos new
41 :       index on str(recno()) + Filenos->file_name to Fin2 for recno() > 50
42 :       close all
43 :       use Filenos new index Fin2
44 :       @ 0,0 say padr("Records should be in RECNO() order but only those > 50...",maxcol())
45 :       browse()
46 :       cls
47 :       ? "Working on third index, a complex FOR condition (range of items)..."
48 :       close all
49 :       use Filenos new
50 :       index on str(recno()) + Filenos->file_name to Fin3 ;
51 :             for recno() > 50 .and. recno() <= 58
52 :       @ 0,0 say padr("Now, here are records 50 to 58....",maxcol())
```

```
 53 :      browse()
 54 :      cls
 55 :      close all
 56 :      use Filenos new index Fin1, Fin2, Fin3
 57 :      Filenos->( dbsetorder(1), dbgotop(), browse() )
 58 :      wait
 59 :      Filenos->( dbsetorder(2), dbgotop(), browse() )
 60 :      wait
 61 :      Filenos->( dbsetorder(3), dbgotop(), browse() )
 62 :      wait
 63 :
 64 :      cls
 65 :      // now use the indexes again and this time, show a gas gauge
 66 :      // after showing the gas gauge, use the WHILE condition to separate
 67 :      // or break out of an index
 68 :
 69 :      ? "This next example builds a Gas Gauge from SAMPLES.LIB and is used"
 70 :      ? "In an EVAL of the index.  Keep in mind that the EVAL of the index"
 71 :      ? "is NOT a code block!"
 72 :
 73 :      */
 74 :
 75 :      aGas := gaugenew(10,0,13,maxcol())
 76 :      close all
 77 :      use Filenos new
 78 :      gaugedisplay( aGas )
 79 :      index on Filenos->file_name to Fin4 ;
 80 :              eval (gaugeupdate(aGas, recno()/lastrec()), pTRUE )
 81 :
 82 :      devpos(maxrow()-1,00)
 83 :      wait
 84 :
 85 :      scroll()
 86 :      @ 8,0 say "Press the ESC key to abort the index!"
 87 :
 88 :      // All of the following code is again, not supported either due to the
 89 :      // WHILE clause or the FOR clause or even.... both....
 90 :
 91 :      /*
 92 :
 93 :      gaugedisplay( aGas := gaugenew(10,0,13,maxcol()) )
 94 :      index on Filenos->file_name to Fin5 ;
 95 :              for recno() < lastrec()/2 ;
 96 :              while ( inkey() != pESC ) ;
 97 :              eval (gaugeupdate(aGas, recno()/lastrec()), pTRUE)
 98 :
 99 :      // And now, let's look at using some of the other clauses with the
100 :      // INDEX command
101 :
102 :      devpos( maxrow()-1,00)
103 :      wait if( lastkey() == pESC, "Index not completely built!", ;
104 :                                  "Index fine and ready for action..." )
105 :
106 :      ? file("Fin5.ntx" )
107 :      wait
108 :
109 :      // The following example is a problem discovered by Troy Hennikof
110 :      // along with the solution.
111 :
112 :      close all
```

```
113 :       use Filenos new
114 :       index on str(recno()) to Fin6 for ODD(recno()) ;
115 :                               eval (nCount := nCount + 1, pTRUE)
116 :       browse()
117 :       cls
118 :       ? "And here are the respective values....(press any key to move on...)"
119 :       Filenos->( qout( lastrec(), lastrec()/2, nCount ) )
120 :
121 :       set index to               // Clear the index list
122 :       nCount := 0                // Reset the index counter
123 :
124 :       index on str(recno()) to Fin6 ;
125 :              for odd(recno()) .and. (nCount++,pTRUE)
126 :
127 :       @ 0,0 say "Now, here are the ODD records and ESC to see the values..."
128 :       browse()
129 :       ?
130 :       ? "And now, these are the values .... "
131 :       Filenos->( qout( lastrec(), lastrec()/2, nCount ) )
132 :
133 :       wait
134 :
135 :       cls
136 :       ? "And now for a descending index..."
137 :       close all
138 :       use filenos new                              // This time use the file
139 :       index on padr(recno(),10) to Find7 descending // and index in reverse
140 :       go top                                       // order and go to the top
141 :       ? recno(), Filenos->file_name, eof()
142 :       skip
143 :       ? recno(), Filenos->file_name, eof()
144 :
145 :       seek padr(lastrec()/2,10)          // an item in the middle w/o
146 :       browse()                           // using the DESCEND() func.
147 :       cls
148 :
149 :       */
150 :
151 :       close all
152 :       ferase( "Fin?." + indexext() )
153 :       ?? "All finished!!!"
154 :
155 :    endif
156 :
157 : // End of File: Ind2.prg
```

On line 9 of IND2.PRG, the formal request for all code for the DBFNDX driver is made. However, making a request for a driver's code is not the same as actually using it in a work area. In implementing the DBFNDX driver, we had to choose one of the two basic ways to use an RDD. We chose not to define DBFNDX on a work area by work area basis, which we could have accomplished with the VIA clause in the USE command:

```
use Clients via "dbfndx"
```

Instead, we have chosen to define a new default driver for the entire application. This is accomplished on line 18 with the DBSETDRIVER( ) function. (We could also have used the RDDSETDEFAULT( ) function, which operates in the same way.) Now, every time a database is opened or an index is built and a driver is not explicitly mentioned, DBFNTX will be used as the default driver.

DBFNDX is a replaceable database driver that aims at dBASE III compatibility. Therefore, it does not support many of the features—and particularly the newer features—of the DBFNTX driver. In IND2.PRG, we have commented out those portions of code that are not supported by the driver and that will cause it to display an "Operation not supported" error message. These features include:

- The FOR clause of the INDEX ON command on lines 41, 51, 95, 114, and 125
- The WHILE clause of the INDEX ON command on line 96
- The DESCENDING keyword of the INDEX ON command on line 139

That a particular device driver may not fully support the syntax of the default DBFNTX driver, however, creates a clear problem. Optimally, we should be able to simply use a particular command or function set, without having to be concerned with whether or not its full functionality is supported by the replaceable database driver. In effect, once defined, the RDD layer should be completely transparent to us. This, however, is still not the case. And because it is not the case, the code for our applications must confront this issue.

Obviously, if an application is designed to use a variety of replaceable database drivers, it may be necessary to alter code. This, however, is the least desirable and practical solution. Instead, the code should be designed to simultaneously accommodate the syntax supported by any replaceable database driver that might be in use. In implementing this approach, the preprocessor can be an important tool that allows conditional code fragments to be built, depending on which RDD is being used. To see this, for example, consider the following program:

```
 1 : // File       Ind6.prg
 2 : // Compile    RMake samprdd /dFILE:ind6
 3 :
 4 : #include "PTValue.ch"   // Power Tools Header file of msc. values.
 5 : #include "PTVerbs.ch"   // Power Tools Header file of commands/statements
 6 : #include "PTInkey.ch"   // Power Tools Header file of ASCII key strokes
 7 : #include "PTFuncs.ch"   // Power Tools Header of pseudofunctions
 8 :
 9 : #define DBFNDX
10 :
11 : #ifdef DBFNDX
12 :    request dbfndx
13 :    #define DRIVER "DBFNDX"
14 : #else
15 :    #ifdef DBFCDX
16 :       request dbfcdx
17 :       #define DRIVER "DBFCDX"
18 :    #else
19 :       #ifdef DBFMDX
20 :          request dbfmdx
21 :          #define DRIVER "DBFMDX"
22 :       #endif
23 :    #endif
24 : #endif
25 :
26 : procedure Main()
27 :
```

```
28 :    local aGas       as array   // Visual Objects compatible
29 :    local nCount := 0 as int    // found in the PTVERBS.CH header file
30 :
31 :    if file( "filenos.dbf" )    // O.k... there is the value...
32 :
33 :       dbsetdriver( DRIVER )
34 :
35 :       cls
36 :       ? "Using the file and building the first index"
37 :       use Filenos new
38 :       set filter to recno() > 50
39 :       go top
40 :       index on str(recno()) + Filenos->file_name to FIn1
41 :       wait
42 :       close all
43 :       use Filenos new index Fin1
44 :       @ 0,0 say padr("Records should be in STR() of RECNO() order...",maxcol())
45 :       browse()
46 :       close all
47 :       cls
48 :
49 :       ? "Working on second index"
50 :       use Filenos new
51 :
52 : #ifdef DBFNDX
53 :       index on if( recno()>50, "0", "1" ) + str(recno()) + ;
54 :               Filenos->file_name to Fin2
55 : #else
56 :       index on str(recno()) + Filenos->file_name to Fin2 for recno() > 50
57 : #endif
58 :
59 :       close all
60 :       use Filenos new index Fin2
61 :       devpos(0,0)
62 :
63 : #ifdef DBFNDX
64 :       devout(padr("Order is all records...",maxcol()))
65 : #else
66 :       devout(padr("Records should be in RECNO() order but only those > ;
67 :                   50...",maxcol()) )
68 : #endif
69 :       devpos(0,0)
70 :       browse()
71 :       cls
72 :       ? "Working on third index, a complex for condition (range of items)..."
73 :       close all
74 :       use Filenos new
75 : #ifdef DBFNDX
76 :       index on if((recno() > 50 .and. recno() <= 58), "0", "1") + ;
77 :               str(recno()) + Filenos->file_name to Fin3
78 :       @ 0,0 say padr("Now, here is are all with those at the top....",maxcol())
79 : #else
80 :       index on str(recno()) + Filenos->file_name to Fin3 ;
81 :               for recno() > 50 .and. recno() <= 58
82 :       @ 0,0 say padr("Now, here are records 50 to 58....",maxcol())
83 : #endif
84 :
85 :       browse()
86 :       cls
87 :       close all
```

```
 88 :        use Filenos new index Fin1, Fin2, Fin3
 89 :        Filenos->( dbsetorder(1), dbgotop(), browse() )
 90 :        wait
 91 :        Filenos->( dbsetorder(2), dbgotop(), browse() )
 92 :        wait
 93 :        Filenos->( dbsetorder(3), dbgotop(), browse() )
 94 :        wait
 95 :
 96 :        cls
 97 :        // now use the indexes again, and this time show a gas gauge
 98 :        // after showing the gas gauge, use the WHILE condition to separate
 99 :        // or break out of an index
100 :
101 :        ? "This next example builds a Gas Gauge from SAMPLES.LIB and is used"
102 :        ? "In an EVAL of the index.  Keep in mind that the EVAL of the index"
103 :        ? "is NOT a code block!"
104 :
105 :        aGas := gaugenew(10,0,13,maxcol())
106 :        close all
107 :        use Filenos new
108 :        gaugedisplay( aGas )
109 :        index on Filenos->file_name to Fin4 ;
110 :              eval (gaugeupdate(aGas, recno()/lastrec()), pTRUE )
111 :
112 :        devpos(maxrow()-1,00)
113 :        wait
114 :
115 :        scroll()
116 :
117 :        // All of the following code is again, not supported either due to the
118 :        // WHILE clause or the FOR clause or even.... both....
119 :
120 :        gaugedisplay( aGas := gaugenew(10,0,13,maxcol()) )
121 :
122 : #ifdef DBFNDX
123 :        @ 8,0 say "Building the index one more time....."
124 :        index on if(recno() <lastrec()/2, "0", "1") + ;
125 :              Filenos->file_name to Fin5 ;
126 :              eval (gaugeupdate(aGas, recno()/lastrec()), pTRUE)
127 : #else
128 :        @ 8,0 say "Press the ESC key to abort the index!"
129 :        index on Filenos->file_name to FIn5 ;
130 :              for recno() < lastrec()/2 ;
131 :              while ( inkey() != pESC ) ;
132 :              eval (gaugeupdate(aGas, recno()/lastrec()), pTRUE)
133 : #endif
134 :
135 :
136 :        // And now, let's look at using some of the other clauses with the
137 :        // INDEX command
138 :
139 :        devpos( maxrow()-1,00)
140 :        wait if( lastkey() == pESC, "Index not completely built!", ;
141 :                                    "Index fine and ready for action..." )
142 :
143 :        ? file("Fin5.ntx" )
144 :        wait
145 :
146 :        close all
```

```
147 :        ferase( "FIn?." + indexext() )
148 :        ?? "All finished!!!"
149 :
150 :     endif
151 :
152 : // End of File: Ind6.prg
```

Although there are differences between each driver's support for the clauses of the INDEX ON command, we can build a program that will work regardless of the driver being used. To start, a nested conditional compiler construct is defined on lines 11 through 24. Here, depending on the driver being defined on line 9, the appropriate REQUEST command is compiled, as is the definition of the DRIVER manifest constant. In other words, if the #define on line 9 is:

```
#define DBFCDX
```

The preprocessor would execute lines 15 through 17, which set up the appropriate REQUEST command and establish the value of the DRIVER manifest constant as "DBFCDX." This value for DRIVER is then used on line 33, which sets the global driver for the application. All that needs to take place for a different driver to be installed is that the value of the manifest constant on line 9 be changed to one of the values tested on lines 11 through 24. Another way to accomplish the same thing would be to delete line 9 and to compile this program using the /D switch to define the correct preprocessor value for the #ifdef directive.

Still, including the proper driver is only one issue that needs to be considered. Some of the drivers do not support the FOR clause, which means that if it is critical to the application, new logic must be used to implement the FOR clause in drivers that do not support it. To see this better, consider the code on lines 52 through 57. If the driver is not DBFNDX, then the FOR condition in the INDEX ON command on line 56 is valid. This will build a conditional index, which means that only those records that meet the FOR condition will be included in the INDEX. However, this feature is not supported in the DBFNDX driver, which necessarily includes all records in the indexes it generates. So a workaround is needed. On line 53, the index is built with a "0" or a "1" character prefix. This means that while all of the records in the database will be included in the index, only those records matching the IF( ) function's condition will appear at the top, while all remaining records will appear at the bottom. Additional code, of course, needs to be written to support this variation, especially in cases of browsing or traversing the database. However, the central point here is that an application can be written to support the use of any driver given enough code and the use of the preprocessor.

## The Clipper 5.2 Database and Index System

Because of Clipper's emergence as an open system, and particularly because of the introduction of Clipper 5.2 and the emphasis on Replaceable Database Drivers that can make differences in file formats transparent to both the user and the developer, it is clear that Clipper's traditional, Xbase-like view of database management must become more general. This means, in part, that the language of database management must change to conform more closely to the generalized features of database management systems, rather than to the peculiarities of the Xbase implementation of those features.

Some of this terminology remains unchanged, and is familiar to anyone who has even a passing familiarity with Clipper. Every index file in Clipper must have a KEY EXPRESSION. This is an expression that is used to create a KEY VALUE for a single record in the associated database file for a particular index. In the standard index file format, this key expression's length must be uniform and consistent for every KEY VALUE in the index file. A KEY VALUE is based on the value(s) contained within one or more database fields or on a computed expression associated with a particular record in a database. KEY EXPRESSIONs do not have to relate explicitly to a field; however, they must relate to something that makes that particular record distinctive. For example, while RECNO( ) is not a particular field in any database, it is a piece of information that may be involved in an index KEY EXPRESSION and thus will alter the KEY VALUE for a particular record.

Because database fields are fixed in length, when a database is opened and an index is created for the first time, Clipper must build a structure of that index file based on the requirements of the RDD involved. This is accomplished regardless of the information in that database. This means that the "phantom record" of every database is used in building the index file. Since the "phantom record" is a blank record of the structure of the database held in memory, it will have no value. This record can be accidentally seen when traversing a database and an attempt is made to go beyond either the EOF( ) or the BOF( ). A blank record will appear on the screen yet, in fact, it does not pertain to any particular or physical record in that database. It is this record that is used to create an index structure and KEY VALUE length. Since all of the field values in a database start off as blank values, they will have no length if they are trimmed. This means that the TRIM( ) of a field or a combination of fields cannot be used in an index KEY EXPRESSION since it will be truncated to a KEY VALUE of 0 length. When the first record is eventually added to a database, no KEY VALUE will be assigned to the index file, and as a result, nothing will every be "found." Therefore, the KEY VALUE must remain constant even upon start-up. This means that in cases where the TRIM( ) of a field or fields is necessary, the PADR( ) or PADL( ) function should be used as well to force a KEY EXPRESSION to have a uniform length.

To these well-known features of Clipper index files, however, Computer Associates has added a number of new concepts and terms to reflect Clipper 5.2's open architecture and its support for replaceable database drivers. The first of these is an IDENTITY, which can be defined as a value that is guaranteed by the structure of the database to uniquely identify each record in the database. Because the standard .DBF file does not automatically prevent the entry of duplicate key values, the IDENTITY for a .DBF is typically the record number. However, using another replaceable database driver, the IDENTITY could be the primary key value. It is in fact not necessary that the data source be a database; in the case of an array, the IDENTITY could be the element's subscript position.

Combining the IDENTITY with a KEY VALUE produces a KEYED-PAIR. This closely corresponds to most standard dBASE-compatible index files, in which a key value is paired with a record number. The KEY VALUE, or the value of the KEY EXPRESSION for that particular record, determines the order in which the record will appear. When a particular KEY VALUE is selected, records are quickly found based on their record numbers because the two form a KEYED-PAIR.

IDENTITY ORDER is a term that describes the natural or physical arrangement of records in a database and is based on their IDENTITY. For .DBF files, for instance, because IDENTITY is defined by record number, IDENTITY ORDER corresponds to the order in which the records were entered. Using the Clipper command SET ORDER TO 0 accesses a database in its IDENTITY ORDER.

An ORDER is an index, or a mechanism for presenting logical views of data based on their KEYED-PAIRS. The ORDER gives the appearance that data is arranged in something other than its IDENTITY ORDER without actually changing the physical arrangement of records in the database.

Since more than one ORDER can be open at a single time, the group of ORDERS open in a work area is called the ORDER LIST; in Clipper, these orders are defined by the SET INDEX TO command or the INDEX keyword of the USE command. However, at any single time, only a single ORDER can control the logical organization of the records in a work area. This active ORDER is termed the CONTROLLING ORDER. The ORDER LIST FOCUS is a pointer to the CONTROLLING ORDER. In general, it indicates the ordinal position of the controlling order in the ORDER LIST. In Clipper, the ORDER LIST FOCUS is the argument used with the SET ORDER TO command to change the controlling order.

A SCOPED ORDER is an ORDER that limits the visibility of the physical records in a database. Clipper's RDD terminology actually distinguishes between two kinds of scoped orders: MAINTAINABLE SCOPED ORDERS are orders whose scoping conditions are stored in the index file header; typically, they are indexes created using the FOR clause. For MAINTAINABLE SCOPED ORDERS, recalling the KEY EXPRESSION will accurately recreate the ORDER. On the other hand, NON-MAINTAINABLE or TEMPORARY ORDERS are scoped orders whose scoping conditions are not stored in the index file header. These orders are typically created using the WHILE, NEXT, and EVAL clauses of Clipper's INDEX ON command; an ORDER BAG is, quite simply, a physical index file.

Each Clipper index (.NTX) file is based on a single key expression and contains one key value for each applicable record in its associated database. For Clipper, each ORDER BAG contains one ORDER. This one-to-one relationship between key expression and index file, however, is not invariable; a number of Xbase products, for instance, can store multiple indexes (or ORDERS) within a single index file (or ORDER BAG). In these cases, TAG is the term used to refer to a single ORDER within a multiple-ORDER index file. The TAG designates a unique KEY EXPRESSION within an ORDER BAG.

Finally, the list of all ORDERS or TAGS within an ORDER BAG is called an ORDER LIST. In the case of the .NTX or .NDX file formats, the ORDER LIST can contain only one ORDER; in this case, the ORDER BAG is also known as a SINGLE-ORDER BAG and does not contain any tags. In the case of .CDX or .MDX files, the ORDER LIST will have as many elements as there are TAGS and is known as a MULTIPLE-ORDER BAG.

The purpose of orders, identities, and order bags is to identify or logically position one of the basic units of database management, the RECORD. Typically, Clipper defines a RECORD as a single row of associated data. This definition, however, is too narrow, since it excludes not only data in some non-Xbase databases, but it also excludes data stored in arrays. To broaden its meaning, a RECORD must instead be seen as a collection of data associated with a single IDENTITY.

In this next example, a few of these terms will be used as we create a few indexes, orders with tag names, order bags and order lists.

```
 1 : // File       Ind3.prg
 2 : // Compile    RMake samprdd /dFILE:Ind3
 3 :
 4 : #include "PTInkey.ch"
 5 : #include "PTVerbs.ch"
 6 : #include "PTValue.ch"
 7 :
 8 : memvar aGas as array
 9 :
10 : #xcommand SET GAUGE   => gaugedisplay(aGas := gaugenew(1,0,3,maxcol()))
11 : #xtranslate SHOW GAUGE => ;
12 :    eval (gaugeupdate(aGas,recno()/lastrec()),pTRUE) every 10
13 :
14 : procedure Main()
15 :
16 :    request dbfcdx
17 :
18 :    if file( "Filenos.dbf" )
19 :       use Filenos new via "dbfcdx"
20 :       cls
21 :       SET GAUGE
22 :       @ 0,0 say "Filename TAG being built"
23 :       index on Filenos->file_name tag names to Filenos SHOW GAUGE
24 :       cls
25 :       SET GAUGE
26 :       @ 0,0 say "File time TAG being built"
27 :       index on Filenos->file_time tag times to Filenos SHOW GAUGE
28 :       cls
29 :       SET GAUGE
30 :       @ 0,0 say "File date TAG being built"
31 :       index on Filenos->file_date tag dates to Filenos ;
32 :           for recno() < 50 ;
33 :           SHOW GAUGE
34 :       cls
35 :       SET GAUGE
36 :       @ 0,0 say "Now, a new order with SUB_NAME as the key..."
37 :       index on Filenos->sub_name tag subs to FileSub SHOW GAUGE
38 :       @ 5,0 say "Press any key to move on...."
39 :       inkey(0)
40 :
41 :       set order to tag names in Filenos
42 :       go top
43 :       cls
44 :
45 :       ShowStuff()
46 :       set order to tag times
47 :       go top
48 :       ShowStuff()
49 :       set order to tag dates
50 :       go top
51 :       ShowStuff()
52 :       set order to tag subs in Filesub
53 :       cls
54 :       go top
55 :       ShowStuff()
56 :
57 :       wait
```

```
 58 :       cls
 59 :       ? "Here is a list of RDDs presently in system using FULL implementation:"
 60 :       aeval( rddlist(1), {|cName| qout( cName )} )
 61 :       ?
 62 :       ? "And here are those with the Import/Export driver only..."
 63 :       aeval( rddlist(2), {|cName| qout( cName )} )
 64 :       ?
 65 :       wait
 66 :
 67 :    endif
 68 :
 69 :
 70 : ********************
 71 :
 72 : static function ShowStuff()
 73 :
 74 :    local cScreen := savescreen()           as char
 75 :    local oBrowse := tbrowsedb(5,2,20,78)   as object
 76 :    local nKey                              as int
 77 :
 78 :    oBrowse:addcolumn( tbcolumnnew( "Record",   {|| Filenos->( recno() ) } ) )
 79 :    oBrowse:addcolumn( tbcolumnnew( "File;name", {|| Filenos->file_name} ) )
 80 :    oBrowse:addcolumn( tbcolumnnew( "File;time", {|| Filenos->file_time} ) )
 81 :    oBrowse:addcolumn( tbcolumnnew( "File;date", {|| Filenos->file_date} ) )
 82 :    oBrowse:addcolumn( tbcolumnnew( "Sub;name", {|| ;
 83 :                       left(Filenos->sub_name,20)}))
 84 :    REPEAT
 85 :
 86 :       oBrowse:forceStable()
 87 :
 88 :       @ 00,00 SAY "   Current order key is: " + ordkey(ordname())
 89 :       @ 01,00 SAY "  Current order name is: " + ordname()
 90 :       @ 02,00 SAY "Current order number is: " + trim(str(ordnumber(ordname())))
 91 :       @ 03,00 SAY "   Current order FOR is: " + ordfor()
 92 :
 93 :       do case
 94 :       case (nkey := inkey(0)) == pESC
 95 :          exit
 96 :
 97 :       case nKey == pDOWN_ARROW
 98 :          oBrowse:down()
 99 :
100 :       case nKey == pUP_ARROW
101 :          oBrowse:up()
102 :
103 :       end case
104 :
105 :    END PROCESS
106 :
107 :    restscreen(,,,,cScreen)
108 :
109 :    VOID
110 :
111 : // End of File: Ind3.prg
```

Before looking at the purpose of lines 10, 11, and 12, a few of the new terms and concepts should be examined. On line 16, the DBFCDX index driver is requested; on line 19, it is loaded in the work area for use with the FILENOS database. Eventually, an index is built on line 23. The name of the ORDER BAG (the index filename) will be FILENOS. Within the

ORDER BAG, there is a new TAG with the key name NAMES. Whenever we want to use that ORDER within that ORDER BAG, we refer to it by the TAG name NAMES. On line 27, we create a second TAG, Times, and on lines 31 through 33, we create the DATES, a SCOPED ORDER TAG. When an ORDER BAG contains multiple ORDERs, we must use the modified SET ORDER command to change the CONTROLLING ORDER. On line 41, the SET ORDER TO command is used to search for the NAMEs TAG within the Filenos ORDER BAG. Finally, the value of RDDLIST( ) is examined on lines 61 and again on line 64, based on two different conditions.

Turn back to the preprocessor directives on lines 10 through 12. There the gas gauge is created and displayed within the compound expression which is assigned to the #xcommand SET GAUGE. Once the array *aGas[ ]* is appropriately established with the GAUGENEW( ) function, it is then passed to the GAUGEDISPLAY( ) function for display purposes. This variable, *aGas[ ]*, must be defined in advance to avoid getting a warning message should the /W switch be used (line 8). Once the gas gauge is established and "stabilized" to the screen, it can be used for the indexing commands. Since the SHOW GAUGE fragment is really an EVAL of an expression, it is easier to redefine the EVAL clause of the INDEX ON command to be simply SHOW GAUGE and to define SHOW GAUGE using the #xtranslate directive, since it will appear not on a line by itself (like the SET GAUGE command) but will always be used within the INDEX ON command (lines 23, 27, 33, and 37). It is important to remember that in order to show a proper gas gauge effect while the index files are being built, the array *aGas[ ]* needs to be rebuilt (or emptied) before each indexing operation. This is why the SET GAUGE command was created and used.

As we noted above, each order must have a distinctive name. In an order bag, that name is called the order's TAG, and it can be used to differentiate one index from other indexes contained within the order bag. In many ways, an order tag is not unlike an alias, which serves as a pointer to the particular work area in which a database resides.

In the sample program IND3.PRG, we used the DBFCDX driver and the INDEX ON...TAG command to create an order bag named FILENOS that contained three tags: NAMES, TIMES, and DATES. We also created another order bag, FILESUB, that contained a single tag, SUBS.

Order tags can be removed as easily as they can be created. The DELETE TAG command is used for this purpose. Its use is illustrated in the following program:

```
 1 : // File      Ind4.prg
 2 : // Compile   RMake samprdd /dFILE:Ind4
 3 :
 4 : #include "PTInkey.ch"
 5 : #include "PTVerbs.ch"
 6 : #include "PTValue.ch"
 7 :
 8 : memvar aGas as array
 9 :
10 : #xcommand SET GAUGE     => gaugedisplay(aGas := gaugenew(1,0,3,maxcol()))
11 : #xtranslate SHOW GAUGE => ;
12 :    eval (gaugeupdate(aGas,recno()/lastrec()),pTRUE) every 10
13 :
14 : procedure Main()
15 :
16 :    request dbfcdx
17 :
```

```
18 :     if file( "Filenos.dbf" )
19 :        use Filenos new via "dbfcdx"
20 :        cls
21 :        SET GAUGE
22 :        @ 0,0 say "Filename TAG being built"
23 :        index on Filenos->file_name tag names to Filenos SHOW GAUGE
24 :        cls
25 :        SET GAUGE
26 :        @ 0,0 say "File time TAG being built"
27 :        index on Filenos->file_time tag times to Filenos SHOW GAUGE
28 :        cls
29 :        SET GAUGE
30 :        @ 0,0 say "File date TAG being built"
31 :        index on Filenos->file_date tag dates to Filenos ;
32 :            for recno() < 50 ;
33 :            SHOW GAUGE
34 :
35 :        cls
36 :        SET GAUGE
37 :        @ 0,0 say "Now, a new order with SUB_NAME as the key..."
38 :        index on Filenos->sub_name tag subs to FileSub SHOW GAUGE
39 :
40 :        cls
41 :        ? "Here are the current list of orders..."
42 :        aeval( OrdList(), {|cName| qout(cName)} )
43 :        wait
44 :
45 :        ? "And here are the remaining ones...."
46 :        delete tag times in Filenos
47 :        aeval( OrdList(), {|cName| qout(cName)} )
48 :
49 :    endif
50 :
51 : *******************
52 :
53 : static function OrdList()
54 :
55 :    local aRetValue := {} as array
56 :    local nOrder           as int
57 :    local nCount    := 1   as int
58 :
59 :    if !empty( alias() ) // There is a database!
60 :       aadd( aRetValue, "RECNO" )
61 :
62 :       nOrder := ordnumber(ordname())
63 :
64 :       PROCESS
65 :
66 :          // first we have to decide if there are TAGS in the order bag
67 :          // and if not, we have to decide if the ORDER BAG can even hold
68 :          // a tag!
69 :
70 :          if empty( ordname(nCount++) )
71 :             exit
72 :          else
73 :             aadd( aRetValue, ordname(nCount-1) )
74 :          endif
75 :
76 :       END PROCESS
77 :
78 :       ordnumber(nOrder)
```

```
79 :
80 :    endif
81 :
82 :    return( aRetValue )
83 :
84 : // End of File: Ind4.prg
```

## Using other RDDs

Each RDD has different characteristics, ranging from its support for unique key values in indexes to support for the FOR condition. The differences among drivers are very important when you are trying to determine under what conditions each driver is best.

### DBFCDX

This driver is the FoxPro 2.x compatible index driver. It supports both compound indexes (including compound structural indexes) and compact indexes. In addition, it generates memo files that are smaller than those created by the traditional .NTX or .NDX drivers. Some individual features of the driver are:

- Implicit record unlocking in single lock mode
- Multiple record locks
- Can support concurrent record locks (depending on available memory)
- Supports Order Management (Order Tags)
- Supports 99 TAGS per Order Bag
- Supports 15 Order Bags per work area
- Supports the conditional FOR clause
- Supports temporary or partial indexes such as those created by the WHILE clause
- Supports descending indexes
- Supports unique indexes
- Supports the EVAL and EVERY clause
- Supports production/structural indexes
- Maximum key expression length is 255 bytes
- Maximum length for a FOR condition is 255 bytes

The DBFCDX driver allows you to both read and write a FoxPro 2.0-compatible database. This RDD carefully mirrors the feature set of Microsoft's own FoxPro product, except that it does not support two FoxPro data types: Float and General. When "F" (Float) is specified as the field type in the DBCREATE( ) command, it is automatically translated into a numeric field. A data type of "G" (for General, a new data type introduced in FoxPro 2.5 to support Object Linking and Embedding) is simply not recognized. The remaining data types, however, are supported by the DBFCDX driver. The following program illustrates the process of database creation with the DBFCDX driver:

```
1 : // File CDX1.PRG
2 :
3 : // Compile   Rmake samprdd /dFILEL:CDX1
4 :
```

```
 5 :     REQUEST DBFCDX
 6 :
 7 :     function main()
 8 :
 9 :         local aStruct := {}
10 :
11 :         aadd(aStruct,{"FName","C",20,0})
12 :         aadd(aStruct,{"LName","C",20,0})
13 :         aadd(aStruct,{"Age","N",3,0})
14 :         aadd(aStruct,{"Comments","M",10,0})
15 :
16 :         dbCreate("FOXDBF",aStruct,"DBFCDX")
17 :
18 :         return(NIL)
```

Note that, in using the DBCREATE( ) function, the value of all four elements that compose a field definition must be explicitly defined. Passing a NIL value, especially for the value of field decimal positions, will cause a syntax error.

The major differences between a Clipper database and a FoxPro database all center on the handling of memo fields:

- In Clipper databases, the first byte of the database header in databases with memo fields is a 83h; FoxPro stores F5h to this position to indicate a memo field.

- Clipper memo fields must have an extension of .DBT, while FoxPro's must have an extension of .FPT.

- While Clipper uses a fix block size of 512 bytes for memo fields, the default block size of FoxPro memo fields is only 64 bytes. (Microsoft FoxPro itself also allows the block size to be defined as a part of the FoxPro environment.) This means that short memo fields in particular will occupy far less disk space and consume far less of the system's resources when an application is running.

- Clipper indicates the end of a memo field entry with the end-of-file marker (ASCII 26). FoxPro, on the other hand, stores the actual length of the memo field entry. This makes the FoxPro memo file more suitable for storing a wide range of binary data (such as executable code, graphic images, etc.).

These differences combine to make the FoxPro database file format superior for applications that rely intensively on handling and manipulating memo fields. In cases that rely extensively on handling data in memo fields, you may want to convert your data from the Clipper database file format to the FoxPro file format. The following short program shows how that might be done by converting TRANS.DBF to a FoxPro file called TRANSF.DBF:

```
 1 :   // File CDX2.PRG
 2 :
 3 :   // Compile  Rmake samprdd /dFILE:CDX2
 4 :
 5 :   REQUEST DBFCDX
 6 :
 7 :   function main()
```

```
 8 :
 9 :     use TRANS new
10 :
11 :     dbCreate("TRANSF",Trans->(dbStruct() ),"DBFCDX")
12 :
13 :     use TRANSF new via "DBFCDX"
14 :     APPEND FROM trans
15 :
16 :     return(NIL)
```

It is worth stressing that, once a FoxPro database file that contains a memo field has been created, it cannot be read using the default Clipper DBFNTX driver. Attempting to do so produces a run-time error, "Corruption detected: <database name>." If a database file does not contain a memo field, however, it can be read by either the NTX or the CDX driver.

Besides providing access to FoxPro databases, the DBFCDX driver allows FoxPro-compatible index files to be generated and read. These index files are of three types:

- .IDX files. This is a *compact* index, which means that indexing information is stored within the file in a compressed format. .IDX files contain a single order per file.
- .CDX files (compound index files). Like .IDX files, .CDX files are compact indexes that are stored in a compressed format. They differ from .IDX files in their ability to contain multiple tags or orders per file.
- Structural compound index files. This is a special kind of .CDX file that is opened automatically when its associated database file is opened. CDX3.PRG, which appears below, is a very simple program that illustrates the use of a compound index file.

```
 1 : // File CDX3.PRG
 2 :
 3 : // Compile  Rmake samprdd /dFILE:CDX3
 4 :
 5 : REQUEST DBFCDX
 6 :
 7 : function main()
 8 :
 9 :     local nCtr
10 :
11 :     cls
12 :
13 :     use TRANSF new via "DBFCDX"
14 :     index on transf->account tag account to transf
15 :     index on transf->adate tag date to transf
16 :     index on transf->now_due tag amount to transf
17 :     close databases
18 :
19 :     use transf new via "DBFCDX"
20 :
21 :     for nCtr := 1 to 3
22 :        qout(ordname(nCtr))
23 :     next
```

```
24 :
25 :      return(NIL)
26 :
27 : // End of File: CDX3.PRG
```

The major advantage offered by both the compact index (.IDX) and compound index (.CDX) files supported by the DBFCDX replaceable database driver is a reduction in size of the index file. The following list, for example, shows the size of some index files, generated from the TRANS database (.IDX and .NTX) with 224 records:

| Key | .IDX Size | .NTX Size | % Reduction |
|---|---|---|---|
| Trans->Account | 3,072 | 6,144 | 50 |
| Trans->Adate | 3,072 | 7,168 | 57.14 |
| Trans->Now_Due | 4,096 | 7,168 | 42.86 |

In general, the DBFCDX driver tends to generate index files that are approximately half the size of the standard .NTX files. In the case of applications that access large database files, this reduced size of index files frequently can be equated with reduced speed and enhanced performance as well.

The structural compound index file also possesses an enormous advantage that makes it one of the more attractive features of the DBFCDX replaceable database driver. By automatically opening all orders within the file whenever its associated database is opened, this feature frees the programmer from the need to explicitly open and close index files. Aside from relieving demands on a programmer's already overloaded memory, it significantly minimizes the possibility that an index file will become corrupted or will fail to correspond to the data in its associated database.

An .IDX file can be created using any of the following syntaxes:

```
INDEX ON <cKeyExpression> TO <cOrderBagName>

OrdCreate(<cOrderBagName>,,<cExpKey>)

dbCreateIndex(<cOrderBagName>,<cExpKey>,<bExpKey>})
```

In other words, when no TAG name is specified, the DBFCDX driver assumes that it is to create a compact single-index file. On the other hand, if the following syntaxes are used, the DBFCDX driver will create a compound index file:

```
INDEX ON <cKeyExpression> TAG <cOrderName> TO <cOrderBagName>

OrdCreate(<cOrderBagName>,<cOrderName>,<cExpKey>)
```

Finally, a structural compound index file is simply a special case of a compound index file. There can only be one structural compound index file per database. The root name of the structural compound index file must be the same as the root name of the database file.

Whether they are single-index files or compound indexes, all DBFCDX index files support all of the new Clipper 5.2 index file enhancements:

- Unique index generated with the UNIQUE keyword
- Conditional indexes generated with the FOR clause
- Conditional indexes generated with the WHILE clause
- Compound indexes (multiple orders per order bag)
- Evaluation of the EVAL clause at the interval specified by the EVERY clause

CDX4.PRG uses the DBFCDX driver to illustrate many of these features and enhancements:

```
 1 :  // File CDX4.PRG
 2 :
 3 :  // Compile  Rmake samprdd /dFILE:CDX4
 4 :
 5 :  #include "PTVALUE.CH"
 6 :  REQUEST DBFCDX
 7 :
 8 :  function main()
 9 :
10 :     local aGas := {}
11 :
12 :     rddsetdefault("DBFCDX")
13 :     cls
14 :
15 :     use transf new        // A Conditional Index
16 :     index on transf->account tag acct5000 to transf ;
17 :         for transf->now_due >= 5000
18 :     browse()
19 :
20 :     transf->(ordsetfocus(0),dbgotop())
21 :     index on transf->now_due tag over5000 to transf ;
22 :         while transf->(recno()) <=100
23 :     browse()
24 :
25 :     aGas := gaugenew(10,0,13,maxcol())
26 :     gaugedisplay( aGas )
27 :     index on if(Transf->paid,"0","1")+str(transf->now_due) ;
28 :         tag owing to transf;
29 :         eval gaugeupdate(aGas, transf->(recno()/lastrec()), pTRUE ) ;
30 :         every 2
31 :     browse()
32 :
33 :     cls
34 :     index on transf->now_due tag balances to transf descending
35 :     browse()
36 :     return(NIL)
37 :
38 :  // End of File: CDX4.PRG
```

There is, however, one anomaly associated with compound index files generated by the DBFCDX driver. When the INDEX ON command or the ORDCREATE( ) function is used to rebuild an existing TAG within a compound index, the space used by the original tag is not released, while the new version of the order tag is build at the end of the file. The result is a "bloated" .CDX that contains large amounts of unused space. This can be freed by using either the REINDEX command or the ORDLISTREBUILD( ) function to "pack" the index file:

```
REINDEX
ORDLISTREBUILD()
```

When opening index files, .CDX and .IDX files can be freely mixed in a particular work area. When indexes are opened, the controlling or master index becomes either that single-order bag that was opened before any other index files, or the first order in the multiple-order bag that was opened before any other indexes. Where a structural compound index file exists, of course, its first order necessarily begins as the controlling index. The controlling index can be changed using any of the following:

```
ORDSETFOCUS(cOrderName>,<cOrderBagName>)

ORDSETFOCUS(nOrder>,<cOrderBagName>)

SET ORDER TO <nOrder> TAG <cOrderName> IN <cOrderBagName>
```

## DBFMDX

DBFMDX is the dBASE IV-compatible index driver. Some of the individual features of the driver are:

- Implicit record unlocking in single lock mode
- Multiple record locks
- Can support concurrent record locks (depending on available memory)
- Supports Order Management (Order Tags)
- Supports 47 TAGS per Order Bag
- Supports 15 Order Bags per work area
- Supports the conditional FOR clause
- Does not support temporary or partial indexes such as those created by the WHILE clause
- Supports descending indexes
- Supports unique indexes
- Does not support the EVAL and EVERY clauses
- Supports production/structural indexes
- Maximum key expression length is 220 bytes
- Maximum length for a FOR condition is 261 bytes

The DBFMDX replaceable database driver allows you both to create and to access dBASE IV-compatible databases. This RDD mirrors the feature set of Borland International's dBASE IV database product, and supports the following field types:

- Character
- Memo

- Numeric
- Float, a data type not present in Clipper that is used to store floating-point numbers
- Date
- Logical

The following program shows how the DBFMDX driver can be used to create a database:

```
 1 : // File MDX1.PRG
 2 :
 3 : // Compile  Rmake samprdd /dFILEL:MDX1
 4 :
 5 : REQUEST DBFMDX
 6 :
 7 : function main()
 8 :
 9 :    local aStruct := {}
10 :
11 :    aadd(aStruct,{"FName","C",20,0})
12 :    aadd(aStruct,{"LName","C",20,0})
13 :    aadd(aStruct,{"Age","N",3,0})
14 :    aadd(aStruct,{"Comments","M",10,0})
15 :    aadd(aStruct,{"Income","F",12,2})
16 :
17 :    dbCreate("DB4DBF",aStruct,"DBFMDX")
18 :
19 :    use DB4DBF new via "DBFMDX"
20 :    aStruct := DB4DBF->(dbstruct() )
21 :    cls
22 :    aeval(aStruct,{|x| qout(x[1],x[2],x[3],x[4])})
23 :
24 :    return(NIL)
25 :
26 : // End of File: MDX1.PRG
```

Database files created by the DBFMDX driver can be read using the standard Clipper DBFNTX driver as long as they do not contain memo fields or float fields; otherwise, the default Clipper DBFNTX driver displays a run-time error message, "Corruption detected: <database name>." This is true as well of DBFCDX, the FoxPro replaceable database driver.

Besides providing access to dBASE IV databases and memo files, the DBFMDX driver also generates and reads dBASE IV-compatible compound index (.MDX) files. However, whereas dBASE IV itself automatically generates a production index file that has the same root name as the database file and that is opened automatically when the database file is opened, the DBFMDX driver does not directly support production indexes. Opening and updating the necessary indexes is the responsibility of the programmer. However, even though the DBFMDX driver will not automatically open the production index (i.e., the index with the same root name as the database), there are several cases in which the driver assumes that a production index exists and, if it cannot find it, will produce a syntax error. This happens, for example, when a new order (or tag) is generated without specifying an index filename.

Note that, although some of the other replaceable database drivers may be able to read the .DBF files generated by the DBFMDX RDD under special conditions, none of the others are able to read the .MDX index files.

The DBFMDX driver supports the creation of .MDX files only; it cannot generate dBASE III-compatible .NDX files. This too places the responsibility on the programmer for keeping track of which orders with which key expressions are to be found in which order bag. The DBFMDX driver will generate a valid .MDX file in each of the following instances, despite their variations in syntax:

```
INDEX ON <xKeyExpression> TO <cOrderBagName>

INDEX ON <xKeyExpression> TAG <cOrderName>

INDEX ON <xKeyExpression> TAG <cOrderName> TO <cOrderBagName>
```

The first code example is confusing, since it adds an order tag that is not explicitly named to an index file. The DBFMDX driver will automatically assign the order tag the same name as <cOrderBagName>. This may, however, not be quite what the programmer intended. The second example can be equally confusing, since although the tag name is present, the index file name is missing. In this case, the DBFMDX driver will *add* the order <cOrderName> to the index file whose root name matches that of its associated database. However, if this index file does not exist, a syntax error will result. Finally, the last code example represents the syntactical form of the INDEX ON command that is least likely to cause confusion. Its use with the DBFMDX driver is highly recommended.

When an .MDX file that contains multiple orders (or tags) is opened, the DBFMDX driver does not automatically recognize a controlling index; the database will be in its natural order. For example, in MDX2.PRG, the index file TRANSMDX1.MDX contains three tags: Now_Due, Account, and Owing. When the index file is opened with either the INDEX argument of the USE command or the SET INDEX TO command, the ORDSETFOCUS( ) function will return a null string, indicating that no index is controlling the logical ordering of the database.

```
 1 : // File MDX2.PRG
 2 :
 3 : // Compile  Rmake samprdd /dFILE:MDX2
 4 :
 5 : #include "PTVALUE.CH"
 6 : REQUEST DBFMDX
 7 :
 8 : function main()
 9 :
10 :    cls
11 :
12 :    qout("Generating database...")
13 :    use TRANS new
14 :    dbCreate("TRANSM",Trans->(dbStruct() ),"DBFMDX")
15 :    use TRANSM new via "DBFMDX"
16 :    APPEND FROM trans
```

```
17 :      close databases
18 :
19 :      qout("Generating indexes...")
20 :      use transm new via "DBFMDX"
21 :      index on transm->now_due tag due to transmdx
22 :      index on transm->account tag account to transmdx
23 :      index on if(!transm->paid,"1","0")+str(transm->now_due) ;
24 :           tag owing to transmdx
25 :      close databases
26 :
27 :      use transm new via "DBFMDX" index transmdx
28 :      qout("Controlling order is " + ordsetfocus() )
29 :
30 :      ordsetfocus(1)
31 :      qout("Controlling order is " + ordsetfocus() )
32 :
33 :      inkey(0)
34 :
35 :      browse()
36 :
37 :      return(NIL)
38 :
39 : // End of File: MDX2.PRG
```

The DBFMDX driver does not support all of the enhancements added to the INDEX...ON command in Clipper 5.2. The features that it does support, which are illustrated in the sample program MDX3.PRG, include the following:

- Unique indexes using the UNIQUE clause
- Conditional indexes using the FOR clause
- Descending indexes using the DESCEND clause

```
 1 : // File MDX3.PRG
 2 :
 3 : // Compile  Rmake samprdd /dFILE:MDX3
 4 :
 5 : #include "PTVALUE.CH"
 6 : REQUEST DBFMDX
 7 :
 8 : function main()
 9 :
10 :      local aGas := {}
11 :
12 :      rddsetdefault("DBFMDX")
13 :      cls
14 :
15 :      use transm new         // A Conditional Index
16 :      index on transm->account tag acct5000 to transm ;
17 :           for transm->now_due >= 5000
18 :      @ 0,0 say "Conditional index with NOW_DUE >= 5000"
19 :      browse()
```

```
20 :
21 :    transm->(ordsetfocus(0),dbgotop())
22 :    index on transm->account tag first100 to transm ;
23 :       while transm->(recno()) <=100
24 :    @ 0,0 say "Conditional index WHILE RECNO() <= 100"
25 :    browse()
26 :
27 :    aGas := gaugenew(10,0,13,maxcol())
28 :    gaugedisplay( aGas )
29 :    index on if(transm->paid,"0","1")+str(transm->now_due) ;
30 :       tag owing to transm;
31 :       eval gaugeupdate(aGas, transm->(recno()/lastrec()), pTRUE ) ;
32 :          every 2
33 :    @ 0,0 say "Index with EVAL"
34 :    browse()
35 :
36 :    cls
37 :    index on transm->now_due tag balances to transm descending
38 :    @ 0,0 say "Descending index with NOW_DUE"
39 :    browse()
40 :    return(NIL)
41 :
42 :    // End of File: MDX3.PRG
```

MDX3.PRG actually illustrates both the features that the DBFMDX driver supports and those that it doesn't support, like the EVAL clause and conditional indexes with the WHILE clause. What is interesting about the driver when it encounters these unsupported clauses, however, is that it does not display a syntax error or terminate program execution. Instead, the program executes "normally," except of course that the indexes generated do not necessarily conform to the indexes requested in the command statement. Insuring that the final indexes are indeed those that were originally requested is therefore the responsibility of the programmer.

## DBFNDX

This driver is the dBASE III compatible index driver. Some of the individual features of the driver are:

- Implicit record unlocking in single lock mode
- Multiple record locks
- Can support concurrent record locks (depending on available memory)
- Supports Order Management
- Supports 1 TAG per Order Bag
- Supports 15 Order Bags per work area
- Does not support the conditional FOR clause
- Does not support temporary or partial indexes such as those created by the WHILE clause
- Does not support descending indexes

- Supports unique indexes
- Does not support the EVAL and EVERY clauses
- Does not support production/structural indexes
- Maximum key expression length is 256 bytes

The DBFNDX driver allows you to both read and write the dBASE III Plus-compatible .DBF file format. Since the default file format supported by Clipper and the DBFNTX replaceable database driver duplicates the dBASE III Plus "standard," any database file created by the DBFNTX driver can be read by the DBFNDX driver, and vice versa.

The differences between the DBFNTX and the DBFNDX drivers center on their index files. An index file generated by one driver cannot be read by the other driver. Nor can indexes generated by the two drivers be open in a single work area. Second, the DBFNDX driver does not allow index files to be generated based on logical keys. For example, we might attempt to generate an index based on the following expression:

```
index on trans->paid to trndx2
```

The DBFNTX driver successfully generates an index based on this logical field; the DBFNDX driver, however, will generate an empty index and display the error message, "ORDCREATE (0) Internal error 1240." Finally, if the goal of using the DBFNDX driver is to allow dBASE III Plus to access Clipper-generated data and index files (rather than to use Clipper to access data that is primarily generated by dBASE III Plus), then special attention must be paid to all key expressions. In particular, the key expression must not contain any function or user-defined function that in any way depends on a function that is not supported by dBASE III Plus.

Finally, the DBFNDX driver does not support the dBASE III Plus file and record locking scheme. Instead, it supports Clipper's own scheme—a logical design decision, since otherwise the DBFNDX driver could never coexist with the DBFNTX driver in a single application. But a major consequence of it is that, because the DBFNDX driver's record locks will be invisible to dBASE III Plus, the two products should never be used to access the same databases simultaneously. If this does happen, corruption of the database could result.

Like DBFNTX, the DBFNDX driver supports only single-tag indexes. Either of the following forms of the INDEX ON command are acceptable for generating an NDX-compatible index file:

```
INDEX ON <xExp> TAG <cTagName> TO <cOrderBag>

INDEX ON <xExp> TO <cOrderBag>
```

The third variation of the INDEX ON command, however, will generate a run-time error:

```
INDEX ON <xExp> TAG <cTagName>
```

Although a tag name can be specified in the INDEX ON command, the tag name is not saved in the header of the index file, and therefore is lost once the file is closed. As a result, for index files created with the INDEX ON...TAG...TO variation of the command, the ORD-

NAME( ) function will return <cTagName> until the index file is first closed. Once it is reopened, the ORDNAME( ) function will return <cOrderBag>, or the index filename.

The DBFNDX driver supports relatively few of the indexing enhancements introduced by Clipper 5.2. It does support the EVAL clause, along with the UNIQUE clause to generate unique indexes. But besides these, it does not support any of the following:

- Conditional indexes created with the FOR clause. The ORDFOR( ) function will return a null string.
- Conditional indexes created with the WHILE clause.
- Descending indexes.

If the DBFNDX driver encounters a request for any of these indexing operations, it produces the following compiler error:

```
Error DBFNDX/0    Operation not supported
```

## DBFNTX

This driver is the standard Clipper index driver. Compared to the other index drivers, some of the features of this driver are:

- Implicit record unlocking in single lock mode
- Multiple record locks
- Can support concurrent record locks (depending on available memory)
- Support TAG/Order Management
- Supports 1 TAG per Order Bag
- Supports 15 Order Bags per work area
- Supports the conditional FOR clause
- Supports temporary or partial indexes such as those created by the WHILE clause
- Supports descending indexes
- Supports unique indexes
- Supports the EVAL and EVERY clauses
- Does NOT support production/structural indexes
- Maximum key expression length is 256 bytes
- Maximum length for a FOR condition is 256 bytes

The DBFNTX driver supports all of the enhanced indexing features introduced in Clipper 5.2, with a single exception: It still supports only single-order bags. But unlike the DBFNDX driver, the standard DBFNTX driver stores the index tag (or order) name in the header of the index file. Therefore, the tag is a permanent part of the index, and becomes the name by which a particular order is known.

NTX files can be created using either of these variations on the INDEX command:

```
INDEX ON <xExp> TAG <cTagName> TO <cOrderBag>
INDEX ON <xExp> TO <cOrderBag>
```

In the second case, since an order name is not specified, the order name will be the same as <cOrderBag>. A third variation of the INDEX ON command will cause an argument error, since the driver does not know the name of the file in which to store the order:

```
INDEX ON <xExp> TAG <cTagName>
```

Because of its support for one tag per order bag, the ORDNAME( ) function will always return the order name rather than the order bag name, where the two differ. Similarly, the ORDERNUMBER( ) requires as a parameter the name of the order. If it is provided the name of the order bag, assuming that the order has a different name, the function will return a 0.

## DBPX

This is the Borland Paradox table and index driver. This format is radically different from any of the drivers previously outlined. Some of the features supported by this driver are

- Implicit record unlocking in single lock mode
- Can support one concurrent record lock (determined by available memory)

All other features are either not supported or not applicable to this driver. While this may appear to be a hinderance, some unique features are found only in this driver.

- Allows the creation that recognizes typical data types as well as Currency ($) and short (S) numbers ranging from -32767 to 32767.
- Creates equally efficient keyed and unkeyed tables.
- Creates, selects, and activates secondary index.

Unlike database files, Paradox stores data in tables consisting of both fields and records. A database in Paradox, is a group of files related to each other rather than just a single file. In addition, Paradox uses the concept of a companion file known as an object. These are related to a table; examples may include report forms, indexes, and data entry forms. A table and any object associated to that table is known as a family. In Paradox, the components of a family all have the same base filename and are distinguished by different file extensions:

| | |
|---|---|
| .DB | Table |
| .PX | Primary index |
| .X?? | Secondary index |
| .Y?? | Secondary index |
| .F | Data entry forms |
| .F?? | Data entry forms |
| .R | Report forms |
| .R?? | Report forms |
| .G | Graph specifications |
| .G?? | Graph specifications |
| .SET | Image settings |
| .VAL | Field validity specifications |

The maximum number of records in a file can be as high as 256 M. In addition, Paradox records in nonkeyed tables can be up to 4000 bytes, while records in keyed tables are limited to 1350 bytes. Each record, regardless of type, can have up to 255 fields with up to 255 characters in each.

What makes a Paradox file or table different from a .DBF file is the concept of an unkeyed or keyed table. In essence, a keyed table is a data file with the index built into it. On the other hand, an unkeyed table is one that will appear in the natural order, or in terms of the .DBF base, the record number order. When a new record is added to an unkeyed table, it will appear at the end of the table and, thus, a new and unique identity (or record) will be recorded. A keyed table works on a different premise. The main premise that is different from traditional xBASE standards is the idea of unique keys as part of the file. In Clipper using the .NTX file, we can have multiple identities (or records) in a data file that will have the same KEY VALUE. Not so in a keyed table using the Paradox driver: All keys must be unique. This makes searching for information incredibly fast, especially when working with table lookups and the like.

To go with this, there are two types of keyed indexes: primary and secondary. A primary index is directly tied to the table and is the initial point of all operations. Think about it: There must be SOME index that is in control so therefore there must be a primary keyed index. Secondary keyed indexes fall more in line with the traditional index file found in Clipper. There is no unique key requirement, and they may be modified without affecting the structure of the table. To make matters even more complicated, there are two types of secondary indexes: incremental (for keyed tables) or independent (for unkeyed tables). Independent indexes are used only for unkeyed tables and therefore are not dynamically maintained in any way. Their accuracy is limited to only the time of their creation. Incremental indexes are created for keyed tables and are automatically maintained, similar to the way primary indexes are maintained except that they do not require a complete rebuild of the table every time a change is made. Therefore, incremental indexes are the preferred method when working with large files.

```
 1 : // File       Ind5.prg
 2 : // Compile    Rmake samprdd /dFILE:ind5
 3 :
 4 : request dbpx
 5 :
 6 : procedure Main()
 7 :
 8 :    local aData := {}
 9 :
10 :    aadd( aData, {"company", "C", 23, 0} )
11 :    aadd( aData, {"datein",  "D", 8, 0} )
12 :    aadd( aData, {"Float",   "S", 10, 0} )
13 :    aadd( aData, {"amount",  "$", 6,2 } )
14 :    dbcreate( "Steve", aData, "dbpx" )
15 :    use Steve new via "dbpx"
16 :    browse()
17 :
18 : // End of File: Ind5.prg
```

## Summary

This is perhaps the most explosive area of Clipper. RDDs allow the core language to work for many different people from different companies, with different needs. This also opens up new consulting possibilities that were once closed to many Clipper users because the language of our choice was restricted to the .DBF file format. Companies that specialize in RDD development will give Clipper the ability to reach out to Sequel Server and a new data format that is faster than all others, with new definable data types, the ability to store arrays and code blocks to disk, and the ability to have fields of varied length.

# 14

# Low-Level File and Binary Functions

## The Basics

In Clipper 5.2, special low-level file functions extend the scope of a Clipper application by allowing us direct control of a file in various formats other than .DBT, .MEM, .DBF, and .NTX. These functions are considered "low-level" because they refer to files via DOS file handles and allow byte for byte manipulation of the file and control of the file pointer; these functions are ordinarily controlled by either the operating system or an applications software package. These functions include FOPEN( ), FCREATE( ), FWRITE( ), FREAD( ), FREADSTR( ), FERASE( ), FERROR( ), FSEEK( ), FCLOSE( ), and FRENAME( ). Most of these functions refer to a file via a DOS file handle that is to be passed to one of these functions to tell the function which file needs to be worked on. There are also the binary functions, which include BIN2I( ), BIN2L( ), BIN2W( ), I2BIN( ), and L2BIN( ). These binary functions are useful in converting floating-point values stored in other formats (normally following IEEE standards).

## DOS and File Handles

Four functions refer to a file by the conventional method using a character string representing the filename. These functions are FERASE( ), FRENAME( ), FOPEN( ), and FCREATE( ). The remaining functions—FWRITE( ), FERROR( ), FREAD( ), FREADSTR( ), FSEEK( ), and FCLOSE( )—refer to a file via the DOS file handle returned from either FOPEN( ) or FCREATE( ). FERASE( ) and FRENAME( ) are individual functions that perform operations similar to most of the low-level file functions. The source of these functions, with the exception of the two just mentioned, is an object module named PHILES.OBJ within EXTEND.LIB.

In working with low-level file functions, remember one common theme: DOS is stupid. Whenever you refer to a file, as in when you issue the command USE (<filename>), Clipper keeps track of the name of the file and goes to DOS and asks for a DOS file handle to open the designated file. Whenever we subsequently refer to that file by its name, it is Clipper that translates our database name to the appropriate DOS file handle.

DOS file handles are allocated sequentially. Normally, in a Clipper application, the first DOS file handle to be allocated is 5, since these file handles are reserved internally by DOS:

| | |
|---|---|
| File Handle 0 | Standard Input Device (CON) Read Only |
| File Handle 1 | Standard Output Device (CON) Write Only |
| File Handle 2 | Standard Error Device (CON) Write Only |
| File Handle 3 | Standard Aux Device (AUX) Read/Write |
| File Handle 4 | Standard Printer Device (PRN) Read/Write |

When a Clipper executable file is opened, it obtains the next sequential file handle number. Because Clipper only keeps track of the relationship between a DOS file handle and the name and makes no other restrictions, files in Clipper (particularly database files) may be opened more than once. For example, an item to be entered into the chart of account files needs to refer to an item in that very file. Instead of maintaining the state of the record pointer and then moving it to seek the dependent record, it is just as easy to open the same database twice, giving a different ALIAS in the second call:

```
use Chart new index Account
use Chart new index Account alias Cons
```

Now, using the CONS work area *only as a lookup area*, it is possible to move the record pointer in that work area independently of the record pointer in the CHART work area.

Clipper can work with up to 250 files (for DOS versions 3.3 and higher). This is in part controlled by the FILES statement within the CONFIG.SYS file or the SET CLIPPER=Fxxx switch on the machine running the Clipper application. If these two numbers do not match, and if the SET CLIPPER switch is used, the Clipper application will recognize whichever value is the lesser of the two. In addition, for some DOS versions, the FILES value should be an odd number if it is greater than 20, to prevent unnecessary memory usage.

Keep in mind that in using the low-level file functions, everything is under the control of the programmer. Whenever the file needs to be opened, the way it is opened is critical; if the file is to be created, it is critical to create the file properly before any data is written to it. These functions give the programmer direct access to a file or a device. The power that stems from these functions should be used cautiously and prudently.

## Low-Level File Functions and RMAKE.EXE

The entire idea of a *touch* program is that you can quickly update the DOS date and time stamp of a file to be later than the object file and, consequently, later than the application's date and time stamp. This allows you to force a total recompile and relink of an application using the RMAKE.EXE utility program; deleting all of the .OBJs of an application would, in many situations, achieve the same effect. However, the comfort margin of deleting files is drastically lower than simply updating the date and time stamp of a group of program files.

```
1 : * File:     Touch.prg
2 :
3 : #include "PTValue.ch"    // Power Tools Header File
4 : #include "PTInkey.ch"    // Power Tools Header File
```

```
 5 :
 6 : ********************
 7 :
 8 : function Main( cFiles )   // Starting point with parameter!
 9 :
10 :    local aDir              // Array of file names that is obtained
11 :
12 :    outstd( pCRLF )         //  Carriage Return/Line Feed
13 :
14 :    if cFiles == NIL        // No DOS parameter came in!
15 :       outstd( "TOUCH <file skeleton>" )
16 :
17 :    else
18 :     if !file( cFiles )  // The specified files don't exist
19 :        outstd( "The files <" )
20 :        outstd( cFiles )
21 :        outstd( "> do not exist." )
22 :
23 :     else
24 :        outstd( "There are " )
25 :        outstd( alltrim( str( len( aDir := directory( cFiles ) ) ) ) )
26 :        outstd( " on the disk to be updated." )
27 :        outstd( pCRLF )
28 :        outstd( "Updating files...." )
29 :
30 :        setcursor( pCURSOR_OFF )
31 :
32 :        aeval( aDir, {|aFile| TouchIt( aFile[1] )} )
33 :
34 :        setcursor( pCURSOR_ON )
35 :
36 :     endif
37 :
38 :    endif
39 :
40 :    outstd( pCRLF )
41 :
42 :    return( NIL )
43 :
44 : ********************
45 :
46 : static function TouchIt( cName )
47 :
48 :    #define pREAD_WRITE   2    // 2 manifest constants to be used
49 :    #define pEND_OF_FILE 2    // just by this function
50 :
51 :    local nFHandle            // The file handle to be TOUCHED
52 :
53 :    outstd( pCRLF )
54 :    outstd( chr( pENTER ) )
55 :    outstd( padr( cName, maxcol() ) )
56 :
57 :    nFHandle := fopen( cName, pREAD_WRITE )     // Open the file
58 :
59 :    // Move the file pointer in nFHandle 0 bytes from the end of the
60 :    // file which, effectively puts the marker on the end of the file
61 :
62 :    fseek( nFHandle, 0, pEND_OF_FILE )
63 :
64 :    fwrite( nFHandle, "", 0 )           // Update the DATE / TIME stamp...
65 :
```

```
66 :     // The last char of the file should be ASCII 26 (^Z). It should not be
67 :     // written over since a NULL byte is being written and that 0 bytes are
68 :     // explicitly passed to the FWRITE() function.  A "" byte to Clipper
69 :     // is 0 in length whereas  a CHR(0)is a character with length of 1.
70 :
71 :     fclose( nFHandle )   // Close the file
72 :
73 :     return( NIL )
74 :
75 :     #undef pREAD_WRITE       // Not necessary but good housekeeping
76 :     #undef pEND_OF_FILE      // practice
77 :
78 : // End of File: Touch.prg
```

Throughout this program, the OUTSTD( ) is used as an alternate method for showing how output may be displayed. OUTSTD( ) stands for output to a standard device; the default standard device is the screen.

If no parameter is passed to the TOUCH program, the value of *cFiles* on line 14 will be NIL and a message will be displayed to the screen. However, if a parameter is passed to the program, the value of *cFiles* will be used in the FILE( ) function on line 18. If no files exist, an appropriate message will be displayed. Otherwise, a count of the number of files matching the *cFiles* skeleton will be displayed on line 25. This is derived from the LEN( ) of the multidimensional array returned from the DIRECTORY( ) function.

Each element in this array is ultimately evaluated and processed by the AEVAL( ) function on line 32. Each array element returned by the DIRECTORY( ) function and passed to the LOCAL parameter *aFiles* in the code block on line 32 is a subarray containing the filename, size, date, time, and attribute returned by the DIRECTORY( ) function. The first element of this subarray is the name of the file, and that value is then passed to the TouchIt( ) function within the code block.

The TouchIt( ) function is STATIC: Only the TOUCH.PRG program file can make a call to it. Within this function, the name of the file to be touched as processed by AEVAL( ) is stored in the LOCAL parameter named *cName*. On lines 57 and 62, the preprocessor is used to help with some of the values of the parameters to the FOPEN( ) and FSEEK( ) functions. A header file named LOWLEVEL.CH has a complete listing of the possible preprocessor values for all the low-level file functions; it is used in later examples in this chapter.

Remember, files are nothing more than numbers to DOS and to the low-level file functions. The variable that will contain the handle of the file that we are about to touch, *nFHandle*, is initialized on line 51. The file is opened in read-write mode by the FOPEN( ) function on line 57. The file pointer is then positioned at the end of the file on line 62; the byte marker to be moved is in the file associated with *nFHandle*, the number of bytes to be moved (either forward or backward) is 0, and the location at which to begin moving the byte marker is at the pEND_OF_FILE. The value of the FSEEK( ) function would be the byte number where the pointer resides after moving. In this particular case, the value of FSEEK( ) and the size of the file would be the same. Once we are at the end-of-file marker, we simply write a NULL byte. This byte has a length of 0 and does not alter the contents of the file, nor does it overwrite an end-of-file marker, if one is present; it simply forces DOS to update the FAT table with a new date and time stamp. If the character written at this position (line 64) were CHR(0), serious trouble would result, since CHR(0) is a character with a length of 1; this would overwrite the end-of-file marker. Once the date and time stamps are appropriately updated, the file associated with *nFHandle* is closed by FCLOSE( ) without the function's return value being used.

## Seeing If a Drive or Path Exists

The low-level file functions are not part of the Clipper run-time error-trapping system. Since they deal with DOS on its native level, they are below interpreterlike operations that may be invoked within a Clipper application at run time. Therefore, it is possible to have the low-level file functions test for such things as whether a drive or path is available, and they can be used in redirecting output to other devices. Since other devices are seen by DOS as nothing more than files, it is possible to do the following:

```
FOPEN( "LPT2", pWRITE_ONLY )
```

For simple communications, it is possible to do this as well:

```
FOPEN( "COM1", pWRITE_ONLY )
```

Simple phone dialers may be built directly into a Clipper application. Redirecting output to a secondary printer (useful in some network environments) and checking the printer status also become possible with the low-level file functions.

The following program shows how to test for a drive and/or path within the Clipper environment. No run-time error will be generated if an invalid drive and/or path is specified.

```
 1 : * File:      Validdr.prg
 2 :
 3 : #include "PTValue.ch"      // Power Tools misc. values
 4 : #include "PTInkey.ch"      // Power Tools key definition table
 5 : #include "PTVerbs.ch"      // Power Tools Commands
 6 :
 7 : #xtranslate SSDREAD() =>( setcursor(1), readmodal(getlist), ;
 8 :                           getlist := {}, setcursor(0), ;
 9 :                           !( lastkey() == 27 ) )
10 :
11 : *******************
12 :
13 : function Main()
14 :
15 :    local cDrive   := "A:"
16 :    local cPath    := padr( "\" + curdir() + "\", 50 )
17 :    local Getlist  := {}                    // This is for the READ/GET
18 :    local lSuccess
19 :
20 :    REPEAT
21 :       scroll()
22 :
23 :       @ 5,5 say "Enter Drive: " GET cDrive PICT "!!"
24 :       @ 6,5 say "        Path: " GET cPath PICT "@K@S30@!"
25 :
26 :       if SSDRead()
27 :
28 :          @ 8,0 SAY "Drive " SAY cDrive   // Enhancement on the old command
29 :
30 :          lSuccess := ValidDrive(cDrive)
31 :
```

**788** *Straley's Programming with Clipper 5.2*

```
32 :        devout( " " + if( lSuccess, "IS READY", "NOT THERE" ) )
33 :
34 :        if ! lSuccess
35 :           qqout( " Error was: " )
36 :           qqout( errorlevel() )
37 :        endif
38 :
39 :        @ 11,0 SAY "Path " SAY cPath SAY " "
40 :
41 :        devout( if( (lSuccess := ValidDrive(,cPath)), ;
42 :                    "Is Fine!", ;
43 :                    "Trouble!") )
44 :
45 :        if ! lSuccess
46 :           qout()
47 :           qout( " Error was: " )
48 :           qqout( errorlevel() )
49 :        endif
50 :
51 :        @ 14,10 say "Press any key to go again or ESC to quit."
52 :        inkey(0)
53 :
54 :     endif
55 :
56 :   UNTIL ( lastkey() == pESC )
57 :
58 :   return( NIL )
59 :
60 : ***********************
61 :
62 : function ValidDrive( cDrive, cPath )
63 :
64 :   local lRetValue := pFALSE    // Default return value
65 :   local nFHandle               // File handle for low-level functions
66 :   local cTempName              // Holds the concatenation of values
67 :
68 :   DEFAULT cDrive TO "", ;
69 :           cPath TO ""
70 :
71 :   // Create the actual file, stripping any double "\\" in case user
72 :   // typed one in.  Default to add them in just in case they are
73 :   // missing.
74 :
75 :   cTempName := strtran( alltrim(cDrive) + "\" + alltrim(cPath) + ;
76 :                         "\LOWFILE.$$$", "\\", "\" )
77 :
78 :   nFHandle := fcreate( cTempName )   // Attemp to create the file
79 :
80 :   if nFHandle > 4            // the file was created!
81 :      ferase( cTempName )     // Erase the file
82 :      errorlevel( 0 )         // set the error level to appropriate value
83 :      fclose( nFHandle )      // Always close the file!
84 :      lRetValue := pTRUE      // Assign the return value of function
85 :   else
86 :
87 :      errorlevel( ferror() )  // Assign the error level to Ferror()
88 :
89 :   endif
90 :
91 :   return( lRetValue )
92 :
93 : // End of File: Validdr.prg
```

In this example, the user-defined command REPEAT and UNTIL <condition> is used; it is found in the header file named PTVERBS.CH. This command allows us to test for a condition at the end of the processing loop rather than at the beginning. In some cases, where the loop is based on the value of the LASTKEY( ) pressed, we have to clear out the keyboard buffer prior to executing the loop, as in this construct:

```
KEYBOARD ""
INKEY()
DO WHILE LASTKEY() != 27    // The ESC key
    * a series of GETS
    * a READ command
ENDDO
```

But with the REPEAT/UNTIL command, we can test the value of the last key pressed for the READ at the end of the loop, which frees us from worrying about the last key that might have been pressed prior to entering the loop.

Line 24 contains a mixed picture function in which the value displayed by the GET will appear until any key is pressed (so long as the cursor is on the first column position), at which time the preexisting GET information is blanked out. This is the "@K" function. All of the letters in the GET on line 24 will be forced to uppercase lettering because of the "@!" function, and the display will scroll horizontally for 30 columns because of the "@S30" picture function.

SSDREAD( ) on line 26 is a pseudofunction introduced on lines 7 through 9 that allows the READ or ReadModal( ) to return a value. In this translation, we see the following:

```
#xtranslate SSDRead() =>> ( setcursor(1), readmodal(getlist), ;
                            getlist := {}, setcursor(0), ;
                            !(lastkey() = 27) )
```

This is one large expression, the value of which is the last evaluation made. Within this expression, the cursor is turned on, a call to the READMODAL( ) function is made with the internal *Getlist[ ]* array, the *Getlist[ ]* is reinitialized at the end of the ReadModal( ) call, the cursor is turned off, and, finally, the value of the mini-expression !(LASTKEY( )=27) becomes the value of the entire expression. Therefore, the GETS are activated, the cursor is turned on and off, the *Getlist[ ]* is cleared out, and the value of the expression SSDREAD( ) becomes a logical true (.T.) if the last key pressed is not the ESC key (ASCII 27).

On line 32, the value of the variable *lSuccess* is the value of the function ValidDrive( ) on line 30. This same function is used on line 41; however, in this second function call, the first parameter is skipped and only the path is passed to it. The definition of this function begins on line 62. If the LOCAL parameter *cDrive* or *cPath* is not passed to the function or is not a character data type, the user-defined command DEFAULT TO is used to assign a NULL byte to each of these parameters. Once each of these two parameters has been verified, a new LOCAL variable named *cTempName* is created on line 75 with the string concatenation of these parameters and a filename, "LOWFILE.$$$". On line 78 the program attempts to create this file on the specified drive and/or path using the low-level file function FCREATE( ). If the file can be created, the drive and/or path specified is a valid value. (A file is considered created if the file handle is greater than 4—the first 5 DOS file handles, 0–4, are reserved, so the next available file handle has to be greater than 4.)

A test to FERROR( ) could be made in addition to this simple test. If the parameters—the drive name, the path name, or both—are invalid, the file LOWFILE.$$$ cannot be created and the value of ERRORLEVEL( ) is set accordingly. Using the ERRORLEVEL( ) function to give additional information to the system other than just what is returned from a function is an ideal use for this function. However, be careful to set ERRORLEVEL( ) for both valid and invalid operations. On line 87, the value of ERRORLEVEL( ) is set to the value of FERROR( ), allowing us to see what error was found by this function outside of its original function call on lines 36 and 48. However, if the call to the function is valid, the value of ERRORLEVEL( ) must also be set accordingly (line 82); otherwise, a preexisting error condition may be evaluated improperly.

In any case, what is important about the ValidDrive( ) function is that it can test for the existence of a drive or path by using the low-level FCREATE( ) function, since the low-level file functions are outside of the run-time error-trapping system in a Clipper application.

## Using the Preprocessor

Along with the standard low-level file functions, there may be a need to extend the function set to include such functions as Feof( ) (similar to EOF( )), Fskip( ) (similar to DBSKIP( )), and Fposition( ) (which reports the current position of the file pointer). All three functions may be better expressed as pseudofunctions and translated by the preprocessor. In the following example, these three functions are used.

```
 1 : * File:     Morelow.prg
 2 :
 3 : #include "PTVerbs.ch"     // Power Tools Command File
 4 : #include "PTLowLvl.ch"
 5 :
 6 : #xtranslate Fposition( <file> ) => fseek( <file>, 0, 1 )
 7 : #xtranslate Feof( <file> ) => ;
 8 :              ( ( _at  := fseek( <file>, 0, 1 ) ), ;
 9 :                ( _ret := fseek( <file>, 0, 2 ) ), ;
10 :                ( fseek( <file>, _at, 0 ) ), ( _ret \< _at ) )
11 :
12 : #xtranslate FSkip( <file>, <number> ) => fseek( <file>, <number>, 1 )
13 :
14 : memvar _at    // This is to prevent a warning message should the file
15 : memvar _ret   // be compiled with the /W since the FEOF() uses these vars.
16 :
17 : *******************
18 :
19 : function Main()
20 :
21 :    local nFhandle
22 :
23 :    scroll()
24 :
25 :    nFhandle := fopen( "Ontap.dbf", pOPEN_READ )
26 :
27 :    if nFhandle > 4     // This is a good file
28 :       while !FEOF( nFhandle )
29 :
30 :          @ 0,0 SAY "Working on byte: "  SAY FPOSITION( nFhandle )
31 :
32 :          FSKIP( nFhandle, 1 )
```

```
33 :      enddo
34 :    endif
35 :
36 :    run dir Ontap.dbf
37 :
38 :    return( NIL )
39 :
40 : // End of File: Morelow.prg
```

In MORELOW.PRG, three pseudofunctions are built. In practice, it is always a good idea to build pseudofunctions as typical user-defined functions first, and then to convert them to pseudofunctions for the preprocessor. Should there be an error within the pseudofunction, either the compile-time or the run-time error that is generated will point to the functions within the pseudofunction, and not to the name of the pseudofunction itself. In other words, without following the approach of first developing the user-defined function and then translating it into a pseudofunction, it will be unclear whether any particular bug is due to the operation of the function itself or to an error in the syntax or the expression used for the preprocessor.

Besides being able to build pseudofunctions, it clearly is important to understand what they are. A pseudofunction is similar to a user-defined function, except that it consists of a translation of the pseudofunction itself into a compound expression. Generally, a pseudofunction is an expression that has been given a single name for readability and that does not place a symbol in the symbol table. In other words, a pseudofunction is nothing more than an elongated expression; the return value of the pseudofunction is the last expression to be evaluated within the compound expression.

For example, the value of the pseudofunction Feof( ) (line 28) is the expression on lines 10. (The "\" is used in the #xtranslation directive to tell the preprocessor that the following character is to be translated literally and is not to be seen as a chunk marker symbol. Therefore, the expression for Feof( ) is really ( _ret < _at ).) Prior to this, the in-line operators are used to assign values to these two variables and to reposition the file pointer (line 10) to its original position prior to the function call. In-line assignments give us the potential to create temporary values and to evaluate them at a later time in that same expression.

## Reading Files

An added benefit of low-level file functions is the ability to read various file formats, write out various formats, and redirect output to various files and devices, including alternate printers.

### TEXT FILES

The individual lines of text files, for the most part, are delimited by CHR(13)+CHR(10). In the next example, files may be read in and dumped out to various devices and/or files.

```
1 : * Name:     Write1.prg
2 :
3 : #include "PTValue.ch"    // Power Tools header file of values
4 : #include "PTInkey.ch"    // and of ASCII values for keys
5 : #include "PTVerbs.ch"    // and user-defined commands
```

```
 6 :
 7 : #include "PTLowLvl.ch"
 8 :
 9 : *********************
10 :
11 : function Main()
12 :
13 :    local cOutput := space(40)
14 :    local cFile   := space(40)
15 :    local getlist := {}
16 :
17 :    REPEAT    // User-Defined Command
18 :
19 :       // The SETKEY() function is the functional form of the SET KEY TO
20 :       // command.  The way this one is being called actually reprograms
21 :       // the SET KEY to accept a user-defined parameter passed and
22 :       // MANIPULATED in the called functions.
23 :
24 :       setkey( pTAB, {|| FilesOnDisk( @cFile )} )
25 :
26 :       cls
27 :
28 :       @ 1,0 say "Press TAB for Files!"
29 :       @ 3,0 say "Enter file name:" get cFile
30 :
31 :       read
32 :
33 :       if !( lastkey() == pESC )
34 :          setkey( pTAB, {|| Output( @cOutput )} )
35 :
36 :          @ 1, 0 say "Press TAB for options!"
37 :          @ 5, 0 say "Direction of output" get cOutput
38 :          read
39 :
40 :          if !( lastkey() == pESC )
41 :
42 :             if !ReadFiles( alltrim(cFile), alltrim(cOutput) )
43 :                outerr( "An error has occurred!  Any key." )
44 :                inkey(0)
45 :             endif
46 :
47 :          endif
48 :
49 :       endif
50 :
51 :    UNTIL lastkey() == pESC
52 :
53 :    VOID
54 :
55 : *********************
56 :
57 : static function ReadFiles( cFile, cOutput )
58 :
59 :    #define pBUFFER 1024    // The buffer size to read in at one time
60 :
61 :    local lRetValue := pFALSE    // Default return value
62 :    local lToExit   := pFALSE    // Condition if while loop is to exit
63 :    local cLine     := ""        // Will hold the individual line of file
64 :    local nFRead                 // DOS file handle to be read
65 :    local nFWrite                // DOS file handle of file written
66 :    local cBytes                 // Individual bytes read in
```

```
 67 :    local cAddBytes              // Any left over bytes from one buffer to next
 68 :
 69 :    if file( cFile )
 70 :
 71 :      nFRead := fopen( cFile, pOPEN_READ )
 72 :
 73 :      do case
 74 :      case cOutput == "CON"       // Go to console
 75 :         nFWrite := fopen( "CON", pOPEN_WRITE )
 76 :
 77 :      case cOutput == "LPT2" // Alternate printer!
 78 :         nFWrite := fopen( "LPT2", pOPEN_WRITE )
 79 :
 80 :      case cOutput == "FILE"  // ALternate file!
 81 :         nFWrite := fcreate( "DUMOUT.TXT", pCREATE_READWRITE )
 82 :
 83 :      otherwise
 84 :         nFWrite := fcreate( cOutput, pCREATE_READWRITE )
 85 :
 86 :      endcase
 87 :
 88 :      while !lToExit
 89 :
 90 :         cBytes   := space( pBUFFER )
 91 :
 92 :         // If the number of bytes read does not match the requested number
 93 :         // to read, then we have reached the end of the file
 94 :
 95 :         lToExit := !( fread( nFRead, @cBytes, pBUFFER ) == pBUFFER )
 96 :
 97 :         cBytes := cLine + cBytes
 98 :
 99 :         REPEAT
100 :
101 :            cAddBytes := if( !( pCRLF $ cBytes ), "", pCRLF )
102 :            cLine := Parse(@cBytes, pCRLF ) + cAddBytes
103 :            fwrite( nFWrite, cLine )
104 :
105 :         UNTIL len( cBytes ) == 0
106 :
107 :         if cOutput == "CON"
108 :            inkey(2)
109 :         endif
110 :
111 :      enddo
112 :
113 :      // Remember to close the files!
114 :      fclose( nFRead )
115 :      fclose( nFWrite )
116 :
117 :      lRetValue := pTRUE
118 :
119 :   endif
120 :
121 :   return( lRetValue )
122 :
123 :   #undef pBUFFER
124 :
125 : *******************
126 :
127 : static function FilesOnDisk( cFile )
```

```
128 :
129 :    static aToSee
130 :
131 :    local nChoice
132 :    local cScreen := savescreen( 4,40,20,60 )
133 :
134 :    if aToSee == NIL
135 :      aToSee := {}
136 :      aeval( directory(), {|aFiles| aadd(aToSee, aFiles[1])} )
137 :    else
138 :      if !( len( directory() ) == len( aToSee ) )
139 :        aToSee := {}
140 :        aeval( directory(), {|aFiles| aadd(aToSee, aFiles[1])} )
141 :      endif
142 :    endif
143 :
144 :    dispbox( 4,40,20,60, pDBAR )
145 :
146 :    if !((nChoice := achoice(5,41,19,59, aToSee)) == 0)
147 :      cFile := padr(aToSee[nChoice], 40)
148 :    endif
149 :
150 :    restscreen( 4, 40, 20, 60, cScreen )
151 :
152 :    VOID
153 :
154 : ********************
155 :
156 : static function Output( cWay )
157 :
158 :    local cScreen  := savescreen( 6, 40, 11, 60 )
159 :    local aOptions := {"LPT2", "CON", "FILE"}
160 :    local nChoice
161 :
162 :    dispbox( 6,40,11,60, pDBAR)
163 :
164 :    if !((nChoice := achoice( 7,41,10,59, aOptions )) == 0)
165 :      cWay := padr( aOptions[nChoice], 40)
166 :    endif
167 :
168 :    restscreen( 6, 40, 11, 60, cScreen )
169 :
170 :    VOID
171 :
172 : ********************
173 :
174 : static function Parse( cString, cBytes ) // To work with this only!
175 :
176 :    local nLocation := at( cBytes, cString )
177 :    local nWidth    := len( cBytes )
178 :    local cTempStr  := if( !empty(nLocation), ;
179 :                           substr(cString, 1, nLocation-1), ;
180 :                           cString )
181 :
182 :    cString   := if( !empty(nLocation), ;
183 :                    substr(cString, nLocation+nWidth), "" )
184 :
185 :    return( cTempStr )
186 :
187 : // End of File: Write1.prg
```

Each line read in by this example program is parsed and output to a "file." Note that a computer's devices are considered files. On lines 73 through 86, based on a previous pop-up selection stored to a variable and passed as the parameter *cOutput*, a file is either opened or created. In the case of the console, the output will go to the file named "CON", which is the console; if the alternate printer was selected as the target of the output, the file "LPT2" will be opened and information will be written to it. This approach can be extended for COM1, as well as for the other devices on a machine.

## .MEM FILES

Using low-level file functions to manipulate files other than text and program files can be extremely valuable when you are building an application. For example, memory variable files (.MEM) are generally used to contain systemwide information that may be needed throughout the life span of an application. In some cases, multiple memory files are necessary to keep general information handy but to keep it separate from module to module. In other words, the system information for a general ledger module is separated from the system information for the accounts payable module, yet both reside within the same application.

Sometimes, especially when memory variables are stored in a series of files, the need to use only one value from another memory variable file is vital. Without low-level file functions to go to that .MEM file and obtain that particular memory variable's value, the entire memory variable file would have to be RESTORED into the system with the ADDITIVE clause, which would burden the memory manager and the system in general—all for one memory variable's value. In the following example, the value of a memory variable is extracted from a memory variable file. This demonstrates the possibility of altering a memory variable value within a .MEM file or of deleting it completely from the .MEM file.

```
 1 : * File:      Write2.prg
 2 :
 3 : #include "PTValue.ch"
 4 : #include "PTInkey.ch"
 5 : #include "PTVerbs.ch"
 6 : #include "PTLowLvl.ch"
 7 :
 8 : #xtranslate SSDREAD() =>( setcursor(1), readmodal(getlist), ;
 9 :                           getlist := {}, setcursor(0), ;
10 :                           !( lastkey() == 27 ) )
11 :
12 : *******************
13 :
14 : function Main()
15 :
16 :    // The following must be private memory variables in order for the
17 :    // SAVE ALL command to work
18 :
19 :    local cVarName
20 :    local getlist := {}      // This is for the GET command
21 :
22 :    private scrdate   := date()
23 :    private scrlog    := pTRUE
24 :    private scrpath   := curdir()
25 :    private scrval    := 1.234
```

```
26 :      private scrpi       := 3.1415926
27 :      private scrwhole := 5
28 :      private scrdrive := "C:"
29 :
30 :      save all like scr* tO TestFile
31 :      clear memory
32 :
33 :      // WAIT scrdate  <<-- That would give a run-time error!
34 :
35 :      REPEAT
36 :         scroll()
37 :
38 :         @ 0,0 say "The following are saved variables" ;
39 :              say "    Press ESC to quit!"
40 :         @ 2,0 say "SCRDATE - SCRLOG - SCRPATH - SCRVAL" ;
41 :              say "  SCRPI - SCRWHOLE - SCRDRIVE"
42 :
43 :         cVarName := space(10)
44 :
45 :         @ 4,0 say "Enter variable name: " get cVarName
46 :
47 :         if SSDRead()
48 :            @ 6,10 SAY "That value is: " ;
49 :                SAY GetVarFromMem( "TESTFILE.MEM", alltrim(cVarName) )
50 :
51 :            @ 8,10 say "Press any key to try again or ESC to quit!"
52 :            inkey(0)
53 :
54 :         endif
55 :
56 :      UNTIL ( lastkey() == pESC )
57 :
58 :      return( NIL )
59 :
60 : *******************
61 :
62 : function Getvarfrommem( cFile, cVariable )
63 :
64 :      // This function and the numeric and date writing portion of this
65 :      // function were written by the Wizard: Essor Maso...
66 :
67 :      local nNumber           // Holds the actual number of the variable
68 :      local cNumValue         // Holds the character of the value
69 :      local cRealVariable     // Holds all data of variable in .mem file
70 :      local cName             // Holds the name of the variable in .mem file
71 :      local cData             // Contains the data for the variable in file
72 :      local cDataType         // Holds the data type of the variable
73 :      local cDataValue        // Holds the data value of the variable
74 :      local nTemp1            // Temporary variable for calculations
75 :      local nTemp2            // Temporary variable for calculations
76 :      local nPower            // Holds the power of the number or date
77 :      local lMinusSign        // Does the variable have a minus sign
78 :      local nMantisa1         // Calculates the mantisa of the number
79 :      local nMantisa2         // Calculates the mantisa of the number
80 :      local nMantisa3         // Calculates the mantisa of the number
81 :      local nMantisa4         // Calculates the mantisa of the number
82 :      local nMantisaTotal     // Holds the total of the mantisa
83 :      local nDataRange        // Holds the data range of the variable
84 :      local nFHandle          // DOS File handle for .MEM file
85 :      local lFileLength       // Length of the .MEM file
86 :      local xRetValue         // Unknown return value, default NIL
```

```
 87 :      local nDecimal           // The number of decimals in value
 88 :
 89 :      IF cFile IS pCHARACTER              // good parameter
 90 :        IF cVariable IS pCHARACTER        // good character
 91 :
 92 :         if file( cFile )                 // .MEM file is found!
 93 :
 94 :            nFHandle    := fopen( cFile, pOPEN_READ )        // open the file
 95 :            lFileLength := FSEEK(nFHandle, 0, pSEEK_EOF)     // Length of file
 96 :
 97 :            fseek( nFhandle, pSEEK_BOF)               // position pointer
 98 :
 99 :            // As long as the variable xRetValue does not return
100 :            // a NIL value, we know that the .MEM file was at least
101 :            // opened.
102 :
103 :            xRetValue := ""
104 :
105 :            if lFileLength < 2    // No items in .MEM file
106 :               fclose(nFHandle)   // close the file!
107 :            else
108 :
109 :               while fseek(nFHandle, 0, pSEEK_CURRENT) + 1 < lFileLength
110 :                  cRealVariable := space(18)
111 :                  fread(nFHandle, @cRealVariable, 18)
112 :
113 :                  cName     := left(cRealVariable, at(chr(0), cRealVariable) - 1 )
114 :                  cData     := substr(cRealVariable, 12, 1)
115 :                  cDataType := bin2w(right(cRealVariable, 2))
116 :                  nDataRange := if( ( cData $ CHR(195) + CHR(204) ), ;
117 :                                    14 + cDataType, 22 )
118 :                  cDataValue := space(nDataRange)
119 :
120 :                  fread(nFHandle, @cDataValue, nDataRange)  // Str value
121 :                  cNumValue := substr(cDataValue, 15)
122 :
123 :                  // If variable exists, continue to process
124 :
125 :                  if upper(trim(cName)) == upper(trim(cVariable))
126 :                    do case
127 :                    case cData == chr(195)    // character data type
128 :                        xRetValue := alltrim(cNumValue)
129 :
130 :                    case cData == chr(204)    // logical data type
131 :                        xRetValue := (asc(cNumValue) == 1)   // 1 for .t.!
132 :
133 :                    case cData = chr(206)         // numeric
134 :                        cDataValue    := substr(cDataValue, 15)
135 :
136 :                       nTemp1 := Modulus(asc(substr(cDataValue,8,1)),128)*16
137 :                       nTemp2 := int(asc(substr(cDataValue,7,1))/16)
138 :                       nPower := nTemp1 + nTemp2 - 1023
139 :                       lMinusSign := int(asc(substr(cDataValue,8,1))/16) >= 8
140 :
141 :                       nMantisa1 := Modulus(asc(substr(cDataValue,7,1)),16)/16
142 :                       nMantisa2 := bin2w(substr(cDataValue, 5, 2)) / ;
143 :                                    (65536*16)
144 :                       nMantisa3 := bin2w(substr(cDataValue, 3, 2)) /;
145 :                                    (65536 * 65536 * 16)
146 :                       nMantisa4 := bin2w(substr(cDataValue, 1, 2)) / ;
147 :                                    (65536 * 65536 * 65536 * 16)
```

```
148 :                      nMantisaTotal := nMantisa1 + nMantisa2 + ;
149 :                                       nMantisa3 + nMantisa4
150 :
151 :                      nNumber := if(lMinusSign, ;
152 :                                  -(1+nMantisaTotal) * (2 ^ nPower), ;
153 :                                   (1+nMantisaTotal) * (2 ^ nPower))
154 :
155 :                      nDecimal := asc(right(cRealVariable, 1))
156 :                      xRetValue := transform(nNumber, "@B")
157 :
158 :                   case cData == chr(196)         // date
159 :                      cDataValue := substr(cDataValue, 15)
160 :
161 :                      nTemp1 := Modulus(asc(substr(cDataValue,8,1)),128)*16
162 :                      nTemp2 := int(asc(substr(cDataValue,7,1))/16)
163 :                      nPower := nTemp1 + nTemp2 - 1023
164 :
165 :                      lMinusSign := int(asc(substr(cDataValue,8,1))/16) >= 8
166 :                      nMantisa1  := Modulus(asc(substr(cDataValue,7,1)),16)/16
167 :
168 :                      nMantisa2  := bin2w(substr(cDataValue,5,2)) / ;
169 :                                    (65536*16)
170 :                      nMantisa3  := bin2w(substr(cDataValue,3,2)) / ;
171 :                                    (65536 * 65536 * 16)
172 :                      nMantisa4  := bin2w(substr(cDataValue, 1, 2)) / ;
173 :                                    (65536 * 65536 * 65536 * 16)
174 :                      nMantisaTotal := nMantisa1 + nMantisa2 + ;
175 :                                       nMantisa3 + nMantisa4
176 :
177 :                      nNumber   := if(lMinusSign, ;
178 :                                   -(1 + nMantisaTotal) * (2 ^ nPower), ;
179 :                                    (1 + nMantisaTotal) * (2 ^ nPower))
180 :
181 :                      nDecimal   := asc(right(cRealVariable, 1))
182 :                      xRetValue := CTOD("01/01/0100") + nNumber - 1757585
183 :
184 :                   otherwise
185 :                      xRetValue := ""
186 :
187 :                   endcase
188 :                   exit     // We have to exit!
189 :
190 :                endif
191 :
192 :             enddo
193 :             fclose( nFHandle )
194 :
195 :          endif
196 :       endif
197 :    endif
198 : endif
199 :
200 : return( xRetValue )
201 :
202 : ********************
203 :
204 : static function Modulus( nNumberator, nDenominator )
205 :
206 :    local nTempValue
207 :    local nRetValue := 0
208 :
209 :    IF nNumberator IS pNUMERIC
```

```
210 :        IF nDenominator IS pNUMERIC    // Both parameters are good!
211 :
212 :           if nDenominator == 0
213 :              nRetValue := nNumberator
214 :
215 :           else
216 :              nTempValue := nNumberator % nDenominator
217 :              nRetValue  := if( nDenominator == 0, ;
218 :                                nNumberator, ;
219 :                                if( nTempValue * nDenominator < 0, ;
220 :                                    nTempValue + nDenominator, ;
221 :                                    nTempValue) )
222 :
223 :           endif
224 :        endif
225 :     endif
226 :
227 :     return( nRetValue )
228 :
229 : // End of File: Write2.prg
```

## .NTX FILES

The expression used in the indexing command appears as is in the header of the .NTX file. This means that if a function is designed to be used for visual purposes (such as graphically displaying a gas gauge while the INDEX ON command is in operation), the name of that function will appear in the first 255 bytes of the file header beginning at byte position 22. While this is visually appealing to the end user, the .NTX file always refers to that function regardless of its operation (so long as the index file is open) and becomes locked into that particular application. Fortunately, low-level file functions can be used to remove an unwanted key from the index file header. However, in order to maintain the integrity of the index file, it is critical that the key expression or function that is removed does not have any effect on the contents of each record's keys. For instance, in the following example, the function always returns a null byte and appears at the end of the index expression:

```
INDEX ON field + BarChart() TO EndXFile

* * * * * * * * * * * * * * * * * *

FUNCTION BarChart()

    // Perform graphical bar chart while indexing

    RETURN( "" )
```

Low-level file functions might also be used to encrypt the name or alias of a database that is associated with a particular index file. This time, the low-level file functions are handy to use in looking at the index key in the index file header and determining the name of the database that is to be opened for the index file to work properly.

```
1 : * File:     Lownames.prg
2 :
3 : #include "PTValue.ch"
4 : #include "PTVerbs.ch"
```

```
 5 : #include "PTLowLvl.ch"
 6 :
 7 : function Main()
 8 :
 9 :    local aNames  := {} // We need TWO arrays, NOT!! two assignments to
10 :    local aInfo   := {} // the same pointer!
11 :    local nChoice := 1
12 :
13 :    private cName
14 :
15 :    cls
16 :    qout( "One moment to index all of the files" )
17 :
18 :    use Ontap new
19 :
20 :    cName := alias()
21 :
22 :    index on Ontap->files + DbfName( "&cName" ) to Lowname1
23 :    index on Ontap->files + Ontap->times + DbfName( "&cName" ) to Lowname2
24 :
25 :    use Clients new
26 :
27 :    cName := alias()
28 :
29 :    index on Clients->account + DbfName( "&cName" ) to Lowname3
30 :    index on Clients->address1 + DbfName( "&cName" ) TO Lowname4
31 :    index on Clients->address2 + DbfName( "&cName" ) TO Lowname5
32 :
33 :    use Trans new
34 :
35 :    cName := alias()
36 :
37 :    index on Trans->account + DbfName( "&cName" ) TO Lowname6
38 :    index on dtos( Trans->adate ) + DbfName( "&cName" ) TO Lowname7
39 :
40 :    dbcloseall()
41 :    scroll()
42 :
43 :    aeval( directory( "Lownam*.ntx"), ;
44 :           {|aFiles| aadd( aInfo, BuildFiles( aFiles[1] )), ;
45 :                     aadd( aNames, aFiles[1]) } )
46 :
47 :    REPEAT
48 :      qqout( "Choose the index file to work with!" )
49 :
50 :      dispbox( 1,0,10,13,pDBAR)
51 :
52 :      if !empty( nChoice := achoice(2,1,9,12, aNames) )
53 :        scroll()
54 :
55 :        // use of the @...SAY...SAY commands
56 :
57 :        @ 0,0 SAY "You selected: " SAY aInfo[nChoice, 1]
58 :        @ 1,0 SAY "Its structure is: " SAY aInfo[nChoice, 2]
59 :        @ 2,0 SAY "Database to be used is: " SAY aInfo[nChoice, 3]
60 :
61 :        @ 3,0 say "Any key to see operation!"
62 :        inkey(0)
63 :
64 :        use (aInfo[nChoice, 3]) new index (aInfo[nChoice, 1])
65 :
66 :        dbedit( 3,0,maxrow(), maxcol() )
```

```
 67 :
 68 :       scroll()
 69 :       dbcloseall()
 70 :    endif
 71 : UNTIL (nChoice == 0)
 72 :
 73 :    cls
 74 :    aeval( aNames, {|cFile| ferase(cFile)} )
 75 :
 76 :    return( NIL )
 77 :
 78 : **********************
 79 :
 80 : static function BuildFiles( cName )
 81 :
 82 :    local nFHandle  := fopen( cName, pOPEN_READ )
 83 :    local cIndexKey := space(255)
 84 :    local cDbfName
 85 :
 86 :    fseek( nFHandle, 22, 0 )    // move the file pointer!
 87 :    fread( nFHandle, @cIndexKey, 255 )
 88 :
 89 :    cIndexKey := upper(cIndexKey) // force it to upper cased lettering
 90 :
 91 :    cDbfName  := substr( cIndexKey, at("DBFNAME(", upper(cIndexKey)) )
 92 :    cIndexKey := alltrim( left( cIndexKey, ;
 93 :                          at("+ " + cDbfName, cIndexKey)-1 ))
 94 :
 95 :    cDbfName  := strtran( alltrim( substr( cDbfName, at("(", cDbfName)+1, ;
 96 :                          at(")", cDbfName ) - at("(", cDbfName)-1 )), ;
 97 :                          '"', "")
 98 :
 99 :    fclose( nFHandle )
100 :
101 :    return( {cName, cIndexKey, cDbfName} )
102 :
103 : **********************
104 :
105 : function DbfName( cName )
106 :
107 :    return( "" )
108 :
109 : // End of File: Lownames.prg
```

## Writing Arrays to Disk

The following example is taken from *Clipper 5.2 Power Tools* and shows how the low-level file functions may be used to assist us in reading and writing multidimensional arrays to and from disk.

```
 1 : /*      Name:  SaveArray.prg
 2 :       Author:  Steve Straley
 3 :       Notice:  Copyright(c) - 1991 by
 4 :                Sirius Software Development, Inc.
 5 :                All Rights Reserved
 6 :                415-399-9810
 7 :         Date:  July 1, 1991
 8 :      Compile:  Clipper SaveArray /m /p /v /w /a /n
 9 :      Version:  Clipper 5.01
10 : Include Path:  \PTools\Include
```

```
11 :     Environment:   f051;
12 :            Link:   N/A
13 :    Library Path:   \Clipper\501
14 :            Note:   This function saves the specified array to the
15 :                    specified file.
16 :
17 : */
18 :
19 : #include "PTVERBS.CH"
20 : #include "PTVALUE.CH"
21 : #include "PTFUNCS.CH"
22 : #include "PTCOLOR.CH"
23 : #include "PTINKEY.CH"
24 :
25 : *******************
26 :
27 : function Main()
28 :
29 :    local aArray := { {1,2,3}, 4, 5, { {6,7}, {8,9} } }
30 :    // local aArray := { 1,2,3, 4, 5, 6,7, 8,9 }
31 :    // local aArray := { 1 }
32 :    local aNew
33 :
34 :    cls
35 :
36 :    SaveArray( aArray, "Saved.arr" )
37 :
38 :    ? "Press any key to continue..."
39 :    inkey(0)
40 :
41 :    aNew := RestoreArray( "Saved.arr" )
42 :
43 :    ? valtype( aNew )
44 :    inkey(0)
45 :    ? len( aNew )
46 :
47 :    ? aNew[1,1], aNew[1,2], aNew[1,3]
48 :    ? aArray[1,1], aArray[1,2], aArray[1,3]
49 :    ?
50 :
51 :    ? aNew[2]
52 :    ? aArray[2]
53 :    ?
54 :
55 :    ? aNew[3]
56 :    ? aArray[3]
57 :    ?
58 :
59 :    ? aNew[4,1,1], aNew[4,1,2]
60 :    ? aArray[4,1,1], aArray[4,1,2]
61 :    ?
62 :
63 :    ? aNew[4,2,1], aNew[4,2,2]
64 :    ?aArray[4,2,1], aArray[4,2,2]
65 :    ?
66 :    inkey(0)
67 :
68 :    VOID
69 :
70 : *******************
71 :
72 : function SaveArray( aArray, cFileName )
```

```
 73 :
 74 :    local lRetValue := pFALSE
 75 :    local nFhandle
 76 :
 77 :    IF aArray IS pARRAY
 78 :
 79 :       IF cFileName IS pCHARACTER
 80 :
 81 :          nFhandle := fcreate( cFileName )
 82 :
 83 :          if nFhandle > 4
 84 :
 85 :             if WriteArray( nFhandle, aArray )
 86 :
 87 :                if empty( ferror() )
 88 :                   lRetValue := pTRUE
 89 :                endif
 90 :
 91 :             endif
 92 :
 93 :             fclose( nFhandle )
 94 :
 95 :          endif
 96 :
 97 :       endif
 98 :
 99 :    endif
100 :
101 :    return( lRetValue )
102 :
103 : *******************
104 :
105 : static function WriteArray( nHandle, xItem )
106 :
107 :    local lRetValue := pFALSE
108 :    local cDataType := valtype( xItem )
109 :    local nLength
110 :    local cString
111 :
112 :    fwrite( nHandle, cDataType, 1 )
113 :
114 :    if empty( ferror() )
115 :      do case
116 :      case cDataType == "A"
117 :         nLength := len( xItem )
118 :         fwrite( nHandle, l2bin(nLength), 4 )
119 :         aeval( xItem, {| xNewItem | WriteArray( nHandle, xNewItem ) } )
120 :
121 :      case cDataType == "C"
122 :         fwrite( nHandle, l2bin( len(xItem) ), 4 )
123 :         fwrite( nHandle, xItem, len(xItem) )
124 :
125 :      case cDataType == "D"
126 :         fwrite( nHandle, l2bin(8), 4 )
127 :         fwrite( nHandle, dtoc( xItem ), 8 )
128 :
129 :      case cDataType == "L"
130 :         fwrite( nHandle, l2bin(1), 4 )
131 :         fwrite( nHandle, if(xItem, "T", "F") )
132 :
133 :      case cDataType == "N"
134 :         nLength := len( cString := str( xItem ) )
```

```
135 :          fwrite( nHandle, l2bin( nLength ), 4 )
136 :          fwrite( nHandle, cString, nLength )
137 :
138 :       otherwise                      // Code Block, NIL, or Object
139 :          fwrite( nHandle, l2bin(3), 4 )
140 :          fwrite( nHandle, "NIL" )
141 :
142 :       endcase
143 :
144 :       lRetValue := empty( ferror() )
145 :
146 :    endif
147 :
148 :    return( lRetValue )
149 :
150 : *******************
151 :
152 : static function RestoreArray( cFileName )
153 :
154 :    local nFhandle
155 :    local aRetValue := {}
156 :
157 :    IF cFileName IS pCHARACTER
158 :
159 :       if file( cFileName )
160 :
161 :          nFHandle := fopen( cFileName )
162 :
163 :          if nFHandle > 4
164 :
165 :             aRetValue := ReadArray( nFhandle )
166 :
167 :          endif
168 :
169 :       endif
170 :
171 :    endif
172 :
173 :    return( aRetValue )
174 :
175 : *******************
176 :
177 : static function ReadArray( nHandle )
178 :
179 :    local cSize     := "    "
180 :    local cDataType := " "
181 :    local nLength
182 :    local xItem
183 :    local nCounter
184 :    local cBuffer
185 :
186 :    fread( nHandle, @cDataType, 1 )
187 :    fread( nHandle, @cSize, 4 )
188 :
189 :    nLength := bin2l( cSize )
190 :
191 :    if cDataType == "A"
192 :       xItem := {}
193 :       for nCounter := 1 to nLength
194 :          aadd( xItem, ReadArray( nHandle ) )
195 :       next
196 :
```

```
197 :      else
198 :         cBuffer := space( nLength )
199 :         fread( nHandle, @cBuffer, nLength )
200 :
201 :         do case
202 :         case cDataType == pCHARACTER
203 :            xItem := cBuffer
204 :
205 :         case cDataType == pDATE
206 :            xItem := ctod( cBuffer )
207 :
208 :         case cDataType == pLOGICAL
209 :            xItem := (cBuffer == "T")
210 :
211 :         case cDataType == pBLOCK
212 :            xItem := NIL
213 :
214 :         case cDataType == pNUMERIC
215 :            xItem := val( cBuffer )
216 :
217 :         endcase
218 :
219 :      endif
220 :
221 :      return( xItem )
222 :
223 : * End of File
```

Since arrays in Clipper can be multidimensional, the method used to save them to disk must take this fact into consideration. To do this, a better look at arrays is needed. Clipper relies on two facts to implement multidimensional arrays: Arrays can hold any valid data type as an element in an array, and arrays are valid data types. This means that a multidimensional array is nothing more than an array in an array. SAVEARRAY.PRG uses this fact to recursively call itself while it is running. For example, after the file that is to hold the array is created on line 81, the file handle *nFhandle*, along with the data set in *aArray*, is passed to the function WriteArray( ). Once inside of this function, the WriteArray( ) stores the data type of the item passed as *xItem* on line 105 to the variable *cDataType*. This variable will hold the one-letter symbol for the data type of the element passed to the function. The value of *cDatatype* is then tested in a series of CASE statements beginning on line 115 and ending on line 142. Within this CASE construct, if the value of *cDataType* is an array (line 116), each element is evaluated through the AEVAL( ) function call on line 119. Within the code block processed by this function, the WriteArray( ) function is called recursively. With the advent of local variables, this is a practical approach to writing an array to disk, especially when arrays can be ragged, can contain other arrays, and can have mixed data types. This technology is not perfect: It will run into problems after the 50th recursive call to the WriteArray( ) function. However, the arrays that we create and deal with are at most four or five levels deep. This is well within the limits of recursive program calling.

## Building New Types of System Files

Rather than using the old .MEM file technology, there is an alternate way in which system-wide information may be saved to the disk other than through a .MEM file or even a database file. Using the ability to save arrays to disk, it is possible to have a function read and write information from a text file where each line in the text file will be an element in a system array. Such an array offers the programmer an easier way to modify and maintain system information: Text files can be reconstructed easier than a .MEM file. The example below begins to outline this approach:

```
 1 : * File:   DocInit.prg
 2 :
 3 : #include "PTValue.ch"
 4 : #include "PTVerbs.ch"
 5 :
 6 : // The system information ...
 7 : #define pSYSTEM_ITEMS       6
 8 : #define pDOCBASE_PATH       1
 9 : #define pDOCBASE_MONO       2
10 : #define pDOCBASE_COLOR      3
11 : #define pDOCBASE_SYSTEM     4
12 : #define pDOCBASE_TABSET     5
13 : #define pDOCBASE_43MODE     6
14 :
15 : *******************
16 :
17 : function Main()
18 :
19 :    local aSystem  // This will be the system information from the file
20 :
21 :    // First, let's make a fake file:
22 :
23 :    if aSystem == NIL  // Not been initialized!
24 :       aSystem := array( pSYSTEM_ITEMS )
25 :       aSystem[ pDOCBASE_PATH ]   := "\" + curdir() + "\"
26 :       aSystem[ pDOCBASE_MONO ]   := .T.
27 :       aSystem[ pDOCBASE_COLOR ]  := "W/N,N/W,,,N/W"
28 :       aSystem[ pDOCBASE_SYSTEM ] := ""   // The system last used is NULL!
29 :       aSystem[ pDOCBASE_TABSET ] := 3
30 :       aSystem[ pDOCBASE_43MODE ] := pFALSE
31 :       WriteIni(aSystem)
32 :    endif
33 :
34 :    cls
35 :    ? "Before memory is cleared:"
36 :    aeval( aSystem, {|xItem| qout( valtype(xItem), xItem )} )
37 :    inkey(0)
38 :
39 :    clear memory
40 :    aSystem := array( pSYSTEM_ITEMS )   // No element values!
41 :
42 :    if file( "DocBase.ini" )            // There is a found .INI file
43 :
44 :       if LoadSystem( @aSystem )        // This loads the System info
45 :          ?
46 :          ? "And now, the information that was read from the file: "
47 :          aeval( aSystem, {|xItem| qout( valtype(xItem), xItem )} )
48 :          qout( replicate( chr(205), maxcol() ) )
49 :          memoedit( memoread("docbase.ini"), row()+1, 0, maxrow(), ;
50 :                                             maxcol(), pFALSE )
51 :
52 :       endif
53 :    endif
54 :
```

```
 55 :    scroll()
 56 :
 57 :    return( NIL )
 58 :
 59 : **********************
 60 :
 61 : static function LoadSystem( aSystem )
 62 :
 63 :    local lLoaded := pFALSE    // Default value that the system is NOT loaded!
 64 :    local nFile                // Low-level file handle
 65 :
 66 :    nFile := fopen( "DocBase.ini" )   // load it and read it into the system
 67 :
 68 :    if nFile > 4                          // There is a file!
 69 :       // Search path
 70 :       aSystem[ pDOCBASE_PATH ]   := FReadLine( nFile )
 71 :       // color or mono
 72 :       aSystem[ pDOCBASE_MONO ]   := (FReadLine( nFile )=="T")
 73 :       // color string
 74 :       aSystem[ pDOCBASE_COLOR ]  := FReadLine( nFile )
 75 :       // system name last used
 76 :       aSystem[ pDOCBASE_SYSTEM ] := FReadLine( nFile )
 77 :       // Tab settings
 78 :       aSystem[ pDOCBASE_TABSET ] := val( FReadLine( nFile ) )
 79 :       // if 43 line mode is supported
 80 :       aSystem[ pDOCBASE_43MODE ] := (FReadLine( nFile )=="T")
 81 :       if !empty( aSystem[ pDOCBASE_PATH ] )
 82 :          aSystem[ pDOCBASE_PATH ] := "\" + curdir() + "\"
 83 :       endif
 84 :       lLoaded := pTRUE
 85 :       fclose( nFile )
 86 :    endif
 87 :
 88 :    return( lLoaded )
 89 :
 90 : ********************
 91 :
 92 : static function WriteIni(aSystem)
 93 :
 94 :    local nFile := ;  // Low-level file handle for INI file!
 95 :               fcreate( "DocBase.ini" )
 96 :
 97 :    if nFile > 4   // No error!
 98 :       FWriteLine( nFile, aSystem[ pDOCBASE_PATH ] )
 99 :       FwriteLine( nFile, StrValue( aSystem[ pDOCBASE_MONO ] ) )
100 :       FWriteLine( nFile, aSystem[ pDOCBASE_COLOR ] )
101 :       FWriteLine( nFile, aSystem[ pDOCBASE_SYSTEM ] )
102 :       FWriteLine( nFile, StrValue( aSystem[ pDOCBASE_TABSET ] ) )
103 :       FwriteLine( nFile, StrValue( aSystem[ pDOCBASE_43MODE ] ) )
104 :       fclose( nFile )
105 :    endif
106 :
107 :    VOID
108 :
109 : // The following functions are part of the Library File called
110 : // Clipper 5.2 Power Tools
111 :
112 : ********************
113 :
114 : static function StrValue( xItem )
```

```
115 :
116 :       local xRetValue := ""
117 :
118 :       if xItem != NIL
119 :
120 :          do case
121 :          case valtype( xItem ) == pCHARACTER
122 :             xRetValue := xItem
123 :
124 :          case valtype( xItem ) == pBLOCK
125 :             xRetValue := StrValue( eval( xItem ) )
126 :
127 :          case valtype( xItem ) == pNUMERIC
128 :             xRetValue := str( xItem )
129 :
130 :          case valtype( xItem ) == pMEMO
131 :             xRetValue := if( (len( xItem ) > (memory(0) * 1024) * .80), ;
132 :                              left(xItem, int( (memory(0) * 1024) * .80)), ;
133 :                              xItem )
134 :
135 :          case valtype( xItem ) == pDATE
136 :             xRetValue := dtoc( xItem )
137 :
138 :          case valtype( xItem ) == pLOGICAL
139 :             xRetValue := if( xItem, "T", "F" )
140 :
141 :          endcase
142 :
143 :       endif
144 :
145 :       return( xRetValue )
146 :
147 : *******************
148 :
149 : static function FReadLine( nFHandle, lRewind )
150 :
151 :      local nLength    := 4096     // length of the buffer
152 :      local cRetValue  := ""       // default starting value of line
153 :      local cBuffer                // character string for the buffer
154 :      local nLocation              // current location of file pointer
155 :      local nBytes                 // number of bytes successfully read
156 :
157 :      DEFAULT lRewind TO pFALSE            // this is to rewind the file!
158 :      DEFAULT nFHandle TO 0
159 :
160 :      if nFHandle > 4              // no error is present
161 :
162 :         cBuffer := space( nLength )
163 :         nBytes  := fread( nFHandle, @cBuffer, nLength )
164 :
165 :         fseek( nFHandle, -(nBytes), 1 )  // reposition pointer in the file
166 :
167 :         nLocation := if( (empty( (nLocation := at( pCRLF, cBuffer )) )), ;
168 :                          nLength, (nLocation - 1) )
169 :
170 :         // move pointer in the file
171 :
172 :         if empty( nLocation )
173 :           if pCRLF == left( cBuffer, 2 )
174 :              fseek(nFHandle, nLocation+2, 1)
175 :              cBuffer := ""
```

```
176 :          nLocation := 1
177 :       else
178 :          fseek(nFHandle, nBytes, 1)
179 :       endif
180 :
181 :    else
182 :       fseek(nFHandle, nLocation+2, 1)
183 :
184 :    endif
185 :
186 :    cRetValue := left(cBuffer, nLocation)
187 :
188 :    if lRewind
189 :       fseek(nFHandle, -(len(cRetValue)+2), 1 )
190 :    endif
191 :
192 : endif
193 :
194 : return( if( len(cRetValue) == nLength, "", cRetValue ) )
195 :
196 : *******************
197 :
198 : static function FWriteLine( nFHandle, cString )
199 :
200 :    local lRetValue := pFALSE    // default return value
201 :
202 :    DEFAULT cString TO ""
203 :
204 :    IF nFHandle IS pNUMERIC
205 :
206 :       if nFHandle > 4
207 :          fwrite( nFHandle, cString, len(cString) )
208 :          if empty( ferror() )
209 :             fwrite( nFHandle, pCRLF, 2 )
210 :             if empty( ferror() )
211 :                lRetValue := pTRUE
212 :             endif
213 :          endif
214 :       endif
215 :
216 :    endif
217 :
218 :    return( lRetValue )
219 :
220 : // End of File: DocInit.prg
```

In the beginning, the array *aSystem[ ]* is not yet defined, only initialized in memory on line 19. Therefore, the value of this variable will be NIL and will cause the IF statement on line 23 to be a logical true (.T.) value. The manifest constants on lines 7 through 13 can be held in a special file for this application. These constants are used to maintain the *aSystem[ ]* array (the pSYSTEM_ITEMS value) as well as the meaning each position in the array is to have. Once all of the items in *aSystem[ ]* are given default values, the array is written to the disk via the WriteIni( ) function on line 31. This array then could be passed to a function that would hold it as a STATIC memory variable, something like this:

```
function System( aArray )

   static aSystem
```

```
if !( aArray == NIL )    //  the parameter was passed
   aSystem := aArray
endif

return( aSystem )
```

Now, the array *aSystem[ ]* is not only written to disk, but all of the elements within the array can be maintained by a special function. To get at one of those values, the function System( ) could be called in conjunction with the manifest constants on lines 8 through 13. For example:

```
cColor := System()[ pDOCBASE_COLOR ]
```

Since the value of the function would be the system array, we can obtain the value of any of the elements within it.

Once the items on the array *aSystem[ ]* are displayed via the AEVAL( ) function call on line 36, all memory variables are cleared, and the array *aSystem[ ]* is reinitialized on line 40. If the file DOCBASE.INI is present, the function LoadSystem( ) will use the low-level file functions to go to the disk, read in each line from the file, and store it to the appropriate element position in the *aSystem[ ]* array. Once again, after this takes place, the array *aSystem[ ]* could be passed to a function called System( ) that would be used to simply hold the values of the array until needed.

Within both the LoadSystem( ) function beginning on line 61 and the WriteIni( ) function beginning on line 92, a couple of the Power Tools functions are used to store the elements of the array to the disk as well as to read them from the disk. Here the function takes each element in the array *aSystem[ ]*, calls the FWriteLine( ) function defined on lines 198 through 218, and writes out each element to the file DOCBASE.INI on lines 98 through 103. As with all low-level file functions, the file should be closed to prevent a loss of a DOS file handle and the potential of a run-time error, DOS error 4: not enough file handles.

The FReadLine( ) function reads the file DOCBASE.INI and parses out any carriage-return/line-feed character on lines 167 and 168. These lines are then the individual elements to the *aSystem[ ]* array that is processed throughout this example.

## Summary

These are just a few examples of the ways that low-level file functions can be used. Other possibilities include .EXE file encryption, protecting a .DBF file, reading information from a Lotus 1-2-3 or Microsoft Excel spreadsheet, packing a .DBT file, and even simple serial communications. Some of the system programs and applications that may be obtained in conjunction with this book use the low-level file functions for these reasons and many others. The potential is vast. Low-level file functions and the binary conversion functions give more raw power to the Clipper language. As a result, the applications that use these special functions will evolve to new plateaus. In addition, the approaches we take to solve programming problems will rely on these functions more and more with each CA-Clipper 5.2 application we write.

# 15

# Code Blocks

## What Are Code Blocks?

A code block is a compiled set of instructions, based on a very distinctive syntax, that will, when pointed to, execute. It is a new data type to Clipper 5.x that contains pointers to instructional statements within the Clipper library or your compiled application. A code block may also contain a parameter list that will be passed to the called subroutines listed in the code block. In essence, it is a block of executable code that may be assigned to a variable and may be processed in various ways. Code blocks, when type checked with the VALTYPE( ) function, will yield "B" for block. You may not use a statement within a code block, but expressions are allowed.

Code blocks are not replacements for macro expansions. They are not the savior to the woes surrounding speed, variable program control, and character macro expansions. They are, however, a significant enhancement to a language that supports the concepts of inheritance, modular programming, and programming an object. If used properly, your functions will take code blocks as parameters; the functions will be very generalized routines, with the data in a code block giving the function the ability to operate in the way you choose.

Code blocks cannot be displayed; their string representations can, however, be expressed as character fields or character memory variables to be later macro-expanded. And code blocks (or the address pointers to them) may be stored to memory variables or to array subscripts. The advantages code blocks have over macros are

1. They execute faster, since macro-expansion involves taking each character in the expression and interpreting what it might mean against the symbol table. A code block is nothing more than an address pointer to a compiled piece of code or a pointer to a location of memory of a previously macro-expanded expression.

2. Code blocks may be passed as parameters to procedures and/or functions, giving a better vehicle to create "black-box" functions that will perform various operations based on the code fragments contained within the code block.

3. Code blocks can help to eliminate naming conflicts between variables. They may also be used to allow LOCAL and STATIC variables to be manipulated within subroutines, thus extending the visibility of these two data-storage classes.

## Syntax for Code Blocks

The general syntax for a code block is

```
{||}
```

The extended syntax is as follows:

```
{ | [<<parm1>> [,<<parm2>> [,...]]] | <<exp1>> [, <<exp2>> [,...]] }
```

Opening and closing bracket symbols with two vertical bars within them delimit a code block. The items within the vertical bars are the parameters passed to the code block. These are LOCAL data-storage class parameters, and they are optional—a code block does not need a parameter list. The items listed after the vertical bars but within the brackets are the expressions that will be executed, one at a time. Keep in mind that there is no comma between the end of the parameter list and the beginning of the first expression that is called.

Code blocks, like formal expressions and functions, have a value. The value of a code block is the value of the last expression in that code block. Any legitimate expression may be evaluated within a code block, so long as the expression has a value.

To help evaluate expressions, remember the extended use of parentheses: They group an expression together and form one single value. For example, consider this coding fragment:

```
xNewValue := ( One(), x := 1 = 1 )
```

In this listing, the function One( ) is called within the expression. Once it has completed its operation, control is returned to the expression. Regardless of the value returned from One( ), the value of the expression will be a logical true (.T.). This happens when *xNewValue* is assigned the value of 1 (an in-line assignment call) and is immediately compared against the value of 1. Since 1 equals 1, the value of the expression will be a logical true (.T.), which in turn becomes the value of *xNewValue*.

Returning to code blocks, the hardest concept to grapple with is programming the parameter list BEFORE declaring what routines are to be called. However, once you fine-tune this adjustment in your programming habits, new rewards will be found. Remember: Code blocks may be stored to variables. These variables will carry the address pointers that will execute the code blocks on demand. Parameter passing will become clearer as we begin to explore its use in conjunction with the EVAL( ) function.

One last advantage of code blocks: They allow LOCAL and STATIC variables and parameters within a procedure or function to be exported to other routines. In essence, you may grant access to a LOCAL or STATIC variable to a subroutine and give it the ability to modify variables that normally would be "out of scope." This is accomplished by having the code block manipulate a LOCAL or STATIC variable. The rule here is that the code block must be defined in the same routine as the LOCAL or STATIC variable or parameter. Later in this chapter there is a complete programming example that demonstrates this. The point to note here is that there may be occasions when a variable or parameter has been defined as LOCAL or STATIC; in programming, it is often critical to manipulate those values within subroutines (such as printer drivers, report writers, and generic list-box functions).

## Code Block Functions for Clipper

In addition to the enhancements made within ASCAN( ) and ASORT( ) to allow code blocks to scan and sort multidimensional arrays, three new functions have been created to expressly work with code blocks. They are

EVAL( )     General-purpose function to evaluate a code block.
AEVAL( )    Evaluates a code block on elements in an array.
DBEVAL( )   Evaluates a code block on records in a database.

Code blocks are essential to the growing capabilities of the language. For example, the DELETE ALL and COUNT TO commands, which appear to be drastically different in nature, are in reality almost identical. Consider these extracts from the standard header file, STD.CH, for DELETE ALL:

```
DBEVAL({|| dbDelete()},<{for}>,<{while}>,<next>,<rec>,<.rest.>)
```

and for COUNT TO <var>:

```
<var> := 0 ;;
DBEVAL( {|| <var>+1}, <{for}>, <{while}>, <next>, <rec>, <.rest.> )
```

Other than requiring two statements to perform the COUNT TO command, the only difference between these two statements is the expressions evaluated within the code blocks that are passed to DBEVAL( ). In the first example, the Clipper function dbDelete( ) is evaluated against every record in a database, subject to a FOR and WHILE condition, with the ancillary NEXT, REC, and REST options. In the second example, the variable expressed as *var* will be set to 0 and then incremented as each record is successfully evaluated by the code block, again subject to a FOR and WHILE condition, with ancillary NEXT, REC, and REST options.

The key to programming with code blocks in Clipper is that you now can build generic functions, or commands, that will work differently based on the code block passed as a parameter. In the past, whenever the role of a function within an application was broadened, additional parameters were added, logic was needed to check the data types of the parameters, or a basic reworking of the logic of the function was required. Now, you can program data to be passed as parameters that tell functions what to do, similar to some of the concepts found in object-oriented programming. To support this, code blocks are used to tell the objects how and what to do in Chapter 16, "Clipper Objects."

## Code Block Usage

### BASIC PROGRAMMING

One of the things that a code block can contain is the name of a procedure or function that will be executed when it is evaluated. One of the ways this can be accomplished without using a code block is using a macro-expanded variable to perform branch operations; this might look something like this:

```
DO Proc&ext
```

Now, variables can contain different code blocks that refer to branching subroutines. In the following example, only one branching routine is called for all of the menu items; but if we were to extend this, we could build a multiple-branching scenario.

```
 1 : * Name:      Cblock1.prg
 2 :
 3 : #include "PTValue.ch"    // Power Tools values
 4 :
 5 : *******************
 6 :
 7 : function Main()
 8 :
 9 :    local nChoice := 1
10 :
11 :    set( pWRAP, pON )              // functional form of SET WRAP ON
12 :    scroll()                       // Clear the screen
13 :    dispbox(9,24,15,50, pDBAR )    // Clear the frame area and set frame
14 :
15 :    while pTRUE
16 :       @ 10,25 prompt padc("Chart of Accounts", 25)
17 :       @ 11,25 prompt padc("Journals", 25)
18 :       @ 12,25 prompt padc("Listings/Reports", 25)
19 :       @ 13,25 prompt padc("End of Period", 25)
20 :       @ 14,25 prompt padc("Quit", 25)
21 :       menu to nChoice
22 :       if !eval( {|nOpt| SubRoutine(nOpt)}, nChoice )
23 :          exit
24 :       endif
25 :    enddo
26 :
27 :    scroll()
28 :    return( NIL )
29 :
30 : *******************
31 :
32 : static function SubRoutine( nOption )
33 :
34 :    local lRetValue := pTRUE
35 :
36 :    if nOption == 0
37 :       lRetValue := pFALSE
38 :
39 :    else
40 :       devpos( maxrow(), 0 )
41 :       devout( "You selected # " )
42 :       devout( nOption )
43 :       devout( "  Any key..." )
44 :       inkey(0)
45 :       lRetValue := !( nOption == 5 )   // Option doesn't equal 5
46 :
47 :    endif
48 :
49 :    // The following command is placed outside of the IF condition so that
50 :    // in case the ESC key is pressed, causing the value of OPTION to be
51 :    // zero, the cursor will still be placed at the bottom of the screen
```

```
52 :    // before the program terminates.
53 :
54 :    scroll( maxrow(), 0 )
55 :
56 :    return( lRetValue )
57 :
58 : // End of File: CBlock1.prg
```

When reading line 22, we must look at it in reverse order, from right to left, where we see that EVAL( ) passes the variable *nChoice* to the code block, where it becomes the LOCAL parameter named *nOpt*. After accepting the value of *nChoice* and giving it to *nOpt*, EVAL( ) will make a call to the function Subroutine( ) and in turn pass the value of *nOpt* to it. Subroutine( ) is a function; therefore it has a return value. That return value will, in this case, become the value of the code block. That value then becomes the value of EVAL( ), which is tested on line 22. It should be obvious that we should expect the value of EVAL( ) to be a logical data type; the value of the code block should be a logical data type; and the value of the lone function called within the code block should be a logical data type. If the value of *nOption* in the function Subroutine( ) (line 32) is 0, the value of *nChoice* is 0, which means that the ESC key was pressed in the MENU TO command. The value of the function in that case will be a logical false (.F.). Otherwise, the option number is displayed on the screen (lines 40 through 43).

Since the DEVOUT( ) function positions the cursor at the end of the displayed expression, in effect moving the cursor position just like the DEVPOS( ) function, the various data types need not be converted for display purposes. In other words, when there is a string, number, and string item to be displayed all together, it is common to convert the numeric data type to a string and concatenate the items for the display. This takes up extra time and memory in the computer when the same effect could be achieved by having multiple calls to the DEVOUT( ) function, one for each different data type, as seen on lines 40 through 43.

Turning back to the rest of the example, if the "Quit" option was selected, the value of *nChoice* will be 5, the value of *nOpt* will be 5, and the value of *nOption* on line 32 will be 5. The value of Subroutine( ) will again be a logical false (.F.), which becomes the value of the expression.

This example shows how EVAL( ) takes the code block as its first parameter and passes to it the parameters optionally passed to the EVAL( ) function, starting with the second parameter.

Code blocks can be very useful when developing a system, not only in helping with the data, but also in helping keep control of the design and user interface portion of an application. Typical applications will have a generic banner across the top complete with system name, program location, date, and possibly a running clock (with the assistance of an ASM or C routine interrupting Clipper to display it). In addition, the application starts off in a standard color setting, and additional settings within the system generally are established all together.

Batching all of these operations together in one subroutine may be the answer, but not always. Consider the idea of wanting to just draw the system border. In the previous example, our border scheme is not programmed with other operations. We either need to duplicate that piece of code in a separate subroutine, or we need to break out each operation from the original subroutine and generate separate procedures or functions for each operation. The trouble with this is that whenever the beginning screen needs to be called, you, the programmer, must know which subroutines to call and in what order to call them. Code blocks can help eliminate this problem.

If each operation is a separate subroutine, to be called individually whenever appropriate, we can batch the individual routines into one code block call. Then, whenever we want the banner to be displayed, all we need to do is EVAL( ) the code block, which in turn makes the individual calls in the order that we need. To see this in action, consider the following example.

```
 1 : * Name:      Cblock2.prg
 2 :
 3 : #include "PTValue.ch"
 4 : #include "PTColor.ch"
 5 : #include "PTVerbs.ch"
 6 : #include "PTFuncs.ch"
 7 :
 8 : #xtranslate SayTitle( <cStr> ) => ;
 9 :          (devpos(3, ((maxcol()/2) - int(len(<cStr>)/2))), devout( <cStr> ))
10 :
11 : static bScreen := {|cName| SetEnv(), DrawBanner(), SayTitle(cName)}
12 :
13 : ********************
14 :
15 : function Main()
16 :
17 :   local nOption := 4   // Start on the 4th item in the list
18 :
19 :   PROCESS       // User-defined command for the WHILE .T. loop
20 :     eval( bScreen, "Main Menu" )
21 :     @ 10,35 prompt " Choice 1 "
22 :     @ 11,35 prompt " Choice 2 "
23 :     @ 12,35 prompt " Choice 3 "
24 :     @ 13,35 prompt " Choice 4 "
25 :     @ 22,00 say "enter your choice or"
26 :     @ 24,00 SAY "Press <ESC> to clear screen"
27 :     menu to nOption
28 :     if nOption == 0    // Exit condition... ESC was pressed
29 :       exit
30 :     endif
31 :
32 :     SayTitle( "You Picked #" + transform(nOption, "9") )
33 :     scroll(10,00)  // Clear from 10,00 to the end of the screen
34 :
35 :     @ maxrow(), 00 say "Press any key to move on..."
36 :     inkey(0)
37 :
38 :   END PROCESS
39 :
40 :   @ maxrow(), 00 say "Press any Key to Draw Banner"
41 :   inkey(0)
42 :
43 :   DrawBanner()
44 :   @ maxrow(), 00 say "Press any Key to move on..."
45 :   inkey(0)
46 :
47 :   SayTitle( "The End" )
48 :   @ maxrow(), 00 say "Press any Key to exit"
49 :   inkey(0)
50 :
51 :   scroll()
```

```
52 :
53 :    VOID       // User-defined command is a return(NIL)
54 :
55 :  *********************
56 :
57 :  static function DrawBanner( cColor )
58 :
59 :    DEFAULT cColor TO MAKECOLOR( pWHITE/pBLUE )
60 :
61 :    scroll()
62 :
63 :    dispbox( 00, 00, 4, maxcol(), pDBAR, cColor )
64 :
65 :    @ 1, 1 say "Cblock2 - Ver. 2.0"
66 :    @ 2, 1 say "Sirius Software Development, Inc"
67 :    @ 1, maxcol() -8 say date()
68 :    @ 2, maxcol()-11 say "F1 for Help"
69 :
70 :    return( NIL )
71 :
72 :  *********************
73 :
74 :  static function SetEnv( lWithClose )    // With a close toggle
75 :
76 :    DEFAULT lWithClose TO pFALSE
77 :
78 :    if lWithClose
79 :       dbcloseall()
80 :       RELEASE ALL
81 :    endif
82 :
83 :    set( pESCAPE, pON )     // set escape on
84 :    set( pDELETED, pON )    // set deleted on
85 :    set( pWRAP, pON )       // set wrap on
86 :    set( pCONFIRM, pOFF )   // set confirm off
87 :
88 :    set( pBELL, !set(pBELL) )   // Toggle the SET BELL command
89 :    setcursor( pCURSOR_ON )     // assign a block size to cursor
90 :
91 :    VOID
92 :
93 :
94 :  // End of File: CBlock2.prg
```

In this example, the variable *bScreen* contains the code block that, when executed, will call the SetEnv( ), DrawBanner( ), and SayTitle( ) routines. Looking at line 11, we can see that the code block takes a LOCAL parameter named *cName*, which will be passed to the SayTitle( ) routine. The value of the code block will be the value of the last expression evaluated within it. In this example, this will be the value of SayTitle( ). On lines 8 and 9, the SayTitle( ) expression is defined as a pseudoexpression. In essence, this expression is a combination call to DEVPOS( ) and DEVOUT( ). Since DEVOUT( ) is the last "real" function called in the expression, it will be the value of the expression. The return value of DEVOUT( ) is NIL; therefore the value of the expression will be NIL, the value of SysTitle( ) will be NIL, and thus, the value of the code block in which SayTitle( ) is called will be NIL.

Each time the main loop on line 19 is executed, the EVAL( ) on line 20 will be called. The string "Main Menu" will be passed to the code block *bScreen*, which means that the string "Main Menu" will be passed to the SayTitle( ) routine. Keep in mind the main point to this:

The standard opening defaults, headers, and title colors are all batched together in the code block, yet they independently retain their operational importance. For example, line 32 makes a call independently to the SayTitle( ) pseudofunction, and on line 43 through 47, each of the main routines in the code block *bScreen* is called individually.

Within the SenEnv( ) function, the SET( ) functions are used in place of the standard SET commands. This shows how the values of the SET( ) functions can be used, toggled, and examined at any time. In the past, memory variables were often used to keep track of the environmental values that help run a program. Here, these values can be accessed by one function: SET( ). For example, on line 88, the value that is passed to the SET( ) function for the BELL operation is the opposite of the current setting of SET BELL, which toggles the setting off if it is on and toggles it on if it is off. (Note, however, that because not all of the values returned by the SET( ) function are logical, this technique cannot be used to reverse all SET( ) values.)

One last point of interest with this example pertains to the file-wide STATIC variable defined on line 11. Since this program module is compiled with the /N switch, the variable *bScreen* can be seen in any of the subroutines within this .PRG file. This means that the Main( ) function (which does make use of the variable), and the static DrawBanner( ) and SetEnv( ) functions can use this variable without a compiler warning message or a run-time error message.

In the previous two examples, the main function that we used to evaluate a code block was the EVAL( ) function. Its general syntax and definition is

```
EVAL( <code block> [, <parameter expression> [,...] ] )
```

As many parameter expressions will be passed to EVAL( ) as there are LOCAL parameters defined in the code block. The value of EVAL( ) is independent of the values passed to the function and their data types.

In the following example, EVAL( ) and code blocks are used to check the data type of a parameter or variable and return its string equivalent.

```
 1 : * Name:      Cblock3.prg
 2 :
 3 : *******************
 4 :
 5 : function Main()
 6 :
 7 :    local bCharBlock := {|cVal| cVal}
 8 :    local bNumbBlock := {|nVal| alltrim( padr(nVal,80) )}
 9 :    local bLogiBlock := {|lVal| if(lVal, "True", "False")}
10 :    local bDateBlock := {|dVal| dtoc( dVal )}
11 :    local cBanner    := "Value"
12 :    local xData
13 :    local nNumber1
14 :    local nNumber2
15 :
16 :    scroll()
17 :
18 :    cBanner += space(28)
19 :
20 :    DispData(0,2,cBanner += "Type of EVAL()       VALTYPE()")
21 :
22 :    xData := "This is a test"
23 :    DispData( 1, 2, eval( bCharBlock, xData ), xData )
```

```
24 :
25 :    xData := 3.1415926
26 :    DispData( 2, 2, eval( bNumbBlock, xData ), xData )
27 :
28 :    xData := ( nNumber1 := 4, nNumber2 := 4, nNumber1 == nNumber2 )
29 :    DispData( 3, 2, eval( bLogiBlock, xData ), xData )
30 :
31 :    xData := date()
32 :    DispData( 4, 2, eval( bDateBlock, xData ), xData )
33 :
34 :    wait
35 :    scroll()
36 :
37 :    return( NIL )
38 :
39 : *******************
40 :
41 : static function DispData( nRow, ;    // Row position of the display
42 :                           nCol, ;    // Column position of the display
43 :                           cSay, ;    // Expression to be seen
44 :                           xData )    // Data
45 :
46 :    devpos( nRow, nCol )
47 :    devout( cSay )
48 :
49 :    if !( xData == NIL )
50 :       devpos(nRow, 35)
51 :       devout( xData )
52 :       devpos(nRow, 55)
53 :       devout( valtype( xData ) )
54 :    endif
55 :
56 :    return( NIL )
57 :
58 : // End of File: CBlock3.prg
```

In this example we pass various code blocks to one function, EVAL( ), to evaluate different data types but return uniform values. Four different variables contain code blocks: *bCharBlock*, *bNumbBlock*, *bLogiBlock*, and *bDateBlock*. These four LOCAL variables are initialized on lines 7 through 10. Each of them will take one parameter, a LOCAL variable which has a root name of *Val*. In the first example, if *cVal* is passed, *cVal* is returned (line 23). If no parameter is passed to *cVal* then the value will be NIL, and that will be the value of the code block. In the second code block, *nVal* is numeric and is converted to a string with the PADR( ) function. In the third example, *lVal* is logical and is converted either to the string "True" or to "False." Finally, if *dVal* is a date, the DTOC( ) function converts it to a string.

The DispData( ) function beginning on line 41 simply displays the values passed to the LOCAL parameters *cSay* and *xData* at the coordinates *nRow,nCol*, which are also passed as parameters. As the variable *xData* changes in type on lines 22, 25, 28, and 31, the value returned from the EVAL( ) and *xData* are passed to the DispData( ) routine along with display row and column coordinates.

On lines 41 through 44, each of the parameters within the function DispData( ) are listed on separate lines, and in-line comments on the side tell what each parameter is used for. This helps to document this subroutine.

More generic functions can be created using the EVAL( ) function to look at the data type of data and to pass the correct block to EVAL( ), thus reducing programming frustrations.

In many places in this book, and in the Clipper manual for that matter, the emphasis has been on distinguishing between LOCALS and STATICS versus PRIVATES and PUBLICS. The main thrust to this is that LOCAL and STATIC variables or parameters are visible in only the procedure or function in which they were declared. However, they may be manipulated in subroutines called by these procedures and/or functions so long as the LOCAL or STATIC variable is manipulated in a code block that will be evaluated in the subroutine. The only qualification is that the code block that will manipulate the values must be declared and initialized in the same procedure or function in which the LOCAL and/or STATIC data variables were declared. Here is a programming example that illustrates this:

```
 1 : * Name:      Cblock4.prg
 2 :
 3 : #include "PTValue.ch"    // Power Tools Header file
 4 :
 5 : function Main()
 6 :
 7 :    local nNumber := 1
 8 :    local bCode   := {|| nNumber--}
 9 :
10 :    scroll()
11 :
12 :    DispValues( nNumber, "  <-- Before the code block" )
13 :    DoBlock( bCode )
14 :    DispValues( nNumber, "  <-- After the code block" )
15 :
16 :    return( NIL )
17 :
18 : **********************
19 :
20 : static function DoBlock( bOperation )
21 :
22 :    local nNumber := 4000   // New local variable with the same name
23 :    local nValue  := eval( bOperation )    // Value of the operation
24 :
25 :    DispValues( nValue, nNumber, "<-- VALUE and NUMBER..." )
26 :
27 :    return( pTRUE )
28 :
29 : ********************
30 :
31 : static function DispValues( xData1, xData2, xData3 )
32 :
33 :    qout( xData1, xData2, "")
34 :    if !( xData3 == NIL )
35 :       qqout( xData3 )
36 :    endif
37 :    qout( "Any key to continue..." )
38 :    inkey(0)
39 :
40 :    return( NIL )
41 :
42 : // End of File: CBlock4.prg
```

This example is simple, yet the implications are dramatic. The variable *nNumber* on line 7 is declared LOCAL; its visibility and life span are limited to the routine that initialized it. On line 8, a code block named *bCode* is created. In it, the LOCAL variable *nNumber* is post-decremented. After the value of *nNumber* is displayed by DispValues( ) on line 12, a call to the DoBlock( ) function passes the code block *bCode* to it. Within this function, two new LOCAL variables are initialized on line 22 and line 23—a new *nNumber* and *nValue*. On line 23, *nValue* becomes the value of EVAL( ), which is 1. It is 1 because the code block, now seen as the parameter *bOperation*, only post-decrements *nNumber*—the *nNumber* from line 7 that starts off with a value of 1. Even though a new LOCAL variable named *nNumber* is initialized to 4000 on line 22, the *nNumber* that is decremented is the variable visible to the code block when it was initialized. In this particular example, this would be the variable *nNumber* on line 7, not the variable on line 22. Since the code block post-decrements *nNumber*, the value assigned to *nValue* is the original value of the first *nNumber* variable (which is 1); and the value of *nNumber* then becomes 0. On returning to the main routine, the value of *nNumber* on line 14 is seen to be 0.

The key here is that the value of a LOCAL or STATIC variable can be visible—and modified if necessary—in a subroutine, provided it is passed within a code block that is initialized in the same procedure or function as the original LOCAL or STATIC variable.

So far, the main focus on a code block is what could be best described as a regular code block: one that evaluates as you would expect. However, with macro-expansion, things may change. Whenever a macro expansion occurs within a code block, we have to be concerned with what is called "early evaluation" versus "late evaluation." In the next example, all three forms of code block evaluation are shown.

```
 1 : * File:    CBlock5.prg
 2 :
 3 : function Main()
 4 :
 5 :    local bBlock1
 6 :    local bBlock2
 7 :    local bBlock3
 8 :    local nCounter
 9 :    local cTemp
10 :
11 :    private cString := "0"    // This variable must be private to be seen
12 :
13 :    // Now, assign the code blocks accordingly
14 :
15 :    bBlock1 := {|cString| cString}      // Regular evaluation
16 :    bBlock2 := {|cString| &cString. }   // Early evaluation
17 :    bBlock3 := {|cString| &(cString) }  // Late evaluation
18 :
19 :    cls
20 :    for nCounter := 1 to 24
21 :       cTemp := str(nCounter)
22 :       qout( eval( bBlock1, cTemp ), valtype( eval( bBlock1, cTemp ) ) )
23 :       qqout( eval( bBlock2, cTemp ), valtype( eval( bBlock2, cTemp ) ) )
24 :       qqout( eval( bBlock3, cTemp ), valtype( eval( bBlock3, cTemp ) ) )
25 :       inkey(.3)
26 :    next
27 :    inkey(0)
28 :
```

```
29 :    scroll()
30 :
31 :    return( NIL )
32 :
33 : // End of File: CBlock5.prg
```

When this program is executed, as shown in Figure 15.1, a series of six items will be displayed for 24 rows. Every two items on the screen is considered a pair. For example, on line 22, two items related to the evaluation of the *bBlock1* variable are displayed. The second column, or second pairing, deals with the *bBlock2* variable, and the final pairing pertains to *bBlock3*. These three code blocks are created on lines 15 through 17. They are not created earlier because the PRIVATE variable *cString* needs to have a value assigned to it prior to the creation of these code blocks. Since the PRIVATE statement cannot come before a LOCAL statement, the LOCAL variables could be declared but not assigned. The key to this example program is that there is a variable with the same name as the parameter being passed into the various code blocks.

The first code block on line 15 is a regular code block; the code block will simply return the value of *cString*, the parameter passed to it. This parameter is the value of the variable *cTemp*, which in turn is the string version of the loop counter, *nCounter*. Hence, through 24 iterations of the FOR...NEXT loop on lines 20 to 26, the code block returns a character string whose value ranges from "1" to "24."

In the second code block on line 16, the variable within the code block, *cString*, is macro-expanded. This is an example of early evaluation: When the code block is created and stored to the variable *bBlock2*, the macro compiler will attempt to evaluate the value of the variable *cString*, and will replace *cString* with "0," its current value at the time the code block is defined. In addition, as part of the macro expansion process, numeric strings are converted into numerics. As a result, the code block returns the numeric constant 0 through all 24 iterations of the loop. Typically, this method of defining what amounts to a constant is not desirable.

Finally, the third code block on line 17 provides an example of late evaluation—*cString*, the local parameter within the code block, is macro-expanded at the point that the code block

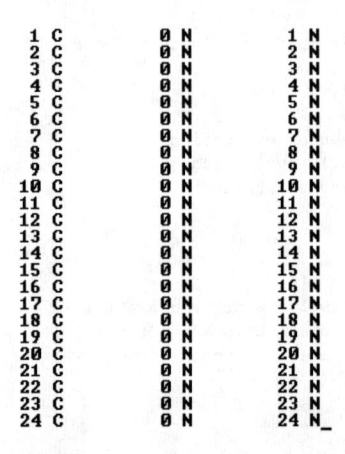

```
 1 C      0 N      1 N
 2 C      0 N      2 N
 3 C      0 N      3 N
 4 C      0 N      4 N
 5 C      0 N      5 N
 6 C      0 N      6 N
 7 C      0 N      7 N
 8 C      0 N      8 N
 9 C      0 N      9 N
10 C      0 N     10 N
11 C      0 N     11 N
12 C      0 N     12 N
13 C      0 N     13 N
14 C      0 N     14 N
15 C      0 N     15 N
16 C      0 N     16 N
17 C      0 N     17 N
18 C      0 N     18 N
19 C      0 N     19 N
20 C      0 N     20 N
21 C      0 N     21 N
22 C      0 N     22 N
23 C      0 N     23 N
24 C      0 N     24 N_
```

**Figure 15.1  Regular, early, and late evaluation of code blocks**

is EVALed, rather than at the point that the code block is created. *cString* in turn represents the string *cTemp*, which is passed to the code block as a parameter. Macro-expanding a numeric string serves to convert it into a numeric value. Consequently, through 24 iterations of the FOR...NEXT loop, the code block *bBlock3* returns a number whose value ranges from 1 to 24.

## INTERMEDIATE PROGRAMMING

In Chapter 10, "Arrays," we have seen the importance of code blocks in relation to the new and powerful AEVAL( ) function. AEVAL( ) will work on every element in the specified array, passing each element to the LOCAL parameter specified in the code block argument list. Again, the code block can accept an element from the array or even a pointer to another array. Whichever is the case, the code block must be properly programmed to accept either single elements from an array or pointers to other arrays. Here is a brief example of a code block working with AEVAL( ).

```
 1 : * Name:      Aevalcb.prg
 2 :
 3 : #include "PTValue.ch"      // Power Tools Header File for values
 4 : #define pFILE_NAME 1       // Position in array for file name
 5 : #define pFILE_SIZE 2       // Position in array for file size
 6 :
 7 : *******************
 8 :
 9 : function Main()
10 :
11 :    local nCounter
12 :    local nValue      := 0
13 :    local aNewValue   := {}
14 :    local bCalc       := {|aFile| ;
15 :                          scroll(1,0,10,40,1), ;
16 :                          setpos(10,0), ;
17 :                          devout( padr(aFile[pFILE_NAME], 20) ), ;
18 :                          devoutpict( aFile[pFILE_SIZE], "999,999,999" ), ;
19 :                          setpos(7,50), ;
20 :                          devoutpict(nValue += aFile[pFILE_SIZE], "999,999,999"),;
21 :                          inkey(.2) }
22 :
23 :    for nCounter := 1 to 10
24 :       aadd( aNewValue, nCounter**2 )
25 :    next
26 :
27 :    cls
28 :
29 :    aeval( aNewValue, {|xItem| qout(xItem)} )
30 :    wait
31 :
32 :    cls
33 :    aeval( directory(), {|aFile| qout( padr( aFile[1], 25 ) ), ;
34 :                         devoutpict( aFile[2], "999,999,999" )} )
35 :    wait
36 :
37 :    cls
38 :    aeval( directory(), bCalc )
39 :    @ maxrow(), 0 say "Press any key"
40 :    inkey(0)
```

```
41 :
42 :    scroll()
43 :    return( NIL )
44 :
45 : // End of File: Aevalcb.prg
```

AEVAL( ) will process each element of an array and pass it to a code block. If the element passed to a code block is a pointer to another array, a nested AEVAL( ) function may be in order, or the code block must be programmed in advance to handle this possibility.

In this programming example, lines 23–25 set up the array *aNewValue[ ]*. Ten elements will be added to this array, each containing the value of *nCounter* to the power of 2. Once the screen is cleared on line 27, a call to AEVAL( ) is made that will evaluate each element in the array and pass it to the literal code block on line 29. In this code block, each subscript position in *aNewValue[ ]* is passed to the LOCAL parameter *xItem*, which is in turn passed to the QOUT( ) function. Remember, this function is the functional equivalent to the ? command; since the ? command must appear on a line by itself, it cannot reside within a code block. In essence, AEVAL( ) will display each element in the array.

In the next call to AEVAL( ), the array created by the DIRECTORY( ) function, which is a multidimensional array with a length determined by the number of files in the current directory and a width of five (filename, file size, file date, file time, and file attribute byte) is passed to AEVAL( ). The code block accepts each element from this array and keeps it in the LOCAL variable *aFile*. Since *aFile* is a pointer to another array, the code block cannot simply display its value. The code block has been programmed to display *aFile[1]* and *aFile[2]*, the name of each file in the current directory and its size.

Finally, in the last call to AEVAL( ) on line 38, the array created by DIRECTORY( ) is passed along with a new variable, *bCalc*, which contains the code block initialized on lines 14 through 21. In it we can see several operations taking place. As each element of the DIRECTORY( ) array is passed to the code block through the LOCAL parameter *aFile* (line 14), each of the following are called in order: the SCROLL( ) function, the SETPOS( ) function, the DEVOUT( ) function, the DEVOUTPICT( ) function, PADR( ) (pad the string on the right), and eventually, the INKEY( ) function. Within the second DEVOUTPICT( ) function call, the value of the variable *nValue,* which is initially assigned the value of 0 on line 12, is incremented with the size of the individual files as passed to the *aFile* parameter. To help make the references to individual elements in the array *aFile* more readable, two manifest constants were used, as defined on lines 4 and 5. Within the code block itself, the SCROLL( ) function defines the display area of the screen and scrolls its contents upward (the fifth parameter, 1, dictates this movement). Next, the cursor is placed at the row, column coordinates 10,0. The name of the passed file is padded to the right with blank spaces so that its total length is 20 characters, and it is displayed. Using the DEVOUTPICT( ) function, the value of the element at the pFILE_SIZE position in *aFile* is converted to a formatted picture. The value of the LOCAL variable *nValue* (initialized on line 12) is incremented by the value of the current file size and is displayed at the row, column position 7,50, again using the DEVOUTPICT( ) function..

The counterpart of AEVAL( ) for arrays is DBEVAL( ) for databases. The DBEVAL( ) function will process every record in the specified database. Its syntax is:

```
DBEVAL(<bBlock>, [<bForCondition>], [<bWhileCondition>], ;
       [<nNextRecords>], [<nRecord>], [<lRest>])
```

## Code Blocks

The function's basic operation, as well as the FOR condition and the WHILE condition, are all expressed in terms of code blocks. In other words, code blocks tell DBEVAL( ) what to do with each record it processes, which records to process, and how long to process them.

That this use of code blocks is a critical part of the focus and direction of the Clipper language can best be seen by examining the traditional database commands in STD.CH. In most cases, the preprocessor translates them into generic DBEVAL( ) calls, with only the code blocks changing.

The following program, DBEVAL1.PRG, illustrates the use of DBEVAL( ) and code block technology:

```
 1 : * Name:      Dbeval1.prg
 2 :
 3 : #include "PTInkey.ch"
 4 : #include "PTValue.ch"
 5 :
 6 : function Main()
 7 :
 8 :    local aRec := {}       // Init an empty array
 9 :
10 :    use FileNos new
11 :    cls
12 :
13 :    dbeval( {|| qqout( Filenos->file_name, Filenos->file_type, ;
14 :                       Filenos->file_size ), qqout( pCRLF ), ;
15 :                       if( Filenos->file_size > 5000, ;
16 :                           aadd( aRec, { Filenos->( recno() ), ;
17 :                                         Filenos->file_name, ;
18 :                                         Filenos->file_size }), ;
19 :                           NIL )},, {|| More()} )
20 :
21 :    wait
22 :    cls
23 :    qout( "Files over 5000 bytes..." )
24 :    aeval( aRec, {|aItem| qout( aItem[1], aItem[2], aItem[3] )} )
25 :    inkey(0)
26 :
27 :    scroll()
28 :
29 :    return( NIL )
30 :
31 : *******************
32 :
33 : static function More()
34 :
35 :    local nKey := inkey()
36 :
37 :    if row() == maxrow() - 2
38 :       @ maxrow(), 00 say "Any key for MORE..."
39 :       inkey(0)
40 :       cls
41 :    endif
42 :
43 :    return( !( nKey == pESC ) )
```

```
44 :
45 : // End of File: DBeval1.prg
```

In this example, the code block defining the operation and the code block for the WHILE parameter are passed to DBEVAL( ) as literals on lines 13 through 19. The QQOUT( ) function, which is the functional equivalent of the ?? command, will be performed on every record. It will display three fields: Filenos->file_name, Filenos->file_type, and Filenos ->file_size. Once these three fields are displayed, the CHR(13)+CHR(10) combination (defined by the manifest constant pCRLF) will be printed as well, forcing a carriage return and line feed to be issued after the line is displayed. The code block also includes a conditional IF( ) function that will be called each time these field values are displayed. In this function, if the value of Filenos->file_size is greater than 5000, then a few items will be dynamically added to the *aRec[ ]* array initialized on line 8. If the record does not meet the condition, a simple NIL value will be returned by the IF( ) function. In essence, the DBEVAL( ) function's code block contains a reference to the local array *aRec[ ]*. The IF( ) function will potentially add elements to this array should the condition be met. This array is then evaluated at a later time (line 24).

The WHILE code block will call the More( ) function on every record. This function simply tests the value of INKEY( ) (line 35) and sees if the display is on row 22 (line 37). (It is assumed that the video will be in a mode in which the value of MAXROW( ) will return 24.) If the cursor is within this region, a special display is issued to the screen at the MAXROW( ) coordinate and a new key is pressed. Eventually, the screen is cleared again, the cursor is placed at the top-left corner of the screen (all via the CLS command), and the function returns a logical flag indicating whether the last key pressed was not ESC.

DBEVAL( ) can be used to do far more than just display records. Remember, the key to unlocking Clipper's power is your ability to creatively mix and match the various new programming tools to achieve newer and bigger effects. In this next example, using DBEVAL( ) to scan records while building an array to be later used by ACHOICE( ) requires very few program lines. This is accomplished to a large degree through the extended use of code blocks.

```
 1 : * Name:      Dbevalcb.prg
 2 :
 3 : #include "PTInkey.ch"
 4 : #include "PTValue.ch"
 5 :
 6 : function Main()
 7 :
 8 :    local aNames    := {}
 9 :    local bDoBlock  := {|| aadd( aNames, {Clients->account, Clients->current} )}
10 :    local bFor      := {|| !empty( Clients->due ) }
11 :    local bWhile    := {|| NoKey() }
12 :    local nChoice   := 1
13 :
14 :    use Clients new
15 :
16 :    Clients->( dbeval( bDoBlock, bFor, bWhile ) )
17 :
18 :    while !( nChoice == 0 )
19 :       dispbegin()
20 :       dispbox(0,0,maxrow(),maxcol(), replicate(chr(178),9) )
```

```
21 :     dispbox(0,0,7,46,pDBAR)
22 :     devpos(0,2)
23 :     devout( "< Enter to choose >" )
24 :     dispend()
25 :
26 :     if !((nChoice := achoice(1,1,6,45,ASingle(aNames) )) == 0 )
27 :       devpos(12,00)
28 :       devout( "Selected Items were: " )
29 :       devout( aNames[nChoice, 1] )
30 :       devout( "   " )
31 :       devout( aNames[nChoice, 2] )
32 :
33 :       @ 14,00 say "Press any key to select another"
34 :       inkey(0)
35 :     endif
36 :   enddo
37 :
38 :   scroll()
39 :   return( NIL )
40 :
41 : *******************
42 :
43 : static function NoKey()
44 :
45 :   return( !( inkey() == pESC ) )
46 :
47 : *******************
48 :
49 : static function ASingle( aArray )
50 :
51 :   // This function turns a multidimensional array into a single-dim array.
52 :
53 :   // AEVAL() could have been used on the LOCAL parameter ARRAY[], but for
54 :   // clarity, the  FOR ... NEXT loop is used instead.
55 :
56 :   local nCounter
57 :   local aRetValue := {}
58 :
59 :   for nCounter := 1 to len( aArray )
60 :     aadd( aRetValue, aArray[nCounter,1] + " === " + ;
61 :                      padr(aArray[nCounter, 2], 10) )
62 :   next
63 :
64 :   return( aRetValue )
65 :
66 : // End of File: DBEvalcb.prg
```

To start with, let us look at the three code blocks that tell DBEVAL( ) what to do. The first block, *bDoBlock*, contains the function call AADD( ) that dynamically adds elements to the array *aNames[ ]*. The element will be an array pointer that contains the value of both Clients->account and Clients->current. The block will be called for every record evaluated by DBEVAL( ). The FOR condition for the DBEVAL( ) is handled by a code block as well. This code block is *bFor* and consists of the expression !EMPTY( Clients->due )—only those records with nonzero values in the Clients->due field will be processed by DBEVAL( ). The WHILE condition in DBEVAL( ) is handled by the NoKey( ) function within the code block *bWhile*. This function always returns a logical true (.T.) if the current key pressed is not the ESC key. If the ESC key is pressed while DBEVAL( ) is being processed, the WHILE code block will return a logical false (.F.) and the function will stop processing. In essence, this routine quickly builds an array of those clients who owe money. This array is then processed within the loop beginning on line 18.

## ADVANCED PROGRAMMING

Code blocks contain address pointers to the operations that will be performed when the code block is evaluated. As such, they may not be displayed, which also means that they may not be saved to disk in a memory variable, an array subscript, or even a database field. However, the string representation of that code block may be stored as a character memory variable, an array subscript value, or even a database field. In other words, what was

```
{|| nVar := nVar + 1}
```

now becomes

```
"{|| nVar := nVar + 1}"
```

It is important to know why the post-incrementing operator, in this example, is not possible. The pre- and post- incrementing and decrementing operators are not available to the macro compiler. The same could be said for any of the in-line operators like += and -=: The macro compiler cannot handle them.

Once this translation is made, the next step is to convert the string into a code block. To do this, the string needs to be macro-expanded and the code block created, as follows:

```
local bCode
private nNumber := 1
private cString := {|| nNumber := nNumber + 1}

bCode := &cString.
```

Once the variable *cString* has been macro-expanded, the run-time library will convert the string into a code block containing the necessary address pointers that refer to compiled sections of code, either in the application or within the Clipper environment itself. In this particular example, the pre-incrementing operation is part of the mathematical run-time library within Clipper. Therefore, when the string is macro-expanded to a code block and stored to the variable *bCode*, it refers to a compiled piece of code—in this case, the mathematical run-time library. Now, all of this does not have to relate to mathematical operations. The real advantage is when strings of code blocks call functions that are located in a pre-linked library (.PLL). These strings can be stored in databases or even text files. This technique allows easy modification of menu options and branching scenarios without recompiling and relinking. So, the advantage of this is not just in the ability to save a code block to disk, but in the faster execution of code blocks.

In this next example, two filters will be initialized 2000 times, the first by a macro-expanded string and the second by a macro-expanded code block.

```
1 : * Name:      Timecb.prg
2 :
3 : function Main()
4 :
```

# Code Blocks 829

```
 5 :    local cVar1
 6 :    local cString
 7 :    local bVar2
 8 :    local nCounter    // Simple counting variable for the FOR...NEXT loop
 9 :    local cScreen     // Temporary screen variable
10 :    local nStart      // Holds the starting time in seconds
11 :
12 :    cls
13 :    use Clients new
14 :
15 :    cVar1 := ' (Clients->status != "6" .and. '
16 :    cVar1 += ' !empty(Clients->address1) .and. recno() < 50) .or. '
17 :    cVar1 += ' deleted() .or. recn() > lastrec()-2 '
18 :
19 :    cString := '{|| (Clients->status != "6" .and. '
20 :    cString += '!empty(Clients->address1) .and. recno() < 50) .or. '
21 :    cString += ' deleted() .or. recno() > lastrec()-2 } '
22 :
23 :    bVar2 := &cString.    // Macro exand to a value
24 :
25 :    @ 0,0 say if( empty( dbfilter() ), "No Filter", dbfilter() )
26 :
27 :    // initialize the seconds
28 :    nStart := seconds()
29 :
30 :    for nCounter := 1 to 2000
31 :      set filter to &cVar1.
32 :      if empty( nCounter % 100 )        // display every 100 records
33 :        @ maxrow(), 00 say nCounter
34 :      endif
35 :    next
36 :    scroll( maxrow(), 00 )              // Clear the screen area
37 :
38 :    @ 1,0 say seconds() - nStart        // Elapsed to the screen
39 :    @ 2,0 say dbfilter()                // display the filter condition
40 :    inkey(0)
41 :    cScreen := savescreen()             // save entire screen before list
42 :
43 :    Clients->( dbgotop() )
44 :
45 :    list    // list the records to the screen....
46 :    inkey(0)
47 :
48 :    dbcloseall()
49 :    use Clients new                     // use again... start fresh
50 :    restscreen(,,,,cScreen)             // Restore the screen
51 :
52 :    @ 10,00 say if( empty( dbfilter() ), "No Filter", dbfilter() )
53 :
54 :    nStart := seconds()
55 :    for nCounter := 1 to 2000
56 :      set filter to eval( bVar2 )
57 :      if empty( nCounter % 100 )        // display every 100 records
58 :        @ maxrow(), 00 say nCounter
59 :      endif
60 :    next
61 :    scroll(maxrow(), 0)
62 :
63 :    @ 11,00 say seconds() - nStart
64 :    @ 12,00 say dbfilter()
```

```
65 :    inkey(0)
66 :
67 :    Clients->( dbgotop() )
68 :
69 :    list
70 :    inkey(0)
71 :
72 :    scroll()
73 :
74 :    return( NIL )
75 :
76 : // End of File: TimeCb.prg
```

The string representation of the code block is initialized on lines 19 through 21. Line 23 is critical: It macro-expands the code block string to form a code block, which is in turn assigned to the *bVar2* variable. Lines 31 and 56 achieve the same effect: A filter is set in the Clients database. However, it takes the SET FILTER TO command on line 31 eight times longer to perform all 2000 iterations than it does the simple EVAL( ) on line 56 (based on an 11-MHz machine). The reason is simple: To macro-expand the string *cVar1* 2000 times means that each character in the string must be expanded and then the value expanded. That process is handled once through the code block; all that needs to be performed on line 56 is the evaluation.

As with the SET FILTER TO command, the INDEX ON command may take macro-expanded variables. We may also add a dummy function call to a display routine as a literal in the index expression; this will add elegance to an otherwise boring operation. (Although, as we have seen in Chapter 13, "Indexes and Replaceable Database Drivers," the EVAL argument of the INDEX ON command can be used for the same purpose.) The thing to keep in mind with any literal expression is that the index header will contain the entire expression, including the reference to the dummy routine used for displays. In a code block, the index expression could change without causing a change to either the key or the header of the file. To show this in action, here is an example:

```
 1 : * Name:      Indexcb.prg
 2 :
 3 : function Main()
 4 :
 5 :    local bIndex := {|nRow| str(recno()) + BarChart(nRow)}
 6 :
 7 :    cls
 8 :    use Filenos new
 9 :    index on str( recno() ) + BarChart(0) to Sample
10 :    qout( indexkey() )
11 :
12 :    use Clients new
13 :    index on str( recno() ) + BarChart(2) to Sample
14 :    qout( indexkey() )
15 :
16 :    use Statcode new
17 :    index on str( recno() ) + BarChart(4) to Sample
18 :    qout( indexkey() )
19 :
20 :    use Statbase new
21 :    index on str( recno() ) + BarChart(6) to Sample
22 :    qout( indexkey() )
23 :
```

```
24 :    use Notap new
25 :    index on str( recno() ) + BarChart(8) to Sample
26 :    qout( indexkey() )
27 :
28 :    wait
29 :    Notap->( DispItem( fieldpos( "files" ) ) )
30 :
31 :    dbcloseall()
32 :
33 :    cls
34 :    use Filenos new
35 :    index on eval( bIndex, 0 ) to Sample
36 :    qout( indexkey() )
37 :
38 :    use Clients new
39 :    index on eval( bIndex, 2 ) to Sample
40 :    qout( indexkey() )
41 :
42 :    use Statcode new
43 :    index on eval( bIndex, 4 ) to Sample
44 :    qout( indexkey() )
45 :
46 :    use Statbase new
47 :    index on eval( bIndex, 6 ) to Sample
48 :    qout( indexkey() )
49 :
50 :    use Notap new
51 :    index on eval( bIndex, 8 ) to Sample
52 :    qout( indexkey() )
53 :
54 :    wait
55 :
56 :    Notap->( DispItem( fieldpos( "files" ) ) )
57 :
58 :    scroll()
59 :
60 :    return( NIL )
61 :
62 : ********************
63 :
64 : static function DispItem( nField )
65 :
66 :    dbgotop()      // Assure that the file is at the top!
67 :
68 :    while !eof()
69 :      @ 23,60 say fieldget( nField )
70 :      scroll(12,0,23,78,1,3)
71 :      dbskip()
72 :    enddo
73 :    wait
74 :
75 :    return( NIL )
76 :
77 : ********************
78 :
79 : static function BarChart( nRow )
80 :
81 :    static nCounter
82 :    static nStartAt
83 :    static nRemainder
```

```
 84 :    static nRecpercol
 85 :
 86 :    // An interesting point about Clipper when it begins an indexing routine:
 87 :    // the value of RECNO() at the very beginning will be 1 greater than the
 88 :    // value of LASTREC().  This is because Clipper will build the index on a
 89 :    // dummy record of blank values.  This coincides with the fact that you
 90 :    // should not index on a TRIM() since the first record is a blank, dummy
 91 :    // record!
 92 :
 93 :    if recno() > lastrec()
 94 :       nRecpercol := maxcol() / lastrec()
 95 :       nStartAt   := nRemainder := 0
 96 :    endif
 97 :
 98 :    nCounter := recno()
 99 :    devpos( nRow, nStartAt )
100 :    devout( replicate( chr(178), nRecpercol ) )
101 :
102 :    nRemainder += (nRecpercol - int( nRecpercol ) )
103 :    nStartAt   += int( nRecpercol )
104 :
105 :    if nRemainder >= 1
106 :       devpos(row(), col() )
107 :       devout( chr(178) )
108 :       nStartAt++
109 :       nRemainder--
110 :    endif
111 :
112 :    if recno() == lastrec()
113 :       devpos(nRow, maxcol())
114 :       devout( chr(178) )
115 :    endif
116 :
117 :    return( "" )
118 :
119 : // End of File: IndexCb.prg
```

The main point to this example is that the index expressions on lines 9, 13, 17, 21, and 25 all refer to the BarChart( ) function, which will therefore appear in the header of the index file SAMPLE.NTX. However, while the code block on line 5 makes a similar reference to this function, the index header for SAMPLE.NTX on lines 35, 39, 43, 47, and 51 will show only a key of EVAL( indexvar, <some value>). After the indexing operation is completed, we simply reassign the value of the variable indexvar that is holding the code block and remove the reference to BarChart( ). Since the return value of the BarChart( ) function is a NULL byte, removing it from the index will play no part in the performance of the application using this index file. Additionally, the keys within the index file will not be corrupted and the header of the index file need not change. So the BarChart( ) function is simply a function to help out with the user interface portion of a program, and at its completion it no longer needs to be retained within the code block.

## GET/SET BLOCK FUNCTIONS

With the introduction of objects, both for browsing and for data entry, there needs to be some easily accessible, automatic way to update a browsing object to reflect the values contained in an array or a database field, and to update the database field or array to reflect changes to the values in the browsing object. Code blocks are vital for this purpose. For example, in a browsing object, a code block controls the display of fields in columns of the object. These are called GET/SET code blocks—they are responsible for automatically obtaining a value from a database field, a memory variable, or an array, and for automatically assigning a value back to a database field, memory variable, or an array.

The GET/SET code block generally takes on the following format:

```
bBlock := {|xItem| if( xItem == NIL, <variable>, <variable> := xItem}
```

When this code block is called, if a piece of data is passed to it, then the value of the variable *xItem* will not be NIL. As a result, *xItem* will be assigned to the specified variable (or array element, or database field). This is the "set" component of the GET/SET code block. An example of this might look something like the following:

```
eval( bBlock, 23 )
```

In this case, the value of the code block, and therefore the value of the EVAL( ) function, would be 23, which would be the value stored to <variable>.

On the other hand, if a value is not specified for *xItem*, the code block will simply obtain the value of <variable>, which might be a database field, a memory variable, or an array element. This use of the "get" component of the GET/SET code block looks like the following:

```
eval( bBlock )
```

In this case, the value of the code block and the value of EVAL( ) is the value of <variable>.

To illustrate how this process might work, let's quickly look at the requirements for converting a field that is to be listed in a browsing column object into a code block. In particular, let's use the Name field in the Clients database. To convert this into a code block, we need to write the following:

```
{|var| IF(EMPTY(PCOUNT())), "+name+", FIELD->"+name+" := var)}
```

This type of code block needs to be built for every field in the browsing object, which is hardly convenient. If it were to be embedded in a function of your own, you would have to build a string representation of the code block with the name of the field passed as a parameter, and then macro-expand that string, thus returning the pointer to the macro-expanded code block. This might look something like the following:

```
FUNCTION FieldBlock( a )

    LOCAL cRetValue := "{|var| IF(EMPTY(PCOUNT())), '+a', FIELD->'+a+' := var)}"

    RETURN( &( cRetValue ) )
```

To make it easier to generate code blocks based on the contents of database fields and memory variables, and also to free the programmer from the need to worry about the correct form and syntax of the GET/SET code block, Clipper provides three functions:

FIELDBLOCK( )  Equivalent to macro-expanding the string representation of a code block involving the specified field.

| | |
|---|---|
| FIELDWBLOCK( ) | Equivalent to macro-expanding the string representation of a code block involving the specified field in a work area that is also specified. |
| MEMVARBLOCK( ) | Similar to FIELDBLOCK( ), except it works with the specified memory variable. |

These functions are specifically intended to be used with the browsing and GET objects that are discussed at length in Chapter 16, "Clipper Objects." It is worth noting, however, that the application of GET/SET code blocks can be far broader. A peculiarity of the code block is that any LOCAL variable visible at the time that the code block is created will remain visible within the code block; therefore, through the code block, they can be passed from subroutine to subroutine and still retain their visibility. We made use of this peculiarity in ARRAY20.PRG, a sample program found in Chapter 10, "Arrays," where we created a GET/SET code block to effectively pass an array element by reference.

An important question that concerns GET/SET code blocks, particularly those that work with database fields, is the work area in which they are to execute. In most of the examples in this chapter, code blocks that work with database fields contained the alias of a field within the code block itself. This means that, regardless of the work area that is current when the code block is evaluated, the code block will know what work area to execute in.

When either the FIELDBLOCK( ) or FIELDWBLOCK( ) function is used to generate a code block, it is important to understand how the code block is generated and which work area it will work in. For example, imagine that we are to create the following code block:

```
Clients->( EVAL( {|| Trans->( DBGOTOP() ) } ) )
```

Here, for example, although our intent is evidently to execute the code block in the Clients work area, the code block itself will move the record pointer to the beginning of the file in the Trans work area.

The point of this is that the FIELDBLOCK( ) function will execute in the current work area or in the aliased work area at the time the code block is evaluated. For example, the following FIELDBLOCK( ) function call creates a GET/SET code block that seems to refer to the Clients work area but actually does not refer to the Clients work area at all:

```
bBlock := Clients->( FIELDBLOCK( "name" ) )
```

In other words, the code block itself contains no reference to the work area in which it is to be evaluated. Therefore, the code block must be evaluated in either of two ways:

```
cName := Clients->( EVAL( bBlock))

cName := EVAL( bBlock)
```

When the code block is executed, it will work successfully if Clients is the current work area (which is assumed by the second call to the EVAL( ) function, if the EVAL( ) function call is preceded by the Clients database's alias (as is our second function call), or if a field named Name exists in the current work area (which is likely to be more a matter of luck than of intent). But if neither of these conditions holds, the EVAL( ) will generate a run-time error. To avoid this possibility, the FIELDWBLOCK( ) function can be used, since it establishes a close relationship within the code block between a field name and a particular work area. The GET/SET code block would be created as follows:

```
bBlock := FIELDWBLOCK( "name" , SELECT("Clients"))
```

It could then simply be evaluated as follows:

```
cName := EVAL(bBlock)
```

Since the name of the database on which the code block should execute is a part of the code block, it is not necessary to use an alias when calling the EVAL( ) function.

## More Advanced Features: Building Generic Subroutines

Code blocks are at the core of the Clipper language. They are one of the major points of departure from the old Xbase way of doing things. With that in mind, we can use code blocks to further enhance the way Clipper behaves by default. Although the following example only reworks one of the common Clipper functions, the concept can be applied in a myriad of other functions.

With the introduction of code blocks comes the question: How do we use them effectively? In all of these examples, many of the features and subtleties are shown, but the real-world use of the code block has yet to be explored. One way to better use a code block is to build a generic function that would in turn use a code block. In the Clipper language, there are several real-world functions that we can attempt to mimic: DBEVAL( ) is a good one for starters. Now, in attempting to build a "better" DBEVAL( ), we need to have new requirements. One new need can be found in the relationship of DBEVAL( ) is it currently exists with the needs of all of our applications. For example, one fact is known about the COUNT, REPLACE ALL, DELETE FOR, AVERAGE, and other commands that translate into the DBEVAL( ) function—they all leave the record pointer at the end of the file. In all applications that use these commands, the record pointer typically has to be repositioned back to the point of origin. It would be nice if DBEVAL( ) did that for us: We are attempting to build a generic function that reflects how we use the function rather than writing code to work with the generic function. Now, to build a "better" DBEVAL( ) that takes on this new property, we can begin to see the use of code blocks, since that is what this function needs in order to operate.

In essence, DBEVAL( ) is a very dumb function. All it does is traverse a database. The specific operation of "what to do" is encapsulated in a code block and passed as a parameter to the DBEVAL( ) to be evaluated at some point in the process. For example, when we want to DELETE a record, that translates into a code block that looks like this:

```
{|| dbdelete() }
```

Hopefully, when this parameter is accepted by the DBEVAL( ) function, it will EVAL( ) this code block before skipping on to the next record rather than the other way around. This is what is meant as "intended behavior": DBEVAL( ) is programmed to EVAL( ) and then SKIP, not the reverse. This means that when we program our version of DBEVAL( ), whether it be a close duplicate or any other generic function, we must come to terms with this phrase:

*It's not what we "do" that matters but "when" we want it done.*

Looking at our example with DBEVAL( ), the "do" is the DELETE operation, but it could be any other operation—like RECALL, COUNT, or REPLACE. That portion of the function is not important, since it is outside DBEVAL( )'s scope. What is critical is when these code blocks get EVAL( )ed: the "when" part of the equation. We found that it is very important to what DBEVAL( ) means that the code block of "do"-ing something take place before the SKIP operation and not the other way around. It is understanding this relationship of code and timing that gets into the behavioral world of object oriented programming, of which code blocks is a very natural first step in the Clipper world.

This next example is an attempt to make an enhanced DBEVAL( ). To avoid getting a run-time warning message, "Public symbol 'DBEVAL' doubly defined," the DBEVAL( ) clone is called DBNetEval( ).

```
 1 : * File:   Dbeval2.prg
 2 :
 3 : #include "PTValue.ch"
 4 : #include "PTVerbs.ch"
 5 :
 6 : function Main()
 7 :
 8 :    local nCount
 9 :
10 :    cls
11 :    use Filenos new
12 :
13 :    Filenos->( dbgoto(4) )
14 :
15 :    ? recno()
16 :
17 :    count to nCount    // This makes a call to DBEVAL()
18 :
19 :    ? recno(), nCount
20 :
21 :    dbgotop()          // we need this in order for the NEXT to work!
22 :    count to nCount next 10
23 :    ? recno(), nCount
24 :
25 :    ? "Here, the DBEVAL() function does not put the record pointer back"
26 :    ? "where it belongs. In the following example, a new DBEVAL() func."
27 :    ? "will be written to add more punch to both function and command"
28 :
29 :    dbcloseall()
30 :
31 :    // let's create the command to do it...
32 : #xcommand COUNT [TO <var>] [FOR <for>] [WHILE <while>] [NEXT <next>] ;
33 :                [RECORD <rec>] [<rest:REST>] [<stay:STAY PUT>] ;
34 :                [MANNER <ext>] [ALL] => ;
35 :                <var> := 0 ;
36 :                ; DBNetEval( {|| <var> := <var> + 1}, ;
37 :                            <{for}>, <{while}>, <next>, <rec>, <.rest.>, ;
38 :                            <.stay.>, <{ext}> )
39 :
40 :    use Filenos new
41 :    Filenos->( dbgoto(4) )
42 :    ? recno()
43 :    count to nCount stay put
44 :
45 :    ? recno(), nCount
```

```
 46 :
 47 :     count to nCount next 10
 48 :     ? recno(), nCount, "And the value of QLock():", QLock()
 49 :
 50 :     return( NIL )
 51 :
 52 : *********************
 53 :
 54 : function DbNetEval( bOperation, ;  // Operation that is to be performed
 55 :                     bFor, ;        // code block for the FOR condition
 56 :                     bWhile, ;      // code block for the WHILE condition
 57 :                     nNext, ;       // number of NEXT records to process
 58 :                     nRecs, ;       // record number to work on exactly
 59 :                     lRest, ;       // Toggle to rewind record pointer
 60 :                     lStay, ;       // Toggle to return to original rec
 61 :                     bWhat )        // Code block of movement in database
 62 :
 63 :    // By writing our own new version of DBEVAL(), the concept of how
 64 :    // to use a code block in a more generic fashion may be seen.  In
 65 :    // addition, it helps to illustrate the phrase "it's not what you
 66 :    // want to do that matters, but when you want to do it".
 67 :
 68 :    local nOriginalRec
 69 :    local nCounter := 0
 70 :
 71 :    if !empty( alias() )  // We are in a work area
 72 :
 73 :       DEFAULT bOperation TO {|| NIL }, ; // Don't do anything!
 74 :               bFor    TO {|| pTRUE}, ;  // The FOR condition of the clause
 75 :               bWhile  TO {|| pTRUE }, ; // The WHILE condition of the clause
 76 :               lRest   TO pFALSE, ;      // if .T., DON'T rewind!
 77 :               lStay   TO pFALSE, ;      // if .F., leave at end
 78 :               nOriginalRec TO recno(), ;
 79 :               bWhat   TO {|| dbskip()}  // What are we going to do?
 80 :
 81 :       IF nRecs IS pNUMERIC   // The record was specified
 82 :          if nRecs > 1 .and. nRecs <= lastrec()  // and it is within range
 83 :             dbgoto( nRecs )
 84 :             if eval( bFor )
 85 :                if rlock()                // attempt to lock the record
 86 :                   eval( bOperation )
 87 :                   QLock( pTRUE )         // Say that the lock was successful
 88 :                   dbunlock()             // Unlock the current record
 89 :                else
 90 :                   QLock( pFALSE )        // Toggle QLock() to show error
 91 :                endif
 92 :             endif
 93 :          endif
 94 :       else   // Assumed all else, use normal path
 95 :
 96 :          if !lRest    // No REST clause so rewind the database
 97 :             dbgotop()
 98 :          endif
 99 :
100 :          DEFAULT nNext TO ( lastrec() - recno() +1 ) // Remaining records
101 :
102 :          if nNext < 1 .or. nNext > lastrec()  // Again, robust and O.B.
103 :             nNext := (lastrec() - recno()+1 )  // Take 2 shot penalty and try
104 :          endif                                 // again, Clayton <sfsf>
105 :
106 :          // This is the main processing loop!
```

```
107 :          while !eof() .and. eval( bWhile )
108 :
109 :             if ++nCounter <= nNext      // we are in range
110 :                if eval( bFor )          // if the FOR condition is true... then...
111 :                   if rlock()            // Attempt to lock record
112 :                      eval( bOperation ) // DO IT!
113 :                      QLock( pTRUE )     // Say that the lock was successful
114 :                      dbunlock()         // Unlock the current record
115 :                   else
116 :                      QLock( pFALSE )    // Toggle QLock()
117 :                      exit               // break out from the range
118 :                   endif
119 :                endif
120 :             endif
121 :
122 :             // default behavior is to skip
123 :             eval( bWhat )
124 :          enddo
125 :
126 :          if lStay     // reposition to original record number
127 :             dbgoto( nOriginalRec )
128 :          endif
129 :
130 :       endif
131 :
132 :    endif
133 :
134 :    return( NIL )
135 :
136 : ******************
137 :
138 : function QLock( lToggle )
139 :
140 :    static lStatus
141 :
142 :    if lStatus == NIL   // Only check this once
143 :       lStatus := !neterr()     // Default is to have everything o.k.
144 :    endif
145 :
146 :    IF lToggle IS pLOGICAL
147 :       lStatus := lToggle
148 :    endif
149 :
150 :    return( lStatus )
151 :
152 : // End of File: DBEval2.prg
```

Lines 17 through 23 show the standard behavior of the COUNT TO command that translates into the DBEVAL( ) function. This can be verified by compiling this program with the /P switch and taking a look at the file DBEVAL2.PPO. On lines 32 through 38, the COUNT TO command is retranslated to use the enhanced DBNetEval( ) function. In addition to the optional clause called STAY PUT, a MANNER option is available. All other options are compatible with Clipper 5.2: We have merely extended the command to be not only backward compatible but forward reaching as well. On line 43, the new command is called using the STAY PUT optional clause. Therefore, since this will translate into the DBNetEval( ) function, the crux of this example lies there.

DBNetEval( ) is defined on lines 54 and following. One of the first rules of building a generic function, especially when using code blocks, is that the function must be robust enough to work in abnormal conditions. In addition, use comments to understand parameters, variable values, and default conditions, as well as program flow. The specific operation that is to take place for the COUNT command is seen on the code block on line 36. The meaning of COUNT is to take the variable specified in the command, which is translated in the regular result marker of *<var>*, and to add 1 to its value. That operation is defined by the command and is passed into the DBNetEval( ) function. Here, the "do" piece of DBNetEval( ) is seen coming from the outside. This code block becomes the parameter *bOperation* on line 54.

Before getting to the point where this code block could be evaluated, the function must test the environment and must ensure that other parameters have default values. Therefore, if there is an open work area active for this function, line 71 will return a logical true (.T.). From here, we have assigned various default values for some of the parameters as well as some of the LOCAL variables. For example, the variable *nOriginalRec* is to contain the value of RECNO( ) (line 78), but if this variable was to have been assigned a value earlier, on line 68 (where the variable is now declared) and if no active work area is available, then an error would exist, making the attempt at being "robust" on line 71 seem foolish.

On line 77 is one of the new enhancements. The parameter lStay is assigned a default value of a logical false (.F.). This variable is designed to tell the function whether to return to the original record position once the function has completed its operation. The default value shows signs of backward compatibility—the default behavior is to stay at the end of the file and not rewind. The STAY PUT optional clause forces the parameter to be either logical true or false; if true, then on line 126 the function will return to the original record, as stored in the variable *nOriginalRec*.

Another enhancement, the MANNER clause, translates into the *bWhat* parameter. This parameter defaults into a code block on line 79 with the DBSKIP( ) function in it. Again, trying to build a function that goes beyond the conventional behavior, we have now allowed record skipping to be controlled outside of the DBNetEval( ) function as well. This means that we can control not only the number of records to be skipped, but also the movement of the record pointer in ancillary databases as well. The only requirement is that the main operation stored in *bOperation* take place before the skipping operation stored in *bWhat*; this is provided for on lines 112 and 123, respectively.

## Summary

Code blocks add new power to the Clipper language. We could build a database of the string representations of code blocks, which would contain all of the operations necessary for a given general function. We could load the database once, macro-expand all of the strings into their code block equivalents, and pass the code blocks to our generic function. These are the beginning steps to creating truly portable and generic functions, routines, and objects. Our list-box routines would be driven by the passed code blocks—an evolutionary step in data-driven programming. The impact of code blocks will be felt in every new application, every command, every function used within the language. Code blocks cannot be avoided; even the simplest command should use them to extend its power. Understanding this, and programming to use code blocks, will extend the power of every procedure, every function, and as a result, every application you write.

# 16

# Clipper Objects

Object-oriented programming is a terminology that is new to the Clipper language. Referring to programming in this fashion in Clipper is not quite correct; "programming Clipper objects" is more appropriate. Before getting into the heart of this subject, one must understand the concept of the structure and use of arrays to build large programming modules. (See Chapter 17, "Windowing, Screens, and Menus.") If the concept of an array structure is understood, the shift to object-oriented programming should be smooth.

Much of the terminology and philosophy of programming Clipper objects finds its roots in object-oriented programming. That method of programming is just a way of attacking and solving the same problems from a different angle. For example, in the past, if in building an application a function stood out as unique and powerful, the desire to add parameters to it, to reprogram it, and thus, extend its use and scope to not just one application but to many others as well, became preeminent. Up to a point, this is fundamentally sound: Building a few generic functions to handle a wide range of services is always desirable. The trouble is that we are reprogramming a function that has previously worked in a specific context. The possibility of breaking a working function is high, and the code of the function slowly becomes bloated as we test for parameters to set up default values.

The introduction of the code block (a memory pointer to a function, procedure, or expression) allows us to program functions in a more generalized way. In other words, the code block allows us to program the data and not specific functions. We can see this in the use of DBEVAL( )—by changing the operation to be performed by this function, the commands SUM, AVERAGE, REPLACE ALL, DELETE ALL, RECALL ALL, and COUNT all go through the same function. The only element that has changed is the code block that is passed to the function. The number of parameters do not change, nor do their data types; the operations that are to be performed on every record within DBEVAL( ) are handled by the instructions formally passed as parameters or as a code block. In many ways, programming objects is similar. The objects will perform differently as they are programmed differently; the parameters passed to them tell them to do things differently.

In the past, programming in the xBASE dialect, and a few other languages as well, meant that we programmed in a top-down fashion. Normally, lower functions were not planned until the need for them became evident. This lead to the problems outlined earlier—finding the better way too late in the coding process. In object-oriented programming, on the other hand, need parallels the development of a system, which means that the design is geared more from the bottom-up. Looking at a system's common denominators before sitting at the keyboard and writing out the first piece of code is a great step toward thinking in this new mind-set. In the future, developers will look at the subcomponents of a system, define their structures, and program them first, layering other structures on top of them.

For example, each report will be defined first and the code written to draw on commonalities across all reports. To get to a report, databases, indexes, relations, and filters must be properly set. All reports require this. A menuing system, structured and uniform across the entire system, must control the end user. In this small example, three new types of structures or objects are outlined. Instead of immediately starting to code, we will take time to define our needs; and we will structure our coding efforts accordingly. This means that object-oriented programming is based on an operational model of the application being designed. If the operation changes, the code changes.

A great deal more time will be spent in the design of an application and in better understanding the needs of the customer. But if this is appreciated, then the far-reaching notion of programming general-ledger objects to be used in a variety of manners becomes more inspiring than taking a general-ledger module written by someone else and tweaking it to fit current needs.

The first term to grapple with from the lexicon of object-oriented programming is the word *classes*. There are four formal classes in Clipper 5.2: GET, TBROWSE, TBCOLUMN, and ERROR. A class is a predefined structure of behaviors and values that describes a specific thing. For example, all GETs will have the same values and behaviors. Whether we choose to program a GET to use a WHEN clause or a VALID clause does not change the fact that any GET can have a WHEN or a VALID. We can look at examples in Chapter 17 on windowing: All of the elements that can describe a window are used in an array, and the structure of that array does not change from window to window. The contents of each window may vary, but the structure itself does not.

In the past, we have worked with the "structure-extended" class. By simply executing this command,

```
CREATE <filename>
```

we will create a structure-extended database. Whether we use all of the contents of this file is immaterial. Every time this command is executed, a file with four fields of fixed names is created.

This is the basic thought behind a class. We can look to parts of an application and point out several classes beyond the four classes provided in Clipper 5.2: MENU, REPORT, DATA ENTRY, COMMUNICATIONS, and so on. Since support for user-defined objects (UDOs) is not present in Clipper 5.2, these may be nothing more than pseudo-classes using arrays to handle the structure of each. This is demonstrated in Chapter 17, "Windowing, Screens, and Menus."

Once a class has been defined, the basic unit of each class is the *object*. An *object* is an abstract data structure that possesses certain characteristics and will respond to certain requests. Objects from the same class will behave and react the same way. Each time a GET command is issued, a unique object in the GET class structure will be generated and stored to an array called *GETLIST[ ]*. While each GET is unique, each shares the same structure and characteristics; whether each attribute in the structure is used or not is immaterial. When a particular object is generated from a specific class, it is said to be an *instance* of that class. The object is a formal data type of an instance of a particular class. The functions that generate the various objects will be specified in a moment; nevertheless, each time these functions are called, an instance of a class is created and is formally stored to an object.

An object, or an instance of a particular class, contains a hard-coded structure with two types of storage locations. One is called an *instance variable*, and the other is called a *method*. Referring to our pseudostructure of a window class in Chapter 17, the instance variables and methods were stored to individual array subscripts. The instance variables contain values that describe the object, while methods prescribe the operations to be performed on the object.

For example, in Chapter 17 some array subscripts contain the screen coordinates of the window, while another subscript contains the code block to execute should that window be opened. The coordinates of the window are held in instance variables; the code block that contains the operations to be performed is a method. In the four predefined objects in Clipper 5.2, some instance variables may be accessed and assigned values. These are known as *exported instance variables*. An operation to be performed on an instance of a class, or an object, is referred to as a method. This will become clearer as examples are shown of this type of storage location.

While objects share the characteristics of their class, each object can differ from other objects of the same class. The *send operator* distinguishes between objects of the same class. To help understand this new operator, consider this programming situation. In an application, there are two open databases (Clients and Invoices), each with a field named "ACCOUNT". The only way to distinguish one field from the other is by using the alias of the work area or database in conjunction with the field pointer operator. In other words, something like this:

```
? Clients->account
? Invoices->account
```

In object-oriented terms, we are sending the message of the alias pointer to the specific field named ACCOUNT. If both of these aliases were of the same class of objects, the above code would look like this:

```
? clients:account
? invoices:account
```

Since the structure of all Clipper objects is predefined and hard-coded, the names of the instance variables and methods are also hard-coded and fixed. To distinguish one method or instance variable in one object from another, the object must be "sent" using the colon (:) operator. What is actually sent is the pointer referring to the object. As a matter of fact, the concept of structure parallels the concept of a predefined structure of array elements. It will be demonstrated in the following examples that the objects follow the same guidelines as arrays when passed from one routine to the next.

# TBROWSE and TBCOLUMN

These two classes depend on one another. Another term used in object-oriented programming is the concept of "browsing." This is an area of the screen that has been defined as a class; the objects that go through that browsing area are defined as columns. There are three functions in Clipper that create either the TBROWSE object or the TBCOLUMN object.

| | |
|---|---|
| TBROWSEDB( ) | Creates a browse object for a database file. |
| TBROWSENEW( ) | Creates a browse object without reference to database files. |
| TBCOLUMNNEW( ) | Creates a column object. |

To create an object of the TBROWSE( ) class, a call to either the TBROWSEDB( ) or TBROWSENEW( ) function is necessary. To do this, the following syntax is used:

```
<variable> := TBROWSEDB(<expN1>, <expN2>, <expN3>, <expN4>)
```

| | |
|---|---|
| <expN1> | Top row coordinate of browsing area |
| <expN2> | Left column coordinate of browsing area |
| <expN3> | Bottom row coordinate of browsing area |
| <expN4> | Right column coordinate of browsing area |

This same syntax applies to TBROWSENEW( ). The return value of this function is a reference to an instance of the TBROWSE class. That instance is stored to the object named in <variable>. The structure of this instance is the following:

### *TBROWSE( ) Class Instance Variables*

| | |
|---|---|
| AUTOLITE | Contains a logical value that, when set to true (.T.) and during stabilization, will highlight the current cell. The default value is a logical true (.T.). This instance variable is assignable. |
| CARGO | Contains any data value that is to be used in conjunction with this particular browsing object. This instance variable is assignable. |
| COLCOUNT | Contains the total number of active columns in the browsing area. For each column, there is an associated column object. This instance variable is not assignable. |
| COLORSPEC | Contains a character string of standard and enhanced colors to be used as a global color index table by the browsing area and all associated columns. The default will be the current value of SETCOLOR( ) when the object is generated. This instance variable is assignable. |
| COLPOS | Contains the current column position of the cursor. This instance variable is assignable. |

| | |
|---|---|
| COLSEP | Contains a character expression used to separate columns in the browsing area. If the TBColumn instance variable *colSep* specifies a column separator, that character string will be used in place of this value. This instance variable is assignable. |
| FOOTSEP | Contains a character expression that defines a footing separator for TBColumn objects not containing a footing separator of their own. |
| FREEZE | Contains the number of columns to freeze on the left side of the browse area. It will freeze the greatest possible number of columns that may be visible in a browsing area. The default value is 0. This instance variable is assignable. |
| GOBOTTOMBLOCK | Contains a code block that instructs the browsing area how to go to the bottom of the current data set. By default, this will be a GO BOTTOM command. This instance variable is assignable. |
| GOTOPBLOCK | Contains a code block that instructs the browsing area how to go to the top of the current data set. By default, this will be a GO TOP command. This instance variable is assignable. |
| HEADSEP | Contains a character string that will be used to separate the data display area in each column from the header display area. If a value is specified for the TBColumn instance variable headSep, it will be used in place of this value. This instance variable is assignable. |
| HITBOTTOM | Contains a logical expression that will be true (.T.) if the browsing object has reached the end-of-file marker while navigating the data set. This instance variable is assignable. |
| HITTOP | Contains a logical expression that will be true (.T.) if the browsing object has reached the top-of-file marker while navigating the data set. This instance variable is assignable. |
| LEFTVISIBLE | Contains a numeric value that indicates the position of the leftmost unfrozen column in the browse object. This instance variable is not assignable. |
| NBOTTOM | Contains a value that specifies the bottom row used by the browsing object. This instance variable is assignable. |
| NLEFT | Contains a value that specifies the leftmost column used by the browsing object. This instance variable is assignable. |
| NRIGHT | Contains a value that specifies the rightmost column used by the browsing object. This instance variable is assignable. |
| NTOP | Contains a value that specifies the top row used by the browsing object. This instance variable is assignable. |

| | |
|---|---|
| RIGHTVISIBLE | Contains a numeric value that indicates the position of the rightmost unfrozen column in the display. This instance variable is not assignable. |
| ROWCOUNT | Contains a value for the number of rows to be used by the data display area. This area does not include the area used by separators, headers, or footers. This instance variable is not assignable. |
| ROWPOS | Contains a numeric value for the current position of the cursor. This instance variable is assignable. |
| SKIPBLOCK | Contains a code block that instructs the browsing object how to "skip." This code block will be evaluated during stabilization. This instance variable is assignable. |
| STABLE | Contains a logical expression. If the value is true (.T.), the browsing object is considered stable and all data elements have been properly displayed. If the value is false (.F.), the object is not stable. This instance variable is assignable. |

### TBROWSE Class Cursor Movement Methods

| | |
|---|---|
| DOWN( ) | Instructs the browse cursor to move down one row. If the cursor is already positioned on the last element, this method will assign a logical true to the *hitBottom* instance variable. |
| END( ) | Instructs the browse cursor to move to the rightmost cell currently visible in the browsing area. |
| GOBOTTOM( ) | Instructs the browsing area to position the data source to the end of the file. |
| GOTOP( ) | Instructs the browsing area to position the data source to the top of the file specified by the *goTopBlock* instance variable. |
| HOME( ) | Moves the browse cursor to the leftmost cell that is not frozen in the browsing area. |
| LEFT( ) | Moves the browse cursor left one column. If a column is present, the columns will pan through the browsing area in an appropriate manner. If there are no more active columns to the left of the cursor, the action will be ignored. |
| PAGEDOWN( ) | Moves the cursor down one full window of row elements. If the data source is currently at the end-of-file marker, this method will assign a logical true (.T.) to the *hitBottom* instance variable. |
| PAGEUP( ) | Moves the cursor up one full window of row elements. If the data source is currently at the top-of-file marker, this method will assign a logical true (.T.) to the *hitTop* instance variable. |

*Clipper Objects* 847

| | |
|---|---|
| PANEND( ) | Moves the cursor to the rightmost column in the browsing area. |
| PANHOME( ) | Moves the cursor to the leftmost column in the browsing area. |
| PANLEFT( ) | Pans the browsing area to the left without altering, if possible, the position of the cursor. |
| PANRIGHT( ) | Pans the browsing area to the right without altering, if possible, the position of the cursor. |
| RIGHT( ) | Moves the cursor to the right one column. If a column is present, the columns will pan through the browsing area in an appropriate manner. If there are no more active columns to the right of the cursor, the action will be ignored. |
| UP( ) | Moves the cursor up one row. If the cursor is currently positioned on the last element, this method will assign a logical true to the *hitTop* instance variable. |

## TBROWSE Class Miscellaneous Methods

ADDCOLUMN( )           ADDCOLUMN( <oColumn> )

    <oColumn>          Column object from TBCOLUMNNEW( )

Adds the column object specified as <oColumn> to the assigned browsing object. This will also increase the value of the *colCount* instance variable by one.

COLORRECT( )           COLORRECT( <aCoords>, <aColors> )

    <aCoords>          Array of window coordinates
    <aColors>          Array of color indexes

Alters the colors of a window region from the top, left coordinates of <aCoords>[1], <aCoords>[2] to coordinates <aCoords>[3], <aCoords>[4]. The color of this region will be directly changed based on a color index specified in the color index table for the corresponding browse object. The color indexes are numeric values and are stored in array <aColors>.

COLWIDTH( )            COLWIDTH( <nColumn> )

    <nColumn>          Number of the column whose width is wanted

This method returns the display width of the <nColumn>th TBColumn contained in the TBrowse class. If <nColumn> is not in the range of columns contained in the TBrowse, then the method will return 0.

CONFIGURE( )           Forces the browsing object to reevaluate all instance variables and column objects. It will also reconfigure the internal settings of the browsing object as applicable.

| | |
|---|---|
| DEHILITE( ) | Instructs the current cell to be de-highlighted. This will not adjust the cursor position. |
| DELCOLUMN( ) | `DELCOLUMN( <nColumn> )` |
|     <nColumn> | Column position |
| | Deletes the column object at position <nColumn> and returns a reference to it. All internal values will be adjusted and restabilization may be needed. |
| FORCESTABLE( ) | This performs a full stabilization of the proper TBrowse class. It does not allow for incremental stabilization in which keystrokes may be trapped. |
| GETCOLUMN( ) | `GETCOLUMN( <nColumn> )` |
|     <nColumn> | Column position |
| | Returns the TBColumn object located at column <nColumn>. |
| HILITE( ) | Instructs the current cell to be highlighted. This will not adjust the cursor position. |
| INSCOLUMN( ) | `INSCOLUMN( <nColumn>,<oColumn> )` |
|     <nColumn> | Column position |
|     <oColumn> | Column object |
| | Inserts the column object <oColumn> at column position <nColumn> and returns a reference to <oColumn>. |
| INVALIDATE( ) | Forces the entire browsing object to be redrawn during the next stabilization. This does not refresh the data rows being displayed. |
| REFRESHALL( ) | Forces a restabilization that will refresh all of the data elements in the browsing area. |
| REFRESHCURRENT( ) | Forces a restabilization only for the row currently activated by the cursor. When stabilization occurs, only those elements in that data row will be reevaluated and redisplayed. |
| SETCOLUMN( ) | `SETCOLUMN( <nColumn>, <oColumn> )` |
|     <nColumn> | Column position |
|     <oColumn> | Column object |
| | Returns the current column object specified in column <nColumn> and replaces it with the column object specified as <oColumn>. |
| STABILIZE( ) | Performs an incremental stabilization. Once an entire browsing area is stable, the method will return a logical true (.T.). If not, it will continue to return a logical false (.F.) value, suggesting further stabilization is required. |

To generate an instance of this class as an object, we could do the following:

```
oB := tbrowsedb(10,10,20,40)
```

This defines the browsing area of the screen at coordinates 10,10 to 20,40 and assigns it to the variable *oB*.

To assign this particular object a heading separator, the following command could be issued:

```
oB:headsep := "==="
```

This is similar to an assignment made to a variable or, in Clipper 5.2, to a field, where *oB* is the alias, ":" is the pointer, and *headSep* is the field.

Once a browsing area has been established, the area must be "stabilized." To do this, a call to a browsing method must be issued and a browsing instance variable must be tested. The method is stabilize( ) and the instance variable is *:stable*. Once a browsing area has been established and the appropriate number of column objects, discussed later, are in place, the browsing area needs to be drawn on the screen, the internal browsing cursor made ready for action, and data displayed in the proper locations.

All of this is handled by the stabilize( ) method. This method activates the appropriate browse object and attempts to perform incremental stabilization on all of the data elements in the browsing area. Because this process occurs in predefined increments, it may be aborted via a keystroke or some other unrelated event. Once the entire browsing area has been stabilized, the value from this method will be a logical true (.T.). As long as more data within the browsing area needs to be stabilized, the value of the method will be a logical false (.F.). Once the browse area is stable, all data will be displayed, the original data source (the database record pointer) is repositioned to the proper location, and the current cell is highlighted on the screen. The method will also assign a logical true (.T.) value to the *:stable* instance variable.

The value of the *:stable* instance variable will switch to a logical false (.F.) when navigational methods are sent to the browsing object. Once the navigational operations are performed and the data redisplayed, the highlighted cell is reactivated and the *:stable* instance variable once again becomes a logical true (.T.). The stabilization process is reactivated via the stabilize( ) method. Once the browse object has stabilized, programming a Browse object concerns keystroke manipulation and the actions to be taken from those keystrokes.

The TBrowse object in turn consists of one or more columns, which are instances of the TBColumn class. Typically, when building a browsing area to work with, once all of the parameters for that area have been defined in instance variables and prior to stabilizing the browsing area, column objects need to be defined and then assigned to a particular browsing object. The assignment portion of this problem is simple. Each browsing object has a dynamic method called ADDCOLUMN( ). Every time a new column object is defined, the object is stored to a particular browsing object in the following fashion:

```
oBrowse:AddColumn( oColumnObject )
```

Think of this as adding an array pointer to another array subscript. In other words, if the array of a browsing structure has 10 elements and the tenth element holds pointers to other columns, we could see the following:

```
aColumnArray := {1, 2, 3}
aBrowseArray[10] := aColumnArray
```

We have yet to tackle the process of creating an instance from the column class. To generate an object of the TBColumn class, there is a function in Clipper 5.2 called TBCO-LUMNNEW( ). The calling convention for this is as follows:

```
<oColumn> := tbcolumnnew( <cHeading>, <bBlock> )
```

<cHeading>    Header expression to be displayed in the column
<bBlock>      Code block to be evaluated for every record in the active database

Each column is a unique object with its own unique structure that consists of unique instance variables particular to the individual column. These instance variables are as follows:

BLOCK         Contains the code block used to retrieve data in a column. The return value of the code block must be an appropriate data type for the column. This instance variable is assignable.

CARGO         A user-defined instance variable that may contain any valid data type associated with a particular column. This instance variable is assignable.

COLORBLOCK    Contains a code block that will be used to determine the color of the items in the column as they are evaluated and displayed. This code block must return an array containing two values. These values are used as pointers/indexes to the general color scheme used in the browsing area associated with this column. This instance variable is assignable.

COLSEP        Contains a character string that is used to draw the vertical separator to the left of the column. If not assigned, the default value will be the value assigned in the corresponding browsing area. This instance variable is assignable.

DEFCOLOR      Contains an array of two values used as pointers/indexes into the color table assigned in the corresponding browsing area. The first value is the unselected color for areas such as headings and footings. The second value is for the selected color, which is for the currently displayed browsing cell. This instance variable is assignable.

FOOTING       Contains the footer string used for a particular column. This instance variable is assignable.

FOOTSEP       Contains the character string used to draw the horizontal lines between the data area and the footer display area. This instance variable is assignable.

| | |
|---|---|
| HEADING | Contains the header string used for a particular column. This instance variable is assignable. |
| HEADSEP | Contains the character string used to draw the horizontal lines between the data area and the header display area. This instance variable is assignable. |
| WIDTH | Contains a numeric value that specifies the width for a particular column. If no value is assigned, the width of the column will be the longest of the width of a particular data element displayed in that column, the width of the header string, or the width of the footer string. This instance variable is assignable. |

The relationship of the TBColumn object to the TBrowse object is similar to the relationship of a single GET to the GET system as a whole. As each new GET is defined, a pointer to that particular GET object is dynamically stored to the *GetList[ ]* array. Similarly, each time a new column object is created, it is dynamically stored to the appropriate browsing object.

## INITIAL STEPS

The steps for setting up a complete browsing window are extensive and tedious, and their order is critical if the desired effect is to be achieved. An area of the screen must be defined as the browsing area. To do this, a call to either TBROWSEDB( ) or TBROWSENEW( ) must be made. This sets up an object for that screen region specified in the parameter list passed to either function.

```
oBrowse := tbrowsedb( 10,10,20,40 )
```

The browsing area is set to window coordinates of 10,10 to 20,40. The object is assigned to the variable *oBrowse*. This means that, in referring to the window region and, in particular, to that browsing object, a reference to *oBrowse* must be made. Once a screen region is defined, one of two things may be established next: the columns to be associated with this particular browsing object or the assignment of specific instance variables for the browsing object, such as the color index and heading separators. To assign values to the instance variables for this particular object, applicable assignments like the following need to be made:

```
oBrowse:headsep    := "==="
oBrowse:freeze     := 1
oBrowse:colorspec  := "W/N, N/R"
```

After the instance variables for a browsing area are defined, the columns to be displayed in that browsing area must be generated and assigned. To generate a column object, a call to TBCOLUMNNEW( ) must be made. The syntax is

```
oColumn := tbcolumnnew( "Header string", {|| Code_block_to_Eval()})
```

Once an individual column has been defined, instance variables within it may be assigned as well. For example, if a footer needs to be defined, it would adhere to the following syntax:

```
oColumn:footing := "This is a;footer"
```

Semicolons in either the header string or the footer string tell the column object, and the associated browsing object as well, that multiple lines are requested for this object's header or footer. Multiple lines for either the header or the footer mean that the number of display rows in the browsing area will be reduced. The following two functions help determine the amount of space used for a footer and for a header in a TBrowse object:

```
/*        Name:    HeaderWidth.prg
        Author:    Steve Straley
        Notice:    Copyright(c) - 1991 by
                   Sirius Software Development, Inc.
                   All Rights Reserved
                   415-399-9810
          Date:    July 1, 1991
       Compile:    Clipper HeaderWidth /m /p /v /w /a /n
       Version:    Clipper 5.01
  Include Path:    \PTools\Include
   Environment:    f051;
          Link:    N/A
  Library Path:    \Clipper\501
          Note:    This returns the width of the header in an TBROWSE()
                   browsing object.

*/

#include "PTVERBS.CH"
#include "PTVALUE.CH"
#include "PTFUNCS.CH"
#include "PTCOLOR.CH"
#include "PTINKEY.CH"

*********************

function HeaderWidth( oObject )

   // get each column, look at each header, determine width

   local oColumn
   local nWidth   := 1
   local nCounter := 1
   local nValue

   for nCounter := 1 TO oObject:colCount  // number of columns!

      oColumn := oObject:getcolumn( nCounter )

      if (nValue := OCCURRENCE( ";", oColumn:heading ) + 1) > nWidth
         nWidth := nValue
      endif

   next

   return( nWidth )
```

```
*******************

function FooterWidth( oObject )

   // get each column, look at each header, determine width

   local oColumn
   local nWidth    := 1
   local nCounter  := 1
   local nValue

   for nCounter := 1 TO oObject:colCount // number of columns!

     oColumn := oObject:getcolumn( nCounter )

     if (nValue := OCCURRENCE( ";", oColumn:footing ) + 1) > nWidth
       nWidth := nValue
     endif

   next

   return( nWidth )

* End of File
```

Once all of the internal settings for a column object have been assigned, the column object needs to be added to a browsing object. This is accomplished with a method sent to the browsing object known as AddColumn( ). Here is an example:

```
oBrowse:AddColumn( oColumn )
```

Once the internal settings for the browsing area have been defined and the individual columns have been defined and assigned to a browsing area/object, the final two steps for creating a functional browsing window are critical: stabilization and keystroke manipulation.

Stabilization is the action that evaluates all of the column objects within the browsing window area and displays their values. Once a browsing object is stable, the evaluation of keystrokes becomes the primary focus. The process of stabilizing a browsing area and processing keystrokes is repeated until the browsing operation is no longer needed. Most of the time will be spent on working out keystroke patterns, operations, and effects within the stabilization loop.

## BASICS

Putting all seven steps together (initialize the browse area, assign browse instance variables, create column objects, assign column instance variables, add columns to browse object, stabilize browse area, and process keys) allows us to create objects whose performance is comparable to functions like DBEDIT( ) and list-box functions. And if TBROWSENEW( ) were used in place of TBROWSEDB( ), the object would function similarly to MEMOEDIT( ) and ACHOICE( ).

To get a complete feel for creating and operating a browsing/columnobject, consider this example.

```
 1 : * File      Ob1.prg
 2 : * Compile   Rmake sample /dFILE:ob1
 3 :
 4 : #include "PTInkey.ch"
 5 : #include "PTColor.ch"
 6 : #include "PTValue.ch"
 7 : #include "PTVerbs.ch"
 8 : #include "PTFuncs.ch"
 9 :
10 : procedure Main()
11 :
12 :    local oBrowse      // Variable holding TBROWSE object
13 :    local oColumn      // Temporary holding var for TBCOLUMN object
14 :
15 :    cls
16 :    use Filenos new
17 :    delete             // Marks the first record for deletion
18 :
19 :    oBrowse := tbrowsedb(5,5,10,40)  // Create a browse area
20 :
21 :    // set up specific instance variables
22 :
23 :    oBrowse:headSep   := replicate( chr(205), 3 )
24 :    oBrowse:colSep    := " " + chr(186) + " "
25 :    oBrowse:colorspec := MAKECOLOR(pWHITE/pBLACK,pBLACK/pWHITE)
26 :
27 :    // And now build the different column objects
28 :    oColumn := tbcolumnnew( " Deleted? ", {|| if( deleted(), " * ", "   ")} )
29 :    oColumn:width := 10
30 :
31 :    oBrowse:addColumn(oColumn)
32 :
33 :    // Now for another column
34 :    oColumn := tbcolumnnew( field(2), fieldblock(field(2)) )
35 :    oColumn:footing := "This is a Field" // alter column instance variable
36 :    oBrowse:addColumn( oColumn )
37 :
38 :    DoIt1( oBrowse )
39 :    Reset( oBrowse ) // This resets the object for the second call. When
40 :                     // restabilization and reconfiguration occurs, the
41 :                     // cursor is shifted.  Normally with the following WAIT
42 :                     // command, it will appear in the top-left corner of the
43 :                     // screen. Calls to certain methods, the cursor is shifted
44 :
45 :    wait "Press any key for next example!"
46 :    cls
47 :    DoIt2( oBrowse )
48 :    cls
49 :    Filenos->( dbgotop(), dbrecall() )
50 :
51 : *********************
52 :
53 : static procedure DoIt1( oTbrowse )
54 :
55 :    local nKey    // ASCII value of key pressed
56 :
57 :    PROCESS
```

```
58 :      while( !oTbrowse:stabilize() ) // incremental stabilization which may be
59 :         if !empty( nKey := inkey() ) // terminated if a key is pressed during
60 :            exit                                   // the process!
61 :         endif
62 :      enddo
63 :
64 :      if oTbrowse:stable              // Once stable, get a key
65 :         nKey := inkey(0)
66 :      endif
67 :
68 :      if nKey == pESC                 // Process keystrokes
69 :         exit
70 :      endif
71 :   END PROCESS
72 :   cls
73 :
74 : *******************
75 :
76 : static procedure DoIt2( oTbrowse )
77 :
78 :   local nKey      // ASCII value of key pressed
79 :
80 :   PROCESS
81 :      oTbrowse:forceStable()   // Not INCREMENTAL stabilization
82 :
83 :      if oTbrowse:stable              // Once stable, get a key
84 :         nKey := inkey(0)
85 :      else
86 :         exit
87 :      endif
88 :
89 :      do case
90 :      case nKey == pESC          // Process keystrokes
91 :         exit
92 :
93 :      case nKey == pRIGHT_ARROW
94 :         oTbrowse:right()
95 :
96 :      case nKey == pLEFT_ARROW
97 :         oTbrowse:left()
98 :
99 :      endcase
100 :
101 :   END PROCESS
102 :   cls
103 :
104 : ******************
105 :
106 : static procedure Reset( oTbrowse )
107 :
108 :      oTbrowse:configure()
109 :      oTbrowse:stable := pFALSE
110 :      oTbrowse:refreshall()
111 :
112 : // End of File: Ob1.prg
```

While going over this coding example, try to identify the seven steps in building and using the browsing object. The first step is to create a browsing object referring to an area of the screen. Since this is to work in conjunction with a database named Clients, the

TBROWSEDB( ) function is called on line 19. The variable *oBrowse* contains the individual object of this instance of the TBROWSE object class. On lines 23 through 25, three instance variables of the browse object are defined: the heading-separator character, the column-separator character, and the global color string. The width of the heading-separator string and the width of the column-separator string should be the same, to prevent screen clutter.

Once the appropriate instance variables are assigned, the associated columns need to be generated. The first column takes shape on lines 28 and 29 with a call to the TBCO-LUMNNEW( ) function. This function takes as parameters the string for the column header and the code block to be performed each time a record is evaluated. The return value of this function is an object of the TBCOLUMN class. To understand the code block passed to this function, try to evaluate the expression mentally on a fictitious record. If the current record being evaluated is marked for deletion, the contents of the cell that is being displayed will be an asterisk surrounded by spaces. If, on the other hand, the record is not marked for deletion, only spaces will be displayed in the cell region.

Once the column object is generated, it is dynamically assigned to a particular TBROWSE object. Line 31 passes the variable *oColumn* that contains the TBCOLUMN object to the AddColumn( ) method for the browse object.

A second column is defined and is again temporarily assigned to a variable named *oColumn*. This does not destroy the previous column, since that column is now a part of the browse object. This is similar in concept to the following:

```
aMainArray      := array(2)
aSubArray       := {2, 3, 1}
aMainArray[1]   := aSubArray
aSubArray       := {3, 2, 1}
aMainArray[2]   := aSubArray
```

Next, one of the instance variables for the TBCOLUMN class is assigned. On line 35, the string "This is a Field" is assigned to the *:footing* instance variable. Following this, the second column is added to the same browsing object. With these steps out of the way, the only thing remaining is to stabilize the browsing object and process the keystrokes. This occurs in both the DoIt1( ) and DoIt2( ) procedures. When the DoIt1 procedure is called, only the name of the object is passed. Objects act like arrays; an array structure parallels the predefined structure found in Clipper objects. Passing the name of the object to a subroutine acts like passing an array by reference to a subroutine. In this case, both the DoIt( ) and DoIt2( ) procedures will have access to all of the methods and instance variables found in the browsing object *oBrowse*.

The DoIt1( ) routine incrementally stabilizes the browsing area. Once it is completely stable, the loop on lines 58 through 62 stops processing and the value of the instance variable *:stable* becomes a logical true (.T.). A call to INKEY(0) (line 65) is then made and the value is stored to the variable *nKey*. With the value of the key pressed stored, that value may then be evaluated. In this case, the only key that is recognized and to which our browse object will respond is the pESC key (found in PTINKEY.CH). No other keystrokes are accepted. A word of caution here is in order: Without an escape route programmed in, the only way to exit this object is to abort the application or to turn off the computer!

Once finished, the DoIt1( ) routine will clear the screen and return program control to line 38. This will then pass the browse object to the Reset( ) subroutine, which calls two methods for this instance of the TBROWSE object and assigns one instance variable. This resets the browsing object for the call to DoIt2( ) on line 47.

Within DoIt2( ), the stabilization process is a bit different. Here, on line 81, the function calls the *:forceStable( )* method, which is the same thing as the incremental stabilization loop in DoIt1( ), except that there is no trapping for a key being pressed. This means that if Clipper cannot stabilize the data in the browsing area, there is no way to stop it short of stopping program execution. Be sure when using this method that the data is intact and can be fully displayed in the browsing region. Once this forced operation takes place, then a keystroke is accepted. In this example, two additional keys are allowed to control the object passed to the procedure: pLEFT_ARROW and pRIGHT_ARROW. When either of these keys are pressed on line 84, they send a message to the Right( ) method or the Left( ) method. This will move the browsing cursor in the appropriate direction. Again, the ESC key will exit this processing loop, clear the screen, and terminate.

The crux of working with objects is programming structures and working with keystrokes that will evaluate either the instance variables or the methods of a particular object. Once all of the parameters for the browsing area and the columns have been defined, all that is left is working with the keystrokes and activating the methods and/or assigning/evaluating the instance variables. This next example builds on the keystroke handling of our previous example to show how a complete browsing area may be controlled.

```
 1 : * File      Ob2.prg
 2 : * Compile   Rmake sample /dFILE:Ob2
 3 :
 4 : #include "PTInkey.ch"   // Power Tools header file with ASCII values
 5 : #include "PTColor.ch"   // Power Tools header file with color settings
 6 : #include "PTValue.ch"   // Power Tools header file with misc values
 7 : #include "PTVerbs.ch"   // Power Tools header file with commands/statements
 8 : #include "PTFuncs.ch"   // Power Tools header file with pseudofunctions
 9 :
10 : procedure Main()
11 :
12 :    local oBrowse
13 :    local oColumn
14 :    local nKey
15 :
16 :    cls
17 :    use Filenos new
18 :    setcursor(pCURSOR_OFF)
19 :    dispbox( 5, 10, 20, 70, pDBAR)
20 :    oBrowse := tbrowsedb( 6, 11, 19, 69 )
21 :
22 :    oBrowse:headSep := replicate( chr(205), 3 )
23 :    oBrowse:colSep  := " " + chr(186) + " "
24 :    oColumn := tbcolumnneW( "Del?", {|| if( deleted(), " * ", "   ")})
25 :    oColumn:width := 5
26 :    oBrowse:addColumn(oColumn)
27 :
28 :    oBrowse:addColumn(tbcolumnnew( "Record;Number", {|| recno()} ))
29 :    oBrowse:addColumn(tbcolumnnew( field(3), fieldblock(field(3))))
30 :
31 :    PROCESS
32 :      oBrowse:forceStable()
33 :      if oBrowse:stable
34 :         devpos(maxrow(), 00 )
35 :         do case
```

```
36 :          case oBrowse:hitbottom
37 :             devout( "End of File" )
38 :
39 :          case oBrowse:hittop
40 :             devout( "Top of File" )
41 :
42 :          otherwise
43 :             devout( "              " )
44 :
45 :          endcase
46 :
47 :          nKey := inkey(0)   // Wait for a key!
48 :       else
49 :          exit               // leave the processing loop
50 :       endif
51 :
52 :       do case
53 :       case ( nKey == pDOWN_ARROW )
54 :          oBrowse:down()
55 :
56 :       case ( nKey == pUP_ARROW )
57 :          oBrowse:up()
58 :
59 :       case ( nKey == pRIGHT_ARROW )
60 :          oBrowse:right()
61 :
62 :       case ( nKey == pLEFT_ARROW )
63 :          oBrowse:left()
64 :
65 :       case ( nKey == pESC )
66 :          exit
67 :
68 :       case ( nKey == pDEL )
69 :          if( deleted(), dbrecall(), dbdelete() )
70 :          oBrowse:refreshCurrent()
71 :          oBrowse:down()
72 :
73 :       endcase
74 :
75 :    END PROCESS
76 :
77 :    setcursor(pCURSOR_ON)
78 :    cls
79 :
80 : // End of File: Ob2.prg
```

This example continues our emphasis on programming the keystrokes and working with the methods of an object. Three columns are defined in this browsing area. One column is first stored to a temporary variable and then assigned to the browsing object. Other columns are generated by immediately storing the TBCOLUMNNEW( ) function's value to the browse object using the AddColumn( ) method. This is done in lines 28 and 29.

After all columns are generated, the final two steps are stabilization and keystroke processing. They are handled within the loop that begins on line 31 and concludes on line 75. The bulk of this routine is dedicated to handling the keystrokes in the massive DO CASE statement beginning on line 52. In addition, if the browse object is stable, two instance variables for the browsing object, *hitBottom* and *hitTop*, are evaluated. If the value of either is a logical true (.T.), the appropriate message will be displayed at the bottom left corner of the screen using the DEVOUT( ) function (line 37 or 40). If the value of neither is true, blank spaces will be displayed at those coordinates (line 43). Once the status of the database has been displayed, the INKEY(0) function is called to read the keyboard.

The keystroke handling routine within this program has been enhanced to support the left and right arrow keys, which will pan the cursor horizontally through the browsing area. One additional key—DEL—is handled by the code beginning on line 68. If the DEL key is pressed, the status of the current record is evaluated. If it is not marked for deletion, it will be deleted; if it is marked for deletion, it will be recalled. Instead of using the DELETE and RECALL commands, the functional equivalents are used in a single function call, the immediate IF( ) on line 69. In either case, the status of the record will change. The deletion status is shown in one of the columns displayed in the browsing area. Therefore, since the status of the current record is altered, whether it is marked for deletion or not, that particular row needs to be redisplayed. To do this, a message is sent to the refreshCurrent( ) method for the browse object in line 70. In addition, the down( ) method on line 71 forces the cursor to jump down to the next cell in the current column. This has the same effect as the following command line:

```
keyboard chr( pDOWN_ARROW )
```

Finally, when all operations have been concluded and the ESC key is pressed, the cursor is turned back on and the screen is cleared.

To further expand on keystroke processing with objects, several factors are worth considering. For example, if a key has been set via a SETKEY( ) function or a SET KEY command, the keystroke section of the program should allow for this. In addition, if WRAP is SET ON or OFF, keystroke processing should work around this value. This example shows some of the possibilities of these programming scenarios.

```
 1 : * File      Ob3.prg
 2 : * Compile   Rmake sample /dFILE:Ob3
 3 :
 4 : #include "PTInkey.ch"   // Power Tools header file with ASCII values
 5 : #include "PTColor.ch"   // Power Tools header file with color settings
 6 : #include "PTValue.ch"   // Power Tools header file with misc values
 7 : #include "PTVerbs.ch"   // Power Tools header file with commands/statements
 8 : #include "PTFuncs.ch"   // Power Tools header file with pseudofunctions
 9 :
10 : #define pDELCHAR    " " + CHR(205)+CHR(16)+" "
11 : #define pUNDELCHAR  SPACE(4)
12 :
13 : #xtranslate BLOCKIFY( <x> ) => <{x}>
14 :
15 : procedure Main()
16 :
17 :    local getlist := {}   // GETLIST array
18 :    local oBrowse         // Browsing object
19 :    local oColumn         // Column object
20 :    local nKey            // ASCII value of key pressed
21 :    local nLock           // Temp var for the GET
22 :
23 :    setkey( pF1, BLOCKIFY( HelpDisp() ) )
24 :    cls
25 :    use Clients new
26 :
```

```
27 :        setcursor( pCURSOR_OFF )
28 :        dispbox( 5, 5, 20, 75, pDBAR )
29 :
30 :        oBrowse := tbrowsedb( 6, 6, 19, 74 )
31 :
32 :        oBrowse:headSep := chr(205) + chr(203) + chr(205)
33 :        oBrowse:colSep  := chr(32) + chr(186) + chr(32)
34 :
35 :        oColumn := tbcolumnnew(" Deleted? ", {|| if( deleted(), pDELCHAR, ;
36 :                                                                pUNDELCHAR)})
37 :
38 :        oBrowse:addColumn(oColumn)
39 :
40 :        oBrowse:addColumn( tbcolumnnew( "Record;Number", {|| recno()} ) )
41 :
42 :        aeval( dbstruct(), ;
43 :           {|aField| (oColumn := tbcolumnnew( aField[1], fieldblock(aField[1])), ;
44 :                      oBrowse:AddColumn(oColumn) )} )
45 :
46 :        oBrowse:freeze := 2
47 :        oBrowse:colPos := oBrowse:freeze+1   // start the cursor off the
48 :                                             // freeze frame
49 :        PROCESS
50 :          @ maxrow(), 50 SAY "Menu Wrap is " SAY if( !set(pWRAP), "On ", "Off")
51 :          while !oBrowse:stabilize()
52 :             if !empty( nKey := inkey() )
53 :                exit
54 :             endif
55 :          enddo
56 :
57 :          if oBrowse:stable
58 :             setpos(maxrow(), 00 )
59 :             do case
60 :             case oBrowse:hitbottom
61 :                if set(pWRAP)         // SET WRAP ON!
62 :                   oBrowse:goTop()
63 :                   oBrowse:refreshAll()
64 :                   loop
65 :                else
66 :                   dispout( "End of File" )
67 :                endif
68 :
69 :             case oBrowse:hittop
70 :                if set(pWRAP)         // SET WRAP ON!
71 :                   oBrowse:goBottom()
72 :                   oBrowse:refreshAll()
73 :                   loop
74 :                else
75 :                   dispout( "Top of File" )
76 :                endif
77 :
78 :             otherwise
79 :                dispout( "             " )
80 :
81 :             endcase
82 :
83 :             nKey := inkey(0)
84 :
85 :          endif
86 :
```

```
 87 :     do case
 88 :     case setkey( nKey ) != NIL
 89 :       eval( setkey( nKey ) )
 90 :
 91 :     case ( nKey == pDOWN_ARROW )
 92 :       oBrowse:down()
 93 :
 94 :     case ( nKey == pUP_ARROW )
 95 :       oBrowse:up()
 96 :
 97 :     case ( nKey == pRIGHT_ARROW )
 98 :       if oBrowse:colPos == oBrowse:colCount
 99 :         oBrowse:panhome()
100 :       else
101 :         oBrowse:right()
102 :       endif
103 :
104 :     case ( nKey == pLEFT_ARROW )
105 :       oBrowse:left()
106 :
107 :     case ( nKey == pESC )
108 :       exit
109 :
110 :     case ( nKey == pDEL )
111 :       if( deleted(), dbrecall() , dbdelete() )
112 :       oBrowse:refreshcurrent()
113 :       oBrowse:down()
114 :
115 :     case ( nKey == pENTER )
116 :       setcursor(pCURSOR_ON)
117 :       nLock := oBrowse:freeze
118 :       @ maxrow(), 00 say "Enter field to lock on: " ;
119 :                  get nLock valid nLock >= 1 .and. nLock <= fcount()
120 :       read
121 :       setcursor(pCURSOR_OFF)
122 :       if lastkey() != pESC
123 :         oBrowse:freeze := nLock
124 :         oBrowse:configure()
125 :         oBrowse:refreshall()
126 :       endif
127 :       @ maxrow(), 00 say space(maxcol())
128 :
129 :     endcase
130 :
131 :     if oBrowse:colpos < (oBrowse:freeze + 1)  // This prevents the
132 :       oBrowse:colPos := oBrowse:freeze + 1    // cursor from going
133 :     endif                                     // into the cell
134 :                                               // marked frozen!
135 :     set( pWRAP, !set(pWRAP) )   // Toggle wrap around
136 :
137 :   enddo
138 :   cls
139 :
140 : *******************
141 :
142 : static function HelpDisp()
143 :
144 :   local cScreen := savescreen(2,20,20,60)
145 :
146 :   dispbox(2,20,20,60, pDBAR)
```

```
147 :      @  2,25 say " Help Screen! "
148 :      @  5,25 say "F1 - This screen"
149 :      @  6,25 SAY chr(24) SAY "- Up One Cell"
150 :      @  7,25 SAY chr(25) SAY "- Down One Cell"
151 :      @  8,25 SAY chr(26) SAY "- Right One Cell (Wrap)"
152 :      @  9,25 SAY chr(27) SAY "- Left One Cell (Wrap)"
153 :      @ 11,25 say "DEL - Will either mark record"
154 :      @ 12,25 say "      for deletion or not based"
155 :      @ 13,25 say "      on record status"
156 :      @ 15,25 say "ENTER - Alter the number of cells"
157 :      @ 16,25 say "        frozen in the display."
158 :      @ 18,25 say "Press any key to continue..."
159 :      inkey(0)
160 :      restscreen( 2, 20, 20, 60, cScreen )
161 :
162 :      VOID
163 :
164 : // End of File: Ob3.prg
```

The SETKEY( ) function is called to set up the F1 key. If it is pressed during a wait state, the HelpDisp( ) routine will be called; however, there is no wait state throughout the programming of the TBROWSE object. Instead, if the browse area is stable and a key is pressed, the value of the *nKey* variable will be evaluated in the DO CASE command beginning on line 87. The keystroke is first evaluated to see if it is a part of the SET KEY internal stack. If it is, the return value of the SETKEY( ) function on line 88 will be a code block (the translation of Blockify( HelpDisp( ) ) ) and therefore will not be NIL. This causes the SETKEY( ) code block to be simply evaluated on line 89 with the EVAL( ) function, which calls the HelpDisp( ) routine.

Column and footer areas may take up more than one line so long as the header string or the footer string contains a semicolon, as seen on line 40. As a result, two rows are used by all column headers. On line 42, the entire structure of the Clients database is evaluated with a nested expression (lines 43 and 44) embedded within a code block called from AEVAL( ). The value of the LOCAL parameter *aField* is a pointer to the array of the structure of the Clients database. The number of times this code block will be called is based on the number of fields in the database.

Finally, the status of the SET( pWRAP ) function is used either to toggle a wraparound condition (wrap either from top to bottom or from bottom to top) or to simply state that the top or bottom of the file has been reached. The browse object can be sensitive to the environment of an application without special setup or preprogramming.

## INTERMEDIATE EXAMPLES

Programming keystroke handling to deal with all of the methods of a TBROWSE object, or to work with the instance variables of a particular TBCOLUMN or TBROWSE object, is perhaps the most intensive task one must undertake. While DBEDIT( ) can be useful, total control of that function is not possible. Having control of all of the operations within a TBROWSE object is possible. The question remains whether the programmer will take the challenge and program with the objects in toto or will avoid the issue entirely and rely on more elementary concepts and versions. The point here is (1) a shift in thinking must take effect; (2) Xbase standards do not apply to objects; and (3) open architecture and the object give more control to the program.

It is this last fact that gets more programmers in trouble: We come to a point where, based on our heritage in interpreters, we want things to be handled for us. Like low-level file functions, if we take on the challenge confronting us in this new technology, we must take them on deliberately and decisively. There is no middle ground, no compromise. It is that harsh. However, if we explore different possibilities and try to broaden our thinking to accept this new technology, our programming assignments will be a challenge to get more out of the computer, more out of the end user, and more out of the compiler.

The following program continues to expand our use of the instance variables for column and browse objects and of the methods for browse objects. In particular, programming the browse object in this example involves panning motions, multiple windows, adjusting the border area of the window, and shifting the order of the columns within the browsing area.

```
 1 : * File       Ob4.prg
 2 : * Compile   Rmake sample /dFILE:Ob4
 3 :
 4 : #include "PTInkey.ch"   // Power Tools header file with ASCII values
 5 : #include "PTColor.ch"   // Power Tools header file with color settings
 6 : #include "PTValue.ch"   // Power Tools header file with misc values
 7 : #include "PTVerbs.ch"   // Power Tools header file with commands/statements
 8 : #include "PTFuncs.ch"   // Power Tools header file with pseudofunctions
 9 :
10 : #define pDELCHAR    " " + CHR(205)+CHR(16)+" "
11 : #define pUNDELCHAR SPACE(4)
12 :
13 : #xtranslate PROMPT( <row>, <col>, <exp>, <mess> ) => ;
14 :             __AtPrompt( <row>, <col>, <exp> ,<mess> )
15 :
16 : #xtranslate MENUTO( <var> ) => ;
17 :             <var> := __MenuTo( {|| <var>}, #<var> )
18 :
19 : procedure Main()
20 :
21 :    local oBrowse    // Holds the TBROWSE object
22 :    local oColumn    // Holds the temp var of the TBCOLUMN object
23 :    local nKey       // ASCII value of the key pressed
24 :    local nLock
25 :    local nCount
26 :    local aSwitch
27 :    local getlist := {}
28 :    local oObject1
29 :    local oObject2
30 :
31 :    cls
32 :    use FileNos new
33 :    setcursor( pCURSOR_OFF )
34 :    dispbox( 5, 5, 20, 75, pDBAR )
35 :
36 :    oBrowse := TBROWSEDB( 6, 6, 19, 74 )
37 :
38 :    oBrowse:headSep := chr(205) + chr(203) + chr(205)
39 :    oBrowse:colSep  := chr(32) + chr(186) + chr(32)
40 :
41 :    oColumn := tbcolumnnew( " Deleted? ", ;
42 :             {|| if( deleted(), pDELCHAR, pUNDELCHAR)})
```

```
 43 :    oColumn:footsep := chr(205) + chr(202) + chr(205)
 44 :    oBrowse:addColumn(oColumn)
 45 :
 46 :    oColumn := tbcolumnnew( "Rec;No.", {|| str(recno(),3)} )
 47 :    oColumn:footsep := chr(205) + chr(202) + chr(205)
 48 :    oColumn:width := 4
 49 :    oBrowse:addColumn( oColumn )
 50 :
 51 :    aeval( dbstruct(), {|aField| oBrowse:AddColumn( AddItem(aField) )} )
 52 :
 53 :    oBrowse:freeze := 2
 54 :    oBrowse:colPos := oBrowse:freeze+1    // start the cursor off the
 55 :                                          // freeze frame
 56 :    PROCESS
 57 :
 58 :       @ maxrow(), 50 SAY "Menu Wrap is " SAY if( !set(pWRAP), "On ", "Off")
 59 :
 60 :       oBrowse:forceStable()
 61 :
 62 :       setpos(maxrow(), 00 )
 63 :
 64 :       do case
 65 :       case oBrowse:hitbottom
 66 :          if set(pWRAP)   // SET WRAP ON!
 67 :             oBrowse:goTop()
 68 :             oBrowse:refreshAll()
 69 :             loop
 70 :          else
 71 :             devout( "End of File" )
 72 :          endif
 73 :
 74 :       case oBrowse:hittop
 75 :          if set(pWRAP)   // SET WRAP ON!
 76 :             oBrowse:goBottom()
 77 :             oBrowse:refreshAll()
 78 :             loop
 79 :          else
 80 :             devout( "Top of File" )
 81 :          endif
 82 :
 83 :       otherwise
 84 :          devout( "            " )
 85 :
 86 :       endcase
 87 :
 88 :       nKey := inkey(0)
 89 :
 90 :       do case
 91 :       case ( nKey == pF1 )
 92 :          DispHelp()
 93 :
 94 :       case ( nKey == pDOWN_ARROW )
 95 :          oBrowse:down()
 96 :
 97 :       case ( nKey == pUP_ARROW )
 98 :          oBrowse:up()
 99 :
100 :       case ( nKey == pRIGHT_ARROW )   // Wrap right to left!
101 :          if oBrowse:colPos == oBrowse:colCount
102 :             oBrowse:panhome()
```

```
103 :        else
104 :           oBrowse:right()
105 :        endif
106 :
107 :     case ( nKey == pLEFT_ARROW )   // Wrap left to right!
108 :        if oBrowse:colPos == oBrowse:freeze+1
109 :           oBrowse:panend()
110 :        else
111 :           oBrowse:left()
112 :        endif
113 :
114 :     case ( nKey == pPGUP )
115 :        oBrowse:pageup()
116 :
117 :     case ( nKey == pPGDN )
118 :        oBrowse:pagedown()
119 :
120 :     case ( nKey == pHOME )
121 :        oBrowse:gotop()
122 :        oBrowse:panhome()
123 :
124 :     case ( nKey == pEND )
125 :        oBrowse:gobottom()
126 :        oBrowse:panhome()
127 :
128 :     case ( nKey == pESC )
129 :        exit
130 :
131 :     case ( nKey == pTAB )
132 :        if Movebox(oBrowse)
133 :           cls
134 :           dispbox(oBrowse:ntop-1, oBrowse:nleft-1, oBrowse:nbottom+1,;
135 :                   oBrowse:nright+1, pDBAR )
136 :
137 :           oBrowse:configure()
138 :           oBrowse:gotop()
139 :           oBrowse:refreshall()
140 :
141 :        endif
142 :
143 :     case ( nKey == pSHIFT_TAB )
144 :        if len(aSwitch := ShiftAround( oBrowse ) ) == 2
145 :
146 :           oObject2 := oBrowse:getColumn(aSwitch[2])
147 :           oObject1 := oBrowse:getColumn(aSwitch[1])
148 :
149 :           oBrowse:setColumn(aSwitch[1], oObject2)
150 :           oBrowse:setColumn(aSwitch[2], oObject1)
151 :
152 :           oBrowse:freeze := 0
153 :           oBrowse:configure()
154 :           oBrowse:gotop()
155 :           oBrowse:refreshall()
156 :           oBrowse:freeze := 1
157 :        endif
158 :
159 :     case ( nKey == pDEL )
160 :        if( deleted(), dbrecall() , dbdelete() )
161 :        oBrowse:refreshcurrent()
162 :        oBrowse:down()
```

```
163 :
164 :       case ( nKey == pENTER )
165 :         setcursor(pCURSOR_ON)
166 :         nLock := oBrowse:freeze
167 :
168 :         @ maxrow(), 00 say "Enter field to lock on: " ;
169 :                   get nLock valid nLock >= 1 .and. nLock <= fcount()
170 :         read
171 :         if lastkey() != pESC
172 :           oBrowse:freeze := nLock
173 :           oBrowse:configure()
174 :           oBrowse:refreshall()
175 :         endif
176 :         @ maxrow(), 00 say space(maxcol())
177 :         setcursor( pCURSOR_OFF )
178 :
179 :     endcase
180 :
181 :     if oBrowse:colpos < (oBrowse:freeze + 1) // This prevents cursor
182 :         oBrowse:colPos := oBrowse:freeze + 1  // from going into
183 :
184 :     endif                                      // marked frozen!
185 :
186 :     set( pWRAP, !set(pWRAP) )
187 :
188 :   END PROCESS
189 :   cls
190 :
191 : *********************
192 :
193 : static function ShiftAround( oBrowse ) // BROWSE object
194 :
195 :   local aHeaders := {}     // THINGS & RETVAL are 2 arrays
196 :   local aRetval  := {}
197 :   local cScreen  := savescreen()
198 :   local nRow
199 :   local nCol
200 :   local nChoice1
201 :   local nChoice2
202 :   local nCount
203 :
204 :   // Gather up the headers for them to be selected!
205 :   for nCount := 1 to oBrowse:colCount
206 :     aadd(aHeaders, padr(ltrim(;
207 :         strtran((oBrowse:getColumn(nCount)):heading, ";"," ")),15))
208 :   next
209 :
210 :   PROCESS
211 :
212 :     nCol := 10
213 :     nRow := 3
214 :     nChoice1 := nChoice2 := 1
215 :
216 :     dispbox(0,0,maxrow()-1, 39, pDBAR)
217 :     dispbox(0,40,maxrow()-1,maxcol(), pDBAR)
218 :     @ 0, 2 say " Switch This Column "
219 :     @ 0,42 say " With This Column "
220 :
221 :     aeval( aHeaders, {|cHeader| PROMPT( nRow++, nCol, cHeader, "" )} )
222 :     MENUTO( nChoice1 )
223 :
```

```
224 :        if !empty( nChoice1 )
225 :           nRow := 3
226 :           nCol += 40
227 :
228 :           aeval( aHeaders, {|cHeader| PROMPT( nRow++, nCol, cHeader, "" )})
229 :           MENUTO( nChoice2 )
230 :
231 :           if !empty( nChoice2 )
232 :              aRetval := {nChoice1, nChoice2}
233 :           endif
234 :
235 :        endif
236 :
237 :        if lastkey() != pESC
238 :          @ maxrow(), 0 say "Is this o.k.?"
239 :          if chr( inkey(0) ) $ "Yy"
240 :             @ maxrow(), 0 say space(20)
241 :             exit
242 :          endif
243 :          @ maxrow(), 0 say space(20)
244 :        else
245 :          exit
246 :        endif
247 :
248 :    END PROCESS
249 :
250 :    restscreen(,,,,cScreen)
251 :
252 :    return( aRetval )
253 :
254 : ********************
255 :
256 : static function DispHelp()
257 :
258 :    local cScreen := savescreen(0,10,20,70)
259 :
260 :    dispbox(0,10,20,70, pDBAR)
261 :
262 :    @  0,15 say " Help Screen! "
263 :    @  1,15 say "F1 - This screen"
264 :    @  2,15 SAY chr(24) SAY "-  Up One Cell"
265 :    @  3,15 SAY chr(25) SAY "-  Down One Cell"
266 :    @  4,15 SAY chr(26) SAY "-  Right One Cell (Wrap)"
267 :    @  5,15 SAY chr(27) SAY "-  Left One Cell (Wrap)"
268 :    @  6,15 say "PgUp - Page Up One Screen"
269 :    @  7,15 say "PgDn - Page Down One Screen"
270 :    @  9,15 say "DEL - Will either mark record for dele-"
271 :    @ 10,15 say "       tion or not based on recordstatus"
272 :    @ 12,15 say "ENTER - Alter the number of cells frozen"
273 :    @ 13,15 say "         in the display."
274 :    @ 15,15 say "TAB - Adjust the frame of the window"
275 :    @ 17,15 say "SHIFT-TAB - Change order of the columns"
276 :    @ 19,15 say "Press any key to continue..."
277 :    inkey(0)
278 :    restscreen( 0,10,20,70, cScreen )
279 :
280 :    VOID
281 :
282 : ********************
283 :
284 : static function MoveBox( oMove )
```

```
285 :
286 :    local nTop       := oMove:nTop-1       // The top corner of the frame
287 :    local nLeft      := oMove:nLeft-1      // Top column of the frame
288 :    local nBottom    := oMove:nBottom+1    // Bottom row of the frame area
289 :    local nRight     := oMove:nRight+1     // Bottom column of the frame area
290 :    local cScreen    := savescreen()       // Saved screen before the move
291 :    local nKey                             // ASCII value of key pressed
292 :
293 :    REPEAT
294 :
295 :       restscreen(,,,, cScreen)
296 :       dispbox( nTop, nLeft, nBottom, nRight, replicate(chr(178),8) )
297 :
298 :       nKey := inkey(0)
299 :
300 :       do case
301 :       case nKey == pDOWN_ARROW
302 :          if nBottom < maxrow()-1
303 :             nBottom++
304 :          endif
305 :
306 :       case nKey == pRIGHT_ARROW
307 :          if nRight < maxcol()-1
308 :             nRight++
309 :          endif
310 :
311 :       case nKey == pUP_ARROW
312 :          if nBottom > nTop+4
313 :             nBottom--
314 :          endif
315 :
316 :       case nKey == pLEFT_ARROW
317 :          if nRight > nLeft+10
318 :             nRight--
319 :          endif
320 :
321 :       endcase
322 :
323 :    UNTIL (nKey == pESC .or. nKey == pENTER )
324 :
325 :    if lastkey() == pENTER
326 :       oMove:ntop     := nTop+1
327 :       oMove:nleft    := nLeft+1
328 :       oMove:nbottom  := nBottom-1
329 :       oMove:nright   := nRight-1
330 :    endif
331 :
332 :    return( lastkey() == pENTER )
333 :
334 : ********************
335 :
336 : static function AddItem( aItem )
337 :
338 :    static nItem
339 :    static nFieldNumber
340 :
341 :    local oColumn := tbcolumnnew( UPPERLOWER(aItem[1]), fieldblock(aItem[1]))
342 :
343 :    if nItem == NIL     // Not yet defined!
344 :       nitem := 3
345 :       nFieldNumber := 1
```

```
346 :     endif
347 :
348 :     oColumn:footsep := chr(205) + chr(202) + chr(205)
349 :     oColumn:footing := "Column:" + transform(nItem++, "999") +;
350 :                  "; Field:" + transform(nFieldNumber++,"999")
351 :
352 :  return( oColumn )
353 :
354 : // End of File: Ob4.prg
```

The first two columns of the browsing area display the deletion status of a record and the record number. Each column object has its own set of instance variables, which may be programmed. In this case, on line 43 and again on line 47, the footing-separator string for each of these columns is programmed before the column is assigned to the browse object. In the second column object created, the width of the column is specified on line 48. Normally, the default size of a column is based on the greatest value of the length of the data element, the length of the header string, or the length of the footer line. But the instance variable :width may instead be explicitly set for each column object.

It should be noted that the column is filled from left to right. Therefore, if the code block for the column object in line 46 referenced just the RECNO( ) function, the width of the column for this object would be 10, since the default width of any numeric data expression is 10. With the width of the column set to 4, the only items that could be seen in each column of the record number would be blank spaces, since the first four columns of a numeric expression of length 10 would be blank. This, of course, applies to record numbers from 1 to 999999: The next record, number 1000000, would appear as a simple 1 in the column.

The remaining columns are initialized and dynamically stored to the browse object by a call to the AEVAL( ) function on line 51 using the value returned by DBSTRUCT( ) in the current work area. The code block evaluated for each item in AEVAL( ) dynamically adds a column to the browse object. That column object is the value returned by the AddItem( ) function, which begins on line 336. The code block for AEVAL( ) has a single local parameter, *aField*, which is the array of structure for each field in the current work area as seen by the DBSTRUCT( ) function. Within the code block, this array is passed to the AddItem( ) function.

AddItem( ) sets up three variables with two different storage classes: LOCAL and STATIC. In essence, as each field structure is passed to this function, the column position and the ordinal position of the field is maintained within the function. These are the STATIC variables.

When AddItem( ) is first called, both *nItem* and *nFieldNumber* are NIL data types. If this is the case, they are assigned the values of 3 and 1, respectively (line 344 and 345). The variable *nItem* keeps track of the number of columns added to the browse object. Since the deletion status of the record is displayed as well as the record number, the first call to the AddItem( ) function is working on the third column of the browse object. In turn, the third column corresponds to the first field; therefore, *nFieldNumber* is assigned the value of 1 (line 345). The other variable, *oColumn*, a LOCAL data storage variable, contains a newly created TBCOLUMN( ) object with the value of *aItem[1]* (the name of the field) as the header of the column.

Before returning the actual object on line 352, the instance variables for this column need to be assigned. The footing separator and the footer message are stored to the column object.

In the process of transforming both the numeric values of *nItem* and *nFieldNumber*, they are appropriately post-incremented (lines 349 and 350) in order to be adjusted for the next call to the AddItem( ) function from the AEVAL( ). Once the footing characters are set and the separator string assigned, the object, like an array pointer, is returned and becomes the value of the function AddItem( ). This value is in turn passed to the *:addColumn( )* method in the browse object called in the code block in AEVAL( ).

This example continues to test outside environmental values by using the SET( ) function to evaluate the WRAP condition. However, the test of the SETKEY( ) stack is not in place. Provided no wait state occurs during the keystroke processing, the SET KEY internal stack will be ignored. As an example, the operation typically associated with the F1 key on line 91 would be totally ignored and is instead superseded by the browsing call to the DispHelp( ) routine. The choice between evaluating the SET KEY stack or not is left to the discretion of the developer.

Other keys that take on new importance in this example are cursor keys like the PAGE UP key tested on line 114 and the PAGE DOWN key tested on line 117. These keys call the browse methods *:pageup( )* and *:pagedown( )*, respectively. The HOME and END keys may also be tested and methods called when they are pressed. In essence, the complete browsing set of keystroke methods are available to be used and called.

Two more keys add new dimensions to this browsing object. The first is the TAB key, tested on line 131; the other is the SHIFT-TAB key combination, tested on line 143. First, looking to the code relating to the TAB key, a call to the Movebox( ) function is made, passing the browse object to it as a parameter. Before looking at this, it is important to remember that passing just the name of an object, like an array, passes the item by reference; any manipulation of any instance variable within the subroutine, like the manipulation of any subscript in an array, will be remembered once the routine has concluded its operation. This includes sending messages to the methods of an object; the methods will be performed. Since objects act in many ways like arrays, passing an object by reference opens up many new programming possibilities.

The Movebox( ) function begins on line 284, where the browse object is now stored to the *oMove* variable. Any reference to the browse object is now made to the LOCAL variable *oMove* instead. Four values are immediately derived from the instance variables for the *oMove* object. The instance variables *:nTop* and *:nLeft* refer to the top, left coordinates of the browsing area; these values are lessened by one to allow for the coordinates of the frame that surrounds the area and stored to LOCAL memory variables. The same is done for the instance variables *:nBottom* and *:nRight*, except that their values are increased by one to allow for the frame coordinates. Using these values, a new border is drawn on line 296 using CHR(178). This highlights the border surrounding the browsing object. Line 298 then pauses the program and awaits a keystroke. If any of the cursor keys are pressed, the value of the corresponding coordinate is either post-incremented or post-decremented, causing the framed area to display a new frame on the next pass through the REPEAT loop.

The REPEAT loop continues UNTIL either the ESC key or the ENTER key is pressed (line 323). If the ENTER key is the last key that was pressed to get out of the loop, the new coordinates adjusted by the end user in the loop are assigned to the instance variables for the *oMove* object. The return value for the Movebox( ) function becomes the evaluation of the expression (LASTKEY( ) == pENTER). If the ENTER key is the exit key, values are changed; if not, values are not changed. Therefore, the value of the Movebox( ) function indicates whether or not the values of the instance variables have changed. Since the ENTER key is the indicator, the expression LASTKEY( ) = pENTER will give the function the ability to return a proper value indicating which of the two possibilities has occurred.

If the ENTER key was pressed, the value of the Movebox( ) function on line 132 will be a logical true (.T.), which will cause lines 133 to 139 to be executed. These lines redraw the border around the browsing area, force the browse object to be reconfigured, adjust all columns accordingly to the new windowed region, reposition the data source pointer to the top of the file, and refresh all of the data displayed within the window region. These operations are performed by three methods: *:configure( )*, *:goTop( )*, and *:refreshAll( )*.

The final keystroke supported within this browsing object is the SHIFT-TAB key combination. The test for it (on line 143, within the massive DO CASE construct evaluating all keystrokes within the browse object) calls the ShiftAround( ) function which begins on line 193, passes the browse object to it, and receives a value back. Looking to line 144, it is possible to conclude that either a character string or an array will be the return value of the ShiftAround( ) function; looking to line 146 quickly drops the notion of *aSwitch* being a character string.

The ShiftAround( ) function, beginning on line 193, stores the browsing object to the LOCAL parameter *oBrowse*. On line 205, a FOR ... NEXT loop starts from 1 to the value of *:colCount*, the instance variable for the *oBrowse* object; the *colCount* instance variable indicates the total number of columns contained within the browse object. The LOCAL variable *aHeaders* will contain the individual headers for each column object within the *oBrowse* object. Think of traversing an array of arrays. Each element in the main array contains a pointer to another array; if we want to look at that array separately, we need to extract it from the total array to a temporary variable. That is the focus here: The column objects are nothing more than nested arrays within the TBrowse object. To get to the pointer to each column object, the :getColumn( ) method is called.

Once each column can be looked at separately, the values of their individual instance variables will be available. Here, on line 207, the heading instance variable is evaluated. The STRTRAN( ) function replaces any semicolon character—used to force the headers onto two lines—with a blank space. Each heading is dynamically stored to an array named *aHeaders[ ]*. Lines 210 through 248 form a large loop that draws two framed windows. Within the frame on the left, the listing of column headings is displayed and put through a Prompt( ) pseudofunction. These become the headers to be selected: They are to be switched with the position of the headers that will be displayed in the right framed area. If both a source header and a destination header are chosen, the position of the columns are stored in an array named *aRetValue*, which is created on line 232. In any other case, the return value of *aRetValue* will be an array with no elements.

Turning back to the original call to the ShiftAround( ) function on line 144, the array containing the two column positions is then stored to the variable *aSwitch*. The individual column object for the column position in *aSwitch[2]* is stored to the variable *oObject2*, and the individual column object for the column position found in *aSwitch[1]* is stored to the variable *oObject1*. The *:getColumn( )* method is used to extract these individual column objects within the browse object. With these two objects extracted—though not removed— from the browse object, the *setColumn( )* method is used to switch the columns. The column object *oObject2* will be stored to the browsing object at column position *aSwitch[1]*, and the column object *oObject1* will be stored to the browsing object at column position *aSwitch[2]*. The columns will effectively switch places with one another. Once the new columns are in place, the browse object needs to be reconfigured, the data source repositioned to the top of the file, and all data elements refreshed, as we did when restructuring the browsing frame.

Programming the keystrokes is a vital task when working with Clipper objects. Nothing can be assumed, nothing can be taken for granted, and yet every possibility must be allowed for. In this next example, the browsing object is enhanced with color and column caching.

```
 1 : * File       Ob5.prg
 2 : * Compile    Rmake sample /dFILE:Ob5
 3 :
 4 : #include "PTInkey.ch"  // Power Tools header file with ASCII values
 5 : #include "PTColor.ch"  // Power Tools header file with color settings
 6 : #include "PTValue.ch"  // Power Tools header file with misc values
 7 : #include "PTVerbs.ch"  // Power Tools header file with commands/statements
 8 : #include "PTFuncs.ch"  // Power Tools header file with pseudofunctions
 9 :
10 : #define pDELCHAR    " " + CHR(205)+CHR(16)+" "
11 : #define pUNDELCHAR SPACE(4)
12 :
13 : procedure Main()
14 :
15 :    local aWindow := {2, 0, 20, maxcol()}
16 :    local oBrowse
17 :    local oColumn
18 :    local nKey
19 :    local cType
20 :    local nLock
21 :
22 :    setcolor( MAKECOLOR( pBRIGHT_WHITE/pBLUE, pCYAN/pBLACK ) )
23 :    cls
24 :    use FileNos new
25 :
26 :    setcursor( pCURSOR_OFF )
27 :    dispbox( 2, 0, 20, MAXCOL(), pDBAR )
28 :
29 :    oBrowse := tbrowsedb( 3, 1, 19, maxcol()-1 )
30 :
31 :    oBrowse:headSep := chr(205) + chr(203) + chr(205)
32 :    oBrowse:colSep  := chr(32) + chr(186) + chr(32)
33 :    oBrowse:colorSpec := ;
34 :      MAKECOLOR( pBRIGHT_WHITE/pBLUE, pCYAN/pBLACK, pRED/pWHITE,;
35 :                 pWHITE/pMAGENTA, pBLACK/pWHITE, pBLUE/pWHITE, ;
36 :                 pBLACK/pCYAN, pWHITE/pRED, pYELLOW/pBLUE )
37 :
38 :    aeval( dbstruct(), {|aField| oBrowse:AddColumn( AddItem(aField) )} )
39 :
40 :    PROCESS
41 :
42 :       oBrowse:forceStable()
43 :
44 :       oColumn := oBrowse:getColumn( oBrowse:colPos )
45 :       cType   := valtype( eval( oColumn:block ) )
46 :
47 :       do case
```

```
 48 :       case cType   == pCHARACTER
 49 :          oBrowse:colorRect( aWindow,{2, 1} )
 50 :       case cType   == pNUMERIC
 51 :          oBrowse:colorRect( aWindow,{4, 3} )
 52 :       case cType   == pLOGICAL
 53 :          oBrowse:colorRect( aWindow,{6, 5} )
 54 :       case cType   == pDATE
 55 :          oBrowse:colorRect( aWindow,{8, 7} )
 56 :       endcase
 57 :
 58 :       @ aWindow[1], aWindow[2]+2 SAY " Column Position: " ;
 59 :                                  SAY str(oBrowse:colPos, 3) ;
 60 :                                  SAY " "
 61 :       InsDel()                     // Just for display purposes!
 62 :
 63 :       nKey := inkey(0)
 64 :
 65 :       do case
 66 :       case ( nKey == pDOWN_ARROW )
 67 :          oBrowse:down()
 68 :
 69 :       case ( nKey == pUP_ARROW )
 70 :          oBrowse:up()
 71 :
 72 :       case ( nKey == pRIGHT_ARROW )
 73 :          oBrowse:right()
 74 :
 75 :       case ( nKey == pLEFT_ARROW )
 76 :          oBrowse:left()
 77 :
 78 :       case ( nKey == pDEL .OR. nKey == pINS )
 79 :          if InsDel( oBrowse )
 80 :             oBrowse:configure()
 81 :             oBrowse:gotop()
 82 :             oBrowse:refreshall()
 83 :          endif
 84 :
 85 :       case ( nKey == pESC )
 86 :          exit
 87 :
 88 :       endcase
 89 :
 90 :    END PROCESS
 91 :
 92 :    setcursor(pCURSOR_ON)
 93 :    cls
 94 :
 95 : ********************
 96 :
 97 : static function InsDel( oBrowse )
 98 :
 99 :    static aCache
100 :
101 :    local nKey      := lastkey()
102 :    local lRetValue := pFALSE
103 :
104 :    if aCache == NIL
105 :       aCache := {}
106 :    endif
107 :
```

```
108 :    if empty( pcount() )
109 :       @ 2,50 SAY " Columns Cached: " SAY str(len(aCache),3) SAY " "
110 :    else
111 :
112 :       if oBrowse:colCount > 1    // there are columns to delete
113 :                                  // We can insert, delete!
114 :          if (nKey == pINS .and. len( aCache ) > 0) .or. nKey == pDEL
115 :             lRetValue := pTRUE
116 :             if nKey == pINS
117 :                oBrowse:insColumn( oBrowse:colPos, aCache[ len(aCache) ] )
118 :                asize( aCache, len(aCache)-1 )
119 :             else
120 :                aadd( aCache, oBrowse:getColumn( oBrowse:colPos ) )
121 :                oBrowse:delColumn( oBrowse:colPos )
122 :             endif
123 :          endif
124 :       endif
125 :    endif
126 :
127 :    return( lRetValue )
128 :
129 : ********************
130 :
131 : static function AddItem( aItem )
132 :
133 :    static nItem
134 :    static nFieldNumber
135 :
136 :    local oColumn := tbcolumnnew( UPPERLOWER(aItem[1]), fieldblock(aItem[1]))
137 :    local cValType
138 :
139 :    if nItem == NIL   // Not yet defined!
140 :       nitem := 3
141 :       nFieldNumber := 1
142 :    endif
143 :
144 :    oColumn:footsep := chr(205) + chr(202) + chr(205)
145 :    oColumn:footing := "Column:" + transform(nItem++, "999") +;
146 :                      "; Field:" + transform(nFieldNumber++,"999")
147 :
148 :    cValType := valtype( eval( fieldblock( aItem[1] ) ) )
149 :
150 :    do case
151 :    case cValType == pCHARACTER
152 :       oColumn:defColor := {1, 2}
153 :    case cValType == pNUMERIC
154 :       oColumn:defColor := {3, 4}
155 :    case cValType == pLOGICAL
156 :       oColumn:defColor := {5, 6}
157 :    case cValType == pDATE
158 :       oColumn:defColor := {7, 8}
159 :    endcase
160 :
161 :    return( oColumn )
162 :
163 : // End of File: Ob5.prg
```

This example uses color and will not work properly if tested on a monochrome monitor. The ISCOLOR( ) function is ineffective since it only tests to see if a color card is present; it does not test for the presence of a color monitor. The system colors are set on line 22, and the screen is cleared with these new colors in place. Every browsing object also contains an instance variable called *colorSpec*. This instance variable contains a basic string that may be used as an index for the columns to draw on when they are created and stored to the browsing object. On line 33 is a color string that, when preprocessed, looks something like this:

```
"W+/B, BG/N, R/W, W/BR, N/W, B/W, N/BG, W/R, GR+/B"
```

While the first two color pairs are used to set the standard and enhanced color palettes, both for background and foreground colors, each pair may be "pointed" to by their individual position within this string. In other words, it is possible to conceive of painting some data item in color item number 4. If this string may be looked at as a color index, the fourth pair in this string is

```
"W/BR"
```

It should be noted that two color pairs make up the color scheme for any column object: one pair for the standard color set and another pair for the enhanced color set. To specify a color palette for a particular screen region, an instance variable in the TBCOLUMNNEW( ) object class is set aside to hold an array. This array will contain two numbers based on the color index string stored in the instance variable *colorSpec* in the browse object: one number for the standard color and the other for the enhanced color. An example of this can be seen on line 152: An array is assigned to the instance variable *:defColor* in the column object. The values 1 and 2 point to the first and second color pairs in the browsing object with which the column object is associated; in this case *oBrowse*.

Within the AddItem( ) function, the data type of each field is evaluated on line 148. Since the name of the field is stored in *aItem[1]*, the FIELDBLOCK( ) function converts this field name into a code block that will return that field's value. The EVAL( ) function will evaluate that code block to give a piece of data. That piece of data is then checked for its data type, which is stored to the variable *cValType*.

Based on the data type of the field in that particular column, the column's color will vary. In the case of a column of character data, the color array will contain 1, 2. Looking at the color index in the *oBrowse:colorSpec* instance variable, that would be "W+/B, BG/N". In the case where the data type of the color is a logical expression, the color for that column will be 5,6, or, in other words, "N/W, B/W". A color specification other than the global color setting will affect individual cell items, which will reflect the color scheme as well as headers and footers, if used. The color change does not affect the color of the column separators, header separators, or footer separators.

In addition to working with the instance variables that handle the color of both a browsing object and a column object, the program illustrates the use of two more methods: *:insColumn( )* and *:delColumn( )*. These methods mean exactly what they say: They allow columns within a browsing region to be deleted and inserted. The keystroke processing tests for the DEL or INS keys. If either key is pressed, the evaluation of those keys on line 78 is true. This will call the InsDel( ) function and pass the browse object to it. This function is defined as STATIC on line 97, with the local parameter *oBrowse* containing the pointer to the browsing object. In addition, a STATIC memory variable named *aCache* is set up to hold deleted column objects. This routine is called in two cases. First, it is called routinely with no parameters on line 61, after the stabilization of the browsing object. The first time that InsDel( ) is called, *aCache* is initialized (line 104), an important detail since the variable is a static that will be visible only within the InsDel( ) function itself. In addition, each regular call to InsDel( ) serves merely to update the video display, which indicates the number of columns currently cached (lines 108–110); once again, this is necessary, since this information is not visible outside of the InsDel( ) routine itself. Besides these regular "maintenance" calls, all other calls to InsDel( ) occur when the INS or DEL keys are pressed and pass the browsing object as a parameter.

On line 112, the number of columns within the *oBrowse* browsing area is looked at. This value is stored in the *:colCount* instance variable and must be greater than 1 to continue. Provided this is the case, a secondary test is made: whether the INS key is pressed and the length of the aCache[ ] array is greater than 0, or the DEL key was pressed. It is the intent that individual column objects may be deleted and inserted in any particular browsing object. In addition, the column that is deleted may be cached and saved for later insertion. However, this test on line 115 does not allow the insertion to be made if no items are in the *aCache[ ]* array. (Incidentally, this shows that objects are formal data types, like character strings, numbers, dates, logicals, code blocks, and even arrays. If not, then the notion of storing an object data type to an array would be inconsistent.)

If the DEL key is pressed, the array *aCache[ ]* is dynamically increased by one element and the object obtained from the *:getColumn( )* method is stored to that array. The position of the column that is obtained is given by the value of the instance variable *:colPos* (line 120). Therefore, if the DEL key is pressed, the column containing the highlighted cell is deleted and placed into the *aCache[ ]* array stack. As items are pushed onto the stack, they are popped off of it if the INS key is pressed. On line 117, following the proper key test on line 116, a column object is inserted in the *oBrowse* browsing object using the *:insColumn( )* method at the current column position stored in *:colPos*. The item that is stored there is the cached column object stored in *aCache[ ]*. The last item in the array is used. The caching method here is LIFO; however, other methods may be employed, such as displaying the headers of the cached columns and allowing the end user to pick the column to be inserted via a PROMPT command. Once the column object is inserted into the *oBrowse* browsing object, the size of *aCache[ ]* is reduced by one, thus removing the last item from the array and resizing it as well.

What makes TBROWSEDB( ) different from TBROWSENEW( ) are the code blocks that are, by default, placed into the object when it is generated. These code blocks are for skipping through a database and for going to the top and bottom of a database. In the past, especially in working with DBEDIT( ), finding the end-of-file marker seemed to take a considerable amount of time, especially with an active filter condition. The major amount of time spent was not in processing keys and evaluating field values; rather, it was spent in the skipping operation—in looking at each record in the database and evaluating it against the active filter.

To get the best performance out of a filter condition, that filter should be a subset of the active index. Allowing end users to pick and choose the precise filter condition without regard to the order of the database, either natural or set by some index, will always take time. However, there is a satisfactory medium in which a predefined index will contain the major filtering order and all "filters" will be natural subsets of the active index. With this, the code blocks used to go to the bottom or the top and the code block used to traverse the database will have enhanced performance. If it is impossible to have a filter condition be the subset of an active index, then all unnecessary indexes should be turned off to prevent those buffers used for indexing from being evaluated while traversing the database.

The actual SET FILTER TO command is preprocessed into a code block. Using a code block to store a filter condition is therefore possible, as is storing that code block to the appropriate browsing object. In this next example, the use of the *cargo* instance variable becomes evident. In addition, the program illustrates the ability to select a column and to SEEK information in that column.

```
 1 : * File       Ob6.prg
 2 : * Compile    Rmake sample /dFILE:ob6
 3 :
 4 : #include "Setcurs.ch"
 5 : #include "Inkey.ch"
 6 :
 7 : #include "PTVerbs.ch"  // Special header file
 8 :
 9 : #xtranslate UPPERLOWER(<exp>)                                    => ;
10 :             ( upper(substr(<exp>,1,1))+lower(substr(<exp>,2)) )
11 :
12 : #define pDELCHAR    " " + chr(205)+chr(16)+" "
13 : #define pUNDELCHAR space(4)
14 :
15 : #define pFILTER 1
16 : #define pCOLUMNS 2
17 :
18 : *******************
19 :
20 : function Main()
21 :
22 :    local nCounter      as int
23 :    local oBrowse       as object // This will hold the TBROWSE object
24 :    local oColumn       as object // This will hold temp TBCOLUMNS before added
25 :    local nKey          as int    // ASCII value of key pressed
26 :    local nLock         as int    // Number of columns to lock
27 :    local nColCount     as int
28 :    local cSearch := "" as char
29 :    local Getlist := {} as array  // To prevent a warning message
30 :
31 :    scroll()
32 :    if !file( "Filenos.dbf" )
33 :       quit
34 :    endif
35 :
36 :    use FileNos new
37 :    index on Filenos->sub_no + Filenos->file_name to File2
38 :    index on Filenos->sub_no + Filenos->file_type to File3
39 :    set index to FileNos1, File2, File3
40 :
41 :    setcursor( SC_NONE )
42 :
43 :    oBrowse := Browse( 1,1,20,75 )
44 :
45 :    oBrowse:headSep := chr(205) + chr(203) + chr(205)
46 :    oBrowse:colSep  := chr(32) + chr(186) + chr(32)
47 :
48 :    // Now, the cargo of this puppy will hold a lot of things!
49 :
```

```
 50 :    oBrowse:cargo     := {}
 51 :    aadd( oBrowse:cargo, { {|| Filenos->sub_no == "  2"}, ;
 52 :                            "Filenos->sub_no == '  2'", ;
 53 :                            "  2" } )
 54 :    aadd( oBrowse:cargo, {} )
 55 :
 56 :    oBrowse:addColumn(tbcolumnnew( " Deleted? ", ;
 57 :                         {|| if( deleted(), pDELCHAR, pUNDELCHAR)} ))
 58 :
 59 :    oBrowse:addColumn( tbcolumnnew( "Record;Number", ;
 60 :                            {|| recno()} ) )
 61 :
 62 :    oBrowse:skipblock     := ;
 63 :           {|nRequest| Filter(nRequest, (oBrowse:cargo)[pFILTER])}
 64 :    oBrowse:gobottomblock := {|| Atbottom(oBrowse:cargo[pFILTER])}
 65 :    oBrowse:gotopblock    := {|| Attop(oBrowse:cargo[pFILTER]) }
 66 :
 67 :    for nCounter := 1 to fcount()
 68 :      oColumn := tbcolumnnew( UPPERLOWER( field(nCounter) ), ;
 69 :                              fieldblock( field(nCounter) ) )
 70 :      do case
 71 :      case field(nCounter) == "FILE_NAME"
 72 :         oColumn:cargo := {|cSearch| dbsetorder(2), dbseek(cSearch) }
 73 :
 74 :      case field(nCounter) == "FILE_TYPE"
 75 :         oColumn:cargo := {|cSearch| dbsetorder(3), dbseek(cSearch) }
 76 :
 77 :      endcase
 78 :      oBrowse:addcolumn(oColumn)
 79 :
 80 :    next
 81 :
 82 :    oBrowse:freeze := 2
 83 :    oBrowse:colPos := oBrowse:freeze + 1
 84 :    oBrowse:gotop()
 85 :
 86 :    while .t.
 87 :
 88 :      if oBrowse:colPos <= oBrowse:freeze      // Can't be on a frozen column
 89 :         oBrowse:colpos := oBrowse:freeze+1
 90 :      endif
 91 :
 92 :      // The following is the visual stuff that is necessary for the
 93 :      // end user... it prevents them from freaking out!!!
 94 :
 95 :      devpos(0,1)
 96 :      devout( "Saved: " )
 97 :      devout( len(oBrowse:cargo[pCOLUMNS]) ) )
 98 :      devout( " ")
 99 :
100 :      devpos(0,20)
101 :      devout( "Locked: " )
102 :      devout( oBrowse:freeze )
103 :
104 :      devpos(oBrowse:nBottom+1, oBrowse:nLeft+1)
105 :      devout( padr(cSearch, oBrowse:nRight-oBrowse:nLeft,chr(205)) )
106 :
107 :      while ( !oBrowse:stabilize() )         // Incremental stabilization
108 :        if !empty( nKey := inkey() )
109 :           exit
```

```
110 :        endif
111 :     enddo
112 :
113 :     if oBrowse:stable
114 :
115 :        do case
116 :        case oBrowse:hitbottom
117 :           devpos(24,00)
118 :           devout("End of File")
119 :
120 :        case oBrowse:hittop
121 :           devpos(24,00)
122 :           devout("Top of File")
123 :
124 :        otherwise
125 :           scroll(24,00)
126 :
127 :        endcase
128 :
129 :        nKey := inkey(0)
130 :
131 :     endif
132 :
133 :     do case
134 :     case ( nKey == K_DOWN )
135 :        oBrowse:down()
136 :
137 :     case ( nKey == K_UP )
138 :        oBrowse:up()
139 :
140 :     case ( nKey == K_RIGHT )
141 :        if oBrowse:colPos = oBrowse:colCount
142 :           oBrowse:panhome()
143 :        else
144 :           oBrowse:right()
145 :        endif
146 :        cSearch := ""    // Re-set the searching string 'cause we moved!
147 :
148 :     case ( nKey == K_LEFT )
149 :        oBrowse:left()
150 :        cSearch := ""    // Re-set the searching string 'cause we moved!
151 :
152 :     case ( nKey == K_PGUP )
153 :        oBrowse:pageup()
154 :
155 :     case ( nKey == K_PGDN )
156 :        oBrowse:pagedown()
157 :
158 :     case ( nKey == K_HOME )
159 :        oBrowse:gotop()
160 :        oBrowse:panhome()
161 :
162 :     case ( nKey == K_END )
163 :        oBrowse:gobottom()
164 :        oBrowse:panhome()
165 :
166 :     case ( nKey == K_ESC )
167 :        exit
168 :
169 :     case ( nKey == K_DEL )
```

```clipper
170 :        if( deleted(), dbrecall(), dbdelete() )
171 :        oBrowse:refreshcurrent()
172 :        oBrowse:down()
173 :
174 :     case ( nKey == K_F5 )    // stuff the current column to the array
175 :        // first see if there are more than the number of frozen
176 :        // columns plus the number we are on in order to freeze
177 :        if oBrowse:freeze + 1 < oBrowse:colCount   // There are
178 :           aadd( oBrowse:cargo[pCOLUMNS], oBrowse:getColumn( oBrowse:colPos ))
179 :           oBrowse:delColumn(oBrowse:colPos)
180 :           oBrowse:configure()
181 :        endif
182 :
183 :     case ( nKey == K_F9 ) // This undoes the static arrays
184 :        // The behavior of this is to take the array that is found in the
185 :        // cargo instance variable, remove it, then put it at the position
186 :        // one column to the right of the frozen field.
187 :        if !empty( oBrowse:cargo[pCOLUMNS] ) // there are items
188 :           oBrowse:insColumn(oBrowse:freeze+1, atail(oBrowse:cargo[pCOLUMNS]) )
189 :           asize(oBrowse:cargo[pCOLUMNS], len(oBrowse:cargo[pCOLUMNS])-1 )
190 :           oBrowse:configure()
191 :        endif
192 :
193 :     case ( nKey == K_TAB )
194 :        if Movebox( oBrowse )
195 :
196 :           scroll()
197 :           dispbox( oBrowse:ntop-1, oBrowse:nleft-1, ;
198 :                    oBrowse:nbottom+1, oBrowse:nright+1, 2 )
199 :
200 :           oBrowse:gotop()
201 :           oBrowse:refreshall()
202 :
203 :        endif
204 :
205 :     case ( nKey == K_F4 )   // Change the width of a column
206 :        ChangeWidth(oBrowse)
207 :
208 :     case ( nKey == K_ENTER )
209 :
210 :        nLock := oBrowse:freeze
211 :
212 :        @ 24,00 say   "Enter field to nLock on: " ;
213 :                get   nLock ;
214 :                valid nLock >= 1 .and. nLock <= int(fcount()/2)
215 :
216 :        read
217 :        if !( lastkey() == K_ESC )
218 :           oBrowse:freeze := nLock
219 :           oBrowse:refreshall()
220 :        endif
221 :
222 :        scroll(24,00)
223 :
224 :     otherwise
225 :        // check to see if the column we are on has a seeking criteria
226 :        // based on it
227 :        if !( (oBrowse:getColumn(oBrowse:colPos)):cargo == NIL )
228 :           // Now, if the key pressed was an alpha key, or if the
229 :           // key pressed was a file extension, or if the key pressed
```

```
230 :            // as the backspace key... process the following!
231 :
232 :            if (nKey == K_BS) .or. (isalpha( chr(nKey) ) .or. chr(nKey) == ".")
233 :              if nKey == K_BS
234 :                if !empty(cSearch)
235 :                   cSearch := left(cSearch, len(cSearch)-1)
236 :                endif
237 :              else
238 :                 cSearch += chr(nKey)
239 :              endif
240 :              if eval( (oBrowse:getColumn(oBrowse:colPos)):cargo, ;
241 :                        oBrowse:cargo[pFILTER, 3] + cSearch )
242 :                 oBrowse:refreshall()
243 :              endif
244 :            endif
245 :
246 :         endif
247 :
248 :      endcase
249 :
250 :   enddo
251 :
252 :   scroll()
253 :
254 :   return( NIL )
255 :
256 : ******************
257 :
258 : static function Browse( nTop, nLeft, nBottom, nRight )
259 :
260 :   scroll(nTop, nLeft, nBottom, nRight)
261 :   dispbox( nTop, nLeft, nBottom, nRight, 2 )
262 :
263 :   return( tbrowsedb( nTop+1, nLeft+1, nBottom-1, nRight-1 ) )
264 :
265 : ******************
266 :
267 : static function Movebox( oMove )
268 :
269 :   local nTop      := oMove:ntop-1                          as int
270 :   local nLeft     := oMove:nleft-1                         as int
271 :   local nBottom   := oMove:nbottom+1                       as int
272 :   local nRight    := oMove:nright+1                        as int
273 :   local cScreen   := savescreen(0, 0, maxrow(), maxcol())  as char
274 :   local nKey                                               as int
275 :
276 :   while .t.
277 :      restscreen( 0, 0, maxrow(), maxcol(), cScreen )
278 :      dispbox( nTop, nLeft, nBottom, nRight, replicate( chr(178), 8 ) )
279 :
280 :      nKey := inkey(0)
281 :
282 :      do case
283 :      case nKey == K_DOWN
284 :         if nBottom < maxrow()-1
285 :            nBottom++
286 :         endif
287 :
288 :      case nKey == K_RIGHT
289 :         if nRight < maxcol()1
```

```
290 :            nRight++
291 :         endif
292 :
293 :      case nKey == K_UP
294 :         if nBottom > nTop+4
295 :            nBottom--
296 :         endif
297 :
298 :      case nKey == K_LEFT
299 :         if nRight > 30    // Due to the visual stuff on the screen
300 :            nRight--       // This has to be locked in at 30
301 :         endif
302 :
303 :      case nKey == K_ESC .or. nKey == K_ENTER
304 :         exit
305 :
306 :      endcase
307 :
308 :   enddo
309 :
310 :   if lastkey() == K_ENTER
311 :      oMove:ntop    := nTop + 1
312 :      oMove:nleft   := nLeft + 1
313 :      oMove:nbottom := nBottom - 1
314 :      oMove:nright  := nRight - 1
315 :   endif
316 :
317 :   return( lastkey() == K_ENTER )
318 :
319 : *********************
320 :
321 : function Filter( nToSkip, aFilter )
322 :
323 :    local nActual := 0 as int
324 :
325 :    if !empty( nToSkip )
326 :      do case
327 :      case nToSkip > 0     // A positive skipping motion
328 :
329 :         while nActual < nToSkip
330 :            dbskip(1)
331 :
332 :            if eof() .or. !eval( aFilter[1] )
333 :               dbskip(-1)
334 :               exit
335 :            endif
336 :            nActual++
337 :         enddo
338 :
339 :      case nToSkip < 0     // A negative skipping motion
340 :
341 :         while nActual > nToSkip
342 :            dbskip(-1)
343 :            if bof() .or. !eval( aFilter[1] )
344 :               dbskip(1)
345 :               exit
346 :            endif
347 :            nActual--
348 :         enddo
349 :
```

```
350 :      endcase
351 :
352 :   endif
353 :
354 :   return( nActual )
355 :
356 : ********************
357 :
358 : function Attop( aCondition )
359 :
360 :   dbseek( aCondition[3] )   // The fourth element has the element to find
361 :
362 :   return( recno() )
363 :
364 : ********************
365 :
366 : function Atbottom( aCondition )
367 :
368 :   local cTemp as char
369 :
370 :   // First, let's take the last byte in the string of the seeking
371 :   // thingie and bump it up one ASCII value
372 :
373 :   cTemp := left( aCondition[3], len(aCondition[3])-1 )
374 :
375 :   cTemp += chr(asc(substr( aCondition[3], len(aCondition[3]), 1 ))+1)
376 :
377 :   dbseek( cTemp, .t. )  // with softseek on
378 :   dbskip(-1)
379 :
380 :   return( recno() )
381 :
382 : ********************
383 :
384 : static function ChangeWidth( oBr )    // Entire obect
385 :
386 :   local nWidth   as int      // Will contain the original width of the column
387 :   local oColumn as object   // Column of the desired object
388 :   local nCol := col() as int     // Row of cursor position
389 :   local nRow := row() as int     // Column of cursor position
390 :   local cScreen        as char   // Screen to be saved for visual puffery
391 :   local nOldWidth      as int    // Temp old width for visual puffery
392 :   local nKey           as int    // ASCII value of key pressed
393 :
394 :   oColumn := oBr:getColumn( oBr:colPos )
395 :   oBr:deHilite()
396 :
397 :   if ( nWidth := oColumn:width ) == NIL
398 :      // Column width must be calculated.... the following function
399 :      // is in honor of Basil....
400 :      nWidth := len( Stringify( eval( oColumn:block ) ) )
401 :
402 :      // Now that we have the length of the data item, let's look at the
403 :      // length of the footer
404 :
405 :      if !(oColumn:footing == NIL)
406 :         nWidth := max(nWidth, GetSize(oColumn:footing))
407 :      endif
408 :
409 :      if !(oColumn:heading == NIL)
```

```
410 :            nWidth := max(nWidth, GetSize(oColumn:heading))
411 :         endif
412 :
413 :     endif
414 :
415 :     REPEAT
416 :        nOldWidth := nWidth
417 :        cScreen   := savescreen(nRow, nCol, nRow, nCol + nOldWidth)
418 :        setpos(nRow,nCol)
419 :        dispout(replicate(chr(178), nWidth))
420 :        nKey := inkey(0)
421 :        do case
422 :        case nKey == K_RIGHT
423 :           if nCol + nWidth < oBr:nRight
424 :              nWidth++
425 :           endif
426 :
427 :        case nKey == K_LEFT
428 :           if nWidth > 1
429 :              nWidth--
430 :           endif
431 :
432 :        endcase
433 :        restscreen(nRow,nCol,nRow,nCol+nOldWidth, cScreen)
434 :
435 :     UNTIL ( nKey == K_ESC .or. nKey == K_ENTER )
436 :
437 :     oBr:Hilite()
438 :     if nKey == K_ENTER   // Accepted width
439 :        oColumn:width := nWidth
440 :        oBr:setColumn( oBr:colPos, oColumn )
441 :        oBr:configure()
442 :        oBr:refreshall()
443 :     endif
444 :
445 :     return( NIL )
446 :
447 : *******************
448 :
449 : static function Stringify( xItem ) // An item of any data type
450 :
451 :     local cReturn as char
452 :
453 :     do case
454 :     case valtype( xItem ) == "C"
455 :        cReturn := xItem
456 :
457 :     case valtype( xItem ) == "L"
458 :        cReturn := if( xItem, "T", "F" )
459 :
460 :     case valtype( xItem ) == "D"
461 :        cReturn := dtoc( xItem )
462 :
463 :     otherwise
464 :        cReturn := str( xItem )
465 :
466 :     endcase
467 :
468 :     return( cReturn )
469 :
```

```
470 :   *******************
471 :
472 :   static function GetSize( cItem ) // This can be either footer or header
473 :
474 :   // First we have to see how many lines are involved with this item
475 :
476 :   local nSize as int           // This is the length of the longest line!
477 :   local cPartial as char       // Hold a partial string value
478 :   local nCounter as int        // Holds the FOR...NEXT counter
479 :   local nTemp    := 0 as int   // Will hold a temporary size!
480 :   local nLines := len(cItem) - len(strtran(cItem, ";", "")) as int
481 :
482 :   if ++nLines == 1             // meaning only one line!
483 :      nSize := len( cItem )
484 :   else
485 :      for nCounter := 1 to nLines
486 :         if ";"$cItem  // There remains a semicolon
487 :            cPartial := left( cItem, at(";", cItem) )
488 :         else
489 :            cPartial := cItem
490 :         endif
491 :         nTemp := max(nTemp, len(cPartial))
492 :         cItem := substr( cItem, at(";", cItem)+1 )
493 :      next
494 :      nSize := nTemp
495 :   endif
496 :
497 :   return( nSize )
498 :
499 : // End of File: Ob6.prg
```

There are ten major points to highlight in this example. First, on line 53 the *:cargo* instance variable of the *oBrowse* object is first initialized to an empty array. Then on lines 51 through 53, a subarray is added: It contains a code block of an expression, the string representation of that code block, and the literal value being tested. Then on line 54, an empty subarray is added to the *:cargo* instance variable. The *:cargo* instance variable now contains an array of values that will be used in various parts of this example. The first element stored to the *:cargo* instance variable will be used to define a FILTER condition. But instead of using conditional indexing or filtering clauses, the only requirement here is that the filter expression be a subset of the controlling index. The controlling index is Filenos1, and its key expression is FILENOS->SUB_NO + FILENOS->FILE_NAME. The "filtering" code block, which is used by the Filter( ) function (which in turn is called when the *skipBlock* instance variable is evaluated) merely checks to insure that the value of Sub_No for a particular record is 2. The second element will be used to store deleted columns. Each element stored to the *:cargo* instance variable, no matter what it may be, is specific to a single purpose.

To help see this better we come to point number two on lines 62 through 65. Here, the various code blocks that control movement of the record pointer are assigned specific values. To understand this better keep in mind that there is a relationship between the methods and the instance variables. To put it simply, TBROWSE does not care what is the source or format of the data set that it is browsing: That specific information is held in various code blocks. What is critical is that there be a relationship between methods and instance variables. For example, when a call is made to move the data pointer to the top of the data set, a "message" to the *:gotop( )* method is sent. This then looks to the *:gotopBlock* instance variable for direction as to what "go top" really means. To a regular database, that means simply to DBGOTOP( ), but to an array, as we will see later, it means something different. Its meaning is defined by the code block contained in the *:skipBlock* instance variable, which is accessed by the *:up( )*, *:down( )*, *:pageUp( )*, and *:pageDown( )* methods. On line 63, we have assigned our own code block to the *skipBlock* instance variable. That code block, when evaluated, will receive a request from a method, *nRequest*, which represents the number of records to be skipped. That request and the array in the *cargo* instance variable at the pFILTER position (a manifest constant defined on line 15), are passed as parameters to the Filter( ) function. Filter( ), in turn, is designed to determine whether the request to skip *nRequest* records is possible and to implemented it. This will become clearer as we examine the operation of the code blocks defined on lines 62 through 65 in depth.

Third, on lines 71 through 75, we are working with the individual column objects before they are stored to the TBROWSE object. When the field that we are working on is the "FILE_NAME" field or the "FILE_TYPE" field, a code block will be assigned to the *cargo* instance variable of the column objects. If, during the course of working with this TBROWSE object, we should come across a column object that has a value of NIL for a *:cargo* instance variable, we know that it is neither one of these columns. The idea of these code blocks is that if a key is pressed when the cursor is in either of these columns, then an on-line SEEK will be performed. These code blocks will select the correct controlling index and perform the DBSEEK( ) function with the character string *cSearch*, which is passed into the code block. Keep in mind that the value of the DBSEEK( ) function will be a logical true (.T.) or false (.F.), based on whether *cSearch* can be found or not. This value will then become the value of the code block, which in turn will be the value of the instance variable, which in turn will be the value of the EVAL( ) function that is making the call. This will be seen shortly.

The fourth point has nothing to do with the previous points outlined other than to show some of the possibilities of the TBROWSE subsystem being built in this example program. Lines 174 through 181 test to see if the F5 key is pressed. The F5 key is to remove the current column object from the browsing area and store it in the second element of the browsing object's *:cargo* instance variable. Since arrays can hold any valid data type, and since an object is a valid data type, it is safe to say that the individual column objects can be stored to the *:cargo* instance variable. Before this can take place, we have to see if there are going to be enough columns left over after one is removed. This test takes place on line 177. As a general rule in this browsing object, the cell pointer must always be positioned at least one column to the right of the total number of frozen columns. If that number should be less than the total number of columns in the browsing area, then the current column can be removed and placed in a safe holding bin. This operation takes place on lines 178 through 180, using the pCOLUMNS manifest constant to define the array element in the *:cargo* instance variable that is used for the column objects.

Fifth, if we are saving deleted columns in the *cargo* instance variable, we want to be able to restore them. The F9 key, which is tested on 183, is used for this purpose, and line 187 tests to make sure that there are saved column objects in the second array element of the *cargo* instance variable. If this latter test returns a logical true (.T.), indicating that column objects have been stored to the array, the ATAIL( ) function is used to get the last column object in the array. This column object is then inserted at the first column adjacent to the browsing object's frozen columns. Note that this latter feature simply reflects the behavior of this particular browsing object; it can be easily modified to better suit your own needs and requirements. The *:insColumn( )* method inserts a column object into the assigned position, moving all other column objects down the stack. This is different from the *:addColumn( )* method, in which a column object is dynamically added to the last position in the TBROWSE object. Once the column object is restored, it has to be removed from the pCOLUMNS array held in the *:cargo* instance variable. This takes place on line 189 and is followed by a :configure( ) message.

Sixth, on lines 205 and 206, if the F4 key should be pressed, the ChangeWidth( ) function is called and the *oBrowse* object passed to it. This function is defined on lines 384 and following. It allows for the width of a column to be adjusted by the cursor keys. If a width has been explicitly assigned to the column, then its *width* instance variable will not be NIL, but will instead reflect the actual width of the column. In most cases, however, *width* will be NIL, and we will have to calculate the value of the width by other means. If the column width has not been explicitly defined, then it will be the largest of the following three values:

- The width of the header
- The width of the footer
- The width of the first data element that appears in the browsing area

For this purpose, line 400 begins with an EVAL( ) of the code block contained in the column's *block* instance variable; since we are working with a database, all data elements will have the same width, so we need not be concerned which particular record is being EVALed. Lines 405 through 407 then determine whether a column footer has been defined. If one is present, the program calculates its width and then takes the maximum of the footer width and the data width. Finally, lines 409 through 411 look for the column's header, calculate its width, and derive the column's actual width. Note that a header or a footer may have multiple lines, which is indicated by the ";" character. We cannot simply compute the total length of the string; instead, we must parse it. The GetSize( ) function does this by examining the *heading* and *footing* instance variables, determining whether multiple rows of text are present, and, if so, calculating the length of the longest row. What follows in the ChangeWidth( ) function is simply a loop that tests whether the right arrow, left arrow, Enter, or ESC key has been pressed and sets the value of *nWidth* accordingly.

Seventh, if the TAB key is pressed, then the entire browsing object is passed to the MoveBox( ) function beginning on line 267. It is important to understand that objects act in so many ways like arrays that it is difficult to consider an object anything but a predefined array structure. (As an interesting aside, an object has a "length" that can be calculated by the LEN( ) function, and items can be attached to an object via the AADD( ) function. While this is not advised, it does shed light to how we can work with objects.) For example, when we pass an array to a subroutine with just the name of the variable holding the array reference, we are passing that array by value. The value of the array is all of the individual items within the array but not the address pointer to the array itself. This means that we could in the subroutine alter the value and contents of any one of the elements in the array—we could even attach items to the array via the AADD( ) function—but we cannot alter the pointer to the array. This means that when the subroutine has finished its operation, all element values will be returned and be visible to the calling routine. Objects passed in the same manner behave in the same way. In the MoveBox( ) function, we will alter the value of four instance variables on lines 311 through 314; once this function returns control to the main routine, those new values will remain attached to the object. This acts like elements in an array in which those elements' values were altered in the subroutine and are now visible in the main routine.

Eighth, note the READ command on line 216 within the TBROWSE subsystem. Here, we are altering the number of locked fields in the TBROWSE object. Keep in mind that only the contiguous leftmost columns can be "frozen." If a column needs to be "frozen" and is not a part of the leftmost block of columns, then it needs to be moved.

Ninth, the user might press a key that is not part of the massive DO CASE construct on lines 133 through 248 that test the value of *nKey*. If this is the case, line 227 tests whether the cursor is currently positioned in a column whose *cargo* instance variable contains some value other than NIL. If so, the program checks to see if the key pressed is the Backspace key, a "." character (reflecting a filename separator), or an alphabetic character. (Of course, this does not include all of the characters that might appear in a filename and file extension. These would have to be added in a working program.). If the Backspace key was pressed and *cString* is not a null string, its last character will be removed. Otherwise, the CHR( ) of the key pressed is added to the end of *cSearch*. This string is then passed to the code block stored in the column's *cargo* instance variable, which is evaluated. If the EVAL( ) returns a logical true (.T.) value, the screen is refreshed. This allows the user, when moving to one of the columns that supports this feature, to enter a file specification and have the browsing object "seek" a matching item. When the end user moves to a new column, lines 146 and 150 reset *cSearch* to a null string.

Tenth, and finally, let's examine the code blocks that are stored to the *goBottomBlock* and *goTopBlock* instance variables on lines 64 and 65. Each calls a special-purpose function that is passed the first (or pFILTER) element of the array stored to the browsing object's *cargo* instance variable. This array element is itself an array, and each function makes use of its third element, a literal that represents the filter string. In the case of the code block stored in *goTopBlock*, the function that it calls, Attop( ) on lines 358–362, simply SEEKs the literal value that corresponds to the filter condition. This will position the record pointer at the top of the database without having to sequentially evaluate all records to insure that they meet the filter condition. The code block stored to *goBottomBlock* calls a function, Atbottom( ) on lines 366 to 380, that increases the ASCII value of the filter string by one and then SEEKs it. Since it does not meet the filter condition, the record pointer is positioned at the end-of-file. Skipping backwards one record then positions the record pointer at the last record in the file without requiring a sequential evaluation of each visible record in the database.

## ADVANCED EXAMPLES

Storing values to a database that will be used in building an object combines the theories and practices of object-oriented programming and data-driven programming. This example shows in addition how effective the INIT PROCEDURE or INIT FUNCTION declaration can be.

```
1 : * File     Ob7.prg
2 :
3 :
```

```
 4 :  #include "PTInkey.ch"   // Power Tools header file with ASCII values
 5 :  #include "PTColor.ch"   // Power Tools header file with color settings
 6 :  #include "PTValue.ch"   // Power Tools header file with misc values
 7 :  #include "PTVerbs.ch"   // Power Tools header file with commands/statements
 8 :  #include "PTFuncs.ch"   // Power Tools header file with pseudofunctions
 9 :
10 :
11 :  #xtranslate AddField( <a>, <b>, <c>, <d>, <e> ) => ;
12 :              AADD( <a>, {<"b">, <"c">, <d>, <e>} )
13 :
14 :  procedure Main()
15 :
16 :     use Trans new index Trans
17 :     use Clients new index Client1
18 :     set relation to Clients->account into Trans additive
19 :     cls
20 :     Clients->( BrowseData("Listbox1") )
21 :     CLS
22 :
23 :     CLOSE DATA
24 :
25 :  *********************
26 :
27 :  procedure BrowseData( cItem1 )
28 :
29 :     local oBrowse1
30 :     local oColumn
31 :
32 :     setcursor( pCURSOR_OFF )
33 :
34 :     if Browdata->( dbseek( cItem1 ) )
35 :        setcolor( trim(Browdata->color) )
36 :        dispbox( Browdata->top-1, Browdata->left-1, Browdata->bottom+1, ;
37 :                 Browdata->right+1, pDBAR )
38 :
39 :        oBrowse1 := tbrowsedb(Browdata->top, Browdata->left, ;
40 :                              Browdata->bottom, Browdata->right)
41 :
42 :        if !empty( Browdata->headlen )
43 :           oBrowse1:headsep := left( Browdata->headsep, Browdata->headlen )
44 :        endif
45 :        if !empty( Browdata->collen )
46 :           oBrowse1:colsep := left( Browdata->colsep, Browdata->collen )
47 :        endif
48 :        oBrowse1:colorSpec := trim( Browdata->color )
49 :        oBrowse1:cargo     := cItem1
50 :
51 :        while Coldata->code == str( Browdata->( recno() ), 10) .and. !eof()
52 :
53 :           oColumn := tbcolumnnew( trim(Coldata->header), ;
54 :                                   &( trim(Coldata->block) ) )
55 :
56 :           oBrowse1:addColumn( oColumn )
57 :           Coldata->( dbskip(1) )
58 :
59 :        enddo
60 :
61 :        if Browdata->freeze < oBrowse1:colCount
62 :           oBrowse1:freeze := Browdata->freeze
63 :           oBrowse1:colPos := Browdata->freeze+1
64 :        endif
```

```
 65 :
 66 :        eval( &( trim(Browdata->keys) ), oBrowse1 )
 67 :
 68 :    endif
 69 :
 70 :    setcursor( pCURSOR_ON )
 71 :
 72 : **********************
 73 :
 74 : function Keys( oBrow )    // Don't have this as a static
 75 :
 76 :    local nKey
 77 :
 78 :    set( pWRAP, pTRUE )    // Set wrap is now on!
 79 :
 80 :    REPEAT
 81 :
 82 :      oBrow:forceStable()
 83 :
 84 :      do case
 85 :      case oBrow:hitbottom
 86 :        if set(pWRAP)            // SET WRAP ON!
 87 :          oBrow:goTop()
 88 :          oBrow:refreshAll()
 89 :          loop
 90 :        endif
 91 :
 92 :      case oBrow:hittop
 93 :        if set(pWRAP)            // SET WRAP ON!
 94 :          oBrow:goBottom()
 95 :          oBrow:refreshAll()
 96 :          loop
 97 :        endif
 98 :
 99 :      endcase
100 :
101 :      nKey := inkey(0)
102 :
103 :      do case
104 :      case ( nKey == pDOWN_ARROW )
105 :        oBrow:down()
106 :
107 :      case ( nKey == pUP_ARROW )
108 :        oBrow:up()
109 :
110 :      case ( nKey == pRIGHT_ARROW )
111 :        if oBrow:colPos == oBrow:colCount
112 :          oBrow:panhome()
113 :        else
114 :          oBrow:right()
115 :        endif
116 :
117 :      case ( nKey == pLEFT_ARROW )
118 :        oBrow:left()
119 :
120 :      case ( nKey == pESC )
121 :        exit
122 :
123 :      case ( nKey == pDEL )
124 :          if( deleted(), dbrecall() , dbdelete() )
```

```
125 :        oBrow:refreshcurrent()
126 :        oBrow:down()
127 :
128 :     endcase
129 :
130 :     if oBrow:colpos < (oBrow:freeze + 1)  // This prevents the cursor
131 :        oBrow:colPos := oBrow:freeze + 1   // from going into the cell
132 :     endif                                 // marked frozen!
133 :
134 :  UNTIL ( nKey == pESC )
135 :
136 :  return( pTRUE )
137 :
138 : *********************
139 :
140 : init procedure Setup
141 :
142 :  REQUEST fieldblock     // Make sure this gets into the system!
143 :
144 :  local aFields := {}
145 :
146 :  if !file( "BROWDATA.DBF" )
147 :     AddField( aFields, Name,    C, 10, 0 )
148 :     AddField( aFields, Area,    C, 10, 0 )
149 :     AddField( aFields, Top,     N,  2, 0 )
150 :     AddField( aFields, Left,    N,  2, 0 )
151 :     AddField( aFields, Bottom,  N,  2, 0 )
152 :     AddField( aFields, Right,   N,  2, 0 )
153 :     AddField( aFields, headsep, C,  5, 0 )
154 :     AddField( aFields, headlen, N,  2, 0 )
155 :     AddField( aFields, colsep,  C,  5, 0 )
156 :     AddField( aFields, collen,  N,  2, 0 )
157 :     AddField( aFields, color,   C, 40, 0 )
158 :     AddField( aFields, freeze,  N,  2, 0 )
159 :     AddField( aFields, keys,    C, 80, 0 )
160 :     dbcreate( "Browdata.dbf", aFields )
161 :     use Browdata new
162 :     index on Browdata->name to Browdata
163 :     use
164 :  endif
165 :
166 :  if !file( "COLDATA.DBF" )
167 :     aFields := {}
168 :     ADDFIELD( aFields, Code,    C, 10, 0 ) // Code of relation
169 :     ADDFIELD( aFields, Header,  C, 60, 0 )
170 :     ADDFIELD( aFields, block,   C, 80, 0 )
171 :     ADDFIELD( aFields, footer,  C, 60, 0 )
172 :     ADDFIELD( aFields, footsep, C,  5, 0 )
173 :     ADDFIELD( aFields, headsep, C,  5, 0 )
174 :     dbcreate( "Coldata.dbf", aFields )
175 :     use Coldata new
176 :     index on Coldata->code to Coldata
177 :     use
178 :  endif
179 :
180 :  use Coldata new index Coldata
181 :  use Browdata new index Browdata
182 :  set relation to str( Browdata->( recno() ), 10 ) into Coldata
183 :
184 :  if empty( Browdata->(lastrec()) )
```

```
185 :        Browdata->( dbappend() )
186 :        Browdata->name     := "Listbox1"
187 :        Browdata->top      := 6
188 :        Browdata->left     := 6
189 :        Browdata->bottom   := 19
190 :        Browdata->right    := 74
191 :        Browdata->area     := "CLIENTS"
192 :        Browdata->headsep  := CHR(205) + CHR(203) + CHR(205)
193 :        Browdata->headlen  := 3
194 :        Browdata->colsep   := CHR(32) + CHR(186) + CHR(32)
195 :        Browdata->collen   := 3
196 :        Browdata->freeze   := 2
197 :        Browdata->color    := Makecolor( pWHITE/pBLUE, pBLACK/pWHITE )
198 :
199 :        Browdata->keys     := "{|x| Keys(x)}"
200 :
201 :        Coldata->( dbappend() )
202 :        Coldata->code   := str( Browdata->( recno() ), 10 )
203 :        Coldata->header := " Deleted? "
204 :        Coldata->block  := "{|| if( Clients->( deleted() ), " +;
205 :                            "CHR(32)+CHR(205)+CHR(16)+CHR(32), " +;
206 :                            "SPACE(4))}"
207 :
208 :        Coldata->( dbappend() )
209 :        Coldata->code   := str( Browdata->( recno() ), 10 )
210 :        Coldata->header := "Record;Number"
211 :        Coldata->block  := "{|| Clients->( RECNO())}"
212 :
213 :        Coldata->( dbappend() )
214 :        Coldata->code   := str( Browdata->( recno() ), 10 )
215 :        Coldata->header := "Account"
216 :        Coldata->block  := "Clients->( FIELDBLOCK( 'Account' ))"
217 :
218 :        Coldata->( dbappend() )
219 :        Coldata->code   := str( Browdata->( recno() ), 10 )
220 :        Coldata->header := "Status"
221 :        Coldata->block  := "Clients->( FIELDBLOCK( 'Status' ))"
222 :
223 :     endif
224 :
225 : // End of File: Ob7.prg
```

This routine uses the INIT PROCEDURE statement to declare the Setup procedure. An INIT routine will be automatically called and executed before any other program code. In addition, multiple INIT routines are allowed and are called one after another as they are defined in the source file, in the order in which those source files are linked together in an application.

In this case, when OBJ7.EXE is executed, program execution will begin at the procedure on line 140. This routine, named Setup( ), is STATIC—it is visible only to the program file in which it is defined. In this particular case, the Setup( ) routine builds an array of a database structure. AddField( ) is a pseudofunction, which is translated into the AADD( ) function. Once the database structure is defined, the database BROWDATA.DBF is generated via the DBCREATE( ) function on line 160. From here, the new database is used and the appropriate index file is generated. After this, an ancillary data file named COLDATA.DBF is generated, if it does not already exist. Once the databases and indexes are generated, a relation is established between them. In addition, data is added to both the Browdata and Coldata databases. The Browdata file is designed to contain information for the TBROWSE( ) class; the Coldata file is designed to contain information for the TBCOLUMN( ) class. Simulating the structure of an object in a database will allow the possibility of data-dictionary technology and data-driven applications.

One item to note is that no formal data storage class is given to a code block in a database; therefore, the string representation of a code block needs to be stored to a character field that, when loaded, will be compiled into a code block at run time. Examples of these are on lines 204 through 206 and again on line 211; the code block that is evaluated for each data cell in a particular column is expressed as a character string.

Once all data is generated, the first line of executable code in the program file, line 16, is finally reached. This simply calls the BrowseData( ) function in the Clients work area. The item that is passed to the BrowseData( ) routine is the name of the data element to pull the object structure from. This is called "Listbox1".

In this routine, the value of the string "Listbox1" is assigned to the variable *cItem1*. This item is sought in the Browdata work area (which was opened by the INIT procedure) with the DBSEEK( ) function on line 34. If the value of *cItem1* is found, that record's fields are used to set the color of the screen (line 35), the coordinates of the frame (lines 36 and 37), and to create an instance of the TBROWSE( ) object using the same coordinates (lines 39 and 40). The instance is stored to the variable *oBrowse1*. Then, if they are present, the heading separator and column separator instance variables are assigned from the Browdata work area. For both the column and header instance variables (*:headSep* and *:colSep*), an associated field is used to determine their length. For example, if the program test was this:

```
IF !EMPTY( Browdata->colsep )
```

and if the column separator was to be CHR(32), the above condition would not be true (because a string with only spaces is considered EMPTY( )) and no setting would be given to this instance variable. Therefore, the secondary fields Browdata->headlen and Browdata->collen are used to set the length of both instance variables. If these values are empty, there are no settings for the *headSep* and *colSep* instance variables.

On lines 51 through 59, a loop traverses the Coldata work area and collects the necessary information on the columns that are to be created by the TBCOLUMNNEW( ) function on lines 53 and 54. For clarity, the variable *oColumn*, which is the newly created column object, can be removed and the return value of TBCOLUMNNEW( ) can be passed directly to the *:addColumn( )* method on line 56. However, if the structure of the Coldata database is changed and additional instance variables are to be assigned from within this database, the initial call to a temporary variable is necessary. It is important to note that the value of the field Coldata->block is a character string representing a code block. Macro-expanding the expression in this field, in effect, compiles a code block at run time.

Once all of the columns are created and assigned to the browsing object, on line 66 the procedure macro-expands the string representation of a code block and evaluates it. This code block is created at run time and is passed to the browsing object that was previously created and stored to the variable *oBrowse1*. This string representation of a code block, stored in the Browdata->keys field, looks like this:

```
{|x| Keys(x)}
```

In essence, the reference to the function Keys( ) resides in the same database as the browsing data information. The procedure BrowData( ) is independent of the keystroke processing loop, which is associated with the very object it, the procedure, creates. This is at the heart of data-driven technology: The database actually builds the browsing and column objects only to call the keystroke processing function, passing to it the objects that were just created. The function Keys( ) is a part of the application; it may even be part of a prelinked library just waiting to be associated with any browsing object. Object-oriented programming lends itself to data-driven programming with very little effort.

And finally, putting a system together using the TBROWSE( ) object as the control center is easy.

```
 1 : * File       Glossary.prg
 2 :
 3 :
 4 : #include "PTInkey.ch"   // Power Tools header file with ASCII values
 5 : #include "PTColor.ch"   // Power Tools header file with color settings
 6 : #include "PTValue.ch"   // Power Tools header file with misc values
 7 : #include "PTVerbs.ch"   // Power Tools header file with commands/statements
 8 : #include "PTFuncs.ch"   // Power Tools header file with pseudofunctions
 9 :
10 : #xtranslate AddField( <a>, <b>, <c>, <d>, <e> ) => ;
11 :             AADD( <a>, {<"b">, <"c">, <d>, <e>} )
12 : #xtranslate Blockify( <x> ) => <{x}>
13 :
14 : procedure Main( cInFile )
15 :
16 :    if file( cInFile )
17 :       aeval( directory( cInFile ), {|aFiles| AddItems(aFiles)} )
18 :    endif
19 :
20 :    Diction->( Perform( tbrowsedb( 3, 3, 20, 75 ) ) )
21 :
22 : ********************
23 :
24 : STATIC FUNCTION Perform( oBrowse )
25 :
26 :    local nHomeKey    := 0
27 :    local nEndKey     := 0
28 :    local cSearch     := ""
29 :    local lDefWay     := pTRUE
30 :    local lInsertMode := readinsert()
31 :    local getlist     := {}
32 :    local cScreen
33 :    local nRow
34 :    local nCol
35 :    local nKey
36 :    local cTemp
37 :    local nAtRecord
38 :
39 :    // If lDefWay is true, then the default way for a DELETE is
40 :    // to go down after the delete.  Pressing ALT_F will flip this
41 :    // and toggle it accordingly
42 :
43 :    set( pDELETED, pOFF )
44 :    set( pSCOREBOARD, pOFF )
45 :    setcursor( pCURSOR_OFF )
46 :    setcolor( MAKECOLOR( pBRIGHT_WHITE/pBLUE, pBLACK/pWHITE ))
```

```
 47 :    scroll()
 48 :    dispbox( oBrowse:ntop-1, oBrowse:nleft-1, ;
 49 :             oBrowse:nbottom+1, oBrowse:nright+1, pDBAR)
 50 :
 51 :    oBrowse:headSep  := chr(205)
 52 :    oBrowse:colSep   := chr(32)
 53 :    oBrowse:colorSpec := makecolor( pBRIGHT_WHITE/pBLUE, pBLACK/pWHITE)
 54 :    oBrowse:addColumn( tbcolumnnew( "DEL", {|| if( deleted(), chr(16),;
 55 :                                                    chr(32))}))
 56 :    aeval( dbstruct(), {|aStru| oBrowse:AddColumn( AColumn(aStru) )})
 57 :    oBrowse:freeze := 2
 58 :    oBrowse:colPos := 3
 59 :
 60 : REPEAT
 61 :
 62 :    oBrowse:forceStable()
 63 :
 64 :    nRow := row()
 65 :    nCol := col()
 66 :
 67 :    @ oBrowse:ntop-1, oBrowse:nleft+2 SAY " " SAY padr(recno(), 5) ;
 68 :                                     SAY   "/" SAY padr(lastrec(), 6)
 69 :
 70 :    @ oBrowse:ntop+2, oBrowse:nleft-1 say if( lDefWay, chr(25), chr(24) )
 71 :    @ oBrowse:nbottom+1, oBrowse:nleft+2 ;
 72 :      SAY " " SAY padr( cSearch + " ", 40, chr(205))
 73 :
 74 :    devpos(maxrow(), 00 )
 75 :
 76 :    do case
 77 :    case oBrowse:hitbottom
 78 :       devout( "End of File" )
 79 :
 80 :    case oBrowse:hittop
 81 :       devout( "Top of File" )
 82 :
 83 :    otherwise
 84 :       devout( "              " )
 85 :
 86 :    endcase
 87 :
 88 :    nKey := inkey(0)
 89 :
 90 :    if nKey != pHOME
 91 :       nHomeKey := 0
 92 :    endif
 93 :    if nKey != pEND
 94 :       nEndKey := 0
 95 :    endif
 96 :
 97 :    devpos(nRow, nCol)
 98 :
 99 :    do case
100 :    case ( nKey == pESC )   // Just a dummy call
101 :
102 :    case ( nKey == pTAB )
103 :       FIELD->tagged := !FIELD->tagged
104 :       oBrowse:refreshcurrent()
105 :       if( lDefWay, oBrowse:down(), oBrowse:up() )
106 :
```

```
107 :        case ( nKey == pSHIFT_TAB )
108 :           if Diction->( dbseek( cSearch ) )
109 :              oBrowse:refreshall()
110 :           else
111 :              alert( "No Match Found!" )
112 :           endif
113 :
114 :        case ( nKey == pF2 )
115 :           Diction->( dbseek( cSearch := "" ) )
116 :           oBrowse:refreshall()
117 :
118 :        case ( nKey == pBKSP )
119 :           Diction->( dbseek( cSearch := left(cSearch, len(cSearch)-1 ) ) )
120 :           oBrowse:refreshall()
121 :
122 :        case ( nKey == pALT_F )    // Flip the toggle
123 :           lDefWay := !lDefWay
124 :
125 :        case ( nKey == pALT_G )   // Global Deletion of string
126 :           if GroupDel()
127 :              oBrowse:refreshall()
128 :              oBrowse:gotop()
129 :           endif
130 :
131 :        case ( nKey == pDOWN_ARROW )
132 :           oBrowse:down()
133 :
134 :        case ( nKey == pUP_ARROW )
135 :            oBrowse:up()
136 :
137 :        case ( nKey == pRIGHT_ARROW )
138 :           if oBrowse:colPos == oBrowse:colCount
139 :              oBrowse:panhome()
140 :           else
141 :              if oBrowse:colPos() == 3
142 :                 oBrowse:right()
143 :              endif
144 :              oBrowse:right()
145 :           endif
146 :
147 :        case ( nKey == pPGUP )
148 :           oBrowse:pageup()
149 :
150 :        case ( nKey == pPGDN )
151 :           oBrowse:pagedown()
152 :
153 :        case ( nKey == pHOME )
154 :           do case
155 :           case ++nHomeKey == 1
156 :              oBrowse:panhome()
157 :           case nHomeKey == 2
158 :              oBrowse:panhome()
159 :              oBrowse:rowPos := 1
160 :           otherwise
161 :              oBrowse:gotop()
162 :              oBrowse:panhome()
163 :              nHomeKey := 0
164 :           endcase
165 :
166 :        case ( nKey == pEND )
```

```
167 :        do case
168 :        case ++nEndKey == 1
169 :           oBrowse:panend()
170 :        case nEndKey == 2
171 :           oBrowse:panEnd()
172 :           oBrowse:rowPos := oBrowse:rowCount
173 :        otherwise
174 :           oBrowse:gobottom()
175 :           oBrowse:panend()
176 :           nEndKey := 0
177 :        endcase
178 :
179 :     case ( nKey == pLEFT_ARROW )
180 :        if oBrowse:colPos() == 5
181 :           oBrowse:left()
182 :        endif
183 :        oBrowse:left()
184 :
185 :     case ( nKey == pF10 )
186 :        if (alert( "Are you sure of this?", {"Yes", "No "}) == 1)
187 :           @ maxrow(), 0 say "Packing the data file.  One moment!"
188 :           pack
189 :           oBrowse:configure()
190 :           oBrowse:refreshall()
191 :           oBrowse:gotop()
192 :           @ maxrow(), 0 say space(maxcol())
193 :        endif
194 :
195 :     case ( nKey == pENTER )
196 :        if oBrowse:colPos == 3   // Edit the entry
197 :           setcolor(MAKECOLOR( pYELLOW/pBLUE, pBRIGHT_WHITE/pRED))
198 :           cTemp := FIELD->word
199 :           @ row(), col() get cTemp
200 :           read
201 :           if lastkey() != pESC
202 :              if updated()
203 :                 FIELD->word := cTemp
204 :                 oBrowse:refreshall()
205 :              endif
206 :           endif
207 :        else             // edit the memo
208 :           cScreen := savescreen( 4, 4, 19, 50 )
209 :           cTemp   := FIELD->define
210 :
211 :           setcursor( if(lInsertMode, 2, 1 ) )
212 :           setcolor(if( empty( cTemp ), MAKECOLOR( pBLACK/pWHITE), ;
213 :                         MAKECOLOR( pBRIGHT_WHITE/pRED ) ))
214 :
215 :           dispbox( 4, 4, 19, 50, pDBAR )
216 :           @ 4, 5 say if( empty(cTemp), " Add Definition ", " Edit Mode " )
217 :           cTemp := memoedit(cTemp, 5, 5, 18, 49, pTRUE )
218 :           if !( lastkey() == pESC )
219 :              FIELD->define := cTemp
220 :           endif
221 :           cTemp := ""
222 :
223 :           setcursor( pCURSOR_OFF )
224 :           restscreen( 4, 4, 19, 50, cScreen )
225 :           oBrowse:refreshcurrent()
226 :
```

```
227 :        endif
228 :        setcolor( oBrowse:colorSpec )
229 :
230 :     case ( nKey == pINS )
231 :        lInsertMode := !lInsertMode
232 :
233 :     case ( nKey == pDEL )
234 :        if( deleted(), dbrecall(), dbdelete() )
235 :        oBrowse:refreshcurrent()
236 :        if( lDefWay, oBrowse:down(), oBrowse:up() )
237 :
238 :     case ( nKey == pALT_P )
239 :        nAtRecord := recno()
240 :        oBrowse:dehilite()
241 :        PrintItems()
242 :        dbgoto( nAtRecord )
243 :        oBrowse:hilite()
244 :
245 :     case ( nKey == pALT_A )
246 :        if AddDiction( oBrowse )
247 :           oBrowse:refreshall()
248 :        endif
249 :
250 :     case ( nKey > 30 .and. nKey < 127 )
251 :        if Diction->( dbseek( cSearch += chr(nKey) ) )
252 :           oBrowse:refreshall()
253 :        else
254 :           alert( "No Match Found!" )
255 :        endif
256 :
257 :     endcase
258 :
259 :     if oBrowse:colpos < (oBrowse:freeze + 1)  // This prevents the cursor
260 :        oBrowse:colPos := oBrowse:freeze + 1  // from going into the cell
261 :     endif                                    // marked frozen!
262 :
263 :  until ( nKey == pESC )
264 :  cls
265 :  setcursor( pCURSOR_ON )
266 :
267 :  return( pTRUE )
268 :
269 : *********************
270 :
271 : static function GroupDel()
272 :
273 :  local cString   := space( 40 )
274 :  local cScreen   := savescreen( 18, 10, 23, 70 )
275 :  local lRetValue := pFALSE
276 :  local getlist   := {}
277 :
278 :  setcolor( MAKECOLOR( pBRIGHT_WHITE/pMAGENTA ) )
279 :  dispbox( 18, 10, 23, 70, pDBAR )
280 :
281 :  @ 20,15 say "Enter String to Remove:" get cString pict "@S30"
282 :  read
283 :  if !( lastkey() == pESC )
284 :     if updated()
285 :        lRetValue := pTRUE
286 :        Diction->( dbsetorder( 0 ) )
```

```
287 :         Diction->( dbeval( BLOCKIFY( RemoveIt(alltrim(cString))),,;
288 :                    BLOCKIFY( ShowRec(22, 50) ) ) )
289 :         Diction->( dbsetorder( 1 ) )
290 :      endif
291 :   endif
292 :
293 :   restscreen( 18, 10, 23, 70, cScreen )
294 :
295 :   return( lRetValue )
296 :
297 : *********************
298 :
299 : static function RemoveIt( cWord )
300 :
301 :    if cWord$FIELD->word
302 :       FIELD->word := stuff(FIELD->word, at(cWord, FIELD->word), len(cWord), "")
303 :    endif
304 :
305 :    return( pTRUE )
306 :
307 : *********************
308 :
309 : static function PrintItems()
310 :
311 :    local nWay := alert("Print Items To...",{"Screen", "Paper", "File"})
312 :    local lTags
313 :    local cScreen
314 :
315 :    if !empty( nWay )
316 :
317 :       lTags := (alert( "Tagged Items will be Printed?" )==1)
318 :
319 :       if nWay == 1     // To the screen
320 :          cScreen := savescreen()
321 :          cls
322 :       else
323 :          cScreen := savescreen( maxrow(), 0, maxrow(), maxcol())
324 :          set( pCONSOLE, pOFF )
325 :          IF nWay == 2
326 :             set( pPRINTER, pON )
327 :          else
328 :             set( pALTERNATE, pON )
329 :             set( pALTFILE, "Glossary.out" )
330 :          endif
331 :       endif
332 :
333 :       Diction->( dbgotop() )
334 :       if lTags
335 :          Diction->( dbeval( BLOCKIFY( Output(nWay) ), BLOCKIFY(FIELD->tagged)))
336 :       else
337 :          Diction->( dbeval( BLOCKIFY( Output(nWay) ), ;
338 :                     BLOCKIFY( (!empty(FIELD->define) .and. ;
339 :                     !deleted() ) )) )
340 :       endif
341 :
342 :       set( pCONSOLE, pON )
343 :       set( pPRINTER, pOFF )
344 :       set( pALTERNATE, pOFF )
345 :       set( pALTFILE, "" )
346 :
```

```
347 :      IF nWay == 1
348 :         restscreen(,,,,cScreen)
349 :      else
350 :         if nWay == 2
351 :            eject
352 :         endif
353 :         restscreen( maxrow(), 0, maxrow(), maxcol(), cScreen)
354 :      ENDIF
355 :   ENDIF
356 :
357 :   return( pTRUE )
358 :
359 : *********************
360 :
361 : static function AddDiction()
362 :
363 :   local cWord       := Diction->( MakeEmpty( 2 ) )
364 :   local cFile       := "User Input"
365 :   local cScreen     := savescreen( 18, 10, 23, 70 )
366 :   local lRetValue   := pFALSE
367 :   local getlist     := {}
368 :
369 :   setcolor( MAKECOLOR( pBRIGHT_WHITE/pMAGENTA ) )
370 :   dispbox( 18, 10, 23, 70, pDBAR )
371 :
372 :   @ 20,12 say "Word/Phrase: " get cWord pict "@S40"
373 :   read
374 :   if !( lastkey() == pESC )
375 :      if updated()
376 :         Diction->( dbappend() )
377 :         Diction->word := cWord
378 :         Diction->file := cFile
379 :         lRetValue     := pTRUE
380 :      endif
381 :   endif
382 :
383 :   restscreen( 18, 10, 23, 70, cScreen )
384 :
385 :   return( lRetValue )
386 :
387 : *********************
388 :
389 : static function Output( nWay )
390 :
391 :   if !( nWay == 1 )     // to the screen
392 :      @ maxrow(), 0 say FIELD->word
393 :   endif
394 :
395 :   qqout( FIELD->word )
396 :   qout()
397 :   qout()
398 :   qqout( hardcr(FIELD->define) )
399 :   qout()
400 :   qout()
401 :
402 :   return( pTRUE )
403 :
404 : *********************
405 :
406 : static function Acolumn( aItem )
```

```
407 :
408 :      local oRetValue
409 :
410 :      do case
411 :      case aItem[2] == "M"
412 :         oRetValue := tbcolumnnew( UPPERLOWER(aitem[1]), ;
413 :                      {|| if( empty(fieldget(4)), space(4), "Memo")})
414 :
415 :      case aItem[2] == "L"
416 :         oRetValue := tbcolumnnew( " ", {|| if( empty(fieldget(1)),,;
417 :                      chr(32), chr(20))} )
418 :
419 :      otherwise
420 :         oRetValue := tbcolumnnew( UPPERLOWER(aitem[1]), fieldblock(aItem[1]))
421 :
422 :      endcase
423 :
424 :      return( oRetValue )
425 :
426 : *********************
427 :
428 : static function AddItems( aFiles )   // A is an array of files
429 :
430 :      #define pBUFFER_SIZE 4096
431 :
432 :      local nReadHandle := fopen( aFiles[1] )
433 :      local nWordCount  := 0
434 :      local cPrior      := ""
435 :      local lExit       := pFALSE
436 :      local cBuffer     := ""
437 :      local cWord
438 :      local cTemp
439 :
440 :      while !lExit
441 :
442 :        cBuffer := space( pBUFFER_SIZE )
443 :        lExit   := !(fread(nReadHandle, @cBuffer, pBUFFER_SIZE) == pBUFFER_SIZE)
444 :
445 :        cBuffer := cPrior + cBuffer  // Add the prior to the buffer!
446 :
447 :        while (" "$cBuffer) .AND. !empty(cBuffer)
448 :
449 :          if pCRLF $ (cWord  := Parse(@cBuffer, " "))
450 :            cTemp   := Parse(@cWord , pCRLF )
451 :            cBuffer := cWord  + cBuffer
452 :            cWord   := cTemp
453 :          endif
454 :
455 :          if !empty( cWord  )
456 :            @ row(), 0 say padr( cWord , maxcol() )
457 :            nWordCount++
458 :            if Diction->( !dbseek( cWord  ) )
459 :              Diction->( dbappend() )   // add word to dictionary
460 :              Diction->word := cWord
461 :              Diction->file := aFiles[1]
462 :              commit
463 :            endif
464 :          endif
465 :        enddo
466 :
```

```
467 :        cPrior  := cBuffer
468 :
469 :    enddo
470 :
471 :    if Diction->( !dbseek( cPrior ) )
472 :       Diction->( dbappend() )    // add word to dictionary
473 :       Diction->word := cPrior
474 :    endif
475 :
476 :    qqout( chr(pENTER) + aFiles[1] + " | Words Viewed:" )
477 :    qqout( padr( nWordCount, 15 ) )
478 :    qout()
479 :    inkey(1)
480 :    fclose( nReadHandle )
481 :
482 :    return( pTRUE )
483 :
484 :    #undef pBUFFER_SIZE
485 :
486 : *******************
487 :
488 : static function Parse( cString, cBytes ) // To work with this only!
489 :
490 :    local nLocation := at( cBytes, cString )
491 :    local nWidth    := len( cBytes )
492 :    local cRetValue := ""
493 :
494 :    cRetValue := if(!empty(nLocation), left(cString, nLocation-1), cString)
495 :    cString   := if(!empty(nLocation), substr(cString, nLocation+nWidth), "")
496 :
497 :    return( cRetValue )
498 :
499 : *******************
500 :
501 : static function makeempty( nNumber )   // Ordinal position of
502 :
503 :    local nOldRecord
504 :    local xRetValue       // Default value is NIL
505 :
506 :    if !empty( alias() )
507 :       if nNumber > 0 .and. nNumber <= fcount() // within range
508 :
509 :          nOldRecord := recno()
510 :          dbgoto( 0 )
511 :          xRetValue := fieldget( nNumber )
512 :          dbgoto( nOldRecord )
513 :
514 :       endif
515 :    endif
516 :
517 :    return( xRetValue )
518 :
519 : *******************
520 :
521 : static function ShowRec( nRow, nCol )
522 :
523 :    local nOldRow := row()
524 :    local nOldCol := col()
525 :
526 :    @ nRow, nCol say padr( recno(), 20 )
```

```
527 :    devpos( nOldRow, nOldCol )
528 :
529 :    return( pTRUE )
530 :
531 : *********************
532 :
533 : init procedure Setup
534 :
535 :    local aFields := {}
536 :
537 :    if !file( "DICTION.DBF" )
538 :       ADDFIELD( aFields, tagged, l, 1, 0 )
539 :       ADDFIELD( aFields, word, c, 45, 0 )
540 :       ADDFIELD( aFields, file, c, 12, 0 )
541 :       ADDFIELD( aFields, define, m, 10, 0 )
542 :       dbcreate( "DICTION.DBF", aFields )
543 :    endif
544 :
545 :    if !file( "DICTION.NTX" )
546 :       use Diction new
547 :       index on Diction->word to Diction
548 :       use
549 :    endif
550 :
551 :    use Diction new index Diction
552 :
553 : // End of File:Glossary.prg
```

In this last TBROWSEDB( ) object, the idea of data manipulation and processing that is controlled from one central point is explored. This program is intended to generate a glossary by scanning one or more text files. The text files to be scanned are brought into the environment by providing a file specification as the parameter that is passed to the program when the program is called, as follows:

```
Glossary *.txt
```

The focus of GLOSSARY.PRG is to build a database with few fields, scan through a predefined set of text files, find new words, place them in the database, and move on. A word is defined in this example as a substring that is CHR(32)delimited. A word may be continued onto the next line in a text file; therefore, these character combinations are removed before the scan for CHR(32)-delimited strings.

All unique words found in all of the files ending with ".TXT" are placed into a database named DICTION.DBF that is created by the INIT PROCEDURE named Setup. In this routine, an index file built on the WORD field is also created.

If a parameter is passed from DOS to this program, the file skeleton or an individual filename is passed to the *cInfile* variable. This is then passed to the DIRECTORY( ) function to iterate each element in the DIRECTORY( ) array and call the AddItems( ) routine. Next, the Perform( ) routine is called, passing to it the browsing object generated by the TBROWSEDB( ) call on line 20. If no parameters are passed to this program, the conditional statement on line 16 would be false and only the call to TBROWSEDB( ) will be made; this allows the user to browse the existing records in the Diction database. This call to the Perform( ) subroutine is made in the Diction work area, which is automatically opened in the INIT PROCEDURE Setup on line 533. Opening necessary and related files to make a specific feature perform within special INIT routines adds greater functionality and scope to the concept of building "black-box" routines and self-defined objects and structures.

The main focus of the Perform( ) subroutine is to handle the browsing object named *oBrowse* and to process keystrokes. It is this routine that becomes the emphasis of the entire application. In this procedure, the keys have been programmed to behave in a fashion similar to Brief(tm): One Home keypress goes to the beginning of the line; two Home keypresses moves to the top left corner of the current screen; three Home keypresses moves to the top of the file. The same pattern applies to the End key as well. To do this, two variables are initialized to 0 on lines 26 and 27. These LOCAL variables, *nHomeKey* and *nEndKey*, will keep track of how many consecutive times each key has been pressed. If, after the browsing object *oBrowse* has been stabilized, the End key is pressed once, the case condition on line 166 will be triggered. Within this case structure, a conditional branch is evaluated; however, in the first comparison, the value of *nEndKey* is pre-incremented. If that value is equal to 1, the *:panEnd( )* method is called. If not, the second evaluation is made on line 170. Since *nEndKey* has been previously incremented on line 166, there is no need to repeat this; therefore, a simple test is conducted. If *nEndKey* is 2, the *:panEnd( )* method is activated and the instance variable *:rowPos* is set to the last row in the *oBrowse* browsing object. Finally, if either condition fails, the End key has to have been pressed three consecutive times; the *:goBottom( )* and *:panEnd( )* methods are activated, and the value of *nEndKey* is reset to 0.

The same process is performed for the Home key, calling different methods and assigning different values. If the key pressed on line 90 is not the Home key, the value of *nHomeKey* is automatically reset to 0; and if it is not the End key, the value of *nEndKey* is set to 0 as well. This insures that the test for either *nHomeKey* or *nEndKey* is made for three consecutive keystrokes.

One way to look at this Perform( ) function is to look at the ReadModal( ) function for the GET system. In essence, once all of the objects in the *GETLIST[ ]* array have been processed, the final operation to be tackled is processing the keys within the GET system. Processing the objects and the end user keystrokes that interact with those objects is the most important concept to grapple with. In the past, DBEDIT( ) handled most of the operations; here, nothing is handled automatically or taken for granted.

Additional features have also been added to this browsing object. For example, whenever an item in the glossary is tagged or marked for deletion, not only is the DBDELETE( ) or DBRECALL( ) function called, but the method to send the cursor to the next cell is also called. Typically, the *down( )* method is called, sending the end user to the next cell. However, by defining a LOCAL variable to act as a toggle, the direction of the cursor can be altered to activate the *up( )* method or the *down( )* method. On line 29, the variable *lDefWay* is set to a logical true (.T.), which means that the browse cursor will move down as the deletion flag is toggled. On line 70, a small indicator is generated to tell the end user in which direction the browsing cursor will move. To change direction, the ALT_F key has been selected on lines 122 and 123 to simply assign to *lDefWay* the inverse of its original value. Then, if the DEL key (line 233) or the TAB key (line 102) is pressed, the IF( ) function is called to test the value of *lDefWay*. Based on that value, either the *:down( )* or *:up( )* method is activated, passing to it the *oBrowse* object.

Keeping track of scanning keys is just as simple. For example, a LOCAL variable named *cSearch* is set to a null character string on line 28. As keys are pressed and assigned to the *nKey* variable, eventually, if all previous tests fail, the test on line 250 will be made. If the key pressed falls within the ASCII range of 30 to 127, a SEEK operation will be performed in the Diction work area. However, before this occurs, an in-line assignment is made to the search variable, which takes on the character string value of the variable *nKey*. If the letter stored to search can be found in the Diction database, the *refreshall( )* method on line 252 is sent to the *oBrowse* object. If not, then the ALERT( ) function is called to inform the end user of the failed match.

As the search variable is modified, its value is displayed to the screen on line 72 after the browsing object *oBrowse* has been stabilized. Individual key values will be added to this string until the backspace key is pressed. Once the backspace key is pressed, the DBSEEK( ) function is called to perform another SEEK operation. The contents of *cSearch* becomes one character shorter. This, in effect, removes the last character from the search string and reissues a SEEK. In all cases, the *:refreshAll( )* method is called.

In processing the keys, if the ENTER key is pressed, data may be entered into the Diction database. If the current column position is 2, the highlighted cell is in the second column, which will be the word column. If so, the system colors are changed and an @ ... GET is called on line 199. If the value of *cTemp* is modified, the field is replaced and the entire browsing screen is refreshed. If the cursor is not on the second column, it will be on the fourth column; this will cause a call to MEMOEDIT( ) to be made. The color of the system will be changed if there is no previous value in the *cTemp* variable, which takes on the value of the field Define on line 209. In either case, when the process is finished, the *:forceStable( )* method will be recalled, forcing the browsing area to become stable once again. In the process, all values of the instance variables are rechecked and evaluated. This will cause the color of the system to change back to the default value assigned to the browsing instance variable *:colorSpec* on line 53.

Finally, this browsing object has the capacity not only to modify and enter data but to print the results as well. If the ALT_P key is pressed, the currently active cell is de-highlighted by the *:dehilite( )* method and the current record number is stored to a variable named *nAtRecord*. Then the PrintItems( ) routine is called on line 241. Once it has finished, the record pointer is repositioned to the value of *nAtRecord* and the cell is once again highlighted.

Within the PrintItems( ) routine starting on line 309, the output may be sent to the screen, to the printer, or to a predefined alternate file. These options are presented to the end user by the ALERT( ) function on line 311—a function that may be used in a wider variety of programming situations than the name may suggest.

Adding records to the database is handled by the ALT-A key, which is tested on line 245. Here, the AddDiction( ) routine is called, passing the browsing object *oBrowse* to it. If the value of the AddDiction( ) function is true, indicating that a record has been added, the browsing area will be refreshed. Inside of the AddDiction( ) routine, a secondary window is drawn with new colors, and the variable *cWord* is set to a blank value by MakeEmpty( ). The parameter passed to the MakeEmpty( ) function is the ordinal field position of the field being evaluated. Since word is the second field in Diction, a 2 is passed to this function. The @ ... SAY ... GET logic on line 372 is then performed and an item, if entered, is eventually added to the Diction work area.

From here it is easy to develop further possibilities. A menuing system nested above the browsing object could guide the end user. The browsing object is self-contained; it has viewing capabilities, data entry possibilities, and printing facilities. In essence, the browsing object is the system/application.

# TBROWSENEW( )

Another browsing function is TBROWSENEW( ). It is identical in structure to TBROWSEDB( ), except that the default code blocks that move the database file pointer and position the file pointer at the top and bottom of the file are not present. This means that TBROWSENEW( ) is geared to displaying nondatabase files and data structures like arrays, memos, and strings.

## BASICS

When working with databases and TBROWSEDB( ), block operations—positioning the pointer to the top or bottom of the data source and calculating the skipping operation of the browsing cursor—are simple; the Clipper database engine is fully equipped with the meaning of GO TOP, GO BOTTOM, and SKIP. However, outside of the database engine, these operations have to be defined for the data set that the browsing object is working on. Sometimes, this can be a difficult task. In the following example, a simple one-dimensional array with seven elements is put through Clipper's browsing object.

```
 1 : * File       Ob8.prg
 2 : * Compile    Rmake sample /dFILE:ob8
 3 :
 4 : #include "PTInkey.ch"
 5 : #include "PTVerbs.ch"
 6 :
 7 : procedure Main()
 8 :
 9 :    local aData := {}
10 :    local nCount
11 :    local oBrowse
12 :    local oColumn
13 :    local nPointer := 1
14 :    local nMoved
15 :    local nKey
16 :
17 :    for nCount := 1 to 7
18 :       aadd( aData, cdow( date()+nCount ) )
19 :    next
20 :
21 :    cls
22 :    oBrowse := tbrowsenew( 5, 10, 18, 25 )
23 :    oBrowse:skipblock := ;
24 :       {|nRequest| nMoved := if( abs(nRequest) >= ;
25 :          if(nRequest >= 0, len(aData)-nPointer,nPointer-1), ;
26 :          if(nRequest >= 0, len(aData)-nPointer,1-nPointer), ;
27 :          nRequest), nPointer+=nMoved, nMoved}
```

```
28 :
29 :      oBrowse:goBottomBlock := {|| nPointer := len(aData)}
30 :      oBrowse:goTopBlock    := {|| nPointer := 1}
31 :      oBrowse:headSep       := chr(205)
32 :
33 :      oColumn := tbcolumnnew( "Days;of;Week",  {|| aData[nPointer]} )
34 :      oColumn:width := 15
35 :
36 :      oBrowse:addColumn( oColumn )
37 :
38 :      REPEAT
39 :         oBrowse:forceStable()
40 :
41 :         if oBrowse:stable
42 :            nKey := inkey(0)
43 :
44 :            do case
45 :            case ( nKey == pDOWN_ARROW )
46 :               oBrowse:down()
47 :
48 :            case ( nKey == pUP_ARROW )
49 :               oBrowse:up()
50 :
51 :            case ( nKey == pEND )
52 :               oBrowse:gobottom()
53 :
54 :            endcase
55 :         else
56 :            exit
57 :         endif
58 :
59 :      UNTIL (lastkey() == pESC)
60 :      cls
61 :
62 : // End of File: Ob8.prg
```

When working with the TBROWSENEW( ) object, there is no internal pointer that will automatically position the cursor to the top or bottom of the array whenever a *goTop( )* or a *goBottom( )* method is called. Additionally, whenever a method to move the cell within the data set is issued, the instance variable *skipBlock* holds the code block that instructs the browsing object what to do. In short, it is possible to move the cursor beyond the end of an array subscript, either at the top or at the bottom.

The array *aData[ ]* contains seven elements. Additionally, a variable named *nPointer* is set to an initial value of 1 (line 13). After all of the elements have been added to the array, the instance for the TBROWSE object is generated and stored to the variable *oBrowse*. On lines 23 through 31, the three instance variables, which will hold the code blocks that tell the browse object how to move the internal pointer *nPointer*, are initialized. Since the variable *nPointer* is available at the time the code block on line 24 is created, the variable can be used in that code block even if the variable is LOCAL.

Before looking at these code blocks, a quick look to the column object is in order. Here, on line 33, it is clear that the value of the cell for this particular column object will be the value of the *aData[ ]* variable at subscript position *nPointer*. As *nPointer* is incremented or decremented by the *skipBlock* instance variable, the value of this cell will vary. Therefore, *nPointer* acts like a record pointer, skipping backward or forward depending on the motion of the method.

The *goBottomBlock* and *goTopBlock* instance variables are easy to understand. If an instruction to go to the top of the current data set is issued, the variable *nPointer* is reset to the value of 1; if the instruction to go to the end of the current data set is issued, the value of *nPointer* is set to the length of *aData[ ]*.

The skipping algorithm, however, is not as straightforward. As with the example in which we used TBROWSEDB( ) to simulate a filter condition, whenever a cursor movement is issued, the code block telling the browsing object how to skip through the data set is evaluated. This code block, when evaluated, is told how many data records or elements are to be skipped. It should always be thought of as a "request to skip," not an actual fact. If the *down( )* method is called, the request to skip is 1, which becomes the value of *nRequest* in the code block beginning on line 24. If the method *up( )* is called, the value of *nRequest* becomes –1.

If the current cell is positioned on the first element in *aData[ ]* and if the :down( ) method is called, the value of *nRequest* is 1. The variable *nMoved* is an intermediate variable to test if the request is allowed. For example, *nMoved* will be set to the value of the following expression:

```
IF( 1 >= IF( 1 >= 0, LEN(aData)-nPointer,nPointer-1), IF(1>=0,
LEN(aData)-nPoint,1-nPointer), 1)
```

Since *nPointer* is also 1 and LEN(*aData*) is 7, we can break this complex expression down to the following:

```
IF( 1 >= IF( 1 >= 0, 7-1, 1-1), IF( 1 >= 0, 7-1,1-1), 1)

nMoved := IF( 1 >= 6, 6, 1 )
```

This value is added to the value of *nPointer* to set the pointing variable to 2, which would be the current value for the next subscript to be evaluated in *aData[ ]*. If, on the other hand, the *up( )* method was called and the last cell in the array subscript was highlighted, the value of *nPointer* is –1, which would result in *nMoved* being set to the following expression:

```
IF(1>=IF( -1>=0, LEN(aData)-nPointer,nPointer-1), IF(-1>=0,
LEN(aData)-nPointer,1-nPointer), -1)
```

or

```
IF( 1 >= IF( -1 >= 0, 7-i,i-1), IF(-1>=0, 7-i, 1-i), -1)
```

and the value of *nPointer* will be 7, which expands to this:

```
IF( 1 >= IF( -1 >= 0, 7-7, 7-1), IF(-1 >= 0, 7-7,7-1), -1)
```

and to

```
nMoved := IF( 1 >= 6, 6, -1 )
```

The value of *nMoved* is then added to *nPointer* to set the new pointer to 6 rather than 7, which represents an upward movement in the object. Besides this small difference, the TBROWSENEW( ) object works the same as the TBROWSEDB( ).

## INTERMEDIATE AND ADVANCED EXAMPLES

Data structures other than arrays can be used with the TBROWSENEW( ) object. For example, these objects can be used in conjunction with the lowlevel file functions that allow large files to be viewed in a browsing area. The time this function takes depends in part on the disk access time for a particular machine. In some cases, loading a file into an array and processing the array will be far faster than working directly with the file. These topics and others are all covered in this example:

```
 1 : * File       Ob9.prg
 2 : * Compile    Rmake sampmore /dFILE:Ob9
 3 :
 4 : #include "PTInkey.ch"   // Power Tools header file with ASCII values
 5 : #include "PTColor.ch"   // Power Tools header file with color settings
 6 : #include "PTValue.ch"   // Power Tools header file with misc values
 7 : #include "PTVerbs.ch"   // Power Tools header file with commands/statements
 8 : #include "PTFuncs.ch"   // Power Tools header file with pseudofunctions
 9 :
10 : #xtranslate DEVRCLEAR(<c>)   => scroll(<c>,,<c>,)
11 : #xtranslate CopyFile(<a>, <b>) => __CopyFile( <a>, <b> )
12 :
13 : #xtranslate MAKESURE() => ALERT("Are you sure of this?", {"Yes", "No "}) == 1
14 :
15 : procedure Main()
16 :
17 :    cls
18 :    setcancel( pOFF )
19 :
20 :    Browse1( DosStru() )
21 :
22 : ******************
23 :
24 : function Browse1( aArray )
25 :
26 :    local oBrowse
27 :    local oColumn
28 :    local bDispBlock
29 :    local nPointer   := 1
30 :    local cFileSpec  := "*.*"
31 :    local cScreen    := savescreen()
32 :    local bDiskBlock
33 :    local cDirName
34 :    local nRow
35 :    local nCol
36 :    local lGoodKey
37 :    local nKey
38 :    local cVerb
39 :    local bExtra
40 :
41 :    private cTemp
42 :
43 :    setcursor( pCURSOR_OFF )
44 :    dispbox(1,0,16,52, pDBAR)
```

```
 45 :      dispbox(1,53,16,79,pDBAR)   // File Information
 46 :      dispbox(17,0,23,79, pDBAR) // Keystroke Area
 47 :
 48 :      oBrowse              := tbrowsenew(2,1,15,51)
 49 :      oBrowse:skipblock    := {|n| ArraySkip(n, @nPointer, len(aArray))}
 50 :      oBrowse:goTopBlock   := {|| nPointer := 1}
 51 :      oBrowse:goBottomBlock := {|| nPointer := len( aArray )}
 52 :
 53 :      bDispBlock := {|| space( OCCURRENCE("\",aArray[nPointer] )-1) + ;
 54 :                                          aArray[nPointer]}
 55 :
 56 :      oColumn := tbcolumnnew( "Directories on Disk", bDispBlock )
 57 :      oColumn:width := 49
 58 :
 59 :      oBrowse:addColumn( oColumn )
 60 :
 61 :      lGoodKey := pTRUE
 62 :      DispKeys1()
 63 :
 64 :      REPEAT
 65 :
 66 :         oBrowse:forceStable()
 67 :
 68 :         do case
 69 :         case oBrowse:hittop
 70 :            nPointer := 1
 71 :         case oBrowse:hitbottom
 72 :            nPointer := len(aArray)
 73 :         endcase
 74 :
 75 :         if lGoodKey
 76 :            DispFiles(cFileSpec, aArray[nPointer])
 77 :         endif
 78 :
 79 :         lGoodKey := pTRUE
 80 :         nKey     := inkey(0)
 81 :
 82 :         do case
 83 :         case ( nKey == pDOWN_ARROW )
 84 :            oBrowse:down()
 85 :
 86 :         case ( nKey == pUP_ARROW )
 87 :            oBrowse:up()
 88 :
 89 :         case ( nKey == pEND )
 90 :            oBrowse:gobottom()
 91 :
 92 :         case ( nKey == pPGUP )
 93 :            oBrowse:pageUp()
 94 :
 95 :         case ( nKey == pPGDN )
 96 :            oBrowse:pageDown()
 97 :
 98 :         case ( nKey == pHOME )
 99 :            oBrowse:gotop()
100 :
101 :         case ( nKey == pENTER ) // Explode the directory!
102 :            oBrowse:dehilite()
103 :            ShowDir( aArray, nPointer, cFileSpec )
104 :            oBrowse:hilite()
105 :            DispKeys1()
```

```
106 :        CLEARESC()
107 :
108 :     case ( nKey == pALT_E ) // Delete the contents
109 :       if MAKESURE()
110 :         DeleteAll(directory( aArray[nPointer]+cFileSpec), aArray[nPointer])
111 :       endif
112 :
113 :     case ( nKey == pALT_R ) // Remove the directory
114 :       if MAKESURE()
115 :         if len( directory( aArray[nPointer]+"*.*","HSD" ) ) > 2
116 :           ErrTone()
117 :           // The following is broken down into two
118 :           // statements in order to fit on the screen.
119 :           @ maxrow(), 00 SAY "Cannot remove a directory with items in it."
120 :           inkey(0)
121 :           DEVRCLEAR(maxrow())
122 :         else
123 :           if CURDIR() == aArray[nPointer]
124 :             run cd ..
125 :           endif
126 :           cTemp := left(aArray[nPointer], len(aArray[nPointer])-1)
127 :           run rd &cTemp.
128 :           adel(aArray, nPointer)
129 :           asize(aArray, len(aArray)-1)
130 :           oBrowse:refreshall()
131 :           oBrowse:gotop()
132 :         endif
133 :       endif
134 :
135 :     case ( nKey == pALT_C ) .or. ( nKey == pALT_M )
136 :       cVerb := IF(nKey == pALT_C, "Copy", "Move")
137 :
138 :       // Pick the subdirectory to move to
139 :       @ maxrow(), 0 SAY cVerb SAY " files from " ;
140 :                           SAY aArray[nPointer]+cFileSpec
141 :       nRow := row()
142 :       nCol := col()
143 :
144 :       cDirName := PickDir( aArray, nPointer )
145 :
146 :       if !empty( cDirName )
147 :         bDiskBlock := {|| devpos( 7, 55 ), devout( "Disk Space" ), ;
148 :                           devoutpict( diskspace(), "9,999,999,999" )}
149 :
150 :         bExtra := IF( cVerb == "Copy", ;
151 :                       {|y| pTRUE}, {|y| ferase(aArray[nPointer]+y)} )
152 :
153 :         @ nRow, nCol SAY " to " SAY cDirName
154 :
155 :         nCol := col()+2
156 :         AEVAL( DIRECTORY(aArray[nPointer]+cFileSpec, "HS"),,;
157 :                {|x| CopyFile( aArray[nPointer]+x[1], ;
158 :                      cDirName+x[1]), eval(bExtra, x[1]),,;
159 :                      eval(bDiskBlock), devpos(nRow,nCol), devout(x[1])} )
160 :
161 :         // copy all files to that subdirectory
162 :       endif
163 :
164 :       DEVRCLEAR(maxrow())
165 :
166 :     case ( nKey == pALT_F ) // Change File Spec
```

```
167 :        oBrowse:dehilite()
168 :        MakeSpec( @cFileSpec )
169 :        oBrowse:hilite()
170 :        DispKeys1()
171 :        CLEARESC()
172 :
173 :     case ( nKey == pESC )
174 :        if alert( "Are you sure you want to Quit?", {"Yes", "No "} ) != 1
175 :           CLEARESC()
176 :        endif
177 :
178 :     otherwise
179 :        lGoodKey := pFALSE
180 :
181 :     endcase
182 :
183 :   UNTIL (lastkey() == pESC)
184 :
185 :   setcursor( pCURSOR_ON )
186 :   restscreen(0,0,maxrow(),maxcol(),cScreen)
187 :
188 :   VOID
189 :
190 : *******************
191 :
192 : static function ShowDir( aArray, nPntr, cFileSpec )
193 :
194 :   local cScreen1  := savescreen(1, 0, 16, 52 )
195 :   local cSearch   := ""
196 :   local aFiles    := directory(aArray[nPntr] + cFileSpec, "HSD")
197 :   local oNewOb    := tbrowsenew(2,1,15,51)
198 :   local nPointer  := 1
199 :   local nTotSize  := 0
200 :   local nTagged   := 0
201 :   local cScreen2  := savescreen( 1,53,16,79 )
202 :   local cDir      := aArray[nPntr]
203 :   local nValue
204 :   local nRow
205 :   local nCol
206 :   local nLimit
207 :   local nForLoop
208 :   local oColumn
209 :   local nKey
210 :   local cDirName
211 :   local cVerb
212 :   local bExtra
213 :   local bDiskBlock := {|| devpos( 7, 55 ), devout( "Disk Space"), ;
214 :                           devoutpict( diskspace(), "9,999,999,999")}
215 :
216 :   aeval( aFiles, {|x| nTotSize += x[2], aadd(x, " ")} )
217 :
218 :   dispbox(1,0,16,52, pSBAR )
219 :   setcolor( MAKECOLOR( pBLACK/pWHITE ) )
220 :   @ 1, 1 say cDir
221 :   setcolor( MAKECOLOR( pWHITE/pBLACK ) )
222 :
223 :   if aFiles != NIL
224 :
225 :     oNewOb:skipblock      := {|n| ArraySkip(n, @nPointer, len(aFiles))}
226 :     oNewOb:goTopBlock     := {|| nPointer := 1}
227 :     oNewOb:goBottomBlock  := {|| nPointer := len( aFiles )}
```

```
228 :
229 :        oColumn := tbcolumnnew(" ", {|| aFiles[nPointer, 6]} )
230 :        oColumn:width := 1
231 :        oNewOb:AddColumn( oColumn )
232 :
233 :        oColumn := tbcolumnnew("File Names", {|| aFiles[nPointer, 1]})
234 :        oColumn:width := 12
235 :        oNewOb:AddColumn( oColumn )
236 :
237 :        oColumn := tbcolumnnew("Sizes",;
238 :                  {|| transform(aFiles[nPointer, 2], "999,999,999")})
239 :        oColumn:width := 13
240 :        oNewOb:AddColumn( oColumn )
241 :
242 :        oColumn := tbcolumnnew( "Date;Stamps", {|| aFiles[nPointer, 3]})
243 :        oColumn:width := 8
244 :        oNewOb:AddColumn( oColumn )
245 :
246 :        oColumn := tbcolumnnew( "Time;Stamps", {|| aFiles[nPointer, 4]})
247 :        oColumn:width := 8
248 :        oNewOb:AddColumn( oColumn )
249 :
250 :        oColumn := tbcolumnnew( " ", {|| aFiles[nPointer, 5]} )
251 :        oColumn:width := 3
252 :        oNewOb:AddColumn( oColumn )
253 :
254 :        DispKeys2()
255 :
256 :        oNewOb:colPos := 2
257 :
258 :        REPEAT
259 :
260 :           oNewOb:forceStable()
261 :
262 :           do case
263 :           case oNewOb:hittop
264 :             nPointer := 1
265 :           case oNewOb:hitbottom
266 :             nPointer := len( aFiles )
267 :           endcase
268 :
269 :           DispFiles(cFileSpec, cDir, if(aFiles= NIL, 0, len(aFiles)),;
270 :                     nTotSize, nTagged, cSearch)
271 :
272 :           nKey   := inkey(0)
273 :
274 :           do case
275 :           case ( nKey == pDOWN_ARROW )
276 :              oNewOb:down()
277 :
278 :           case ( nKey == pUP_ARROW )
279 :              oNewOb:up()
280 :
281 :           case ( nKey == pEND ,
282 :              oNewOb:gobottom()
283 :
284 :           case ( nKey == pPGUP )
285 :              oNewOb:pageUp()
286 :
287 :           case ( nKey == pPGDN )
288 :              oNewOb:pageDown()
```

```
289 :
290 :         case ( nKey == pHOME )
291 :           oNewOb:gotop()
292 :
293 :         case ( nKey == pALT_T )
294 :           if aFiles[nPointer, 6] != chr(16)
295 :             nTagged++
296 :             aFiles[nPointer, 6] := chr(16)
297 :             oNewOb:refreshcurrent()
298 :           endif
299 :           oNewOb:down()
300 :
301 :         case ( nKey == pALT_R )
302 :           IF MAKESURE()
303 :             DeleteAll( aFiles, cDir )
304 :
305 :             // The following must be done this way because when the ADEL()
306 :             // function works it removes the element and leaves the last
307 :             // element NIL.  Therefore, the LIMIT range must be decreased
308 :             // and the position of X must be re-executed.  For this reason,
309 :             // the FOR ... NEXT loop is more efficient than an AEVAL().
310 :
311 :             nLimit := len(aFiles)
312 :             for nForLoop := 1 to nLimit
313 :               if aFiles[nForLoop, 6] == CHR(16)
314 :                 adel(aFiles, nForLoop--)
315 :                 nLimit--
316 :               endif
317 :             next
318 :             asize(aFiles, len(aFiles)-nTagged)
319 :             nTagged := 0
320 :             oNewOb:refreshall()
321 :             oNewOb:gotop()
322 :           endif
323 :
324 :         case ( nKey == pALT_E )
325 :           if MAKESURE()
326 :             aFiles[nPointer, 6] := chr(16)
327 :             DeleteAll( directory(cDir+aFiles[nPointer, 1]), cDir )
328 :             adel(aFiles, nPointer)
329 :             asize(aFiles, len(aFiles)-1)
330 :             oNewOb:refreshall()
331 :           endif
332 :
333 :         case ( nKey == pBKSP )
334 :           if !empty( cSearch )
335 :             cSearch := left(cSearch, len(cSearch)-1)
336 :             if !empty( nValue := ascan( aFiles, {|x| x[1] == cSearch}))
337 :               nPointer := nValue
338 :               oNewOb:refreshall()
339 :             endif
340 :           endif
341 :
342 :         case ( nKey == pENTER )
343 :           if aFiles[nPointer, 5] != "D"
344 :             oNewOb:dehilite()
345 :             ShowFile( cDir + aFiles[nPointer, 1], aFiles[nPointer, 2] )
346 :             oNewOb:hilite()
347 :             CLEARESC()
348 :           endif
349 :
```

```
350 :        case nKey == pALT_U
351 :           if aFiles[nPointer, 6] != chr(32)
352 :             nTagged--
353 :             aFiles[nPointer, 6] := chr(32)
354 :             oNewOb:refreshcurrent()
355 :           endif
356 :           oNewOb:down()
357 :
358 :        case ( nKey == pALT_K )
359 :           @ maxrow(), 00 say "Copy tagged files to "
360 :           nRow := row()
361 :           nCol := col()
362 :
363 :           if !empty( cDirName := PickDir( aArray, nPntr )  )
364 :
365 :              @ nRow, nCol SAY " to " SAY cDirName
366 :
367 :              aeval( aFiles, {|x| IF( x[6] == chr(16) .and. x[5] != "D", ;
368 :                  (CopyFile( cDirName+x[1], cDirName+x[1]), eval(bDiskBlock), ;
369 :                    devpos(nRow,nCol), devout(cDirName+x[1])),NIL)} )
370 :           endif
371 :
372 :           DEVRCLEAR(maxrow())
373 :
374 :        case ( nKey == pALT_M ) .OR. ( nKey == pALT_C)
375 :           cVerb := if(nKey == pALT_C, "Copy", "Move")
376 :           @ maxrow(), 00 SAY cVerb SAY " file " SAY aFiles[nPointer, 1]
377 :           nRow := row()
378 :           nCol := col()
379 :
380 :           cDirName := PickDir( aArray, nPntr )
381 :
382 :           if !empty( cDirName ) .and. aFiles[nPointer, 5] != "D"
383 :
384 :              bExtra := if( cVerb == "Copy", {|| pTRUE}, {|x| FERASE(cDirName + ;
385 :                  x[1])})
386 :              @ nRow, nCol SAY " to " SAY cDirName
387 :              nCol := col()+2
388 :
389 :              CopyFile(cDir+aFiles[nPointer, 1], cDirName+aFiles[nPointer, 1])
390 :
391 :              eval(bExtra, aFiles[nPointer])
392 :              eval(bDiskBlock)
393 :              @ nRow, nCol say cDirName + aFiles[nPointer, 1]
394 :
395 :           endif
396 :
397 :           DEVRCLEAR(maxrow())
398 :
399 :        otherwise
400 :           cSearch += upper( chr(nKey) )
401 :           nValue := ascan( aFiles, {|aFileStuff| aFileStuff[1] == cSearch} )
402 :           if !empty( nValue )
403 :              nPointer := nValue
404 :              oNewOb:refreshall()
405 :           endif
406 :
407 :        endcase
408 :
409 :     UNTIL (LASTKEY() == pESC)
410 :
```

```
411 :      else
412 :        ErrTone()
413 :        @ 3, 5 say "No Files Match!"
414 :        DispKeys2()
415 :        inkey(0)
416 :      endif
417 :
418 :      restscreen( 1, 0, 16, 52, cScreen1 )
419 :      restscreen( 1,53, 16, 79, cScreen2 )
420 :
421 :      VOID
422 :
423 : ********************
424 :
425 : static function ShowFile( cFile, nSize )
426 :
427 :      local oShowOb  := tbrowsenew(2,1,15,51)
428 :      local cScreen1 := savescreen(1, 0, 16, 52 )
429 :      local nBuffer  := int( len( cScreen1 ) / 2 )
430 :      local nFhandle := fopen( cFile )
431 :      local nLength  := FLength( nFhandle )
432 :      local nPointer := 1
433 :      local oColumn
434 :      local nKey
435 :
436 :      oShowOb:skipblock     := {|n| ArraySkip(n, @nPointer, nLength)}
437 :      oShowOb:goTopBlock    := {|| nPointer := 0}
438 :      oShowOb:goBottomBlock := {|| nPointer := nLength }
439 :
440 :      oColumn := tbcolumnnew( "", {|| left(Freadline(nFhandle, nPointer), 50)} )
441 :      oColumn:width := 50
442 :
443 :      oShowOb:addColumn( oColumn )
444 :
445 :      dispbox( 1, 0, 16, 52, replicate( chr(178), 8 ) + chr(32) )
446 :      @ 1, 2 say " " + cFile + " "
447 :
448 :      REPEAT
449 :
450 :        oShowOb:forceStable()
451 :
452 :        do case
453 :        case oShowOb:hittop
454 :          nPointer := 1
455 :        case oShowOb:hitbottom
456 :          nPointer := nLength
457 :        endcase
458 :
459 :        nKey   := INKEY(0)
460 :
461 :        do case
462 :        case ( nKey == pDOWN_ARROW )
463 :          oShowOb:down()
464 :
465 :        case ( nKey == pUP_ARROW )
466 :          oShowOb:up()
467 :
468 :        case ( nKey == pEND )
469 :          oShowOb:gobottom()
470 :
471 :        case ( nKey == pPGUP )
```

```
472 :        oShowOb:pageUp()
473 :
474 :      case ( nKey == pPGDN )
475 :        oShowOb:pageDown()
476 :
477 :      case ( nKey == pHOME )
478 :        oShowOb:gotop()
479 :
480 :    endcase
481 :
482 :  UNTIL (lastkey() == pESC)
483 :
484 :  fclose( nFhandle )
485 :  restscreen( 1, 0, 16, 52, cScreen1 )
486 :
487 :  VOID
488 :
489 : *******************
490 :
491 : static function ShowString( nFhandle, nPointer )
492 :
493 :    // read a string, move the file pointer, strip CHR(13)+CHR(10)
494 :    // character combinations, adjust pointer, and move on.
495 :
496 :    local cBuffer := space(50)
497 :
498 :    fseek(nFhandle, nPointer, 0)
499 :    fread(nFhandle, @cBuffer, 50)
500 :
501 :    if pCRLF $ cBuffer
502 :      cBuffer := left(cBuffer, at(pCRLF, cBuffer)-1 )
503 :    endif
504 :
505 :    nPointer += LEN(cBuffer)
506 :
507 :    return(cBuffer)
508 :
509 : *******************
510 :
511 : static function MakeSpec( cFileSpec )
512 :
513 :    local cScreen := savescreen(17,0,23,79)
514 :    local getlist := {}
515 :
516 :    cFileSpec := padr(cFileSpec, 12)
517 :
518 :    dispbox(17,0,23,79, pSBAR)
519 :
520 :    @ 19,10 say "Enter New File Spec: " get cFileSpec pict "@K@!"
521 :    read
522 :    cFileSpec := alltrim( cFileSpec )
523 :
524 :    restscreen(17,0,23,79,cScreen)
525 :
526 :    VOID
527 :
528 : *******************
529 :
530 : static function DeleteAll( aFiles, cPath )
531 :
532 :    local bProcess
```

```
533 :      local bDiskBlock := {|| devpos( 7, 55 ), devout( "Disk Space" ),;
534 :                       devoutpict( diskspace(), "9,999,999,999")}
535 :
536 :      if len( aFiles[1] ) == 6 // This has tagged files!
537 :         bProcess := {|x| if(!empty(x[6]) .and. x[5] != "D", ;
538 :                        (devpos(maxrow(),00), devout( "Deleting: "+;
539 :                         padr(x[1], maxcol()))), ;
540 :                         ferase(cPath+x[1]), eval(bDiskBlock)),NIL)}
541 :      else
542 :         bProcess := {|x| if( x[5] != "D", (devpos(maxrow(),00), ;
543 :                         devout("Deleting: " + padr(x[1], ;
544 :                         maxcol())), ferase(cPath+x[1]), ;
545 :                         eval(bDiskBlock)), NIL)}
546 :      endif
547 :
548 :      aeval( aFiles, bProcess )
549 :
550 :      @ maxrow(), 0 say "All Finished.  Any key to continue."
551 :      inkey(0)
552 :      DEVRCLEAR(maxrow())
553 :
554 :      VOID
555 :
556 : *********************
557 :
558 : static function DispFiles( cSpec, cDirName, nFiles, nSizes, ;
559 :                                               nTagged, cSeekItem)
560 :
561 : #define DRAWBAR CHR(199) + REPLICATE( CHR(196), 25)  + CHR(182)
562 : #xtranslate PutBar(<x>) => ( DEVPOS(<x>, 53), DEVOUT( DRAWBAR ) )
563 :
564 :     local aTemp
565 :
566 :     static cVolume
567 :
568 :     if cVolume == NIL
569 :       aTemp    := directory("*.*", "V")
570 :       cVolume  := if(empty(len(aTemp)), "None", aTemp[1] )
571 :     endif
572 :
573 :     @ 2, 55 SAY "File Spec: " SAY padr(cSpec, 13)
574 :     PUTBAR(3)
575 :
576 :     @ 4, 55 say "Directory Name"
577 :     @ 5, 55 say padr(cDirName, 24)
578 :     PUTBAR(6)
579 :
580 :     @ 7, 55 say "Disk Space"
581 :     devoutpict( diskspace(), "9,999,999,999" )
582 :     PUTBAR(8)
583 :
584 :     @ 9, 55 say "Number of Files"
585 :     if( nFiles == NIL, devout("        "), devoutpict( nFiles, "99999" ))
586 :     PUTBAR(10)
587 :
588 :     @ 11, 55 SAY "Volume Label:" SAY cVolume
589 :     PUTBAR(12)
590 :
591 :     @ 13, 55 say "Dir. Size: "
592 :     if !( nSizes == NIL )
593 :        devoutpict( nSizes, "999,999,999" )
```

```
594 :    endif
595 :
596 :    PUTBAR(14)
597 :    @ 15, 55 say "Tagged Files: "
598 :    if nTagged != NIL
599 :       devoutpict( nTagged, "99999" )
600 :    endif
601 :
602 :    if !( cSeekItem == NIL )
603 :       devpos(16,2)
604 :       if !empty( cSeekItem )
605 :          devout( "Search: " )
606 :       endif
607 :       devout( padr(cSeekItem,30, chr(196)) )
608 :    endif
609 :
610 :    VOID
611 :
612 : *******************
613 :
614 : static function DispKeys1()
615 :
616 :    dispbox(17,0,23,79,pDBAR)
617 :
618 :    @ 18, 5 SAY "ENTER - Select a Directory      " ;
619 :            SAY "ALT-E - Erase directory contents "
620 :    @ 19, 5 SAY "ALT-R - Remove a directory      " ;
621 :            SAY "ALT-C - Copy Directory Contents  "
622 :    @ 20, 5 SAY "ALT-M - Move Directory Contents " ;
623 :            SAY "All Cursor Keys as expected      "
624 :    @ 21, 5 SAY "ALT-F - Change the File Spec    " ;
625 :            SAY "ESC - Quit "
626 :
627 :    VOID
628 :
629 : *******************
630 :
631 : static function DispKeys2()
632 :
633 :    dispbox(17,0,23,79,pSBAR)
634 :
635 :    @ 18, 5 SAY padr("ALT-E - Erase a file", 38) ;
636 :            SAY "ENTER - View a File         "
637 :    @ 19, 5 SAY padr("ALT-M - Move a File", 38) ;
638 :            SAY "ALT-T - Tag a file          "
639 :    @ 20, 5 SAY padr("ALT-C - Copy a File", 38) ;
640 :            SAY "ALT-U - Untag a File        "
641 :    @ 21, 5 SAY padr("ALT-R - Remove tagged files", 38) ;
642 :            SAY "  ESC - Quit                "
643 :    @ 22, 5 SAY padr("ALT-K - Copy Tagged Files", 38) ;
644 :            SAY "All Cursor Keys as expected "
645 :
646 :    VOID
647 :
648 : ********************
649 :
650 : static function ArraySkip( nRequest, nPointer, nLength )
651 :
652 :    local nCount
653 :
654 :    nCount := if( abs(nRequest) >= ;
```

```
655 :                    if(nRequest >= 0, nLength-nPointer, nPointer-1 ),;
656 :                    if(nRequest >= 0, nLength-nPointer, 1-nPointer), nRequest )
657 :
658 :    nPointer += nCount
659 :
660 :    return( nCount )
661 :
662 : *********************
663 :
664 : static function PickDir( aDirs, nAtWhat )
665 :
666 :    local cScreen    := savescreen(1,0,16,52)
667 :    local cRetValue := ""
668 :    local nPointer   := 1
669 :    local oColumn
670 :    local oBrow
671 :    local bDispBlock
672 :    local nKey
673 :
674 :    setcolor( MAKECOLOR( pBLACK/pWHITE, pWHITE/pBLACK ) )
675 :    dispbox(2,1,15,51,pDBAR)
676 :
677 :    @ 2,2 SAY " Current Dir: " SAY left(aDirs[nAtWhat], 20)
678 :
679 :    oBrow              := tbrowsenew(3,2,14,50)
680 :    oBrow:skipblock    := {|n| ArraySkip(n, @nPointer, len(aDirs))}
681 :    oBrow:goTopBlock   := {|| nPointer := 1}
682 :    oBrow:goBottomBlock := {|| nPointer := len( aDirs )}
683 :
684 :    bDispBlock := {|| space( OCCURRENCE("\",aDirs[nPointer] )-1 ) + ;
685 :                     aDirs[nPointer]}
686 :
687 :    oColumn := tbcolumnnew( "Directories on Disk", bDispBlock )
688 :    oColumn:width := 48
689 :
690 :    oBrow:addColumn( oColumn )
691 :
692 :    REPEAT
693 :
694 :      oBrow:forceStable()
695 :
696 :      do case
697 :      case oBrow:hittop
698 :         nPointer := 1
699 :      case oBrow:hitbottom
700 :         nPointer := len(aDirs)
701 :      endcase
702 :
703 :      nKey := inkey(0)
704 :
705 :      do case
706 :      case ( nKey == pENTER )
707 :         cRetValue := aDirs[nPointer]
708 :         exit
709 :
710 :      case ( nKey == pDOWN_ARROW )
711 :         oBrow:down()
712 :
713 :      case ( nKey == pUP_ARROW )
714 :         oBrow:up()
715 :
```

```
716 :        case ( nKey == pEND )
717 :           oBrow:gobottom()
718 :
719 :        case ( nKey == pPGUP )
720 :           oBrow:pageUp()
721 :
722 :        case ( nKey == pPGDN )
723 :           oBrow:pageDown()
724 :
725 :        case ( nKey == pHOME )
726 :           oBrow:gotop()
727 :
728 :        endcase
729 :
730 :     until (lastkey() == pESC)
731 :     setcolor( MAKECOLOR( pWHITE/pBLACK, pBLACK/pWHITE ) )
732 :
733 :     restscreen(1,0,16,52,cScreen)
734 :     CLEARESC()
735 :
736 :     return( cRetValue )
737 :
738 : ********************
739 :
740 : function DosStru( cFiles )
741 :
742 :    local nCounter := 0
743 :    local aDir     := {"\"}
744 :    local cScreen  := savescreen(maxrow(), 0, maxrow(), maxcol())
745 :    local aSubs
746 :
747 :    setpos( maxrow(), 0 )
748 :
749 :    while ++nCounter <= len( aDir )
750 :
751 :      if !empty( len( aSubs := Getdirs( aDir[nCounter], cFiles ) ) )
752 :         aeval(aSubs, {|x| aadd(aDir, x)} )
753 :      endif
754 :
755 :    enddo
756 :
757 :    restscreen(maxrow(), 0, maxrow(), maxcol(), cScreen)
758 :
759 :    return( asort(aDir) )
760 :
761 : ******************
762 :
763 : static function Getdirs( cPattern )
764 :
765 :    local aRet := {}
766 :
767 :    aeval( directory(cPattern + "*.*", "D"), ;
768 :           {|aFIles| if( aFIles[5] == "D" .and. ;
769 :                      !("."==aFIles[1] .or. ".."==aFIles[1]),;
770 :                      ( qqout(chr(13)+padr(cPattern+aFIles[1]+"\", maxcol()) ),;
771 :                      aadd(aRet, cPattern + aFIles[1] + "\")), "" )} )
772 :
773 :    return( aRet )
774 :
775 : *****************
776 :
```

```
777 : static function ErrTone()
778 :
779 :    tone(164.80, 4)
780 :    tone(130, 1)
781 :
782 :    VOID
783 :
784 : ********************
785 :
786 : static function FLength( nFHandle )
787 :
788 :    // This function is designed to figure out the number of lines in a
789 :    // file based on CHR(13)+CHR(10) character combinations
790 :
791 :    #define pBUFFER_SIZE 4096
792 :
793 :    local lExit     := pFALSE
794 :    local nPointer  := 0
795 :    local counter   := 0
796 :    local cBuffer
797 :    local nBegin
798 :    local nLocation
799 :
800 :    fseek( nFHandle, 0 )
801 :    while !lExit
802 :       cBuffer := space( pBUFFER_SIZE )
803 :       lExit   := !( fread(nFHandle, @cBuffer, pBUFFER_SIZE ) == pBUFFER_SIZE )
804 :       nBegin  := 1
805 :
806 :       while pTRUE
807 :          if !empty( nLocation := at( pCRLF, substr(cBuffer, nBegin ) ) )
808 :             nPointer++
809 :             nBegin += nLocation+1
810 :          else
811 :             exit
812 :          endif
813 :       enddo
814 :    enddo
815 :
816 :    return( ++nPointer )
817 :
818 : ********************
819 :
820 : static function Freadline( nFHandle, cLine )
821 :
822 :    local lExit     := pFALSE
823 :    local cRetValue := space( pBUFFER_SIZE )
824 :    local nPointer  := 0
825 :    local cBuffer
826 :    local nBegin
827 :    local nLocation
828 :
829 :    fseek( nFHandle, 0 )
830 :
831 :    while !lExit
832 :       cBuffer := space( pBUFFER_SIZE )
833 :       lExit   := !( fread(nFHandle, @cBuffer, pBUFFER_SIZE ) == pBUFFER_SIZE )
834 :       nBegin  := 1
835 :
836 :       while pTRUE
```

```
837 :
838 :        nLocation := at( pCRLF, substr(cBuffer, nBegin) )
839 :
840 :        if !empty( nLocation )
841 :           if ++nPointer == cLine
842 :              cRetValue := substr(cBuffer, nBegin, nLocation-1)
843 :              exit
844 :           endif
845 :           nBegin += nLocation+1
846 :        else
847 :           exit
848 :        endif
849 :     enddo
850 :  enddo
851 :
852 :  return( cRetValue )
853 :
854 : // End of File:Ob9.prg
```

Typically, the ALT-C key combination will terminate a Clipper application; however, if this key is deactivated by the SETCANCEL( ) function, thus shutting off ALT-C as a termination key, it will return a regular INKEY( ) value of 302. This value is assigned to a manifest constant within the header file PTINKEY.CH. This is also true for the ALT-D key, which ordinarily activates the debugger. If ALT-D(0) is used to disable ALT-D as the activation key for the debugger, ALT-D will also return an INKEY( ) value of 288.

After the necessary preprocessor directives, the screen is cleared, the cancellation key (Alt-C or Ctrl-Break) is turned off, and the Browse1( ) function is called, passing it the value returned by the user-defined function DosStru( ).

DosStru( ), which begins on line 740, returns an array containing the directory structure of the currently logged drive. As it executes, however, it displays the name of each directory as it is scanned an entered into the array returned by the function. Once DosStru( ) terminates, control returns to Browse1( ), the central browsing routine in OB9.PRG.

To help show the purpose and direction of this programming example, listed below are the various support functions and their purpose:

| | |
|---|---|
| Browse1( ) | The main browsing routine. |
| ShowDir( ) | Creates an object to view the files within a selected subdirectory. |
| ShowFile( ) | Creates an object to view a file using the low-level file functions. |
| ShowString( ) | Returns a string of a specific line. |
| MakeSpec( ) | Contains the GET for changing the skeleton of the file specification. |
| DeleteAll( ) | A generic function that deletes files from a subdirectory or deletes files tagged for deletion. |
| DispFiles( ) | Displays general file information regardless of which browsing object is active. This includes disk space, file specification, number of files in a directory, number of tagged files within a subdirectory, and the size of a directory. |
| DispKeys1( ) | Displays the available key strokes for the first object that lists directories on the currently logged drive. |

| | |
|---|---|
| DispKeys2( ) | Displays the available key strokes for the second object that lists individual files in a subdirectory. |
| IsStable( ) | Used by all of the objects to stabilize the object and to return a stable state for keystroke processing. |
| ArraySkip( ) | Used by all of the objects to move the element pointer for the SKIPBLOCK instance variable in the various objects. |
| PickDir( ) | A secondary call to the DOS tree structure; allows the end user to pick a subdirectory to copy or move files to. |
| DosStru( ) | Returns an array of the directory structure on the currently logged drive. |
| GetDirs( ) | A supporting function for the DosStru( ) function. |
| ErrTone( ) | Generates an error sound. |
| FLength( ) | Returns the number of lines in a file. |
| Freadline( ) | Returns a specific line from a file. |

The Browse1( ) routine creates a browsing object for *aArray[ ]*, the array returned from DosStru( ). Within this routine, two important variables are initialized and assigned values: *nPointer* and *cFileSpec*. *cFileSpec* is a string variable that contains the file specification that will be used throughout this subroutine. The *nPointer* variable is just that—it points to an element within *aArray[ ]* as the methods and code blocks within instance variables are referenced.

To help understand how to set up a browsing area for an array, picture a small screen region that will contain elements from the array. Each element of the array will occupy one cell in the browsing object's column. In the *bDispBlock* variable on line 53, the contents of *aArray[ ]* at subscript position *nPointer* will be expressed. Whatever the value of *nPointer* is, that particular element in *aArray[ ]* will be displayed to the screen for each cell in this particular column.

When a skip is to be performed, the pointer variable is manipulated by the code block in the *skipBlock* instance variable. This is initialized on line 49 and refers to the ArraySkip( ) function. ArraySkip( ), which begins on line 650, has a LOCAL parameter *nCount* whose value is passed to the function from the browsing object and which represents the number of elements in the data set that are to be skipped. In other words, if the *down( )* method is called, it requests that +1 item be skipped. This value is then passed to the *skipBlock* instance variable, which will check to see if the requested number of items to skip is permitted and, if so, will perform it. If the *up( )* method is called for the *oBrowse* browsing object, a request to skip –1 item is made to the *skipBlock* instance variable, and this becomes the value of *nCount*. One of these values, based on the method that is performed, is passed to the ArraySkip( ) function, which simply adjusts the value of *nPointer* according to the value of *nCount* (the number of data elements to be skipped) and the total number of elements available, represented by the value of LEN(*aArray*). The value of *nPointer*, though LOCAL, is passed by reference to the ArraySkip( ) function, which allows any adjustment made to this variable to be visible to the calling routine once the ArraySkip( ) function has completed its task.

In addition, the *goTopBlock* instance variable on line 50 contains the code to assign the *nPointer* variable to 1, and the *goBottomBlock* instance variable on line 51 contains the code to assign the *nPointer* variable to the length (the total number of elements) of *aArray[ ]*. When a *goTop( )* method is performed, the *goTopBlock* instance variable is evaluated and the browsing area is repositioned to the top of the data set. When the *goBottom* method is evaluated, the *goBottomBlock* instance variable is evaluated and the browsing area is repositioned to the end of the data set.

These instance variables, and consequently the code block, are the fundamental force behind getting the browsing object to work with a data set other than a database. In working with a database, the functions to move the record pointer are inherent in the language: GO TOP, GO BOTTOM, and SKIP operations tell the internal mechanisms of the database engine what to do. Here, there is none of this, which means the capability has to be programmed into the data set. These operations and code assignments, in essence, define for an array what GO TOP, GO BOTTOM, and SKIP means to a database.

Once the column object has been established and related to the *oBrowse* browsing object, the keystroke processing loop begins on line 64, and forced stabilization occurs on line 66. The variable *lGoodKey*, used on line 75, is designed to be a toggle; if an invalid key is pressed, there is no need to recall the DispFiles( ) function on line 76, since no operation has taken place. If, on the other hand, a valid key has been pressed, the information displayed to the screen may be about to change. The OTHERWISE command on line 178 simply sets the value of *lGoodKey* to a logical false (.F.). This is the final statement in the large DO CASE command structure that processes all of the keystrokes for the *oBrowse* browsing object and it basically handles keystrokes that have no assigned purpose. The initial value of *lGoodKey* is set to a logical true (.T.), which is also the default value each time this processing loop is activated.

To maintain the *nPointer* variable in case the end or the beginning of the data set has been reached, the respective instance variables are tested on lines 68 through 73, and, if true (.T.), the value of *nPointer* is adjusted. This is to prevent a blank cell from appearing at either the top or the bottom of the data set assigned to the *oBrowse* object.

The keys that cause the most complicated activities are the ENTER key, tested on line 101, and the ALT-C or ALT-M keys, beginning on line 135. The ENTER key branches off to other operations, whereas the ALT-C and ALT-M options are limited to a few lines of code.

Frequently, several operations in a program may be very similar. For example, in our sample program, ALT-C copies all files from one subdirectory to another, whereas the ALT-M key moves all files from one subdirectory to another. The only difference between the two tasks is that moving files involves a deletion process in addition to the copy process. On line 136, the LOCAL variable *cVerb*, which will be used as a display message, is initialized with either the string "Copy" or the string "Move." *cVerb* also is used to condition the assignment of a code block beginning on line 150. Here, if the value condition of the variable *cVerb* is the string "Copy", the code block assigned to the variable *bExtra* is nothing more that a logical true (.T.)—in essence, a dummy code block. However, if the value of *cVerb* is not "Copy", the code block assigned to *bExtra* involves a call to the FERASE( ) function. On lines 156–159, the code block will always copy the files from a subdirectory to another, but the code block assigned to the variable *bExtra* performs the deletion, thus completing the "move" task. Since this is a "copy" operation, the amount of available disk space may be altered. Instead of waiting for the operation to be completed, the code that is used to position the cursor at the appropriate screen location as well as to display the amount of available disk space is stored to a code block variable. This variable, *bDiskBlock*, defined on lines 147 and 148, is included in the code block evaluated by the AEVAL( ) on lines 156–159. It will be evaluated for each file that is to be copied or moved.

Before the copy or move operation begins, the name of the subdirectory to which files are to be copied or moved needs to be obtained. This comes from the PickDir( ) function, which generates yet another object containing the directory structure originally obtained from the DosStru( ) function. The variable *cDirName* on line 144 holds the name of this subdirectory; if no value is in *cDirName*, no selection was made from the PickDir( ) function and the operation is aborted. However, if there is a value in *cDirName*, the AEVAL( ) function call beginning on line 156 begins the iterative process. The DIRECTORY( ) function uses the file specification to build an array containing the names of the files in the selected directory (*aArray[nPointer]*). This array will include hidden and system files, but will exclude directories. Each element of this array is passed to the code block and becomes the value of *x*. The DIRECTORY( ) function returns an array with only the names of the files. The path of each file, originally stored in *aArray[nPointer]*, needs to be concatenated with each filename processed by the code block in the AEVAL( ) function. This string is passed to the pseudo-function CopyFile( ), which simply copies the file from the subdirectory currently highlighted in the *oBrowse* browsing area to the subdirectory named in the variable *cDirName*.

Once the copy process is completed, the evaluation of both the *bExtra* code block and the *bDiskBlock* code block occurs. In the first call to EVAL( ), the value of *x[1]* is the name of the file that was just copied. This then becomes the value of *y* in the code block, provided the "move" operation was selected. If the "copy" selection was made, the code block ignores the attempt to pass a parameter and performs, in essence, no operation other than returning a logical true (.T.) value (line 159). The second call to EVAL( ) using the *bDiskBlock* variable causes the value of the DISKSPACE( ) function to be redisplayed to the appropriate screen location. Using code blocks within code blocks is an efficient way to group similar operations without too much extra coding.

The other key to consider is the ENTER key, tested on line 101. Here, the current cell is de-highlighted using the *dehilite( )* method. Then, a call to the ShowDir( ) function is made, passing to it the array of the directory structure, the value of *cFileSpec*, and the current subscript position stored in the variable *nPointer*. ShowDir( ), beginning on line 192, explodes the file information found in the highlighted subdirectory. A new array is built that contains all of the files in the selected subdirectory based on the value of the parameter *cFileSpec*. The value of *nPointer* from Browse1( ) is stored in the variable *nPntr*. *nPointer* in Browse1( ) is not to be confused with the new LOCAL variable also named *nPointer*—because they are LOCAL variables, variables with identical names may be used in separate procedures or functions without affecting one another. The LOCAL variable *aFiles* is a derivative of the original array selection.

ShowDir( ) generates a new browsing object, *oNewOb*, that will contain more than just one column of information. Before the column objects are defined, the array *aFiles[ ]* is further manipulated on line 216, where two operations are performed. First, the total number of bytes used by the files in the selected subdirectory is stored to the variable *nTotSize*, based on the size of each file scanned by the code block in the AEVAL( ) function. This in-line assignment sums the value of the sizes of all files including hidden, system, and directories. In addition, since the value of *x* in the code block on line 216 is nothing more than a pointer to another array, the second dimension of that array is dynamically increased by one element and a blank space is stored at that location. The reason for this will become clear in a moment.

As with the first object named *oBrowse*, the data elements for *oNewOb* are found in an array; but this array will contain more than one dimension. However, the basic code blocks (that is to say those code blocks used to position the variable pointer to the appropriate location) also may be used for this browsing object. The first column object to be added to this new browsing object contains the newly installed elements of the second dimension of the array *aFiles[ ]*. This column will have a single space as the header and the value of the sixth subscript position of *nPointer* in the *aFiles[ ]* array. Each column after this contains one of the subarrays from the second dimension of the *aFiles[ ]* array. For example, the second column will display the names of the files obtained by the DIRECTORY( ) function on line 196 and stored to the first element in each subarray in the *aFiles[ ]* array.

From here, the same basic principle of browsing stabilization and keystroke processing takes effect. If the ALT-T or ALT-U keys are pressed, the element found in the sixth position of the subarray at the *nPointer* position of *aFiles[ ]* is manipulated. On line 294, for example, if the value of this element is not equal to CHR(16), the tagged variable counter is incremented and a CHR(16) is stored to this element. This newly added subscript position thus becomes a special subscript used for tagging and untagging files in this browsing object. A similar operation is performed by the ALT-U keystroke, which will untag tagged files.

Within this browsing object, some additional keystrokes are supported: ENTER, ALT-R, and any alphabetic character, including the BKSP character. If the ALT-R key is pressed, files that were tagged are removed from the directory. However, this does not remove the names of those files from the array currently being displayed in the *oNewOb* browsing area. In this case, however, it is much easier to work with a FOR ... NEXT loop to traverse and update the array than it is to use the AEVAL( ) function. The number of files in the directory before any files were deleted is stored to the variable *nLimit* on line 311. This variable is used instead of the direct call to the LEN( ) function, since the number of elements in the *aFiles[ ]* array is about to fluctuate. A call to ADEL( ) will remove the element at position *nForLoop*. It will in turn move all remaining elements in the *aFiles[ ]* array up one position, leaving the last element in the array as NIL. This means two things. First, the elements at the end of the array *aFiles[ ]* do not need to be processed and compared (line 313) since they have a NIL value. Second, with the ADEL( ) function, the value of the element at the *nForLoopth* position after a deletion is now new and needs to be reprocessed. For these reasons, the values of limit and *nForLoop* need to be decremented by 1 each time a call to ADEL( ) is made. This takes place on lines 314 and 315. Programming this algorithm for AEVAL( ) would have been more complicated than it is worth. Once all elements have been removed from the array, the array *aFiles[ ]* is resized, the variable *nTagged* is reset, and the browsing area is refreshed and repositioned to the top of the data set.

The BKSP keystroke works with the *cSearch* variable. Here, alphabetic keys are processed by the OTHERWISE statement on line 399. The character strings of the ASCII values are added to *cSearch*. Then, the ASCAN( ) function is used to search for the first occurrence of *cSearch* in the *aFiles[ ]* array. The code block on line 401 is used to process the first element in each nested array in *aFiles[ ]*. If there is a match, *nValue* will contain subscript position of that item. The variable *nPointer* is then assigned this value, and the browsing object *oNewOb* on line 404 is refreshed. If the BKSP character is pressed, this same process takes place, but on a string with the last character removed; on line 335, the value of *cSearch* is decremented one character.

The final keystroke deals with yet another object. In the first two examples, the browsing objects have used either single dimensional or multidimensional arrays as their data elements. Another possibility is to have the browsing objects access a file on the disk. This is slow to process; however, there is no memory limitation since the file in question is not brought entirely into memory. If the ENTER key is pressed in the keystroke processing loop for the *oNewOb* object (line 342) and if the highlighted element is not a directory, the ShowFile( ) function is called. The first parameter passed is the name of the file preceded by its directory path; the second parameter is the file size.

The ShowFile( ) function on line 425 uses the low-level file function FOPEN( ) to open the file. The FLength( ) function calculates the number of lines in that file based on the assumption of a CHR(13)+CHR(10) line terminator. This value is stored to the variable length and acts as the LEN( ) function for the previously manipulated arrays. The length of the file is needed to position the pointer variable on the correct line. Again, a new LOCAL variable, *nPointer*, is used; instead of pointing to subscript positions, this will point to actual lines in a text file. The same type of code blocks are then assigned to the various instance variables for the newly created instance of the browsing object, *oShowOb*. The column displayed will be a single line, with no more than 50 characters of that line being shown in a cell region. The smaller the line width, the faster this object will process the information; however, it will handle all types of files of all sizes, regardless of internal memory constraints.

Object-oriented programming can be a challenge. We have to think in terms of the relation of the cells to the columns, the columns to the browsing area, and the browsing area to the data set that is involved. However, this type of programming allows new avenues to be explored and, as a result, new applications to be developed.

## An Advanced Example Using DICT( )

As seen in example OB6.PRG, we used the *:cargo* instance variable to hold values that the TBROWSE object would need. With more and more things being stored to that one slot, it becomes important to come up with a mechanism that will allow unlimited items (within reason) to be stored to that one slot without confusion. The idea is known as a data dictionary; several functions in the Clipper arsenal come with the right functions to handle the task. In the example below, a multidimensional array is browsed with both the dataset and the data pointer stored to a data dictionary held in the :cargo instance variable.

```
1 : * File      Ob10.prg
2 : * Compile   Clipper Ob10
3 : * Link      RtLink fi ob10 lib Samples P11 Base52
```

```
  4 :  #include "PTInkey.ch"    // Power Tools header file with ASCII values
  5 :  #include "PTColor.ch"    // Power Tools header file with color settings
  6 :  #include "PTValue.ch"    // Power Tools header file with misc values
  7 :  #include "PTVerbs.ch"    // Power Tools header file with commands/statements
  8 :  #include "PTFuncs.ch"    // Power Tools header file with pseudofunctions
  9 :
 10 :  *******************
 11 :
 12 :  function Main()
 13 :
 14 :     scroll()
 15 :
 16 :     DirNames( directory() )
 17 :
 18 :     return( NIL )
 19 :
 20 :  *******************
 21 :
 22 :  function DirNames( aDirs )
 23 :
 24 :     #define pDATADICT oBrowArray:cargo
 25 :
 26 :     local oBrowArray
 27 :     local oColumn
 28 :     local nKey     := 0
 29 :     local cScreen  := savescreen(4,10,17,70)
 30 :     local k
 31 :
 32 :     setcursor( pCURSOR_OFF )
 33 :
 34 :     dispbox( 4, 10, 17, 70, pDBAR )
 35 :
 36 :     oBrowArray                := tbrowsenew(5,11,16,69)
 37 :
 38 :     oBrowArray:cargo          := dictnew()
 39 :     dictput( pDATADICT, "POINTER", 1 )      // First element position
 40 :     dictput( pDATADICT, "DATA", aDirs )     // Second element position
 41 :
 42 :     oBrowArray:headSep        := "==="
 43 :     oBrowArray:colSep         := " | "
 44 :     oBrowArray:SkipBlock      := ;
 45 :        { |n| k := if( abs(n) >= ;
 46 :                    if( n >= 0, ;
 47 :                        len( dictat( pDATADICT, "DATA") ) - ;
 48 :                            dictat(pDATADICT,"POINTER"), ;
 49 :                            dictat(pDATADICT,"POINTER") - 1), ;
 50 :                    if(n >= 0, dictat( pDATADICT, "DATA") - ;
 51 :                            dictat(pDATADICT,"POINTER"), ;
 52 :                            1 - dictat(pDATADICT,"POINTER")), n), ;
 53 :          dictput(pDATADICT,"POINTER", dictat(pDATADICT,"POINTER") + k), k}
 54 :
 55 :     oBrowArray:goTopBlock    := {|| dictput( pDATADICT, "POINTER", 1 ) }
 56 :     oBrowArray:goBottomBlock := ;
 57 :        {|| dictput( pDATADICT, "POINTER", len( dictat( pDATADICT, "DATA")) )}
 58 :
 59 :     oColumn := tbcolumnnew("File Name", ;
 60 :        {|| dictat( pDATADICT, "DATA" )[dictat( pDATADICT, "POINTER"), 1] } )
 61 :     oColumn:width := 14
 62 :     oBrowArray:addColumn(oColumn)
```

```
 63 :
 64 :      oColumn := tbcolumnnew("File Size", ;
 65 :         {|| dictat( pDATADICT, "DATA" )[dictat( pDATADICT, "POINTER"), 2] } )
 66 :      oColumn:width := 10
 67 :      oBrowArray:addColumn(oColumn)
 68 :
 69 :      oColumn := tbcolumnnew("File Date", ;
 70 :         {|| dictat( pDATADICT, "DATA" )[dictat( pDATADICT, "POINTER"), 3] } )
 71 :      oColumn:width := 10
 72 :      oBrowArray:addColumn(oColumn)
 73 :
 74 :      oColumn := tbcolumnnew("File Time", ;
 75 :         {|| dictat( pDATADICT, "DATA")[dictat( pDATADICT, "POINTER"), 4] } )
 76 :      oColumn:width := 10
 77 :      oBrowArray:addColumn(oColumn)
 78 :
 79 :   PROCESS
 80 :
 81 :      if dictat( pDATADICT, "POINTER") > len( dictat( pDATADICT, "DATA") )-2
 82 :         oBrowArray:gotop()
 83 :         loop
 84 :      endif
 85 :
 86 :      oBrowArray:forceStable()
 87 :
 88 :      if !RegularKeys( (nKey := inkey(0)), oBrowArray )
 89 :
 90 :         if nKey == pESC
 91 :            exit
 92 :         endif
 93 :
 94 :      endif
 95 :
 96 :   END PROCESS
 97 :
 98 :   restscreen(  4, 10, 17, 70, cScreen)
 99 :
100 :   setcursor( pCURSOR_ON )
101 :
102 :   VOID
103 :
104 : *******************
105 :
106 : static function RegularKeys( nKey, oObject )
107 :
108 :    local lRetValue := pTRUE
109 :
110 :    do case
111 :    case nKey == pDOWN_ARROW
112 :       oObject:Down()
113 :
114 :    case nKey == pUP_ARROW
115 :       oObject:Up()
116 :
117 :    case nKey == pRIGHT_ARROW
118 :       oObject:Right()
119 :
120 :    case nKey == pLEFT_ARROW
121 :       oObject:Left()
```

```
122 :
123 :        case nKey == pHOME
124 :           oObject:colPos := 1
125 :           oObject:refreshCurrent()
126 :
127 :        case nKey == pEND
128 :           oObject:colPos := 4
129 :           oObject:refreshCurrent()
130 :
131 :        case nKey == pPGUP
132 :           oObject:colPos := 1
133 :           oObject:pageUp()
134 :
135 :        case nKey == pPGDN
136 :           oObject:colPos := 1
137 :           oObject:pageDown()
138 :
139 :        otherwise
140 :           lRetValue := pFALSE
141 :
142 :        endcase
143 :
144 :        return( lRetValue )
145 :
146 : // Ob10.prg
```

Functionally, this works like the previous example program, using the *:cargo* instance variable of the *oBrowArray* object. However, rather than forcing the array of information held in *:cargo* to be rigid and inflexible, the various data dictionary functions found in SAMPLES.LIB are used. First, on line 38, a new dictionary array is created and stored to the *:cargo* instance variable via the DICTNEW( ) function. Then, two entries are created via the DICTPUT( ) function. This function not only places the first entry into the data dictionary, but will act as a replacement function should any of the values within the dictionary need to be updated. The first entry will have a tag name of "POINTER" and will default to a value of 1 (line 39); the second entry will be called "DATA" and will contain the multidimensional array *aDirs[ ]*, as passed into the DirNames( ) function on line 22. The manifest constant pDATADICT refers to the *oBrowArray:cargo* slot as seen on line 24. This way, it is easier to refer to the dictionary location rather than constantly coding in the *:cargo* instance variable for this particular browsing object.

A simple example of using these functions can be seen on line 55, where goTopBlock is assigned a code block. Here, going to the top means resetting the pointer variable to 1: This is when the code block calls the DICTPUT( ) function and tells the "POINTER" slot to store a 1 to it. A more complex version of this can be seen on the next line. Here, going to the bottom means taking the number of elements in the dataset and storing that to the pointer position. Within this code block, the DICTAT( ) function retrieves the item known as "DATA" within the data dictionary slot pDATADICT. The length of this value is then used to pass back to the DICTPUT( ) function for the item known as "POINTER". Complex? Take time to understand the complexity of the *:skipBlock* code block on lines 44 through 53: It is the manipulation of the dictionary functions, treating the :cargo slot in terms of key words and multiple values.

# The GET Object

The GET object is easier to handle than the TBROWSE object. Instead of working with a complete screen region with related TBCOLUMN objects panning through it, the GET object deals with only one particular area on the screen in which data may be entered by the end user. For a browsing object, the cell is the smallest unit; this is also the focus of the GET object. There are differences, which serve to distinguish this new object. Every GET command generates an identical instance of the GET object; the values of various instance variables may differ based on which clauses in the GET command are used.

Two functions can be used to generate a GET object. The first is an internal function, while the second is documented.

_GET_( )     Creates a new GET object to a variable.
GETNEW( )    Creates a new GET object to a variable.

The creation of an instance of a GET object is handled by the preprocessor whenever an @ ... GET command is issued. A typical @ ... GET command is translated into the following statement:

```
SetPos(<row>, <col>) ;;
AAdd( GetList, _GET_(<var>, <(var)>, <pic>, <{valid}>, <{when}>):display() )
```

Once the cursor has been placed at the assigned coordinates by the SETPOS( ) function, an instance of the GET class is dynamically stored to the *GetList[ ]* array. Once contained in this array, the ReadModal( ) function, which is the translated READ command, merely processes each GET object in this array as an individual element. (The ReadModal( ) function consists of pure Clipper code and may be found in the GETSYS.PRG program file.) When an instance is generated, the current cursor position is taken into consideration, and the values for ROW( ) and COL( ) are immediately assigned to some of the instance variables within the GET object structure for that particular object.

The syntax for this internal function is

```
<variable> := _GET_( <expC1>, "<expC1>", <expC2>, <expB3>, <expB4> ):display()
```

<expC1>     The variable that is to participate in the GET
"<expC1>"   The string of the name of the variable participating in the GET
<expC2>     The PICTURE template to be used in the GET
<expB3>     A post-validation code block for the GET
<expB4>     A pre-validation code block for the GET

A documented function, GetNew( ), also creates a GET object. Its syntax is the following:

```
<variable> := GETNEW([<expN1> [,<expN2> [,<expB3>
[,<expC4> [,<expC5> [,<expC6>]]]]]])
```

<expN1>     The row position of the GET object.
<expN2>     The column position of the GET object.
<expB3>     The code block used to SET/GET the value of the GET variable.
            Do not use MEMVARBLOCK for arrays in a GET.

&lt;expC4&gt;    The variable in the GET/SET code block.
&lt;expC5&gt;    The PICTURE clause.
&lt;expC6&gt;    The COLOR string.

The structure of this object class is the following:

### GET Instance Variables

BADDATE    Contains a logical true (.T.) value if the variable being edited in the edit buffer is a date data type and if the value is invalid. This instance variable will contain a logical false (.F.) value if the variable is not a date data variable or if the date entered is valid. This is not an assignable instance variable.

BLOCK    Contains the code block that is used to set or to get the individual value of a GET variable. This is typically set via the MEMVARBLOCK( ) function. The code block assigned to this instance variable may take an optional parameter argument that will assign the value of the variable. If no parameter is specified, the code block should return the current value of the variable. This is an assignable instance variable.

BUFFER    Contains a character value that defines the editing buffer used by the GET object. Once the object has input focus, the contents of this variable will be any data type other than NIL. This is an assignable instance variable.

CARGO    Contains any data value that is to be used in conjunction with this particular GET object. This instance variable is assignable.

CHANGED    Will be assigned a true (.T.) value if the specified buffer has changed in value since the GET object received input focus. This is not an assignable instance variable.

CLEAR    This contains a logical value that indicates whether the editing buffer should be cleared before any value is entered. This is set to a logical true (.T.) via the :*setfocus( )* method as well as the :*undo( )* method.

COL    Contains the numeric value of the column coordinate of the GET object that is displayed. This is an assignable instance variable.

COLORSPEC    Contains the character string used to define the video attribute bytes for the GET object. The string must have two color patterns. The first is used to set the unselected color that is used when the GET object does not have input focus. The second is used to set the selected color that is used when the GET object has input focus. This is an assignable instance variable.

DECPOS    Contains a numeric value that specifies the position of the decimal point within the editing buffer. This is not an assignable instance variable.

EXITSTATE       Contains the numeric value that represents the state by which a GET was exited. The following table is used to set the values of this instance variable:

0   No exit performed
1   The up arrow key
2   The down arrow key
3   The top of the GET buffer
4   The bottom of the GET buffer
5   The ENTER key
6   A formal write exit
7   The ESC key was pressed
8   The WHEN clause is not satisfied

This is an assignable instance variable.

HASFOCUS        Will be assigned a logical true (.T.) value should the GET object have input focus. This is not an assignable instance variable.

MINUS           Contains a logical value indicating that a minus sign has been added to the editing buffer. This will only be a logical true (.T.) if the data type of the variable involved with this GET object is numeric.

NAME            Contains the name of the variable involved with the GET object. This is an assignable instance variable.

ORIGINAL        Contains the original value of the GET object. Disregard this variable. Use the *varGet( )* and *varPut( )* methods for the GET object.

PICTURE         Contains a character string that defines the PICTURE template and picture formatting functions used to control the editing of the GET object. This is an assignable instance variable.

POS             Indicates the position of the cursor within the editing buffer. If the GET object does not yet have input focus, this instance variable will be a NIL data value. This is not an assignable instance variable.

POSTBLOCK       Contains the code block used to validate a GET object after completion of input focus. If the newly entered value should complete the GET object, this code block should evaluate to a logical true (.T.) value. This is an assignable instance variable.

PREBLOCK        Contains the code block used to validate a GET object prior to receiving input focus. When evaluated, this code block should return a logical true (.T.) if the GET object is to obtain input focus. This is an assignable instance variable.

READER          Contains a code block that defines special behavior for a READ. This is an assignable instance variable.

REJECTED        Contains a logical true (.T.) value if the last character specified in either the INSERT or OVERSTRIKE method was rejected. This is not an assignable instance variable.

*Clipper Objects* 935

ROW — Contains the numeric value of the row coordinate of the GET object that is displayed. This is an assignable instance variable.

SUBSCRIPT — Contains the subscript position of the element in an array involved with a particular GET. If the reference is to a position in a single-dimension array, the value of this instance variable will be the value representing that subscript position. This is an assignable instance variable.

TYPE — Contains the single character string that represents the data type of the GET variable. This is not an assignable instance variable.

TYPEOUT — Contains a logical true (.T.) value should the most recent message/method attempt to move the cursor out of the editing buffer. This will also contain a logical true (.T.) value should no editable position exist in the edit buffer. This is not an assignable instance variable.

## *GET Methods*

ASSIGN( ) — Assigns the contents of the edit buffer to the GET variable by evaluating the BLOCK instance variable. This will have purpose only when the GET object has input focus.

BACKSPACE( ) — Moves the cursor to the left one position and deletes that character as it moves.

COLORDISP( ) — Changes a GET object's color and redisplays it.

DELETE( ) — Deletes the character directly under the cursor.

DELEND( ) — Deletes the characters directly under the cursor position to the end of the GET buffer.

DELLEFT( ) — Deletes the character to the left of the cursor without moving the position of the cursor.

DELRIGHT( ) — Deletes the character to the right of the cursor without moving the position of the cursor.

DELWORDLEFT( ) — Deletes one word to the left of the cursor position.

DELWORDRIGHT( ) — Deletes one word to the right of the cursor position.

DISPLAY( ) — Displays the contents of the BUFFER instance variable of the GET object on the screen so long as the GET object has been granted input focus. Otherwise, the BLOCK instance variable is evaluated and the results are displayed.

END( ) — Moves the cursor to the rightmost editable position in the edit buffer.

HOME( ) — Moves the cursor to the leftmost editable position in the edit buffer.

| | |
|---|---|
| INSERT( ) | Allows the specified character to be inserted into the editing buffer at the current cursor position, shifting the existing contents of the editing buffer to the right. |
| KILLFOCUS( ) | Terminates the input focus of a GET object. |
| LEFT( ) | Moves the cursor to the left one position within the editing buffer. |
| OVERSTRIKE( ) | Allows the specified character to be inserted into the editing buffer at the current cursor position, overwriting the existing contents of the buffer. |
| RESET( ) | Resets the GET object's internal information so long as the GET object has been granted input focus. |
| RIGHT( ) | Moves the cursor to the right one position within the editing buffer. |
| SETFOCUS( ) | Gives input focus to the specified GET object. It will create and initialize all the GET object's internal information and will display the contents of the editing buffer on the screen. |
| TODECPOS( ) | Moves the cursor to the immediate right of the decimal point position within the edit buffer. This will take place if there is a numeric value in the edit buffer. |
| UNDO( ) | Sets the value of the original GET value and redisplays the GET edit buffer. |
| UNTRANSFORM( ) | Converts the character value in the editing buffer back to the data type of the original value. |
| UPDATEBUFFER( ) | Updates the edit buffer and redisplays the current GET value. |
| VARGET( ) | Returns the current value of the GET variable. |
| VARPUT( ) | Assigns the GET variable the value that is passed as a parameter to this method. |
| WORDLEFT( ) | Moves the cursor one word to the left within the edit buffer. |
| WORDRIGHT( ) | Moves the cursor one word to the right within the edit buffer. |

The purpose of the edit buffer is to grant input focus to a particular GET object. This is in principle the same as stabilizing a browsing area, which sets up the hard task of programming the keystroke possibilities. Once focus is granted to the GET object, there is a direct connection between the end user, keyboard, and the variable in the application. Without focus, there is no GET system. The GET system is discussed at length in Chapter 18, "Data Entry Options."

## The Error Object

The fourth object provided with Clipper 5.2 pertains to the error-handling system in a Clipper application. Errors fall into a class by themselves; all errors behave in a similar manner. In a later chapter of this book is a complete error handling system that may be linked into a

Clipper application to provide additional error handling and reporting capabilities (Chapter 19).

The basic function that will create an error object is

```
<variable> := ErrorNew()
```

where <variable> contains an object of the Error class instance.

The ERRORBLOCK( ) function is used within a Clipper application to set a code block to be processed by the error-handling system. This is not a part of the Error system; rather, it is a hook into that system that will work with the application and not against it.

The structure of this object class is the following:

## ERRORNEW( ) Instance Variables

| | |
|---|---|
| ARGS | An array that contains arguments that will be supplied to an operator or to a function when an argument error has occurred. For all other error types, the value will be a NIL. This is an assignable instance variable. |
| CANDEFAULT | Contains a logical true (.T.) value if there is an error recovery system available for the error. A logical false (.F.) value will otherwise be stored to this slot. This is an assignable instance variable. |
| CANRETRY | Contains a logical true (.T.) value if the application's subsystem is allowed to retry the operation that originally caused the error. If the CANSUBSTITUTE instance variable contains a logical true (.T.) value, this instance variable will not contain a logical true (.T.) value. This is an assignable instance variable. |
| CANSUBSTITUTE | Contains a logical true (.T.) value if a new result can be substituted for the operation that originally produced the error condition. This is an assignable instance variable. |
| CARGO | Contains any data value that is to be used in conjunction with this particular error object. This is an assignable instance variable. |
| DESCRIPTION | Contains a string that describes the error condition. This is an assignable instance variable. |
| FILENAME | Contains a character string that has the name of the original file in which the error occurred. This is an assignable instance variable. |
| GENCODE | Contains an integer that represents a Clipper generic error code. The preprocessor definitions for these numeric values are<br>  1  EG_ARG<br>  2  EG_BOUND<br>  3  EG_STROVERFLOW<br>  4  EG_NUMOVERFLOW<br>  5  EG_ZERODIV<br>  6  EG_NUMERR |

*(continued)*

| | | |
|---|---|---|
| GENCODE *(continued)* | 7 | EG_SYNTAX |
| | 8 | EG_COMPLEXITY |
| | 11 | EG_MEM |
| | 12 | EG_NOFUNC |
| | 13 | EG_NOMETHOD |
| | 14 | EG_NOVAR |
| | 15 | EG_NOALIAS |
| | 16 | EG_NOVARMETHOD |
| | 17 | EG_BADALIAS |
| | 18 | EG_DUPALIAS |
| | 19 | EG_CYCLICAL |
| | 20 | EG_CREATE |
| | 21 | EG_OPEN |
| | 22 | EG_CLOSE |
| | 23 | EG_READ |
| | 24 | EG_WRITE |
| | 25 | EG_PRINT |
| | 30 | EG_UNSUPPORTED |
| | 31 | EG_LIMIT |
| | 32 | EG_CORRUPTION |
| | 33 | EG_DATATYPE |
| | 34 | EG_DATAWIDTH |
| | 35 | EG_NOTABLE |
| | 36 | EG_NOORDER |
| | 37 | EG_SHARED |
| | 38 | EG_UNLOCKED |
| | 39 | EG_READONLY |
| | 40 | EG_APPENDLOCK |

OPERATION     Contains a character string that describes the operation that was attempted when the error took place. This is an assignable instance variable.

OSCODE     Contains an integer that represents the DOS error code associated with the error condition. This is an assignable instance variable.

SEVERITY     Describes the severity of the error condition, using a numeric value. The following table is used to describe the value of the possible error severity. The manifest constants in the far right column may be found in the ERROR.CH header file, as follows:

| | | |
|---|---|---|
| 0 | No error, not important | ES_WHOCARES |
| 1 | Warning | ES_WARNING |
| 2 | General error | ES_ERROR |
| 3 | Fatal error | ES_CATSTROPHIC |

SUBCODE     Contains an integer that represents the subsystem-specific error code. This is an assignable instance variable.

SUBSYSTEM         Contains a string that represents the name of the internal subsystem that generated the error.

TRIES             Contains a number that represents the number of times the operation has been attempted and failed. This is not an assignable instance variable.

## Conclusion

The conclusions to be drawn from these examples are, at best, staggering to our previous programming consciousness. Our limited view of the world served the community well in an era of limited storage capacity, limited computer power, and limited programming possibilities. However, a new dawn has broken, and object-oriented programming is not only here before us, but it is here to evolve onto a new plateau. The concept of a linear approach to programming for a graphical user interface is difficult, if not overwhelming. Object-oriented programming lends itself to building more and more complex problem-solving routines by building on the instances and methods of preexisting object models. Every application we write has some degree of commonality and, until now, we have been reprogramming those commonalities to fit the end user. Now, the object we create can infer information and data from other preexisting objects. As a result, larger and larger systems will be constructed in far less development time. This is the age that allows the code of a programmer to blossom into a programming idea, which in turn builds many applications that reflect this idea. We are one step away from user-definable objects. When that step has been taken, the bridge between the hypothetical and reality will be built on our abilities to dream, to hope, and to create.

# 17

# Windowing, Screens, and Menus

After the databases have been properly defined, relations mapped out, indexes built, and reports defined and sketched out, the final step of application development is that part which interfaces with the end user. This includes designing banners and titles, menus, colors, sounds, and, finally, windows. In Clipper 5.2, the advent of arrays and code blocks as formal data types greatly helps the development of these interface objects.

## Basic Screen Control

When an application is being developed, there are two basic considerations besides menus and windows. The first is screen layout. This includes colors, banners, and titles: the color of the basic screen, the shape of the banner for each menu item to be selected, and the title and position of each. The preprocessor and code blocks can be used in conjunction with one another to help with this process. The second consideration is the interface chosen for escape paths (normally the ESC key), the placement of error messages, and sounds generated for any condition or situation.

To start, individual functions and pseudofunctions may be used to build a standard banner interface. These functions and pseudofunctions may be called individually or collectively as a batch of operations. The concept comes from the idea of Clipper being able to call functions like commands and the idea of an extended expression containing several suboperations. For example, this one expression would develop a banner:

```
xDummy := (scroll(), dispbox(0,0,4,maxcol()), Title())
```

The value of the last function within the expression, Title( ), is simply stored to a variable dummy, which can be ignored. In the meantime, three different operations have been batched together to make a banner.

Code blocks may also be used to give a formal name to this batch operation, which adds meaning, purpose, and clarity to the code:

```
bBanner := {|| scroll(), dispbox(0,0,4,maxcol()), Title() }
```

Now, whenever the banner needs to be displayed, a simple call to EVAL( ) with the proper code block, *bBanner*, will generate the right results. In addition, parameters may be passed to the code block to provide for specific items to be used in one (or more) of the functions within the code block. For example, the Title( ) function could accept a character string as the title to be displayed. Passing that string to the code block must be planned in advance.

```
bBanner := {|cName| scroll(), dispbox(0,0,4,maxcol()), Title(cName)}
```

In this code block example, a string that is a local parameter called *cName* will be passed to the code block. It in turn will be passed to the Title( ) function. Using the EVAL( ) function to call the code block and passing the proper string to it, the call would look something like this:

```
eval( bBanner, "Main Menu" )
```

The string "Main Menu" is then passed to the code block that is passed to the TITLE( ) function.

However, to someone reading the source code, this call to EVAL( ) does not easily and graphically describe what this code block does. Instead, we can use the preprocessor to translate the stale EVAL( ) into something more meaningful.

```
#xtranslate BANNER( <b>, <string> ) => eval( <b>, <string> )
```

Now, a call to BANNER( ) is nothing more than a preprocessed call to EVAL( ). This may be extended one additional step: Since the same code block is used repeatedly for each banner to be displayed, the preprocessor can reference the code block as well:

```
#xtranslate BANNER( <string> ) => ;
            eval( {|cName| scroll(), dispbox(0,0,4,maxcol()), ;
            Title(cName)}, <string> )
```

Besides banners and titles, the same concept may be used to display error messages, prompts, and dialog boxes.

```
 1 : * File      Banner1.prg
 2 : * Compile   Rmake sample /dFILE:Banner1
 3 :
 4 : #include "PTValue.ch"   // Power Tools' Header file of misc. values
 5 : #include "PTColor.ch"   // Power Tools' Header file of color
 6 : #include "PTInkey.ch"   // Power Tools' Header file of ASCII values
 7 : #include "PTFuncs.ch"   // Power Tool's Header file of pseudofunctions
 8 : #include "PTVerbs.ch"   // Power Tool's Header file of commands/statements
 9 :
10 : #xtranslate BANNER(<exp>) => eval({|cTitle| dispbox(0,0,4,maxcol(),pDBAR), ;
11 :     devpos(1, 1), devout(cAppName), devpos(2, 1), devout(cAppVer), ;
12 :     devpos(1,60), devout(padl(date(), 19)),;
13 :     devpos(2,60), devout(padl(cAppDev, 19)), TITLE(cTitle)}, <exp>)
14 :
15 : #xtranslate MESSAGES( <exp> ) => ;
16 :         ( scroll(maxrow(),0,maxrow(),maxcol()), devpos(maxrow(),0), ;
17 :         devout( <exp> ), inkey(0) )
18 :
```

## Windowing, Screens, and Menus

```
19 : #xtranslate PALETTE() => ( setcolor( "B/W" ), ;
20 :                dispbox(0,0,maxrow(),maxcol(), replicate( chr(178), 9 ) ), ;
21 :                setcolor( "W/B, N/W,,, W/B" ) )
22 :
23 : #xtranslate ASKYESNO( <exp> ) => eval( {|x| YesNo(x, maxrow(), 0)}, <exp> )
24 :
25 : #xtranslate TITLE( <item> ) => ;
26 :              ( devpos(3, int( (maxcol()-2-len(<item>)) / 2 ) ),;
27 :                devout( <item> ), pTRUE )
28 :
29 : procedure Main()
30 :
31 :    local cAppName := "Call Tracking System"
32 :    local cAppVer  := "1.0"
33 :    local cAppDev  := "Sirius Software"
34 :
35 :    cls
36 :    BANNER( "Main Menu" )
37 :    MESSAGES( "Press any key for next frame" )
38 :
39 :    setcolor( MAKECOLOR( pBLACK/pWHITE ) )
40 :    BANNER( "Utility Menu" )
41 :    MESSAGES( "Press any key for Palette!" )
42 :
43 :    PALETTE()
44 :    BANNER( "Call Tracking's Main Menu" )
45 :    if ASKYESNO( "Do you want to continue? " )
46 :      BANNER( "Second Screen" )
47 :      MESSAGES( "Final screen... any key to continue..." )
48 :    endif
49 :    scroll()
50 :
51 : *********************
52 :
53 : static function YesNo( cString, nRow, nCol )
54 :
55 :    local cOption := ""
56 :    local lRetVal := pFALSE
57 :
58 :    scroll( nRow, nCol, nRow, maxcol() )
59 :
60 :    REPEAT
61 :
62 :      devpos( nRow, nCol )
63 :      devout( cString )
64 :      devpos( row(), col()+1 )
65 :
66 :      cOption := chr(inkey(0))
67 :
68 :      if cOption$"YyNn"
69 :         devout( if( lRetVal:= (cOption$"Yy"), "Yes", "No ") )
70 :      endif
71 :
72 :    UNTIL lastkey() == pENTER
73 :
74 :    return( lRetval )
75 :
76 : // End of File: Banner1.prg
```

The key here is that most of the standard interface for an application can be set up in a header file. In this particular example, the interface for this program is standardized around lines 10 through 28, in lines for the preprocessor that may also reside in a separate include file. Each application can have a separate and unique interface, but the overhead to create and support such an interface is minimal—the preprocessor handles most of the work. There are five pseudofunctions; three of the five use the DEVPOS( ) and DEVOUT( ) functions, simple screen functions, and the EVAL( ) function. In the case of the Banner( ) pseudofunction, a call to another defined pseudofunction helps clear up the meaning of certain words and function calls.

Once the screen is cleared on line 35, a call to the standard BANNER( ) interface is made, using the string "Main Menu" as the title for the banner area. This in turn is translated as a call to EVAL( ) with the code block coded directly by the preprocessor. Nested within this code block is a call to the pseudofunction named Title( ). This, too, is translated to the proper expression. Once the banner is drawn, the message "Press any key for next frame" is displayed at the proper location, and the program waits for a keystroke. These three lines of code are translated into this:

```
Scroll() ; SetPos(0,0)

eval({|cTitle| dispbox(0,0,4,maxcol(),"ÉÍ»°¼°ÍÈ"), devpos(1, 1), ;
   devout(cAppName), devpos(2, 1), devout(cAppVer), devpos(1,60), ;
   devout(padl(date(), 19)), devpos(2,60), devout(padl(cAppDev, 19)), ;
   ( devpos(3, int( (maxcol()-2-len(cTitle)) / 2 ) ), ;
   devout( cTitle ),  .T. )}, "Main Menu")

( scroll(maxrow(),0,maxrow(),maxcol()), devpos(maxrow(),0), ;
   devout( "Press any key for next frame" ), inkey(0) )
```

In fact, in our example, there is only one "real" function: YesNo( ). All of the others are pseudofunctions. These use the preprocessor to translate expressions that may be used in building an application with a standard interface.

Screen colors are another consideration in an application. More color monitors are in place on personal computers, and effective use of color is vital if an application is to be well received. For example, a cyan background with red letters is not appealing under most data entry conditions. Some suggest the best color is the simplest color—a black background with white letters. However, this is generally too straining on the eyes. Softer background colors are more pleasing; contrasting colors, whether highlighted or not, make for easier reading.

In Clipper, color options and screen selections are simple to implement with the SETCOLOR( ) function. This function allows not only the standard and enhanced color set to be established (the color for the SAYs and the color for the GETs), but also the color set for unselected items in either a GET or a MENU TO. In addition, the colors selected, along with a REPLICATE( ) function, can soften the palette of a monitor and offer the visual effect of three dimensions.

```
1 : * File      Banner2.prg
2 : * Compile   Rmake sample /dFILE:Banner2
3 :
4 : #include "PTValue.ch"   // Power Tools' Header file of misc. values
5 : #include "PTColor.ch"   // Power Tools' Header file of color
6 : #include "PTInkey.ch"   // Power Tools' Header file of ASCII values
7 :
8 : #xtranslate BANNER(<exp>) => eval({|cTitle| dispbox(0,0,4,maxcol(),pDBAR), ;
```

```
 9 :     devpos(1, 1), devout(cAppName), devpos(2, 1), devout(cAppVer), ;
10 :     devpos(1,60), devout(padl(date(), 19)),;
11 :     devpos(2,60), devout(padl(cAppDev, 19)), Title(cTitle)}, <exp>)
12 :
13 : #xtranslate TITLE( <item> ) => ;
14 :             ( devpos(3, int( (maxcol()-2-len(<item>)) / 2 ) ),;
15 :               devout( <item> ), pTRUE )
16 :
17 : #xtranslate MESSAGES( <exp> ) => ;
18 :             ( scroll(maxrow(),0,maxrow(),maxcol()), devpos(maxrow(),0), ;
19 :               devout( <exp> ), inkey(0) )
20 :
21 : #xtranslate PALETTE() => ( setcolor( "B/W" ), ;
22 :               dispbox(0,0,maxrow(),maxcol(), replicate( chr(178), 9 ) ), ;
23 :               setcolor( "W/B, N/W,,, W/B" ) )
24 :
25 : procedure Main()
26 :
27 :     local cAppName := "Call Tracking System"
28 :     local cAppVer  := "1.0"
29 :     local cAppDev  := "Sirius Software"
30 :     local nChoice  := 1
31 :     local getlist  := {}          // This is for the @...SAY...GET stuff
32 :
33 :     set( pSCOREBOARD, pOFF )   // Turn off the scoreboard
34 :
35 :     PALETTE()
36 :     BANNER( "Change Banner Values" )
37 :     dispbox(10,10,16,70,pSBAR)
38 :
39 :     @ 12,15 say "Enter Application Name:" get cAppName
40 :     @ 13,15 say "          Version Number:" get cAppVer
41 :     @ 14,15 say "             Development:" get cAppDev
42 :     read
43 :
44 :     PALETTE()
45 :     BANNER( "New Values" )
46 :
47 :     dispbox(10,30,16,50,pSBAR)
48 :     @ 11, 31 prompt padc("General Ledger", 19)
49 :     @ 12, 31 prompt padc("Payroll", 19)
50 :     @ 13, 31 prompt padc("Inventory", 19)
51 :     @ 14, 31 prompt padc("Purchasing", 19)
52 :     @ 15, 31 prompt padc("Order Entry", 19)
53 :     menu to nChoice
54 :     scroll()
55 :
56 : // End of File: Banner2.prg
```

In this example, the use of the Palette( ) pseudofunction to generate a soft-background textured screen gives the illusion of a three-dimensional interface. The bordered region around either the data entry area (line 37) or the menuing system (line 47) can be highlighted with a shadow line, especially one that draws a true shadow line (a gray shadow). In addition, since the Palette( ) pseudofunction on lines 21 through 23 sets the system to a specific color, it also sets the unselected color of the system. The last color string on line 23 sets the unselected color of all GET items to be the same as the color string used for the standard color set. This means that only the currently selected GET will be a color of "N/W".

## Menus

Once the banners, titles, messages, colors, and keystrokes have been established, the next thing to select is the menuing system to be used. There are three basic styles of menus, and all three can be created with Clipper's @ ... PROMPT and MENU TO commands. These three styles are called "bounce-bar," "Lotus-like," and "pull-down" (or "Mac-like") menus. Each can be used effectively to guide an end user to the proper destination within the application. However, it is important to note that improper menuing is just as easy to create as a proper menuing scheme. The end user should be kept in mind at all times, and a particular interface should never be "fallen in love" with when it causes the end user to be totally lost. Menus are personal matters; menus for a programmer may not be applicable to an end user. Over the course of software development, these three "styles" have stood out as acceptable interfaces between your code, your customer, and your customer's machine.

### BOUNCE-BAR MENUS

```
 1 : * File       Menu1.prg
 2 : * Compile    Rmake sample /dFILE:Menu1
 3 :
 4 : #include "PTValue.ch"   // Power Tools' Header file of misc. values
 5 : #include "PTInkey.ch"   // Power Tools' Header file of ASCII values
 6 : #include "PTVerbs.ch"   // Power Tools' Header file of commands/statements
 7 :
 8 : #define pMENU_ALONE  0
 9 : #define pMENU_LEFT   1
10 : #define pMENU_RIGHT  2
11 : #define pMENU_CENTER 3
12 :
13 : #xtranslate Prompt( <row>, <col>, <exp>, <mess> ) => ;
14 :             __AtPrompt( <row>, <col>, <exp> ,<mess> )
15 :
16 : #xtranslate MenuTo( <var> ) => ;
17 :             <var> := __MenuTo( {|_1| if(PCount() == 0, ;
18 :                                 <var>, <var> := _1)}, #<var> )
19 :
20 : #xtranslate BLOCKIFY( <item> ) => <{item}>   // This is a test!
21 :
22 : #xtranslate BANNER(<exp>) => eval({|cTitle| dispbox(0,0,4,maxcol(),pDBAR), ;
23 :     devpos(1, 1), devout(cAppName), devpos(2, 1), devout(cAppVer), ;
24 :     devpos(1,60), devout(padl(date(), 19)),;
25 :     devpos(2,60), devout(padl(cAppDev, 19)), Title(cTitle)}, <exp>)
26 :
27 : #xtranslate PALETTE() => ;
28 :             ( setcolor( "N/W" ), ;
29 :               dispbox(0,0,maxrow(),maxcol(), replicate( chr(178),9 ) ), ;
30 :               setcolor( "W/N" ) )
31 :
32 : #xtranslate TITLE( <item> ) => ;
33 :             ( devpos(3, int( (maxcol()-2-len(<item>)) / 2 ) ),;
34 :               devout( <item> ), pTRUE )
35 :
36 : #xtranslate BOXSAVE( <t>, <l>, <b>, <r>, <s> ) => ;
37 :             ( M->cTemp := savescreen( <t>, <l>, <b>, <r> ), ;
38 :               dispbox( <t>, <l>, <b>,<r> , <s> ), M->cTemp )
39 :
```

```
 40 : static cAppName := "Random House Menu Program"
 41 : static cAppVer  := "1.0"
 42 : static cAppDev  := "Sirius Software"
 43 :
 44 : *******************
 45 :
 46 : procedure Main()
 47 :
 48 :    local aMainMenu    := {}
 49 :    local nMainOption  := 0
 50 :    local cMainscr     := ""
 51 :
 52 :    AddMenu( aMainMenu, 10,10, " 1> Chart of Accounts",    ;
 53 :            "Work with Chart of Account Information",      ;
 54 :            Blockify(Domenu11()), 24, pMENU_RIGHT )
 55 :    AddMenu( aMainMenu, 13,10, " 2> Transactions",         ;
 56 :            "Add/Edit/Scan/Delete Transactions",           ;
 57 :            Blockify(Domenu12()), 24, pMENU_RIGHT )
 58 :    AddMenu( aMainMenu, 16,10, " 3> Posting & Balancing", ;
 59 :            "Post Transactions / Balance Chart of Accounts", ;
 60 :            Blockify(Domenu13()), 24, pMENU_RIGHT )
 61 :    AddMenu( aMainMenu, 19,10, " 4> Transfers",            ;
 62 :            "Transfer Data to Mainframe",                  ;
 63 :            Blockify(Domenu14()), 24, pMENU_RIGHT )
 64 :    AddMenu( aMainMenu, 10,46, " 5> Print",                ;
 65 :            "Generate Lists and Reports",                  ;
 66 :            Blockify(Domenu15()), 24, pMENU_RIGHT )
 67 :    AddMenu( aMainMenu, 13,46, " 6> Checks",               ;
 68 :            "Print Checks",                                ;
 69 :            Blockify(Domenu16()), 24, pMENU_RIGHT )
 70 :    AddMenu( aMainMenu, 16,46, " 7> Utilities",,, 24, pMENU_RIGHT)
 71 :    AddMenu( aMainMenu, 19,46, " 8> End of Period",;
 72 :            "End of Period Processing",                    ;
 73 :            Blockify(Domenu18()), 24, pMENU_RIGHT )
 74 :
 75 :    set( pWRAP, pON )
 76 :    set( pMESSAGE, 21 )
 77 :    set( pMCENTER, pON )
 78 :
 79 :    scroll()   // Just clear the screen since we will be drawing
 80 :    PALETTE()
 81 :
 82 :    cMainscr := BOXSAVE( 7,2,22,77, pDBAR )
 83 :
 84 :    REPEAT
 85 :      BANNER( "Main Menu" )
 86 :      nMainOption := MakeMenu( aMainMenu, nMainOption )
 87 :    UNTIL empty( nMainOption )
 88 :
 89 :    restscreen(7, 2, 22, 77, cMainscr)
 90 :    scroll()
 91 :
 92 : *******************
 93 :
 94 : static procedure Domenu11()
 95 :
 96 :    local aMenu    := {}
 97 :    local cScreen  := BOXSAVE(9,39,19,73, pDBAR)
 98 :
 99 :    AddMenu( aMenu, 11, 44, " 1> Enter Account     " )
100 :    AddMenu( aMenu, 13, 44, " 2> Edit an Account   " )
```

```
101 :     AddMenu( aMenu, 15, 44, " 3> Examine an Account" )
102 :     AddMenu( aMenu, 17, 44, " 4> Delete an Account " )
103 :
104 :     REPEAT
105 :        BANNER( "Chart of Accounts" )
106 :     UNTIL empty( MakeMenu( aMenu )  )
107 :
108 :     restscreen( 9,39,19,73, cScreen )
109 :
110 : ********************
111 :
112 : static procedure Domenu12
113 :
114 :     local aMenu   := {}
115 :     local cScreen := BOXSAVE(10,41,18,68,pDBAR)
116 :
117 :     AddMenu( aMenu, 12, 44, " 1> Enter Transaction  " )
118 :     AddMenu( aMenu, 14, 44, " 2> Edit a Transaction " )
119 :     AddMenu( aMenu, 16, 44, " 3> Delete Transaction " )
120 :
121 :     REPEAT
122 :        BANNER( "Transaction Sub-Menu" )
123 :     UNTIL empty( MakeMenu( aMenu )  )
124 :
125 :     restscreen(10,41,18,68,cScreen)
126 :
127 : ********************
128 :
129 : static procedure Domenu13
130 :
131 :     local aMenu   := {}
132 :     local cScreen := BOXSAVE( 13, 40, 19, 65, pDBAR )
133 :
134 :     AddMenu( aMenu, 15, 42, " 1> Post Transactions " )
135 :     AddMenu( aMenu, 17, 42, " 2> Balance Accounts  " )
136 :
137 :     REPEAT
138 :        BANNER( "Post/Balance Sub-Menu" )
139 :     UNTIL empty( MakeMenu( aMenu )  )
140 :
141 :     restscreen( 13, 40, 19, 65, cScreen )
142 :
143 : ********************
144 :
145 : static procedure Domenu14
146 :
147 :     local aMenu   := {}
148 :     local cScreen := BOXSAVE( 8, 38, 18, 70, pDBAR )
149 :
150 :     AddMenu( aMenu,10, 41, " 1> Accounts Receivable " )
151 :     AddMenu( aMenu,11, 41, " 2> Payroll             " )
152 :     AddMenu( aMenu,12, 41, " 3> Accounts Payable    " )
153 :     AddMenu( aMenu,13, 41, " 4> Inventory           " )
154 :     AddMenu( aMenu,14, 41, " 5> Other Systems       " )
155 :     AddMenu( aMenu,15, 41, " 6> Outside Systems     " )
156 :     AddMenu( aMenu,16, 41, " 7> Post Transfers      " )
157 :
158 :     REPEAT
159 :        BANNER( "Transfer Data Sub-Menu" )
160 :     UNTIL empty( MakeMenu( aMenu )  )
```

```
161 :
162 :     restscreen( 8, 38, 18, 70, cScreen )
163 :
164 : ********************
165 :
166 : static procedure Domenu15
167 :
168 :     local aMenu    := {}
169 :     local cScreen := BOXSAVE( 8, 5, 18, 40, pDBAR )
170 :     local nOption := 1
171 :
172 :     AddMenu( aMenu, 10, 10, " 1> Chart of Account Data   ",, ;
173 :             Blockify( Domenu151() ) )
174 :     AddMenu( aMenu, 12, 10, " 2> Print/Reprint Checks    ",, ;
175 :             Blockify( Domenu152() ) )
176 :     AddMenu( aMenu, 14, 10, " 3> Transaction Information ",, ;
177 :             Blockify( Domenu153() ) )
178 :     AddMenu( aMenu, 16, 10, " 4> Heading Listings        ",, ;
179 :             Blockify( Domenu154() ) )
180 :
181 :     REPEAT
182 :       BANNER( "Print Sub-Menu" )
183 :     UNTIL empty( nOption := MakeMenu( aMenu, nOption )  )
184 :
185 :     restscreen( 8, 5, 18, 40, cScreen )
186 :
187 : ******************
188 :
189 : static procedure Domenu151
190 :
191 :     local aMenu    := {}
192 :     local cScreen := BOXSAVE( 14, 42, 22, 69, pDBAR )
193 :
194 :     AddMenu( aMenu, 16, 46, " 1> Account Listing " )
195 :     AddMenu( aMenu, 18, 46, " 2> Account History " )
196 :     Addmenu( aMenu, 20, 46, " 3> Budget Listing " )
197 :
198 :     REPEAT
199 :       BANNER( "Print Chart of Account Sub-Menu" )
200 :     UNTIL empty( MakeMenu( aMenu )  )
201 :
202 :     restscreen( 14, 42, 22, 69, cScreen )
203 :
204 : ******************
205 :
206 : static procedure Domenu152
207 :
208 :     local aMenu    := {}
209 :     local cScreen := BOXSAVE( 12, 42, 20, 73, pDBAR )
210 :
211 :     AddMenu( aMenu, 14, 46, " 1> Print Checks         " )
212 :     AddMenu( aMenu, 16, 46, " 2> Reprint Checks       " )
213 :     AddMenu( aMenu, 18, 46, " 3> Print Check Register " )
214 :
215 :     REPEAT
216 :       BANNER( "Print Checks" )
217 :     UNTIL empty( MakeMenu( aMenu )  )
218 :
219 :     restscreen( 12, 42, 20, 73, cScreen )
220 :
```

```
221 : *******************
222 :
223 : static procedure Domenu153
224 :
225 :    local aMenu    := {}
226 :    local cScreen := BOXSAVE( 9, 42, 21, 74, pDBAR )
227 :
228 :    AddMenu( aMenu, 11, 46, " 1> By Transaction Code     " )
229 :    AddMenu( aMenu, 13, 46, " 2> By Transaction Source   " )
230 :    AddMenu( aMenu, 15, 46, " 4> By Date of Transaction  " )
231 :    AddMenu( aMenu, 17, 46, " 5> By Account Order        " )
232 :    AddMenu( aMenu, 19, 46, " 6> All Transactions        " )
233 :
234 :    REPEAT
235 :       BANNER( "Print Transaction Information" )
236 :    UNTIL empty( MakeMenu( aMenu )  )
237 :
238 :    restscreen( 9, 42, 21, 74, cScreen )
239 :
240 : *******************
241 :
242 : static procedure Domenu154
243 :
244 :    local aMenu    := {}
245 :    local cScreen := BOXSAVE( 13, 40, 21, 76, pDBAR )
246 :
247 :    AddMenu( aMenu, 15, 43, " 1> List Mast/Sub Masters      ")
248 :    AddMenu( aMenu, 17, 43, " 2> List Subheadings/Subtotals ")
249 :    AddMenu( aMenu, 19, 43, " 3> List all                   ")
250 :
251 :    REPEAT
252 :       BANNER( "Print Heading Listing" )
253 :    UNTIL empty( MakeMenu( aMenu )  )
254 :
255 :    restscreen( 13, 40, 21, 76, cScreen )
256 :
257 : *******************
258 :
259 : static procedure Domenu16
260 :
261 :    local aMenu    := {}
262 :    local cScreen := BOXSAVE( 11, 5, 19, 39, pDBAR )
263 :
264 :    AddMenu( aMenu, 13, 8, " 1> Print Trial Balance        " )
265 :    AddMenu( aMenu, 15, 8, " 2> Print Statement of Income  " )
266 :    AddMenu( aMenu, 17, 8, " 3> Print Balance Sheet        " )
267 :
268 :    REPEAT
269 :       BANNER( "Printing of Reports" )
270 :    UNTIL empty( MakeMenu( aMenu ) )
271 :
272 :    restscreen( 11, 5, 19, 39, cScreen )
273 :
274 : *******************
275 :
276 : static procedure Domenu18
277 :
278 :    local aMenu    := {}
279 :    local cScreen := BOXSAVE( 10, 8, 18, 35, pDBAR )
280 :
```

```
281 :     AddMenu( aMenu, 12, 12, " 1> End of Month    " )
282 :     AddMenu( aMenu, 14, 12, " 2> End of Quarter  " )
283 :     AddMenu( aMenu, 16, 12, " 3> End of Year     " )
284 :
285 :     REPEAT
286 :       BANNER( "End of Period Processing Sub-Menu" )
287 :     UNTIL empty( MakeMenu( aMenu )  )
288 :
289 :     restscreen( 10, 8,18,35, cScreen )
290 :
291 : // The following functions are the support functions for this program.
292 : // These functions could be removed and placed into the function library of
293 : // choice, or added to the functions from the UDF chapter
294 :
295 : **********************
296 :
297 : static function MakeMenu( aStructure, nStartAt )
298 :
299 :     // This function will display a menu from top-to-bottom, left-to-right.
300 :
301 :     local nChoice   := 1
302 :     local nColumns  := 1
303 :     local nCount                              // For the FOR...NEXT loop
304 :     local bOld_left
305 :     local bOld_right
306 :
307 :     DEFAULT nStartAt TO 1
308 :
309 :     for nCount := 2 to len( aStructure )
310 :        if aStructure[nCount,1] < aStructure[nCount-1,1] .and. ;
311 :           aStructure[nCount,2] > aStructure[nCount-1,2]
312 :
313 :           nColumns++   // Adjust counter
314 :
315 :        endif
316 :     next
317 :
318 :     if !( nColumns == 1 )
319 :        bOld_left  := setkey( pLEFT_ARROW )
320 :        bOld_right := setkey( pRIGHT_ARROW )
321 :        setkey( pLEFT_ARROW,  Blockify( ;
322 :           PanAcross(int(len(aStructure)/nColumns)) ) )
323 :        setkey( pRIGHT_ARROW, Blockify( ;
324 :           PanAcross(int(len(aStructure)/nColumns)) ) )
325 :     ENDIF
326 :
327 :     aeval( aStructure, {|aItem| Prompt(aItem[1], aItem[2], ;
328 :                        MenuPad(aItem[3], aItem[6], aItem[7]), aItem[4]) } )
329 :
330 :     if !empty( nChoice := MENUTO( nStartAt )  )
331 :        IF aStructure[nChoice,5] IS pBLOCK
332 :           eval( aStructure[nChoice,5] )
333 :        endif
334 :     endif
335 :
336 :     if !( nColumns == 1 )
337 :        setkey( pLEFT_ARROW, bOld_left)
338 :        setkey( pRIGHT_ARROW, bOld_right )
339 :     endif
340 :
```

```
341 :    return( nChoice )
342 :
343 : *********************
344 :
345 : static procedure PanAcross( cStuffing )
346 :
347 :    KEYBOARD( replicate( chr(pDOWN_ARROW), cStuffing ) )
348 :
349 : *********************
350 :
351 : static function MenuPad( cPrompt, ;   // is the prompt string
352 :                         nWidth, ;     // is the prompt's width
353 :                         nDir )        // is the padding direction from the #define
354 :
355 :    local cRetVal := cPrompt
356 :
357 :    if !( nDir == 0 ) .and. !( nWidth == 0 )
358 :       do case
359 :       case nDir == 1                          // Pad left
360 :          cRetVal := padl(cPrompt, nWidth)
361 :       case nDir == 2                          // Pad Right
362 :          cRetVal := padr(cPrompt, nWidth)
363 :       otherwise                               // Pad Center
364 :          cRetVal := padc(cPrompt, nWidth)
365 :       endcase
366 :    endif
367 :
368 :    return( cRetVal )
369 :
370 : *********************
371 :
372 : static function AddMenu(aArray, nRow, nCol, cItem, cString, bBlock, ;
373 :                         nWidth, nPadway)
374 :
375 :    /* This function could also be a preprocessor pseudofunction but since
376 :       there is a test on a parameter, namely the STRING variable, this needs
377 :       to be a formal function instead.
378 :
379 :       PADWAY is a numeric toggle that says how things will be padded
380 :          in the MakeMenu() function.  A 0 says leave alone; 1 is
381 :          to pad left, 2 is to pad right, 3 is to pad center, and
382 :          the width that is used passed by WIDTH
383 :    */
384 :
385 :    DEFAULT cString TO "", ;
386 :            nWidth TO 0, ;
387 :            nPadway TO 0
388 :
389 :    aadd( aArray, {nRow, nCol, cItem, cString, bBlock, nWidth, nPadway})
390 :
391 :    return( pTRUE )
392 :
393 : // End of File: Menu1.prg
```

In this menuing example, the bounce-bar menu provides that the menu items will be highlighted and will wrap around from top to bottom or from bottom to top. In addition, a general rule to follow is this: If a selected item is on the left side of the screen and it should open up a submenu, then place the submenu close to the menu choice, leaving it visible, yet overlaying the submenu on the opposite side of the screen. This layered effect can be nested to as many submenus as necessary; each layer opens on the opposite side of the choice and leaves the previous choice visible. Compiling this example and trying a few of the options will demonstrate this feature.

To start with, the standard banner and general interface is handled by pseudofunctions on lines 22 through 38. The new pseudofunction BOXSAVE( ) combines the SAVESCREEN( ) function that saves the current screen to the variable *ctemp* with the DISPBOX( ) function that draws the border. These operations are within a complete expression; the value of the expression becomes the value of the variable *M->cTemp*. In addition, a special pseudofunction is used to help convert typical function calls into function calls within code blocks. This pseudofunction is the BLOCKIFY( ) function on line 20. In some of the following functions, a code block is required as a parameter. Instead of trying to get the syntax of a code block just right, the preprocessor can be used instead. In this particular example, the simple function call is turned into a code block.

The concept underlying this example is that a menu, no matter what its style, can be preprogrammed with the use of an array. Each array item will itself be an array that contains a row and column coordinate value, a PROMPT message string, an optional MESSAGE string, a code block to be performed if that menu item should be selected, the width of each item, and an indication of how the PROMPT string should be filled out. This last option is set by the four preprocessor #define statements on lines 8 through 11. In essence, a structure of menu items is established, with the AddMenu( ) function acting like a formal method to build this array. The array *aMainMenu[ ]*, starts off on line 48 as an empty array. The AddMenu( ) function simply dynamically adds elements to the array specified as its first parameter. Default values are also added to skipped parameters (lines 372 through 391). For example, on lines 52 through 73, the menu to be created will be based on the structure of the items in the array *aMainMenu[ ]*.

Once the structure of the menu is built, the main processing loop to get things going is relatively simple. In the past, a typical menu system would look like this:

```
WHILE .T.

    @ 10,10 PROMPT " 1> Chart of Accounts    " MESSAGE ;
                   "Work with Chart of Account Information"
    @ 13,10 PROMPT " 2> Transactions         " MESSAGE ;
                   "Add/Edit/Scan/Delete Transactions"
    @ 16,10 PROMPT " 3> Posting & Balancing  " MESSAGE ;
                    "Post Transactions / Balance Chart of Account"
    @ 19,10 PROMPT " 4> Transfers            " MESSAGE ;
                   "Transfer Data to Mainframe"
    @ 10,46 PROMPT " 5> Print                " MESSAGE ;
                   "Generate Lists and Reports"
    @ 13,46 PROMPT " 6> Checks               " MESSAGE ;
                   "Print Checks"
    @ 16,46 PROMPT " 7> Utilities"
    @ 19,46 PROMPT " 8> End of Period        " MESSAGE ;
                   "End of Period Processing"

    MENU TO choice

    DO CASE
```

```
            CASE choice = 1
               Domenu11()
            CASE choice = 2
               Domenu12()
            CASE choice = 3
               Domenu13()
            CASE choice = 4
               Domenu14()
            CASE choice = 5
               Domenu15()
            CASE choice = 6
               Domenu16()
            CASE choice = 7
               Domenu17()
            CASE choice = 8
               Domenu18()
            OTHERWISE
               EXIT
         ENDCASE

      ENDDO
```

Now, all of that code is handled by the contents of the array *aMainMenu[ ]*, which is passed to the MakeMenu( ) function. Therefore, the code to do everything listed above is now:

```
   nMainOpt := MakeMenu( aMainMenu, nMainOpt )
```

The crux of the application is the MakeMenu( ) function, which takes the structure defined by the parameters passed to the AddMenu( ) function and processes the information to build a bounce-bar menu system. The MakeMenu( ) function, which begins on line 297, takes two parameters: an array that contains the menu structure, and the beginning element number in the array to start the menu bar on. The default for this parameter is 1, which is handled by the DEFAULT TO command on line 307 that is defined in the PTVERBS.CH header file.

The first operation performed by the MakeMenu( ) function is to calculate the number of columns that will be generated by the array structure. It is considered standard to have menu items go from top to bottom completely before moving from right to left. With this as a standard operating procedure, certain assumptions may be made with confidence. When calculating columns, if the current value of the row and column coordinates of the menuing array *aStructure[ ]* is less than the previous row and column coordinates, a new column must be present. If so, the IF condition on lines 310 and 311 will be true, and the value of the variable *nColumns* will be incremented. At the end of this FOR ... NEXT loop, if the value of columns is not equal to 1 (meaning that there are multiple columns), the left and right arrow keys will be set to simulate column-wise movement on lines 318–325. With the PROMPT command, the down arrow key and the right arrow key perform the same action; the same is true of the up arrow and left arrow keys. Since there are multiple columns, end users will instinctively use the right arrow key to move from the left to the right column, even though it will do nothing more than advance the PROMPT bar one item. If that key were set to simulate going over to the next column by stuffing the keyboard with enough down arrow keys, the end user would be none the wiser. Lines 319 through 323 attempt to do this. The left and right arrow keys are set to the same subroutine, PanAcross( ), but the number of keys to be stuffed is handled by the expression "INT(LEN(structure)/columns)" on lines 322 and 324.

Once the keys are set, a simple AEVAL( ) will process the menu structure, calling the pseudofunction Prompt( ) found at the top of the file on lines 13 through 16, and finally calling the MenuTo( ) pseudofunction, found on lines 16 to 18. If a choice is made, the value of *nChoice* will be not empty (as tested on line 330). If this is the case, and if there is a code block assigned to that menu item, that code block will be evaluated on line 332. This, in essence, replaces the massive DO CASE statement from the previous coding example. The code block to perform, or the subroutine to branch to, is held in the same array structure along with the row and column coordinates, the message string for the prompt, and even the prompt string itself. All menus of this nature can be set up in advance within an array and passed to one generic function, which will create the standard user interface needed to communicate effectively with the end user.

But we can do more than create bounce-bar menus; using the same structure and techniques, a Lotus-like menu is just as simple.

## LOTUS-LIKE MENUS

```
 1 : * File       Menu2.prg
 2 : * Compile    Rmake sample /dFILE:Menu2
 3 :
 4 : #include "PTValue.ch"    // Power Tools' Header file of misc. values
 5 : #include "PTInkey.ch"    // Power Tools' Header file of ASCII values
 6 : #include "PTVerbs.ch"
 7 :
 8 : #xtranslate PROMPT( <row>, <col>, <exp>, <mess> ) => ;
 9 :              __AtPrompt( <row>, <col>, <exp> ,<mess> )
10 :
11 : #xtranslate MENUTO( <var> ) => ;
12 :              <var> := __MenuTo( {|_1| if(PCount() == 0, ;
13 :                                <var>, <var> := _1)}, #<var> )
14 :
15 : #xtranslate Blockify( <item> ) => <{item}>
16 :
17 : #xtranslate LOTUSBANNER(<x>) => ;
18 :        eval({|val| scroll(0,0,3,maxcol()), ;
19 :              devpos(0, 0), devout( val ), ;
20 :              devpos(2, 0), devout( replicate( chr(205), maxcol()) ) ,;
21 :              devpos(0,69), devout( "ESC to Quit" )}, <x> )
22 :
23 : #xtranslate LotusNew( <t>, <l> ) => { <t>, <l> }
24 :
25 : procedure Main()
26 :
27 :    local aMainMenu := LOTUSNEW(1,0)
28 :    local nOption   := 1
29 :
30 :    set( pMESSAGE, 3 )
31 :    set( pWRAP, pON )
32 :    scroll()
33 :
34 :    AddLotus( aMainMenu, "Files", ;
35 :       "Work with chart of account information", Blockify( Domenu11() ) )
```

```
 36 :     AddLotus( aMainMenu, "Data", ;
 37 :         "Add/Edit/Scan/Delete Transactions", Blockify( Domenu12() ) )
 38 :     AddLotus( aMainMenu, "Balancing & Post", ;
 39 :         "Post Transactions / Balance COA", Blockify( Domenu13() ) )
 40 :     AddLotus( aMainMenu, "Move", "Move Sub-Menu", Blockify( Domenu14() ) )
 41 :     AddLotus( aMainMenu, "Print", "Generate Lists & Charts", ;
 42 :                             Blockify( Domenu15() ) )
 43 :     AddLotus( aMainMenu, "Reports", "Print Statements and Reports",;
 44 :                             Blockify( Domenu16() ) )
 45 :     AddLotus( aMainMenu, "EOP", "Perform End of Period Processing",;
 46 :                             Blockify( Domenu17() ) )
 47 :     REPEAT
 48 :        LOTUSBANNER( "Main Menu" )
 49 :     UNTIL empty( nOption := LotusMenu( aMainMenu, nOption ) )
 50 :     scroll()
 51 :
 52 : *********************
 53 :
 54 : static procedure Domenu11
 55 :
 56 :    local aMenu := LotusNew(1,0)
 57 :
 58 :    AddLotus( aMenu, "Add", "Add COA Information" )
 59 :    AddLotus( aMenu, "Edit", "Edit COA Information" )
 60 :    AddLotus( aMenu, "Scan", "Scan COA Information" )
 61 :    AddLotus( aMenu, "Delete", "Delete/Recall COA Information" )
 62 :
 63 :    REPEAT
 64 :       LOTUSBANNER( "Files Menu" )
 65 :    UNTIL empty( LotusMenu( aMenu ) )
 66 :
 67 : *********************
 68 :
 69 : static procedure Domenu12
 70 :
 71 :    local aMenu := LotusNew(1,0)
 72 :
 73 :    AddLotus( aMenu, "Add", "Add Journal Transaction" )
 74 :    AddLotus( aMenu, "Edit", "Edit Journal Trnasaction" )
 75 :    AddLotus( aMenu, "Delete", "Delete up-posted Transaction"    )
 76 :
 77 :    REPEAT
 78 :       LOTUSBANNER( "Data Menu" )
 79 :    UNTIL empty( LotusMenu( aMenu ) )
 80 :
 81 : *********************
 82 :
 83 : static procedure Domenu13
 84 :
 85 :    local aMenu := LotusNew(1,0)
 86 :
 87 :    AddLotus( aMenu, "Post", "Post Journal Transactions to COA" )
 88 :    AddLotus( aMenu, "Balance", "Balance Posted Transaction" )
 89 :
 90 :    REPEAT
 91 :       LOTUSBANNER( "Balancing and Posting Menu" )
 92 :    UNTIL empty( LotusMenu( aMenu ) )
 93 :
 94 : *********************
 95 :
```

```
 96 :   static procedure Domenu14
 97 :
 98 :      local aMenu := LotusNew(1,0)
 99 :
100 :      AddLotus( aMenu, "1> A/R", "Transfer A/R Information" )
101 :      AddLotus( aMenu, "2> Payroll", "Transfer Payroll Information" )
102 :      AddLotus( aMenu, "3> A/P", "Transfer A/P Information" )
103 :      AddLotus( aMenu, "4> Inventory", "Transfer Inventory Information" )
104 :      AddLotus( aMenu, "5> Other", "Transfer Other Sirius Software Data" )
105 :      AddLotus( aMenu, "6> Post", "Post Transferred Data" )
106 :
107 :      REPEAT
108 :         LOTUSBANNER( "Move Menu" )
109 :      UNTIL empty( LotusMenu( aMenu )   )
110 :
111 : *******************
112 :
113 : static procedure Domenu15
114 :
115 :      local aMenu := LotusNew(1,0)
116 :
117 :      AddLotus( aMenu, "Account", "Chart of Account Listings / Printings", ;
118 :                       Blockify( Domenu151() ) )
119 :      AddLotus( aMenu, "Checks", "Print / Reprint Checks", ;
120 :                       Blockify( Domenu152() ) )
121 :      AddLotus( aMenu, "Transactions", ;
122 :         "Print out all transactional information", Blockify( Domenu153() ) )
123 :      AddLotus( aMenu, "Headings", "Print out heading information",;
124 :                       Blockify( Domenu154() ) )
125 :
126 :      REPEAT
127 :         LOTUSBANNER( "Print Menu" )
128 :      UNTIL empty( LotusMenu( aMenu )   )
129 :
130 : *******************
131 :
132 : static procedure Domenu151
133 :
134 :      local aMenu := LotusNew(1,0)
135 :
136 :      AddLotus( aMenu, "Listing", "Print Account Listing" )
137 :      AddLotus( aMenu, "History", "Print Account History" )
138 :      AddLotus( aMenu, "Budget", "Print Budget Listing" )
139 :
140 :      REPEAT
141 :         LOTUSBANNER( "Print Account Information Menu" )
142 :      UNTIL empty( LotusMenu( aMenu )   )
143 :
144 : *******************
145 :
146 : static procedure Domenu152
147 :
148 :      local aMenu := LotusNew(1,0)
149 :
150 :      AddLotus( aMenu, "Print", "Print Checks" )
151 :      AddLotus( aMenu, "Reprint", "Reprint Checks" )
152 :      AddLotus( aMenu, "Register", "Print Check Register" )
153 :
154 :      REPEAT
155 :         LOTUSBANNER( "Print Checks Menu" )
```

```
156 :     UNTIL empty( LotusMenu( aMenu )  )
157 :
158 : *********************
159 :
160 : static procedure Domenu153
161 :
162 :    local aMenu := LotusNew(1,0)
163 :
164 :    AddLotus( aMenu, "Code","Transaction List by Transaction Code" )
165 :    AddLotus( aMenu, "Source", "Transaction List by Transaction Source")
166 :    AddLotus( aMenu, "Date", "Transaction List by Date of Transaction")
167 :    AddLotus( aMenu, "Order", "Transaction List by Account Order" )
168 :    AddLotus( aMenu, "All", "Print All Transaction" )
169 :
170 :    REPEAT
171 :       LOTUSBANNER( "Print Transaction Menu" )
172 :    UNTIL empty( LotusMenu( aMenu )  )
173 :
174 : *********************
175 :
176 : static procedure Domenu154
177 :
178 :    local aMenu := LotusNew(1,0)
179 :
180 :    AddLotus( aMenu, "Master/Sub Masters", "List Masters and/or Sub-Masters")
181 :    AddLotus( aMenu, "Subheadings/Subtotals", ;
182 :                     "List Subheadings and/or Subtotals" )
183 :    AddLotus( aMenu, "All", "List All" )
184 :
185 :    REPEAT
186 :       LOTUSBANNER( "Print Headings Menu" )
187 :    UNTIL empty( LotusMenu( aMenu )  )
188 :
189 : *********************
190 :
191 : static procedure Domenu16
192 :
193 :    local aMenu := LotusNew(1,0)
194 :
195 :    AddLotus( aMenu, "Trial Balance")
196 :    AddLotus( aMenu, "Statement of Income" )
197 :    AddLotus( aMenu, "Balance Sheet" )
198 :
199 :    REPEAT
200 :       LOTUSBANNER( "Reports Menu" )
201 :    UNTIL empty( LotusMenu( aMenu )  )
202 :
203 : *********************
204 :
205 : static procedure Domenu17
206 :
207 :    local aMenu := LotusNew(1,0)
208 :
209 :    AddLotus( aMenu, "Month", "End of Month Processing" )
210 :    AddLotus( aMenu, "Quarter", "End of Quarter Processing" )
211 :    AddLotus( aMenu, "Year", "End of Year Processing" )
212 :
213 :    REPEAT
214 :       LOTUSBANNER( "End of Period Menu" )
215 :    UNTIL empty( LotusMenu( aMenu )  )
```

```
216 :
217 : *******************
218 :
219 : static function AddLotus( aArray, cTag, cItem, bChoice )
220 :
221 :    DEFAULT cItem TO "", ;
222 :            bChoice TO {|| NIL}
223 :
224 :    aadd( aArray, {" " + cTag + " ", cItem, bChoice} )
225 :
226 :    return( pTRUE )
227 :
228 : *******************
229 :
230 : static function LotusMenu( aArray, nChoice )
231 :
232 :    local nRow
233 :    local nCol
234 :    local cItem
235 :    local cMessage
236 :    local nCount
237 :
238 :    DEFAULT nChoice TO 1
239 :
240 :    devpos( aArray[1], aArray[2] )
241 :
242 :    for nCount := 3 to len( aArray )
243 :       nRow     := row()
244 :       nCol     := col()
245 :       cItem    := aArray[nCount,1]
246 :       cMessage := aArray[nCount,2]
247 :       PROMPT( nRow, nCol, cItem, cMessage )
248 :       devpos( nRow, nCol + 2 + len(cItem) )
249 :    next
250 :
251 :    if !empty( nChoice := MENUTO( nChoice )  )
252 :       IF aArray[nChoice+2,3] IS pBLOCK
253 :          eval(aArray[nChoice+2,3])
254 :       endif
255 :    endif
256 :
257 :    return( nChoice )
258 :
259 : // End of File: Menu2.prg
```

In this example, the array structure for this menu is generated by the pseudofunction LotusNew( ). The parameters to this function are the row and column coordinates for the beginning menu item for the Lotus-like menu. This menu will be based on the idea that every menu item will go from left to right, with one additional column space between each item. The beginning coordinates mark the beginning seed position. These values are placed in an array. In essence, the pseudofunction LotusNew( ) is nothing more than an array. Just like the AddMenu( ) from the previous example, this program uses the array created on line 27 and adds elements to it. The structure of the array is as follows:

| aArray[1]   | = beginning row coordinate |
| aArray[2]   | = beginning column coordinate |
| aArray[x+1] | = array of Lotus menu structure |

```
           aArray[x+1,1]      = menu item
                 [x+2,2]      = menu item message string
                 [x+3,3]      = code block of operation to perform if selected
```

As with the previous example, once the entire Lotus-like menu structure is built, one function call, LotusMenu( ) on line 49, will create the desired menu.

## PULL-DOWN MENUS

The third basic menu style is the pull-down menu, which is commonly found on the Macintosh. These types of windows require far more coding to make them functional; however, the power of Clipper extends itself here as well.

```
 1 : * File        Menu3.prg
 2 : * Compile     Rmake sample /dFILE:Menu3
 3 :
 4 : #include "PTValue.ch"   // Power Tools' Header file of misc. values
 5 : #include "PTInkey.ch"   // Power Tools' Header file of ASCII values
 6 : #include "PTFuncs.ch"
 7 : #include "PTVerbs.ch"
 8 :
 9 : #xcommand CLEAR MESSAGE => setpos( SET(pMESSAGE), 0 )
10 : #xtranslate SETMESSAGE() => (set(pMESSAGE, maxrow()), set(pMCENTER, pON ))
11 :
12 : static nScreenLevel := 0   // File wide static rather than a PUBLIC!
13 : static aScreens[10]        // FIle wide static rather than a PUBLIC
14 :
15 : procedure Main()
16 :
17 :    local nOption := 1
18 :
19 :    cls
20 :    set( pSCOREBOARD, pOFF )
21 :    set( pWRAP, pON )
22 :    SETMESSAGE()
23 :
24 :    KEYBOARD( chr( pENTER ) )
25 :
26 :    @ 0, 0 say "General Ledger Main Menu"
27 :    @ 0,68 say "ProCount(tm)"
28 :    @ 3, 0 say replicate(chr(205), maxcol())
29 :
30 :    UpScreen(0, 0,24,79, pTRUE,pFALSE)
31 :
32 :    while !empty( nOption )
33 :       setkey( pDOWN_ARROW, {|| Topkey_on1()} )
34 :
35 :       SETMESSAGE()
36 :
37 :       @  2, 1 prompt " Accounts "    message ;
38 :             "Information Pertaining to the Ledger's Chart of Accounts"
39 :       @  2,11 prompt " Transactions " message ;
40 :             "Record Transactions based on Chart of Accounts"
41 :       @  2,25 prompt " Importing "   message ;
42 :             "Transfer Data from Other Modules/Systems"
43 :       @  2,36 prompt " Lists "       message ;
```

```
 44 :                            "Print General Accounting Information"
 45 :         @  2,43 prompt " Checks "      message "Print General Checks"
 46 :         @  2,51 prompt " Reports "     message ;
 47 :                            "Print Reports for Business Activities"
 48 :         @  2,60 prompt " Utilities " message "File and Program Utilities"
 49 :         @  2,71 prompt " Period "      message "End of Period Processing"
 50 :
 51 :         menu to nOption
 52 :         setkey( pDOWN_ARROW, NIL )
 53 :         UpScreen(0,0,24,79,pFALSE,pFALSE)
 54 :         CLEAR MESSAGE
 55 :
 56 :         if empty( nOption )
 57 :            @  2, 1 say " Accounts "
 58 :            @  2,11 say " Transactions "
 59 :            @  2,25 say " Importing "
 60 :            @  2,36 say " Lists "
 61 :            @  2,43 say " Checks "
 62 :            @  2,51 say " Reports "
 63 :            @  2,60 say " Utilities "
 64 :            @  2,71 say " Period "
 65 :            @  4, 1 say "Are you sure you would like to Quit? "
 66 :            if Verify()
 67 :               @  4, 1 say "All Files Closed, Returning to Operating System      "
 68 :               @  6, 0 say ""
 69 :            else
 70 :               scroll(4,0)
 71 :               nOption := 1
 72 :            endif
 73 :
 74 :         else
 75 :            ArrowKeys( pON )
 76 :            setkey( pDOWN_ARROW, NIL )
 77 :
 78 :            eval( &("{|| Glmen1" + transform(nOption, "9") + "() }") )
 79 :
 80 :         endif
 81 :         ArrowKeys( pOFF )
 82 :      enddo
 83 :
 84 : ********************
 85 :
 86 : procedure Glmen11    // this section is the Chart of Account Sub-Menu
 87 :                      // This must remain a PUBLIC function since it is
 88 :                      // involved in the macro-expanded code block
 89 :
 90 :      local nOption := 1
 91 :
 92 :      UpScreen( 3, 1,12, 11, pFALSE, pFALSE)
 93 :      @ 9,1 say chr(199) + replicate(chr(196), 9) + chr(182)
 94 :      UpScreen( 0,0,24,79,pTRUE,pFALSE)
 95 :
 96 :      while !empty( nOption )
 97 :
 98 :         ArrowKeys( pON )
 99 :         SETMESSAGE()
100 :
101 :         @  4, 2 prompt " Enter    "    message ;
102 :                        "  Enter a Ledger Account to the Chart of Accounts "
103 :         @  5, 2 prompt " Change   "    message ;
```

```
104 :                    " Change Existing Chart of Account Information"
105 :         @  6, 2 prompt " Scan     "   message ;
106 :                    "Scan Through Existing Chart of Account Information"
107 :         @  7, 2 prompt " Delete   "   message ;
108 :                    "   Delete Existing Chart of Account Information"
109 :         @  8, 2 prompt " Balance  "   message ;
110 :                    "Balance Chart of Account Information"
111 :         @ 10, 2 prompt " Finder   "   message "Information About the Finder"
112 :         @ 11, 2 prompt " Quit     "   message "Exit Program Completely"
113 :
114 :         menu to nOption
115 :
116 :         ArrowKeys( pOFF )
117 :         CLEAR MESSAGE
118 :
119 :         if nOption == 7
120 :            keyboard chr(pESC) + chr(pESC)
121 :            DownScreen()
122 :            return                                  // NOTE! Escape route!
123 :         endif
124 :
125 :      enddo
126 :      DownScreen()
127 :
128 : *******************
129 :
130 : procedure Glmen12
131 :
132 :      // that this section is the Transaction Sub-Menu
133 :
134 :      local nOption := 1
135 :
136 :      UpScreen( 3,11, 8,20, pTRUE,pFALSE)
137 :
138 :      while !empty( nOption )
139 :
140 :         ArrowKeys( pON )
141 :         SETMESSAGE()
142 :
143 :         @ 4,12 prompt " Enter  "    message ;
144 :                    "Enter Transaction into General Ledger"
145 :         @ 5,12 prompt " Change "    message ;
146 :                    "Change Existing Transaction(s) on file"
147 :         @ 6,12 prompt " Delete "    message ;
148 :                    "Delete Existing Transaction(s) of file"
149 :         @ 7,12 prompt " Post   "    message ;
150 :                    "Post Transactions to General Ledger Accounts"
151 :         menu to nOption
152 :
153 :         ArrowKeys( pOFF )
154 :         CLEAR MESSAGE
155 :
156 :         if nOption <= 4 .and. nOption > 0
157 :            Glmen121( nOption, {"Enter","Change","Delete", "Post"}[nOption] )
158 :         endif
159 :
160 :      enddo
161 :      DownScreen()
162 :
163 : *******************
```

```
164 :
165 : static procedure Glmen121(nBaseCount, cExtra)
166 :
167 :    local nOption := 1
168 :
169 :    UpScreen( 4+nBaseCount, 13, 13+nBaseCount,36, pTRUE, pTRUE)
170 :
171 :    while !empty( nOption )
172 :
173 :       @ 5+nBaseCount,14 prompt " 1> General Journal     " ;
174 :          message cExtra + " General Journal Transactions"
175 :       @ 6+nBaseCount,14 prompt " 2> Cash Disbursement   " ;
176 :          message cExtra + " Cash Disbursement Transactions"
177 :       @ 7+nBaseCount,14 prompt " 3> Cash Receipt        " ;
178 :          message cExtra + " Cash Receipt Transactions"
179 :       @ 8+nBaseCount,14 prompt " 4> Payroll             " ;
180 :          message cExtra + " Payroll Transactions"
181 :       @ 9+nBaseCount,14 prompt " 5> Sales Journal       " ;
182 :          message cExtra + " Sales Transactions"
183 :       @10+nBaseCount,14 prompt " 6> Purchases Journal   " ;
184 :          message cExtra + " Purchase Transactions"
185 :       @11+nBaseCount,14 prompt " 7> Operator Error      " ;
186 :          message cExtra + " Operator Error Transactions"
187 :       @12+nBaseCount,14 prompt " 8> User-Defined        " ;
188 :          message cExtra + " User-Defined Transactions"
189 :
190 :       menu to nOption
191 :       CLEAR MESSAGE
192 :
193 :    enddo
194 :    DownScreen()
195 :
196 : ********************
197 :
198 : procedure Glmen13  // that this section is the Transfer Sub-Menu
199 :
200 :    local nOption := 1
201 :
202 :    UpScreen( 3, 25, 10, 50, pTRUE, pFALSE)
203 :
204 :    while !empty( nOption )
205 :
206 :       ArrowKeys( pON )
207 :       SETMESSAGE()
208 :
209 :       @ 4,26 prompt " 1> Accounts Receivable " message ;
210 :                  "Transfer Accounts Receivable Information"+ ;
211 :                  " into General Ledger"
212 :       @ 5,26 prompt " 2> Payroll             " message ;
213 :                  "Transfer Payroll Information into General Ledger"
214 :       @ 6,26 prompt " 3> Accounts Payable    " message ;
215 :                  "Transfer Accounts Payable Information "+ ;
216 :                  "into General Ledger"
217 :       @ 7,26 prompt " 4> Inventory           " message ;
218 :                  "Transfer Inventory Information into General Ledger"
219 :       @ 8,26 prompt " 5> Other Systems       " message ;
220 :                  "Transfer Other Accounting Information from "+ ;
221 :                  "Other System into General Ledger"
222 :       @ 9,26 prompt " 6> Post Transfers      " message ;
223 :                  "Post Transferred Transaction to the Chart"+ ;
```

```
224 :                      " of Account Balances"
225 :         menu to nOption
226 :
227 :         ArrowKeys( pOFF )
228 :         CLEAR MESSAGE
229 :         set( pMESSAGE, pOFF )
230 :
231 :         if nOption == 5
232 :            Other_sys()
233 :         endif
234 :
235 :      enddo
236 :      DownScreen()
237 :
238 : *******************
239 :
240 : procedure Glmen14 // this is for the Printing of Lists
241 :
242 :    local nOption := 1
243 :
244 :    UpScreen( 3, 36, 7,61,pTRUE,pFALSE)
245 :
246 :    while !empty( nOption )
247 :
248 :       ArrowKeys( pON )
249 :       set message to maxrow() center
250 :       @ 4,37 prompt " Chart of Account Info. "    message ;
251 :             "Print General Ledger Chart of Account Information"
252 :       @ 5,37 prompt " Transaction Information"   message ;
253 :             "Print Basic Transaction Information in General Ledger"
254 :       @ 6,37 prompt " Headings Listings       "  message ;
255 :             "Print General Ledger's Headings for Chart of Accounts"
256 :
257 :       menu to nOption
258 :
259 :       ArrowKeys( pOFF )
260 :       CLEAR MESSAGE
261 :
262 :       do case
263 :       case nOption == 1
264 :          Glmen141()
265 :       case nOption == 2
266 :          Glmen142()
267 :       case nOption == 3
268 :          Glmen143()
269 :       endcase
270 :    enddo
271 :
272 :    DownScreen()
273 :
274 : *******************
275 :
276 : static procedure Glmen141
277 :
278 : #define pTHISMESS "Print a listing of Chart of Account"
279 :
280 :    local nOption := 1
281 :
282 :    UpScreen( 5,37, 9,58,pTRUE,pTRUE)
283 :
```

```
284 :    while !empty( nOption )
285 :
286 :       SETMESSAGE()
287 :
288 :       @  6,38 prompt " 1> Account Listing  " message ;
289 :                  pTHISMESS + " General Information"
290 :       @  7,38 prompt " 2> Account History  " message ;
291 :                  pTHISMESS + " History Information"
292 :       @  8,38 prompt " 3> Budget Listing   " message ;
293 :                  pTHISMESS + " Budget Information"
294 :       menu to nOption
295 :
296 :       CLEAR MESSAGE
297 :
298 :       if nOption == 3
299 :          Glmen1413()
300 :       endif
301 :
302 :    enddo
303 :    DownScreen()
304 :
305 : #undef pTHISMESS
306 :
307 : ********************
308 :
309 : static procedure Glmen1413
310 :
311 :    local nOption := 1
312 :
313 :    UpScreen( 9,38,13,58, pTRUE,pTRUE)
314 :
315 :    while !empty( nOption )
316 :
317 :       SETMESSAGE()
318 :
319 :       @ 10,39 prompt " One Account      " message ;
320 :                      "   Select a Single Account for the Budget Listing "
321 :       @ 11,39 prompt " Range of Accounts " message ;
322 :                      "Select a Range of Accounts for the Budget Listing"
323 :       @ 12,39 prompt " All Accounts     " message ;
324 :                      "    Select All Account for the Budget Listing    "
325 :       menu to nOption
326 :       CLEAR MESSAGE
327 :    enddo
328 :    DownScreen()
329 :
330 : ********************
331 :
332 : static procedure Glmen142
333 :
334 :    local nOption := 1
335 :    local cNewmess := "Print a list of"
336 :
337 :    UpScreen( 6,37,13,65, pTRUE,pTRUE)
338 :
339 :    while !empty( nOption )
340 :
341 :       SETMESSAGE()
342 :
343 :       @  7,38 prompt " 1> By Transaction Number  " message ;
```

```
344 :                    cNewmess+" Specified Transaction Number"
345 :           @  8,38 prompt " 2> By Transaction Source    " message ;
346 :                    cNewmess+" Specific Transaction G/L Source Code"
347 :           @  9,38 prompt " 3> By Date of Transaction   " message ;
348 :                    cNewmess+" Transaction Codes in Date Order"
349 :           @ 10,38 prompt " 4> By Account Order         " message ;
350 :                    cNewmess+" Transactions in Account Order"
351 :           @ 11,38 prompt " 5> All Transactions         " message ;
352 :                    cNewmess+" All Transactions"
353 :           @ 12,38 prompt " 6> By Posted or Edited      " message ;
354 :                    cNewmess+" Transactions Posted, Edited, or Both"
355 :           menu to nOption
356 :           CLEAR MESSAGE
357 :
358 :      enddo
359 :      DownScreen()
360 :
361 : *******************
362 :
363 : static procedure Glmen143
364 :
365 :      local nOption := 1
366 :
367 :      UpScreen( 7,38,11,62, pTRUE,pTRUE)
368 :
369 :      while !empty( nOption )
370 :         SETMESSAGE()
371 :
372 :         @  8,39 prompt " Master/Sub-Masters    " message ;
373 :                    "Print a Listing of Master and Sub-Master Headings"
374 :         @  9,39 prompt " Subheadings/Subtotals " message ;
375 :                    "Print a Listing of Subheadings and Subtotals"
376 :         @ 10,39 prompt " All                   " message ;
377 :                    "Print a Listing of Master, Sub-Master, "+ ;
378 :                    "Subheadings, and Subtotals"
379 :         menu to nOption
380 :         CLEAR MESSAGE
381 :      enddo
382 :      DownScreen()
383 :
384 : *******************
385 :
386 : procedure Glmen15
387 :
388 :      local nOption := 1
389 :
390 :      UpScreen( 3,43, 7,60, pTRUE,pFALSE)
391 :
392 :      while !empty( nOption )
393 :         ArrowKeys( pON )
394 :         SETMESSAGE()
395 :
396 :         @ 4,44 prompt " Print Checks   " message ;
397 :                    "Print General Ledger Check for Cash Disbursements"
398 :         @ 5,44 prompt " Reprint Checks " message ;
399 :                    "Reprint Checks Previously Printed from "+ ;
400 :                    "Cash Disbursements"
401 :         @ 6,44 prompt " Check Register " message ;
402 :                    "Generate a Check Register for Printed Checks"
403 :         menu to nOption
404 :         ArrowKeys( pOFF )
```

```
405 :        CLEAR MESSAGE
406 :     enddo
407 :     DownScreen()
408 :
409 : *******************
410 :
411 : procedure Glmen16 // this is Printing Reports on General Ledger
412 :
413 :    local nOption := 1
414 :
415 :    UpScreen( 3,51, 7,73, pTRUE, pFALSE)
416 :
417 :    while !empty( nOption )
418 :       ArrowKeys( pON )
419 :       SETMESSAGE()
420 :       @ 4,52 prompt " Trial Balance        " message ;
421 :                     "   Generate a Trial Balance   "
422 :       @ 5,52 prompt " Statement of Income " message ;
423 :                     "Generate a Statement of Income"
424 :       @ 6,52 prompt " Balance Sheet       " message ;
425 :                     "   Generate a Balance Sheet   "
426 :       menu to nOption
427 :       ArrowKeys( pOFF )
428 :       CLEAR MESSAGE
429 :    enddo
430 :    DownScreen()
431 :
432 : *******************
433 :
434 : procedure Glmen17
435 :
436 :    // that this is for the Utility Sub-Menu
437 :
438 :    local nOption := 1
439 :
440 :    UpScreen( 3,35,19,71, pTRUE,pFALSE)
441 :
442 :    while !empty( nOption )
443 :
444 :       SETMESSAGE()
445 :       ArrowKeys( pON )
446 :
447 :       @  4,36 prompt " 1> Backup/Recover Data Files      ";
448 :               message "Transfer Data onto Floppy Disks"
449 :       @  5,36 prompt " 2> Create Basic Chart of Accounts ";
450 :               message "Generate Sample Chart of Account "+ ;
451 :                       "Listings Based on Profession"
452 :       @  6,36 prompt " 3> Recreate Data Files            ";
453 :               message "Generates All New Data Files"
454 :       @  7,36 prompt " 4> Change System Password         ";
455 :               message "Allows Password to Be Changed"
456 :       @  8,36 prompt " 5> Change System Date             ";
457 :               message "Changes the System Date"
458 :       @  9,36 prompt " 6> Output Data                    ";
459 :               message "Output Data Files in ASCII Format"
460 :       @ 10,36 prompt " 7> Change G/L Defaults            ";
461 :               message "Change Basic General Ledger Settings"
462 :       @ 11,36 prompt " 8> Change Screen Defaults         ";
463 :               message "Change Screen & File Settings"
464 :       @ 12,36 prompt " A> Change Working Directory       ";
465 :               message "Change Current Working Directory for all Files"
```

```
466 :        @ 13,36 prompt " B> Un-mark Marked Data         ";
467 :               message "Un-Tagged Those Records Tagged to be Removed from Files"
468 :        @ 14,36 prompt " C> Change Header Information    ";
469 :               message "Change General Ledger, Chart of "+ ;
470 :                       "Account Header Information"
471 :        @ 15,36 prompt " D> Layout Check Design          ";
472 :               message "Design a Check Format"
473 :        @ 16,36 prompt " E> Remove Marked Data           ";
474 :               message "Remove Records Marked for Deletion"
475 :        @ 17,36 prompt " F> Re-sort Data Files           ";
476 :               message "Recreate Index File and File Order"
477 :        @ 18,36 prompt " G> Status of Files/Disk         ";
478 :               message "Display Statistical Information on "+ ;
479 :                       "Data Files and Disk"
480 :        menu to nOption
481 :        ArrowKeys( pOFF )
482 :        CLEAR MESSAGE
483 :
484 :     enddo
485 :     DownScreen()
486 :
487 : *******************
488 :
489 : static procedure Topkey_on1
490 :
491 :    KEYBOARD( chr(pENTER) )
492 :
493 : *******************
494 :
495 : procedure Glmen18 // this is the End of Period on General Ledger
496 :
497 :    local nOption    := 1
498 :    local cNewmess   := "Perform End of the"
499 :    local cAnotMess  := "Processing on Chart of Accounts"
500 :
501 :    UpScreen( 3,58, 7,78,pTRUE,pFALSE)
502 :
503 :    while !empty( nOption )
504 :
505 :       SETMESSAGE()
506 :       ArrowKeys( pON )
507 :
508 :       @ 4,59 prompt " 1> End of Month    " message ;
509 :          cNewmess +" Month "+ cAnotMess
510 :       @ 5,59 prompt " 2> End of Quarter  " message ;
511 :          cNewmess +" Quarter "+ cAnotMess
512 :       @ 6,59 prompt " 3> End of Year     " message ;
513 :          cNewmess +" Year "+ cAnotMess
514 :       menu to nOption
515 :
516 :       ArrowKeys( pOFF )
517 :
518 :    enddo
519 :    DownScreen()
520 :
521 : *******************
522 :
523 : static function Verify(cString)
524 :
525 :    local cInerTemp := ""
526 :    local lRetValue := pFALSE
```

```
527 :
528 :    DEFAULT cString TO "YyNn"
529 :
530 :    set console off
531 :    while !( cInerTemp$cString )
532 :      wait to cInerTemp
533 :    enddo
534 :    set console on
535 :
536 :    if upper(cInerTemp) = upper(left(cString,1))
537 :       if upper(left(cString,1)) == "Y"
538 :          ?? "Yes"
539 :          lRetValue := pTRUE
540 :       else
541 :          ?? "No "
542 :       endif
543 :    endif
544 :
545 :    inkey(1)
546 :
547 :    return( lRetValue )
548 :
549 : ********************
550 :
551 : static procedure Other_sys
552 :
553 :    local nOption := 1
554 :
555 :    UpScreen( 9,27,18,58,pTRUE,pTRUE)
556 :
557 :    while !empty( nOption )
558 :       @ 10,28 prompt " On-Time Legal Billing          "
559 :       @ 11,28 prompt " In-Time General Billing        "
560 :       @ 12,28 prompt " The Rent Property Management  "
561 :       @ 13,28 prompt " Master Controller              "
562 :       @ 14,28 prompt " Property Manager               "
563 :       @ 15,28 prompt " DAC Easy Accounting            "
564 :       @ 16,28 prompt " Dollar and Sense Accounting    "
565 :       @ 17,28 prompt " Star's Accounting Partner      "
566 :       menu to nOption
567 :
568 :    enddo
569 :    DownScreen()
570 :
571 : ********************
572 :
573 : static procedure Rightside
574 :
575 :    KEYBOARD( chr(pESC) + chr(pDOWN_ARROW) + chr(pENTER) )
576 :
577 : ********************
578 :
579 : static procedure Upright
580 :
581 :    KEYBOARD( chr(pESC) + chr(pRIGHT_ARROW) + chr(pENTER) )
582 :
583 : ********************
584 :
585 : static procedure Upleft
586 :
587 :    KEYBOARD( chr(pESC) + chr(pUP_ARROW) + chr(pENTER) )
```

```
588 :
589 : **********************
590 :
591 : static procedure Leftside
592 :
593 :    KEYBOARD( chr(pESC) + chr(pUP_ARROW) + chr(pENTER) )
594 :
595 : **********************
596 :
597 : static procedure UpScreen(nTop, nLeft, nBottom, nRight, lWSave, lFullscr)
598 :
599 :    if !(nTop + nLeft == 0) .and. !(nBottom + nRight == 103)
600 :       dispbox( nTop, nLeft, nBottom, nRight, ;
601 :                if( !lFullscr, left(pDBAR, 8), pDBAR) )
602 :    endif
603 :
604 :    if lWSave
605 :       nScreenLevel++
606 :       aScreens[nScreenLevel] := savescreen()
607 :    endif
608 :
609 : **********************
610 :
611 : static procedure Downscreen
612 :
613 :    nScreenLevel := IF( nScreenLevel-- <= 0, 0, nScreenLevel)
614 :
615 :    restscreen(,,,,aScreens[nScreenLevel])
616 :
617 : **********************
618 :
619 : static procedure ArrowKeys( lWay )
620 :
621 :    if lWay
622 :       setkey(pRIGHT_ARROW, {|| Upright()} )
623 :       setkey(pLEFT_ARROW,  {|| Upleft()} )
624 :    else
625 :       setkey( pRIGHT_ARROW, NIL )
626 :       setkey( pLEFT_ARROW, NIL )
627 :    endif
628 :
629 : // End of File: Menu3.prg
```

## Virtual Screens

Virtual screens are possible in Clipper by using two functions within CLIPPER.LIB: DISPBEGIN( ) and DISPEND( ). By issuing a DISPBEGIN( ) prior to sending any output to the screen, a beginning marker is established for the virtual screen. All direct video output will be stored in an area of memory established by the call to DISPBEGIN( ). Making a call to the DISPEND( ) will close the virtual screen and cause it to be immediately displayed. To acquaint yourself better with this programming technique, try this example program.

```
1 : * File       Dispbgn.prg
2 : * Compile    Rmake sample /dFILE:dispbgn
3 :
4 : #define pCRLF CHR(13)+CHR(10)
5 :
6 : procedure Main()
7 :
```

```
 8 :    cls
 9 :    @  1, 1 say "press any key to get the rest of the screen"
10 :    dispbegin()
11 :    @ 10,10 say "Hello world"
12 :    @ 11,10 say "Good bye there..."
13 :    inkey(0)
14 :    dispend()
15 :    wait "Press any key to continue..."
16 :    cls
17 :    dispbegin()   // This begins the virtual screen in which all output
18 :                  // through the normal device driver is displayed.
19 :
20 :    outstd("Using the OUTSTD() function, the virtual screen")
21 :    outstd( pCRLF )
22 :    outstd("may be built without concern for what is being placed")
23 :    outstd( pCRLF )
24 :    outstd("into the virtual screen.  Press any key to find out!")
25 :    setcursor(0)
26 :    devpos(10,10)
27 :    devout("Isn't this fun!  This means that additional screens")
28 :    devpos(11,10)
29 :    devout("may be built at the same time as regular screens")
30 :    devpos(12,10)
31 :    devout("through the OUTSTD() and devpos()/devout() functions")
32 :    inkey(0)
33 :
34 :    dispend()    // This ends and paints the virtual screen
35 :
36 :    wait "Press any key to end..."
37 :    cls
38 :
39 : // End of File: DispBgn.prg
```

The important point here is that some functions for output are not affected by the DISPBEGIN( )... DISPEND( ) construct. On line 10, the virtual screen is established, and the following two lines of direct output are written to that screen. In fact, the screen continues to display a prior message, and the cursor will sit waiting for any key to be pressed, as prescribed by the INKEY(0) function. When any key is pressed, the virtual screen is quickly thrown up on the screen via a call to the DISPEND( ) function. Then a virtual screen is created again via the DISPBEGIN( ) function. However, the calls to the OUTSTD( ) functions direct all output to the standard DOS device, which is not controlled by the virtual screen. Therefore, the text on lines 20 through 24 will still appear without being stored to the virtual screen. The DEVPOS( ) and DEVOUT( ) functions (which are the preprocessor equivalents for the @ ... SAY command) are stored to the virtual screen.

The major advantage of a virtual screen is its ability to pop in screens with a snap and with flair. Take a few moments to go over this example and see how a virtual screen may add spice to an application with the blahs.

In this next example, a method for saving a virtual screen is demonstrated. This will allow a screen to be built in advance and to be popped onto the monitor quickly. In addition to the virtual screen, the GET stack is also saved; therefore, a complete data entry screen may be drawn in the background and displayed at any given moment.

```
1 : * File      Virtpnt.prg
2 : * Compile   Rmake sample /dFILE:Virtpnt
3 :
4 : #include "PTValue.ch"  // Power Tools' Header file of misc. values
```

```
  5 :
  6 : memvar GETLIST    // This is for the @...GET stuff
  7 :
  8 : procedure Main()
  9 :
 10 :    local nCount     := 1
 11 :    local cName      := curdir()
 12 :    local aOldScreen
 13 :    local aVirtual1
 14 :    local aVirtual2
 15 :    local aNewScreen
 16 :
 17 :    cls
 18 :    aOldScreen := BeginVirtual()    // Set the current screen up
 19 :    @ 10,10 say "Enter a New Value: " get nCount
 20 :    aVirtual1   := EndVirtual( aOldScreen ) // Giving back the old screen!
 21 :    aNewScreen  = BeginVirtual()
 22 :    @ 12,20 say "Enter Subdirectory: " get cName
 23 :    aVirtual2   := EndVirtual( aNewScreen )  // Storing this virtualscreen!
 24 :    wait "Press any key for popping of virtual screens!"
 25 :    cls
 26 :    ShowVirtual( aVirtual1 )   // Activate this virtual screen
 27 :    read
 28 :    ShowVirtual( aVirtual2 )   // And this one with GET stack!
 29 :    read
 30 :
 31 :    cls
 32 :    qout( "This is the value of NCOUNT: ", nCount )
 33 :    qout( "         the value of CNAME: ", cName )
 34 :
 35 : *******************
 36 :
 37 : static function BeginVirtual
 38 :
 39 :    local cScreen := savescreen()
 40 :
 41 :    clear gets
 42 :    dispbegin()
 43 :
 44 :    return( { cScreen, getlist } )
 45 :
 46 : *******************
 47 :
 48 : static function EndVirtual( aArray )
 49 :
 50 :    local cScreen := savescreen()
 51 :    local aGets1  := getlist
 52 :
 53 :    clear gets
 54 :    restscreen(,,,,aArray[1])
 55 :    getlist := aArray[2]
 56 :
 57 :    dispend()
 58 :
 59 :    return( {cScreen, aGets1} )
 60 :
 61 : *******************
 62 :
 63 : static procedure ShowVirtual( aArray )
 64 :
```

```
65 :    restscreen(,,,, aArray[1])
66 :    getlist := aArray[2]
67 :
68 : // End of File: Virtpnt.prg
```

In this example, three functions were created to help handle the creation and display of a virtual screen: BeginVirtual( ), EndVirtual( ), and ShowVirtual( ). The return value of the BeginVirtual( ) function is the contents of the screen prior to the call to DISPBEGIN( ) and the value of the *GetList[ ]* array. Both values are stored to an array, which becomes the return value of the BeginVirtual( ) function. On line 19, a GET is displayed to the virtual screen because the BeginVirtual( ) function triggered the DISPBEGIN( ) function. This display is not seen. When the EndVirtual( ) function is called on line 20, the original screen and *GetList[ ]* values are restored to the system, and the virtual values, both the screen and *GetList[ ]*, are saved to temporary variables. The DISPEND( ) function is called to turn off the virtual screen, and the EndVirtual( ) function concludes by returning an array containing the virtual screen and virtual *GetList[ ]*. This process is repeated on lines 21 through 23, and the virtual array is finally stored to a new variable named *aVirtual2[ ]*.

After the WAIT command on line 24, the ShowVirtual( ) function simply takes the array *aVirtual1[ ]* and uses it to restore the virtual screen, now visible because the RESTSCREEN( ) function is called with the value from the first subscript position in the array. In addition, the value of the internal variable *GetList[ ]* is set to the value of *aVirtual1[2]*. This, in essence, restores the GET that was originally called, but not seen, on line 19. The READ on line 29 then activates this GET. The same thing takes place for the array *aVirtual2[ ]*, which contains the second virtual screen and *GetList[ ]*.

This example strongly suggests not only the use of pop-up utilities and functions, but the idea of drawing all of the screens to a system at the beginning of the application. This will add some additional time to the load-up procedure of an application but will, through the course of an application's life span, save time during processing.

## Windows

A window is different from a virtual screen. To start with, the entire monitor is considered the largest possible window. The borders for all things to be displayed will lie between coordinates 0,0 and MAXROW( ),MAXCOL( ). A window, or what is commonly viewed as a window, is really a subvideo monitor that isolates an area of the original window (the entire screen) and instructs all video output to appear within those coordinates. Windows, as referred to here, are not the same thing as the Microsoft Windows package, although the concepts are similar. There, programs and applications can run in a windowed region tied to an icon that replaces the DOS prompt. In Windows programming, hooks to the Windows operating environment allow the application to dynamically change the characteristics of its open window. While the hooks for such an event are not present in Clipper at this time, these concepts can be employed and the results simulated. A windowing structure can be created so that if a particular window region is isolated, all video output will be dynamically altered. For example, what would normally place the cursor at 0,0 on the full screen would only place the cursor at 10,0 if the window region were isolated at those coordinates. In other words (through some defined functions for supporting windowing), whenever a window region is changed, so are all of the coordinates associated with that particular window. So, instead of programming exact screen coordinates, relative coordinates take effect.

With this in mind, a window structure is built in the same manner as a menu structure. Whenever structures (or pseudoobjects) are built, the items that define the structure must be laid out in advance. In this particular case, a window consists of, but is not limited to, the following items:

1. Actual screen coordinates
2. Border string
3. Color
4. Title
5. Menu
6. Shadow toggle
7. Exploding toggle
8. Actual saved portion of screen
9. Actual saved coordinates
10. Operational code block

In Chapter 16, "Clipper Objects," many parallels are drawn to support the concept that an object is nothing more than an array structure. Individual array elements that contain values can be thought of as instance variables; and the elements that hold code blocks or other structures can be thought of as methods. The key is that every window has the same structure. In a database of invoices, for example, not every field will contain a value, but the record for a particular invoice has the capability of accessing and using those fields. The same is true here: Not every window will have a title, but the opportunity to have a title is there. Whenever entities have the same structure, both in operations and in values, they can be batched together to make an array structure. As demonstrated in Chapter 16, this is a "class."

Notice that we are beginning to look at application development in new terms. No longer will we be programming in a linear fashion: We will be programming objects that we merged together with other objects to form an application. Programming a window environment is one such element in this philosophy.

The methodology chosen for building a window structure determines the type of windowing structure that will be built and how the windows will be established, created, and displayed. The first way is to save the screen region before the window area is drawn; the other is to draw the window first and then save its image. The difference is subtle but staggering. Saving the screen region before drawing a new window creates a window stack on which windows will be "pushed" and "popped" as they are called. This is a very simple and straightforward windowing scheme. Whenever a window is popped, the previous-screen region (which was covered up by the window that was removed) will be quickly restored to the screen. The other way creates each window as a stack item. Since the previous-screen region is not tied to the current window being drawn, windows can be pushed, moved, and even deleted. Since the previous screen's image is not tied to any particular window saved, windows may simply be removed from the screen.

The main thing to consider when applying this second approach is that all windows, starting with the first, must be redrawn up to the point of the current window. This redrawing effect is sometimes visible and is not as crisp as the first methodology; however, it is far more flexible. In this chapter, focus will be given to the first windowing technology: saving the video screen before drawing and creating a window.

```
 1 : * File       Window.prg
 2 : * Compile    Rmake sample /dFILE:Window
 3 :
 4 : #include "PTValue.ch"   // Power Tools' Header file of misc. values
 5 : #include "PTVerbs.ch"   // Power Tools' Header file of commands/statements
 6 : #include "PTInkey.ch"   // Power Tools' header file of ASCII values
 7 :
 8 : #xtranslate Prompt( <row>, <col>, <exp>, <mess> ) => ;
 9 :               __AtPrompt( <row>, <col>, <exp> ,<mess> )
10 :
11 : #xtranslate MenuTo( <var> ) => ;
12 :               <var> := __MenuTo( {|_1| if(PCount() == 0, ;
13 :                                  <var>, <var> := _1)}, #<var> )
14 :
15 : #xtranslate PALATE() => ;
16 :                 ( setcolor( "N/W" ), ;
17 :                   dispbox(0,0,maxrow(),maxcol(), replicate(chr(178),9)), ;
18 :                   setcolor( "W/N" ) )
19 :
20 : #xtranslate Blockify( <item> ) => <{item}>
21 :
22 : #define pMENU_ALONE 0
23 : #define pMENU_LEFT 1
24 : #define pMENU_RIGHT 2
25 : #define pMENU_CENTER 3
26 :
27 : static nWinLevel := 0
28 : static aWinStack := {}           // Items for the windowing
29 :
30 : procedure Main()
31 :
32 :    local bMenu := { || MainMenu() }
33 :
34 :    cls
35 :    PALATE()
36 :
37 :    Wset(0,0,maxrow(),maxcol(),SETCOLOR(),0,,,"",pFALSE)
38 :    Wset( 2,2,10,40,,,pDBAR,,"Main Menu", pTRUE, bMenu)
39 :    Wset( 4,3,14,41,,,pSBAR,,"Second Menu", pFALSE, bMenu )
40 :    Wset( 6,7,13,45,,,pDBAR,,"Third Menu",pTRUE,bMenu )
41 :
42 :    Wposition( Wfind( "Main Menu" ) )
43 :    Wopen()
44 :
45 :    Wposition( Wfind( "Second Menu" ) )
46 :    Wopen()
47 :    Wposition( Wfind( "Third Menu" ) )
48 :    Wopen()
49 :    Wclose()
50 :    inkey(3)   // 3 seconds later, the second screen will be closed
51 :    Wclose()
52 :    inkey(3)
53 :    Wclose()
54 :    scroll()
55 :
56 : ********************
57 :
```

```
 58 : static function MainMenu()
 59 :
 60 :    local aMenu   := {}
 61 :    local nOption := 1
 62 :    local bPerform
 63 :
 64 :    // the following is a code block of operations to be performed
 65 :    // if an item should be selected.  The value of X in the code
 66 :    // is the numeric value from the menu choice when evaluated in
 67 :    // the MakeMenu() function.
 68 :
 69 :    bPerform := {|x| ( Wclear(), ;
 70 :        devpos(Wrow(1), Wcol(2)), ;
 71 :        devout( padc("You picked option number", Wwidth()-1 ) ), ;
 72 :        devpos(Wrow(3), Wcol(2)), ;
 73 :        devout( padc(alltrim(str(x)), Wwidth()-1 ) ), ;
 74 :        devpos(Wrow(5), Wcol(2)), ;
 75 :        devout(padc("Press any key to move on...", Wwidth()-1 ) ),;
 76 :        inkey(0), Wclear() ) }
 77 :
 78 :    AddMenu( aMenu, Wrow(2), Wcol(8), " 1> Add",,bPerform, 15, pMENU_RIGHT)
 79 :    AddMenu( aMenu, Wrow(3), Wcol(8), " 2> Edit",,bPerform, 15, pMENU_RIGHT)
 80 :    AddMenu( aMenu, Wrow(4), Wcol(8), " 3> Scan",,bPerform, 15, pMENU_RIGHT)
 81 :    AddMenu( aMenu, Wrow(5), Wcol(8), " 4> Delete",,bPerform, 15, pMENU_RIGHT)
 82 :
 83 :    REPEAT
 84 :    UNTIL empty( nOption := MakeMenu( aMenu, nOption )  )
 85 :
 86 :    RETURN( pTRUE )
 87 :
 88 : ******************
 89 :
 90 : static function Wposition( nValue )
 91 :
 92 :    DEFAULT nValue TO nWinLevel
 93 :
 94 :    nValue := if( nValue > len(aWinStack), nWinLevel, nValue )
 95 :    nValue := if( nValue < 1, nWinLevel, nValue )
 96 :
 97 :    return( nWinLevel := nValue )
 98 :
 99 : ******************
100 :
101 : static function Wfind( cString )
102 :
103 :    local nCount     // This is for the FOR...NEXT loop
104 :
105 :    for nCount := 1 to len( aWinStack )
106 :      if cString == aWinStack[nCount,14]
107 :          exit
108 :      endif
109 :    next
110 :
111 :    return( if( nCount > len(aWinStack), 0, nCount ) )
112 :
113 : ******************
114 :
115 : static function Wclose( nLevel )
116 :
117 :    DEFAULT nLevel TO nWinLevel
```

```
118 :
119 :     nLevel := if( nLevel >=0 .and. nLevel <= nWinLevel, nLevel, nWinLevel )
120 :
121 :     // restore the screen and decrement the master pointer value
122 :
123 :     restscreen(aWinStack[nLevel,5], aWinStack[nLevel,6], ;
124 :                aWinStack[nLevel,7], aWinStack[nLevel,8], ;
125 :                aWinStack[nLevel,9] )
126 :
127 :     nLevel--
128 :     nWinLevel--
129 :
130 :     setcolor( aWinStack[nWinLevel,13] )
131 :
132 :     return( nWinLevel )
133 :
134 : *******************
135 :
136 : static function WOpen( nLevel )
137 :
138 :     DEFAULT nLevel TO nWinLevel
139 :
140 :     nLevel := if( nLevel >=0 .and. nLevel <= nWinLevel, nLevel, nWinLevel )
141 :
142 :     // save the screen at the current screen coordinates to the
143 :     //      current array stack, set the color and draw the stuff
144 :
145 :     setcolor( aWinStack[nLevel,13] )
146 :
147 :     aWinStack[nLevel,9] := savescreen(aWinStack[nLevel,5], ;
148 :                           aWinStack[nLevel,6], ;
149 :                           aWinStack[nLevel,7], ;
150 :                           aWinStack[nLevel,8] )
151 :
152 :     dispbox( aWinStack[nLevel,5], aWinStack[nLevel,6], ;
153 :       aWinStack[nLevel,7], aWinStack[nLevel,8], aWinStack[nLevel,11])
154 :
155 :     if aWinStack[nLevel,15]
156 :        if empty( aWinStack[nLevel,11] )
157 :           @ Wrow(0), Wcol(0) say aWinStack[nLevel,14]
158 :        else
159 :          @ aWinStack[nLevel,5], Wcol(0) + (Wwidth()/2) - ;
160 :            (len(aWinStack[nLevel,14])/2) say aWinStack[nLevel,14]
161 :        endif
162 :     endif
163 :
164 :     IF aWinStack[nLevel,16] IS pBLOCK
165 :        eval( aWinStack[nLevel,16] )
166 :     endif
167 :
168 :     return( nWinLevel )
169 :
170 : *****************
171 :
172 : static function Wset(nTop, ;
173 :                      nLeft, ;
174 :                      nBottom, ;
175 :                      nRight, ;
176 :                      cColor, ;
177 :                      nShadow, ;
```

```
178 :                         cBorder, ;
179 :                         lExplode, ;
180 :                         cTitle, ;
181 :                         lToggle, ;
182 :                         bBlock )
183 :
184 :   local aData
185 :
186 :   DEFAULT nTop TO 0, ;
187 :           nLeft TO 0, ;
188 :           nBottom TO 0, ;
189 :           nRight TO 0, ;
190 :           cColor TO setcolor(), ;
191 :           nShadow TO 0, ;
192 :           cBorder TO space(9), ;
193 :           lExplode TO pFALSE, ;
194 :           cTitle TO "", ;
195 :           lToggle TO pFALSE, ;
196 :           bBlock TO {|| ""}
197 :
198 :   nWinLevel++
199 :
200 :   // test for shadow and for explode default border
201 :
202 :   aData := {nTop, nLeft, nBottom, nRight}   // Subscripts 1 - 4
203 :
204 :   // if shadow, now coordinates based on type
205 :
206 :   aadd(aData, nTop )       // Subscript 5
207 :   aadd(aData, nLeft )      // Subscript 6
208 :   aadd(aData, nBottom )    // Subscript 7
209 :   aadd(aData, nRight )     // Subscript 8
210 :
211 :   // if !EMPTY(border) then re-adjust the coordinates within the screen.
212 :
213 :   if !empty(cBorder)
214 :      aData[1] := nTop + 1
215 :      aData[2] := nLeft + 1
216 :      aData[3] := nBottom - 1
217 :      aData[4] := nRight - 1
218 :   endif
219 :
220 :   // An empty subscript position must be given to the screen that
221 :   // is to be saved when the window is opened!
222 :
223 :   aadd(aData, "" )   // Subscript 9
224 :
225 :   aadd(aData, nShadow )    // Subscript 10
226 :   aadd(aData, cBorder )    // Subscript 11
227 :   aadd(aData, lExplode )   // Subscript 12
228 :   aadd(aData, cColor )     // Subscript 13
229 :   aadd(aData, cTitle )     // Subscript 14
230 :   aadd(aData, lToggle )    // Subscript 15
231 :   aadd(aData, bBlock )     // Subscript 16
232 :
233 :   aadd( aWinStack, aData ) // Add this windows that is set to the
234 :                            // the WINDOWS array!
235 :
236 :   return( nWinLevel )
237 :
```

```
238 : *******************
239 :
240 : static function Wclear(nLevel)
241 :
242 :    DEFAULT nLevel TO nWinLevel
243 :
244 :    nLevel := if( nLevel >=0 .and. nLevel <= nWinLevel, nLevel, nWinLevel )
245 :
246 :    setcolor( aWinStack[nLevel,13] )
247 :
248 :    scroll( aWinStack[nLevel,1], aWinStack[nLevel,2], ;
249 :            aWinStack[nLevel,3], aWinStack[nLevel,4] )
250 :
251 :    return( pTRUE )
252 :
253 : *******************
254 :
255 : static function Wdepth(nLevel)
256 :
257 :    DEFAULT nLevel TO nWinLevel
258 :
259 :    nLevel := if( nLevel >=0 .and. nLevel <= nWinLevel, nLevel, nWinLevel )
260 :
261 :    return( aWinStack[nLevel,3] - aWinStack[nLevel,1] )
262 :
263 : *******************
264 :
265 : static function Wwidth(nLevel)
266 :
267 :    DEFAULT nLevel TO nWinLevel
268 :
269 :    nLevel := if( nLevel >=0 .and. nLevel <= nWinLevel, nLevel, nWinLevel )
270 :
271 :    return( aWinStack[nLevel,4] - aWinStack[nLevel,2] )
272 :
273 : *******************
274 :
275 : static function Wrow(nRow)
276 :
277 :    DEFAULT nRow TO 0
278 :
279 :    return( aWinStack[nWinLevel,1] + nRow )
280 :
281 : *******************
282 :
283 : static function Wcol(nCol)
284 :
285 :    DEFAULT nCol TO 0
286 :
287 :    return( aWinStack[nWinLevel,2] + nCol )
288 :
289 : *******************
290 :
291 : static function MakeMenu( aStructure, nStartAt )
292 :
293 :    // This function will display a menu from top-to-bottom, left-to-right.
294 :
295 :    local nChoice  := 1
296 :    local nColumns := 1
297 :    local nCount                              // For the FOR...NEXT loop
```

```
298 :    local bOld_left
299 :    local bOld_right
300 :
301 :    DEFAULT nStartAt TO 1
302 :
303 :    for nCount := 2 to len( aStructure )
304 :      if aStructure[nCount,1] < aStructure[nCount-1,1] .and. ;
305 :         aStructure[nCount,2] > aStructure[nCount-1,2]
306 :
307 :          nColumns++   // Adjust counter
308 :
309 :      endif
310 :    next
311 :
312 :    if !( nColumns == 1 )
313 :      bOld_left  := setkey( pLEFT_ARROW )
314 :      bOld_right := setkey( pRIGHT_ARROW )
315 :      setkey( pLEFT_ARROW,  Blockify( ;
316 :         PanAcross(int(len(aStructure)/nColumns)) ) )
317 :      setkey( pRIGHT_ARROW, Blockify( ;
318 :         PanAcross(int(len(aStructure)/nColumns)) ) )
319 :    ENDIF
320 :
321 :    aeval( aStructure, {|aItem| Prompt(aItem[1], aItem[2], ;
322 :                       MenuPad(aItem[3], aItem[6], aItem[7]), aItem[4]) } )
323 :
324 :    if !empty( nChoice := MENUTO( nStartAt )  )
325 :      IF aStructure[nChoice,5] IS pBLOCK
326 :         eval( aStructure[nChoice,5], nChoice )
327 :      endif
328 :    endif
329 :
330 :    if !( nColumns == 1 )
331 :      setkey( pLEFT_ARROW, bOld_left)
332 :      setkey( pRIGHT_ARROW, bOld_right )
333 :    endif
334 :
335 :    return( nChoice )
336 :
337 : *********************
338 :
339 : static procedure PanAcross( cStuffing )
340 :
341 :    KEYBOARD( replicate( chr(pDOWN_ARROW), cStuffing ) )
342 :
343 : *********************
344 :
345 : static function MenuPad( cPrompt, ;   // is the prompt string
346 :                          nWidth, ;    // is the prompt's width
347 :                          nDir )       // is the padding direction from the #define
348 :
349 :    local cRetVal := cPrompt
350 :
351 :    if !( nDir == 0 ) .and. !( nWidth == 0 )
352 :      do case
353 :        case nDir == 1                   // Pad left
354 :          cRetVal := padl(cPrompt, nWidth)
355 :        case nDir == 2                   // Pad Right
356 :          cRetVal := padr(cPrompt, nWidth)
357 :        otherwise                        // Pad Center
```

```
358 :        cRetVal := padc(cPrompt, nWidth)
359 :     endcase
360 :   endif
361 :
362 :   return( cRetVal )
363 :
364 : ********************
365 :
366 : static function AddMenu(aArray, nRow, nCol, cItem, cString, bBlock, ;
367 :                 nWidth, nPadway)
368 :
369 :   /* This function could also be a preprocessor pseudofunction but since
370 :      there is a test on a parameter, namely the STRING variable, this needs
371 :      to be a formal function instead.
372 :
373 :      PADWAY is a numeric toggle that says how things will be padded
374 :         in the MakeMenu() function.  A 0 says leave alone; 1 is
375 :         to pad left, 2 is to pad right, 3 is to pad center, and
376 :         the width that is used passed by WIDTH
377 :   */
378 :
379 :   DEFAULT cString TO "", ;
380 :           nWidth  TO 0, ;
381 :           nPadway TO 0
382 :
383 :   aadd( aArray, {nRow, nCol, cItem, cString, bBlock, nWidth, nPadway})
384 :
385 :   return( pTRUE )
386 :
387 : // End of File: Window.prg
```

This example combines both the window technology and the menu technology previously outlined. Here, four separate windows are "set" or created in memory. As a window is set, the Wset( ) function dynamically adds an element to the file-wide STATIC array variable *aWinStack[ ]*. The variable *nWinLevel* sets a pointer to the current window being set. The basic operation is that the attributes of windows are defined, and then they are opened when appropriate. The initial window, the one without any background information, is considered the first window created. This takes place on line 37, immediately after the screen has been cleared and the basic palette has been drawn. In essence, four windows are initialized. The second window has the title "Main Menu" and is toggled to be displayed when the window is opened. In addition, the last parameter passed to the Wset( ) function is code to be performed when the window is opened. The variable *bMenu* contains the code block referring to the MainMenu( ) procedure. Within this procedure is the menu structure previously outlined. And as each window is opened, the menu system outlined in the MainMenu( ) routine will be repositioned accordingly.

The difference between the second and third window areas is not only in position but in border string and in title. In addition, the third window is set to not display its title, even though it is assigned one. This title, whether displayed or not, is used in searching for the window to be displayed. Once all of the windows are set in memory, a dual call is made to the Wposition( ) and Wfind( ) functions.

The return value of the Wfind( ) function is the subscript position of the window whose title matches a string. Regardless of whether the title is to be displayed or not, the position of the window in the *aWinStack[ ]* array is the value of this function. This value is then passed to the Wposition( ) function, which "points" to the proper window structure. That particular window is then opened. When it is opened with the attributes prescribed in the Wset( ) call on line 38, the array contents for this window are used by the Wopen( ) function on line 43. Within the Wopen( ) function, the 16th element in this particular array structure—the element that contains the code block of operations assigned to this window—is tested. In other words, once the color of the window is set (line 145), once the screen region for the window is saved (lines 147 through 150), once the border and screen region are drawn (lines 152 and 153), once the title is displayed (or not), the code block stored to the window structure is finally evaluated (line 165).

Once the window is opened, the routine MainMenu( ) is called. Within this routine, a code block named *bPerform* is set to a complex expression. This expression is to be performed each time a menu item is selected. However, within this expression, reference to the relative position of the currently opened window is made in the form of calls to the Wrow( ) and Wcol( ) functions. This code block is passed to each menu item of the menu structure array named *aMenu[ ]*. In this example, there is a new twist: The MakeMenu( ) function, when evaluating this code block, will pass to it the value of the MenuTo( ) pseudofunction (line 324).

This exercise should open up new avenues of programming possibilities, including the concept of chained list boxes, dialog boxes, and much more.

## Conclusion

The ergonomics of an application often determines the first impression an end user has of a system. If little or no time is given to properly developing screens, titles, banners, colors, keystrokes, and menuing styles, the end user will tend to give a disproportionate amount of time to learning the application. Alienating any end user means that the hidden joys of the system—those programming marvels deeply embedded within—will never be experienced and appreciated due to the failure to make that end user feel comfortable. Clipper 5.2 has the ability, with code blocks, objects, arrays, and the preprocessor, to create standard user interfaces with very little effort. In addition, menus and windows can take on new levels of sophistication and power—their structures can be created to run and govern an entire system. This power is simply an extension of the concepts of object-oriented programming.

# 18

# Data Entry Options

Perhaps the most important aspect of application development is the complex of issues surrounding data entry, data validation, and subsequent data verification and updating. The data entry module must be carefully thought out with the end user in mind. That might mean an extensive use of error messages and data and keystroke-trapping algorithms, or it might mean a heavy reliance on colors and sounds. Whatever the choice, make certain that the audience is receptive to the features they will confront in all data entry modules. The entire point of getting data out of an application is making sure that the data gets into the system in an orderly and proper fashion.

## Parts of a GET

In Clipper 5.2, a GET is a particular object class, and it is stored in a predefined array named *GETLIST[ ]*. This array is dynamically built with the AADD( ) function each time a new GET is generated. Generating a GET is not the same thing as activating it; the activation of a GET takes place with the READ command (or READMODAL( ) function). It is possible, however, to build an entire data entry system in advance as individual arrays to be swapped to the *GETLIST[ ]* array when they need to be activated; more on this in a moment. However, understanding all of the parts that can affect the GET and the data being entered into the GET's location is vital. Each of the following Clipper features can have a direct impact on the location of the data on the screen, the format of the data, and the data itself, both while it is being entered and after it has been entered. These features are

@ <row>, <col>
Memory variable field for the GET
Picture clause for the GET
WHEN clause
VALID clause

```
READ ( ReadModal() )
SET KEY TO
GET Objects
```

## ROWS AND COLUMNS

The row and column location of a GET is determined either by the actual values of the @ <row>, <col> GET statement or by a relative position if it is in an @ <row>, <col> SAY <exp> GET command statement.

If the SAY clause precedes the GET statement, the relative position of the GET will begin one column to the right of the ending position of the expression in the SAY clause. This can be clearly seen in the standard header file (STD.CH):

```
#xcommand @ <row>, <col> SAY <sayxpr> [<sayClauses,...>];
          GET <var> [<getClauses,...>] => ;
          @ <row>, <col> SAY <sayxpr> [<sayClauses,...>] ;;
          @ Row(), Col()+1 GET <var> [<getClauses,...>]
```

Be careful with the screen location of the GET variable: It must be within the boundaries determined by the values in MAXROW( ) and MAXCOL( ). If the width of the GET area is a concern, this may be controlled with a picture template function, which will be discussed later.

## MEMORY VARIABLES AND FIELDS

Never work directly from a field in a database. Working directly on a database seriously jeopardizes the integrity of that database for future operations, especially in a network environment.

All data entry should be performed on memory variables or on array elements. Choosing between the two is purely a question of style and taste; memory variables may emulate the name of the field being worked on in the database, whereas the array subscript position may be tied to the ordinal position of that field in the database. As a general rule, when an entire record needs to be updated, an array is more efficient than individual memory variables. On the other hand, if the data entry section is limited to just a few fields, memory variables may be a better choice.

Data entry does not mean just that data which is to be placed in a database; data entry is any type of data needed to process information in an application. For example, there may be a situation in which the data is in the file and the end user wishes to get at it. One possible scenario is to ask for just the account number or name, taking that piece of information to obtain the complete record. While the complete record might work from arrays and their subscripts, the simple inquiry function may look like this:

```
cAcct := MakeEmpty( Chart->account )
cDesc := MakeEmpty( Chart->desc )
if Getacct(6,24, @cAcct, 6, 47, @cDesc )
    // Edit the record
endif
```

Here, the Getacct( ) function actually performs a READ and a SEEK all in one place. If either the account number or description is used, the Getacct( ) function will return a logical true (.T.), allowing the rest of the edit procedure to take place. The ROW( ), COL( ) coordinates for the *cAcct* variable are 6,24, while the ROW( ), COL( ) coordinates for the *dDesc* variable are 6,47. The MakeEmpty( ) function simply makes a blank variable for a given field. Again, the focus of this operation is on the use of memory variables for data entry rather than on the use of arrays.

In Clipper 5.2, the concept of arrays is important. The idea of simulating a structure with an array is equally, if not more, important. The advantages arrays have over individual memory variables are simple. First, there can be a one-to-one relationship between the ordinal field position in the database and the subscript of an array. In other words, it does not matter that the first field is named "LASTNAME," just that it is the first field and is therefore the first element in the array. Second, altering the names of fields in a database as well as its structure has less impact on an array-based data entry system than on a memory-variable based system. And finally, the code that stores values from a database to an array and replaces them can be located in one subroutine for all data-entry screens. This subroutine can include the appropriate record-locking requirements for a multiuser application.

However, programming for an array-based system takes some time to get used to. Here is some code that takes this approach:

```
if !lArCust .or. nRecord > 0
    @ 06,17 get aCust[2]  pict cArpict valid if( Mustfill( aCust[2], ;
 cScrErrRow, cScrErrCol1), NoDupe("Customer", aCust[2], nRecord),.F. )
else
    aCust[2] := "NEW       "
endif
@ 06,35 get aCust[3] pict if( lArUpper,"@K@!","@K" ) ;
valid MustFill(aCust[3], cScrErrRow, cScrErrCol)
@ 07,17 get aCust[6]   pict if( lArUpper,"@K@!","@K" ) ;
valid if(substr(cReqList,6,1) == "N",.T.,Mustfill(aCust[6], ;
cScrErrRow, cScrErrCol) )
@ 07,49 get aCust[7]   pict if( lArUpper,"@K@!","@K" ) ;
valid if( substr(lReqList,7,1) == "N",.T., Mustfill(aCust[7], ;
cScrErrRow, cScrErrCol) )
@ 08,17 get aCust[8]   pict if( lArUpper,"@K@!","@K" ) ;
valid if(substr(lReqList,8,1) == "N",.T., Mustfill(aCust[8], ;
cScrErrRow, cScrErrCol) )
@ 08,43 get aCust[10] pict "!!" ;
valid Intable("aCust[10]","Artable","TAXES",;
"TAX_STATE","21/23","",08,43,.F.) .and.  BlankVal("aCust[10]") ;
.and. !( lastkey() == pESC )
```

There are two disadvantages to using an array-based data entry scheme. First, it is not as easy to code for; it may be easier to understand and alter the code of an application where the names of the database fields are similar to the names of the variables containing their information. (For example, some conventions used in the past include using the letter "m" along with the field name to signify a memory variable reference rather than a field reference.) Second, array elements may not be passed by reference to data validation subroutines in either a WHEN clause or a VALID clause. It is possible to emulate this feature, but this requires additional programming in the validation subroutines.

## PICTURE CLAUSES FOR FORMATTING

The picture clause for formatting the information of the GET can be just as important to manage the data as the functions in the WHEN and VALID clauses. Some of the more important functions include @!, @K, and @Sxxx.

## WHEN AND VALID CLAUSES

These two clauses allow expressions to be resolved before executing a GET and after completing a GET, respectively. Each is independent of the other and is not restricted to the data surrounding that particular GET. For example, it is possible to have the expression in the WHEN clause of a GET work from data previously entered, and it is equally plausible to have the expression in a VALID clause set up data that may be needed farther in that particular GET stream. Similarly, particular GETs may not be invoked if information in previous GETs was not entered (e.g., no zip code GET if the city and state GETs are left blank). The VALID clause provides for data validation after the item has been entered; consequently, list boxes may not automatically pop up prior to a GET being executed.

Another clause that is similar to the VALID clause is the RANGE clause. It contains the two extremes of a numeric, an alphanumeric, or a date GET. It also produces a message that is displayed in a fixed location at the top of the screen. Verification is handled after the GET has been performed and may not be altered. Given these limitations, the RANGE clause can be better controlled in a user-defined function working from a VALID clause.

## THE READ COMMAND AND READMODAL( ) FUNCTION

The preprocessor translates the READ command into the READMODAL( ) function, which is pure Clipper code; it is in an object module in CLIPPER.LIB named GETSYS. The source code for GETSYS.OBJ is in a program file that comes with the distribution disks. Within this program file is the source code for working with the GET object found in the *GetList[ ]* array. In addition, if you understand the *GetList[ ]* array, you can see that it is possible to suspend a GET to activate a new GET. Consider the possibility of entering an order in an order-entry application when the inventory item being ordered is not yet in the system. Suspending that particular GET, saving all of the information entered, and then quickly entering an inventory item and permitting the order-entry application to proceed are vital in a practical application. In addition to working directly with the GET structure or "object class" (covered in Chapter 16), it is equally critical to know how and when to process keys within the READ command. All of the keystroke manipulation is handled by this function; and since this function is written in Clipper, it is possible to customize a GET and the performance of the READ command. This means that time-out conditions may be built into the GET system, and that the position and direction of the cursor can also be customized and programmed.

## THE SET KEY COMMAND AND SETKEY( ) FUNCTION

Being able to execute a different procedure and/or function while executing a GET (or a MENU TO) has been an integral part of Clipper and of building an application. Pop-up calculators and calendars can be assigned to keys that, when pressed during a GET, can activate them. The data within these subroutines may manipulate the active GET, or they may have nothing to do with the GET. When the subroutine is called, the location of the cursor within the GET is remembered and may be restored to its original position. In addition, the size of the cursor may be changed based on whether or not the insert key is pressed. Additional possibilities include passing the GET variable by reference, if the variable is a regular memory variable, or passing the name representation of the array element.

### OBJECT-ORIENTED PROGRAMMING

The GET system is a particular predefined GET object class. This means that all GETs work the same way and have the same requirements. What we choose to do with those options does not make one particular GET any different from another. Not every GET requires a WHEN, a VALID, a RANGE, or a PICTURE clause. But because all GETs can have these programming features, the entire GET system can be grouped together to form a *class*. The concepts surrounding object-oriented programming, classes, instance variables, and methods are all discussed in Chapter 16 and, more important, are handled automatically by both the preprocessor and CLIPPER.LIB.

## The Basic Data Screen

To see the impact of all of the various options available for data entry, let's start with a simple data entry program. In this example, memory variables for a data entry system are used.

```
 1 : * File       Dentry1.prg
 2 : * Compile    RMake sample /dFILE:Dentry1
 3 :
 4 : #include "PTValue.ch"
 5 : #include "PTColor.ch"
 6 : #include "PTFuncs.ch"
 7 : #include "PTInkey.ch"
 8 :
 9 : procedure Main()
10 :
11 :    local getlist := {}    // This is the variable used by all of the GET stuff.
12 :    local cStatus          // These are the four variables used to get and
13 :    local cAccount         // set information to and from a database.
14 :    local cName
15 :    local cAaddress1
16 :
17 :    use Clients new
18 :
19 :    cStatus    := Clients->( space(dbstruct()[1,3]) )   // Initialize the vars
20 :    cAccount   := Clients->( space(dbstruct()[2,3]) )   // based on the struct
21 :    cName      := Clients->( space(dbstruct()[3,3]) )   // of the database.
22 :    cAaddress1 := Clients->( space(dbstruct()[4,3]) )
23 :
24 :    setcolor( MAKECOLOR( pWHITE/pBLUE ) )
25 :
26 :    cls
27 :
28 :    @ 1,0 say "Adding to Clients with memory variables"
29 :
30 :    @ 3,5 say "    Status: " get cStatus
```

```
31 :      @ 4,5 say "     Account: " get cAccount
32 :      @ 5,5 say "        Name: " get cName
33 :      @ 6,5 say "Address One: " get cAaddress1
34 :      read
35 :
36 :      setcolor( MAKECOLOR( pWHITE/pBLUE, pBLACK/pWHITE,,, pWHITE/pBLUE ) )
37 :
38 :      cls
39 :
40 :      @ 1,0 say "Adding to Clients with memory variables"
41 :
42 :      @ 3,5 say "      Status: " get cStatus
43 :      @ 4,5 say "     Account: " get cAccount
44 :      @ 5,5 say "        Name: " get cName
45 :      @ 6,5 say "Address One: " get cAaddress1
46 :      read
47 :
48 :      if !( lastkey() == pESC )
49 :         Clients->( dbappend() )
50 :         Clients->status   := cStatus
51 :         Clients->account  := cAccount
52 :         Clients->name     := cName
53 :         Clients->address1 := cAaddress1
54 :      endif
55 :      cls
56 :      Clients->( dbedit() )   // Check to see if the record is there!
57 :      cls
58 :
59 : // End of File: Dentry1.prg
```

In this example, the DBSTRUCT( ) function is used to obtain the length of each of the fields, which is then used with the SPACE( ) function. These values are then assigned to each of the four variables on lines 19 through 22. With the first series of GETs, the screen is set to a blue background with white lettering. With the second series of GETs, the colors are slightly adjusted to take advantage of the unselected color option. On line 36, the color of the active GET will be a white background with black lettering; however, all unselected GETs will have white lettering with a blue background. Using the unselected GET colors lets the end user know instantly what GET is active without searching across an entire data entry screen for the cursor (which may accidentally disappear). Lines 50 through 53 are in-line assignments from a memory variable to a field; when the in-line assignments are used instead of the REPLACE command, the FIELD statement or the database alias must be used. Once the record is added, DBEDIT( ) is called within the Client's work area.

In this example, taking the concepts from the previous example, arrays are now used in a data entry screen.

```
1 : * File       Dentry2.prg
2 : * Compile    Rmake sample /dFILE:dentry2
3 :
4 : #include "PTValue.ch"
5 : #include "PTColor.ch"
6 : #include "PTFuncs.ch"
7 : #include "PTInkey.ch"
8 : #include "PTVerbs.ch"
9 :
```

```
10 :  memvar GETLIST    // To prevent a warning... use a PUBLIC symbol.
11 :
12 :  procedure Main()
13 :
14 :     local aData      // Array holds a record of information.
15 :     local nCount     // For the FOR...NEXT loop
16 :
17 :     use Clients new
18 :
19 :     aData := Clients->( GetRecord( 0 ) )
20 :     setcolor( MAKECOLOR( pWHITE/pBLUE ) )
21 :     scroll()
22 :     @ 0,0 say "Adding to Clients via Array!"
23 :     for nCount := 1 to Clients->( fcount() )
24 :        @ nCount,5 say padl( Clients->( field(nCount) ), 15 ) get aData[nCount]
25 :     next
26 :     read
27 :
28 :     setcolor( MAKECOLOR( pWHITE/pBLUE, pBLACK/pWHITE, , ,pWHITE/pBLUE) )
29 :     scroll()
30 :
31 :     @ 0,0 SAY "Adding to Clients via Array!"
32 :     for nCount := 1 to Clients->( fcount() )
33 :        @ nCount,0 say padl( Clients->(field(nCount)), 15 ) get aData[nCount]
34 :     next
35 :     read
36 :
37 :     if !( lastkey() == pESC )
38 :
39 :       nCount := 1
40 :       Clients->( dbappend(), ;
41 :                  aeval( aData, {|xField| fieldput(nCount++, xField)} ) )
42 :     endif
43 :
44 :     Clients->( dbedit() )  // Check to see if the record is there!
45 :     scroll()
46 :
47 : *******************
48 :
49 : static function GetRecord( nRecord )
50 :
51 :     local nOldRecord := recno()     // Save current record position.
52 :     local aRetValue  := {}          // Build default return value
53 :     local nCount                    // for the FOR...NEXT loop.
54 :
55 :     DEFAULT nRecord TO 0            // Phantom Record is DEFAULT!!!
56 :
57 :     if !empty( alias () )   // Robust enough... testing to see if valid area
58 :        dbgoto(nRecord)      // got to requested record
59 :        for nCount := 1 to fcount()        // Process through each field in
60 :           aadd( aRetValue, fieldget(nCount) ) // the data structure.
61 :        next
62 :     endif
63 :
64 :     dbgoto( nRecord )
65 :
66 :     return( aRetValue )
67 :
68 : // End of File: Dentry2.prg
```

This example uses arrays instead of memory variables. The focus of this example is the GetRecord( ) function, which works within the Client's work area (line 19). This function returns an array with either blank values for each field in the database or the values for a specific record. Since a 0 is passed to this function, the function will return blank values. Looking to this function's definition on line 49 and following, the array *aRetValue[ ]* will be dynamically built based on the number of fields reported by FCOUNT( ) on line 59. The FIELDGET( ) function is used to get the value of the fields; however, if the record pointer is placed on RECORD 0, Clipper's phantom record will cause the FIELDGET( ) function to return blank values, since there are no values in any field at record 0. Once the array is built for each field, the original record position is restored and the array *aRetValue[ ]* is returned.

Once the array is obtained, a simple FOR ... NEXT loop beginning on line 23 and again on line 32 displays the name of each field as well as the contents of the array *aData[ ]* for each corresponding subscript position. In other words, there is a one-to-one relationship between the name of the first field and the value of the first subscript in the *aData[ ]* array. In application development, the concept of names becomes foreign if this data entry scheme is implemented; only the ordinal position of a field is vital. Changing a field name, therefore, will not violate the integrity of the system; you can make a change without having to make changes to existing code. However, since everything is based on sequential and ordinal positions, adding fields to an existing database requires that the fields be added to the end of the database structure, thus maintaining the integrity of previously defined arrays and GET streams. Once the items are entered into the GETs, the replacement algorithm is handled by line 41, which simply scans through each element in the array named *aData[ ]* and passes each element to the code block, which in turn calls the FIELDPUT( ) function, which actually replaces the values in the database. The variable *nCount* maintains the one-to-one relationship between the iteration of AEVAL( ) and the field position.

## WORKING WITH VALID CLAUSES

The VALID expression has been part of the language from the beginning. It is, in many ways, an extension of the RANGE clause. The concept of an expression that has a value to trigger the VALID expression was a revolutionary idea back when Clipper was being created. Today, individual GET validation is not only necessary—it is expected.

The VALID clause is simply a post-data-entry validation expression. Once the GET has been completed, the VALID expression is checked. If the value of the expression in the VALID clause is a logical false (.F.), the VALID clause is considered to be false (.F.) and the cursor will remain on that particular GET. If, on the other hand, the expression in the VALID clause is a logical true (.T.), the VALID clause is true (.T.) and the GET is completed to allow either for the next GET to be processed or for the READ to be completed.

There are a couple of things to keep in mind when working with the VALID clause. While list box technology, discussed at length later in this chapter, seems optimal to use in conjunction with the VALID expression, it may present certain problems. The main problem is with the information within a GET. Consider the scenario of a VALID expression that would change the value of the GET variable, as a list box should. If the expression returns a logical true (.T.), such as in a return value from a UDF (user-defined function), the screen on which the GET appears would not automatically be refreshed. While the variable may be altered and the VALID condition considered true (.T.), the end user might see old data; the new data would not appear until the cursor moved to that GET to reactivate it.

The second thing to keep in mind when working with the VALID clause is the issue of escape routes. Make certain that all escape routes are allowed for. This means that, since an end user, while working on the third GET variable in a series of GETs, may decide to alter the value of the first GET variable, you must allow for the up arrow key within the VALID expression of the third GET. If the data within the third GET is not VALID and if the up arrow key is not allowed, the end user may be forced to perform an unwanted action (such as entering bogus information just to satisfy the VALID) before being allowed to alter a previous GET value. Programming is not for the programmer—it is for the end user.

In this example, the VALID clause—or post-validation block—is used to help validate the data being entered on each individual GET. The use of arrays is continued.

```
 1 : * File       Dentry3.prg
 2 : * Compile    Rmake sample /dFILE:dentry3
 3 :
 4 : #include "PTValue.ch"
 5 : #include "PTColor.ch"
 6 : #include "PTFuncs.ch"
 7 : #include "PTInkey.ch"
 8 : #include "PTVerbs.ch"
 9 :
10 : memvar GETLIST
11 :
12 : procedure Main()
13 :
14 :    local aData
15 :    local nTimes := 0
16 :    local nCount
17 :
18 :    use Clients new
19 :
20 :    REPEAT              // User-Defined Command
21 :       aData := Clients->( GetRecord( nTimes ) )
22 :       setcolor(MAKECOLOR(pWHITE/pBLUE, pBLACK/pWHITE,,,pWHITE/pBLUE))
23 :       scroll()
24 :       aData[2] := if(empty(aData[2]), "Enter Account Number",aData[2] )
25 :       @ 0,0 say "Adding to Clients via Array!"
26 :
27 :       @ 1,0 say " Status:" get aData[1] pict "!" valid aData[1] $ "ABCDEF"
28 :       @ 2,0 say " Account:" get aData[2] pict "@K" valid ;
29 :             (( !empty( aData[2] ) .and. alltrim( aData[2]) != ;
30 :             "Enter Account Number") .or. lastkey() == pUP_ARROW )
31 :       @ 3,0 say "    Name:" get aData[3] valid MustFill( aData[3], ;
32 :             maxrow(),0,, pTRUE )
33 :       @ 4,0 say " Address:" get aData[4] pict "@S10" valid MustFill(;
34 :             aData[4],,40,,pTRUE )
35 :       read
36 :       if !(lastkey() == pESC )
37 :
38 :          Clients->( if( nTimes == 0, dbgobottom(), dbgoto(nTimes) ) )
39 :          nCount := 1
40 :          aeval( aData, {|xItem| fieldput(nCount++, xItem) } )
41 :          Clients->( dbedit(6,0,maxrow(), maxcol() ) )
42 :
```

```
 43 :      endif
 44 :
 45 :   UNTIL ++nTimes == 2
 46 :   scroll()
 47 :
 48 : *******************
 49 :
 50 : static function MustFill( xItem, ;  // Item to be tested
 51 :                           nRow, ;  // Row for the display
 52 :                           nCol, ;  // Column for the display
 53 :                           cSaying, ;  // Saying for the display
 54 :                      lWithSound)    // Toggle for the sound
 55 :
 56 :   static cScreen   // The screen for message is remembered!
 57 :
 58 :   local lRetValue := pTRUE
 59 :
 60 :   DEFAULT nRow TO row(), ;
 61 :           nCol TO col()+1, ;
 62 :           cSaying TO "This must be filled", ;
 63 :           lWithSound TO pFALSE
 64 :
 65 :   if !( lastkey() == pUP_ARROW )  // Escape Routes MUST be allowed.
 66 :     if empty( xItem )             // This is the beginning of the test.
 67 :       if cScreen == NIL
 68 :         cScreen := savescreen(nRow, nCol, nRow, nCol+len(cSaying) )
 69 :       endif
 70 :       lRetValue := pFALSE
 71 :       @ nRow, nCol say cSaying
 72 :
 73 :       if lWithSound
 74 :         tone(164.80, 4)
 75 :         tone(130, 1)
 76 :       endif
 77 :     endif
 78 :   endif
 79 :
 80 :   if lRetValue           // Clear out the screen area!
 81 :     if !( cScreen == NIL )
 82 :       restscreen( nRow, nCol, nRow, nCol+len(cSaying), cScreen )
 83 :       cScreen := NIL
 84 :     endif
 85 :   endif
 86 :
 87 :   return( lRetValue )
 88 :
 89 : *******************
 90 :
 91 : static function GetRecord( nRecord )
 92 :
 93 :   local nOldRecord := recno()    // Save current record position.
 94 :   local aRetValue := {}          // Build default return value
 95 :   local nCount                   // for the FOR...NEXT loop.
 96 :
 97 :   DEFAULT nRecord TO 0           // Phantom Record is DEFAULT!!!
 98 :
 99 :   if !empty( alias() )  // Robust enough... testing to see if valid area
100 :     dbgoto(nRecord)     // got to requested record
101 :     for nCount := 1 to fcount()            // Process through each field in
102 :       aadd( aRetValue, fieldget(nCount) )  // the data structure.
103 :     next
```

```
104 :    endif
105 :
106 :    dbgoto( nRecord )
107 :
108 :    return( aRetValue )
109 :
110 :    // End of File: Dentry3.prg
```

The REPEAT command on line 20 is a user-defined command from the PTVERBS.CH file. The second element in the *aData[ ]* array is altered to have a default value of "Enter Account Number" if the element is empty (line 24). Once this quick setup step is finished, each individual GET is processed with unique validation requirements. In the first GET, only the letters A, B, C, D, E, and F are allowed to be in *aData[1]*. The expression is considered to be either a logical true (.T.) or false (.F.); in the case of the latter, the GET is not completed.

On the next GET, there is a compound expression in the VALID clause. First, *aData[2]* must not be empty, and it must not equal the default string "Enter Account Number." This string would be blanked out immediately if any noncursor key is pressed in this GET while the cursor is on the first position; this is the essence of the @K picture function. If neither is true, the GET is considered invalid and will not be completed. However, if the up arrow key is pressed, the GET will be completed and the default action performed. This is an escape route—plan for them so that they work with rather than against the end user.

In the next two GET commands, the VALID clause is working in conjunction with a user-defined function named MustFill( ). This generic user-defined function tests to see if the item passed to it is EMPTY or not; if not, it displays a message at the specified row and column coordinates and makes an optional error sound. Again, the escape route is provided for: If the last key pressed is not the up arrow key, the function will continue to process. If, on the other hand, the last key pressed is the up arrow key, the function returns its default value of true. This value is assigned on line 58 and is returned on line 87. This value becomes the value of the function, which in turn becomes the value of the VALID clause, which determines whether the GET is completed or not.

## WORKING WITH WHEN CLAUSES

The WHEN clause is similar to the VALID clause, with a slight exception. The WHEN clause is a prevalidation block; the WHEN clause is expressed and resolved before the GET is processed. If the expression within the WHEN clause is true, the GET associated with that particular WHEN expression will be processed. If, on the other hand, the expression within the WHEN clause is false, the WHEN clause is considered false and the GET is not processed. If this should take place, a VALID expression, if present, is never considered or processed; the operation will proceed to the next GET or, if there is none, conclude the READ. The WHEN clause works independently of the VALID. This may be seen in the file GETSYS.PRG, which is the READ command in pure Clipper code. This file comes with the distribution disks and is discussed at length later in this chapter.

One of the extensions of the WHEN clause, in addition to automatic pick-list functions and conditional GET variables based on previous conditions or values, is the implementation of a context-sensitive message system tied to each individual GET, similar to the MESSAGE clause in the @ ... PROMPT command. This example begins to explore that possibility. Keep in mind that an expression may be made up of several other expressions, and that the last expression to be evaluated will be the value of the main or master expression.

```
 1 : * File       Dentry4.prg
 2 : * Compile    Rmake sample /dFILE:dentry4
 3 :
 4 : #include "PTValue.ch"
 5 : #include "PTColor.ch"
 6 : #include "PTFuncs.ch"
 7 : #include "PTInkey.ch"
 8 : #include "PTVerbs.ch"
 9 :
10 : memvar getlist
11 :
12 : procedure Main()
13 :
14 :    local aData
15 :    local nTimes := 0
16 :    local aWhens := {}
17 :    local nCount
18 :
19 :    aadd( aWhens, "This is the Status Field: A through F" )
20 :    aadd( aWhens, "The Account Field on Record" )
21 :    aadd( aWhens, "This is the person's full name and must have value" )
22 :    aadd( aWhens, "Enter Address; only 10 characters will appear!")
23 :    aadd( aWhens, "There is no 5th element" )
24 :    aadd( aWhens, "Enter City.  Leave Blank for NO Zip or State!" )
25 :    aadd( aWhens, "Enter 2 letter abbreviation for state!" )
26 :    aadd( aWhens, "Enter Zip+4 code" )
27 :    aadd( aWhens, "Enter Current Amount Due!" )
28 :
29 :    use Clients new
30 :
31 :    REPEAT      // User-Defined Command
32 :      set(pMESSAGE, maxrow())
33 :      if nTimes == 0
34 :         set(pMCENTER, pTRUE )
35 :      endif
36 :      aData := Clients->( GetRecord( nTimes ) )
37 :
38 :      setcolor(MAKECOLOR( pWHITE/pBLUE, pBLACK/pWHITE,,,pWHITE/pBLUE))
39 :      scroll()
40 :      aData[2] := if(empty(aData[2]), "Enter Account Number",aData[2] )
41 :      @ 0,0 say "Adding to Clients via Array!"
42 :
43 :      @ 1,0 say "  Status:" get aData[1] pict "!" when SayIt( aWhens[1] ) ;
44 :                                            valid aData[1] $ "ABCDEF"
45 :      @ 2,0 say " Account:" get aData[2] pict "@K" when SayIt( aWhens[2] ) ;
46 :             valid (( !empty( aData[2] ) .and. alltrim(aData[2]) !=;
47 :                "Enter Account Number") .or. lastkey() == pUP_ARROW )
48 :      @ 3,0 say "    Name:" get aData[3] when SayIt( aWhens[3] ) ;
49 :             valid MustFill( aData[3], maxrow()-1, 0,, pTRUE )
50 :      @ 4,0 say " Address:" get aData[4] pict "@S10" ;
51 :             when SayIt( aWhens[4] ) valid MustFill( aData[4],,40,,pTRUE )
52 :      @ 5,0 say "    City:" get aData[6] when SayIt( aWhens[6] )
53 :      @ 6,0 say "   State:" get aData[7] pict "!!" ;
54 :             when SayIt( aWhens[7] ) .and. !empty( aData[6] )
55 :      @ 7,0 say "     Zip:" get aData[8] pict "@R 99999-9999" ;
56 :             when SayIt( aWhens[8] ) .and. !empty( aData[6] )
57 :      @ 8,0 say "  Amount:" get aData[9] pict "@R 999,999,999,999.99";
```

```
 58 :             when SayIt( aWhens[9] )
 59 :       read
 60 :       if !(lastkey() == pESC )
 61 :
 62 :          Clients->( if( nTimes == 0, dbgobottom(), dbgoto(nTimes) ) )
 63 :          nCount := 1
 64 :
 65 :          aeval( aData, {|xItem| fieldput(nCount++, xItem) } )
 66 :          Clients->( dbedit(10,0,maxrow(), maxcol() ) )
 67 :       endif
 68 :
 69 :    UNTIL ++nTimes == 2
 70 :    scroll()
 71 :
 72 : ********************
 73 :
 74 : static function SayIt( cSaying )
 75 :
 76 :    local cColor := setcolor(MAKECOLOR(pBLACK/pCYAN))
 77 :
 78 :    devpos( set( pMESSAGE), 0 )
 79 :    devout( if( !set(pMCENTER), padr(cSaying, maxcol()+1),;
 80 :                               padc(cSaying, maxcol()+1) ) )
 81 :
 82 :    setcolor( cColor ) // Reset the color to what it was!
 83 :
 84 :    return( pTRUE )
 85 :
 86 : ******************
 87 :
 88 : static function MustFill( xItem, ; // Item to be tested
 89 :                           nRow, ;  // Row for the display
 90 :                           nCol, ;  // Column for the display
 91 :                           cSaying, ; // Saying for the display
 92 :                           lWithSound)  // Toggle for the sound
 93 :
 94 :    static cScreen   // The screen for message is remembered!
 95 :
 96 :    local lRetValue := pTRUE
 97 :
 98 :    DEFAULT nRow TO row(), ;
 99 :            nCol TO col()+1, ;
100 :            cSaying TO "This must be filled", ;
101 :            lWithSound TO pFALSE
102 :
103 :    if !( lastkey() == pUP_ARROW ) // Escape Routes MUST be allowed.
104 :      if empty( xItem )           // This is the beginning of the test.
105 :         if cScreen == NIL
106 :            cScreen := savescreen(nRow, nCol, nRow, nCol+len(cSaying) )
107 :         endif
108 :         lRetValue := pFALSE
109 :         @ nRow, nCol say cSaying
110 :
111 :         if lWithSound
112 :            tone(164.80, 4)
113 :            tone(130, 1)
114 :         endif
115 :      endif
116 :    endif
117 :
118 :    if lRetValue         // Clear out the screen area!
```

```
119 :        if !( cScreen == NIL )
120 :           restscreen( nRow, nCol, nRow, nCol+len(cSaying), cScreen )
121 :           cScreen := NIL
122 :        endif
123 :     endif
124 :
125 :     return( lRetValue )
126 :
127 : *******************
128 :
129 : static function GetRecord( nRecord )
130 :
131 :     local nOldRecord := recno()    // Save current record position.
132 :     local aRetValue  := {}         // Build default return value
133 :     local nCount                   // for the FOR...NEXT loop.
134 :
135 :     DEFAULT nRecord TO 0           // Phantom Record is DEFAULT!!!
136 :
137 :     if !empty( alias () )    // Robust enough... testing to see if valid area
138 :        dbgoto(nRecord)       // got to requested record
139 :        for nCount := 1 to fcount()          // Process through each field in
140 :           aadd( aRetValue, fieldget(nCount) ) // the data structure.
141 :        next
142 :     endif
143 :
144 :     dbgoto( nRecord )
145 :
146 :     return( aRetValue )
147 :
148 : // End of File: Dentry4.prg
```

To simulate the MESSAGE TO condition within the WHEN clause, an element in an array of GETs and the corresponding element from an array of strings need to be displayed. On lines 19 through 27, the array *aWhens[ ]* is dynamically built, with a string added to each newly created subscript position. And in keeping with the goal of simulating a MESSAGE in the WHEN clause, the message row and location are set on lines 32 through 35. If the value of *nTimes* is 0, the message for PROMPTs will be set to MAXROW( ) and all MESSAGE clauses will be centered; otherwise, the messages will still be on MAXROW( ) but they will be left-justified.

Again, the GetRecord( ) function on line 36 will get a complete record of information and return an array to the variable *aData[ ]*. This operation will be performed in the Clients work area because of Clipper's extended use of expressions—being able to point to the work area the expression is to work in. When this takes place, Clipper will automatically select the correct work area, evaluate the expression, deselect the work area, return the value from the expression, and return to the original work area. All of this takes place on line 36. The value of *nTimes* tells the function to get a blank record (if the value is 0) or to retrieve a specific record. As with previous examples, the colors are set, this time with a pseudofunction processed by the preprocessor and defined in the header file PTFUNCS.CH. This is designed to combine setting the screen's colors with the clear screen operation. Once completed, the program will eventually begin to build the array stack as each GET is processed. Once the GETs are activated, processing of the WHEN clauses, the individual GET operations, and the VALID clauses begins.

Lines 43 and 44 start the first GET. It contains both a WHEN and a VALID clause. It is important to note that the WHEN clause comes after the GET statement. (If you are ever unsure of the syntax of a command, refer to STD.CH, the Standard Header File for all Clipper commands.) The WHEN clause will call the SayIt( ) function, passing to it the value of the *aWhens[1]* element. When the SayIt( ) function returns a logical true (.T.), the GET on *aData[1]* will be performed, with the VALID clause beginning the validation operation once the ENTER key is pressed, the down arrow key is pressed, or the GET has been completed. If, on the other hand, it were possible that the value returned from the SayIt( ) function might be a logical false (.F.), the WHEN clause would tell the READMODAL( ) function (which processes the READ) to skip this GET and move on to the next one. This would cause the WHEN clause on line 45—the WHEN for the second GET—to be evaluated. Keep this in mind: The GET will still appear on the screen; however, it will not have focus (the object-oriented method). This was discussed at length in Chapter 16, "Clipper Objects."

A detailed look at the SayIt( ) function is in order, to get a better understanding of the potential of the WHEN clause. The definition of SayIt( ) begins on line 74, where the string from the *aWhens[ ]* array is stored to the local parameter *cSaying*. First, the current system color is stored to the LOCAL variable *cColor*. Then, the color is set to a different color. Next, the value from the SET( ) function on line 78 is used to position the cursor. The operation of this function depends on the value of the first parameter, the manifest constant pMESSAGE. However, if we were to turn to the PTVALUE.CH file, we would find the following #define statements:

```
#define pMESSAGE        36
#define pMCENTER        37
```

In other words, this file's manifest constants may be used within our own programs as well—in this case, to tell the SET( ) function to return the value of the row position for the MESSAGE strings for all @ ... PROMPT commands. This should be the same value as MAXROW( ). In addition, by passing the numeric value of 37 to the SET( ) function, which is the constant value of _SET_MCENTER, a test can be made to see if the CENTER flag is on or not. If it is on, the string *cSaying* will be centered via the PADR( ) function to be displayed at MAXROW( ), 0. If CENTER is off, the string *cString* will be left-justified at the same coordinates, with the PADR( ) function on line 80 padding the string with enough spaces on the right side to fill it out to MAXCOL( )+1. Once this has finished, the color of the screen is reset to the original value of *cColor* (line 83), and the function returns the manifest constant pTRUE, as defined in PTVALUE.CH. Since the function will always return a logical true (.T.), each of the WHEN clauses that depends on this function will always be true, which in turn will cause the corresponding GETs to be always activated.

The WHEN clause may also take multiple expressions, as seen on line 54. Here, SayIt( ) will be called and will return a logical true (.T.); however, another expression is to be considered. If the value of *aData[6]* is EMPTY( ), the value for the WHEN clause will be false (.F.) and the GET will not be activated, regardless of the value of the SayIt( ) function. Another way line 54 could have been written is the following:

```
54 :        when ( SayIt( aWhens[7] ), !empty( aData[6]) )
```

The complete expression is defined by the outer set of parentheses, and each expression within this set is to be individually processed. However, the value of the expression is not based on the value of SayIt( ), since that function will always return a logical true (.T.). The real consideration is whether *aData[6]* is EMPTY( ) or not. Grouping expressions together like this causes the individual functions to be called and executed, yet it is the last expression's value in this grouping that makes the difference.

One might consider the possibility of setting up alternate files and then opening additional databases and indexes that are context-sensitive to the individual GET. It is possible to extend this example so that all WHEN clauses contain only the following expression:

```
WHEN EVAL( block, parameters )
```

This way, the expression for the WHEN clause is not hard-coded. Comparing this with the previous example, it is possible to take the expression and convert it to a code block that will be processed by a simple EVAL( ). Consider this:

```
bBlock := {|| ( SayIt( aWhens[7] ), !empty( aData[6] ) )}

54:      when eval( bBlock )
```

Now we have assigned the expression we want processed to a variable. This code block could be in string format, which would in turn make our code look like this:

```
cString := "{|| ( SayIt( aWhens[7] ), !empty( aData[6]) ) }"

    bBlock    := &cString.

54:      when eval( bBlock )
```

This strongly suggests that the expression to be processed by the WHEN clause (and the VALID clause) may reside in a text file to be read in and parsed, or even in a database, so that the character field containing the string representation of a code block may be macro-expanded and processed by the EVAL. This should be considered a possible alternative to hard-coding an application, a process that requires more time to maintain than does basing an application on a data dictionary.

## WORKING WITH THE SET KEY TO COMMAND

The SET KEY command can manipulate data in a GET; it can also be used to assist the end user in entering proper data the first time through, or to offer additional related information. The procedure assigned to a key will automatically be passed three values: the procedure name, the line number, and the name of the variable being processed by the GET. If this is an array, only the name of the array will be passed. Looking to STD.CH, it is clear how this command operates:

```
#command  SET KEY <n> TO <proc>         => ;
          SetKey( <n>, {|p, 1, v| <proc>(p, 1, v)} )
```

Data Entry Options 999

In essence, the SETKEY( ) function is called, the internal SET KEY array is dynamically grown (if the key has yet to be assigned), and the name of the procedure is converted to a function call with the values of *p*, *l*, and *v* passed as parameters. We will take a further look at this operation. First, consider this simple SET KEY command using the TAB key as a "hot key."

```
 1 : * File        Dentry5.prg
 2 : * Compile     Rmake sample /dFILE:dentry5
 3 :
 4 : #define CLIPPER    // This is to re-set the power tools header files
 5 :                    // so they will look at the Clipper SET KEY stuff and
 6 :                    // not the Power Tools stuff.
 7 :
 8 : #include "PTValue.ch"
 9 : #include "PTColor.ch"
10 : #include "PTFuncs.ch"
11 : #include "PTInkey.ch"
12 : #include "PTVerbs.ch"
13 :
14 : memvar getlist
15 :
16 : procedure Main()
17 :
18 :    local cFile := space(15)
19 :
20 :    setcolor( MAKECOLOR( pWHITE/pBLUE ) )
21 :
22 :    set scoreboard off
23 :    set key pTAB to Listing
24 :    set key pINS to InsToggle
25 :
26 :    REPEAT
27 :       scroll()
28 :       @ 1, 0 SAY "Enter name of file to look at.   " ;
29 :               SAY "Press TAB for DIR listing!"
30 :       @ 2,33 SAY "     INS for Insert Toggle!"
31 :
32 :       @ 4,5 say "Filename: " get cFile
33 :       read
34 :       if !(lastkey() == pESC )
35 :          if file( alltrim( cFIle ) )
36 :             @ 4, 40 say "Use Cursor Keys to view, ESC to quit!"
37 :             memoedit( memoread( alltrim(cFile) ), 6, 0, maxrow(), maxcol(), ;
38 :                       pFALSE )
39 :             CLEARESC()           // Pseudo-function!!!
40 :          endif
41 :       endif
42 :
43 :    UNTIL lastkey() == pESC
44 :
45 : *********************
46 :
47 : static procedure Listing
48 :
49 :    local cScreen := savescreen()
50 :
51 :    cls
```

```
52 :     aeval( directory(), {|aFiles| qqout( padr(aFiles[1], 15) ), Position()} )
53 :
54 :     @ maxrow(), 0 say "Press any key to return to GET!"
55 :     inkey(0)
56 :
57 :     restscreen(,,,,cScreen)
58 :
59 : *********************
60 :
61 : static function Position
62 :
63 :    devpos( row() + 1, col() - 15 )
64 :    if row() > maxrow()-4
65 :       devpos( 0, col() + 15 )
66 :       if col() > maxcol()-15
67 :          devpos(maxrow(), 0)
68 :          devout( "Press any key for next screen!" )
69 :          inkey(0)
70 :          cls
71 :       endif
72 :    endif
73 :
74 :    return( pTRUE )
75 :
76 : *********************
77 :
78 : static procedure InsToggle
79 :
80 :    setcursor( if( readinsert( !readinsert() ), 3, 1 ) )
81 :
82 : // End of File: Dentry5.prg
```

## List Boxes

A prime enhancement of the WHEN and VALID clauses is the use of a list box (or a pick list) to assist the end user in the daily task of data entry. List boxes are areas of the screen that will contain information, such as related data or values, that the user may pick or select for any given GET variable or field. In the past, list boxes were somewhat difficult to program because of certain limiting factors in the language. These factors have been removed; because of certain changes within Clipper 5.2, we now can have context-sensitive list boxes, list boxes that pass variables by reference, automatic list boxes, and list boxes in other work areas. One change is the preprocessor, which will be looked at shortly. Another is the advent of the WHEN clause.

In the following example, the same function used for data validation with the VALID clause of a GET command is used for prevalidation with the WHEN clause. This will create automatic list boxes from GETs if necessary. In the past, a NULL GET would force the VALID clause to be executed. The NULL GET would be passed by reference, and the function within the VALID clause would see this and automatically generate the list box. Now, we have the WHEN clause to do this for us.

```
1 : * File       Dentry6.prg
2 : * Compile    Rmake sample /dFILE:dentry6
3 :
4 : #define CLIPPER    // This is to re-set the power tools header files
5 :                    // so they will look at the Clipper SET KEY stuff and
```

```
  6 :                         // not the Power Tools stuff.
  7 :
  8 : #include "PTValue.ch"
  9 : #include "PTColor.ch"
 10 : #include "PTFuncs.ch"
 11 : #include "PTInkey.ch"
 12 : #include "PTVerbs.ch"
 13 :
 14 : memvar getlist
 15 :
 16 : procedure Main()
 17 :
 18 :    local cFIle := space(15)
 19 :    local nSize := 0
 20 :    local dDate := ctod("")
 21 :
 22 :    setcolor( MAKECOLOR( pWHITE/pBLUE ) )
 23 :
 24 :    set scoreboard off
 25 :    set key pINS to InsToggle
 26 :
 27 :    PROCESS
 28 :      scroll()
 29 :      @ 1,0 SAY "Enter name of file to look at.   " ;
 30 :           SAY "Press INS for Insert Toggle!"
 31 :
 32 :      @ 4,5 say " Filename: " get cFile ;
 33 :           when  GoodFile(@cFile, @nSize, @dDate, pTRUE ) ;
 34 :           valid GoodFile(@cFile, @nSize, @dDate, pFALSE )
 35 :
 36 :      @ 5,5 say "    size: " get nSize PICT "@B"
 37 :      @ 6,5 say "    date: " get dDate
 38 :      read
 39 :      if !( lastkey() == pESC )
 40 :         @ 10,10 say "YOUR VALUES ARE: "
 41 :         @ 12,10 get cFile
 42 :         @ 12,35 get nSize
 43 :         @ 12,55 get dDate
 44 :         clear gets
 45 :         wait
 46 :         cFIle := space(15)
 47 :         nSize := 0
 48 :         dDate := ctod("")
 49 :         cls
 50 :      else
 51 :         exit
 52 :      endif
 53 :
 54 :    END PROCESS
 55 :
 56 : *********************
 57 :
 58 : static function GoodFile( cName, nFileSize, dFileDate, lWhenToggle )
 59 :
 60 :    local cScreen
 61 :    local nChoice
 62 :    local lRetValue:= pTRUE
 63 :
 64 :    static aFiles
 65 :
 66 :    if !( lastkey() == pUP_ARROW )    // The ESC route!
```

```
 67 :      // It's a WHEN statement and the WHENTOGGLE is EMPTY or when the file
 68 :      // entered in A is not found!  But first, build the array of the files
 69 :      // to be used in the ACHOICE() to follow.
 70 :
 71 :      if aFIles == NIL
 72 :        aFiles := {}
 73 :        aeval( directory(), {|aFile| aadd(aFiles, padr(aFile[1], 15)+ ;
 74 :                                    padr(aFile[2],20) + padr(aFile[3],10))})
 75 :      endif
 76 :
 77 :      if (empty(cName) .and. lWhenToggle) .or. !file( alltrim(cName))
 78 :        cScreen := savescreen(5, 33, 15,79 )
 79 :        dispbox(5,33,15,79,pDBAR)
 80 :        nChoice := achoice(6,34,14,78, aFiles)
 81 :        if !empty( nChoice )
 82 :          cName := substr(aFiles[nChoice], 1, 15)
 83 :          nFileSize := val( substr( aFiles[nChoice], 16,36 ) )
 84 :          dFileDate := ctod( substr( aFiles[nChoice], 37 ) )
 85 :          aeval( getlist, {|oGet| oGet:display()} )
 86 :
 87 :          if !lWhenToggle // This is the VALID clause.
 88 :            lRetValue := pFALSE   // Force the GET to be refreshed.
 89 :            keyboard pENTER
 90 :          endif
 91 :
 92 :        else
 93 :          if !lWhenToggle
 94 :            lRetValue := pFALSE
 95 :          endif
 96 :        endif
 97 :        restscreen(  5, 33, 15,79, cScreen )
 98 :      endif
 99 :    endif
100 :
101 :    return( lRetValue )
102 :
103 : *********************
104 :
105 : static procedure InsToggle
106 :
107 :    setcursor( if( readinsert( !readinsert() ), 3, 1 ) )
108 :
109 : // End of File: Dentry6.prg
```

This example continues to use many of the coding techniques used previously, such as the user-defined command PROCESS and the MakeColor( ) pseudofunction defined in PTFUNCS.CH. In addition, the SET KEY command is used to toggle the size of the cursor in the InsToggle( ) procedure. But the main point of the program is the first GET on lines 32 through 34. Here, the same function, GoodFile( ), is used for the WHEN clause as well as for the VALID clause. In both cases, the three variables involved in the READ are passed by reference, allowing the GoodFile( ) function to manipulate them directly. Remember, avoid manipulating variables directly in the subroutine; if a value needs to be altered in a subroutine, pass it by reference. This is particularly true when you are working with LOCAL variables such as these three variables. The only difference between these two function calls is the fourth parameter: One is a logical true (.T.), and the other is a logical false (.F.). (The logical values are manifest constants defined in the PTVALUE.CH file.)

In the GoodFile( ) function, defined on line 58 and following, the fourth parameter is clear. It is a flag that tells the function which part of the GET the function is being called from—either the VALID clause or the WHEN clause. The function is defined as STATIC, which means that only this particular example program can call this function. As with any function used with the GET command, plan for the escape route. In this case, as long as the last key pressed was not the up arrow key, the rest of the GoodFile( ) function will operate. If the last key pressed is the up arrow, program flow will fall all the way through to line 99 and then on to line 101, where the function returns a logical true (.T.), the default value of *lRetValue*.

Planning for one entry point and one exit point in a function is good structured programming and should be attempted; however, it should never be maintained as the gospel. Remember, write code that works and is easy to maintain. If you have to go out of your way to avoid a LOOP statement or to have only one exit point, do not bother.

Turning back to this example, if the program flow falls into lines 77 through 99, several operations begin. First, the variable *aFiles* is tested against the value NIL. This variable is originally initialized as a STATIC variable on line 64, which means that at that particular point in the program its value is NIL. Therefore, the value is then set to an empty array on line 72. This array is then dynamically built as the AEVAL( ) function on lines 73 and 74, works through the DIRECTORY( ) array, and builds the *aFiles[ ]* array by concatenating the filenames, the sizes, and the date stamps. Since the *aFiles[ ]* array was initialized as STATIC, once the GoodFile( ) function completes its operation, the array will remain in memory. This means that in the second call to this function, *aFiles[ ]* will not be equal to NIL (as tested on line 71) and thus, the array need not be rebuilt. Unless a file has been added to the disk between calls to this function, using the STATIC storage class for this array will save on processing time beginning with the second call to the function.

Once this step has been completed, the LOCAL parameter *cName* (which is the variable *cFile* passed by reference) and the value of *lWhenToggle* are evaluated. In addition, the existence of the file *cFile* is also evaluated. In other words, if the function is in a "when" state because the value of *lWhenToggle* is a logical true (.T.) and if the value of *cName* is EMPTY( ), line 77 and following will be executed. If this is not the case, but if the name of a file expressed in the variable *cName* is not found, the lines are also executed. So at the beginning of this example program, the value of *cFile* is EMPTY( ) and the value of *lWhenToggle* is a logical true (.T.), which will force these lines of code (lines 77 through 92) to initiate an automatic list box. If, on the other hand, the name of the file specified in *cFile* (which is passed to the variable *cName*) is not found, the same list box will also be drawn. The same list box function is being used to pop up a list box automatically for the WHEN clause every time the value of *cFile* is EMPTY( ) and for the VALID clause every time the name of the file in *cFile* is not found. Using the same function for both pre- and post-validation extends the viability of a function, allows for easier program maintenance, and saves memory.

List boxes are a fact of life. After the first end user used a list box, it became necessary for every application. A list box, as in the previous example, may be a list from an array. This array can have been previously built or, as we have seen, built within the list-box function. In addition, list boxes may be databases, either in part or in whole. Table-oriented programming and data-dictionary programming are just extensions of the same philosophy.

In this next example, list-box technology, seeking initial values, working from memory variables, and using arrays are all combined to show that the real power of Clipper 5.2 is not in just one idea, one command, or one function; rather, it is in the combination of several ideas, several commands, or several functions.

```
 1 : * File      Dentry7.prg
 2 : * Compile   Rmake sample /dFILE:dentry7
 3 :
 4 : #include "PTValue.ch"
 5 : #include "PTColor.ch"
 6 : #include "PTFuncs.ch"
 7 : #include "PTInkey.ch"
 8 : #include "PTVerbs.ch"
 9 :
10 : memvar GETLIST
11 :
12 : procedure Main()
13 :
14 :    local cFiles
15 :    local aData
16 :    local nCount
17 :
18 :    use Notap new readonly index Notap alias Check
19 :    use Notap new index Notap
20 :
21 :    PROCESS
22 :       cls
23 :       cFiles := space(12)
24 :       if GetFileName( 6, 5, @cFiles )
25 :
26 :          aData := Notap->( dbseek( cFiles ), GetRecord( recno() ) )
27 :          for nCount := 2 to len( aData )      // edit the record
28 :             @ 6+nCount, 0 say padr(field(nCount),15) get aData[nCount]
29 :          next
30 :          read
31 :          if !( lastkey() == pESC )
32 :             Notap->( PutRecord( aData, recno() ) )
33 :          endif
34 :       else
35 :          exit
36 :       endif
37 :
38 :    END PROCESS
39 :
40 : *********************
41 :
42 : static function GetFileName( nRow, nCol, cName )
43 :
44 :    local lRetValue := pFALSE
45 :
46 :    @ nRow, nCol say "Enter File Name: " get cName ;
47 :                  pict "@!" valid Check->( OnFile( @cName ) )
48 :    read
49 :    if !( lastkey() == pESC )
50 :       lRetValue := Check->( dbseek( cName ) )
51 :    endif
52 :
53 :    return( lRetValue )
54 :
```

```
 55 : ********************
 56 :
 57 : static function OnFile( xItem )
 58 :
 59 :   local lRetValue := pTRUE
 60 :   local cScreen   := savescreen( 6,40, 18,70 )
 61 :
 62 :   if !dbseek(xItem)
 63 :     lRetValue := pFALSE
 64 :     dispbox(6,40,18,70,pDBAR)
 65 :     dbgotop()    // MUST BE to avoid internal 5333 w/ field
 66 :     dbedit(7,41,17,69)
 67 :
 68 :     if lastkey() == pENTER
 69 :       xItem := FIELD->files
 70 :       keyboard pENTER
 71 :     endif
 72 :   endif
 73 :
 74 :   restscreen( 6,40,18,70, cScreen )
 75 :   return( lRetValue )
 76 :
 77 : ********************
 78 :
 79 : static function GetRecord( nRecord )
 80 :
 81 :   local nOldRecord := recno()    // Save current record position.
 82 :   local aRetValue  := {}         // Build default return value
 83 :   local nCount                   // for the FOR...NEXT loop.
 84 :
 85 :   DEFAULT nRecord TO 0           // Phantom Record is DEFAULT!!!
 86 :
 87 :   if !empty( alias () )  // Robust enough... testing to see if valid area
 88 :     dbgoto(nRecord)      // got to requested record
 89 :     for nCount := 1 to fcount()           // Process through each field in
 90 :       aadd( aRetValue, fieldget(nCount) ) // the data structure.
 91 :     next
 92 :   endif
 93 :
 94 :   dbgoto( nRecord )
 95 :
 96 :   return( aRetValue )
 97 :
 98 : ********************
 99 :
100 : static function PutRecord( aData, nRecord )
101 :
102 :   local nOldRecord := recno()    // Save current record position
103 :   local nCount                   // for the FOR...NEXT loop.
104 :   local lRetValue  := pFALSE
105 :
106 :   DEFAULT nRecord TO 0           // Phantom Record is DEFAULT!!!
107 :
108 :   if !empty( alias () )  // Robust enough... testing to see if valid area
109 :     if empty( nRecord )
110 :       dbappend()
111 :     else
112 :       dbgoto(nRecord)           // got to requested record
113 :     endif
114 :     for nCount := 1 to fcount()             // Process through each field in
```

```
115 :            fieldput(nCount, aData[nCount] ) // the data structure.
116 :         next
117 :         lRetValue := pTRUE
118 :      endif
119 :
120 :      dbgoto( nRecord )
121 :
122 :      return( lRetValue )
123 :
124 : // End of File: Dentry7.prg
```

Since Clipper is not an interpreter, the error-trapping mechanism commonly found in interpreters that prevents an end user from opening the same database more than once is not present. This means that under program control, the same file can be opened more than once, using a different alias for each work area. It is important to keep this in perspective; opening the same file can be dangerous as well as advantageous. Using the secondary file for looking up information is acceptable; altering data in either file is hazardous to the integrity of the application. Here, the same database file is opened twice, with the alias of one of the work areas set to the name "Check." Once this file is opened, the main processing loop begins on line 21, the screen is cleared, and *cFiles*, the memory variable used for lookup, is set to an empty value. At this point, the GetFileName( ) function is called, and the variable *cFiles* is passed to it by reference. (The other two parameters for this function are the row and column coordinates to be used for an @ ... SAY ... GET command using the passed parameter *cFiles*.) This is a lookup function that is used to find a record in the Notap database. If the record is found, the GetFileName( ) function will return a logical true (.T.); if not, a logical false (.F.) will be returned, causing the EXIT command on line 35 to be called, thus terminating the loop.

At the time of the call to the GetFileName( ) function, the currently selected work area is Notap. The validation clause of the GET on lines 46 and 47, however, points to the Check work area. When the VALID clause calls the OnFile( ) function, Clipper will automatically deselect the Notap work area and select the Check work area. Even though this is the same database, each work area maintains its own set of file and record pointers, filter conditions, and so on. In addition, the local parameter *cName*, which is the variable *cFiles* passed by reference, is then passed to the OnFile( ) function by reference as well. Without moving the file pointer in the Notap work area, the Check work area validates the value of *cName*; if the value of *cName* is in the Check work area (Notap database), the VALID clause returns a logical true (.T.), which in turn causes the DBSEEK( ) function in line 50 to return a true value in *lRetValue*. This then is the value of the function GetFileName( ).

In the OnFile( ) function, the list box is used with a simple generic DBEDIT( ) call. This may be replaced by the TBROWSE( ) object, as discussed in Chapter 16. If the ENTER key is pressed while the DBEDIT( ) function is active, the function will terminate and the expression on line 68 will be evaluated. Since this will be a true condition, the variable *xItem*, which is the variable *cName* passed by reference and which in turn is the variable *cFiles* passed by reference, is altered with the value from the *cFiles* field. The FIELD alias is used instead of the alias Check. This allows the function OnFile( ) to be called for any work area; it is not hard-coded and thus is not tied to one specific work area. This increases the modularity and portability of this function. Of course, the work area would have to contain a field named *cFiles*; however, this too may be programmed for using the FIELDGET( )

function, along with an additional numeric parameter passed to this routine pointing to the desired field. Once the field value is stored to the variable *xItem*, the keyboard is stuffed with the ENTER key and the function passes a return value of false (.F.) back to the VALID clause on line 47. If an item should be selected, the variable in the GET (line 46) is modified and must be displayed to the end user. Here, however, the value is altered but not seen; stuffing the keyboard with an ENTER key and returning a logical false (.F.) allows Clipper to naturally refresh the GET buffer, which in turn redisplays the contents of the variable that has been altered. Stuffing the ENTER key eliminates the need for the end user to do it.

Once the GetFileName( ) function returns a logical true (.T.), the value of *cFiles* will be valid. Now we come to line 26, a complex expression. First, the expression will be evaluated in the Notap work area, and the value of the expression will be the last expression within it that is evaluated. This is the GetRecord( ) function. However, before this function is called, a call is made to the DBSEEK( ) function. This positions the record pointer in the Notap work area to the proper record. Once positioned, the GetRecord( ) function is called using the current RECNO( ) value as positioned by the DBSEEK( ) function. The FOR ... NEXT loop on lines 27 through 29 displays the entire record in the array *aData[ ]*. Once READ is active, the record is returned to the Notap database via the PutRecord( ) function.

Keep in mind that while the same database is used twice, only one work area, one database, and one index file are updated. The other work area is used simply for data validation and record positioning.

## Saving GETs

Sometimes in data entry, items from one database depend on the existence of items in another database. One scenario, for example, is an order-entry system where items to be ordered depend on the existence of items in inventory. However, in the real world, there may be times while entering an order a clerk will discover that the inventory item is not on file. In the past, third-party libraries had to be purchased or special tricks had to be resorted to that allowed you to suspend a GET, process a new GET, and then return to the old GET to continue. This was called nesting GETs, or the ability to SAVE and RESTORE GETs at will.

Before showing how this can be accomplished with Clipper 5.2, we must turn once again to the Clipper Standard Header file, STD.CH. To help us see Clipper's potential, here is the extract of how the READ command and a simple @ ... GET command are translated:

```
#command READ => ReadModal(GetList) ; GetList := {}

#command @ <row>, <col> GET <var> [PICTURE <pic>] [VALID <valid>];
         [WHEN <when>]   => ;
         SetPos(<row>, <col>) ;
         AAdd( GetList, ;
              _GET_(<var>, <(var)>, <pic>, <{valid}>, <{when}>):display())
```

In the case of the READ command, the READMODAL( ) function is called and a variable called *GetList* is passed to it. Once the READMODAL( ) function has finished its operation, the *GetList* variable is reinitialized to an empty array. Looking at the @ ... GET command, the cursor is positioned at the proper coordinates with the SETPOS( ) function, then the same variable, *GetList[ ]*, is passed to the AADD( ) function to have an element dynamically allocated to it. The function _GET_( ) generates the GET object that is stored to the element subscript position allocated by the AADD( ) function. In other words, the entire GET system is one array processed by either an AADD( ) and a _GET_( ) or by the READMODAL( ) function.

If the GETs of a system are held in this internal variable called *GetList[ ]*, how difficult would it be to write a user-defined command that will temporarily assign that GET to a new variable, allowing a new GET system to be called? Consider these two user-defined commands that may be found in the header file called PTVALUE.CH.

```
#xcommand SAVE GET TO <var> => <var> := M->GetList ; M->GetList := {}

#xcommand RESTORE GET FROM <var> => M->GetList := <var>
```

The first command takes the current array in M->GetList[ ] and assigns it to the variable used in the source application. It then clears out the *M->GetList[ ]* array and is ready for a new set of @ ... GET commands. The next command then takes the variable containing the previous GET and restores the *M->GetList[ ]* array to that value.

Here is an example program that implements this technology.

```
 1 : * File      Dentry8.prg
 2 : * Compile   Rmake sample /dFILE:dentry8
 3 :
 4 : #include "PTValue.ch"
 5 : #include "PTColor.ch"
 6 : #include "PTFuncs.ch"
 7 : #include "PTInkey.ch"
 8 : #include "PTVerbs.ch"
 9 :
10 : memvar GETLIST
11 :
12 : procedure Main()
13 :
14 :    local nTimes := 0
15 :    local aWhens := {}
16 :
17 :    private aData
18 :
19 :    use Statcode new
20 :    index on Statcode->status to Statcode
21 :    use Clients new
22 :    index on Clients->status to ClieStat
23 :
24 :    set(pMESSAGE, maxrow())
25 :    set(pMCENTER, pON )
26 :
27 :    aadd( aWhens, "This is the Status Field: TAB to add one!" )
28 :    aadd( aWhens, "The Account Field on Record" )
29 :
30 :    setkey( pTAB, {|| Statcode->( AddStat() ) } )
31 :
32 :    REPEAT
33 :
34 :       aData := Clients->( GetRecord( nTimes++ ) )
35 :       setcolor(MAKECOLOR(pWHITE/pBLUE, pBLACK/pWHITE,,,pWHITE/pBLUE))
36 :       scroll()
37 :       @ 0,0 say "Press TAB to Add STATUS Code"
38 :
```

```
39 :      @ 1,0 say " Status:" get aData[1] pict "!" when SayIt( aWhens[1] ) ;
40 :                        valid Statcode->( GoodStat( "aData[1]" ) )
41 :      @ 2,0 say " Account:" get aData[2] when SayIt( aWhens[2] ) ;
42 :                        valid MustFill( aData[2] )
43 :      read
44 :      if !(lastkey() == pESC)
45 :        Clients->( PutRecord( aData, nTimes ), dbedit(10,0,maxrow(),maxcol()) )
46 :      endif
47 :
48 :    UNTIL nTimes == 5
49 :    cls
50 :
51 : *********************
52 :
53 : static function Goodstat( xItem )
54 :
55 :    local cScreen
56 :    local lRetValue:= pTRUE
57 :    local lIsArray := IsAnArray( xItem )
58 :    local aData
59 :
60 :    if !dbseek( lIsArray, &xItem., xItem )
61 :      lRetValue := pFALSE
62 :      cScreen   := savescreen( 4,40,20,65 )
63 :      dbgotop()
64 :      dispbox( 4,40,20,65, pDBAR )
65 :      dbedit( 5,41,19,64 )
66 :      if lastkey() == pENTER   // an item is selected!
67 :        if lIsArray
68 :          &xItem.   := fieldget(1)
69 :          aData[2] := fieldget(2)
70 :        else
71 :          xItem    := fieldget(1)
72 :        endif
73 :      endif
74 :      restscreen( 4,40,20,65, cScreen )
75 :
76 :    endif
77 :
78 :    setcursor( pCURSOR_ON )
79 :
80 :    return( lRetValue )
81 :
82 : *********************
83 :
84 : static function IsAnArray( xThing )
85 :
86 :    local nLeft
87 :    local nRight
88 :    local lRetValue := pFALSE
89 :
90 :    IF xThing IS pCHARACTER
91 :
92 :      if "["$xThing .and. "]"$xThing
93 :        nLeft  := at("[", xThing)
94 :        nRight := at("]", xThing)
95 :        if nLeft < nRight
96 :          lRetValue := (val( substr(xThing, nLeft+1, nRight-nLeft-1)) > 0)
97 :        endif
98 :      endif
```

```
 99 :    endif
100 :
101 :    return( lRetValue )
102 :
103 : **********************
104 :
105 : static procedure AddStat
106 :
107 :    local nRow    := row()
108 :    local nCol    := col()
109 :    local cScreen := savescreen( 13,0,17, maxcol() )
110 :    local aData   := GetRecord()
111 :    local aCurrentGet
112 :
113 :    SAVE GET TO aCurrentGet      // User-Defined Command !
114 :
115 :    dispbox(13,0,17,maxcol(),pDBAR)
116 :
117 :    @ 14,1 say "Enter Status Code: " get aData[1] pict "!" ;
118 :           valid MustFill(aData[1], maxrow()-1)
119 :
120 :    @ 15,1 say "       Description: " get aData[2] pict "@!" ;
121 :           valid MustFill(aData[1], maxrow()-1)
122 :    read
123 :    if !( lastkey() == pESC )
124 :      PutRecord( aData, 0 )
125 :      dbedit(13,0,17,maxcol())
126 :    endif
127 :
128 :    RESTORE GET FROM aCurrentGet
129 :
130 :    restscreen( 13,0,17,maxcol(), cScreen )
131 :
132 :    setcursor( pCURSOR_ON )
133 :    devpos( nRow, nCol )
134 :
135 : *********************
136 :
137 : static function SayIt( cSaying )
138 :
139 :    local cColor := setcolor(MAKECOLOR(pBLACK/pCYAN))
140 :
141 :    devpos( set( pMESSAGE), 0 )
142 :    devout( if( !set(pMCENTER), padr(cSaying, maxcol()+1),;
143 :                                padc(cSaying, maxcol()+1) ) )
144 :
145 :    setcolor( cColor ) // Reset the color to what it was!
146 :
147 :    return( pTRUE )
148 :
149 : *******************
150 :
151 : static function MustFill( xItem, ; // Item to be tested
152 :                           nRow,  ; // Row for the display
153 :                           nCol,  ; // Column for the display
154 :                           cSaying, ; // Saying for the display
155 :                           lWithSound)   // Toggle for the sound
156 :
157 :    static cScreen  // The screen for message is remembered!
158 :
```

```
159 :    local lRetValue := pTRUE
160 :
161 :    DEFAULT nRow TO row(), ;
162 :            nCol TO col()+1, ;
163 :            cSaying TO "This must be filled", ;
164 :            lWithSound TO pFALSE
165 :
166 :    if !( lastkey() == pUP_ARROW ) // Escape Routes MUST be allowed.
167 :      if empty( xItem )            // This is the beginning of the test.
168 :        if cScreen == NIL
169 :          cScreen := savescreen(nRow, nCol, nRow, nCol+len(cSaying) )
170 :        endif
171 :        lRetValue := pFALSE
172 :        @ nRow, nCol say cSaying
173 :
174 :        if lWithSound
175 :          tone(164.80, 4)
176 :          tone(130, 1)
177 :        endif
178 :      endif
179 :    endif
180 :
181 :    if lRetValue          // Clear out the screen area!
182 :      if !( cScreen == NIL )
183 :        restscreen( nRow, nCol, nRow, nCol+len(cSaying), cScreen )
184 :        cScreen := NIL
185 :      endif
186 :    endif
187 :
188 :    return( lRetValue )
189 :
190 : ********************
191 :
192 : static function GetRecord( nRecord )
193 :
194 :    local nOldRecord := recno()   // Save current record position.
195 :    local aRetValue  := {}        // Build default return value
196 :    local nCount                  // for the FOR...NEXT loop.
197 :
198 :    DEFAULT nRecord TO 0          // Phantom Record is DEFAULT!!!
199 :
200 :    if !empty( alias () )   // Robust enough... testing to see if valid area
201 :      dbgoto(nRecord)       // got to requested record
202 :      for nCount := 1 to fcount()            // Process through each field in
203 :        aadd( aRetValue, fieldget(nCount) ) // the data structure.
204 :      next
205 :    endif
206 :
207 :    dbgoto( nRecord )
208 :
209 :    return( aRetValue )
210 :
211 : ********************
212 :
213 : static function PutRecord( aData, nRecord )
214 :
215 :    local nOldRecord := recno()   // Save current record position
216 :    local nCount                  // for the FOR...NEXT loop.
217 :    local lRetValue   := pFALSE
218 :
```

```
219 :    DEFAULT nRecord TO 0        // Phantom Record is DEFAULT!!!
220 :
221 :    if !empty( alias () )    // Robust enough... testing to see if valid area
222 :       if empty( nRecord )
223 :          dbappend()
224 :       else
225 :          dbgoto(nRecord)          // got to requested record
226 :       endif
227 :       for nCount := 1 to fcount()        // Process through each field in
228 :          fieldput(nCount, aData[nCount] ) // the data structure.
229 :       next
230 :       lRetValue := pTRUE
231 :    endif
232 :
233 :    dbgoto( nRecord )
234 :
235 :    return( lRetValue )
236 :
237 : // End of File:Dentry8.prg
```

Before getting into the crux of this example, several unique features need to be pointed out. On line 30 there is a call to the SETKEY( ) function; this is the main function at the heart of the SET KEY command. In this example, the TAB key is assigned to the code block that, when evaluated, will automatically deselect the current work area and select the Statcode work area. At that point, a call to the AddStat( ) procedure is made. When the AddStat( ) procedure has finished processing, Clipper will automatically deselect the Statcode work area and return to the calling area.

Next comes the REPEAT command. This is a user-defined command that is similar to the PROCESS and the WHILE .T. commands, with one small exception. Here, the UNTIL command contains the condition which determines how many times this loop beginning on line 32 will be processed. The test for the exit condition is at the bottom of the loop rather than at the top (e.g., WHILE !EOF( )). Consider this possible WHILE command:

```
WHILE LASTKEY( ) != 27   /// the ESC key
```

We have to make certain before executing this command that the last key pressed prior to this command was not the ESC key if we want to make sure that the loop executes at least once. This means that we have to clear out the keyboard buffer before entering the loop. Similar examples can be found in every Clipper application—often, the exit condition needs to be evaluated at the bottom of the WHILE loop rather than at the top.

Now, returning to working with nested GETs, consider the @ ... SAY ... GET commands on lines 39 through 42. They are activated by the READ command or the READMODAL( ) function. If the TAB key is pressed when the GET is active, program flow will jump to the AddStat procedure, defined beginning on line 105, which works in the Statcode work area. When a SET KEY command or SETKEY( ) function causes a procedure to be called from a READ statement, it is important to preserve the environment. Here, the first thing that happens is that the row and column position of the cursor within the READ command is saved to the variables *nRow* and *nCol*. Once the cursor position is obtained, the current GET system is saved to a LOCAL variable called *aCurrentGet[ ]*. Once the screen is saved as well and a new border is drawn, an array called *aData[ ]* is declared that contains an array of empty elements based on the structure of the database in the current work area, Statcode. Do not get this *aData[ ]* array confused with the previously called *aData[ ]* array—this array is LOCAL to the AddStat function and is independent of the previous array. Then, a new series of @ ... SAY ... GET commands is issued. Here, the values of the array elements are entered and eventually added to the database in the current work area via the PutRecord( ) function on line 124. To show that the items were placed into the database, a simple DBEDIT( ) call is made. Regardless of this operation, once the controlling IF command with the READ is complete, the previous GET is restored from the variable *aCurrentGet[ ]*. The screen is restored as well, and the cursor is turned on (it could have been turned off by the DBEDIT( ) function) and is placed back at the precise row and column on which it was originally positioned.

The significance of the AddStat procedure is that if a value entered for the GET on lines 39 through 41 does not appear in the Statcode work area, as determined by the GoodStat( ) function in the VALID clause, the TAB key can be pressed to quickly add the item to the database and allow this GET to be completed.

One more item needs to be pointed out in this example. When you are working with array elements, it is important to remember that individual array subscripts cannot be passed by reference to a function; they can only be passed by value. To simulate this, the string representation of the individual array element is passed to the GoodStat( ) function (line 40) instead. Here, it becomes the local parameter *xItem*, which contains the string of the array element, and it in turn is passed to the IsAnArray( ) function to determine, as best it can, whether this variable, *xItem*, is an array element passed as a string or a regular memory variable. The result of this test is stored to another LOCAL variable named *lRetValue*.

The DBSEEK( ) function as well as the replacement commands in lines 60 through 76 are all based on either macro-expanding the string representation of the array element, which would in essence pass the array element by reference, or treating it as a simple memory variable. This technique of macro-expanding the string value of an array subscript allows functions to view an array element passed as a string in the same manner as a regular parameter passed by reference.

## SET KEY Applications

In previous programming examples we have seen how the SET KEY command and the SETKEY( ) function can aid in the task of data entry. In the past, it was only a dream to be able to automatically select a work area from a SET KEY. Only dreamers thought of passing values directly to the routine called by the SET KEY, and even fewer thought of context-sensitive SET KEY statements. On the surface, these still are only far-off notions; however, with a little help from the STD.CH file, we can see that more is offered to us than just the simple SET KEY command.

In the past, unstructured programming techniques allowed private variables to be manipulated at lower levels of the program. In particular, a procedure called by the SET KEY command could manipulate any of the PRIVATE variables in the calling routine. However, this meant that the procedure called by the SET KEY command was tied to that specific routine; the ability to use the procedure with the SET KEY command in other places was limited unless massive amounts of programming muscle were used, such as CASE statements and evaluating the *v* variable (the variable name of the GET, which was automatically passed to the SETKEY routine).

While this reliance on PRIVATE variables and its resulting programming technique will still work under Clipper 5.2, Clipper 5.2 at the same time offers a number of new features that together suggest that the old programming techniques are no longer viable and that a new approach is needed. First of all, LOCAL variables make it impossible to manipulate variables in lower, dependent routines (and, as a result, make it impossible to accidentally modify the values of variables in dependent routines). Clipper also allows you to pass a variable by reference to a function by simply preceding the variable name with the "@" character. It is also possible to call a function within a code block. The SETKEY( ) function requires that a code block, along with the ASCII value of the "hot key," be passed to it. Instead of passing the program name, the line number, and the variable name to the function within the code block, consider passing the GET variables by reference, as you would to a VALID or a WHEN clause. The following example program shows this in action:

```
 1 : * File        Dentry9.prg
 2 : * Compile     Rmake sample /dFILE:Dentry9
 3 :
 4 : #include "PTValue.ch"
 5 : #include "PTInkey.ch"
 6 : #include "PTVerbs.ch"
 7 :
 8 : procedure Main()
 9 :
10 :    local getlist := {}
11 :    local cFIle
12 :    local nSize
13 :
14 :    setkey( pTAB, {|| FilesOnDisk( @cFile, @nSize, getlist )} )
15 :
16 :    PROCESS
17 :       cls
18 :       cFile := space(40)
19 :       nSize := 0
20 :
21 :       @ 1,0 say "Press TAB for Files!"
22 :       @ 3,0 say "Enter File Name: " get cFile
23 :       @ 4,0 say "             Size: " get nSize
24 :       read
25 :       if !( lastkey() == pESC )
26 :          @ 6,5 say "Values are: " get cFile
27 :          @ 7,5 say "             " get nSize
28 :          clear gets
29 :          wait
30 :       else
31 :          exit
32 :       endif
33 :
34 :    END PROCESS
35 :
36 : *********************
37 :
38 : static function FilesOnDisk( cFileName, nFileSize, aGetList )
39 :
40 :    static aTheFiles
41 :    static aTheSizes
42 :
43 :    local nVar
44 :    local cScreen := savescreen( 4,40,20,60 )
```

```
45 :
46 :      if aTheFiles == NIL    // Both variables cannot go to the same
47 :                             // array pointer because they are different!
48 :         aTheFiles := {}
49 :         aTheSizes := {}
50 :         aeval( directory(), {|aDir| aadd(aTheFiles, aDir[1]), ;
51 :                                     aadd(aTheSizes, aDir[2]) } )
52 :      endif
53 :      dispbox(4,40,20,60,pDBAR)
54 :
55 :      if !empty( nVar := achoice(5,41,19,59,aTheFiles)  )
56 :         cFileName := padr( aTheFiles[nVar], 40 )
57 :         nFileSize := aTheSizes[nVar]
58 :         aeval( aGetList, {|oGet| oGet:display()} )
59 :      endif
60 :
61 :      restscreen( 4, 40, 20, 60, cScreen )
62 :
63 :      return( NIL )
64 :
65 : // End of File: Dentry9.prg
```

Here the TAB key is set to execute the code block, which in turn executes the function FilesOnDisk( ). Two parameters are passed to this function by reference: *cFile* and *nSize*. Both are LOCAL memory variables (lines 11 and 12) that are involved in the GET commands beginning on lines 22 and 23. One other variable initialized on line 10 is the local array *GetList[ ]*. This means that the @...GET commands will be dynamically adding values to this array rather than the PUBLIC variable *GETLIST[ ]*. This is how we can limit the scope and visibility of the *GetList[ ]* array to a single subroutine. If the TAB key is pressed while the READ command (line 24) is active, a call to FilesOnDisk( ) is made. The address pointers to *cFile*, *nSize*, and *GetList[ ]* are then passed to the local parameters *cFileName*, *nFileSize*, and *aGetList[ ]* on line 38. If the STATIC arrays *aTheFiles[ ]* and *aTheSizes[ ]* have yet to be created, they are generated on lines 48 through 51 by using the AEVAL( ) function in conjunction with the DIRECTORY( ) function. Once they are built (or if they exist from a previous call), a simple ACHOICE( ) is made on line 55.

Note that this line of code is a nested expression: The value of the ACHOICE( ) function is first stored to the *nVar* variable, which in turn is evaluated by the EMPTY( ) function. If an element is selected from this array, the value of *nVar* will not be empty; the program will then store the corresponding values from both the *aTheFiles[ ]* and *aTheSizes[ ]* arrays to the local parameters *cFileName* and *nFileSize*. Since these were passed by reference, the values of *cFile* and *nSize* should then be altered. Now, since the values are altered, and since we passed the contents of the original *GETLIST[ ]* down to this subroutine, we can call the individual GET objects within each array element and force the newly updated values to be re-painted to the screen. Line 58 does just this: It refreshes the entire *GETLIST[ ]* array, passed as *aGetList[ ]*, and calls the *:display( )* method on each GET object.

## Working with User-Defined Readers

Our discussion of the GET system so far in this chapter has focused on customizing the behavior of individual GETs without altering the general or default behavior of the GET system as a whole. Now, however, we want to look at a way of adding new behaviors to individual GETs without modifying the GET system as defined in GETSYS.PRG. These are behaviors that the GET system itself ordinarily does not support.

The following is an extract from GETSYS.PRG that is within the looping mechanism, prior to granting input focus to a GET. It provides a hook that allows the behavior of individual GETs to be modified:

```
// Read the GET
IF ( VALTYPE( oGet:reader ) == "B" )
   EVAL( oGet:reader, oGet )    // Use custom reader block
ELSE
   GetReader( oGet )            // Use standard reader
ENDIF
```

What this line should tell us is that there is an instance variable named *:reader* that is important enough to have a piece of code referring to it. Should the instance variable be a code block, it will be evaluated, with the individual GET object passed to it. Now come two questions: What is supposed to be in this code block, and how are we going to get it into the GET system? The latter is the easier of the two to answer. Again, looking at code within the GETSYS.PRG file, we see that the GET object being looked at in conjunction with the *:reader* instance variable is the same GET object passed to the code block within the *:reader* when it is evaluated. Therefore, a piece of code outside of the GETSYS.PRG file probably looks something like this:

```
oGet:reader := {|oG| SomeFunc(oG)}
```

Now comes the question: How to get this code block assigned to the GET object at the appropriate time? This is what the SEND clause of the @ ... GET command is meant to do. This little documented clause allows us to "send a message" to the GET object just defined via the _GET_( ) function, which is the @ ... GET command. This clause is not just for the *:reader* instance variable: Any assignable instance variable that is part of the GET object structure can be specified in this way. So, a code block can be assigned to the *:reader* that would in turn be EVAL( )'d within the GET system. This might look something like this:

```
@ 10,10 get nDate send reader := {|oG| SomeFunc(oG)}
```

This leads us to plan what is the essence of the "SomeFunc( )" function. This function is to be designed to trap the keys from the input and process them accordingly. Again, looking to GETSYS.PRG, we can see that if no code block is assigned, the GET system uses a function called GETREADER( ). It is a safe bet that that function can be used as a template for our own function; one we can build from to add new readers to our GET system.

Before examining GETREADER( ), we must plan what our new reader is to do. To start, let's plan a reader that might be used for a General Ledger. Most ledger systems allow the end user to put the format code of the account into the system. Typically, these codes look like "LL-1221.11" which means that if used as a PICTURE clause, the characters "XA-.!9" are valid input characters. If the end user could place into the system the format characters that would in turn be used as General Ledger formatting codes, one of two options is available to us. First, we could build a user-defined function to be used in conjunction with the VALID clause that would test the validity of the data after they are input into the GET variable. The other option would be to restrict every key other than those acceptable from getting into the

GET variable in the first place. This would then free up the VALID clause for some other validation expression. To implement the latter, start by taking the GETREADER( ) function, copying it, and renaming it.

```
procedure GetGLRead( oGet )

  if ( GetPreValidate( oGet ) )  // Read GET if WHEN condition

    oGet:setFocus()              // Activate the GET for reading

    while ( oGet:exitState == GE_NOEXIT )

      if ( oGet:typeOut )   // Check for (no editable positions)
        oGet:exitState := GE_ENTER
      endif

      while ( oGet:exitState == GE_NOEXIT ) // Apply keystrokes
        GetGLApKey( oGet, inkey( 0 ) )
      enddo

      // Disallow exit if the VALID condition is not satisfied
      if ( !GetPostValidate( oGet ) )
        oGet:exitState := GE_NOEXIT
      endif
    enddo

    // De-activate the GET
    oGet:killFocus()

  endif

// End of function
```

Almost all of this is identical to the GETREADER( ) function within the GETSYS.PRG file. The only exception is the function called to directly apply the keys. This function, typically called GETAPPLYKEY( ), is also renamed as GetGLApKey( ) and, in turn, needs to be copied and modified. It is this function that processes the keys and, thus, needs to restrict all of the inappropriate keys. Now, here is that function modified:

```
static procedure GetGLApKey( oGet, nKey )

  local cKey       := chr(nKey)    // character version of key pressed
  local bKeyBlock                  // used to hold block from SETKEY()

  if !( ( bKeyBlock := setkey( nKey ) ) == NIL ) // Check for SET KEY first
    GetDoSetKey( bKeyBlock, oGet )
  else

    do case
    case ( nKey == K_UP )
      oGet:exitState := GE_UP

    case ( nKey == K_SH_TAB )
      oGet:exitState := GE_UP
```

```
case ( nKey == K_DOWN )
  oGet:exitState := GE_DOWN

case ( nKey == K_TAB )
  oGet:exitState := GE_DOWN

case ( nKey == K_ENTER )
  oGet:exitState := GE_ENTER

case ( nKey == K_ESC )
  if ( set( _SET_ESCAPE ) )
    oGet:undo()
    oGet:exitState := GE_ESCAPE
  endif

case ( nKey == K_PGUP )
  oGet:exitState := GE_WRITE

case ( nKey == K_PGDN )
  oGet:exitState := GE_WRITE

case ( nKey == K_CTRL_HOME )
  oGet:exitState := GE_TOP

case ( nKey == K_CTRL_W ) // Both ^W and ^End terminate the READ
  oGet:exitState := GE_WRITE

case ( nKey == K_INS )
  set( _SET_INSERT, !set( _SET_INSERT ) )
  // ShowScoreboard()   // This is remarked 'cause it ain't a PUBLIC
                        // function!

case ( nKey == K_UNDO )
  oGet:undo()

case ( nKey == K_HOME )
  oGet:home()

case ( nKey == K_END )
  oGet:end()

case ( nKey == K_RIGHT )
  oGet:right()

case ( nKey == K_LEFT )
  oGet:left()

case ( nKey == K_CTRL_RIGHT )
  oGet:wordRight()

case ( nKey == K_CTRL_LEFT )
  oGet:wordLeft()

case ( nKey == K_BS )
  oGet:backSpace()

case ( nKey == K_DEL )
  oGet:delete()

case ( nKey == K_CTRL_T )
  oGet:delWordRight()
```

```
       case ( nKey == K_CTRL_Y )
         oGet:delEnd()

       case ( nKey == K_CTRL_BS )
         oGet:delWordLeft()

       otherwise
         if cKey $ "9XA.-!,"
           if ( SET( _SET_INSERT ) )
             oGet:insert( cKey )
           else
             oGet:overstrike( cKey )
           endif

           if ( oGet:typeOut )
             if ( set( _SET_BELL ) )
               qqout( chr(7) )
             endif

             if ( !set( _SET_CONFIRM ) )
               oGet:exitState := GE_ENTER
             endif
           endif

         endif

       endcase

     endif
```

Within this function is a massive DO CASE construct which processes the key that was pressed within the GetGLRead( ) function. For this operation, the restricting keys are isolated under the OTHERWISE statement. There, only the keys that match the pattern are allowed into the GET buffer either in insert mode or overstrike mode. In addition, some of the other code constructs that appear in the GETAPPLYKEY( ) function were removed, since this function does not have to be "compatible" with any predecessor.

And now, putting all of this together, we would have the following:

```
 1 : #include "Set.ch"
 2 : #include "Inkey.ch"
 3 : #include "Getexit.ch"
 4 :
 5 : function Main()
 6 :
 7 :    local cGlPict := space(10)
 8 :    local getlist := {}          // This is for the @...GET command.
 9 :
10 :    scroll()
11 :
12 :    @ 10,5 say "Enter General Ledger Picture Format: " get cGlPict ;
13 :       when (devpos(maxrow(), 0), devout( "Only '9X.,-!' are valid" ), .t.) ;
14 :       send reader := {|oGet| GetGLRead(oGet)}
15 :
16 :    read
17 :
18 :    @ 12,5 say "Value of the 'cGlPict' variable: "
19 :    devout( alltrim( cGlPict ) )
20 :
21 :    return( NIL )
```

```
22 :
23 : //   And now for the special readers!
24 :
25 : #define K_UNDO           K_CTRL_U    // This is for the special ^U key
26 :
27 : procedure GetGLRead( oGet )    // to handle General Ledger format codes!
28 :
29 :    if ( GetPreValidate( oGet ) ) // Read GET if WHEN condition
30 :
31 :       oGet:setFocus()            // Activate the GET for reading.
32 :
33 :       while ( oGet:exitState == GE_NOEXIT )
34 :
35 :          if ( oGet:typeOut )  // Check for (no editable positions).
36 :             oGet:exitState := GE_ENTER
37 :          endif
38 :
39 :          while ( oGet:exitState == GE_NOEXIT ) // Apply keystrokes
40 :             GetGLApKey( oGet, inkey( 0 ) )
41 :          enddo
42 :
43 :          // Disallow exit if the VALID condition is not satisfied
44 :          if ( !GetPostValidate( oGet ) )
45 :             oGet:exitState := GE_NOEXIT
46 :          endif
47 :       enddo
48 :
49 :       // De-activate the GET
50 :       oGet:killFocus()
51 :
52 :    endif
53 :
54 : static procedure GetGLApKey( oGet, nKey )
55 :
56 :    local cKey         := chr(nKey)      // character version of key pressed
57 :    local bKeyBlock                      // used to hold block from SETKEY()
58 :
59 :    if !( ( bKeyBlock := setkey( nKey ) ) == NIL ) // Check for SET KEY first
60 :       GetDoSetKey( bKeyBlock, oGet )
61 :    else
62 :
63 :       do case
64 :       case ( nKey == K_UP )
65 :          oGet:exitState := GE_UP
66 :
67 :       case ( nKey == K_SH_TAB )
68 :          oGet:exitState := GE_UP
69 :
70 :       case ( nKey == K_DOWN )
71 :          oGet:exitState := GE_DOWN
72 :
73 :       case ( nKey == K_TAB )
74 :          oGet:exitState := GE_DOWN
75 :
76 :       case ( nKey == K_ENTER )
77 :          oGet:exitState := GE_ENTER
78 :
79 :       case ( nKey == K_ESC )
80 :          if ( set( _SET_ESCAPE ) )
81 :             oGet:undo()
82 :             oGet:exitState := GE_ESCAPE
```

```
 83 :         endif
 84 :
 85 :      case ( nKey == K_PGUP )
 86 :         oGet:exitState := GE_WRITE
 87 :
 88 :      case ( nKey == K_PGDN )
 89 :         oGet:exitState := GE_WRITE
 90 :
 91 :      case ( nKey == K_CTRL_HOME )
 92 :         oGet:exitState := GE_TOP
 93 :
 94 :      case ( nKey == K_CTRL_W )  // Both ^W and ^End terminate the READ.
 95 :         oGet:exitState := GE_WRITE
 96 :
 97 :      case ( nKey == K_INS )
 98 :         set( _SET_INSERT, !set( _SET_INSERT ) )
 99 :         // ShowScoreboard()   // This is remarked 'cause it ain't a PUBLIC
100 :                               // function!
101 :
102 :      case ( nKey == K_UNDO )
103 :         oGet:undo()
104 :
105 :      case ( nKey == K_HOME )
106 :         oGet:home()
107 :
108 :      case ( nKey == K_END )
109 :         oGet:end()
110 :
111 :      case ( nKey == K_RIGHT )
112 :         oGet:right()
113 :
114 :      case ( nKey == K_LEFT )
115 :         oGet:left()
116 :
117 :      case ( nKey == K_CTRL_RIGHT )
118 :         oGet:wordRight()
119 :
120 :      case ( nKey == K_CTRL_LEFT )
121 :         oGet:wordLeft()
122 :
123 :      case ( nKey == K_BS )
124 :         oGet:backSpace()
125 :
126 :      case ( nKey == K_DEL )
127 :         oGet:delete()
128 :
129 :      case ( nKey == K_CTRL_T )
130 :         oGet:delWordRight()
131 :
132 :      case ( nKey == K_CTRL_Y )
133 :         oGet:delEnd()
134 :
135 :      case ( nKey == K_CTRL_BS )
136 :         oGet:delWordLeft()
137 :
138 :      otherwise
139 :         if cKey $ "9XA.-!,"
140 :            if ( SET( _SET_INSERT ) )
141 :               oGet:insert( cKey )
142 :            else
143 :               oGet:overstrike( cKey )
```

```
144 :             endif
145 :
146 :             if ( oGet:typeOut )
147 :                if ( set( _SET_BELL ) )
148 :                   qqout( chr(7) )
149 :                endif
150 :
151 :                if ( !set( _SET_CONFIRM ) )
152 :                   oGet:exitState := GE_ENTER
153 :                endif
154 :             endif
155 :
156 :          endif
157 :
158 :       endcase
159 :
160 :    endif
161 :
162 : // End of File
```

We are not restricted to working only with this reader. We could now build date readers that are Quicken-compatible, GET readers that act like calculators, GET readers that are mouse sensitive, GETs that allow the user to type in characters from right-to-left, and password readers as well.

## Modifying GETSYS.PRG

Why even bother with this thought, right? Well, for the most part, GETs behave the same way they have for the past 10 years, yet new demands are constantly being placed upon us by end users and their needs. To a C programmer, the concept of rebuilding a predefined behavior is not uncommon: The C programmer expects to take charge for any changes and, thus, assume responsibility. Clipper programmers have longed for respect from their C counterparts; however, when a Clipper programmer accepts the status-quo in fear of changing something that may not be supported in the future, most C programmers shake their heads. The goal is to build a program that (a) best suits the needs of the end user and (b) requires as little effort as possible on our part to implement and maintain. For the past six years, Clipper programmers were promised that the Extend system would not change, and yet it has changed with each new version since Autumn '86. Our goal should be to look at the base language and to fix what is not right or what works against us in a typical programming environment.

For example, let's say we want to have the cursor size altered from within a GET based on whether the GET was in insert mode or in overstrike mode. To do this without touching GETSYS.PRG, we need to use the following SET KEY command:

```
SET KEY pINS TO FlipIns()
```

and then we have to write the following:

```
function FlipIns()

   setcursor( if( readinsert( !readinsert() ), 3, 1 ) )

   return( NIL )
```

This function would have to be a PUBLIC function, thus using more symbol space and more load memory, and the SET KEY assignment would have to be turned on and off again each and every time a data entry screen was about to be called up. If this feature is wanted throughout all of our data entry screens, would it not be prudent to just give that behavior to GETSYS.PRG rather than issuing hundreds of lines of code or issuing user-defined readers on every GET? It comes down to what makes sense. If a particular feature should be used systemwide, application to application, then giving that behavior to GETSYS.PRG makes all the sense in the world. We are taking responsibility for our environment, for our applications, and for the needs of our clients. But then again, that's the way it should be, right?

While modifying the GET system may sound dangerous, it is not if you follow certain guidelines. The main guideline is to document all changes made to the system. This can help future versions of modifications as our needs increase.

As seen in the section on making your own reader in which we took much of our code from GETAPPLYKEY( ), there was a reference to a function called SHOWSCOREBOARD( ) which, if allowed into our user-defined reader, would give us an error. This is because SHOWSCOREBOARD( ) is defined as a STATIC procedure and needs either to be duplicated in our reader functions or to be converted to a PUBLIC function. The point to all of this is to show that there are ample reasons why GETSYS.PRG might best serve our programming needs if modified.

The key to this approach is to determine what is a new behavior that you want to give to the GET system. From Clipper version 5.1 to 5.2, a new option to position the element number specifically was included. This is important for those multiple-page data entry screens that allow the end user to press the UP key on the first GET of the second page of GETs and let them now be positioned on the last GET of the first page. However, with this addition to the READMODAL( ) function (the main function within the GET system), there is no modification to the READ command to allow for this new enhancement that might look something like this:

```
READ STARTING AT 3
```

The "STARTING AT 3" would be an optional clause and would therefore not be in any older code but could be added to work with the new version of Clipper. So keep in mind that as new behaviors are added to GETSYS.PRG, there may be a requirement to add new optional clauses to command definitions.

The first thing we would want to do is list on paper and then eventually in the header of the GETSYS.PRG file all of the global changes we want to make, giving each alteration a key number and code name to tell us at a later date who made the change, when, and why. Obviously, one of the first things we might want to do is make SHOWSCOREBOARD( ) a public function, or we might just remove that function from the system in order to prevent having that little display box appear within the frames of our banner. Another option if the SHOWSCOREBOARD( ) function were made PUBLIC would be to offer parameters for row and column positioning, defaulting to the predictable 0,60. Another simple addition would be to modify the cursor size if in insert mode or overstrike mode. This would remove one more SETKEY( ) definition and remove a few more lines of code that would need support from the application. We might also add the option to globally toggle off the operation of the SETKEY( ) function. In other words, if there are times when predefined

SET KEY assignments need to be turned off prior to a data entry screen and then turned back on at the conclusion, it might be easier to toggle a global flag that would tell the GETSYS program not to apply SETKEY( ) assignments. This value would have to be visible in case of user-defined readers: That is a part of the scope of the plan as modifications are being made. A good rule to go by is to make changes to the GET system that make sense for someone else: to make the GETSYS.PRG file robust, compatible, reusable, and modifiable.

We might also want to toggle off the Page Up and Page Down keys to prevent them from being used in our data entry screens. Rather than programming in user-defined readers for each "normal" GET, why not plan it into the GET system?

Below is a modified GET system with many of these changes plus a few more. Where there is a need, a few commands and functions are added to make programming the GET system even easier.

Before looking at the modified GET system, here is a header file called PTVERBS.CH that is used in the modified GET system, GTSIRIUS.PRG. It is a slightly modified version of the header file PTVERBS.CH found in Appendix 3.

```
// File:    PtVerbs.ch
// Date:    March 18, 1993
// By:      Steve Straley
// Rem:     This is a special header file with modified commands from
//          the Power Tools Library for the modified GET System.

#xcommand DEFAULT <exp> TO <value> [, <expN> TO <valN> ] => ;
            <exp> := if(( valtype(<exp>)==valtype(<value>) .and. (<exp> != nil)), ;
            <exp>, <value>) ;
            [; <expN> := if(( valtype(<expN>)==valtype(<valN>) .and. (<expN> != ;
            nil)), <expN>, <valN>) ]

#xcommand SET <var> WITHIN <bottom> TO <top> BASE <value> => ;
            if !(<var> >= <bottom> .and. <var> <= <top> ) ;;
               <var> := <value> ;;
            endif

//% 007 The following is a modified command that is important to use
//      to allow the implementation of the TIMEOUT and EXECUTE operations
//      to work smoothly.

#xcommand READ [STARTING AT <npos>] ;
               [TIMEOUT <secs> [EXECUTE <block>]] ;
               [POST EXECUTE <code> ] => ;
            readmodal( getlist, <npos>, <secs>, <{block}>, <code> ) ;;
            getlist := {}

#xcommand local int    <*exp*>     => local <exp>
#xcommand local char   <*exp*>     => local <exp>
#xcommand local double <*exp*>     => local <exp>
#xcommand local date   <*exp*>     => local <exp>
#xcommand local logical <*exp*>    => local <exp>
#xcommand local float  <*exp*>     => local <exp>
#xcommand local array  <*exp*>     => local <exp>
#xcommand local block  <*exp*>     => local <exp>
#xcommand local object <*exp*>     => local <exp>
#xcommand local glob   <*exp*>     => local <exp>    // This is for unknown vars.

// End of File: PTverbs.ch
```

## And now for the new GET system:

```
// File:    GtSirius.prg
// Date:    March 18, 1993
// Author:  Steve Straley
// Based:   Getsys.prg
//          Standard Clipper 5.2 GET/READ Subsystem
//          Copyright (c) 1991-1993, Computer Associates International, Inc.
//          All rights reserved.
// Comp:    /a /m /w /v /p /es2
//          This could be compiled with the compiler switch
//          /DpTEST
// Link:    This file, if compiled in test mode, cannot be linked with the
//          BASE52 pre-linked library.

//% 001 sjs Add the size of the cursor change to the INS toggle.
//          This means that the cursor size must be saved and turned
//          on within the main ReadModal() function as well as being
//          toggled within the file.
//% 002 sjs Make a file-wide static for the SETKEY() lookup toggle and
//          write a function that will act like a toggle for that
//          variable.
//% 003 sjs Altered the naming convention of the GETLIST array to fit
//          the Hungarian convention rules
//% 004 sjs Pass more information into the code block of the user-defined
//          reader just in case it is needed.
//% 005 sjs Make the large DO CASE construct of key strokes for a GET
//          variable into a separate function that is called by the
//          GetApplyKey() function.  This will allow custom readers to
//          use those keystrokes and offer changes to only those
//          that would fit the OTHERWISE section.
//% 006 sjs Make a file-wide static for the PageUP and PageDown keys to
//          be toggled as part of the standard default keys.
//% 007 sjs Make a timeout option with a code block to execute should the
//          timeout be true.
//% 008 sjs Build a RefreshGets() function
//% 009 sjs Allow for a calculation code block

#include "Inkey.ch"
#include "Getexit.ch"
#include "PTverbs.ch"    // Special header from Power Tools' Commands

#define K_UNDO        K_CTRL_U
#define pTRUE  .t.                       // Special manifest constants
#define pFALSE .f.                       // for clarity

// State variables for active READ

static sbFormat
static slUpdated          := pFALSE
static slKillRead
static slBumpTop
static slBumpBot
static snLastExitState
static snLastPos
static soActiveGet
static scReadProcName
static snReadProcLine

static slSetKeyToggle     := pTRUE   //% 002 this is compatible w/ past
```

```
static slPgKeys            := pTRUE   //% 006 this is compatible w/ past
static slTimedOut          := pFALSE  //% 007 Start off so that no timeout yet

//
// Format of array used to preserve state variables
//
#define GSV_KILLREAD        1
#define GSV_BUMPTOP         2
#define GSV_BUMPBOT         3
#define GSV_LASTEXIT        4
#define GSV_LASTPOS         5
#define GSV_ACTIVEGET       6
#define GSV_READVAR         7
#define GSV_READPROCNAME    8
#define GSV_READPROCLINE    9

#define GSV_COUNT           9

#ifdef pTEST

function Main()

   local array getlist := {}
   local char  cTemp   := space(20)
   local int   nTemp   := 1
   local date  dTemp   := date()

   local double nTotal    := 0.00
   local double nAmount   := 0.00
   local int    nQty      := 1
   local double nDiscount := 0.00
   local double nShipping := 0.00
   local double nTax      := 0.00

   // The code block for the calculation needs to be created AFTER all of the
   // other local variables are initialized.

   local block bCalc    := {|aList, nPos| ;
                            (nTotal := (nAmount * nQty) - nDiscount + ;
                            nShipping + nTax ), RefreshGets( aList ), ;
                            devpos(15,21), ;
                            devout(nTotal, "9999.99", "GR+/B" )}

   set key -9 to TempDisp

   PageKeysToggle( pFALSE )

   cls
   @  8,10 say "The PageUP and PageDOWN keys have been disabled"
   @  9,10 say "Press the F10 key for display"
   @ 10,10 get cTemp
   @ 11,10 get nTemp
   @ 12,10 get dTemp
   READ STARTING AT 2 TIMEOUT 30 EXECUTE TempDisp()

   cls
   PageKeysToggle( !PageKeysToggle() )  // Toggles value of the page keys
   SetKeyToggle( pFALSE )    // turn off the looking at the SETKEY stuff
   @  7,10 say "The PageUP and PageDOWN keys are now back on-line"
   @  8,10 say "The value of setkey() is: "
```

```
   devout( valtype( setkey(-9) ) )
   @ 9,10 say "The F10 key for display has been turned off in GET Stack"
   @ 10,10 get cTemp
   @ 11,10 get nTemp
   @ 12,10 get dTemp
   read

   scroll()
   PageKeysToggle( !PageKeysToggle() )    // Toggles value of the page keys
   @  7,10 say "Enter in values and watch the calculations"
   @ 10,10 say " Enter Amount: " get nAmount   pict "99999.99"
   @ 11,10 say "      Quantity: " get nQty     pict "99"
   @ 12,10 say "      Shipping: " get nShipping pict "99999.99"
   @ 13,10 say "           Tax: " get nTax     pict "99999.99"
   @ 14,10 say "less Discount: " get nDiscount pict "99999.99"
   @ 15,10 say "     TOTAL "

   READ POST EXECUTE bCalc

   return( NIL )

*******************

function TempDisp()

   local char cScreen := savescreen()

   scroll(10,15,12,65)
   dispbox(10,15,12,65,2)   // issue a double line
   @ 11,17 say "F10 key was pressed and we're inside GET system"

   inkey(5)

   restscreen(,,,,cScreen)

   return( NIL )

#endif

function readmodal( aGetList, ;     //% 003 Array of get objects
                    nPos, ;         //  Optional starting position
                    nSeconds, ;     //% 007 Number of seconds to allow
                    bTimeout, ;     //% 007 for a timeout and a code block
                    bCalc )         //% 009 this for the calculating GETS

   local object oGet
   local array  aSavGetSysVars
   local int    nCursor := setcursor(1)   //% 001

   //% 007  Set the default number of seconds to use
   DEFAULT nSeconds TO 0, ;
           bCalc    TO {|| NIL}

   if ( valtype( sbFormat ) == "B" )
     eval( sbFormat )
   endif

   if empty( aGetlist )         // no items are in the array
     setpos( maxrow() -1, 0 )   // S'87 compatibility
     setcursor(nCursor)         //% 001 turn back the cursor
```

```
      return( pFALSE )           // NOTE: This should not be like this.
   endif

   aSavGetSysVars := ClearGetSysVars()  // Preserve state variables.

   scReadProcName := procname( 1 )   // Set these for use in SET KEYs
   snReadProcLine := procline( 1 )   // Set these for use in SET KEYs

   if !( valtype( nPos ) == "N" .and. nPos > 0 ) // Set initial GET read
      nPos := settle( aGetlist, 0 )
   endif

   while !( nPos == 0 )

      GetTimeOut( pFALSE )   //% 007 Set the timeout off for each GET

      // Get next GET from list and post it as the active GET
      PostActiveGet( oGet := aGetlist[ nPos ] )

      if ( valtype( oGet:reader ) == "B" )        // Read the GET
         //% 004  Custom reader
         //% 007  Pass it the number of seconds to wait for
         eval( oGet:reader, oGet, aGetlist, @nPos, nSeconds )
      else
         //% 007 Pass it the number of seconds to wait for
         GetReader( oGet, nSeconds )     // Use standard reader
      endif

      //% 007 Check to see if not a timed out condition
      if !slTimedOut

         eval( bCalc, aGetlist, nPos )    //% 009 This performs the calc!

         nPos := Settle( aGetlist, nPos )   // next GET based on exit cond.

      else
         if valtype( bTimeout ) == "B"     // Yes a code block was passed.
            eval( bTimeout, aGetlist, nPos )  // Pass it the getlist and position.
         endif
         exit
      endif

   enddo

   RestoreGetSysVars( aSavGetSysVars )  // Restore state variables.

   setpos( maxrow() - 1, 0 )          // S'87 compatibility
   setcursor(nCursor)                 //% 001 turn back the cursor

   return( slUpdated )

*******************

procedure GetReader( oGet, ;    // Standard modal read of a single GET
                     nSeconds )   //% 007 This is the number of seconds

   local int nKey     //% 007 Holds the value of the key pressed

   if ( GetPreValidate( oGet ) ) // Read the GET if the WHEN condition is satisfied.
```

```
      // Activate the GET for reading
      oGet:setFocus()

      while ( oGet:exitState == GE_NOEXIT )

        if ( oGet:typeOut )              // Check for initial typeout.
           oGet:exitState := GE_ENTER
        endif

        // Apply keystrokes until exit
        while ( oGet:exitState == GE_NOEXIT )
          if !empty( nKey := inkey(nSeconds) )  //% 007 Adding the timeout
             GetApplyKey( oGet, nKey )
          else
             //% 007 We need to make a function grant access to this file-wide
             //      static variable because custom readers will need to have it
             //      as well.
             GetTimeOut( pTRUE )     // It timed out.
             exit
          endif

        enddo

        if !slTimedOut    //% 007 no time out so validate the GET
           // Disallow exit if the VALID condition is not satisfied
           if ( !GetPostValidate( oGet ) )
              oGet:exitState := GE_NOEXIT
           endif
        else
           exit
        endif
      enddo

      oGet:killFocus()    // De-activate the GET

   endif

   return

*********************

procedure GetApplyKey( oGet, ;    // Get object having focus
                       nKey )     // ASCII value of key pressed

   local char   cKey := chr( nKey )     // CHR of the key pressed
   local block  bKeyBlock               // holds temp assigned key block

   //% 002  Check the file-wide static to see if allows for the set
   //       key stack to be checked.

   if slSetKeyToggle    // Check for SET KEY first
     if !( ( bKeyBlock := setkey( nKey ) ) == NIL )
        GetDoSetKey( bKeyBlock, oGet )
        return                                  // NOTE
     endif
   endif

   //% 005 This function returns a logical true (.T.) if the key pressed
   //      was part of the massive DO CASE test of "normal" keystrokes.
```

```
      if ! GetDefKeys( oGet, nKey )
        if ( nKey >= 32 .and. nKey <= 255 )
          if ( oGet:type == "N" .and. ( cKey == "." .OR. cKey == "," ) )
            oGet:toDecPos()
          else
            if ( set( _SET_INSERT ) )
              oGet:insert( cKey )
            else
              oGet:overstrike( cKey )
            endif

            if ( oGet:typeOut )
              if ( set( _SET_BELL ) )
                qqout( chr(7) )
              endif

              if ( !set( _SET_CONFIRM ) )
                oGet:exitState := GE_ENTER
              endif
            endif
          endif
        endif
      endif

      return

*********************

function GetPreValidate( oGet )    // Test for the WHEN clause

   local logical lSavUpdated
   local logical lWhen := pTRUE     // default return value

   if !( oGet:preBlock == NIL )

      lSavUpdated := slUpdated

      lWhen := eval( oGet:preBlock, oGet )

      oGet:display()

      ShowScoreBoard()
      slUpdated := lSavUpdated

   endif

   do case
   case ( slKillRead )
      lWhen := pFALSE
      oGet:exitState := GE_ESCAPE        // Provokes ReadModal() exit

   case ( !lWhen )
      oGet:exitState := GE_WHEN          // Indicates failure

   otherwise
      oGet:exitState := GE_NOEXIT        // Prepares for editing

   endcase

   return ( lWhen )

************************
```

## Data Entry Options

```
function GetPostValidate( oGet )     // This is for the VALID clause.

  local logical lSavUpdated
  local logical lValid := pTRUE      // Default return value

  if ( oGet:exitState == GE_ESCAPE )
    return( pTRUE )                  // NOTE
  endif

  if ( oGet:badDate() )
    oGet:home()
    DateMsg()
    ShowScoreboard()
    return( pFALSE )                 // NOTE
  endif

  if ( oGet:changed )  // If editing occurred, assign new value to var.
    oGet:assign()
    slUpdated := pTRUE
  endif

  oGet:reset() // Reform edit buffer, set cursor to home, redisplay.

  if !( oGet:postBlock == NIL ) // Check VALID condition if specified.
    lSavUpdated := slUpdated

    setpos( oGet:row, oGet:col + len( oGet:buffer )) // S'87 compatibility

    lValid := eval( oGet:postBlock, oGet )

    setpos( oGet:row, oGet:col ) // Reset S'87 compatibility cursor position.

    ShowScoreBoard()
    oGet:updateBuffer()

    slUpdated := lSavUpdated

    if ( slKillRead )
      oGet:exitState := GE_ESCAPE       // Provokes ReadModal() exit
      lValid := pTRUE
    endif
  endif

  return( lValid )

*********************

procedure GetDoSetKey( bKeyBlock, ;   // Code block from SETKEY()
                       oGet )         // Individual GET object

  local logical lSavUpdated

  if ( oGet:changed )    // If editing has occurred, assign variable.
    oGet:assign()
    slUpdated := pTRUE
  endif

  lSavUpdated := slUpdated

  eval( bKeyBlock, scReadProcName, snReadProcLine, readvar() )

  ShowScoreboard()
```

```
      oGet:updateBuffer()

      slUpdated := lSavUpdated

      if ( slKillRead )
        oGet:exitState := GE_ESCAPE      // provokes ReadModal() exit
      endif

      return

/* The following functions and procedures are support routines that are
   noted as "READ SERVICES".
*/

*********************

static function Settle( aGetList, ;    //% 001  Array of GET objects
                        nPos )         //             Subscript position
/***
*  Returns new position in array of Get objects, based on:
*      - current position
*      - exitState of Get object at current position
*
*  NOTES: Return value of 0 indicates termination of READ
*         exitState of old Get is transferred to new Get.
*/

   local int nExitState

   if ( nPos == 0 )
     nExitState := GE_DOWN
   else
     nExitState := aGetList[ nPos ]:exitState       //% 001
   endif

   if( nExitState == GE_ESCAPE .or. nExitState == GE_WRITE )
     return( 0 )                // NOTE
   endif

   if !( nExitState == GE_WHEN )
     // Reset state info
     snLastPos := nPos
     slBumpTop := pFALSE
     slBumpBot := pFALSE
   else
     // Re-use last exitState, do not disturb state info
     nExitState := snLastExitState
   endif

   //
   // Move
   //
   do case
   case ( nExitState == GE_UP )
     nPos--

   case ( nExitState == GE_DOWN )
     nPos++

   case ( nExitState == GE_TOP )
     nPos         := 1
```

```
      slBumpTop    := pTRUE
      nExitState   := GE_DOWN

   case ( nExitState == GE_BOTTOM )
      nPos         := len( aGetList )        //% 001
      slBumpBot    := pTRUE
      nExitState   := GE_UP

   case ( nExitState == GE_ENTER )
      nPos++

   endcase

   //
   // Bounce
   //
   do case
   case ( nPos == 0 )                            // Bumped top
      if ( !readexit() .and. !slBumpBot )
         slBumpTop    := pTRUE
         nPos         := snLastPos
         nExitState   := GE_DOWN
      endif

   case ( nPos == len( aGetList ) + 1 )   //% 001   Bumped bottom

      if ( !ReadExit() .and. !( nExitState == GE_ENTER ) .and. !slBumpTop )
         slBumpBot    := pTRUE
         nPos         := snLastPos
         nExitState   := GE_UP
      else
         nPos := 0
      endif
   endcase

   snLastExitState := nExitState      // Record exit state

   if !( nPos == 0 )
      aGetList[ nPos ]:exitState := nExitState
   endif

   return( nPos )

********************

static procedure PostActiveGet( oGet )

   GetActive( oGet )
   ReadVar( GetReadVar( oGet ) )
   ShowScoreBoard()

   return

static function ClearGetSysVars()
/*
*   Save and clear READ state variables. Return array of saved values.
*
*   NOTE: 'Updated' status is cleared but not saved (S'87 compatibility).
*/

   local array aSavSysVars[ GSV_COUNT ]
```

```
    // Save current sys vars
    aSavSysVars[ GSV_KILLREAD ]     := slKillRead
    aSavSysVars[ GSV_BUMPTOP ]      := slBumpTop
    aSavSysVars[ GSV_BUMPBOT ]      := slBumpBot
    aSavSysVars[ GSV_LASTEXIT ]     := snLastExitState
    aSavSysVars[ GSV_LASTPOS ]      := snLastPos
    aSavSysVars[ GSV_ACTIVEGET ]    := GetActive( NIL )
    aSavSysVars[ GSV_READVAR ]      := ReadVar( "" )
    aSavSysVars[ GSV_READPROCNAME ] := scReadProcName
    aSavSysVars[ GSV_READPROCLINE ] := snReadProcLine

    // Re-init old ones
    slKillRead      := pFALSE
    slBumpTop       := pFALSE
    slBumpBot       := pFALSE
    snLastExitState := 0
    snLastPos       := 0
    scReadProcName  := ""
    snReadProcLine  := 0
    slUpdated       := pFALSE

    RETURN ( aSavSysVars )

/***
*
*   RestoreGetSysVars()
*
*   Restore READ state variables from array of saved values.
*
*   NOTE: 'Updated' status is not restored (S'87 compatibility).
*
*/
static procedure RestoreGetSysVars( aSavSysVars )

    slKillRead      := aSavSysVars[ GSV_KILLREAD ]
    slBumpTop       := aSavSysVars[ GSV_BUMPTOP ]
    slBumpBot       := aSavSysVars[ GSV_BUMPBOT ]
    snLastExitState := aSavSysVars[ GSV_LASTEXIT ]
    snLastPos       := aSavSysVars[ GSV_LASTPOS ]

    GetActive( aSavSysVars[ GSV_ACTIVEGET ] )

    readvar( aSavSysVars[ GSV_READVAR ] )

    scReadProcName  := aSavSysVars[ GSV_READPROCNAME ]
    snReadProcLine  := aSavSysVars[ GSV_READPROCLINE ]

    return

********************

static function GetReadVar( oGet )

    local char cName := upper( oGet:name )
    local int  nCounter                       // For the FOR loop

    // The following code includes subscripts in the name returned by
    // this FUNCTIONtion, if the get variable is an array element
    //
    // Subscripts are retrieved from the oGet:subscript instance variable.
```

```
      //
      // NOTE: Incompatible with Summer '87.
      //
      if !( oGet:subscript == NIL )
        for nCounter := 1 to len( oGet:subscript )
          cName += "[" + ltrim( str( oGet:subscript[nCounter] ) ) + "]"
        next
      endif

      return( cName )

   /***
    *            System Services
    */

   *******************

   procedure __SetFormat( bCode )     // for the SET FORMAT TO

      sbFormat := if( valtype( bCode ) == "B", bCode, NIL )

      return

   *******************

   procedure __KillRead()     // CLEAR GET service

      slKillRead := pTRUE

      return

   *******************

   function GetActive( oGet )    // Retrieves currently active GET object

      local object oOldActive := soActiveGet

      if !( oGet == NIL )
        soActiveGet := oGet
      endif

      return( oOldActive )

   *******************

   function Updated()

      return( slUpdated )

   *******************

   function ReadExit( lNew )

      return( set( _SET_EXIT, lNew ) )

   *******************

   function ReadInsert( lNew )

      return( set( _SET_INSERT, lNew ) )
```

```
/***
*                  Wacky Compatibility Services
*/

// Display coordinates for SCOREBOARD
#define SCORE_ROW      0
#define SCORE_COL      60

/***
*
*  ShowScoreboard()
*
*/
static procedure ShowScoreboard()

  local int nRow
  local int nCol

  if ( set( _SET_SCOREBOARD ) )
    nRow := row()
    nCol := col()

    setpos( SCORE_ROW, SCORE_COL )
    dispout( if( set( _SET_INSERT ), "Ins", "   " ) )
    setpos( nRow, nCol )
  endif

  return

/***
*
*  DateMsg()
*
*/
static procedure DateMsg()

  local int nRow
  local int nCol

  if ( set( _SET_SCOREBOARD ) )
    nRow := row()
    nCol := col()

    setpos( SCORE_ROW, SCORE_COL )
    dispout( "Invalid Date" )
    setpos( nRow, nCol )

    while ( nextkey() == 0 )
    enddo

    setpos( SCORE_ROW, SCORE_COL )
    dispout( space( 12 ) )
    setpos( nRow, nCol )

  endif

  return

/***
*
*  RangeCheck()
*
```

```
*   NOTE: Unused second param for 5.00 compatibility.
*
*/
function RangeCheck( oGet, ;
                     junk, ;
                     lo, ;
                     hi )

  local char cMsg
  local int  nRow
  local int  nCol
  local glob xValue    // Could be of any data type

  if ( !oGet:changed )
    return( pTRUE )             // NOTE
  endif

  xValue := oGet:varGet()

  if ( xValue >= lo .and. xValue <= hi )
    return( pTRUE )             // NOTE
  endif

  if ( set(_SET_SCOREBOARD) )
    cMsg := "Range: " + ltrim( transform( lo, "" ) ) + ;
            " - " + ltrim( transform( hi, "" ) )

    if ( len( cMsg ) > maxcol() )
      cMsg := substr( cMsg, 1, maxcol() )
    endif

    nRow := row()
    nCol := col()

    setpos( SCORE_ROW, min( 60, maxcol() - len( cMsg ) ) )
    dispout( cMsg )
    setpos( nRow, nCol )

    while ( nextkey() == 0 )
    enddo

    setpos( SCORE_ROW, min( 60, maxcol() - len( cMsg ) ) )
    dispout( space( len( cMsg ) ) )
    setpos( nRow, nCol )

  endif

  return( pFALSE )

********************

function ReadKill( lKill )

  local logical lSavKill := slKillRead

  if !( lKill == NIL )  // A parameter is passed.
    slKillRead := lKill
  endif

  return( lSavKill )

********************
```

```
function ReadUpdated( lUpdated )

  local logical lSavUpdated := slUpdated

  if !( lUpdated == NIL )
    slUpdated := lUpdated
  endif

  return( lSavUpdated )

*******************

function ReadFormat( bCode )

  local block bSavFormat := sbFormat

  if !( bCode == NIL )
    sbFormat := bCode
  endif

  return( bSavFormat )

//% 002 The following function toggles the file-wide static 'slSetKeyToggle'
//      that will be used in the apply key section.

function SetKeyToggle( lValue )

  // toggles the value of the file-wide static and returns the old status
  // of the value

  local logical lOldValue := slSetKeyToggle

  if valtype( lValue ) == "L"   // a logical was passed
    slSetKeyToggle := lValue
  endif

  return( lOldValue )

//% 006 The following function toggles the file-wide static 'slPgKeys'
//      that will be used in the apply key section.

function PageKeysToggle( lValue )

  // toggles the value of the file-wide static and returns the old status
  // of the value

  local logical lOldValue := slPgKeys

  if valtype( lValue ) == "L"   // a logical was passed
    slPgKeys := lValue
  endif

  return( lOldValue )

//% 007 This function grants access to the file-wide static variable for
//      timeout conditions and considerations.

function GetTimeOut( lValue )

  local logical lOldValue := slPgKeys
```

```
      if valtype( lValue ) == "L"   // a logical was passed
        slTimedOut := lValue
      endif

      return( lOldValue )

//% 005 This function tests to see if the key pressed within the passed
//      GET object was a part of the "default" set.

********************

function GetDefKeys( oGet, ;    // Object of the GET that has input focus
                    nKey )     // ASCII value of the key pressed

   local logical lMember := pTRUE  // Default is a true to be altered
                                   // in the OTHERWISE at the end.

   do case
   case ( nKey == K_UP )
      oGet:exitState := GE_UP

   case ( nKey == K_SH_TAB )
      oGet:exitState := GE_UP

   case ( nKey == K_DOWN )
      oGet:exitState := GE_DOWN

   case ( nKey == K_TAB )
      oGet:exitState := GE_DOWN

   case ( nKey == K_ENTER )
      oGet:exitState := GE_ENTER

   case ( nKey == K_ESC )
      if ( set( _SET_ESCAPE ) )
         oGet:undo()
         oGet:exitState := GE_ESCAPE
      endif

   case ( nKey == K_PGUP )
      if slPgKeys                    //% 006 This is the test of the file-
         oGet:exitState := GE_WRITE  //      wide static variable.
      endif

   case ( nKey == K_PGDN )
      if slPgKeys                    //% 006 This is the test of the file-
         oGet:exitState := GE_WRITE  //      wide static variable.
      endif

   case ( nKey == K_CTRL_HOME )
      oGet:exitState := GE_TOP

   case ( nKey == K_CTRL_END )
      oGet:exitState := GE_BOTTOM

   case ( nKey == K_CTRL_W )
      oGet:exitState := GE_WRITE

   case ( nKey == K_INS )
      setcursor( if(set( _SET_INSERT, ;
                    !set( _SET_INSERT ) ), 1, 3 ) )   //% 001
```

```
        ShowScoreboard()

    case ( nKey == K_UNDO )
      oGet:undo()

    case ( nKey == K_HOME )
      oGet:home()

    case ( nKey == K_END )
      oGet:end()

    case ( nKey == K_RIGHT )
      oGet:right()

    case ( nKey == K_LEFT )
      oGet:left()

    case ( nKey == K_CTRL_RIGHT )
      oGet:wordRight()

    case ( nKey == K_CTRL_LEFT )
      oGet:wordLeft()

    case ( nKey == K_BS )
      oGet:backSpace()

    case ( nKey == K_DEL )
      oGet:delete()

    case ( nKey == K_CTRL_T )
      oGet:delWordRight()

    case ( nKey == K_CTRL_Y )
      oGet:delEnd()

    case ( nKey == K_CTRL_BS )
      oGet:delWordLeft()

    otherwise
      lMember := pFALSE

    endcase

    return( lMember )

//% 008 This function is designed to refresh the GETLIST function.

function RefreshGets( aGetlist )

    if valtype( aGetlist ) == "A"        // O.k.... it's an array.
      if !empty( aGetlist )              // There are items to be processed.
        aeval( aGetlist, ;
              {|xItem| if( valtype( xItem ) == "O", ;
                          xItem:display(), ;
                          NIL )} )
      endif
    endif

    return( NIL )

// End of File: GtSirius.prg   // Modified Get System
```

## Summary

We could go farther with the modifications to include MESSAGES, positioning for the MESSAGES, hot keys, PRE EVALUATE conditions, display code blocks for a clock, mouse support, and many other options. We could even go farther and offer a SAY pseudoobject that, when joined with the GET object through a SayList ability gives us the chance to build all of the data entry screen without being forced into the following:

```
while condition
   // design data entry screens
   read
   // the read command destroys the GETLIST array
   if lastkey() != K_ESC
      // Update information
   else
      exit
   endif
   // Only to rebuild the GETLIST on the second pass
enddo
```

If we could put the GET information and the SAY information together in a single array to be processed by our modified GET system, we could avoid the process of building arrays only to destroy them time after time.

The basic reasons for modifying the GETSYS.PRG file are to build more power into our programming needs, have easier ways to modify existing code, and to offer enhanced performance.

Data entry is the most serious part of application development. With user-defined commands, enhanced SETKEY( ) functions, and SET KEY support, context messages can be added to each and every GET; some actions can be performed before the GET is active, independent of other GETS; the data can be validated before and after it is entered; the appearance of the data on the screen can be modified and configured; keystroke processing can be modified; and a GET can be aborted based on a timing variable. All are possible with Clipper 5.2.

# 19

# *The Help and Error Systems*

In this chapter are two self-contained modules that can be used in your next Clipper 5.2 application. The first module is a help system complete with editing and viewing capabilities. The second module is an error-trapping and logging system. Both modules have associated test programs that may be used to get a better understanding of these systems.

## The Help System

Whenever a module named Help is linked with an application, the F1 key will automatically activate the Help routine if it is pressed during a standard Clipper wait state. When it is invoked in this fashion, the help routine is passed the following parameters:

- The name of the program or routine that was active at the time the F1 key was pressed
- Assuming that the program was compiled without the /L switch, the line number that was executing when the F1 key was pressed
- If F1 was pressed during a GET, the name of the variable that had the input focus

This information makes it possible to provide four basic kinds of help to the users of a Clipper application:

- General Help
- Context-sensitive Help
- Topic-oriented Help (based on a menu)
- User-defined Help

The following example program sets up a GET stack with array items. The Help system provided shows how the subscript of the GET can be trapped within the Help system itself.

```
 1 : * File      THelp1.prg
 2 : * Compile   Rmake THelp1
 3 :
 4 : // SET KEY 28 TO Help
 5 :
 6 : request OnLineHelp
 7 :
 8 : memvar getlist
 9 :
10 : procedure Main()
11 :
12 :    local aData   := {1, 2, 3}
13 :    local nNumber := 1
14 :
15 :    scroll()
16 :
17 :    if empty( gete( "EDITHELP" ) )
18 :       @ 7,10 say "issue -> SET EDITHELP=YES   to invoke the ability to edit"
19 :    endif
20 :    if empty( gete( "MAKEHELP" ) )
21 :       @ 6,10 say "issue -> SET MAKEHELP=YES   to invoke the ability to make"
22 :    endif
23 :
24 :    @  9,10 say "Press F1 for HELP on each GET variable!"
25 :    @ 10,10 get aData[1]
26 :    @ 11,10 get aData[2]
27 :    @ 12,10 get aData[3]
28 :    @ 13,10 get nNumber
29 :    read
30 :
31 : // End of File: THelp1.prg
```

And now, here is the Help program used in conjunction with this example program.

```
 1 : * File      Help1.prg
 2 : * Compile   RMake THelp1
 3 : * Notes     This is a totally self-contained HELP module.  It can be linked
 4 : *           into the application as a help system.  If an item cannot be
 5 : *           found, then the environment must be set with MAKEHELP in order
 6 : *           to have this routine add items to the file.  If an item exists
 7 : *           and is displayed, and if the environment has EDITHELP, then the
 8 : *           item may be edited<N>which is also included in this module.
 9 : *           The last point uses the technique of recursion.  In addition,
10 : *           this routine uses the technique of an INIT procedure to create
11 : *           and to use the necessary HELP files.  The name of the help file
12 : *           can be changed within this module.
13 :
14 : #include "PTValue.ch"
15 : #include "PTVerbs.ch"
16 : #include "PTFuncs.ch"
17 : #include "PTInkey.ch"
18 :
19 : #xtranslate DEVRCLEAR(<x>,<y>) => (scroll(<x>, <y>, <x>, maxcol()))
20 :
21 : memvar GETLIST    // This is for the SAVE GET command.
22 :
23 : announce OnLineHelp
```

```
24 :
25 : procedure Help( cName, nLines, cVariable )
26 :
27 :    local oGetObject := getactive()
28 :    local cPattern   := ""
29 :    local nCol       := col()
30 :    local nRow       := row()
31 :    local lScore     := set( pSCOREBOARD )
32 :    local cHColor    := setcolor()
33 :    local cTempScreen
34 :
35 :    // First, prevent recursion of the help key!
36 :
37 :    if !empty( select("HELP") )
38 :
39 :       // First, add other names to the NAME variable as well as
40 :       // testing to see if the subscript is being used.  The LINES
41 :       // variable should NOT be used in case line numbers are not
42 :       // used.
43 :
44 :       IF oGetObject IS pOBJECT
45 :          cVariable := oGetObject:name
46 :          IF oGetObject:subscript IS pARRAY
47 :             if !empty( len( oGetObject:subscript ) )
48 :                cVariable += StrScript( oGetObject:subscript )
49 :             endif
50 :          endif
51 :       endif
52 :
53 :       // In case the HELP key is pressed on a function from a library the
54 :       // name of the procedure will not necessarily change.  However, by
55 :       // tracing back two or three levels into the program the chances are
56 :       // sounder of making a more solid match.
57 :
58 :       cName := procname(2)+procname(3)+procname(4)
59 :
60 :       if !empty( cName )     // No name, no going any further!
61 :
62 :          cPattern := cName + cVariable
63 :
64 :          if Help->( dbseek( cPattern ) )
65 :            if !empty( gete( "EDITHELP" ) )        // Recursion!
66 :               setkey( pF1, NIL )            // Turn off the key.
67 :               cTempScreen := savescreen()
68 :               Help->( EditHelp( cPattern ) )
69 :               setkey( pF1, {|cProc, nLine, cVar| Help(cProc, nLine, cVar)} )
70 :            else
71 :               Help->( DisplayHelp() )
72 :               setkey( pF1, {|cProc, nLine, cVar| Help(cProc, nLine, cVar)} )
73 :               if !( cTempScreen == NIL )
74 :                  restscreen(,,,,cTempScreen)
75 :               endif
76 :            endif
77 :
78 :          else
79 :             // Offer to enter the help screen provided there is
80 :             // an environmental switch to toggle the help system!
81 :             if !empty( gete( "MAKEHELP" ) )
82 :                Help->( MakeHelp( cPattern ) )
83 :             endif
84 :          endif
```

```
 85 :        endif
 86 :     endif
 87 :
 88 :     // Re-set the cursor position of the original screen and re-
 89 :     // set the scoreboard area of the screen.
 90 :
 91 :     setpos( nRow, nCol )
 92 :     set( pSCOREBOARD, lScore )
 93 :     setcolor( cHColor )
 94 :     CLEARESC()
 95 :
 96 : ********************
 97 :
 98 : static function DisplayHelp()
 99 :
100 :    local nWidth   := Help->right - Help->left
101 :    local cScreen  := savescreen( Help->top, Help->left, ;
102 :                                  Help->bottom, Help->right)
103 :    local nKeyVal  := setkey( pF10 )
104 :    local nCursor  := setcursor()
105 :    local cColor   := setcolor()
106 :    local nTop     := Help->top
107 :    local nLeft    := Help->left
108 :    local nBottom  := Help->bottom
109 :    local nRight   := Help->right
110 :
111 :    // The variables nTop, nLeft, nBottom, and nRight are used to house the
112 :    // old help screen coordinates in order to re-adjust the screen prior to
113 :    // any maneuver brought on by an EDIT.
114 :
115 :    setcolor( alltrim(Help->color) )
116 :    setcursor( pCURSOR_ON )
117 :    dispbox( Help->top, Help->left, Help->bottom, Help->right, pDBAR )
118 :
119 :    if !empty( Help->title )
120 :      if Help->showtitle
121 :         setpos( Help->top, Help->left+1 )
122 :         dispout( " " + left( alltrim(Help->title), nWidth ) + " " )
123 :      endif
124 :    endif
125 :    setpos( Help->bottom, Help->left+1 )
126 :    dispout( left( " ESC to quit ", nWidth ) )
127 :    memoedit( Help->text, Help->top+1, Help->left+1, Help->bottom-1,;
128 :              Help->right-1, pFALSE )
129 :
130 :    restscreen( nTop, nLeft, nBottom, nRight, cScreen )
131 :
132 :    setcursor( nCursor )
133 :    setcolor( cColor )
134 :
135 :    VOID
136 :
137 : ********************
138 :
139 : static function MakeHelp( cItem, lAtItem )   // The item to ADD
140 :
141 : #define pBAR1 REPLICATE(CHR(176),8)+CHR(32)
142 : #define pBAR2 REPLICATE(CHR(178),8)+CHR(32)
143 :
144 :    local cScreen     := savescreen()
```

```
145 :    local nCursor     := setcursor( pCURSOR_OFF )
146 :    local lScore      := set( pSCOREBOARD, pOFF )
147 :    local cColor      := setcolor()
148 :    local lShowTitle  := pFALSE
149 :    local nTop        := 8
150 :    local nLeft       := 20
151 :    local nBottom     := 12
152 :    local nRight      := 60
153 :    local cText       := ""
154 :    local cTitle      := space(40)
155 :    local nKey
156 :    local aTempGet
157 :    local bTempBlock
158 :    local cNewColor
159 :
160 :    DEFAULT lAtItem TO pFALSE    // Forcing things to add
161 :
162 :    if lAtItem
163 :       cText      := Help->text
164 :       nTop       := Help->top
165 :       nLeft      := Help->left
166 :       nBottom    := Help->bottom
167 :       nRight     := Help->right
168 :       cTitle     := Help->title
169 :       lShowTitle := Help->showtitle
170 :    endif
171 :
172 :    REPEAT    // move the window region
173 :       restscreen(,,,,cScreen )
174 :       dispbox(nTop,nLeft,nBottom,nRight,cScreen)
175 :       setpos(maxrow(), 0)
176 :       dispout("Press TAB, <T>op, <L>eft, <B>ottom, <R>ight,or ESC ")
177 :       nKey := inkey(0)
178 :
179 :       do case
180 :       case nKey == pTAB
181 :          DragBox(@nTop, @nLeft, @nBottom, @nRight, cScreen)
182 :
183 :       case chr(nKey) $ "tT"
184 :          MoveHorizontal( pTRUE, @nTop, @nLeft, @nBottom, @nRight, cScreen )
185 :
186 :       case chr(nKey) $ "bB"
187 :          MoveHorizontal( pFALSE, @nTop, @nLeft, @nBottom, @nRight, cScreen )
188 :
189 :       case chr(nKey) $ "lL"
190 :          MoveVertical( pTRUE, @nTop, @nLeft, @nBottom, @nRight, cScreen )
191 :
192 :       case chr(nKey) $ "rR"
193 :          MoveVertical( pFALSE, @nTop, @nLeft, @nBottom, @nRight, cScreen )
194 :
195 :       endcase
196 :
197 :    UNTIL ( nKey == pESC .or. nKey == pENTER )
198 :
199 :    if !( nKey == pESC )
200 :
201 :       SAVE GET TO aTempGet
202 :
203 :       DEVRCLEAR(maxrow(),0)
204 :       cNewColor := ColorChoice( cScreen )
```

```
205 :
206 :         if !( lastkey() == pESC )
207 :            setcursor( pCURSOR_ON )
208 :            dispbox( nTop, nLeft, nBottom, nRight, pBAR2 ) // Add text to the item.
209 :            setpos( maxrow(), 0 )
210 :            dispout( "Press F10 to save, ESC to quit" )
211 :            bTempBlock := setkey( pF10 )
212 :            setcolor( cNewColor )
213 :            setkey( pF10, {|| KEYBOARD( chr( pCTRL_W ) )} )
214 :            cText := memoedit(cText, nTop+1, nLeft+1, nBottom-1, nRight-1, pTRUE )
215 :            setkey( pF10, bTempBlock )
216 :            setcolor( cColor )
217 :
218 :            if lastkey() == pCTRL_W
219 :               DEVRCLEAR( maxrow(), 0 )
220 :               @ maxrow(), 0 say "Enter Title: " get cTitle
221 :               read
222 :               if !( lastkey() == pESC )
223 :                  DEVRCLEAR( maxrow(), 0 )
224 :                  @ maxrow(), 0 say "Show Title? " get lShowTitle pict "Y"
225 :                  read
226 :                  if !( lastkey() == pESC )
227 :                     if !lAtItem
228 :                        Help->( dbappend() )
229 :                     endif
230 :                     Help->search   := cItem
231 :                     Help->top      := nTop
232 :                     Help->left     := nLeft
233 :                     Help->bottom   := nBottom
234 :                     Help->right    := nRight
235 :                     Help->title    := cTitle
236 :                     Help->color    := cNewColor
237 :                     Help->showtitle := lShowTitle
238 :                     Help->screen   := cScreen
239 :                     Help->text     := cText
240 :                  endif
241 :               endif
242 :            endif
243 :         endif
244 :
245 :         RESTORE GET FROM aTempGet
246 :
247 :      endif
248 :      restscreen(,,,,cScreen )
249 :      setcursor( nCursor )
250 :      setcolor( cColor )
251 :      set( pSCOREBOARD, lScore )
252 :
253 :      VOID
254 :
255 : *******************
256 :
257 : static function Dragbox( nTop, nLeft, nBottom, nRight, cScreen )
258 :
259 :      local nOldTop    := nTop
260 :      local nOldLeft   := nLeft
261 :      local nOldBottom := nBottom
262 :      local nOldRight  := nRight
263 :      local nKey
264 :
```

```
265 :    REPEAT
266 :       restscreen(,,,,cScreen)
267 :       setpos(maxrow(),0)
268 :       dispout("Cursor Keys to drag, ENTER to Set, ESC to quit")
269 :       dispbox(nTop, nLeft, nBottom, nRight, pBAR1)
270 :
271 :       nKey := inkey(0)
272 :
273 :       do case
274 :       case nKey == pUP_ARROW
275 :          if( nTop != 0, ( nTop--, nBottom-- ), NIL )
276 :
277 :       case nKey == pDOWN_ARROW
278 :          if( nBottom != maxrow(), (nTop++,nBottom++), NIL )
279 :
280 :       case nKey == pLEFT_ARROW
281 :          if( nLeft != 0, (nLeft--, nRight--), NIL )
282 :
283 :       case nKey == pRIGHT_ARROW
284 :          if( nBottom != maxrow(), (nLeft++,nRight++), NIL )
285 :
286 :       case nKey == pESC
287 :          nTop     := nOldTop
288 :          nLeft    := nOldLeft
289 :          nBottom  := nOldBottom
290 :          nRight   := nOldRight
291 :
292 :       endcase
293 :
294 :    UNTIL ( nKey == pESC .or. nKey == pENTER )
295 :
296 :    CLEARESC()
297 :
298 :    VOID
299 :
300 : *********************
301 :
302 : static function MoveHorizontal( lIsTop, nTop, nLeft, nBottom, nRight, cScreen )
303 :
304 :    local nOldTop    := nTop
305 :    local nOldLeft   := nLeft
306 :    local nOldBottom := nBottom
307 :    local nOldRight  := nRight
308 :    local nKey
309 :
310 :    REPEAT
311 :       restscreen(,,,,cScreen)
312 :       setpos(maxrow(),0)
313 :       dispout("Up / Down Arrows, ENTER to Set, ESC to quit")
314 :       dispbox(nTop, nLeft, nBottom, nRight, pBAR1)
315 :
316 :       nKey := inkey(0)
317 :
318 :       do case
319 :       case nKey == pUP_ARROW
320 :          if( lIsTop, if( (nTop-1 != 0), nTop--, NIL ), ;
321 :                      if( nBottom != nTop-1 , nBottom--, NIL ) )
322 :
323 :       case nKey == pDOWN_ARROW
324 :          if( lIsTop, if( (nTop+1 != nBottom), nTop++, NIL ), ;
```

```
325 :                     if( nBottom+1 != maxrow(), nBottom++, NIL ) )
326 :
327 :        case nKey == pESC
328 :           nTop    := nOldTop
329 :           nLeft   := nOldLeft
330 :           nBottom := nOldBottom
331 :           nRight  := nOldRight
332 :
333 :        endcase
334 :
335 :     UNTIL ( nKey == pESC .or. nKey == pENTER )
336 :
337 :     CLEARESC()
338 :
339 :     VOID
340 :
341 : *******************
342 :
343 : static function MoveVertical( lIsLeft, nTop, nLeft, nBottom, nRight, cScreen )
344 :
345 :     local nOldTop    := nTop
346 :     local nOldLeft   := nLeft
347 :     local nOldBottom := nBottom
348 :     local nOldRight  := nRight
349 :     local nKey
350 :
351 :     REPEAT
352 :        restscreen(,,,,cScreen)
353 :        setpos(maxrow(),0)
354 :        dispout("Left / Right Arrows, ENTER to Set, ESC to quit")
355 :        dispbox(nTop, nLeft, nBottom, nRight, pBAR1)
356 :
357 :        nKey := inkey(0)
358 :
359 :        do case
360 :        case nKey == pLEFT_ARROW
361 :           if( lIsLeft, if( nLeft != 0, nLeft--, NIL ), ;
362 :                        if( nRight-1 != nLeft, nRight--, NIL ) )
363 :
364 :        case nKey == pRIGHT_ARROW
365 :           if( lIsLeft, if( nLeft+1 != nRight, nLeft++, NIL ), ;
366 :                        if( nRight != maxcol(), nRight++, NIL ) )
367 :
368 :        case nKey == pESC
369 :           nTop    := nOldTop
370 :           nLeft   := nOldLeft
371 :           nBottom := nOldBottom
372 :           nRight  := nOldRight
373 :
374 :        endcase
375 :
376 :     UNTIL ( nKey == pESC .or. nKey == pENTER )
377 :
378 :     CLEARESC()
379 :
380 :     VOID
381 :
382 : #undef pBAR1
383 : #undef pBAR2
384 :
```

```
385 : ********************
386 :
387 : static function ColorChoice( cScreen )
388 :
389 :    local nChoice1 := 1
390 :    local nChoice2 := 8
391 :    local cColor    := setcolor()       // Old color status
392 :    local lConfirm := set(pCONFIRM)     // Old confirm status
393 :    local aGround
394 :    local aWords
395 :    local bOperation
396 :    local bIsGood
397 :
398 :    aWords := {" 1> BLACK"," 2> BLUE", " 3> GREEN", " 4> CYAN",;
399 :              " 5> RED", " 6> MAGENTA", " 7> BROWN", " 8> WHITE",;
400 :              " 9> GRAY", "10> BRIGHT BLUE", "11> BRIGHT GREEN",;
401 :              "12> BRIGHT CYAN", "13> ORANGE","14> YELLOW",;
402 :              "15> BRIGHT WHITE"}
403 :
404 :    aGround := {"N","B","G","BG","R","RB","GR","W","N+","B+",;
405 :                "G+","BG+","R+","GR+","W+"}
406 :
407 :    DEVRCLEAR(maxrow(),0)
408 :
409 :    bOperation := {|| ( dispbox(7,62,23,maxcol(), pDBAR), devpos(8,63),;
410 :              aeval(aWords, {|cName| (devout(cName), devpos(row()+1,63))}), ;
411 :              setcolor( cColor )) }
412 :
413 :    bIsGood := {|| ( DEVRCLEAR(maxrow(),0), setpos(maxrow(),00), ;
414 :                  devout("Is this o.k.? "), chr(inkey(0))$"Yy" )}
415 :
416 :    eval( bOperation )
417 :
418 :    REPEAT
419 :
420 :      @ maxrow(),00 say "What is the color of the background? " ;
421 :                   get nChoice1 pict "##"
422 :      read
423 :      if lastkey() != pESC
424 :        @ maxrow(), 00 say "What is the color of the foreground? ";
425 :                     get nChoice2 PICT "##"
426 :        read
427 :        if lastkey() != pESC
428 :          setcolor( aGround[nChoice2] + "/" + aGround[nChoice1] )
429 :          eval( bOperation )
430 :        endif
431 :      endif
432 :
433 :    until lastkey() == pESC .or. eval( bIsGood )
434 :
435 :    restscreen(,,,, cScreen )
436 :
437 :    return( aGround[nChoice2] +"/"+ aGround[nChoice1] )
438 :
439 : ********************
440 :
441 : static function EditHelp( cItem, cScreen )
442 :
443 :    MakeHelp( cItem, Help->( found() ) )
444 :    restscreen(,,,,cScreen)
```

```
445 :
446 :    keyboard chr(pESC)
447 :
448 :    VOID
449 :
450 : ********************
451 :
452 : static function StrScript( aArray )
453 :
454 :    local cRetValue := ""
455 :
456 :    aeval( aArray, { |cItem| cRetValue += "[" + alltrim(str(cItem)) + "]"} )
457 :
458 :    return( cRetValue )
459 :
460 : ********************
461 :
462 : init function Helpsetup()
463 :
464 :    local cHelpName := "Sjshelp"
465 :    local aStru := {}
466 :
467 :    if !file( cHelpName + ".DBF" )
468 :       aadd( aStru, {"SEARCH",   "C", 80, 0} )
469 :       aadd( aStru, {"TOP",      "N",  2, 0} )
470 :       aadd( aStru, {"LEFT",     "N",  2, 0} )
471 :       aadd( aStru, {"BOTTOM",   "N",  2, 0} )
472 :       aadd( aStru, {"RIGHT",    "N",  2, 0} )
473 :       aadd( aStru, {"COLOR",    "C", 15, 0} )
474 :       aadd( aStru, {"TITLE",    "C", 40, 0} )
475 :       aadd( aStru, {"SHOWTITLE","L",  1, 0} )
476 :       aadd( aStru, {"SCREEN",   "M", 10, 0} )
477 :       aadd( aStru, {"TEXT",     "M", 10, 0} )
478 :       dbcreate( cHelpName + ".dbf", aStru )
479 :    endif
480 :
481 :    if !file( cHelpName + indexext() )
482 :       use (cHelpName) new alias Help
483 :       index on Help->search to (cHelpName)
484 :       use
485 :    endif
486 :
487 :    use (cHelpName) new index (cHelpName) alias Help
488 :
489 :    VOID
490 :
491 : ********************
492 :
493 : exit procedure CloseHelp()
494 :
495 :    select Help
496 :    use
497 :
498 : // End of File: Help1.prg
```

And the RMAKE file that was used to create the example program:

```
1 : // This is an RMAKE script file for the THelp1.prg program.
2 :
3 : .prg.obj:
```

```
 4 :    clipper $* /m /n /a /w /v /p /b /es2
 5 :
 6 : thelp1.obj         :       thelp1.prg
 7 : help1.obj          :       help1.prg
 8 :
 9 : thelp1.exe         :       thelp1.obj help1.obj
10 :    if not errorlevel 1 rtlink fi thelp1, help1
11 :
12 : // End of THelp1.rmk
```

This example is geared toward building a context-sensitive help system, rather than a general help system or a menu-driven, topic-oriented help system. It also illustrates a technique for building a help system on the fly by using an external database to contain the context-sensitive help information. In this particular case, help information is stored in a database called SJSHELP. By modifying line 464, however, the filename can be modified to better conform to a particular environment or application.

Note that the program THELP1.PRG begins with a REQUEST statement on line 6. Similarly, the ANNOUNCE statement is used to assign the label OnLineHelp to the HELP1.PRG module on line 23 of HELP1.PRG. This ensures that, should the help module within HELP1.PRG reside in an external library or object file, it will nevertheless be linked with the application. Because of this, the INIT FUNCTION HelpSetup( ) beginning on line 462 of HELP1.PRG will automatically be called before the first line of THELP1.PRG executes. This routine ensures that the necessary help file exists before the main part of the program begins, and opens it for the main program module to use. Similarly, the EXIT PROCEDURE CloseHelp beginning on line 493 of HELP1.PRG makes sure that all help files are closed when the program terminates. While the simple USE command is used by both the INIT and EXIT procedures, additional instructions could be added to make the program more robust and to ensure the integrity of the help file for later use.

The successful operation of the program relies on two DOS environmental variables. In order to create the context-sensitive Help system illustrated by THELP1.PRG, a DOS environmental variable named MAKEHELP must be defined. This can be done at the DOS prompt with the following statement:

```
SET MAKEHELP=<anything>
```

Similarly, in order to allow existing help information to be edited, a DOS environmental variable named EDITHELP must be defined as follows:

```
SET EDITHELP=<anything>
```

If MAKEHELP is defined, the F1 is pressed when a particular GET is active, and there is no help information available for a particular topic, then the help system will prompt for the location, color, and title of the help window corresponding to the particular GET. It then prompts for the help text itself. If EDITHELP is defined, the F1 key is pressed, and help information is available for that particular GET, the program will allow the location, color, and title of the window to be redefined. It will then display the help text, which can be changed. Finally, if neither DOS variable is defined and the F1 key is pressed when a particular GET is active, any available help text corresponding to it will be displayed.

We could extend the concept in this simple example to tackle issues like hypertext help and chaining help from one item to the next. We could allow for the Help system to be sensitive to individual menu items on the screen. We could even allow the Help system to be programmable. All of these ideas are expanded upon in the Helios Library, which is referenced in the back of this book.

In THELP1.PRG and its associated programs, we used DOS environmental variables to control the creation and display of help information. In the following sample program, however, the process of constructing the program is more carefully integrated into the program. While the F1 key is used to display help, F3 is used to define context-sensitive help for either menu items or for active GETs. If desired, the ability to use F3 to define help information can be enabled or disabled by removing the comment symbols from lines 21 and 23 and using the preprocessor for conditional compilation. In this case, the following command would enable MakeHelp( ), the routine that generates help information:

```
RMAKE THELP2 /Dwithmakehelp
```

On the other hand, in order to disable the program's ability to modify its help files, simply invoke RMAKE as follows:

```
RMAKE THELP2
```

What follows is the main program that illustrates the use of the help creation and Help display modules:

```
 1 : * File       THelp2.prg
 2 : * Compile    Rmake THelp2
 3 :
 4 : #define CLIPPER          // Default to use the Clipper SETKEY stuff!
 5 :
 6 : #include "PTInkey.ch"    // Power Tools Header file of ASCII values
 7 : #include "PTVerbs.ch"    // Power Tools Header file of commands/statements
 8 : #include "PTValue.ch"    // Power Tools Header file of misc values
 9 :
10 : request OnLineHelp
11 :
12 : procedure Main()
13 :
14 :    local nChoice := 1         // This is for the MENU TO stuff.
15 :
16 : //  HelpName( "HELIOS" )      // Enter the name of the NEW database!
17 : //  ReBuildHelp()             // And this re-creates the data files
18 :
19 :    set key pF1 to DispHelp    // This is only for displaying the help.
20 :
21 : //#ifdef WITHMAKEHELP         // Only add this if it is compiled as such!
22 :    set key pF3 to MakeHelp    // This is now for making the help!
23 : //#endif
24 :
25 :    scroll()
26 :    dispbox(0,0,4,maxcol(),pDBAR)
27 :    @ 1,1 say padc("The following HELP system is a subset of the system found", maxcol()-1 )
28 :    @ 2,1 say padc("in the Helios Library published by Sirius Software.", maxcol()-1 )
29 :    @ 3,1 say padc("-] Details in the back of this book [- ", maxcol()-1 )
30 :
31 :    PROCESS
32 :
33 :    dispbox(5,30,11,50, pDBAR)
```

```
34 :        HelpRowCol( pON )                    // Turn on the row and column settings.
35 :
36 :        @  6,31 prompt padr( "General Ledger", 19 )
37 :        @  7,31 prompt padr( "Payroll", 19 )
38 :        @  8,31 prompt padr( "Inventory", 19 )
39 :        @  9,31 prompt padr( "Accounts Payable", 19)
40 :        @ 10,31 prompt padr( "Supervisor", 19 )
41 :        menu to nChoice
42 :        HelpRowCol( pOFF )
43 :
44 :        do case
45 :        case nChoice == 0
46 :          exit
47 :
48 :        otherwise
49 :          NextStep()
50 :
51 :        endcase
52 :
53 :    END PROCESS
54 :    scroll()
55 :
56 : ******************
57 :
58 : static function NextStep()
59 :
60 :    local aData   := {1, 2, 3}
61 :    local nNumber := 1
62 :    local getlist := {}
63 :    local cScreen := savescreen()
64 :
65 :    dispbox( 9,20,14,60,pSBAR)
66 :    @ 10,25 say "Enter a value: " get aData[1]
67 :    @ 11,25 say "   and another: " get aData[2]
68 :    @ 12,25 say "          -----> " get aData[3]
69 :    @ 13,25 say "   And now a #: " get nNumber
70 :    read
71 :
72 :    restscreen(,,,,cScreen)
73 :
74 :    VOID
75 :
76 : // End of File: THelp2.prg
```

One of the features built into this routine is the ability to reprogram the name of the Help database. The default will be SJSHELP.DBF; however, this is not always wanted—especially if more than one application is using the same Help subsystem. Here on lines 16 and 17, two lines that are commented out in this version of the program, a call to the HelpName( ) function, which is defined within the HELPINIT.PRG file, defines a STATIC variable and then attempts to rebuild a Help database with this name. If not specified, then the INIT routine listed in the next file simply sets up the default database and index files.

While displaying Help is always desired, the ability to make Help on the fly is to be used in rare occasions. In the previous example, we used the GETE( ) function to set DOS environmental variables to toggle on and off the ability to display and/or edit on-line/context-sensitive Help screens. Here, the ability to display a Help screen is "burned" into the application on line 19. If the comment markings were removed on line 21 and again on line

23, a conditional compile could be used so that, if the manifest constant WITHMAKEHELP is defined, the SET KEY command would turn on the ability to make help on the fly.

This version of the Help system also toggles on and off the program's ability to recognize the row and column position of the cursor when the F1 key was originally pressed. In particular, it is toggled on line 34, before the MENU TO command on line 41 can execute. This allows the Help program modules—on lines 37-40 of HELPMAKE.PRG and lines 33-36 of HELPDISP.PRG—to use these row and column coordinates as a part of the search criteria for the correct help information. If the ability to detect the row and column positions of the cursor were toggled off, the program would support the display of only general help information when a menu is active. This is the case because the information passed to the help routines would be the same regardless of which menu item was highlighted at the point that the F1 key was pressed; the value of the program name would be MAIN in each case, and the active variable for each PROMPT item would be *nChoice*.

Finally, the technique used to determine what search strings are to be used in locating help information is worth noting. Often, the user may attempt to get help in the middle of a generic routine, such as a listbox function, that may be used in a variety of locations within an application. In this case, we do not want help on the listbox itself, and therefore we do not want to search for help based on the procedure or variable active at the time the F1 key was pressed. In our sample program, one of a number of possible techniques to solve this problem is used in the HelpIndex( ) function; previous procedures form the basis for the search string, rather than the name of the module active at the point that the Help module was called.

Here is the HELPINIT.PRG file that holds all of the generic routines for the Help system as well as the INIT and EXIT routines:

```
 1 : * File      HelpInit.prg
 2 : * Compile   Rmake THelp2
 3 : * Note      This file is nothing more than a file to hold information for the
 4 : *           Help system.  This is based on the Helios Library Help System
 5 : *           which is available from Sirius Software: details in back of
 6 : *           book.
 7 :
 8 : #include "PTInkey.ch"     // Power Tools Header file of ASCII values
 9 : #include "PTVerbs.ch"     // Power Tools Header file of commands/statements
10 : #include "PTValue.ch"     // Power Tools Header file of misc values
11 :
12 : announce OnLineHelp
13 :
14 : *******************
15 :
16 : procedure ReBuildHelp()    // This simply rebuilds the Help file should
17 :                            // the name of the file be rebuilt!
18 :    select Help
19 :    use
20 :    MakeHelp()              // Now, recreate a new file!
21 :
22 : *******************
23 :
24 : init procedure HelpSetup
25 :
26 :    MakeHelp()
27 :
28 : *******************
29 :
```

## The Help and Error Systems 1057

```
30 : static procedure MakeHelp()
31 :
32 :    local cHelpName := HelpName()
33 :    local aStru     := {}
34 :
35 :    if !file( cHelpName + ".DBF" )
36 :       aadd( aStru, {"SEARCH",    "C", 200, 0} )
37 :       aadd( aStru, {"TOP",       "N",   2, 0} )
38 :       aadd( aStru, {"LEFT",      "N",   2, 0} )
39 :       aadd( aStru, {"BOTTOM",    "N",   2, 0} )
40 :       aadd( aStru, {"RIGHT",     "N",   2, 0} )
41 :       aadd( aStru, {"COLOR",     "C",  15, 0} )
42 :       aadd( aStru, {"TITLE",     "C",  40, 0} )
43 :       aadd( aStru, {"SHOWTITLE", "L",   1, 0} )
44 :       aadd( aStru, {"SCREEN",    "M",  10, 0} )
45 :       aadd( aStru, {"TEXT",      "M",  10, 0} )
46 :       dbcreate( cHelpName + ".dbf", aStru )
47 :    endif
48 :
49 :    if !file( cHelpName + indexext() )
50 :       use (cHelpName) new alias Help
51 :       index on Help->search to (cHelpName)
52 :       use
53 :    endif
54 :
55 :    use (cHelpName) new index (cHelpName) alias Help
56 :
57 : *******************
58 :
59 : exit procedure CloseHelp()
60 :
61 :    select Help
62 :    use
63 :
64 : // The following are functions used by either the DispHelp() or the
65 : // MakeHelp() routines.
66 :
67 : *******************
68 :
69 : function HelpName( cName )
70 :
71 :    static cFileName
72 :
73 :    DEFAULT cFileName TO "SJSHELP"
74 :
75 :    IF cName IS pCHARACTER
76 :       cFileName := cName    // Assign static value name of file.
77 :    ENDIF
78 :
79 :    return( cFileName )
80 :
81 : *****************
82 :
83 : function HelpRowCol( lToggle )
84 :
85 :    static lSetting
86 :
87 :    DEFAULT lSetting TO pFALSE
88 :
89 :    IF lToggle IS pLOGICAL
90 :       lSetting := lToggle
```

```
 91 :      ENDIF
 92 :
 93 :      return( lSetting )
 94 :
 95 : ********************
 96 :
 97 : function HelpIndex()
 98 :
 99 :      // This function was originally found in Clipper 5.2 Power Tools Book
100 :      // which, along with the source code, is available from Sirius.  Details
101 :      // in the back of the book.
102 :
103 :      local cItem    := ""
104 :      local nCounter := 2
105 :
106 :      REPEAT
107 :
108 :         if !("_" $ procname(nCounter) .or. "(b)" $ procname(nCounter) )
109 :            do case
110 :            case procname(nCounter) == "READMODAL"
111 :            case procname(nCounter) == "GETDOSETKE"
112 :            case procname(nCounter) == "GETAPPLYKE"
113 :            case procname(nCounter) == "GETREADER"
114 :            otherwise
115 :               cItem += procname(nCounter)
116 :            endcase
117 :         endif
118 :
119 :      UNTIL empty( procname( ++nCounter ) )
120 :
121 :      return( cItem )
122 :
123 : ********************
124 :
125 : function StrScript( aArray )
126 :
127 :      local cRetValue := ""
128 :
129 :      aeval( aArray, { |cItem| cRetValue += "[" + alltrim(str(cItem)) + "]"} )
130 :
131 :      return( cRetValue )
132 :
133 : // End of File: Helpinit.prg
```

Separate files are used to make the Help entries or display the Help entries. First, the file that displays the Help entries:

```
 1 : * File       HelpDisp.prg
 2 : * Compile    Rmake THelp2
 3 :
 4 : #include "PTInkey.ch"    // Power Tools Header file of ASCII values
 5 : #include "PTVerbs.ch"    // Power Tools Header file of commands/statements
 6 : #include "PTValue.ch"    // Power Tools Header file of misc values
 7 :
 8 : procedure DispHelp( cProgram, nLine, cVariable )
 9 :
10 :      local oGetObject := getactive()
11 :      local cSearch
12 :      local nRow       := row()
13 :      local nCol       := col()
14 :
```

```
15 :      // Do not allow recursion.
16 :      if !( cProgram == "DISPHELP" .or. cProgram == "MAKEHELP" )
17 :        if !empty( select("HELP") )      // Means that there is a database for it
18 :
19 :          // First, let's work with the name of the variable!
20 :          IF oGetObject IS pOBJECT
21 :            cVariable := upper(oGetObject:name)
22 :            IF oGetObject:subscript IS pARRAY
23 :              if !empty( len( oGetObject:subscript ) )
24 :                cVariable += StrScript( oGetObject:subscript )
25 :              endif
26 :            endif
27 :          endif
28 :
29 :          // Rather than taking the procname, let's take a complete
30 :          // index of the subroutines.
31 :          cSearch := HelpIndex() + cVariable
32 :
33 :          if HelpRowCol()
34 :             cSearch += alltrim(str(nRow))
35 :             cSearch += alltrim(str(nCol))
36 :          endif
37 :
38 :          if Help->( dbseek( cSearch ) )
39 :             Help->( DisplayItem() )
40 :          endif
41 :
42 :        endif
43 :      endif
44 :
45 : *******************
46 :
47 : static function DisplayItem()
48 :
49 :      local nWidth  := Help->right - Help->left
50 :      local cScreen := savescreen( Help->top, Help->left, ;
51 :                                   Help->bottom, Help->right)
52 :      local nKeyVal := setkey( pF10 )
53 :      local nCursor := setcursor()
54 :      local cColor  := setcolor()
55 :      local nTop    := Help->top
56 :      local nLeft   := Help->left
57 :      local nBottom := Help->bottom
58 :      local nRight  := Help->right
59 :
60 :      setcolor( alltrim(Help->color) )
61 :      setcursor( pCURSOR_ON )
62 :      dispbox( Help->top, Help->left, Help->bottom, Help->right, pDBAR )
63 :
64 :      if !empty( Help->title )
65 :        if Help->showtitle
66 :           setpos( Help->top, Help->left+1 )
67 :           dispout( " " + left( alltrim(Help->title), nWidth ) + " " )
68 :        endif
69 :      endif
70 :      setpos( Help->bottom, Help->left+1 )
71 :      dispout( left( " ESC to quit ", nWidth ) )
72 :      memoedit( Help->text, Help->top+1, Help->left+1, Help->bottom-1,;
73 :                Help->right-1, pFALSE )
74 :
75 :      restscreen( nTop, nLeft, nBottom, nRight, cScreen )
```

```
76 :
77 :    setcursor( nCursor )
78 :    setcolor( cColor )
79 :
80 :    VOID
81 :
82 : // End of File: Helpdisp.prg
```

And now for the file responsible for making Help entries:

```
 1 : * File       HelpMake.prg
 2 : * Compile    Rmake THelp2
 3 :
 4 : #include "PTInkey.ch"     // Power Tools Header file of ASCII values
 5 : #include "PTVerbs.ch"     // Power Tools Header file of commands/statements
 6 : #include "PTValue.ch"     // Power Tools Header file of misc values
 7 : #include "PTFuncs.ch"     // Power Tools header file of pseudo-functions
 8 :
 9 : memvar getlist
10 :
11 : #xtranslate DEVRCLEAR(<x>,<y>) => (scroll(<x>, <y>, <x>, maxcol()))
12 :
13 : procedure MakeHelp( cProgram, nLine, cVariable )
14 :
15 :    local oGetObject := getactive()
16 :    local cSearch
17 :    local nRow        := row()
18 :    local nCol        := col()
19 :    local lScore      := set( pSCOREBOARD )
20 :    local chColor     := setcolor()
21 :
22 :    if !( cProgram == "DISPHELP" .or. cProgram == "MAKEHELP" )
23 :      if !empty( select("HELP") )      // Means that there is a database for it
24 :
25 :         // First, let's work with the name of the variable!
26 :         IF oGetObject IS pOBJECT
27 :           cVariable := upper(oGetObject:name)
28 :           IF oGetObject:subscript IS pARRAY
29 :             if !empty( len( oGetObject:subscript ) )
30 :               cVariable += StrScript( oGetObject:subscript )
31 :             endif
32 :           endif
33 :         endif
34 :
35 :         cSearch := HelpIndex() + cVariable
36 :
37 :         if HelpRowCol()
38 :           cSearch += alltrim(str(nRow))
39 :           cSearch += alltrim(str(nCol))
40 :         endif
41 :
42 :         Help->( MakeIt( cSearch, dbseek( cSearch ) ) )
43 :
44 :      endif
45 :    endif
46 :
47 :    setpos( nRow, nCol )
48 :    set( pSCOREBOARD, lScore )
49 :    setcolor( chColor )
50 :    CLEARESC()
```

```
 51 :
 52 : *********************
 53 :
 54 : static function MakeIt( cItem, lAtItem )   // The item to ADD
 55 :
 56 : #define pBAR1 REPLICATE(CHR(176),8)+CHR(32)
 57 : #define pBAR2 REPLICATE(CHR(178),8)+CHR(32)
 58 :
 59 :    local cScreen     := savescreen()
 60 :    local nCursor     := setcursor( pCURSOR_OFF )
 61 :    local lScore      := set( pSCOREBOARD, pOFF )
 62 :    local cColor      := setcolor()
 63 :    local lShowTitle  := pFALSE
 64 :    local nTop        := 8
 65 :    local nLeft       := 20
 66 :    local nBottom     := 12
 67 :    local nRight      := 60
 68 :    local cText       := ""
 69 :    local cTitle      := space(40)
 70 :    local nKey
 71 :    local aTempGet
 72 :    local bTempBlock
 73 :    local cNewColor
 74 :
 75 :    DEFAULT lAtItem TO pFALSE   // Forcing things to add
 76 :
 77 :    if lAtItem
 78 :       cText      := Help->text
 79 :       nTop       := Help->top
 80 :       nLeft      := Help->left
 81 :       nBottom    := Help->bottom
 82 :       nRight     := Help->right
 83 :       cTitle     := Help->title
 84 :       lShowTitle := Help->showtitle
 85 :    endif
 86 :
 87 :    REPEAT   //  Move the window region.
 88 :       restscreen(,,,,cScreen )
 89 :       dispbox(nTop,nLeft,nBottom,nRight,cScreen)
 90 :       setpos(maxrow(), 0)
 91 :       dispout("Press TAB, <T>op, <L>eft, <B>ottom, <R>ight,or ESC ")
 92 :       nKey := inkey(0)
 93 :
 94 :       do case
 95 :       case nKey == pTAB
 96 :          DragBox(@nTop, @nLeft, @nBottom, @nRight, cScreen)
 97 :
 98 :       case chr(nKey) $ "tT"
 99 :          MoveHorizontal( pTRUE, @nTop, @nLeft, @nBottom, @nRight, cScreen )
100 :
101 :       case chr(nKey) $ "bB"
102 :          MoveHorizontal( pFALSE, @nTop, @nLeft, @nBottom, @nRight, cScreen )
103 :
104 :       case chr(nKey) $ "lL"
105 :          MoveVertical( pTRUE, @nTop, @nLeft, @nBottom, @nRight, cScreen )
106 :
107 :       case chr(nKey) $ "rR"
108 :          MoveVertical( pFALSE, @nTop, @nLeft, @nBottom, @nRight, cScreen )
109 :
110 :       endcase
```

```
111 :
112 :      UNTIL ( nKey == pESC .or. nKey == pENTER )
113 :
114 :      if !( nKey == pESC )
115 :
116 :         SAVE GET TO aTempGet
117 :
118 :         DEVRCLEAR(maxrow(),0)
119 :         cNewColor := ColorChoice( cScreen )
120 :
121 :         if !( lastkey() == pESC )
122 :            setcursor( pCURSOR_ON )
123 :            dispbox( nTop, nLeft, nBottom, nRight, pBAR2 ) // Add text to the item.
124 :            setpos( maxrow(), 0 )
125 :            dispout( "Press F10 to save, ESC to quit" )
126 :            bTempBlock := setkey( pF10 )
127 :            setcolor( cNewColor )
128 :            setkey( pF10, {|| KEYBOARD( chr( pCTRL_W ) )} )
129 :            cText := memoedit(cText, nTop+1, nLeft+1, nBottom-1, nRight-1, pTRUE )
130 :            setkey( pF10, bTempBlock )
131 :            setcolor( cColor )
132 :
133 :            if lastkey() == pCTRL_W
134 :              DEVRCLEAR( maxrow(), 0 )
135 :              @ maxrow(), 0 say "Enter Title: " get cTitle
136 :              read
137 :              if !( lastkey() == pESC )
138 :                DEVRCLEAR( maxrow(), 0 )
139 :                @ maxrow(), 0 say "Show Title? " get lShowTitle pict "Y"
140 :                read
141 :                if !( lastkey() == pESC )
142 :                  if !lAtItem
143 :                    Help->( dbappend() )
144 :                  endif
145 :                  Help->search    := cItem
146 :                  Help->top       := nTop
147 :                  Help->left      := nLeft
148 :                  Help->bottom    := nBottom
149 :                  Help->right     := nRight
150 :                  Help->title     := cTitle
151 :                  Help->color     := cNewColor
152 :                  Help->showtitle := lShowTitle
153 :                  Help->screen    := cScreen
154 :                  Help->text      := cText
155 :                endif
156 :              endif
157 :            endif
158 :         endif
159 :
160 :         RESTORE GET FROM aTempGet
161 :
162 :      endif
163 :      restscreen(,,,,cScreen )
164 :      setcursor( nCursor )
165 :      setcolor( cColor )
166 :      set( pSCOREBOARD, lScore )
167 :
168 :      VOID
169 :
170 : *********************
```

```
171 :
172 : static function Dragbox( nTop, nLeft, nBottom, nRight, cScreen )
173 :
174 :    local nOldTop     := nTop
175 :    local nOldLeft    := nLeft
176 :    local nOldBottom  := nBottom
177 :    local nOldRight   := nRight
178 :    local nKey
179 :
180 :    REPEAT
181 :      restscreen(,,,,cScreen)
182 :      setpos(maxrow(),0)
183 :      dispout("Cursor Keys to drag, ENTER to Set, ESC to quit")
184 :      dispbox(nTop, nLeft, nBottom, nRight, pBAR1)
185 :
186 :      nKey := inkey(0)
187 :
188 :      do case
189 :      case nKey == pUP_ARROW
190 :         if( nTop != 0, ( nTop--, nBottom-- ), NIL )
191 :
192 :      case nKey == pDOWN_ARROW
193 :         if( nBottom != maxrow(), (nTop++,nBottom++), NIL )
194 :
195 :      case nKey == pLEFT_ARROW
196 :         if( nLeft != 0, (nLeft--, nRight--), NIL )
197 :
198 :      case nKey == pRIGHT_ARROW
199 :         if( nBottom != maxrow(), (nLeft++,nRight++), NIL )
200 :
201 :      case nKey == pESC
202 :         nTop     := nOldTop
203 :         nLeft    := nOldLeft
204 :         nBottom  := nOldBottom
205 :         nRight   := nOldRight
206 :
207 :      endcase
208 :
209 :    UNTIL ( nKey == pESC .or. nKey == pENTER )
210 :
211 :    CLEARESC()
212 :
213 :    VOID
214 :
215 : *******************
216 :
217 : static function MoveHorizontal( lIsTop, nTop, nLeft, nBottom, nRight, cScreen )
218 :
219 :    local nOldTop     := nTop
220 :    local nOldLeft    := nLeft
221 :    local nOldBottom  := nBottom
222 :    local nOldRight   := nRight
223 :    local nKey
224 :
225 :    REPEAT
226 :      restscreen(,,,,cScreen)
227 :      setpos(maxrow(),0)
228 :      dispout("Up / Down Arrows, ENTER to Set, ESC to quit")
229 :      dispbox(nTop, nLeft, nBottom, nRight, pBAR1)
230 :
```

```
231 :      nKey := inkey(0)
232 :
233 :      do case
234 :      case nKey == pUP_ARROW
235 :         if( lIsTop, if( (nTop-1 != 0), nTop--, NIL ), ;
236 :                     if( nBottom != nTop-1 , nBottom--, NIL ) )
237 :
238 :      case nKey == pDOWN_ARROW
239 :         if( lIsTop, if( (nTop+1 != nBottom), nTop++, NIL ), ;
240 :                     if( nBottom+1 != maxrow(), nBottom++, NIL ) )
241 :
242 :      case nKey == pESC
243 :         nTop    := nOldTop
244 :         nLeft   := nOldLeft
245 :         nBottom := nOldBottom
246 :         nRight  := nOldRight
247 :
248 :      endcase
249 :
250 :   UNTIL ( nKey == pESC .or. nKey == pENTER )
251 :
252 :   CLEARESC()
253 :
254 :   VOID
255 :
256 : *******************
257 :
258 : static function MoveVertical( lIsLeft, nTop, nLeft, nBottom, nRight, cScreen )
259 :
260 :    local nOldTop    := nTop
261 :    local nOldLeft   := nLeft
262 :    local nOldBottom := nBottom
263 :    local nOldRight  := nRight
264 :    local nKey
265 :
266 :    REPEAT
267 :       restscreen(,,,,cScreen)
268 :       setpos(maxrow(),0)
269 :       dispout("Left / Right Arrows, ENTER to Set, ESC to quit")
270 :       dispbox(nTop, nLeft, nBottom, nRight, pBAR1)
271 :
272 :       nKey := inkey(0)
273 :
274 :       do case
275 :       case nKey == pLEFT_ARROW
276 :          if( lIsLeft, if( nLeft != 0, nLeft--, NIL ), ;
277 :                       if( nRight-1 != nLeft, nRight--, NIL ) )
278 :
279 :       case nKey == pRIGHT_ARROW
280 :          if( lIsLeft, if( nLeft+1 != nRight, nLeft++, NIL ), ;
281 :                       if( nRight != maxcol(), nRight++, NIL ) )
282 :
283 :       case nKey == pESC
284 :          nTop    := nOldTop
285 :          nLeft   := nOldLeft
286 :          nBottom := nOldBottom
287 :          nRight  := nOldRight
288 :
289 :       endcase
290 :
```

```
291 :    UNTIL ( nKey == pESC .or. nKey == pENTER )
292 :
293 :    CLEARESC()
294 :
295 :    VOID
296 :
297 : #undef pBAR1
298 : #undef pBAR2
299 :
300 : ********************
301 :
302 : static function ColorChoice( cScreen )
303 :
304 :    local nChoice1 := 1
305 :    local nChoice2 := 8
306 :    local cColor   := setcolor()       // Old color status
307 :    local lConfirm := set(pCONFIRM)    // Old confirm status
308 :    local aGround
309 :    local aWords
310 :    local bOperation
311 :    local bIsGood
312 :
313 :    aWords := {" 1> BLACK"," 2> BLUE", " 3> GREEN", " 4> CYAN",;
314 :               " 5> RED", " 6> MAGENTA", " 7> BROWN", " 8> WHITE",;
315 :               " 9> GRAY", "10> BRIGHT BLUE", "11> BRIGHT GREEN",;
316 :               "12> BRIGHT CYAN", "13> ORANGE","14> YELLOW",;
317 :               "15> BRIGHT WHITE"}
318 :
319 :    aGround := {"N","B","G","BG","R","RB","GR","W","N+","B+",;
320 :                "G+","BG+","R+","GR+","W+"}
321 :
322 :    DEVRCLEAR(maxrow(),0)
323 :
324 :    bOperation := {|| ( dispbox(7,62,23,maxcol(), pDBAR), devpos(8,63),;
325 :                aeval(aWords, {|cName| (devout(cName), devpos(row()+1,63))}), ;
326 :                setcolor( cColor )) }
327 :
328 :    bIsGood := {|| ( DEVRCLEAR(maxrow(),0), setpos(maxrow(),00), ;
329 :                     devout("Is this o.k.? "), chr(inkey(0))$"Yy" )}
330 :
331 :    eval( bOperation )
332 :
333 :    REPEAT
334 :
335 :       @ maxrow(),00 say "What is the color of the background? " ;
336 :                  get nChoice1 pict "##"
337 :       read
338 :       if lastkey() != pESC
339 :          @ maxrow(), 00 say "What is the color of the foreground? ";
340 :                     get nChoice2 PICT "##"
341 :          read
342 :          if lastkey() != pESC
343 :             setcolor( aGround[nChoice2] + "/" + aGround[nChoice1] )
344 :             eval( bOperation )
345 :          endif
346 :       endif
347 :
348 :    until lastkey() == pESC .or. eval( bIsGood )
349 :
350 :    restscreen(,,,, cScreen )
```

```
351 :
352 :     return( aGround[nChoice2] +"/"+ aGround[nChoice1] )
353 :
354 : // End of File:Helpmake.prg
```

And finally, here is the .RMK file that can be used to put this entire program together:

```
 1 : // This is an RMAKE script file for the THelp1.prg program.
 2 :
 3 : .prg.obj:
 4 :   clipper $* /m /n /a /w /v /p /b /es2
 5 :
 6 : thelp2.obj       :       thelp2.prg
 7 : helpinit.obj     :       helpinit.prg
 8 : helpdisp.obj     :       helpdisp.prg
 9 : helpmake.obj     :       helpmake.prg
10 :
11 : thelp2.exe       :       thelp2.obj helpinit.obj helpdisp.obj helpmake.obj
12 :    if not errorlevel 1 rtlink fi thelp2, helpinit, helpdisp, helpmake
13 :
14 : // End of THelp2.rmk
```

Consider this: Since the screens of the application as well as the text information for Help are stored together, it is possible to write another program that could take the data stored in these files and build a user manual, based on the on-line help that the application would provide. This is the type of vehicle that makes the end user a part of the application development cycle.

## The Error System

Programming for potential errors in an application can be one of the most difficult and more time-consuming adventures. There are some basic things to consider when programming either the Error Object or the entire Error System.

The first step in understanding errors is that you can program an escape route directly into the application should an error occur. This means that you can attempt to plan for errors to take place as a part of the application. Admittedly, it is difficult to plan for mistakes—it's easy to plan for the expected, but to program the unexpected is a different matter. To get a better feel for this, consider the following example program:

```
 1 : * File      Terr1.prg
 2 : * Compile   Rmake sample /dFILE:terr1
 3 :
 4 : procedure main()
 5 :
 6 :    local bError := errorblock({|oError| break(oError)})
 7 :
 8 :    cls
 9 :    ? "This program is designed to show you how the basic logic of the"
10 :    ? "BEGIN SEQUENCE...RECOVER...END SEQUENCE structure works".
11 :
12 :    begin sequence
13 :
14 :       ? "String compared to a number" == 23
15 :
16 :    recover
17 :
```

```
18 :        ?
19 :        ?
20 :        ? "If this line printed, then there was an error and this is the"
21 :        ? "recovery!"
22 :
23 :     end sequence
24 :
25 : // End of File: Terr1.prg
```

The first thing to keep in mind is that you have to tell the underlying error system that in case of an error, it should not take over but, instead, should break back to the application and search for the associated RECOVER statement. The BEGIN SEQUENCE statement on line 12 gives the Error system the beginning of a base to refer back to. On line 14 there is an obvious type mismatch error. Had line 6 been omitted from the program, the Error system would retain control once line 14 is processed, and a pop-up dialog box describing the error would appear on the screen. Instead, should an error be detected (which it will be), the BREAK( ) instruction within the error block processed by the Error system tells Clipper to send the flow of the program to the statements following the associated RECOVER statement on line 16. As a result, the information on lines 18 through 21 is displayed.

It is also important to note that the END SEQUENCE on line 23 is necessary to prevent a compiler error informing you of an unbalanced structure. The END SEQUENCE (or just END) statement is needed to balance the BEGIN SEQUENCE statement.

It is also possible that information can be sent back to the main program to be processed. This is accomplished by the RECOVER statement along with the USING clause. The next example illustrates this point. The output shown from running this program appears in Figure 19.1.

```
 1 : * File       Terr2.prg
 2 : * Compile    Rmake sample /dFILE:terr2
 3 :
 4 : procedure main()
 5 :
 6 :    local bError := errorblock({|oError| break(oError)})
 7 :    local oRecover   // Error object returned from error system
 8 :
 9 :    cls
10 :    ? "This program is designed to show you how the basic logic of the"
11 :    ? "BEGIN SEQUENCE...RECOVER...END SEQUENCE structure works".
12 :
13 :    begin sequence
14 :
15 :       ? "String compared to a number" == 23
16 :
17 :    recover using oRecover
18 :
19 :       ?
20 :       ? "Here is some detailed information coming back from the error object:"
21 :       ?
22 :       ? "Argument is: ", valtype(oRecover:args)
23 :       ? "Can default: ", oRecover:canDefault
24 :       ? "  Can retry: ", oRecover:canRetry
25 :       ? " Substitute: ", oRecover:canSubstitute
26 :       ? "Description: ", oRecover:description
27 :       ? "  File Name: ", oRecover:filename
28 :       ? "   Gen Code: ", oRecover:gencode
```

1068  Straley's Programming with Clipper 5.2

```
This program is designed to show you how the basic logic of the
BEGIN SEQUENCE...RECOVER...END SEQUENCE structure works

Here is some detailed information coming back from the error object:

Argument is:   A
Can default:   .F.
  Can retry:   .F.
 Substitute:   .T.
Description:   Argument error
  File Name:
   Gen Code:           1
  Operation:          ==
    OS Code:           0
   Severity:           2
   Sub Code:        1070
 Sub System:   BASE
      Tries:           0
```

**Figure 19.1   Information returned by *oRecover***

```
29 :        ? "  Operation: ", oRecover:operation
30 :        ? "    OS Code: ", oRecover:osCode
31 :        ? "   Severity: ", oRecover:severity
32 :        ? "   Sub Code: ", oRecover:subCode
33 :        ? " Sub System: ", oRecover:subSystem
34 :        ? "      Tries: ", oRecover:tries
35 :
36 :     end sequence
37 :
38 : // End of File: Terr2.prg
```

Each item listed on lines 22 through 34 is an instance variable of the error object *oRecover*. Together, they accurately indicate the cause of the error. Using these values to determine the error is the beginning of building a robust Error subsystem. This next example continues to do just that.

```
 1 : * File       Terr3.prg
 2 : * Compile    Rmake sample /dFILE:terr3
 3 :
 4 : procedure main()
 5 :
 6 :    local nValue := "Wrong value assigned"
 7 :    local bError := errorblock({|oError| Test(oError,@nValue)})
 8 :    local oRecover  // Error object returned from error system
 9 :
10 :    while .t.
11 :       cls
12 :       ? "This program is designed to show you how the basic logic of the"
13 :       ? "BEGIN SEQUENCE...RECOVER...END SEQUENCE structure works".
14 :
15 :       begin sequence
16 :
17 :          ? 23 == nValue
18 :          wait
19 :          ? nValue == 23
20 :
21 :       recover using oRecover
22 :
23 :          ?
```

```
24 :        ? "Here is some detailed information coming back from the error object".
25 :        ?
26 :        ? "Argument is: ", valtype(oRecover:args)
27 :        ? "Can default: ", oRecover:canDefault
28 :        ? "  Can retry: ", oRecover:canRetry
29 :        ? " Substitute: ", oRecover:canSubstitute
30 :        ? "Description: ", oRecover:description
31 :        ? "  File Name: ", oRecover:filename
32 :        ? "   Gen Code: ", oRecover:gencode
33 :        ? "  Operation: ", oRecover:operation
34 :        ? "    OS Code: ", oRecover:osCode
35 :        ? "   Severity: ", oRecover:severity
36 :        ? "   Sub Code: ", oRecover:subCode
37 :        ? " Sub System: ", oRecover:subSystem
38 :        ? "      Tries: ", oRecover:tries
39 :        inkey(0)
40 :        loop
41 :
42 :      end sequence
43 :      exit                    // Leave the loop!
44 :
45 :    enddo
46 :
47 : *********************
48 :
49 : static function Test( oError, nNumber )
50 :
51 :    static nTries := 1
52 :
53 :    if nTries++ == 2
54 :       nNumber := 34       // Reassign the number of the variable.
55 :    else
56 :       break( oError )    // Now, find the RECOVER statement.
57 :    endif
58 :
59 :    return( nNumber )
60 :
61 : // End of File: Terr3.prg
```

This example is a bit different from the rest since a user-defined function named Test( ) is called by the Error system's error block. In that function, the variable *nValue* is passed by reference, which means that the function Test will be used to recover from the potential error on line 17, and that the function can alter the value of the variable directly to make it now work on line 17 should the process be reexecuted.

The program flow of this example is simple. Within the main loop beginning on line 10 is a BEGIN SEQUENCE ... END SEQUENCE construct. It is important to understand that the EXIT statement on line 43 could not be placed within the code between the BEGIN SEQUENCE and the END SEQUENCE statements. If you do you will get a compiler error message. In the first pass, there is an error on line 17, which means that the program will go through the default error system and find a reference to a function called Test( ). The program will then jump to that program and start execution. There, two parameters are received: the error object containing all of the error information, and the variable *nValue*, passed by reference and available for modification. As long as the value of the STATIC variable *nTries* within the Test( ) function is not equal to 2, the function will simply perform a BREAK( ), passing back the error object that was originally passed to it, unchanged. This will then cause the program to jump to the RECOVER statement on line 21. If no parameter is passed to the BREAK( ) function (or if the BREAK command is used instead), another error would take place because on line 21 we are expecting an error object to be returned. Once all of the information on the error is displayed, the INKEY(0) on line 39 waits for a key to be pressed. Once a key is pressed, the LOOP statement takes the program flow back to the top of the loop to start reexecuting. Again, an error will take place because the value of the variable *nValue* is a character string and it is being compared with a numeric. On this second pass through the error, the function Test( ) will take over again. Now the value of the STATIC variable *nTimes* is equal to 2, which causes *nNumber* to be set to a numeric on line 54. Now, the BREAK( ) operation does not take effect and the function Test( ) returns 34 to the screen and causes the rest of the program on lines 18 and 19 to be executed. Since there is no LOOP instruction in this segment of the application, program flow will jump to the end of the BEGIN SEQUENCE, which is on line 42, and to the following EXIT statement, causing the program to leave the loop and, ultimately, the program as well.

Without exaggerating, a complete book could be written on the subject of errors and recovery tactics. These few examples are just hints of the complexity needed to build a robust Error system. One of the main points to keep in mind is your approach: Most error recovery schemes are considered reactionary—they take place after the error is engaged. A good tactic is one that combines this scheme with a preventive Error system—one that automatically recovers from the error and continues the operational flow of the application without the end user being aware of a problem. Such a system requires a balance between code in the application to handle the error and a reprogrammed Error system. Below is a crude example of how an error system could be programmed and how it is linked in an application. First, the example program that will cause the error:

```
 1 : * File      Testerr.prg
 2 : * Compile   Rmake Testerr
 3 :
 4 : procedure Main()
 5 :
 6 :    local nNumber := 1
 7 :
 8 :    private dSysDate := date()
 9 :    private cSysName := "Sirius Software Development"
10 :
11 :    use Notap new
12 :    use Ontap new index Ontap
13 :    set filter to recno() > 20
14 :
15 :
16 :    run dir /w
17 :    ? cHelp
18 :
19 : // End of File: Testerr.prg
```

The modified Error system looks like this:

```
 1 : * File      Errorsys.prg
 2 : * Compile   Rmake Testerr
 3 : * Note      This is a complete error trapping system that not only
 4 : *           logs the error through the error object; it creates
 5 : *           a special LOG file, writes out information concerning
```

```
 6 : *              any and all open databases, filters, indexes,relations;
 7 : *              it strips the attribute bytes and dumps the screen to
 8 : *              the file, and finally, it writes out the values of all
 9 : *              PRIVATE and PUBLIC variables, not to mention the values
10 : *              of the internal environmental variables.
11 :
12 : #include "PTValue.ch"   // Power Tools Header file of misc values
13 : #include "PTVerbs.ch"   // Power Tools header file of commands/statements
14 :
15 : #include "fileio.ch"
16 :
17 : procedure Errorsys
18 :
19 :    // As seen in the previous examples, this now reroutes the error to a
20 :    // function called LogError() passing to it the Error Object.
21 :
22 :    Errorblock( {|oError| LogError(oError)} )
23 :
24 : *********************
25 :
26 : static function LogError( oErr )
27 :
28 :    local cScreen    := savescreen()   // The entire screen before error
29 :    local cLogFile   := "Error.log"    // Log file to hold error processing
30 :    local nWorkArea := select()        // Numeric work area number
31 :    local nRange     := (maxcol()+1)*2 // Width of the display area
32 :    local nStart     := 1
33 :    local nFhandle                     // Low-level file handle to write to log
34 :    local nCount                       // for the FOR...NEXT loop
35 :    local nForLoop                     // Another variable for an inside FOR loop
36 :    local nMemHandle                   // DOS file handle for .MEM file
37 :    local nMemLength                   // Length/Size of the .MEM file
38 :    local nMemWidth                    // The width of the buffer range
39 :    local nMemCount                    // Contains the memory variable
40 :    local cOutstring
41 :    local cSubstring
42 :    local cVarName                     // Name of the variable in the mem file
43 :    local cVarType                     // Data type of the memor variable
44 :    local cTemp                        // Temp string holding the value
45 :    local nLenTemp                     // Length of the temp string buffer
46 :    local nBytes                       // The number of bytes processed
47 :    local cVarRec
48 : //   local nVars
49 :
50 :    alert( "An Error Has Occurred.  Information Will be Written!")
51 :
52 :    nFhandle := fcreate( cLogFile, FC_NORMAL )  // Create file
53 :
54 :    if nFhandle < 4  // We have an error in creating the file!
55 :      cls
56 :      devout( "Due to an error, unable to write information to file!  " )
57 :
58 :    ELSE
59 :
60 :      FWriteLine( nFhandle, padc(" Error Log File ", 79, "*"   ) )
61 :      FWriteLine( nFhandle, "" )
62 :
63 :      FWriteLine( nFhandle, "" )
64 :      FWriteLine( nFhandle, "" )
65 :      FWriteLine( nFhandle, "              Date: " + dtoc( date()) )
```

```
 66 :      FWriteLine( nFhandle, "           Time: " + time() )
 67 :      FWriteLine( nFhandle, "Available Memory: " + StrValue(memory(0)) )
 68 :      FWriteLine( nFhandle, "   Current Area: " + StrValue(select()) )
 69 :      FWriteLine( nFhandle, PADC( " Environmental Information", 79, "-" ) )
 70 :      FWriteLine( nFhandle, "" )
 71 :      FWriteLine( nFhandle, "        Exact is: " + StrValue(set(pEXACT), pTRUE))
 72 :      FWriteLine( nFhandle, "        Fixed is: " + StrValue(set(pFIXED), pTRUE))
 73 :      FWriteLine( nFhandle, "Decimals is at: " + StrValue(set(pDECIMALS)))
 74 :      FWriteLine( nFhandle, "Path is set to: " + StrValue(set(pPATH)))
 75 :      FWriteLine( nFhandle, " Default is at: " + StrValue(set(pDEFAULT)))
 76 :      FWriteLine( nFhandle, "        Epoch is: " + StrValue(set(pEPOCH)))
 77 :      FWriteLine( nFhandle, "Date Format at: " + StrValue(set(pDATEFORMAT)))
 78 :      FWriteLine( nFhandle, "   Alternate is: " + StrValue(set(pALTERNATE),pTRUE))
 79 :      FWriteLine( nFhandle, " Alter File is: " + StrValue(set(pALTFILE)))
 80 :      FWriteLine( nFhandle, "      Console is: " + StrValue(set(pCONSOLE), pTRUE))
 81 :      FWriteLine( nFhandle, "   Margin is set: " + StrValue(set(pMARGIN)))
 82 :      FWriteLine( nFhandle, "      Printer is: " + StrValue(set(pPRINTER), pTRUE))
 83 :      FWriteLine( nFhandle, "   Printer File: " + StrValue(set(pPRINTFILE)))
 84 :      FWriteLine( nFhandle, "   Device is at: " + StrValue(set(pDEVICE)))
 85 :      FWriteLine( nFhandle, "         Bell is: " + StrValue(set(pBELL), pTRUE ))
 86 :      FWriteLine( nFhandle, "      Confirm is: " + StrValue(set(pCONFIRM), pTRUE))
 87 :      FWriteLine( nFhandle, "Delimiters are: " + StrValue(set(pDELIMITERS),pTRUE))
 88 :      FWriteLine( nFhandle, " Delimit Chars: " + StrValue(set(pDELIMCHARS)))
 89 :      FWriteLine( nFhandle, "   Escape is set: " + StrValue(set(pESCAPE), pTRUE))
 90 :      FWriteLine( nFhandle, "   Intensity is: " + StrValue(set(pINTENSITY),pTRUE ) )
 91 :      FWriteLine( nFhandle, "   Scoreboard is: " + StrValue(set(pSCOREBOARD),pTRUE ) )
 92 :      FWriteLine( nFhandle, "     Wrap is set: " + StrValue(set(pWRAP), pTRUE ) )
 93 :      FWriteLine( nFhandle, "   Message line: " + StrValue(set(pMESSAGE)))
 94 :      FWriteLine( nFhandle, "Message Center: " + StrValue(set(pMCENTER), pTRUE) )
 95 :      FWriteLine( nFhandle, "   Exclusive is: " + StrValue(set(pEXCLUSIVE),pTRUE ) )
 96 :      FWriteLine( nFhandle, "    Softseek is: " + StrValue(set(pSOFTSEEK), pTRUE) )
 97 :      FWriteLine( nFhandle, "      Unique is: " + StrValue(set(pUNIQUE), pTRUE) )
 98 :      FWriteLine( nFhandle, "     Deleted is: " + StrValue(set(pDELETED, pTRUE)) )
 99 :
100 :      // write SET stuff
101 :      FWriteLine( nFhandle, "" )
102 :      FWriteLine( nFhandle, "" )
103 :      FWriteLine( nFhandle, padc( " Detailed Work Area Items", maxcol(), "=" ) )
104 :      FWriteLine( nFhandle, "" )
105 :
106 :      for nCount := 1 to 55
107 :         if !empty( (nCount)->( alias() ) )
108 :            (nCount)->(FWriteLine( nFhandle, "  Work Area No.: " + StrValue( select())))
109 :            (nCount)->(FWriteLine( nFhandle, "     Alias Name: " + alias() ))
110 :            (nCount)->(FWriteLine( nFhandle, "  Current Recno.: " + Strvalue( recno())))
111 :            (nCount)->(FWriteLine( nFhandle, "  Current Filter: " + dbfilter() ))
112 :            (nCount)->(FWriteLine( nFhandle, "    Relation Exp.: " + dbrelation() ))
113 :            (nCount)->(FWriteLine( nFhandle, "     Index Order: " + StrValue( indexord())))
114 :            (nCount)->(FWriteLine( nFhandle, "      Active Key: " + indexkey( indexord())))
115 :            (nCount)->(FWriteLine( nFhandle, "" ))
116 :         endif
117 :      next
118 :
119 :      FWriteLine( nFhandle, "" )
120 :      FWriteLine( nFhandle, padc( " Internal Error Handling Information ", maxcol(), "+") )
121 :      FWriteLine( nFhandle, "" )
122 :      FWriteLine( nFhandle, "Subsystem call: " + oErr:subsystem() )
123 :      FWriteLine( nFhandle, "    System code: " + StrValue(oErr:subcode()) )
124 :      FWriteLine( nFhandle, "Default Status: " + StrValue(oErr:candefault ) )
125 :      FWriteLine( nFhandle, "   Description: " + oErr:description() )
```

```
126 :       FWriteLine( nFhandle, "      Operation: " + oErr:operation() )
127 :       FWriteLine( nFhandle, " Involved File: " + oErr:filename() )
128 :       FWriteLine( nFhandle, "DOS Error Code: " + StrValue(oErr:oscode()) )
129 :       fwrite( nFhandle, " Trace Through: " )
130 :
131 :       nCount := 1
132 :       while !empty( procname( ++nCount) )
133 :          FWriteLine( nFhandle, padr(procname(nCount), 20) + ": " +;
134 :                                padr(procline(nCount), 20) )
135 :          fwrite( nFhandle, "                     " )
136 :       enddo
137 :       FWriteLine( nFhandle, "" )
138 :
139 :       FWriteLine( nFhandle, "" )
140 :       FWriteLine( nFhandle, padc( " Video screen Dump ", maxcol(), "+" ) )
141 :       FWriteLine( nFhandle, "" )
142 :       FWriteLine( nFhandle, "" )
143 :       FWriteLine( nFhandle, "+"+replicate("-",maxcol()+1)+"+" )
144 :
145 : //    nWidth := maxcol()
146 :       for nCount := 1 to maxrow()
147 :          cOutString := ""
148 :          cSubString := substr(cScreen, nStart, nRange )
149 :          for nForLoop := 1 to nRange step 2
150 :             cOutString += substr(cSubString, nForLoop, 1)
151 :          next
152 :          FWriteLine( nFhandle, "|"+cOutString+"|" )
153 :          nStart += nRange
154 :       next
155 :       FWriteLine( nFhandle, "+"+replicate("-",maxcol()+1)+"+" )
156 :       FWriteLine( nFhandle, "" )
157 :
158 :       FWriteLine( nFhandle, "" )
159 :       FWriteLine( nFhandle, padc( " Available Memory Variables", maxcol(), "+"))
160 :       FWriteLine( nFhandle, "" )
161 :
162 : //    SELECT( nWorkArea )
163 :
164 :       save all like * to Errormem
165 :
166 :       nMemHandle := fopen( "Errormem.mem", FO_READWRITE )
167 :       nMemLength := fseek( nMemHandle, 0, 2)
168 :       fseek(nMemHandle,0)
169 :
170 :       nCount := 1   // Reset the variable.
171 :
172 :       while fseek(nMemHandle, 0, 1)+1 < nMemLength
173 :
174 :         nMemWidth := space(18)
175 :         fread(nMemHandle, @nMemWidth, 18)   // Get the variable specific information.
176 :
177 :         cVarName := left(nMemWidth, at(chr(0), nMemWidth)-1)
178 :         cVartype := substr(nMemWidth, 12, 1)
179 :         cVarRec  := bin2w(right(nMemWidth,2))
180 :
181 :         nMemCount := if( cVarType $ chr(195)+chr(204), 14+cVarRec, 22 )
182 :
183 :         fseek(nMemHandle, nMemCount, 1)
184 :
185 :         cTemp := left(cVarName + space(10), 10)
```

```
186 :
187 :        cTemp += "   TYPE " + type(cVarName)
188 :        cTemp += "   " + if( type(cVarName) == pCHARACTER, ;
189 :                         ["] + &cVarName + ["], StrValue( &cVarName ))
190 :        nBytes:=0
191 :        do case
192 :        case type(cVarName) == pCHARACTER
193 :           nBytes += ( nLenTemp := len( &cVarName. ) )
194 :
195 :        case type(cVarName) == pNUMERIC
196 :           nBytes += ( nLenTemp := 9 )
197 :
198 :        case type(cVarName) == pLOGICAL
199 :           nBytes += ( nLenTemp := 2 )
200 :
201 :        case type(cVarName) == pDATE
202 :           nBytes += ( nLenTemp := 9 )
203 :
204 :        endcase
205 :
206 :        fwrite( nFhandle, "        " + transform(nLenTemp, "9999999") + ;
207 :                          " bytes -> ")
208 :        FWriteLine( nFhandle, "        " + cTemp )
209 :
210 :     enddo
211 :
212 :     fclose(nMemHandle)
213 :     ferase( "Errormem.mem" )
214 :     fclose( nFhandle )
215 :
216 :   endif
217 :
218 :   errorlevel( 1 )
219 :   cls
220 :   close all
221 :   quit
222 :
223 :   return( pFALSE )
224 :
225 : *******************
226 :
227 : static function StrValue( cString, lOnOff )
228 :
229 :   local cRetValue := ""
230 :
231 :   DEFAULT lOnOff TO pFALSE
232 :
233 :   do case
234 :   case valtype( cString ) == pCHARACTER
235 :      cRetValue := cString
236 :
237 :   case valtype( cString ) == pNUMERIC
238 :      cRetValue := alltrim( str( cString ) )
239 :
240 :   case valtype( cString ) == pMEMO
241 :      cRetValue := if( (len(cString) > (memory(0) * 1024) * .80), ;
242 :                       left(cString, int(memory(0)*1024*.80)), cString )
243 :
244 :   case valtype( cString ) == pDATE
245 :      cRetValue := dtoc( cString )
```

```
246 :
247 :    case valtype( cString ) == pLOGICAL
248 :       cRetValue := if( lOnOff, if(cString, "On", "Off"), ;
249 :                   if(cString, "True", "False") )
250 :
251 :    endcase
252 :
253 :    return( cRetValue )
254 :
255 : ********************
256 :
257 : static function FWriteLine( nHandle, cString )
258 :
259 :    // This is a STATIC function rather than a pseudo-function because as
260 :    // such, circular definition was incorrectly detected and no switch to
261 :    // over-ride could be issued.
262 :
263 :    fwrite( nHandle, cString )
264 :    fwrite( nHandle, chr(13) )   // Carriage return
265 :    fwrite( nHandle, chr(10) )   // Line feed!
266 :
267 :    VOID
268 :
269 : // End of File: Errorsys.prg
```

Finally, there is the RMAKE script file to put these two items together:

```
 1 : // This is an RMAKE script file for the TestErr.prg program.
 2 :
 3 : .prg.obj:
 4 :    clipper $* /m /n /a /w /v /p /b
 5 :
 6 : testerr.obj       :       testerr.prg
 7 : errorsys.obj      :       errorsys.prg
 8 :
 9 : testerr.exe       :       testerr.obj errorsys.obj
10 :    if not errorlevel 1 rtlink fi testerr, errorsys
11 :
12 : // End of Testerr.rmk
```

The key thing to remember in all of this is that the low-level file functions do not adhere to the Error system, which means that they may be used to help print out information regarding any error detected.

## Conclusion

With programmable replacements for the Error system and the GET system, and with the capacity of adding a customized Help system, Clipper 5.2 provides a powerful, open-ended system for application development.

# 20

# *Epilogue*

As we await the release of CA-Visual Objects, a product that will take Clipper applications into the Windows environment, the Clipper language is beginning to be the base upon which all applications, either in DOS or Windows, will be built. And this book has tried to place CA-Clipper 5.2 within that broader perspective, and to allow you to use Clipper today to build applications for the future. One relatively minor indication of this is the attempt to make Clipper code Visual Object aware, as seen in the PTVERBS.CH header file. In essence, this book is not just a rewrite of old examples and techniques: It is an attempt to make all of the efforts uniform and consistent. It is important to completely document the language, the concepts, and the techniques in order to be immediately productive and profitable; and this book has certainly attempted to do this. However, an eye to the future is also used in many of the examples, making Clipper an evolving language and not just a stagnant language.

It is this combination that makes this the best of all possibilities. We must accept that doing business in the '90s and beyond means rethinking our problem solving techniques and seeing how the language can best be utilized to achieve the desired end results. Relying on old postulates is one thing: using them without exploring other ideas derived from them is another. We must build a business plan for how to write code, how code should look, and what our programming approaches will be to solve basic coding problems. However, we must also understand that none of these techniques and ideas should be used at the cost of losing a client, a customer, or an account.

Programming is an art and not just a science. We must constantly balance the high wire between end-user wants and needs with language constraints and restrictions. Knowing that the restrictions and constraints are greatly reduced in the Clipper language (as opposed to others) is fine only if we accept the responsibility to look for the new ways in which we can walk that tightrope to safety and customer satisfaction.

In all of the years I have tried to support this language and to share it with you, the future has never been more exciting and filled with new adventures and ideas. While it may appear to some to be the best of times and the worst of times, it is from this perspective, the ideal of times. We are now developing the models from which the applications of tomorrow will come, and our new ideas, changed models and paradigms, and broadening base of concepts mean that the need for our services can only increase. So while it will appear frustrating at times, it will ultimately prove to be profitable—and quite frankly, no matter what else is said, that is the "bottom line"—to enjoy the work, to create something which did not exist before, and to make a living in the process. From that it can only be the best of times.

I wish you all the best as you begin to explore the potential and the power of the Clipper language.

# Part III

*Appendixes*

# Appendix 1

# *Data Generation Program*

In each previous edition of this book, we provided a program that, when compiled, linked, and executed, would generate all of the other files needed by the various program modules and examples throughout the book. This is also the purpose of the following program. However, whether through its improved internal documentation or through the textual discussion which follows the source code, it is our hope that this program can also serve as an educational tool.

```
 1 : * File:      Makedata.prg
 2 :
 3 : #include "PTVerbs.ch"    // User-defined commands from Power Tools
 4 : #include "PTValue.ch"    // Misc. values from Power Tools Header file
 5 : #include "PTColor.ch"    // Colors from the Power Tools Header file
 6 : #include "PTFuncs.ch"    // Pseudo-function defs in Power Tools
 7 : #include "PTInkey.ch"    // Contains ASCII key values in Power Tools
 8 :
 9 : #define pTHEFILES {"Ontap", "Clients", "Trans", "Statcode", "Disknos",;
10 :                   "Filenos", "Statbase", "Notap"}
11 : #define pFRAME1 chr(213)+chr(205)+chr(184)+chr(179)+chr(190)+chr(205)+;
12 :                 chr(212)+chr(179)+chr(32)
13 :
14 : #xtranslate ADDFIELD(<field>, <type>, <len>, <dec>) => ;
15 :             aadd(aData, { <(field)>, <type>, <len>, <dec> } )
16 :
17 : #xtranslate ADDINDEX( <exp>, <file> ) => ;
18 :             aadd(aIndex, { <(exp)>, <(file)> } )
19 :
20 : #xcommand ADD <area> STRUCTURE TO <array> => ;
21 :             aadd( <array>, { <(area)>, aData, aIndex } ) ;;
22 :             aData  := {} ;;
23 :             aIndex := {}
24 :
25 : static cColor              // Color palate to be used
26 : static aWindows := {}      // Array of windows
27 : static cFilePath           // contains the file path to be globally used
28 :
```

```
29 : function Main(cPath)
30 :
31 :    local cText
32 :    local cScreen   := savescreen()   // save original screen
33 :    local nRow      := row()          // save original row position
34 :    local nCol      := col()          // save original columns position
35 :    local nCurs     := setcursor(0)   // turn off the cursor and save old val.
36 :
37 :    // work on the path to write things out to...
38 :    DEFAULT cPath TO curdir()
39 :    cFilePath := strtran("\"+cPath+"\", "\\", "\" )
40 :
41 :    scroll()
42 :
43 :    // set the file-wide static variable accordingly
44 :    cColor := if( IsMono(12,20), ;
45 :       MAKECOLOR( pWHITE/pBLACK, pBRIGHT_WHITE/pBLACK, pWHITE/pBLACK, ;
46 :       pWHITE/pBLACK, pBLACK/pWHITE ), MAKECOLOR( pWHITE/pBLUE, ;
47 :       pRED/pCYAN, pWHITE/pBLUE, pBLACK/pCYAN, pYELLOW/pBLUE ) )
48 :    dispbox(0,0,maxrow(), maxcol(), replicate(chr(178),9), cColor )
49 :
50 :    // Generate a window warning of the CONFIG.SYS FILES= statement
51 :    cText := "Please be certain that your;"
52 :    cText += "'FILES=' statement in your CONFIG.SYS;"
53 :    cText += "file is set to at least 79"
54 :
55 :    // Display a message
56 :    if !(alert( cText, {"Continue", "Quit"}, AColor()[3] ) == 2)
57 :
58 :       cText := "In addition, please make certain;"
59 :       cText += "that the CLIPPER switch from DOS;"
60 :       cText += "is set to 79 files as well."
61 :
62 :       if !(alert( cText, {"Continue", "Quit"}, AColor()[3] ) == 2 )
63 :
64 :          Phase1()
65 :
66 :       endif
67 :    endif
68 :
69 :    scroll()
70 :    devpos(0,0)
71 :    if !( errorlevel() == 0 )   // There was an error!
72 :       devout("Error in process: ")
73 :       devout( errorlevel() )
74 :    else
75 :       devout("Files are now generated. ")
76 :       qout()
77 :       devout("Now closing the files...." )
78 :       dbcloseall()
79 :       qout()
80 :       devout("Operation completed.  Any key to continue...")
81 :       inkey(0)
82 :       restscreen(,,,,cScreen)
83 :       setpos(nRow,nCol)
84 :    endif
85 :
86 :    setcursor( nCurs )
87 :
88 :    VOID
89 :
```

```
 90 : *******************
 91 :
 92 : static function Phase1()
 93 :
 94 :    local cColor := AColor()[3]
 95 :
 96 :    cColor += ","                            // Add the comma separator
 97 :    cColor += RevColor( AColor()[3] )        // Reverse the selected color
 98 :
 99 :    dispbox(0,0,2,maxcol(), pDBAR, cColor )   // The Banner
100 :    @ 1,11 say ;
101 :       "Straley's Programming With Clipper 5.2 - MakeData Program" ;
102 :       color cColor
103 :
104 :    WindowOpen( 4,1,23,40, cColor )  // Opens a window
105 :    @ WRow(0), WCol(0) say "Building Table of Structures" color cColor
106 :
107 :    DataStructures()          // Call function w/o parms
108 :    Phase2(cColor, 1)         // Start the call to the first data element
109 :    Phase3(cColor)            // Put information into the databases
110 :
111 :    WindowClose()
112 :
113 :    VOID
114 :
115 : ******************
116 :
117 : static function Phase2(cColor, nLevel)
118 :
119 :    local xStruct := DataStructures( pTHEFILES[nLevel] )
120 :
121 :    WindowClear()
122 :    @ WRow(0 + nLevel), WCol(0) SAY "Now, creating " +xStruct[1]+ ;
123 :                             " database--->" COLOR cColor ;
124 :
125 :
126 :    if xStruct != NIL  // Which means we have a structure
127 :       ShowStructure(5,40,22,75,xStruct )
128 :       MakeDbf( xStruct )
129 :       ShowStructure()
130 :       if !(nLevel == len( pTHEFILES ))   // We've recursed far enough!
131 :          Phase2(cColor, ++nLevel)
132 :       endif
133 :    else
134 :       errorlevel(1)  // Set the error level
135 :    endif
136 :
137 :    VOID
138 :
139 : ******************
140 :
141 : static function ShowStructure( nTop, nLeft, nBottom, nRight, aStru )
142 :
143 :    local cColor := AColor()[4]
144 :    local nRow
145 :
146 :    cColor += ","
147 :    cColor += AColor()[2]
148 :
149 :    if nTop == NIL  //
150 :       WindowClose()
```

```
151 :    else
152 :       nRow := nTop + 1
153 :       dispbegin()
154 :       WindowOpen(nTop, nLeft, nBottom, nRight, cColor )
155 :       @ WRow(-1), WCol(1) SAY " " +aStru[1]+ " " COLOR AColor()[2]
156 :       aeval( aStru[2], {|aField| devpos(nRow++, nLeft+1), ;
157 :                                  devout( padr(aField[1], 11), AColor()[2] ), ;
158 :                                  devout( padr(aField[2], 3 ), AColor()[2] ), ;
159 :                                  devout( padr(aField[3], 5 ), AColor()[2] ) , ;
160 :                                  devout( padr(aField[4], 4 ), AColor()[2] ) } )
161 :       dispend()
162 :    endif
163 :
164 :    VOID
165 :
166 : ********************
167 :
168 : static function DataStructures( cFile )
169 :
170 :    // If cFile is not passed, then it is assumed that the data structures
171 :    // are to be created; otherwise, the file is seeked and the array is
172 :    // then return.
173 :
174 :    // The structure of the array will be as follows:
175 :
176 :    static aStructure
177 :
178 :    local aIndex := {}      // This will contain the index keys and files
179 :    local aData  := {}      // This will contain the individual structures
180 :    local xRetValue         // Starts off as NIL which is o.k.
181 :    local nPosition         // Variable for the ASCAN() function
182 :
183 :    if aStructure == NIL  // Hasn't been assigned yet...
184 :       aStructure := {}   // Give it an empty array
185 :    endif
186 :
187 :    if cFile == NIL        // Generate the array of structures
188 :
189 :       // Build the data structure for the ONTAP database
190 :
191 :       ADDFIELD( FILES,      pCHARACTER, 12, 0 )
192 :       ADDFIELD( SIZES,      pNUMERIC,   10, 0 )
193 :       ADDFIELD( DATESTAMP,  pDATE,       8, 0 )
194 :       ADDFIELD( TIMES,      pCHARACTER,  8, 0 )
195 :       ADDFIELD( NOTES,      pMEMO,      10, 0 )
196 :       ADDINDEX( Ontap->files, Ontap )
197 :       ADD Ontap STRUCTURE TO aStructure
198 :
199 :       ADDFIELD( STATUS,    pCHARACTER,   1,  0 )
200 :       ADDFIELD( ACCOUNT,   pCHARACTER,  25,  0 )
201 :       ADDFIELD( NAME,      pCHARACTER,  25,  0 )
202 :       ADDFIELD( ADDRESS1,  pCHARACTER,  20,  0 )
203 :       ADDFIELD( ADDRESS2,  pCHARACTER,  20,  0 )
204 :       ADDFIELD( CITY,      pCHARACTER,  15,  0 )
205 :       ADDFIELD( STATE,     pCHARACTER,   2,  0 )
206 :       ADDFIELD( ZIP,       pCHARACTER,   9,  0 )
207 :       ADDFIELD( CURRENT,   pNUMERIC,    16,  2 )
208 :       ADDFIELD( DUE ,      pNUMERIC,    16,  0 )
209 :       ADDFIELD( PHONE,     pCHARACTER,  14,  0 )
210 :       ADDFIELD( CONTACT,   pCHARACTER ,  5,  0 )
211 :       ADDFIELD( INDATE,    pDATE ,       8 , 0 )
```

```
212 :        ADDFIELD( ACTIVE,    pCHARACTER,    1,   0 )
213 :        ADDFIELD( PAIRED,    pLOGICAL,      1 , 0 )
214 :        ADDFIELD( CALC,      pCHARACTER,  100,   0 )
215 :        ADDINDEX( Clients->status, Client1 )
216 :        ADDINDEX( Clients->account, Client2 )
217 :        ADD Clients STRUCTURE TO aStructure
218 :
219 :        ADDFIELD( ACCOUNT,   pCHARACTER,    6,   0 )
220 :        ADDFIELD( ADATE,     pDATE,         8,   0 )
221 :        ADDFIELD( NOW_DUE,   pNUMERIC,     10,   2 )
222 :        ADDFIELD( PAID,      pLOGICAL,      1,   0 )
223 :        ADDFIELD( NOTES,     pMEMO,        10,   0 )
224 :        ADDINDEX( Trans->account, Trans )
225 :        ADD Trans STRUCTURE TO aStructure
226 :
227 :        ADDFIELD( STATUS,    pCHARACTER,    1,   0 )
228 :        ADDFIELD( DESCRIPT,  pCHARACTER,   20,   0 )
229 :        ADD Statcode STRUCTURE TO aStructure
230 :
231 :        ADDFIELD( DISK_NO,   pCHARACTER,   10,   0 )
232 :        ADDFIELD( SUB_NO,    pCHARACTER,    3,   0 )
233 :        ADDFIELD( DISK_NAME, pCHARACTER,   50,   0 )
234 :        ADDFIELD( DISK_COMM, pCHARACTER,   40,   0 )
235 :        ADDFIELD( DATE_ADD,  pDATE,         8,   0 )
236 :        ADDFIELD( DATE_UP,   pDATE,         8,   0 )
237 :        ADDFIELD( DISK_LABEL, pMEMO ,      10,   0 )
238 :        ADDFIELD( BYTES_LEFT, pNUMERIC,    10,   0 )
239 :        ADDFIELD( HARDFLOP,  pLOGICAL,      1,   0 )
240 :        ADDFIELD( DRIVELET,  pCHARACTER,    2,   0 )
241 :        ADDINDEX( Disknos->disk_no, Disknos )
242 :        ADD Disknos STRUCTURE TO aStructure
243 :
244 :        ADDFIELD( DISK_NO,   pCHARACTER,   10,   0 )
245 :        ADDFIELD( SUB_NO,    pCHARACTER,    3,   0 )
246 :        ADDFIELD( SUB_NAME,  pCHARACTER,   40,   0 )
247 :        ADDFIELD( FILE_NO,   pCHARACTER,    5,   0 )
248 :        ADDFIELD( FILE_NAME, pCHARACTER,   12,   0 )
249 :        ADDFIELD( FILE_TYPE, pCHARACTER,    3,   0 )
250 :        ADDFIELD( FILE_SIZE, pNUMERIC,     10,   0 )
251 :        ADDFIELD( FILE_DATE, pDATE,         8,   0 )
252 :        ADDFIELD( FILE_TIME, pCHARACTER,   10,   0 )
253 :        ADDFIELD( FILE_COMM, pCHARACTER,   50,   0 )
254 :        ADDFIELD( IS_ARC,    pLOGICAL,      1,   0 )
255 :        ADDINDEX( Filenos->sub_no + Filenos->file_name, Filenos1 )
256 :        ADDINDEX( Filenos->sub_no + Filenos->sub_name, Filenos2 )
257 :        ADDINDEX( Filenos->sub_no + Filenos->file_type, Filenos3 )
258 :        ADD Filenos STRUCTURE TO aStructure
259 :
260 :        ADDFIELD( STATE,  pCHARACTER,    2,   0 )
261 :        ADDFIELD( ZPRE,   pCHARACTER,    1,   0 )
262 :        ADDFIELD( PPRE,   pCHARACTER,    3,   0 )
263 :        ADD Statbase STRUCTURE TO aStructure
264 :
265 :        ADDFIELD( FILES,     pCHARACTER,   12,   0 )
266 :        ADDFIELD( SIZES,     pNUMERIC,     12,   0 )
267 :        ADDFIELD( DATESTAMP, pDATE,         8,   0 )
268 :        ADDFIELD( TIMES,     pCHARACTER,    8,   0 )
269 :        ADDFIELD( COMMENT,   pMEMO,        10,   0 )
270 :        ADDFIELD( FILE_USE,  pCHARACTER,   40,   0 )
271 :        ADDFIELD( SUBDRIVE,  pCHARACTER,   50,   0 )
272 :        ADDFIELD( PER_USED,  pNUMERIC,      8,   4 )
```

```
273 :         ADDINDEX( Notap->files, Notap )
274 :         ADD Notap STRUCTURE TO aStructure
275 :
276 :     else    // Search for the field
277 :        nPosition := ascan( aStructure, {|aItem| upper(aItem[1]) == upper(cFile)} )
278 :        if !(nPosition == 0 )
279 :           xRetValue := aStructure[nPosition]
280 :        endif
281 :
282 :     endif
283 :
284 :     return( xRetValue )
285 :
286 : *********************
287 :
288 : static function MakeDbf( aStru )
289 :
290 :     // aStru[1]    is the name of the area
291 :     // aStru[2]    is the data structure
292 :     // aStru[3]    is the index structure
293 :
294 :     local nCounter     // This is for the FOR...NEXT loop
295 :
296 :     dbcreate( cFilePath + aStru[1], aStru[2] )
297 :     if !empty( aStru[3] )            // there are defined index keys
298 :        use (cFilePath + aStru[1]) new        // This uses the file!
299 :        for nCounter := 1 to len( aStru[3] )
300 :           // add the indexing statements
301 :           index on &(aStru[3,nCounter,1]) to (cFilePath + aStru[3,nCounter,2])
302 :        next
303 :     endif
304 :
305 :     VOID
306 :
307 : *********************
308 :
309 : static function Phase3( cColor )
310 :
311 :     local nCounter     // Counter for the FOR..NEXT loop
312 :     local xStru        // Contains a reference to data structure
313 :     local nIndex       // Counter for the INDEX loop
314 :     local aDirs        // Array of subdirectories found
315 :
316 :     dbcloseall()
317 :     for nCounter := 1 to len( pTHEFILES )
318 :        xStru := DataStructures( pTHEFILES[nCounter] )
319 :        use (cFilePath + xStru[1]) new
320 :        for nIndex := 1 to len( xStru[3] )
321 :           dbsetindex( cFilePath + xStru[3,nIndex,2] )
322 :        next
323 :     next
324 :
325 :     WindowClear()
326 :     @ WRow(10), WCol(0) say "Adding Information to first file" color cColor
327 :
328 :     // Add information into the ONTAP database
329 :     Ontap->( aeval( directory(), {|aFile| AddOntap(aFile, cColor)} ) )
330 :
331 :     WindowClear()
332 :     @ WRow(11), WCol(0) say "Adding stuff now to CLIENTS" color cColor
333 :     Clients->( WithTwo() )
```

```
334 :
335 :    WindowClear()
336 :    @ WRow(12), WCol(0) say "Add transactions fo the file!" color cColor
337 :    Trans->( WithThree() )
338 :
339 :    WindowClear()
340 :    @ WRow(13), WCol(0) say "Storing Code information...." color cColor
341 :    Statcode->( WithFour() )
342 :
343 :    WindowClear()
344 :    @ WRow(14), WCol(0) say "Making the help files....." color cColor
345 :    MakeHelp()
346 :
347 :    WindowClear()
348 :    @ WRow(15), WCol(0) say "Searching through the drive:" color cColor
349 :    aDirs := SubDirs()
350 :
351 :    WindowClear()
352 :    @ WRow(0), WCol(0) say "Adding file names to databases" color cColor
353 :    Disknos->( aeval( aDirs, ;
354 :                {|cDirName, nPos| PutDirName(cDirName, nPos, cColor)} ) )
355 :
356 :    WindowClear()
357 :    @ Wrow(1), WCol(0) say "Now adding state information" color cColor
358 :    Statbase->( StatBase() )
359 :
360 :    WindowClear()
361 :    @ WRow(1), WCol(0) say "Now adding the final piece..." color cColor
362 :    Notap->( aeval( directory(), {|aFiles| Final(aFiles, cColor)} ) )
363 :
364 :    VOID
365 :
366 : // From this point in the file are the anciliary functions/procedures that
367 : // have the task of adding information to the various database
368 :
369 : ********************
370 :
371 : static procedure AddOntap( aFiles, cColor )
372 :
373 :    dbappend()
374 :    @ WRow(17), WCol(0) SAY "FILE: " +padr(aFiles[1], 30) COLOR cColor
375 :    Ontap->files     := aFiles[1]
376 :    Ontap->sizes     := aFiles[2]
377 :    Ontap->datestamp := aFiles[3]
378 :    Ontap->times     := aFiles[4]
379 :
380 : ********************
381 :
382 : static procedure WithTwo()
383 :
384 :      Adding("3", "100000", "Nantucket Corporation", "GONE ARE THE DAYS!!", ;
385 :             "", "Los Angeles","CA", "90066", 1000.00, 23.00, "1-800-231-1521",;
386 :             "Ray", DATE(), "", pFALSE)
387 :      Adding("1", "200000", "Sirius Software Develop.", "564 Mission St.", ;
388 :             "Suite 343", "San Francisco", "CA", "941052", 210000.00, 10.00, ;
389 :             "1-415-399-9810", "Steve", DATE(), "", pFALSE)
390 :      Adding("1", "200000", "Stephen Straley & Assoc.", "319 Barrow Street", ;
391 :             "Suite 7A", "Jersey City", "NJ", "07302", 230000.00, 12.00, ;
392 :             "1-201-432-8189", "Steve", DATE(), "", pFALSE)
393 :      Adding("6", "200001", "Falcon Software, Ltd.", "319 Barrow - Ste 7A", ;
394 :             "", "Jersey City", "NJ", "07302", 200.00, 2.00, "1-201-432-8189", ;
```

```
395 :                    "Steve", DATE(), "", pTRUE)
396 :      Adding("1", "200010", "Number One Software", "", "", "", "", "", 2.00, ;
397 :              1221.00, "", "", DATE(), "", pFALSE )
398 :      Adding("3", "300000", "Ashton-Tate", "", "", "", "", "", 23.00, 13.00, ;
399 :              "", "", DATE(), "", pFALSE)
400 :      Adding("1", "323333", "Lotus Development", "", "", "", "", "", 14525.00, ;
401 :              2313.00, "", "", DATE(), "", pTRUE)
402 :      Adding("1", "352231", "Microsoft Corp.", "", "", "", "", "", 7472374.00, ;
403 :              8482348.00, "", "", DATE(), "", pFALSE)
404 :      Adding("1", "400000", "IBM", "", "", "", "", "", 8237.00, 76674.00, "", ;
405 :              "", DATE(), "", pFALSE)
406 :      Adding("2", "511001", "Panasonic", "", "", "", "", "", 1625.00, ;
407 :              95945.00, "", "", DATE(), "", pTRUE)
408 :      Adding("1", "610000", "Sony", "", "", "", "", "", 0.00, 0.00, "", "", ;
409 :              DATE(), "", pTRUE)
410 :      Adding("2", "714442", "Tandy International", "", "", "", "", "", 0.00, ;
411 :              0.00, "", "", DATE(), "", pTRUE)
412 :      Adding("1", "740000", "Texaco Limited", "", "", "", "", "", 0.00, 0.00, ;
413 :              "", "", DATE(), "", pFALSE)
414 :      Adding("4", "830000", "Magnus Production", "", "", "", "", "", 0.00, ;
415 :              0.00, "", "", DATE(), "", pFALSE)
416 :      Adding("1", "831000", "Macintosh Corp.", "", "", "", "", "", 0.00, ;
417 :              0.00, "", "", DATE(), "", pFALSE)
418 :      Adding("1", "845500", "Hayes Microcomputer", "", "", "", "", "", 0.00, ;
419 :              0.00, "", "", DATE(), "", pFALSE)
420 :      Adding("8", "860000", "Sharp Images", "", "", "", "", "", 0.00, ;
421 :              0.00, "", "", DATE(), "", pFALSE)
422 :      Adding("2", "900000", "Ford Motorcars", "", "", "", "", "", 0.00, ;
423 :              0.00, "", "", DATE(), "", pFALSE)
424 :      Adding("9", "910000", "Chrysler Corporation", "", "", "", "", "", 0.00, ;
425 :              0.00, "", "", DATE(), "", pFALSE)
426 :      Adding("9", "920000", "General Motors", "", "", "", "", "", 0.00, 0.00, ;
427 :              "", "", DATE(), "", pFALSE)
428 :      Adding("9", "930000", "Nissan Motors", "", "", "", "", "", 0.00, 0.00, ;
429 :              "", "", DATE(), "", pFALSE)
430 :      Adding("9", "931000", "Toyota", "", "", "", "", "", 0.00, 0.00, "", "", ;
431 :              DATE(), "", pFALSE)
432 :      Adding("9", "933100", "Isuzu", "", "", "", "", "", 0.00, 0.00, "", "", ;
433 :              DATE(), "", pFALSE)
434 :      Adding("9", "935000", "Honda Motorcars", "", "", "", "", "", 0.00, ;
435 :              0.00, "", "", DATE(), "", pFALSE)
436 :      Adding("9", "939300", "Subaru", "", "", "", "", "", 0.00, 0.00, "", "", ;
437 :              DATE(), "", pFALSE)
438 :      Adding("9", "940000", "ABC", "", "", "", "", "", 0.00, 0.00, "", "", ;
439 :              DATE(), "", pFALSE)
440 :      Adding("9", "945000", "Fox Television", "", "", "", "", "", 0.00, 0.00, ;
441 :              "", "", DATE(), "", pFALSE)
442 :      Adding("9", "950000", "NBC", "", "", "", "", "", 0.00, 0.00, "", "", ;
443 :              DATE(), "", pFALSE)
444 :      Adding("9", "955000", "CBS", "", "", "", "", "", 0.00, 0.00, "", "", ;
445 :              DATE(), "", pFALSE)
446 :
447 : *******************
448 :
449 : stati procedure Adding( cStatus, cAccount, cName, cAddress1, ;
450 :                         cAddress2, cCity, cState, cZip, nCurrent, ;
451 :                         nDue, cPhone, cContact, dInDate, lActive, ;
452 :                         lPaired, cCalc )
453 :
454 :    dbappend()
455 :    @ WRow(17), WCol(0) SAY cAccount + " " + padr(cName, 20)
```

```
456 :
457 :      // Doubling up on the assignment in an expression to save on visual
458 :      // space.  This should only be done if one is comfortable with the
459 :      // concept of an expression executing as-is.
460 :
461 :    ( Clients->status    := cStatus,   Clients->account  := cAccount  )
462 :    ( Clients->name      := cName,     Clients->address1 := cAddress1 )
463 :    ( Clients->address2  := cAddress2, Clients->city     := cCity    )
464 :    ( Clients->state     := cState,    Clients->zip      := cZip     )
465 :    ( Clients->current   := nCurrent,  Clients->due      := nDue     )
466 :    ( Clients->phone     := cPhone,    Clients->contact  := cContact )
467 :    ( Clients->indate    := dInDate,   Clients->active   := lActive  )
468 :      Clients->paired    := lPaired
469 :      Clients->calc      := 'Trans->(Field_tot("Trans->now_due", '+;
470 :        '"TRIM(Trans->account) = TRIM([" + Clients->account + "])")'
471 :
472 : *******************
473 :
474 : static procedure WithThree()   // This adds transactions to the TRANS
475 :                                //  workarea
476 :
477 : #xtranslate %%(<acc1>, <date1>, <value1>, <acc2>, <date2>, <value2>) => ;
478 :           AddIt( #<acc1>, ctod(#<date1>), <value1>, .f. ) ;;
479 :           AddIt( #<acc2>, ctod(#<date2>), <value2>, .f. )
480 :
481 :    %%(100000, 02/18/90, 25452.23, 200000, 02/18/90, 54512.23)
482 :    %%(200001, 02/18/90, 545213.23, 200010, 02/18/90, 5412.23)
483 :    %%(300000, 02/18/90,   512.23, 323333, 02/18/90,  5412.23)
484 :    %%(352231, 02/18/90,  5122.32, 400000, 02/18/90,     2.33)
485 :    %%(511001, 02/18/90,    52.36, 610000, 02/18/90,     3.54)
486 :    %%(714442, 02/18/90,     1.25, 740000, 02/18/90,     0.01)
487 :    %%(830000, 02/18/90,   221.22, 831000, 02/18/90,    84.50)
488 :    %%(845500, 02/18/90,  7014.00, 860000, 02/18/90,    21.00)
489 :    %%(900000, 02/18/90,     7.01, 910000, 02/18/90,    10.25)
490 :    %%(920000, 02/18/90,     2.50, 930000, 02/18/90,     6.00)
491 :    %%(931000, 02/18/90,    10.00, 933100, 02/18/90,     0.01)
492 :    %%(935000, 02/18/90,    24.12, 939300, 02/18/90,    15.24)
493 :    %%(940000, 02/18/90,     0.12, 945000, 02/18/90,     5.21)
494 :    %%(950000, 02/18/90,    48.21, 955000, 02/18/90,     4.21)
495 :    %%(100000, 02/18/90,    47.21, 200000, 02/18/90,     4.21)
496 :    %%(200001, 02/18/90,    42.65, 200010, 02/18/90,     2.21)
497 :    %%(300000, 02/18/90,     4.84, 323333, 02/18/90,     5.21)
498 :    %%(352231, 02/18/90,     2.14, 400000, 02/18/90,    78.21)
499 :    %%(511001, 02/18/90,    43.26, 610000, 02/18/90,    32.12)
500 :    %%(714442, 02/18/90,    34.21, 740000, 02/18/90,  3721.12)
501 :    %%(830000, 02/18/90,    34.71, 831000, 02/18/90, 29482.72)
502 :    %%(845500, 02/18/90,    31.43, 860000, 02/18/90,   273.13)
503 :    %%(900000, 02/18/90,   243.13, 910000, 02/18/90,   234.73)
504 :    %%(920000, 02/18/90,  2156.83, 930000, 02/18/90,    22.09)
505 :    %%(931000, 02/18/90,   542.56, 933100, 02/18/90,  4273.26)
506 :    %%(935000, 02/18/90,     4.32, 939300, 02/18/90,    36.14)
507 :    %%(940000, 02/18/90,     5.78, 945000, 02/18/90,     4.95)
508 :    %%(950000, 02/18/90,     1.23, 955000, 02/18/90,    64.51)
509 :    %%(100000, 02/18/90,    24.20, 200000, 02/18/90,  2314.21)
510 :    %%(200001, 02/18/90,     0.15, 200010, 02/18/90,     4.26)
511 :    %%(300000, 02/18/90,     1.23, 323333, 02/18/90,     1.24)
512 :    %%(352231, 02/18/90,     7.25, 400000, 02/18/90,     8.14)
513 :    %%(511001, 02/18/90,     0.26, 610000, 02/18/90,     7.19)
514 :    %%(714442, 02/18/90,     8.23, 740000, 02/18/90,    47.20)
515 :    %%(830000, 02/18/90,    47.21, 831000, 02/18/90,     7.23)
516 :    %%(845500, 02/18/90,    47.51, 860000, 02/18/90,     8.32)
```

1090  *Appendix 1*

```
517 :    %%(900000, 02/18/90,    47.22, 910000, 02/18/90,      1.00)
518 :    %%(920000, 02/18/90,    23.32, 930000, 02/18/90,      8.00)
519 :    %%(931000, 02/18/90,     0.23, 933100, 02/18/90,      0.32)
520 :    %%(935000, 02/18/90,     0.32, 939300, 02/18/90,      5.32)
521 :    %%(940000, 02/18/90,     0.32, 945000, 02/18/90,      3.32)
522 :    %%(950000, 02/18/90,     3.32, 955000, 02/18/90, 334273.13)
523 :    %%(100000, 02/18/90,     2.73, 200000, 02/18/90,   2342.37)
524 :    %%(200001, 02/18/90, 32134.13, 200010, 02/18/90,     27.43)
525 :    %%(300000, 02/18/90, 2831314.32, 323333, 02/18/90,  3382.34)
526 :    %%(352231, 02/18/90,   231.38, 400000, 02/18/90,     32.32)
527 :    %%(511001, 02/18/90,     1.00, 610000, 02/18/90,      2.00)
528 :    %%(714442, 02/18/90,     3.00, 740000, 02/18/90,      6.00)
529 :    %%(830000, 02/18/90,     4.00, 831000, 02/18/90,      5.00)
530 :    %%(845500, 02/18/90,     7.00, 860000, 02/18/90,     85.00)
531 :    %%(900000, 02/18/90,   212.00, 910000, 02/18/90,    236.00)
532 :    %%(920000, 02/18/90,     0.31, 930000, 02/18/90,   2323.00)
533 :    %%(931000, 02/18/90,    25.12, 933100, 02/18/90,    241.74)
534 :    %%(935000, 02/18/90,    32.96, 939300, 02/18/90,      5.28)
535 :    %%(940000, 02/18/90,     7.23, 945000, 02/18/90, 425412.36)
536 :    %%(950000, 02/18/90,  2475.92, 955000, 02/18/90,      3.65)
537 :    %%(100000, 02/18/90,     0.13, 200000, 02/18/90,    542.13)
538 :    %%(200001, 02/18/90,    23.00, 200010, 02/18/90,     64.13)
539 :    %%(300000, 02/18/90,   267.13, 323333, 02/18/90,    264.13)
540 :    %%(352231, 02/18/90,   721.29, 400000, 02/18/90,   1542.73)
541 :    %%(511001, 02/18/90, 126437.13, 610000, 02/18/90,    267.13)
542 :    %%(714442, 02/18/90, 2642373.16, 740000, 02/18/90,     2.31)
543 :    %%(830000, 02/18/90,  3165.23, 831000, 02/18/90,  16432.31)
544 :    %%(845500, 02/18/90,     9.03, 860000, 02/18/90,    121.24)
545 :    %%(900000, 02/18/90,    37.12, 910000, 02/18/90,     31.13)
546 :    %%(920000, 02/18/90, 27912.42, 930000, 02/18/90,   7325.12)
547 :    %%(931000, 02/18/90,    14.72, 933100, 02/18/90, 331324.72)
548 :    %%(935000, 02/18/90,    38.53, 939300, 02/18/90,   4237.13)
549 :    %%(940000, 02/18/90,    24.72, 945000, 02/18/90, 312337.52)
550 :    %%(950000, 02/18/90,     3.15, 955000, 02/18/90,     67.22)
551 :    %%(100000, 02/18/90,  3328.53, 200000, 02/18/90,  21234.53)
552 :    %%(200001, 02/18/90, 28231.23, 200010, 02/18/90,    825.12)
553 :    %%(300000, 02/18/90, 35268.03, 323333, 02/18/90,   1234.72)
554 :    %%(352231, 02/18/90, 31235.22, 400000, 02/18/90,  38321.28)
555 :    %%(511001, 02/18/90,    32.12, 610000, 02/18/90,  37235.23)
556 :    %%(714442, 02/18/90, 423832.13, 740000, 02/18/90,  21328.22)
557 :    %%(830000, 02/18/90, 31325.23, 831000, 02/18/90,   1235.12)
558 :    %%(845500, 02/18/90, 3279513.22, 860000, 02/18/90,   321.23)
559 :    %%(900000, 02/18/90,   423.12, 910000, 02/18/90,  31564.23)
560 :    %%(920000, 02/18/90, 167232.13, 930000, 02/18/90,     6.12)
561 :    %%(931000, 02/18/90,   313.23, 933100, 02/18/90,     24.28)
562 :    %%(935000, 02/18/90,   742.25, 939300, 02/18/90,     12.32)
563 :    %%(940000, 02/18/90, 56412.23, 945000, 02/18/90,  52141.23)
564 :    %%(950000, 02/18/90,    25.23, 955000, 02/18/90,      1.25)
565 :    %%(100000, 02/18/90,     2.23, 200000, 02/18/90,     62.36)
566 :    %%(200001, 02/18/90,     5.21, 200010, 02/18/90,     42.23)
567 :    %%(300000, 02/18/90,   102.12, 323333, 02/18/90,     32.20)
568 :    %%(352231, 02/18/90,   315.08, 400000, 02/18/90,      1.70)
569 :    %%(511001, 02/18/90,     9.10, 610000, 02/18/90,      9.72)
570 :    %%(714442, 02/18/90,  3084.02, 740000, 02/18/90,   5137.13)
571 :    %%(830000, 02/18/90,   568.23, 831000, 02/18/90,      2.23)
572 :    %%(845500, 02/18/90,    24.02, 860000, 02/18/90,    645.73)
573 :    %%(900000, 02/18/90, 3426723.12, 910000, 02/18/90, 3309725.31)
574 :    %%(920000, 02/18/90, 328321.02, 930000, 02/18/90,  38235.13)
575 :    %%(931000, 02/18/90, 28322.13, 933100, 02/18/90,    283.13)
576 :    %%(935000, 02/18/90,  2832.13, 939300, 02/18/90,   2831.03)
577 :    %%(940000, 02/18/90,   283.13, 945000, 02/18/90,    235.73)
```

```
578 :        %%(950000, 02/18/90,   123.03, 955000, 02/18/90,   2137.30)
579 :        %%(100000, 02/18/90,   231.23, 200000, 02/18/90,  23023.00)
580 :        %%(200001, 02/18/90,  1543.23, 200010, 02/18/90,     23.03)
581 :        %%(300000, 02/18/90, 22354.03, 323333, 02/18/90, 273123.00)
582 :        %%(352231, 02/18/90,  3231.30, 400000, 02/18/90,    212.21)
583 :        %%(511001, 02/18/90,     4.12, 610000, 02/18/90,      1.12)
584 :        %%(714442, 02/18/90,     3.20, 740000, 02/18/90,      3.12)
585 :        %%(830000, 02/18/90,    34.02, 831000, 02/18/90,      3.23)
586 :        %%(845500, 02/18/90,     0.23, 860000, 02/18/90,      1.03)
587 :        %%(900000, 02/18/90,     0.23, 910000, 02/18/90,    157.53)
588 :        %%(920000, 02/18/90,     0.90, 930000, 02/18/90,      0.12)
589 :        %%(931000, 02/18/90,     0.40, 933100, 02/18/90,      0.27)
590 :        %%(935000, 02/18/90,     0.12, 939300, 02/18/90,     23.00)
591 :        %%(940000, 02/18/90,    24.13, 945000, 02/18/90,   3212.42)
592 :        %%(950000, 02/18/90,    37231.42, 955000, 02/18/90,   337.43)
593 :
594 : *******************
595 :
596 : static procedure AddIt( xField1, xField2, xField3, xField4 )
597 :
598 :    // This routine will work for the TRANS, STATCODE, and STATBASE
599 :    // work areas!
600 :
601 :    local cColor := AColor()[4]
602 :
603 :    cColor += ","
604 :    cColor += RevColor( AColor()[4] )
605 :
606 :    dbappend()
607 :    @ WRow(17), WCol(0) say padr(xField1, 30) color cColor
608 :
609 :    fieldput(1, xField1)
610 :    fieldput(2, xField2)
611 :
612 :    if xField3 != NIL        // It was passed!
613 :       fieldput(3, xField3)
614 :    endif
615 :    if xField4 != NIL        // It was passed!
616 :       fieldput(4, xField4)
617 :    endif
618 :
619 : *********************
620 :
621 : static procedure WithFour()
622 :
623 :    ( AddIt( "1", "Normal Account"),    AddIt("2", "Inventory Account") )
624 :    ( AddIt("3", "Special"),            AddIt("4", "Fortune 500") )
625 :    ( AddIt("5", "Premire Account"),    AddIt("6", "Gold Card Member") )
626 :    ( AddIt("7", "Inventory Control"),  AddIt("8", "Unassigned") )
627 :    ( AddIt("9", "Development"),        AddIt("A", "Additional Account") )
628 :    AddIt("T", "Tax Account")
629 :
630 : *******************
631 :
632 : static procedure MakeHelp()
633 :
634 : #define SOFTCR chr(141)+chr(10)
635 :
636 :    local cString := "Pressing the ESC Key will abort "
637 :
638 :    cString += SOFTCR
```

```
639 :       cString += "the window of PROMPTS and return "
640 :       cString += SOFTCR
641 :       cString += "you to the main DBEDIT() window  "
642 :       memowrit( cFilePath + "Helptxt1.txt", cString )
643 :
644 :       // now for the next string...
645 :       cString := "Pressing F1 in most systems will " + SOFTCR
646 :       cString += "generate some type of help.  In this " + SOFTCR
647 :       cString += "example, TOPIC ORIENTED HELP is " + SOFTCR
648 :       cString += "the main focus.  With this, the user " + SOFTCR
649 :       cString += "can identify what area of help is " + SOFTCR
650 :       cString += "required BEFORE actually viewing text " + SOFTCR
651 :       cString += "on it."
652 :       memowrit(cFilePath + "Helptxt2.txt", cString )
653 :
654 :       // And now for the file HELP file
655 :       cString := "Pressing the F10 key on the first field " + SOFTCR
656 :       cString += "will mean that another DBEDIT() will be " + SOFTCR
657 :       cString += "called showing all of the legitimate " + SOFTCR
658 :       cString += "account names for the coded values entered." + SOFTCR + SOFTCR
659 :       cString += "Pressing the F10 key on any other field " + SOFTCR
660 :       cString += "will show the account balance DUE from " + SOFTCR
661 :       cString += "that customer."  + SOFTCR + SOFTCR
662 :       cString += "This means that keystrokes may not only be" + SOFTCR
663 :       cString += "manipulated, but they may be by field location" + SOFTCR
664 :       cString += "as well."
665 :       memowrit(cFilePath + "Helptxt3.txt", cString)
666 :
667 : #undef SOFTCR      // Undefining the Manifest Constant to help with memory
668 :                    // for the preprocessor.
669 :
670 : ******************
671 :
672 : static procedure PutDirName(cDirName, nPosition, cColor)
673 :
674 :    dbappend()    // add a record
675 :
676 :    @ WRow(16), WCol(0) SAY "ADDING: " + padr(cDirName, 28) COLOR cColor
677 :
678 :    Disknos->disk_no   := transform(1, replicate("9", len( Disknos->disk_no )))
679 :    Disknos->sub_no    := transform(nPosition, "999")
680 :    Disknos->disk_name := "Master Disk"
681 :    Disknos->date_add  := Disknos->date_up := date()
682 :    Disknos->bytes_left := diskspace()
683 :    Disknos->hardflop   := pTRUE
684 :    Disknos->drivelet   := "C:"
685 :
686 :    Filenos->( aeval( directory(cDirName+"*.*", "DSH"), ;
687 :              {|aFiles, nPos| RestOfIt(aFiles, nPos, cDirName, cColor)}))
688 :
689 : ********************
690 :
691 : static procedure RestOfIt( aFiles, nPos, cDirName )
692 :
693 :    dbappend()
694 :
695 :    @ WRow(17), WCol(0) SAY "FILES: " + padr(aFiles[1], 23) COLOR cColor
696 :
697 :    Filenos->disk_no   := Disknos->disk_no
698 :    Filenos->sub_no    := Disknos->sub_no
699 :    Filenos->sub_name  := cDirName
```

```
700 :    Filenos->file_no   := transform(nPos, "99999")
701 :    Filenos->file_name := aFiles[1]
702 :    Filenos->file_type := aFiles[5]
703 :    Filenos->file_size := aFiles[2]
704 :    Filenos->file_date := aFiles[3]
705 :    Filenos->file_time := aFiles[4]
706 :    Filenos->is_arc    := (".ARC"$aFiles[1]) .or. (".ZIP"$aFiles[1])
707 :
708 : *********************
709 :
710 : static procedure StatBase()
711 :
712 :    (AddIt("AR", "4", "501"), AddIt("AZ", "9", "602"), AddIt("AK", "9", "907"))
713 :    (AddIt("AL", "3", "205"), AddIt("CO", "8", "303"), AddIt("CT", "0", "203"))
714 :    (AddIt("DE", "1", "302"), AddIt("HA", "9", "808"), AddIt("NM", "7", "505"))
715 :    (AddIt("MD", "1", "301"), AddIt("ME", "0", "207"), AddIt("OE", "9", "503"))
716 :    (AddIt("UT", "8", "801"), AddIt("WV", "2", "304"), AddIt("WY", "6", "307"))
717 :    AddIt("ND", "6", "701")
718 :
719 : ***********************
720 :
721 : static procedure Final( aFiles, cColor )
722 :
723 :    dbappend()
724 :    @ WRow(17), WCol(0) SAY "File: " + aFiles[1] COLOR cColor
725 :
726 :    Field->files     := aFiles[1]
727 :    Field->sizes     := aFiles[2]
728 :    Field->datestamp := aFiles[3]
729 :    Field->times     := aFiles[4]
730 :    Field->per_used  := (aFiles[2] / diskspace()) * 100
731 :    Field->subdrive  := curdir()
732 :
733 : *******************
734 :
735 : static function SubDirs()
736 :
737 :    // This function is designed to go through the entire directory
738 :    // structure of the logged drive and to return an array of those
739 :    // subdirectories.
740 :
741 :    local aRetValue := {"\"}    // Return value of the array
742 :    local nCounter  := 0        // Pointer to select the correct subdir
743 :    local aSubs                 // The array of found subdirectories
744 :
745 :    while ++nCounter <= len(aRetValue)
746 :
747 :       if !empty( aSubs := GetDirs( aRetValue[nCounter] ) )
748 :          aeval( aSubs, {|cDir| aadd( aRetValue, cDir )} )
749 :       endif
750 :
751 :    enddo
752 :
753 :    return( asort( aRetValue ) )
754 :
755 : *******************
756 :
757 : static function GetDirs( cPattern )
758 :
759 :    local aRetValue := {}
760 :
```

```
761 :     aeval( directory( cPattern + "*.*", "D" ), ;
762 :          {|aFiles| if( (aFiles[5] == "D" .and. ;
763 :                        !(aFiles[1] == "." .or. aFiles[1] == ".." )), ;
764 :                        (aadd( aRetValue, cPattern + aFiles[1] + "\"), ;
765 :                        devpos( WRow(17), WCol(0) ), ;
766 :                        devout( padr(cPattern + aFiles[1] + "\", 30) )), ;
767 :                        NIL )} )
768 :
769 :     return( aRetValue )
770 :
771 : // The following functions are modified functions from the Power Tools
772 : // Library and are issued specifically for this program file.
773 :
774 : *******************
775 :
776 : static function WindowOpen( nTop, nLeft, nBottom, nRight, cColor )
777 :
778 :     dispbegin()    // turn on the virtual screen
779 :     aadd( aWindows, {nTop, nLeft, nBottom, nRight, ;
780 :                     savescreen(nTop, nLeft, nBottom, nRight), cColor} )
781 :
782 :     dispbox(nTop, nLeft, nBottom, nRight, pFRAME1, cColor )
783 :     // Shadow stuff
784 :     dispend()
785 :
786 :     return( NIL )
787 :
788 : *******************
789 :
790 : static function WindowClear()
791 :
792 :     local aWin := atail( aWindows )
793 :
794 :     dispbegin()
795 :     dispbox( aWin[1], aWin[2], aWin[3], aWin[4], pFRAME1, aWin[6] )
796 :     dispend()
797 :
798 :     return( NIL )
799 :
800 : *******************
801 :
802 : static function WindowClose()
803 :
804 :     local aWin := atail(aWindows)   // last window on the stack
805 :
806 :     asize(aWindows, len(aWindows)-1)
807 :     restscreen(aWin[1], aWin[2], aWin[3], aWin[4], aWin[5])
808 :
809 :     return( NIL )
810 :
811 : *******************
812 :
813 : static function WRow(nRow)
814 :
815 :     DEFAULT nRow TO 0
816 :
817 :     return( atail(aWindows)[1]+nRow+1)
818 :
819 : *******************
820 :
```

```
821 :   static function WCol(nCol)
822 :
823 :      DEFAULT nCol TO 0
824 :
825 :      return( atail(aWindows)[2]+nCol+1 )
826 :
827 :   // The following functions are a part of the Power Tools Library
828 :
829 :   *********************
830 :
831 :   static function AColor()
832 :
833 :      local nOffset           // Numeric offset position of "," character
834 :
835 :      static aColors
836 :
837 :      if aColors == NIL
838 :         aColors := {}
839 :
840 :         while !empty( nOffset := at( ",", cColor ) )   // there are commas
841 :            aadd( aColors, left( cColor, nOffset-1 ) )
842 :            cColor := alltrim(substr(cColor, nOffset+1 ))
843 :         enddo
844 :         aadd( aColors, cColor )   // Add the last item
845 :      endif
846 :
847 :      return( aColors )
848 :
849 :   *********************
850 :
851 :   static function RevColor( cColor )
852 :
853 :      local cFront := left( cColor, at("/", cColor)-1 )
854 :      local cBack  := substr( cColor, at("/", cColor)+1 )
855 :
856 :      return( cBack + "/" + cFront )
857 :
858 :   *********************
859 :
860 :   static function IsMono(nRow,nCol)
861 :
862 :      local cKey                 // Character string of key pressed
863 :      local cLastKey := chr(1)   // keeps track of the old lastkey
864 :
865 :      DEFAULT nRow TO maxrow(), nCol TO maxcol()
866 :
867 :      scroll(nRow, nCol, nRow )         // Clear the line!
868 :      PROCESS
869 :         dispbegin()                    // Turn on the virtual screen
870 :         setpos(nRow, nCol)
871 :         devout( "Do you want MONOCHROME colors? " )
872 :         dispend()
873 :
874 :      do case
875 :      case (cKey := upper(chr(inkey(0)))) == chr(pENTER)
876 :         // Enter key was prressed so exit
877 :         exit
878 :
879 :      case cKey == "Y"    // For yes!
880 :         devout( "Yes" )
```

```
881 :
882 :        case cKey == "N"      // For No!
883 :           devout( "No " )
884 :
885 :        endcase
886 :        cLastKey := cKey      // store the last key and NOT the ENTER key
887 :
888 :     END PROCESS
889 :
890 :     scroll(nRow,nCol,nRow)    // Clear the line again
891 :
892 :     return( cLastKey == "Y" )
893 :
894 : // End of File: Makedata.prg
```

On lines 3 through 7, an entire battery of header files is used. These header files define new commands (PTVERBS.CH), pseudofunctions (PTFUNCS.CH), and miscellaneous values (PTVALUE.CH). Once we have used the #include preprocessor directive to read all of the general definitions that we have stored in external header files, we can define all of the translations that are specific to this program and therefore are best not placed in any of our five header (.CH) files. Those definitions—of manifest constants using the #define directive, of commands using the #xcommand directive, and of pseudofunctions using the #xtranslate directive—follow the inclusion of the header files and are found on lines 9 through 23. On line 9 there is a manifest constant called pTHEFILES which is nothing more than a literal array of the names of the files that will be generated by this program. This will be used in two critical areas of the program.

Next, a manifest constant called pFRAME1 is used to define the frame typically used for the @...BOX command or its functional equivalent, DISPBOX( ).

Lines 14 through 23 define supporting functions for specific variables. For example, on lines 14 and 15, the ADDFIELD( ) pseudofunction adds elements to the *aData[ ]* array variable, while the ADDINDEX( ) pseudofunction on lines 17 and 18 adds elements to the *aIndex[ ]* array variable. Rather than coming up with a more generic function/pseudofunction that would use either variable so long as it was passed to the expression, these "dedicated" pseudofunctions are used to make coding a bit easier. In other words, the ADDFIELD( ) pseudofunction can never be used for anything other than adding a subarray to the *aData[ ]* array. And in similar manner, the ADD ... STRUCTURE TO command on lines 20 and 21 specifically refers to both the *aData[ ]* and *aIndex[ ]* arrays.

Finally, on lines 25 through 26, three filewide STATIC variables are defined. For these three variables to be considered as "filewide," this program module must be compiled with the /N switch.

The main part of this program starts on line 28 with the function called Main( ), which takes a local parameter called *cPath*. The intent here is to allow this program to be called like this:

```
MakeData
```

in which a directory is not specified and the value of *cPath* will be NIL. If that should be the case, the user-defined command DEFAULT on line 38 will assign the value of CURDIR( ) to the variable *cPath*. If, however, the program is called like this:

```
MakeData \pwc\straley\test
```

then the value of *cPath* will be the string "\pwc\straley\test," which will be the path used for creating all data files. Also noteworthy is the string handling that we have used to prevent an error. Although our second method of invoking the MAKEDATA program uses the backslash as the first character of the path, we cannot be sure that the user will always include it. And of course, a backslash is not used to terminate the path name. This, however, might cause an error if we concatenate a filename to the path name. For example, if the filename CLIENTS.DBF is added to this string, the result would be the following:

```
\pwc\straley\testCLIENTS.DBF
```

To prevent this, line 38 adds a backslash to both the beginning and end of *cPath*. But this can create another error; if a backslash was already present either at the beginning or at the end of *cPath*, a double backslash ("\\") would result. To avoid the syntax error that would result from this, line 38 also uses the STRTRAN( ) function to remove all occurrences of "\\" and replace them with "\". Once *cPath* has been properly formatted in this way, the value returned by the STRTRAN( ) function is stored to the variable *cFilePath*. It is this variable that will be used within the program's subroutines and will be combined with individual filenames.

The first operation within Main( ) is the call to the IsMono( ) function on line 44. This function, which is statically defined beginning on line 860, prompts whether the user wants to use monochrome or color. If the value of this function is a logical true (if the "Y" key is pressed followed by the ENTER key), then the color string defined on line 45 will be assigned to the filewide static variable *cColor*. If not, then the value of the color string defined on line 46 will be assigned to the variable. The pseudofunction MAKECOLOR( ) takes the individual color pairs defined on each of these lines and surrounds them with quotation marks. In essence, the color pairs are converted into a string which in turn is assigned to *cColor*. While *cColor* is a filewide static variable, it first comes into play on line 56 in the call to the AColor( ) function. Here, the ALERT( ) function is used to produce a dialog box that displays the contents of the concatenated string *cText* (defined on lines 51 through 53) in the center of the screen and offers the user the option to "Continue" or to "Quit." This dialog is displayed in the colors returned from the AColor( ) function. This function's value is an array, and the third element is used for the ALERT( ) function.

The AColor( ) function itself is defined beginning on line 831. In essence, if the static array *aColors[ ]* has not yet been defined within the function, it will have a NIL value. If so, it is first initialized to a blank array on line 837 and then the WHILE loop on lines 840 through 843 parses the string stored in *cColor* and stores each color pair to the *aColors[ ]* array. If the AColor( ) function is called again, the array *aColors[ ]* will not have a NIL value, and the function will simply return the value of the array. The idea of this function is to take a color string or color index, not just limited to five color pairs but to any number of color pairs, and to convert each as an element of a color table or array. This function simply keeps track of that array.

Eventually, after the user responds to all of the questions, the Phase1( ) function is called on line 64. In the Phase1( ) function beginning on line 92, a new color option is stored to the local variable *cColor*, and the reverse of this color string is concatenated on line 97. Even though there is a file-wide static variable with the same name as the LOCAL variable, all references to the *cColor* variable within the Phase1( ) function will be to the LOCAL variable

1098    *Appendix 1*

defined on line 94. Within this function a banner is drawn and some simple text is displayed on lines 100 through 102. Then, a primitive windowing function is called on line 104. Eventually, a call to the DataStructures( ) function is made on line 107.

Within the DataStructures( ) function, beginning on line 168, the various data file structures along with their filenames and ancillary index keys are defined. Like the AColor( ) function, this function uses a static array to keep track of the various data files, their structures, and the index information.

In essence, the array *aStructure[ ]* defined on line 176 will hold all of the information for the various files generated by this program. The individual data structures will be stored to the LOCAL variable *aData[ ]*, while index information will be stored to the LOCAL variable *aData[ ]*. Line 183 tests to see if *aStructure[ ]* has been initialized; if not, a blank array is assigned to the variable on line 184. Since no formal parameter was passed to this function when it was called on line 107, the value of *cFile*, as tested on line 187, will be a NIL. As a result, the function attempts to define the various file structures. Beginning on line 191, the pseudofunction ADDFIELD( ) is used. As seen on lines 14 and 15, this pseudofunction attempts to dynamically build an array of field information and store it to the LOCAL array named *aData[ ]*. In essence, this pseudofunction has no purpose outside of the DataStructures( ) function, since this is the only function within this program module that explicitly defines a variable named *aData[ ]*. In addition, to make life easier, the first parameter passed to the AADDFIELD( ) pseudofunction is just a word that might look like a variable name; however, the definition of ADDFIELD( ) says to transform the contents of the first parameter into a string. This means that the first item in the array that will be stored to *aData[ ]* will be the name of the database field, which has been converted to a string via the dumb-stringify result marker in the preprocessor. By line 195, all of the fields of our first database are defined. Just as the ADDFIELD( ) pseudofunction explicitly uses the *aData[ ]* array, the ADDINDEX( ) pseudofunction uses the *aIndex[ ]* array. The first parameter to ADDINDEX( ) is the index key, while the second parameter is the name of the index file that will hold this key. If there were more indexes to be defined, additional ADDINDEX( ) pseudofunctions could appear, as in lines 215 through 217, which defines indexes for the Clients database.

Once the two arrays—the array of file structures and the array of index information—are fully defined, they need to be dynamically added to the *aStructure[ ]* array. Each element of the *aStructure[ ]* array is itself an array that contains information about a particular database file. The first element of this subarray contains the name of the database file that the program is to create. The second element of the subarray is itself an array that contains the structure of the database; in this case, the array contains the *aData[ ]* array. Finally, the third element of the subarray contains the index information from the *aIndex[ ]* array; if no index files are associated with the database, this array element will be empty.

```
aStructure[] -> array of all data files

    aStructure[x] -> array of information about a database

        aStructure[x,1] -> Alias name of the database
        aStructure[x,2] -> Array of the file's structure
            aStructure[x,2,y] -> Array of field information
                aStructure[x,2,y,1] -> Name of the y$^{th}$ field
```

```
              aStructure[x,2,y,2] -> Data type of the y^th field
              aStructure[x,2,y,3] -> Length of the y^th field
              aStructure[x,2,y,4] -> Number of decimals in the y^th field
aStructure[x,3]   -> Array of index information
     aStructure[x,3,y]   -> Array of information for the y^th index file
              aStructure[x,3,y,1] -> Character key of y^th index
              aStructure[x,3,y,2] -> Name of y^th index file
```

Note that the first element of the second dimension of each subarray (i.e., *aStructure[x,1]*) contains the name of the database file. Our intent here, as we shall see shortly, is that we can scan the first element in the second dimension of each element in *aStructure[ ]* for an alias that corresponds to the name of the database with which we want to work. Once we have found it, the value of *x* becomes a pointer to the larger array structure that we have defined and that we can use to create the database and index files. Once the data structures are defined and maintained within the DataStructures( ) function, control is returned to the Phase1( ) function on line 107, and the Phase2( ) function on line 108 is called.

The second parameter to the Phase2( ) function call on line 108 is a numeric 1. This value is passed to the Phase2( ) function on line 117 and becomes the value of *nLevel*. This variable is designed to be a pointer into the literal array defined on lines 9 and 10 as pTHEFILES. So on line 119, the value of the array element at position *nLevel* or position 1 is obtained. This value, which is "Ontap," is then passed to the DataStructures( ) function, where it becomes the value of *cFile*.

Since the parameter *cFile* is formally passed to the DataStructure( ) function, line 187 is false. As a result, the code on lines 191 through lines 274 will be skipped, while the code on lines 276 through 280 will be executed. On line 277, the first element of the subarray in each element of the static array *aStructure[ ]* is scanned for a string that matches the value of *cFile*. If it is found, the position of the element in the *aStructure[ ]* array is stored to the variable *nPosition*. *nPosition* then becomes a pointer used to obtain the entire array of database and index file information for file *cFile*; this array structure becomes the return value of the DataStructures( ) function and is stored to the variable *xStruct[ ]* on line 119.

On line 126, if the value returned by DataStructures( ) and stored to *xStruct[ ]* is not NIL, the code on lines 126 through 132 will execute. First, the structure of the database that is about to be created will be displayed to the screen by the ShowStructure( ) function. Following this, the MakeDbf( ) function is called, and *xStruct[ ]*, the array of database information, is passed to it. Again, in this case it is the information relating to the "Ontap" file.

The MakeDbf( ) function begins on line 288. And on line 296 we can begin to see the use of this array structure. First, the name of the database (the same one used as the search string in the DataStructures( ) function is found in *aStru[1]*. This value is joined with the filewide static variable *cFilePath* to give a filename with directory path. The second parameter to DBCREATE( ) must be a multidimensional array containing the field information for the database we are about to create. This is stored in the variable *aStru[2]*. On line 297, the third element of *aStruc[ ]* is evaluated to determine if indexing information is present. If there is no index information, the element will be EMPTY( ), and lines 296 through 302 will be skipped. Otherwise, the newly created database file needs to be used (line 298), and then one at a time, the information contained in *aStru[3]* is used to create the indexes. This takes place on line 301.

Once the database and applicable indexes are created, control is returned to the Phase2( ) function, and we come to the ShowStructure( ) function call on line 129. This closes the window that was opened in order to show the data structure. Here, the parameter *nLevel* comes back into play. If the value of this parameter, originally set to 1, is not equal to the number of files listed in the array pTHEFILES[ ], then the Phase2( ) function is called again recursively, with the value of the *nLevel* parameter preincremented. Since the number of files in pTHEFILES is finite (and relatively small), the use of recursion is appropriate. Eventually, all of the files in the array pTHEFILES will be generated in the same manner as Ontap was. When this happens, all calls to the Phase2( ) function will terminate, and the program will naturally return to the original calling function, Phase1( ), on line 108.

Finally, the data needs to be stored in the various databases. This operation takes place in the function called Phrase3( ) which is called on line 109.

# Appendix 2

# *STUBSTD.CH*

The following is the source code for a file called STUBSTD.CH, a modified STD.CH file that only deals with those commonly used commands that have no functional equivalent or that are easier to use in their command-based form rather than in their functional equivalents. Using STUBSTD.CH will speed up the compiling process.

This file only supports the following:

- END SEQUENCE
- Most SET operations
- ? or ??
- EJECT
- CLS / CLEAR SCREEN
- @ ... SAY ... GET (RANGE clause not supported)
- READ / CLEAR GETS
- MENU TO / @ ... PROMPT
- WAIT / CLEAR TYPEAHEAD / SET TYPEAHEAD
- SET KEY
- REQUEST
- USE
- SET FILTER
- DELETE
- RECALL
- PACK
- ZAP
- SET RELATION
- CLOSE FORMAT
- INDEX ON
- DELETE TAG / REINDEX / SET ORDER / SET INDEX

To use STUBSTD.CH, simply use the /U compiling switch to substitute an alternate header file for STD.CH. This can be done in either of two ways. The first is interactively from the command line:

```
CLIPPER <program_name> /uSTUBSTD.CH
```

The second is to store the /U switch to the CLIPPERCMD environmental variable, as follows:

```
SET CLIPPERCMD=/Ustubstd.ch
```

Of course, CLIPPERCMD can also contain any other compiling switches that you might use regularly. For instance:

```
CLIPPERCMD=/m /n /p /v /w /a  /uSTUBSTD.CH
```

Once the CLIPPERCMD environmental variable has been defined, you can simply compile without any switches:

```
CLIPPER <program_name>
```

To indicate that it is reading definitions from an alternate header file, Clipper will display the following message when compiling:

```
Loading standard defs from stubstd.ch
```

Note that we *strongly advise against* renaming (or, even worse, deleting) STD.CH, and renaming STUBSTD.CH so that it becomes the "new" STD.CH.

```
* File:         Stubstd.ch
* Note:         This is a stub of the STD.CH file that is part of the
*               Clipper compiler which is....
*
*               Copyright (c) 19901993, Computer Associates International, Inc.
*               All rights reserved.
*

/***
*   Definitions from Set.ch are used in SET commands
*/
#ifndef _SET_CH
   #include "Set.ch"
#endif

/***
*   Basic statement synonyms
*/

#command END SEQUENCE           => end
#command ENDSEQUENCE            => end

/***
*   System SETs
*/

#command SET EXACT <x:ON,OFF,&>      => Set( _SET_EXACT, <(x)> )
#command SET EXACT (<x>)             => Set( _SET_EXACT, <x> )

#command SET FIXED <x:ON,OFF,&>      => Set( _SET_FIXED, <(x)> )
#command SET FIXED (<x>)             => Set( _SET_FIXED, <x> )
```

```
#command SET DECIMALS TO <x>                  => Set( _SET_DECIMALS, <x> )
#command SET DECIMALS TO                      => Set( _SET_DECIMALS, 0 )

#command SET PATH TO <*path*>                 => Set( _SET_PATH, <(path)> )
#command SET PATH TO                          => Set( _SET_PATH, "" )

#command SET DEFAULT TO <(path)>              => Set( _SET_DEFAULT, <(path)> )
#command SET DEFAULT TO                       => Set( _SET_DEFAULT, "" )

/***
*   Date format SETs
*/

#command SET CENTURY <x:ON,OFF,&>             => __SetCentury( <(x)> )
#command SET CENTURY (<x>)                    => __SetCentury( <x> )
#command SET EPOCH TO <year>                  => Set( _SET_EPOCH, <year> )
#command SET DATE FORMAT [TO] <c>             => Set( _SET_DATEFORMAT, <c> )

#define _DFSET(x, y)  Set( _SET_DATEFORMAT, if(__SetCentury(), x, y) )

#command SET DATE [TO] AMERICAN               => _DFSET( "mm/dd/yyyy", "mm/dd/yy" )
#command SET DATE [TO] ANSI                   => _DFSET( "yyyy.mm.dd", "yy.mm.dd" )
#command SET DATE [TO] BRITISH                => _DFSET( "dd/mm/yyyy", "dd/mm/yy" )
#command SET DATE [TO] FRENCH                 => _DFSET( "dd/mm/yyyy", "dd/mm/yy" )
#command SET DATE [TO] GERMAN                 => _DFSET( "dd.mm.yyyy", "dd.mm.yy" )
#command SET DATE [TO] ITALIAN                => _DFSET( "ddmmyyyy", "ddmmyy" )
#command SET DATE [TO] JAPANESE               => _DFSET( "yyyy/mm/dd", "yy/mm/dd" )
#command SET DATE [TO] USA                    => _DFSET( "mmddyyyy", "mmddyy" )

/***
*   Terminal I/O SETs
*/

#command SET ALTERNATE <x:ON,OFF,&>           => Set( _SET_ALTERNATE, <(x)> )
#command SET ALTERNATE (<x>)                  => Set( _SET_ALTERNATE, <x> )

#command SET ALTERNATE TO                     => Set( _SET_ALTFILE, "" )

#command SET ALTERNATE TO <(file)> [<add: ADDITIVE>]                    ;
       => Set( _SET_ALTFILE, <(file)>, <.add.> )

#command SET CONSOLE <x:ON,OFF,&>             => Set( _SET_CONSOLE, <(x)> )
#command SET CONSOLE (<x>)                    => Set( _SET_CONSOLE, <x> )

#command SET MARGIN TO <x>                    => Set( _SET_MARGIN, <x> )
#command SET MARGIN TO                        => Set( _SET_MARGIN, 0 )

#command SET PRINTER <x:ON,OFF,&>             => Set( _SET_PRINTER, <(x)> )
#command SET PRINTER (<x>)                    => Set( _SET_PRINTER, <x> )

#command SET PRINTER TO                       => Set( _SET_PRINTFILE, "" )

#command SET PRINTER TO <(file)> [<add: ADDITIVE>]                      ;
       => Set( _SET_PRINTFILE, <(file)>, <.add.> )


#command SET DEVICE TO SCREEN                 => Set( _SET_DEVICE, "SCREEN" )
#command SET DEVICE TO PRINTER                => Set( _SET_DEVICE, "PRINTER" )

/***
*   "Console" / printer output
*/
```

## Appendix 2

```
#command ?   [ <list,...> ]        => QOut( <list> )
#command ??  [ <list,...> ]        => QQOut( <list> )

#command EJECT                     => __Eject()

/***
*   Clear screen
*/
#command CLS                                                            ;
      => Scroll()                                                       ;
       ; SetPos(0,0)

#command CLEAR SCREEN                                                   ;
      => CLS

/***
*   @..BOX
*/

/***
*   @..SAY
*/

#command @ <row>, <col> SAY <xpr>                                       ;
                        [PICTURE <pic>]                                 ;
                        [COLOR <color>]                                 ;
                                                                        ;
      => DevPos( <row>, <col> )                                         ;
       ; DevOutPict( <xpr>, <pic> [, <color>] )


#command @ <row>, <col> SAY <xpr>                                       ;
                        [COLOR <color>]                                 ;
                                                                        ;
      => DevPos( <row>, <col> )                                         ;
       ; DevOut( <xpr> [, <color>] )

/***
*   GET SETs
*/
#command SET BELL <x:ON,OFF,&>     => Set( _SET_BELL, <(x)> )
#command SET BELL (<x>)            => Set( _SET_BELL, <x> )

#command SET CONFIRM <x:ON,OFF,&>  => Set( _SET_CONFIRM, <(x)> )
#command SET CONFIRM (<x>)         => Set( _SET_CONFIRM, <x> )

#command SET ESCAPE <x:ON,OFF,&>   => Set( _SET_ESCAPE, <(x)> )
#command SET ESCAPE (<x>)          => Set( _SET_ESCAPE, <x> )

#command SET INTENSITY <x:ON,OFF,&> => Set( _SET_INTENSITY, <(x)> )
#command SET INTENSITY (<x>)        => Set( _SET_INTENSITY, <x> )

#command SET SCOREBOARD <x:ON,OFF,&> => Set( _SET_SCOREBOARD, <(x)> )
#command SET SCOREBOARD (<x>)        => Set( _SET_SCOREBOARD, <x> )

#command SET DELIMITERS <x:ON,OFF,&> => Set( _SET_DELIMITERS, <(x)> )
#command SET DELIMITERS (<x>)        => Set( _SET_DELIMITERS, <x> )

#command SET DELIMITERS TO <c>          => Set( _SET_DELIMCHARS, <c> )
#command SET DELIMITERS TO DEFAULT      => Set( _SET_DELIMCHARS, "::" )
#command SET DELIMITERS TO              => Set( _SET_DELIMCHARS, "::" )
```

```
/***
*   @..GET
*/

#command @ <row>, <col> GET <var>                                       ;
                        [PICTURE <pic>]                                 ;
                        [VALID <valid>]                                 ;
                        [WHEN <when>]                                   ;
                        [SEND <msg>]                                    ;
                                                                        ;
       => SetPos( <row>, <col> )                                        ;
        ; AAdd(                                                         ;
             GetList,
             _GET_( <var>, <(var)>, <pic>, <{valid}>, <{when}> ):display();
             )                                                          ;
        [; ATail(GetList):<msg>]



/***
*   @..SAY..GET
*/

#command @ <row>, <col> SAY <sayxpr>                                    ;
                        [<sayClauses,...>]                              ;
                        GET <var>                                       ;
                        [<getClauses,...>]                              ;
                                                                        ;
       => @ <row>, <col> SAY <sayxpr> [<sayClauses>]                    ;
        ; @ Row(), Col()+1 GET <var> [<getClauses>]



// @..GET COLOR

#command @ <row>, <col> GET <var>                                       ;
                        [<clauses,...>]                                 ;
                        COLOR <color>                                   ;
                        [<moreClauses,...>]                             ;
                                                                        ;
       => @ <row>, <col> GET <var>                                      ;
                        [<clauses>]                                     ;
                        SEND colorDisp(<color>)                         ;
                        [<moreClauses>]
/***
*   READ
*/

#command READ SAVE                                                      ;
       => ReadModal(GetList)

#command READ                                                           ;
       => ReadModal(GetList)                                            ;
        ; GetList := {}

#command CLEAR GETS                                                     ;
       => __KillRead()                                                  ;
        ; GetList := {}
```

```
/***
 *  Refinement...
 */

#command @ [<clauses,...>] COLOUR [<moreClauses,...>]              ;
       => @ [<clauses>] COLOR [<moreClauses>]

/***
 *  MENU TO
 */

#command SET WRAP <x:ON,OFF,&>   => Set( _SET_WRAP, <(x)> )
#command SET WRAP (<x>)          => Set( _SET_WRAP, <x> )

#command SET MESSAGE TO <n> [<cent: CENTER, CENTRE>]               ;
       => Set( _SET_MESSAGE, <n> )                                 ;
        ; Set( _SET_MCENTER, <.cent.> )

#command SET MESSAGE TO                                            ;
       => Set( _SET_MESSAGE, 0 )                                   ;
        ; Set( _SET_MCENTER, .f. )

#command @ <row>, <col> PROMPT <prompt> [MESSAGE <msg>]            ;
       => __AtPrompt( <row>, <col>, <prompt> , <msg> )

#command MENU TO <v>                                               ;
       => <v> := __MenuTo( {|_1| if(PCount() == 0, <v>, <v> := _1)}, #<v> )




/***
 *  SAVE / RESTORE SCREEN
 */

/***
 *  Modal keyboard input
 */

#command WAIT [<c>]              => __Wait( <c> )
#command WAIT [<c>] TO <var>     => <var> := __Wait( <c> )


#command KEYBOARD <c>            => __Keyboard( <c> )
#command CLEAR TYPEAHEAD         => __Keyboard()
#command SET TYPEAHEAD TO <n>    => Set( _SET_TYPEAHEAD, <n> )

#command SET KEY <n> TO <proc>                                     ;
       => SetKey( <n>, {|p, l, v| <proc>(p, l, v)} )

#command SET KEY <n> TO <proc> ( [<list,...>] )                    ;
       => SET KEY <n> TO <proc>

#command SET KEY <n> TO <proc:&>                                   ;
                                                                   ;
         => if ( Empty(<(proc)>) )                                 ;
          ;    SetKey( <n>, NIL )                                  ;
          ; else                                                   ;
          ;    SetKey( <n>, {|p, l, v| <proc>(p, l, v)} )          ;
          ; end

#command SET KEY <n> [TO]                                          ;
       => SetKey( <n>, NIL )
```

```
/***
 *  Declaration
 */

#command REQUEST <vars,...>           => EXTERNAL <vars>

/***
 *  DB SETs
 */

#command SET EXCLUSIVE <x:ON,OFF,&>   => Set( _SET_EXCLUSIVE, <(x)> )
#command SET EXCLUSIVE (<x>)          => Set( _SET_EXCLUSIVE, <x> )

#command SET SOFTSEEK <x:ON,OFF,&>    => Set( _SET_SOFTSEEK, <(x)> )
#command SET SOFTSEEK (<x>)           => Set( _SET_SOFTSEEK, <x> )

#command SET UNIQUE <x:ON,OFF,&>      => Set( _SET_UNIQUE, <(x)> )
#command SET UNIQUE (<x>)             => Set( _SET_UNIQUE, <x> )

#command SET DELETED <x:ON,OFF,&>     => Set( _SET_DELETED, <(x)> )
#command SET DELETED (<x>)            => Set( _SET_DELETED, <x> )

/***
 *  DB
 */


#command USE                          => dbCloseArea()

#command USE <(db)>                                                     ;
         [VIA <rdd>]                                                    ;
         [ALIAS <a>]                                                    ;
         [<new: NEW>]                                                   ;
         [<ex: EXCLUSIVE>]                                              ;
         [<sh: SHARED>]                                                 ;
         [<ro: READONLY>]                                               ;
         [INDEX <(index1)> [, <(indexn)>]]                              ;
                                                                        ;
      => dbUseArea(                                                     ;
              <.new.>, <rdd>, <(db)>, <(a)>,                            ;
              if(<.sh.> .or. <.ex.>, !<.ex.>, NIL), <.ro.>              ;
             )                                                          ;
                                                                        ;
      [; dbSetIndex( <(index1)> )]                                      ;
      [; dbSetIndex( <(indexn)> )]

#command PACK                 => __dbPack()
#command ZAP                  => __dbZap()

#command SET RELATION TO      => dbClearRel()

#command SET RELATION                                                   ;
      [<add:ADDITIVE>]                                                  ;
      [TO <key1> INTO <(alias1)> [, [TO] <keyn> INTO <(aliasn)>]]       ;
                                                                        ;
   => if ( !<.add.> )                                                   ;
      ;    dbClearRel()                                                 ;
      ; end                                                             ;
                                                                        ;
      ; dbSetRelation( <(alias1)>, <{key1}>, <"key1"> )                 ;
     [; dbSetRelation( <(aliasn)>, <{keyn}>, <"keyn"> )]
```

```
#command  SET FILTER TO            =>  dbClearFilter(NIL)
#command  SET FILTER TO <xpr>      =>  dbSetFilter( <{xpr}>, <"xpr"> )

#command  SET FILTER TO <x:&>                                               ;
      =>  if ( Empty(<(x)>) )                                               ;
       ;    dbClearFilter()                                                 ;
       ;  else                                                              ;
       ;    dbSetFilter( <{x}>, <(x)> )                                     ;
       ;  end

#command  DELETE                   =>  dbDelete()
#command  RECALL                   =>  dbRecall()


// NOTE:  CLOSE <alias> must precede the others
#command  CLOSE FORMAT             =>  __SetFormat(NIL)

/***
*   ORD    Ordering commands
*/
#command  INDEX ON <key> [TAG <(cOrderName)> ] TO <(cOrderBagName)>         ;
          [FOR <for>]                                                       ;
          [<all:ALL>]                                                       ;
          [WHILE <while>]                                                   ;
          [NEXT <next>]                                                     ;
          [RECORD <rec>]                                                    ;
          [<rest:REST>]                                                     ;
          [EVAL <eval>]                                                     ;
          [EVERY <every>]                                                   ;
          [<unique: UNIQUE>]                                                ;
          [<ascend: ASCENDING>]                                             ;
          [<descend: DESCENDING>]                                           ;
      =>  ordCondSet( <"for">, <{for}>,                                     ;
                      [<.all.>],                                            ;
                      <{while}>,                                            ;
                      <{eval}>, <every>,                                    ;
                      RECNO(), <next>, <rec>,                               ;
                      [<.rest.>], [<.descend.>] )                           ;
       ;  ordCreate(<(cOrderBagName)>, <(cOrderName)>,                      ;
                    <"key">, <{key}>, [<.unique.>]      )

#command  INDEX ON <key> TAG <(cOrderName)> [TO <(cOrderBagName)>]          ;
          [FOR <for>]                                                       ;
          [<all:ALL>]                                                       ;
          [WHILE <while>]                                                   ;
          [NEXT <next>]                                                     ;
          [RECORD <rec>]                                                    ;
          [<rest:REST>]                                                     ;
          [EVAL <eval>]                                                     ;
          [EVERY <every>]                                                   ;
          [<unique: UNIQUE>]                                                ;
          [<ascend: ASCENDING>]                                             ;
          [<descend: DESCENDING>]                                           ;
      =>  ordCondSet( <"for">, <{for}>,                                     ;
                      [<.all.>],                                            ;
                      <{while}>,                                            ;
                      <{eval}>, <every>,                                    ;
                      RECNO(), <next>, <rec>,                               ;
                      [<.rest.>], [<.descend.>] )                           ;
       ;  ordCreate(<(cOrderBagName)>, <(cOrderName)>,                      ;
                    <"key">, <{key}>, [<.unique.>]      )
```

```
#command INDEX ON <key> TO <(file)> [<u: UNIQUE>]                      ;
      => dbCreateIndex(                                                 ;
                      <(file)>, <"key">, <{key}>,                       ;
                      if( <.u.>, .t., NIL )                             ;
                    )

#command DELETE TAG <(cOrdName1)> [ IN <(cOrdBag1)> ]                   ;
                  [, <(cOrdNameN)> [ IN <(cOrdBagN)> ] ]                ;
        => ordDestroy( <(cOrdName1)>, <(cOrdBag1)> )                    ;
        [; ordDestory( <(cOrdNameN)>, <(cOrdBagN)> ) ]

#command REINDEX                                                        ;
          [EVAL <eval>]                                                 ;
          [EVERY <every>]                                               ;
        => ordCondSet(,,,, <{eval}>, <every>,,,,,,,)                    ;
         ; ordListRebuild()


#command REINDEX                    => ordListRebuild()

#command SET INDEX TO [ <(index1)> [, <(indexn)>]] [<add: ADDITIVE>]    ;
                                                                        ;
          => if !<.add.> ; ordListClear() ; end                          ;
                                                                        ;
          [; ordListAdd( <(index1)> )]                                   ;
          [; ordListAdd( <(indexn)> )]


#command SET ORDER TO <xOrder>                                          ;
           [IN <(cOrdBag)>]                                             ;
                                                                        ;
          => ordSetFocus( <xOrder> [, <(cOrdBag)>] )


#command SET ORDER TO TAG <(cOrder)>
;
           [IN <(cOrdBag)>]                                             ;
                                                                        ;
          => ordSetFocus( <(cOrder)> [, <(cOrdBag)>] )

#command SET ORDER TO               => ordSetFocus(0)
```

# Appendix 3

# RMAKE Script Files

There are two basic script files that were used to compile the various sample programs. One script file does not link in the SAMPLES.LIB file while the other one does. Additionally, there is a script file to make a more encompassing .PLL file taking into consideration that various functions in SAMPLES.LIB as well as EXTEND.LIB and CLIPPER.LIB. Please check with the headers of each program to see which script file is needed to make an executable file.

### SAMPLE.RMK

```
.prg.obj:
    clipper $(FILE) /m /n /p /w /a /v /es2

.obj.exe:
    if not errorlevel 1 rtlink fi $(FILE) pll base52

$(FILE).obj      :      $(FILE).prg
$(FILE).exe      :      $(FILE).obj
```

### SAMPMORE.RMK

```
.prg.obj:
    clipper $(FILE) /m /n /p /w /a /v /es2

.obj.exe:
    if not errorlevel 1 rtlink fi $(FILE) pll base52 lib samples

$(FILE).obj      :      $(FILE).prg
$(FILE).exe      :      $(FILE).obj
```

## SAMPRDD.RMK

```
// File              Samprdd.rmk
// Purpose           To be a general script file for the SAMPLES library
//                   as well as the RDD libraries

.prg.obj:
    clipper $(FILE) /m /n /p /w /a /v /es2 /b

.obj.exe:
    if not errorlevel 1 rtlink fi $(FILE) lib dbfndx, \
dbfntx, samples, dbfcdx, dbfmdx, dbpx, samples

$(FILE).obj       :      $(FILE).prg
$(FILE).exe       :      $(FILE).obj

// End of file: Samprdd.rmk
```

## SAMPNDX.RMK

```
.prg.obj:
    clipper $(FILE) /m /n /p /w /a /v /es2 /b

.obj.exe:
    if not errorlevel 1 rtlink fi $(FILE) lib dbfndx, dbfntx, samples, dbfcdx

$(FILE).obj       :      $(FILE).prg
$(FILE).exe       :      $(FILE).obj
```

## FULLBASE.LNK

```
#
# FULLBASE.LNK for CAClipper 5.2
#

PRELINK

##################################
# Remove below comment marker if you want to create a FULLBASE.OVL
# file for all the Clipper-compiled portion of the libraries
#
# DYNAMIC INTO fullbase.ovl
#
##################################

OUTPUT fullbase
VERBOSE

LIB extend
LIB clipper
LIB terminal
```

```
LIB samples
lib dbfntx

refer _MAIN,_VOPS,_VMACRO
refer _VTERM,_VPICT,_VGETSYS,_VDBG
refer __ACCEPT,DISPBOX,__GET,RANGECHECK
refer __ATPROMPT,DBAPPEND,__DBAPP,__KILLREAD
refer __MCLEAR,__KEYBOARD,DBCLOSEARE,DBCOMMITAL
refer __DBCONTIN,__DBCOPYST,__DBCOPYXS,__DBCOPY,__DBCREATE, dbf
refer __DBLIST,__DBPACK, __DBSORT,__DBSORT,__DBTOTAL
refer DBDELETE,__EJECT,DBSEEK
refer DBGOTO,DBGOTOP,DBGOBOTTOM,DBCREATEIN,__ACCEPTST,__DBJOIN
refer __LABELFOR,__DBLOCATE,__MENUTO,__QUIT,DBRECALL
refer __MXRELEAS,__MRELEASE,__REPORTFO,__MRESTORE,RESTSCREEN,__RUN
refer __MSAVE,DBSELECTAR,__SETCENTU,DBSETFILTE,__SETFORMA,__SETFUNCT
refer DBCLEARIND,DBSETINDEX,SETKEY,DBSETORDER,DBCLEARREL,DBSETRELAT
refer DBSKIP, __TEXTSAVE,__TEXTREST,__TYPEFILE
refer __COPYFILE,DBUNLOCK,DBUNLOCKAL,__DBUPDATE,DBUSEAREA,__WAIT,__DBZAP
refer __ATCLEAR,__BOXD,__BOXS,__DIR,__CLEAR,_VDBG,SETTYPEAHE,__GETA
refer DISPBEGIN,DISPEND

refer   memory
refer   achoice,acopy,adel,adir,afields,afill,ains
refer   ascan,asort,bin2i,bin2l,bin2w
refer   curdir,dbedit,dbfilter,descend,diskspace,doserror
refer   dbrelation,dbrselect,readinsert,setcancel,readexit
refer   errorlevel,fclose,fcreate,ferror,fopen,fread,freadstr
refer   fseek,fwrite,gete,hardcr,header,i2bin,isalpha
refer   indexext,indexord,islower,isupper,isprinter
refer   l2bin,lupdate,memoedit,memoline,memoread,memotran
refer   memowrit,mlcount,mlpos,neterr,nextkey,left
refer   rat,savescreen,scroll,recsize
refer   setcolor,setprc,soundex,strtran,stuff,tone

refer   aclone,aeval,array,asize,dbcreate,dbeval
refer   dbstruct,directory,errorblock,ferase
refer   frename,isdigit,maxcol,maxrow,padl,padc,padr,qout,qqout
refer   readmodal,setcursor,setkey
refer   getnew,tbrowsenew,tbrowsedb,browse,setmode,setblink,fieldput
refer   fieldget,getenv,version,fieldblock,fieldwbloc

refer ablock, abrowse, acomp, amax, amin, dimensions, asserttest
refer boxmenu, boxshadow, addmonth, arrayasdat, dateasage, dateasarra
refer dateisleap, dmy, mdy, ntod, dictat, dicteval, dictnew, dictput
refer dictputpai, dictremove, filebase, filedrive, fileext, filepath
refer fullpath, getpath, setall, gaugedispl, gaugenew, gaugeupdat
refer collect, extract, ieval, inkeywait, addrec, fillock, netuse
refer reclock, basetobase, ceiling, dtor, floor
refer numascurre, numaslog10, numgetdeci, numgetlen, rtod, sign
refer printcodes, scrollbard, scrollbarn, scrollbaru
refer stackisemp, stacknew, stackpop, stackpush, stacktop
refer statusnew, statusupda, citystate, listasarra, occurs, proper
refer secondsasd, timeasampm, timeasseco, timeasstri, timediff
refer timeisvali, valedit
```

```
refer ordbagext, ordbagname, ordcreate, orddestroy, ordfor, ordkey
refer ordlistadd, ordname, ordnumber, rddlist, rddname

# Remove the below comment if you have your own ERRORSYS.OBJ module.
#
# exclude errorsys
```

# Appendix 4

# *Include Files*

This appendix lists the header files used by all of the example programs in this book. These header files are updates of the header files found in *Clipper 5.2 Power Tools*. The objective was to use a common set of header files, thus reducing the need for redundant files cluttering up your hard disk.

Although we are trying to draw upon a common set of header files for our sample programs, there are two major kinds of compatibility problems that are likely to arise:

- These header files are revised and updated versions of the ones published in *Clipper 5.2 Power Tools*. That means that, if you are currently using the header files that accompanied the Power Tools diskette, some of the sample programs in this book may not work. To minimize this difficulty, we have noted in the text which lines in each header file have changed.

- Many of the user-defined commands and pseudofunctions defined in these header files in turn call functions that are contained within the Power Tools library. And in particular, the Power Tools library contains a number of alternate subsystems that are intended to replace and enhance the standard subsystems supplied with Clipper. If you do not have the Power Tools library, these translations will not work properly. Consequently, we have noted which lines of a header file are likely to cause trouble. If you do not have the Power Tools library, the sample programs in this book will still work successfully if you comment out these offending lines of code.

These header files are constantly being updated and improved and are used by other programs and products, including The Pleiades, Helios, and Hermes, all published by Sirius Software Development, Inc. To obtain the most up-to-date versions of these header files, please see the coupon in the back of the book.

# PTCOLOR.CH

```
/*       Name:    PTcolor.ch
       Author:    Steve Straley
       Notice:    Copyright(c) 1991-1993 - Sirius Software Development, Inc.
                  All Rights Reserved  --  415-399-9810
         Date:    July 1, 1991
      Compile:    N/A
      Version:    Clipper 5.01
 Include Path:    \PTools\Include
  Environment:    f051;
         Link:    N/A
 Library Path:    \Clipper\501
         Note:    This is the header file for the Colors for the Power
                  Tools Library

*/

#stdout Using PTColor.ch

#define pBLACK              N
#define pBLUE               B
#define pGREEN              G
#define pCYAN               BG
#define pRED                R
#define pMAGENTA            RB
#define pBROWN              GR
#define pWHITE              W
#define pUNDERLINE          U
#define pINVERSE            I
#define pBLANK              X

* Bright colors

#define pGREY               N+
#define pGRAY               N+
#define pBRIGHT_BLUE        B+
#define pBRIGHT_GREEN       G+
#define pBRIGHT_CYAN        BG+
#define pORANGE             R+
#define pYELLOW             GR+
#define pBRIGHT_WHITE       W+

* Blinking colors

#define pBLACK_BLINK        N*
#define pBLUE_BLINK         B*
#define pGREEN_BLINK        G*
#define pCYAN_BLINK         BG*
#define pRED_BLINK          R*
#define pMAGENTA_BLINK      RB*
#define pBROWN_BLINK        GR*
#define pWHITE_BLINK        W*
```

* Bright colors blinking

```
#define pGRAY_BLINK           N+*
#define pGREY_BLINK           N+*
#define pBRIGHT_BLUE_BLINK    B+*
#define pBRIGHT_GREEN_BLINK   G+*
#define pBRIGHT_CYAN_BLINK    BG+*
#define pORANGE_BLINK         R+*
#define pYELLOW_BLINK         GR+*
#define pBRIGHT_WHITE_BLINK   W+*
```

* default colors

```
#define pMONO_NORMAL '7/0, 0/7'
#define pCOLR_NORMAL '7/1, 1/7'
```

* End of File

## PTINKEY.CH

```
/*      Name:  PTInkey.ch
      Author:  Steve Straley
      Notice:  Copyright(c) 1991-1993 - Sirius Software Development, Inc.
               All Rights Reserved  --  415-399-9810
        Date:  July 1, 1991
     Compile:  N/A
     Version:  Clipper 5.01
Include Path:  \PTools\Include
 Environment:  f051;
        Link:  N/A
Library Path:  \Clipper\501
        Note:  This header file contains all of the manifest constants
               for the inkey values within the Clipper environment for
               the Power Tools Library

*/

#stdout Using PTInkey.ch

* The following is the basic function key listing

#define pF1  -28
#define pF2  -1
#define pF3  -2
#define pF4  -3
#define pF5  -4
#define pF6  -5
#define pF7  -6
#define pF8  -7
#define pF9  -8
#define pF10 -9
#define pF11 -40
```

*Appendix 4*

```
#define pF12 -41
#define pSHIFT_F1 -10
#define pSHIFT_F2 -11
#define pSHIFT_F3 -12
#define pSHIFT_F4 -13
#define pSHIFT_F5 -14
#define pSHIFT_F6 -15
#define pSHIFT_F7 -16
#define pSHIFT_F8 -17
#define pSHIFT_F9 -18
#define pSHIFT_F10 -19
#define pSHIFT_F11 -42
#define pSHIFT_F12 -43
#define pSHIFT_TAB -271

#define pCTRL_F1 -20
#define pCTRL_F2 -21
#define pCTRL_F3 -22
#define pCTRL_F4 -23
#define pCTRL_F5 -24
#define pCTRL_F6 -25
#define pCTRL_F7 -26
#define pCTRL_F8 -27
#define pCTRL_F9 -28
#define pCTRL_F10 -29
#define pCTRL_F11 -44
#define pCTRL_F12 -45
#define pALT_F1 -30
#define pALT_F2 -31
#define pALT_F3 -32
#define pALT_F4 -33
#define pALT_F5 -34
#define pALT_F6 -35
#define pALT_F7 -36
#define pALT_F8 -37
#define pALT_F9 -38
#define pALT_F10 -39
#define pALT_F11 -46
#define pALT_F12 -47

* The following is a listing of other ALT keys

#define pALT_1 376
#define pALT_2 377
#define pALT_3 378
#define pALT_4 379
#define pALT_5 380
#define pALT_6 381
#define pALT_7 382
#define pALT_8 383
#define pALT_9 384
#define pALT_0 385
#define pALT_WHITE_MINUS 386
#define pALT_GREY_MINUS 330
#define pALT_EQUAL 387
#define pALT_ENTER 332
```

```
#define pALT_BKSP 270
#define pALT_TAB 421
#define pALT_WHITE_SLASH 309
#define pALT_GREY_SLASH 420
#define pALT_ASTERISK 311
#define pALT_Q 272
#define pALT_W 273
#define pALT_E 274
#define pALT_R 275
#define pALT_T 276
#define pALT_Y 277
#define pALT_U 278
#define pALT_I 279
#define pALT_O 280
#define pALT_P 281
#define pALT_A 286
#define pALT_S 287
#define pALT_D 288
#define pALT_F 289
#define pALT_G 290
#define pALT_H 291
#define pALT_J 292
#define pALT_K 293
#define pALT_L 294
#define pALT_Z 300
#define pALT_X 301
#define pALT_C 302
#define pALT_V 303
#define pALT_B 304
#define pALT_N 305
#define pALT_M 306

* And now for other keyboard mappings

#define pBKSP               8
#define pHOME               1
#define pPGUP               18
#define pPGDN               3
#define pEND                6
#define pLEFT_ARROW         19
#define pUP_ARROW           5
#define pDOWN_ARROW         24
#define pRIGHT_ARROW        4
#define pDEL                7
#define pINS                22
#define pSPACE_BAR          32
#define pCTRL_PGUP          31
#define pCTRL_PGDN          30
#define pCTRL_END           23
#define pCTRL_HOME          29
#define pCTRL_ENTER         10
#define pCTRL_RIGHT_ARROW   2
#define pCTRL_LEFT_ARROW    26
#define pCTRL_BKSP          127    // Ctrl-Backspace
#define pCTRL_TAB           404
#define pENTER         13
```

## Appendix 4

```
#define pTAB              9
#define pESC              27
#define pKEYPAD_5         332
#define pCTRL_UP_ARROW    397
#define pCTRL_DOWN_ARROW  401
#define pGREY_PLUS        43
#define pGREY_MINUS       45

#define pCTRL_A  1
#define pCTRL_B  2
#define pCTRL_C  3
#define pCTRL_D  4
#define pCTRL_E  5
#define pCTRL_F  6
#define pCTRL_G  7
#define pCTRL_H  8
#define pCTRL_I  9
#define pCTRL_J  10
#define pCTRL_K  11
#define pCTRL_L  12
#define pCTRL_M  13
#define pCTRL_N  14
#define pCTRL_O  15
#define pCTRL_P  16
#define pCTRL_Q  17
#define pCTRL_R  18
#define pCTRL_S  19
#define pCTRL_T  20
#define pCTRL_U  21
#define pCTRL_V  22
#define pCTRL_W  23
#define pCTRL_X  24
#define pCTRL_Y  25
#define pCTRL_Z  26
#define pCTRL_SLASH         405
#define pCTRL_GREY_MINUS    398
#define pCTRL_WHITE_MINUS   31
#define pCTRL_ASTERISK      406

* End of File
```

PTINKEY.CH includes two new INKEY( ) translations not found on the original Power Tools diskette:

```
#define pGREY_PLUS    43
#define pGREY MINUS   45
```

# PTVALUE.CH

```
/*    Name:    PTValue.ch
      Author:  Steve Straley
      Notice:  Copyright(c) 1991-1993 - Sirius Software Development, Inc.
               All Rights Reserved  --  415-399-9810
```

```
         Date:   July 1, 1991
      Compile:   N/A
      Version:   Clipper 5.01
 Include Path:   \PTools\Include
  Environment:   f051;
         Link:   RTLink FI
 Library Path:   \Clipper\501
         Note:   This header file is for the Clipper Power Tools Library
                 for all of the needed manifest constants.

*/
#stdout Using PTValue.ch

// Miscelaneous manifest constants

#define RETURN return
#define return return
#define pCRLF chr(13)+chr(10)
#define pTRUE .t.
#define pFALSE .f.
#define pPI 3.1415926535897932384
#define pON .t.
#define pOFF .f.

// The following are the manifest constants for the register for the
// INTERUPT86() function

#define pREGISTERS aRegister
#define pAX aRegister[1]
#define pBX aRegister[2]
#define pCX aRegister[3]
#define pDX aRegister[4]
#define pSI aRegister[5]
#define pDI aRegister[6]
#define pBP aRegister[7]
#define pDS aRegister[8]
#define pES aRegister[9]
#define pREG_FLAG aRegister[10]

#define pAX_REG 1
#define pBX_REG 2
#define pCX_REG 3
#define pDX_REG 4
#define pSI_REG 5
#define pDI_REG 6
#define pBP_REG 7
#define pDS_REG 8
#define pES_REG 9
#define pFLAG_REG 10

#define pMOUSE_REGISTERS MouseStat()[1]
#define pMOUSE_XCOORD     MouseStat()[2, 1]
#define pMOUSE_YCOORD     MouseStat()[2, 2]
#define pMOUSE_HORZONTAL MouseStat()[2, 3]
```

```
#define pMOUSE_VERTICLE    MouseStat()[2, 4]
#define pMOUSE_STATUS      MouseStat()[2, 5]

#define DOS_INT     33
#define MOUSE_INT   51

// The following are manifest constants for graphic keys
#define pDBAR       "CBHDAEH"
#define pSBAR       "SRVTQUV"

// The following are manifest constants for the setcursor() function
#define pCURSOR_OFF    0
#define pCURSOR_ON     1
#define pCURSOR_LOWER  2
#define pCURSOR_BLOCK  3
#define pCURSOR_UPPER  4

// The following manifest constants are for the various data
// types in the Clipper language

#define pARRAY      "A"
#define pBLOCK      "B"
#define pCHARACTER  "C"
#define pDATE       "D"
#define pLOGICAL    "L"
#define pMEMO       "M"
#define pNUMERIC    "N"
#define pOBJECT     "O"

// The following manifest constants pertain to the SET() function
// and the various environmental values.

#define pEXACT         1
#define pFIXED         2
#define pDECIMALS      3
#define pDATEFORMAT    4
#define pEPOCH         5
#define pPATH          6
#define pDEFAULT       7
#define pEXCLUSIVE     8
#define pSOFTSEEK      9
#define pUNIQUE        10
#define pDELETED       11
#define pCANCEL        12
#define pDEBUG         13
#define pTYPEAHEAD     14
#define pCOLOR         15
#define pCURSOR        16
#define pCONSOLE       17
#define pALTERNATE     18
#define pALTFILE       19
#define pDEVICE        20
#define pEXTRA         21
#define pEXTRAFILE     22
```

```
    #define pPRINTER         23
    #define pPRINTFILE       24
    #define pMARGIN          25
    #define pBELL            26
    #define pCONFIRM         27
    #define pESCAPE          28
    #define pINSERT          29
    #define pEXIT            30
    #define pINTENSITY       31
    #define pSCOREBOARD      32
    #define pDELIMITERS      33
    #define pDELIMCHARS      34
    #define pWRAP            35
    #define pMESSAGE         36
    #define pMCENTER         37
    #define pSCROLLBREAK     38
    #define pCOUNT           38

    * End of File
```

## PTFUNCS.CH

This header file contains all of the pseudofunctions and expressions seen throughout the book. This is so even though a case could be made for placing some of the pseudofunctions in other header files. MAKECOLOR( ), for instance, could legitimately be placed in the PTCOLOR.CH header file; instead, we have chosen to place it here.

```
/*        Name:  PTFuncs.ch
        Author:  Steve Straley
        Notice:  Copyright(c) 1991-1993 - Sirius Software Development, Inc.
                 All Rights Reserved  --  415-399-9810
          Date:  July 1, 1991
       Compile:  N/A
       Version:  Clipper 5.01
  Include Path:  \PTools\Include
   Environment:  f051;
          Link:  N/A
  Library Path:  \Clipper\501
          Note:  This is a header file for the Clipper Power Tools
                 Library and includes all pseudofunctions and expressions

*/

#stdout Using PTFuncs.ch

//% 001 sjs Added new pseudofunctions for 1.1 version

#xtranslate DBZAP()                                                    => ;
            ( if( !empty(alias()), (__dbzap(), (lastrec()==0)), .f. ) )

#xtranslate DBCONTINUE()                                               => ;
            ( __dbContinue(), found() )

#xtranslate DBLOCATE( <for> [, <while> [, <next> [, <rec> [, <rest:REST>]]]] ) =>;
            ( __dbLocate( <{for}>, <{while}>, <next>, <rec>, <.rest.> ), found() )
```

## Appendix 4

```
#xtranslate NOFERROR()                                          => ;
            ( FERROR() == 0 )

#xtranslate SETFILTER( <exp>, <move> )                          => ;
            ( dbSetFilter( <{exp}>, <"exp"> ), dbGotop(), dbfilter() )

#xtranslate SETFILTER( <exp> )                                  => ;
            ( dbSetFilter( <{exp}>, <"exp"> ), dbfilter() )

#xtranslate SETFILTER()                                         => ;
            ( dbClearFilter( NIL ), dbfilter() )

#xtranslate ISWRAP()                                            => ;
            ( SET( _SET_WRAP ) )

#xtranslate WHATAREA(<x>)                                       => ;
            <x>->(SELECT())

#xtranslate APPEND()                                            => ;
            ( IF( !EMPTY(ALIAS()), ( dbAppend(), .T.), .F.) )

#xtranslate EJECT()                                             => ;
            ( __Eject(), .T. )

#xtranslate UPPERLOWER(<exp>)                                   => ;
            ( upper(substr(<exp>,1,1))+lower(substr(<exp>,2)) )

#xtranslate FILECOPY( <source>, <destination> )                 => ;
            ( __CopyFile( <(source)>, <(destination)> ) )

#xtranslate KEYBOARD([<exp>])                                   => ;
            ( __Keyboard(<exp>), .T. )

#xtranslate SAY( <row>, <col>, <exp> [, <color> ] )             => ;
            ( setpos(<row>, <col>), devout( <exp>, <color> ) )

#xtranslate SAYPICT( <row>, <col>, <exp>, <pict> [, <color> ] ) => ;
            ( setpos(<row>, <col>), devoutpict( <exp>, <pict>, <color> ) )

#xtranslate GET( <var> [, <pict>, <bValid>, <bWhen>] )          =>;
        aadd( getlist, _get_( <var>, <(var)>, <pict>, <bValid>, <bWhen> ) )
#xtranslate GET( <var> [, <pict>, <bValid>] )                   =>;
        aadd( getlist, _get_( <var>, <(var)>, <pict>, <bValid>, ) )
#xtranslate GET( <var> [, <pict>, , <bWhen>] )                  =>;
        aadd( getlist, _get_( <var>, <(var)>, <pict>,, <bWhen> ) )
#xtranslate GET( <var> [, <pict> ] )                            =>;
        aadd( getlist, _get_( <var>, <(var)>, <pict>,, ) )
#xtranslate GET( <var>, [,<bValid> [, <bWhen>]] )               =>;
        aadd( getlist, _get_( <var>, <(var)>,, <bValid>, <bWhen> ) )
#xtranslate GET( <var>, ,[, <bWhen>] )                          =>;
        aadd( getlist, _get_( <var>, <(var)>, , , <bWhen> ) )

#xtranslate WAIT( [<c>] )                                       => ;
            ( WaitKey( <c> ) )

#xtranslate VALIDPARM(<x>, <y>)                                 => ;
            ( IF( <x> == NIL, <y>, IF( VALTYPE(<x>) != VALTYPE(<y>), <y>, <x> )))

#xtranslate CLS()                                               => ;
            ( scroll(), setpos(0,0) )
```

```
#xtranslate OCCURRENCE( <a>, <b> )                              => ;
            ( INT(LEN( <b> )-LEN(STRTRAN(<b>, <a>, ""))) / LEN(<a>) )

#xtranslate DAYS( <secs> )                                      => ;
            ( int( <secs> ) / 86400 )

#xtranslate DBF()                                               => ;
            alias()

#xtranslate TSTRING( <secs> )                                   => ;
            ( StringZeros( int( Modulus( <secs>/3600, 24)), 2, 0 ) + ":" + ;
              StringZeros( int( Modulus( <secs>/  60, 60)), 2, 0 ) + ":"  + ;
              StringZeros( int( Modulus( <secs>,     60)), 2, 0 ) )

#xtranslate SECS( <time> )                                      => ;
            ( val( <time> ) * 3600 + val( substr( <time>, 4 ) ) * 60 + val( substr( <time>, 7 ) ) )

#xtranslate LENNUM( <number> )                                  => ;
            ( len( alltrim( str( <number> ) ) ) )

#xtranslate ODD( <number> )                                     => ;
            ( !empty( <number> % 2 ) )

#xtranslate EVEN( <number> )                                    => ;
            ( empty( <number> % 2 ) )

#xtranslate FORCEBETWEEN(<x>,<y>,<z>)   => ;
              (if(<x>\>=<y>.and.<x>\<=<z>, <x>, max(min(<y>, <z>), <x>)))

#xtranslate LOWBYTE( <byte> ) => ( int( <byte> % 256 ) )
#xtranslate HIGHBYTE( <byte> ) => ( int( <byte> / 256 ) )
#xtranslate HIGHBIT( <number> ) => (<number> * ( 2**8 ) )

#xtranslate COLDBOOT() => ReBoot(0)
#xtranslate WARMBOOT() => ReBoot(1)

#xtranslate MAKECOLOR( <c,...> ) => #<c>

#xtranslate CLEARESC() => ( __keyboard(chr(0)), inkey() )

#xtranslate SETCENTURY( [<x>] )   => __SetCentury( <x> )

#xtranslate PTREAD() => ( setcursor(1), ptreadmodal( getlist ), getlist := {},
setcursor(0), lastkey() != 27 )

#xtranslate DOSFILEPATH(<c>) => substr( <c>, 1, rat("\", <c>) )
#xtranslate DOSFILENAME(<c>) => substr( <c>, rat("\",<c>)+1 )

#xtranslate DATEREADR()          => ;
            {|oGet, nTime, lTimeOut, bExceptions, aList, nPos| ;
             DateReader(oGet,nTime, lTimeOut, bExceptions, aList, nPos)}

#xtranslate RLREADER()           => ;
            {|oGet, nTime, lTimeOut, bExceptions, aList, nPos| ;
             R2LReader(oGet,nTime, lTimeOut, bExceptions, aList, nPos)}

#xtranslate MEMBLOCK(<x>)        => { {|a| if(a=nil, <x>, <x>:=a)}, <(x)> }
#xtranslate MEMPACK()            => memory(-1)
#xtranslate MEMSEGS()            => memory(101)
```

# Appendix 4

```
#xtranslate MEMHEAP()            =>  memory(102)
#xtranslate MEMREAL()            =>  memory(104)

#xtranslate SOFTFOUND()          =>  ( !found() .and. !eof() )

#xtranslate CalcOnGet([<row>,<col>,<color>])  => ;
            {|cName,nLine,cVar,oGet,aList,nPos| oGet:varput( ;
               Calculator(,{<row>,<col>,<color>}) )}

#xtranslate SetPrinter()         =>  set( 23 )
#xtranslate SetConsole()         =>  set( 17 )
#xtranslate SetDevice()          =>  set( 20 )
#xtranslate SetConfirm()         =>  set( 27 )
#xtranslate SetAlternate()       =>  set( 18 )
#xtranslate SetDeleted()         =>  set( 11 )
#xtranslate SetMargin()          =>  set( 25 )
#xtranslate SetWrap()            =>  set( 35 )

#xtranslate MAKEDATE( <cDate> )  =>  ctod( #<cDate> )

//% 001 sjs This pseudofunction is for the 1.1 release
#xtranslate DOSFILEEXT( <exp> )  =>  substr( <exp>, rat(".", <exp>) + 1 )

* End of File
```

The following pseudofunction is new to PTFUNCS.CH:

```
#xtranslate DOSFILEEXT( <exp> )  =>  substr( <exp>, rat(".", <exp>) + 1 )
```

In addition, the pseudofunctions listed below make calls to the Power Tools library that accompanies the book *Clipper 5.2 Power Tools*. Unless you have this software, therefore, these pseudofunctions should not be used in your code. The pseudofunctions are listed in the order in which they occur in PTFUNCS.CH:

    WAIT( )
    TSTRING( )
    COLDBOOT( )
    WARMBOOT( )
    PTREAD( )
    DATEREADR( )
    RLREADER( )
    CALCONGET( )

## PTVERBS.CH

The header file PTVERBS.CH implements the collection of user-defined commands and statements found in *Clipper 5.2 Power Tools*.

```
/*      Name:     PTVerbs.ch
        Author:   Steve Straley
        Notice:   Copyright(c) 1991-1993 - Sirius Software Development, Inc.
                  All Rights Reserved   --   415-399-9810
        Date:     July 1, 1991
        Compile:  N/A
        Version:  Clipper 5.01
```

## Include Files  1127

```
     Include Path:   \PTools\Include
      Environment:   f051;
             Link:   N/A
     Library Path:   \Clipper\501
             Note:   This is the header file for the Clipper Power Tools
                     Library for all of the commands

*/

#stdout Using PTVerbs.ch

//% 001 sjs Added new commands to the standard 1.0 release

#xtranslate VOID => return( NIL )

#xcommand PROCESS => while .T.
#xcommand END PROCESS => end

#xcommand REPEAT => while .t.
#xcommand UNTIL <exp> => if <exp> ; exit ; end ; end

#xcommand DEFAULT REGISTERS => aRegister := array(10)

#xcommand DO SWITCH => do case
#xcommand SWITCH <exp> [ PERFORM <act> ] => case <exp> [; <act>]
#xcommand END SWITCH => endcase

#xcommand SAVE GET TO <var>        => ;
          <var> := aclone( getlist ) ; getlist := {}
#xcommand RESTORE GET FROM <var> => getlist := <var>

#xtranslate (<var> IS <type>)         => ( valtype(<var>) = <type> )
#xtranslate (<var> IS NOT <type>)     => ( valtype(<var>) != <type> )

#xcommand IF <var> IS <type>          => if valtype(<var>) = <type>
#xcommand IF <var> IS NOT <type>      => if valtype(<var>) != <type>
#xcommand IF <ele> IS IN <array>      => if !(len( <array> ) \< <ele> )
#xcommand IF <ele> IS NOT IN <array>  => if len( <array> ) \< <ele>

#xtranslate @@<exp>          => {|x| if( x == nil, <exp>, <exp> := x)}
#xtranslate (<x> !$ <y>) => !( <x> $ <y> )

#xcommand WAITKEY [<c>]                           => WaitKey( <c>, .t. )
#xcommand WAITKEY  [<c>] TO <var>                 => WaitKey( <c>, .t.,,, @<var>, <(var)> )
#xcommand WAITKEY  AT <row>, <col> [<c>]          => WaitKey( <c>, .t.,<row>, <col> )
#xcommand WAITKEY  AT <row>, <col> [<c>] TO <var> => WaitKey( <c>, .t.,<row>, <col>,
@<var>, <(var)> )

#ifndef CLIPPER
#xcommand SET KEY <n> TO <proc>              [DESCRIPT <name>]         =>;
          SETKEYTABLE( <n>, {|p,l,v,oGet,aList,nPos| <proc>(p,l,v,oGet,aList,nPos)}, <name> )
#xcommand SET KEY <n> TO <proc>( [<list,...>] ) [DESCRIPT <name>]      =>;
                                   SETKEYTABLE( <n>, {|| <proc>(<list>) }, <name> )
#xcommand SET KEY <n> [TO]                        => SETKEYTABLE( <n>, NIL )
#xcommand SET KEY RESET                           => SETKEYTABLE(,,,.t.)
#xcommand SET KEY <n> TO BLOCK <block> [DESCRIPT <name>] => SETKEYTABLE( <n>, <block>,
<name> )
#xcommand SET KEY STACK TO <var>                  => <var> := SETKEYTABLE()
#xcommand SET KEY STACK FROM <var>                => SETKEYTABLE(,,,,<var>)
#endif
```

## 1128  Appendix 4

```
#xcommand INIT MASTER          => local lMaster
#xcommand BEGIN MASTER         => begin sequence
#xcommand EXIT MASTER          => lMaster := .t.
#xcommand END MASTER           => end; if lMaster != NIL ; exit ; end
#xcommand SET MASTER TO <key>  => setkey( <key>, {|| Break(NIL)}, "Return to master key" )

#xcommand DEFAULT <exp> TO <value> [, <expN> TO <valN> ] => ;
          <exp> := if(( valtype(<exp>)==valtype(<value>) .and. (<exp> != nil)), <exp>, <value>) ;
              [; <expN> := if(( valtype(<expN>)==valtype(<valN>) .and. (<expN> != nil)), <expN>, <valN>) ]

#xtranslate NEWREADER <exp> [WITH <var>] => ;
            send reader := {|x| <exp>(x [,<var>])}

#xcommand INIT DATA <exp> => <exp> := { {}, {}, {|| NIL}, {|| NIL} }

#xcommand INIT DATA <exp> PRE <block> => ;
                    <exp> := { {}, {}, <block>, {|| NIL} }

#xcommand INIT DATA <exp> POST <block> => ;
                    <exp> := { {}, {}, {|| NIL}, <block> }

#xcommand INIT DATA <exp> PRE <block1> POST <block2> => ;
                    <exp> := { {}, {}, <block1>, <block2> }

#xcommand DEFINE DATA <array> GET <get> ;
               AT <row>, <col> ;
               [COLOR <color>] ;
               [PICT <pict>] ;
               [MESSAGE <message> [MSGCOLOR <newcolor>][AT <mRow>, <mCol>] ] ;
               [KEYSET <key> [TO <block>] [<offkey: ONLY>]] ;
               [READER <reader> ] ;
               [WHEN <when>] ;
               [VALID <valid>] => ;
                                       ;
   BuildGetSystem(<array>, , ;
     {<get>, {|a| if(a=nil, <get>, <get>:=a)}, <(get)>, ;
             <row>, ;
             <col>, ;
             <color>, ;
             <pict>, ;
             <message>, ;
             <newcolor>, ;
             <mRow>, ;
             <mCol>, ;
             <reader>, ;
             <key>, ;
             <block>, ;
             <.offkey.>, ;
             <{when}>, ;
             <{valid}> } )

#xcommand DEFINE DATA <array> SAY <say> ;
               AT <row>, <col> ;
               [PICT <pict>] [COLOR <color>] ;
               [GET <get> [AT <gRow>, <gCol>] ;
               [COLOR <gColor>] ;
               [PICT <gPict>] ;
               [MESSAGE <message> [MSGCOLOR <newcolor>][AT <mRow>, <mCol>] ] ;
```

```
                            [KEYSET <key> [TO <block>][<offkey: ONLY>]] ;
                            [READER <reader> ] ;
                            [WHEN <when>] ;
                            [VALID <valid>] ] => ;
                                                             ;
        BuildGetSystem( <array>, ;
                    {<row>, <col>, <say>, <pict>, <color>, ;
                      {|cPict, cColor| setpos(<row>, <col>), ;
                         if(cPict == NIL, ;
                             devout(<say>, <color> ), ;
                             devoutpict( <say>, cPict, <color> ) ;
                                                 ) ;
                                 } } ;
                    [, {<get>, ;
                         {|a| if(a=nil, <get>, <get>:=a)}, ;
                         <(get)>, ;
                         <gRow>, ;
                         <gCol>, ;
                         <gColor>, ;
                         <gPict>, ;
                         <message>, ;
                         <newcolor>, ;
                         <mRow>, ;
                         <mCol>,;
                         <reader>, ;
                         <key>, ;
                         <block>, ;
                         <.offkey.>, ;
                         <{when}>, ;
                         <{valid}> } ] )

#xcommand BUILD VIEWER TO <var> [COLOR <color>,...>] => ;
         <var> := { { {}, {,}, {,},<(var)>,#<color>,,}, {}, {}, {}, {}, {}, {} }

#xcommand VIEW <var> NAME <name> => <var>\[1,4] := <"name">

#xcommand VIEW <var> SAVE FILE <name> => ;
          <var>\[1,7] := <name>

#xcommand VIEW <var> AT <top>, <left>, <bottom>, <right> => ;
          <var>\[1,1] := {<top>, <left>, <bottom>, <right>}

#xcommand VIEW RELATION <key> INTO <alias> TO <var> => ;
          <var>\[1,2,1] := {|lBefore| if( lBefore, ;
                                  (dbClearRel(), ;
                                   dbSetRelation( <(alias)>, <{key}>, <"key">)), ;
                                   dbClearRel() ) } ;;
          <var>\[1,2,2] := "{ '"+ <(alias)> + "', {|| " + <(key)> + "}, '" + <"key"> + "'}"

#xcommand VIEW ITEM <header>, <thing> [WIDTH <width>] [SEARCH <block>] IN <var> => ;
          aadd(<var>\[2], <header>) ;;
          aadd(<var>\[3], <thing>) ;;
          aadd(<var>\[4], <width>) ;;
          aadd(<var>\[5], <"thing"> ) ;;
          aadd(<var>\[6], <block> ) ;;
          aadd(<var>\[7], <"block"> )

#xcommand VIEW <var> [WITH <block>][DISPLAY <aDisp>] => ;
            ViewModal(<var> [, {|nKey, oView, aData| <block>(nKey, oView, aData)}][, <aDisp>] )
```

```
#xcommand VIEW <var> TO <item> [WITH <block>][DISPLAY <aDisp>] => ;
          <item> := ViewModal(<var> [, {|nKey, oView, aData| <block>(nKey, oView,
aData)}][, <aDisp>])

#xcommand VIEW <var> [EXCEPTION <block>] [DISPLAY <aDisp>] => ;
          ViewModal(<var> [, <{block}> ][, <aDisp>] )

#xcommand VIEW <var> TO <item> [EXCEPTION <block>][DISPLAY <aDisp>] => ;
          <item> := ViewModal(<var> [, <{block}> ][, <aDisp>])

//% 001 These are the items to be released in Version 1.1

#xcommand for <x> := <nStart> up to <nEnd> [step <value>] => ;
          for <x> := <nStart> to <nEnd> [step <value>]

#xcommand FOR <x> := <nStart> DOWN TO <nEnd> STEP <value> => ;
          for <x> := <nStart> to <nEnd> step (-1 * <value>)

#xcommand FOR <x> := <nStart> DOWN TO <nEnd> => ;
          for <x> := <nStart> to <nEnd> step -1

#xcommand FOR <x> = <*rest*> => for <x> := <rest>

#xcommand @ <row>, <col> [SAY <xpr> [PICTURE <pic>] [COLOR <color>]] ;
       => DevPos( <row>, <col> )                                     ;
         [; DevOutPict( <xpr>, <pic>, <color> )]

#xcommand @ <row>, <col> [ SAY <exp> [COLOR <color>] ] => ;
          devpos( <row>, <col> ) ;
          [; devout( <exp>, <color> ) ]

#xcommand local <exp,...> as int     => local <exp>
#xcommand local <exp,...> as char    => local <exp>
#xcommand local <exp,...> as double  => local <exp>
#xcommand local <exp,...> as date    => local <exp>
#xcommand local <exp,...> as logical => local <exp>
#xcommand local <exp,...> as float   => local <exp>
#xcommand local <exp,...> as array   => local <exp>
#xcommand local <exp,...> as block   => local <exp>
#xcommand local <exp,...> as object  => local <exp>
#xcommand local <exp,...> as glob    => local <exp>

#xcommand static <exp,...> as int     => static <exp>
#xcommand static <exp,...> as char    => static <exp>
#xcommand static <exp,...> as double  => static <exp>
#xcommand static <exp,...> as date    => static <exp>
#xcommand static <exp,...> as logical => static <exp>
#xcommand static <exp,...> as float   => static <exp>
#xcommand static <exp,...> as array   => static <exp>
#xcommand static <exp,...> as block   => static <exp>
#xcommand static <exp,...> as object  => static <exp>
#xcommand static <exp,...> as glob    => static <exp>

#xcommand private <exp,...> as int     => private <exp>
#xcommand private <exp,...> as char    => private <exp>
#xcommand private <exp,...> as double  => private <exp>
#xcommand private <exp,...> as date    => private <exp>
#xcommand private <exp,...> as logical => private <exp>
#xcommand private <exp,...> as float   => private <exp>
```

```
#xcommand private <exp,...> as array   => private <exp>
#xcommand private <exp,...> as block   => private <exp>
#xcommand private <exp,...> as object  => private <exp>
#xcommand private <exp,...> as glob    => private <exp>

#xcommand public <exp,...> as int      => public <exp>
#xcommand public <exp,...> as char     => public <exp>
#xcommand public <exp,...> as double   => public <exp>
#xcommand public <exp,...> as date     => public <exp>
#xcommand public <exp,...> as logical  => public <exp>
#xcommand public <exp,...> as float    => public <exp>
#xcommand public <exp,...> as array    => public <exp>
#xcommand public <exp,...> as block    => public <exp>
#xcommand public <exp,...> as object   => public <exp>
#xcommand public <exp,...> as glob     => public <exp>

#xcommand global <exp,...> => public <*exp*>
#xcommand memvar <exp,...> as <*stuff*> => memvar <exp>

#xcommand SET <var> WITHIN <bottom> TO <top> BASE <value> => ;
          if !(<var> >= <bottom> .and. <var> <= <top> ) ;;
             <var> := <value> ;;
          endif

#xcommand REPLACE [ <f1> WITH <x1> [, <fn> WITH <xn> ] ] [FOR <for>] ;
          [WHILE <while>] [NEXT <next>] [RECORD <rec>] [<rest:REST>] ;
          [<stay: STAY PUT>] [ALL] => ;
  DBNetEval( {|| _FIELD-><f1> := <x1> [, _FIELD-><fn> := <xn>]}, ;
             <{for}>, <{while}>, <next>, <rec>, <.rest.>, <.stay.> )

#xcommand REPLACE <f1> WITH <v1> [, <fN> WITH <vN> ] => ;
  _FIELD-><f1> := <v1> [; _FIELD-><fN> := <vN>]

#xcommand COUNT [TO <var>] [FOR <for>] [WHILE <while>] [NEXT <next>] ;
          [RECORD <rec>] [<rest:REST>] [<stay:STAY PUT>] [ALL] =>    ;
  <var> := 0 ;;
    DBNetEval( {|| <var> := <var> + 1}, ;
             <{for}>, <{while}>, <next>, <rec>, <.rest.>, <.stay.>)

#xcommand SUM [ <x1> [, <xn>]  TO  <v1> [, <vn>] ] [FOR <for>] ;
          [WHILE <while>] [NEXT <next>] [RECORD <rec>] [<rest:REST>] ;
          [<stay:STAY PUT>] [ALL] => ;
  <v1> := [ <vn> := ] 0 ;;
    DBNetEval( {|| <v1> := <v1> + <x1> [, <vn> := <vn> + <xn> ]}, ;
             <{for}>, <{while}>, <next>, <rec>, <.rest.>, <.stay.> )

#xcommand AVERAGE [ <x1> [, <xn>] TO  <v1> [, <vn>] ] [FOR <for>] ;
          [WHILE <while>] [NEXT <next>] [RECORD <rec>] [<rest:REST>] ;
          [<stay:STAY PUT>] [ALL] => ;
  M->__Avg := <v1> := [ <vn> := ] 0 ;;
    DBNetEval( {|| M->__Avg := M->__Avg + 1, ;
               <v1> := <v1> + <x1> [, <vn> := <vn> + <xn>] }, ;
             <{for}>, <{while}>, <next>, <rec>, <.rest.>, <.stay.> ) ;;
  <v1> := <v1> / M->__Avg [; <vn> := <vn> / M->__Avg ]

#xcommand DELETE [FOR <for>] [WHILE <while>] [NEXT <next>] [RECORD <rec>] ;
          [<rest:REST>] [<stay:STAY PUT>] [ALL] =>  ;
    DBNetEval( {|| dbDelete()}, ;
             <{for}>, <{while}>, <next>, <rec>, <.rest.>, <.stay.> )
```

```
#xcommand RECALL [FOR <for>] [WHILE <while>] [NEXT <next>] [RECORD <rec>] ;
         [<rest:REST>] [<stay:STAY PUT>] [ALL] =>  ;
  DBNetEval( {|| dbRecall()}, ;
           <{for}>, <{while}>, <next>, <rec>, <.rest.>, <.stay.> )

#xcommand DELETE                  =>   dbDelete()
#xcommand RECALL                  =>   dbRecall()

// End of File
```

A number of changes have been made to PTVERBS.CH since the original publication of *Clipper 5.2 Power Tools*. Many of these enhancements have centered on the introduction of syntax—like variable typing or the FOR...UP TO and FOR...DOWN TO statements—that is expected to be appear in a Windows-based version of Clipper known as CA-Visual Objects for Clipper.

In the version of PTVERBS.CH published in *Clipper 5.2 Power Tools*, a number of commands appeared that translated the standard Clipper WAIT command into a call to the Power Tools WaitKey( ) function. These included the following #xcommand directives:

```
#xcommand WAIT [<c>]                      => WaitKey( <c>, .t. )
#xcommand WAIT [<c>] TO <var>             => WaitKey( <c>, .t.,,, @<var>, <(var)> )
#xcommand WAIT AT <row>, <col> [<c>]      => WaitKey( <c>, .t.,<row>, <col> )
#xcommand WAIT AT <row>,<col> [<c>] TO <var> => WaitKey( <c>, .t.,<row>, <col>, @<var>,
<(var)> )
```

Because the net effect of this directive is to replace the Clipper WAIT command, which is defined in STD.CH, with the Power Tools WaitKey( ) function, these lines have been modifed as follows for this book:

```
#xcommand WAITKEY [<c>]                      => WaitKey( <c>, .t. )
#xcommand WAITKEY [<c>] TO <var>             => WaitKey( <c>, .t.,,, @<var>, <(var)> )
#xcommand WAITKEY AT <row>, <col> [<c>]      => WaitKey( <c>, .t.,<row>, <col> )
#xcommand WAITKEY AT <row>,<col> [<c>] TO <var> => WaitKey( <c>,.t.,<row>,<col>,
@<var>,<(var)>)
```

Those who already own the Power Tools library and prefer the enhancements offered by WaitKey( ), however, should leave these lines of code in the original version of PTFUNCS.CH intact.

In addition, the following commands and statements have been added to PTVERBS.CH:

FOR...UP TO
FOR...DOWN TO
LOCAL...AS INT
LOCAL...AS CHAR
LOCAL...AS DOUBLE
LOCAL...AS DATE
LOCAL...AS LOGICAL
LOCAL...AS FLOAT
LOCAL...AS ARRAY
LOCAL...AS BLOCK
LOCAL...AS OBJECT

LOCAL...AS GLOB
STATIC...AS INT
STATIC...AS CHAR
STATIC...AS DOUBLE
STATIC...AS DATE
STATIC...AS LOGICAL
STATIC...AS FLOAT
STATIC...AS ARRAY
STATIC...AS BLOCK
STATIC...AS OBJECT
STATIC...AS GLOB
PRIVATE...AS INT
PRIVATE...AS CHAR
PRIVATE...AS DOUBLE
PRIVATE...AS DATE
PRIVATE...AS LOGICAL
PRIVATE...AS FLOAT
PRIVATE...AS ARRAY
PRIVATE...AS BLOCK
PRIVATE...AS OBJECT
PRIVATE...AS GLOB
PUBLIC...AS INT
PUBLIC...AS CHAR
PUBLIC...AS DOUBLE
PUBLIC...AS DATE
PUBLIC...AS LOGICAL
PUBLIC...AS FLOAT
PUBLIC...AS ARRAY
PUBLIC...AS BLOCK
PUBLIC...AS OBJECT
PUBLIC...AS GLOB
GLOBAL
MEMVAR...AS
SET...WITHIN...TO...BASE

Finally, enhanced versions of a number of standard Clipper commands are included. These include:

REPLACE
COUNT TO
SUM
AVERAGE
DELETE
RECALL

## PTLOWLVL.CH

Originally called LOWLEVEL.CH, this header file is not found in the original Clipper 5.2 Power Tools Library. It contains translations that make Clipper's low-level file functions easier to use.

```
/*            Name:  PTLowLvl.ch
            Author:  Steve Straley
            Notice:  Copyright(c) 1991-1993  - Sirius Software Development, Inc.
                     All Rights Reserved     - 415-399-9810
              Date:  July 1, 1991
           Compile:  N/A
           Version:  Clipper 5.3
      Include Path:  \PTools\Include
       Environment:  f051;
              Link:  N/A
      Library Path:  \Clipper\52
              Note:  This is the header file for the Clipper Power Tools
                     Library for all low-level file functions
*/
#stdout Using PTLowLvl.ch

#define pSEEK_BOF                   0           // FSEEK( handle, 0, bytes )
#define pSEEK_CURRENT               1           // FSEEK( handle, 1, bytes )
#define pSEEK_EOF                   2           // FSEEK( handle, 2, bytes )

#define pOPEN_READ                  0           // FOPEN( file, 0 )
#define pOPEN_WRITE                 1           // FSEEK( file, 1 )
#define pOPEN_READWRITE             2           // FSEEK( file, 2 )

#define pOPEN_EXCLUSIVE_READ        16          // FOPEN( file, 16 )
#define pOPEN_EXCLUSIVE_WRITE       17          // FOPEN( file, 17 )
#define pOPEN_EXCLUSIVE_READWRITE   18          // FOPEN( file, 18 )

#define pOPEN_NOWRITE_READ          32          // FOPEN( file, 32 )
#define pOPEN_NOWRITE_WRITE         33          // FOPEN( file, 33 )
#define pOPEN_NOWRITE_READWRITE     34          // FOPEN( file, 34 )

#define pOPEN_NOREAD_READ           48          // FOPEN( file, 48 )
#define pOPEN_NOREAD_WRITE          49          // FOPEN( file, 49 )
#define pOPEN_NOREAD_READWRITE      50          // FOPEN( file, 50 )

#define pOPEN_SHARED_READ           64          // FOPEN( file, 64 )
#define pOPEN_SHARED_WRITE          65          // FOPEN( file, 65 )
#define pOPEN_SHARED_READWRITE      66          // FOPEN( file, 66 )

#define pCREATE_READWRITE           0           // FCREATE( file, 0 )
#define pCREATE_READ                1           // FCREATE( file, 1 )
#define pCREATE_SHARED_WRITE        2           // FCREATE( file, 2 )
#define pCREATE_SHARED_READWRITE    4           // FCREATE( file, 4 )

* End of File
```

The following files are not a part of *Clipper 5.2 Power Tools*. They are carried over from the last version of this book and used strictly for the sake of backward compatibility.

## WORDS.CH

```
* File:     Words.ch

#xtranslate PRE-INCREMENT <n>          => ++<n>
#xtranslate POST-INCREMENT <n>         => <n>++
#xtranslate PRE-DECREMENT <n>          => --<n>
#xtranslate POST-DECREMENT <n>         => <n>--
#xtranslate ADD <n> TO <y>             => <y>+=<n>
#xtranslate SUBTRACT <n> FROM <y>      => <y>-=<n>
#xtranslate MULTIPLY <n> TO <y>        => <y>*=<n>
#xtranslate DIVIDE <n> FROM <y>        => <y>/=<n>
#xtranslate REMAINDER <n> OF <y>       => IF(<n> = 0, 0, <y>%=<n>)
#xtranslate RAISE <y> TO POWER OF <n>  => <y>^=<n>
#xtranslate WHAT IS <n,...>            => Qout( <n> )

// End of File: Words.ch
```

## MOREDEFS.INC

```
* File:     Moredefs.inc

#include "newdefs.inc"

// First the extra definitions

#define pF10 -9
#define pBLACK N
#define pWHITE W
#define pBLUE B

#xtranslate ABORTED() => (lastkey() == 27)
#xtranslate COLOR( <exp,...> ) => (#<exp>)

// End of File: Moredefs.inc
```

## NEWDEFS.INC

```
* File:     Newdefs.inc

#define pESC 27

#xtranslate PAUSE() => ( qout("Press any key..."), inkey(0) )

memvar getlist    // In case any GET is used!

// End of File: Newdefs.inc
```

## SIRIUS.INC

```
// The standard 5 header files that are typically used by Sirius
// Software Development.

#include "PTInkey.ch"   // Deals with all of the ASCII values of keys
#include "PTFuncs.ch"   // Contains the standard Pseudofunctions
#include "PTVerbs.ch"   // Contains the standard command set
#include "PTValue.ch"   // Holds general values
#include "PTColor.ch"   // Deals with all of the color codes

// End of File: Sirius.inc
```

# Appendix 5

# ASCII Codes and the IBM Extended Character Set

| | | | | | | | | | | | |
|---|---|---|---|---|---|---|---|---|---|---|---|
| 0 | NUL | 1 | ☺ SOH | 2 | ☻ STX | 3 | ♥ ETX | 4 | ♦ EOT | 5 | ♣ ENQ |
| 6 | ♠ ACK | 7 | • BEL | 8 | ◘ BS | 9 | ○ HT | 10 | ◙ LF | 11 | ♂ VT |
| 12 | ♀ FF | 13 | ♪ CR | 14 | ♫ SO | 15 | ☼ SI | 16 | ► DLE | 17 | ◄ DC1 |
| 18 | ↕ DC2 | 19 | ‼ DC3 | 20 | ¶ DC4 | 21 | § NAK | 22 | ▬ SYN | 23 | ↨ ETB |
| 24 | ↑ CAN | 25 | ↓ EM | 26 | → SUB | 27 | ← ESC | 28 | ∟ FS | 29 | ↔ GS |
| 30 | ▲ RS | 31 | ▼ US | 32 | | 33 | ! | 34 | " | 35 | # |
| 36 | $ | 37 | % | 38 | & | 39 | ' | 40 | ( | 41 | ) |
| 42 | * | 43 | + | 44 | , | 45 | - | 46 | . | 47 | / |
| 48 | 0 | 49 | 1 | 50 | 2 | 51 | 3 | 52 | 4 | 53 | 5 |
| 54 | 6 | 55 | 7 | 56 | 8 | 57 | 9 | 58 | : | 59 | ; |
| 60 | < | 61 | = | 62 | > | 63 | ? | 64 | @ | 65 | A |
| 66 | B | 67 | C | 68 | D | 69 | E | 70 | F | 71 | G |
| 72 | H | 73 | I | 74 | J | 75 | K | 76 | L | 77 | M |
| 78 | N | 79 | O | 80 | P | 81 | Q | 82 | R | 83 | S |
| 84 | T | 85 | U | 86 | V | 87 | W | 88 | X | 89 | Y |
| 90 | Z | 91 | [ | 92 | \ | 93 | ] | 94 | ^ | 95 | _ |
| 96 | à | 97 | a | 98 | b | 99 | c | 100 | d | 101 | e |
| 102 | f | 103 | g | 104 | h | 105 | i | 106 | j | 107 | k |
| 108 | l | 109 | m | 110 | n | 111 | o | 112 | p | 113 | q |
| 114 | r | 115 | s | 116 | t | 117 | u | 118 | v | 119 | w |
| 120 | x | 121 | y | 122 | z | 123 | { | 124 | | | 125 | } |

*(continued)*

*(continued)*

| | | | | | | | | | |
|---|---|---|---|---|---|---|---|---|---|
| 126 | ~ | 127 | ⌂ | 128 | Ç | 129 | ü | 130 | é |
| 131 | â | 132 | ä | 133 | à | 134 | å | 135 | ç |
| 136 | ê | 137 | ë | 138 | è | 139 | ï | 140 | î |
| 141 | ì | 142 | Ä | 143 | Å | 144 | É | 145 | æ |
| 146 | Æ | 147 | ô | 148 | ö | 149 | ò | 150 | û |
| 151 | ù | 152 | ÿ | 153 | Ö | 154 | Ü | 155 | ¢ |
| 156 | £ | 157 | ¥ | 158 | ₧ | 159 | ƒ | 160 | á |
| 161 | í | 162 | ó | 163 | ú | 164 | ñ | 165 | Ñ |
| 166 | ª | 167 | º | 168 | ¿ | 169 | ⌐ | 170 | ¬ |
| 171 | ½ | 172 | ¼ | 173 | ¡ | 174 | « | 176 | ░ |
| 177 | ▒ | 178 | ▓ | 179 | │ | 180 | ┤ | 181 | ╡ |
| 182 | ╢ | 183 | ╖ | 184 | ╕ | 185 | ╣ | 186 | ║ |
| 187 | ╗ | 188 | ╝ | 189 | ╜ | 190 | ╛ | 191 | ┐ |
| 192 | └ | 193 | ┴ | 194 | ┬ | 195 | ├ | 196 | ─ |
| 197 | ┼ | 198 | ╞ | 199 | ╟ | 200 | ╚ | 201 | ╔ |
| 202 | ╩ | 203 | ╦ | 204 | ╠ | 205 | ═ | 206 | ╬ |
| 207 | ╧ | 208 | ╨ | 209 | ╤ | 210 | ╥ | 211 | ╙ |
| 212 | ╘ | 213 | ╒ | 214 | ╓ | 215 | ╫ | 216 | ╪ |
| 217 | ┘ | 218 | ┌ | 219 | █ | 220 | ▄ | 221 | ▌ |
| 222 | ▐ | 223 | ▀ | 224 | α | 225 | β | 226 | Γ |
| 227 | π | 228 | Σ | 229 | σ | 230 | μ | 231 | τ |
| 232 | Φ | 233 | Θ | 234 | Ω | 235 | δ | 236 | ∞ |
| 237 | φ | 238 | ε | 239 | ∩ | 240 | ≡ | 241 | ± |
| 242 | ≥ | 243 | ≤ | 244 | ⌠ | 245 | ⌡ | 246 | ÷ |
| 247 | ≈ | 248 | ° | 249 | · | 250 | • | 251 | √ |
| 252 | ⁿ | 253 | ² | 254 | ■ | 255 | NULL | | |

# INKEY() Chart

The INKEY( ) chart is made up of the ASCII characters listed above, plus some special key values. Below is a list of those function, directional, and control keys along with their ASCII values.

## SPECIAL KEYS

| | | | | |
|---|---|---|---|---|
| F1 | 28 | Left Arrow | 19 |
| F2 | -1 | Right Arrow | 4 |
| F3 | -2 | Home | 1 |

## SPECIAL KEYS *(continued)*

| | | | |
|---|---|---|---|
| F4 | -3 | End | 6 |
| F5 | -4 | PgUp | 18 |
| F6 | -5 | PgDn | 3 |
| F7 | -6 | EOF Character | 26 |
| F8 | -7 | Reform | 2 |
| F9 | -8 | Esc | 27 |
| F10 | -9 | Enter | 13 |
| F11 | -40 | Tab | 9 |
| F12 | -41 | Backspace | 8 |
| Up Arrow | 5 | Del | 7 |
| Down Arrow | 24 | Ins | 22 |

## CONTROL KEYS

| | | | | | |
|---|---|---|---|---|---|
| Ctrl-A | 1 | Ctrl-T | 20 | Ctrl-- (white) | 31 |
| Ctrl-B | 2 | Ctrl-U | 21 | Ctrl-- (gray) | 398 |
| Ctrl-C | 3 | Ctrl-V | 22 | Ctrl-+ (gray) | 400 |
| Ctrl-D | 4 | Ctrl-W | 23 | Ctrl-5 (gray) | 399 |
| Ctrl-E | 5 | Ctrl-X | 24 | Ctrl-\ | 28 |
| Ctrl-F | 6 | Ctrl-Y | 25 | Ctrl-[ | 27 |
| Ctrl-G | 7 | Ctrl-Z | 26 | Ctrl-] | 29 |
| Ctrl-I | 8 | Ctrl-F1 | -20 | Ctrl-Tab | 404 |
| Ctrl-H | 9 | Ctrl-F2 | -21 | Ctrl-Backspace | 127 |
| Ctrl-J | 10 | Ctrl-F3 | -22 | Ctrl-Prtsc | 406 |
| Ctrl-K | 11 | Ctrl-F4 | -23 | Ctrl-Left Arrow | 26 |
| Ctrl-L | 12 | Ctrl-F5 | -24 | Ctrl-Right Arrow | 2 |
| Ctrl-M | 13 | Ctrl-F6 | -25 | Ctrl-Home | 29 |
| Ctrl-N | 14 | Ctrl-F7 | -26 | Ctrl-End | 23 |
| Ctrl-O | 15 | Ctrl-F8 | -27 | Ctrl-PgUp | 31 |
| Ctrl-P | 16 | Ctrl-F9 | -28 | Ctrl-PgDn | 30 |
| Ctrl-Q | 17 | Ctrl-F10 | -29 | Ctrl-Enter | 10 |
| Ctrl-R | 18 | Ctrl-F11 | -44 | | |
| Ctrl-S | 19 | Ctrl-F12 | -45 | | |

## SHIFT KEYS

| | | | | | |
|---|---|---|---|---|---|
| Shift-Tab | 271 | Shift-F5 | -14 | Shift-F10 | -19 |
| Shift-F1 | -10 | Shift-F6 | -15 | Shift-F11 | -42 |
| Shift-F2 | -11 | Shift-F7 | -16 | Shift-F12 | -43 |
| Shift-F3 | -12 | Shift-F8 | -17 | | |
| Shift-F4 | -13 | Shift-F9 | -18 | | |

## ALT KEYS

| | | | | | |
|---|---|---|---|---|---|
| Alt-A | 286 | Alt-U | 278 | Alt-- (gray) | 330 |
| Alt-B | 304 | Alt-V | 303 | Alt-+ (gray) | 334 |
| Alt-E | 274 | Alt-W | 273 | Alt-* (gray) | 311 |
| Alt-F | 289 | Alt-X | 301 | Alt-- (white) | 386 |
| Alt-G | 290 | Alt-Y | 277 | Alt-= | 387 |
| Alt-H | 291 | Alt-Z | 301 | Alt-1 | 376 |
| Alt-I | 279 | Alt-F1 | -30 | Alt-2 | 377 |
| Alt-J | 292 | Alt-F2 | -31 | Alt-3 | 378 |
| Alt-K | 293 | Alt-F3 | -32 | Alt-4 | 379 |
| Alt-L | 294 | Alt-F4 | -33 | Alt-5 | 380 |
| Alt-M | 306 | Alt-F5 | -34 | Alt-6 | 381 |
| Alt-N | 305 | Alt-F6 | -35 | Alt-7 | 382 |
| Alt-O | 280 | Alt-F7 | -36 | Alt-8 | 383 |
| Alt-P | 281 | Alt-F8 | -37 | Alt-9 | 384 |
| Alt-Q | 272 | Alt-F9 | -38 | Alt-0 | 385 |
| Alt-R | 275 | Alt-F10 | -39 | Alt-\ | 299 |
| Alt-S | 287 | Alt-F11 | -46 | Alt-[ | 282 |
| Alt-T | 276 | Alt-F12 | -47 | Alt-] | 283 |
| Alt-ESC | 257 | Alt-. | 308 | Alt-/ | 309 |
| Alt-à | 297 | Alt-, | 307 | Alt-D | 288 |
| Alt-C | 302 | | | | |

# Appendix 6

# *Color Tables*

The following table is a generic listing of the colors and their associated color codes used in Clipper 5.2 for a color monitor. For more detail on the use of these codes in Clipper commands and functions, see the sections on SETCOLOR( ) in the function reference and SET COLOR TO in the command reference.

| Color | Letter | Number |
| --- | --- | --- |
| Black | U,N or " " | 0 |
| Blue | B | 1 |
| Green | G | 2 |
| Cyan | BG | 3 |
| Red | R | 4 |
| Magenta | RB | 5 |
| Brown | GR | 6 |
| White | W | 7 |
| Gray | N+ | 8 |
| Bright Blue | B+ | 9 |
| Bright Green | G+ | 10 |
| Bright Cyan | BG+ | 11 |
| Bright Red | R+ | 12 |
| Bright Magenta | RB+ | 13 |
| Yellow | GR+ | 14 |
| Bright White | W+ | 15 |
| Inverse | I | |
| Blank | X | |

The following table is for a monochrome monitor.

| Color | Letter | Number |
|---|---|---|
| Black | N,N+ or " " | 0, 8 |
| Underline | U,B | 1 |
| White | W | 7 |
| Bright Underline | B+ | 9 |
| Bright White | W+ | 15 |
| Inverse | I | |
| Blank | X | |

Following is a table of numeric attribute values and their corresponding color values if called with the user-defined function SetColor(*cString*) found in this book.

| Attribute Byte | Letters | / | Background |
|---|---|---|---|
| 0 | Black | / | Black |
| 1 | Blue | / | Black |
| 2 | Green | / | Black |
| 3 | Cyan | / | Black |
| 4 | Red | / | Black |
| 5 | Magenta | / | Black |
| 6 | Brown | / | Black |
| 7 | White | / | Black |
| 8 | Gray | / | Black |
| 9 | Bright Blue | / | Black |
| 10 | Bright Green | / | Black |
| 11 | Bright Cyan | / | Black |
| 12 | Bright Red | / | Black |
| 13 | Bright Magenta | / | Black |
| 14 | Yellow | / | Black |
| 15 | Bright White | / | Black |
| 16 | Black | / | Blue |
| 17 | Blue | / | Blue |
| 18 | Green | / | Blue |
| 19 | Cyan | / | Blue |
| 20 | Red | / | Blue |
| 21 | Magenta | / | Blue |
| 22 | Brown | / | Blue |
| 23 | White | / | Blue |

| Attribute Byte | Letters | / | Background |
|---|---|---|---|
| 24 | Gray | / | Blue |
| 25 | Bright Blue | / | Blue |
| 26 | Bright Green | / | Blue |
| 27 | Bright Cyan | / | Blue |
| 28 | Bright Red | / | Blue |
| 29 | Bright Magenta | / | Blue |
| 30 | Yellow | / | Blue |
| 31 | Bright White | / | Blue |
| 32 | Black | / | Green |
| 33 | Blue | / | Green |
| 34 | Green | / | Green |
| 35 | Cyan | / | Green |
| 36 | Red | / | Green |
| 37 | Magenta | / | Green |
| 38 | Brown | / | Green |
| 39 | White | / | Green |
| 40 | Gray | / | Green |
| 41 | Bright Blue | / | Green |
| 42 | Bright Green | / | Green |
| 43 | Bright Cyan | / | Green |
| 44 | Bright Red | / | Green |
| 45 | Bright Magenta | / | Green |
| 46 | Yellow | / | Green |
| 47 | Bright White | / | Green |
| 48 | Black | / | Cyan |
| 49 | Blue | / | Cyan |
| 50 | Green | / | Cyan |
| 51 | Cyan | / | Cyan |
| 52 | Red | / | Cyan |
| 53 | Magenta | / | Cyan |
| 54 | Brown | / | Cyan |
| 55 | White | / | Cyan |
| 56 | Gray | / | Cyan |
| 57 | Bright Blue | / | Cyan |
| 58 | Bright Green | / | Cyan |
| 59 | Bright Cyan | / | Cyan |
| 60 | Bright Red | / | Cyan |

*(continued)*

*(continued)*

| Attribute Byte | Letters | / | Background |
|---|---|---|---|
| 61 | Bright Magenta | / | Cyan |
| 62 | Yellow | / | Cyan |
| 63 | Bright White | / | Cyan |
| 64 | Black | / | Red |
| 65 | Blue | / | Red |
| 66 | Green | / | Red |
| 67 | Cyan | / | Red |
| 68 | Red | / | Red |
| 69 | Magenta | / | Red |
| 70 | Brown | / | Red |
| 71 | White | / | Red |
| 72 | Gray | / | Red |
| 73 | Bright Blue | / | Red |
| 74 | Bright Green | / | Red |
| 75 | Bright Cyan | / | Red |
| 76 | Bright Red | / | Red |
| 77 | Bright Magenta | / | Red |
| 78 | Yellow | / | Red |
| 79 | Bright White | / | Red |
| 80 | Black | / | Magenta |
| 81 | Blue | / | Magenta |
| 82 | Green | / | Magenta |
| 83 | Cyan | / | Magenta |
| 84 | Red | / | Magenta |
| 85 | Magenta | / | Magenta |
| 86 | Brown | / | Magenta |
| 87 | White | / | Magenta |
| 88 | Gray | / | Magenta |
| 89 | Bright Blue | / | Magenta |
| 90 | Bright Green | / | Magenta |
| 91 | Bright Cyan | / | Magenta |
| 92 | Bright Red | / | Magenta |
| 93 | Bright Magenta | / | Magenta |
| 94 | Yellow | / | Magenta |
| 95 | Bright White | / | Magenta |
| 96 | Black | / | Brown |
| 97 | Blue | / | Brown |

| Attribute Byte | Letters | / | Background |
|---|---|---|---|
| 98 | Green | / | Brown |
| 99 | Cyan | / | Brown |
| 100 | Red | / | Brown |
| 101 | Magenta | / | Brown |
| 102 | Brown | / | Brown |
| 103 | White | / | Brown |
| 104 | Gray | / | Brown |
| 105 | Bright Blue | / | Brown |
| 106 | Bright Green | / | Brown |
| 107 | Bright Cyan | / | Brown |
| 108 | Bright Red | / | Brown |
| 109 | Bright Magenta | / | Brown |
| 110 | Yellow | / | Brown |
| 111 | Bright White | / | Brown |
| 112 | Black | / | White |
| 113 | Blue | / | White |
| 114 | Green | / | White |
| 115 | Cyan | / | White |
| 116 | Red | / | White |
| 117 | Magenta | / | White |
| 118 | Brown | / | White |
| 119 | White | / | White |
| 120 | Gray | / | White |
| 121 | Bright Blue | / | White |
| 122 | Bright Green | / | White |
| 123 | Bright Cyan | / | White |
| 124 | Bright Red | / | White |
| 125 | Bright Magenta | / | White |
| 126 | Yellow | / | White |
| 127 | Bright White | / | White |

Use the same values followed by "*" to get the same color pair but in flashing letters.

# Appendix 7

# Table of Tones

Following is a table of the values that, if passed to the TONE( ) function, will generate a specific common sound. The second parameter is duration. The value of 18, used in this table, represents one full second of sound.

| Common Note | | Tone( ) Call |
|---|---|---|
| Low | C | TONE( 130.80,18 ) |
| | C# | TONE( 138.60,18 ) |
| | D | TONE( 146.80,18 ) |
| | D# | TONE( 155.60,18 ) |
| | E | TONE( 164.80,18 ) |
| | F | TONE( 174.60,18 ) |
| | F# | TONE( 185.00,18 ) |
| | G | TONE( 196.00,18 ) |
| | G# | TONE( 207.70,18 ) |
| | A | TONE( 220.00,18 ) |
| | A# | TONE( 233.10,18 ) |
| | B | TONE( 246.90,18 ) |
| Mid | C | TONE( 261.70,18 ) |
| | C# | TONE( 277.20,18 ) |
| | D | TONE( 293.70,18 ) |
| | D# | TONE( 311.10,18 ) |
| | E | TONE( 329.60,18 ) |
| | F | TONE( 349.20,18 ) |

*(continued)*

*(continued)*

| Common Note | | Tone( ) Call |
|---|---|---|
| Mid | F# | TONE( 370.00,18 ) |
| | G | TONE( 392.00,18 ) |
| | G# | TONE( 415.30,18 ) |
| | A | TONE( 440.00,18 ) |
| | A# | TONE( 466.20,18 ) |
| | B | TONE( 493.90,18 ) |
| High | C | TONE( 523.30,18 ) |

# Appendix 8

# *DOS Error Messages*

Following is a list of DOS error numbers and their meanings. Those numbers that are not listed are reserved for the operating system.

| | |
|---|---|
| 1 | Invalid function number |
| 2 | File not found |
| 3 | Path not found |
| 4 | Too many open files |
| 5 | File access denied |
| 6 | Invalid file handle |
| 7 | Memory control blocks destroyed |
| 8 | Insufficient memory |
| 9 | Invalid memory block address |
| 10 | Invalid environment |
| 11 | Invalid format |
| 12 | Invalid access code |
| 13 | Invalid data |
| 15 | Invalid drive specified |
| 16 | Attempt to remove the current directory |
| 17 | Not same device |
| 18 | No more files |
| 19 | Attempt made to write on a write-protected disk |
| 20 | Unknown unit |
| 21 | Drive not ready |
| 22 | Unknown command |
| 23 | Data error (CRC) |
| 24 | Bad request structure length |

*(continued)*

| | |
|---|---|
| 25 | Seek error |
| 26 | Unknown media type |
| 27 | Sector not found |
| 28 | Printer out of paper |
| 29 | Write fault error |
| 30 | Read fault error |
| 31 | General failure |
| 32 | Sharing violation |
| 33 | Lock violation |
| 34 | Invalid disk change |
| 35 | FCB unavailable |
| 36 | Sharing buffer overflow |
| 50 | Network request not supported |
| 51 | Remote computer not responding |
| 52 | Duplicate name on network |
| 53 | Network name not found |
| 54 | Network is busy |
| 55 | Network device no longer present |
| 56 | Network BIOS command limit exceeded |
| 57 | Network adapter hardware error |
| 58 | Incorrect response from network |
| 59 | Unexpected network error |
| 60 | Incompatible remote adapter |
| 61 | Print queue full |
| 62 | Not enough space for print file |
| 63 | Print file deleted (lack of space) |
| 64 | Network name deleted |
| 65 | Access denied |
| 66 | Network device type incorrect |
| 67 | Network name not found |
| 68 | Network name limit exceeded |
| 69 | Network BIOS session limit exceeded |
| 70 | Temporarily paused |
| 71 | Network request not accepted |
| 72 | Print or disk redirection paused |
| 80 | File already exists |
| 82 | Cannot make directory entry |
| 83 | Fail on INT 24H |
| 84 | Too many redirections |
| 85 | Duplicate redirection |
| 86 | Invalid password |
| 87 | Invalid parameter |
| 88 | Network device fault |

# Appendix 9

# Warning and Error Messages

## Compiler Warning Messages

| | |
|---|---|
| C1001 | Returns statement with no value in function |
| C1002 | Procedure returns a value |
| C1003 | Ambiguous variable reference |
| C1004 | Ambiguous variable reference, assuming MEMVAR |
| C1005 | Redefinition or duplicate definition of #define |
| C1007 | Function does not end with RETURN |

## Compiler Error Messages

| | |
|---|---|
| C2001 | Syntax error |
| C2002 | Statement unterminated at end of line |
| C2003 | Syntax error in statement |
| C2004 | Illegal character |
| C2005 | Statement not recognized |
| C2006 | Statement not allowed outside procedure or function |
| C2007 | Unterminated string |
| C2009 | Invalid use of @ (pass-by-reference) operator |
| C2010 | Incorrect number of arguments |
| C2011 | EXIT statement with no loop in sight |
| C2012 | LOOP statement with no loop in sight |
| C2013 | EXIT statement violates enclosing SEQUENCE |
| C2014 | LOOP statement violates enclosing SEQUENCE |

*(continued)*

| | |
|---|---|
| C2015 | Illegal initializer |
| C2016 | Name conflicts with previous declaration |
| C2017 | Duplicate variable declaration |
| C2018 | Outer block variable out of reach |
| C2019 | CALL of CA-Clipper procedure or function |
| C2020 | Mistreatment of CALLed symbol |
| C2021 | Redefinition of CA-Clipper procedure or function |
| C2022 | Redefinition of predefined function |
| C2023 | CA-Clipper definition of CALLed symbol |
| C2024 | Unclosed control structures |
| C2025 | ELSE does not match IF |
| C2026 | ELSEIF does not match IF |
| C2027 | ENDIF does not match IF |
| C2028 | ENDDO does not match WHILE |
| C2029 | NEXT does not match FOR |
| C2030 | ENDCASE does not match DO CASE |
| C2031 | CASE or OTHERWISE is not immediately within DO CASE |
| C2032 | TEXT statement error |
| C2033 | Missing ENDTEXT |
| C2034 | Formal parameters already declared |
| C2035 | Invalid declaration |
| C2036 | Mayhem in CASE handler |
| C2037 | Invalid procedure name in DO statement |
| C2038 | Invalid target name in CALL statement |
| C2039 | Invalid selector in send |
| C2040 | Invalid unary in-line operator |
| C2041 | Invalid binary operator |
| C2042 | Invalid lvalue |
| C2043 | Invalid alias expression |
| C2044 | Invalid function name |
| C2045 | Target name was used previously in non-CALL context |
| C2046 | SEQUENCE nesting error |
| C2047 | GET contains complex macro |
| C2048 | GET contains both macro and declared symbol references |
| C2049 | Code block contains complex macro |
| C2050 | Code block contains both macro and declared symbol references |
| C2051 | LOCAL declaration follows executable statement |
| C2052 | MEMVAR declaration follows executable statement |
| C2053 | FIELD declaration follows executable statement |
| C2054 | STATIC declaration follows executable statement |
| C2055 | Syntax error in #define |
| C2056 | Unexpected end of file in #define |

| | |
|---|---|
| C2057 | Label missing in #define |
| C2058 | Comma or right parenthesis missing in #define |
| C2059 | Missing => in #translate/#command |
| C2060 | Unknown result marker in #translate/#command |
| C2061 | Label error in #translate/#command |
| C2062 | Bad match marker in #translate/#command |
| C2063 | Bad result marker in #translate/#command |
| C2064 | Bad restricted match marker in #translate/#command |
| C2065 | Empty optional clause in #translate/#command |
| C2066 | Unclosed optional clause in #translate/#command |
| C2067 | Too many nested #ifdefs |
| C2068 | Error in #ifdef |
| C2069 | #endif does not match #ifdef |
| C2070 | #else does not match #ifdef |
| C2071 | Error in #undef |
| C2072 | Ambiguous match pattern in #translate/#command |
| C2073 | Result pattern contains nested clauses in #translate/#command |
| C2074 | Error message displayed by #error |
| C2075 | Too many locals |
| C2076 | Too many parameters |
| C2077 | Too many parameters |
| C2078 | Circular #define |
| C2079 | Circular #translate/#command |
| C2086 | RETURN violates enclosing SEQUENCE |

## Compiler Fatal Error Messages

| | |
|---|---|
| C3001 | Out of memory |
| C3002 | Input buffer overflow |
| C3003 | Can't open intermediate file |
| C3004 | Bad command line option |
| C3005 | Bad command line parameter |
| C3006 | Can't create preprocessed output file |
| C3007 | Can't open #include file |
| C3008 | Bad filename in #include |
| C3009 | Too many nested #includes |
| C3010 | Invalid name follows # |
| C3011 | Can't open standard rule file |
| C3012 | Too many standard rules |
| C3013 | Expression stack overflow |
| C3014 | Expression stack underflow |

*(continued)*

| | |
|---|---|
| C3015 | Control stack overflow |
| C3016 | Control stack underflow |
| C3017 | Error reading or opening script file |
| C3018 | Too many symbols |
| C3019 | Too many publics |
| C3020 | Too many segments |
| C3021 | Too many fixups |
| C3022 | Too many external references |
| C3023 | Too many labels |
| C3024 | Too many procs |
| C3025 | Too many proc requests |
| C3026 | Segment too big |
| C3027 | Proc too big |
| C3028 | Symbol table too big |
| C3029 | Write error to intermediate file |
| C3030 | Write error to OBJ |
| C3031 | Can't create OBJ |
| C3032 | Can't create intermediate file |
| C3039 | Phase error |
| C3040 | Unexpected end of intermediate file |

## .RTLink Warning Messages

| | |
|---|---|
| wrt0003 | Memory model mismatch in COMMENT record... |
| wrt0004 | Duplicate start address (using the first one we saw...) |
| wrt0005 | No Stack Segment |
| wrt0009 | Unrecognized map type '<char>' .... ignored |
| wrt0011 | Public symbol '<symbol>' redefined |
| wrt0012 | Prelinked Library symbol '<symbol>' redefined |
| wrt0014 | Cannot define linker reserved symbol '<symbol>'... |
| wrt0022 | .EXE may not execute properly—undefined symbols |
| wrt0031 | RTLUTILS.LIB is an automatically loaded reserved library |

## .RTLink Error Messages

| | |
|---|---|
| ert0004 | Duplicate stacks |
| ert0005 | Filename portion of output file '<filename>' too long... |
| ert0010 | Overlay Area Nesting Area |
| ert0011 | PRELOAD command must have active section |
| ert0013 | Input terminated with area left open |
| ert0014 | Overlays not supported in Prelinked Library |

| | |
|---|---|
| ert0015 | Bad format binary number '<number>' |
| ert0016 | Bad format octal number '<number>' |
| ert0017 | Bad format decimal number '<number>' |
| ert0018 | Bad format hexadecimal number '<number>' |
| ert0024 | Cannot open .RTLink configuration file '<filename>' |
| ert0025 | Cannot open script file '<filename>' |
| ert0026 | Output Name not specified or implied |
| ert0028 | Cannot find transfer file '<filename>' |
| ert0029 | Cannot open transfer file '<filename>' |
| ert0030 | Disallowed symbol '<symbol>' already loaded in .PLL... |
| ert0032 | User-level .PLL transferred to RTLink producing .PLL |
| ert0033 | Invalid format in transfer (.PLT) file '<filename>'... |
| ert0035 | Cannot find object file '<filename>' |
| ert0041 | Unrecognized option '<option>' |
| ert0044 | Illegal STACK size |
| ert0045 | Cannot create transfer file '<filename>' |
| ert0048 | Only one Output Name should be specified |
| ert0049 | Cannot create map file '<map>' |
| ert0052 | Attempt to load module defining symbol '<symbol>' |
| ert0054 | Cannot find library file '<library>' |
| ert0055 | Cannot seek within library dictionary |
| ert0056 | Read of random library table failed |
| ert0061 | Input/output error on output file <filename> |
| ert0066 | Write to map file <filename> failed |
| ert0067 | Not enough characters in command '<option>' to guarantee... |
| ert0077 | Cannot find startup code 'RTLINKST.COM' |
| ert0078 | Error reading RTLINKST.COM |
| ert0083 | Cannot find RTLINK.DAT (free-format parser data) |
| ert0084 | Cannot read RTLINK.DAT header (free-format parser data) |
| ert0085 | Free-format parser tables too big to fit in memory |
| ert0086 | Cannot read RTLINK.DAT data (free-format parser data) |
| ert0088 | Illegal information level <level> requested |
| ert0092 | Cannot find RTLINK.HLP |
| ert0097 | Invalid MAP flag <type> |
| ert0112 | Filename <filename> is more than <length> characters long |
| ert0166 | Wrong version of RTUTILS.LIB |

## .RTLink Miscellaneous Error Messages

| | |
|---|---|
| eut0003 | Not enough free memory |
| eut0006 | Need to swap but nothing is on the swap list |

*(continued)*

1156   Appendix 9

| eut0007 | Cannot open work file '<filename>' |
| eut0009 | Write of <number> chars to work file <filename> at position... |
| eut0015 | Write to buffered output file '<filename>' at position 0x... |
| eut0016 | Open of buffered output file '<filename>' failed |
| eut0019 | Bad format object or library file '<filename>' |
| eut0032 | Invalid Index 0x90 passed to get_block |
| eut0035 | Write to expanded (EMS) or extended (XMS) memory failed |

## Run-Time Error Messages

| BASE/1001 | Undefined function |
| BASE/1002 | Undefined alias |
| BASE/1003 | Undefined variable |
| BASE/1004 | No exported method |
| BASE/1005 | No exported variable |
| BASE/1065 | Argument error: & |
| BASE/1066 | Argument error: conditional |
| BASE/1067 | Argument error: array dimension |
| BASE/1068 | Argument error: array access |
| BASE/1069 | Argument error: array assign |
| BASE/1070 | Argument error: == |
| BASE/1071 | Argument error: = |
| BASE/1072 | Argument error: <> |
| BASE/1073 | Argument error: < |
| BASE/1074 | Argument error: <= |
| BASE/1075 | Argument error: > |
| BASE/1076 | Argument error: >= |
| BASE/1077 | Argument error: .NOT. |
| BASE/1078 | Argument error: .AND. |
| BASE/1079 | Argument error: .OR. |
| BASE/1080 | Argument error: - |
| BASE/1081 | Argument error: + |
| BASE/1082 | Argument error: - |
| BASE/1083 | Argument error: * |
| BASE/1084 | Argument error: / |
| BASE/1085 | Argument error: % |
| BASE/1086 | Argument error: ++ |
| BASE/1087 | Argument error: -- |
| BASE/1088 | Argument error: ^ |
| BASE/1089 | Argument error: ABS |
| BASE/1090 | Argument error: INT |

| | |
|---|---|
| BASE/1091 | Argument error: WORD |
| BASE/1092 | Argument error: MIN |
| BASE/1093 | Argument error: MAX |
| BASE/1094 | Argument error: ROUND |
| BASE/1095 | Argument error: LOG |
| BASE/1096 | Argument error: EXP |
| BASE/1097 | Argument error: SQRT |
| BASE/1098 | Argument error: VAL |
| BASE/1099 | Argument error: STR |
| BASE/1100 | Argument error: TRIM |
| BASE/1101 | Argument error: LTRIM |
| BASE/1102 | Argument error: UPPER |
| BASE/1103 | Argument error: LOWER |
| BASE/1104 | Argument error: CHR |
| BASE/1105 | Argument error: SPACE |
| BASE/1106 | Argument error: REPLICATE |
| BASE/1107 | Argument error: ASC |
| BASE/1108 | Argument error: AT |
| BASE/1109 | Argument error: $ |
| BASE/1110 | Argument error: SUBSTR |
| BASE/1111 | Argument error: LEN |
| BASE/1112 | Argument error: YEAR |
| BASE/1113 | Argument error: MONTH |
| BASE/1114 | Argument error: DAY |
| BASE/1115 | Argument error: DOW |
| BASE/1116 | Argument error: CMONTH |
| BASE/1117 | Argument error: CDOW |
| BASE/1118 | Argument error: DTOC |
| BASE/1119 | Argument error: CTOD |
| BASE/1120 | Argument error: DTOS |
| BASE/1121 | Argument error: TYPE |
| BASE/1122 | Argument error: TRANSFORM |
| BASE/1123 | Argument error: AADD |
| BASE/1124 | Argument error: LEFT |
| BASE/1131 | Bound error: array dimension |
| BASE/1132 | Bound error: array access |
| BASE/1133 | Bound error: array assign |
| BASE/1187 | Bound error: AADD |
| BASE/1209 | String overflow: + |
| BASE/1210 | String overflow: - |

*(continued)*

1158 Appendix 9

| BASE/1233 | String overflow: SPACE |
| BASE/1234 | String overflow: REPLICATE |
| BASE/1340 | Zero divisor: / |
| BASE/1341 | Zero divisor: % |
| BASE/1449 | Syntax error: & |
| BASE/1513 | Operation too complex: & |
| BASE/2005 | Open error (RESTORE command) |
| BASE/2006 | Create error (SAVE command) |
| BASE/2011 | Open error (TYPE command) |
| BASE/2012 | Open error (COPY FILE command) |
| BASE/2016 | Write error (COPY FILE command) |
| BASE/2017 | Argument error (AEVAL function) |
| BASE/2018 | Open error (DISKSPACE( ) function) |
| BASE/2020 | Argument error (SET( ) function) |
| BASE/5300 | Memory low |

## TERM Error Messages

| TERM/2013 | Create error (SET ALTERNATE command) |
| TERM/2014 | Create error (SET PRINTER command) |
| TERM/2015 | Open error (TO FILE clause) |

## DBFNTX Error Messages

| DBFNTX/1001 | Open error (.DBF) |
| DBFNTX/1002 | Open error (.DBT) |
| DBFNTX/1003 | Open error (index) |
| DBFNTX/1004 | Open error (creating .DBF) |
| DBFNTX/1005 | Open error (creating .DBT) |
| DBFNTX/1006 | Create error (creating index) |
| DBFNTX/1010 | Read error |
| DBFNTX/1011 | Write error |
| DBFNTX/1012 | Corruption detected |
| DBFNTX/1020 | Data type error |
| DBFNTX/1021 | Data width error |
| DBFNTX/1022 | Lock required |
| DBFNTX/1023 | Exclusive required |
| DBFNTX/1024 | Append lock failed |
| DBFNTX/1025 | Write not allowed |
| DBFNTX/1026 | Data width error |
| DBFNTX/1027 | Limit exceeded |

## DBFNDX Error Messages

| | | |
|---|---|---|
| DBFNDX/1001 | Open error (.DBF) |
| DBFNDX/1002 | Open error (.DBT) |
| DBFNDX/1003 | Open error (index) |
| DBFNDX/1004 | Open error (creating .DBF) |
| DBFNDX/1005 | Open error (creating .DBT) |
| DBFNDX/1006 | Create error (creating index) |
| DBFNDX/1010 | Read error |
| DBFNDX/1011 | Write error |
| DBFNDX/1012 | Corruption detected |
| DBFNDX/1020 | Data type error |
| DBFNDX/1021 | Data width error |
| DBFNDX/1022 | Lock required |
| DBFNDX/1023 | Exclusive required |
| DBFNDX/1024 | Append lock failed |
| DBFNDX/1025 | Write not allowed |
| DBFNDX/1026 | Data width error |
| DBFNDX/1027 | Limit exceeded |

## DBCMD Error Messages

| | |
|---|---|
| DBCMD/1001 | Argument error |
| DBCMD/1003 | Argument error |
| DBCMD/1004 | Argument error |
| DBCMD/1005 | Argument error |
| DBCMD/1006 | Argument error |
| DBCMD/1007 | Argument error |
| DBCMD/1008 | Argument error |
| DBCMD/1009 | Argument error |
| DBCMD/1010 | Illegal characters in alias |
| DBCMD/1011 | Alias already in use |
| DBCMD/1101 | Syntax error |
| DBCMD/2001 | Work area not in use |
| DBCMD/2019 | Argument error |

## Run-Time Unrecoverable Error Messages

| | |
|---|---|
| 24 | Write error |
| 331 | String/array memory overflow |
| 332 | String/array memory overflow |

*(continued)*

| | |
|---|---|
| 415 | Cannot open overlay file |
| 5302 | Conventional memory exhausted |
| 5304 | Conventional memory exhausted |
| 5306 | Conventional memory exhausted |
| 5312 | Conventional memory exhausted |

## RMAKE Warning Messages

| | |
|---|---|
| R1001 | Ignoring redefinition of command-line macro |
| R1002 | Target does not exist: '<file>' |
| R1003 | Ignoring text: '<text>' |

## RMAKE Execution Error Messages

| | |
|---|---|
| R2001 | Exit n: '<action line>' |

## RMAKE Fatal Error Messages

| | |
|---|---|
| R3001 | Too many make files |
| R3002 | Can't open: '<file>' |
| R3003 | Invalid option: '<option>' |
| R3004 | Out of memory |
| R3005 | Internal workspace exhausted |
| R3006 | Symbol table exhausted |
| R3007 | String too large |
| R3008 | String table exhausted |
| R3009 | File table exhausted |
| R3010 | Too many actions |
| R3011 | Too many dependencies |
| R3012 | Syntax error: '<token>' |
| R3013 | Unbalanced parentheses |
| R3014 | #else without if |
| R3015 | #endif without if |
| R3016 | Open conditionals |
| R3017 | Unrecognized directive: '<directive>' |
| R3018 | Dependency does not exist: '<file>' |
| R3019 | Circular dependency |
| R3020 | Environment overflows workspace |
| R3021 | Error in redirection |
| R3022 | Can't execute '<action line>' |

# Index

AADD( ) function, 328, 632, 672
   initializing arrays and, 626
   operation of, 633
ABLOCK( ) function, 329
Aborting loops, 246
ABROWSE( ) function, 329–330
ABS( ) function, 330–331
Absolute value, 330–331
ACCEPT command, 217–218
ACHOICE( ) function,
   331–334, 632
   action keys for, 332–333
   arrays and, 672
   operation of, 633–642
   used with DIRECTORY( )
     function, 637–638
ACLONE( ) function, 334, 632
   operation of, 642–643
AColor( ) function, 667
   code for, 666–667
ACOMP( ) function, 334–335
ACOPY( ) function, 335–336,
   632
   operation of, 643–645
Action keys
   for ACHOICE( ) function,
     332–333
   for DBEDIT( ) function,
     374–375

Activating light-bar menu
   selection, 215–216
Actual variables, 187
ADDCOLUMN( ) method, 847,
   849–850
Addition, in-line, 155–159
ADDITIVE clause, of SET
   RELATION command, 732
ADDMONTH( ) function, 338
ADDREC( ) function, 338
Addresses, converting into
   strings, 359
ADEL( ) function, 336, 632
   operation of, 645–646
ADIR( ) function, 336–337, 632
AEVAL( ) function, 339, 632,
   672, 813
   building program and text
     editor with, 702–716
   code blocks and, 823–824
   DOS command line
     parameters and, 200–201
   operation of, 646–652
AFIELDS( ) function, 339–340,
   632
AFILL( ) function, 340, 632
   operation of, 652–653
AINS( ) function, 341, 632
   operation of, 653–655

ALERT( ) function, 341–342
ALIAS( ) area pointer, 185
ALIAS( ) function, 342–343
Aliased fields, 164–165
Aliased memory variables,
   164–165, 182–185
Aliases
   expressions and, 610–621
   obtaining work area numbers
     for, 514
   of work areas, 342–343, 377
ALL command, in Debugger, 587
ALLTRIM( ) function, 120,
   343–344
Alphabetic characters, as first
   characters of strings, 445
ALT-C key, toggling as cancel
   key, 520–521
ALTD( ) function, 344
Alternate data formats, building
   databases from, 744–745
Alt keys, 1140
AMAX( ) function, 344–345
AMIN( ) function, 345
& character, designating macros
   with, 601
AMPM( ) function, 345–346
AM/PM format, time strings in,
   345–346

ANIMATE command, in
    Debugger, 586, 594
Animate mode
    for Debugger, 594
    setting speed of, 599
Annotating source code, 269
ANNOUNCE command, 218
ANNOUNCE statement,
    204–205
ANSITERM.LIB file, contents
    of, 73–74
APPEND BLANK command,
    131, 218–219
    memo fields and, 685
APPEND FROM command,
    219–222
Appending blank records to
    files, 218–219
Appending blank records to
    work areas, 338
Appending records to databases,
    219–222, 367–368
Applications
    without batch files, 565–578
    exiting from, 406–407
    SET KEY, 1013–1015
Application screens, displaying
    with Debugger, 598
APP SCREEN command, in
    Debugger, 586
ARGS instance variable, 937
Arithmetic operators. *See*
    Mathematical operators
ARRAY( ) function, 346, 632
    initializing arrays and,
        626–628
    operation of, 655–656
ARRAYASDATE( ) function,
    347
Array-based functions, 632–662
Array elements
    passing by reference, 676–678
    passing to subroutines,
        197–198
Array operators, 149–150
Arrays, 171, 623–683
    adding elements to, 328, 633
    applying code blocks to,
        360–361

of available RDDs, 493
browsing objects and,
    906–931
browsing two-dimensional,
    329–330
building program and text
    editor and, 702–716
calculating dimensions of,
    396–397
changing sizes of, 348–349,
    658–659
Clipper 5.2 and, 623–625
comparing elements in,
    334–335
converting dates to, 366
converting delimited strings
    to, 451–452
converting into dates, 347
copying elements in,
    335–336
creating empty databases
    from, 370–372
creating GET/SET code
    blocks for elements of, 329
creating multidimensional,
    387–388
creating public, 273–274
data dictionaries and,
    394–395
data types and, 624–625
declaring and defining in
    macros, 603–604
declaring public and private,
    264–265
declaring sizes of, 346,
    655–656
defining for GET command,
    183–184
deleting elements from, 336,
    645–646
denoting subscript markers
    of, 118
displaying window list boxes
    of items in, 331–334,
    633–642
duplicating multidimensional,
    334, 642–643
enlarging with NIL values,
    341, 653–655

evaluating subscript elements
    of, 339, 646–652
filling with a single value,
    340, 652–653
filling with database field
    information, 339–340
filling with directory
    information, 336–337,
    397–399
gauge arrays, 430
independent functions for,
    662–668
initializing, 237–238,
    626–630
initializing local, 261–262
initializing static, 314
matching criteria, 410
memory variables and,
    624–625
multidimensional, 623–624
nested, 678–683
notation for, xxxiii
obtaining maximum numeric
    values from, 344–345
obtaining minimum numeric
    values from, 345
obtaining number of
    initialized positions in, 450
obtaining rightmost elements
    of, 351
one-dimensional, 623–624
parallel, 636–637
parameter passing and,
    631–632
passing as parameters,
    194–199
scanning for specific
    expressions, 348, 656–658
for scrollbars, 511
secondary, 636–637
sorting, 349–350, 659–662
writing to disk, 801–805
ArraySkip( ) function, 924
Array structures, pictures of, 683
ASC( ) function, 347
ASCAN( ) function, 348, 632,
    667
    operation of, 656–658
Ascending index keys, 253

Index 1163

ASCII (American Standard Code for Information Interchange)
    applying ASCII values of keys to GET objects, 432–433
    converting numeric values to characters in, 358–359
    obtaining values of characters in, 347
ASCII codes, 1137–1140
ASIZE( ) function, 348–349, 632
    initializing arrays and, 626
    operation of, 658–659
ASORT( ) function, 349–350, 632
    operation of, 659–662
Assembly language, executing subroutines in, 223–224
ASSIGN( ) method, 935–936
Assignment operators, 155–159
/A switch, 5
AT( ) function, 350
    memo fields and, 686
ATAIL( ) function, 351, 632
@...BOX command, 211–212
@...CLEAR...TO command, 212–213
@...GET command, 213–215
@...PROMPT command, 215–216
    establishing message row for, 305–306
    wrapping in menus, 311
@...SAY command, 216
    directing output from, 299
@ symbol
    passing array elements by reference and, 676
    passing arrays and, 197
    passing variables by reference and, 194
@...TO command, 217
AUTOEXEC.BAT file, 201
AUTOLITE instance variable, 844
Automatic declaration, of variables, 5

AVERAGE command, 222
Averaging numeric fields, 222

BACKSPACE( ) method, 935–936
BADCACHE switch, 20
BADDATE instance variable, 933
BarChart( ) function, 832
    code for, 831–832
Bar charts, 832
Base 10 logarithms, 473
BASE52.LNK file, 38–39
Bases of numbers, converting numeric values from one to another, 351–352
BASETOBASE( ) function, 351–352
/BATCH command, 30
Batch compiling, 15–17
Batch files
    building applications without, 565–578
    executing, 210
BEGINAREA command, 31
Beginning-of-file condition, testing for, 353–354
Beginning virtual screens, 400
BEGIN SEQUENCE command, 223
    controlled break-out from, 356
Bell, toggling, 294
BIN2I( ) function, 352, 783
BIN2L( ) function, 352, 783
BIN2W( ) function, 352–353, 783
Binary functions, 783–810
Binary numbers, converting to integers, 352, 783
Blank records
    appending to databases, 218–219
    appending to work areas, 338
Blank spaces
    strings of, 527
    trimming from strings, 343–344, 453, 505–506, 551
Blinker, 88

Blinking condition, setting, 519–520
BLOCKIFY( ) function, 953
Blockifying, 119
Blockify result token, 119
BLOCK instance variable, 850, 933
BOF( ) function, 353–354
    managing index files and, 723
Boolean expressions, concise, 163–164
Boolean operators. See Logical operators
Borders, drawing, 217
Bounce-bar menus, creating, 946–955
Boxes
    clearing and drawing frames in, 212–213
    drawing, 211–212, 400–401
    painting menus inside, 354–355
    shadowing, 356
BOXMENU( ) function, 354–355
BOXSHADOW( ) function, 356
BP command, in Debugger, 594
Branching subroutines, 814–815
Branch operations, 242–243
    conditional, 251–252
BREAK( ) function, 356
BREAK command, creating command sequences for, 223
BREAKPOINT command, in Debugger, 587
BreakPoints, 589
    deleting, 595
    inserting, 594
    listing, 597
    running programs in Debugger with, 596
BROWSE( ) function, 356–357
Browse1( ) function, 923, 924
Browse objects
    creating and operating, 853–862
    generating with defaults, 538–540

## 1164  Index

Browse objects (*continued*)
   generating without defaults, 540–542
   keystroke actions for, 862–888
Browsing, 844–931
   of arrays, 329–330
   of data, 356–357
   of databases and work areas, 373–376
Browsing areas, 849
Browsing functions, 844–931
   TBROWSE( ) and TBCOLUMN( ), 844–906
   TBROWSENEW( ), 906–931
Browsing windows, setting up, 851–853
/B switch, 5
B-tree algorithm, index files and, 722–723
B+-tree style index structure, 747
BUFFER instance variable, 933
Bytes, reading from files, 424

Cache( ) function, 671
   code for, 669–670
CALL command, 223–224
   converting numeric parameters of, 559–560
CALLSTACK command, in Debugger, 586, 595
Callstack window, 582
   displaying, 595
   keystroke assignments for, 591
CANCEL command, 225
Cancel key, ALT-C key as, 520–521
CANDEFAULT instance variable, 937
CANRETRY instance variable, 937
CANSUBSTITUTE instance variable, 937
Capitalizing words in strings, 490
CARGO instance variable, 844, 850, 933, 937
Carriage returns, 438–439
   before expressions, 210–211
   formatting strings with, 462–463

CASE SENSITIVE command, in Debugger, 585
Case sensitivity, of #define command, 97–98
CA-Visual Objects, 1077
CDOW( ) function, 357
.CDX files, 770
CEILING( ) function, 357–358
Centering expressions within strings, 483–484
Century digits in a date, toggling, 294
CGACURS switch, 20
CHANGED instance variable, 933
Character expressions. *See also* Strings
   converting to lowercase, 452–453
   converting to uppercase, 554–555
   extracting leftmost substrings from, 449
   extracting rightmost substrings from, 502–503
   finding previous occurrences of, with Debugger, 598
   obtaining lengths of, 450
   repeating, 501–502
Character fields
   concatenating, 168
   in databases, 721
Characters
   converting dates to, 403–404
   converting to numeric values, 555–556
   writing to files, 429
Character strings, finding next occurrences of, in Debugger, 597
Character variables, assigning user input to, 217–218
.CH files, 93–94
CHR( ) function, 358–359
CITYSTATE( ) function, 359
C language, executing subroutines in, 223–224
Classes, objects and, 842–843

CLEAR ALL command, 173, 225–226
CLEAR command, 225
CLEAR GETS command, 226
Clearing boxes, 212–213
Clearing GET objects, 225
Clearing GET/READ stack, 226
Clearing Order List, 479
Clearing the keyboard buffer, 228
Clearing the screen, 225
Clearing the stack, 401
Clearing the video screen, 228
CLEAR instance variable, 933
CLEAR MEMORY command, 173, 226–227
CLEAR SCREEN | CLS command, 228
CLEAR TYPEAHEAD command, 228
CLIP files, 15–17, 580
Clipper
   future prospects of, 1077–1078
   obtaining version number of, 559
Clipper 5.2
   arrays in, 623–625
   code block functions for, 813
   converting to, xxiii–xxviii
   database and index system for, 761–768
   debugging programs in, 579–600
   disk configurations for, xxviii–xxix
   enhancements for, xxix–xxxi
   functions in, 327–561
   linkers available for, 88
   standard commands in, 209–325
Clipper Browse objects. *See* Browse objects
CLIPPERCMD variable, 18–19
Clipper Column objects. *See* Column objects
Clipper Debugger. *See* Debugger
Clipper environment, controlling, 672–676

Clipper error messages, 23
CLIPPER.LIB file, 37–39
   contents of, 41–63
Clipper objects, 841–939
*clipper* public variable, 173–174
CLIPPER switches, 20–22
   using, 23
CLIPPER variable, 20–22
CLOSE command, 228–229
Closing databases, 228–229
Closing files, 228–229, 369, 411
Closing index files, 368
.CLP files, 15–17, 27, 580
CMONTH( ) function, 359–360
Code block format, writing text in, 119
Code block functions, 813
Code blocks, 171, 811–839
   advanced features of, 835–839
   advanced programming with, 828–832
   advantages of, 812–813
   AEVAL( ) function and, 646–652
   applying to arrays, 360–361
   ASCAN( ) function and, 656–658
   basic programming with, 813–823
   creating, 329
   Debugger and, 580–581
   defined, 811–812
   evaluating, 394, 409, 440, 822–823
   evaluating against data dictionary array, 394
   executing, 433
   generating for fields, 414–415
   generating for specific field values, 417–418
   getting and setting for FORMAT file, 494–495
   "hot keys" and, 672
   intermediate programming with, 823–828
   macros and, 604–608, 811, 828–830
   for memory variables, 463–464

object-oriented programming and, 841–843
passing array elements by reference and, 676–678
passing arrays and, 198–199
for run-time errors, 407
sorting arrays and, 659–662
syntax for, 812–813
CODEBLOCK TRACE command, in Debugger, 588
Code window, 582
   displaying files in, with Debugger, 600
   displaying source code in, with Debugger, 599
   keystroke assignments for, 590
COL( ) function, 360
COLCOUNT instance variable, 844
COL instance variable, 933
COLLECT( ) function, 360–361
Colon-equal (:=) operator, xxxiv
Color
   establishing system, 294–295
   setting and evaluating current screen color, 521
COLOR( ) pseudofunction, 122–123
Color adapter cards, testing for, 445
COLORBLOCK instance variable, 850
COLORDISP( ) method, 935–936
Color monitors, testing for, 445
COLORRECT( ) method, 847
Colors, activating attributes of, 361
COLORS command, in Debugger, 588
COLORSELECT( ) function, 361
COLORSPEC instance variable, 844, 933
Color tables, 1141–1145
COLPOS instance variable, 844
COLSEP instance variable, 845, 850
Column locations, of GETs, 984

Column objects, creating, 543
Columns
   obtaining maximum number of, 454–455
   putting text in, 700–702
   setting display mode for column width, 523–524
COLWIDTH( ) method, 847
COMMAND.COM file, 201
#command command, 116–125
   user-defined commands and, 129
Commands, 209–325
   creating sequences of, 223
   debugging, 592–600
   multiple, 125
   in RMAKE.EXE utility, 565–566
   user-defined, 129–130, 138–139
Command statements, in RMAKE.EXE utility, 566–568
Command window, 582
   keystroke assignments for, 590
COMMIT command, 229
Communication libraries, xxx
Compact indexes, 770
Compiler, defined, 3–4
Compiler directives, 18–19
Compiler error messages, 1151–1153
Compiler fatal error messages, 1153–1154
Compiler warning messages, 1151
Compiling files, 308
Compiling switches, 4–14
   standard, 14–15
Compound index files, 770
COMSPEC environmental variable, 201
Conditional branch operations, 251–252
Conditional compilation, 102–111
Conditional statements, 149–169
Conditions, testing, 441–442

## 1166    Index

CONFIG.SYS file, 201
   FILES statement in, 784
CONFIGURE( ) method, 847
Console display, toggling, 296
CONTINUE command, 229
Control keys, 1139
Controlling index, obtaining
   numeric position of, 443
Controlling index order, setting,
   306, 386
Controlling order, 763, 766
COPY FILE command, 230
Copying array elements,
   335–336
Copying database structures,
   230, 231
Copying files, 230
COPY STRUCTURE
   command, 230
COPY STRUCTURE
   EXTENDED command,
   231
COPY TO command, 231–233
COUNT command, 233–234
Counting passed parameters,
   486–487
Counting records, 233–234
COUNT TO command, 813
CREATE command, 234–236
   in creating .DBF files,
   725–727
CREATE FROM command,
   236–237
Creating files, 411–412
Creating orders, 476
Creating windows, 973–982
Credits, listing of, 5
/CREDIT switch, 5
Criteria, arrays matching, 410
CTOD( ) function, 362
CURDIR( ) function, 362–363
Cursor
   defining shape of, 522
   movement methods for,
   846–847
   moving to a position, 524–525
   moving with Debugger, 596
   obtaining current column
   position of, 360

   obtaining current row position
   of, 504–505
   obtaining row/column
   coordinates in memos and
   strings, 468–470
   positioning, 392–393
   toggling, 296
Cursor methods, in GET objects,
   436

Data
   browsing, 356–357
   displaying at specified device
   coordinates, 216
   READ command changes of,
   554
Database buffers, updating, 370
Database fields, memory
   variables and, 182–185
Database files. *See* Databases
Database generation and
   maintenance programs, 579
Database management, rules and
   tips for, 723–725
Databases, 719–745. *See also*
   .DBF files; .DBT files;
   Files; .NXT files
   appending records to,
   219–222
   appending records to database
   files, 367–368
   browsing, 373–376
   building from alternate data
   formats, 744–745
   checking for presence in work
   areas, 555
   clearing relations in, 369
   closing, 228–229, 369
   copying records between,
   231–233
   copying structures of, 230,
   231
   counting fields in, 411
   counting records in, 499
   creating a STRUCTURE
   EXTENDED database file,
   234–236
   creating files for, 725–729
   creating from arrays, 370–372

   creating from STRUCTURE
   EXTENDED database
   files, 236–237
   creating index files for,
   252–254, 372–373
   creating multidimensional
   arrays from database
   structures, 387–388
   deleting all records from, 325
   deleting records from,
   238–239
   displaying records of a
   database file, 241
   establishing database drivers
   for work areas, 384–385
   evaluating records in, 376–377
   field structures of, 720–721
   files to manage, 719–721
   filling arrays with field
   information from, 339–340
   highlighting records marked
   for deletion from, 298
   joining, 255–256
   locating values in, 247–248
   management of, 719–745
   marking records for deletion
   from, 238–239, 373
   moving record pointer to a
   specific location in a
   database, 378
   moving record pointer to
   bottom of a database, 378
   moving record pointer to top
   of a database, 379
   object-oriented programming
   and, 888–906
   obtaining date of last update
   to, 453
   obtaining number of records
   in, 449
   obtaining relations between,
   380
   opening with retry, in
   networks, 471
   parent and child, 732
   relating by keys and record
   numbers, 386
   removing records marked for
   deletion from, 269–271

sorting, 312–313
toggling exclusive/shared use of, 301
traversing, 738–739
unmarking records marked for deletion from, 278, 379
updating, 321–322
using database files, 322–324
using database files in work areas, 389
working with, 729–732
Data-caching system, building, 668–672
Data dictionaries, removing items from, 396
Data dictionary arrays, evaluating code blocks against, 394
Data dictionary functions, creating arrays for, 394–395
Data dictionary key words
adding, paired with items, 395–396
entering and replacing, 395
obtaining associated values of, 393
Data entry, 983–1040
Data entry programming, basic, 987–1000
Data generation program, 1081–1100
Data storage classes, 172–182
Data types, 171–172
AFILL( ) function and, 653
arrays and, 624–625
of expressions, 553
validating, 557–559
DATE( ) function, 363–364
DATEASAGE( ) function, 364–365
DATEASARRAY( ) function, 366
Date fields, in databases, 721
DATEISLEAP( ) function, 366
Dates
adding months to, 338
converting arrays into, 347
converting date of birth to a specific age, 364–365

converting elapsed seconds into days, 367
converting into month values, 468
converting numeric values into, 472–473
converting strings to, 362
converting to arrays, 366
converting to characters, 403–404
converting to string format, 402
converting to strings, 404–405, 456
converting year portion to a numeric value, 560–561
deriving day of the week from, 357
obtaining larger of two, 454, 464
obtaining names of months from, 359–360
obtaining numeric day of the month, 366–367
obtaining numeric day of the week, 403
obtaining system, 363–364
operators for, 152–155
setting base year for, 299–300
setting formats for, 296–297
testing date for leap year, 366
toggling century digits in, 294
DAY( ) function, 366–367
Day of the week, 357, 403
Days
converting elapsed seconds into, 367
converting seconds to, 513–514
obtaining numeric day of the month, 366–367
obtaining numeric value of day of the week, 403
DAYS( ) function, 367
DBAPPEND( ) function, 367–368
DBCLEARFILTER( ) function, 368

DBCLEARINDEX( ) function, 368
DBCLEARRELATION( ) function, 369
DBCLOSEALL( ) function, 369
DBCLOSEAREA( ) function, 369
DBCMD error messages, 1159
DBCOMMIT( ) function, 370
DBCOMMITALL( ) function, 370
DBCREATE( ) function, 370–372
in creating .DBF files, 728–729
DBCREATEINDEX( ) function, 372–373
DBDELETE( ) function, 373
DBEDIT( ) function, 373–376
action keys for, 374–375
building program and text editor with, 702–716
handling keystroke exceptions with, 638
DBEVAL( ) function, 123, 376–377, 813
code blocks and, 824–828, 835–839
traversing databases with, 738–739
using, 739–744
DBF( ) function, 377
DBFCDX driver, 765, 766, 768–773
DBFCDX.LIB file, contents of, 70–73
.DBF files, 719–720. See also Databases
header structure of, 720
updating, 321–322
DBFILTER( ) function, 377–378
DBFMDX driver, 773–777
DBFMDX.LIB file, contents of, 69–70
DBFNDX driver, 754–755, 757–758, 777–779
error messages for, 1159
DBFNDX.LIB file, contents of, 69

DBFNTX driver, 744–745, 753–755, 779–780
  error messages for, 1158
  RDDs and, 750–752
DBFNTX.LIB file, 37–39
  contents of, 68–69
DBGOBOTTOM( ) function, 378
DBGOTO( ) function, 378
DBGOTOP( ) function, 379
DBNetEval( ) function, 838
  code for, 837–838
DBPX driver, 780–781
DBPX.LIB file, contents of, 74–86
DBRECALL( ) function, 379
DBREINDEX( ) function, 379–380
DBRELATION( ) function, 380
DBRLOCK( ) function, 381
DBRLOCKLIST( ) function, 381
DBRSELECT( ) function, 381–382
DBRUNLOCK( ) function, 383
DBSEEK( ) function, 383–384
DBSELECTAREA( ) function, 384
DBSETDRIVER( ) function, 384–385, 754, 757
DBSETFILTER( ) function, 385
DBSETINDEX( ) function, 385
DBSETORDER( ) function, 386
  managing index files and, 724
DBSETRELATION( ) function, 386
DBSKIP( ) function, 386–387, 839
DBSTRUCT( ) function, 387–388
  arrays and, 632
  building program and text editor with, 702–716
  creating databases and, 726–727
  multidimensional arrays and, 667
.DBT files, 171, 719. *See also* Memo files
  header structure of, 722
  memo fields and, 685

DBU.EXE program, 579
  creating databases with, 725
DBUNLOCK( ) function, 388
DBUNLOCKALL( ) function, 388–389
DBUSEAREA( ) function, 389
/DEBUG command, 29
Debugger, 579–600
  calling, 581–588
  exiting from, 598
  invoking, 344
  keyboard interface for, 589–593
  menu options in, 584–588
  restarting, 598
  restrictions on, 580–581
  windows for, 582–584, 589–593
Debugger windows, modifying the attributes of, 582–583
Debugging, preparing code for, 580–581
Debugging commands, 592–600
Debugging information, 5
Debugging points, 589
Debugging screens, displaying, 598
Decimal places
  determining, 474
  setting, 297, 302
Declaration statements, 182–186
DECLARE command, 237–238
DECLARE statement, 174
  arrays and, 626
DECPOS instance variable, 933
/DEFAULTLIBRARYSEARCH command, 30
DEFAULT...TO command, arrays and, 671
DEFCOLOR instance variable, 850
#define command, 95–101
Degrees
  converting radians to, 505
  converting to radians, 404
DEHILITE( ) method, 848
DELCOLUMN( ) method, 848
DELEND( ) method, 935–936
DELETE( ) method, 935–936

DeleteAll( ) function, 923
DELETE ALL command, 813
DELETE command, 238–239
  in Debugger, 587, 595
DELETED( ) function, 390
DELETE FILE command, 239
DELETE TAG command, 239–240
Deleting all records from a database, 325
Deleting array elements, 336, 645–646
Deleting files, 239, 244–246, 412–413
Deleting records, 238–239, 278
Deletion flag, testing for, 390
Delimiters, table of, 149–150
DELLEFT( ) method, 935–936
DELRIGHT( ) method, 935–936
DELWORDLEFT( ) method, 935–936
DELWORDRIGHT( ) method, 935–936
DESCEND( ) function, 390–391
  indexing in descending order without, 753
Descending index keys, 253, 390–391
Descending index order, 753
DESCRIPTION instance variable, 937
DEVOUT( ) function, 391, 817
  arrays and, 672
  programming techniques with, 145
DEVOUTPICT( ) function, 392
DEVPOS( ) function, 392–393, 817
  arrays and, 672
  programming techniques with, 144–145
Dialog boxes
  creating modal, 341–342
  in Debugger, 583–584
  keystroke assignments for, 592
DICTAT( ) function, 393
DICTEVAL( ) function, 394

DICT functions, browsing objects and, 928–931
DICTNEW( ) function, 394–395
DICTPUT( ) function, 395
DICTPUTPAIR( ) function, 395–396
DICTREMOVE( ) function, 396
Digit characters, as leftmost characters in strings, 445–446
DIMENSIONS( ) function, 396–397
Dimensions of arrays, calculating, 396–397
DIR command, 240–241
Directories
  creating multidimensional arrays of directory information, 397–399
  filling arrays with information from, 336–337
  obtaining name of current directory, 362–363
DIRECTORY( ) function, 397–399, 682, 786
  AEVAL( ) function and, 647–649, 651
  arrays and, 632
  ASCAN( ) function and, 658
  ASORT( ) function and, 662
  DOS command line parameters and, 200–201
  used with ACHOICE( ) function, 637–638
Directory names, displaying, 240–241
Disk configurations, for Clipper 5.2, xxviii–xxix
Disk drives. *See also* Drives; Hard disk
  calculating available space on, 399–400
DISKSPACE( ) function, 399–400
DISPBEGIN( ) function, 400, 970–973
DISPBOX( ) function, 400–401
DISPCOUNT( ) function, 401

DISPEND( ) function, 401, 970–973
DispFiles( ) function, 923, 925
DispKeys1( ) function, 923
DispKeys2( ) function, 924
DISPLAY( ) method, 935–936
Display areas, 309
DISPLAY command, 241
Displaying data, 216
Displaying directory names, 240–241
Displaying expressions, 491
Displaying file information, 240–241
Displaying labels, 257–259
Displaying records of a database file, 241
Displaying reports, 282–284
Displaying text, 316–317
Displaying values, 391, 402
  with picture templates, 392
Displaying windows, 973–982
Display mode, setting for depth and width, 523–524
DISPOUT( ) function, 402
Division
  in-line, 155–159
  by zero, 168
Division operator, 168
DMY( ) function, 402
DO CASE...ENDCASE command, 242–243
DOCBASE.EXE utility, 579
DOCBASE.INI file, 810
DO commands, 242
  subroutines and, 191–194
DOS (Disk Operating System), file handles and, 783–784
DOS ACCESS command, in Debugger, 585
DOS command, in Debugger, 595
DOS command line, obtaining values from, 199–201
DOS commands, executing, 210, 286–287
DOS environment, 18–23
  obtaining settings for, 433–434

DOS environmental variables, 18–23
DOSERROR( ) function, 402–403
DOS ERRORLEVEL, 23
  setting, 6–7
DOS error messages, 1149–1150
DOS errors, returning last, 402–403
DOS SET INCLUDE command, 7
DOS shell, entering, 595
DosStru( ) function, 923, 924
Double-equal (==) operator, xxxiv, 167
  sample program to demonstrate, 153–154
Double semicolon (;;) operator, 166
DOW( ) function, 403
DO WHILE...ENDDO command, 243
DOWN( ) cursor movement method, 846
Drawing borders, 217
Drawing boxes, 211–212, 400–401
Drive letters for filenames, 419
Drives. *See also* Disk drives; Hard disk
  determining the existence of, 787–790
/D switch, 5–6
DTOC( ) function, 403–404
DTOR( ) function, 404
DTOS( ) function, 404–405
Dumb stringify result tokens, 118
Duplicating arrays, 334, 642–643
/DYNAMIC command, 28
Dynamic overlays, 34–35
  Virtual Memory Manager (VMM) and, 91
DYNF: switch, 20

E: switch, 20–21
Early evaluation of code blocks, 822–823

Editing, with MEMOEDIT( )
function, 698–699, 702–716
Editing methods
in GET objects, 436
Editing numeric values, 556–557
Editing strings and memos,
456–459
Editors, xxxi
Education, for Clipper 5.2, xxxi
EJECT command, 244
Elapsed time
calculating, 405
in seconds from midnight, 513
ELAPTIME( ) function, 405
#else directive, 102–111
EMPTY( ) function, 405–406
Empty condition, in expressions,
405–406
Empty stack array, testing for,
528
Encryption, of database names,
799
END( ) cursor movement
method, 846
END( ) method, 935–936
ENDAREA command, 31
#endif directive, 102–111
End-of-file condition, testing
for, 406
End-of-file markers, 137–138
Entry methods, in GET objects,
437
Environment. *See also* Clipper
environment;
DOS environment;
SET environment;
Work areas
changing and evaluating
settings for, 515–519
getting and setting SET( )
values for, 519
resetting, 225–226
Environmental control, arrays
and, 672–676
Environmental variables. *See
also* Variables
obtaining values from,
201–203
in RMAKE.EXE utility, 569

for RTLink, 32–34
setting, 18–23, 201–203
ENVIRONMENT
PROCEDURE command,
147–148
EOF( ) function, 406
managing index files and, 723
ERASE command, 244–246
Erasing files, 412–413
ERRORBLOCK( ) function,
407
ERROR class, 842
#error command, 125–126
ERRORINHANDLER( )
function, 406–407
ERRORLEVEL( ) function,
407–408, 790
Error-level status, evaluating,
407–408
Error messages, 23, 1151–1153.
*See also* Fatal error
messages
.RTLink miscellaneous,
1155–1156
DBCMD, 1159
DBFNDX, 1159
DBFNTX, 1158
from preprocessor, 125–126,
127
RMAKE execution, 1160
RMAKE fatal, 1160
.RTLink, 1154–1155
run-time, 1156–1158
run-time unrecoverable,
1159–1160
TERM, 1158
ERRORNEW( ) function,
408–409
ERRORNEW( ) instance
variables, 937–939
Error objects, 936–939
generating, 408–409
Errors
outputting lists to standard
error device, 482
posting code blocks for
run-time errors, 407
returning last-encountered
DOS error, 402–403

Error status, of low-level file
functions, 413–414
Error system, 1066–1075
Error trapping, 787
ErrTone( ) function, 924
/ES2 switch, 183
ESC key, toggling, 300
/ES switch, 6–7
EVAL( ) function, 409, 813
building program and text
editor with, 702–716
code blocks and, 815–816,
818, 819
EVAL clause, of INDEX ON
command, 752–753
Evaluating array subscripts, 339,
646–652
Evaluating records, 376–377
Exact matches for strings,
toggling, 300–301
EXCHANGE SCREENS
command, in Debugger, 588
! command, 210
! operator, 167
/EXCLUDE command, 30
Exclusive use of databases,
toggling, 301
Executing commands, 210
Executing menu bars, 265–269
Executing subroutines, 223–224
.EXE files, RMAKE.EXE utility
and, 565
EXIT command, 246
in Debugger, 585
Exiting from applications,
406–407
Exit keys for GETs, 295
EXIT PROCEDURE statement,
204
Exit severity level, setting, 6–7
EXITSTATE instance variable,
934
EXP( ) function, 409–410
Exponentials, calculating,
409–410
Exported instance variables,
defined, 843
Expressions, 608–621
aliases and, 610–621

Index  1171

centering within strings, 483–484
converting into dates, 472–473
converting numbers into strings with leading zeros, 533–535
determining number of whole numbers in, 474
displaying, 491
displaying values of, 402
displaying with Debugger, 594
empty condition in, 405–406
evaluating, 169
evaluating and outputting, 210–211
extended use of, 610–621
fields and, 610
formatting with picture templates, 547–551
left-justifying within strings, 484–485
macro-expanded, 609–610
obtaining data types of, 553
obtaining larger of two, 454, 464
parentheses and, 608–609
right-justifying expressions within, 485
scanning arrays for, 348, 656–658
tips on, 163–169
validating data types of, 557–559
in work areas, 610–621
/EXTDICTIONARY command, 30
Extending libraries, xxix
EXTEND.LIB file, 37–40
contents of, 63–68
Extensions, for filenames, 419–420
EXTERNAL command, 185–186, 246–247
External programs, executing, 286–287
External subroutines, 185–186
specifying, 246–247, 284–285
EXTRACT( ) function, 410

F: switch, 21
Fatal error messages, 1153–1154
RMAKE, 1160
FCLOSE( ) function, 411, 783
FCOUNT( ) function, 411
uses of, 735
FCREATE( ) function, 411–412, 783, 789–790
FEOF( ) pseudofunction, 137–138
FERASE( ) function, 412–413, 783
FERROR( ) function, 413–414, 783, 790
FIELD( ) function, 414
uses of, 735–737
Field-> alias pointer, 185
FIELDBLOCK( ) function, 414–415, 833–835
uses of, 735–738
FIELD command, 247
Field definitions, copying to database files, 231
Field delimiters, defining and toggling, 298–299
FIELDGET( ) function, 415
arrays and, 667, 668
uses of, 735–737
FIELDNAME( ) function, 415–416
arrays and, 668
uses of, 735–737
Field names
copying to database files, 231
declaring lists of, 247
FIELDPOS( ) function, 416
FIELDPUT( ) function, 416–417
arrays and, 668
uses of, 735–737
Fields
aliased, 164–165
assigning values to, 166–167, 280–282
averaging numeric, 222
counting, 411
expressions and, 610
filling arrays with information about, 339–340

generating code blocks for, 414–415, 417–418
GETs and, 984–985
in initial STRUCTURE EXTENDED databases, 725
notation for, xxxiii
obtaining names of, 414, 415–416
obtaining values of, 415
ordinal positions of, 416
placing values into, 416–417
structure of, in databases, 720–721
summing numeric, 315
totaling numeric fields based on key values, 317–319
working with, 735–738
FIELD statement, 184–185
Field statements, order of, 186–187
FIELDWBLOCK( ) function, 417–418, 834–835
uses of, 735–738
FILE( ) function, 418
FILEBASE( ) function, 418–419
File directory search list, including, 7
FILEDRIVE( ) function, 419
FILEEXT( ) function, 419–420
File functions, low-level, 783–810
File handles, DOS and, 783–784
File menu, in Debugger, 585
FILENAME instance variable, 937
FILEPATH( ) function, 420
Files. *See also* Batch files; CLIP files; Databases; Format files; Header files; INCLUDE files; Index files; Memo files; Object files; Swap files; System files; Text files
appending blank records to, 218–219
appending records to database files, 367–368
closing, 228–229, 369, 411
closing index files, 368

Files (*continued*)
  converting to strings, 461
  copying, 230
  creating, 411–412
  creating index files for databases, 252–254
  database-management related, 719–723
  deleting, 239, 244–246
  displaying information about, 240–241
  displaying with Debugger, 600
  erasing, 412–413
  error status of low-level file functions, 413–414
  finding end-of-file markers in, 137–138
  finding in search paths, 437
  format files for READ command, 302–303
  including in programs, 111–116
  internal information in, 732–735
  joining database files, 255–256
  lengths of headers of, 439
  locating records in, 262–264
  locking, 420, 421–422
  memo files, 685–686
  obtaining drive letters associated with, 419
  obtaining extensions of index modules, 442
  obtaining full path of, 427–428
  obtaining paths for, 420
  obtaining three-letter extensions of, 419–420
  opening, 422–423
  opening index files, 303–304
  outputting to alternate, 293–294
  positioning pointers in, 427
  reading, 791–801
  reading bytes from, 424
  reading strings from, 424–425
  renaming, 280, 425–426
  restoring contents of memory variable files, 285
  root names of, 418–419
  saving memory variables to, 289–291
  searching for indexed records in, 291–292
  specifying for compilation, 308
  specifying search paths for, 307
  switches for, xxxiv
  temporary, 12, 19
  testing for beginnings of, 353–354
  testing for ends of, 406
  testing for existence of, 418
  typing contents of, 320
  unlocking, 320–321
  using database, 322–324
  writing characters to, 429
  writing strings and memo fields to, 463
FILES statement, 784
Filewide static variables, 181–182
FILLOCK( ) function, 420
Filter conditions for work areas
  clearing, 368
  establishing, 385
  obtaining, 377–378
  setting, 301–302
Filters
  code blocks and, 828–830
  databases and, 732
FIND command, 247–248
  with databases, 730
  in Debugger, 585, 596
Finding values in databases, 247–248
FKLABEL( ) function, 421
FKMAX( ) function, 421
FLength( ) function, 924
FLOCK( ) function, 421–422
FLOOR( ) function, 422
Flushing memory buffer, 370
Flushing the memory buffer, 229
Focus
  for orders in Order List, 481
  validating GET objects and, 437, 438
FOOTING instance variable, 850
FOOTSEP instance variable, 845, 850
FOPEN( ) function, 422–423, 783
FORCESTABLE( ) method, 848
FOR conditions, DBEVAL( ) function and, 741–744
FOR expresions, of orders, 477–478
Form( ) function, MEMOEDIT( ) function and, 700–702
Format files, for READ command, 302–303
Formatted lines, counting, 464–465
Formatting, of GETs, 986
Formatting rules, with GET functions and templates, 214–215
Form-feed command, 244
FOR...NEXT command, 248
  basic programming techniques with, 141–142
FOUND( ) function, 423
Frames, drawing, 212–213
FREAD( ) function, 424, 783
Freadline( ) function, 924
FREADSTR( ) function, 424–425, 783
/FREEFORMAT command, 28
Freeformat interface, 28
  command structure for invoking, 31
Free memory, calculating, 461–462
FREEZE instance variable, 845
FRENAME( ) function, 425–426, 783
FSEEK( ) function, 427, 783
FULLBASE.LNK program, 1112–1114
FULLPATH( ) function, 427–428
FUNCTION command, 249
Function keys
  assigning character strings to, 330
  in Debugger, 589–590

obtaining names of, 421
setting maximum number of, 421
Functions, 327–561
  array-based, 632–662
  assigning to keys, 304–305
  in code blocks, 813–814
  creating user-defined, 116–125
  declaring subroutines as user-defined functions, 249
  low-level file and binary, 783–810
  for memo handling, 686–699
  in networks, 470
  obtaining line numbers of, 488
  obtaining names of, 488–490
  passing parameters to, 187–199
  user-defined, 129–130, 205–206
FWRITE( ) function, 429, 783

"Garbage collection," 90–91
Gas gauge display, 766
Gauge arrays, creating, 430
GAUGEDISP( ) function, 429–430
GAUGEDISPLAY( ) function, 766
GAUGENEW( ) function, 430, 766
Gauges
  displaying on screens, 429–430
  updating information on, 430–432
GAUGEUPDAT( ) function, 430–432
GENCODE instance variable, 937–938
Generic subroutines, building, 835–839
_GET_( ) function, 932
GETACTIVE( ) function, 432
GETAPPLYKEY( ) function, 432–433
GET class, 842–843
GETCOLUMN( ) method, 848

GET command
  exit keys for, 295
  programming techniques with, 143
  toggling enhanced display for, 304
GetDirs( ) function, 924
GETDOSETKEY( ) function, 433
GETE( ) function, retrieving environmental strings with, 201–202
GETENV( ) function, 433–434
GET functions, formatting rules with, 214
GET instance variables, 933–935
GETLIST array
  activating READ on, 498
  killing active, 497
*GETLIST[ ]* array, 983–984
GET methods, 935–936
GETNEW( ) function, 434–437, 932
GET objects, 181, 932–936
  applying ASCII values of keys to, 432–433
  clearing, 225
  creating and displaying, 213–215
  generating, 434–437
  killing active, 497
  obtaining currently active, 432
  parts of, 983–987
  reading, 438
  saving, 1007–1013
  testing values of variables in, 492
  validating, 437, 438
GETPATH( ) function, 437
GETPOSTVALIDATE( ) function, 438
GETPREVALIDATE( ) function, 437
GETREADER( ) function, 438
GET/READ stack, clearing, 226
GET/SET block functions, 832–835

GET/SET code blocks, 199
  creating for array elements, 329
GETSYS.PRG file, modifying, 1022–1040
GET system, 983–1041
  activating current, 275–277
GET templates, formatting rules with, 215
GOBOTTOM( ) cursor movement method, 846
GOBOTTOMBLOCK instance variable, 845
GO command, 250–251
  in Debugger, 586, 596
GOTO command, in Debugger, 596
GOTO LINE command, in Debugger, 585
GOTOP( ) cursor movement method, 846
GOTOPBLOCK instance variable, 845
Graphics library, xxix–xxx

Hard carriage returns, replacing soft carriage returns with, 438–439
HARDCR( ) function, 438–439
  memo fields and, 686, 688
Hard disk. *See also* Disk drives; Drives
  deleting files from, 244–246, 412–413
  writing arrays to, 801–805
  writing on, 229, 370
HASFOCUS instance variable, 934
HEADER( ) function, 439
Header files, 12–13
  notation for, xxxiii
  preprocessor and, 94
Headers, lengths of, 439
HEADING instance variable, 851
HEADSEP instance variable, 845, 851
HELIOS.CH program, code for, 115–116

/HELP command, 29
HELP command, in Debugger, 596
Help menu, in Debugger, 588
Help system, 1043–1066
Help window (Debugger), 582
   keystroke assignments for, 591
HERMES.RMK file, 574–578
HILITE( ) method, 848
HITBOTTOM instance variable, 845
HITTOP instance variable, 845
HOME( ) cursor movement method, 846, 935–936
"Hot keys," arrays and, 672

I2BIN( ) function, 439–440, 783
IBM extended character set, 1137–1140
Iconizing windows, 582
Identifiers, 118
IDENTITY in index files, 762–763
.IDX files, 770
IEVAL( ) function, 440
IF( ) function, 441–442
#ifdef directive, 102–111
IF...ENDIF command, 251–252
#ifndef directive, 102–111
/IGNORECASE command, 30
#include command, 111–116
INCLUDE files, 19–20, 1115–1136
   #include command and, 111–116
INCLUDE variable, 19–20
/INCREMENTAL command, 29–30
Incremental linking, 35–36
Index buffers, updating, 370
INDEX command, 252–254
Indexes
   rebuilding open, 379–380
   using the minus operator on strings in, 168
INDEXEXT( ) function, 442

Index files, 747–781. *See also* .CDX files; .IDX files; .MDX files; .NDX files; .NTX files
   adding to work areas, 385
   closing, 368
   compact, 770
   compound, 770
   creating, 252–254
   creating for databases, 372–373
   database management and, 722–723
   header structure of, 747–748
   ITEM entry structure and, 748
   key page structure of, 748
   keys for, 253–254, 390–391
   locating records with, 383–384
   midpoints of, 722–723
   nonunique keys in, 310–311
   obtaining key expressions of, 442
   opening, 303–304
   rebuilding, 278–279, 379–380
   searching for indexed records in files, 291–292
   setting controlling index order for, 306, 386
   structural compound, 770
   working with, 729–732
INDEXKEY( ) function, 442
Index keys, managing databases and, 722–725
Index modules, obtaining file extensions of, 442
INDEX ON command
   code blocks and, 830
   with databases, 729
   DBFMDX driver and, 776
   DBFNDX driver and, 778–779
   DBFNTX driver and, 779–780
   EVAL clause of, 752–753
INDEXORD( ) function, 443
Index order, controlling, 306, 386
INFO switch, 21–22

InitArray( ) function, 667, 672
   code for, 665, 670
Initializing arrays, 237–238, 626–630
INIT PROCEDURE statement, 203–204
INKEY( ) chart, 1138–1140
INKEY( ) function, 443
INKEYWAIT( ) function, 444
In-line assignments, 166–167
In-line operators, 155–159
   rules of precedence for, 159–163
Input, assigning user input to a character variable, 217–218
INPUT command, 254–255
   in Debugger, 597
INSCOLUMN( ) method, 848
INSERT( ) method, 936
INS key, toggling in READ and MEMOEDIT( ), 495–496
Instance variables
   in Browse objects, 538–539, 541
   in Column objects, 543
   defined, 843
   in GET objects, 434–435
   in TBROWSE class, 844–846
INT( ) function, 444
Integers
   converting binary numbers to, 352
   converting 16–bit binary numbers to, 352–353
   converting 32–bit binary numbers to, 352
   converting to 16–bit binary numbers, 439–440
   converting to 32–bit binary numbers, 454
   obtaining integer portion of a numeric value, 444
   obtaining largest in a base range, 422
   obtaining smallest integer greater than a passed parameter, 357–358
Interfaces, with RTLink, 28

Internal file information, looking at, 732–735
INVALIDATE( ) method, 848
ISALPHA( ) function, 445
ISCOLOR( ) function, 445
ISDIGIT( ) function, 445–446
ISLOWER( ) function, 446
ISPRINTER( ) function, 446
IsStable( ) function, 924
ISUPPER( ) function, 447
/I switch, 7
ITEM entry structure, for index files, 748
Iterations, in loops, 248
JOIN command, 255–256

Keyboard
 assigning strings to function keys, 330
 stuffing strings to, 256–257
Keyboard buffer
 clearing, 228
 obtaining next key in, 472
KEYBOARD command, 256–257
 MEMOEDIT( ) function and, 698
Keyboard interface, with Debugger, 589–593
Keyboard values, manifest constants and, 97
KEYED-PAIR in index files, 762–763
KEY EXPRESSION in index files, 762–763
Key expressions
 for index files, 442
 of orders, 478
Key fields, relating work areas by, 308–309, 386
Key movements within READ command, 275–276
Key page structure, of index files, 748
Keys
 for ACHOICE( ) function, 332–333
 alt, 1140

assigning functions and procedures to, 304–305
assigning to subroutines, 522–523
control, 1139
for exiting from READ, 496–497
for index files, 253–254, 390–391
MEMOEDIT( ) function and key handling, 695–697
nonunique, 310–311
obtaining code for key pressed, 443, 444
obtaining value of last, 447–448
shift, 1140
special, 1138–1139
KEYS( ) function, handling keystroke exceptions with, 641–642
Keystroke actions, for browse objects, 862–888
Keystroke exceptions, handling with array functions, 638–642
Keystrokes, programming browse objects for, 906–931
KEY VALUE in index files, 762
Key values, totaling numeric fields based on, 317–319
Keywords, 117, 118
 adding key word/item pairs to data dictionary, 395–396
 entering and replacing in data dictionary, 395
 obtaining associated values from data dictionary, 393
KILLFOCUS( ) method, 936

L2BIN( ) function, 454, 783
LABEL FORM command, 257–259
Label generation programs, 579
Labels, displaying, 257–259
Languages
 customizing, 145–148
 inventing, 127–148

simulating with Clipper preprocessor, 147–148
Large strings, working with, 685–690
LASTKEY( ) function, 447–448
LASTREC( ) function, 449
Late evaluation of code blocks, 822–823
.LBL files, 579
Leap year, testing dates for, 366
LEFT( ) cursor movement method, 846
LEFT( ) function, 449
LEFT( ) method, 936
Left-justifying expressions within strings, 484–485
LEFTVISIBLE instance variable, 845
LEN( ) function, 450, 682
LENNUM( ) function, 451
Levels in expressions, 159–163
.LIB files, 4, 26
 RMAKE.EXE utility and, 565
Libraries, 41–88
 ANSITERM.LIB, 73–74
 Clipper compiler and, 4
 CLIPPER.LIB, 41–63
 DBFCDX.LIB, 70–73
 DBFMDX.LIB, 69–70
 DBFNDX.LIB, 69
 DBFNTX.LIB, 68–69
 DBPX.LIB, 74–86
 EXTEND.LIB, 63–68
 NOVTERM.LIB, 86
 PCBIOS.LIB, 86
 prelinked, 36–41
 SAMPLES.LIB, 86–88
 TERMINAL.LIB, 68
Library files, 26
Library utility, 575
Light-bars on menus, activating, 215–216
Line continuations, multiple commands for, 165–166
Line feeds, formatting strings with, 462–463
Line numbers, suppressing, 7–8

LINE NUMBERS command, in Debugger, 587
Line numbers in source code, displaying with Debugger, 597
Linkers, xxx–xxxi, 25–27. *See also* RTLink
Linking
 ideas for, 88
 incremental, 35–36
LISTASARRAY( ) function, 451–452
List boxes
 for array items, 331–334, 633–642
 using, 1000–1007
LIST command, 259–261
 in Debugger, 597
Listing records, 259–261
List match markers, 117
Lists
 outputting to standard device, 482–483
 outputting to standard error device, 482
Literals, 117, 118
.LNK files, 27–28
LOCAL command, 261–262
 in Debugger, 587
LOCALE.TXT file, 574
Local variables, xxxiii, 172, 176–178, 179, 683
 arrays and, 678
 code blocks and, 812–813, 820, 821
 initializing, 261–262
 initializing arrays as, 626–631
 lifespan and visibility of, 180
 macros and, 602–603
 MEMOEDIT( ) function and, 697
 subroutines and, 190–191
LOCATE command, 262–264
LOCATE FOR command, resuming searches by, 229
Locate menu, in Debugger, 585
Locating records, 262–264
Locating values in databases, 247–248

Locking files, 420, 421–422
Locking records, 381, 500
 in work areas, 503
LOG( ) function, 452
Logarithms
 calculating natural, 452
 calculating to base 10, 473
Logical data format, writing text in, 119
Logical fields, in databases, 721
Logical operators, 151
 rules of precedence for, 159–163
Logifying, 119
Logify result tokens, 119
Lookup( ) function, 678
LOOP command, 264
Loops
 aborting, 246
 executing, 243, 248
 going to the tops of, 264
Lotus-like menus, creating, 955–960
LOWER( ) function, 452–453
Lowercase characters
 converting strings to, 452–453
 as leftmost characters in strings, 446
Low-level file functions, 783–810
 error status of, 413–414
 reading files with, 791–801
 RMAKE.EXE utility and, 784–787
LPT1 port, testing, 446
/L switch, 7–8
LTRIM( ) function, 120, 453
LUPDATE( ) function, 453

Macro operators, 149
Macros, 601–608
 array declarations and definitions and, 603–604
 code blocks and, 604–608, 811, 828–830
 Debugger and, 580–581
 expanding expressions as, 609–610

 illegal substitutions in, 602–603
 RMAKE.EXE utility and, 566–568, 570–573, 574–578
Macro substitutions, guidelines for, 602–603
Main procedure, suppressing automatic, 8–10
Main( ) routine, 682
Maintainable scoped orders, 763
MAKECOLOR( ) pseudofunction, 136
MAKEDATE( ) pseudofunction, 136
MakeEmpty( ) function, 667
 code for, 665–666, 670–671
MakeSpec( ) function, 923
Manifest constants
 conditional compilation and, 102–111
 defining, 5–6, 95–101
 naming of, 97
 notation for, xxxiii
 undefining, 101–102
MANNER clause, 839
/MAP command, 29
Margin offset, setting left, 305
Match tokens, 117
Mathematical operators, 150–151, 155–159
 rules of precedence for, 159–163
MAX( ) function, 454
MAXCOL( ) function, 454–455
Maximum numeric values, 344–345
MAXROW( ) function, 455–456
.MDX files, 775
MDY( ) function, 456
.MEM files
 alternatives to, 805–810
 reading, 795–799
MEMOEDIT( ) function, 456–459, 691–702
 basics of, 691–695
 building program and text editor with, 702–716
 as a display routine, 693

handling keys and, 695–697
handling keystroke exceptions with, 638
large strings and, 685–686
performing program changes with, 579
restricting the size of, 698–699
toggling display area for, 309
toggling INS key for, 495–496
window for, 691
Memo fields, 171
basics of handling, 685–686
in databases, 721
functions for handling, 686–699
writing to files, 463
Memo files, 685–686. *See also* .DBT files; .MEM files; Memos
database management and, 721–722
MEMOLINE( ) function, 460, 686
columnizing text and, 702
MEMOREAD( ) function, 461, 686, 690, 692
Memory, 89–90
calculating free, 461–462
garbage collection in, 90–91
swapping, 90
MEMORY( ) function, 461–462
large strings and, 685
Memory buffer, flushing, 229, 370
Memory variables. *See also* Private variables; Public variables; Variables
aliased, 164–165
arrays and, 624–625
clearing all, 226–227
for code blocks, 463–464
creating private, 271–272
creating public, 273–274
database fields and, 182–185
declaring public and private, 264–265
GETs and, 984–985
initializing, 261–262
initializing static, 314

local, 176–178
releasing, 279–280
restoring contents of files of, 285
saving to files, 289–291
Memos. *See also* Memo files
counting formatted lines in, 464–465
editing, 456–459
extracting substrings from, 460
obtaining row/column coordinates of characters in, 465–466
obtaining row/column coordinates of cursor for, 468–470
MEMOTRAN( ) function, 462–463, 686, 688–689
MEMOWRIT( ) function, 463, 686, 692
MEMVARBLOCK( ) function, 463–464, 834–835
MEMVAR command, 182–184, 264–265
MENU BAR command, in Debugger, 588
Menu bars, executing, 265–269
Menu options, in Debugger, 584–588
Menus
activating light-bars on, 215–216
creating bounce-bar menus, 946–955
creating Lotus-like menus, 955–960
creating pull-down menus, 960–970
for Debugger, 585–588
painting inside boxed regions, 354–355
wrapping PROMPTs in, 311
MENU TO command, 265–269
obtaining current variables from, 499
Message rows, establishing for PROMPTs, 305–306

Metasymbols, xxxiii
Methods
in Browse objects, 539–540, 541–542
in GET objects, 436
Midpoint value, of an index file, 723
MIN( ) function, 464
Minimum numeric values, 345
Minus (–) operator
sample program to demonstrate, 153–155
using on strings in indexes, 168
MINUS instance variable, 934
Mixed data types in arrays, 624–625
MLCOUNT( ) function, 464–465
columnizing text and, 702
memo fields and, 686
MLCTOPOS( ) function, 465–466
memo fields and, 686
MLPOS( ) function, 467
memo fields and, 686
MOD( ) function, 467–468
Modal dialog boxes, creating, 341–342
MODULE command, 31
Module identifiers, declaring, 218
Modulus of two numbers, 467–468
Modulus operator, 168
Monitor menu, in Debugger, 587
Monitor window, 582
keystroke assignments for, 591
Monochrome monitor, color table for, 1142
MONO DISPLAY command, in Debugger, 588
MONTH( ) function, 468
Months
adding to dates, 338
converting date expressions into, 468
obtaining names of, 359–360
obtaining numeric day of the month, 366–367

MOREDEFS.INC file, 1135
Moving windows, 583
MPOSTOL( ) function, memo fields and, 686
MPOSTOLC( ) function, 468–470
/M switch, 8
Multidimensional arrays, 623–624
   AEVAL( ) function and, 646–647
   duplicating, 334, 642–643
   filling with a single value, 652–653
   QuArray( ) function and, 682
   scanning, 813
   sorting, 662, 813
   writing to disk, 801–805
Multiple commands, 125
Multiplication, in-line, 155–159

NAME instance variable, 934
Natural logarithms, 452
NBOTTOM instance variable, 845
.NDX files, 747
   RDDs and, 749
Nested arrays, 678–683
NETERR( ) function, 470
NETNAME( ) function, 471
NETUSE( ) function, 471
Network functions, testing, 470
Networking library, xxx
Networks, opening databases and, 471
Network station names, obtaining, 471
NEWDEFS.INC file, 1135
NEXT command, in Debugger, 585, 597
NEXTKEY( ) function, 472
NEXT ROUTINE command, in Debugger, 586
NG.EXE program, 579
NIL data type, 171, 174
   ADEL( ) function and, 645–646
   ASIZE( ) function and, 658–659
   enlarging arrays with NIL values, 341, 653–655

NLEFT instance variable, 845
/NOBATCH command, 30
/NODEFAULTLIBRARYSEARCH command, 30
/NOEXTDICTIONARY command, 30
NOIDLE switch, 22
/NOIGNORECASE command, 30
/NOINCREMENTAL command, 30
Non-maintainable orders, 763
Normal stringify result tokens, 118
Norton Instant Access engine, 579
NOSNOW( ) function, 472
NOTE command, 269
NOVTERM.LIB file, contents of, 86
NRIGHT instance variable, 845
/N switch, 8–10, 181
NTOD( ) function, 472–473
NTOP instance variable, 845
.NTX files, 719, 722–723, 763
   format of, 747–748
   header structure of, 747–748
   RDDs and, 749
   reading, 799–801
NUMASCURRENCY( ) function, 473
NUMASLOG10( ) function, 473
NUM command, in Debugger, 597
Numeric attribute values, color values for, 1142–1145
Numeric expressions
   obtaining lengths of, 451
   rounding off, 503–504
Numeric fields
   averaging, 222
   in databases, 721
   summing, 315
   totaling based on key values, 317–319
Numeric values
   converting characters to, 555–556
   converting from one base to another, 351–352

   converting into strings, 532–533
   converting numbers into strings with leading zeros, 533–535
   converting years to, 560–561
   displaying with Debugger, 594
   formatting with picture templates, 547–551
   obtaining integer portions of, 444
   obtaining maximum, 344–345
   obtaining minimum, 345
   one-time editing of, 556–557
   signs of, 526
NUMGETDECIMALS( ) function, 474
NUMGETLEN( ) function, 474

Object files
   preprocessor and, 94
   specifying, 10–11
Object modules, names of, 41–88
Object-oriented programming, 841–843
   databases and, 888–906
   GET system and, 987
Objects, 841–939
   classes of, 842–843
   defined, 842–843
.OBJ files, 26
   incremental linking and, 36
   preprocessor and, 94
   RMAKE.EXE utility and, 565
   specifying, 10–11
OCCURRENCE( ) pseudofunction, 690
OCCURS( ) function, 474–475
ODD( ) pseudofunction, 753
One-dimensional arrays, 623–624
One-time editing of numeric values, 556–557
One-to-many relationships, between databases, 732
One-to-one relationships, between databases, 732
ON KEY command, 147–148

OPEN command, in Debugger, 585
Opening files, 422–423
Opening index files, 303–304
Opening Watch window, 600
Opening work areas, 322–324, 389
Operating system, obtaining name of, 481
OPERATION instance variable, 938
Operators, 149–169
 aliasing and, 164–165
 Boolean, 163–164
 division by zero and, 168
 evaluating expressions and, 169
 fields and in-line assignments and, 166–167
 for line continuation, 165–166
 mathematical, 155–159
 negation and ==, 167
 rules of precedence for, 159–163
 sample program to demonstrate, 151–152
 for strings and dates, 152–155
 for strings in indexes, 168
 table of, 149–151
 tips on, 163–169
Optional clauses, 118
Options menu, in Debugger, 587–588
ORDBAGEXT( ) function, 475
ORDBAGNAME( ) function, 475–476
ORDCREATE( ) function, 476
ORDDESTROY( ) function, 477
Order Bag, 763, 766
 creating orders in, 476
 obtaining extension for, 475
 obtaining name of, 475–476
 removing orders from, 239–240, 477
Order List, 763
 adding orders to, 478–479
 clearing, 479
 obtaining order names in, 480
 obtaining order positions in, 480
 rebuilding orders in, 479
 setting focus to orders in, 481
Orders
 key expressions for, 478
 obtaining FOR expressions for, 477–478
Order tags, 763, 766
 removing, 239–240
ORDFOR( ) function, 477–478
Ordinal positions of fields, 416
ORDKEY( ) function, 478
ORDLISTADD( ) function, 478–479
ORDLISTCLEAR( ) function, 479
ORDLISTREBUILD( ) function, 479
ORDNAME( ) function, 480
ORDNUMBER( ) function, 480
ORDSETFOCUS( ) function, 481
ORIGINAL instance variable, 934
OS( ) function, 481
OSCODE instance variable, 938
/O switch, 10–11
OUTERR( ) function, 482
OUTPUT command, in Debugger, 598
Output pattern, 118
OUTSTD( ) function, 482–483, 786
Overlays, 34–35
OVERSTRIKE( ) method, 936
.OVL files, 35

PACK command, 269–271
PADC( ) function, 483–484
PADL( ) function, 484–485
PADR( ) function, 485
PAGEDOWN( ) cursor movement method, 846
Page frames, 90
Pages, of memory, 91
PAGEUP( ) cursor movement method, 846
PANEND( ) cursor movement method, 847
PANHOME( ) cursor movement method, 847
PANLEFT( ) cursor movement method, 847
PANRIGHT( ) cursor movement method, 847
Paradox table and index driver, 780–781. *See also* DBPX driver
Parallel arrays, 636–637
Parameter passing, 187–203
 arrays and, 631–632
 by reference, 191–194, 676–678
 by value, 187–191
Parameters
 counting number of passed, 486–487
 obtaining from the DOS command line, 199–201
 passing arrays as, 194–199
PARAMETERS command, 271
PARAMETERS statement, 174
Parameter variables, declaring private, 271
Parentheses
 expressions and, 608–609
 passing variables by reference and, 194
 segregating levels in expressions with, 159–163
Parsing program, 108–111
"Pass-through" mode, 579
PATH environmental variable, 201
Paths, 420, 427–428
 determining the existence of, 787–790
 finding files in search paths, 437
 specifying, 307
Pausing program execution, 324–325
PCBIOS.LIB file, contents of, 86
PCOL( ) function, 485–486
PCOUNT( ) function, 486–487
 DOS command line parameters and, 199
PE.EXE program editor, 579
Phone dialers, 787
Pick boxes, using, 1000–1007
PickDir( ) function, 924

Picture clauses, for formatting GETs, 986
PICTURE instance variable, 934
Picture templates
 displaying values with, 392
 formatting values and expressions with, 547–551
/PLL command, 30–31
.PLL files, 36–41, 828
 adding calls to, 40
Pointers, positioning in files, 427
Point menu, in Debugger, 586–587
POS instance variable, 934
/POSITIONAL command, 28
Positional interface, 28
 command structure for invoking, 31
Positioning cursor and printhead, 392–393
POSTBLOCK instance variable, 934
Post-decrement operators, 155–159
Post-increment operators, 155–159
.PPO files, 580
 preprocessor and, 94
PREBLOCK instance variable, 934
Precedence, rules of, 159–163
Pre-decrement operators, 155–159
Pre-increment operators, 155–159
/PRELINK command, 31
Prelinked libraries, 35–41
PRELOAD command, 31
PREPROCESSED CODE command, in Debugger, 587
Preprocessed output listing, generating, 11
Preprocessor
 line continuations for, 165–166
 overview of, 93–95
 using, 790–791
Preprocessor commands, 95–127
Preprocessor output file, 580

PREV command, in Debugger, 598
PREVIOUS command, in Debugger, 585
.PRG files, 26, 181
 functions and procedures and, 206
 preprocessor and, 94
PRINTCODES( ) function, 487–488
Printer
 advancing to top of form, 244
 formatting text for, with MEMOEDIT( ) function, 700–702
 sending printer codes to, 487–488
 setting row and column position of, 525
 toggling, 307–308
 typing contents of a file to, 320
Printer codes, 487–488
Printhead
 obtaining relative column position of, 485–486
 obtaining relative row position of, 490–491
 positioning, 392–393
PRIVATE command, 271–272
 in Debugger, 587
PRIVATE statement, 174–176
 arrays and, 626
Private variables, 172, 174–176. See also Memory variables; Variables
 clearing all, 226–227
 creating, 271–272
 declaring, 264–265, 271
 lifespan and visibility of, 180
 macros and, 602
 releasing, 279–280
 subroutines and, 190–191
PROCEDURE command, 272–273
Procedures
 assigning to keys, 304–305
 in code blocks, 813–814

 declaring user-defined, 272–273
 functions and, 205–206
 obtaining line numbers of, 488
 obtaining names of, 488–490
 passing parameters to, 187–199
PROCLINE( ) function, 488
 arrays and, 663
PROCNAME( ) function, 488–490
 arrays and, 663
Program editors, 579
 building, 702–716
Programming
 object-oriented, 841–843
 top-down, 842
Programming operators, 149–169
 table of, 149–151
Programming techniques
 advanced, 145–147
 basic, 139–142
 intermediate, 142–145
Program modules, compiling specified, 8
Programs
 compiling, 308
 executing, 210
 executing external, 286–287
 executing loops in, 243
 pausing, 324–325
 terminating execution of, 225, 274–275
PROMPT command
 building program and text editor and, 702–716
 toggling enhanced display for, 304
PROPER( ) function, 490
PROW( ) function, 490–491
Pseudocode, 3
Pseudofunctions, 130–138, 790–791
 advantages of, 131–132
 building, 790–791
 combining commands and functions into, 137–138
 creating user-defined, 116–125

defining, 100–101
disadvantages of, 132
undefining, 101–102
user-defined commands and, 129
/P switch, 11, 94
PTCOLOR.CH file, 1116–1117
PTFUNCS.CH file, 1123–1126
PTINKEY.CH file, 1117–1120
PTLOWLVL.CH file, 1134
PTVALUE.CH file, 1120–1123
PTVERBS.CH file, 1126–1133
PUBLIC command, 273–274
  in Debugger, 587
PUBLIC statement, 173–174
  arrays and, 626
Public variables, 172. *See also*
  Memory variables;
  Variables
  clearing all, 226–227
  creating, 273–274
  declaring, 264–265
  lifespan and visibility of, 180
  macros and, 603
  releasing, 279–280
Pull-down menus, creating, 960–970

QOUT( ) function, 25, 491
  AEVAL( ) function and, 648
  programming techniques with, 142
QQOUT( ) function, 491
  programming techniques with, 142
/Q switch, 11
QuArray( ) function, 678–683
? command, 210–211
  in Debugger, 594
  programming techniques with, 142
?? command, 211
  programming techniques with, 142
Quiet mode, 11, 581
QUIT command, 274–275
  in Debugger, 598
QU program, 678–683

Radians
  converting degrees to, 404
  converting to degrees, 505
RANGECHECK( ) function, 492
RAT( ) function, 492
RDDLIST( ) function, 493
RDDNAME( ) function, 493
RDDs (replaceable database drivers), 749–761
  arrays of available, 493
  DBFCDX driver for, 768–773
  DBFMDX driver for, 773–777
  DBFNDX driver for, 777–779
  DBFNTX driver for, 779–780
  DBPX driver for, 780–781
  getting and setting default, 493–494
  obtaining names of active, 493
RDDSETDEFAULT( ) function, 493–494, 754, 757
READ command, 275–277
  activating format files for, 302–303
  current GETLIST array and, 498
  determining if data was changed by, 554
  exiting from, 494
  GETs and, 986
  getting and setting internal updated status of, 498
  key movements within, 275–276
  obtaining current variables from, 499
  obtaining value of keys for exiting from, 496–497
  toggling display area for, 309
  toggling ESC key for, 300
  toggling status of INS key in, 495–496
READER instance variable, 934
Readers, user-defined, 1015–1022
READEXIT( ) function, 494
READFORMAT( ) function, 494–495
Reading files, with low-level file functions, 791–801

Reading GET objects, 438
READINSERT( ) function, 495–496
READKEY( ) function, 496–497
READKILL( ) function, 497
READMODAL( ) function, 498, 789
  GETs and, 986
  toggling ESC key for, 300
READUPDATED( ) function, 498
READVAR( ) function, 499
  arrays and, 662
Real memory, 89
Real numbers, exponentials of, 409–410
Rebuilding index files, 278–279, 379–380
RECALL command, 123, 278
RECCOUNT( ) function, 499
RECLOCK( ) function, 500
RECNO( ) function, 500
  arracys and, 671
Record numbers, relating work areas by, 308–309
Record pointer
  moving, 311–312, 386–387
  moving to a specific location in a database, 378
  moving to bottom of a database, 378
  moving to top of a database, 379
  positioning, 250–251
Records
  appending blank, 338
  appending to a database from a database, 219–222
  appending to database files, 367–368
  copying between databases, 231–233
  counting, 233–234, 499
  displaying, 241
  evaluating, 376–377
  highlighting records marked for deletion, 298
  listing on screen, 259–261
  locating with indexes, 383–384
  locking, 381, 500, 503

Records (*continued*)
  marking for deletion, 238–239, 373
  obtaining current record number or identity, 500
  obtaining lists of locked, 381
  obtaining number of records in a work area or database, 449
  obtaining sizes of, 501
  placing values into specified fields in, 416–417
  relating work areas by record numbers, 386
  removing all, 325
  removing records marked for deletion, 269–271
  searching for indexed, 291–292
  sequential searches for, 262–264
  testing deletion flags of, 390
  unlocking, 320–321, 383, 388–389
  unmarking records marked for deletion, 278, 379
RECSIZE( ) function, 501
/REFER command, 31
Reference
  passing array elements by, 676–678
  passing parameters by, 191–194
Reference periodicals, xxxi
REFRESHALL( ) method, 848
REFRESHCURRENT( ) method, 848
Regular evaluation of code blocks, 822–823
Regular match markers, 117
Regular result tokens, 118
REINDEX command, 278–279
  building index files and, 723
REJECTED instance variable, 934
Relations
  clearing, 369
  between databases and indexes, 729–732

obtaining dependent work areas in, 381–382
RELEASE command, 173, 279–280
Releasing variables, 279–280
Removing orders, 477
RENAME command, 280
Renaming files, 280, 425–426
REPEAT command, 141
Repeating character expressions, 501–502
Repeating clauses, 119
REPLACE command, 280–282
REPLICATE( ) function, 501–502
REPORT command, 282–284
Report generation programs, 579
Reports
  displaying, 282–284
  MEMOEDIT( ) function and, 693–695
REQUEST command, 284–285
REQUEST statement, 186
  ANNOUNCE statement and, 204–205
RESET( ) method, 936
/RESIDENT command, 28–29
RESTART command, in Debugger, 586, 598
RESTORE FROM command, 285
RESTORE SCREEN command, 285–286
RESTORE SETTINGS command, in Debugger, 588
Restoring saved screens, 285–286
Restoring screen areas, 502
Restoring windows, 583
Restricted match markers, 117
RESTSCREEN( ) function, 502
Result markers, 118
Result tokens, 118–119
RESUME command, in Debugger, 585, 599
RETURN command, 286
RIGHT( ) cursor movement method, 847, 936

RIGHT( ) function, 502–503
Right-justifying expressions within strings, 485
RIGHTVISIBLE instance variable, 846
RL.EXE program, 579
  make file for, 572
RLOCK( ) function, 503
RL.RMK file, 572–573
RMAKE execution error messages, 1160
RMAKE.EXE utility, 565–578
  command statements in, 566–568
  commands used with, 565–566
  creating a screen editor with, 573–574
  environmental variables in, 569
  invoking, 568
  low-level file functions and, 784–787
  macros and, 566–568, 570–573, 574–578
  operation of and rules for, 569–578
  optional switches in, 566
  using, 573–578
RMAKE fatal error messages, 1160
RMAKE script files, 1111–1114
RMAKE warning messages, 1160
.RMK files, 566, 568, 572–573
ROLLBACK AT command, 671, 672
Root names of files, 418–419
ROUND( ) function, 504–505
Rounding off numeric expressions, 503–504
ROW( ) function, 504–505
ROWCOUNT instance variable, 846
ROW instance variable, 935
Row locations, of GETs, 984
ROWPOS instance variable, 846

Rows
  obtaining maximum number of, 455–456
  setting display mode for row depth, 523–524
.RPT files, 579
/R switch, 12
RTLink, 25–91
  defined, 27–28
RTLink command summary, 28–32
RTLink error messages, 1154–1155
RTLink files, 27
RTLink miscellaneous error messages, 1155–1156
RTLink warning messages, 1154
RTOD( ) function, 505
RTRIM( ) function, 505–506
RUN command, 286–287
Run menu, in Debugger, 586
Running commands, programs, and batch files, 210
Run-time error messages, 1156–1158
Run-time unrecoverable error messages, 1159–1160

SAMPLE.RMK program, 1111
SAMPLES.LIB file, contents of, 86–88
SAMPMORE.RMK program, 1111
SAMPNDX.RMK program, 1112
SAMPRDD.RMK program, 1112
SAVESCREEN( ) function, 506–508
SAVE SCREEN command, 287–289
SAVE SETTINGS command, in Debugger, 588
SAVE TO command, 289–291
Saving screens, 287–289, 506–508
Scoped orders, 763

Screen
  clearing, 225
  displaying labels on, 257–259
  displaying preprocessor messages on, 126–127
  listing records on, 259–261
  setting and evaluating current color of, 521
Screen colors
  manifest constants and, 96
  memory variables and, 100
Screen control, 941–945
Screen editor, creating with RMAKE.EXE utility, 573–574
Screens, 941–945
  beginning virtual, 400
  clearing, 228
  for data entry, 987–1000
  displaying application screen with Debugger, 598
  displaying gauges on, 429–430
  obtaining column position of cursors on, 360
  obtaining row positions of cursors on, 504–505
  restoring areas of, 502
  restoring saved, 285–286
  saving, 287–289, 506–508
  scrolling in, 508–510
  terminating virtual, 401
  typing contents of files to, 320
  updating status indicator arrays for, 531–532
  virtual, 970–973
Script files, Debugger and, 597
SCROLL( ) function, 138–139, 508–510
SCROLLBARDISPLAY( ) function, 510
SCROLLBARNEW( ) function, 511
Scrollbars, 510–513
  arrays for, 511
  displaying, 510
  updating information in, 511–513

SCROLLBARUPDATE( ) function, 511–513
Scrolling in screens, 508–510
  scrollbars for, 510–513
Search drives and directories, establishing, 297–298
Search operations, determining success of, 423
Search paths, specifying, 307
Secondary arrays, 636–637
Seconds
  converting into days, 367, 513–514
  converting into time strings, 545, 551–553
  converting time to, 544
  elapsed from midnight, 513
  elapsed from system time, 514
SECONDS( ) function, 513
SECONDSASDAYS( ) function, 513–514
SECS( ) function, 514
SECTION command, 31
SEEK command, 291–292
  with databases, 730
Seek conditions, toggling, 309–310
SE.EXE file, 573–574
Segmented Virtual Object Store (SVOS), 90–91
Segments, 89
SELECT( ) function, 514
SELECT command, 292–293
Selecting work areas, 292–293
Semicolon (;), line continuations with, 165–166
Send operator, defined, 843
SET( ) function, 515–519, 818
SET( ) values for environment, 519
SETALL( ) function, 519
SET ALTERNATIVE command, 293–294
SET BELL command, 294, 818
SETBLINK( ) function, 519–520
SETCANCEL( ) function, 520–521
SET CENTURY command, 294

SETCOLOR( ) function, 521
    arrays and, 667
SETCOLOR( ) pseudofunction, 136
SET COLOR command, 294–295
Set Color window, 582
SETCOLUMN( ) method, 848
SET command
    environmental variables and, 201–202
    programming techniques with, 143–144
SET CONFIRM command, 295
SET CONSOLE command, 296
SETCURSOR( ) function, 522
SET CURSOR command, 296
SET DATE command, 296–297
SET DECIMALS command, 297
SET DEFAULT command, 297–298
SET DELETED command, 298
    databases and, 732
SET DELIMITERS command, 298–299
SET DEVICE command, 299
SET environment, arrays and, 672
SET EPOCH command, 299–300
SET ESCAPE command, 300
SET EXACT command, 300–301
SET EXCLUSIVE command, 301
SET FILTER command, 301–302
    databases and, 732
SET FILTER TO command,
    code blocks and, 830
SET FILTER TO expression, 163–164
SET FIXED command, 302
SETFOCUS( ) method, 936
SET FORMAT command, 302–303
SET FUNCTION command, 303
SET INDEX command, 303–304
    with databases, 729–730
SET INTENSITY command, 304

SETKEY( ) function, 206, 522–523
    arrays and, 672
    GETs and, 986–987
SET KEY applications, 1013–1015
SET KEY command, 304–305
    GETs and, 986–987
SETKEY stack, arrays and, 672
SET KEY stack operations, 444
SET KEY TO command
    MEMOEDIT( ) function and, 695
    working with, 998–1000
SET LIB command, 33
SET MARGIN command, 305
SET MESSAGE command, 305–306
SETMODE( ) function, 523–524
SET OBJ command, 33–34
SET ORDER command, 306
SET PATH command, 307
SET PLL command, 33
SETPOS( ) function, 524–525
SETPRC( ) function, 525
SETPRINTER( ) pseudofunction, 135
SET PRINTER command, 307–308
SET PROCEDURE command, 308
SET RELATION command, 308–309
    ADDITIVE clause for, 732
    with databases, 730
SET RTLINKCMD command, 32–33
SETS command, in Debugger, 586
SET SCOREBOARD command, 309
SET SOFTSEEK command, 309–310
SET TMP command, 33
SETTYPEAHEAD( ) function, 525
SET TYPEAHEAD command, 310

SET UNIQUE command, 310–311
SET WRAP command, 311
SEVERITY instance variable, 938
Shadowed boxes, 356
Shared use of databases, toggling, 301
SHELL command, 201
Shift keys, 1140
"Shortcutting" optimization, suppressing, 14
ShowDir( ) function, 923
ShowFile( ) function, 923
ShowString( ) function, 923
SIGN( ) function, 526
Sign of a number, obtaining, 526
/SILENT command, 29
Single step mode, executing programs in, with Debugger, 599
SIRIUS.INC file, 1136
16–bit binary numbers
    converting integers to, 439–440
    converting to integers, 352–353
Sizes of arrays
    changing, 348–349, 658–659
    declaring, 346, 655–656
    setting, 237–238
Sizing windows, 582
SKIPBLOCK instance variable, 846
SKIP command, 311–312
    RDDs and, 749
Smart stringify result token, 118
Snow condition, toggling, 472
Soft carriage returns, replacing with hard carriage returns, 438–439
SORT command, 312–313
    in Debugger, 587
Sorting arrays, 349–350, 659–662
Sorting databases, 312–313
Sorting index keys, 253, 390–391

SOUNDEX( ) function, 526–527
Sounds-like calculations, 526–527
Source code, annotating, 269
Source pattern, 117
SPACE( ) function, 527
Special keys, 1138–1139
SPEED command, in Debugger, 586, 599
Split screens, 581
SQRT( ) function, 528
Square root, calculating, 528
/S switch, 12
Stabilization, 853
STABILIZE( ) method, 848, 849
STABLE instance variable, 846
Stack, clearing, 401
Stack array
  adding elements to, 529
  first item in, 530
  generating new, 528–529
  removing elements from, 529–530
  testing for empty, 528
/STACK command, 30
STACKISEMPTY( ) function, 528
STACKNEW( ) function, 528–529
STACKPOP( ) function, 529–530
STACKPUSH( ) function, 529
STACKTOP( ) function, 530
Statements, 203–205
STATIC command, 314
  in Debugger, 587
Static functions, MEMOEDIT( ) function and, 695–696
STATIC FUNCTION statement, 203
Static overlays, 34–35
STATIC PROCEDURE statement, 203
Static variables, xxxiii, 172, 176, 177, 179–182
  arrays and, 668, 671
  code blocks and, 812–813, 820, 821
  filewide, 181–182
  initializing, 314
  initializing arrays as, 626–631
  lifespan and visibility of, 180
  subroutines and, 190–191
Station names, in networks, 471
Status indicators
  creating new, 531
  updating arrays for, 531–532
STATUSNEW( ) function, 531
STATUSUPDATE( ) function, 531–532
STD.CH file, 93–94
  saving GETs and, 1007
#stdout command, 126–127
STEP command, in Debugger, 586, 599
StoreArray( ) function, code for, 665, 671
STORE command, 124, 314–315
STR( ) function, 532–533
Stringifying, 118
Strings. See also Character expressions; Dates; Time strings
  alphabetic characters in, 445
  assigning to function keys, 330
  of blank spaces, 527
  capitalizing words in, 490
  centering expressions within, 483–484
  converting city, state, and zip-code into, 359
  converting dates to, 404–405, 456
  converting dates to string format, 402
  converting delimited strings to arrays, 451–452
  converting files to, 461
  converting numbers into strings with leading zeros, 533–535
  converting numeric values into, 532–533
  converting to dates, 362
  converting to lower case, 452–453
  converting to upper case, 554–555
  counting formatted lines in, 464–465
  determining number of occurrences of substrings in, 474–475
  digit characters in, 445–446
  editing, 456–459
  exact matches for, 300–301
  extracting leftmost substrings of, 449
  extracting rightmost substrings of, 502–503
  extracting substrings from, 460, 537–538
  formatting with carriage returns and line feeds, 462–463
  large, 685–690
  left-justifying expressions within, 484–485
  locating substrings in, 350, 492
  locating with Debugger, 596
  lowercase characters in, 446
  MEMOEDIT( ) function and, 691
  obtaining positions of lines in, 467
  obtaining row/column coordinates of characters in, 465–466
  obtaining row/column coordinates of cursor for, 468–470
  operators for, 152–155
  reading from files, 424–425
  right-justifying expressions within, 485
  sample program to demonstrate, 153–154
  stuffing into other strings, 535–536

Strings (*continued*)
  stuffing keyboard with, 256–257
  system time as a string, 543–544
  translating substring values within, 533
  trimming blank spaces from, 343–344, 453, 505–506, 551
  uppercase characters in, 447
  validating as time strings, 545–546
  writing to files, 463
STRTRAN( ) function, 533
  DOS command line parameters and, 200
  memo fields and, 686, 688–689, 690
Structural compound index files, 770
Structure, 624
Structure-extended classes, 842
STRUCTURE EXTENDED
  databases, 725–727
  copying, 231
  creating, 234–236
  creating new databases from, 236–237
STRZERO( ) function, 533–535
STUBSTD.CH file, 1101–1109
STUFF( ) function, 535–536
  memo fields and, 686, 688–689
Stuffing keyboard with strings, 256–257
Stuffing strings into other strings, 535–536
SUBCODE instance variable, 938
Subroutines
  assigning keys to, 522–523
  beginning procedural, 242
  building generic, 835–839
  declaring as user-defined functions, 249
  DO commands and, 191–194
  executing, 223–224
  external, 185–186
  obtaining names of, 488–490

  passing arrays to, 631–632
  passing parameters to, 187–199
  specifying external, 246–247, 284–285
  terminating execution of, 286
SUBSCRIPT instance variable, 935
Subscripts of arrays, evaluating, 339, 646–652
SUBSTR( ) function, 537–538
  memo fields and, 686
Substrings
  extracting, 537–538
  extracting leftmost, 449
  extracting rightmost, 502–503
  locating in strings, 350, 492
  translating within strings, 533
SUBSYSTEM instance variable, 939
Subtraction, in-line, 155–159
SUM command, 315
Summer '87, converting from, xxiii–xxviii
Summing numeric fields, 315
Swap files, 90
SWAPK: switch, 22
SWAP ON INPUT command, in Debugger, 588
SWAPPATH: switch, 22
Switches
  for the debugger, 581
  in RMAKE.EXE utility, 566
Symbolic code, 3
Syntax checking, 12
Syntax of code blocks, 812–813
  checking, 812
System color, establishing, 294–295
System date, 363–364
System files, building new types of, 805–810
System time
  seconds from, 514
  as a string, 543–544

TAB WIDTH command, in Debugger, 588

TBCOLUMN class, 842
TBCOLUMNNEW( ) function, 543, 844, 850
TBCOLUMN object, 844–906
TBROWSE class, 842, 844–906
  cursor movement methods for, 846–847
  instance variables in, 844–846
  methods for, 846–848
  miscellaneous methods for, 847–848
TBROWSEDB( ) function, 538–540, 844, 906–931
  setting up browsing windows with, 851–853
TBROWSENEW( ) function, 540–542, 682, 844, 906–931
  setting up browsing windows with, 851–853
TBROWSENEW objects, 906–931
Templates, formatting values and expressions with, 547–551
Temporary files, 12, 19
Temporary orders, 763
TEMPPATH: switch, 22
TERM error messages, 1158
TERMINAL.LIB file, 37–38, 39
  contents of, 68
Terminating program execution, 225
Terminating virtual screens, 401
TERM object module, 37
Text
  displaying blocks of, 316–317
  fomatting for printer, 700–702
  MEMOEDIT( ) function handling of, 699
  stringifying, 118
TEXT command, 316–317
Text editor, building, 702–716
Text files, reading, 791–795
32–bit binary numbers
  converting integers to, 454
  converting to integers, 352

Time
  calculating elapsed, 405
  converting to seconds, 544
  converting to 12–hour format, 544
  obtaining system time as a string, 543–544
TIME( ) function, 543–544
TIMEASAMPM( ) function, 544
TIMEASSECONDS( ) function, 544
TIMEASSTRING( ) function, 545
TIMEDIFF( ) function, 545
TIMEISVALID( ) function, 545–546
Time strings
  in AM/PM format, 345–346
  calculating difference between, 545
  converting seconds into, 551–553
  converting seconds to, 545
  validating, 545–546
TITLE user-defined command, 125
TMP variable, 19
TO CURSOR command, in Debugger, 586
TODECPOS( ) method, 936
Toggling bell, 294
Toggling console display, 296
Toggling cursor, 296
Toggling printers, 307–308
Toggling seek conditions, 309–310
Toggling snow condition, 472
Tokens, 4
  literal, 117, 118
TONE( ) function, 546–547
Tones
  generating, 546–547
  table of, 1147–1148
Top-down programming, 842
Top of form, advancing to, 244
TOTAL command, 317–319
Totaling numeric fields based on key values, 317–319

Touch programs, 784
TP command, in Debugger, 599
TRACE command, in Debugger, 586
TRACEPOINT command, in Debugger, 587
TracePoints, 589
  deleting, 595
  listing, 597
  running programs in Debugger with, 596
  tracing expressions and, 599
Training, for Clipper 5.2, xxxi
Transaction rollback, 668–672
TRANSFORM( ) function, 547–551
#translate command, 116–125
  user-defined commands and, 129
TRIES instance variable, 939
TRIM( ) function, 120, 551
  index files and, 725
TSTRING( ) function, 551–553
/T switch, 12
12–hour format, converting time to, 544
TYPE( ) function, 553
  return values from, 171–172
Typeahead buffer
  setting, 525
  setting size of, 310
TYPE command, 320
TYPE instance variable, 935
TYPEOUT instance variable, 935
Typing contents of files, 320

Unaliased references, resolving, 182–185
#undef command, 101–102
UNDO( ) method, 936
UNLOCK command, 320–321
Unlocking files, 320–321
Unlocking records, 320–321, 383, 388–389
Unresolved external references, 12

UNTRANSFORM( ) method, 936
UP( ) cursor movement method, 847
UP and DOWN arrow keys, toggling for exits from READ, 494
UPDATEBUFFER( ) method, 936
UPDATE command, 321–322
UPDATED( ) function, 554
Updating databases, 453
Updating .DBF files, 321–322
Updating index and database buffers, 370
UPPER( ) function, 554–555
Uppercase characters
  converting strings to, 554–555
  as leftmost characters in strings, 447
USE command, 322–324
  with databases, 729
USED( ) function, 555
User-defined commands, 129–130, 138–139
  pseudofunctions and, 129
User-defined functions, 129–130, 205–206, 249
User-defined procedures, declaring, 272–273
User-defined readers, working with, 1015–1022
/U switch, 12–13
Utility programs, 565–600

VAL( ) function, 555–556
VALEDIT( ) function, 556–557
VALID clauses
  of GETs, 986
  working with, 990–993
VALTYPE( ) function, 557–559
  code blocks and, 811
  macro-expanding arrays and, 603
  return values for, 172
Value, passing parameters by, 187–191
VARGET( ) method, 936

Variable initialization, 172–182
Variables. *See also* Character variables; Environmental variables; Local variables; Memory variables; Private variables; Public variables; Static variables
  accessing DOS environmental, 201–203
  actual, 187
  aliased, 164–165
  automatic declaration of, 5
  clearing, 226–227
  clearing all, 225–226
  code blocks and, 812–813, 820, 821
  creating private, 271–272
  creating public, 273–274
  displaying with Debugger, 594
  entering values into, 254–255
  initializing static, 314
  manifest constants and, 96
  obtaining from MENU TO or READ commands, 499
  releasing, 279–280
  resolving ambiguous references to, 13, 14
  storing values to, 314–315
  testing values of, in GET objects, 492
Variable statements, order of, 186–187
VARPUT( ) method, 936
/VERBOSE command, 29
VERSION( ) function, 559
VIEW command, in Debugger, 600
View menu, in Debugger, 586
View Sets window, 582
View Work Area window, 582
  keystroke assignments for, 591–592
Virtual memory, 89, 91
Virtual Memory Manager (VMM), 89–91
  dynamic overlays and, 91
Virtual screens, 970–973
  beginning, 400
  terminating, 401

Visual Objects, 1077
/V switch, 13, 183

WAIT command, 324–325, 579–580
Warning messages, 1151
  RMAKE, 1160
  RTLink, 1154
WATCHPOINT command, in Debugger, 586–587
WatchPoints, 589
  deleting, 595
  listing, 597
Watch window, 582
  keystroke assignments for, 591
  opening, 600
WHEN clauses
  of GETs, 986
  working with, 993–998
WHILE command, basic programming techniques with, 140–142
WHILE conditions, DBEVAL( ) function and, 741–744
Whole numbers. *See also* Digit characters; Integers
  determining number of, 474
WIDTH instance variable, 851
Wild match markers, 118
Window list boxes, for array items, 331–334, 633–642
Window menu, in Debugger, 588
Windows
  creating and displaying, 973–982
  for Debugger, 582–584, 589–593
  iconizing, 582
  moving, 583
  restoring, 583
  sizing, 582
  zooming, 583
WORD( ) function, 559–560
WORDLEFT( ) method, 936
WORDRIGHT( ) method, 936
Words, defined, 118
WORDS.CH file, 1135

Work areas
  adding indexes to, 385
  appending blank records to, 338
  browsing, 373–376
  changing, 384
  checking for presence of databases in, 555
  clearing database relations in, 369
  clearing filter conditions for, 368
  closing database files in, 369
  closing open files in, 369
  establishing database drivers for, 384–385
  establishing filter conditions for, 385
  evaluating records in, 376–377
  expressions in, 610–621
  generating code blocks for specific field values in, 417–418
  locking records in, 503
  moving record pointer in, 311–312, 386–387
  obtaining alias names of, 342–343, 377
  obtaining current record number in, 500
  obtaining database relations in, 380
  obtaining dependent, 381–382
  obtaining filter expressions in, 377–378
  obtaining number of records in, 449
  obtaining positions of controlling indexes of, 443
  obtaining work area numbers for aliases, 514
  opening, 322–324, 389
  opening index files for, 303–304
  ordinal positions of fields in, 416
  relating by key fields or record numbers, 308–309, 386

selecting, 292–293
setting filter conditions for, 301–302
WORKAREAS command, in Debugger, 586
WP command, in Debugger, 600
Wrapping PROMPTs, 311
Writing on hard disk, 370
Writing on the hard disk, 229
/W switch, 14, 183

X: switch, 22
#xcommand command, 116–125
#xtranslate command, 116–125

Year
converting to a numeric value, 560–561
setting base, 299–300
testing dates for leap year, 366
YEAR( ) function, 560–561

ZAP command, 325
Zeros
converting numbers into strings with leading zeros, 533–535
working with, 168
Zip codes, converting into strings, 359
Zooming windows, 583
/Z switch, 14